Malaysia
Singapore & Brunei

THE ROUGH GUIDE

YO-BDB-114

There are more than one hundred Rough Guide titles
covering destinations from Amsterdam to Zimbabwe

Forthcoming titles include
Bangkok • Barbados • Edinburgh
Japan • Jordan • Syria

Rough Guide Reference Series
Classical Music • The Internet • Jazz • Opera
Reggae • Rock Music • World Music

Rough Guide Phrasebooks
Czech • French • German • Greek • Hindi & Urdu • Indonesian • Italian
Mandarin Chinese • Mexican Spanish • Polish • Portuguese • Russian
Spanish • Thai • Turkish • Vietnamese

Rough Guides on the Internet
http://www.roughguides.com
http://www.hotwired.com/rough

ROUGH GUIDE CREDITS

Text editor: Helena Smith
Series editor: Mark Ellingham
Editorial: Martin Dunford, Jonathan Buckley, Samantha Cook, Jo Mead, Kate Berens, Amanda Tomlin, Ann-Marie Shaw, Paul Gray, Vivienne Heller, Sarah Dallas, Chris Schüler, Julia Kelly, Caroline Osborne, Judith Bamber (UK); Andrew Rosenberg (US)
Production: Susanne Hillen, Andy Hilliard, Judy Pang, Link Hall, Nicola Williamson, Helen Ostick

Cartography: Melissa Flack, David Callier, Maxine Burke
Online Editors: Alan Spicer (UK); Geronimo Madrid (US)
Finance: John Fisher, Celia Crowley, Catherine Gillespie
Marketing & Publicity: Richard Trillo, Simon Carloss, Niki Smith (UK), Jean-Marie Kelly, SoRelle Braun, (US)
Administration: Tania Hummel, Alexander Mark Rogers

ACKNOWLEDGEMENTS

The editor would like to thank Jo Mead and Kate Berens for their patient help; Maxine Burke for the maps; and Helen Ostick and Nicola Williamson in production.

The authors would like to thank the following people:

Charles: David de Ledesma and Fiona Murray.

Mark: In Sarawak, I am greatly indebted to Jean-Christophe Robles-Espinoza and Caroline Bintang Kanyan of the Sarawak Tourism Board; Philip Yong and Florence Apu at Borneo Adventures; Audrey Wan Ullok at Kuching's *Telang Usan Hotel*; Dayang Rokaiyah Abang Hj. Naim at the *Riverside Majestic*, Kuching; and to Mike Reed and Wayne Tarman for advice and nights out. Countless thanks, also, to Frankie Ting in Sibu; to Shep Bala in the Kelabit Highlands; and to my friend Thomas Ngang in Miri for an unforgettable five days in Mulu. In Sabah, thanks must go to Alice Yap and the Sipadan Dive Centre in Kota Kinabalu; to Jerry Kamijan at the *Shangri-La Tanjung Aru Resort*, to Hildy Angkangon, William Fletcher and Rudy Tangit Kinajil of the *Borneo Rainforest Lodge*; and to Gerald for the footie ticket. Thank you also to Royal Brunei, and to Rex Garratt from the London branch of Tourism Malaysia. At home, much love, as ever, goes to Selwyn, Dinah, Chris and Peter Lewis, Jane Hart and Jo Peggie for their continued support and encouragement; thanks also to STA's Craig Anderson for assistance in London; and – last but not least – to Helena for fine, unflappable and good-natured editing.

Pauline: Anuar and Badriah; Jack and Fatimah; Helena on Sibu; Simon from HTD; Pim and Liz; Nana; and Ross.

Simon: I'd like to thank Rex Garratt and the staff at Tourism Malaysia in London for pre-travel arrangements and fact checking; Cindy Lim and Razally Hussin at the KL head office of Tourism Malaysia for their support, Chandra Sehgaran at MATIC and all the staff members of the various tourist offices I badgered around the country. Special thanks to Sarah Loftus at Smi Hotels and Resorts who pulled out all the stops to arrange accommodation, and to Donny Ewe at Berjaya Hotels and Resorts, Elizabeth Soo at *The Legend*, Esther Wai at *The Datai*, Joyce Mah at the *Hyatt Regency Kuantan*, and Peter Bucher at the *Pangkor Laut Resort*. Stevie, Vincent and all the staff at KL's *Backpackers Traveller's Lodge* deserve special thanks for their unstinting kindness and help, as does Daniel in Tanah Rata, and Anuar and Badriah in Kota Bharu; thanks also to Tony Champion at Magic of the Orient and Michael Hill at Specific Performance. Kean Wong and Faridah Stephens at *Men's Review* helped give me an insight into the modern face of Malaysia, as did Karim Raslan and Johnni Wong. Special thanks to Katy Manuel, Philip Ross, Lindsay Tait and Gillian Sharp and all other fellow travellers I met along the way, and mercilessly interrogated. Finally, thanks to Donna for her support, her unique insight into KL, and for giving me a home when I needed it most.

PUBLISHING INFORMATION

This second edition published September 1997 by Rough Guides Ltd, 1 Mercer St, London WC2H 9QJ. Distributed by the Penguin Group:

Penguin Books Ltd, 27 Wrights Lane, London W8 5TZ
Penguin Books USA Inc., 375 Hudson Street, New York 10014, USA
Penguin Books Australia Ltd, 487 Maroondah Highway, PO Box 257, Ringwood, Victoria 3134, Australia
Penguin Books Canada Ltd, 10 Alcorn Avenue, Toronto, Ontario, Canada M4V 1E4
Penguin Books (NZ) Ltd, 182–190 Wairau Road, Auckland 10, New Zealand

Typeset in Linotron Univers and Century Old Style to an original design by Andrew Oliver.
Printed in the UK by Clays Ltd, St Ives PLC
Illustrations in Part One and Part Three by Edward Briant.
Illustrations on p.1 & p.595 by Henry Iles

Malaysia
Singapore & Brunei

THE ROUGH GUIDE

written and researched by

Charles de Ledesma, Mark Lewis and Pauline Savage

with additional accounts by

Simon Richmond

THE ROUGH GUIDES

THE ROUGH GUIDES

TRAVEL GUIDES • PHRASEBOOKS • MUSIC AND REFERENCE GUIDES

 We set out to do something different when the first Rough Guide was published in 1982. Mark Ellingham, just out of university, was travelling in Greece. He brought along the popular guides of the day, but found they were all lacking in some way. They were either strong on ruins and museums but went on for pages without mentioning a beach or taverna. Or they were so conscious of the need to save money that they lost sight of Greece's cultural and historical significance. Also, none of the books told him anything about Greece's contemporary life – its politics, its culture, its people, and how they lived.

So with no job in prospect, Mark decided to write his own guidebook, one which aimed to provide practical information that was second to none, detailing the best beaches and the hottest clubs and restaurants, while also giving hard-hitting accounts of every sight, both famous and obscure, and providing up-to-the-minute information on contemporary culture. It was a guide that encouraged independent travellers to find the best of Greece, and was a great success, getting shortlisted for the Thomas Cook travel guide award,

and encouraging Mark, along with three friends, to expand the series.

The Rough Guide list grew rapidly and the letters flooded in, indicating a much broader readership than had been anticipated, but one which uniformly appreciated the Rough Guide mix of practical detail and humour, irreverence and enthusiasm. Things haven't changed. The same four friends who began the series are still the caretakers of the Rough Guide mission today: to provide the most reliable, up-to-date and entertaining information to independent-minded travellers of all ages, on all budgets.

We now publish 100 titles and have offices in London and New York. The travel guides are written and researched by a dedicated team of more than 100 authors, based in Britain, Europe, the USA and Australia. We have also created a unique series of phrasebooks to accompany the travel series, along with an acclaimed series of music guides, and a best-selling pocket guide to the Internet and World Wide Web. We also publish comprehensive travel information on our two web sites:

http://www.hotwired.com/rough
and http://www.roughguides.com

HELP US UPDATE

We've gone to a lot of effort to ensure that this new edition of The Rough Guide to Malaysia, Singapore and Brunei is accurate and up-to-date. However, things change — places get "discovered", opening hours are notoriously fickle, restaurants and rooms raise prices or lower standards, extra buses are laid on or off. If you feel we've got it wrong or left something out, we'd like to know, and if you can remember the address, the price, the time, the phone number, so much the better.

We'll credit all contributions, and send a copy of the next edition (or any other Rough Guide if you prefer) for the best letters. Please mark letters: "Rough Guide Malaysia, Singapore and Brunei Update" and send to:
Rough Guides, 1 Mercer St, London WC2H 9QJ, or
Rough Guides, 375 Hudson St, 9th floor, New York NY 10014.
Or send email to: mail@roughguides.co.uk
Online updates about this book can be found on Rough Guides' website at
http://www.roughguides.com

THE AUTHORS OF THE ROUGH GUIDE TO MALAYSIA, SINGAPORE & BRUNEI

Freelance journalist **Charles de Ledesma** was born in Sarawak, and spent his first formative year there. Charles is an inveterate music enthusiast with a special expertise in Asian and Brazilian music, knowledge which he put to good use as a contributor to the *Rough Guide to World Music*. When not in London, Charles travels the globe in search of carnivals and music festivals.

After graduating from the University of Bristol in 1989, **Mark Lewis** spent a year teaching English in Singapore, during which time he regularly contributed book reviews to the *Singapore Straits Times*. Having spent the best part of the next year exploring Southeast Asia, he returned to England and began work on the first edition of this guide. Mark is also author of the *Rough Guide to Singapore*, and co-author of the *Rough Guide to Vietnam*.

After leaving university, **Pauline Savage** travelled extensively throughout Asia. Although she now works as a desk-bound editor in London, she maintains a keen interest in the area and returns whenever she has the opportunity.

READERS' LETTERS

Thanks from the authors of this book, to all the people who wrote in with comments on the previous edition of the guide, and suggestions for this edition:

Trish Adams, Paul & Loretta Arcangeli, Frances Beasley, Ingrid Beazely, D. G. Blakemore, Daniel Bleed, Douglas Brook, Catherine Bruzzone, Paul Calthorpe, Khian Chye, Anne Cody, Roy R. Crockett, Michel J. van Dam, Liam Fitzpatrick, Aleksandra Golebiowska, Lise Gunderson, Richard Henderson, John Hillman, Andrew Hutter, Graham Kenyon, David Leggett, Louise Nutt, Tina Ottman, Bernardo Pavolini, Mrs A. Peckham, Pauline Pow, Steve Prior, Renee Renjel, Martin Russell, Fiona Waters & Jonathan Cope, Rona Williams, Terence Yeung.

CONTENTS

Introduction x

PART ONE BASICS 1

Getting there from Britain 3
Getting there from Ireland 7
Getting there from North America 8
Getting there from Australia
  and New Zealand 13
Getting there from Southeast Asia 16
Visas and red tape 18
Insurance 21
Information and maps 22
Travellers with disabilities 25
Costs, money and banks 26
Health matters 29

Getting around 34
Accommodation 42
Eating and drinking 45
Communications: post, phones
  and the media 52
Police and emergencies 55
Peoples 56
Religions, temples and social conventions 62
Festivals 66
Opening hours and public holidays 69
Shopping and souvenirs 70
Outdoor pursuits 72

PART TWO THE GUIDE 77

- ## CHAPTER 1: KUALA LUMPUR AND AROUND 79–130

Arrival and information 83
City transport 86
Accommodation 88
The Colonial District 95
Chinatown 100
Little India 104

Eating 109
Drinking and nightlife 114
The arts and entertainment 115
Markets and shopping 117
Listings 118
Around KL 120

- ## CHAPTER 2: THE WEST COAST 131–203

Fraser's Hill 134
Cameron Highlands 137
Ipoh and around 147
Pulau Pangkor 152
Kuala Kangsar 157

Taiping and Maxwell Hill 160
Penang 163
Georgetown 166
Alor Setar 188
Langkawi 192

- ## CHAPTER 3: THE INTERIOR 204–239

Taman Negara 208
Kuala Lipis 225

Kenong Rimba State Park 228
Gua Musang 231

Jelawang Country Park 232
Tasek Chini 235

Tasek Bera 237

• CHAPTER 4: THE EAST COAST 240—281

Kota Bharu 241
Pulau Perhentian 253
Merang 257
Pulau Redang 258
Kuala Terengganu 259

Marang 266
Pulau Kapas 268
Rantang Abang 269
Cherating 272
Kuantan 274

• CHAPTER 5: THE SOUTH 282—336

Seremban 283
Sri Menanti 287
Melaka 290
Gunung Ledang 309

Johor Bahru 311
Mersing 317
Pulau Tioman and the Seribuat Archipelago 319
Endau Rompin National Park 332

• CHAPTER 6: SARAWAK 337—421

Kuching 344
Bako National Park 362
Batang Lupar and Batang Ai 368
Sibu 373
The Rajang 378
Kapit 380
Belaga 385

Mukah 388
Bintulu 390
Niah National Park 395
Miri 387
Marudi 406
Gunung Mulu National Park 407
The Kelabit Highlands 414

• CHAPTER 7: SABAH 422—476

Kota Kinabalu 426
Tunku Abdul Rahman Park 436
Keningau 440
Beaufort 444
Pulau Labuan 447
The Kudat Peninsula 452

Kinabalu National Park 454
Sandakan 460
Turtle Islands National Park 466
Danum Valley Conservation Area 471
Pulau Sipadan 472
Tawau 473

• CHAPTER 8: BRUNEI 477—498

Bandar Seri Begawan 483
Brunei Muara 492
Temburong district 494

Tutong 495
Belait district 496

Arrival and information 508
City transport 511
Accommodation 515
Downtown Singapore 522
The Colonial District   523
Orchard Road 534
Chinatown 537
The Financial District 545
Little India 547

Northern Singapore 553
Eastern Singapore 558
Western Singapore 561
Sentosa and the southern isles 566
Eating 569
Drinking and nightlife 583
The arts and culture 587
Shopping 590
Listings 592

PART THREE CONTEXTS 595

The historical framework 597
Cutting down the rainforest 613
Wildlife 617
Malaysian music 621

Books 625
Language 631
Glossary 635

Index 638

LIST OF MAPS

Malaysia, Singapore and Brunei	x–xi	Kuala Kangsar	158
Southeast Asia	17	Taiping	160
The Malaysian Train Network	36	Pulau Penang	164
Chapter divisions	77	Georgetown	167
Kuala Lumpur and around	80	Central Georgetown	170–171
Kuala Lumpur Transport System	87	Batu Ferringhi	183
Kuala Lumpur	92–93	Alor Setar	189
The Colonial District and Chinatown	100	Pulau Langkawi	193
Jalan Ampang and the Golden Triangle	103	Pantai Tengah and Pantai Cenang	196
Little India and Jalan Tar	106–107	Pantai Kok	198
Bangsar	108	**The Interior**	206–207
The West Coast	132–133	Jerantut	211
Fraser's Hill	135	Kuala Tahan & Resort	212
Cameron Highlands	138	Day trips and short trails	215
Tanah Rata	142	Taman Negara	219
Ipoh	148	Kuala Lumpur to the northeast coast	224
Pulau Pangkor	153	Kuala Lipis	226

Kenong Rimba State Park	229
Gua Musang	231
Temerloh	238
The East Coast	242–243
Kota Bharu	245
Around Kota Bharu	251
Pulau Perhentian	254
Kuala Terengganu	260
Marang	267
Pulau Kapas	269
Cherating	273
Kuantan	275
Pekan	280
The South	284–285
Seremban	286
Melaka	291
Central Melaka	297
Johor Bahru	312
Mersing	318
Pulau Tioman	320
Tekek and Air Batang	324
Salang	326
Juara	327
The Seribuat Archipelago	330
Sarawak	338–339
Kuching	345
Central Kuching	350

Bako National Park	363
Sibu	374
Kapit	381
Mukah	389
Bintulu	392
Niah National Park	395
Miri	398
Limbang	403
Gunung Mulu National Park	408
Kelabit Highlands	415
Sabah	423
Kota Kinabalu	427
Beaufort	445
Pulau Labuan	448
Mount Kinabalu	456
Sandakan	460–461
Tawau	474
Brunei	478–479
Bandar Seri Begawan	484
Singapore	500–501
The MRT system	512
Hotels around Bencoolen Street	517
Central Singapore	524–525
The Colonial District	527
Orchard Road	536–537
Chinatown	540–541
Little India and the Arab quarter	548–549

MAP SYMBOLS

▬▬	Railway	∴	Ruins	⅏	Marshland	
▭	Motorway	☥	Public Gardens	ⓘ	Tourist Office	
═══	Road	Λ	Campsite	⊠	Post Office	
-----	Path	☗	Refuge	ℭ	Telephone	
– – –	Ferry route	◉	Hotel	⅄	Golf Course	
———	Waterway	▣	Restaurant	■	Building	
▬▬▬	Chapter division boundary	◠	Cave	◲	Church	
▬·▬·▬	International borders	▲	Peak	⁺⁺⁺	Christian Cemetery	
▬▬▪	County boundary	⅏	Viewpoint	ᵞᵞᵞ	Muslim Cemetery	
⊠	Mosque	★	Bus Stop	▒	Park	
♠	Buddhist Temple	✕	Airport	▦	National Park	
♣	Hindu Temple	⅄	Lighthouse	▬	Pedestrianised area	
✿	Synagogue	⚓	Waterfall	▨	Area Market	
♜	Castle					

INTRODUCTION

A t first glance there seems little to link **Malaysia**, **Singapore** and **Brunei**, not even geographical proximity. It's almost two thousand kilometres from the Malay Peninsula, across the South China Sea, to the separate Malay state of Sabah at the northern tip of Borneo. And Bangkok is as close to Kuala Lumpur and Singapore as is the Bruneian capital Bandar Seri Begawan. But all three countries are born of a common history and ethnic composition that links the entire Malay archipelago, from Indonesia to the Philippines. Each became an important port of call on the trade route between India and China, the two great markets of the early world, and later formed the colonial lynchpins of the Portuguese, Dutch and British empires. However, Malaysia, Singapore and Brunei have only existed in their present form since 1963, when the federation of the eleven Peninsular states and the two Bornean territories of Sarawak and Sabah became known as Malaysia. Singapore, an original member of this union, left in 1965 to gain full independence, and Brunei, always content to maintain its own enclave in Borneo, lost its British colonial status in 1984.

Since then, Malaysia, Singapore and Brunei have been united by their **economic dominance** of Southeast Asia. While the tiny Sultanate of Brunei is locked into a paternalistic regime, using its considerable wealth to guarantee its citizens an enviable standard of living, the city-state of Singapore has long been a model of free-market profi-

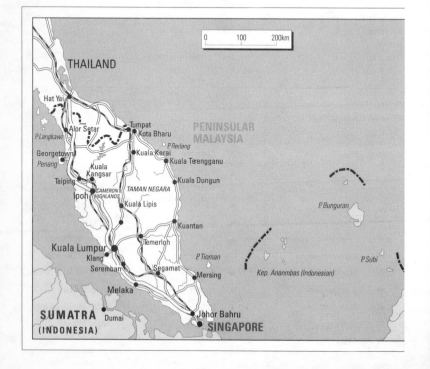

teering, transformed from a tiny port with no natural resources into one of the world's capitalist giants. Malaysia is the relative newcomer to the scene, publicly declaring itself well on the way to First World status in an ambitious manifesto, whose aim is to double the size of the economy and increase personal income four-fold by the year 2020, massively expanding tourism in the process. That Malaysia is taking giant steps towards realizing its ambitions is manifest in the fact that it has been awarded the 1998 Commonwealth Games.

Malaysia, Singapore and Brunei do not have the grand, ancient ruins of neighbouring Thailand. However, their rich **cultural heritage** is apparent, with traditional architecture and crafts thriving in the rural kampung (village) areas, and on display in cultural centres and at exhibitions throughout the modern cities. The dominant cultural force in the region has undoubtedly been the Malay adoption of **Islam** in the fourteenth century, while in Singapore, **Buddhism** has held sway since its foundation. But it's the commitment to religious plurality – most markedly in Malaysia and Singapore – that is so attractive, often providing startling juxtapositions of mosques, temples and churches. What's more, the region's diverse **population**, a blend of indigenous Malays (*bumiputras* or "sons of the soil"), Chinese and Indians, has spawned a huge variety of annual **festivals** as well as a wonderful mixture of **cuisines**.

As well as a rich cultural life, the region has astonishing **natural beauty**. With parts of Thailand starting to suffer from overexposure to tourism, it comes as a welcome surprise to discover Peninsular Malaysia's unspoiled east coast **beaches**, while both the Peninsula and the Bornean states have some of the world's oldest tropical **rainforest**. The national parks are superb for cave exploration, river-rafting and wildlife-watching,

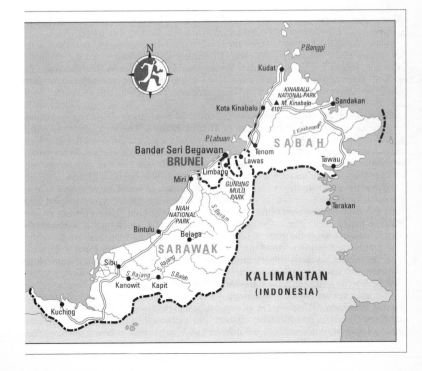

and provide challenging **treks**, including that to the peak of Southeast Asia's highest mountain, Mount Kinabalu in Sabah.

Malaysia

Malaysia's fast-growing capital, **Kuala Lumpur** (or just KL) makes much the same initial impression as does Singapore, with high-rise hotels and air-conditioned shopping malls, and characterful ethnic areas like Chinatown and Little India. The seat of government for the federation, KL is also the social and economic driving force of a nation eager to better itself, a fact reflected in the growing number of designer bars and restaurants in the city, and in the booming manufacturing industries surrounding it. A light rail transit system around KL is the latest sign that it is gearing up for a mass influx of visitors for the 1998 Commonwealth Games. But this is a city firmly rooted in tradition, where modern Malay executives might have a cellular phone to hand, but will never miss Friday prayers. And although the city is changing quickly – the **skyline** appears to be redesigned annually – life on the busy streets still has a raw feel, with markets and food stalls crowded in amongst new banks and businesses.

Less than three hours south of the capital lies the birthplace of Malay civilization, **Melaka**, a must on anybody's itinerary. Much further up the **west coast** is the first British settlement, the island of **Penang**, with old colonial buildings and a vibrant Chinatown district adorning its capital, **Georgetown**. In between KL and Melaka is a string of old tin-mining towns, such as **Ipoh** and **Taiping**, which provided the engine of economic change in the nineteenth century. For a taste of Old England, head for the hill stations of **Fraser's Hill**, **Cameron Highlands** and **Maxwell Hill**, where cooler temperatures and lush countryside provide ample opportunities for walks, rounds of golf and cream teas. North of Penang, there's a more Malay feel to the country, with **Alor Setar** forming the last stronghold before the Thai border. This far north, the premier tourist destination is **Pulau Langkawi**, a popular duty-free island.

Routes down the Peninsula's **east coast** are more relaxing, running past the sleepy kampungs of the mainland – **Merang**, **Cherating** and **Marang** – and the stunning islands of **Pulau Perhentian**, **Pulau Redang** and **Pulau Tioman**. The state capitals of **Kota Bharu**, near the northeastern Thai border, and **Kuala Terengganu**, further south, are showcases for the best of Malay traditions, craft production and performing arts.

Crossing the Peninsula's mountainous interior by road or rail allows you to venture into the unsullied tropical rainforests of **Taman Negara**. The park's four thousand square kilometres has enough to keep you occupied for weeks: trails, salt-lick hides for animal-watching, a high canopy walkway, limestone caves and waterfalls. Other interior routes can take in a ride on the **jungle railway**, which links east and west coasts, and visits to the southern **lakes**, which retain communities of indigenous Malays.

Across the sea from the Peninsula are the **Bornean** states of Sarawak and Sabah. For most travellers, their first taste of **Sarawak** is **Kuching**, the old colonial capital, and then the Iban **longhouses** of the Batang Ai and Batang Lupar river systems, or the Bidayuh longhouses close to the Kalimantan border. **Sibu**, much further to the north on the Rajang river, is the starting-point for the most exciting trips, to more authentic Iban longhouses. In the north of the state, **Gunung Mulu National Park** is the principal destination, its extraordinary razor-sharp limestone needles providing demanding climbing. More remote still are the rarely explored **Kelabit Highlands**, further to the east, where the mountain air is refreshingly cool and flora and fauna is abundant.

The main reason for a trip to **Sabah** is to conquer the 4101-metre granite peak of **Mount Kinabalu**, which is set in its own national park, though the lively modern capital **Kota Kinabalu** and its idyllic offshore islands have their moments, too. Beyond this, Sabah is worth a visit for its **wildlife**: turtles, orang-utans, proboscis monkeys and hornbills are just a few of the exotic residents of the jungle, while oceanic Pulau Sipadan has a host of sharks, fishes and turtles.

Singapore

For many first-time travellers to Asia, **Singapore** is the ideal starting point, with Western standards of comfort and hygiene, and dazzling consumerism, alongside traditional Chinese, Malay and Indian enclaves and the architectural remnants of the state's colonial past. Singapore also rightly holds the title of Asia's **gastronomic capital**, with snacks at simple hawker stalls, high tea at **Raffles**, and exquisite Chinese banquets united in their high quality. Most people find a few days in the metropolis is long enough to see the sights, fill shopping bags and empty pockets, before moving on.

Brunei

Few travellers venture into **Brunei**, which lies between Sabah and Sarawak, perhaps put off by the high transport and accommodation costs. Certainly you'd do better to wait until you reach the east Malaysian states if you intend to visit longhouses, forests or river systems. For those who do pass through, however, there are few more stirring sights than the spectacle of the main mosque in the capital **Bandar Seri Begawan**, towering over the water village below, which is culturally a million miles away from the state's latest attraction, the Disneyland-style **Jerudong Playground**.

When to go

Temperatures vary little in Malaysia, Singapore and Brunei, constantly hovering around 30°C (22°C in highland areas), while humidity is high all year round. The major distinction in the seasons is marked by the arrival of the **monsoon** (officially termed the "rainy season" to avoid deterring travellers), which affects the east coast of Peninsular Malaysia, the northeastern part of Sabah, Brunei, and the western end of Sarawak from November to February. The Peninsula's west coast experiences thunderstorms during the months of April, May and October. Monsoon brings heavy and prolonged downpours, sometimes lasting two or three hours and prohibiting more or less all activity for the duration; boats to most of the islands in affected areas will not attempt the sea swell during the height of the rainy season. It's worth noting, too, that tropical climates are prone to showers all year round, often in the mid-afternoon, though these short, sheeting downpours clear up as quickly as they arrive. In mountainous areas like the Cameron Highlands, the Kelabit Highlands and any of the hill stations, you may experience more frequent rain as the high peaks gather clouds more or less permanently. See the climate chart overleaf for more precise information about temperature and rainfall.

The **ideal time** to visit is during the first half of the year, between March and July, thereby avoiding the worst of the rains. Arriving just after the monsoon – say, in early March – affords the best of all worlds: an abundant water supply, verdant countryside and bountiful waterfalls. If you brave the heavy showers, the months of January and February are particularly rewarding for **festivals**, especially Chinese New Year and the Hindu celebration of Thaipusam. By sticking to Singapore and the west coast of the Peninsula, you not only miss the rains but, coincidentally, find yourself in the most important areas for Chinese and Hindu culture. Arrive in Sabah a little later, in May, and you'll be able to take in the Sabah Fest, a week-long celebration of Sabahan culture. In Sarawak, June's Gawai festival is well worth attending, when longhouse doors are flung open for two weeks of rice-harvest merry-making, with dancing, eating, drinking and music. Similarly, the pre-monsoon month of September, just around harvest time, is a fruitful time for the Malaysian east coast in terms of cultural activity.

CLIMATE CHART

Average daily temperatures (°C, max and min) and monthly rainfall (mm)

	Jan	Feb	March	April	May	June	July	Aug	Sept	Oct	Nov	Dec
Bandar Seri Begawan												
max °C	30	30	31	32	32.5	32	31.5	32	31.5	31.5	31	31
min °C	23	23	23	23.5	23.5	23.5	23.5	23.5	23	23	23	23
rainfall mm	133	63	71	124	218	311	277	256	314	334	296	241
Cameron Highlands												
max °C	21	22	23	23	23	23	22	22	22	22	22	21
min °C	14	14	14	15	15	15	14	15	15	15	15	15
rainfall mm	120	111	198	277	273	137	165	172	241	334	305	202
Kota Bharu												
max °C	29	30	31	32	33	32	32	32	32	31	29	29
min °C	22	23	23	24	24	24	23	23	23	23	23	23
rainfall mm	163	60	99	81	114	132	157	168	195	286	651	603
Kota Kinabalu												
max °C	30	30	31	32	32	31	31	31	31	31	31	31
min °C	23	23	23	24	24	24	24	24	23	23	23	23
rainfall mm	133	63	71	124	218	311	277	256	314	334	296	241
Kuala Lumpur												
max °C	32	33	33	33	33	32	32	32	32	32	31	31
min °C	22	22	23	23	23	23	23	23	23	23	23	23
rainfall mm	159	154	223	276	182	119	120	133	173	258	263	223
Kuching												
max °C	30	30	31	32	33	33	32	33	32	32	31	31
min °C	23	23	23	23	23	23	23	23	23	23	23	23
rainfall mm	683	522	339	286	253	199	199	211	271	326	343	465
Mersing												
max °C	28	29	30	31	32	31	31	31	31	31	29	28
min °C	23	23	23	23	23	23	22	22	22	23	23	23
rainfall mm	319	153	141	120	149	145	170	173	177	207	359	635
Penang												
max °C	32	32	32	32	31	31	31	31	31	31	31	31
min °C	23	23	24	24	24	24	23	23	23	23	23	23
rainfall mm	70	93	141	214	240	170	208	235	341	380	246	107
Singapore												
max °C	31	32	32	32	32	32	31	31	31	31	31	30
min °C	21	22	23	23	23	23	22	22	22	22	22	22
rainfall mm	146	155	182	223	228	151	170	163	200	199	255	258

THE

BASICS

GETTING THERE FROM BRITAIN

Most visitors to the region fly either to Kuala Lumpur (KL) or Singapore. There are regular daily flights to both cities from Britain and the cheapest return tickets start at around £420 in the low season (Jan–June). It's more expensive to reach East Malaysia – Sarawak or Sabah – since this involves a change of planes in KL or Singapore, though connections are at least very frequent. Direct services are more limited, and even pricier, to Brunei.

For all flights, you're best off booking through an established **discount agent**, which can usually undercut airline prices significantly: there's a list of reliable specialist agents on p.5; or consult the ads in the national Sunday papers (particularly the *Observer* and the *Sunday Times*), London's *Evening Standard* newspaper or *Time Out* magazine, or major regional newspapers and listings magazines, like the Manchester-based *City Life*. It's worth noting that the occasional ludicrously low ad price – £350 to KL – is more often than not a myth, designed to get you to call in the first place. If you are a **student or under 26**, you may be able to get further discounts on flight prices – consult Campus Travel or STA in the first instance – but for this part of the world, there's little difference between a youth fare and a regular discounted one.

If you're seeing Malaysia or Singapore as part of a longer Southeast Asian trip, then look at discounted flights to Bangkok in Thailand, which can be up to £50 cheaper than to KL; from Bangkok, you can then travel overland by train to Malaysia

and Singapore – see "Getting There From Southeast Asia" (p.16) for all the details. You might also consider a **Round-the-World ticket** (RTW), including KL and Singapore, which start at around £700. If this sounds too ambitious, you could at least enquire about **open-jaw tickets**, which allow you, say, to fly into Singapore, travel overland to Bangkok, and then fly home from there. There's an increasing number of **package holidays** and **adventure tours** available, ranging from fly-drive holidays to Malaysia and specialist trekking trips in Sarawak to city-based breaks in Singapore. Although usually not the cheapest way of travelling, these can be worthwhile if you have a specific interest or a tight itinerary (see p.6).

FLIGHTS TO MALAYSIA

The quickest flights to Malaysia are the thirteen-hour **non-stop scheduled services** to Kuala Lumpur **from London** (Heathrow) with either Malaysia Airlines (MAS) or British Airways. These, however, can be extremely expensive: the most flexible PEX fare (valid for a minimum of 7 days and a maximum of 6 months, refundable with the payment of a £50 cancellation fee) can run to as much as £899 return in high season (mid-July to Sept), around £100 or so cheaper during the rest of the year. You can buy less expensive scheduled tickets, called Superpex, for around £659–679 return, though these are much more restrictive, valid for only two months and allow no date change and no refund. Add-on fares are also available from **regional British airports** – MAS quotes a total fare of around £780 on the Manchester–London–KL route.

Most people, in fact, pay nothing like these prices for a ticket to Malaysia, since several airlines fly **indirectly** to KL, which is considerably cheaper but can take up to eight hours longer – it also, of course, offers the chance of a stopover in another country. Options include Air India (via Delhi), KLM (via Amsterdam), Qantas (via Singapore), Thai (via Bangkok) and Gulf Air (via Bahrain). Any reliable specialist agent can sell you a ticket on one of these routes, which usually cost £420–500, though you might find prices higher between June and September. In terms of price, there's little to choose between the airlines.

It's worth bearing in mind that KLM offers fares to KL from regional British airports such as Teeside, Aberdeen and Cardiff, via Amsterdam, for the same price as its London–KL deals.

If you're headed directly for **Sarawak** or **Sabah**, you have to get there via KL or Singapore, connecting with an MAS internal flight. Current MAS Superpex return fares from London are £670–790 to Kuching, £700–799 to Kota Kinabulu, and the total flight time can vary enormously, depending on what day (and what time of day) you fly. There are at least ten daily flights leaving Kuala Lumpur for Kuching and the best connection adds another 1 hour 40 minutes to your journey; Kota Kinabulu receives the same number of daily flights from KL, with a best journey time of 2 hours 30 minutes. However, as not all flights from KL to either destination are direct, you could be looking at more like three to four hours on top of the journey time from London. Although BA can quote you a through-fare from

Britain to Kuching or Kota Kinabulu, it's prohibitively expensive – it's much cheaper to buy your onward MAS ticket in KL. Alternatively, consider buying an MAS **Malaysia Pass** – only available in conjunction with an MAS ticket into or out of Malaysia; see "Getting Around" on p.39, for more details.

FLIGHTS TO SINGAPORE

Non-stop scheduled flights to Singapore **from London** Heathrow take thirteen hours, with either Singapore Airlines, British Airways, Royal Brunei or Qantas. These scheduled services are relatively expensive with the most flexible PEX tickets going for as much as £899 return in high season (mid-July to Sept). There are cheaper scheduled APEX fares for £659–679 return, but these carry the usual restrictions – a minimum stay of seven nights in Singapore, maximum of two months and no changes or refunds allowed.

AIRLINES

Air India, 17 New Bond St, London W1 (☎0171/491 7979). One flight a week to KL (with a 6-hr stopover in Delhi). Also three direct flights a week to Singapore.

Air Lanka, 22 Regent St, London SW1 (☎0171/930 4688). Four flights weekly to Singapore and twice a week to KL, all with overnight stops in Colombo.

British Airways, 156 Regent St, London W1 (☎0345/222111). Daily London to Singapore flights, plus five flights weekly to KL.

Finnair, 14 Clifford St, London W1 (☎0171/408 1222). Three flights a week from London to Singapore, via Helsinki.

Gulf Air, 10 Albermarle St, London, W1X 4LS (☎0171/408 1717). Several flights a week, routed through Bahrain, to Singapore.

KLM, 8 Hanover St, London W1 (☎0181/750 9000). Flies via Amsterdam at least three times a week to KL and once daily to Singapore.

Kuwait Airways, 16 Baker St, London, W1 (☎0171/412 0007). Three weekly flights to Singapore.

Malaysia Airlines (MAS), 191 Askew Rd, London W12 (☎0181/862 0800). The efficient Malaysian national airline, with two daily non-stop to KL (2 on Sat). Regular connections on to

Kuching, Kota Kinabulu and Penang; less frequently to Brunei.

Pakistan International Airways, 1–15 King St, London (☎0171/734 5544). Three flights a week to Singapore, via Karachi.

Qantas, 182 The Strand, London W1 (☎0345/747767). Daily non-stop flights to Singapore; three times a week these flights have connections to KL within two hours of landing.

Royal Brunei Airlines, 49 Cromwell Rd, London SW7 (☎0171/584 6660). Flies from London Heathrow to Brunei daily with short stops in Dubai and Singapore.

Singapore Airlines, 143–147 Regent St, London W1 (☎0181/747 0007). Twice-daily flights to Singapore on the comfortable national carrier, with some immediate connections to KL, Penang and Brunei. Break your journey in Bombay, and you can travel overland to another part of the region – say, Lahor or Katmandu – and push east from there.

Thai International, 41 Albermarle St, London, W1 (☎0171/499 9113). Daily flights to Bangkok, connecting with regional trips to KL and Singapore.

Turkish Airlines, 11 Hanover St, London W1 (☎0171/499 4499). Flies to Singapore three times a week, via Istanbul.

DISCOUNT FLIGHT AGENTS

Campus Travel, 52 Grosvenor Gardens, London SW1 (☎0171/730 3402); 541 Bristol Rd, Selly Oak, Birmingham (☎0121/414 1848); 61 Ditchling Rd, Brighton BN1 4SD (☎01273/570226); 37–39 Queen's Rd, Clifton, Bristol BS8 1QE (☎0117/929 2494); 5 Emmanuel St, Cambridge (☎0223/324283); 53 Forest Rd, Edinburgh (☎0131/668 3303); 166 Deansgate, Manchester (☎0161/2731721); 105–106 St Aldates, Oxford OX1 1DD (☎01865/242067). Student/youth travel specialists, with branches also in YHA shops and on university campuses all over Britain.

Council Travel, 28a Poland St, London W1 (☎0171/437 7767). Flights and student discounts.

South Coast Student Travel, 61 Ditchling Rd, Brighton (☎01273/570226). Student experts but plenty to offer non-students as well.

STA Travel, 74 Old Brompton Rd, London W7 (☎0171/937 9962); 25 Queen's Rd, Bristol (☎0117/929 3399); 38 Sidney St, Cambridge (☎01223/66966); 75 Deansgate, Manchester

(☎0161/834 0668); 88 Vicar Lane, Leeds (☎0113/244 9212); 36 George St, Oxford, OX1 2OJ (☎01865/792800); and offices at the universities of Birmingham, London, Kent and Loughborough. Discount fares, with particularly good deals for students and young people.

Trailfinders, 42–50 Earls Court Rd, London W8 (☎0171/938 3366); 194 Kensington High St, London W8 (☎0171/938 3939); 58 Deansgate, Manchester (☎0161/839 6969); 254–284 Sauchiehall St, Glasgow G2 3EH (☎0141/353 2224); 22–24 The Priory, Queensway, Birmingham B4 6BS (☎0121/236 1234); and 48 Corn St, Bristol BS1 1HQ (☎0117/929 9000). One of the best informed and most efficient agents dealing with Southeast Asia; good for RTW tickets, too.

Travel Bug, 125a Gloucester Rd, London, SW7 4SF (☎0171/835 2000); 597 Cheetham Hill Rd, Manchester (☎0161/721 4000). Large range of discounted tickets.

Qantas do sometimes have some better deals than this. Add-on costs from **regional British airports** are around £60 return to London.

You'll be able to pick up a ticket for much less than this from an agent – usually £420–500 (often a little more in July, August and December), with either Air India (via Delhi), KLM (via Amsterdam), Finnair (via Helsinki), Pakistan International Airways (via Karachi), Turkish Airlines (via Istanbul), Thai International (via Bangkok or Gulf Air (via Bahrain); Pakistan International Airways and Finnair are usually among the cheapest. Most of these indirect services will take around seventeen hours in total to reach Singapore, though the route can take as long as 22 hours.

FLIGHTS TO BRUNEI

The only airline that flies **directly to Brunei** is their national carrier, Royal Brunei Airlines, which flies daily **from London** Heathrow to the capital Bandar Seri Begawan, a fourteen-hour flight, with stops in Dubai and Singapore. Fares, even from a discount agent, are high – from £610 return low season to £750 high season – though the tickets are fairly flexible and allow changes and refunds. It's worth noting that flights in July and December are particularly busy. The only way to undercut

these prices is to pick up the cheapest possible fare to KL or Singapore and fly on from there with Royal Brunei, Singapore Airlines or MAS, though the second part of the journey is still going to cost at least another £150–200 return.

You can also fly from London to Bandar Seri Begawan with MAS, but the connections are poor and involve spending the night in KL. Singapore Airlines flights from London have better connections, with usually only a short wait in Singapore before you can catch an onward flight to Brunei. However, both the MAS or Singapore Airlines through-fares to Brunei are very expensive, and rarely worth considering.

RTW TICKETS

The cheapest **Round-the-World tickets** through STA start from around £700 in low season (Jan–June & Sept to early Dec). A typical one-year open ticket would depart and return to London, taking in Singapore, Bangkok, Bali, Sydney, Auckland, Tahiti, Los Angeles and New York, allowing you to cover the Singapore–Bagkok and Los Angeles–New York legs overland. Some of the agents listed above specialize in RTW tickets; remember that you should always confirm onward reservations at every stage. The Qantas

"Triangle" ticket, for about £630, is a return from London which includes three **Asian stops** – in Bangkok, Singapore and Hong Kong, taken in any order. For students and under-26s, Campus Travel has a similar deal for £589 during low season. Another option is an **open-jaw** ticket – flying into one airport, say KL, and making your own way overland to Singapore for the return leg. There are occasionally very good deals on a route like this, sometimes as low as £499, though £550–600 is more usual.

ORGANIZED TOURS AND PACKAGE HOLIDAYS

There is an increasing number of **organized tours** and **package holidays** available to both Singapore and Malaysia, and the main operators are listed in the box below. For **city breaks**, five nights in Singapore, including flights but with and room-only accommodation in a three-star hotel, go for around £600 (£800 in high season), a figure which rises to £800–1000 for two weeks.

SPECIALIST TOUR OPERATORS

Abercrombie & Kent Travel, Sloane Square House, Holbein Place, London SW1W 8NS (☎0171/730 9600). Experts in compiling top-of-the-range, tailor-made tours, including both city/resort trips and adventure itineraries. Nine-day self-drive tours start at £1392, while fourteen days in Sarawak and Sabah run to £2500.

Asia World Travel, third floor, Waterloo House, 11–17 Chertsey Rd, Woking, Surrey GU21 5AB (☎01483/730808). City-based holidays in Singapore, fly-drive holidays, trips to Taman Negara, Sarawak and Mount Kinabalu in Sabah, and tours of both west and east coast Malaysia. Recommended, but not budget-priced.

Bales Tours, Bales House, Junction Rd, Dorking, Surrey RH4 3HB (☎01306/885991). Especially recommended for guided tours in Sarawak and Sabah, as well as tailor-made trips incorporating the Eastern & Oriental trip from Singapore to Bangkok.

British Airways Holidays, Pacific House, Hazelwick Ave, Crawley, West Sussex RH10 1NP (☎01293/723170). Five-night city stays in Singapore, KL or Penang for £600–800.

Eastern & Oriental Express, Sea Containers House, 20 Upper Ground, London SE1 (☎0171/928 6000). Tours incorporating one of the most exclusive train journeys in the world (see p509), but at correspondingly high prices.

Exodus Expeditions, 9 Weir Rd, London SW12 0LT (☎0181/675 5550). Their seven-week overland Southeast Asia jaunt from Bangkok to Bali (around £1000 plus flights) incorporates three weeks in the Peninsula.

Explore Worldwide, 1 Frederick St, Aldershot, Hants, GU11 1LQ (☎01252/319448). Known for its adventure trips to Sarawak, where a two-week tour, including nights in a longhouse and white-water rafting, runs from £830 (excluding flights) on a twin-sharing basis: the "Head-hunters' trail" tour takes you to Mulu.

Hayes & Jarvis, Hayes House, 152 Kings St, London W6 0QU (☎0181/222 7822). Various Malaysian tours including visits to Taman Negara and Gunung Mulu parks.

Imaginative Traveller, 14 Barley Mow Passage, Chiswick, London W4 4PH (☎0181/742 3113). UK agents for Intrepid, offering small-group adventure holidays ranging from the fifteen-day "Malay Peninsula tour" (£600) to the more demanding eighteen-day "Head-hunter's trail" (£825) and the sixteen-day "Borneo Adventure" (£840); recommended.

Kuoni Worldwide, Kuoni House, Dorking, Surrey RH5 4AZ (☎01306/740888). Hotel-based city, Peninsular and East Malaysia tours.

Magic Of The Orient, 2 Kingsland Court, Three Bridges Rd, Crawley, West Sussex, RH10 1HL (☎01293/537700). Varied adventure tours in East Malaysia to suit most budgets; specialists in fly-drive packages on the Peninsula. Recommended.

MAS, 247 Cromwell Rd, London SW5 9GA (☎0171/341 2020). The Malaysian national airline operates seven-day fly-drive holidays from £350 per person, based on two people travelling together, including car and hotels (flight extra). Also arranges trekking trips or seven-day river rafting from £400 per person (flights extra).

Reliance Holidays Asia, 12 Little Newport St, London WC2 (☎0171/437 0503). Well represented in Malaysia and offering numerous tours of varying length.

Thomas Cook Holidays, PO Box 5, 12 Conigsby Rd, Peterborough PE3 8XP (☎01733/332255). Varied escorted and independent tours to all points in the region – fly-drives, city breaks and beach holidays.

Standard two-week **packages to Malaysia** usually include nights in KL, Cameron Highlands, Melaka, Penang and Kota Bharu, ending up (or starting) in Singapore, again for a price of just over £1000 in high season, perhaps £150–200 cheaper in winter.

Specialist operators can also arrange itineraries which include trekking through the rainforest, guided adventure tours in the national parks, and even a ride on the extremely swish Eastern & Oriental Express train from Singapore to Bangkok. All these tours tend to be expensive, but may include activities that would be very difficult or impossible to arrange for yourself. Operators like Explore Worldwide and Imaginative Traveller usually have competitive prices: Explore's "Borneo Adventure" is a two-week trip to Sarawak and Sabah, including visits to a longhouse and various national parks, costs £825 (excluding flights); Imaginative Traveller offers fourteen- to eighteen-day itineraries in Peninsular Malaysia, Sabah and Sarawak, that cost from £600 to £850. MAS, the Malaysian national airline, can arrange river-rafting trips starting at around £400 per person for six nights (air fares extra). If you're concerned about

the cost, you can usually arrange less expensive local tours to all the parks and sights on the ground **in Kuala Lumpur, Sabah and Sarawak** – local tour operators, details and prices are given where appropriate in the guide.

Several companies – including MAS – also offer **fly-drive** packages to Malaysia and Singapore, with the standard fourteen-day route starting in Singapore and visiting Melaka, Kuala Lumpur, the Cameron Highlands, Penang, Kota Bharu and Kuantan. An itinerary like this costs around £1000–2000, including return flight, the use of a small car and pre-booked accommodation in three-star hotels. Some companies – like Magic of the Orient and Asia Worldwide – are usually willing to organize a tailor-made fly-drive tour, which gives you the chance to get a little off the beaten track and visit the interior and Taman Negara. Again, two weeks, inclusive of flights, accommodation and car, starts at around £1000 per person.

If you just want to organize renting a car in Malaysia, and not the flights and accommodation, too, see "Getting Around" (p.40) for details of car rental.

GETTING THERE FROM IRELAND

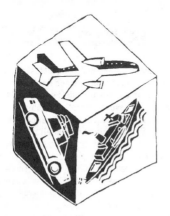

There are no non-stop flights from Ireland to Malaysia or Singapore, though both Singapore Airlines and MAS will quote you through-fares via London. Students, under- **26s and independent travellers should consult USIT (see box on p.8 for address) in the first instance, since they can usually offer the best deals.**

From Dublin to KL, the cheapest fares with BA/MAS range from IR£550–710, depending on the season; there's a IR£20 add-on for the first leg if you're starting from Shannon or Cork. The daily flights **to Singapore** from Dublin, Cork or Shannon with Aer Lingus/Singapore Airlines can usually be had for about IR£610 return, though an agent ought to be able to get you a slightly better deal travelling on airlines like Thai Airways or even Aeroflot, which operates a once-weekly service from Shannon to Singapore, via Moscow, with fares starting from around IR£540 return. **From Belfast** to KL or Singapore, flights to London with BA or British Midland can be combined with onward flights with MAS or Singapore Airlines for a total price of roughly £690–790, depending on the season.

AIRLINES

Aer Lingus, Northern Ireland reservations ☎0645/737 747; 40–41 O'Connell St, Dublin 1; 13 St Stephen's Green, Dublin 2 and 12 Upper St George's St, Dun Laoghaire all use centralized reservations at Dublin airport (☎01/844 4777); 2 Academy St, Cork (☎021/327 155); 136 O'Connell St, Limerick (☎061/474 239).

British Airways, 9 Fountain Centre, College St, Belfast BT1 6ET (☎01232/899 131 or 0345/222 111); reservations in the Republic ☎1800/626

747. BA don't have a Dublin office; *Aer Lingus* acts as their agents.

British Midland, Northern Ireland reservations ☎0345/554554; Nutley, Merrion Rd, Dublin 4 (☎01/283 8833).

MAS, 20 Upper Merrion St, Dublin (☎01/676 1561).

Ryanair, 3 Dawson St, Dublin (☎01/677 4422).

Singapore Airlines, third floor, 29 Dawson St, Dublin (☎01/671 0722).

AGENTS AND OPERATORS

Joe Walsh Tours, 34 Grafton St, Dublin 2 (☎01/671 8751); 69 Upper O'Connell St , Dublin 2 (☎01/872 2555); 8–11 Baggot St, Dublin 2 (☎01/676 3053); 117 St Patrick St, Cork (☎021/277 959). Discounted flight agent.

USIT, Fountain Centre, College St, Belfast BT1 6ET (☎01232/324073); 10–11 Market Parade,

Patrick St, Cork (☎021/270900); 33 Ferryquay St, Derry (☎01504/371888); Aston Quay, Dublin 2 (☎01/602 1600); Victoria Place, Eyre Square, Galway (☎091/565177); Central Buildings, O'Connell St, Limerick (☎061/415064); 36–37 Georges St, Waterford (☎051/872601). Ireland's main outlet for youth and student fares.

Alternatively, you could take advantage of the cheap air fares between Ireland and Britain, and pick up an onward flight from London with another airline (see "Getting There From Britain" above). Aer Lingus, British Midland or Ryanair fly from Dublin to London with fares rising from IR£80; from Belfast, there are British Airways or British Midland flights for around £80–100. Any travel agent can sell you a ticket on these routes.

GETTING THERE FROM NORTH AMERICA

The cheapest fares and the greatest choice of flights are to Singapore and Kuala Lumpur (KL). Other options include Penang (on the Malaysian west coast), Kuching (in Sarawak), Kota Kinabulu (in Sabah) and Bandar Seri Begawan (in Brunei).

Malaysia and Singapore are roughly halfway around the world from the East Coast, which means that whether you plan on flying east or west you're going to have a **long flight** with at least one stopover. However, the eastbound (transatlantic) route is more direct because the usual stopover cities aren't as far out of the way, which makes it quicker – about 21 hours' total travel time – and cheaper. From the West Coast, it's faster to fly westwards (over the Pacific) – Los Angeles to

Singapore can be done in as little as nineteen hours – although flying via Europe may not cost that much more, if that suits your itinerary better.

Air fares from North America to Southeast Asia are highest from around early June to late August, and again from early December to early January. All other times are considered low season. The price difference between high season and low season is only about $200 on a typical round-trip fare, but bear in mind that you have to

MAJOR AIRLINES IN NORTH AMERICA

Air Canada (☎1-800/776-3000; 1-800/555-1212 for local toll-free number). Non-stop four to five times a week (depending on the season) to Hong Kong or Seoul from Vancouver, Montréal and Toronto; arrangements with other carriers to Singapore and KL.

Air France (☎1-800/237-2747; Canada ☎1-800/667-2747). Daily non-stop to Paris from Toronto, Montréal, Chicago, New York, Los Angeles, San Francisco, Houston, Miami and Washington DC; connections to Singapore and KL.

Air India (☎1-800/237-2747). Daily non-stop to Paris from Toronto, Montréal, Chicago, New York, Los Angeles, San Francisco, Houston, Miami and Washington DC; connections to Singapore and KL.

Asiana Airlines (☎1-800/227-4262). Daily flights to Singapore via Seoul from Seattle, Los Angeles, San Francisco, Honolulu, Detroit and New York.

British Airways (☎1-800/247-9297). Daily non-stop service from eighteen US gateway cities. Also from Montréal, Toronto and Vancouver, with connections to Singapore and KL.

Canadian Airlines (☎1-800/426-7000). Daily flights from Montréal/Toronto and Vancouver to Hong Kong or Tokyo; agreements with other carriers to Singapore and KL. Twice-weekly direct flights to KL from Vancouver via Taipei.

Cathay Pacific (☎1-800/233-2742; Canada ☎1-800/555-1212). Daily flights to Hong Kong from Vancouver, Toronto, Los Angeles, New York, with connections to KL and Singapore.

China Air Lines (☎1-800/227-5118) Daily flights to Taipei from New York, Los Angeles, San Francisco, Honolulu and Anchorage, with connections to KL and Singapore.

Delta Airlines (☎1-800/241-4141). Daily direct service to Singapore from New York via Frankfurt.

EVA Airlines (☎1-800/695-1188). Daily flights to Singapore from New York, Seattle, San Francisco, Los Angles and Honolulu via Taipei.

Garuda Air (☎1-800/342-7832). Daily flights from Los Angles to Singapore and KL via Jakarta or Denpasar.

Japan Airlines (☎1-800/525-3663). Daily flights to Hong Kong from Los Angeles, San Francisco (16hr), New York (19hr) and Vancouver via Tokyo (15hr).

KLM (☎1-800/374-7747; Canada ☎1-800/361-5073). Daily non-stops to Amsterdam from eleven US cities and major Canadian cities; connections to KL and Singapore.

Korean Airlines (☎1-800/438-5000). Daily flights to Singapore and three times a week to KL via Seoul from New York, Los Angeles, San Francisco, Chicago, Dallas, Washington DC, Atlanta, Vancouver and Toronto.

Lufthansa (☎1-800/645-3880; Canada 1-800/563-5954). Daily flights to Frankfurt from many US cities and major Canadian cities, with connections to KL and Singapore.

Malaysia Airlines (☎1-800/552-9264). Daily flights from Los Angeles and twice-weekly from Vancouver to KL, connections to Singapore, Penang, Kuching, Kota K, Bandar Seri Begawan.

Northwest Airlines (☎1-800/447-4747). Daily flights to Singapore via Tokyo from New York, Los Angeles, San Francisco, Chicago, Seattle, Detroit and Minneapolis.

Philippine Airlines (☎1-800/435-9725). Los Angeles and San Francisco to Manila, with connections to KL and Singapore.

Pakistan International Airlines (PIA) (☎1-800/221-2552). Daily flights from New York, Chicago, Washington DC and Toronto to Karachi, with connections to Singapore.

Singapore Airlines (☎1-800/742-3333). Daily to Singapore from San Francisco, Los Angeles, Vancouver and New York, connections to KL, Penang, Kuching, Kota K, Bandar Seri Begawan.

Thai International (☎1-800/426-5204; Canada ☎1-800/668-8103). Four weekly flights to Hong Kong from Los Angeles with connections to KL, Penang and Singapore.

United Airlines (☎1-800/538-2929). Daily flights from major US and Canadian cities to Hong Kong and Tokyo and onto Singapore and KL.

DISCOUNT AGENTS, CONSOLIDATORS AND TRAVEL CLUBS IN NORTH AMERICA

Air Brokers International, 323 Geary St, San Francisco, CA 94102 (☎1-800/883-3273). Email: airbroker@aimnet.com

Council Travel Head Office, 205 E 42nd St, New York, NY 10017 (☎1-800/743-1823). Nationwide US student travel organization with branches in San Francisco, Washington DC, Boston, Austin, Seattle, Chicago and Minneapolis.

Discount Travel International Ives Bldg, 114 Forrest Ave, Suite 205, Narberth, PA 19072 (☎1-800/334-9294). 169 West 81st St, New York, NY 10024 (☎212/362-3636, fax 212-362-3236).Discount travel club.

Educational Travel Center, 438 N. Frances St Madison, WI 53703. (☎1-800/747-5551). Student/youth discounts.

Flight Centre, South Granville St, Vancouver, BC (☎604/739-9539). Discount airfares from Canada.

Gateway Express, 3488 Columbia Center, Seattle, WA (☎206/-624-3400). Discounts on flights to Asia.

High Adventure Travel Inc., 253 Sacramento Street, Suite 600, San Francisco, CA 94111. (☎1-800/428-8735). Email: airtreks@highadv.com. World Wide Web site: http://www.highadv.com

Last Minute Travel, 132 Brookline Ave, Boston, MA 02215 (☎1-800/LAST-MIN). Discount air fares, hotel packages.

Moment's Notice, 425 Madison Ave, New York, NY 10017 (☎212/486-0503). Discount travel club.

Now Voyager, 74 Varick St, Suite 307, New York, NY 10013 (☎212-431-1616, fax 212-334-5243). Courier flight broker.

Overseas Tours, 475 El Camino Real, Room 206, Millbrae, CA, 94030 (☎1-800/323-8777). Discount tickets and tours.

Pan Express Travel, 6 Wellesley St E., Suite 303, M41-186, Toronto, Canada (☎416/964-6888). Discount airfares.

STA Travel, 48 East 11th St, New York, NY 10003 (☎J-800/777-0112; nationwide). Worldwide specialist in independent travel with branches in the Los Angeles, San Francisco and Boston areas and offices in KL and Singapore.

Travel Cuts, 187 College St, Toronto, ON M5T 1P7 (☎416/979-2406). Canadian student travel organization with branches all over the country.

Worldtek Travel, 111 Water St, New Haven, CT 06511 (☎1-800/243-1723). Discount travel agency.

make your reservation further in advance during the high season or you could get stuck paying a higher fare than you'd counted on. Note that flying at weekends ordinarily adds about $100 to the round-trip fare; price ranges quoted in the sections below assume midweek travel.

Local **travel agents** should be able to access airlines' up-to-the-minute fares, although in practice they may not have time to thoroughly research all the possibilities – occasionally you'll turn up better deals by calling the **airlines** directly (be sure to ask about seasonal promotions).

Whatever the airlines have on offer, however, there are any number of specialist travel agents which will set out to beat it. These are the outfits you'll see advertising in the Sunday newspaper travel sections, and they come in several varieties. **Consolidators** buy up large blocks of tickets to sell on at a discount. They don't normally impose advance purchase requirements (although in busy periods you'll want to book ahead to be sure of getting a seat), but they do often charge

very stiff fees for date changes. Note that airlines generally won't alter tickets after they've gone to a consolidator, so you can only make changes through the consolidator. **Discount agents** also wheel and deal in blocks of tickets off-loaded by the airlines, but typically offer a range of other travel-related services such as insurance, youth and student ID cards, car rentals, tours and the like. They tend to be most worthwhile to students and under-26s. **Discount travel clubs**, offering money off air tickets, car rental and the like, are an option if you travel a lot. Most charge annual membership fees.

Don't automatically assume that tickets purchased through a travel specialist will be the cheapest available – once you get a quote, check with the individual airlines and you may be able to turn up an even better deal. Be advised also that the pool of travel companies is swimming with sharks – *never* deal with a company that demands cash up front or refuses to accept payment by credit card.

FLIGHTS TO MALAYSIA

Malaysia Airlines (MAS) and Singapore Airlines operate the only **direct services** between North America and Kuala Lumpur, and also have the only connections to other cities in Malaysia. MAS's flights depart from Los Angeles via Tokyo and Taipei. Singapore Airlines flies east out of New York (via Frankfurt) and west out of LA/San Francisco (via Tokyo, Taipei or Hong Kong). Both airlines can arrange connecting flights from other US or Canadian cities on other carriers.

Many other airlines can get you to Malaysia if you don't mind changing planes in their hub cities. Korean Airlines offers some of the **cheapest flights** to KL via Seoul, especially if you go through a discount travel agent. Korean offers flights from New York, Los Angeles, San Francisco, Chicago, Dallas, Washington DC and Atlanta. From the East Coast you can also fly with KLM, Lufthansa, British Airways, Air France and Air India. Westbound, Thai International, China Airlines, Cathay Pacific, EVA, Garuda, Philippines and Japan Airlines all make connections to KL.

The cheapest **fares** from New York, Miami, Chicago and Atlanta **to KL** run from about $875 in the low season to $1229 in the high season. From Houston you're looking at $949-$1229, whole from Los Angeles, San Francisco or Seattle fares run from $775 to $1034. Penang and Kuching are common-rated with KL, which means it doesn't cost any extra for the **internal** connecting flight if you book with MAS or Singapore Airlines. Fares to Kota Kinabulu run $100–$150 higher. **Airpasses** allowing up to five flights in Malaysia are available from MAS in conjunction with round-trip tickets. Prices are either $99 and $199, depending on the type of pass.

FROM CANADA

Canadian Airlines has daily flights from Montréal/Toronto and Vancouver to Hong Kong or Tokyo; with connecting flights onwards with other carriers to Singapore and KL. There are twice-weekly **direct flights** to KL from Vancouver via Tapei, and connections via China Air on other days. From Vancouver, Malaysia Airlines offers twice-weekly flights via Taipei. Korean Air also operates flights out of Vancouver and Toronto (via Chicago) to Seoul and onto Singapore and KL. Fares from Vancouver range from C$1000 to C$1200 and from Toronto and Montréal, C$1100 to C$1300.

FLIGHTS TO SINGAPORE

Singapore Airlines offers the most **frequent departures**, with direct flights from New York (via Frankfurt), and Los Angeles (San Francisco via Tokyo, Taipei or Hong Kong). Delta Airlines also offers a direct daily flight from New York via Frankfurt. Taking an indirect flight with another airline, or using a combination or airlines won't necessarily increase your journey time, and can often be a cheaper option. The cheapest flights are on Asiana Airlines and Korean Airlines, which make connections via Seoul from New York, Los Angeles, San Francisco, Seattle, Chicago, Dallas, Washington DC, Atlanta, Detroit and Honolulu. Many other airlines offer a **stopover** in Hong Kong or another Asian city for $50–75 extra on a round-trip fare. Singapore Airlines, for instance, charge $50 to stop in Hong Kong or Tokyo on routes continuing on to Singapore. Korean Air and Asiana allow a Seoul stopover for an extra $50. From New York, Miami, Chicago and Atlanta, the cheapest fares range from $875 in the low season to $1114 in the high season; from Houston $949–$1114; from Los Angeles, San Francisco and Seattle $775–$1005.

FROM CANADA

Canadian Airlines have daily flights from Montréal/Toronto and Vancouver to Hong Kong or Tokyo and connections with other carriers to Singapore. Singapore flies from Vancouver via Seoul. Korean Air also flies via Seoul from Vancouver and Toronto. Other airlines, such as EVA and Northwest, have connections via Taipei and Tokyo. Fares from Vancouver range from C$1000 to C$1200; from Toronto and Montréal; C$1100 to C$1300.

BRUNEI

Brunei is pretty much off the beaten track, and that's reflected in the air fares. Only MAS and Singapore Airlines fly directly there from North America. You could conceivably pick up a cheap ticket to London, Singapore or KL, and fly on from there with Royal Brunei Airlines, MAS or Singapore Airlines (see "Getting There from Britain" p.5), but discount agents are unlikely to be able to sell you a ticket for the final leg. Apex fares with MAS or Singapore from New York are in the $1400–1575 range; from Los Angeles, $1165–1350; from Vancouver, $1870–2000.

RTW AND COURIER FLIGHTS

Discounters such as Airbrokers International (☎1-800/883-3273) or High Adventure Travel Inc. (☎1-800/428-8735) can supply **Round-the-World** and **Circle-Pacific** fares with Singapore and Malaysia stopovers starting at around $1400 (add around $200 more for Canadian departures). A sample route might be New York–Los Angeles–Singapore–Bangkok–Hong Kong and back to New York. A good way to get familiar with routes and fares is to check out High Adventure's World Wide Web site (see box) which lists hundreds of possible combinations and sample fares.

Round-trip **courier flights** to Singapore and Kuala Lumpur cost $300–500, with last-minute specials booked within three days of departure as low as $150. For information about courier flights, contact The Air Courier Association, 191 University Blvd. Suite 300, Denver, 80206 (☎303/279-3600) or Now Voyager, 74 Varick St, Suite 307, New York, NY 10013 (☎212/431-1616, fax 334-5243).

NORTH AMERICAN TOUR OPERATORS

Abercrombie & Kent, 1520 Kensington Rd, Oak Brook, IL 60521 (☎1-800/323-7308). Deluxe tours built around the Eastern & Oriental Express.

Adventure Center, 1311 63rd St, Suite 200, Emeryville, CA 94608 (☎1-800/227-8747). Adventure tours and hikes combining Singapore, Malaysia and Thailand. Fourteen-day "Head-hunter's Trail" jungle tour, including Brunei, for $1335 plus airfare.

Adventures Abroad, Suite 2148-20800 Westminster Highway, Richmond BC, Canada V6V2W3 (☎1-800/665-3998); Email: adabroad@infoserve.net. Small-group adventure tours to Malaysia. Eight-day trip jungle trip, for $2995, including airfare from the west coast.

Asian Affair Holidays, Singapore Airlines (☎1-800/742-3333). Packages including airfare from the USA, hotels and sightseeing. Three-day Singapore or KL package, from $1200.

Boulder Adventures, PO Box 1279, Boulder, CO 80306. Southeast Asia specialists. Sixteen-day Borneo package $2695 plus airfare.

Cathay Pacific Holidays, (☎1-800/762-8181). City-break packages, discounts on hotels. Four-day Singapore package $299.

Cox & Kings, 511 Lexington Ave, Suite 355, New York, NY 10017 (☎1-800/999-1758). Deluxe sightseeing and wildlife tours.

Creative Adventure Club, PO Box 1918, Costa Mesa, CA 92628 (☎1-800/544-5088). Hiking/nature tours and scuba diving in Sarawak, Sabah and Peninsular Malaysian.

Earthwatch, 680 Mt. Auburn St Watertown, MA 02272-9104. (☎1-800/776-0188). Volunteer conservation programs. Ten-day research trip in Brunei's rainforest canopy costs $2070 plus airfare.

Japan & Orient Tours, 3131 Camino del Rio North, Suite 1080, San Diego, CA 92108 (☎1-800/377-1080). Regional tours, KL/Penang/Singapore city breaks, cruises, fly-drives, E&O Express.

Journeyworld International, 119 West 57th St, Penthouse North, New York, NY 10019 (☎1-800/635-3900). General Malaysian vacations.

Nature Expeditions International, 474 Wilamette St, Eugene, OR 97440 (☎503/484-6529). Sarawak/Sabah wildlife tours.

Overseas Adventure Travel, 349 Broadway, Cambridge, MA 02139 (☎1-800/221-0814). Trekking in Sarawak and Sabah.

Pacific Bestour, 228 River Vale Rd, River Vale, NJ 07675 (☎1-800/688-3288). Regional tours, Singapore city breaks, E&O Express.

Pacific Holidays, 2 West 45th St Suite 1101, New York, NY 10036-4212 (☎1-800/355-8025). Inexpensive group tours. Eight-day Singapore trip for $1580 including airfare from the West Coast.

Saga Holidays, 222 Berkeley St, Boston, MA 02116. (☎1-800/234-8220). Inexpensive coach tours. Ten-day "Orient Tour" including Singapore costs $2199 including airfare from the USA.

TBI Tours (☎415/668-0964). Allied with Northwest, JAL, United Air and Malaysia Airlines; offers a variety of packages in Singapore and Malaysia. Seven-day Singapore tour, $1520 including airfare from the West Coast.

United Vacations, United Airlines (☎1-800/835-7253). Escorted tours, short city stay packages with purchase of UA ticket. Three-day Singapore package for $274.

Vacationland, 150 Post St, Suite 680, San Francisco, CA 94108 (☎1-800/245-0050). Malaysia Airlines' tour arm; extensive range of city breaks, fly-drives, regional tours, sightseeing add-ons, plus golf itineraries.

PACKAGES AND ORGANIZED TOURS

Tours in Malaysia and Singapore range from sweaty jungle treks through to five-star city breaks and sightseeing excursions to opulent splendour aboard the **Eastern & Oriental Express** train. Inevitably, these packaged journeys are more expensive than they would be if done independently, but, particularly if you're short of time, they can be worth it for a hasslefree exprience.

Including airfare, a two-week adventure vacation taking in Malaysian Borneo (Sabah and Sarawak) will cost around $3000. A two-week package tour including Kuala Lumpur, the Malay Peninsula and Singapore will run to around $2300 including airfare. A week in Singapore, including airfares, hotels and some sightseeing, will cost around $1300. Three and four-day independent travel packages, including hotels, airport transport, some meals and some sightseeing, start at around $290. The Eastern & Oriental train (see p.37 for more information) is the ultimate in expense – tours, which invariably throw in several days' worth of luxurious side trips along with the two-night train journey from Singapore to Bangkok, start at $1300 per person. North American operators don't really offer budget tours, although **fly-drive** packages, starting at around $1800, at least allow you to keep costs down by giving you more independence.

Note that your local travel agent should be able to book any tour for you at no additional cost. For a list of North American tour companies, see box.

GETTING THERE FROM AUSTRALIA & NEW ZEALAND

or flying somewhere else first – like Thailand or Indonesia – and continuing **overland** from there.

All the **fares** quoted below are for travel during low or shoulder seasons, and exclude airport taxes; flying at peak times (primarily Dec to mid-Jan) can add substantially to these prices. Whatever kind of ticket you're after, your first call should be one of the **specialist travel agents** listed in the box below, which can fill you in on all the latest fares and any special offers. If you're a **student** or **under 26**, you may be able to undercut some of the prices given here; STA is a good place to start.

FLIGHTS

There's a fair amount of choice of flights to **Malaysia, Singapore and Brunei from Australia or New Zealand, with each country regularly served by its own national airline, Malaysian Airlines (MAS), Singapore Airlines or Royal Brunei, as well as by other carriers.**

Increased competition on the Singapore routes means that this is generally the cheapest gateway to the region, with the most frequent flights. Many people plan to see Malaysia and Singapore as part of a longer trip, in which case you'll either be looking at a **Round-the-World** (RTW) ticket

MAS, Singapore Airlines and Qantas all have regular services **from Australia** to Malaysia: prices for a return flight **to Kuala Lumpur** from Sydney or Melbourne are around A$1100, with slightly cheaper fares (A$999) for stays up to a maximum of 35 days; leaving from Perth, fares are about A$200 less. Flying **into Singapore** tends to be cheaper, and you can always take the train into Malaysia (Singapore to KL only takes six hours – see "Getting Around", p.35, for details). Fares with the major airlines range from A$849 to 949, but rock-bottom return fares start from A$549 for flights from Perth, rising to around A$600 for Sydney departures, and A$770 for flights from

Air New Zealand, 5 Elizabeth St, Sydney (local-call rate ☎13 2476); Level 18, 1 Queen St, Auckland (☎09/366 2400).

British Airways, Level 26, 201 Kent St, Sydney (☎02/9258 3300); 154 Queen St, Auckland (☎09/356 8690).

Egypt Air, 630 George St, Sydney (☎02/9267 6979). No NZ office.

Garuda, 55 Hunter St, Sydney (☎02/9334 9944); 120 Albert St, Auckland (☎09/366 1855).

Malaysian Airlines, 16 Spring St, Sydney (local-call rate ☎13 2627); Level 12, Swanson Centre, 12–26 Swanson St, Auckland (☎09/373 2741).

Merpati, 12 West Lane, Darwin (☎08/8985 3268). No NZ office.

Qantas, 70 Hunter St, Sydney (local-call rate ☎13 1211); Qantas House, 154 Queen St, Auckland (☎09/357 8900).

Royal Brunei Airlines, Suite 5208, MLC Centre, 19 Martin Place, Sydney (☎02/9223 1566); Unit 9, 25 Mary St, Brisbane (☎07/3221 7757). No NZ office.

Singapore Airlines, 17–19 Bridge St, Sydney (local-call rate ☎13 1011); Lower Ground Floor, West Plaza Building, corner of Customs and Albert streets, Auckland (☎09/379 3209).

Thai Airways, 75–77 Pitt St, Sydney (☎02/9844 0999; toll-free ☎1-800/422 020); Kensington Swan Building, 22 Fanshawe St, Auckland (☎09/377 3886).

Anywhere Travel, 345 Anzac Parade, Kingsford, Sydney (☎02/9663 0411).

Asian Travel Centre, 126 Russell St, Melbourne (☎03/9654 8277).

Brisbane Discount Travel, 260 Queen St, Brisbane (☎07/3229 9211).

Budget Travel, 16 Fort St, Auckland; other branches around the city (☎09/366 0061, toll-free ☎0800/808 040).

Flight Centres Australia: Level 11, 33 Berry St, North Sydney (☎02/9241 2422); Bourke St, Melbourne (☎03/9650 2899), plus other branches nationwide. New Zealand: National Bank Towers, 205–225 Queen St, Auckland (☎09/309 6171); Shop 1M, National Mutual Arcade, 152 Hereford St, Christchurch (☎03/379 7145); 50–52 Willis St, Wellington (☎04/472 8101); other branches countrywide.

J.W. Asean Travel Specialists, Suite 206, 2 Pembroke St, Epping, Sydney (☎02/9869 5199).

Northern Gateway, 22 Cavenagh St, Darwin (☎08/8941 1394).

San Michele Travel, 81 York St, Sydney (☎02/9299 1111, toll-free ☎1-800/222 244); branches in Melbourne and Perth.

Singapore Travel, 141 Queen St Mall, Brisbane (☎07/3221 4599).

STA Travel, Australia: 702–730 Harris St, Ultimo, Sydney; 256 Flinders St, Melbourne; other offices in state capitals and major universities (nearest branch ☎13 1776; telesales ☎1300/360 960). New Zealand: Travellers' Centre, 10 High St, Auckland (☎09/309 0458); 233 Cuba St, Wellington (☎04/385 0561); 90 Cashel St, Christchurch (☎03/379 9098); other offices in Dunedin, Palmerston North, Hamilton and major universities. World Wide Web site: www.statravelaus.com.au; Email: traveller@statravelaus.com.au.

Thomas Cook, Australia: 321 Kent St, Sydney; 257 Collins St, Melbourne; branches in other state capitals (all branches local-call rate ☎13 1771, or call Thomas Cook direct toll-free ☎1-800/064 824) New Zealand: 96–98 Anzac Ave, Auckland (☎09/379 3920).

Tymtro Travel, 314 Victoria Ave, Chatswood, Sydney (☎1300/652 969).

Brisbane, Melbourne and Adelaide. The real bargains are often with Middle Eastern airlines keen to fill flights for the leg to Singapore before they head for home; Egypt Air, for example, flies twice a week from Sydney for $A589. Royal Brunei flies to Singapore or Kuala Lumpur **via Brunei** from Brisbane (return fares start at $840), Perth and Darwin (A$750–800).

From New Zealand, Air New Zealand, British Airways, Garuda, Qantas and Singapore Airlines, among others, fly direct to Singapore, with fares starting at NZ$1210. Fares to Kuala Lumpur are

NZ$50–100 more, while a side-trip to Brunei adds around NZ$550 to the total cost.

Finally, if you're flying with MAS, it's worth remembering the **Malaysia Pass**, which allows discounted flights within Malaysia when booked with your international ticket (see "Getting Around" on p.39 for more).

OPEN-JAW AND RTW TICKETS

An **open-jaw ticket**, which enables you to fly into Kuala Lumpur and out of Singapore, saves on backtracking and doesn't add hugely to the cost – around A$1120 out of Sydney, flying with Qantas.

Given enough time to make the most of them, **Round the World** tickets offer greater flexibility and represent good value compared to straightforward return flights. Virtually any combination of stops is possible, as more and more airlines enter into partnerships to increase their global coverage: a sample itinerary from Adelaide to Singapore to London to New York to Denver to Los Angeles to Auckland to Adelaide costs from A$2180; and a round trip to Brunei from Singapore or Kuala Lumpur will add an extra A$450 to the basic price. Ultimately your choice will depend on where you want to travel before or after Malaysia and Singapore – again, a good travel agent is your best ally in planning a route to suit your preferences.

OVERLAND OPTIONS

If you're determined to arrive overland, flying to **Thailand** is a possibility, though fares can be higher than for comparable direct flights, especially those to Singapore. The cheapest return flights to Bangkok begin at around A$700 from Sydney or Brisbane, A$770 from Melbourne, A$859 from Perth, A$920 from Adelaide – though these tend to impose restrictions on your length of stay or carry other conditions; more flexible fares with the major airlines such as ANZ or Thai will be nearer the A$1000 mark. Return flights from Auckland start at NZ$1310. Coming through **Indonesia**, the cheapest fares are on the twice-weekly Merpati flight from Darwin to Timor (A$350 return), where you're poised for some Indonesian island-hopping, but services to other Indonesian gateways such as Denpasar or Jakarta are back up in the region of A$750 from Perth, A$900–1000 from the east coast of Australia, and NZ$1225 from New Zealand.

See "Getting There from Southeast Asia" (pp.16–18) for details of your options from Bangkok and the Indonesian archipelago.

PACKAGES, CITY BREAKS AND SPECIALIST TOURS

If you can only manage a short visit and are happy to base yourself in one city or resort, package holidays can be an economical and hassle-free way of sampling the delights of this part of Asia. Inexpensive five-night **packages** in Penang from eastern Australia start at $979 through STA Travel, including return airfare, transfers, twin-share accommodation and breakfast. **City stays**, **fly-drive** options and **coach tours** are offered by a whole host of operators, including Ansett Australia Holidays, Creative Tours, Asian Explorer Holidays and Qantas Holidays; most can also arrange add-on trips to resort islands, Sabah and Sarawak, cruises from Singapore, and can book accommodation in regional Malaysia. Sample city-break prices are four nights in Singapore for A$1099–1400, or seven nights in Kuala Lumpur (A$1149–1215), with the exact price depending on the level of accommodation chosen; two-night extensions to Langkawi or Tioman cost A$267–300; to Sarawak, approximately A$400; and to Sabah, A$650 (all including air transfers from KL). Package holidays departing from Perth or Darwin, where available, generally cost about A$200 less per person.

Extended journeys through the region cater to all tastes – from those in search of thrills and adventure to those who simply prefer to tour in a group. Operators such as Explore Worldwide (book though Adventure World – see box below) and Intrepid have a range of itineraries covering Peninsular Malaysia, Singapore and Brunei. The options with Explore run from thirteen days taking in Langkawi, Penang, the Cameron Highlands, Melaka and Singapore (A$1270, airfare extra) to seventeen days in Sabah and Sarawak, including some trekking and the chance to stay in a long-house (A$1760, again excluding airfare from Australia). Intrepid offers comparable trips, plus some longer jaunts such as 29-day treks in Borneo (A$3000, including all airfares); they can also make "land-only" arrangements for independent travellers (for example, 8 days from Penang to Singapore for A$495) and homestays with Malaysian families (from A$195 for 3 days).

SPECIALIST TOUR OPERATORS

Most travel agents offer a range of holidays and tours, so check out those listed in the box on p.14 as well as the following:

Adventure World, 73 Walker St, North Sydney (☎02/9956 7766, toll-free ☎1-800/221 931); Level 3, 33 Adelaide St, Brisbane (☎07/3229 0599); 8 Victoria Ave, Perth (☎08/9221 2300); 101 Great South Rd, Remuera, Auckland (☎09/524 5118).

Ansett Australia Holidays, 19 Pitt St, Sydney, and branches throughout Australia (local-call rate ☎13 1767); 2/50 Grafton Rd, Auckland (☎09/796 409).

Asian Explorer Holidays, 6 Watts St, Box Hill, Melbourne (☎03/9245 0777).

Creative Tours, Level 3, 55 Grafton St, Woollahra, Sydney (☎02/9386 2111).

Exodus Expeditions, Suite 5, Level 5, 1 York St, Sydney (☎02/9251 5430, toll-free ☎1-800/800 724).

Intrepid, 246 Brunswick St, Melbourne (☎03/9416 2655).

Qantas Holidays, 141 Walker St, North Sydney (toll-free ☎1-800/808 506).

GETTING THERE FROM SOUTHEAST ASIA

If you are not too restricted by time, it can be cheaper to get a flight to another Southeast Asian city and then continue your journey from there. Flights to Bangkok can often be particularly good value, and from there, as well as from Jakarta and Hong Kong, there are frequent daily flights to KL, Singapore and other local destinations. While obviously more time-consuming, its cheaper to travel overland by train from Bangkok – the main line runs down the west coast of Malaysia (for Penang and KL) and ends in Singapore.

There are, of course, other possible routes into either Malaysia or Singapore from Southeast

Asia: by ferry, bus or taxi from various southern Thai towns, by sea from points in Sumatra (Indonesia), or by road from Indonesian Kalimantan to Sarawak. There's a round-up below of the most popular border crossings, and details of the routes are included in the text throughout.

FROM THAILAND

The most popular way of getting to Malaysia from Thailand is to catch the **train** from Bangkok. Trains leave Bangkok's Hualamphong station (book at least a day in advance at the station ticket office) four times a day for **Hat Yai**, where the line divides. One daily train goes south via the Malaysian border town of Padang Besar (see p.35) and on to Butterworth (p.37) for the Malaysian **west coast route**, which continues on to KL (24hr; around £50/US$75 one-way) and Singapore (28hr; £60/US90 one-way). Two daily trains from Hat Yai follow an **easterly route** to the Thai border town of Sungei Golok, from where it's a short walk to the Malaysian border crossing at Rantau Panjang (see p.35) – from there, you can catch a local bus or taxi the 30km to Kota Bharu – the total journey from Bangkok taking around twenty hours and costing £45/US$70.

There are also frequent **flights from Bangkok** on Thai Airways International to KL (2 daily; one-way £140/US$224), Penang (daily; £109/US$174), Singapore (3 daily; £248/US$396) and Brunei (3 weekly; £220/US$330); but no direct flights to

Sarawak or Sabah. **From Phuket**, you can fly to Penang (3 weekly; £44/US$77), KL (3 weekly; £80/US$128) and Singapore (1 daily; £160/US$256); while **from Hat Yai**, there are services to KL (2 weekly; £66/US$105) and Singapore (1 daily; £157/US$251). Other services from Bangkok are with MAS to Kuala Lumpur and Penang.

Tickets are available from **travel agents** in Bangkok; students and under-26s will probably be able to undercut these prices by booking through STA, which has an office in the Thai Hotel, 78 Prajathipatai Rd, Banglamphu (☎02/281 5314); or try Trade Travel Service, c/o Vieng Thai Hotel, 42 Thani Rd, Banglamphu (☎02/281 5788).

By **ferry**, there are scheduled services from the most southwesterly Thai town of **Satun** to the Malaysian west coast towns of Kuala Perlis (boats leave when full; 30min) and Langkawi (3 daily; 1hr). Other options include the once-daily ferry from the Thai resort of **Phuket**: to Penang. The easiest **road access** from Thailand is via the rail junction town of **Hat Yai**, from where buses and shared taxis run regularly to Butterworth and Penang, around a six-hour trip. From the interior Thai town of **Betong** on route 410 there's a road across the border to the Malaysian town of Keroh, which provides access to Butterworth and the west coast; shared taxis run along the route. There's also an east coast route from the southeastern Thai town of **Ban Taba**, from where taxi is the only efficient means of transport for the few kilometres to Kota Bharu.

SOUTHEAST ASIA

FROM INDONESIA

There are frequent Garuda flights from **Jakarta** to either Singapore (1 daily; 3hr) or KL (1 daily; 3hr); as well as services from **Pontianak** to Kuching (1 daily; 1hr) and Singapore, and from **Medan** to Penang (1 daily; 20min) and Singapore (3 weekly; 2hr).

A **ferry** service operates four times a week from **Medan** in northern Sumatra to Penang (4hr) and, from **Dumai** further south, there's a daily service to Melaka (2hr 30min). There are also shorter thirty-minute services twice-daily from **Pulau Batam** in the Riau archipelago (accessible by plane or boat from Sumatra or Jakarta) to either Johor Bahru (p.311) or Singapore; and a minor ferry crossing from **Tanjung Balai** (3 weekly; 45min) to Kukup (see p.311), just to the southwest of JB.

By **road**, it's possible to reach **Sarawak** from Indonesian Kalimantan on various routes, the easiest the nine-hour bus trip from the western city of Pontianak to the border town of Entikong; from here, you cross the border to the Sarawak town of Tebedu (p.368) and then travel onwards another four hours to the Sarawak capital, Kuching (p.344) by bus. There's a once-daily SJS bus company departure from Pontianak at 6am (around £12/US$18), arriving at the border at 3pm with ample time to catch an onward bus to Kuching. Alternatively, there's a once-daily through-bus through to Kuching (£25/US$40) run by the Damry company; information and tickets for both departures from the ticket offices at Pontianak bus station at Batu Layang.

Finally, there's a daily **ferry** from Tarakan in eastern Kalimantan to **Tawau** (p.473) in Sabah, which costs around £22/US$35 and takes four hours or so; or more expensive **flights** from Tarakan to Tawau depart three times a week.

FROM HONG KONG

There are daily non-stop **flights** from Hong Kong to KL on Cathay Pacific and MAS, and up to six daily flights to Singapore with Cathay Pacific and Singapore Airlines. Fares aren't particularly good value, but for the best deals, visit one of the following **travel agents** in Hong Kong: China Travel Service, fourth floor, CTS House, 78-83 Connaught Rd, Central (☎2853 3533); or Hong Kong Student Travel, tenth floor, Room 1021, Star House, Salisbury Rd, Tsim Sha Tsui (☎730 3269).

VISAS AND RED TAPE

Below are detailed the entry requirements for Malaysia, Singapore and Brunei; in most cases visas aren't required for visits of less than three months. If you're unsure about whether or not you require a visa, or any other documentation, your first call should be to the relevant embassy or consulate in your own country, whose main offices are given below.

MALAYSIA

British citizens and those of the Republic of Ireland, Australia, New Zealand, Canada, Switzerland, the United States and the Netherlands do not need a **visa** to enter Malaysia. Citizens of most European countries need visas only for visits of more than three months (which cost $20); French nationals require a visa for stays of over one month. Japanese citizens will need to apply in advance for a visa if their visit exceeds three months, and will have to pay $50 per month. All other nationals should

MALAYSIAN EMBASSIES AND CONSULATES ABROAD

Australia 7 Perth Ave, Yarralumla, Canberra, ACT 2600 (☎06/2731543).

Brunei 437 Kg Pelambayan, Jalan Kota Batu, PO Box 2826, Bandar Seri Begawan (☎02/228410).

Canada 60 Boteler St, Ottawa, Ontario KlN 8Y7 (☎613/237 5182).

Indonesia 17 Jalan Imam Bonjol, 10310 Jakarta Pusat (☎021/336438).

Ireland No office.

Netherlands Runtenburweg 2, 2517 KE, The Hague (☎070/3506506).

New Zealand 10 Washington Ave, Brooklyn, Wellington (☎04/852439).

Singapore 301 Jervois Rd, Singapore 1024 (☎2350111).

Thailand 35 South Sathorn Rd, Bangkok 10120 (☎02/2861390).

UK 45 Belgrave Square, London SW1X 8QT (☎0171/235 8033).

USA 2401 Massachusetts Ave NW, Washington DC 20008 (☎202/328 2700); Two Grand Central Tower, 140 45th St, 43rd Floor, New York, NY 10017 (☎212/490 2722); 350 Figueroa St, Suite 400, World Trade Centre, Los Angeles, CA 90071 (☎213/621 2991).

contact their local Malaysian embassy for details of visa requirements. **Passports** must be valid for three months beyond your date of departure, and for six months if you're going to Sabah or Sarawak.

On **arrival**, you're stamped in for two months. Should you need to extend your stay, it's a straightforward matter taken care of at immigration department offices in (among other places) Kuala Lumpur (p.79), Penang (p.163) and Johor Bahru (p.311) – though from JB it's simpler just to cross into Singapore and back. In theory, visitors can extend their stay for up to six months in total, although this is subject to the discretion of the official you encounter. In practice, there's rarely a problem with extending your stay to three months.

Tourists travelling from the Peninsula to **East Malaysia** (Sarawak and Sabah) must carry a valid passport and be cleared again by immigration; visitors to Sabah can remain as long as their original two-month stamp is valid. Visitors to Sarawak – whether from Sabah or from the mainland – will receive a new, one-month stamp which is rarely extendable. If you start your trip in Sarawak and then fly to the mainland, be sure to go to the immigration office in Kuching (p.344) and have your passport stamped with the usual two-month pass. You'll also need special **travel permits** for certain trips within Sarawak – where applicable details are given in the text.

Malaysia's **duty-free** allowances let you bring in 200 cigarettes, 50 cigars or 250g of tobacco, and wine, spirits or liquor not exceeding 75cl. In addition, no duty is paid on electrical goods, cameras, watches, cosmetics and perfumes. There's no customs clearance for passengers travelling from Singapore or Peninsular Malaysia to East Malaysia, nor for people passing between Sabah and Sarawak.

DRUGS: A WARNING

In Malaysia, Singapore and Brunei, the possession of drugs – hard or soft – carries a hefty **prison sentence** and trafficking is punishable by the **death penalty**. If you are caught smuggling drugs into or out of the country, at the very best you are facing a long stretch in a foreign prison; at worst, you could be hanged. This is no idle threat, as the Malaysians have, in the recent past, shown themselves to be prepared to pass the death sentence on Western travellers. The simple answer, of course, is not to have anything to do with drugs in any of these countries; and never agree to carry anything through customs for a third party.

SINGAPORE

British citizens, and those of the Republic of Ireland, the United States, Canada and New Zealand don't need a **visa** to enter Singapore. Nationals of Australia and most major European countries and Japan need visas only for stays of over three months. Regulations change from time to time, though, so check with the relevant embassy before departure. Unless you specify how long you intend staying in Singapore, you'll normally be stamped in for fourteen days. Extending for up to three months is possible, at the discretion of the Immigration Department (see p.593 for details); extensions beyond three months are not unknown, but are less common. If you have any problems with extending your stay, there's always the option of taking a bus up to Johor Bahru, across the border in Malaysia, and then coming back in again.

Entering from anywhere other than Malaysia (with which there are no duty-free restrictions), you can bring in 1 litre each of spirits, wine and beer duty-free; duty is payable on all tobacco. Other **duty-free** goods in Singapore include electronic and electrical items, cosmetics, cameras, clocks, watches, jewellery, and precious stones and metals.

BRUNEI

British nationals with the right of abode in the UK, as well as Singaporeans and Malaysians, don't need a **visa** for visits of up to thirty days; US citizens can stay up to three months without a visa; Canadian, French, Dutch, German, Swedish, Norwegian, Swiss and Belgian citizens can stay for fourteen days without a visa; all other visitors require visas, which can be obtained at local Brunei diplomatic missions (see below) or, failing that, at a British consulate. Visas are normally for two weeks, but renewable in Brunei. Officials may ask to see either an onward ticket, or proof of sufficient funds to cover your stay, when you arrive.

Visitors may bring in 200 cigarettes, 50 cigars or 250 grams of tobacco, and 60ml of perfume; non-Muslims over 17 can also import two quarts of liquor and twelve cans of beer for personal consumption – any alcohol brought into the country must be declared upon arrival.

SINGAPOREAN EMBASSIES AND CONSULATES ABROAD

Australia 17 Forster Crescent, Yarralumla, Canberra, ACT 2600 (☎06/273 3944).

Brunei 5th floor, RBA Plaza, Jalan Sultan, Bandar Seri Begawan (☎02/227583).

Canada 1305–999 Hastings St, Vancouver BC V6C 2W2 (☎604/669 5115).

Indonesia Block X/4 Kav No. 2, Jalan H.R. Rasuna Said, Kuningan, Jakarta 12950 (☎021/520 1489).

Ireland No office.

Malaysia 209 Jalan Tun Razak, Kuala Lumpur 50400 (☎03/261 6277).

Netherlands Rotterdam Plaza, Weena 670 3012 CN Rotterdam (☎020/404 2111).

New Zealand 17 Kabul St, Khandallah, Wellington, PO Box 13-140 (☎4/4792076).

Thailand 129 South Sathorn Rd, Bangkok (☎02/2862111).

UK 9 Wilton Crescent, London SW1X 8SA (☎0171/235 8315).

USA 3501 International Place NW, Washington DC, 20008 (☎202/537 3100); 2424 SE Bristol, Suite 320, Santa Ana Heights, CA 92707 (☎714/476 2330).

BRUNEIAN EMBASSIES AND CONSULATES ABROAD

Australia 16 Bulwarra Close, O'Mally ACT 2606, Canberra (☎06/290 1801).

Canada *Les Suite Hotel*, Ottowa, Ontario, KIN 9M9 (☎613/236 5657)

Indonesia Wisma Bank Central Asia Building, eighth floor, Jalan Jendral Sudirman, KAV 22-23, Jakarta (☎021/5712124).

Ireland No office.

Malaysia 8th floor, Wisma Sin Heap Lee, Jalan Tun Razak, Kuala Lumpur (☎03/261 2800).

New Zealand No office.

Singapore 325 Tanglin Rd (☎7339055).

Thailand 154, Soi E Kamai 14, Su Khumvit 63, Bangkok (☎02/515766).

UK 19/20 Belgrave Square, London SW1X 8PG (☎0171/581 0521).

USA Watergate, Suite 300, 2600 Virginia Avenue, NW, Washington DC, 20037 (☎202/342 0159

INSURANCE

Since there are no reciprocal health agreements between Malaysia, Singapore or Brunei and any other country, costs for medical services and hospital care must be borne by the visitor. Consequently, it's essential to arrange travel insurance before you leave, which will cover you for medical expenses incurred, as well as for loss of luggage, cancellation of flights and so on.

If you're going trekking or river rafting in Sabah or Sarawak, check that your policy covers you for these sorts of outdoor pursuits. Always keep receipts for medical treatment and drugs, as they will have to be surrendered to the insurance company in the event of a claim, along with a copy of a police report for any stolen goods.

UK INSURANCE

A certain level of insurance is often included if you pay for your trip by credit card. However, any bank or travel agent can issue you with a policy, or check out those offered by a specialist travel firm like Campus Travel or STA (see p.5 for addresses), or by the low-cost **insurers** Endsleigh Insurance (97–107 Southampton Row, London WC1; ☎0171/436 4451) or Columbus Travel Insurance (17 Devonshire Square, London EC2; ☎0171/375 0011). Two weeks' cover starts at around £36; a month costs from £50. For trips of up to four months, or if this is one of many short trips in one year, you may be better off with a frequent traveller policy, which offers twelve

months of cover for around £100 – details from the companies listed above. Remember that certain activities, like scuba diving, mountain climbing and other **dangerous sports**, are unlikely to be covered by most policies, although by paying an extra premium of around £25 you can usually get added cover for the time period in which these activities are taking place.

AUSTRALIAN INSURANCE

In **Australia**, CIC Insurance, offered by Cover-More Insurance Services (Level 9, 32 Walker St, North Sydney; ☎02/202 8000; branches in Victoria and Queensland), has some of the widest cover available and can be arranged through most travel agents. It costs from A$140 for 31 days.

NORTH AMERICAN INSURANCE

In the USA and Canada, insurance tends to be much more expensive, and may offer medical cover only. Before buying a policy, check that you're not already covered by existing insurance plans. **Canadians** are usually covered by their provincial health plans; holders of ISIC cards and some other student/teacher/youth cards are entitled to $3000 worth of accident coverage and sixty days ($100 per diem) of hospital in-patient benefits for the period during which the card is valid. **Students** will often find that their student health coverage extends during the vacations and for one term beyond the date of their last enrolment. Bank and credit cards (particularly American Express) often have certain levels of medical or other insurance included, and travel insurance may also be included if you use a major credit or charge card to pay for your trip. **Homeowners'** or **renters'** insurance often covers theft or loss of documents, money and valuables while overseas, though conditions and maximum amounts vary from company to company.

After exhausting the possibilities above you might want to contact a specialist travel insurance company; your travel agent can usually recommend one. Travel insurance offerings are quite comprehensive, anticipating everything from charter companies going bankrupt to delayed or lost baggage, by way of sundry illnesses and accidents. **Premiums** vary widely, from the very reasonable ones offered primarily through student/youth agencies to those so expensive that the cost for anything more than two months of coverage will probably equal the cost of the worst possible combination of disasters. Note also that very few insurers will arrange on-the-spot payments in the event of a major expense or loss; you will usually be reimbursed only after going home. Basic travel insurance packages are available starting at around $65 for two-week trip and $85 for three weeks to a month. Try Access America, PO Box 90310, Richmond, VA 23230, (☎1-800/284-8300) or Carefree Travel Insurance, The Berkeley Group, 120 Mineola

Blvd, PO Box 310, Mineola, NY 11501 (☎1-800/645-2424).

None of these policies insures against **theft** of anything while overseas. North American travel policies apply only to items **lost** from, or **damaged** in, the custody of an identifiable, responsible third party – hotel porter, airline, luggage consignment, etc. Even in these cases you will have to contact the local police within a certain time limit to have a complete report made out so that your insurer can process the claim. If you are travelling via London it might be better to take out a British policy, available instantly and easily (though making the claim may prove more complicated).

INFORMATION AND MAPS

You can get plenty of information before you leave by calling or writing to the relevant national tourist organizations, which have offices in most foreign countries. Much of the information on Malaysia is fairly general, though you should be able to get hold of good maps and lots of glossy brochures. For Singapore, it's easier to get hold of information in advance of your trip, right down to bus timetables and museum opening hours.

For hard information on more remote areas – especially on Sarawak and Sabah – you'll have to wait until you get there, though even in the places themselves you'll often be frustrated by the lack

of available information; the MATIC office in KL (p.85) is a good first stop. Specific tourist office opening hours throughout the region are given in the text where appropriate.

TOURIST OFFICES AND INFORMATION

The **Malaysian Tourism Promotion Board** (MTPB) is the government tourist organization, often referred to as Tourism Malaysia. It operates a **tourist office** in most major towns, usually open Monday to Friday 8am–12.45pm and 2–4.15pm, Saturday 8am–12.45pm; though in the Muslim east coast states offices close on Friday and open Sunday instead. As a rule, the offices are more than happy to furnish you with glossy brochures and leaflets, organized on a state-by-state basis, but are less helpful for hard information about areas off the beaten track. Best publication is the *Malaysia Travel Planner*, which rounds up all thirteen states' attractions as well as listing practical information (like train timetables). It's best to get this from Tourism Malaysia offices abroad. In most cases, the offices maintain local accommodation lists, though this doesn't necessarily guarantee any particular standard. There'll always be someone on hand who can speak at least some English. All of Malaysia's **national parks** also have information offices (Taman Negara even has a public library) stocked with maps and leaflets, and staffed by English speakers. Most, however, won't be able to give you

TOURISM MALAYSIA OFFICES ABROAD

Australia 56 William St, Perth, WA 6000
(☎09/481 0400, fax 321 1421); 65 York St,
Sydney, NSW 2000 (☎02/299 4441, fax 02/262
2026).

Canada 830 Burrard St, Vancouver, BC, V6Z 2K4
(☎604/689 8899, fax 689-8804).

Ireland No office.

New Zealand No office.

France 29 Rue des Pyramides, 75001 Paris
(☎331/4297 4171, fax 4297 4169).

Germany Rossmarkt 11, 603110 Frankfurt Am
Main (☎069/283782, fax 285215).

Holland c/o MAS, Weteringschans 24A, 1017
SG Amsterdam (☎020/6381146).

UK 57 Trafalgar Square, London WC2N 5DU
(☎0171/930 7932, fax 930 9015).

USA 595 Madison Ave, New York, NY 10022
(☎212/754-1117, fax 754-1116).

SINGAPORE TOURIST BOARD

Australia 8th floor, St Georges Court, 16 St
Georges Terrace, Perth WA 6000 (☎09/3235
8578); Level 11, AWA Building, 47 York St,
Sydney NSW 2000 (☎02/9290 2888).

Canada Standard Life Centre, 121 King St West,
Suite 1000, Toronto, Ontario M5H 3T9
(☎416/363-8898).

France Centre d'Affaires Le Louvre, 2 Place du
Palais-Royal, 75044 Paris (☎01/4297 1616).

Germany Hockstrasse 35–37, 60313, Frankfurt
(☎069/9207700).

Ireland No office.

New Zealand 3rd floor, 43 High St, Auckland
(☎09/3581191).

UK 1st floor, Carrington House, 126–130 Regent
St, London W1R 5FE (☎0171/437 0033).

USA 12th floor, 590 Fifth Ave, New York, NY
10036 (☎212/302-4861); Prudential Plaza, 180 N
Stetson Ave, Suite 1450, Chicago, IL 60601
(☎312/938-1888); 8484 Wiltshire Blvd, Suite 510,
Beverly Hills CA 90210 (☎213/852-1901).

much in-depth information, the exceptions being Sarawak's Bako National Park, where photocopied scientific reports are available, and the parks in Sabah, for which extensive fold-out brochures are published by the Sabah Parks office (see p.429).

In Singapore, information is put out by the **Singapore Tourist Promotion Board** (STPB), which has two downtown branches with English-speaking staff and toll-free information lines (see p.510 for details). Each branch has a huge range of handouts, the biggest and best of which is the *Singapore Official Guide*, featuring good maps. You can also pick up the free *Map of Singapore*, which the Singapore Hotel Association endorses.

Brunei barely has a tourist industry, and the only offering from the Economic Development Board (see p.485), which handles tourism and maintains a booth at the airport, is the lacklustre *Explore Brunei* booklet. For information prior to departure, contact your local Bruneian embassy or consulate.

MAPS

Maps of **Malaysia** are widely available abroad, the best general maps either Macmillan's

1:2,000,000 *Malaysia Traveller's Map* or the more detailed *Nelles* 1:650,000 *West Malaysia* (not including Sabah and Sarawak) – both include plans of Singapore and major Malaysian towns. The 1:2,000,000 Bartholomew *Singapore & Malaysia World Travel Map* shows the entire region, though check that this (and other maps) is a recent edition – some don't yet show the North–South Highway, for example. Better road maps are available once you get there and, if **driving**, you'll want to arm yourself with the free 1:1,000,000 *Road Map of Malaysia*, available from any tourist office. The excellent Petronas *Heritage Mapbook of Peninsular Malaysia* has 43 double pages showing the Malaysian road system from town to town, with descriptions of all points of interest on the route. In theory, it's available from the larger Petronas service stations, though, in practice, it can be quite hard to come by. Easier to get hold of is the *PLUS Guide to Peninsular Malaysia*.

Good maps of Sarawak and Sabah can be difficult to find, both at home and abroad. For a detailed relief map of **Sarawak**, you'll be hard pressed to find one better than the Land and

MAP OUTLETS IN THE UK

Maps by **mail or phone order** are available from *Stanfords* (☎0171/836 1321).

London
National Map Centre, 22–24 Caxton St, SW1 (☎0171/222 4945).

Stanfords, 12–14 Long Acre, WC2 (☎0171/836 1321).

The Travel Bookshop, 13–15 Blenheim Crescent, W11 2EE (☎0171/229 5260).

Glasgow
John Smith and Sons, 57–61 St Vincent St (☎0141/221 7472).

MAP OUTLETS IN NORTH AMERICA

Rand McNally now has 24 stores across the USA; call ☎1-800/333-0136 (ext 2111) for the address of your nearest store, or for **direct mail** maps.

Chicago
Rand McNally, 444 N Michigan Ave, IL 60611 (☎312/321-1751).

New York
The Complete Traveler Bookstore, 199 Madison Ave, NY 10016 (☎212/685-9007).

Rand McNally, 150 52nd St, NY 10022 (☎212/758-7488).

Traveler's Bookstore, 22 52nd St, NY 10019 (☎212/664-0995).

San Francisco
The Complete Traveler Bookstore, 3207 Fillmore St, CA 92123 (☎415/923-1511).

Rand McNally, 595 Market St, CA 94105 (☎415/777-3131).

Santa Barbara
Map Link Inc, 30 S La Petera Lane, Unit 5, Santa Barbara, CA 93117 (☎805/692-6777).

Seattle
Elliot Bay Book Company, 101 South Main St, WA 98104 (☎206/624-6600).

Wide World Books and Maps, 1911 North 45th St, Seattle 98103 (☎206/634-3453).

Toronto
Open Air Books and Maps, 25 Toronto St, M5R 2C1 (☎416/363-0719).

Vancouver
World Wide Books and Maps, 1247 Granville St (☎604/687-3320).

Washington DC
Rand McNally, 1201 Connecticut Ave NW, Washington DC 20036 (☎202/223-6751).

MAP OUTLETS IN AUSTRALIA

Adelaide
The Map Shop, 16a Peel St, Adelaide, SA 5000 (☎08/231 2033).

Brisbane
Hema, 239 George St, Brisbane, QLD 4000 (☎07/221 4330).

Melbourne
Bowyangs, 372 Little Bourke St, Melbourne, VIC 3000 (☎03/670 4383).

Sydney
Travel Bookshop, 20 Bridge St, Sydney, NSW 2000 (☎02/241 3554).

Perth
Perth Map Centre, 891 Hay St, Perth, WA 6000 (☎09/322 5733).

Survey Department's 1:500,000 issue, available in the bookshop at the Kuching *Holiday Inn* (see Sarawak, p.358); also good is the *Periplus* 1:1,000,000 Sarawak map. The best coverage of **Sabah** is on maps produced by Nelles. The **hiking maps** provided by information offices in places like Cameron Highlands and Taman Negara are barely adequate, but they are the best you'll find since there are no proper Ordnance Survey maps of the areas – not available to the

general public anyway. If you're following hiking routes marked on sketch maps (including those in this book), it's always wise to ask local advice before setting off.

The best available map of **Singapore** is the 1:22,500 Nelles *Singapore*, though the *Singapore Street Directory*, from all bookshops, is a must if you're renting a car.

There are few specific maps of **Brunei** available; the coverage on general maps of East

Malaysia/Borneo tends to be rather scant. The Bruneian government, however, does produce a map of Bandar Seri Begawan and its environs, which is available in the capital's bookshops and stationers; a countryside map is in the pipeline.

TRAVELLERS WITH DISABILITIES

Of the three countries, Singapore is the most accessible to travellers with disabilities; hefty tax incentives are provided for developers who include access features for the disabled in new buildings. In contrast, Malaysia makes few provisions for its own disabled citizens, a state of affairs that clearly affects the tourist with disabilities.

In both countries, life is made a lot easier if you can afford to pay for more upmarket hotels (which usually have specially adapted elevators) and to shell out for taxis and the odd domestic

CONTACTS FOR TRAVELLERS WITH DISABILITIES

BRITAIN

Holiday Care Service, second floor, Imperial Building, Victoria Rd, Horley, Surrey RH6 7PZ (☎01293/774535). Provides free lists of accessible accommodation abroad – European, American and long-haul destinations – plus a list of accessible attractions in the UK. Information on financial help for holidays available.

RADAR (Royal Association for Disability and Rehabilitation), 12 City Forum, 250 City Rd, London EC1V 8AF (☎0171/250 3222; Minicom ☎0171/250 4119). Produces an annual holiday guide for the UK (£7 includes p&p) and separate guides for long-haul and for Europe (both £5 inc. p&p) alternate years.

Tripscope, The Courtyard, Evelyn Rd, London W4 5JL (☎0181/994 9294). This registered charity provides a national telephone information service offering free advice on international transport and travel for those with a mobility problem.

NORTH AMERICA

The Council on International Education Exchange, 205 East 42nd St, New York, NY 10017-5706 (☎212/661-1414 ext 1108).

Information Center for People with Disabilities, Fort Point Place, 27–43 Wormwood St, Boston, MA 02210 (☎617/727-5540). Clearing house for information, including travel.

Jewish Rehabilitation Hospital, 3205 Place Alton Goldbloom, Montréal, Québec H7V 1R2 (☎514/688-9550, ext 226). Guidebooks and travel information.

Kéroul, 4545 Ave Pierre de Coubertin, CP 1000 Station M, Montréal H1V 3R2 (☎512/252-3104). Travel for mobility-impaired people.

Mobility International USA, Box 10767, Eugene, OR 97440 (☎503/343-1284). Information, access guides, tours and exchange programmes.

Society for the Advancement of Travel for the Handicapped (SATH), 347 Fifth Ave, New York, NY 10016 (☎212/447-7284). Information on suitable tour operators and travel agents.

Travel Information Service, Moss Rehabilitation Hospital, 1200 Tabor Rd, Philadelphia, PA 19141 (☎215/456-9600). Telephone information service and referral.

The Travlin' Talk Network, PO Box 3534, Clarksville TN 37043. (☎615/552-6670). Provides information and services for disabled travelers, publishes *Travlin' Talk*, a directory of travel and tour agencies specializing in travel for people with disabilities and publishes a newsletter with updates on tours, trips and other activities.

AUSTRALIA AND NEW ZEALAND

Australia
ACROD, PO Box 60, Curtain, ACT 2605 (☎06/682 4333).

Barrier Free Travel, 36 Wheatley St, North Bellingen, NSW 2454 (☎066/551733).

New Zealand
Disabled Persons Assembly, PO Box 10–138, The Terrace, Wellington (☎04/472 2626).

flight. Similarly, the more expensive international **airlines** tend to be better equipped to get you there in the first place: MAS, British Airways, KLM and Qantas all carry aisle wheelchairs and have at least one toilet adapted for disabled passengers. However, few, if any, tour operators offering holidays in the region accommodate the needs of those with disabilities.

The **Singapore Council of Social Service**, at 11 Penang Lane, Singapore, can provide you with a free copy of *Access Singapore*, a thorough and informative brochure detailing amenities for the disabled in Singapore's hotels, hospitals, shopping centres, cinemas and banks. Access is improving, slowly, and most hotels now make some provision for disabled guests, though often there will only be one specially designed bedroom in an establishment – always call first for information, and book in plenty of

time. Getting around the city is less straightforward: buses are not accessible to wheelchairs and there are no elevators in the MRT system. However, one taxi company, TIBS (see p.514 for details), has several cabs big enough to take a wheelchair, and there are acoustic signals at street crossings.

In Malaysia, wheelchair users will have a hard time negotiating the uneven pavements in most towns and cities, and will find it difficult to board buses, trains and ferries, none of which have been adapted for wheelchairs. Although most modern hotels in KL and Georgetown have good access, much budget accommodation is located up narrow stairways and presents difficulties for the disabled. Also, do not expect people to respond quickly to requests for help, as strict Muslims particularly avoid bodily contact with non-Muslims as a tenet of their faith.

COSTS, MONEY AND BANKS

Those entering Malaysia from Thailand will find their daily budget remains pretty much unchanged; approaching from Indonesia, on the other hand, costs will take a step up. Once in the region, daily necessities like food, drink and travel are marginally more expensive in Singapore than in Malaysia; over in East Malaysia, room rates tend to be a little higher than on the Peninsula, and you'll also find yourself forking out for river trips and nature tours.

Travelling as a couple will help keep accommodation and eating costs down. The region affords no savings for senior citizens, though an **ISIC student card** might occasionally pay dividends. However, **bargaining** is *de rigueur* throughout Malaysia and Singapore, especially when shopping or renting a room for the night – it's always worth trying to haggle, though note that you don't bargain for meals. In addition, most tourist attractions offer discounted entrance fees for **children**, while Malaysia's **public transport** network has a variety of special deals on tickets that help keep costs down (see "Getting Around" for more).

TAKING MONEY ABROAD

The safest and most convenient method of carrying your money is as **travellers' cheques** – either sterling or US dollar cheques are acceptable, though check with your bank before you buy for the latest advice. Available at a small commission from most banks, and from branches of American Express and Thomas Cook, these can be cashed at Malaysian, Singaporean and Bruneian banks, licensed moneychangers and some hotels, upon presentation of a passport. Some shops will

Malaysia, Singapore and Brunei all call their basic unit of currency the **dollar** (see relevant sections below for more details), written throughout this book as $. When it's necessary to distinguish between the currencies, we've used the following:

M$ = Malaysian dollar.

S$ = Singaporean dollar.

B$ = Bruneian dollar.

US$ = US dollar.

even accept travellers' cheques as cash. Major **credit cards** are widely accepted in the more upmarket hotels, shops and restaurants throughout the region, but beware of the illegal surcharges levied by some establishments – check before you pay that there's no surcharge; if there is, contact your card company and tell them about it. Banks will often **advance cash** against major credit cards; moreover, with American Express, Visa and Mastercard, it's possible to withdraw money from **automatic teller machines** (ATMs) in Singapore and major Malaysian cities – get details from your card company before you leave home.

If your funds run out, you can arrange for cash to be transferred from home. **Wiring money** – which can take anything from two to seven working days – incurs a small fee in Southeast Asia and a larger one back home. You'll need, first, to supply your home bank with details of the local branch to which the money should be sent, after which it'll be issued to you upon presentation of some form of ID.

For lost or stolen travelers checks or credit cards contact: **Visa** in Malaysia (☎800-1060), in Singapore (☎1-800/345-1345); **Master Card** in Malaysia (☎800-804594), in Singapore (☎800-1100-113); **American Express**, collect from anywhere outside the USA (☎1-910-333-3211).

MALAYSIA

Basic food, accommodation and public transport costs in **Peninsular Malaysia** are extremely reasonable and if you're prepared to live frugally – staying in the most spartan lodging houses, roughing it on local transport, and eating and drinking at roadside stalls – it's quite feasible to manage on £8/US$12 a day. You'll not want to live like this for too long, though, and once you

start to treat yourself to a few luxuries, the figures soon add up: an air-conditioned room, a meal at a decent restaurant, and a beer to round off the day could easily bump your **daily budget** up to a more realistic £18/US$27 a day. From there, the sky's the limit, with Malaysia's plush hotels, swanky restaurants and exclusive nightclubs well capable of emptying even the fullest wallet. You'll find living costs roughly similar in **East Malaysia**, though you can expect room rates to be up to 50 percent more expensive than on the mainland. Moreover, just getting around in Sarawak and Sabah can be fairly expensive, since you'll often have to organize your own transport; there are more details at the beginning of the relevant chapters.

Malaysia's unit of **currency** is the Malaysian **Ringgit**, divided into 100 sen. You'll also see the ringgit written as "RM", or – as in this book – simply as "$" (M$), and often hear it called a "dollar". **Notes** come in M$1, M$5, M$10, M$20, M$50, M$100, M$500 and M$1000 denominations; **coins** are minted in 1 sen, 5 sen, 10 sen, 20 sen, 50 sen and $1 denominations.

At the time of writing, the **exchange rate** was around M$3.90 to £1, M$2.60 to US$1. It's a relatively stable currency, but more up-to-the-minute rates are posted daily in banks and exchange kiosks, and published in the *New Straits Times*. There is no black market in Malaysia, and no limit to the amount of cash you can take in or out of the country.

Banking hours are generally Monday to Friday 10am–3pm and Saturday 9.30–11.30am, though in the largely Muslim states of Kedah, Perlis, Kelantan and Terengganu, Friday is a holiday and Sunday a working day.

Major banks represented in Malaysia include the United Malayan Banking Corporation, Maybank, Bank Bumiputra, Oriental Bank, Hong Kong Bank, and Standard Chartered; Ban Hin Lee Bank (BHL) doesn't charge any commission for changing American Express Travellers' Cheques, but can only be found in major cities. Licensed **moneychangers**' kiosks, found in bigger towns all over the country, tend to open later, until around 6pm, with some opening at weekends and until 9pm, too; some hotels will exchange money at all hours. Exchange rates tend to be more generous at banks, but once you've paid their (often extortionate) commission fees, using a moneychanger often works out cheaper. It's not generally difficult to change money in Sabah or Sarawak, though if you are travelling along a river in the interior for any length of time, it's a wise idea to carry a fair amount of cash, in smallish denominations.

SINGAPORE

As in neighbouring Malaysia, if money is no object, you'll be able to take advantage of hotels, restaurants and shops as sumptuous as any in the world. But equally, with budget dormitory accommodation in plentiful supply, and both food and internal travel cheap in the extreme, you'll find it possible to live on less than £8/US$12 a day. Upgrading your lodgings to a private room in a guest house, eating in a restaurant and having a beer or two gives a more realistic **daily budget** of £21/US$32 a day. Once you are housed, fed and watered, Singapore has much of interest that costs nothing at all.

The currency is **Singapore dollars**, written simply as $ (or – occasionally in this book – S$ to distinguish it from Malaysian currency) and divided into 100 cents. **Notes** are issued in denominations of $1, $2, $5, $10, $20, $50, $100, $500, $1000 and $10,000; **coins** are in denominations of 1, 5, 10, 20 and 50 cents, and $1. The current **exchange rate** is around $2.30 to £1, $1.50 to US$1. Singaporean dollars are not accepted in Malaysia, but are legal tender in Brunei (see below).

Singapore **banking hours** are generally Monday to Friday 10am–3pm and Saturday 11am–1pm, outside of which you'll have to go to a moneychanger in a shopping centre (see p.592 for locations), or to a hotel. **Major banks** represented include the Overseas Union Bank, the United Overseas Bank, the OCBC, the Development Bank of Singapore, Standard Chartered Bank, Hong Kong and Shanghai Bank and Citibank; of these, the OCBC and the Overseas Union Bank usually offer the best rates, while the Standard Chartered charges a hefty $15 fee for currency transactions. No black market operates in Singapore, nor are there any restrictions on carrying currency in or out of the state.

BRUNEI

Costs for everything except accommodation in Brunei are roughly the same as in Singapore. However, there's only one budget place to stay in the capital and if you can't get in there, you're looking at around £20/US$30 minimum per night in a hotel, which means an average **daily budget** in Brunei is likely to start at around £25–30/US$37–45. In addition, if you want to see anything of the surrounding countryside, you are dependent on expensive taxis since the public transport network is minimal.

Brunei's currency is the **Brunei dollar**, which is divided into 100 cents; you'll see it written as B$, or simply as $. The Bruneian dollar has parity with the Singapore dollar and both are legal tender in either country. Notes come in $1, $5, $10, $50, $100, $500, $1000 and $10,000 denominations; coins come in denominations of 1, 5, 10, 20 and 50 cents.

Brunei **banking hours** are Monday to Friday 9am–3pm and Saturday 9–11am, with **banks** represented in Bandar including the International Bank of Brunei, Citibank, Standard Chartered Bank and the Overseas Union Bank – all of which charge a few dollars transaction fee for cashing travellers' cheques.

HEALTH MATTERS

There are no inoculations required for visiting Malaysia, Singapore or Brunei, although the immigration authorities may require proof of a yellow fever vaccination (administered within the last ten years) if you're arriving from a country that has a long history of this disease.

However, it's a wise precaution to visit your doctor no less than two months before you leave to check that you are up to date with your **polio**, **typhoid**, **tetanus** and **hepatitis A** inoculations, and to check the malarial status of the areas you are visiting. If you're travelling for a long time, or in rural areas, your doctor may also recommend protection against **Japanese B encephalitis**, **hepatitis B**, **tuberculosis** and **rabies**.

IMMUNIZATION

North Americans will have to pay for these inoculations, available at an **immunization centre** – there's one in every city of any size – or most local clinics. Most general practitioners in the **UK** have a travel surgery from which you can obtain advice and certain vaccines on prescription, though they may not administer some of the less common immunizations.

For up-to-the-minute information, make an appointment at a specialized **travel clinic**. All these clinics sell travel-associated **accessories**, including mosquito nets and first-aid kits (if you want to make up your own, see below).

A TRAVELLERS' FIRST-AID KIT

Among items you might want to carry with you – especially if you're planning to go trekking (see "Outdoor Pursuits", p.72, for more details) – are:

Antiseptic cream.

Plasters/Band Aids.

Lints and sealed bandages.

Knee supports.

A course of flagyl antibiotics.

Immodium (lomotil) for emergency diarrhoea treatment.

Paracetamol/aspirin (useful for combating the effects of altitude).

Multi-vitamin and mineral tablets.

Rehydration sachets.

Hypodermic needles and sterilized skin wipes (more for the security of knowing you have them, than any fear that a local hospital would fail to observe basic sanitary precautions).

MEDICAL PROBLEMS

The levels of hygiene and medical care in Malaysia and Singapore are higher than in much of the rest of Southeast Asia and with any luck, the most serious thing you'll go down with is a cold or an upset stomach.

It's wise, though, to take a few precautions and know about the dangers beforehand. In a tropical climate it's especially important to be vigilant about **personal hygiene**. Wash your hands often, especially before eating, keep all cuts clean, treat them with iodine or antiseptic, and cover them to prevent infection. Be fussier about sharing things like drinks and cigarettes than you might be at home; never share a razor or toothbrush. It is also inadvisable to go around barefoot – and best to wear flip-flop sandals even in the shower. In addition, make sure you eat *enough* – an unfamiliar diet may reduce the amount you eat – and **get enough sleep** and rest – it's easy to get run-down if you're on the move a lot, especially in a hot climate.

HEAT PROBLEMS

Travellers unused to tropical climates periodically suffer from **sunburn** and **dehydration**. The eas-

MEDICAL RESOURCES FOR TRAVELLERS

BRITAIN AND IRELAND

British Airways Travel Clinic, 156 Regent St, London W1 7RA (Mon–Fri 9.30am–5.15pm, Sat 10am–4pm; ☎0171/439 9584), no appointment necessary; there are also appointment-only branches at 101 Cheapside, London EC2 (Mon–Fri 9–11.45am & 12.15–4.45pm; ☎0171/606 2977) and at the *BA* terminal in London's Victoria Station (8.15–11.30am & 12.30–3.40pm; ☎01276/685040). *BA* also operate around forty regional clinics throughout the country (call ☎0171/831 5333 for the one nearest to you); airport locations at Gatwick and Heathrow.

Hospital for Tropical Diseases, St Pancras Hospital, 4 St Pancras Way, London NW1 0PE (☎0171/388 9600). Travel clinic and recorded message service (☎0839/337733; 39–49p per minute) which gives hints on hygiene and illness prevention as well as listing appropriate immunisations.

MASTA (Medical Advisory Service for Travellers Abroad), London School of Hygiene and Tropical Medicine (☎0891 224100; 39–49p per minute). Operates a Travellers' Health Line 24 hours a day, Seven days a week, giving written information tailored to your journey by return of post.

Travel Medicine Services, PO Box 254, 16 College St, Belfast 1 (☎01232/315220).

Tropical Medical Bureau, Grafton St Medical Centre, 34 Grafton St, Dublin 2 (☎01/671 9200); Dun Laoghaire Medical Centre, 5 Northumberland Ave, Dun Laoghaire, Co. Dublin (☎01/280 4996).

USA AND CANADA

Canadian Society for International Health, 170 Laurier Ave West, Suite 902, Ottawa, ON K1P 5V5 (☎613/230-2654). Distributes a free pamphlet, "Health Information for Canadian Travellers", containing an extensive list of travel health centres in Canada.

International Association for Medical Assistance to Travellers (IAMAT), 417 Center St, Lewiston, NY 14092 (☎716/754-4883) and 40 Regal Rd, Guelph, ON N1K 1B5 (☎519/836-0102). A non-profit organization supported by donations, it can provide a list of English-speaking doctors, climate charts and leaflets on various diseases and inoculations.

International SOS Assistance, PO Box 11568, Philadelphia, PA 19116 (☎1-800/523-8930). Members receive pre-trip medical referral info, as well as overseas emergency services designed to complement travel insurance coverage.

Travel Medicine, 351 Pleasant St, Suite 312, Northampton, MA 01060 (☎1-800/872-8633). Sells first-aid kits, mosquito netting, water filters and other health-related travel products.

Travelers Medical Center, 31 Washington Square, New York, NY 10011 (☎212/982-1600). Consultation service on immunizations and treatment of diseases for people travelling to developing countries.

AUSTRALIA AND NEW ZEALAND

Auckland Hospital, Park Rd, Grafton (☎09/379 7440).

Travel Health and Vaccination Clinic, 114 Williams St, Melbourne (☎03/9670 2020).

Travellers Immunization Service, 303 Pacific Hwy, Sydney (☎02/9416 1348).

Travellers' Medical and Vaccination Centre, Level 7, 428 George St, Sydney (☎02/9221 7133); Level 3, 393 Little Bourke St, Melbourne (☎03/9602 5788); Level 6, 29 Gilbert Place, Adelaide (☎08/8212 7522); Level 6, 247 Adelaide St, Brisbane (☎07/3221 9066); 1 Mill St, Perth (☎08/9321 1977).

iest way to avoid this is to restrict your exposure to the midday sun, use high-factor sun screens, wear sunglasses and a hat. You should also drink plenty of water (see below) and, if you do become dehydrated, keep up a regular intake of fluids; weak black tea and clear soups are useful for mineral salts, or a rehydration preparation such as Dioralyte also does the trick – the DIY version is a handful of sugar with a good pinch of salt added to a litre of water, which creates roughly the right mineral balance. **Heat stroke** is more serious: it is indicated by a high temperature, dry red skin and a fast pulse and can require hospitalization. To prevent **heat rashes**, **prickly heat** and **fungal infections**, use a mild antiseptic soap and dust yourself with prickly heat talcum powder, which you can buy all over Malaysia and Singapore.

WATER PURIFICATION

Contaminated water is a major cause of sickness due to the presence of micro-organisms which cause diseases such as diarrhoea and gastroenteritis, typhoid, cholera, dysentery, poliomyelitis, hepatitis A, giardiasis and bilharziasis – these can be present even when water looks clean and safe to drink. If you're trekking in the back of beyond, or travelling upriver in deepest Sarawak, all drinking water should be regarded with caution.

Apart from **bottled water**, there are various methods of treating water, whether it is from a tap or from a river or stream. Boiling is the time-honoured method which will be effective in sterilizing water, although it will not remove unpleasant tastes. A minimum **boiling** time of ten minutes (longer at higher altitudes) is sufficient to kill micro-organisms.

Chemical sterilization can be carried out using either chlorine or iodine tablets or a tincture of iodine liquid. With tablets it is essential to follow the manufacturer's dosage and contact time,

whilst, with tincture of iodine, you add a couple of drops to one litre of water and leave to stand for twenty minutes. Iodine tablets are preferable to chlorine as the latter leave an unpleasant taste in the water and are not effective in preventing such diseases as amoebic dysentery and giardiasis. If you are using sterilizing tablets, a water filter is useful, not least to improve the taste. However, note that a water filter alone will not remove viruses which, due to their microscopic size, will pass through into the filtered water.

Purification, a two-stage process involving both filtration and sterilization, gives the most complete treatment. Portable water purifiers range in size from units weighing as little as 60 grams which can be slipped into a pocket, to 800 grams for carrying in a backpack. Some of the best water purifiers on the market are made in Britain by **Pre-Mac**, available in the UK from British Airways Travel Clinics and specialist outdoor equipment retailers (call ☎01732/460333 for details of local stockists).

All Water Systems Ltd, 126 Ranelagh, Dublin 6, Ireland (☎496 4598).

Outbound Products, 1580 Zephry Ave, Box 56148, Hayward CA 94545-6148, USA (☎510/429-0096).

Outbound Products, 8585 Fraser St, Vancouver, BC V5X 3Y1, Canada (☎604/321-5464).

STOMACH PROBLEMS: FOOD AND WATER

The most common complaint is a **stomach problem**, which can range from a mild dose of diarrhoea to full-blown dysentery. Since stomach bugs are usually transmitted by contaminated food and water, steer clear of raw vegetables and unpeeled fruit, and stick to freshly cooked foods. The amount of money you pay for a meal is no guarantee of its safety; in fact, food in top hotels has often been hanging around longer than food cooked at roadside stalls. Use your common sense – eat in places that look clean, avoid reheated food and be wary of shellfish.

Tap water is drinkable throughout Malaysia, Singapore and Brunei (and in major towns in Sarawak and Sabah), but in rural areas you should buy bottled water, which is available everywhere. If you're going trekking in the national parks, or travelling upriver in Sarawak, you might want to invest in a **water purifier** (see box above). In addition, drinking excessive amounts of alcohol is

a common cause of diarrhoea, and in a tropical climate your tolerance level is likely to be much lower than it would be at home. But however careful you are, spicy or just different food can sometimes upset your system, in which case, try to stick to bland dishes such as rice and noodles and avoid fried food. Ninety-five percent of stomach bugs will be of this unpleasant, but basically unthreatening, type. However, if you notice blood or mucus in your stools, then you may have amoebic or bacillary **dysentery**, in which case you should seek medical help immediately.

MALARIA AND OTHER DISEASES

Although the risk of catching **malaria** in Malaysia, Singapore or Brunei is pretty low, if you're planning to travel for a long time or think you might be staying in remote areas, then you should consider protection. Malaria begins with flu-like symptoms, with a fluctuating high fever; it cannot be passed directly from one person to another. The prevention of mosquito bites is the most reliable way to avoid the disease: apply **insect repellent** at regular intervals and sleep with a mosquito net where possible – some places provide these but it is safer to take your own. Mosquito coils (which you light) are very cheap and widely available in shops throughout Malaysia and Singapore. Most doctors will advise the additional use of **malaria tablets** and although they aren't completely effective, taking them can help reduce the symptoms should you develop malaria. You have to start taking them one week before you leave and continue taking them throughout your trip as well as for four weeks when you return; if you don't complete the course, you won't be protected. Your GP will be able to advise you as to which course of tablets is most effective for the region you intend to visit – currently a combination of chloroquine and palu-drine is recommended for Peninsular Malaysia's deeply-forested regions; while mefloquine (sold as Larium, and recently exposed as triggering some nasty side-effects) is best for Sabah.

It's highly unlikely that you'll catch anything very serious while in Malaysia and Singapore, though long-term travellers may have brought something with them from elsewhere, so it's important to recognize the early stages of some possible diseases. **Dengue fever** belongs to a family of viruses which are transmitted by the mosquito bite in a similar way to malaria, and tends to occur seasonally and in epidemics. While it is a very common cause of fever and non-spe-cific flu-like symptoms in Southeast Asia, gener-ally speaking the disease is not serious – deaths in adults are very rare. However, the symptoms – severe headache, bone pain (especially of the back), fever and often a fine, red rash over the body – can be serious enough to keep you in bed for a few days. There's no specific treatment, just plenty of rest, adequate fluid intake and painkillers when required.

Typhoid is a lethal disease that is spread by contact with infected water or food. It begins with a headache and a consistently high fever, fol-lowed by red spots on the chest and back, dehy-dration and occasional diarrhoea. If you think you have these symptoms you should seek immediate medical treatment.

Hepatitis is an inflammation of the liver, which may manifest itself as jaundice – a yellow discolouration of the skin and eyes – though extreme tiredness is a common characteristic.

While there are many causes of hepatitis (includ-ing drug and alcohol abuse), that caused by virus is most commonly hepatitis A or B, both of which can be prevented by vaccination. A new and rather expensive vaccine, *Havrix*, provides immu-nity against hepatitis A for up to ten years; one jab is required. Hepatitis A is one of the most like-ly infections to be encountered in Asia and is spread via contaminated food and water. Rest, lots of fluids and a total abstinence from alcohol are the major elements in the cure, as well as a simple, bland diet. Hepatitis B is rarer; it is com-monly transmitted through infected blood and blood products, so intravenous drug-users, together with those who have had unprotected sex, are most at risk. The Hepatitis B vaccine (three jabs over six months, plus a booster after five years) is recommended to anyone falling into one of these high-risk categories, and to those travelling in rural areas with access to only basic medical care.

From time to time, outbreaks of **cholera** are reported in Malaysia; however the vaccine is con-sidered so ineffectual nowadays that there's little point in having it. Cholera is caught by contact with infected water and food, and begins with fever, severe vomiting and diarrhoea, followed by weakness and muscle cramps – seek medical help immediately and watch out for dehydration.

Rabies is spread by the bite or even the lick of an infected animal – most commonly a dog or cat. If you suspect that you have been bitten by a rabid animal, wash the wound immediately and thor-oughly with antiseptic and seek medical help. Even if you have been inoculated, you'll require further injections.

CUTS, BITES AND STINGS

Wearing protective clothing when swimming, snorkelling or diving can help avoid sunburn and protect against any sea stings. **Sea lice**, minute creatures which cause painful though harmless bites are the most common hazard; more danger-ous are **jellyfish**, whose stings must be doused with vinegar to deactivate the poison before you seek medical help. **Coral** can also cause nasty cuts and grazes. Any wounds should be cleaned vigorously since retained coral particles are a common cause of prolonged deep infection. After cleaning, make sure you keep the wound as dry as possible until it's properly healed. The only way to avoid well-camouflaged **urchins** and **stone fish** is by not stepping on the sea bed, since even thick-soled shoes don't provide total protection against long, sharp spines. If you do step on one, spines can be removed by softening the skin – although you should try to get a professional to do this.

Jungle trekking presents a few health problems, too. Poisonous **snakes** are rare, but if you are bitten you must remain absolutely still and calm until help arrives. Meanwhile, get someone to clean and disinfect the wound thoroughly (alcohol will do if nothing else can be found), and apply a bandage with gentle pressure to the affected area. It helps if you can kill the snake and take it to be identified. Poisonous **spiders** are relatively rare; as with snake bites, keep calm and seek medical help as soon as possible. **Leeches** are a far more common bother and though harmless, cause an unpleasant sensation. Long trousers and socks help deter them, but once on your skin, they can be hard to remove. If flicking or pulling them off doesn't work, burning leeches off with a lighter or cigarette is effective, as is rubbing them with alcohol or tobacco juice. See "Outdoor pursuits", p.73, for more.

TREATMENT: PHARMACIES, DOCTORS AND HOSPITALS

Medical services in Malaysia, Singapore and Brunei are excellent, with staff almost everywhere speaking good English and using up-to-date techniques. Throughout the guide, in the

To call an **ambulance**, dial ☎999 or 991 in Malaysia, ☎995 in Singapore and ☎991 in Brunei.

"Listings" sections of major towns, you'll find details of local pharmacists and hospitals; major hospitals are often marked on our maps, too.

In **Malaysia**, there's always a **pharmacy** in main towns, which are well stocked with familiar brand-name drugs; pharmacists can also recommend products for skin complaints or simple stomach problems, though if you're in any doubt, it always pays to get a proper diagnosis. Opening hours are usually Monday to Saturday 9.30am–7pm (except in Kelantan, Terengganu, Kedah and Perlis states, where Friday and not Sunday is the closing day). Private **clinics** are found even in the smallest towns – your hotel or the local tourist office will be able to recommend a good English-speaking doctor. A visit costs around M$30, not including the cost of any prescribed medication. Don't forget to keep the receipts for insurance claim purposes. Finally, the emergency department of each town's **General Hospital** will see foreigners (usually allowing you to jump the queue) for the token fee of $1, though obviously costs rise rapidly if continued treatment or overnight stays are necessary.

Services in **Singapore** are broadly similar –for the location of Singapore pharmacies and hospitals, turn to p.593.

GETTING AROUND

Details of specific **routes** and **journey times** between towns are given at the end of each chapter in "Travel Details". Look, too, for the boxed "Leaving" sections in each major town account, which provide useful hints on the most convenient local routes and services.

Malaysia, Singapore or Brunei, especially since internal transport costs tend to be fairly low.

BUSES

Apart from in Sarawak, the national **bus** network is the easiest and quickest way of getting around Malaysia, with regular services between all major towns. Inter-state destinations are covered by comfortable, air-conditioned **express buses**. In addition to the government-run *Transnational* and individual state bus companies, a large number of private companies operate services along specific routes; each has an office in the town's bus station which is where you buy your ticket. The departure time of the company's next bus is usually displayed and since prices are fairly similar on all routes, it matters little which company you opt for. Buses for long-distance routes (those over 3hr) typically leave in clusters in the early morning and late evening, while shorter or more popular routes are served regularly throughout the day. In most cases you can just turn up immediately prior to departure, though on some of the more popular routes – Kuala Lumpur to Penang, or Kuantan to Singapore – it's advisable to **reserve a ticket** at least a day in advance at the relevant ticket office (particularly during the major holiday periods of Christmas, Easter and Hari Raya. **Fares** are eminently reasonable: the eight-hour run from KL to Georgetown, for example, costs $18.50; for other fares, see the box below. Many towns and cities have more than one bus station, serving different regions or companies; the text and maps detail where you should go to catch your bus.

Local buses usually, though not always, operate from a separate station. They serve routes within the state and are consequently cheaper, but also slower, less comfortable and without air-conditioning. It's not possible to book a seat – buy your ticket on the bus.

Public transport in the region is extremely reliable, though not as cheap as in other Southeast Asian countries. Most of your travelling, particularly on the Peninsula, will be by bus or long-distance taxi, though the Malaysian train system has its uses, especially on the long haul up the west coast from Singapore and into Thailand. By and large, the roads in Peninsular Malaysia are reasonable and if you're driving, new road construction continues to speed up journey times: the North–South highway runs the length of the west coast from Johor Bahru to Bukit Kayu Hitam, while the East–West highway connects Kota Bahru with Penang.

Sabah and Sarawak have their own travel peculiarities – in Sarawak, for instance, you'll be reliant on boats, and occasionally planes, for most long-distance travel; there are more details given below and turn to p.342 (Sarawak), p.424 (Sabah) and p.482 (Brunei) for further information. The main thing to note is that there is no boat service between Peninsular Malaysia or Singapore and East Malaysia; consequently, you have to fly from the mainland to Sabah, Sarawak or Brunei. In Singapore there's a comprehensive city and island-wide **public transport system** – all the details are covered on p.511–515.

Many foreigners hitch while in Malaysia, particularly along the east coast, and some consider it to be a valuable way of meeting local people. However, this guide does not recommend hitching as a means of getting around any part of

SAMPLE EXPRESS BUS ROUTES AND FARES

All fares are given in Malaysian dollars.

Kuala Lumpur to:

Alor Setar	8hr	$21
Butterworth	7hr	$17
Cameron Highlands	4hr	$12
Ipoh	4hr	$10
Johor Bahru	7hr	$17
Kota Bharu	7hr	$25
Kuala Lipis	4hr	$8
Kuantan	5hr	$12
Lumut	5hr 30min	$13
Melaka	2hr	$7
Singapore	8hr	$22

Several buses ply the long-distance routes across **Sabah**, but they are heavily outnumbered by the **minibuses** that buzz around the state, which generally leave from the same terminals. Faster and slightly more expensive than the scheduled bus services, minibuses only leave when jam-packed and are often very uncomfortable as a result; from Kota Kinabulu to Kudat costs around $10, to Sandakan $15–20. Also prevalent in Sabah are **landcruisers**, outsized jeeps which take only eight passengers and whose fares are priced somewhere between those of a bus and a taxi.

Modern air-con buses in **Sarawak** ply the trans-state coastal road between Kuching and the Brunei border, serving Sibu, Bintulu and Miri en route. The trip from Kuching to Miri costs $70, from Kuching to Sibu around $30. In addition, more rickety local buses serve the satellite towns and villages around the state's main settlements.

TRAINS

The Peninsula's **train** service, operated by Keretapi Tanah Melayu (KTM), is limited in scope, relatively expensive and extremely slow, making it for the most part an unappealing alternative to the bus. However, it is virtually the only way to reach some of the more interesting places in the interior and there's still a certain thrill in arriving at some of the splendidly solid colonial stations, built when the train was the prime means of transport.

ROUTES AND SERVICES

There are only two main lines through Peninsular Malaysia, both originating in Thailand at the southern town of Hat Yai. The **west coast** route from Thailand via Padang Besar on the Malaysian border runs south through Butterworth (for Penang), Ipoh, Tapah Road (for the Cameron Highlands) and KL, where you usually have to change trains before continuing on to Singapore. Between KL and Singapore the train route splits at **Gemas**, 58km northeast of Melaka, from where a second line runs north through the mountainous interior – a section known as the **jungle railway** – via Kuala Lipis and skirting Kota Bharu (nearest station is at Wakaf Bharu) to the northeastern border town of Tumpat. If you want to get to Thailand by train this way, you have to get off at Pasir Mas and catch a bus or taxi to the border crossing at Rantau Panjang, since the Malaysian branch line to the border is no longer used (see p.244 for more details).

East Malaysia's only rail line is the 55-kilometre, narrow-gauge link between Kota Kinabalu and Tenom in **Sabah**. The service is slow and jarring, and only really worth following between Beaufort and Tenom, when it traces a dramatic path along Sungei Padas; all the details are on p.446.

There are two types of train: **express trains**, running on the west coast line only and stopping at principal stations, and **ordinary trains** (labelled *M* on the timetables), which run on both lines and stop at virtually every station. Where there's a choice, you'll find that the only real difference between them is the speed of the journey, since they are both divided into three classes with the option of air-con. Choosing an express train, however, on a west coast route can knock anything up to three hours off your journey time. You don't need to book in advance for ordinary trains, but you may want to reserve a day or two in advance (which incurs a small charge) for express trains, particularly if you require an overnight berth. This must be done at the station – reservations are not accepted over the phone.

On the **west coast** there are three trains a day between Singapore and KL, and five between KL and Padang Besar; of these, only one is an ordinary train. In addition, there is a once-daily *Kedah Line* service, running between Butterworth and Arau, and one **international express** a day between Butterworth and Bangkok, for which additional charges apply (see below). Thus to

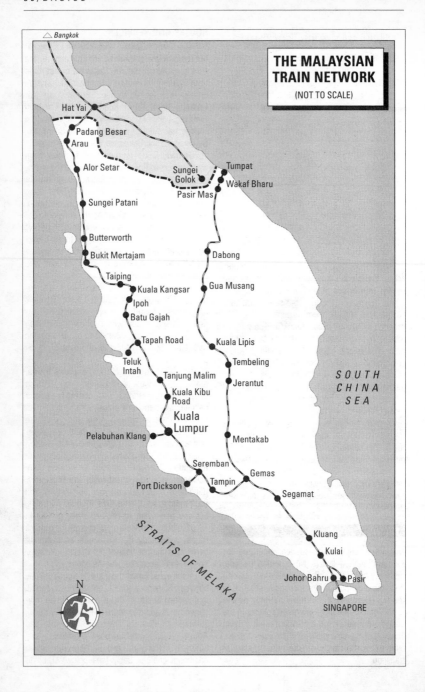

△ Bangkok

THE MALAYSIAN TRAIN NETWORK
(NOT TO SCALE)

Hat Yai
Padang Besar
Arau
Alor Setar
Sungei Patani
Butterworth
Bukit Mertajam
Taiping
Kuala Kangsar
Ipoh
Batu Gajah
Tapah Road
Teluk Intah
Tanjung Malim
Kuala Kibu Road
Kuala Lumpur
Pelabuhan Klang
Seremban
Port Dickson
Tampin

Sungei Golok
Tumpat
Wakaf Bharu
Pasir Mas
Dabong
Gua Musang
Kuala Lipis
Tembeling
Jerantut
Mentakab
Gemas
Segamat
Kluang
Kulai
Johor Bahru
Pasir
SINGAPORE

SOUTH CHINA SEA

STRAITS OF MELAKA

N

travel from Singapore to Bangkok involves changing at both KL and Butterworth, unless you catch the once-daily **Ekspres Raykat** train (ER on the timetable) from Singapore, which stops briefly at KL before continuing on to Butterworth – though you'll still have to wait there until the next day to pick up the Bangkok connection. Two daily services between Kluang and Singapore, and one daily between Gemas and Singapore, augment the west coast schedule. All the trains on the **interior route** are ordinary trains, with the exception of the *Tumpat Express* which runs three times weekly between Singapore and Tumpat. There's also a once-daily train from Gemas to Tumpat.

A free **timetable** for the whole country is available from the train station in Kuala Lumpur and other major towns; it details all the services on the various routes except for some additional local services on the jungle railway; all stations have departure and arrival times posted near the platform.

TICKETS AND PASSES

Fares vary according to class of travel and type of train; for main routes and prices see the box below. Second-class is usually roomy and comfortable enough for most journeys, and the only real advantage of first-class travel is the air-conditioning; first-class tickets are almost twice the price. Third-class, although only around half as much as second, is inevitably more crowded, with fewer comforts.

On **overnight sleepers**, there's only first- and second-class available, though you can opt for aircon or not in second class. A berth on the **international express** between Butterworth and Bangkok (see above) costs $22.70 first-class, from $18.10 in second-class air-con and from $8.10 in non-air-con, depending on whether you want an upper or lower berth. Charges for berths on all other overnight trains are marginally higher.

Eurotrain International offers an **Explorer Pass** to all under 26 years, students and people under 30 holding either an International Student Identity Card, Hostelling International membership card, or Young Scot card, but you'll have to be prepared to travel almost exclusively by train to get your money's worth. This is valid for unlimited second-class train travel on *KTM* in Peninsular Malaysia and Singapore for 7 (£25/US$40), 14 (£33/US$52) or 21 (£41/US$66) days; the pass includes the cost of seat reservations but not sleeper berth charges; it's also not valid on the Sabah train line. It's available from Campus Travel in London (see p.5 for address), or from student-orientated travel agents in Kuala Lumpur and Singapore, where it costs roughly the same in the local currencies.

TRANS-MALAYSIAN ROUTES

Other than the Malaysian journeys, one long-distance route you might consider is the train ride **from Singapore to Bangkok**, which takes a minimum of fifty hours. While there is only one through-connection from Singapore to Butterworth (the *Ekspres Raykat*), you never usually have to wait longer than an hour in KL to catch an onward service, although unfortunately none of the trains to Butterworth connect conveniently with the international express to Bangkok, involving either an overnight stop in Butterworth or, at best, a six-and-a-half-hour wait. It's a tiring journey done in one go, particularly if you don't book a berth on the overnight leg between Butterworth and Bangkok (see above for charges), but is the quickest way (other than flying) to travel right through Malaysia. **One-way tickets** for the whole route, from Singapore to Bangkok, cost M$206.80 first-class and M$91.70 second-class, though an Explorer Pass (see above) is valid on the Malaysian leg of the journey.

Following the same route in considerably more luxury, the **Eastern & Oriental Express** departs every Sunday from Singapore to Bangkok (returning on Thursday), stopping at Kuala Lumpur and Butterworth (for Penang); the trip takes fifty hours, includes two nights on the train and costs from £890/US$1424 per person, depending on the type of cabin. **Bookings** can be made at Eastern & Oriental Express, Sea Containers House, 20 Upper Ground, London SE1 (☎0171/928 6000); through some of the North American tour operators listed on p.12; in Singapore at E&O Services, 05/01 Carlton Building, 90 Cecil St (☎02/323 4390); or in Bangkok through Sea Tours Co. Ltd, Room 413/4, fourth floor, Siam Centre, 965 Ramal Rd (☎02/251 4862).

If you want to sample the luxury of colonial-era train travel, but can't afford the Eastern & Oriental Express, a good alternative is the **Peninsular Line**, which runs daily between Singapore and Tampin, near Melaka. The train departs from Singapore at 8.20am and arrives in Tampin at 1.50pm, where there is a bus transfer to Melaka. The return service leaves Tampin at 3pm and

SAMPLE TRAIN ROUTES AND FARES

All fares are given in Malaysian dollars.	EXPRESS			ORDINARY		
	1st	2nd	3rd	1st	2nd	3rd
Kuala Lumpur to:						
Alor Setar	79.00	37.00	23.00	70.50	30.60	17.40
Butterworth	67.00	34.00	19.00	58.50	25.40	14.40
Gemas	35.00	20.00	11.00	27.00	11.70	6.70
Ipoh	40.00	22.00	12.00	31.50	13.70	7.80
Kuala Lipis	–	–	–	61.50	26.70	15.20
Padang Besar	89.00	42.00	26.00	81.00	35.10	20.00
Taiping	53.00	28.00	16.00	45.00	19.50	11.10
Tapah Road	32.00	19.00	10.00	23.30	10.10	5.80
Tumpat	–	–	–	106.50	46.20	26.20
Singapore	68.00	34.00	19.00	60.00	26.00	15.00
Singapore to:						
Alor Setar	139.00	69.00	37.00	130.50	56.60	32.20
Butterworth	127.00	60.00	34.00	118.50	51.40	29.20
Gemas	43.00	23.00	13.00	34.00	15.00	8.50
Kuala Lipis	–	–	–	67.50	29.30	16.70
Kuala Lumpur	68.00	34.00	19.00	60.00	26.00	15.00
Padang Besar	148.00	69.00	39.00	139.00	60.50	34.40
Tumpat	–	–	–	112.50	48.80	27.70

arrives in Singapore at 9.20pm. For the section between Gemas and Tampin, the carriages are pulled by the only working steam locomotive on the Malaysian rail system. Fares start at $260 one-way, which includes all meals aboard the train. For bookings contact Specific Performance, Mezzanine floor, KL Railway Station, Jalan Sultan Hishamuddin, Kuala Lumpur (☎03/273 9118; fax 03/273 9634). There are plans to extend the service to cover the rest of the Peninsula.

LONG-DISTANCE TAXIS

Most towns have a long-distance **taxi rank** (usually right next to the express bus station). The four-seater taxis charge fixed-price, per-person fares on long-distance routes throughout the country; you can usually reckon on paying between 50 and 100 percent more than the regular bus fare. Prices are chalked up on a board in the station, so there's no danger of being ripped off – in fact, taxis are generally very reliable and a lot quicker than the buses. From Kuala Lumpur you're looking at around $30 to Butterworth, $17

to Ipoh and $35 to Kota Bharu. You'll have to wait until the car has its full complement of four passengers before departure, but in most major towns this should never be more than thirty minutes. As a foreigner you may be pressured to charter the whole car (at four times the one-person fare), making it expensive unless you're in a group.

FERRIES AND BOATS

Ferries sail to all the major islands off Malaysia's east and west coasts, though the traditional **bumboats** – originally used for fishing – are rapidly being replaced by faster, sleeker express models; if you want to experience an old-style bumboat ride, you can still do so in Singapore (p.515). On all ferries, you can buy your ticket in advance from booths at the jetty, though you can usually pay on the boat as well. All the relevant details are given in the text. There's a reduced service to the east coast Perhentian islands and to Redang, Kapas, Tioman and the rest of the Seribaut archipelago between the **monsoon**

months of November and February. The only regular **inter-island** connection is between Penang and Langkawi, a daily service taking two hours (p.192); there's a regular catamaran service between **Singapore and Pulau Tioman** (p.319). There are plans for a ferry service between Singapore and Johor Bahru. Boats also run from Langkawi to Thailand (see "The West Coast" p.192).

There are no ferry services across the South China Sea from the Peninsula to East Malaysia; you'll have to fly. Once in **Sarawak**, the most usual method of travel is by long, turbo-charged **express boat** along the widespread river systems. These low-lying craft are the lifeline of the people who live along the rivers in the interior and run to a regular timetable – buy your ticket on the boat. Once on the smaller tributaries, travel is by **longboat**, which often turns out to be more expensive since you may have to charter the whole vessel on some routes. For more details on getting around Sarawak by boat, see p.342.

Sabah has no express boats, but regular ferries connect Pulau Labuan with Kota Kinabalu, Sipitang and Menumbok on the west coast; details are given in the text. In **Brunei**, there are occasional boat services, including the speedboat service from the capital, Bandar Seri Begawan, to Bangar and the regular boats from Bandar to Lawas or Limbang in Sarawak and Pulau Labuan in Sabah; see p.486 for all the details.

PLANES

The Malaysian national airline, **MAS**, operates a comprehensive range of domestic flights, though services between major towns on the Peninsula are often routed via Kuala Lumpur, making them long-winded and uneconomical. But some routes are definitely worth considering: although expensive, the flight from KL to Langkawi (M$135 one-way) takes just 55 minutes, thus saving a lengthy eleven-hour bus journey followed by an hour's ferry ride.

Special fares offer considerable discounts to tourists. For example, designated **night tourist flights** can reduce the price of a one-way flight between KL and Alor Setar from $113 to $57; similar reductions are available on any night flights. In addition, **one-way** and **return excursion** fares operate between Johor Bahru and Kota Kinabulu, Kuching and Penang, and between KL and Kota Kinabulu, Kuching, Labuan and Miri, representing savings of 10–15 percent. **Family fares** within Malaysia (but excluding Singapore and Brunei) apply to a return trip made within thirty days: if one family member pays the full fare, the accompanying spouse and/or children get a 25 percent discount. Two types of **group fares** are in operation: between Peninsular Malaysia and East Malaysia and between Sabah and Sarawak, three or more passengers travelling together receive a 50 percent discount; for other routes in Malaysia, a 25 percent discount applies. To qualify, participants must stay between four and thirty days and full payment must be made at least seven days prior to departure. **Blind or disabled** passengers are entitled to a 50 percent discount, with a 25 percent reduction for a companion. There are **no student reductions** for anyone studying outside Malaysia.

One other way to keep internal flight costs down is to buy a **Discover Malaysia Pass**, which is only available in conjunction with an international MAS international sector ticket of some description. These cost approximately £62/US$99 for flights within one of Malaysia's three sectors (Sarawak, Sabah and the Peninsula) and £125/$199 for flights in any of these three. The passes are valid on a specific pre-booked itinerary for 28 days, although, after the first flight, dates of subsequent flights can be changed for free and the route can be changed at US$25 per change. The pass is valid for five "sectors", which gives you up to five free flights: from KL to most Peninsular destinations counts as one sector. When you buy the pass you must book your first internal connection: you can leave the dates open for the rest of the itinerary. See the "Getting There" sections above for details of MAS tickets and offices in your own country.

MAS has **booking offices** in every major town and city on the Peninsula, as well as in Sarawak, Sabah and Singapore; addresses and phone numbers are given throughout the text.

MAIN ROUTES

The most frequent service is the shuttle **between KL and Singapore**, on either MAS or Singapore Airlines, with departures every half-hour at peak times for a standard one-way fare of M$119 (S$111); the journey takes 55 minutes. There's also an hourly service **to Penang** (45min; M$104) from KL, and a Singapore Airlines service from Singapore (3 daily; S$340 return). In addition, the MAS subsidiary, Pelangi Air, operates Twin-Otter planes to the **islands** of Tioman and Pangkor from Kuala Lumpur, Kuantan and Singapore, as well as to the interior around Taman Negara (see relevant sections for details) – spectacular flights all. The Singapore Airlines subsidiary, SilkAir, also connects Singapore with Tioman, Langkawi and Kuantan.

Flights to East Malaysia operate mainly out of Kuala Lumpur, with Johor Bahru providing additional services to Kuching and Kota Kinabalu (see p.314 for more information). Note that flight times from KL to either Kuching or Kota Kinabalu can take longer than you think. Although direct services take roughly 1 hour 40 minutes to Kuching, and 2 hours 30 minutes to Kota Kinabalu, many flights are routed via Johor Bahru, with some Sabah-bound flights then making several more stops in Sarawak on the way. **Within Sarawak and Sabah**, the numerous nineteen-seater Twin-Otter flights help maintain communications with the remote provinces. There are regular rural air services **from Kuching** to most Sarawak towns, **from Kota Kinabalu** to Kudat, Lawas, Limbang, Miri and Sandakan, and **from Lawas** to Ba Kalalan and Limbang, among many others, though the more remote areas are susceptible to delays and cancellations due to weather conditions.

DRIVING AND VEHICLE RENTAL

The condition of the **roads** in Peninsular Malaysia is generally excellent, making driving there a viable prospect for tourists, though not so in Sabah, Sarawak and Brunei where the roads are rougher and highly susceptible to flash flooding.

On the Peninsula, the pristine **North–South Highway** (the only toll road in the country; see below) from Singapore runs nearly 900km up the west coast to the border with Thailand, with Route 1, its predecessor, shadowing it virtually all the way. At Kuala Lumpur, Route 2, a notorious accident blackspot, cuts through the central region to connect the capital with the east coast town of Kuantan, while much further to the north, the **East–West Highway** (Route 4) traces the Thai border to link Butterworth with Kota Bharu. The mountainous interior is sliced in two by the narrow and winding Route 8, which leaves Route 2 roughly 50km from Kuala Lumpur, passing through Kuala Lipis and Kuala Kerai before reaching Kota Bharu. The east coast is served by Route 3, a relatively traffic-free road that begins in Kota Bharu and terminates in Johor Bahru, 700km to

CAR RENTAL AGENCIES	
Britain	
Avis	☎0990/900500
Budget	☎0800/181181
Hertz	☎0990/996699
North America	
Avis	☎1-800/331-1212
Budget	☎1-800/527-0700
Hertz	☎1-800/654-3131
National Car Rental	☎1-800/227-7368
Australia	
Avis toll-free	☎1800/225 533
Budget local-call rate	☎13 2727
Hertz local-call rate	☎13 3039
New Zealand	
Avis	☎09/526 2847
Budget	☎09/375 2222
Hertz	☎09/309 0989

the south. As far as **journey times** go, you can reckon on a two-and-a-half-hour journey between Kuala Lumpur and Melaka, and about seven to Penang.

Note that the streets of **major cities** like Kuala Lumpur, Kuantan and Georgetown are particularly traffic-snarled, with confusing one-way systems to boot, not ideal for the disorientated driver.

With main roads so hassle-free, **fly-drive holidays** on the Malaysian Peninsula are a popular option. Several travel agencies (see "Getting There" sections above) offer pre-booked routes, or you can choose your own route, booking accommodation in hotels as you go.

CAR AND BIKE RENTAL

To **rent a vehicle** in Malaysia, Singapore and Brunei, you must be 23 or over and have held a clean driving licence for at least a year; a national driving licence, particularly if written in English, should be sufficient, though there's no harm in acquiring an International Driving Licence.

The major international **car rental agencies** represented in Malaysia and Singapore are Avis, Budget, Hertz and National, and you'll find at least one of their offices in each major town and at the airports; there is also a handful of local companies, which charge about the same. Useful addresses and phone numbers are given in the

A DRIVING VOCABULARY

Utara	North
Selatan	South
Barat	West
Timur	East
Awas	Caution
Ikut Kiri	Keep left
Kurangkan Laju	Slow down
Jalan Sehala	One way
Lencongan	Detour
Berhenti	Stop
Beri Laluan	Give way
Had Laju .../jam	Speed limit .../ per hour
Dilarang Memotong	No Overtaking
Dilarang Melatak Kereta	No Parking
Lebuhraya	Expressway

accounts of major cities. Note that the international rental agencies need at least two days' notice if you're booking and paying locally, or between three and seven days for a pre-paid booking before you leave your home country (see box for telephone numbers).

In **Malaysia**, rates begin at around M$165 (£42/US$68) per day for a basic Proton Saga, including unlimited mileage, personal insurance and usually a collision damage waiver of up to $2000; where this isn't included, an additional charge of around M$15 per day is levied. Rates for periods over three days are better value: a week's rental costs around M$700–800 (£175–200/US$262–300). If you want to take the car into Singapore, a surcharge of US$20 a day applies.

In **Singapore**, rental deals vary according to whether the three percent tax and collision damage waiver is included, but the rate, again for a Proton Saga, averages around S$140 (£56/US$84) a day, from S$730–830 (£317–360/US$507–576) a week. To take the car into Malaysia incurs a surcharge of S$25 per day. Offices usually require two days notice and a deposit of around S$100; this can be avoided by pre-booking abroad.

Motorbike rental is much more informal, usually offered by Malaysian guesthouses and shops in more touristy areas. You'll probably need to leave your passport as a deposit, but it's unlikely you'll have to show any proof of eligibility – officially you must be over 21 and have an appropriate driving licence. Wearing helmets is compulsory. Costs vary from M$20 to M$30 per day, while **bicycles** can be rented for around M$4 a day. For bike rental in Singapore, see p.514.

RULES OF THE ROAD AND OTHER MATTERS

Malaysia, Singapore and Brunei follow the UK system of **driving on the left**: most road signs are recognizable, and wearing seat belts in the front is compulsory. One confusing habit that Malaysian drivers have adopted is that they **flash their headlights** when they are claiming the right of way, *not* the other way around, as is common practice in the West.

On highways, the **speed limit** is 110km/hr, and 90km/hr on trunk roads, while in built-up areas it's 50km/hr; you'd be wise to stick religiously to these limits, since speed traps are commonplace and mandatory **fines** are a hefty $200. There are plenty of **garages** throughout Malaysia and Singapore; in any case, the rental agency will supply you with emergency numbers to call in the event of a **breakdown**.

Fuel is readily available in Malaysia and costs just over M$1 (25p/38 sen) a litre, slightly more in Singapore. The North–South Highway is the only **toll road** – you can reckon on paying approximately M$1 for every 7km travelled.

CITY TRANSPORT

Most Malaysian towns have some kind of **bus** service and details are given in the text wherever appropriate. Fares are always very cheap even if some of the systems – in places like KL and Georgetown – initially appear absolutely unfathomable to visitors. In KL, there are also the Komuter train and LRT (Light Rail Train) systems (see p.86). It's usually easier to jump in a **taxi** and sometimes that's the only way to reach certain local sights. Taxis are always metered, but meters not always used, despite this being illegal. Taxi drivers in KL often refuse to go to certain destinations, especially if the traffic is likely to be heavy or if it is raining. Drivers don't always speak English, so it's not a bad idea to have your destination written down on a piece of paper.

Trishaws (bicycle rickshaws), seating two people, are seen less and less these days, made redundant by the chaotic traffic systems in most towns. But they are still very much part of the tourist scene in places like Melaka, Penang and Kota Bharu, though in most cases they're not much cheaper than taking a taxi – bargain hard to fix the price in advance. You can expect to pay a minimum of $3 for a short journey, while chartering by the hour can be as much as $15. Taking a

trishaw tour in Georgetown and Melaka can be a useful introduction to the town and the drivers often provide interesting, anecdotal information. Subject to bargaining, these tours usually cost around $20 for an hour's ride. **Singapore** also has trishaws, as well as other methods of getting around – from river trips to helicopter rides; see p.511 for all the details.

ACCOMMODATION

While accommodation in Malaysia and Singapore is not the cheapest in Southeast Asia, in most places you can still get pretty good deals on simple rooms: in Malaysia, double rooms for under M$30 (£5/US$7.50) are common; under S$25 (£11/US$16.50) in Singapore. East Malaysia is more expensive, particularly in Sabah where you'll often pay M$25–30 (£6–7/US$9–10.50) for a very ordinary place, though the longhouses in Sarawak can be quite economical.

The very cheapest form of accommodation is in a dormitory bed at a guesthouse or lodge, but these generally only exist in the more obvious tourist spots – Singapore, Georgetown, Kota Bharu and Cherating. At the other end of the scale, the region's luxury hotels offer a level of comfort and style to rank with any in the world. Prices in these, relatively speaking, aren't too outrageous, and you have the chance of staying in some of the world's most famous colonial hotels, like the *Raffles* in Singapore and the *E&O* in Georgetown (closed for renovation until 1998).

At the budget end of the market you'll have to share a bathroom, which in most cases will feature a shower and either a squat or Western-style toilet. Older places, or those in rural areas, some-times have *mandis* instead of showers, a large basin of cold water which you throw over yourself with a bucket or ladle; it's very bad form to get soap in the basin or, worse still, get in it yourself. While **air-conditioning** is standard in the smarter hotels, some at the budget end also have special, slightly more expensive air-con rooms.

Room rates remain relatively stable throughout the year, though they can rise dramatically during the major holiday periods – Christmas, Easter and Hari Raya. It's always worth bargaining during the monsoon lull (from November to February). When asking for a room, note that a **single** room usually means it will contain one double bed, while a **double** has two double beds or two single beds, a **triple** three, and so on, making most rooms economical for families and groups; baby cots are usually available only in more expensive places.

In popular resorts, you'll often be accosted by people at bus or train stations advertising rooms: it's rarely worth going with them (especially since it's hard to turn down the room if you don't like it), although they can be useful in securing you a room in the peak holiday season, saving you a lot of fruitless trudging around.

GUESTHOUSES, HOMESTAYS AND HOSTELS

The mainstay of the travellers' scene in Malaysia and Singapore are the **guesthouses**, located in popular tourist areas and usually good places to meet other people and pick up information. They can range from simple beachside A-frame huts to modern multistorey apartment buildings complete with a TV and video room. Their advantage for the single traveller on a tight budget is that almost all offer **dormitory beds**, which can cost as little as M$7–8 a night (S$7). There are always basic double rooms available, too, usually with a fan and possibly a mosquito net, and averaging M$15 (S$20). Fierce competition on the Malaysian east coast means that prices there occasionally drop as low as M$10 for a double room, though this is somewhat offset by the pricier huts and chalets on the islands in the south, where you'll be hard pushed to find anything for under M$25.

In certain places – Kota Bharu especially – **homestay** programmes are available, whereby you stay with a Malaysian family, paying for your bed and board. The facilities are modest, and although some people find staying with a family too restrictive, it can be a good way of sampling Malay home cooking and culture. Local tourist offices have details of participants in the scheme.

Official **youth hostels** in Malaysia and Singapore are often hopelessly far-flung and no cheaper than dorms and rooms in the guesthouses – the rare exceptions are noted in the text. As a rule, it's not worth becoming an HI member just for the trip to Malaysia or Singapore, though if you're travelling further afield it might pay for itself eventually. Each major town generally also has both a **YMCA** and a **YWCA** which, like the youth hostels, are rarely conveniently located. Although facilities are better than those at the youth hostels, they cost around M$40 a night,

making them poor value compared to the budget hotels.

HOTELS

The cheapest **hotels** in Malaysia and Singapore are usually Chinese-run and cater for a predominantly local clientele. They're generally clean and well kept – though often housed in antiquated buildings – and there's never any need to book in advance: just go to the next place around the corner if your first choice is full. Ordinary rooms go for around M$20 ($25–30 in Singapore) and are usually divided by thin, partition walls; there'll always be a washbasin, table and ceiling fan, though never a mosquito net; mattresses are usually rock hard. In the better places – often old converted mansions – you may also be treated to beautifully polished wooden floors and antique furniture. You'll often have the choice of air-con rooms as well, though the noisy rattle may not seem worth the extra $10 or so. Showers and toilets (squat-style almost everywhere) are shared and can be pretty basic. The other consideration is the noise level, which can be very considerable since most places are on main streets. A word of **warning**: most of the hotels at the cheaper end of the scale also function as brothels and you should pick and choose carefully, particularly if you're a woman travelling alone. Those which use the Malay term *Rumah Persinggahan* usually double as brothels.

If you can't stand the noise in the cheaper places, then the **mid-range hotels** are your only alternative in most towns, though they're rarely better value than a well-kept budget place. The big difference is in the comfort of the mattress – nearly always sprung – and getting your own Western-style bathroom. Prices range from M$40–150 (S$40–150 in Singapore), and for this you can expect a carpeted room with air-con and TV, and, towards the upper end of the range, a telephone and refrigerator. In these places, too, a genuine distinction is made between single rooms and doubles.

Also in the mid-range category are **Government Resthouses** (*Rumah Rehat*), which once provided accommodation for visiting colonial officials, though a lot of the old buildings have been replaced by more modern ones. Facilities, varying from the antiquated to the modern, are generally excellent value: rooms are large and well equipped, usually with a separate lounge area and always with private bathrooms. Each resthouse has its own restaurant as well. In many towns the resthouses have been replaced by *Seri Malaysia* hotels, which offer a uniformly good standard of accommodation for around $100 per night, including breakfast.

Moving to the top of the scale, the **high-class hotels** are as comfortable as you might expect, many with state-of-the-art facilities. Recently, the trend in Malaysia has been to reflect local traditions with the incorporation of kampung-style architecture – low-level timber structures with saddle-shaped roofs and open-sided public areas – though such hotels still feature all the usual trappings of swimming pools, air conditioning and business facilities. While prices can be as reasonable at M$150 per room (S$200), rates in popular destinations such as Penang can rocket to M$400 and above – though this is still relatively good value compared to hotels of an equivalent standard in London or New York. Having said that, famous hotels, like the *Raffles* in Singapore, can virtually charge what they like. Don't forget that the price quoted by the hotel rarely includes the compulsory 10 percent **service charge** and 5 percent **government tax** (4 percent in Singapore), often signified by "++" after the price. It is always cheaper to stay at top hotels if you're on a pre-booked package – ask your travel agent if you want to stay at a specific hotel.

LONGHOUSES

The most atmospheric accommodation in Malaysia is in the wood-and-bamboo stilted **longhouses**, found only on the rivers of **Sarawak** and **Sabah**. These can house dozens of families, and usually consist of three elevated sections reached by a simple ladder. A long, open verandah is used for jobs like drying rice and washing clothes, behind is a longroom where the families eat, dance, talk and play music and games, and further in are the private quarters of each family, usually just one room with an open fire for cooking. Of course, each tribe has its idiosyncratic variations on this basic pattern. Large mats are stored in the rafters and brought down to sleep or sit on. Contemporary longhouses are built increasingly of more durable material like stone and hardwoods, and furnished with corrugated iron roofs, although some built in the traditional manner still exist and some of these are accessible to visitors, too. Most tourists stay at longhouses as part of an organized tour, and these are inevitably more commercial, but if you're interested, it's actually quite easy to travel along the rivers and, with a minimal command of Malay, be directed to communities off the beaten track which seldom see visitors.

Traditionally, there's no charge to stay in a longhouse, though it is good manners to bring **gifts** such as exercise books and pens and pencils for children, or to give a donation of, say, $10 a head. Once there, you can participate in many activities including learning to weave, cook, use a blowpipe, fish, help in the agricultural plots, and perhaps go out on a wild boar hunt. All the details, including a rundown of longhouse etiquette, are given on p.343 and p.371.

CAMPING

Despite the rural nature of most of Malaysia, there are few official opportunities for **camping**, perhaps because guesthouses and hotels are so reasonable. Where there are campsites, they charge around $10, and facilities are very basic. If you go trekking in the more remote regions, for example in Endau-Rompin National Park, camping is about your only option – note that, even if you're on an organized trip, equipment is rarely included in the advertised price. In **Singapore**, camping is confined to Pulau Ubin and Pulau Sentosa (see p.516); there are no official campsites in Brunei.

EATING AND DRINKING

One of the best reasons to come to Malaysia and Singapore (even Brunei, to a lesser extent) is for the food. The countries' cuisines are inspired by the heritage of their three main communities, Malay, Chinese and Indian. From the ubiquitous hawker stalls to the restaurants in world-class hotels, the standard of cooking is extremely high and food everywhere is remarkably good value.

Basic noodle- or rice-based meals at a stall will rarely come to more than a few Malaysian or Singaporean dollars, and even a full meal with drinks in a reputable restaurant should rarely run to more than M$40–S$30 a head – though if you develop a taste for delicacies such as shark's-fin or bird's-nest soup, the sky is the limit. The most renowned culinary centres are Singapore, Georgetown, KL, Melaka and Kota Bharu, although other towns, like Johor Bahru, Ipoh, Kuching and Sibu all have their own distinctive dishes.

THE CUISINES

As well as mainstream dishes from the principal ethnic cuisines – Malay, Chinese and Indian –

hawker stalls, cafés and restaurants throughout the region serve up a variety of regional dishes that reflect the pattern of immigration over the last five hundred years. The most familiar Chinese cooking style is Cantonese, but all over Malaysia and Singapore you can also sample Szechuan, Hokkien, Beijing and other regional Chinese specialities. Indian food splits into northern, southern or Muslim styles of cooking, while even the indigenous Malay cuisine mixes various elements from other Asian cuisines. The main oddity for the visitor is that there is no such thing as specifically Singaporean cuisine – there, and in the former Straits Settlement towns in Malaysia like Georgetown and Melaka, a hybrid cuisine known as Nonya evolved from the mixed-race marriages of early Chinese immigrants and local Malays. Below are accounts of the different cuisines, while for a rundown of the most popular dishes, turn to the food glossary on p.49.

MALAY FOOD

Surprisingly perhaps, good **Malay** cuisine can be hard to find, with the best cooking often confined to the home. On the positive side, the Malay restaurants that do exist are of a universally high standard, presenting dishes with a loving attention to detail. The cuisine is based on rice, often enriched with *santan* (coconut milk), which is served with a dizzying variety of curries and *sambal*, a condiment comprising pounded chillies blended with *belacan* (shrimp paste), onions and garlic. Other spices which characterize Malay cuisine include ginger and *galangal* (a ginger-like root), coriander, lemon grass and lime leaves.

The most famous **dish** is satay – virtually Malaysia's national dish – which is skewers of barbecued meat (chicken, mutton or beef) dipped in spicy peanut sauce. The classic way to sample Malay curries is to eat *nasi campur*, a buffet (usually served at lunchtime) of steamed rice supplemented by any of up to two dozen accompanying dishes, including *lembu* (beef), *kangkong* (greens), fried chicken and fish steaks and curry sauce, and various vegetables. Other popular dishes include *nasi goreng* (mixed fried rice with meat, seafood and vegetables), and *rendang*. Pork, of course, is taboo to all Muslims, but it has been married with Malay cooking in Nonya dishes, for which see below. For **breakfast**, the most popular Malay dish is *nasi lemak*, rice cooked in coconut milk and served with *sambal ikan bilis* (tiny crisp-fried anchovies in hot chilli paste), fried peanuts and slices of fried or hard-boiled egg.

Much of the diet of the indigenous groups living in settled communities in **East Malaysia** tends to revolve around standard Malay and Chinese dishes. But in the remoter regions, or at festival times, you may have an opportunity to sample ethnic cuisine. In Sabah's Klias Peninsula and in **Brunei**, villagers still produce *ambuyat*, a glue-like, sago starch porridge that's dipped in sauce; or there's the Murut speciality of *jaruk* – raw wild boar, fermented in a bamboo tube, and definitely an acquired taste. Most famous of Sabah's dishes is *hinava*, or raw fish pickled in lime juice. In Sarawak, you're most likely to eat with the Iban or Kelabit, sampling wild boar with jungle ferns and sticky rice.

NONYA FOOD

The earliest Chinese immigrants settled in the Straits Settlements of Melaka, Penang and Singapore and intermarried with local Malays, their descendants – the Peranakans – evolving their own particular culture and cuisine, called **Nonya**, from the name given to women of Straits Chinese families (men were called Babas). There's more information on Peranakan culture on p.302 and p.536.

Typical Nonya **dishes** incorporate elements and ingredients from Chinese, Indonesian and Thai cooking, the end product tending to be spicier than Chinese food. Chicken, fish and seafood form the backbone of the cuisine, and unlike Malay food, pork is used. Noodles (*mee*) flavoured with chillies, and rich curries made from rice flour and coconut cream, are common. A popular dish is *laksa*, noodles in spicy coconut soup served with seafood and finely chopped beansprouts, lemon grass, pineapple, pepper, lime leaves and chilli; *assam laksa* is the version served in Penang, its fish stock giving it a sharper taste. Other popular Nonya dishes include *ayam buah*

keluak, chicken cooked with Indonesian "black" nuts; and *otak-otak*, fish mashed with coconut milk and chilli paste and steamed in a banana leaf.

CHINESE FOOD

Chinese food dominates in Singapore and Malaysia, with perhaps only the cooking in Hong Kong reaching a higher standard – fish and seafood is nearly always outstanding, with prawns, crab, squid and a variety of fish on offer almost everywhere. Noodles, too, are ubiquitous, and come in wonderful variations – thin, flat, round, served in soup (wet) or fried (dry).

The dominant style of Chinese cookery is **Cantonese** – as it is in most foreign countries, echoing the pattern of immigration from southern China – but later groups of settlers from **other regions** of China spread Foochow, Hokkien, Hainanese, Teochow and Szechuan dishes throughout Peninsular Malaysia, East Malaysia and Singapore. Of these, Hokkien and Teochow are dominant, especially in Singapore where Hokkien fried *mee* (noodles with pork, prawn and vegetables) and *char kuey teow* (spicy flat noodles mixed with meat, fish and egg) are available almost everywhere. The classic Cantonese lunch is *dim sum* (literally "to touch the heart"), a variety of steamed and fried dumplings served in bamboo baskets in cafés and restaurants. Other popular lunch dishes are Hainan chicken rice (not surprisingly, rice cooked in chicken stock and topped with tender steamed or fried chicken) or rice topped with *char siew* (roast pork); while standard dishes available everywhere include chicken in chilli or with cashew nuts; buttered prawns, or prawns served with a sweet and sour sauce; spare ribs; and mixed vegetables with tofu (beancurd) and beansprouts. For something a little more unusual, try a **steamboat**, a Chinese-style fondue filled with boiling stock in which you cook meat, fish, shellfish, eggs and vegetables; or a **claypot** – meat, fish or shellfish cooked over a fire in an earthenware pot.

INDIAN FOOD

In the same way as the Chinese, immigrants from north and south **India** brought their own cuisines with them, which vary in emphasis and ingredients, though all utilize *daal* (lentils), chutneys, yoghurts and sweet or sour *lassis* (yoghurt drinks); neither north nor south Indians eat beef. North Indian food tends to rely more on meat, especially mutton and chicken, and uses breads – *naan*, *chapatis*, *parathas* and *rotis* – rather than rice to great effect. The most famous style of north Indian cooking is *tandoori* – named after the clay oven in which the food is cooked – and you'll commonly come across *tandoori* chicken marinated in yoghurt and spices and then baked. A favourite **breakfast** is *roti canai* (pancake and *daal*) or *roti kaya* (pancake spread with egg and jam).

Southern Indian (and Sri Lankan) food tends to be spicier and more reliant on vegetables. Its staple is the *dosai* (pancake), often served at breakfast time as a *masala dosai*, stuffed with onions, vegetables and chutney, and washed down with *teh tarik*, a sweet, frothy milky tea. Indian Muslims serve the similar *murtabak*, a grilled *roti* pancake with egg, onion and minced meat.

Many south Indian cafés turn to serving *daun pisang* at lunchtime, usually a vegetarian meal where rice is served on banana leaves and small, replenishable heaps of various vegetable curries are placed alongside; in some places, meat and fish side dishes are on offer, too. It's normal to eat a **banana leaf** meal with your right hand, though restaurants will always have cutlery if you can't manage. As with the other immigrant cuisines, the Indian food available in Malaysia and Singapore has adapted to Malay tastes and to the availability of ingredients over the years: banana leaf curry, for example, is more widely available in Malaysia and Singapore than in India, while another Malay Indian staple, *mee goreng* – fried egg noodles with spices and chillies – isn't known at all in India.

HAWKER STALLS

To eat inexpensively in Malaysia or Singapore you go to **hawker stalls**, traditionally simple wooden stalls on the roadside, with a few stools to sit at. In Singapore, Kuala Lumpur and some other major cities, the trend is to corral hawker stalls in neat, air-conditioned food centres where you can pick different dishes from a variety of stalls, but in most of Malaysia the old-style stalls still dominate the streets.

Wherever you find the stalls, you don't have to worry too much about **hygiene**: most are scrupulously clean, with the food cooked instantly in front of you. Avoid dishes that look as if they've been standing around for a while, or have been reheated, and you should be fine. The standard of

---

VEGETARIANS AND VEGANS

Vegetarians will find specialist Chinese and Indian restaurants in larger towns and cities; details are given in the text. If you're going to more remote areas, things get trickier – the Chinese barely class chicken and pork as meat, and anyway, meat stock forms the basis of many Chinese dishes. It's wise to say "I only eat vegetables" (in Bahasa Malay: *saya hanya makan sayuran*) and steel yourself for a diet of vegetables and rice.

Vegans really have their work cut out: tell your waiter, "I do not eat dairy products or meat" (*saya tidak makanan yang di perbuat dari susu atau daging*) and keep your fingers crossed.

---

cooking at hawker stalls is high and they are very popular; politicians and pop stars crowd in with the locals to eat at the cramped tables.

Most hawker stalls serve standard Malay **noodle and rice dishes**, satay and, in many places, more obscure regional delicacies. The influence of the region's immigrants also means you'll encounter Chinese noodle and seafood dishes, Indian specialities and Indonesian food. At modern food centres, particularly in Singapore, you'll increasingly come across Western food like burgers, and steak and eggs, or even Japanese and Korean food.

Hawker stalls don't have menus, though most have signs in English detailing their specialities; otherwise point at anything you like the look of. When you **order** a dish, make it clear if you want a small, medium or large portion – or else you'll get the biggest and most expensive one. You don't have to sit close to the stall you're patronizing: find a free table, and the vendor will track you down when your food is ready. Meals are paid for when they reach your table.

Most hawker stalls are closed at breakfast time, as Malays tend to eat before they go to work, and Chinese and Indians head for the coffee houses and cafés. Most outdoor stalls open instead at around midday, usually offering the day's *nasi campur* selection; prices are determined by the number of dishes you choose on top of your rice; most stalls (and cafés) charge around $1–1.50 per portion. Hawker stalls usually close well before midnight; any open after this time will be limited to fried noodles and soups. Hawker centres will usually have a hot and cold drinks stall on hand; in Singapore, you'll always be able to get a **beer**, too.

KEDAI KOPIS

Few streets exist without a **kedai kopi** (a coffee house or café), usually run by Chinese or Indians. Most open at 8am or 9am; closing times vary from 6pm to midnight. Basic Chinese coffee houses serve noodle and rice dishes all day, and feature a decent selection of cakes and cookies. The culinary standard is never spectacularly high, but you're unlikely to spend more than two or three dollars for a filling one-plate meal. Some cafés are a little more adventurous and serve full meals of meat, seafood and vegetables, for which you'll pay from around $5 per person; Malay-run cafés, where you can find them, usually serve a midday spread of *nasi campur* dishes. Indian cafés tend to be a bit livelier and – especially in the Indian quarters of Singapore, Kuala Lumpur, Georgetown and Melaka – decidedly theatrical. Here you can watch the Muslim *mamak* men at work, making the frothy *teh tarik* (tea) by pouring liquid from a height from one vessel into another, and pounding and moulding the *roti* into an oily, bubble-filled shape.

It's worth noting that the Chinese *kedai kopis* are often the only places you'll be able to get a beer in the evening; this is especially true in towns along Malaysia's largely Muslim east coast.

RESTAURANTS

On the whole, proper **restaurants** are either places you go to be seen or to savour particular delicacies found nowhere else, like **fish-head curry** (a famous Singaporean dish), Chinese specialities like **shark's-fin dishes** and **bird's-nest soup**, and high-quality seafood. In many restaurants, the food is not necessarily superior to that served at a good café or hawker stall – you're just paying the (often considerable) extra for air-con and tablecloths. One reason to splash out, though, is to experience a **cultural show** of music and dance, often performed in larger restaurants in the main cities – in Singapore, several of the large Chinese seafood restaurants put on displays. Some of the best of the shows are detailed in the text.

Both Malaysia and Singapore do have a tradition of **haute cuisine**, usually available in new restaurants decorated in traditional kampung-style, or in the top-notch hotels. All the best hotel-restaurants in Kuala Lumpur, Singapore and Georgetown boast well-known chefs, drawing in the punters with well-received French, Thai and Japanese food as well as more local delicacies.

Unless you're in a Muslim restaurant, or anywhere in Brunei, you'll be able to wash down your meal with a glass of cold **beer**; wine is less common, though smarter establishments will normally retain a modest choice. Few **desserts** feature on Southeast Asian restaurant menus, but the region's bounty of tropical **fruit** more than compensates: the glossary on p.51 lists some of the less familiar fruits you may come across.

Tipping is not expected and bills arrive complete with service charge and (in Malaysia and Singapore) government tax. In the main, restaurants are open from 11.30am to 2.30pm and from 6 to 10.30pm. Making yourself understood is rarely a problem, and nor is negotiating a menu: many are written in English, especially in Singapore.

DRINKING

Tap water is safe to drink in Malaysia and Singapore, though it's wise to stick to bottled water when travelling in rural areas (and in Sarawak and Sabah), widely available for around $2 a litre. Using ice for drinks is generally fine, too, making the huge variety of seasonal **fresh fruit drinks**, available in hawker centres and street corners, even more pleasant; always specify that you want them without sugar, unless you like your fruit juice heavily laced with syrup. Sugar-cane mangles can be found on many street corners, producing a watery, sweet drink that's very cloying yet still manages to be invigorating. The usual range of **soft drinks** is available everywhere for around $1.20 a can/carton, with the F&N and Yeo companies providing more unusual flavours, and Pokka making cans of decent fruit juices. Saccharine-filled drinks of fruit juice in boxes with a straw can be handy for journeys, again costing about $1 a piece; soya milk in cartons is another popular local choice.

Tea and coffee are as much national drinks as they are in the West, though you'll often find that sweet condensed milk is added unless you ask for it without (*teh-o* is tea without milk, *kopi-o* for coffee). If you don't like the often over-

A FOOD AND DRINK GLOSSARY

Many menus, especially in Singapore, are written in English, but it's worth noting that transliterated spellings are not standardized throughout Malaysia and Singapore – you may well see some of the following dishes written in a variety of ways; we've used the most widely accepted spellings. For a full rundown of the various cuisines available in Malaysia and Singapore, see pp.45–47.

NOODLES (*MEE*) AND NOODLE DISHES

Bee hoon Thin rice noodles, like vermicelli; *mee fun* is similar.

Char kuey teow Flat noodles with any combination of prawns, Chinese sausage, fishcake, egg, vegetables and chilli.

Foochow noodles Steamed and served in soy and oyster sauce with spring onions and dried fish.

Hokkien fried mee Yellow noodles fried with pieces of pork, prawn and vegetables.

Kang puan mee A rich Sibu speciality – noodles cooked in lard.

Kuey teow Flat noodles, comparable to Italian tagliatelle; *hor fun* is similar.

Laksa Noodles, beansprouts, fishcakes and prawns in a spicy coconut soup.

Mee Standard round yellow noodles that look like spaghetti and are made from wheat flour.

Mee goreng Indian fried noodles.

Mee suah Noodles served dry and crispy.

Sar hor fun Flat rice noodles served in a chicken stock soup, to which prawns, fried shallots and beansprouts are added; a speciality in Ipoh.

Wan ton mee Roast pork, noodles and vegetables served in a light soup containing dumplings.

RICE (*NASI*) DISHES

Biriyani Saffron-flavoured rice cooked with chicken, beef or fish; a North Indian speciality.

Claypot Rice topped with meat (as diverse as chicken and turtle), cooked in an earthenware pot over a fire to create a smoky taste.

Daun pisang Malay term for banana leaf curry, a southern Indian meal with chutneys and curries, served on a mound of rice, and presented on a banana leaf with *popadums*.

Hainan chicken rice Singapore's unofficial national dish: steamed or boiled chicken slices on rice cooked in chicken stock, and served with chicken broth, and chilli and ginger sauce.

Kunyit Rice cooked in turmeric; a side dish.

Lemang Glutinous rice stuffed into lengths of bamboo.

Nasi campur Rice served with an array of meat, fish and vegetable dishes.

Nasi goreng Fried rice with diced meat and vegetables.

Nasi kerabu Purple, green or blue rice with a dash of vegetables, seaweed and grated coconut; a Kota Bharu speciality.

Nasi lemak A Malay classic: *ikan bilis* (fried anchovies), cucumber, peanuts and fried or hard-boiled egg slices served on coconut rice.

Nasi puteh Plain boiled rice.

MEAT, FISH AND BASICS

Ayam	Chicken	*Kepiting*	Crab	*Sup*	Soup
Babi	Pork	*Kambing*	Mutton	*Tahu*	Tofu (beancurd)
Daging	Beef	*Sayur*	Vegetable	*Telor*	Egg
Ikan	Fish	*Sotong*	Squid	*Udang*	Prawn

GENERAL TERMS

Assam	Sour	*Istimewa*	Special (as in	*Manis*	Sweet
Garam	Salt		"today's special")	*Minum*	Drink
Goreng	Fried	*Kari*	Curry		
Gula	Sugar	*Makan*	Food		*Continued over*

Continued over

Continued from over

OTHER SPECIALITIES

Ayam goreng Malay-style fried chicken.

Ayam percik Barbecued chicken with a creamy coconut sauce; a Kota Bharu speciality.

Bak kut teh Literally "pork bone tea", a Chinese dish of pork ribs in soya sauce, ginger, herbs and spices.

Char siew pow Cantonese steamed bun stuffed with roast pork in a sweet sauce.

Chay tow kueh Also known as "carrot cake", this is actually an omelette made with white radish and spring onions.

Congee Rice porridge, cooked in lots of water and eaten with slices of meat and fish; sometimes listed on menus as "porridge".

Coto makassar A meat broth boosted with chunks of rice cake.

Dim sum Chinese titbits – dumplings, rolls, chicken's feet – steamed or fried and served in bamboo baskets.

Dosai Southern Indian pancake, made from ground rice and lentils, and served with *daal* (lentils) and spicy dips.

Fish-head curry The head of a red snapper (usually), cooked in a spicy curry sauce with tomatoes and okra; a contender for the title of Singapore's most famous dish.

Gado gado Malay/Indonesian salad of lightly cooked vegetables, boiled egg, slices of rice cake and a crunchy peanut sauce.

Ikan bilis Deep-fried anchovies.

Kai pow Similar to *char siew pow*, but contains chicken and boiled egg.

Kerupuk Crackers.

Kongbian Chinese-style bagels, found only in Sibu.

Midin Stir-fried jungle fern, native to Sarawak.

Murtabak Thick Indian pancake, stuffed with onion, egg and chicken or mutton.

Otak-otak Fish mashed with coconut milk and chilli paste and steamed in a banana leaf; a Nonya dish.

Popiah Chinese spring rolls, filled with peanuts, egg, beanshoots, vegetables and a sweet sauce; sometimes known as *Lumpia*.

Rendang Dry, highly spiced coconut curry with beef, chicken or mutton.

Rojak Indian fritters dipped in chilli and peanut sauce; the Chinese version is a salad of greens, beansprouts, pineapple and cucumber in a peanut-and-prawn paste sauce, similar to *gado gado*.

Roti canai Light, layered Indian pancake served with a thin curry sauce or *daal*; sometimes called *roti pratha*.

Roti john Simple Indian dish of egg, onion and tomato sauce spread on bread and heated.

Satay Marinated pieces of meat, skewered on small sticks and cooked over charcoal; served with peanut sauce, cucumber and *ketupat* (rice cake).

Sop kambing Spicy Indian mutton soup.

Steamboat Chinese equivalent of the Swiss fondue: raw vegetables, meat or fish and other titbits dunked into a steaming broth until cooked.

Umai Raw fish salad, mixed with shallots and lime, found in East Malaysia and Brunei.

Yam basket Sarawak speciality: meat, vegetables and soya beancurd in a fried yam pie crust.

DESSERTS

Bubor cha cha Sweetened coconut milk with pieces of sweet potato, yam and tapioca balls.

Cendol Coconut milk, palm sugar syrup and pea-flour noodles poured over shaved ice.

Es kachang Shaved ice with red beans, cubes of jelly, sweetcorn, rose syrup and evaporated milk.

Pisang goreng Fried banana fritters.

Pisang murtabak Banana pancake.

DRINKS

Air minum	Water.	*Teh*	Tea.
Bir	Beer.	*Teh-o*	Black tea.
Jus	Fruit juice.	*Teh susu*	Tea with milk.
Kopi	Coffee.	*Teh tarik*	Sweet, milky tea, poured between two cups to produce a frothy drink.
Kopi-o	Black coffee.		
Kopi susu	Coffee with milk.		
Lassi	Sweet or sour yoghurt drink of Indian origin.		

brewed tea or coffee, most cafés have *milo*, the ubiquitous hot chocolate drink.

ALCOHOLIC DRINKS

Only in Brunei (officially a dry state) and certain places on the east coast of the Malaysian Peninsula is drinking **alcohol** outlawed. Elsewhere in Malaysia and Singapore, despite the Muslim influence, alcohol is available in bars, restaurants, Chinese *kedai kopis* and supermarkets.

Anchor and Tiger **beer** (lager) are locally produced (see p.565 for more) and are probably the best choice, though you can also get other Western beers, as well as the Chinese Tsingtao and a variety of stouts (like Guinness) – including the Singaporean ABC, which is truly horrible. It's best drunk mixed with a Tiger beer, which is what you'll see many people doing.

Locally produced **whisky** and **rum** are cheap enough, too, though it's pretty rough stuff and can well do with mixing with Coke. The **brandy**, which is what the local Chinese drink, tends to be better. In the more upmarket restaurants, you can get cocktails and imported **wine**, the latter hideously expensive (at least M$60 a bottle) and often not very good at all. Only on Pulau Langkawi and Sabah's Pulau Labuan, both duty-free islands, can wine be bought from the supermarkets at prices roughly equivalent to the West (approximately M$20 for the least expensive bottle).

WHERE TO DRINK

In **Malaysia**, there is a thriving **bar scene** in KL (mainly in the Golden Triangle and Bangsar) and its modern suburb, Petaling Jaya, popular with

---

TROPICAL FRUIT

The more familiar fruits available in Malaysia and Singapore include forty varieties of banana, known locally as *pisang*; coconut (*kelapa*); seven varieties of mango; three types of pineapple (*nanas*); and watermelon (*tembiki*).

Chempedak This smaller version of the *nangka* (see below) is normally deep-fried, enabling the seed, which tastes like new potato, to be eaten too.

Ciku Looks like an apple; varies from yellow to pinkish brown when ripe, with a soft, pulpy flesh.

Durian Malaysia and Singapore's most popular fruit has a greeny-yellow, spiky exterior and grows to the size of a football from March to May, June to August, and November to February. It has thick, yellow-white flesh and an incredibly pungent odour likened to a mixture of mature cheese and caramel.

Guava A green, textured skin and flesh with five times the vitamin C content of orange juice.

Jackfruit This large, pear-shaped fruit, also known as *nangka*, grows up to 50cm long and has a greeny-yellow exterior with sweet flesh inside.

Langsat Together with its sister fruit, the *duku*, this looks like a small, round potato, with juicy white flesh which can be anything from sweet to sour.

Longgan Similar to the lychee, this has juicy white flesh and brown seeds.

Mangosteen Available from June to August and November to January, it has a sweet though slightly acidic flavour. Its smooth rind deepens to a distinctive crimson colour when ripe.

Markisa Known in the West as passion fruit, this has purple-brown dimpled skin with a rich flavour; it's a frequent ingredient in drinks.

Papaya Better known as *betik*, this milky orange-coloured flesh is a rich source of vitamins A and C.

Pomelo The pomelo, or *limau bali*, is the largest of all the citrus fruits and looks rather like a grapefruit, though it is slightly drier and has less flavour.

Rambutan The bright red rambutan's soft, spiny exterior has given it its name – *rambut* means "hair" in Malay. Usually about the size of a golf ball, it has a white, opaque fruit of delicate flavour, similar to a lychee.

Salak Teardrop-shaped, the *salak* has a skin like a snake's and a tart taste.

Star fruit Also known as *carambola*, this waxy, pale-green star-shaped fruit is said to be good for high blood pressure; the yellower the fruit, the sweeter its flesh.

Zirzat Inside its bumpy, muddy green skin is smooth white flesh like blancmange, hence its other name, custard apple; also known as sour-sop (and described by Margaret Brooke, wife of Sarawak's second Rajah, Charles, as "tasting like cotton wool dipped in vinegar and sugar").

fashionable youths and yuppies. Other towns have less of a scene, though in most of the places popular with Western tourists, you'll be able to get a beer in something approaching a bar – otherwise, go to a Chinese *kedai kopi* for a bottle of beer. Fierce competition keeps **happy hours** a regular feature in most bars (usually daily 5–7pm), bringing the beer down to around M$4.50 a glass, though spirits still remain pricey; look out for "all-night" discounts that appear from time to time. While there are some bars which open all day (11am–11pm), most tend to double as clubs, opening in the evenings until 3 or 4am.

In **Singapore**, bars are much the same, although the variety is even wider, ranging from those run on an English pub theme, featuring occasional guest beers from the UK, through to early evening karaoke bars – all the details are on p.583. The more glitzy places often introduce a cover charge (around $8–25) from 10pm onwards at weekends. Bars open from 7pm to midnight, though some also cater for the lunchtime crowd by offering bargain meals.

COMMUNICATIONS: POST, PHONES AND THE MEDIA

The communications network in Malaysia and Singapore is generally fast and efficient, though you can occasionally experience difficulties in making local phone calls in Malaysia (particularly in the states of Sabah and Sarawak), and some of the smaller offshore islands still have no phone network. Mobile phones are in evidence everywhere, and in many remote areas, this can be the only way of keeping in touch.

You can send mail *to* Malaysia, Singapore and Brunei care of the poste restante/general delivery section of the local GPO (see below); when picking up mail, be sure to have the staff check under first names as well as family names – misfiling is common.

POSTAL SERVICES

In **Malaysia**, the postal service is well organized, with overseas mail taking four to seven days to reach its destination. Postcards to anywhere in the world require a 50 sen stamp, while aerogrammes cost a uniform 50 sen; you can buy stamps in post offices. Packages are expensive to send, with surface/sea mail taking around two months to Europe, longer to the USA, and even air mail taking a few weeks. It's worth noting that if you leave your letter or package **unsealed**, the postage will be cheaper. There's usually a shop near the post office which will wrap your parcel for $5 or so. Each Malaysian town has a **General Post Office** (GPO) with a **poste restante/general delivery** section, where mail will be held for two months. If you're having mail sent there, make sure your surname is in capitals or underlined, and that the letter is addressed as follows: name, Poste Restante, GPO, town or city, state (optional). GPOs will also forward mail (for one month), free of charge, if you fill in the appropriate form. Usual post office **opening hours** are Monday to Saturday 8am–6pm (except for the east coast states, where Friday is closing day).

In **Singapore**, the GPO, housing the poste restante counter, is on Robinson Road; see p.593 for more details and opening hours. There are other post offices across the state, with usual hours of Monday to Friday 8.30am–5pm and Saturday 8.30am–1pm, though postal services are available until 9pm at the Comcentre on

Killiney Road (Mon–Fri). Singapore's postal system is predictably efficient, with letters and cards often reaching their destination within three days. Stamps are available at post offices (some have vending machines operating out of hours), and at some stationers and hotels. Airmail letters to Europe and the US start at 75c, aerogrammes to all destinations cost 35c and postcards cost 30c. You'll find fax and telex facilities in all major post offices, too, while if you want to make up a parcel, postpacs (cardboard cartons) are available in varying sizes. Surface mail is the cheapest means of sending a parcel home: a parcel under 10kg costs $43 to the UK, $74 to the USA and $35 to Canada and Australasia; there's a wrapping counter at the GPO.

Post offices in **Brunei** are open Monday to Thursday and Saturday 7.45am–4.30pm; see p.492 for details of the GPO. Some hotels can also provide basic postal facilities. Postcards to anywhere in the world cost 30c, aerogrammes 45c; overseas letters cost 90c for every 10g.

TELEPHONES

For dialling to and from the region, see the box below for all the relevant **dialling code** information. Note that Singapore has no **area codes**; both Malaysia and Brunei do, and they are included in the telephone numbers given throughout the book – omit them if dialling locally. It's also worth pointing out that many businesses in Malaysia and Singapore have **mobile phone numbers** – usually prefixed ☎011 or 010 – these are very expensive to call. Finally, you can use your BT or AT&T **chargecard** in both Malaysia and Singapore.

MALAYSIA

There are **public telephone** boxes in most towns in Malaysia; local calls cost just 10 sen for an unlimited time. For long-distance calls, it makes sense to use a **card phone**, which are as common as coin-operated phones. There are three companies operating card phones: the ubiquitous Uniphone – whose yellow phones tend to be the most expensive – Cityphone, whose phones are green and are found mainly in the bigger cities, and the government Kadfon network (of blue phone boxes), which are the most widespread. Check the card phone can be used to make international calls before you start dialling

– there's usually an international logo on the phone booth. Cards come in denominations of $5, $10, $20 and $50 and can be purchased from Shell and Petronas service stations and most *7-Eleven* outlets. Before inserting the card, press button *2 and the instructions will appear in English. If your card runs out during the call, press * when you hear the tones to eject the card, and you can insert a new card without losing the connection.

Although there is an international direct-dial (IDD) facility from most phone boxes, you cannot make **collect** (reverse charge) **calls** from them. For these (and for long-distance calls) it's best to go to a **Telekom** office, located in most towns (and detailed in the text throughout), where – if you haven't called collect – you pay the cashier after your call. Telekom offices are generally only open during normal office hours, which can make international calls tricky, though there are 24-hour offices in KL, Penang and Kota Kinabulu.

In KL, Penang and Kota Kinabalu there are also **Home Country Direct** phones – press the appropriate button and you'll be connected with your home operator, who can either arrange a collect call, or debit you; if you're paying, settle your bill with the cashier after the call.

SINGAPORE

Local calls from private phones in Singapore cost next to nothing; calls from public phones cost 10c for three minutes, with the exception of Changi Airport's free courtesy phones. Singapore has **no area codes** – the only time you'll punch more than seven digits for a local number is if you're dialling a toll-free (☎1800-) number. **Card phones** are taking over from payphones in Singapore: cards, available from the **Comcentre** (see p.593) and post offices, as well as *7-Elevens*, stationers and bookshops, come in denominations from $2 upwards. **International calls** can be made 24 hours a day from booths at the Comcentre and from all public card phones.

Some booths are equipped with **Home Country Direct** phones – see "Malaysia" above for the procedure. Otherwise, use a card- or credit card phone – the following numbers will put you through to your home country's operator: UK ☎8004400; USA ☎8000011; Australia ☎8006100; Canada ☎8001000; New Zealand ☎8006400. For directory enquiries, dial ☎00.

PHONING ABROAD

From the UK: dial ☎00 60 (Malaysia), ☎00 65 (Singapore), or ☎00 673 (Brunei) + area code
     minus first 0 (except Singapore) + number

From the USA: dial ☎011 60 (Malaysia), ☎011 65 (Singapore), or ☎011 673 (Brunei) + area code
     minus first 0 (except Singapore) + number

FROM MALAYSIA
Dial ☎007 + IDD country code (see below) + area code minus first 0 + subscriber number

FROM SINGAPORE
Dial ☎001 + IDD country code (see below) + area code minus first 0 + subscriber number

FROM BRUNEI
Dial ☎01 + IDD country code (see below) + area code minus first 0 + subscriber number

IDD CODES

Australia ☎61	Ireland ☎353	UK ☎44
Canada ☎1	New Zealand ☎64	USA ☎1

TIME
Malaysia, Singapore and Brunei are 8 hours ahead of GMT, 16 hours ahead of US Pacific Standard
Time, 13 ahead of Eastern Standard Time, and 2 hours behind Sydney.

BRUNEI

Local calls from phone boxes in **Brunei** cost 10c, and are free if made from private phones. **International** (IDD) calls can be made through hotels, in booths at the Telekom office in the capital, or from card phones in shopping centres and other public places. Phone cards rise in value from $10, and can be bought from the Telekom office and post offices.

NEWSPAPERS AND MAGAZINES

Malaysia has three daily English-language **newspapers**, another which comes out in the afternoon, and a weekly tabloid, all of which are indirectly owned by the government. *The New Straits Times* – sister to the *Singapore Straits Times*, but to all intents a separate company – is a thick broadsheet with blatantly government-slanted political news and wide arts coverage. *The Business Times* covers finance throughout Southeast Asia, while *The Star* is a news-focused tabloid. The afternoon *Malay Mail* has an extensive "what's on" section and the daily tabloid, *The Sun*, is strong on populist columns about all things Malaysian and has an excellent weekly listings magazine – *Time Out* – on Thursdays. All four daily papers have Sunday editions as well.

There are also Chinese-, Tamil- and Malay-language newspapers and a variety of weekly and monthly **English-language magazines**, the best being the current affairs *Asiaweek* (available worldwide; *Aliran Monthly*, which treats economic and political issues from a less centralized, more independent perspective; the weekly listings magazine *Day & Night*; the monthly style/features *Men's Review*, and *Journal One*.

TV AND RADIO

Two of **Malaysia**'s three **television channels**, RTM1 and RTM2, are broadcast in Malay and are government-owned, but they broadcast some material in Chinese and English. The third station, TV3, is run commercially and shows English-language news and documentaries, Chinese kung fu, and Tamil, British and American films and soaps. In KL there is also another commercial station, Metrovision. The country is in the process of setting up an extensive range of satellite TV stations, but government censorship is likely to affect the broadcast content of such stations.

In **Singapore**, the Television Corporation of Singapore (TCS) screens programmes in English, Chinese, Malay and Tamil on Channels 5, 8 and 12 – Channel 5 features the most English-language programmes, Channel 8 specializes in Chinese soap operas, and the newer Premier 12 features English-language movies and documentaries, and sport from around the globe. Most Singaporean TV sets also receive Malaysia's RTM1, RTM2 and TV3 channels, In southern Malaysia it's possible to pick up Singaporean TV and radio. **Brunei** has a more limited range. Radio and Television Brunei (RTB) broadcasts daily on a single channel – many of its programmes are imported, and there's English-language news at 7pm each evening.

The six main Malaysian **radio stations** are also government-run, and include one devoted to pop music, and others broadcasting in Malay, Chinese and Tamil. The BBC World Service can be received on shortwave (in Johor, you might be able to pick it up on FM), as can Voice of America. In **Singapore**, the Radio Corporation of Singapore (RCS) broadcasts several English-language radio shows daily: Radio 1 (90.5FM), an information and music channel; Heart (91.3FM), offering music and "infotainment"; The Place to Relax (92.4FM), featuring classical music; Perfect 10 (98.7FM), playing pop music; Class (95FM), playing middle of the road hits; and Power (98FM), with light pop music. There's also a decent pirate radio station operating from Indonesia's Batam island, and BBC World Service (88.9FM) broadcasts 24 hours a day. For locals, there are daily shows in Chinese (95.8FM), Malay (94.2FM) and Tamil (96.8FM). For listings, check in the daily newspapers, or in *8 Days* magazine. In **Brunei**, RTB broadcasts two channels a day on the medium wave and FM bands – one in Malay, the other in English and Chinese. More surprisingly, London's Capital Radio can be received across the state.

POLICE AND EMERGENCIES

If you lose something in Malaysia and Singapore, you're more likely to have someone running after you with it than running away. Nevertheless, you shouldn't become complacent – muggings have been known to occur and theft from dormitories by other tourists is a common complaint.

Most people carry their passport, travellers' cheques and other valuables in a concealed money belt, and guesthouses and hotels will often have a safety deposit box. Always keep a separate record of the numbers of your traveller's cheques, together with a note of which ones you've cashed. It's probably worth taking a photocopy of the relevant pages of your passport, too, in case it's lost or stolen. In the more remote parts of Sarawak or Sabah there is little crime, and you needn't worry unduly about carrying cash – in fact, the lack of banks means that you'll probably have to carry more than you might otherwise.

It's worth repeating here that it is very unwise to have anything to do with **drugs** of any description in Malaysia and Singapore. The penalties for trafficking drugs in or out of either country are severe in the extreme – foreigners have been executed in the past – and if you are arrested for drugs offences you can expect no mercy and little help from your consular representatives.

MALAYSIA

If you do need to report a crime in Malaysia, head for the nearest police station (marked on the maps and included in the text), where there'll invariably be someone who speaks English – you'll need a copy of the police report for insurance purposes. In many major tourist spots, there are specific **tourist police stations** which are geared up to problems faced by foreign travellers. The police are generally more aloof than in the West, dressed in blue trousers and white short-sleeved shirts, and armed with small handguns. While you're likely to be excused any minor misdemeanour as a foreigner, it pays to be deferential if caught on the wrong side of the law.

In the predominantly **Muslim** east coast states of Kelantan and Terengganu, restrictions such as "close proximity" between people of the opposite sex and eating in public during daylight hours in the Ramadan month apply to Muslims only, and are customary rather than legal in nature. However, it's courteous to observe restrictions like this where possible and there's advice throughout the guide on how to avoid giving offence. Lastly, if you're **driving**, watch out for police speed traps – if you're caught speeding there's a spot fine of $200.

SINGAPORE

Singapore is known locally as a "fine city". There's a fine of $500 for smoking in public places such as cinemas, trains, lifts, air-conditioned restaurants and shopping malls, and one of $50 for "jaywalking" – crossing a main road within 50m of a pedestrian crossing or bridge. Littering carries a $1000 fine, with offenders now issued Corrective Work Orders and forced to do litter-picking duty, while eating or drinking on the MRT could cost you $500. Other fines include those for urinating in lifts (legend has it that some lifts are fitted with urine detectors), not flushing a public toilet and chewing gum (which is outlawed in Singapore). It's worth bearing all these offences in mind, since foreigners are not exempt from the various Singaporean punishments – as American Michael Fay discovered early in 1994, when he was given four strokes of the cane for vandalism.

Singapore's **police**, who wear dark blue, keep a fairly low profile, but are polite and helpful when approached. For details of the main police station, and other emergency information, check the relevant sections of "Listings", p.593.

PEOPLES

Largely because of their pivotal position on the maritime trade routes between the Middle East, India and China, the present-day countries of Malaysia, Singapore and Brunei have always been a cultural melting-pot. During the first millennium Malays crossed from present-day Sumatra and Indians arrived from India and Sri Lanka, while later the Chinese migrated from mainland China and Hainan island. But all these traders and settlers arrived to find that the region already contained a gamut of indigenous tribes, thought to have migrated here around 50,000 years ago from the Philippines, which was then connected by a land bridge to Borneo and Southeast Asia. Indeed, the indigenous tribes which still exist on the Peninsula are known as the Orang Asli, Malay for "the first people".

First people they may have been, but the descendants of the various indigenous groups now form a small minority of the overall **populations** of the three countries. Over the last 150 years a massive influx of Chinese and Indian immigrants, escaping poverty, war and revolution, has swelled the population of **Malaysia**, which now stands at nearly 18.2 million: on the Peninsula, the Malays still form the majority of the population at just over 50 percent, the Chinese number nearly 38 percent, Indians 10 percent and the Orang Asli around 1 percent; in Sarawak, on the other hand, the indigenous tribes account for almost 50 percent of the population, the Chinese 30 percent, with the other 20 percent divided amongst Malays and Indians; while in Sabah, the indigenous groups represent around 55 percent, the Chinese 30 percent, with the remainder a mix of Malays, Indians and, latterly, Filipino immigrants.

Brunei's population of around 280,000 is heavily dominated by Malays, with minorities of Chinese, Indians and indigenous peoples. In **Singapore**, there were only tiny numbers of indigenes left on the island by the time of the arrival of Raffles. They have no modern-day presence in the state and more than three-quarters of the 2.8-million strong population are of Chinese extraction, while around 15 percent are Malay, and 6.5 percent Indian.

THE MALAYS

The **Malays**, a Mongoloid people believed to have originated from the meeting of Central Asians with Pacific islanders, first moved to the west coast of the Malaysian Peninsula from Sumatra in early times. Known as Orang Laut (sea people), they sustained an economy built around fishing, boat-building and, in some communities, piracy. Strong in present-day Indonesia during the first millennium, it was the growth in power of the Malay sultanates from the fifteenth century onwards (see p.599) – coinciding with the arrival of Islam – that established Malays as a force to be reckoned with in the Malay Peninsula and in Borneo. They developed an aristocratic tradition, courtly rituals and a social hierarchy (for more on which, see p.298) which have an influence even today. The rulers of the Malaysian states still wield immense social and economic power, reflected in the sharing of the appointment of the *agong*, a pre-eminent sultan nominated on a five-year cycle. Although it's a purely ceremonial position, the *agong* is seen as the ultimate guardian of Malay Muslim culture and, despite recent legislation to reduce his powers, is still considered to be above the law. The situation is even more pronounced in **Brunei**, to which many Muslim Malay traders fled after the fall of Melaka to the Portuguese in 1511. There, the sultan is still the supreme ruler (as his descendants have been, on and off, for over 500 years), his powers verging on the autocratic.

Even though Malays have been Muslims since the fifteenth century, the region as a whole is not **fundamentalist** in character. Only in Brunei is alcohol banned, for instance, and while fundamentalist groups do hold sway in the eastern states of Kelantan and Terengganu, their influence is rarely oppressive.

The main contemporary change for Malays in Malaysia was the introduction of the **bumiputra** policy – a Malay word meaning "sons of the soil" – initiated after independence to separate those inhabitants of Peninsular and Sabah and Sarawak who had cultural affinities indigenous to the region from those who originated from outside. The policy was designed to make it easier for the Malays, the Orang Asli of the Peninsula, and the various Malay-related indigenous groups in Sarawak and Sabah, to compete in economic and educational fields against the Chinese and Indians, who – since the large-scale immigration of the nineteenth century – had traditionally tended to be the higher achievers.

These days, certain **privileges**, mostly financial or status-enhancing, are offered to a *bumiputra* which are not available to the non-*bumiputra*, although in practice these privileges are only fully extended to Muslim Malays. Malaysian companies are supposed to employ a Malay at a senior level and all companies must have at least a 51-percent Malay shareholder profile, although the rapid development of the economy in recent years has led to a relaxing of such rules. Also, Malays get discounts on buying houses and find it much easier to get loans from the banks. As a consequence, Malays tend to take the top positions in government, state-owned companies and prestigious private firms.

Although tensions between Malays and the Chinese have led occasionally to unrest, the worst example being the race riots of 1969, the overall effect of stimulating Malay opportunities, mostly at the expense of the Chinese, seems to have been positive. Some critics have likened the *bumiputra* policy to a form of apartheid, but as long as the modern Malaysian economic miracle continues to enrich the whole community, those excluded from the policy rarely complain in public. The situation is slightly different in **Singapore**, where the policy doesn't hold sway: despite being greatly outnumbered by their Chinese compatriots, Singapore's Malay community appears content to stay south of the causeway and enjoy the state's higher standard of living.

THE CHINESE AND STRAITS CHINESE

Chinese traders began visiting the region in the seventh century, but it was in Melaka in the fifteenth century that the first significant community established itself. However, the ancestors of the majority of Chinese now living in Peninsular Malaysia emigrated from southern China in the nineteenth century to work in the burgeoning tin-mining industry. In Sarawak, Chinese from Foochow, Teochew and Hokkien provinces played an important part in opening up the interior, establishing pepper and rubber plantations along Sungei Rajang; while in Sabah, Hakka Chinese labourers were recruited by the British North Borneo Chartered Company to plant rubber, and many stayed on, forming the base of the Chinese business community there.

Although many Chinese in the Peninsula came as labourers, they graduated quickly to shopkeeping and business ventures, both in established towns like Melaka and fast-expanding centres like KL, Penang and Kuching. Chinatowns developed throughout the region, even in Malay strongholds like Kota Bharu and Kuala Terengganu, while **Chinese traditions**, religious festivities, theatre and music became an integral part of a wider Malayan, and later Malaysian, multiracial culture. On the political level, the Malaysian Chinese are well represented in parliament and occupy around a quarter of the current ministerial positions. By way of contrast, **Chinese Bruneians** are not automatically classed as citizens and suffer a fair amount of discrimination at the hands of the majority Malay population.

Singapore's nineteenth-century trade boom drew large numbers of Cantonese, Teochew, Hokkein and Hakka Chinese traders and labourers, who quickly established a Chinatown on the south bank of the Singapore river. Today, the Chinese account for 78 percent of the state's population and are the most economically successful racial group in Singapore. As the proportion of Singaporean Chinese born on the island increases, the government's efforts to cultivate a feeling of Singaporean national identity are beginning to show signs of working, especially among the younger generation. Consequently, the main difference between the Chinese in Singapore and those in Malaysia is that Singapore's Chinese majority prefers to think of itself simply as Singaporean. Nevertheless, as in Malaysia, they still display their traditional work ethic and spurn none of their cultural heritage.

One of the few examples of regional intermarrying is displayed in the **Peranakan** or "Straits-born Chinese" heritage of Melaka, Singapore and, to a lesser extent, Penang. When male Chinese immigrants settled in these places from the sixteenth century onwards to work as miners or commercial entrepreneurs, they often married local Malay women, whose male offspring were termed "Baba" and the females "Nonya". **Baba-Nonya** society, as it became known, adapted elements from both cultures to create its own traditions: the descendants of these sixteenth-century liaisons have a unique culinary and architectural style (for more on which see p.302). Although Baba-Nonyas dress as Malays – the men in stiff-collared tunics and *songkets* and the women in sarongs and fitted, long-sleeved blouses – most follow Chinese Confucianism as their religion and speak a distinct Malay dialect.

THE INDIANS

The second-largest non-*bumiputra* group in Malaysia, the **Indians**, first arrived as traders more than two thousand years ago, although few settled and it wasn't until the early fifteenth century that a small community of Indians (from present-day Tamil Nadu and Sri Lanka) was based in Melaka. But, like the majority of Chinese, the first large wave of Indians – Tamil labourers – arrived in the nineteenth century as indentured workers, to build the roads and railways and to work on the European-run rubber estates. But an embryonic entrepreneurial class from north India soon followed and set up businesses in Penang and Singapore; because most were Muslims, these merchants and traders found it easier to assimilate themselves within the existing Malay community than the Hindu Tamils did.

Although Indians comprise only 10 percent of Malaysia's population (7 percent in Singapore) their impact is felt everywhere. The Hindu festival of Thaipusam (see p.64) is celebrated annually at KL's Batu Caves by upwards of a million people (with a smaller, but still significant celebration in Singapore); the festival of Deepavali is a national holiday; and Indians are increasingly competing with Malays in the arts, and dominate certain professional areas like medicine and law. And then, of course, there is the culinary area – very few Malaysians these days could do without a daily dose of *roti canai*, so much so that this north Indian snack has been virtually appropriated by Malay and Chinese cafés and hawkers.

Despite this influence, in general Indians are at the bottom of the economic ladder, a situation which has its origins in the colonial system. Even today, many Tamils work on private plantations and are unable to reap many of the benefits of Malaysia's economic success. Indians' political voice has also traditionally been weak, although there are signs that a younger generation of political leaders from the two Indian-dominated political parties, the Malaysian Indian Congress and the Indian Progressive Front, are asserting the community's needs more effectively.

THE ORANG ASLI

The **Orang Asli** – the indigenous peoples of Peninsular Malaysia – mostly belong to three distinct groups, within which various tribes are related either by geography, language or physiological features.

The largest of the groups is the **Senoi** (the Asli word for person), who number about 40,000. They live in the large, still predominantly forested interior, within the states of Perak, Pahang and Kelantan, and divide into two main tribes, the Semiar and the Temiar, which still live a traditional lifestyle, following animist customs in their marriage ceremonies and burial rites. On the whole they follow the practice of shifting cultivation – a regular rotation of jungle-clearance and crop-planting – although government resettlement drives have successfully persuaded many to settle and farm just one area.

The **Semang** (or Negritos), of whom there are around 2000, live in the northern areas of the Peninsula. They comprise six distinct, if small, tribes, related to each other in appearance – they are mostly dark-skinned and curly haired – and share a traditional nomadic, hunter-gatherer lifestyle. However, most Semang nowadays live in settled communities and work within the cash economy, either as labourers or selling jungle produce in markets. Perhaps the most frequently seen Semang tribe are the Batek, who live in and around Taman Negara.

The third group, the so-called **Aboriginal Malays**, live south of the Kuala Lumpur–Kuantan road. Some of the tribes in this category, like the Jakun who live around Tasek Chini and the Semelais of Tasek Bera, have vigorously retained their animist religion and artistic traditions despite living in permanent villages near Malay communities and working within the regular economy. These are among the easiest of the Orang Asli to approach, since some have obtained employment in the two lakes' tourist industries; others are craftspeople selling their wares from stalls beside the water. See p.235 for more details.

These three main groupings do not represent all the Orang Asli tribes in Malaysia. One, the Lanoh in Perak, are sometimes regarded as Negritos, but their language is closer to that of the Temiar. Another group, the semi-nomadic Che Wong, of whom just a few hundred still survive on the slopes of Gunung Benom in central Pahang, are still dependent on foraging to survive and live in temporary huts made from bamboo and rattan. Two more groups, the Jah Hut of Pahang and the Mah Meri of Selangor, are particularly fine carvers, and it's possible to buy their sculptures at regional craftshops.

The tribes of Tasek Chini and Tasek Bera apart, it's difficult to visit most Orang Asli communities. Many live way off the beaten track and can only be reached if you go on a tour (some operators do visit Orang Asli settlements in Tasek Bera or Endau Rompin National Park). It's most unlikely that visitors would ever chance upon a remote Orang Asli village, though you will sometimes pass tribe members in the national parks or on inaccessible roads in eastern Perak, Pahang and Kelantan. To learn more about the disappearing Asli culture, the best stop is KL's Orang Asli Museum (see p.122).

SARAWAK'S PEOPLES

In direct contrast to the Peninsula, indigenous groups make up a substantial chunk of the population in Sarawak, which is what attracts many visitors there in the first place – see the Sarawak chapter for all the details. Although the Chinese comprise 29 percent of the state's population and the Malays and Indians around 24 percent together, the remaining 47 percent are made up of various indigenous **Dyak** groups – a word derived from the Malay for "up-country".

The largest Dyak groups are the Iban, Bidayuh, Melanau, Kayan, Kenyah, Kelabit and Penan tribes, all of which have distinct cultures, although most have certain things in common, including a lifestyle predominantly based outside towns. Many live in **longhouses** (for more, see p.353) along the rivers or on the sides of hills in the mountainous interior, and maintain a proud cultural legacy which draws on animist religion (see p.62 for more on this), arts and crafts production, jungle skills and a rich tradition of **festivals**. The tribal dances are seldom seen these days, their traditions rapidly being absorbed into wider Malay art forms, but the culturally stronger groups in Sarawak are slowly exerting their distinct identities. The *ngajat*, a dance traditionally performed by warriors on their return from battle, is now more commonly performed in the longhouses, albeit in a milder, truncated form. Spectacular costumes featuring large feathers are worn by the dancers who, arranged in a circle, perform athletic leaps to indicate their virility.

The **Iban**, a stocky, rugged people, make up nearly one-third of Sarawak's population. The Iban originated hundreds of miles south of present-day Sarawak, in the Kapuas valley in Kalimantan, and migrated north in the sixteenth century, coming into conflict with the Kayan and Kenyah tribes and, later, the British, over the next two hundred years. Nowadays, Iban longhouse communities are found in the Batang Ai river system in the southwest, and along the Rajang, Katibas and Baleh rivers in the interior – though tribe members tend to migrate to Kuching and Miri, looking for work. These communities are quite accessible, their inhabitants always hospitable and keen to illustrate aspects of their culture like traditional dance, music, textile-weaving, blow-piping, fishing and game-playing. For the Iban, the planting and cultivation of rice – their staple crop – is intimately connected with human existence, a relationship which underpins their animist beliefs. In their time, the Iban were infamous head-hunters and some longhouses are still decorated with authentically collected – then shrunken – heads. These days, though, the tradition of head-hunting has been replaced by that of *berjelai*, or "journey", whereby a young man leaves the community to prove himself in the outside world – returning to their longhouses with television sets, generators and outboard motors, rather than heads. For more details about the Iban, see p.370.

The most southern of Sarawak's indigenous groups are the **Bidayuh** (see p.367), who – unlike most Dyak groups – traditionally lived away from the rivers, building their longhouse on the sides of hills. Culturally, they are similar to the Iban, although in temperament they are much milder and less gregarious, keeping themselves to themselves in their inaccessible homes on Sarawak's mountainous southern border with Kalimantan.

The **Melanau** are a coastal people, living north of Kuching in a region dominated by mangrove swamps. Few roads have been built in this area and not many visitors venture here. Many Melanau, however, now live in towns, preferring the kampung-style houses of the Malays to the elegant longhouses of the past. They are expert fishermen and cultivate sago as an alternative to rice. Many Melanau died in the battles that followed when the Iban first migrated northwards, and the survival of their communities owes much to the first White Rajah, James Brooke, who protected them in the last century. He had a soft spot for the Melanau, thinking them the most attractive of the state's ethnic peoples and employing many as boat-builders, labourers and domestic servants.

The **Kelabit** people live on the highland plateau which separates north Sarawak from Kalimantan. Like the Iban, they live in longhouses and maintain a traditional lifestyle, but differ from the other groups in that they are Christian; they were converted just after World War II, during which the highlands had been used by British and Australian forces to launch attacks on the occupying Japanese. The highlands were totally inaccessible before the airstrip at Bario was built; now the area has become popular for hikers, since within a few days' walk of Bario are many longhouses which welcome visitors (see p.415 for more).

The last main group is the semi-nomadic **Penan**, who live in the upper Rajang and Limbang areas of Sarawak in temporary lean-tos or small huts. They rely, like some of the Orang Asli groups in the Peninsula, on hunting and gathering and collecting jungle produce for sale in local markets. They also have the lightest pigment of all the ethnic groups of Sarawak, largely because they live within the shade of the forest, rather than on the rivers and in clearings. In recent years the state government has tried to resettle the Penan in small villages, a controversial policy not entirely unconnected with the advance of logging in traditional Penan land, which has caused opposition from the Penan themselves and criticism from international groups. Some tour operators now have itineraries which include visiting Penan communities in the Baram river basin and in the primary jungle that slopes away from the Kelabit Highlands.

Most of the other groups in Sarawak fall into the catch-all ethnic classification of **Orang Ulu** (people of the interior), who inhabit the more remote inland parts of the state, further north than the Iban, along the upper Rajang, Balui and Linau rivers. The most numerous, the **Kayan** and the **Kenyah**, are closely related and in the past often teamed up to defend their lands from the invading Iban. But they also have much in common with their traditional enemy, since they are longhouse-dwellers, animists and shifting cultivators. The main difference is the more hierarchical social structure of their communities, with one leader, a *penghulu*, who has immense influence over the other inhabitants of the longhouse. Nowadays, many Kayan are Christians – converted after contact with missionaries following World War II – and their longhouses are among the most prosperous in Sarawak. Like the Iban, they maintain a tradition of *berjelai*, and the return of the youths from their wanderings is always an excuse for a big party, at which visitors from abroad or from other longhouses are always welcome. There's more information on both the Kenyah and Kayan on p.386.

SABAH'S PEOPLES

Sabah has a population of around 1.6 million, made up of more than thirty distinct racial groups, between them speaking over eighty different dialects. Most populous of these groups are the **Dusun**, who account for around a third of Sabah's population. Traditionally agriculturists (the word *Dusun* means "orchard"), the sub-groups of the Dusun inhabit the western coastal plains and the interior of the state. These days they are known generically as **Kadazan/Dusun**, although strictly speaking "Kadazan" refers only to the Dusun of Penampang. Other branches of the Dusun include the **Lotud** of Tuaran and the **Rungus** of the Kudat Peninsula, whose convex longhouses are all that remain of the Dusun's longhouse tradition. Although most Dusun are now Christians, remnants of their animist past are still evident in their culture, most obviously in the harvest festival, or *pesta kaamatan*, when their *bobohizans*, or priestesses, perform rituals to honour the *bambaazon*, or rice spirit. In the s*amazau* dance – almost the national dance of East Malaysia – the costumes worn are authentically Kadazan. Two rows of men and women dance facing each other in a slow, rhythmic movement, flapping their arms to the pulse of the drum, their hand gestures mimicking the flight of birds. Not to be outdone, the women of the Kwijau community have their own dance, the *buloh*, which features high jumping steps to the percussive sounds of the gong and bamboo.

The mainly Muslim **Bajau** tribe drifted over from the southern Philippines some two hundred years ago, and now constitute Sabah's second largest ethnic group, accounting for around 10 percent of the population. Their penchant for piracy quickly earned them the sobriquet "Sea Gypsies", though nowadays they are agriculturists and fishermen, noted for their horsemanship and their rearing of buffalo. The Bajau live in the northwest of Sabah and occasionally appear on horseback at Kota Belud's market (see p.451).

Sabah's third sizeable tribe is the **Murut**, which inhabits the area between Keningau and the Sarawak border, in the southwest. Their name means "hill people", though they prefer to be known by their individual tribal names, such as Timugon, Tagal and Nabai. The Murut farm rice and cassava by a system of shifting cultivation and, at times, still hunt using blowpipes and poison darts. Though their head-hunting days are over, they retain other cultural traditions, such as the construction of brightly adorned grave huts to house the graves and belongings of the dead. Another tradition that continues is the consumption at ceremonies of *tapai* or rice wine, drawn from a ceremonial jar using bamboo straws. Although the Murut are now eschewing longhouse life, many villages retain a ceremonial hall, complete with a *lansaran*, or bamboo trampoline, for festive dances and games.

RELIGION, TEMPLES AND SOCIAL CONVENTIONS

Three great religions – Islam, Buddhism and Hinduism – are represented in Malaysia and Singapore, and they play a vital role in the everyday lives of the population. Indeed, some religious festivals, like Muslim Hari Raya and Hindu Thaipusam, have been elevated to such stature that they are among the main cultural events in the regional calendar.

In Malaysia, the vast majority of people are **Muslims**, while in Singapore – where three-quarters of the population are Chinese – **Buddhism** is the main religion. There's a smaller, but no less significant, **Hindu** Indian presence in both countries, while the other chief belief system is **animism**, followed by many of the indigenous ethnic peoples of Malaysia – including the Orang Asli in the Peninsula and the various Dyak groups in Sarawak. However, the main tribal group in Sabah, the Kadazan, is **Christian**, as are the Kelabit in Sarawak, though this is otherwise a minority religion in much of Malaysia and Singapore, practised primarily by the Eurasian community. The other main feature of religion in the region is that both Islam and Buddhism in Malaysia and Singapore are syncretic adaptations of the religions as practised elsewhere, partly due to the influence of animist elements which over the centuries have been integrated from the indigenous peoples' beliefs.

It's not uncommon to see the **temples** of different creeds happily existing side by side, each providing a social as well as a religious focal point for the corresponding community; in the early days, the temple formed an essential support network for newcomers to Malaysia and Singapore. Architectural traditions mean that the Chinese and Indian temples, built out of brick, have long outlasted the timber Malay mosque, making them the oldest structures you're likely to see in the region.

Although Malaysians and Singaporeans in general are hospitable, friendly and tolerant of visitors, it helps to know about the region's customs and to try to abide by the main rules of **etiquette**. Most are related to tenets of the various religions, though in East Malaysia – especially during stays in a longhouse – you're exposed to more subtle customs to do with status and social behaviour.

ANIMISM

The first principle of **animism** is that everything in nature has a soul or spirit (*semangat*), which inhabits mountains, trees, rocks and lakes, and has to be mollified as it controls the forces of nature. Although many of Malaysia's ethnic groups are now nominally Christian or Muslim, many of their old beliefs and ceremonies still survive. Birds, especially the **hornbill**, are of particular significance to the Iban and the Kelabit peoples in Sarawak. Many Kelabit depend upon the arrival of migrating flocks to decide when to plant their rice crop, while Iban hunters still interpret sightings of the hornbill and other birds as good or bad omens. In the Iban male rite-of-passage ceremony, a headdress made of hornbill feathers adorns the young man's head.

For the Orang Asli groups in the interior of the Peninsula, most of their remaining animist beliefs centre on healing and funereal ceremonies. A sick person, particularly a child, is believed to be invaded by a bad spirit, and drums are played and incantations performed to persuade the spirit to depart. The death of a member of the family is followed by a complex process of burial and reburial – a procedure which, hopefully, ensures an easy passage for the person's spirit.

An important link between the animism still practised by the tribal groups and Islam is provided by the **bomoh** (medicine man), who can still be found in Malay villages and some towns performing tasks like calling on the elements to bring rain during droughts or preventing rain from ruining an important ceremony. A central part of the *bomoh*'s trade is recitation, often of sections of the Koran, while – like his Orang Asli counterparts – he uses various healing techniques, including herbs, localized burning and chants to cure or ease pain and disease. Although there are still quite a few *bomoh* in Malaysia, they are a vanishing breed, largely because there are fewer younger men willing to continue the tradition and the Muslim establishment frowns on the practice.

ISLAM

The first firm foothold **Islam** made in Malaysia was the conversion of Paramesvara, the ruler of Melaka, in the early fifteenth century. The commercial success of Melaka accelerated the process of Islamicization and, one after another, the powerful Malay court rulers took to Islam, adopting the title sultan ("ruler"), either because of sincere doctrinal conversion or because they took a shrewd view of the practical advantages to be gained by embracing the new faith. On a wider cultural level, too, Islam had great attractions; its revolutionary concepts of equality in subordination to Allah freed people from the feudal Hindu caste system which had previously dominated parts of the region.

With the fall of Melaka in 1511, the migration of Muslim merchants to Brunei strengthened the hold of Islam in the region. The first wave of Islamic missionaries were mostly **Sufis**, the mystical and generally more liberal wing of Islam. Sufi Islam integrated some animist elements and Hindu beliefs: the tradition of pluralist deity worship which is central to Hinduism continued, and accounts for the strong historical and cultural importance of **festivals** like Deepavali and Thaipusam, where powerful deities are commemorated.

However, in the early nineteenth century the dominance of Sufism declined when a more puritanical Islamic branch, the **Wahabi**, captured Mecca. The return to the Koran's basic teachings became identified with a more militant approach, leading to several *jihads* (holy wars) in Kedah, Kelantan and Terengganu against the Malay rulers' Siamese overlords and, subsequently, the British. The British colonial period inevitably drew Christian missionaries to the region, but they had more success in Borneo than on the Peninsula. Indeed, the British, in a bid to avoid further unrest among the Malays, were restrained in their evangelical efforts and Islam continued to prosper.

Islam in Malaysia today is a mixture of Sufi and Wahabi elements and as such is relatively liberal. Although most Muslim women wear traditional costume, especially headscarves, very few adopt the veil and some taboos, like not drinking alcohol, are ignored by a growing number of Malays (though public consumption of alcohol is banned in Brunei). There are stricter, more fundamentalist Muslims – in Kelantan the local government is dominated by them – but in general Islam here has a modern outlook, blending a vibrant, practising faith with a business-minded approach.

The most important point of the Islamic year is **Ramadan**, the ninth month of the Muslim lunar calendar, when the majority of Muslims fast from the break of dawn to dusk, and also abstain from drinking and smoking. The reason for the fast is to intensify awareness of the plight of the poor and to identify with the hungry. During Ramadan many hawker stalls sell cakes and fruit, and families often break their fast at the stalls, although the most orthodox Muslim families tend to eat privately during this period. The end of Ramadan is marked by the two-day national holiday, **Hari Raya Puasa**, at which point the fast stops and the festivities begin. By tradition, royal palaces (*istanas*) are open over the holiday – usually the only days in the year when they are – and Malay families invite friends and business associates into their houses for food and refreshments.

VISITING A MOSQUE

While only a small proportion of the faithful attend the **mosque** every day, on Friday – the Muslim day of prayer – Malays converge on their nearest mosque (*masjid*), with all employers providing an extended three-hour lunch break to provide time for prayers, lunch and the attendant socializing. In Malaysia, every town, village and hamlet has a mosque, with loudspeakers strapped to the minaret to call the faithful to prayer. The capital city of each state is the site of the *Masjid Negeri*, the state mosque, always more grandiose than its humble regional counterparts – an ostentatious statement of Islam's significance to the Malay people. Designs reflect religious conservatism, and you'll rarely see contemporary mosques varying from the standard square building topped by onion domes and minaret – though there were some notable flirtations with obscure geometrics and fibreglass in the 1960s. Only in Melaka state, where Malaysia's oldest mosques are located, does the architecture become more interesting, revealing unusual **Sumatran influences**.

Once at the mosque, the men wash their hands, feet and faces three times in the outer chambers, before entering the prayer hall to recite sections of the **Koran**. After this initial period, an **Iman** will lead prayers and, on occasions, deliver a sermon, where the teachings of Allah will be applied to a contemporary context. Women cannot enter the main prayer hall during prayers and must congregate in a chamber to the side of the hall. Visitors are welcome at certain times (it's always worth checking first with the local tourist office) and must wear acceptable clothing – long trousers and shirt for men, and a long cloak and headdress, which is provided by most mosques, for women. No non-Muslim is allowed to enter a mosque during prayer time or go into the prayer hall at any time, although it's possible to stand just outside and look in.

HINDUISM

Hinduism arrived in Malaysia long before Islam, brought by Indian traders more than a thousand years ago. Its central tenet is the belief that life is a series of rebirths and reincarnations that eventually leads to spiritual release. An individual's progress is determined by *karma*, very much a law of cause and effect, where negative decisions and actions slow up the process of upward reincarnation and positive ones accelerate it. A whole variety of **deities** are worshipped, which on the surface makes Hinduism appear complex, but with only a loose understanding of the *Vedas* – the religion's holy books – the characters and roles of the main gods quickly become apparent. The deities you'll come across most often are the three manifestations of the faith's supreme divine being: Brahma the Creator, Vishnu the Preserver and Shiva the Destroyer.

The earliest Hindu **archeological remains** are in Kedah (see p.188) and date from the tenth century, although the temples found here indicate a synthesis of Hindu and Buddhist imagery. Although almost all of the region's Hindu past has been obliterated, elements live on in the popular arts like *wayang kulit* (shadow plays), where

sacred texts like the *Ramayana* (see below) form the basis of the stories.

There was a Hindu **revival** in the late nineteenth century when immigrants from southern India arrived to work on the Malaysian rubber and palm oil plantations and built temples to house popular idols. The Hindu celebration of Rama's victory – the central theme of the epic *Ramayana* – in time became the national holiday of **Deepavali** (the festival of lights), reflecting the Malaysian policy of religious tolerance, while another Hindu festival, **Thaipusam**, when Lord Subramaniam and elephant-headed Ganesh, the sons of Shiva, are worshipped, has become the single largest religious gathering in the region.

Visitors are welcome in Malaysia and Singapore's Hindu **temples**, and are expected to remove their shoes before entering. Step over the threshold and you enter a veritable Disneyland of colourful gods and fanciful creatures. The style is typically Dravidian (South Indian), as befits the largely Tamil population, with a soaring *gopuram*, or entrance tower, teeming with sculptures and a central courtyard leading to an inner sanctum to the presiding deity. In the temple precinct, there are always busy scenes – incense burning, the application of sandalwood paste, and the *puja* (ritualistic act of worship). However, as most Hindu temples are run by voluntary staff, it's often impossible to find anyone to give you a guided tour of the temples' abundant carvings and sculptures.

CHINESE RELIGIONS

Most visitors will be more aware of the region's **Chinese** religious celebrations than of the Muslim or Hindu ones, largely because the festivals themselves are particularly welcoming of tourists and are often exciting. Most are organized by *kongsis*, or clan houses, which are the cornerstone of all immigrant Chinese communities in Malaysia and Singapore and traditionally provided housing, employment and a social structure for the newly arrived (see p.176).

More so than Islam, Chinese religion shares animist beliefs with the ethnic groups. Chinese pioneers, while opening out the rivers of Sarawak for trade, could understand the beliefs and practices (except the head-hunting!) of the Iban and Melanau tribesmen they were dealing with, partly because they could identify with the animist ideas that were a driving force in their own lives.

Malaysian and Singaporean Chinese usually consider themselves either **Buddhist**, **Taoist** or **Confucianist**, although in practice they are often a mixture of all three. These different strands in Chinese religion ostensibly lean in very different directions: Confucianism began as a philosophy based on piety, loyalty, humanitarianism and familial devotion, and has transmuted into a set of principles that permeate every aspect of Chinese life; Taoism places animism within a philosophy which propounds unity with nature as its chief tenet; and Buddhism is primarily concerned with the attainment of a state of personal enlightenment, *nirvana*. But in practice, the combination of the three comprises a system of belief which is first and foremost pragmatic. The Chinese use their religion to ease their passage through life, whether in the spheres of work or family, while temples double as social centres, where people meet and exchange views.

CHINESE TEMPLES

The rules of geomancy, or *feng shui* (wind and water), are rigorously applied to the construction of Chinese **temples**, so that the building is placed in such a geographical position as to render it free from evil influences. Visitors wishing to cross the threshold of a temple have to step over a kerb that's intended to trip up evil spirits, and walk through doors painted with fearsome door gods; fronting the doors are two stone lions, whose roars provide yet another defence. Larger temples typically consist of a front entrance hall opening onto a walled-in courtyard, beyond which is the hall of worship, where joss (luck) sticks are burned below images of the deities. The most important and striking element of a Chinese temple is its **roof** – grand, multi-tiered affairs, with low, overhanging eaves, the ridges alive with auspicious creatures such as dragons and phoenixes and, less often, with miniature scenes from traditional Chinese life and legend. Temples are also normally constructed around a framework of huge, lacquered timber beams, adorned with intricately carved warriors, animals and flowers. More figures are moulded onto outer walls, which are dotted with octagonal, hexagonal or round grille-worked windows. *Feng shui* comes into play

again inside the temple, with auspicious room numbers and sizes, colour and sequence of construction. Elsewhere in the temple grounds, you'll see sizeable ovens, stuffed constantly with paper money, prayer books and other offerings; or a pagoda – a tall, thin tower thought to keep out evil spirits.

Chinese temples, too, play an important part in Chinese community life and many have weekly musical and theatrical performances, which can be enjoyed by visitors as well as locals. Most temples are open from early morning to early evening and devotees go in when they like, to make offerings or to pray; there are no set prayer times. Visitors are welcome and all the larger temples have janitors who will show you round, although only a few speak good English.

SOCIAL CONVENTIONS AND ETIQUETTE

The main **domestic rules** when entering a home are: always take your shoes off; dress modestly – for women that means below-knee-length skirts or shorts, a bra and sleeved T-shirts, for men, long trousers; never help yourself to food without first being offered it; and if eating with your hands or chopsticks, avoid using your left hand, which in Islamic culture is considered unclean.

In most respects Malaysia and Brunei are not particularly strict Muslim societies but certain public acts which are quite acceptable in most non-Muslim countries are looked down upon here. Among these are kissing or cuddling, arguing, raising one's voice, pointing, or drinking in public.

Other, more subtle, **points of etiquette** include not touching the head of a Malaysian, Muslim or otherwise, as the head is considered sacred in Eastern culture; and not shaking hands unless the host has offered theirs.

Taking a small present to a Malay home, like flowers, fruit or chocolates, is always appreciated. When travelling to longhouse communities in East Malaysia, or to Orang Asli villages in the Peninsula, it's a good idea to bring some little **gifts**, and notebooks and pens for the children will come in useful. For the finer points of longhouse etiquette, see p.371.

FESTIVALS

With so many ethnic groups and religions represented in Malaysia, Singapore and Brunei, you'll be unlucky if your trip doesn't coincide with some sort of festival, either secular or religious. Religious celebrations range from exuberant, family-oriented pageants to blood-curdlingly gory displays of devotion. Secular events might comprise a carnival with a cast of thousands, or just a local market with a few cultural demonstrations laid on. If you're keen to see a major religious festival, it's best to make for a town or city where there is a large population of the particular ethnic group involved –

all the relevant details are given in the list of festivals and events below, and are backed up by special accounts throughout the text.

If you're particularly interested in specifically **Malay festivities**, it's worth noting that in the northeastern Malaysian towns of Kota Bharu and Kuala Terengganu, cultural centres have been established as a platform for traditional Malay pastimes and sports – there's more information in the "East Coast" chapter. **Chinese religious festivals** – in particular, the Festival of Hungry Ghosts – are the best times to catch a free performance of a Chinese opera, or *wayang*, in which characters act out classic Chinese legends, accompanied by crashing cymbals, clanging gongs and stylized singing.

Bear in mind that the major festival periods may play havoc with even the best-planned travel itineraries. Over Ramadan in particular, transport networks and hotel capacity are stretched to their limits, as countless Muslims engage in *balik kampung* – the return to one's home village; Chinese New Year wreaks similar havoc. Some, but by no means all, festivals are also public holidays (when everything closes); check the lists below in "Opening Hours and Public Holidays" for those.

Most of the festivals have **no fixed dates**, but change annually according to the lunar calendar. We've listed rough timings, but for specific dates each year it's a good idea to check with the local tourist office.

A FESTIVAL AND EVENTS CALENDAR

JANUARY–FEBRUARY

Perlis Bird Singing Competition Bird-lovers and bird-owners from Malaysia and beyond gather at Kangar to hear the region's most melodious songbirds do battle (early Jan).

Thaiponggal A Tamil thanksgiving festival marking the end of the rainy season and the onset of spring; offerings of food are made at Hindu temples such as Singapore's Sri Srinivasa Perumal Temple on Serangoon Road (mid-Jan).

Procession of Kwong Teck Choon Ong Scores of cultural troupes perform lion dances and operas, and process around Kuching to honour this Chinese deity (Jan).

Chinese New Year Chinese communities spring spectacularly to life, to welcome in the new year. Old debts are settled, friends and relatives visited, and red envelopes (*hong bao*) containing money are given to children; Chinese operas and lion and dragon dance troupes perform in the streets, while ad hoc markets sell sausages and waxed ducks, pussy willow, chrysanthemums and mandarin oranges. Colourful parades of stilt-walkers, lion dancers and floats along Singapore's Orchard Road and through the major towns and cities of west coast Malaysia celebrate the *Chingay* holiday, part of the new year festivities (Jan–Feb).

Continued...

Chap Goh Mei The fifteenth and climactic day of the Chinese New Year period, and a time for more feasting and firecrackers; women who throw an orange into the sea at this time are supposed to be granted a good husband; the day is known as *Guan Hsiao Chieh* in Sarawak (Feb).

Thaipusam Entranced Hindu penitents carry elaborate steel arches (*kavadi*), attached to their skin by hooks and skewers, to honour Lord Subriaman. The biggest processions are at Kuala Lumpur's Batu Caves and from the Sri Srinivasa Perumal Temple to the Chettiar Hindu Temple in Singapore (Jan/Feb).

Birthday of the Monkey God To celebrate the birthday of one of the most popular deities in the Chinese pantheon, mediums possessed by the Monkey God's spirit pierce themselves with skewers; elsewhere street operas and puppet shows are performed. Make for Singapore's Monkey God Temple on Seng Poh Road, or look out for ad hoc canopies erected near Chinese temples (Feb & Sept).

Regatta Lipa-Lipa *Lipa Lipa* – elegant square-rigged fishing boats – race at Semporna, on Sabah's east coast (Feb).

Brunei National Day The sultan and 35,000 other Bruneians watch parades and fireworks at the Sultan Hassanal Bolkiah National Stadium, just outside Bandar Seri Begawan; the rest watch on TV (Feb 23).

MARCH–MAY

Ramadan Muslims spend the ninth month of the Islamic calendar fasting in the daytime, and breaking their fasts nightly with delicious Malay sweetmeats served at stalls outside mosques. See p.63 for more details (Jan–April).

Le Tour de Langkawi A ten-day international bicycle race which, despite its name, covers most of Peninsular Malaysia before finishing in Langkawi (March).

Hari Raya Puasa The end of Ramadan, which Muslims celebrate by feasting, and by visiting family and friends; this is the only time the region's royal palaces are open to the public (March/April), including Brunei's, where the holiday is known as *Hari Raya Aidilfitri*.

Easter Candle-lit processions held on Good Friday at Christian churches like St Peter's in Melaka and St Joseph's in Singapore (March/April).

Qing Ming Ancestral graves are cleaned and restored, and offerings made by Chinese families at the beginning of the third lunar month – signals the beginning of spring and a new farming year (April).

Singapore Film Festival Annual bash showcasing the sorts of movies that would otherwise never muscle their way into the local cinemas' Arnie- and kung-fu-dominated programmes.

Vesak Day Saffron-robed monks chant prayers at packed Buddhist temples, and devotees release caged birds to commemorate the Buddha's birth, enlightenment and the attainment of Nirvana (May).

Pesta Kaamatan Celebrated in the villages of Sabah's west coast and interior, the harvest festival of the Kadazan/Dusun people features a ceremony of thanksgiving by a *bobohizan* (high priestess), followed by lavish festivities; the festival culminates in a major celebration in Kota Kinabalu (May).

Birthday of the Third Prince Entranced mediums cut themselves with swords to honour the birthday of the Buddhist child god Ne Zha; their blood is wiped on much sought-after paper charms. It's a ritual observed at various Chinese temples throughout the region (May).

Sabah Fest A week of events in Kota Kinabalu, offering a chance to experience Sabah's food, handicrafts, dance and music (late May).

Brunei Armed Forces Day The formation of Brunei's armed forces is celebrated with parades and displays on the padang (May 31).

Hari Raya Haji An auspicious day for Muslims, who gather at mosques to honour those who have completed the Haj, or pilgrimage to Mecca; goats are sacrificed, and their meat given to the needy. Known as *Hari Aidiladha* in Brunei (April–July).

JUNE–AUGUST

Yang di-Pertuan Agong's Birthday Festivities are held in KL to celebrate the *Agong's* birthday – see p.57 (June 4).

Malaysia International Kite Festival A showcase of kite-flying and design, held at Tumpat in Kelantan (June).

Gawai Dayak Sarawak's Iban and Bidayuh peoples celebrate the end of harvesting with extravagant longhouse feasts – aim to be in an Iban longhouse on the Rajang river (June).

Singapore Festival of the Arts Biennial celebration of world dance, music, drama and art, utilizing venues around the state (June).

Continued...

Feast of Saint Peter Melaka's Eurasian community decorate their boats to honour the patron saint of fishermen (June 24).

Dragon Boat Festival Rowing boats, bearing a dragon's head and tail, race in Penang, Melaka, Singapore and Kota Kinabalu, to commemorate a Chinese scholar who drowned himself in protest against political corruption (June/July).

Singapore Food Festival The whole island goes into an eating frenzy for a month, with outlets from hawker stalls to hotel restaurants staging events, tastings and special menus (July).

His Majesty the Sultan of Brunei's Birthday Celebrations Starting with a speech by the sultan on the Padang, celebrations continue for two weeks with parades, lantern processions, traditional sports competitions and fireworks – see local press for details (15 July).

Pesta Rumbia The uses of the *rumbia*, or sago palm, in handicrafts, housing, food and traditional medicines are demonstrated by the villagers of Kuala Penyu, in Sabah (late July).

Kelantan Cultural Week Kelantan citizens celebrate their heritage through cultural performances and handicraft demonstrations; particularly good in Kota Bharu (July–Aug).

Flower Festival Based in the Cameron Highlands, with a display of floral arrangements and a competition for the best flower-covered float (Aug).

Sarawak Extravaganza Kuching hosts a month of arts and crafts shows, street parades, food fairs and traditional games, all celebrating the culture of Sarawak (Aug).

Singapore National Day Singapore's independence is celebrated with a huge show at the National Stadium, featuring military parades and fireworks (Aug 9).

Malaysia National Day Parades in KL, Kuching and Kota Kinabalu to mark the formation of the state of Malaysia (Aug 31).

Festival of the Hungry Ghosts *Yue Lan*, held to appease the souls of the dead released from Purgatory during the seventh lunar month, when Chinese street operas are held, and joss sticks, red candles and paper money burnt outside Chinese homes (late Aug).

SEPTEMBER–DECEMBER

Malaysia Fest Fifteen-day festival in Kuala Lumpur, showcasing the best of Malaysian food, handicrafts and culture (Sept).

Moon Cake Festival Also known as the Mid-Autumn Festival (held on the 15th day of the 8th moon), when Chinese people eat and exchange moon cakes (made from sesame and lotus seeds and stuffed with a duck egg) to honour the fall of the Mongol Empire, plotted, so legend has it, by means of messages secreted in cakes. After dark, children parade with gaily coloured lanterns. Chinatowns are the obvious places to view the parades, but Singapore's Chinese Gardens and Kuching's Reservoir Park also have particularly good displays (Sept).

Navarathiri Hindu temples devote nine nights to classical dance and music in honour of the consorts of the Hindu gods, Shiva, Vishnu and Brahman; one reliable venue is Singapore's Chettiar Temple (Sept–Oct).

Thimithi Hindu firewalking ceremony in which devotees prove the strength of their faith by running across a pit of hot coals; best seen at the Sri Mariamman Temple in Singapore (Sept–Nov).

Festival of the Nine Emperor Gods The nine-day sojourn on earth of the Nine Emperor Gods – thought to bring good health and longevity – is celebrated in Singapore at the Kiu Ong Yah Temple (Upper Serangoon Rd) by Chinese operas and mediums cavorting in the streets (Oct).

Pilgrimage to Kusu Island Locals visit Singapore's Kusu Island in their thousands to pray for good luck and fertility at the Tua Pekong Temple and the island's Muslim shrine (Oct/Nov).

Kota Belud Tamu Besar Sabah's biggest annual market, attended by Bajau tribesmen on horseback, features cultural performances and handicraft demonstrations (Oct/Nov).

Deepavali Hindu festival celebrating the victory of Light over Dark: oil lamps are lit outside homes to attract Lakshmi, the Goddess of Prosperity, and prayers are offered at all temples (Oct/Nov).

Christmas Shopping centres in major cities compete to create the most spectacular Christmas decorations (Dec 25).

OPENING HOURS AND PUBLIC HOLIDAYS

Specific opening hours are given throughout the text, but check below for the general opening hours of businesses and offices in Malaysia, Singapore and Brunei. It's worth noting that in Malaysia's more devout Muslim states, Friday – not Sunday – is the day of rest. Businesses and offices close after lunch on Thursday to accommodate this, while government offices in Brunei close on Fridays *and* Sundays.

Singapore and Malaysia share several common **public holidays**, as well as each having their own. Transport becomes a headache on these days, though you're only likely to be really inconvenienced around Chinese New Year (Jan–Feb) and the month of Ramadan (Jan–April),

when hotels are bursting at the seams and restaurants, banks and shops all close. Local tourist offices can tell you exactly which dates these holidays fall upon annually. In Malaysia, a further complication is that public holidays vary from state to state, depending on each state's religious make-up.

Below, we've listed only the most widely celebrated holidays; in addition, countless localized **state holidays** mark the birthdays of sultans and governors. Don't be surprised to turn up somewhere and find everything closed for the day.

MALAYSIA AND BRUNEI

In **Malaysia**, **shops** are open daily 9.30am–7pm and shopping centres typically open daily

PUBLIC HOLIDAYS

For an explanation of the festivities associated with some of the holidays, see "Festivals", above.

SINGAPORE

January 1: New Year's Day
January/February: Chinese New Year (2 days)
March/April: Hari Raya Puasa
March/April: Good Friday
May 1: Labour Day

May: Vesak Day
May/July: Hari Raya Haji
August 9: National Day
November: Deepavali
December 25: Christmas Day

MALAYSIA

January 1: New Year's Day
February: Thaipusam
January/February: Chinese New Year (2 days)
March/April: Hari Raya Puasa
May: Pesta Kaamatan (Sabah only)
May 1: Labour Day
May/July: Hari Raya Haji

June: Gawai Dayak (Sarawak only)
June 4: Yang di-Pertuan Agong's birthday
June/July: Maal Hijrah (marking Mohammed's journey from Mecca to Medina)
August: Birthday of the Prophet Mohammad
August 31: National Day
November: Deepavali
December 25: Christmas Day

BRUNEI

January 1: New Year's Day
February: Israk Mikraj
January/February: Chinese New Year
February 23: National Day
February/March: First Day of Ramadan
March/April: Anniversary of Revelation of the Koran

March/April: Hari Raya
June 1: Armed Forces' Day
May/July: Hari Raya Haji
June/July: First Day of Hijrah
July 15: Sultan's Birthday
August: Birthday of the prophet Mohammed
December 25: Christmas Day

10am–9pm. Government **offices** tend to work Monday to Thursday 8am–12.45pm & 2–4.15pm, Friday 8am–12.15pm & 2.45–4.15pm, Saturday 8am–12.45pm; however, in the states of Kedah, Kelantan and Terengannu, on Thursday the hours are 8am–12.45pm, they're closed on Friday and open on Sunday. **Banks** open Monday to Friday 10am–3pm and Saturday 9.30am–1.30pm; as with government offices, Thursday is a half-day and Friday a holiday in the states of Kedah, Kelantan and Terengganu. It's impossible to give general opening hours for **temples, mosques and museums** – check the text for specific hours, given where appropriate.

Government offices in **Brunei** open 7.45am–12.15pm & 1.30–4.30pm, except Friday and Sunday; **shopping centres** daily 10am–10pm; and **banks** Monday to Friday 9am–3pm and Saturday 9–11am.

SINGAPORE

In Singapore, **shopping centres** open daily 10am–10pm; **banks** are sure to open at least Monday to Friday 10am–3pm, Saturday 11am–1pm and sometimes longer; while **offices** generally work Monday to Friday 8.30am–5pm and sometimes on Saturday mornings. In general, Chinese **temples** open daily from 7am to around 6pm, Hindu temples from 6am to noon and 5 to 9pm and **mosques** from 8am to 1pm; specific opening hours for all temples and museums are given in the text.

SHOPPING AND SOUVENIRS

Southeast Asia offers real shopping bargains, with electrical equipment, cameras, clothes, fabrics, tapes and CDs all selling at competitive prices. What's more, the region's ethnic diversity means you'll be spoilt for choice when it comes to souvenirs and handicrafts.

Unless you're in a department store, prices are negotiable, so be prepared to **haggle**. If you're planning to buy something pricey in Singapore – a camera, say, or a stereo – it's a good idea to pay a visit to a fixed-price store and arm yourself with the correct retail price; this way, you'll know if you're being ripped off. Asking for the "best price" is always a good start to negotiations; from there, it's a question of technique, but be realistic – shopkeepers will soon lose interest if you offer an unreasonably low price. Moving towards the door of the shop often pays dividends – it's surprising how often you'll be called back. If you do buy any electrical goods, make sure you get an international **guarantee**, and that it is endorsed by the shop.

Throughout the guide, good buys and bargains are picked out and there are features on the best things to buy in specific regions. Malaysian pastimes throw up some interesting purchases: *wayang kulit* (shadow play) puppets, portraying characters from Hindu legend, are attractive and light to carry; equally colourful but completely impractical if you have to carry them around are the Malaysian kites, which can be several metres long. There's a round-up below of the other main souvenir items you might want to bring back. For specific details of shopping and **shops in Singapore**, see p.590.

FABRICS

The art of producing **batik** cloth originated in Indonesia, but today batik is available across Southeast Asia and supports a thriving industry in Malaysia. Batik is made by applying hot wax to a piece of cloth with either a pen or a copper stamp; when the cloth is dyed, the wax resists the dye and a pattern appears, a process that can be repeated many times to build up colours. Batik is used to create shirts, skirts, bags and hats, as well as traditional **sarongs** – rectangular lengths of cloth wrapped around the waist and legs to form a sort of skirt worn by both males and females. These start at around $20 and are more expensive, depending on how complex and colourful the design is. In some of the Malaysian east coast towns, little cottage industries have sprung up enabling tourists to make their own batik clothes; we've given details where relevant.

The exquisite style of fabric known as **songket** is a big step up in price from batik; made by hand-weaving gold and silver thread into plain cloth, *songket* is used to make sarongs, headscarves and the like. Expect to pay at least $100 for a sarong-length of cloth, and $300–400 for the most decorative pieces. The other thing you'll be able to buy in Indian enclaves everywhere is primary coloured silk **sarees** – look in Little India in Singapore and Kuala Lumpur for the best bargains. Prices start at around $80.

METALWORK AND WOODCARVING

Of the wealth of metalwork on offer, **silverware** from Kelantan is among the finest and most intricately designed; it's commonly used to make earrings, brooches and pendants, as well as more substantial pieces. Selangor state is renowned for its **pewter** – a refined blend of tin, antimony and copper, which makes elegant vases, tankards and ornaments. Prices for pewter are fixed throughout Malaysia. Over in Brunei, the speciality is **brassware** – cannons, kettles (called *kiri*) and gongs – decorated with elaborate Islamic motifs.

Natural resources from the forest have traditionally been put to good use, with rattan, cane, wicker and bamboo used to make baskets, bird cages, mats, hats and shoulder bags. **Woodcarving** skills, once employed to decorate the palaces and public buildings of the early sultans, are today used to make less exotic articles such as mirror frames. However, it's still possible to see one of the dynamic **statues** created by the Orang Asli tribes at cultural shows and festivals in Kuala Lumpur and Kuantan. As animists, Orang Asli artists draw upon the natural world – animals, trees, fish, as well as more abstract elements like fire and water – for their imagery.

Of particular interest are the **carvings** of the Mah Meri of Selangor, which are improvisations on the theme of *moyang*, literally "ancestor", which is the generic name for all spirit images. Dozens of *moyang*, each representing a different spirit, are incorporated into the Meri's beliefs and inspire the wooden-face sculptures which they carve. Also popular are *topeng*, or face masks.

EAST MALAYSIAN HANDICRAFTS

In East Malaysia, the craft shops of Kota Kinabalu in **Sabah** have a wide variety of ethnic handicrafts native to the state. Most colourful of these are the *tudong duang*, a multicoloured food cover that looks more like a conical hat, and the painstakingly elaborate, beaded necklaces of the Runggus tribe. Also available are the bamboo, rattan and bark haversacks that locals use in the fields. For more unusual mementoes, look out for the *sumpitan*, a type of blowpipe, or the *sompoton*, a musical instrument consisting of eight bamboo pipes inserted into a gourd, which sounds like a harmonica.

Sarawak's peoples also produce a wide range of handicrafts using raw materials from the forest, with designs that are inspired by animist beliefs. Unique to Sarawak is *pua kumbu* (in Iban, "blanket"), a textile whose complex designs are created using the *ikat* method of weaving (see p.371 for more details). Look out too, for the exquisite wood carving (many or them representing slender rice-gods) sold along Kuching's waterfront. In longhouses, you may also see blowpipes and tools being made.

OUTDOOR PURSUITS

With some of the oldest tropical rainforest in the world and countless beaches and islands, trekking, snorkelling and scuba diving are common pursuits in Malaysia, while Singapore is only a short step away from these diversions. The more established resorts on the islands of Penang, Langkawi and Tioman offer more elaborate sports such as jet skiing and paragliding, while Cherating (the budget travellers' centre on the east coast), with its exposed, windy bay, is a hot spot for windsurfers. Although all these places and activities are covered in more detail in the relevant chapters, below are some pointers to consider.

If you intend to take up any of these pursuits, check that your travel **insurance policy** covers you (see "Insurance", p.21); and see "Health Matters" (p.29) for details of any problems you might encounter out in the Malaysian wilds.

SNORKELLING, DIVING AND WINDSURFING

The crystal-clear waters of Malaysia and its abundance of tropical fish and coral make snorkelling and diving a must for any underwater enthusiast. This is particularly true of Sabah's Pulau Sipadan and the Peninsula's east coast, where islands like Perhentian, Redang, Kapas and Tioman are turning their natural resources into a lucrative business. **Pulau Tioman** offers the most choice for schools and dive sites – though some damage has already been caused to the coral reefs by over-eager visitors. However tempting the coral looks, don't remove it as a souvenir: this can cause irreparable damage and upset the delicate underwater ecosystem.

Most beachside guesthouses have **snorkelling equipment** for rent (though flippers are rare) and rates are very reasonable at $10–15 per day – check before you set out that the mask makes a secure seal against your face. **Dive shops** offer courses ranging from a five-day beginner's open water course, typically around M$650, right through to the dive master certificate, a fourteen-day course costing about M$1200. Make sure that the shop is registered with PADI (Professional Association of Diving Instructors), and it's a good idea to ascertain the size of the group, as well as that the instructor speaks good English. All equipment and tuition should be included in the price: it's worth checking the condition of the gear before signing on the dotted line.

Windsurfing has yet to take off in all but the most expensive resorts in Malaysia, with the notable exception of Cherating (p.272). Its large, open bay and shallow water provide near-perfect conditions for the sport and a few local entrepreneurs are catching on by renting out equipment – usually for around M$15 per hour – but don't expect expert coaching.

TREKKING

The majority of **treks**, either on the Malaysian Peninsula or in Sarawak and Sabah, require some forethought and preparation. As well as the fierce sun, the tropical climate can unleash torrential rain without any warning, which rapidly affects the condition of trails or the height of a river – what started out as a ten-hour trip can end up taking twice as long. That said, the time of year is not a hugely significant factor when planning a trek. Although the **rainy season** (Nov–Feb) undoubtedly slows your progress on some of the trails, conditions are less humid and the parks and adventure tours not oversubscribed.

Most visitors trek in the large **national parks** to experience the remaining primary jungle and rainforest at first hand. Treks in the parks often require that you go in a group with a **guide**, although it's quite possible to go to most parks on your own and then join a group once there. Costs and conditions vary from park to park: there's a check list of the

NATIONAL PARKS: A ROUND-UP

Bako	(p.362)
Endau Rompin	(p.332)
Gunung Gading	(p.366)
Gunung Mulu	(p.407)
Kenong Rimba	(p.288)
Kinabulu	(p.454)
Kubah	(p.360)
Lambir Hills	(p.401)
Niah	(p.395)
Similajau	(p.394)
Taman Negara	(p.208)

national parks covered in this guide given below, and each account contains full practical and trekking details. For inexperienced trekkers, Taman Negara is probably the best place to start, boasting the greatest variety of walks; for the more experienced, the parks in Sarawak, especially Gunung Mulu, should offer sufficient challenges for most tastes; the largely inaccessible Endau Rompin park is for serious expedition fiends only. **Tour operators** in your home country (see the various "Getting There" sections), and those based in Kuala Lumpur (p.119), Kuching (p.359), Miri (p.401) and Kota Kinabalu (p.435), are the best places for more information on conditions and options in the parks – Malaysia's tourist

offices aren't much help, although there is a national parks section at MATIC in KL.

Basic **clothing and equipment** for all treks, be they three hours or ten days, should comprise loose cotton trousers and long-sleeved shirts which protect against sun and sharp thorns; good hiking boots, preferably canvas ones which dry out quickly; hats which shield both the front and the back of the head from the sun; and as small and comfortable a rucksack as you can get by with. (Never take all your possessions on a trek if you can leave some safely behind.) There's a trekking **equipment check list** below, which should see you through most of the treks you're likely to undertake in Malaysia.

For many people, the ubiquitous **leech** – whose bite is not actually harmful or painful – is the most irritating aspect to jungle trekking. When there's been a heavy rainfall, you can rely upon the leeches to come out. Always tuck your trousers into your socks and tie your boot laces tight. The best anti-leech socks are made from calico and can be bought for around $10 from the Malaysian Nature Society, 17 Jalan Tanjung, SO 13/2 Seri Damansara, KL (☎03/632 9422, 635 8773). If you find the leeches are getting through, the best remedy is to soak the outside of your socks and your boots in insect repellent, or dampen tobacco and apply it in between your socks and shoes. It's best to get into the habit of checking your feet and legs every twenty minutes or so for leeches.

CHECK LIST OF TREKKING EQUIPMENT

The check list below assumes you'll be staying in hostels and lodges. This may not always be possible and if you plan to camp, you'll need more, not least your own tent (since most tours don't include camping equipment).

ESSENTIALS	CLOTHING AND FOOTWEAR	OTHER USEFUL ITEMS
Backpack	Shirts/T-shirts	Plastic bag (to rainproof your pack)
Sleeping bag	Trousers	Candles
Mosquito net	Skirt/dress (mid-calf length is best)	Emergency snack food
		Spare bootlaces
Water bottle	Woolly sweater	Sewing kit
Toiletries and toilet paper	Gloves	Small towel
Torch	Rainproof plastic coat or poncho	Soap powder
Pocket knife	Cotton hat with brim	Insulation mat
Sunglasses (UV protective)	Jacket	Large mug and spoon
Sun block and lip balm	Trekking boots	Basic first aid kit (see p.29)
Insect repellent	Cotton and woollen socks	
Compass		

DIRECTORY

AIRPORT TAXES From Malaysia, an airport tax of M\$5 is levied on all domestic flights and on flights to Brunei or Singapore, and M\$40 on international flights. Singapore charges a S\$15 airport tax on all international flights. Brunei charges B\$5 to Malaysia and Singapore, B\$12 to other destinations.

CHILDREN The general levels of hygiene in Malaysia, Singapore and Brunei make travelling with children a viable prospect. Asian attitudes towards the young are far more tolerant than they are in the West, though children inevitably attract a great deal of attention, too, which can be both tiring and stressful for the child. Remember also that children dehydrate much more quickly than adults, particularly if they have diarrhoea, so keep up their fluid intake. Everything you might need is readily available, with the exception of fresh milk – though even this can be found in supermarkets. Disposable nappies and powdered milk are easy to find, and bland Chinese soups and rice dishes are ideal for systems unaccustomed to spicy food. The biggest problem is likely to be in the evening, for only the smartest hotels have a baby-sitting service, though every restaurant or *kedai kopi* will have a high chair. Only upmarket hotels will provide baby cots, though others may be able to rustle something up if given advance warning. However, rooms in the cheaper hotels usually come with an extra bed (see "Accommodation", p.43), for little extra cost. Children under 12 get into most attractions for half-price, and even at the most basic resorts, there'll be a children's playground.

CONTRACEPTIVES Oral contraceptives are available from all pharmacists in Malaysia, Singapore and Brunei, as are spermicidal gels. Condoms are also obtainable.

DUTY-FREE GOODS Duty-free products in Singapore include electronic and electrical goods, cosmetics, cameras, clocks, watches, jewellery, precious stones and metals. Malaysia has no duty on cameras, watches, cosmetics or electronic goods; in addition, perfumes, cigarettes and liquors are duty-free. Pulau Labuan and Pulau Langkawi are both duty-free islands, though neither has a particularly impressive range of products.

ELECTRICITY Mains voltage in Malaysia, Singapore and Brunei is 220 volts, so any equipment which uses 110 volts will need a converter. Malay plugs have three prongs like British ones. If your appliance has a different type of plug, take an adapter.

GAY AND LESBIAN LIFE Though homosexuality is officially outlawed in Singapore, and punishable by from ten years to life imprisonment, a discreet but thriving scene does exist. In Malaysia, homosexuality is no longer illegal, although the relaxation of the statutes has not led to any significant liberalization of general attitudes. There is a gay scene particularly in KL and Penang, but it's fairly low-key and not especially accessible to visiting tourists. The prime minister's daughter Marina Mahathir has raised the profile of the gay community through her work in AIDS education. There is a Pink Triangle Malaysia group based in KL.

LAUNDRY Most towns will have a public launderette, where clothes can be washed cheaply. In addition, some budget hostels have washing machines available for guests for a small charge or offer a laundry service for around M\$7/S\$5. Otherwise, small sachets of soap powder (50c) are readily available from general stores if you prefer to hand-wash, though they tend to have a bleaching effect on strongly coloured clothing. Dry-cleaning services are less common, though any hotel of a decent standard will be able to oblige.

TIME DIFFERENCES Malaysia, Singapore and Brunei are 8 hours ahead of GMT, 16 hours ahead of US Pacific Standard Time, 13 ahead of Eastern Standard Time, and 2 hours behind Sydney.

WOMEN Women in Muslim Malaysia and Brunei have a lower public profile than elsewhere. For the tourist, this manifests itself in the need to dress modestly in conservative and rural areas (particularly in Kelantan and Terengganu) by covering legs and upper arms, though headscarves are not necessary. Most Malay women outside the larger cities dress in long, brightly coloured skirts and headscarves, covering all traces of their limbs, hair and neck – even school children are clothed this way. As a foreigner, there's no need to cover up to this extent – Chinese women don't adhere to these rules – but it's always wise to respect local customs. In the strictly Muslim areas of Peninsular Malaysia, you should think twice about stripping off and swimming outside resort areas; Muslim women go into the water fully clothed. Muslim women enter the mosque by a separate entrance and worship from behind a screen; non-Muslim women may be forbidden entrance altogether, though some places allow women inside provided they wear a long cloak (supplied at the door). Sexual harassment in Malaysia and Singapore is minimal, and certainly no more than you might encounter at home – the level of contact rarely strays beyond the odd whistle or shy giggles. Irritating though it can be, you have to expect some attention both as a foreigner and as a woman, but it's often no more than pure curiosity and your novelty value.

WORKING Unless you've got a prearranged job and a work permit, opportunities for working in Malaysia and Singapore are few and far between. Helping hands are often required in guesthouses; wages are low, but often include free board and lodgings. Work is also occasionally available teaching in language schools, though you're far more likely to secure employment if you have a TEFL (Teaching English as a Foreign Language) qualification, or at least some experience in the field. With the construction boom in Malaysia and the push to develop industries linked to new technology, opportunities are also available to those with engineering and computing skills.

THINGS TO TAKE

A universal electric plug adapter and a universal sink plug.

A mosquito net.

A sheet sleeping bag.

A small torch.

Earplugs (for street noise in hotel rooms).

High-factor sun block.

A pocket alarm clock (for those early-morning departures).

An inflatable neck rest, to help you sleep on long journeys.

A multipurpose penknife.

A needle and some thread.

Plastic bags (to sort your baggage, make it easier to pack and unpack, and keep out damp and dust).

Multi-vitamin and mineral tablets.

Suggestions for a general **first-aid kit** are listed on p.29; for **trekking**, see the list on p.73.

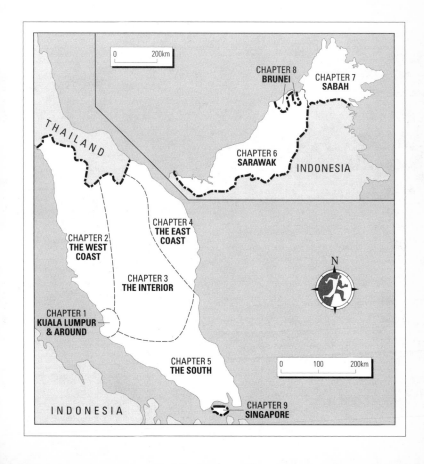

KUALA LUMPUR AND AROUND

K uala Lumpur, or KL as it's known to residents and visitors alike, is the youngest Southeast Asian capital and, these days, the most economically successful after Singapore. Founded as late as the mid-nineteenth century, signs of growth abound – it's almost impossible to walk through the city without taking detours around vast holes in streets crammed with building works, while city maps are out of date before the ink's dry. The city is a jigsaw of various periods and styles, the few remaining colonial buildings rubbing shoulders with chic, modern banks designed to look like traditional Malay houses; other buildings have a futuristic, mega-buck look which wouldn't be out of place in Hong Kong or New York. But then KL never had a coherent style. The first grand structures around Merdeka Square dating from the 1880s were eccentric mishmashes themselves, British engineers bringing together a zestful conglomeration of Moorish, Moghul, Malay and Victorian architectural elements. You never quite know what's round the next corner – or whether what you saw one day will still be in one piece the next.

Some people are disappointed by KL. It's not particularly charming, and doesn't have the narrow alleys, bicycles and mahjong games of Melaka or Kota Bharu. Untrammelled development has given the city more than its share of featureless buildings, follies and failures, terrible traffic snarl-ups and visible, urban poverty. But on the whole it's a safe and sociable place, where most of the 1.4 million inhabitants are friendly, and there are enough interesting monuments to keep visitors busy for a week at least. The classic tour of KL includes the colonial core around **Merdeka Square** and the enclaves of **Chinatown** and **Little India**, followed either by a trip north up Jalan Tunku Abdul Rahman to the warren of plankboard passages known as **Chow Kit Market**, or south to the **Muzium Negara** (National Museum).

But, heading at random in almost any direction is just as rewarding, not least for the contact this brings with KL street life. At the last count, there were 86 **markets** in the city, some, like the wet fish market in between Jalan Tun H.S. Lee and Jalan Petaling, with entrances you would miss if you blinked at the wrong moment. And everywhere are hawker centres, and soya milk and fresh fruit and juice stalls – the latter a necessity, since KL's **humidity** can fell even the most hardened tropical traveller. You'll soon become aware, too, of the **pollution**, which on some days hangs above KL in malevolent clouds. The price paid for the city's rapid development can best be assessed by a trip out to the Klang Valley, west of the city, where craters and half-built structures line the highways, soon to become factories, oil and gas terminals, and timber- and rubber-processing plants. But despite the building boom, KL still has a fair amount of greenery – it's easy to escape the heat, pollution, dust and noise in the gentle sanctuary of the **Lake Gardens** and **Lake Titiwangsa**, while the wider expanses of **Templer Park** or the modern hill station of the **Genting Highlands** are both only an hour's bus ride away.

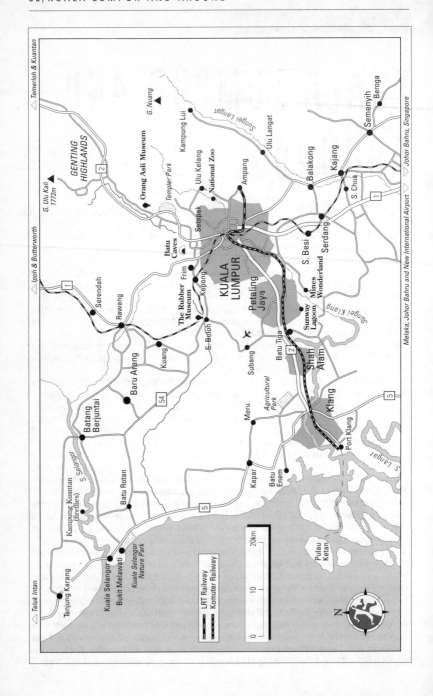

ACCOMMODATION PRICE CODES

Throughout the Malaysia chapters we've used the following **price codes** to denote the cheapest available room for two people. Single occupancy should cost less than double, though this is not always the case. Some guesthouses provide dormitory beds, for which the dollar price is given.

① $20 and under	④ $61–80	⑦ $161–240
② $21–40	⑤ $81–100	⑧ $241–400
③ $41–60	⑥ $101–160	⑨ $401 and above

KL's unique, evenly balanced cultural and **ethnic mix** of Malays, Chinese and Indians makes itself felt throughout the city: in conversations on the street, in the variety of food for sale, in the good manners, patience and insouciance shown to visitors, and in the sheer number of mosques, Buddhist temples and Hindu shrines. In particular, the rugged limestone **Batu Caves**, on the city's northern boundary, contain the country's most sacred Hindu shrine, focus of a wild celebration during the annual Thaipusam religious festival.

Kuala Lumpur is probably the most liberal **Islamic** city in the world, where dress-code strictness is tempered by Malay patterned headscarfs and Indian sarees, and citizens clutch the Koran in one hand and a cellular phone in the other. There is, however, a more traditional side to the city: in the early morning or evening, the sound of the muezzin's call to prayer, *Allah-hu-Akbar*, drifts across from the minarets of the three main mosques, while at Friday lunchtime especially, you can't avoid the thousands of white-robed men converging on the mosques to fulfil their religious duties. Take another look at the architecture, too, and you'll often notice a peculiarly Islamic aesthetic at work in buildings like the Maybank and the Dayabumi Complex, which fuse the modern with the traditional. This is at it's most pronounced in KL's most celebrated new building – for the time being the tallest in the world – the **Petronas Towers**, whose two soaring towers consciously echo minarets.

A little history

Kuala Lumpur (Malay for "muddy estuary") was founded in 1857 when the chief of Selangor State, Rajah Abdullah, sent a party of Chinese prospectors to explore the area around the confluence of the Klang and Gombak rivers for extractable deposits of tin – a metal that had already brought great wealth to the northern town of Ipoh. Although many died from malaria as they hacked through the dense, swampy jungle, the pioneers' reward came with the discovery of rich deposits near **Ampang**, 6km from the confluence, which grew into a staging post for Chinese labourers who arrived to work in the mines. The first Chinese **towkays** (merchants) set up two secret societies in Ampang and fierce competition for the economic spoils soon developed, boiling over into angry confrontations between rivals, effectively restraining the growth of Ampang towards the current centre of KL until the 1870s. But the arrival of an influential Chinese merchant, **Yap Ah Loy** – who had a fearsome reputation as a secret society boss in mainland China – helped unify the divergent groups. Ah Loy's career was a symbol of the Eldorado lifestyle of KL's early years. Starting out as a minor gangster, he became a local hero when he organized the protests in the Negeri Sembilan miners' rebellion of the mid-1860s (see p.283), on the back of which he invested in gambling dens and tin. By the time Ah Loy was 30 he had become KL's *Kapitan Cina*, or headman. But the precarious rule of the pioneers was swept rudely aside during the settling of the Selangor Civil War (see p.128) through British gunboat diplomacy, and in 1880 the British Resident of Selangor State, **Frank Swettenham**, took command.

KL became the capital of the state and, in 1896, the capital of the Federated Malay States.

Until the 1880s, KL was little more than a shantytown of wooden huts precariously positioned on the edge of the river bank. Reaching the settlement was a tough job in itself. Small steamers could get within 30km of the town along Sungei Klang, but from there onwards, the rest of the trip was either by shallow boat or through the roadless jungle. To get to the tin mines was even worse. In his memoirs, *Footprints in Malaya*, Swettenham remembered it being ". . . a twelve-hour effort and very strenuous and unpleasant at that, for there was no discernible path and much of the distance we travelled up to our waist in water. Torn by thorns, poisoned by leech bites and stung by scores of blood-sucking insects, the struggle was one long misery." And yet people were drawn to the town like bees to honey. Early British investors, Malay farmers, Chinese *towkays* and workers – and in the first years of the twentieth century – Indians from Tamil Nadu, all arrived in the search for something better, whether it was work in the tin mines, on surrounding rubber estates or, later, on roads and railway construction.

Swettenham demolished most of the wooden huts and imported **British architects** from India to design solid, grand edifices, suitable for a new capital. He faced an initial setback in 1881 when fire destroyed all the buildings; rebuilding was slow and the governor described the sanitary conditions the following year as "pestilential". Nevertheless, by 1887 the city had five hundred brick buildings and by the turn of the century eight times that amount. The population, which grew from four thousand to forty thousand, was predominantly Chinese, but was swollen by the arrival of the Tamils. The seeds of KL's staggering modern growth had been sown.

Development continued steadily in the first quarter of the twentieth century. Catastrophic floods in 1926 inspired a major engineering project which straightened the course of Sungei Klang, confining it within reinforced, raised banks and successfully preventing future flooding. By the time the **Japanese invaded** in December 1941, overrunning the British army's positions with devastating speed, the commercial zone around Chinatown had grown to eclipse the original colonial area, and the *towkays*, enriched by the rubber boom, were already installed in opulent townhouses along today's Jalan Tunku Abdul Rahman and Jalan Ampang. Although the Japanese bombed the city, they missed their main targets and little physical damage occurred beyond a general looting of stores and the blowing up of bridges by the retreating British army. But the invasion had a radical psychological impact on each of the ethnic communities in the city. The Japanese ingratiated themselves with some Malays by suggesting their loyalty would be rewarded with independence after the war, while inflicting terrible repression on their historic enemies, the Chinese – at least five thousand were killed in the first few weeks of the invasion alone. The Indians also suffered, with thousands sent to Burma to build the infamous railway; very few survived.

At the end of the war, following the **Japanese surrender** in September 1945, the British were once more in charge in the capital, but found they couldn't pick up where they had left off. Nationalist demands had replaced the Malays' former acceptance of the colonizers, while for some of the Chinese population, identification with Mao's revolution in 1949 led to a desire to see Malaya become a communist state. The following period of unrest, which stopped just short of Civil War, lasted twelve years (1948–60), and is known as the **Emergency**. Although very few incidents occurred in KL itself during the Emergency – the guerrillas aware that they couldn't actually take the capital – the atmosphere in the city remained tense. Malaysian independence – **Merdeka** – finally came in 1957, but tensions between the Malays and the Chinese later spilled over into **race riots** in the city in 1969. Tunku Abdul Rahman, the first prime minister, was forced to set an agenda for development which aimed to give all Malaysia's ethnic groups an equal slice of the economic cake.

The look of the city changed, too, during this postwar period, with the nineteenth-century buildings which had dominated KL – the Sultan Abdul Samad Building, the Railway Station and other government offices – gradually being overshadowed by a plethora of **modern developments**. Likewise, interracial hostilities have been transformed in the last twenty years, galvanized into an all-hands-on-deck approach to quicken the pace of economic progress. In recent years the Klang Valley, which runs west from KL to Klang through Petaling Jaya and Shah Alam, has become a thriving industrial zone, feeding the manufacturing sectors of this expansion, while the peripheral towns to the north and south have been converted into residential and industrial satellites.

> The **telephone code** for KL is ☎03.

Arrival and information

KL is at the hub of Malaysia's transport systems. It has the main international airport, where you'll have to change if you're flying on to Sarawak or Sabah, while buses from all over Peninsular Malaysia converge on one of four bus stations. The train station doubles as a tourist sight, a magnificent building fusing Moorish architectural flourishes with British colonial design. For departures, see the box on p.84.

By air

The dated but efficient **Sultan Abdul Aziz Shah International Airport** at Subang is 30km west of the centre. Bus #47 (every 30min, 6am–9pm; $1.60) leaves from the bay on the left outside the Terminal 1 departure hall; buy your ticket on board the bus. The journey takes around forty minutes and goes via the Railway Station to the terminus on Jalan Sultan Mohammed, opposite the Klang bus station (see below). This is close to Central Market at the southern edge of Chinatown, the main area for budget accommodation. **Taxis** into the centre cost around $40 – buy a coupon from the desk outside the arrival hall, and present it to the driver. You'll doubtless be approached by taxi

---

KUALA LUMPUR'S NEW AIRPORT

On January 1, 1998, the ten-billion-dollar **Kuala Lumpur International Airport** (KLIA) will begin operations at Sepang, 33km south of KL. The opening is likely to be a "soft" one – a trial run while glitches are sorted out or, as is the case with KLIA, facilities are still being built. It is an important point of pride for the Malaysian government, however, to have the airport up and running in time for the Commonwealth Games, being hosted in September 1998. Once the airport is fully operational, the Sultan Abdul Aziz Shah International Airport at Subang will most likely close to commercial flights and become a military facility.

The publicity for KLIA at Sepang promises an "airport in the forest, a forest in the airport." This does not mean that planes will be crash-landing in jungle, but that the overall environment is being designed to be as green and leafy as possible, with indigenous vegetation both inside and outside the terminal building. Apart from the futuristic greenhouse-like terminal, there will two parallel runways and a satellite terminal, which will cater for up to 2.5 million passengers a year. The eventual aim is that people will be whisked into the heart of KL in 35 minutes along a new **high-speed rail link**, connecting with the city's LRT system. Buses and cars will drive along a new highway linking KL and Sepang in about 45 minutes.

For the addresses and telephone numbers of airlines, foreign consulates, travel agencies and tour operators in KL, see pp.118–119.

Airport
The easiest way to get to the **airport** is to call a taxi from your hotel or lodge, which will cost around $40; taxis flagged down on the street tend not to want to go out that far. Otherwise, bus #47 ($1.60) leaves from the Jalan Sultan Mohammed terminus, opposite Klang bus station, every thirty minutes from 6am to 10pm. It's a forty-minute journey – allow for delays in rush hour. Most international flights depart from Terminal 1. Terminal 2 handles flights to Singapore, while Terminal 3 is for domestic services. For flight enquiries call ☎746 1235 or 746 1014.

Trains
The information kiosk in the **Railway Station** has up-to-date train timetables; ☎274 7443 or 273 8000 for information and reservations. You must book, preferably at least three days in advance, for the night sleeper to Singapore or Butterworth; booking isn't necessary for most other routes. Most of the large hotels can book train tickets for you, but the tourist offices can't.

Buses and long-distance taxis
Most long-distance buses and taxis leave from inside **Pudu Raya bus station** (☎230 0145), reached by the footbridge over Jalan Pudu. Buses also operate from outside the terminus – you can't miss the hawkers touting these services – and although these are legitimate, check when the driver is leaving as he may wait for the bus to fill up, which could take a while. Long-distance taxi journeys – to destinations like Penang, Melaka and Kuantan – are a good deal, seldom much more than twice the price of the bus, but again the drivers wait for a full car-load before departing.

For some departures you'll need one of the other bus stations: Putra (☎442 9530) by the Putra World Trade Centre for east coast buses; Klang (☎230 7694) on Jalan Sultan Mohammed for services west of KL in Selangor State; and Pekeliling (☎442 1256) on Jalan Raja Laut for the east coast and interior. For **bus route information** the *Infoline* (see "Information and Maps" below) is useful.

Ferries
Ferries to Tanjung Balai and Belawan (for Medan) in Sumatra depart daily, except Monday, from **Port Klang**, 38km southwest of KL. Take the Komuter train or a bus from the Klang bus station on Jalan Sultan Mohammed to the port (see p.86 for details).

touts, but stick to the official coupon system or you could find yourself seriously out of pocket.

All the major **car rental** firms have offices at the airport, though if you're seeing Malaysia by car you'd be best advised to pick it up on your last day in KL – a short drive downtown can take years off your life. There are money exchange outlets at the airport, and a tourist office in the arrival hall, where you can pick up a map of the city.

By train, bus and taxi

Chinatown is ten minutes' walk north of Kuala Lumpur's striking **Railway Station** (see p.96) is on Jalan Sultan Hishamuddin – follow the covered walkway starting outside the east side of the station and finishing across from Central Market; the National Art Gallery is opposite and the Muzium Negara another ten minutes' walk further south. There's a good information kiosk (daily 8am–8pm) in the station concourse which has hotel lists and train timetables. Hotels near the Putra World Trade Centre can be reached by Komuter train, while for those in the Golden Triangle area, catch a bus or taxi.

Most long-distance buses arrive at the giant **Pudu Raya bus station**, an island of concrete in the middle of Jalan Pudu, just to the east of Chinatown. It looks chaotic, but is actually quite an efficient place, with hundreds of buses setting off day and night for most of the main destinations on the Peninsula. The buses draw into ground-floor bays, while the ticket offices are on the floor above, along with dozens of stalls selling food, and a left-luggage office. **Long-distance taxis** also arrive at Pudu Raya, on the second floor above the bus ticket offices. Chinatown hotels are within walking distance of here, and for the Golden Triangle, take bus #29, which goes to the Lot 10 Shopping Centre.

Some buses from the east coast end up instead at **Putra bus station**, a smaller, more modern terminus to the northwest of the city centre, just beside the Putra World Trade Centre. This is handy for the budget hotels on Jalan Raja Laut and in the Chow Kit area, but it's quite a way from Chinatown, 2km to the southeast; to head downtown, walk from the bus station down Jalan Putra to *The Mall* shopping centre. From here, either catch a bus to Central Market on Jalan Hang Kasturi – you'll have to ask to make sure you get on the right one – or walk a little further south to the Putra Komuter Station, where trains run to both Bank Negara and the main train station at least every thirty minutes.

There are two other bus stations at which you might arrive. Services from Kuantan or from the interior stop at **Pekeliling bus station** at the northern end of Jalan Raja Laut; from here, regular buses head south to Chinatown. Finally, the **Klang bus station** on Jalan Sultan Mohammed, just south of Central Market, is used by Klang Valley buses to and from Port Klang (where **ferries** arrive from Belawan, in Sumatra, see the box on "Leaving KL"), Klang, Shah Alam and Kuala Selangor.

Information and maps

As well as the information office in the train station and at the airport, KL has lots of **tourist information centres**, each of which hands out excellent free **maps** listing places to visit and useful telephone numbers. The biggest tourist office is **MATIC** (Malaysian Tourist Information Complex) at 109 Jalan Ampang (daily 9am–9pm; ☎264 3929), east of the centre close to the junction with Jalan Sultan Ismail. Housed in a beautiful old colonial building that was originally a tin *towkay*'s house, the main desk here hands out various free city maps and brochures, as well as holding details of accommodation in KL and throughout the country; another desk takes bookings for Taman Negara National Park (see p.283). Cultural shows are held on the first floor (Tues, Thurs, Sat & Sun at 3.30pm; $2).

The **KL Visitors' Centre** (Mon–Fri & Sun 8am–5pm, Sat 8am–12.45pm; ☎274 6063) is at 3 Jalan Sultan Hishamuddin, to the left of the main entrance to the train station. There is also a Tourism Malaysia office just outside the train station booking hall. The most extensive selection of brochures is at the **Malaysian Tourism Promotion Board** (Mon–Fri 9am–4.30pm, Sat 9am–6pm; ☎441 1295), Level 2, Putra World Trade Centre on Jalan Putra, close to *The Mall*.

You can pick up a city **bus service map** from the Dewan Bandaraya (KL City Hall) just north of Merdeka Square on Jalan Raja Laut. There's also an English-speaking **Infoline** (☎230 0300), worth trying mainly for long-distance bus timetables. For **entertainment listings**, check the weekly magazine *Day and Night*, the "Time Out" section in Thursday's edition of the *Sun* newspaper, and the "Metro" section in the tabloid *Malay Mail*, which lists concerts, cinema, theatre, clubs, fashion shows and art exhibitions. The bi-monthly magazine *Vision Kuala Lumpur* is also a useful source of information and features on the city.

City transport

Most of the city centre – the **Colonial District**, Chinatown and Little India – is easy to cover on foot, though take care as neither cars nor motorbikes can be trusted to stop at traffic lights or pedestrian crossings. In any case, it's inadvisable to walk everywhere, because you will soon become exhausted by the combined effects of humidity and traffic fumes. When you can, either take the **LRT**, jump on a **bus** – avoiding if possible the rush hour periods (8–10am & 4.15–6pm) – or take a **taxi**. These, although plentiful and fairly inexpensive (if the driver puts on the meter), can be tricky to hire during rush hour, and during the frequent downpours of rain. For sights outside the city, use the modern **Komuter train** system.

Light Rail Transit

The latest attempt to ease KL's chronic traffic problem is the **Light Rail Transit (LRT)** system, the first twelve-kilometre stretch of which is already in operation. Running between Ampang and Jalan Sultan Ismail, the LRT trains cut through Chinatown at Pudu Raya bus station, and past Merdeka Square up to the Mara Building. They're easy to spot in the city centre since they run on raised concrete ramps above the main roads. Trains operate from 6am to midnight, every three to five minutes during peak periods, and every eight to fifteen minutes at other times. Tickets are purchased from the ticket office outside of each station, and are passed through an electronic gate. Stored-value tickets (either $20 or $50) are returned at the gate, with the remaining amount on the ticket displayed on the machine. Fares start at 75 sen; for journeys between central KL Hang Rakyat and Sultan Ismail stations, the minimum fare is $1.25. The second stage of the system, scheduled to be partly in operation during 1998, will extend Phase 1 north to Sentul and Phase 2 for 30km between Gombak, northeast of KL, to the People's Park beyond Petaling Jaya. It will include a five-kilometre underground stretch from Central Market to Yow Chuan Plaza. A map and booklet on the system can be picked up from each station, or you can call the Customer Service Hotline (☎03/298 4977) during office hours.

Buses

KL's **bus** services are comprehensive, quick and inexpensive. For visitors, the downside is that they're extremely difficult to fathom, because none of the services run in straight lines or seem to start from a particular point. The old system of blue buses run by Sri Jaya and independent pink minibuses is being phased out. These are being replaced by new buses run by the government Intrakota company. However, until early 1998 you may still see blue and pink minibuses; the bus route numbers given here apply to both the old buses, and the new Intrakota ones.

The main depots are the Pudu Raya bus station on Jalan Pudu, the Jalan Sultan Mohammed terminus (opposite Klang bus station) and Lebuh Ampang, on the northern edge of Chinatown. Fares are based on the distance you are travelling and range from 50 sen to $2 a journey; if the bus has a conductor, you don't need to have the exact change, but otherwise you will. Services start running at around 6am and operate regularly throughout the day until midnight.

Taxis

Many visitors depend completely on **taxis** to get around and you'll seldom pay more than $15 for any journey within the city. Taxi fares start at $1.50 and rise 30 sen for every kilometre travelled, so you've got to be going quite a distance for the price to mount up. However, as KL's traffic is so congested, it's often faster to get out and walk.

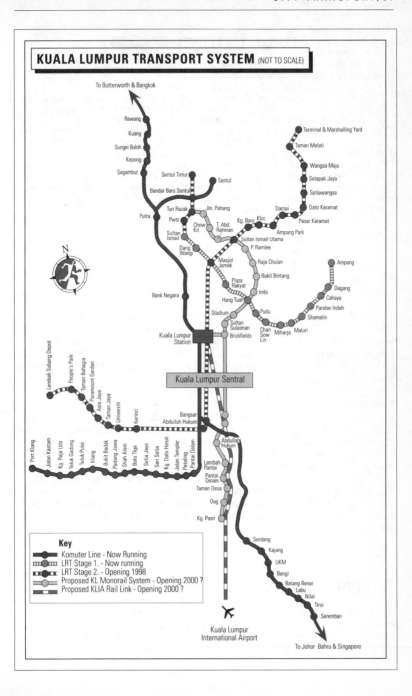

KUALA LUMPUR TRANSPORT SYSTEM (NOT TO SCALE)

To Butterworth & Bangkok

Rawang
Kuang
Sungei Buloh
Kepong
Segambut

Sentul Timur
Sentul
Bandar Baru Sentul

Tun Razak
Jln. Pahang
Putra
Pwtc
Chow Kit
T. Abd. Rahman
Kg. Baru
Klcc
Sultan Ismail
Dang Wangi
Sultan Ismail Utama
Ampang Park
P. Ramlee
Masjid Jamek
Raja Chulan
Bukit Bintang
Plaza Rakyat
Imbi
Bank Negara
Hang Tuah
Stadium
Pudu
Sultan Sulaiman
Chan Sow Lin
Miharja
Maluri
Kuala Lumpur Station
Brickfields

Terminal & Marshalling Yard
Taman Melati
Wangsa Maju
Setapak Jaya
Setiawangsa
Dato Keramat
Damai
Pasar Keramat

Ampang
Dagang
Cahaya
Pandan Indah
Shamelin

Kuala Lumpur Sentral

Lembah Subang Depot
People's Park
Taman Bahagia
Paramount Garden
Asia Jaya
Taman Jaya
Universiti
Kerinci

Bangsar
Abdullah Hukum

Port Klang
Jalan Kastam
Kg. Raja Uda
Teluk Gadong
Teluk Pulai
Klang
Bukit Badak
Padang Jawa
Shah Alam
Batu Tiga
Setia Jaya
Seri Setia
Kg. Dato Harun
Jalan Templer
Petaling
Pantai Dalam

Abdullah Hukum
Lembah Pantai
Pantai Delam
Taman Desa
Oug
Kg. Pasir

Serdang
Kajang
UKM
Bangi
Batang Benar
Labu
Nilai
Tiroi
Seremban

Key

- Komuter Line - Now Running
- LRT Stage 1. - Now running
- LRT Stage 2. - Opening 1998
- Proposed KL Monorail System - Opening 2000 ?
- Proposed KLIA Rail Link - Opening 2000 ?

Kuala Lumpur International Airport

To Johor Bahru & Singapore

N

TRANSPORT SYSTEMS

As Malaysia's economy has boomed so has the population of KL, rising at a steady 3 per cent annually to a current total of around 1.4 million. With the demand for private cars constantly rising, and a predicted 1.4 million vehicles on the roads across the country by the year 2000, the government knows it has a growing problem on its hands and has been making efforts to combat it. During 1997, KL's notorious pollution-spewing pink minibuses are being phased out and replaced with sleek, air-conditioned buses. The idea is to co-ordinate the buses with the Komuter trains and new LRT lines that run across the city, and eventually offer an integrated travel ticket valid on all modes of transport. Sometime before the year 2000, the ultra-modern Sentral station at Brickfields will open, with its high-speed rail link to the new international airport at Sepang and connections with all the other rail lines. This will include an elevated monorail system running through the heart of the city. More streets will be pedestrianized and an elevated highway over Sungei Gombak is planned. But with land at a premium in KL and a never-ending flow of new cars on to the roads, it's already become clear that the city will not totally solve its traffic problems unless it goes some way down the dictatorial route taken by Singapore, virtually banning vehicles from the city centre.

Many of the taxi drivers can't speak English, and some don't know their way around the city, so it's best to carry a map, and have your destination and the name of some main thoroughfares written down. Some may also refuse to take you to a destination, unless you pay way over the meter price. This is illegal, but happens to locals as well as tourists. There are numerous taxi ranks around the city, usually situated beside bus stops; it's a good idea to wait on the correct side of the road for the direction you want to go in since taxi drivers often refuse to turn their cab round. Alternatively you can simply flag one down and jump in – bashful visitors will usually be overlooked in the melee. If you **telephone** for a taxi (see "Listings", p.119, for companies), an extra $1 is added to the fare.

Komuter trains

For getting around the centre of KL, the **Komuter** train is of limited use, although the section between Putra, near the Putra World Trade Centre, and KL's main train station can be handy for travel between these two points. Where the system really does come into its own is for travel to and from sights outside the city. There are two lines – one running from Rawang to Seremban, the other from Sentul to Port Klang. Both connect at the central KL stations of Putra, Bank Negara and Kuala Lumpur Railway Station. The trains are modern and run smoothly at thirty-minute intervals, with extra services during the early-morning and evening rush hours. Tickets, which start at $1, can be purchased from the stations and automatic machines at the stops. There are various saver passes for periods of one week up to one year, but the best value for the visitor is the $5 day ticket (valid Mon–Fri after 9.30am) for unlimited travel on the network. For further information, ring ☎272 2828.

Accommodation

Accommodation prices in KL are reasonable by international standards, except for the high rates charged in hotels in the Golden Triangle, east of the centre. All the other main areas – Chinatown, Little India, along Jalan TAR and around Pudu Raya – contain a wide range of choices, from travellers' hostels and lodges to expensive hotels. You shouldn't need to book in advance unless you're opting for one of the more popular old-style hotels, like the *Coliseum*, or arriving at the weekends or during holiday seasons when the best budget accommodation fills up quickly. KL's tourist offices all have accommodation lists, though the very cheapest places won't be listed.

Most travellers head for **Chinatown**, though in recent years **Little India** has become a valid alternative, with entrepreneurs opening up both budget and mid-range places to cater for KL's steady increase in visitors. As you'd expect, inexpensive places also proliferate close to the Pudu Raya bus station around **Jalan Pudu**, most sited in Jalan Pudu Lama, just off the main road. Further east, the **Golden Triangle** is where the first-class hotels are situated, alongside fashionable malls and nightclubs. West and north of Little India and Chinatown, the hotels along the two-kilometre stretch of **Jalan TAR** include some of the sleaziest and most famous in town. **Brickfields** also has a range of good-value accommodation (and a large *YMCA*) but is south of the city, way beyond walking distance from the centre, though there are plenty of buses that link the area with the Klang bus station near Central Market.

Chinatown

All the following lodges, hotels and hostels are marked on the map on pp.92–93.

Backpackers Travellers Inn, second floor, 60 Jalan Sultan (☎238 2473, fax 202 1855). Centrally located, on the eastern edge of Chinatown, with small, clean single and double rooms, some with air-con, and a dorm. Manager Stevie has added some nice touches like a book exchange, games and colour TV. ①.

Backpackers Travellers Lodge, first floor, 158 Jalan Tun H.S. Lee (☎201 0889, fax 238 1128). Second operation for Stevie's family, run by brother Vincent and his friendly staff. A range of clean rooms, some with air-con, as well as cramped four-bed. Videos shown every night and there's no curfew. Recommended. Dorms $8. ①.

City Inn, 11 Jalan Sultan (☎238 9190, fax 441 9864). Mid-range modern hotel, with small, but spotless air-con rooms with bathroom. ④.

Furama, Kompleks Selangor, Jalan Sultan (☎230 1777, fax 230 2110). This is a modern air-con hotel with small but comfortable, well-equipped rooms. ⑤.

Leng Nam, 165 Jalan Tun H.S. Lee (☎230 1489). Beside the Sri Mahamariamman Temple, and close to Chinatown's most picturesque street, Jalan Petaling, this traditional Chinese hotel has a great atmosphere. Small rooms come with two large beds; toilets and shower are shared. ②.

Lok Ann, 113a Jalan Petaling (☎238 9544). Neat hotel, offering rather charmless rooms with full facilities, although better value than others at the same price. ④.

Malaya, Jalan Hang Lekir (☎232 7722, fax 230 0980). One of the most expensive hotels in Chinatown, but excellent for the price. The deluxe rooms have all the trimmings, and the café is renowned. ⑥.

Mandarin, 2–8 Jalan Sultan (☎230 3000, fax 230 4363). Chinatown's largest hotel, boasting a coffee house, 24-hour room service and even a hair salon and health centre. Rooms are big with full facilities. ⑥.

Swiss Inn, 62 Jalan Sultan (☎232 3333, fax 201 6699). Comfortable, modern hotel in the heart of Chinatown complete with a café that does cheap breakfasts and a terrace overlooking Jalan Petaling. ⑥.

Sun Kong, 210 Jalan Tun H.S. Lee (☎230 2308). One of the cheapest and smallest Chinese hotels in the area. Run by a friendly family; it has a shrine in the hall and dark polished wood floors. ②.

Travellers Moon Lodge, 36b Jalan Silang (☎230 6601). Just south of Jalan Tun Perak, this popular lodge includes a rather grotty dorm, small two- and three-bed rooms and a roof terrace. The management is friendly; there's a fine collection of maps, pamphlets and books. ①.

YWCA, 12 Jalan Hang Jebat (☎230 1623, fax 201 7753). This delightful hostel – safely away from the noise of Chinatown – only rents its clean, comfortable singles and doubles to women, couples and families. It's a great deal if you qualify, with the added advantage of a lovely sitting room. ②.

Wan Kow, 16 Jalan Sultan (☎238 2909). Rather unpromising entrance leads to an airy lobby and traditional Chinese hotel box rooms. Cheap and clean. ②.

Near the train station

All the following lodges and hotels are marked on the map on pp.92–93.

The Heritage Station Hotel, Kuala Lumpur Railway Station, Jalan Sultan Hishamuddin (☎273 5588, fax 273 2842). Ideal if you've an early-morning train to catch. The lobby and rickety lift retain some of the atmosphere of a colonial hotel, but the functional rooms are a bit of a disappointment. ⑥.

Kuala Lumpur International Youth Hostel, 21 Jalan Kampung Attap (☎273 6870, fax 274 1115). From the train station, follow Jalan Sulaiman around to the Police Co-op building and then turn right down Jalan Kampung Attap. The hostel is at the end of the block in a very quiet location. There are only dorms with four, six and ten beds, a café and a laundry service. The atmosphere is rather sterile. Dorms $8. ①.

Riverside Lodge, 80a Jalan Rotan (☎201 1210). Just off Jalan Kampung Attap. A dingy, but popular dorm, set in a quiet area within walking distance of Chinatown. Dorms $18. ②.

Little India

All the following lodges and hotels are marked on the map on pp.92–93.

Champagne, 141 Lorong Bunus, off Jalan Masjid India (☎298 6333). This hotel, popular with the Indian elite is associated with the *Chamtan*, but is not as nice. ④.

Chamtan, 62 Jalan Masjid India (☎293 0144, fax 293 2422). Smaller than the *Champagne*, but the rooms are slightly better and have TVs and attached bathrooms. ④.

City Skyline, 74a Jalan Masjid India (☎294 9877, fax 294 3098). One of the cheaper hotels in the area, but the rooms, although carpeted and clean, smell a bit musty. ③.

Empire, 48b Jalan Masjid India (☎ & fax 293 6890). Cheaper than the better-known *Champagne* and *Chamtan*, this is a good deal with well-equipped rooms and discounts for longer stays. ②.

Palace, 40 Jalan Masjid India (☎298 6122, fax 293 7528). Top-of-the-range with sumptuous, but small rooms, featuring all mod cons. ⑥.

TI Lodge, 104 Jalan Masjid India (☎293 0261). Friendly, brightly painted place that's the best of the budget bunch. Also has slightly more expensive air-con rooms with attached bathrooms. ②.

Along Jalan TAR and near Putra World Trade Centre

All the following lodges and hotels are marked on the map on pp.92–93.

City Villa Kuala Lumpur, 69 Jalan Haji Hussein (☎292 6077, fax 292 7734). This long-established hotel has good, small rooms with bath and air-con. Its location within Chow Kit Market makes it noisy early in the morning though. ⑥.

Coliseum, 98 Jalan TAR (☎292 6270). KL's most famous old-style hotel. It can be a bit noisy, but oozes atmosphere, from the moment you swing through the Western saloon-style door into the bar. The café serves great steaks and gravy. ②.

Kowloon, 142 Jalan TAR (☎293 4246, fax 292 6548). In the middle of a small red-light district – with a good coffee house. The rooms are small, but good value. ⑥.

The Legend, Putra Place, 100 Jalan Putra (☎442 9888, fax 441 1030). One of KL's most luxurious hotels, offering comfortable rooms and an excellent range of restaurants, some of which have fantastic views across the city. Handy for *The Mall* next door and the Putra World Trade Centre across the road. ⑧.

Rex, 102 Jalan TAR(no phone). Clean Chinese cheapie; the bathrooms are shared. ②.

Tivoli, 136 Jalan TAR (☎292 4108). Another low-budget place overlooking KL's traffic-clogged thoroughfare. Not as friendly as the *Rex*, with clean rooms and shared shower and toilet. ②.

Transit Villa, 36 Jalan Chow Kit (☎441 0443). Popular with young Malaysians, this vibrant place is not really designed for travellers, but has rooms from dorms to triples. Dorms $8. ①–②.

Around Pudu Raya

All the following lodges and hotels are marked on the map on pp.92–93.

Katari, 38 Jalan Pudu (☎201 7777, fax 201 7911). Bang opposite the bus station, this new upmarket business hotel has a coffee house and small, clean rooms with the usual facilities. ⑥.

Kawana Tourist Inn, 68 Jalan Pudu Lama (☎238 6714, fax 230 2120). Neat, small rooms in a modern, rather bare place, but extremely good value and only ten minutes' walk from the bus station. ②.

KL City Lodge, 16 Jalan Pudu (☎230 5275, fax 201 3725). Convenient, although avoid the rooms which look over busy Jalan Pudu. Dorms and air-con rooms; useful extras include the laundry service and free lockers. Dorms $8. ①.

Pudu Raya, 4th floor, Pudu Raya bus station (☎232 1000, fax 230 5567). Well-positioned for arriving late or leaving town early, but obviously a noisy area. The small rooms are good, with bath and air-con. ⑥.

The Golden Triangle
All the following lodges and hotels are marked on the map on pp.92–93.

Concorde, 2 Jalan Sultan Ismail (☎244 2200, fax 244 1628). The trendiest of the area's hotels, housing the *Hard Rock Café* and fashionable boutiques, including Armani and Issey Miyake. It has large rooms with full facilities, phone and fridge. ⑦.

Federal, 35 Jalan Bukit Bintang (☎248 9166, fax 248 2877). Patronized mostly by Malaysians, this unflashy old hotel offers large, comfortable rooms and a revolving rooftop restaurant. ⑦.

Equatorial, Jalan Sultan Ismail, opposite the MAS building (☎261 7777, fax 261 9020). Vast three-hundred-room hotel with four-hundred-metre swimming pool, shops and some good restaurants and cafés. ⑧.

Holiday Inn On The Park, Jalan Pinang (☎248 1066, fax 248 1930). Set back from the noisy street, the large rooms here are comfortably furnished and well-equipped. ⑧.

Istana, 73 Jalan Raja Chulan (☎244 1445). From the moment you walk into its glittering lobby you know you're in one of KL's best hotels. Palace-like decor, tropical plants, swimming pool and the booking office for Taman Negara National Park Resort, also run by the same hotel group. The rooms are of a high standard, too. ⑨.

The Lodge, Jalan Sultan Ismail (☎242 0122, fax 241 6819). One of the best-value deals in the Triangle area, with motel-style rooms, swimming pool and an outdoor restaurant. ⑤.

Park Royal, Jalan Imbi, corner of Jalan Sultan Ismail (☎242 5588, fax 241 4281). Undistinguished modern building, but larger than usual rooms. ⑧.

The Regent, 160 Jalan Bukit Bintang (☎241 8000, fax 242 1441). A prestigious, expensive hotel, with a large swimming pool, massive rooms and immensely luxurious suites. ⑨.

The Renaissance, 130 Jalan Ampang (☎262 2233, fax 263 1122). One of the city's newest luxury hotels, sharing facilities, including a swimming pool, gym and restaurants – with the adjacent *New World* hotel, which is slightly cheaper. ⑨.

The Shuttle Inn, 112b Jalan Bukit Bintang (☎245 0828). The cheapest decent hotel in the area, located right by the main shopping complexes. Small, but clean air-con rooms with attached bathrooms. ④.

Brickfields
Lido, 7a Jalan Marsh, opposite the YMCA (☎274 1258). This place is a good deal; the large rooms have bath and air-con, and there are much cheaper rooms with shared bathrooms. ②–③.

New Winner, 11 Jalan Thambapillai, off Jalan Tun Sambanthan (☎273 3766, fax 273 3762). Average hotel, aimed at business people. The air-con rooms have all the usual facilities. ④.

Quee Ping, 13–15 Jalan Thumbapillai (☎274 3505, fax 273 8288). Standard Chinese hotel, whose small, neat rooms have full facilities. ④.

YMCA, 95 Jalan Padang Belia (☎274 0045, fax 274 0559). Best to book ahead for these small, but spotless rooms. On offer are language lessons, a resource centre, gym, laundry, barber and more. Rates include breakfast. ②–④.

The City

KUALA LUMPUR is constantly being reshaped – the most spectacular example being the levelling of the city's second largest hill, south of the centre, to make way for the new Merdeka Stadium. The earth which was removed was used to fill in the valley below the National Mosque. But despite the changes to the landscape and architecture over the last twenty years, the centre at least has its attractions: the tranquillity of Merdeka Square and its colonial surroundings, the commercial zeal of Chinatown, and the silty

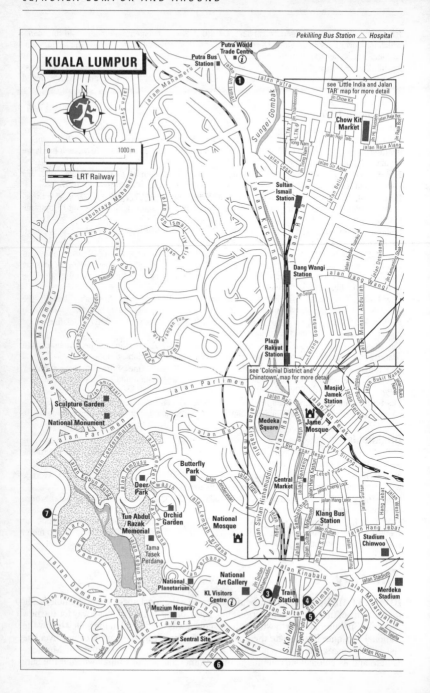

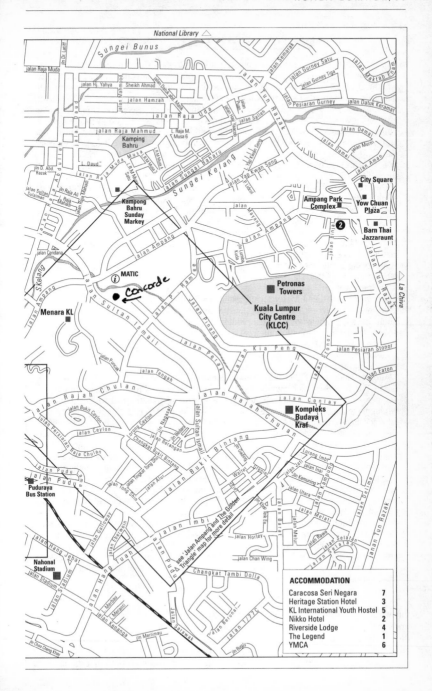

ACCOMMODATION

Caracosa Seri Negara	7
Heritage Station Hotel	3
KL International Youth Hostel	5
Nikko Hotel	2
Riverside Lodge	4
The Legend	1
YMCA	6

THE NEW ARCHITECTURE

Since the 1970s, KL's construction boom has given Malaysian **architects** untold opportunities both to experiment with new styles and confront certain questions – in particular, whether climate should be the governing factor in building design, or if cultural or religious elements should be paramount. The resultant new buildings in KL – the Maybank, Tabung Haji, the Dayabumi and the National Library – have seen traditional elements interacting with innovative architectural expressions, often with strikingly original effect. Some architects have looked to the past and combined the archetypal sloping Malay roof and Islamic arches with the latest functionalist thinking; others have incorporated solar panelling for heating and water concourses to regulate the internal temperature. In addition, KL's architects have started to work closely with new sculptors, integrating two- and three-dimensional artworks into their designs; see pp.115–116 for more on this.

The architect who best demonstrates the contemporary fusing of essentially religious motifs with new design is **Hijjas Kasturi**, who was responsible for the Maybank and Tabung Haji buildings. The **Maybank Building** (p.116) is perhaps his most impressive work, where the dominance of the colour white denotes purity while the smooth, cool contours of the building and it's height are reminiscent of a mosque's minaret. In the **Tabung Haji**, on Jalan Tun Razak at the intersection with Jalan Ampang, the five columns which support the structure represent the five pillars of Islam, the single tower symbolizing unity with God. Appropriately, the building is the headquarters of the Islamic Bank of Malaysia.

The new **National Library** on Jalan Tun Razak is a good example of a building which reinterprets traditional Malay forms. Although the library is dominated by a gleaming roof covered in large blue ceramic tiles, architect Shamsuddin Mohammed's starting point was a typical east coast house, which are built on stilts and encompass an intimate space, more often than not made from a warm material like wood. Within the library he incorporated everyday cultural symbols, using the shapes of traditional earthenware pots for the interior sculpture, and the patterns of *songket* headscarves worn by Malay women on the walls.

Another leading architect, **Ken Yeang**, considers Malay culture and religion as a side issue. For him the chief consideration is climate, and his **Menara Measiniaga** skyscraper – on the way to Subang Airport – is the latest in a string of tropical buildings which make maximum use of natural light and ventilation. His intention is to make it possible for the occupants to experience as much of the country's natural climate as possible: the windows are shaded to reduce heat, plants spiral up the walls in what is known as vertical landscaping, while energy efficiency, like solar panelling, is integral to the design.

Nik Mohammed's **Dayabumi Complex** (p.96), combines both ecological and Islamic ideas, although at heart it's much more functional than any of the later buildings, with office space more important than cosmetic flourishes. Nevertheless, as one of the earliest new buildings, it set the standard by being unmistakably Malaysian, modern and different. The most spectacular new building in KL – Cesar Pelli's **Petronas Towers** –wasn't designed by a Malaysian, though it strongly stresses Islamic themes. Standing at just over 490m high, it is the tallest building in the world (until China's Chongqing Tower tops out). Tapered twin towers resembling minarets are joined by a bridge 41 floors up, forming a megalithic gateway, while the interior design is a profusion of squares and circles symbolizing harmony and strength. Here is the ultimate expression of Malaysia's intention to stand at the economic heart of modern Southeast Asia, while maintaining its traditions and faith.

brown wash of the Sungei Klang. Much of KL's appeal – markets, temples and historic mosques – is untouched by the new construction, though the inevitable by-products of headlong development, such as exhaust and industrial pollution, have grown considerably worse in the last few years. KL now has at least four times the number of cars joining the multi-lane highways and edging through its narrow streets than it did in 1988.

The city centre is quite compact, with the colonial district centred on **Merdeka Square**; close by, across the river and to the south, is **Chinatown**, with **Little India** just to its north – these are the two main traditional commercial districts. One of the most prominent (and busiest) of KL's central streets, **Jalan Tunku Abdul Rahman** (or Jalan TAR), runs due north from Merdeka Square for 2km to **Chow Kit Market**; closer in, west of the square, are the **Lake Gardens**, Parliament House and the National Monument, while to the south, lie the **Masjid Negara** (National Mosque), the landmark **Railway Station** and the **Muzium Negara** (National Museum).

Everything else of interest in central KL lies to the east of the colonial district. From Merdeka Square, the congested **Jalan Tun Perak** leads southeast to the Pudu Raya bus station, a kilometre further east of which is the **Golden Triangle**. This consumer sector is delineated by three main roads – Jalan Bukit Bintang, Jalan Imbi and Jalan Sultan Ismail – and contains most of the city's expensive hotels, modern malls, night-clubs, and the lofty **Menara and Petronas Towers**. Just to the north of here, **Jalan Ampang** – leading east out of the city – was one of the first streets to be developed as a residential area for rich tin *towkays* and colonial administrators at the turn of the century.

All this is confined within the **Jalan Tun Razak** ring road, which encircles the city. Most of what you come to see in KL is inside the ring road, but there are popular spots just outside in the **suburbs** – including Lake Titiwangsa, the important Thean Hou Temple and the National Zoo.

The Colonial District

The small **Colonial District** (see map on p.100), which developed around the confluence of the Gombak and Klang rivers in the 1880s, is unlike any other area of KL, its eccentric fusion of building styles at extreme odds with the rest of the city. The district is centred on the beautifully tended, two-hundred-metre-long **Merdeka Square** on the west bank of the Klang. Once both English cricket field and Malay padang (field), it's now the most famous stretch of green in Malaysia, as it was here that Malaysian independence – simply called *merdeka* (freedom) – was proclaimed on August 31, 1957. On the eastern edge of the square the 95-metre-high flagpole, the tallest in the world, and nearby a large video screen which displays advertisements and religious messages, reflecting Malaysia's twin creeds – consumerism and Islam. On Saturday evenings locals flock to the square to parade beside the fairy lights of the Sultan Abdul Samad Building (see below), and watch the latest TV drama on the video screen.

The **Royal Selangor Club** on the square was the British elite's favourite watering hole. Colonial wags used to refer to the low, black-and-white mock-Tudor building as "the Spotted Dog" in memory of the club mascot, a dalmatian, which a former member used to tie up at the steps. Dating from 1890, the club is now theoretically open to anyone who can afford membership, though old colonial prejudices die hard – the rule barring women from the bar is still in force and it's only possible to visit if invited by a member. To the north, the Anglican **St Mary's Church** (1894) welcomed the city's European inhabitants every Sunday before they repaired to the club; it's usually open during the day.

Across Jalan Sultan Hishamuddin, the **Sultan Abdul Samad Building** was among the earliest of the capital's Moorish-style buildings; Moorish architecture dominated the work of British architects between 1890 and 1920. Designed by Anthony Norman (also responsible for St Mary's) and finished in 1897, the building is contemporary with the Railway Station, its two-storey grey-and-red-brick facade dominated by a forty-metre-high clock tower and curved colonnades topped with impressive copper cupolas. Norman's brief was to design buildings suitable for the new State Secretariat, and his grand construction still serves KL in a public capacity. The Sultan Abdul Samad

Building is now the High Court; nearby, to the north stands the black-domed old **City Hall**, and to the south the **National Museum of History** (daily 9am–6pm; free). Once the workplace of banker John Major in his pre-prime ministerial days, the Moorish-style cream-coloured building on the corner of Jalan Raja was converted in 1996 from government offices into a museum. It provides an informative romp through the main points of the nation's history, spanning everything from the geological formation of the Malay Peninsula to Prime Minister Mahathir's Vision 2020 programme. The three floors can be covered in half an hour and the final section of the museum on the ground floor is devoted to displays on all the Commonwealth countries. On the opposite corner is the original Public Works Department, which has striped brickwork and keyhole archways. These days this houses **Infokraft** (daily 9am–5pm; free). Most of the items in this crafts museum are commercially made and the main idea is for visitors to buy rather than browse.

South of Merdeka Square

South of Merdeka Square along **Jalan Sultan Hishamuddin** is the unmissable 35-storey **Dayabumi Complex** on your left. Built in the 1970s, it was the first modern building in KL to incorporate Islamic principles in its design. Malay architect Nik Mohammed took modern mosque architecture as his model and produced a sky-scraper whose high-vaulted entrance arches and glistening white open-fretwork has become characteristic of progressive Malaysian city architecture. The complex is home to the national oil company, Petronas, which maintains an excellent gallery, Galeri Petronas, on the ground floor, displaying contemporary Malaysian art (see p.116).

The **GPO** is next door, while a couple of hundred metres further down, on the opposite side of Jalan Sultan Hishamuddin, stands the seventy-metre-high minaret and geometric lattice work of the **Masjid Negara**, the National Mosque (daily 9am–6pm except Fri 2.45–6pm), which opened in 1965. It's an impressive building, with sweeping rectangles of white marble bisected by pools of water, and a grand hall which can accommodate up to ten thousand worshippers. In the prayer hall, size gives way to decorative prowess, the star-shaped dome adorned with eighteen points signifying the five pillars of Islam and the thirteen states of Malaysia. To enter (which you can only do when prayers are over), you need to be properly dressed: robes can be borrowed from the desk at the mosque entrance. The **Islamic Exhibition Centre** (daily 9am–5pm; free) – opposite the mosque on Jalan Perdana – houses a collection of Islamic manuscripts, pottery, coins and other *objets d'art*, as well as a library and bookshop.

The Railway Station

A hundred metres south of the mosque, the **Railway Station**, probably the city's most famous building, could have come straight out of the *Arabian Nights*. KL's first train station stood on a site close to Merdeka Square, but was superseded in 1911 by the current building, designed on a grand scale by a British architect, A.B. Hubbock, and built to last. Hubbock had previously lived in India and had been inspired by North Indian Islamic architecture, something reflected here in his meshing of spires, minarets and arches with a hardy iron roof. Hubbock had already tried out some of these flourishes on the Jame Mosque which he'd completed in 1909 (see p.99). Amazingly, colonial administrators insisted that the station's roof be built to withstand six feet of snow; today there is talk of putting a swimming pool up here for the hotel which has opened in the northwest corner of the station. For the best views, walk past the station and turn left on to Jalan Kinabalu. Standing on the bridge here, you can see the station's seven minarets in their full glory, positioned between two thirty-metre-high domes, an incongruous sight with the futuristic Dayabumi and other skyscrapers dominating the sky-line behind.

The National Art Gallery

Across from the station, next to the railway administration offices, what was once the colonial *Majestic Hotel* now houses the country's **National Art Gallery** (daily 10am–6pm; free). The ground floor is given over to temporary exhibitions, usually of painting, sculpture or photography from Malaysia and other Southeast Asian countries, with the permanent collection occupying the second and third floors. If you were hoping to expand your knowledge of Malaysian artists, you'll be disappointed by the poorly referenced collection, which provides only the artists' names and dates of the works. However, it is instructive to wander from the more contemporary canvases on the second floor – which include several colourful abstract works, some inspired by Islamic design – to the more traditional works on the top floor. Here, landscapes and portraits offer historical insights and reveal images of another, more rural Malaysia, where handicraft-making and music-playing predominate. There's a possibility that the building will once again become a luxury hotel to service, among others, passengers on the Eastern and Oriental Express. This depends, however, on a new location being found for the gallery.

The Muzium Negara

Past the art gallery, ten minutes' walk along Jalan Damansara brings you to the **Muzium Negara**, Malaysia's National Museum (daily 9am–6pm; $1), built in 1963, with a sweeping roof, characteristic of Sumatran Minangkabau architecture, and an exit flanked by Italianate mosaics showing scenes from the Malaysia's history and culture. Much of the museum's original collection, housed in the old Selangor Museum, was destroyed by World War II bombing, but the extensive ethnographic and archeological exhibits on display are still impressive.

The museum's entrance is at the back of the building, past the reproduction of the Pinitu Malim archway, from a Malay fort in Kedah. The **ground floor** is mostly taken up with tacky life-size dioramas depicting various aspects of traditional Malaysian life, from the prosaic activities of the Malay kampung (village) – fishing, farming and weaving – to the pomp and ritual of a wedding or a Malay circumcision ceremony. At the end of the room, a cross-section of a Melaka *Baba* house is revealed, loaded with mahogany furniture, intricate carpets and ornaments made from silver, brass and gold. Also on the ground floor are Wayang Kulit (shadow play) displays, which show how the wooden puppets used in this ancient artistic tradition differ in design and colour depending on their provenance.

On the **upper floor**, a large but uninspiring section of stuffed birds and animals needn't detain you long, certainly not if you're waylaid by the much more impressive collection of weapons, including a large number of *kris* daggers, *parangs* (machetes), swords and miniature cannons. Finally, there's a fabulous section on traditional musical instruments: the *serunai*, a reed with a multicoloured end; the *rebab*, a kind of fiddle played like a cello; numerous two-metre-long Kelantanese drums and smaller *rebana* drums; and Chinese lutes, gongs and flutes. Although Malay instruments are still in common use at festivals and ceremonies, traditional Chinese music in Malaysia was virtually extinct by independence, but has now been partially revived – if you're interested in hearing the music produced by these instruments, check out the venues listed on p.117.

The Lake Gardens and around

Once at the National Museum you're only a short walk from the **Lake Gardens**, one hundred hectares of close-cropped lawns, gardens and hills originally laid out in the

1890s by the British state treasurer to Malaya, Alfred Venning, though much of the spectacular landscaping has been completed within the last twenty years. Spread around a lake (Tasek Perdana), the park incorporates a number of sights – the National Monument, the Butterfly House and Bird Park, Orchid and Hibiscus Gardens, the National Planetarium and the colonial mansions of the former Governor of the Malay States – while just beyond, on the northern edge, is Malaysia's Parliament House.

From the Muzium Negara, you can take the footbridge across Jalan Damansara which leads to the entrance of the National Planetarium. Alternatively, head along Jalan Damansara for about 50m, looking out for the small pathway leading into a tunnel at the junction with Jalan Kebun Bunga. This takes you to the southern edge of the gardens, from where it's a good twenty-minute walk along the lake and up the hill to the bird park and flower gardens. From Chinatown, the nearest entrance is past the National Mosque on Jalan Perdana. The main entrance is a thirty-minute walk due west of Merdeka Square along Jalan Parlimen; you can take either bus #21 or bus #48 from Jalan Sultan Mohammed.

In the gardens

Opposite the main entrance, off Jalan Parlimen, 50m along Jalan Tamingsabi, is the **National Monument**, a great bronze sculpture designed by Felix de Weldon, better known for his work on the Iwo Jima Memorial in Washington DC. The fifteen-metre-high shiny slab was constructed in 1966 to commemorate the nation's heroes, yet strangely, the seven military figures protruding from it appear to be European rather than from any of the various Malaysian ethnic groups who fought in World War II and during the Emergency (see p.82). Reached by a path leading up from the car park, the monument stands surrounded by a moat with fountains and ornamental pewter water lilies – a tranquil spot. Back at the car park, looking down on Jalan Parlimen, is the **Taman Asean sculpture garden**, to which neighbouring countries have contributed abstract works in marble, iron, wood and bamboo.

The **Butterfly House** (daily 9am–5pm; $5) – first left from the National Monument inside the Lake Gardens – holds a diverse collection of butterflies (dead and alive), though more likely to hold your attention is the excellent **Bird Park** (daily 9am–6pm; $3); retrace your steps from the Butterfly House to the main road and turn left uphill, following the road for 200m to the Bird Park entrance. Modelled on Singapore's Jurong Bird Park, walkways loop around streams and pools taking in the habitats of indigenous species such as hornbills, the Brahminy Kite and the Hawk Eagle, and specimens of the largest pheasant in the world, the Argus Pheasant. You may as well nip into the **Orchid** and **Hibiscus Gardens** (daily 9am–6pm; free) opposite, where hundreds of plants are grown and sold; the hibiscus section especially provides a wonderful assault on the senses.

The main road through the gardens then weaves down past a field of deer, to the **Tun Abdul Razak Memorial**, a house built for the second Malaysian prime minister – his motorboat and golf trolley are ceremonially positioned outside. Beyond is the **lake** itself, where you can rent boats and pedaloes and buy food and drink from a number of stalls. It takes nearly an hour to walk all the way round the lake, and from here you're only twenty minutes from the southern entrance (for access to the Muzium Negara).

On a hill to the east of the lake is the **National Planetarium** (Tues–Sun 10am–7pm; $1). This joint venture between Malaysia and Japan is housed in a building strongly reminiscent of a mosque, with a blue-domed roof, minaret tower and fountains cascading water along an imposing stairway. The displays illuminate the Islamic origins of astronomy as well as Malaysia's modern-day thrust for the stars via various satellite launches. For an extra $6, you can enter the Space Theatre and watch one film from a daily changing programme of special wide-screen movies. Those with cast-iron stomachs may also care to experience zero gravity in the Shuttle Spaceball ($1), where the would-be astronaut is spun in three directions within a man-sized gyroscope – to the amusement of all onlookers. The viewing gallery on the fourth floor provides a panoramic view of Kuala Lumpur's skyline and the surrounding Lake Gardens.

Up a winding hill road to the west of the lake stands KL's most exclusive – and expensive – hotel, **Caracosa Seri Negara** (☎282 1888, fax 282 7888; ⑨). The former colonial residence of the British Governor of the Malay States comprises two elegant white-washed mansions – the *Caracosa* built in 1904 for Sir Frank Swettenham and the *Seri Negara*, formerly called the "Kings House" which was used for guests. The buildings were only returned to the Malaysian government in 1987, and in 1989, after a visit by Queen Elizabeth II, became a hotel. The hotel has since played host to virtually all visiting heads of state, but is also open to the public for lunch, dinner and an affordable high tea (daily 3.30–6pm; around $30). All the suites – there are no single rooms here – come with their own butler, who meets guests at the airport and is on hand during their entire stay.

Parliament House

If you coincide with the parliamentary sessions (March–Aug Mon–Thurs 2.30–6.30pm; Oct–Dec Mon–Thurs 2.30–6.30pm), you might want to tie in a visit to the gardens with one to **Parliament House**, 300m further down Jalan Parlimen from the main entrance. Here, two white buildings – the House of Representatives, an ultra-modern highrise, and the Senate, a lower building with a curved roof and protruding circular windows – emerge from a lush green hill and command an excellent view of the Lake Gardens. You need to get prior written permission for your visit by contacting the Sectretary to the Parliament, Bangunan Parlimen, Jalan Parlimen, 50680 KL (☎03/232 1955, fax 230 0986). Make sure you're properly dressed: women in long sleeves, trousers or long dresses, and men in long-sleeved shirts and long trousers.

East of Merdeka Square: Jame Mosque to Central Market

At the southern end of Merdeka Square, Lebuh Pasar Besar runs over KL's busiest bridge, connecting the Colonial District with the commercial sector. Just north of here, on a promontory at the confluence of the Klang and Gombak rivers, stands KL's most attractive devotional building, the **Jame Mosque**. It's a site replete with significance, since it was here – on a section of dry land carved out from the enveloping forest – that the pioneers from Klang searching for tin in the 1850s, established a base that soon turned into a boom town. The mosque itself formed part of the second great period of expansion in KL, completed in 1909 by the British architect A.B. Hubbock, and incorporating features he had copied from Moghul mosques in North India – pink brick walls and arched colonnades, topped by oval cupolas and squat minarets. There's an intimacy at work here that isn't obvious at the much larger national mosque (which replaced the Jame as the centre of Muslim faith in KL), and the grounds, bordered by palms, are a pleasant place to sit and rest. The main entrance is on Jalan Tun Perak.

Head south down Jalan Benteng, over the junction with Lebuh Pasar Besar, and you reach the Art-Deco **Central Market** (daily 9am–10pm). Backing onto Sungei Klang, this large pastel-coloured brick hangar was built in the 1920s as the capital's wet market, but now houses restaurants, craft shops and stalls selling anything from T-shirts to porcelain statues of Hindu and Chinese deities. The ground floor has batik textiles, hand-painted shadow-play masks, silk scarves, hats, bags, baskets and wooden Orang Asli sculptures. The first and second floors feature hawker stalls (busiest 1–3pm & 6–8pm), while directly outside the market, on the west side, are more cafés. Opposite the northern end of the market, the primary-coloured building houses the Central Market Annex, containing some funky gift shops, cafés and a cinema. Cultural performances are held both inside and outside the market, usually during the evening from Thursday to Sunday.

Chinatown

Spreading out from Central Market is **Chinatown**, KL's commercial kernel dating from the arrival of the first traders in the 1860s. Bordered by Jalan Petaling to the east and Jalan Tun Perak to the north, the area had adopted its current borders by the late-nineteenth century, with southern-Chinese shophouses, coffee shops and temples springing up along narrow streets such as Jalan Tun H.S. Lee and Jalan Sultan. Little has changed: there are still traditional apothecaries displaying medicines on the street corners, though other shops are as likely to stock computers and sound systems as tools and pots and pans, and what remains of the early architecture is dwarfed by the surrounding skyscrapers. For the moment, family businesses still predominate, but the few remaining genuinely old sites, like the **wet market** between Jalan Petaling and Jalan Tun H.S. Lee, may well soon be cleared for development. In the meantime, a stroll down Chinatown's narrow lanes still reveals dilapidated shops and Chinese pharmacies, and large baskets of cured and dried meats alternate with the street-vendors' ranks of brightly coloured sweet drinks, soya milk and cigarette lighters.

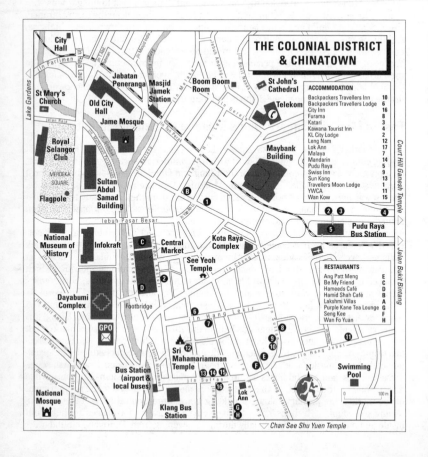

THE COLONIAL DISTRICT & CHINATOWN

ACCOMMODATION

Backpackers Travellers Inn	10
Backpackers Travellers Lodge	6
City Inn	16
Furama	3
Katari	4
Kawana Tourist Inn	8
KL City Lodge	2
Leng Nam	12
Lok Ann	17
Malaya	7
Mandarin	14
Pudu Raya	5
Swiss Inn	9
Sun Kong	13
Travellers Moon Lodge	1
YWCA	11
Wan Kow	15

RESTAURANTS

Ang Patt Meng	E
Be My Friend	C
Hameeds Café	D
Hamid Shah Café	B
Lakshmi Villas	A
Purple Kane Tea Lounge	G
Seng Kee	F
Wan Fo Yuan	H

In the early years of this century, **Jalan Petaling** was home to brothels and gambling dens. Nowadays, dozens of colourful umbrellas shield the street vendors from the fierce sun, and tourists spend their time bartering for mock Gucci watches, bric-a-brac and clothes. At numbers 86, 90 and 96 you can buy beads, stones, necklaces, masks, sculptures and conches. After 6pm the street is closed to vehicles and the entire area is transformed into a pasar malam (night market), where food stalls offer *loong kee* (rectangular slices of pork) and deep-fried bananas and expert hagglers can pick up bags, sunglasses, clothes and crafts at bargain prices.

See Yeoh and Chan See Shu Yuen temples

Just past the junction of Jalan Tun H.S. Lee and Jalan Cheng Lock is the **See Yeoh Temple**, founded by Yap Ah Loy, KL's early headman (see p.81), who became the temples' chief deity when he died in 1885. The temple is atmospheric but not particularly interesting, though it comes to life on festival days. You're better off visiting the area's largest temple, **Chan See Shu Yuen**, at the very southern end of Jalan Petaling. The main deity here is Chong Wah, a Sung-dynasty emperor. The inner shrine is covered in gold-painted scenes of lions, dragons and mythical creatures battling with warriors. Statues representing the temples' three deities stand behind a glass wall, with a mural of a brilliant yellow sun above them. From outside, you can see the intricately carved roof, its images depicting more monumental events in Chinese history and mythology, and decorating the edge of the pavilion are blue ceramic vases and small statues of peasants – the guardians of the temple – armed with poles crowned with lanterns.

Sri Mahamariamman Temple

Oddly perhaps, KL's main Hindu temple is also located in the heart of Chinatown, on Jalan Tun H.S. Lee, between the two main Buddhist temples. Outside the pyramid-shaped entrance to the **Sri Mahamariamman Temple**, garland-makers sell their wares, and sweetmeats and other delicacies are often available. The earliest temple on this site was built in 1873 by Tamil immigrants and named after the Hindu deity, Mariamman, whose intercession was sought to provide protection against sickness and "unholy incidents". In the case of the Tamils, who had arrived to build the railways or to work on the plantations, they needed all the solace they could find from the appalling rigours of their working life. Significant renovation of the temple took place in the 1960s when sculptors from India were commissioned to design idols to adorn the five tiers of the gate tower – these now shine with gold embellishments, precious stones and exquisite Spanish and Italian tiles. Above the gate is a hectic profusion of Hindu gods, frozen in dozens of scenes from the *Ramayana*.

During the Hindu **Thaipusam** festival, the temple's golden chariot is paraded through the streets on its route to the Batu Caves, on the northern edge of the city (see p.120). For the rest of the year, the chariot is kept in a building at the side of the temple, and can be seen if you walk along Jalan Hang Lekir, the first street on the left back along Jalan Tun H.S. Lee from the temple. The temple is always open to the public and is free to visit, although you may want to contribute a dollar or so towards its upkeep.

Chinatown's eastern edge

Chinatown's main west–east thoroughfares, Jalan Tun Perak and Jalan Cheng Lock (the latter the route of the original rail track through KL) converge at the Pudu Raya roundabout, just off which stands the **Malay Banking (Maybank) Building**. Built in the late 1980s by Hijjas Kasturi, it's a structure typical of the new KL, designed with Islamic principles in mind. Unlike many of the other modern skyscrapers, there's actually a reason to venture inside – to visit either the excellent art gallery or the **Nurismatic Museum** (Mon–Sat 10am–6pm; free), both on the main lobby floor. This is an unusually interesting collection, arranged in chronological fashion, starting with pre-coinage artefacts once used for transactions in Southeast Asia – tin ingots, gold dust and bars of silver or, for what the caption describes as "ordinary people", cowrie shells, rice and beads. Coins were gradually introduced into the region along with the arrival of the various colonizing powers; early sixteenth-century Portuguese coins on display here are delicately engraved with miniatures of the Malay Peninsula and tiny kites billowing in the air. The first mass-produced coins were those issued by the East India Company which bore the company's coat of arms – a practice seen until the late eighteenth century when tokens were minted by timber and rubber companies to pay their expanding labour pool. The very first notes were produced by a private bank in 1694, although they were only issued officially at the end of the nineteenth century. During the Japanese invasion, the occupying administration produced its own notes which, after the Japanese surrender, the British diligently collected and stamped "not legal tender" and "specimen only".

Across the Pudu Raya roundabout from the Maybank the bus station inhabits an oblong island in the wide road. North of here, a little street, Jalan Pudu Lama, leads to KL's second most important Hindu shrine, the **Court Hill Ganesh Temple**, a small and often crowded place, with dozens of stalls outside selling garlands, incense, sweet-meats and charms. This was a favoured stop for visitors on their way to KL's original law courts, once sited nearby. Supplicants prayed to the chief deity, Lord Ganesh, who specializes in the removal of all obstacles to prosperity, peace and success.

Menara KL, Jalan Ampang and the Golden Triangle

Heading north from the Pudu Raya roundabout you'll reach Jalan Raja Chulan and the Neoclassical fronted headquarters of the state telephone company A five-minute walk east along here brings you to the **Menara Kuala Lumpur** (daily 10am–10pm; $8). When it officially opened in October 1996, this tower, standing at 421 metres, was the tallest in Asia and the third tallest in the world. These rankings are no longer assured, but the tower remains a striking addition to the KL skyline, nearly a match for the near-by Petronas Towers, and is the best lookout from which to piece together the disparate parts of the city and its surroundings.

Designed in the shape of the *gasing*, or Malaysian spinning top, the Menara serves as a telecommunications tower as well as a tourist attraction. The foyer has the usual souvenir shops as well as a moneychanger, a POS Malaysia booth, a *McDonald's* serving a special Menara version of the Big Mac (four burgers in a bun), and a video room screening an informative film about the tower's construction. The entrance to the high-speed lifts is decorated with ornate tiles and mirrors, courtesy of craftsmen from Isfahan in Iran, one of KL's twin cities. The viewing gallery is on Level One, at the base of the bulbous portion at the tower's top. Immediately above it is *Seri Angkasa*, a revolving buffet-style restaurant which has to qualify as the city's most glittering dinner-date destination. To get here from Central Market take bus #60 to Jalan P. Ramlee and walk up Jalan Punchak towards the tower. The road up Bukit Nanas, on which the Menara stands, is a steep hike.

Running along one side of Bukit Nanas, **Jalan Ampang** swings east out of the city, jumping back a century as it goes. Mansions were built here with profits from the tin industry by Chinese *towkays* and British businessmen and administrators, whose archi-tectural inspiration ranged from Islam to Art Deco. One mansion is now the informa-tion office, MATIC, at no. 109 (see p.85), while a little further along on the same side of the road, another became *Le Coq D'Or* restaurant (p.112), supposedly built by one tin baron to impress another, who had refused to let his daughter marry him because he had once been too poor. Other surviving period residences along here are now for-eign embassies and high commissions, although many of those further out along Jalan

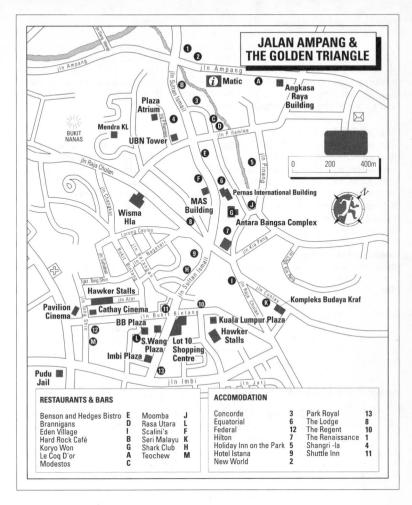

JALAN AMPANG &
THE GOLDEN TRIANGLE

ℹ️ Matic

Angkasa
Raya
Building

Plaza
Atrium

Mendra KL

BUKIT
NANAS

UBN Tower

0   200   400m

MAS
Building

Pernas International Building

Wisma
Hla

Antara Bangsa Complex

Hawker Stalls

Pavilion
Cinema

Cathay Cinema

BB Plaza

Kompleks Budaya Kraf

Kuala Lumpur Plaza

Hawker
Stalls

S.Wang
Plaza

Lot 10
Shopping
Centre

Imbi Plaza

Pudu
Jail

RESTAURANTS & BARS

Benson and Hedges Bistro	E	Moomba	J
Brannigans	D	Rasa Utara	L
Eden Village	I	Scalini's	F
Hard Rock Café	B	Seri Malayu	K
Koryo Won	G	Shark Club	H
Le Coq D'or	A	Teochew	M
Modestos	C		

ACCOMODATION

Concorde	3	Park Royal	13
Equatorial	6	The Lodge	8
Federal	12	The Regent	10
Hilton	7	The Renaissance	1
Holiday Inn on the Park	5	Shangri -la	4
Hotel Istana	9	Shuttle Inn	11
New World	2		

Ampang were pulled down in the 1980s to make way for more modern developments, like the Ampang Shopping Complex, Yuan Chuan Plaza and City Square, all at the junction with Jalan Tun Razak, around 3km from the centre. Buses #23, #24, #173, #186 and #176 from the Central Market come out this way, to the junction of Jalan Ampang and Jalan Tun Razak.

In the section of Jalan Ampang between Jalan Sultan Ismail and Jalan Tun Razak is a huge building site, from which a gleaming city of steel and glass is rising. At its centre is the **Petronas Towers**, the tallest building – for the time being – in the world. The entire site, built on the former Selangor Turf Club, is called the **Kuala Lumpur City Centre (KLCC)** and is designed as a testament to Malaysia's booming economic power. The Petronas Towers will house the offices of the national petroleum company, and several other multinational companies. Critics already sneer that one of the towers is leaning, but the gleaming multifaceted facade of this twenty-first-century complex is undeniably impressive. The **Podium** at the base of the towers will include the Petronas Concert Hall, an interactive Petroscience education centre, an art gallery containing the largest private art collection in Malaysia and a public library. Beside several other skyscrapers, a luxury hotel and shopping centre, KLCC will also have a twenty-acre public park and garden at its heart and a new mosque, decorated with mosaics created by craftsmen from Uzbekistan. The LRT will eventually stop at the KLCC when the second section of the system is finished in 1998.

The Golden Triangle

The grid of roads south of Jalan Ampang – with Jalan Sultan Ismail and Jalan Bukit Bintang at its heart – comprises what locals refer to as the **Golden Triangle**, the only area of the city which keeps really late hours. Here, among the hotels, shopping malls, neon signs and nightclubs, smartly dressed KL youth and thousands of expats drift from bar to club to shop, taking in the arts and handicraft stalls and food centres along the way. One reason for visiting the area during the day is the **Kompleks Budaya Kraf** (daily 10am–6pm; free), at the end of Jalan Conlay. Once you've worked your way past the concessionary shops, you'll find the actual museum at the back of the complex, with two floors devoted to the country's wide range of arts and crafts, including silver, pewter and brass ware, batik, wood carvings and ceramics. This is a good opportunity to see excellent examples of Malaysia's crafts in one place, and to do some serious souvenir shopping. There's also a café which overlooks a feeble attempt at landscaped gardens.

Heading west back towards Chinatown on the corner of Jalan Imbi and Jalan Hang Tuah is **Pudu Jail**. The prison's outside walls are covered with what is claimed to be the longest mural in the world – the wall painting of lush jungles and lazy beaches is the work of the prisoners, who used their hands, not brushes, to apply the paint. Unfortunately, the mural is in a sorry state and will disappear completely when the building, which has stood on the site since 1896, is demolished in the near future.

Little India to Chow Kit Market

Just to the north of Chinatown, **Little India** – the commercial centre for KL's Indian community – lies on the site of a Malay kampung dating from the very earliest days of the settlement. Although covering a much smaller area than Chinatown, Little India is equally fascinating and is the main area in the city for buying silk goods, especially *sarees*, *songkets*, scarves and skull caps, as well as handmade jewellery.

Turning into **Jalan Masjid India** from Jalan Tun Perah, it's soon clear you've entered the Tamil part of the city, with *poori* and *samosa* vendors and cloth salesmen vying for positions on the crowded streets outside the cafés and hotels. Ten minutes' walk north, Lorong Bunus branches off to the right and leads to a small market where you'll see **garland-makers** busy at their craft. There's another nightly pasar malam here: a good place to come to eat tandoori chicken and other dishes.

Along Jalan TAR

KL's largest day market, Chow Kit, is 2km north of Little India, along **Jalan Tunku Abdul Rahman** (or **Jalan TAR** as it's always known). The street – named after the first prime minister of independent Malaysia – is at its most interesting at its extremities, so having dawdled around the southern end, catch a bus north. In an (unsuccessful) attempt to ease the city's chronic traffic congestion, Jalan TAR only carries one-way traffic southbound, so you have to skip over a block to the northbound Jalan

Raja Laut for the bus – virtually every bus heading north will take you towards Chow Kit.

If you're walking along Jalan TAR you'll pass the plain facade of the **Coliseum Hotel** where the British owners of the rubber plantations once met to drink tumblers of whisky and water (*stengahs*) and eat steak. It's still one of KL's most fashionable places, serving up hearty if overpriced meals (see p.114) and ice-cold beers; the adjacent *Coliseum Cinema* puts on a strict diet of kung fu films, and Indian and Malay romances and dramas.

On Saturday nights this whole section of Jalan TAR becomes a **pasar malam** (7pm–midnight), where blind street musicians and Filipino rock bands entertain the crowds. It's KL's longest and busiest street market, selling clothes and toys, but it is strongest on food, soft drinks and kitchenware.

Another five minutes' walk up Jalan TAR from the *Coliseum*, down narrow Jalan Medan Tunku, **Wisma Loke** (Mon–Fri 10am–6.30pm, Sat 10am–5pm) occupies a beautiful colonial building, once the home of Loke Yew, a Chinese business baron, and now an antique and handicraft gallery, also known as the *Artequarium*. Its display pieces – sandalwood and mahogany furniture, pewter and ceramic pots and jars – are rather overpriced, but looking them over at least gives you an excuse to poke around the white two-storey building, taking in the sumptuous interior with its ornate ceiling, blue floor tiles and exotic pillars.

Chow Kit Market

At the northern end of Jalan TAR, the entrance to **Chow Kit Market** (daily 9am–5pm) is announced by a gaggle of stalls crowding the pavements – the best place in KL to buy cheap second-hand clothes, such as checked shirts and trousers. Inside, in the city's largest market, precarious plankways lead past stalls laden with meat, fish, vegetables, spices, tofu and fruit. You'll be pressed to buy worms squirming in baskets (you eat them, if you were wondering), while crabs and lobsters crawl around in near-empty tubs of water. In addition to food there are clothes, shoes, cassettes and fabrics on sale, and at the northern end of the market, food stalls serve up excellent *roti canai*, *tehtarek* and high-quality *nasi campur*. This all adds up to one of the most interesting markets in the city, though more lurid accounts suggest it's also the haunt of pickpockets and drug addicts. The Malaysian government for one believes its own warnings, and the police regularly trawl the area for illegal aliens (usually Indonesians) supposedly orchestrating nefarious activities; the police sweep through the warren of narrow paths in the early morning, checking everyone's passes and throwing the unlucky ones into jail.

To reach the market from Jalan Raja Laut, get out of the bus at Jalan Haji Taib and walk east for ten minutes, crossing Jalan TAR to the market entrance.

Kampung Bahru

Ten minutes' walk east of Chow Kit Market along Jalan Raja Alang is the oldest Malay residential area in KL, **Kampung Bahru**, founded in 1899 and the site of another well-known weekly pasar malam. On the way, you'll pass Kuala Lumpur's main Sikh temple (not open to the public), a red-and-white brick building, its facade reminiscent of the city's prewar shophouses, most of which have now been demolished. At the junction of Jalan Raja Alang and Jalan Abdullah – the kampung's main street – the district's **mosque** was built in 1924, a strong concrete structure at odds with most of the surrounding traditional Malay wooden houses.

Continuing along Jalan Raja Alang, at the junction with Jalan Raja Muda Musa, a narrow twist of lebuhs houses Saturday's night market, the **Pasar Minggu**. It's also known

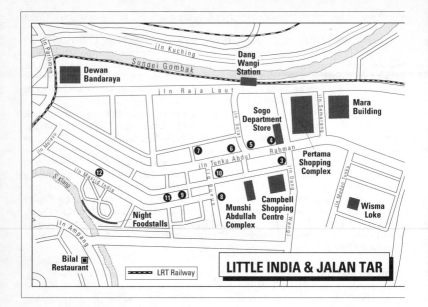

as the **Sunday market** because it runs from 6pm to 1am. There's a thoroughly Malay atmosphere here, and poking around turns up a number of jewellery, handicraft and fabric shops, alongside the usual hawker stalls. In particular, there are two excellent handicraft shops located where the main, narrow market street branches off from Jalan Raja Muda Musa, as well as a number of stalls which sell batik and *songket* fabrics at knock-down prices.

Out from the centre

KL's urban sprawl is infamous. Main drags south like Jalan Syed Putra and Jalan Tun Sambanthan are choked solid at rush hour and, increasingly, at other times of the day as well. Most visitors take one look at the traffic and decide to stay put, within the confines of the city centre, until it's time to move on. It's worth venturing into the suburbs, though, for a couple of destinations, not least **Lake Titiwangsa**, a couple of kilometres north of Chow Kit, and the terrific **Thean Hou Temple**, just to the south of the city. Slightly further south, the Indian area of **Brickfields** and adjacent **Bangsar** are both excellent places to come and eat. Further out than all of these is KL's zoo, north of the city, and the Rubber Museum, neither exactly must-see attractions but diverting enough if you have a couple of hours to kill.

Lake Titiwangsa

Set in a small park close to Jalan Pahang, 2km north of Chow Kit, **Lake Titiwangsa** is an oval-shaped lake, usually swamped with locals who come here to rent boats ($5 an hour) and fool around on the water. There are concrete walkways through the landscaped park, but most people don't do anything too energetic. The best thing by far is to head for one of the numerous hawker stalls, though many people eat instead at the *Lake Titiwangsa Restaurant*, at the northwestern edge of the lake (see p.113).

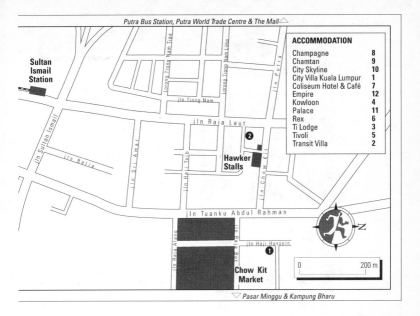

Putra Bus Station, Putra World Trade Centre & The Mall△

Sultan Ismail Station

Jln Tiong Nam

Jalan Nam Tiga

Lorong Tiong Nam Lima

Jln Putra

ACCOMMODATION

Champagne	8
Chamtan	9
City Skyline	10
City Villa Kuala Lumpur	1
Coliseum Hotel & Café	7
Empire	12
Kowloon	4
Palace	11
Rex	6
Ti Lodge	3
Tivoli	5
Transit Villa	2

Jln Tiong Nam

Jln Raja Laut

Jln Sultan Ismail

Jln Belia

Jln Sri Amar

Jln Haji Taib

Jln Chow Kit

❷

Hawker Stalls

Jln Tuanku Abdul Rahman

Jln Raja Alang

Jln Haji Hussein

❶

0 ────── 200 m

Chow Kit Market

▽ Pasar Minggu & Kampung Bharu

To get to the lake, catch buses #172, #169 or #170 from Lebuh Ampang on the northern edge of Chinatown; ask for the lake stop, and you'll be dropped off opposite Jalan Titiwangsa. Walk along here for ten minutes then turn right onto Jalan Kuantan – the lake is 100m up on the left.

Thean Hou Temple

KL's huge and colourful Buddhist temple, the **Thean Hou Temple** (daily 9am–6pm; free), was completed in 1987 and is located on a hilltop 1.5km south of the city centre, between a sacred bodhi tree and a one hundred-year-old Buddhist shrine. The temple is always busy, with busloads of tourists descending for the marvellous views north over the city and south to the satellite town of Petaling Jaya. It's also the most popular place in KL for Chinese marriages, and has its own registry office on the first floor of the temple complex.

The main focus of excitement is the pagoda, in whose inner temple stands the shrine to Thean Hou's main deity, Kuan Yin, the Goddess of Mercy, who – legend has it – appears on earth in a variety of forms and can be identified by the precious dew flask which she always holds. The decor is as ornate as you'd expect, with a ceiling whose intricate patterns contain hundreds of green lanterns. In the centre of the line of sculpted deities sits Thean Hou, with Kuan Yin to her right, in front of whom visitors gather to burn offerings of joss sticks and paper money.

The easiest way to get here is by bus #27 or #52 from Klang bus station, getting off at the Jalan Kelang Lama junction on Jalan Syed Putra (ask the driver for the temple). From there, the temple is five minutes' walk up a steep hill on the right.

Brickfields and Bangsar

Located on either side of Jalan Tun Sambanthan and around 3km south of the city centre, **Brickfields** was first settled by Tamils employed to build the railways, and named

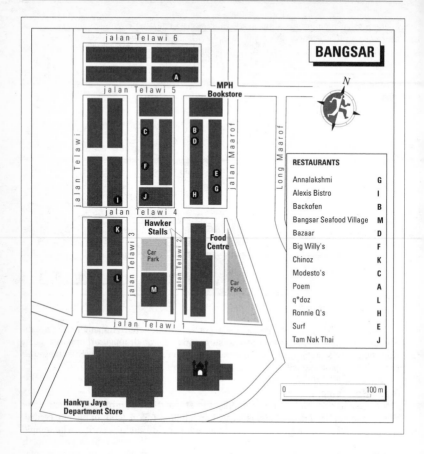

BANGSAR

N

RESTAURANTS

Annalakshmi	**G**
Alexis Bistro	**I**
Backofen	**B**
Bangsar Seafood Village	**M**
Bazaar	**D**
Big Willy's	**F**
Chinoz	**K**
Modesto's	**C**
Poem	**A**
q*doz	**L**
Ronnie Q's	**H**
Surf	**E**
Tam Nak Thai	**J**

after the brick yards which lined the railway tracks. The main street runs along the back of the original rail line and many of the turn-of-the-century buildings still remain. However, all this may change over the next few years as Brickfields finds itself at the centre of the **Sentral**: the new station and business district (see "Transport Systems" box on p.88). It's a great place to come to eat (see "Eating" below), while you might also venture this far afield for the Temple of Fine Arts (daily 11am–9pm; free; see also p.117) at 116 Jalan Berhala, which features monthly Indian concerts and special events during Hindu festivals; music and dance lessons in the early evening; and a café. Also, behind the YMCA, is one of KL's best second-hand bookshops, *Skoob Books*, at 88 Jalan Padang Belia. The shop also has an art gallery, performance space and café. To get to Brickfields, take any of the frequent Bangsar buses from Central Market and get off at Jalan Travers, which is a short walk from Jalan Tun Sambanthan, Brickfield's main thoroughfare.

Four kilometres further south, along Jalan Bangsar, is **Bangsar** itself. Until the early 1990s, this small grid of streets was a quiet, middle-class residential area with a few good cafés and a popular pasar malam. Nowadays, it's the trendiest area in KL to eat and drink in the evening, with dozens of excellent restaurants, two hawkers' areas – one inside a giant hangar, the other in the adjoining street. The beauty of Bangsar is that there are so many places to go within easy walking distance of each other. There are several good bookshops, and a couple of Internet-linked cafés. The pasar malam is held every Saturday and is one of the most fashionable in the Klang Valley area, selling fresh food, hardware, kitchenware and clothing. The last bus back to Central market is around 11pm, but if you miss it, a taxi should be no more than $3.

The National Zoo

Malaysia's **National Zoo**, the Zoo Negara (daily 9am–6pm; $6), is 14km north of the city centre, beyond Jalan Tun Razak on Jalan Ulu Klang; buses #17 and #174 run regularly from Lebuh Ampang. Set in large grounds, you'll need to devote at least three hours to the zoo if you want to see everything, unless you take advantage of the shuttle bus ($1) which drops you off at main spots like the tiger and lion enclosures. The zoo is particularly strong on indigenous species including the musang fox, civet, tiger, bearded pig and rhino. There is also an exceptional collection of **snakes**, including the Sumatran pit viper and the Indian rock python. However, several of the cages and fenced areas are almost devoid of vegetation, and many of the animals look cramped and ill at ease, an exception being the little island containing two smooth-coated otters, who appear to adore the attention. An **aquarium** is located at the back of the zoo proper and although rather dark is worth venturing into to catch a glimpse of rare species and various coral reef fishes.

The Rubber Museum

The Malaysian rubber story began in 1877 with an Englishman, Henry Wickham, who collected seventy thousand seeds from Brazil and took them to Kew Gardens in London, where they were germinated. Of these, 22 were sent to Singapore and nine to Kuala Kangsar, where they were planted in Resident Hugh Low's garden. By the 1930s, thousands of square kilometres were under production and Malaya's rubber industry had dwarfed that of Brazil.

You can trace the development of the industry in the city's **Rubber Museum** (Mon–Thurs 8.30am–12.30pm & 2pm–4pm, Fri & Sat 8.30am–noon; $1), in the grounds of the Rubber Research Institute, 40km northwest of KL in a kampung called Sungei Buloh. Very few people make the effort to visit the museum – mainly because it's so far out – and it may be necessary to pick up the keys from the manager, who lives in the adjacent bungalow. Inside the museum, photographs, diagrams and drawings record in great detail various changes in technology, from manual distillation techniques to large-scale automation. More intriguing is the information on the lives of the tens of thousands of immigrants – mostly Tamil Indians and Teochew Chinese – who worked on the vast estates, clearing malarial swamps for plantation.

From KL, catch bus #144 or #145 from stands 21–23 at Pudu Raya bus station, which leave about every forty minutes (a 70-min journey); ask for the Rubber Research Institute (RRI) and you'll be dropped at the gates.

Eating

KL boasts an extraordinary number of hawker stalls, coffee shops and restaurants, all of which boast a high standard of cuisine, and many of which are very cheap. The vast majority of places to eat serve **Malay**, **Chinese or Indian food**; international cuisine is also becoming more popular with Italian, Japanese, Thai, Korean, and fast-food outlets rapidly multiplying.

Locals make little distinction between eating at inexpensive **hawker stalls** and pricier **restaurants** – the quality of food at a stall is usually just as good, and many

> Outside the city, don't forget the large choice of excellent hawker stalls, cafés and restaurants in **Petaling Jaya**, the southwestern satellite of KL – see p.124 for all the details.

offer regional dishes which aren't available elsewhere. There is, though, a difference between the stalls themselves. Traditionally, they were open-air and many still line the traffic-choked roads in little enclaves throughout the city, but increasingly stalls are found grouped together in food courts inside buildings, where the food is usually no more expensive but the surroundings are air-conditioned. Good as the stalls can be, for really special local cuisine you'll need to dine out at one of the big hotels, since most Malay restaurants in KL serve a limited range of dishes. The exception is at festival times when the stops are pulled out and imaginative Malay cuisine is available throughout the city – look out for hotels offering special buffets. Finding good Chinese or Tamil and North Indian food is much easier; it's served in cafés and restaurants in both Chinatown and Little India. In Little India especially, the cafés and hawkers do a manic trade at lunchtime in excellent banana leaf curries, *murtabak*, *dosai* and *roti*.

Hawker stalls

Indoor hawker stalls tend to be in shopping malls and complexes and open all day between 10am and 10pm. Outdoor stalls don't usually start business until 6pm or 7pm, but then stay open until 2am or so; exceptions are noted below.

Indoor

Ampang Shopping Complex, Jalan Ampang at junction with Jalan Tun Razak. The food court in this hi-tech mall is a mix of international and Asian tastes, designed to please Ampang's abundant middle class. Bus #15 from the Central Market.

Central Market, first and second floors, Jalan Hang Kasturi. Best are the superb Malay stalls on the top floor where plates of *nasi campur* cost just $2.

Hilton Hotel, Jalan Sultan Ismail. Just behind the hotel, this opens late morning for *nasi campur*, Malay salad (*ulam*), Chinese noodles, Indian and Malay curries and fried fish, There are also fresh juice and beer vendors here.

Medan Hang Tuah, basement and fourth floor, *The Mall*, Jalan Putra. Here, dozens of stalls sell everything from burgers to Chinese "steamboats" of fish, meat and vegetables. In the basement is a mix of Chinese noodle dishes and Malay *nasi* options. Closes at around 10pm.

Naan Corner, 200m from the International School, Ampang. A long trawl by bus #23 from Lebuh Ampang, but this Indian hawker centre serves sensational north Indian food and is good for parties. Probably the best-quality Indian in KL after *Annalakshmi* in Bangsar (see below).

Pudu Raya bus station, first floor, Jalan Pudu. A dozen stalls serving a mix of Chinese, Malay and Indian *nasi*, *roti* and noodles. This has longer hours than many, and a few stalls are open all night.

Semua House, basement, Jalan Masjid India. Very popular and crowded lunchtime spot, where you can opt for a fabulous *nasi campur*, or an equally good banana leaf curry.

Sungei Wang Plaza Hawker Centre, fourth floor, Jalan Bukit Bintang. KL's oldest mall, with a crowded food centre selling Malay and Chinese fast food.

Jalan Telawi Tiga Food Centre, Jalan Telawi Tiga, Bangsar. Compared to the glitzy surroundings, this is a rather unatmospheric building, but the food is great with the Indian tandoori stalls outstanding. Take any Bangsar bus from outside Central Market.

Outdoor

Bangsar Hawkers, Jalan Telawi Tiga, Bangsar. Behind the *Jalan Telawi Tiga Food Centre* (see above) are a dozen or so excellent stalls including Korean, north Indian tandoori and Malay. Take any Bangsar bus from outside Central Market. Open from 6pm.

Brickfields Hawkers, Jalan Thambapillai, Brickfields. A cluster of predominantly Chinese cafés, though *Sri Vani's Corner* – just beside the *YMCA* – is renowned as the best tandoori hawker in KL. Plenty of buses from Klang station pass by the area. Stalls open 6pm; closed Mon.

Chinatown, Jalan Tun H.S. Lee and Jalan Petaling market. Essentially a wet fish (and meat and veg) market, there are some great Chinese noodle stalls in this warren of plankways reached via narrow openings halfway down either street. Open early morning till 7pm.

Chow Kit Market, Jalan Sultan. At the top end of Chow Kit Market there are some good *roti canai* hawkers, and tucked away in a building just south of Jalan Sultan Suleiman some *nasi campur* stalls. Open 8am–7pm.

Golden Triangle, Jalan Alor. A wide street with lots of Chinese cafés which put tables out into the street after dark. If you like fried chicken wings, this is the best place to go in KL. Open from 7pm.

Little India, Jalan Masjid India. Along the main street there are dozens of excellent food stalls, not only Indian. Although lunchtime is best, there's still plenty to eat up until 11pm.

Restaurants and cafés

All the **restaurants and cafés** listed below are open daily from 11am or noon until midnight, unless otherwise stated. Most restaurants stay open throughout the year, though note that everything will be closed during the two-day Hari Raya festival (Feb/March), and most Malay restaurants close during Ramadan (Feb). It's difficult to be precise about **prices** at restaurants in KL, save to say that you'll generally spend more than at a hawker stall, but rarely have to fork out more than $50 per person. That said, even in top-class restaurants it's possible to sit down and just order a plate of noodles at lunchtime; the reviews give an idea of how much you can generally expect to pay for an decent meal. It's also worth looking out for buffets and special deals at the top hotels (see the "Time Out" section of Thursday's edition of *The Sun* and the weekly *Day & Night* magazine for tips).

Phone numbers are given below for restaurants where it's necessary to reserve a table in advance – or just call in earlier in the day. If you're staying outside the Golden Triangle, the best way to get there is to take any bus from outside Central Market which runs east to the centre of the district, to the junction of Jalan Sultan Ismail and Jalan Bukit Bintang. Coming back, after midnight, you'll have to take a cab.

> The **telephone code** for KL is ☎03.

Central KL

Ang Patt Meng Café, 97 Jalan Petaling, Chinatown. There are many cheap Chinese cafés like this, serving morning noodles and, after midday, *nasi campur* with meat, fish and vegetable dishes.

Bilal Restaurant, 33 Jalan Ampang. At the western, city-centre, end of Jalan Ampang, this is one of KL's most revered north Indian restaurants, and is particularly popular for its chicken and mutton curries and *naans*. Prices are reasonable, at about $20 for two.

Be My Friend Café, Central Market Annex. Sandwiches, salads, jacket potatoes and beer in stylish surroundings. Good terrace from which to watch the comings and goings around the market.

Coliseum Café, 98 Jalan TAR. Colonial hotel-restaurant famous for it's shuffling service and sizzling steaks. Also offering chicken, fish, salad and Chinese dishes. Steak meals are overpriced at around $30 per person.

Hameeds Café, ground floor, Central Market, Jalan Hang Kasturi, Chinatown. Superb, busy, north Indian cafe serving tandoori chicken, curries and rice dishes. Open when the market's open – a good air-conditioned spot for *roti* in the morning.

Hamid Shah Café, 30 Jalan Silang, Chinatown. Excellent, busy, café for Malay and North Indian curries and *roti*. Very good value at around $10–12 for two. Open 8am–6pm.

Kenanga Seafood Restaurant, first floor, MARA Building, Jalan Raja Laut. Malay restaurant noted for its squid, crab and prawn dishes – from around $20 a head.

Lakshmi Villas, Lebuh Ampang, Little India. On the edge of Chinatown, this is the best south Indian café in KL. The ground floor serves various *dosai*; the first floor specializes in banana leaf curries, with extra meat and vegetable curries from midday; a bargain at around $6 for two. Closes at 7pm.

Purple Kane Tea Lounge, Lebuh Sultan, Chinatown. This Chinese tea outlet has a shop stocking all manner of infusions on the corner of Jalan Sultan and a tea lounge for sampling the wares on the third floor of a building further down the street. Good opportunity to learn about different types of tea and try sticky Chinese sweets.

Seng Kee Restaurant, 100 Jalan Petaling, Chinatown. Frenetically busy restaurant with great prawn and duck dishes; well priced at around $25 for two.

Wan Fo Yuan Vegetarian Restaurant, Lebuh Sultan, Chinatown. The area's best-known vegetarian restaurant serving excellent tofu and vegetable dishes.

Golden Triangle

Benson & Hedges Bistro, ground floor, Life Centre, Jalan Sultan Ismail. Ultra-trendy European-style café with a terrace, a wide and wild range of coffees and international food including sandwiches and pasta dishes; around $15 a head.

Eden Village, 260 Jalan Raja Chulan (☎241 4027). Popular family restaurant, with dozens of types of fish cooked Cantonese-style. A meal for costs around $50.

Golden Phoenix, at the *Hotel Equatorial*, Jalan Sultan Ismail (☎261 7777). Top-of-the-range Chinese restaurant specializing in exotic seafood dishes; expect to spend over $30 a head.

Hard Rock Café, *Concorde Hotel*, 2 Jalan Sultan Ismail. The usual burgers, steaks and salad for around $20 a head (drinks extra), accompanied by loud music and related pop and rock artefacts.

Koryo-Won, Antara Bangsa Complex, 37 Jalan Sultan Ismail (☎242 0425). Top Korean restaurant, next to the *KL Hilton*, specializes in chilli-hot meat and fish dishes. Expensive, but makes a nice change.

Le Coq D'Or, 121 Jalan Ampang (☎242 9732). Housed in a converted tin *towkay*'s mansion full of atmosphere, it's worth coming for a drink on the verandah, even if you don't want to eat. The French, Malay and Chinese dishes aren't bad and shouldn't set you back more than $40 a head. Dress smartish.

Modestos, Lorong Perak, just off Jalan P. Ramlee (☎248 9924). This sprawling pizza and pasta joint also has a lively bar.

Moomba, UOA Centre, 19 Jalan Pinang (☎262 8226). Passable effort at cutting-edge Australian cuisine – barramundi fillets, mud crabs, baby lamingtons for dessert – in a split-level, design-heavy space. Expect to pay around $25 a head.

Rasa Utara, BB Plaza, Jalan Bukit Bintang. A northern Malay menu characterizes this busy restaurant; try the *ayam percik*, a hot, sour chicken dish from the state of Kelantan. Moderately priced.

Scalini's, 19 Jalan Sultan Ismail (☎245 3211). The most stylish Italian restaurant in town, raised on a hill above the traffic of the Golden Triangle. *Al fresco* dining an option, as is just a drink at the long wooden bar. Around $40 a head.

Seri Angkasa, Menara KL (☎208 5055). Revolving restaurant which serves an excellent lunch, high tea and dinner buffets atop KL's landmark tower. Breathtaking views guaranteed. Smart dress (no shorts and sandals) essential for dinner, which costs around $55 a head.

Shang Palace, *Shangri-La Hotel*, Jalan Sultan Ismail (☎241 6572). One of the most popular places in KL for *dim sum*; dinner, too, is highly regarded but not cheap.

Teochew Restaurant, 272 Jalan Pudu. Well-known and extremely busy Chinese restaurant, noted especially for its high-quality *dim sum* (served daytime only) at around $50 for two.

North of the centre

Cili Padi Thai Restaurant, second floor, *The Mall*, Jalan Putra. Excellent, moderately priced Thai restaurant, good on Bangkok-style cuisine, including elaborate chicken and seafood dishes.

Hoshigaoka Restaurant, *The Mall*, Jalan Putra. Superb Japanese food at reasonable prices – sushi is around $6 a portion and set meals are from $12. There's a more central branch at *Lot 10 Shopping Centre*, Jalan Bukit Bintang, in the Golden Triangle.

Museum Restaurant, *The Legend Hotel*, 100 Jalan Putra (☎442 9888). Award-winning Chinese restaurant serving Cantonese and Teochew cuisine amid beautifully displayed antiques and paintings. Also worth checking out is the same hotel's Japanese *Gen* restaurant, which does good-value set lunches.

Nelayan Titiwangsa Restaurant, Jalan Kuantan, off Jalan Pahang, Lake Titiwangsa (☎422 8600). Built on a floating platform, this seafood-based restaurant includes Malay and Chinese dishes. Although overpriced at around $50 for two, this includes a cultural show of Malaysian singing and dancing. Take bus #172, #169 or #170 from Lebuh Ampang in Chinatown.

Bangsar

For map of Bangsar, see p.108.

Annalakshmi, 46 Jalan Maarof (☎282 3799). Most people opt for the as-much-as-you-can-eat buffet, with delicious vegetable curries, *daal* and pastries at this excellent south Indian vegetarian restaurant. It's a fine place and reasonably priced at around $20 a head.

Alexis Bistro, 29 Jalan Telawi Tiga (☎284 2880). Big helpings of designer food for the cappuccino set. Lots of magazines to read if you want to pass some time. You can eat well for around $25 per head.

Backofen, 16 Jalan Telawi Dua. This Austrian bakery is a good spot for breakfast and stays open until 8pm serving simple, cheap meals.

Bangsar Seafood Village, Jalan Telawi Tiga. Over-expensive seafood specialists attractively located in a large garden.

Bazaar, 18 Jalan Telawi Dua (☎282 4492). Turkish cuisine in a restaurant that successfully captures a Mediterranean feel. Around $20 a head.

Big Willy's Bar & Bistro, 14 Jalan Telawi Tiga (☎283 1136). Bustling hang-out for expats and KL yuppies, which dishes up gigantic pizzas and other hearty meals like beef stew cooked with Guinness. Also has a big video screen showing football and other sports programmes.

Chinoz, 43 Jalan Telawi Tiga (☎283 1231). A mix of Eastern and Western dishes, including gourmet sandwiches. A little on the expensive side (around $30 per head) for what it does.

Modesto's, 12a Jalan Telawi Tiga. Bangsar outlet of the pasta, pizza and party joint. There's a pool table and seats outside for watching the passing parade.

Poem, 38a Jalan Telawi Lima (☎284 1977). Cool, stylish cyber-café, with several terminals on which to surf the Internet at $6 for thirty minutes. Set dinner is $20, with cheaper snacks and drinks available.

q*doz, 57 Jalan Telawi Tiga (☎284 3699). Perhaps Bangsar's most stylish restaurant with adventurous dishes and a good selection of wine. Not cheap (around $40 upward) but worth splashing out on.

Surf, 54 Jalan Maarof. The interior waterfall at this cyber-café provides a tranquil atmosphere in which to plug into the information highway at $15 per hour. Western food and beer available.

Tam Nak Thai, 27 Jalan Telawi Tiga. One of a chain of Thai restaurants that are popular with locals. Offers vegetarian and spicy *tom yam* dishes at reasonable prices.

Brickfields

For bus details to Brickfields, see pp.107–108.

Ikan Bakar, Jalan Thunbapillai. Specializes in seafood – you choose your fish and watch it being cooked at the pavement kitchen. The barbecued stingray in banana leaves is delicious, but check prices before agreeing your order.

Ghandi, Jalan Thunbapillai. Recommended Indian vegetarian restaurant where you can also buy cooking ingredients.

Puteri Restaurant, 146 Jalan Tun Sambanthan. One of a number of good north Indian cafés in Brickfields with fine *roti canai* and curries.

Sri Devi Restaurant, Jalan Travers. Brickfields' best, selling excellent banana leaf curries from midday onwards and wonderful *dosais* all day. Extremely cheap.

Drinking and nightlife

KL has a growing number of excellent bars and fashionable clubs and discos, especially in the more monied districts along Jalan Bukit Bintang and Jalan Ampang. **Bars** here are often called pubs, a hangover from the British colonial presence and a draw for the British and Australian expats in the city. Many of the larger places feature live music, usually performed by Filipino bands, although a seemingly insatiable appetite for **karaoke** has engulfed KL recently. Beer is relatively expensive throughout KL – usually $6–7 a glass – but many places have "happy hours" where the price drops by a couple of dollars. Most bars are open throughout the day from noon onwards, and close after midnight; karaoke bars tend to open from 9pm to 1 or 2am, and don't have a cover charge.

The daily "Metro" section in *The Star* newspaper has **club** listings and the leaflets sometimes given out in Central Market advertise new places. The most fashionable – and most interesting – events are usually unpublicized, so unless you meet an in-the-know local you're unlikely to get to hear of them. Doors usually open at around 9pm, though nothing much tends to happen before midnight, with clubs closing at 3am. Entrance charges are high, around $20 including one drink, which makes them the preserve of expats and the Malaysian middle class. Most also have "ladies' nights" during the week, when entrance and certain drinks are free for women. The music played is a diverse mix of international and Malay pop, soul and rock, although KL is increasingly moving into the international dance music circuit with Western club DJs making guest appearances at clubs. For more on the Malaysian music scene, see Contexts, p.621.

Concerts featuring Malay pop stars or visiting big names from other Southeast Asian countries (and further afield) play large-scale venues like Merdeka Stadium or the Civic Centre in Petaling Jaya (see p.125) outside the city. Concerts are always over early – by 11pm – to ensure that everybody can get home easily by public transport. Ticket prices start at around $20 and tickets are available either by going to the venue itself or to a ticket agency; the easiest one to find is the *Horizon Music Centre* (☎274 6778) on the ground floor of Central Market.

Bars and pubs

Brannigans, Lorong Perak, just off Jalan P. Ramlee. Unsubtle two-floor bar and disco, popular with the expat crowd. Open 5pm–2am, 3am on weekends when there's a $10 cover charge.

Bull's Head, Central Market, Jalan Benteng. A very busy bar, popular with expats, tourists and business people alike. Closes at midnight.

Coliseum Hotel, 98 Jalan TAR. Always busy, the *Coliseum* bar has a rich history and relaxed atmosphere. The cartoonist, Lat (see p.116), drinks here and his work is on the walls. Open 10am–10pm.

Lai-Lai Karaoke Lounge, Sungei Wang Plaza, Jalan Sultan Ismail, Golden Triangle. Close to the junction with Jalan Bukit Bintang, this is the best karaoke bar, especially at around 10pm, when you're likely to get a turn yourself.

London Pub, Lorong Hampshire, off Jalan Ampang (behind the *Ming Court Hotel*). A lively stomping ground for British expats, perfect if you want to play darts and drink draught beer.

Modestos, Lorong Perak, just off Jalan P. Ramlee. The bar is as close as the Golden Triangle gets to raging on most nights of the week. There's a section with table-top football, pool and darts, too.

The Pub, *Shangri-La Hotel*, Jalan Sultan Ismail. Non-residents can drink in *The Pub*, which is better than most hotel bars offering a good atmosphere and a chance to look round KL's most opulent hotel.

Riverbank, Central Market, Jalan Benteng. Well-placed bar, opposite the river, with occasional music – handy for the cultural performances at the nearby bandstand.

Ronnie Q's, 32 Jalan Telawi Dua, Bangsar. You'll love this long-running bar if you're into watching re-runs of football matches on small portable TV screens and rubbing shoulders with KL's older expat businessmen.

Shark Club, 23 Jalan Sultan Ismail. Lively sports bar and restaurant at the heart of the Golden Triangle, which is open 24 hours and has a long happy hour 5–9pm.

Discos and clubs

Baze-2, Plaza Yow Chuan, Jalan Tun Razak. Happening club frequented by KL's well-heeled youth; soul, reggae and dance music are played. Open 5pm–3am.

Blue Moon, *Hotel Equatorial*, Jalan Sultan Ismail (opposite the MAS Building). Popular with KL's gay crowd, the only place where you'll hear Malaysian golden oldies from the 1950s, French schmaltz and a famous singer, the golden-voiced baritone, P. Ramlee. Open 7pm–midnight.

Boom Boom Room, 11 Lebuh Ampang. Another gay hangout, where thumping house music and a twice-nightly drag show create a winning combination at KL's most off-beat night club. Convenient if you're based in Chinatown.

Fire, 8 Lorong P. Ramlee, off Jalan P. Ramlee (behind the *Shangri-La Hotel*). Fashionable club which plays Western dance music. High door prices and crowds of punters. Open 9pm–4am.

The Jump, 241 Jalan Tun Razak. Gets rave revues as one of the best dance clubs in KL. Ladies' night is on Wednesday, with free entrance and free drinks for women.

Live music

Barn Thai Jazzaraunt, 370b Jalan Tun Razak (☎244 6699). Spicy Thai food followed by some of the best live jazz that KL offers.

Hard Rock Café, *Concorde Hotel*, 2 Jalan Sultan Ismail. Features well-known rock bands and gets absolutely packed on Friday and Saturday nights – you don't have to eat if you've come to see the band, but you will have to pay a cover charge. Open 11am–midnight.

La Chiva, 1b Jalan U-Thant. If you're into lively South American and Caribbean music, this is the top dance spot in KL. Also serves salsa-type food to match the music.

Merdeka Stadium, Jalan Hang Jebat. Stages occasional large concerts, mostly of visiting Western rock acts, ballad singers and (a must-see) Malay heavy metal-bands – look for posters around town.

The arts and entertainment

Culturally speaking, KL has a fairly provincial feel, although the performing arts scene is improving. Contemporary dance is very much in its infancy, as is theatre, and the only time you can really guarantee seeing traditional theatre, dance and music is at festivals. Otherwise, you'll have to depend on the **cultural shows** performed in some restaurants and other venues, which combine such activities, though often to lame and inauthentic effect. There are bright spots, though, including a number of promising theatre companies, including the Five Arts Centre, Straits Theatre Company and Instant Café Theatre which has caused a stir recently with its satirical treatment of Malaysian life, and which now has its own performing space at Menara SMI, Lorong P. Ramlee, in the Golden Triangle. Unfortunately, there is no national theatre in KL and companies have to hunt for appropriate space when they want to stage something.

Cinema is popular, but of limited interest to most visitors since the majority of movies are either Western ones which have been hacked by the censor or dubbed into Malay, Cantonese or Tamil, or domestic movies made in those languages. Listings appear in *The New Straits Times*, *The Star*, *The Sun* and *The Malay Mail*; tickets cost $10–15. There are occasional festivals of English-language films but the government's draconian censorship laws usually mean that many are cut to shreds.

Where KL is strongest is in the **visual arts**, with numerous private galleries stocked with new work and visiting exhibitions, notably from Southeast Asian countries. Banks and oil companies – like the state-owned Petronas which runs the gallery in the Dayabumi Complex – sponsor art and sculpture in KL, which in the case of the Maybank's pioneering ground-floor gallery has led to dozens of Malay (and increasingly Indian and Chinese) artists selling work and gaining international reputations.

LAT

Malaysia's most famous artist is **Lat**, a cartoonist who, more than any fiction writer or essayist, successfully holds his culture's foibles up for forensic examination. Now in his early forties, Lat has published four books and is seldom out of the country's most influential English-language newspaper, *The New Straits Times*. In his first book, *Kampung Boy*, he used bright watercolour sketches to draw a contrast between his traditional Malay upbringing in the kampung and modern life in the city suburbs. The pictures he creates are full of wit, depicting, for example, how the boys in the kampung were so proud of their shorts, despite the fact that the inner linings of the pockets were made from flour sacks and carried the words "Best Quality".

Lat quickly became a national institution and it's a commonly held view in Malaysia that he can get away with criticizing contemporary society in his work, which the government wouldn't tolerate coming from anyone else. Banks and galleries display his work, despite the fact that in many of his drawings the holders of Malaysia's purse strings are cleverly caricatured. As with any great cartoonist, Lat draws out the prime characteristics of his subject, so most Malay women are covered by a headscarf, but some – the ambitious urban generation – power dress and wear high heels. Likewise, Malay men are mostly drawn in relaxed, even lazy, demeanour, sitting about in their sarongs, while others are sketched as power-hungry, attention-seeking egotists. Malaysians see themselves in Lat's cartoons – if often as grotesques – and visitors interested in Malaysian society can get an instant and accessible sociological update from his work.

Top talents include colourful abstract painters like Ismael Latiff, S. Chandhiran and Tajuddin Ismail, and more naturalistic artists whose work reflects everyday life: Rahmat Ramli, Maamor Jantan and Sani Mohammed Dom. **Sculpture** in public places is also a growth area, with impressive works including Lee Kiew Sing's *Vision 2020* outside the Public Bank on Jalan Raja Laut, and Syed Ahmaed Jamal's iron and marble figures at the UNBC Building on Jalan Kuching.

Art galleries

Art Folio, second floor, City Square, 182 Jalan Tun Razak. Stacks of watercolours, oil paintings and ceramics, at high prices.

Art House, second floor, Wisma Stephens, Jalan Raja Chulan, Golden Triangle. Specializes in Chinese ink brush paintings and ceramics.

Collectors' Focus, Lot T, 137, third floor, City Square, 182 Jalan Tun Razak. A good place to check out affordable works of art.

Galeri Petronas, ground floor, Dayabumi Complex, Jalan Sultan Hishamuddin. Large space with excellent temporary exhibitions, often on naturalistic themes such as the rainforest or the oceans.

Impression Arts, first floor, Wisma Stephens, Jalan Raja Chulan, Golden Triangle. Another commercial outlet for KL's artistic talent.

Maybank Building, ground floor, Pudu Raya roundabout. KL's most influential art gallery, with shows that change monthly – the best place to gain an insight into contemporary Malaysian art.

National Art Gallery, Jalan Sultan Hishamuddin. Fairly poor at displaying new work, but the temporary exhibitions on the ground floor are usually worth seeing.

Valentine Willie Fine Art (☎245 1262). Ex-lawyer turned leading KL curator of private art exhibitions. This is his own gallery, specializing in southeast Asian art works, open by appointment only.

Cinemas

Cathay, Jalan Bukit Bintang, opposite the *Federal Hotel* (☎242 9942). Screens thoroughly mainstream material, from Malay epics to Chinese kung fu.

Central Market Cineplex, third floor, Central Market Annex (☎230 8548). Three screens which show mainly US movies.

Coliseum, Jalan TAR, next to the *Coliseum Hotel* (☎292 5995). Shows the latest Cantonese and Taiwanese blockbusters.

Federal, Jalan Raja Laut, at corner of Jalan Sultan Ismail (☎442 5041). Specializes in Malay cinema, which ranges from corny romances to historical epics.

Odeon, Jalan TAR, corner of Jalan Dang Wangi (☎292 0084). Shows a wide range of material, including Indian musicals.

Pavilion, Jalan Pudu at the junction with Jalan Bukit Bintang (no phone). Shows Malay, Chinese and Tamil films.

President, Sungei Wang Plaza, Jalan Sultan Ismail (☎248 0084). Screens English-language films, usually a few months behind US and European release. There are several other cinemas within this shopping complex.

Rex, Jalan Sultan (☎238 3021). Single screen in the heart of Chinatown showing a mixture of local and US movies.

Cultural shows, dance and traditional music

Malaysian Tourist Information Complex (MATIC), 109 Jalan Ampang (☎243 4929). Costumed shows (Tues, Thurs, Sat & Sun at 3.30pm; $2). There are occasional shows held in the gardens outside, too.

Nelayan Titiwangsa Restaurant, Jalan Kuantan, off Jalan Pahang, Lake Titiwangsa. Atmospheric location overlooking the lake, though featuring a rather tame song-and-dance troupe.

Sri Melayu, Jalan Conlay, behind the *KL Hilton*. A traditional Malay-style house, a regular and enthusiastic cast which perform Chinese, Indian and Malay dances, and delicious buffet meals make this the best option for an all-round cultural evening out.

Temple of Fine Arts, 116 Jalan Berhala, Brickfields (☎274 3709). Arts organization which preserves Tamil Hindu culture by promoting dance, theatre, folk, classical music and craft-making.

Markets and shopping

Most of KL's malls are open daily from 10am to 10pm; elsewhere, shops are usually open daily from 9am to 6pm. Although **handicrafts** are best picked up outside KL, there are some outlets worth visiting in the city. Pewter production is of a very high standard, and a visit to the Royal Selangor Pewter Factory shows the scale and sophistication of the production process, and provides an opportunity to buy items at lower prices than in the shops. You can also pick up batik products in the city, including textiles, bags, belts and hats, as well as carvings, artwork and sculpture – check the list of shops below for the best deals.

However, the unchallenged top shopping activity for most locals is to visit the **night markets** – the pasar malams – where goods of all sorts are sold at competitive prices, bargains are easy to come by and the atmosphere is always gregarious, almost like a festival. Most markets have already been covered in *The Guide*, but there's a round-up below.

Markets

Central Market, Jalan Hang Kasturi, Chinatown (daily 9am–10pm). See p.99.

Chow Kit, Jalan Haji Hussein, off Jalan TAR (daily 9am–5pm). See p.104.

Pasar Minggu, Jalan Raja Muda Musa, Kampung Bharu (Sat 6pm–1am). See pp.105–106.

Jalan Petaling, Chinatown (daily 9am–10pm). See p.101.

Pudu Market, bordered by Jalan Yew, Jalan Pasar and Jalan Pudu, 2km southeast of the centre (Mon–Sat 8am–4pm). A massive market selling mostly food. Bus from Central Market.

Jalan TAR (Sat 7pm–midnight). See p.104.

Tun Razak, Jalan Jujur, at the intersection with Jalan Tun Razak. Saturday night market including cut-price clothing.

Batiks, pewter and handicrafts

Aked Ibu Kota, Jalan TAR, opposite the *Coliseum*. A shopping centre on KL's busiest main street which sells local handicrafts, including batiks.

Central Market, Jalan Hang Kasturi. Some of the craftsmen actually work here, so you can buy batik clothing and handicrafts, including bags, caps, kites and masks which you've just watched being made.

Chin Li, 13 Jalan Tun Mohammed. Stocks a wide range of painting, sculptures and finely made furniture at steep prices.

Dai-Ichi Arts and Crafts, 122 mezzanine floor, *Park Royal Hotel*, Jalan Sultan Ismail. An impressive collection of highly priced pewter products.

Infokraft, Jalan Sultan Hishamuddin. A decent range of crafts from government-sponsored manufacturers – they aren't cheap.

Kompleks Budaya Kraf, Jalan Conlay. All of Malaysia's crafts under one roof, beside the museum.

Jalan Masjid India, Little India. Excellent for sarees and other colourful Indian fabrics. Also religious paraphernalia, metalware and handicrafts from the Middle East, Indonesia and north Asia.

Royal Selangor Pewter Factory, 4 Jalan Usahawan, Sentul, 4km northeast of the centre. It's worth visiting in working hours (Mon–Fri 9am–6pm, Sat 9am–noon) to see how pewter is made. Take bus #167 or #169 from Lebuh Ampang.

Wisma Batek, Jalan Tun Perak. Offers a wide selection of shirts, sarongs, blouses, trousers, bags and local drawings and paintings, with prices cheaper than in the Central Market.

Shopping malls

BB Plaza, Jalan Bukit Bintang, Golden Triangle. The mall with the most frequent price reductions; excellent deals on cameras, electronic equipment and shoes.

Imbi Plaza, Jalan Imbi, Golden Triangle. Specializes in computers, with hardware and software on sale.

Lot 10 Shopping Centre, junction of Jalan Bukit Bintang and Jalan Sultan Ismail, Golden Triangle. One of the area's trendy shopping venues, which specializes in designer clothes, sportswear and music, and includes an outlet of the Japanese department store *Isetan*.

The Mall, Jalan Putra. Besides the food centres in the basement and on the fourth floor, the main attraction is the Japanese store, *Yaohan*, on the first and second floors. It incorporates the best bookshop in the city and the widest range of designer clothing in KL.

Metrojaya, City Square, Jalan Tun Razak. Malaysia's most popular chainstore has pride of place here, with brand-name clothing at reasonable prices and in Western sizes.

Sogo Pernas Department Store, Jalan TAR. Apparently the largest department store in Southeast Asia, this has an excellent supermarket in its basement as well as an entertaining musical clock in its lobby.

Star Hill, Jalan Bukit Bintang. The cutting edge of KL shopping centres – until the one at KLCC is finished – and the place to hang out with the beautiful people, shopping at upmarket Western clothes stores.

Wisma Stephens, Jalan Raja Chulan, Golden Triangle. A complex which includes bars, an art gallery, music stores, clothes shops and cafés.

Yow Chuan Plaza, Jalan Tun Razak. Specializes in arts and crafts, and also has a couple of nightclubs.

Listings

Airlines Most airlines have offices in and around the Golden Triangle. Major airlines include: Aeroflot, Ground floor, 1 Jalan Perak (☎261 3331); American Airlines, Angkasa Raya Building, 123 Jalan Ampang (☎242 4311); Bangladesh Airlines, Subang Airport (☎248 3765); British Airways, Wisma Merlin, Jalan Sultan Ismail (☎242 6177); Cathay Pacific, UBN Tower, 10 Jalan P. Ramlee (☎238 3377); China Airlines, Level 3, Amoda Building, 22 Jalan Imbi (☎242 7344); Delta Airlines, UBN Tower, 10 Jalan P. Ramlee (☎291 5490); Garuda, first floor, Angkasa Raya Building, 123 Jalan Ampang (☎262 2811); Japan Airlines, first floor, Pernas International Building, Lot 1157, Jalan

Sultan Ismail (☎261 1728); KLM, Shop 7, Ground floor, President House, Jalan Sultan Ismail (☎242 7011); MAS, MAS Building, Jalan Sultan Ismail (☎261 0555); Pelangi Air, c/o MAS (☎262 4448); Qantas, UBN Tower, 10 Jalan P. Ramlee (☎238 9133); Royal Brunei, first floor, Wisma Merlin, Jalan Sultan Ismail (☎230 7166); Singapore Airlines, Wisma SIA, 2 Jalan Sang Wangi (☎292 3122); Thai International, Kuwasa Building, 5 Jalan Raja Laut (☎293 7100); United Airlines, MAS Building, Jalan Sultan Ismail (☎261 1433).

Banks and exchange Main branches are: Bank Bumiputra, Jalan Melaka; Bank of America, first floor, Wisma Stephens, Jalan Raja Chulan; Chase Manhattan, first floor, Pernas International Building, Jalan Sultan Ismail; Hongkong Bank, 2 Lebuh Ampang; Maybank, 100 Jalan Tun Perak; Standard Chartered Bank, 2 Jalan Ampang; United Malayan Banking Corporation, UMBC Building, Jalan Sultan Sulaiman. Almost all of their branches change money (Mon–Fri 10am–4pm, Sat 9am–12.30pm), but you get better rates from official moneychangers, of which there are scores in the main city areas; the kiosk below the General Post Office, on Jalan Sultan Hishamuddin, also gives good rates.

Bookshops For English-language books try *Berita Book Centre*, Bukit Bintang Plaza; *MPH*, Jalan Telawi Lima, Bangsar and at BB Plaza, Jalan Bukit Bintang; *Times Books*, Yow Chuan Plaza, Jalan Ampang; *Minerva Book Store*, 114 Jalan TAR; *Yaohan Book Store*, second floor, *The Mall*, Jalan Putra.

Car rental All main companies have offices at the airport; or contact Avis, 40 Jalan Sultan Ismail (☎241 7144); Budget, 29 Jalan Yap Kwan Seng (☎242 5166); Hertz, International Complex, Jalan Sultan Ismail (☎243 3433); National Car Rental, Wisma HLA, Jalan Raja Chulan (☎248 0522); Pacific, Wisma MCA, Jalan Ampang (☎263 7748).

Embassies and consulates Australia: 6 Jalan Yap Kwan Seng (☎242 3122); Brunei: 113 Jalan U Thant (☎261 2820); Canada: seventh floor, MBF Plaza, 172 Jalan Ampang (☎261 2000); China: 229 Jalan Ampang (☎242 8495); Indonesia: 233 Jalan Tun Razak (☎984 2011); Japan: 11 Persiaran Stonor (☎242 7044); Laos: 108 Jalan Damai (☎248 3895); Netherlands: 4 Jalan Mesra, off Jalan Damai (☎248 5151); New Zealand: 193 Jalan Tun Razak (☎238 2533); Philippines: 1 Jalan Changkat Kia Peng, (☎248 4233); Thailand: 206 Jalan Ampang (☎248 8333); UK: 185 Jalan Ampang (☎248 2122); US: 376 Jalan Tun Razak (☎248 9011), Vietnam: 4 Persiaran Stonor (☎248 4036).

Emergencies Dial ☎999 for ambulance, police or fire. For the Tourist Police Unit call ☎241 5522 or ☎241 5243.

Hospitals and clinics General Hospital, Jalan Pahang (☎292 1044); Assunta Hospital, Petaling Jaya (☎792 3433); Pantai, Jalan Pantai, off Jalan Bangsar, Bangsar (☎282 5077); Tung Shin Hospital, Jalan Pudu (☎232 1655). There are 24-hour casualty wards at all of the above.

Immigration At third floor, Jalan Pantai Bahru, off Jalan Damansara (Mon–Fri 9am–4.30pm; ☎757 8155). This is where you come for visa extensions.

Laundry Most hotels, guest houses and lodges will do your laundry for you for a few dollars.

Left-luggage office At Pudu Raya bus station, Jalan Pudu (daily 8am–10pm; $2 per item).

Police The Chinatown police station is at the southern end of Jalan Tun H.S. Lee (☎232 5044). You can report stolen property and claim your insurance form here.

Post office The GPO is on Jalan Sultan Hishamuddin, opposite Central Market (Mon–Fri 8am–4pm, Sat 8am–2pm); poste restante/general delivery mail comes here.

Sports Bowling at Federal Bowl, Federal Hotel, Jalan Bukit Bintang (daily 10am–11pm; $10); golf at Kelab Golf Negara, Subang, near the airport (green fees $60–100); most large hotels have swimming pools, open to residents only. There are public pools in Chinatown, near Chinwoo Stadium, off Jalan Hang Jebat (daily 10am–12.50pm & 3–8pm) and at Bangsar Sports Complex, Jalan Bangsar, Bangsar (daily 8am–10pm; $8 adults, $4 children; ☎254 6065), where there are also squash, tennis and badminton courts. Finally, you can play tennis at Kelanga Sports Complex, Jalan Padan Belia, Brickfields (daily 8am–10pm; $12 an hour).

Taxis To call a cab, use one of the following numbers: Comfort Radio Taxi Service (☎733 0507); Koteksi (☎781 5352); Radio Teksi (☎442 0848).

Telephone offices The cheapest places to make international calls are the Telekom Malaysia offices dotted around the city. The largest is the one in Wisma Jothi, Jalan Gereja; and there's also Kedai Telekom (an outlet of Telecom Malaysia) at Subang International Airport. Making calls from the major hotels costs at least fifty percent more.

Tour operators The larger tour operators listed here are all able to organize tailor-made adventure trips across Malaysia: Angel Tours, Lower ground floor, City Tower, Jalan Alor (☎241 7018); Asian

Overland Services, 35 Jalan Dewan Sultan Sulaiman (☎292 5637); Borneo Travel, Lot 36–37, The Arcade, Hotel Equatorial, Jalan Sultan Ismail (☎261 2130); Fairwind Travel, Lot T, Sungei Wang Plaza, Jalan Sultan Ismail (☎248 6920); Insight Travel, 9th floor, Plaza MBF, Jalan Ampang (☎261 2488).

Travel agencies MSL Travel, Asia Hotel, 69 Jalan Haji Hussein, (☎298 9722); Reliance Travel, third floor, Sungei Wang Plaza, (☎248 6022); Semestra Travel, 52 Jalan Bulan, Jalan Bukit Bintang (☎243 4802); STA, fifth floor, Magnum Plaza, 128 Jalan Pudu (☎248 9800); Tina Travel, first floor, Holiday Inn, Jalan Raja Laut (☎457 8877).

Around KL

The biggest attractions around KL are north of the city, where limestone peaks rise up out of the forest and the roads narrow as you pass through small kampungs. There is dramatic scenery as close as 13km from the city, where the Hindu shrine at the **Batu Caves** attracts enough visitors to make it one of Malaysia's main tourist attractions. Further north, the **Forest Institute of Malaysia** and **Templer Park** encompass the nearest portion of primary rainforest to the capital, while some distance beyond – 50km northeast of KL – the much-hyped **Genting Highlands** is the first, and least inspiring, of the country's hill stations.

Frankly, once you've visited the northern hills, you've seen the best of the country-side surrounding the city. Travelling southwest along Route 2 into the state of Selangor, you enter one of the most polluted and ugliest parts of Malaysia, with much of the **Klang Valley** from KL to Klang itself resembling a vast building site with half-built structures marooned in seas of gashed earth and puddles of water. Three towns spread along the valley, all effectively outsize satellites of KL. At **Petaling Jaya** (PJ), a large conurbation easily the size of central KL, the renowned restaurants and nightlife attract locals and visitors from the capital. If you haven't had enough of the amusements at the Genting Highlands there are several more **theme parks** around PJ. The National Mosque at adjacent **Shah Alam** is the biggest in Southeast Asia and you can combine a visit here with seeing the neighbouring agricultural park, an interesting blend of environmental protection, educational displays and commercial good sense. Perhaps the most alluring single destination, though, is Selangor's first capital, **Klang**, whose old centre retains a warehouse now turned into a fascinating tin museum, and one of the country's most atmospheric mosques. Another appealing day-trip is to the quaint Chinese fishing village of Pulau Ketam, an hour's ferry ride from Port Klang.

Finally, northwest of the city, close to **Kuala Selangor**, itself a historic town of some repute, the coastal **Kuala Selangor Nature Park** and the spectacle of the nearby fire-flies might tempt those with time to spare, although these are tricky destinations to reach by bus and you'll need either a rented car or taxi.

See the map on p.80 for the location of destinations around Kuala Lumpur.

The Batu Caves

Long before you reach the entrance to the **Batu Caves**, you can see them ahead: small, black holes in the vast limestone thumbs which comprise a ridge of hills 13km north of the city centre. The caves were first discovered by the American explorer William Hornaby, and ten years later, in 1891, local Indian dignitaries convinced the British colonial authorities that the caves were ideal for worship. Soon devotees were visiting the caves in ever increasing numbers to pay homage to the shrine established here to Lord Muruga – better known as **Lord Subramaniam**. The temple complex was later expanded to include a shrine to the elephant-headed deity **Ganesh**, while today the caves and shrines are surrounded, too, by the full panoply of religious commercialism, with shops selling Hindu idols, pamphlets, bracelets, postcards and cassettes. The caves are incredibly popular, and always packed with visitors, but the numbers most days are nothing compared to the hundreds of thousands of devotees who descend here during the three-day **Thaipusam festival** held at the beginning of every year.

The caves are just off the old Gombak road, which branches off from Jalan Pahang beyond Lake Titiwangsa – catch **bus** #11 from the Pertama Shopping Centre or #68 or #70 from Lebuh Ampang in Chinatown, for the forty-minute journey. On the way, the bus passes **Pak Ali's House** (daily 9am–6pm; $3), a good example of a traditional Malay stilt house, common in Kuala Lumpur in the early years of the century. It was built in 1917, using timber hewn from the nearby jungle, its verandah, stairs and roof carved with opulent shapes and ornate designs – you'll get a fleeting view from the bus.

During **Thaipusam**, extra buses operate services to the caves and it's advisable to get there early – say 7am – for a good view of the proceedings. Although there are numerous cafés at the caves, you should also take plenty of water and snacks with you as the crowds are horrendous.

The caves

To the left of the brick staircase leading up to the main Temple Cave, a small path strikes off to the so-called **Art Gallery** (daily 8.30am–7pm; $1), which contains dozens of striking multicoloured statues of deities, portraying scenes from the Hindu scriptures. As well as these psychedelic dioramas – including a naked goddess astride a five-headed snake, flanked by figures with goats' heads carrying tools – flamboyant murals line the damp walls of the cave depicting jungle settings, mythic battles and abstract designs.

Climbing to the top of the main staircase there's a clear view through to the **Subramaniam Swamy Temple** (daily 8am–7pm), set deep in a large cave around 100m high and 80m deep, and illuminated by shafts of light from gaps in the ceiling high above. The cave walls are lined with idols representing the six lives of Lord Subramaniam and, in the small inner temple, devoted to Lord Subramaniam and the deity Rama, a dome is densely sculpted with more scenes from the scriptures. Two figures stand guard at its entrance, their index fingers pointing upwards towards the light. In a chamber at the back of the temple is a statue of Rama, who watches over the well-being of all immigrants, adorned with silver jewellery and a silk sarong. If you want to look closely at the inner sanctum, the temple staff will mark a small red dot on your forehead, giving you a spiritual right to enter.

Templer Park

Another 10km or so north of the Batu Caves, **Templer Park** (daily 8am–6pm; free) makes a great day out from the city, boasting a number of beautiful waterfalls, small trails and abundant bird life. Opened in the 1950s, and named after Sir Gerald Templer (the last of Malaya's British High Commissioners), it's the closest you'll get to primary rainforest if you haven't got time to visit the state parks in the interior. Coming from the city, take bus #66 from Pudu Raya bus station; the trip takes a little over thirty minutes and costs around $1.50. Alternatively, you can combine visiting the park with a trip to the Batu Caves, from where you catch the #11 minibus out to the main Ipoh road and then wait for the red Tanjung Malim bus (#66), on its way from KL.

The park is at its busiest at weekends, when trippers arrive from the capital, but you don't need to make too much of an effort to escape the crowds. The park covers over a square kilometre of primary forest, dominated by a belt of limestone outcrops set into a valley, cutting through the hills for five kilometres. A narrow road winds from the entrance to an artificial lake, 300m to the east, before shrinking to a narrow path, which

THAIPUSAM AT THE BATU CAVES

The most important festival in the Malaysian Hindu calendar, **Thaipusam** honours the Hindu deity Lord Subramaniam. Originally a Tamil festival from southern India, it's a day of penance and celebration, held during full moon in the month of "Thai" (between January 15 and February 15), when huge crowds arrive at the Batu Caves – a site chosen a century ago as a centre for the devotions, probably because its spectacular geography was thought to be reminiscent of the sacred Himalayas. What was originally intended to be a day of penance for past sins has now become a major tourist attraction, with both Malaysians and foreigners flocking to the festival every year.

Thaipusam starts with the early-morning passage of a golden chariot bearing a statue of Subramaniam which makes a seven-hour procession from KL's Sri Mahamariamman Temple to the caves, with thousands of devotees following on foot. At the caves, the statue is placed in a tent before being carried up to the temple cave by the devotees. As part of their penance – and in a trance-like state – the devotees carry numerous types of *kavadi* ("burdens" in Tamil), the most popular being milk jugs decorated with peacock feathers placed on top of the head, which are connected to the penitents' flesh by hooks. Others wear wooden frames with sharp spikes protruding from them which are carried on the back and hooked into the skin; trident-shaped skewers are placed through some devotees' tongues and cheeks. This rather grisly procession – which now only occurs in Malaysia, Singapore and Thailand – has its origins in India, where most of Lord Subramaniam's temples were sited on high ridges, which devotees would walk up, carrying heavy pitchers or pots to honour the deity. At Batu, the 272-step climb up to the main chamber expresses the idea that you cannot reach God without expending effort.

Once in the temple cave the devotees participate in ceremonies and rituals to Subramanian and Ganesh, finishing with a celebration for Rama, when milk from the *kavadi* bowl can be spilt as an offering – incense and camphor is burned as the bearers unload their devotional burdens. The festival takes many hours to complete and the atmosphere becomes so highly charged that police are needed to line the stairs and protect onlookers from the entranced *kavadi*-bearers and their instruments of self-flagellation.

snakes up into the forest. This trail leads back and forth across the shallow, five-metre-wide Sungei Templer, reaching a dramatic waterfall after an hour's walk. From here you can follow the riverside path through primary jungle for another hour or so, but you'll have to return by the same route. An alternative is to leave the main path on a trail to the left of the waterfall, from where a one-hour trek hugs the edge of the hillside and later meets the concrete road near the park entrance. Other paths snake up into the forested hills and pass natural swimming lagoons and waterfalls. The highest point is **Bukit Takun** (740m) rising on the western side of the river in the northern corner of the park. Few animals can now be seen in the park, as what is left of the jungle here is surrounded by development, which has frightened off much of the wildlife.

The park authorities permit **camping**, although there isn't an official campsite, or any toilets, washing or cooking facilities. As long as you're prepared to rough it, it's a rewarding experience.

The Orang Asli Museum

Like Templer Park, KL's **Orang Asli Museum** (Mon–Thurs & Sun 9am–5.30pm; free) holds a certain interest if this is as far into rural Malaysia as you're going to get. Located 24km north of the city, the museum, which is organized and run by the government-sponsored Centre for Orang Asli Affairs, provides a fine illustration of the cultural richness and demographic variety of the Orang Asli (Malay for "the first people") – Malaysia's indigenous inhabitants (see Basics, p.58). As you enter the unobtrusive timber building, a large map of west Malaysia shows that the separate Orang Asli groups are found, in varying numbers, in just about every part the region, which may well surprise visitors who often see little sign of them during their travels. Many of the Orang Asli maintain a virtually pre-industrial lifestyle – some still rely on blowpipes for hunting – and pursue their traditional occupations in some isolation, whether it's hunting and gathering in the fast-depleting forests, fishing along the increasingly polluted Johor coastline, or carving their extraordinary handicrafts. Partly, too, it's believed that the Orang Asli try to keep out of the way because they see that their culture is under threat, and too much exposure to modern Malaysia is likely to do them more harm than good.

Although the museum is small, a lot is crammed into it. There's an explanation of the incidence of the groups of Orang Asli, while various displays vividly portray the tools of their trade – from fishing nets and traps to guns and blowpipes. More interestingly, hidden in an annexe are examples of traditional handicrafts including the **head carvings** made by the Mah Meri tribe from the swampy region on the borders of Selangor and Negeri Sembilan, and the Jah Hut from the slopes of Gunung Benom in central Pehang; the carvings are around 50cm high and fashioned from a particularly strong, heavy hardwood. They still have religious significance – the central image used, the animist deity Moyang, represents the spirit of the ancestors – and are prevalent in contemporary religious ceremonies, when the masks are worn during dances honouring a pantheon of gods. The Orang Asli's **animist religion** is influenced by early Hindu beliefs, and the carvings here show similarities with those of some Hindu deities. At the far end of the museum's main room are photographs of Orang Asli militia commandeered by the government to fight the Communist guerrillas in the 1950s (see p.205), while other displays describe the changes forced on the Orang Asli over the past thirty years – some positive, like the eradication of serious disease and the development of health and school networks, others less encouraging, like the erosion of the family system as young men drift off to look for seasonal work.

Bus #174 leaves Lebuh Ampang in Chinatown every thirty minutes; the fifty-minute trip along the old Gombak road passes the International Islamic University. Two rundown shops are located at the museum stop, and the entrance is 50m to the right along a narrow, steep road (ask the driver to tell you when you've arrived as it's not obvious). For the return trip, wait outside the shops for the bus.

The Forest Institute of Malaysia

If you don't make it out to Taman Negara and its canopy walkway, you can stroll through the tree tops at the **Forest Institute of Malaysia (FRIM)** (daily 8am–6.30pm ☎03/635 9578), about an hour's bus ride out from the Kota Raya Shopping Centre on bus #148 ($1.60). The canopy walkway here, which takes about twenty minutes to traverse and provides a unique view of KL's skyscrapers through the trees, is open from Tuesday to Saturday and on one Sunday of each month. Booking ahead is essential, so guides can be arranged and visitors briefed on forest conditions before they start their trek. You should prepare as you would for any other jungle trek: bring along plenty of drinking water and insect repellent and wear laced shoes. There are plenty of other treks within FRIM's fifteen square kilometres and, for those who wish to learn more about Malaysia's ecological heritage, a museum which contains details of the institute's research as well as an eclectic range of wood-based antiques and implements including an intricately carved boat, treasure chests and a four-poster bed.

The Genting Highlands

Of the three hill stations located on the western side of the Banjaran Titwangsa mountain range north of KL, the **Genting Highlands** is the odd one out. Whereas Fraser's

Hill (p.134) and the Cameron Highlands (p.137) feature short treks, visits to waterfalls and colonial tranquillity, Genting – 50km northeast of the city – can be stress-inducing in the extreme. Although the highlands themselves are eminently attractive – something that's obvious from the journey there, as the bus zigzags its way gingerly up the road – upon arrival you're deposited at a brain-numbingly noisy, concrete resort, perched on top of the hill, where the focus of attention is a quadrangle of highrise hotels, with their shopping arcades and restaurants. An exclusive golf course is the main "green" recreation the hill station has to offer, besides horse riding, and you'd be hard pushed to find any trails reaching out from the hotels. Before the early 1980s, when the development began, the whole area was covered in forest, but now Malaysians flock here from the city in their thousands to frequent the only casino in the country and to spoil their families in the fast-food outlets, swimming pools and theme park.

On the way up to the top, the bus passes the Awana Golf Club and Country Resort on the right; to the left a **cable car** (Mon 12.15–8.30pm, Tues–Sun 8.30am–9.30pm; every 20min; $5) offers an alternative and precipitous journey up the remaining few kilometres to the resort hotel at the top. By bus, you are deposited in the bowels of the eighteen-storey Genting Highlands Resort Hotel (☎03/211 1118; ⑥), where one-armed bandits and computer games vie for your attention. Two floors above is the **casino** (open 24hr; minimum age 21), where the chips start at $10. Outside, 20m from the concrete forecourt which is usually full of exhaust-belching buses, there's a **swimming pool** and a small area set aside for picnicking. The other hotels include *The Awana Towers* (☎03/211 3015; ⑥), the *Theme Park Hotel* (☎03/262 2666, fax 211 3535; ⑤) and *The Highlands* (☎03/211 2812; ⑤), all of which also have overpriced restaurants. There is no budget accommodation.

Transport here is by the Genting **bus** from either the Pudu Raya (tickets from booth 43) or Pekeliling stations, (hourly 8am–7pm; journey time 1hr; $5). Getting a seat on a return bus can be hard, and often involves competing for space with a crowd of young Malaysians – get to the stop at the *Genting Highlands Resort Hotel* early. You can take a shared taxi for $40 per taxi from the second floor at Pudu Raya.

The Klang Valley

Three hundred years before KL was founded, the **Klang Valley** which is southwest of the modern capital, was one of the most important regions in Malaysia and the sultans of Selangor were based at the royal town of **Klang**. In the late nineteenth century, with the discovery of new tin deposits further inland, Klang lost its importance, but the valley remained ripe for development as KL expanded rapidly. The first road linking Klang to KL wasn't built until the 1920s – previously all goods were carried along a narrow horse track or went by river – but a decade later the rail line between the two towns came into existence, and today it serves as a commuter line. Road transport is along Route 2, which cuts from the capital to the coast, running through the modern satellite towns of **Petaling Jaya** and **Shah Alam**. If you're based in KL, you may fancy a day out in these parts, though the destinations aren't of huge interest in themselves. Ferries to Sumatra leave from **Port Klang**, 8km southwest of Klang.

Petaling Jaya
PETALING JAYA, or PJ as it's known locally, is 12km southwest of the city centre, covering a sprawling area divided into 25 different planned sections. Originally conceived as an overspill suburb for KL, it provided low-cost, modern housing for those who flocked to the city to find work in the 1970s, when the Malaysian economy began to expand rapidly. Now it's virtually a separate city, with a manufacturing base rooted in electronics, computers and textiles, and a population of well over quarter of a million.

KL's cash-rich middle class come to eat in PJ's swanky restaurants and sample the booming nightlife; some of the best places are covered below.

The town is split into sections, the main ones being "State", "Damansara Utama", "Bandar Utama" and the Orwellian "Section 2" (or SS2). **State** is the closest thing PJ has to a municipal centre and boasts an enormous Civic Centre which stages large-scale concerts and exhibitions. **SS2** is probably the most interesting section for foreign visitors, with its terrific pasar malam, held every night (6pm–midnight) around a massive square known locally as "glutton square". Here, you'll find hawkers selling *satukeping* – delicious pancakes layered with brown sauce and shredded vegetables. **Bandar Utama** is host to Malaysia's largest shopping mall, 1 Utama, and includes a mammoth food court, offering Japanese, Vietnamese and western cuisine, alongside Malaysian favourites. Later at night, the focus shifts to **Damansara Utama**, a massive rectangular spread of shop fronts incorporating dozens of restaurants and nightclubs along its four sides, which stay open until 4am over the weekend.

PRACTICALITIES

From KL, **buses** #28, #30, #33 and #35 from Klang bus station (every 10min), run to State in about twenty minutes, where you change for buses to other sections of town. Addresses in PJ can be confusing at first glance, though once you appreciate that the city was planned on a grid system, and that streets have numbers and not names, you're halfway there.

PJ's main **eating** area is based around the hawker stalls at SS2, offering a mixture of food including burgers, pizza and Korean food, but also with plenty of Chinese and Malay noodle and rice dishes too. For specific restaurants, try *Out of Africa* – decorated with stuffed wildlife trophies – at 1 Jalan Sultan close to the Petaling Jaya Hilton. Other good restaurants are found in Damansara Utama, where most of the **nightlife** is too. *Ecstasy* at 16 Jalan Sultan SS 21/39 (5pm–2am; $20; ☎03/717 5800) is home to the country's most innovative musical artistes, such as Amir Yussof and Julian Mokhtar. The *Longhorn Pub* (7pm–2am; $10 after 11pm), is KL's foremost country and western spot, where local groups perform classic numbers. Many of the big acts which make it to Malaysia usually play at the **PJ Civic Centre**, Jalan Penchala, in State (☎03/757 1211), a state-of-the-art venue which puts on rock and classical concerts, musicals and exhibitions.

Sunway Lagoon, Wet World Water Park and Mines Wonderland are three recently-built **theme parks** in the Klang Valley, between PJ and Shah Alam. In an increasingly affluent nation, these parks are springing up to fill the leisure time of middle-class Malaysians, and should keep kids happy for a few hours. **Sunway Lagoon** (Mon, Wed & Thurs noon–9pm, Fri noon–10.30pm, Sat & Sun 10am–10.30pm; $45 for all three sections), close to PJ, is the most hyped of the three parks. Its "Adventure Park" and "Fort Lagoon Wild West" ($32) are tame in comparison to some Western theme parks. Perhaps the best reason for visiting is to cool off in the "Waterpark" ($18), which includes a wave pool, lots of water slides, and water-based roller coasters. To reach the park, take bus #4, #51 or #252 from Klang bus station. **Wet World Water Park** (Tues–Fri noon–8pm, Sat 10am–8pm; $7 plus $6 for an inflatable inner tube needed for the best rides) is really for children, although it does have the "Monsoon Blaster", allegedly the world's longest uphill water coaster. Take buses #5, #222 and #338 from Klang bus station near Central Market. One of the strangest sensations in sultry Malaysia is on offer at the **Mines Wonderland** (daily 4pm–11pm; $18). Here you can experience a mini-world covered in machine-generated snow in the "Snow House", once the site of the world's largest open-cast tin mining lake. After dark, there are various laser and light shows, plus some mildly thrilling fire-eating and snake-wrestling displays. The park is at Sungei Besai. Take bus #110 from Pudu Raya or #17 and #18 from Kota Raya.

PUTRAJAYA

A former rubber plantation, 25km south of KL, is to be the site of Malaysia's twenty-first-century city – Putrajaya. This "environmentally benign" city will form one end of a "Multimedia Super Corridor" (MSC) – the other being the KLCC. The plan sees Malaysia developing as an information technology hub, with everything from software engineers and electronic publishing to telemedicine. Despite such promotional puff by the government, the idea was dealt a serious blow on August 3, 1996, when the whole country suffered a twelve-hour power blackout. This second nationwide power cut in four years has left some wondering if Malaysia is ready for the information age. Still, Prime Minister Mahathir characteristically plans to lead the way by making his department a paperless office when it moves out to Putrajaya in 1998.

Shah Alam

Further downvalley is **SHAH ALAM**, designated the state capital of Selangor in 1982. Much of its ultra-modern centre is generally devoid of interest, the exception being the stunning **Sultan Salahuddin Abdul Aziz Shah Mosque** (Thurs–Sat 10am–noon & 2–4pm). Completed in 1988 at a cost of $162 million, this is the largest mosque in Southeast Asia, a vast complex incorporating massive blue marble pillars and set in an expanse of shining concrete and glistening water – the prayer hall alone holds sixteen thousand people. The 92-metre-high dome was designed by computer and has a striking blue and white design, its main panels emblazoned with Koranic inscriptions. The dome itself is porous – when rain falls between the joints of the outer panels, it's collected in a special channel, flows into a storage tank and is pumped up into one of the four minarets. Worshippers taking their ablutions before prayers trigger the flow of water from the tank by breaking a photo-electric beam.

To visit the mosque, women must wear a *tudong* (plain headscarf) and a long dress or trousers, and men long-sleeved shirts and long trousers. Take any Shah Alam bus from KL's Klang bus station, which leave every thirty minutes; you'll need to ask for the mosque, though most services will drop you right outside. The Komuter train also stops at Shah Alam, but you'll have to catch a bus or a taxi from the station to the mosque.

The Agricultural Park

Three kilometres west of Sham Alam, the **Bukit Cahaya Sri Alam Agricultural Park** (Tues–Sun 8.30am–6pm; $2) presents traditional Malaysian agrarian activities in a beautiful natural setting. It's aimed particularly at school groups, but it doesn't make a bad day out if you're interested in tropical horticulture and agro-forestry. Four roads fan out from the **park headquarters**, where you can pick up a map and brochures describing the park activities. The road going northeast leads past a rice field, an aviary, and mushroom, spice and orchid gardens, to a dam and a freshwater fish-breeding centre. To the north, there's a campsite and another dam, from where there is a short, well-signposted pathway into primary jungle. Other roads lead to food stalls, an open-air theatre, insect house, a tropical fruits plantation, and even a small Orang Asli village – whose inhabitants no longer pursue a traditional lifestyle. You can **camp** or rent **chalets** in the park (park headquarters has the details), though in truth you'd do better at almost any minor stop in the interior.

Hourly buses – either the #222 or #338 from Klang bus station (around $4) – take eighty minutes to reach the park. The bus drops you within sight of the park entrance, with the headquarters a further ten minutes' walk beyond. Coming back, either walk back outside the park to the main road and wait for the #222 or #338, or catch the (less regular) Shah Alam town bus, which leaves from next to the park HQ and runs to the PNKS Complex in Shah Alam, from where the #206 or #222 run on to KL.

Klang

The highway running the length of the Klang Valley comes to an end in **KLANG**, 30km southwest of KL. As erstwhile royal seat and historic capital of Selangor State, Klang is hundreds of years older than KL, and from the early sixteenth century onwards was at the centre of one of the most important tin-producing areas in Malaysia, its development inextricably bound up with the gradual expansion of tin production. But in this was sown the seeds of its own decline. It was from Klang that the expedition up Sungei Klang to seek new tin deposits was organized, the success of which led to the founding of Kuala Lumpur in the 1850s (see p.81). In 1880, KL superseded Klang as state capital (more than a century later it moved again to Shah Alam) and the old river port ceased to have any political or ceremonial importance.

Although still a bustling, commercial centre, whose main industry is fishing, Klang's historic buildings – the tin museum, the mosque, the government offices and the old istana (palace) – reflect a more dignified, graceful past, where the call to prayer dictated the pace of life. Most of these buildings are found in the **old quarter** of town – to get here, follow the main road past the bus station and cross the bridge over Sungei Klang. If you arrive by train, you'll already be on this side of the river. Immediately below you, on your right, is the Gedung Rajah Abdullah, an old tin warehouse built in 1856 and now housing the **National Tin Museum** (daily 9am–4pm; Fri closed noon–2.45pm; free) within its black sloping roof and whitewashed walls. The warehouse was built by Rajah Abdullah – the Sultan of Selangor's son – both as a home and storehouse for the tin he owned; it was at Abdullah's prompting that the pioneers rafted up Sungei Klang in 1857 to look for new sources of tin. As well as an extensive photographic record detailing the history of tin and the town, the museum contains examples of currency made from tin, including tortoise-shaped ingots, and various pieces of production equipment. Try and catch the hourly video show, which briefly covers the history of tin production in the region.

To reach the istana and mosque follow Jalan Besar, which runs under the bridge opposite the museum, deeper into the old part of Klang. The road passes well-maintained Chinese terraced shops and cafés, before reaching the main street, Jalan Istana, which leads to the nineteenth-century **istana**, another 200m to the north. As is usual, you can only visit the magnificent palace during the two-day Hari Raya festival (at the end of Ramadan in March or April), but the walk up the road past well-tended plants, trees and flowerbeds offers a ravishing prospect, with the main golden spire of the palace gleaming. If you return the way you came and take the first right onto Jalan Kota Raja past the padang; you'll reach Klang's mosque, the intimate and atmospheric **Masjid Sultan Suleiman** ten minutes further on. It has seven yellow domes and grey stone outer walls. Low, arched entrances set into the walls lead into narrow passages where the worshippers sit and read the Koran. Further, into the inner prayer room, stained-glass windows provide luminous light.

PRACTICALITIES

The Komuter train runs at least every thirty minutes to Klang from KL's main station ($3.60 one way). There are hourly **buses** – the #51, #58 or #225 – from Klang bus station in KL, which take an hour to reach Klang. If you don't want to return directly to the capital, services from Klang's bus station head north on Route 5 to Kuala Selangor and its nature park (see below) – though realistically, given the paucity of facilities in both towns, you're only going to continue in this direction if you have your own transport.

Port Klang and on to Indonesia

The main reason for continuing the 8km on to **PORT KLANG** is to catch a ferry to Indonesia, although ferry services also run to **PULAU KETAM**, a quaint Chinese fishing village, on the most westerly of the islands opposite the port.

The Komuter train stops directly opposite the main jetty while buses off-load their passengers 200m further along the road. Comfortable air-conditioned boats leave for Tanjung Balai in Sumatra (daily Tues–Sun 11am; 6hr 30min), and for Belawan, close to Medan (Thurs & Sat, 10am 8hr 30min). You will need a prearranged visa for Tanjung Balai, but not for Belawan. The jetty complex at Port Klang includes the *Port View* restaurant, some duty-free shops and a moneychanger. Tickets to Tanjung Balai are $100 one-way, and to Belawan $110 one-way; $15 departure tax is payable on both tickets. The ticket to Belawan includes the onward bus journey at the other end to Medan. If you're stuck in Port Klang for a while, apart from the *Port View*, there's also the *Sri Thankashmi Villas*, opposite the bus stop, which serves excellent *masala dosai* and, close to the train terminus, a colourful Indian temple.

PULAU KETAM

An hour's ferry ride from Port Klang through the mangrove swamps is the fishing village of **Pulau Ketam**, meaning Crab Island. The village has been a Chinese stronghold since three fishermen established a community here at the turn of the century. Today, it is most appealing for its clapboard houses built on stilts, its lack of cars, and its delicious seafood restaurants.

Bicycles can be rented at the *Sea Lion Villa Lodge* next to the jetty for $3 an hour, but everything on the island is within easy walking distance. The *Hock Leng Keng* temple at the end of Jalan Merdeka – the main shopping street with old painted movie banners strung across it to provide shade – is worth checking out, as is the local Chinese Association hall, the balcony of which provides a pleasant view across the village. Rather less pleasant is the pollution in the water around the houses, all too apparent at low tide.

It's possible to stay on the island at the *Sea Lion Villa Lodge* (☎03/351 4121; ②) and the *Pulau Ketam Lodge* (☎03/351 4200; ②) on Jalan Merdeka, although there is little to do in the evening. The reasonably priced seafood is worth sampling though. Not surprisingly, the speciality is crab, best eaten at the *Kuai Lok Hian* restaurant by the jetty (around $13), where the sea breeze will keep you cool as you watch the fishing boats plough up and down the estuaries between the islands.

Ferries to Pulau Ketam leave from the jetty to the right of the Port Klang rail terminus (Mon–Fri hourly 9.40am–5.40pm, extra services Sat & Sun 8.40am & 6.40pm; $6 return). If you miss the ferry or wish to go out fishing around the island, speedboats can be hired in the village, starting at around $70 for the journey back to Port Klang.

Kuala Selangor and around

The other main target around KL is the former strategic royal town of **KUALA SELANGOR**, 67km to the northwest, lying on the banks of Sungei Selangor. Today, the town is no more than one main street of two-storey concrete buildings and is really only worth a stop if you're on your way to either of the local natural attractions (see below). All that remains of Kuala Selangor's more glorious past are the remnants of two forts overlooking the town, the largest of which, **Fort Altingberg** (daily 9am–4.30pm; free), recalls a period in Malaysian history when this part of the country changed hands, bloodily, on several occasions. Originally called Fort Melawati, Altingberg was built by local people during the reign of Sultan Ibrahim of Selangor in the eighteenth century, but was later captured by the Dutch (who renamed it) as part of an attempt to wrestle the tin trade from the sultans. Later, the fortress was partly destroyed during local skirmishes in the Selangor Civil War (1867–73). Within the grounds of the fort is a cannon, reputed to be from the Dutch era, and a rock used for executions. Bukit Melawati, the hill on which the fort is based, also has a lighthouse and a resthouse built during the British colonial period.

Kuala Selangor is reached on hourly bus #141 from bay 23 at Pudu Raya bus station; the ninety-minute trip costs around $4.

Kuala Selangor Nature Park

Eight kilometres southeast of Kuala Selangor by road – although directly below the fort – is the **Kuala Selangor Nature Park** (daily 8am–7pm), opened in 1987. Among the different habitats in this reclaimed mangrove swamp are mud flats, lakes and a small patch of forest which holds around 150 species of birds, with thirty more passing along the coastline annually. This is the only site in Malaysia where the spoonbilled sandpiper has been sighted. Silver leaf monkeys live in the forest, and along the coast the mangroves provide a home for a variety of crabs and fish.

There are several clearly marked **trails** in the park, but none are more than a few hundred metres long. **Accommodation** here ranges from sturdy A-frame tents for around $20, to small three-bed chalets for $40, either of which can be booked through the Malaysian Nature Society (☎03/791 2185) or directly at the park (daily 9am–5pm; ☎03/889 2294). Weekends are always busy, but during the week you could probably just turn up. Buses run here up Route 5 from Klang; get off the bus at the Mobil petrol station 8km before Kuala Selangor and follow Jalan Klinik 200m to the park entrance.

Kampung Kuantan

Most people make the trip to Kuala Selangor to see the **luminous fireflies** (see box) which glow spectacularly in the early evening along the banks of the Sungei Selangor, around 10km inland of Kuala Selangor itself, at a small village called **KAMPUNG KUANTAN**. To enter the village costs $1, while sampans are $24 (bookings on ☎03/889 2403) and hold up to four people. The boats are rowed upriver for forty minutes for passengers to observe the extraordinary fireflies and glow-worms, which have developed a striking synchronized flashing pattern. The best time to view the flies is on a dry night between 8pm and midnight, after which time they will have found a mate and stopped glowing.

There's no public transport to Kampung Kuantan, and you'll have to take a taxi which will cost around $100 from KL, or $50 from Kuala Selangor, for the return trip. A couple of kilometres back towards Kuala Selangor is a small fishing village with riverside restaurants which is an excellent place to stop for seafood dishes. Try the *New River View* at 1 Jalan Besar, Pasir Penambang for the speciality calamari.

FIREFLIES

The firefly display at **Kampung Kuantan** is one of Malaysia's **eco-tourism** success stories. Known locally as *kelip kelip*, fireflies are not really flies, but six-millimetre long beetles which belong to the *Lampyridae* species. This rhythmic flashing only occurs in the region stretching from India to the Philippines and Papua New Guinea, and is becoming an increasingly rare sight, as their natural habit – **mangrove swamps** – is hacked back for development. During the day, the fireflies rest on blades of grass behind the mangroves. After sunset they move to mangrove trees to feed on nectar from the leaves and attract mates with their synchronized flashing. The flashes are at a rate of three per second and all the male fireflies flash within one-thirtieth of a second of each other. The females also produce a bright light, but they don't flash in the same flamboyant way as the males. It's important for visitors to remain quiet during viewing of the firefly display and not to take flash photographs, since such behaviour will scare the insects away. Scientists are still trying to work out exactly why the fireflies flash in unison, but for the visitor it helps create the Christmas lights effect that Kampung Kuantan has become famous for.

travel details

Trains

Kuala Lumpur to: Alor Setar (4 daily; 10hr); Butterworth (4 daily; 8hr); Gemas (5 daily; 4hr); Ipoh (4 daily; 3hr Singapore (4 daily; 6hr 30min); Tapah Road (4 daily; 2hr).

Buses
Kuala Lumpur

Pudu Raya station to:
Alor Setar (9 daily; 9hr); Butterworth (every 30min; 7hr); Cameron Highlands (hourly; 4hr 30min); Fraser's Hill (hourly; 4hr); Genting Highlands (hourly; 1hr); Ipoh (every 30min; 4hr); Johor Bahru (5 daily; 6hr); Kampar (4 daily; 4hr); Kuala Kedah (6 daily; 8hr); Kuala Perlis (6 daily; 9hr); Lumut (6 daily; 4hr); Melaka (every 30min; 2hr); Mersing (1 daily; 8hr); Muar (4 daily; 3hr); Penang (every 30min; 8hr); Seremban (8 daily;

1hr); Singapore (7 daily; 7hr); Tanjong Bidara (3 daily; 2hr; Taiping (9 daily; 5hr).

Pekeliling station to:
Jerantut (4 daily; 3hr 30min); Kuala Kuba Bharu (8 daily; 2hr); Kuala Lipis (4 daily; 4hr).

Putra station to:
Kota Bharu (7 daily; 10hr); Kuala Terengganu (3 daily; 7hr); Kuantan (every 30min; 5hr); Temerloh (hourly; 3hr).

Planes

Kuala Lumpur to: Alor Setar (6 daily; 50min); Ipoh (5 daily; 35min); Johor Bahru (8 daily; 45min); Kota Bharu (6 daily; 50min); Kota Kinabalu (10 daily; 2hr 35 min); Kuala Terengganu (2 daily; 45min); Kuantan (4 daily; 40min); Kuching (10 daily; 1hr 45 min); Langkawi (4 daily; 55min); Penang (18 daily; 45min); Singapore (18 daily; 55min).

Market stall, Jalan Petaling, KL

The Petronas Towers, KL

Sultan Abdul Samad building, KL

Pulau Ketam

Batu Caves

The gleaming dome of one of Malaysia's hundreds of mosques.

Canopy walkway, Taman Negara

Butterfly farm, Penang

SIMON RICHMOND

Kek Lok Si Temple, Penang

VICKI COUCHMAN

Street scene, Penang

CHAPTER TWO

THE WEST COAST

T he west coast of the Malaysian Peninsula, from Kuala Lumpur north to the Thai border, is the most industrialized and densely populated – not to mention cosmopolitan – part of the whole country. Its considerable natural resources have long brought eager traders and entrepreneurs here, but it was the demand for the region's tin in the late nineteenth century that spearheaded Malaysia's phenomenal economic rise. Immigrant workers, most of whom settled in the region for good, bestowed a permanent legacy in the predominantly Chinese towns that punctuate the route north. Perak State – once boasting the richest single tin field in the world – and its capital, the old tin-boom city of Ipoh, are still littered with reminders of the recent industrial past. But even when the light industry surrounding Malaysia's other major commodity, rubber, took over from the dying tin trade in the 1950s, it didn't quite obliterate the essentially agricultural nature of much of the region. The state of Kedah, along with Perlis, tucked into the northern border, shares the distinction of being the historical jelapang padi, or "rice bowl", of Malaysia, where rich, emerald paddy fields and jutting limestone outcrops form the Peninsula's most dramatic scenery.

This is the area in which the **British** held most sway, attracted by the political prestige of controlling such a strategic trading region. Although the British had claimed administrative authority since 1826 through the Straits Settlements (which included Singapore and Melaka as well as Penang), it was the establishment here of the Federated Malay States of Perak, Pahang, Selangor and Negeri Sembilan fifty years later that extended colonial rule to the whole Peninsula.

Most visitors are too intent on the beckoning delights of Thailand to bother stopping at anything other than the major destinations. But nowhere are the rural delights of the country more apparent than at the **hill stations** north of KL, designed as cool retreats for colonial administrators. **Fraser's Hill** is closest to the capital, though it's easily overshadowed by the **Cameron Highlands** 95km further north, Malaysia's largest hill station and one of the most significant tourist spots in the country. Both are justifiably popular mountain retreats, with opportunities for forest treks and indulgence in the traditional British comforts of crackling log fires and cream teas.

Due west of here, tiny **Pulau Pangkor**, though not as idyllic as the islands of the Peninsula's east coast, is an increasingly visited resort, with the best beaches in the area. However, the fastest development is on its far northern rival, **Pulau Langkawi**, the largest island in the glittering and largely unpopulated Langkawi archipelago. Most travellers wisely give the port of **Butterworth** a wide berth, just using it for access to the island of **Penang**, whose vibrant capital **Georgetown** combines modern shopping malls with ancient Chinese shophouses.

These main destinations aside, there's a whole host of intriguing and under-visited places off the beaten track, such as **Ipoh**, 200km north of Kuala Lumpur which has elegant colonial buildings and mansions at every turn, and its northern neighbour the royal town of **Kuala Kangsar**, a quiet place of architectural interest. The route north also passes through the old mining town of **Taiping**, whose small hill station, **Maxwell Hill**, is now fading gently into insignificance. The state capital of Kedah is **Alor Setar**, the last major town before the border (and the last significant stop other than Pulau Langkawi). Long a stamping ground for successive invaders, the region still reveals a

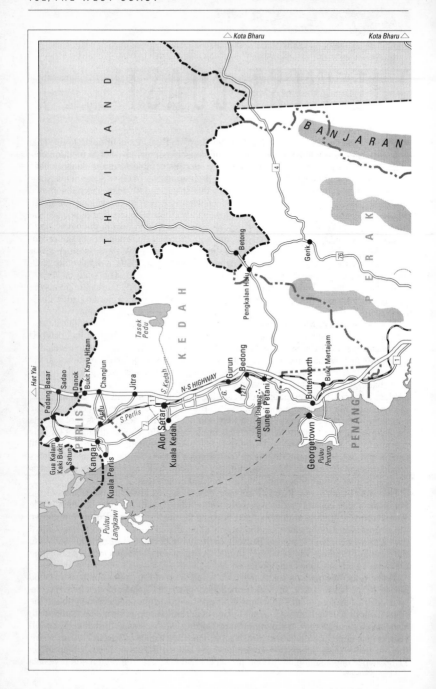

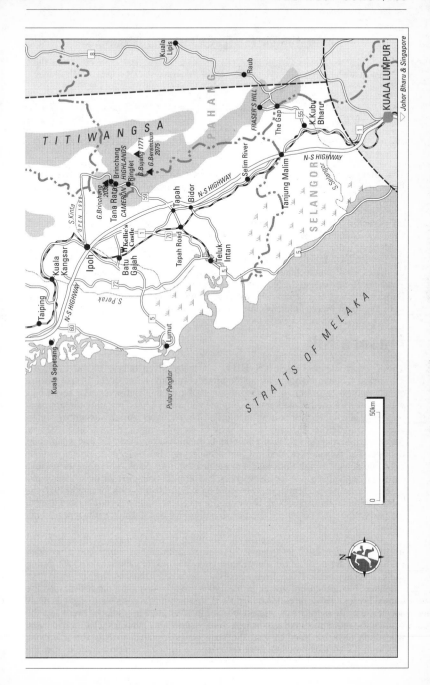

Thai influence in its cuisine, although Alor Setar itself is a staunch Muslim stronghold. From here it's a short hop from any of the **border towns** – Kuala Perlis, Kangar and Arau – into Thailand itself.

Because of its economic importance, the west coast has a well-developed transport infrastructure. The newly completed **North–South Highway**, pristine and little used, virtually shadows the already adequate **Route 1**, and runs from Singapore all the way to Malaysia's northern border at Bukit Kayu Hitam. The **train line**, which runs more or less parallel to these roads, is used less, though its border crossing at Padang Besar facilitates easy connections with Hat Yai, the transport crossroads of southern Thailand. Both roads and train line pass through all the major towns – Ipoh, Taiping, Butterworth and Alor Setar – with **express buses** providing the backbone of the services and **local buses** linking to the hills and the coast.

Fraser's Hill

The development at **FRASER'S HILL** – actually seven hills – 1500m up in the Titiwangsa mountain range, was built to provide welcome relief for the British expatriate community from humid Kuala Lumpur, 100km to the southwest. The seven hills which comprise the hill station were originally known as *Ulu Tras*, until the arrival in the 1890s of a solitary British pioneer, called James Fraser. An accountant by profession, he travelled to Australia at the peak of its gold rush and then on to Malaya. Although gold wasn't found in any quantity in the hills here, Fraser did find plentiful **tin** deposits. The tin was excavated by Chinese miners and hauled by mule along a perilous hill route down through thick jungle to the nearest town, Raub, where Fraser set up a camp and a gambling den for his workers. But after 25 years, Fraser mysteriously disappeared, and when a search party trekked up into the area to look for him in 1917, the camp and mines were deserted. However, the excellent location recommended itself to the party, who soon convinced the British authorities that it would make a perfect hill station.

Fraser Hill was never as popular as the much larger Cameron Highlands to the north, and even today it feels remote. The surrounding mountainous jungle provided perfect cover for some of the Communist guerrillas' secret camps (see p.205) during the Emergency in the 1950s, from where they launched strikes on British-owned plantations and neighbouring towns. In the 1960s the area saw a partial revival, and the annual Fraser's Hill International Bird Race, in which teams compete to sight as many species of birds as they can, was established in 1988. Held in June, the event sets the tone for the rather reserved atmosphere here: visitors are mainly from KL, and tourists, who don't have the time to visit the state parks, come in manageable numbers. Although it's possible to come here on a day-trip from KL, it's preferable to stay the night at one of the hotels or lodges around the hill station.

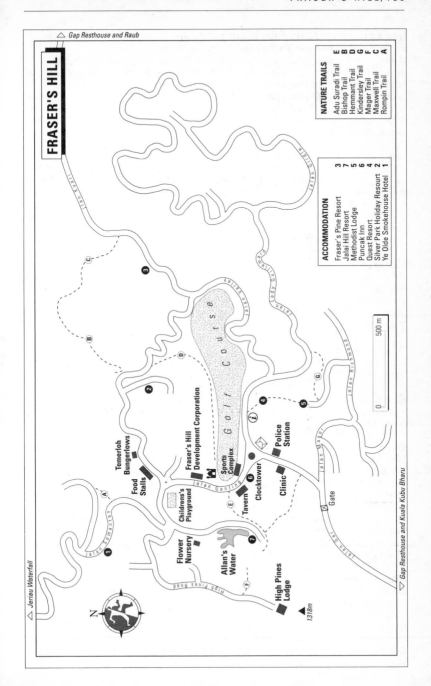

△ *Gap Resthouse and Raub*

FRASER'S HILL

NATURE TRAILS

Adu Suradi Trail	E
Bishop Trail	B
Hemmant Trail	D
Kindersley Trail	G
Mager Trail	F
Maxwell Trail	C
Rompin Trail	A

ACCOMMODATION

Fraser's Pine Resort	3
Jalai Hill Resort	7
Methodist Lodge	5
Puncak Inn	6
Quest Resort	4
Silver Park Holiday Resourt	2
Ye Olde Smokehouse Hotel	1

△ *Jeriau Waterfall*

Temerloh Bungerlows

Food Stalls

Fraser's Hill Development Corporation

Children's Playground

Golf Course

Sports Complex

Police Station

Clocktower

Clinic

Tavern

Allan's Water

Flower Nursery

High Pines Lodge

▲ *1318m*

Jalan Semantan

Jalan Genting

Jalan Girdle

Jalan Kuala

Jalan Richmond

Jalan Mager

Jalan Lady

High Pines Road

N

0 ____ 500 m

Gate

▽ *Gap Resthouse and Kuala Kubu Bharu*

Getting there: via Kuala Kubu Bharu and Raub

From KL, you need to catch the Kuala Kubu Bharu bus from bay 21 at Pudu Raya bus station, which leaves hourly and costs around $3.50. Aim to leave KL by 9am, and you'll get to the attractive small town of **KUALA KUBU BHARU**, 60km northeast of KL, in time to have a quick look round – before the up-country Fraser's Hill bus leaves at noon. It's another 40km to Fraser's Hill and the bus takes an hour. There is an earlier bus service at 8am, though you're unlikely to want to stay overnight here just to catch this. Alternatively, you could charter a taxi ($40) from the taxi rank at the KKB bus station. If all else fails, there's a daily bus service to Raub at 2.30pm (it's usually late) which can drop you at the Gap (see below). If you are killing time in KKB, there's a good Indian Muslim café, close to the bus station.

Coming from the interior, via **Raub** (see p.225), get off the bus at the junction with **the Gap**, the narrow, twisting eight-kilometre road which leads up to Fraser's Hill. At the junction, there's a hotel, *The Gap Rest House* (☎09/362 2227; ③), where you can wait for the Kota Kubu Bahru–Fraser's Hill bus, although many people choose to walk from here. This colonial-style building needs some repair but has elegant rooms, great views and a fine dining room – not a bad place to stay the night.

Halfway up the road from KKB to the Gap you'll see a sign, "Emergency Historical Site", marking the spot where **Sir Henry Gurney**, the British High Commissioner for Malaya during the height of the Communist insurgency in 1951, was ambushed and killed. The guerrillas hadn't known how important their quarry was; their aim had been only to steal guns, ammunition and food, but when Gurney strode towards them demanding that they put down their weapons, they opened fire.

The hill station and trails

None of the **trails** takes more than two hours to cover so you can walk them all within a couple of days. The Fraser's Hill Development Corporation has named each of the trails (see map) and plans more in the future. They're not always clearly marked, but you're unlikely to get lost. This isn't primary jungle and you'll see few mammals, although Fraser's Hill is particularly renowned for its **bird life** – look out for flycatchers, woodpeckers and hornbills. There's a more comprehensive account of the region's flora and fauna in the "Wildlife" section of Contexts, p.617.

The two main routes which loop around the hills start from the clocktower marking the centre of the hill station, with shorter trails snaking off on all sides. Heading north, Jalan Gentry winds up a beautiful hill, and in fifteen minutes reaches the *Temerloh Bungalows*. From here you can continue along Jalan Lady Maxwell to the Bishop's House, the start of the Bishop's Trail. This uphill route joins the Maxwell trail and takes about an hour, before running into Jalan Kuari. For a longer walk, turn left at the fork after the children's playground and go past *Ye Olde Smokehouse Hotel* to reach the **Jeriau Waterfall**, around 4km (1hr) from the clocktower. Next to the waterfall is a concrete-encased swimming area – the water is freezing cold – and tables for picnicking. If you follow the narrow road opposite the turn-off to *Ye Olde Smokehouse Hotel*, you soon reach a flower nursery and beyond that a small **lake** where you can rent rowing boats ($4 for 15min).

Probably the most scenic route is the Mager trail to *High Pines Lodge*, which weaves along the side of a hill buzzing with cicadas and flying beetles. After around thirty minutes the trail drops down Jalan High Pines leading to the lodge, which is a good vantage point for bird-spotting.

Another good road walk starts at the information office: take Jalan Lady Guillemard past the information office and stick to it until it joins the loop road, Jalan Girdle. This leads to the most remote section of the hill station. bordering **Ulu Tramin Forest Reserve**, with private bungalows hidden down driveways. Completing the circle, all the way round and back to the information office, takes around ninety minutes.

Practicalities

Right by the clocktower is the Fraser's Hill **information office** (daily 8am–7pm; ☎09/362 2201). Here you can pick up a map, **rent bicycles** ($4 per hr) and check on accommodation availability. The Fraser Hill Development Corporation office (☎09/362 2248, fax 362 2273) is further up the hill past the mosque; there are plans to create a nature education centre here. Green fees for the nine-hole golf course are $30 a day during the week and $40 at the weekend, with a $15 charge for renting clubs. There's a small Maybank branch outside the *Quest Resort* (see below) where you can change money. The two **return bus services** to Kuala Kubu Bharu leave at 10am and 2pm.

Accommodation, eating and drinking

Some of the hotels listed below have restaurants, but cheaper options for **eating** are the small row of cafés opposite the clocktower, which sell rice and noodle dishes, and the **food stalls**, which are found at the northern end of Jalan Genting. The best place for a **drink** is *The Tavern*, opposite the Sports Centre. In addition to the **accommodation** listed here, the Development Corporation also rents out several bungalows, from around $100 a night, and has plans to open the *Jalai Hill Resort* (⑤), overlooking Allan's Water — enquire at the information office for details.

Fraser's Pine Resort, Jalan Kuari (☎09/362 2122, fax 783 6108). One of the largest developments in the area, unobtrusively positioned in a valley between two hills. As well as rooms, the resort rents out apartments during the week. ⑧.

Methodist Lodge (☎09/362 2236, KL office ☎03/232 0477). South of the information office, it's around thirty minutes' walk along Jalan Mager, then Jalan Richmond to the turning for the lodge. Alternatively, you can take the Kindersley Trail going uphill, off Jalan Lady Guillemard. The view is breathtaking and the double rooms very good value. ④.

Puncak Inn, Jalan Genting (☎09/362 2055). The most central and cheapest place, opposite the clocktower. The rooms are very basic, and at weekends the karaoke in the golf club opposite can keep going until the early hours. ②.

Quest Resort, Jalan Lady Guillemard (☎09/362 2300, fax 362 2284). This ugly concrete block is on the hill above the information office. Some of its rooms have the saving grace of a pleasant view across the golf course and there is a coffee shop and Chinese restaurant (dishes around $13). ⑥

Silverpark Holiday Resort, Jalan Ledegham (☎09/362 2888, fax 362 2887). New and expensive accommodation with mock-Tudor towers and spectacular views. ⑦.

Ye Olde Smokehouse, Jalan Semantan (☎09/362 2226, fax 362 2035). Designed along the lines of an English Tudor country cottage, this small place caters for a wealthy clientele and has a faded colonial elegance. ⑦.

Cameron Highlands

Amid the lofty peaks of Banjaran Titiwangsa, the various outposts of the **CAMERON HIGHLANDS** (1524m) form Malaysia's most extensive hill station, which took its name from William Cameron, a government surveyor who stumbled across the plateau in 1885 during a mapping expedition. Cameron actually failed to mark his find on a map, and it wasn't until the 1920s that the location of the plateau was officially confirmed. Sir George Maxwell, a senior civil servant, saw the same potential for a hill station here when he visited in 1925 as he'd seen at Fraser's Hill. Others, too, were quick to see the benefits of the region, and early tea planters were followed by Chinese vegetable farmers and wealthy landowners in search of a weekend retreat – a spate of development that culminated in today's hotels and luxury apartments.

Despite seventy years of tourism, William Cameron's early, glowing descriptions of the plateau's gentle contours and dramatic peaks still apply. Although tall condominiums occasionally punctuate the landscape, a quintessential English character remains

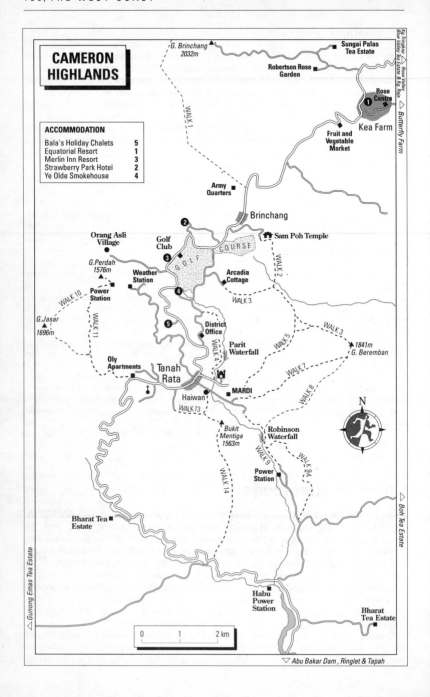

CAMERON HIGHLANDS

ACCOMMODATION

Bala's Holiday Chalets	5
Equatorial Resort	1
Merlin Inn Resort	3
Strawberry Park Hotel	2
Ye Olde Smokehouse	4

G. Brinchang 2032m

Sungai Palas Tea Estate

Robertson Rose Garden

Rose Centre

Kea Farm

Fruit and Vegetable Market

WALK 1

Army Quarters

Brinchang

Sam Poh Temple

Orang Asli Village

Golf Club

GOLF COURSE

WALK 2

G.Perdah 1576m

Weather Station

Arcadia Cottage

Power Station

WALK 10

WALK 3

G.Jasar 1696m

WALK 11

WALK 3

1841m G. Bereman

District Office

Parit Waterfall

WALK 5

WALK 4

WALK 7

Oly Apartments

Tanah Rata

MARDI

WALK 8

Haiwan

WALK 13

Bukit Mentiga 1563m

Robinson Waterfall

N

WALK 9

WALK 9A

Power Station

WALK 14

Bharat Tea Estate

Habu Power Station

Bharat Tea Estate

◁ *Gunong Emas Tea Estate*

▷ *Boh Tea Estate*

Kg. Tringkap ▷
Rose Valley,
Blue Valley Tea Estate & Kg. Raja ▷

▷ *Butterfly Farm*

| 0 | 1 | 2 km |

▽ *Abu Bakar Dam , Ringlet & Tapah*

with rolling green fields dotted with country cottages, farms and a golf course. While weekenders flock here in their thousands, it's not difficult to avoid the crowds. Leisure activities tend to be rather wholesome, with the emphasis on fresh air and early nights. The vast plateau and surrounding hills and forests are ideal for **walking**, and the climate is cool. Other pleasures are simple – in fact, there's precious little to do here, particularly in the evenings when **eating** provides just about the sole diversion. The Highlands' colonial past means you can round off a day of walking with an English cream tea, followed by dinner incorporating the local speciality, the steamboat. This is the Malaysian equivalent of the Swiss *fondue*, which involves dipping raw fish, meat, noodles and vegetables in a steaming broth until cooked – a filling (and lengthy) meal.

The highlands encompass three small towns: **Ringlet**, a rich agricultural area and site of the famous tea plantations; 13km beyond and 300m higher, **Tanah Rata**, the principal settlement of the highlands; and 5km further north, **Brinchang**, renowned for its farms, most of which are located to the north towards the kampungs of Tringkap and Raja.

The best accommodation is situated in Tanah Rata and Brinchang; they're also convenient for tours of the farms and tea estates, since many operators will collect you from your hotel or guesthouse. If you're travelling in a group and plan to stay for some time, you could try the **bungalows** and **apartments** for rent dotted around the region. **Prices** soar at peak holiday times when you can expect to add at least $20 to the price of an ordinary room; book ahead if you can. It's always worth bargaining out of season. You need to make sure that there is hot water provided, since it can be very chilly in the early mornings and evenings. Some places also have real fires, which can make no end of difference to an otherwise uninspiring hotel.

Tours of the whole region are organized by the Tanah Rata tourist office (3-hr; $15) and though a bit "whistle-stop" in character, do at least cover all the main sights and destinations in one swoop; the inevitable shopping stop at the end is mercifully low-key.

The **weather** in the Cameron Highlands is as British as the countryside, and you can expect rainstorms even in the dry season. It makes sense to avoid the area during the monsoon itself, and at major holiday times (Christmas, Easter and Hari Raya) if you want to avoid the crowds. Temperatures drop dramatically at night – whatever the season – so you'll need socks and a jumper as well as waterproofs.

Approaches to the highlands

The road and rail routes north towards the Cameron Highlands pass through pale green splashes of endless **rubber plantations**. It's a fairly monotonous stretch, but for the Peninsula's main mountain range, the 350-kilometre **Banjaran Titiwangsa**, which rises up away to the east.

If you have time to spare and your own transport, a more idiosyncratic itinerary would be to follow the coastal Route 5 from Kuala Lumpur, running through low-lying marshland almost all the way to **TELUK INTAN**, 157km northwest of the capital. Here you can stop off at the leaning pagoda-like clocktower and grab a bowl of noodles, before taking the minor back roads to Bidor, to connect with the North–South Highway and Route 1. North of Bidor is **TAPAH**, from where Route 59 leads east to the highlands.

Tapah is hardly more than a crossroads but is the main jumping-off point for the Cameron Highlands; local bus services run from the **bus station** on Jalan Raja off the town's main street. For long-distance services including those to Hat Yai in Thailand, you can buy a ticket from one of the express bus agencies in town, such as the *Kah Mee* opposite the bus station, or *Caspian* on the main road. They'll either tell you where to catch your bus or, more than likely, will flag it down for you, since express buses only stop briefly in Tapah to allow new passengers to join. The **train station**, for routes up and down the west coast, is a few kilometres west of town (the station is called "Tapah Road"), but it's easy enough to get from the station into town by the hourly local bus (70 sen) or taxi ($6).

You're unlikely to get stuck in Tapah, as it's only a two-hour journey from Kuala Lumpur and buses run hourly (8.15am–6.15pm) on the further two-hour trip up to Tanah Rata in the Cameron Highlands. However, if you need to stay there are some reasonable **hotels**: the *Bunga Raya* (☎05/401 1436; ①) on the corner of the main street and Jalan Raja is pretty basic, while the *Utara* (☎05/401 2299; ②) on Jalan Stesen, parallel to Jalan Raja, is a bit more comfortable. Much better value all round is the *Timuran* (☎05/401 1092; ①) further along Jalan Stesen, which is very clean; all the rooms here have attached bathrooms. There are a number of cheap but nondescript Indian and Chinese **restaurants** dotted around town.

Ringlet

There's not much to **RINGLET**, the first settlement in the Cameron Highlands. The area to the north of town is dominated by the immense Sultan Abu Bakar Dam, its glittering blue water contrasting with the deep green of the forest. While there are places

---

WALKING IN THE CAMERON HIGHLANDS

The Cameron Highlands feature a number of **walks** of varying difficulty. While the forest sometimes obscures the view, the trails here take in some of the most spectacular scenery in Malaysia, encompassing textured greenery and misty mountain peaks. Some of the walks are no more than casual strolls, while others veer off into what seems like the wild unknown, giving a sense of isolation rarely encountered in lowland Malaysia. You're unlikely to come across much wildlife on the trails, perhaps the odd wild pig or squirrel, but the **flora** at all times of the year is prolific, including ferns, pitcher plants and orchids.

Unfortunately, the trails are often badly signposted and maintained, though there are various sketch **maps** on sale at the Tanah Rata tourist office and at many of the hotels which – despite their apparent vagueness – do make some sort of sense on the ground. The best is the black-and-white sketch map available for 50 sen (sometimes free at hostels), which has all the walks fairly clearly marked, although some of them no longer exist. There used to be more official trails but many were closed during the 1970s due to the supposed threat of Communist guerrillas hanging out in the undergrowth. Even now, if you want to attempt any **unofficial routes**, a guide recommended by the tourist office is essential and you must also obtain a permit from the District Office which is tricky and expensive (see "Listings", p.144).

However, the **official trails**, detailed below (and marked on the map on p.138) are varied enough for most tastes and energies. The timings given are for one-way walks for people with an average level of fitness. You should always inform someone, preferably at your hotel, where you are going and what time you expect to be back. On longer trips take warm clothing, water, a torch and a cigarette lighter or matches for basic survival should you get lost. If someone else doesn't return and you suspect they may be in **trouble**, inform the District Office immediately. It's not a fanciful notion that the hills and forests are dangerous. The most notorious incident to date concerns the American silk entrepreneur Jim Thompson, who came on holiday here in Easter 1967 and disappeared in the forest. The services of Orang Asli trackers, dogs and even mystics failed to provide any clue to his fate – a warning to present-day trekkers of the hazards of jungle life.

to stay in town, including one deluxe hotel, *The Lakehouse* (☎05/495 6152, fax 495 6213; ⑦), this is a somewhat isolated place to base yourself. There are several **tea plantations**, of which the best known is the **Boh Tea Estate** (Tues–Sun 11am–3pm), 8km northeast of town, which has free tours. You'll be able to see the whole process – from the picking to the packing of the tea, which you cannot do at the estate's more frequented **Palas** division (☎05/496 1146), north of Brinchang (see p.145).

Buses from Tapah stop on the main road in Ringlet before moving on to Tanah Rata. There are buses from Ringlet to the Boh Tea Estate daily at 6.30am, 11.30am, 3.15pm and 5.15pm, with return journeys at 7.20am, 12.20pm, 3.45pm and 6pm. It's easy enough to get to Ringlet from Tanah Rata, since there are buses every thirty minutes throughout the day. From Tanah Rata, the quickest way to get to the tea estate is to take a taxi ($8 one-way).

Tanah Rata

The tidy town of **TANAH RATA** is the highlands' main development, a genteel, place festooned with hotels, white balustraded buildings, flowers and parks. It comprises little more than one street (officially called Jalan Pasar, but usually just known as "Main

Walk 1 (1hr) A short, but tough walk, starting just north of Brinchang, up a rarely used and unmaintained track by the army quarters north of Brinchang. You must come back the same way.

Walk 2 (1hr 30min) Begins just before the Sam Poh Temple below Brinchang – it's not clearly marked and you have to walk through someone's garden first. Often a scramble rather than a straight footpath, you'll need to be reasonably fit and well prepared. The route undulates severely and eventually merges with Walk 3.

Walk 3 (2hr 30min) Starts at *Arcadia Cottage* to the southeast of the golf course, crossing streams and climbing quite steeply to reach the peak of Gunung Beremban (1841m). Moderately arduous.

Walk 4 (20min) Starts south of the golf course and goes to Parit Waterfall, which is a disappointing and rubbish-strewn picnic spot, but leads on to a watchtower with good views over Brinchang.

Walk 5 (1hr) Branches off from Walk 3 and ends up at the Malaysian Agriculture Research and Development Institute (MARDI). It's an easy walk through peaceful woodland, and then you can cut back up the road to Tanah Rata.

Walk 6 The official numbering system falls down here – this walk doesn't exist.

Walk 7 (2hr) Starts near MARDI and climbs steeply to Gunung Beremban (see

Walk 3), an arduous hike and best recommended as a descent route from Walk 3.

Walk 8 (3hr) Another route to Gunung Beremban, a tough approach from Robinson Waterfall, but not as tough as 7.

Walks 9 & 9a (1hr) The descent from Robinson Waterfall to the power station is reasonably steep and strenuous; the station caretaker will let you through to the road to Boh. Walk 9a branches off from the main route to emerge in a vegetable farm on the Boh road and is less steep than Walk 9.

Walks 10 & 11 (2hr–2hr 30min) Starts just behind the Oly Apartments for the fairly strenuous climb to Gunung Jasar (1696m). The only problem is that the end of the route is now blocked by a power station – you'll have to return the way you came or go along the less challenging (and slightly shorter) Walk 11 which bypasses the summit.

Walk 12 Now replaced by a road to the power station.

Walk 13 (1hr) A trail which starts thirty minutes behind the *Cameronian Holiday Inn* in Tanah Rata and eventually merges with Walk 14.

Walk 14 (3hr) A tricky and initially steep route via Bukit Mentiga (1563m), with great views. It begins at Haiwan (vet centre) and continues south, joining the road 8km from Tanah Rata. It's best not to do this one alone.

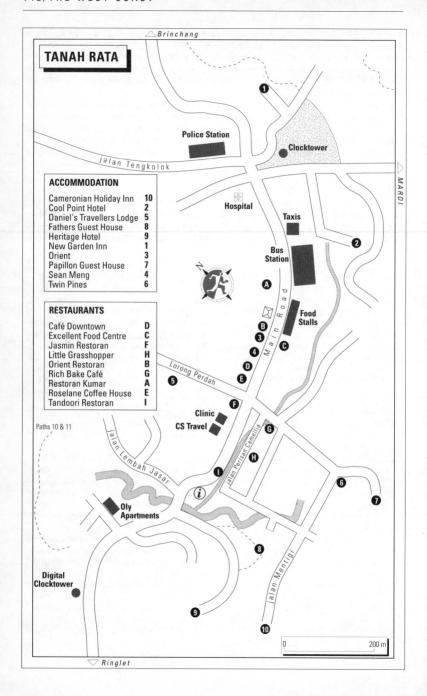

△ Brinchang

TANAH RATA

MARDI ▷

Police Station

Clocktower

Jalan Tengkolok

ACCOMMODATION

Cameronian Holiday Inn	**10**
Cool Point Hotel	**2**
Daniel's Travellers Lodge	**5**
Fathers Guest House	**8**
Heritage Hotel	**9**
New Garden Inn	**1**
Orient	**3**
Papillon Guest House	**7**
Sean Meng	**4**
Twin Pines	**6**

RESTAURANTS

Café Downtown	**D**
Excellent Food Centre	**C**
Jasmin Restoran	**F**
Little Grasshopper	**H**
Orient Restoran	**B**
Rich Bake Café	**G**
Restoran Kumar	**A**
Roselane Coffee House	**E**
Tandoori Restoran	**I**

Hospital

Taxis

Bus Station

Food Stalls

Main Road

Lorong Perdah

Clinic

CS Travel

Jalan Perisan Camellia

Paths 10 & 11

Jalan Lembah Jasar

Oly Apartments

Jalan Mentigi

Digital Clocktower

0   200 m

▽ Ringlet

Road"), which is where you'll find most of the hotels, banks and other services, as well as some of the best restaurants in the Cameron Highlands, all lined up in a half-kilometre stretch. Since the street also serves as the main thoroughfare to the rest of the region, it suffers from the constant honking of departing buses during the day, but at night becomes the centre of the Cameron Highlands' social life, with restaurants spilling their tables out onto the pavement.

All the local and long-distance **buses** go only as far as Tanah Rata; to move onto Brinchang and other destinations you'll have to change here. The helpful **tourist office** (Mon–Sat 8am–4pm) is at the southern end of town and has a small local history museum attached. The **bus station** is about halfway along the main road, 250m from the tourist office, and Tanah Rata's **taxi rank** is just a little further along. At the far end of town, past the hospital and the police station, the road bends round to the left to continue on to Brinchang.

Since many of the Cameron Highlands' **walks** start from nearby (see box, pp.140–41), Tanah Rata is an ideal base; a couple of waterfalls, a mosque and three reasonably high mountain peaks are all within hiking distance. Several of the walks pass through, or close to, the **Malaysian Agriculture Research and Development Institute** (MARDI, ☎05/491 1255) a couple of kilometres east of town, which is open for tours by appointment, though it's rather dry for anyone other than a specialist. This is the location for the annual **Flower Festival** held every August, when colourful floats compete for prizes.

Accommodation

The places strung along the main road can be a bit noisy – the best are picked out below. For more solitude you'll have to pay the higher prices charged at the comfortable hotels out on the Brinchang road, or rent one of the **apartments** or cottages in the locality. There are places advertised in shop windows in Tanah Rata – rates quoted are usually per day, and a residential cook or caretaker is often offered at an additional cost. Try the *Golf View Villa* (☎05/491 1624), a six-room bungalow for $280; the *Lutheran Bungalow* (☎05/491 1584) which sleeps twenty at $20 a head; *Rose Cottage* (☎05/491 1173) which has two rooms and costs $230; or *Country Lodge* (☎05/491 1811) which sleeps six to nine people for $200–360. All the accommodation below is marked on either the Tanah Rata map or the main map of the highlands. Many of the budget hostels have touts at the bus station in Tanah Rata waiting to escort you.

Cameronian Holiday Inn, 16 Jalan Mentigi (☎05/491 1327). The self-proclaimed "Home of the Budgets", this secluded hostel is relatively luxurious, and there's a sitting room and small library. Recommended. ①.

Cool Point, just off the main road behind the Shell station (☎05/491 4914, fax 491 4070). A new hotel in a quiet location, but the large rooms tend to be dark and damp. ⑥.

Daniel's Travellers Lodge, 9 Lorong Perdah (☎05/491 5823, fax 491 5828). One of the newest budget places in town, with clean rooms and good hot showers. Can get a bit rowdy. ①.

Father's Guest House (☎05/491 2484, fax 491 5484). This long-running place retains a loyal following. Just before the bridge as you enter town from Ringlet, take the road on the right which curves around the bottom of the convent hill and follow the stone steps to the top. Basic corrugated iron bunkers with shared kitchen facilities and free tea. ①.

Heritage, Jalan Gereja (☎05/491 3888, fax 491 5666). Set on a hill at near the approach road from Ringlet, the most upmarket hotel in Tanah Rata is very comfortable and has several upmarket restaurants. ⑦.

New Garden Inn (☎05/491 5170, fax 491 5169). Take the road on the right just past the clocktower. Recently renovated, it has many rooms with balconies and excellent bathrooms. Weekly cultural shows in the garden food court. ⑦.

Orient, 38 Main Rd (☎05/491 1633). Very good value with thoughtfully furnished airy rooms, although it can be noisy during holiday periods. ①.

Papillon Guest House, 8 Jalan Mentigi (☎05/491 4427). Follow the road left after the *Twin Pines* to reach this friendly, clean hostel. The dorms are a bit cramped, but there's a pleasant lounge. Dorms $8. ①.

Seah Meng, 39 Main Rd (☎05/491 1618). Clean, well-kept rooms; one of the best-value hotels. ②.

Twin Pines, 2 Jalan Mentigi (☎05/491 2169). Set back from the main road, this blue-roofed building has small rooms but an attractive patio garden and books full of travellers' tips. ①

ON THE BRINCHANG ROAD

Bala's Holiday Chalets (☎05/491 1660, fax 491 4500). A kilometre or so towards Brinchang, this English-style country house has rooms, including small dorms, as well as a lounge and two dining rooms, a real fire and beautiful gardens. A great spot for afternoon tea. Dorms $8. ①.

Merlin Inn Resort (☎05/491 1211, fax 491 1178). More promising from the outside than inside. Standard, bland rooms, some overlooking the golf course, and a pool/snooker room. ⑦.

Strawberry Park (☎05/491 1166, fax 491 1949). A high-class hotel in a superb location at the top of a hill, which makes it rather inaccessible; you're reliant on the hotel minibus. There's an indoor swimming pool ⑦.

Ye Olde Smokehouse (☎05/491 1215, fax 491 1214). Twelve suites, most with four-poster beds, just on the tasteful side of kitsch. Leaded windows and wooden beams belie the fact that this country pub is only sixty years old. ⑨.

Eating and drinking

There are a number of places in Tanah Rata offering Western dishes, particularly pepper steak, but nothing especially imaginative. Much cheaper than the restaurants, and often more satisfying, are the Malay **food stalls** along the main road. Open in the evening, they serve *satay*, *tom yam* (spicy Thai soup) and the usual rice and noodle combinations, for about $2 per dish.

Café Downtown, 41 Main Rd. Good spot for breakfast and lunch. Does tasty pastries and cakes as well as set meals.

Excellent Food Centre, on the main road opposite the post office. Lives up to its name with a large, inexpensive menu of Western and Asian dishes – it's great for breakfast. Open during the day only. In the adjacent *Fresh Milk Corner*, you can get wonderful shakes and *lassis* (yoghurt drinks).

Jasmine Restoran, 45 Main Rd. Popular with German and Dutch travellers for its *rijstafel* set meals. It has karaoke in the evenings, which can get a bit rowdy.

Little Grasshopper, 57b Persiran Camellia 3. On the second floor above the new shophouses. Excellent value steamboats, starting at just $6, served by friendly staff in a tasteful setting. Also has traditional Chinese tea.

Orient Restoran, 38 Main Rd. Standard Chinese food in the restaurant below the hotel. The set meals are reasonable value, as are the steamboats.

Restoran Kumar, Main Rd. Along with *Thanam* next door, the *Kumar* specializes in clay pot rice.

Rich Bake Café, Main Rd. Bright jazzy spot on the corner, which sometimes has live music; serves good pancakes.

Roselane Coffee House, 44 Main Rd. The various set menus and low-price meat grills here make up for the twee decor.

Tandoori Restoran, Main Rd Tasty, good-value Indian food, including *naan* breads and *tandoori* dishes. The food can take time to arrive.

Ye Olde Smokehouse (☎05/491 1215). Halfway to Brinchang; the hotel opens its restaurant to non-residents – intimate surroundings for a romantic splash-out. The traditional English menu features a choice of roast meat dinners for around $70, and other dishes start at $20. You'll need to book in advance. Afternoon tea is $11.

Listings

Banks All situated on the main road and open during standard banking hours.

District office 39007 Tanah Rata (Mon–Thurs 8.30am–12.30pm & 2–3.50pm, Fri 8.30am–noon & 2.45–3.50pm, Sat 8.30–11am; ☎05/491 1066, fax 491 1843). Contact immediately if you suspect someone has got lost on a walk. Also call here to obtain permits for unofficial trails.

Hospital Main Rd, opposite the park (☎05/491 1966). There's also a clinic at 48 Main Rd (8.30am–12.30pm, 2–5.30pm & 8–10pm). Ring doorbell after clinic hours.

Laundry *Highlands Laundry*, Main Rd (☎05/491 1820) is reasonably priced, but most hostels also offer this service.

Police station Main Rd, opposite the *Garden Inn* (☎05/491 1222).

Post office Main Rd (☎05/491 1051); pick up poste restante/general delivery mail here.

Service station There are service stations in both Tanah Rata and Brinchang.

Sport Cameron Highlands Golf Club (☎05/491 1126) has an eighteen-hole course ($45 for half a day, $90 at weekends, equipment rental extra); there's a strict dress code. Tennis courts at the golf club ($4 per hr for court, $5 for racket).

Taxi station Main Rd (☎05/491 1234).

Travel agent CS Travel, Main Rd (☎05/491 1200), is an agent for express bus tickets from Tapah to all major destinations.

Brinchang and around

After Tanah Rata, **BRINCHANG**, 5km or so further north, seems rather scruffy. Sprawling around a central square and the main road through town, it lacks the charm of its neighbour, although its saving grace is the lively **night market** which opens at about 4pm on Saturdays and holidays. In the holiday periods, you may have to resort to Brinchang as an alternative to Tanah Rata in order to find a room – not a major disaster since some of the walks are easily approached from here too, and reaching the farms and tea estates to the north is quicker. A more challenging alternative to the local trails is to hike to the summit of **Gunung Brinchang** (2032m), the highest peak in Malaysia accessible by road. This takes two to three hours from Brinchang and although the road is sealed, it's an extremely steep and exhausting climb. On a clear day though, the views back down the broad valley are wonderful. You can also walk to the **Sam Poh Temple**, 1km southeast of Brinchang, a gaudy modern place with a monastery which was built in 1965.

Buses leave Tanah Rata for Brinchang and Kampung Raja, the furthest point north, every hour or so between 6.40am and 6pm. A taxi from Tanah Rata to Brinchang costs around $2.50. You can also head direct to the Sungei Palas Tea Estate (see below) from Brinchang's own **bus station** just south of the square, at 9.30am, 11.45am and 1.45pm. If you take the 1.45pm bus, you'll have to make your own way back to the main road (a 20-min walk) to pick up the more regular Brinchang-bound bus from Kampung Raja, since the last Palas bus returns at 2.20pm.

Sungai Palas Tea Estate

The **Sungai Palas Tea Estate** (Tues–Sun 8.30am–3pm, tours roughly every 10min; free) is set high in the hills and doesn't attract crowds of people. Despite the romantic imagery used on the packaging, handpicking – though the best method for producing highest quality tea – is now far too labour intensive to be economical. Instead, the Tamil, Bangladeshi and Malay workers who live on the estates pick the small, green leaves with shears. Once in the factory, the full baskets are emptied into large wire vats where the leaves are withered by alternate blasts of hot and cold air for sixteen to eighteen hours; this removes around fifty percent of their moisture. They are then sifted of dust and impurities and rolled by ancient, bulky machines. This breaks up the leaves and releases the moisture for the all-important process of **fermentation**, when they begin to emit their distinctive, pungent smell. After ninety minutes of grinding in another machine, the soggy mass is fired at 90°C in what is effectively a spin-dryer, to halt the fermentation process, and the tea turns black. After being sorted into grades, the tea matures for three to six months before being packaged and transported to market.

How much you glean of this process from your guide is dependent on your hearing, as parts of the factory are so deafening that all sound save the roar of the dryers is obliterated. Some areas of the building are also made extremely dusty by the tea impurities, so take a handkerchief to cover your mouth and nose. There's a **pleasant café and garden** where you can enjoy a drink of tea before or after the tour.

The farms and other attractions

All over the Cameron Highlands – but especially north of Brinchang – you'll pass small sheds or greenhouses by the roadside, selling cabbages, leeks, cauliflower, mushrooms and strawberries. These come from various fruit and vegetable **farms** where you should find someone willing to show you the cultivation process. Narrow plots are cut out of the sheer hillsides to increase the surface area for planting, forming giant steps all the way up the slopes. However, such ingenious terrace farming poses a problem for the transportation of the harvested crop, since the paths between the terraces are only wide enough for one nimble-footed person. This has been solved by the introduction of a **cable system**, initially operated by brute force but now powered by diesel engine, which hoists the large baskets of vegetables from the terraces to trucks waiting by the roadside high above, from where they are taken to market – over forty percent of the produce is for export to Singapore, Brunei and Hong Kong.

A couple of more specific targets might entice you out into the countryside north of Brinchang. You could easily pass on the **Butterfly Farm** (daily 8am–6pm; $3), 5km to the north at Kea Farm, where butterflies fly amongst the flowers and ponds; the Kampung Raja bus from Brinchang passes outside. Better is the **Robertson Rose Garden** (daily 10am–4pm; free), 2km to the northwest of Brinchang on the way to the Sungai Palas Tea Estate; a visit is rewarded by superb views of the sculpted sweep of the surrounding hills. Rose bushes aside, the shop here sells honey and cordials, as well as attractive dried flower arrangements. Flower lovers are also well served by **Rose Valley** (daily 8am–6pm; $3) on the way to Tringkap, which has over 450 varieties of roses on display, as well as many other blooms, most displayed in covered terraces. The **Rose Centre** at Kea Farm (daily 8am–6pm; $3) is similar, but spread over a larger area with a spectacular view of the surrounding valleys from its summit, crowned in surreal fashion by a colourful Mother Hubbard-like boot. The sculptures here were created by Burmese craftsmen and do a lot to liven up a potentially dull attraction.

Accommodation

Most of the hotels in Brinchang line the east and west sides of the central square, and although the numbering system leaves much to be desired, you shouldn't have too much difficulty locating them.

Brinchang, 36 Main Rd (☎05/491 1755, fax 491 1246). Good-sized rooms with colour TV and phone. ③.

East Garden, (☎05/491 3280, fax 491 2262). On the northwest corner of the square, rooms are clean with well-equipped bathrooms, but overpriced for what you get. ③.

Equatorial Resort, Kea Farm, (☎05/496 1777, fax 496 1333). The Cameron Highland's newest luxury resort, about 2km north of Brinchang, near the Rose Centre. The hotel's towers are perched precariously on the edge of the mountain; planned facilities include a cineplex and bowling alley. ⑧.

Kowloon, 34–35 Main Rd (☎05/491 1366, fax 491 1803). Small, comfortable rooms; quads are good value. ③.

Parkland, 45 Main Rd (☎05/491 1299, fax 491 1803). Run by the same management as the *Kowloon*. Thirty plush rooms with great views over town. ④.

Pines and Roses (☎05/491 2203). Friendly, clean and simple accommodation set back from the main road. All rooms have TV and attached bathrooms. ③.

Rafflesia Inn, Lot 30 Main Rd (☎05/491 2859, fax 491 2859). This new backpacker operation is the only real budget accommodation in town. Has a comfy TV lounge, but the dorm beds are a bit hard. ①.

Rosa Passadena, 1 Bandar Baru Brinchang (☎05/491 2288, fax 491 2688). Large modern hotel. Rooms have all the usual features but are not really worth the price. ⑥.

Sentosa, 38 Main Rd (☎05/491 1907). This friendly hotel is basic but clean. Some rooms have attached bathrooms. ①.

Silverstar, 10 Main Rd (☎05/491 1387). Fifteen basic, fair-sized rooms with *mandi*. Rates are subject to negotiation and sometimes drop as low as $10 per person in a shared room. ②.

Eating and drinking

As well as the Malay **food stalls** in the central square, the following cafés and restaurants are worth a try.

Hong Kong, Main Rd, west side of square. Looks more upmarket than it actually is and serves the usual Chinese dishes and steamboats.

Kowloon, 34–35 Main Rd. Smart, efficient restaurant with prices to match. The dishes from the very large Chinese menu are worth the extra cost.

Parkland, 45 Main Rd. Part of the hotel, this pleasant, airy restaurant has good views over town but is fairly pricey for the bland, international cuisine it serves.

Restoran Sakaya, Main Rd. Near the *Hong Kong*, this is one of three good budget Chinese eating houses (along with *You ho* and *Kuan Kee*), with buffet lunches on offer from $3 for three dishes, including rice.

Ipoh and around

Eighty kilometres north of Tapah in the Kinta Valley is **IPOH**, the state capital of Perak and third biggest city in Malaysia. It grew rich on the tin trade, which transformed it within forty years from a tiny kampung in a landscape dominated by dramatic limestone outcrops to a sprawling boomtown. Now a metropolis of over half a million people, Ipoh – whose name comes from the *upas* tree which thrived in the area and whose sap was used by the Orang Asli for arrow-head poison – is a far cry from the original village on this site. Perak had been renowned for its rich tin deposits since the sixteenth century, which made it vulnerable to attempts from rival chiefs to seize the throne and thus gain control of the lucrative tin trade. However, it wasn't until the discovery of a major field in 1880 that Ipoh's fortunes turned; before long it became a prime destination for pioneers, merchants and fortune-seekers from all over the world, and a cosmopolitan city, something reflected in the broad mix of cultures today. To accommodate the rapidly increasing population, the city expanded across Sungei Kinta between 1905 and 1914 into a "new town" area, its economic good fortune reflected in a multitude of **colonial buildings** and Chinese **mansions**. Despite the later decline in demand for tin, when Malaysia turned to oil to resurrect its hopes of prosperity, the export of tin is the fifth largest earner of foreign currency in the country, and Ipoh is still a major player in Malaysia's meteoric rise to the top of the Southeast Asian economic league table.

Yet despite its historical significance and present-day administrative importance, Ipoh is a disappointment to many visitors – the colonial parts of Georgetown, for example, are far more interesting. In fact, the main reason people stop is to visit the outlying attractions – the Chinese cave temples of **Sam Poh Tong** and **Perak Tong**, the anachronistic ruin of **Kellie's Castle** and the unique development at the **Tambun Hot Springs** – though to do these justice you're likely to have to spend at least one night in the city.

The City

The layout of central Ipoh is reasonably straightforward since the roads form, more or less, a grid system. What *is* confusing is that some of the old colonial **street names** have been changed in favour of something more Islamic, though the street signs

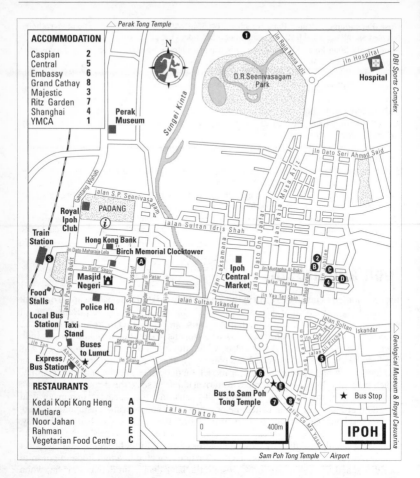

△ *Perak Tong Temple*

ACCOMMODATION

Caspian	2
Central	5
Embassy	6
Grand Cathay	8
Majestic	3
Ritz Garden	7
Shanghai	4
YMCA	1

RESTAURANTS

Kedai Kopi Kong Heng	A
Mutiara	D
Noor Jahan	B
Rahman	E
Vegetarian Food Centre	C

D.R.Seenivasagam Park

Hospital

Perak Museum

PADANG

Royal Ipoh Club

Hong Kong Bank

Train Station

Birch Memorial Clocktower

Masjid Negeri

Ipoh Central Market

Food Stalls

Police HQ

Local Bus Station

Taxi Stand

Buses to Lumut

Express Bus Station

Bus to Sam Poh Tong Temple

★ Bus Stop

0   400m

IPOH

Sam Poh Tong Temple ▽ *Airport*

haven't always caught up; hence, Jalan C.M. Yusuf instead of Jalan Chamberlain, Jalan Mustapha Al-Bakri for Jalan Clare and Jalan Bandar Timar for Jalan Leech, although in practice, people will know either name. The muddy and lethargic **Sungei Kinta** cuts the centre of Ipoh neatly in two; most of the hotels (see below) are situated east of the river, whilst the **old town** is on the opposite side between the two major thoroughfares, Jalan Sultan Idris Shah and Jalan Sultan Iskander.

Although most of what might attract you to Ipoh is located on its outskirts, there are a few diversions here that are worth at least a cursory glance. The most prominent reminder of Ipoh's economic heyday, the **train station** was built in 1917 at the height of the tin boom, a typical example of the British conception of "East meets West", with its Moorish turrets and domes and a verandah that runs the entire two-hundred-metre length of the building. Like other colonial train stations, in KL and Hong Kong, it sported a plush hotel (see p.150) in which the planters, traders and administrators sank cocktails.

The modernist **Masjid Negeri** on Jalan Sultan Iskander is one of the more conspicuous landmarks in the centre of town, all tacky Sixties' cladding, with a minaret that rises over

40m above its mosaic-tiled domes – evidence that despite the maelstrom of immigrants to the city, Ipoh has retained a buoyant Islamic population. Directly opposite the mosque, on the parallel Jalan Dato' Sagor, stands the **Birch Memorial Clocktower**, a square white tower incorporating a portrait bust of J.W.W. Birch, the first British Resident of Perak, who was murdered in 1874. When Birch was installed as Resident, his abrupt manner and lack of understanding of Malay customs quickly offended Sultan Abdullah, who resented Birch's attempts to control rather than advise – a crucial distinction laid out in the Pangkor Treaty (see p.152) earlier that year. Birch's manner proved to be an insult to the sensibilities of the Perak royalty for which he paid with his life – on November 2 he was shot while bathing in the river at Kuala Kangsar, on a trip to post notices of his own reforms.

Walk around any of the streets north of the clocktower and you'll encounter many other buildings which show the influence of colonial and Straits Chinese architecture, the most impressive of which is the white stucco **Hong Kong Bank** on Jalan Dato' Maharaja Lela, with its Corinthian columns and unusual pillared tower. Turning right from the bank into Jalan Sultan Yusuf, you're on the outskirts of **Chinatown**, of equal architectural note, although many of the pastel-coloured nineteenth-century shophouses along the streets to the east are looking rather tatty nowadays.

The **Perak Museum** (daily 9am–5pm; free) is housed in an elegant, former tin miner's mansion and is only a short walk north from the station. Covering two floors, the museum has evocative photos of Ipoh's glory days during the tin boom, but otherwise the displays lack imagination.

Ipoh's **Geological Museum** (Mon–Thurs 8am–4.15pm, Fri 8am–12.15pm, Sat 8am–12.45pm; free) on Jalan Sultan Azlan Shah on the far eastern outskirts of the city ($5 by taxi), does its best to make tin appear interesting, but other than granting a perfunctory insight into what made the city rich, the only achievement here is comprehensiveness – over six hundred samples of minerals and an array of fossils and precious stones are displayed, which is about as fascinating as it sounds.

Practicalities

All the transport facilities are located in roughly the same area. The **train station** is on Jalan Panglima Bukit Gantang Wahab (or just Jalan Panglima), west of the old town, with the **GPO** practically next door. Just south of the train station, at the junction of Jalan Tun Abdul Razak and Jalan Panglima is the **local bus station**. Opposite you'll find the **taxi stand**; **express buses** operate from behind a bank of ticket booths across the road. Buses to **Lumut** (the departure point for Pulau Pangkor; see p.152) leave from a separate forecourt, beside a row of shops, a little further along Jalan Tun Abdul Razak. You might conceivably fly into Ipoh – the Sultan Azlan Shah **airport** is 5km from the city (☎05/312 2459 for information).

There are two **tourist offices**. The best is in the State Economic Planning Unit close to the train station on Jalan Tun Sambanthan (Mon–Thurs 8am–12.45pm & 2–4.15pm, Fri 8am–12.15pm & 2.45–4.15pm, Sat 8am–12.45pm; ☎05/241 2958) and can also provide information on all of Perak State. The local Tourist Association office is at the rather inconveniently sited *Royal Casuarina* hotel, 18 Jalan Gopeng, at the eastern end of town (same hours as above; ☎05/255 5555 ext 8123). The main **banks** are on Jalan Sultan Idris Shah and Jalan Yang Kalsom. For **car rental**, contact Avis (☎05/313 6586) or Budget (☎05/313 4558), both with offices at the airport.

Accommodation

Most of the **places to stay** in Ipoh are found east of the river, around Jalan C.M. Yusuf and Jalan Mustapha Al-Bakri; the latter has a more seedy feel, though it's generally much quieter. The best-known place in town is the elegant *Majestic* on the third floor of the train station.

Caspian, 6–10 Jalan Jubilee (☎05/254 3224). Good rooms with air-con and hot water. ③.

Central, 20–26 Jalan Ali Pitchay (☎05/255 0142). All the rooms come with TV and balcony – excellent for the price. ③.

Embassy, Jalan C.M. Yusuf (☎05/254 9496). This is better than most; all rooms have attached bathrooms. ②.

Grand Cathay, 88–94 Jalan C.M. Yusuf (☎05/241 9685). The best option at the lower end of the scale, this is a typical Chinese hotel with a very knowledgeable manager. ②.

Majestic, (☎05/255 5605, fax 255 3393) third floor of the train station, off Jalan Panglima. The recent renovation recaptures the fine colonial style which made this place so sought-after in its prime, but the cheaper rooms are pretty much standard. ⑥.

Ritz Garden, C.M. Yusuf (☎05/254 7777, fax 254 5222). This has large rooms, and the price includes breakfast. ⑥.

Shanghai, 85 Jalan Mustapha Al-Bakri (☎05/241 2070). Standard Chinese hotel which is pleasant enough for the money. ②.

YMCA, 211 Jalan Raja Musa Aziz (☎05/254 0809). Too far out of the centre to be useful, although the bargain $8 dorm beds may be a draw for some. ③.

Eating and drinking

Many of Ipoh's **restaurants** close in the evenings, so you may have to resort to the **hawker stalls** near the train station or those at the top of Jalan C.M. Yusuf. At lunchtime, however, the choice is much more extensive. Regional specialities available at most Chinese restaurants in Ipoh include *kuey teow* (a chicken-based dish in soup or fried form) and *sar hor fun*, flat rice noodles served in a chicken stock soup, to which prawns, fried shallots and beansprouts are added.

On Jalan Mustapha Al-Bakri are the very clean *Mutiara* and the *Vegetarian Food Centre*, a rare treat in meat-orientated Malaysia, while Jalan C.M. Yusuf has the *Grand Cathay* restaurant which is very popular with Chinese locals, and the *Rahman*, an extremely friendly Indian restaurant. Around Jalan Bandar Timar in the old town are several Chinese restaurants, the oldest and best known of which is the *Kedai Kopi Kong Heng* (lunchtime only) where you wander round the bustling stalls and pick your dish; someone else will then offer you drinks at your table. There are also several **bakeries** in town serving lovely fresh bread and pastries; try the *Noor Jahan* on Jalan Raja Ekram.

Around Ipoh

Much of Ipoh's striking surroundings have been marred by unsightly manufacturing industries. Nevertheless, it's not long before you escape the industrialization and find yourself in the heart of extensive rubber plantations, typical of so much of this part of the country. To the north and south of Ipoh are craggy limestone peaks; those nearest to the city are riddled with caves where Ipoh's immigrant workers established Buddhist temples, now popular pilgrimage centres, particularly during the Chinese New Year celebrations.

The Perak Tong and Sam Poh Tong temples

The **Perak Tong Temple** (daily 8am–6pm; free), situated 6km north of Ipoh, is the more impressive of the two Chinese cave temples just outside the city, housed in dramatic surroundings and doubling as a centre for Chinese art. Take bus #141 (to Kuala Kangsar) from the local bus station; it's a twenty-minute ride. The gaudiness of the temple's exterior – bright red and yellow pavilions flanked by feathery willows and lotus ponds – gives you no hint of the eerie atmosphere inside, where darkened cavern upon cavern honeycombs up into the rock formation. The huge first chamber is dominated by a fifteen-metre-high golden statue of the Buddha, plump and smiling, while two startled-looking companions on either side dance and play instruments. A massive bell, believed to be more than a century old, fills the chamber with booming echoes from time to time, rung by visiting devotees to draw attention to the donation they've just offered. Walking past the bell into the next chamber, as your eyes become more accustomed to the gloom you'll notice the decorated walls, covered with complex calligraphy and delicate flower paintings. Towards the back of this musty hollow, a steep flight of 385 crudely fashioned steps climbs up and out of the cave to a sort of balcony, with excellent views over the valley, studded with great limestone outcrops and ugly factory buildings.

The **Sam Poh Tong Temple** (daily 8am–4.30pm; free) just south of the city is also a popular place of pilgrimage for Chinese Buddhists. Built into a rock face, the huge limestone caverns open towards the rear to give more impressive views over the surrounding suburbs and hills. Unfortunately, the upkeep of the temple leaves a lot to be desired; the place is covered with litter and graffiti. There's an expensive bar nearby and a good Chinese vegetarian restaurant. A visit to the temple makes an easy half-morning's trip: catch the green "Kinta" bus #66 or #73 (to Kangar) from the local bus station, or from the roundabout near the *Embassy* hotel; it's a ten-minute journey.

Kellie's Castle

If you only have time for one trip from Ipoh then make it **Kellie's Castle**, a mansion situated in a four square kilometres of the Kinta Kelas Rubber Estate, 12km south of Ipoh. It stands as a symbol of the prosperity achieved by many an enterprising foreigner who saw the potential of the rubber market in the early 1900s. The mansion, with its weighty rectangular tower and apricot-coloured bricks, was to have been the second home of William Kellie Smith, a Scottish entrepreneur, who settled here in order to make his fortune. Designed with splendour in mind, there were even plans for a lift to be installed, the first in Malaysia. However, during the mansion's construction in the 1920s, an epidemic of Spanish influenza broke out, killing many of the Tamil workers. In an act of appeasement, Smith had a Hindu temple built near the house and here, among the deities represented on its roof, you can see a figure dressed in a white suit and pith helmet, presumably Smith himself. While work resumed on the "castle", Smith left on a trip to England in 1925 and never returned; he fell ill and died in Portugal. The crumbling, warren-like remains, set in lush, hilly countryside are now covered in graffiti dating back to 1941 which records the passage of tourists down the years.

Getting to the castle from Ipoh is best done by taxi (about $5); by bus it requires some determination. You need to take bus #36 or #37 from the local bus station for the thirty-minute journey to Batu Gajah (departures every 1hr 20min or so), and either walk the remaining 4km on the A8 road (clearly marked) or catch bus #67 which passes the castle fairly frequently. It's easiest to take a taxi from Batu Gajah – around $4.

Tambun Hot Springs

At the **Tambun Hot Springs** (Tues–Sun 4–9pm; $11), 8km northeast of Ipoh, you can indulge in hot, mineral-rich soaks in the two thermal swimming pools, one cooler than the other, which are fed naturally by hot springs – no mean feat of engineering, as the enthusiastic owner will probably tell you. All around you, steaming slimy water breaks through the surface of the earth. For a further $5.50 you can crawl into the corner of a nearby limestone cave for a natural sauna (not for the claustrophobic), or amuse yourself with a game of snooker or ten-pin bowling using the four-lane alley ingeniously built into the principal cave. Another of the surrounding caves was once inhabited by Japanese monks and later by Japanese soldiers hiding out during World War II who left painted characters on some of the cave walls. There are rather expensive **hotel rooms** (☎05/545 4407; ⑤) round the pools, whose bathrooms are – of course – fed by the natural hot water supply.

To reach the hot springs, take the "Rambutan" bus from Ipoh's local bus station for about thirty minutes until you see the signpost for "Resort Air Panas", off to the right of the main road; the springs are a further kilometre down a dirt track.

Pulau Pangkor

PULAU PANGKOR is one of the west coast's more appealing islands, with some of the best beaches to be found on this side of the Malay Peninsula. It's also one of the most accessible, lying just a thirty-minute ferry ride from the port of Lumut (85km southwest of Ipoh), a short hop which has turned Pangkor into an increasingly popular weekend resort. This is naturally affecting the levels of both development and prices on the island. There's an airport (currently closed for repairs and expected to be open again in November in 1998) and three international-standard hotels, while the adjacent island of Pangkor Laut, just off the southwest coast of Pulau Pangkor, is privately owned and home to one of Malaysia's most exclusive resorts. These facilities are disproportionate to Pangkor's small size and at odds with its quiet, almost genteel, atmosphere. The inhabitants still live largely by fishing and boat-building rather than tourism – although development around Teluk Nipah looks set to tip the balance. Most of the thriving local villages lie in a string along the east coast, while tourist accommodation and the best beaches are on the west side of the island. The interior is mountainous and dense with jungle, inaccessible but for a few tiny trails and one main road that connects the two coasts, but there's plenty to occupy you around the rim, from superb stretches of sand to historical sites including a seventeenth-century Dutch fort and several temples.

The island played an important part in the development of modern Malaysia, witnessing the signing of the ground-breaking **Pangkor Treaty** of January 20, 1874. Until this time, British involvement in Malay affairs had been unofficial, but late in 1873, Raja Abdullah of Perak (in which state Pangkor lies) invited the new Governor of the Straits Settlements, Andrew Clarke, to appoint a Resident (colonial officer) to Perak, in exchange for Abdullah being recognized as the Sultan of Perak instead of his rival, the intractable Sultan Ismail. This held some appeal for the British – eager to foster stability and facilitate economic progress in the region – and the Pangkor Treaty was signed by Clarke and Abdullah, who agreed to accept the advice of the Resident "on all questions other than those touching Malay religion and custom". It is doubtful that the Malays had any idea of the long-term consequences of the treaty. The original version indicated that the decision-making process would be collective, much like the Malays' own courts; more significantly, the political and religious distinction was from the start a nonsensical concept to the Malays, for whom all action was dictated by the laws of Islam. Sultan Abdullah, bent on acquiring local power and status, therefore inadvertently provided a foot in the door for the British which eventually led to their full political intervention in the Peninsula.

Getting there: Lumut

The airport is currently closed for repairs – enquire with Tourism Malaysia as to the state of play. Most people still cross to Pulau Pangkor by ferry from the quiet coastal town of **LUMUT**. Once a relatively obscure fishing village, it has since become the main base of the Royal Malaysian Navy, whose towering apartment buildings dominate the coastline from the sea. In an attempt to cash in on the success of Pulau Pangkor, Lumut too has seen its own spate of development, but this is still low-key. The town manages to retain its charm, with multicoloured fishing boats bobbing in the tiny marina, and stores specializing in the shell and coral handicrafts for which Lumut is famed locally. However, all this is a mere diversion from your main purpose, which is to jump straight onto one of the numerous ferries to Pulau Pangkor.

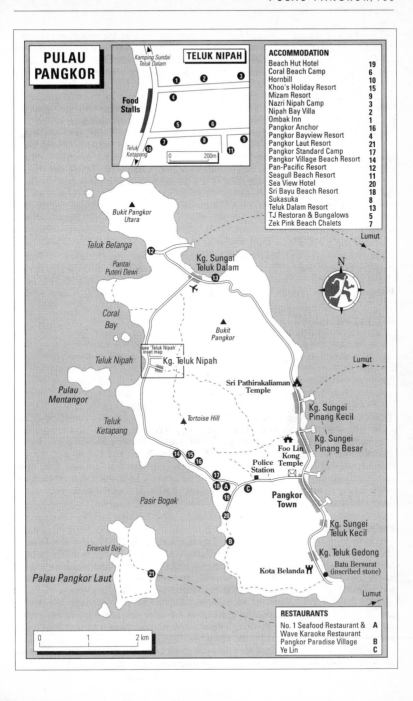

PULAU PANGKOR

Kamping Sundai
Teluk Dalam

TELUK NIPAH

Food
Stalls

① ② ③
④
⑤ ⑥
⑦ ⑧ ⑨
Teluk ⑩
Ketapang ⑪

0   200m

ACCOMMODATION

Beach Hut Hotel	19
Coral Beach Camp	6
Hornbill	10
Khoo's Holiday Resort	15
Mizam Resort	9
Nazri Nipah Camp	3
Nipah Bay Villa	2
Ombak Inn	1
Pangkor Anchor	16
Pangkor Bayview Resort	4
Pangkor Laut Resort	21
Pangkor Standard Camp	17
Pangkor Village Beach Resort	14
Pan-Pacific Resort	12
Seagull Beach Resort	11
Sea View Hotel	20
Sri Bayu Beach Resort	18
Sukasuka	8
Teluk Dalam Resort	13
TJ Restoran & Bungalows	5
Zek Pink Beach Chalets	7

Lumut

▲ Bukit Pangkor
Utara

Teluk Belanga

⑫

Kg. Sungai
Teluk Dalam

⑬

Pantai
Puteri Dewi

Coral
Bay

▲ Bukit
Pangkor

see 'Teluk Nipah'
inset map

Teluk Nipah   Kg. Teluk Nipah

Pulau
Mentangor

Teluk
Ketapang

▲ Tortoise Hill

Sri Pathirakaliaman
Temple

Kg. Sungei
Pinang Kecil

Kg. Sungei
Pinang Besar

⑭ ⑮
⑯
⑰
⑱ Ⓐ
Ⓒ
⑲

Foo Lin
Kong
Temple

Police
Station

Pasir Bogak

⑳

Ⓑ

**Pangkor
Town**

Kg. Sungei
Teluk Kecil

Emerald Bay

Kg. Teluk Gedong

Batu Bersurat
(inscribed stone)

㉑

Kota Belanda

Palau Pangkor Laut

Lumut

0   1   2 km

N

RESTAURANTS

No. 1 Seafood Restaurant &	Ⓐ
Wave Karaoke Restaurant	
Pangkor Paradise Village	Ⓑ
Ye Lin	Ⓒ

Lumut's **bus station** is behind the public gardens opposite the jetty; there are services from Ipoh roughly every hour, which take ninety minutes. If you're coming from the Cameron Highlands or from the south, there's a twice-daily direct bus from Tapah ($9), but it originates in Kuala Lumpur and is often full. There's a branch of Maybank in Pangkor Town on Pulau Pangkor but it can be difficult to change travellers' cheques, so it's best to **change money** first at one of the several moneychangers in Lumut. In front of the bus station is the Tourism Malaysia office (Mon–Sat 9am–5pm; ☎ & fax 05/683 4057) and several offices representing the larger resorts on Pangkor.

You'd have to be very unlucky to need to **spend the night** in Lumut, but late arrivals could try either the *Phin Lum Hooi*, 93 Jalan Panjang (☎05/683 5641; ①), the cheapest place in town, or the *Indah*, 208 Jalan Iskander Shah (☎05/683 5064; ③), which makes reductions for single travellers; they're both very close to the jetty. There's also a small *Government Rest House* (☎05/683 6687; ③) on the seafront, east of the jetty. There isn't much choice when it comes to **eating** – the *Phin Lum Hooi* has a decent restaurant, or there are some hawkers' stalls in the bus station.

FERRIES

The **express ferries to Pulau Pangkor** run approximately every twenty minutes (daily 6.45am–7.30pm; $1.50 each way), calling at Kampung Sungei Pinang Kecil before reaching the main jetty at Pangkor Town. Seven boats a day also run to the *Pan Pacific Resort* at the north end of the island (Pan Silver ☎05/683 5541; $8 return). Ferries to **Pangkor Laut** are arranged by the private resort and are not available to day visitors.

Around the island

Pulau Pangkor has a sealed **road** of varying quality all the way around its circumference. Owing to the mountainous interior this only crosses the island at one point, from Pangkor Town where the ferry docks, to the tourist developments at Pasir Bogak on the west coast, 2km away. **Renting** a motorbike or pushbike in Pangkor Town or from a hotel or guesthouse on the west coast costs around $30 and $10 respectively per day; the *Pangkor Standard Camp* has a good selection. As Pulau Pangkor is only 3km by 9km, a trip **around the island** is easily accomplished in a day. You could see all the sights by motorbike in about five hours, stopping en route for lunch – add another few hours if you're travelling by pushbike. Otherwise the only other means of transport are the **minibus taxis** ($4 to Pasir Bogak, $10 to Teluk Nipah and $24–30 for a round-island trip), and the **local buses**, which run hourly between 8am and 6pm from Pangkor Town to Pasir Bogak. It might only be a couple of kilometres from Pangkor Town across to the west coast, but don't think of walking it in the heat of the day – there's no shade.

Pangkor Town

The ferry from Lumut drops you at the jetty in **PANGKOR TOWN**, the island's principal settlement, whose few dusty streets feature *kedai kopis* graced with Nonya marble-topped tables and antique clocks. The best part of the town by far is the lively port, where the early-morning catch is packed into boxes of crushed ice to be despatched to the mainland. The island is particularly renowned for *ikan bilis* (anchovies).

Other than to stretch your legs once you've got off the ferry, there's very little reason to stop long; buses and taxis to the beaches on the other side of the island leave from the jetty. There are, though, a couple of reasonably attractive **places to stay**: the *Chuan Full*, 60 Main Rd (☎05/685 1123; ①), with a rear balcony overlooking the water has lots of character; nearer the jetty, *Hotel Min Lian* at no. 1a (☎05/685 1294; ②) is basic for the price. There are a number of Chinese **restaurants** which cater to the locals.

South to Teluk Gedong

Following the coastal road south out of town, after 1.5km you'll come to pretty **KAM-PUNG TELUK GEDONG**, a gathering of traditional wooden stilted houses named after the bay in which they are cradled. Here, set back from the road on the right, is the **Kota Belanda**, or Dutch Fort, originally built in 1670 to store tin supplies from Perak and keep a check on piracy in the Straits, but destroyed in 1690 by the Malays, discontent with Dutch rule. The fort was rebuilt in 1743 but only remained in use for a further five years, when the Dutch finally withdrew after several further attacks. The abandoned site was left to decay, and the disappointing half-built structure that you see today is, unbelievably, a recent reconstruction.

A few metres further along the road on the left lies the **Batu Bersurat**, a huge boulder under a canopy. The year 1743 is inscribed beside a drawing which, if you use your imagination, depicts a tiger mauling a child – a grisly memorial to a Dutch child who disappeared while playing near the rock. A more plausible account of the incident is that the infant was kidnapped by the Malays, in retribution for the continuing Dutch presence.

Pasir Bogak

A two-kilometre road connects the east and west coasts of Pulau Pangkor, terminating in the holiday village of **PASIR BOGAK**, the biggest and most upmarket development on the island. If you've come to Pangkor for the beaches – and most people do – then you'll be disappointed by what's on offer here. A narrow strip of grubby sand, the beach is virtually nonexistent when the tide is high, a fact that seems to have escaped the notice of the chalet owners, who continue to renovate and upgrade their accommodation to cater for the weekend trade. If you plan to stay, it's worth shopping around because some places are grossly overpriced, and rates can rocket everywhere at weekends.

ACCOMMODATION

Only a few of the **chalets** front the beach itself; most line the road that continues north along the west coast, but even so, they're all reasonably close to the sea. All the hotels here have **restaurants** attached, with the exception of *Pangkor Standard Camp*, which does, however, have the basic *Pangkor Restaurant* right behind it. By far the best value is *Ye Lin*, slightly away from the principal cluster, on the cross-island road, which offers huge plates of excellent Chinese food, while the finest view belongs to the *Pangkor Paradise Village* up a dirt track to the south of the main strip, whose beachfront restaurant – on stilts over the water – is great for a beer at sunset. Otherwise, the food here (like the accommodation) is overpriced. Back in the thick of things, the *No. 1 Seafood Restaurant* and adjacent *Wave Karaoke Restaurant* (only open in the evenings) both serve large dishes of Chinese food for $6–7.

Beach Hut, Pasir Bogak (☎ & fax 05/685 1159). At the southern end of Pasir Bogak, this has clean but uninspiring rooms. ③.

Khoo's Holiday Resort, Pasir Bogak (☎05/685 1164). A long-running, increasingly upmarket place with comfortable mosquito-proof chalets, hot water, fantastic views and an indoor badminton court. ⑤.

Pangkor Anchor, Pasir Bogak (☎05/685 1363). A run-down establishment with A-frame huts. ②.

Pangkor Standard Camp, Pasir Bogak (☎05/685 1878). About the cheapest place at Pasir Bogak, with A-frame huts. ②.

Pangkor Village Beach Resort, Pasir Bogak (☎ & fax 05/685 2227). Has a wide choice of accommodation, including budget tents ($12.50), huts ($33) and expensive chalets.

Sea View, Pasir Bogak (☎05/685 1605, fax 685 1970). Up a significant notch in price and comfort, with a good beachside location. ⑥.

Sri Bayu Beach Resort, Pasir Bogak (☎05/685 1929, fax 685 1050). Come here if money is no object; the beautiful complex in extensive grounds is popular with KL's in-crowd. ⑥.

Teluk Ketapang and Teluk Nipah

Much better beaches than those at Pasir Bogak are to be found about 2km further north at **TELUK KETAPANG**, a bay which has been known to harbour the increasingly rare giant leatherback turtle (Teluk Ketapang means "Turtle Bay") which swims thousands of miles to lay its eggs on Malaysia's beaches. Although the turtles normally favour the Peninsula's eastern coast (see p.270), you might be lucky with a few sightings here between May and September. Otherwise, take the opportunity to stretch out on white sand beaches – edged by palm trees – which are slightly less crowded than Pasir Bogak and much wider and cleaner.

Since there's no accommodation at Teluk Ketapang, you'll have to make do with either staying in Pasir Bogak or, better, continuing north a couple more kilometres to **TELUK NIPAH**, which is becoming something of a boom town, and where there are some splendid beaches. Of these, **Coral Bay** is the best – a perfect cove with crystal-clear sea and smooth white sand, backed by dense jungle climbing steeply to one of the island's three peaks, Bukit Pangkor. The bay is inaccessible by road and to reach it you have to climb over the rocks at the northern end of Teluk Nipah – watch the tide or you might have to swim back. If you haven't the energy for this, the main bay of Teluk Nipah more than suffices.

Much of the recent development on Pangkor has focused on Teluk Nipah because of its beaches. There are new places opening all the time, and although the atmosphere during the week can still be quite informal there are crowds at times, and the tranquillity is occasionally punctuated by the thud of construction. The best-value accommodation on this stretch is the friendly *TJ Restoran and Bungalows*. **Food stalls** are lined up along the beach before the next road into the kampung.

ACCOMMODATION

Coral Beach Camp (☎05/685 2711). Chalet accommodation about five minutes' walk from the coast road. ⑤.

Hornbill (☎05/685 2005, fax 685 2006). The first place reached on the coast road from Teluk Ketapang, where all the wooden-floored rooms have balconies and a view of the beach. ⑤.

Mizam Resort (☎ & fax 05/685 3359). The last stop along the road is run by friendly people, but is overpriced and a long walk from the beach. ⑤.

Nazri Nipah Camp (☎05/685 2014, fax 685 3730). At the end of the second turning as you go north on the coastal road, this well-maintained place has A-frames, more sophisticated accommodation, and a café. ①–③.

Nipah Bay Villa (☎05/685 2198, fax 685 2386). Back towards the beach on the same side as the *Nazri Nipah Camp*, this place includes all meals in its price, but is still not a great bargain. ⑥.

Ombak Inn. Run-down chalets on the second turn-off going north on the coast road. It has very cheap accommodation in basic tents. ①.

Pangkor Bayview Resort (☎05/685 3540, fax 685 1308). Near the beach and opposite the inn, these are nicely-designed, spacious chalets. ⑤.

Seagull Beach Resort (☎05/685 2878, fax 685 2857). Down a dirt road beyond *Sukasuka*, where the cheapest rooms consist of nothing more than a mattress on the floor and a fan. ②.

Sukasuka (no phone). Just along from the pink chalets, on the same side of the road, these are reasonably priced, attractive huts with *atap* roofs. ②.

TJ Restoran and Bungalows (☎05/685 3477). About 200m from the coast road on the left, this offers the best-value accommodation along this stretch. The café is a good deal too, with tables named after different countries. ②.

Zek Pink Beach Chalets (☎05/685 3529). Close to the coast road, these pink-painted chalets live up to their name; even the furniture is in rosy shades. ④.

The north coast

The road cuts inland from Teluk Nipah and crosses to the northeastern tip of the island, where it branches off left to the high-class *Pan Pacific Resort* (☎05/685 1091, fax

685 2390; ⑤), situated in secluded **TELUK BELANGA**. You can get here directly by ferry from Lumut, though unless you're staying at the resort you'll be charged $40 (collected at the entrance gate) to use the beach, for which price they include a snack. The bonus is the good sports facilities here, including a golf course, and the beach, **Pantai Puteri Dewi** ("Beach of the Beautiful Princess") – a fine stretch of crunchy white sand.

Doubling back to the junction with the main road, you'll pass the airport and come to the pleasant Teluk Dalam Resort (☎05/685 5000, fax 685 4000; ⑤). Large chalets are set around a quiet bay, with a couple of restaurants. Continue up the steep hill and craggy headland for 3km before descending into the first bay on the east coast. There's not much to see on this side of the island until you reach **KAMPUNG SUNGEI PINANG KECIL**, which is little more than a few straggling dwellings by the roadside and the first stop for the ferry from Lumut. The **Sri Pathirakaliaman** Hindu temple just before the village, overlooking the sea, is only worth a cursory glance before the more substantial **KAMPUNG SUNGEI PINANG BESAR**, less than 1km away. Here, down a small turning to the right, you'll find the **Foo Lin Kong** temple, a cross between a place of worship and a theme park. Inside the dim, rather spooky room that houses the shrine are some authentic-looking shrunken heads designed to ward off evil spirits, and a few incongruous Guinness bottles as offerings. Surrounding the temple itself is a miniature Great Wall of China spreading up the hillside, a small children's playground and a dismal zoo. Back on the main road, a few hundred metres more brings you back to Pangkor Town.

Other islands: Pulau Pangkor Laut and Pulau Sembilan

There are several small islands around Pulau Pangkor to which some of the hotels arrange fishing and snorkelling **day-trips** for around $10 a head. No accommodation is available except on **PULAU PANGKOR LAUT**, off the southwest coast, a privately owned island which is the exclusive domain of the **Pangkor Laut Resort** (☎05/699 1100, fax 699 1200; ⑤). With its sympathetically designed accommodation and top-class restaurants, this luxurious resort is well worth visiting for Emerald Bay alone, whose superb sand and waters make it one of the most beautiful beaches in Malaysia. Transport to the island is arranged by the resort from Lumut on eight daily ferries.

PULAU SEMBILAN, an archipelago of nine islands two hours south by boat from Pulau Pangkor, is the setting for an annual **fishing safari**, a competitive event held in conjunction with the lavishly celebrated Lumut Pesta Laut (in Lumut), a popular festival that takes place every August. Only one island in the clump, Pulau Lalang, has fresh water and accessible beaches, and at present there is nowhere to stay. You can charter a boat from Lumut jetty or Pasir Bogak for around $300.

Kuala Kangsar

While Ipoh is the state administrative capital of Perak, **KUALA KANGSAR** – 50km to the northwest – is its royal town, home to the Sultans of Perak since the fifteenth century, and with monuments to match. Built at a grandiose sweep of Sungei Perak, it's a neat, attractive town of green parks and flowers, which sees few tourists – another reason to make time for at least a couple of hours' stopover between Ipoh and Taiping. Nineteenth-century accounts of Kuala Kangsar rhapsodized about its situation: Ambrose B. Rathborne in his *Camping and Tramping in Malaya* (1883) wrote that it had "one of the prettiest views in the Straits . . . overlooking Sungei Perak, up whose beautiful valley an uninterrupted view is obtained". Rathborne camped and tramped through the jungle on an elephant, which was the only way to reach Kuala Kangsar in the nineteenth century.

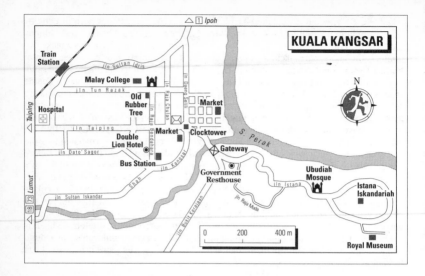

With the planting of nine **rubber plant** seedlings here at the beginning of Hugh Low's Residency (see box) in 1877, Kuala Kangsar was in at the start of colonial Malaya's most important industry (one of the original rubber trees survives in a compound next to the District Office). Despite the town's one-time importance as an administrative centre, not much has survived from that period, but a clutch of monuments on the outskirts of town provide a snapshot of Kuala Kangsar's indigenous royal and religious importance.

Heading east from the clocktower in the centre of town, follow Jalan Istana as it curves around the fast-moving river, passing through the ornamental gateway that straddles the street. After about 2km, as you begin to notice the gentle gradient of Bukit Chandan, you'll reach the **Ubudiah Mosque**, whose large gold onion domes soar skywards. Squashed out of proportion to its width, it looks like Islam's answer to Cinderella's castle. Built in 1917, its construction was interrupted several times, most dramatically when two elephants belonging to Sultan Idris rampaged all over the imported Italian marble floor. Non-Muslims should ask permission before entering.

A fifteen-minute walk up the same road brings you to the imposing white marble **Istana Iskandariah**, the sultan's ultra-modern official palace. It's closed to the public, but stroll round to the left of the huge gates and you'll get a good view down the river. An early legend associated with Sungei Perak explains why there is no crown in the sultan's regalia. A former prince was caught in a severe storm while sailing on the river. Throwing his crown overboard to calm the waves, he saved the sinking ship but not his headgear. Since that day, new Sultans have been enthroned to the sound of drumming rather than by being crowned.

Close by, off to the left as you circle the palace to rejoin the road, the **Royal Museum** (Muzium di Raja; Mon–Wed, Sat & Sun 9.30am–5pm, Thurs 9.30am–12.45pm; free) is of greater architectural significance. This former royal residence, the erstwhile Istana Kenangan, is a traditional stilted wooden structure – apparently built without the use of a single nail – with intricate friezes and geometric-patterned wall panels. Inside, the

THE RESIDENTIAL SYSTEM

The creation of the **Residential System** formed the backbone of the Pangkor Treaty of 1874 and furthered the notion of indirect British rule. The British Resident – one for each state – was to have an advisory role in Malay affairs of state in return for a sympathetic observance of their own customs and rituals. The interpretation of the newly created post was in the hands of **Hugh Low** (1824–1905), the very first Resident, whose jurisdiction of Perak (1877–1889) was based in Kuala Kangsar. The personable Low lived modestly by British standards in the Residency building (no longer extant) and, together with his two pet chimpanzees for company, kept open house during his ten-hour working day. Together with his assistant George Maxwell, Low's adroit linguistic skills won him favour with the local chiefs with whom he could soon converse fluently, and whose practices he quickly understood. Having spent nearly thirty years in Borneo, Low had become great friends with Charles and James Brooke (see p.605) and sought to replicate their benign system of government.

The approval of the Malay nobility – by no means guaranteed, as the Birch incident shows (see p.604) – was vital to the success of the Residency scheme, and was secured principally with compensation for the income they had lost from taxes and property. This suited the Sultans well, for not only did they establish financial security for themselves by virtue of their healthy stipends, they were also protected from other rivals. As time went on, lesser figures were given positions within the bureaucracy, thus weaving the Malays into the fabric of the administration, of which the cornerstone was the **State Council**. Although the Sultan was the ceremonial head, it was the Resident who chose the constituent members and who set the political agenda, in consultation with his deputies, the **District Officers**, and the Governor.

The increasing power of central government soon began to diminish the consultative side of the Resident's role, and by the 1890s fewer and fewer meetings of the council were being held. Religious matters were the only things exempt from British control, but even here the goal posts were often moved to suit British purposes. Furthermore, there were few Residents as talented and sympathetic as Hugh Low and so, predictably, the involvement of the British in Malay affairs became less to instruct their subjects in new forms of government and more to affirm British status.

museum displays a collection of royal artefacts (medals, costumes and so on), although the photographs of past and present royalty in Perak are of more interest.

Back in town, the most evocative memory of colonial days is provided by the **Malay College** on Jalan Tun Razak, its elegant columns and porticoes visible as you approach the centre from the train station. Founded in January 1905, it was conceived by British administrators as a training ground for the sons of Malay nobility, an "Eton of the East", where discipline and tradition was more English than in England – although the schoolboys were required to wear formal Malay dress. The success of many of the college's pupils in finding good jobs in the newly created Malay Administrative Service left parents clamouring for places for their offspring and started a craze for English education elsewhere in the country.

Practicalities

The **train station** is on the northwestern outskirts of town, a twenty-minute walk from the clocktower in the centre of town. Buses from Ipoh, Butterworth and Taiping pull up at the **bus station** at the bottom of Jalan Raja Bendahara, close to the river. Although you won't necessarily want to stay in Kuala Kangsar, there are a couple of choices if you do get stuck. Opposite the bus station is the *Double Lion*, at 74 Jalan Kangsar (☎05/861010; ②), while a quieter option, on the way to the Ubudiah Mosque, is the *Government Rest House* (☎05/863 872; ③), whose decor and facilities don't match its stately riverside location.

Taiping and Maxwell Hill

Set against the backdrop of the mist-laden Bintang hills, **TAIPING** – like so many places in Perak – has its origins in the discovery of tin here in the first decades of the nineteenth century. As a mining centre, overrun by enthusiastic prospectors, its early history was predictably turbulent. Originally known as Larut, the town was torn apart in 1871 by violent wars between various Chinese secret societies whose members had come to work in the mines. A truce was finally declared in 1874, after British intervention as a result of the Pangkor Treaty, and the town was somewhat hopefully renamed Taiping, meaning "everlasting peace" – which, incidentally, makes it the only sizeable town in Malaysia today with a Chinese name.

From these shaky beginnings Taiping thrived, and its expanding prosperity helped fund many firsts at a time when Kuala Lumpur was barely on the map: the first railway in the country to facilitate the export of the tin, connecting Taiping with the coastal port of Fort Weld (now Kuala Sepetang); the first English-language school in 1878; the first museum in 1883; and the first English-language newspaper (the *Perak Pioneer*) in 1894. With the establishment of the nearby hill station of **Maxwell Hill** (now Bukit Larut) as a retreat for its administrators, Taiping was firmly at the forefront of the colonial devel-

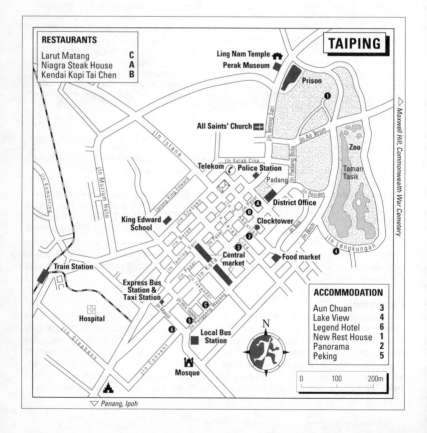

TAIPING

RESTAURANTS

Larut Matang	C
Niagra Steak House	A
Kendai Kopi Tai Chen	B

Ling Nam Temple
Perak Museum
Prison
All Saints' Church
Maxwell Hill, Commonwealth War Cemetery
Zoo
Taman Tasik
Telekom
Police Station
Padang
District Office
King Edward School
Clocktower
Central market
Food market
Train Station
Express Bus Station & Taxi Station
Hospital
Local Bus Station
Mosque
Jln Istana
Jln Muzium Hulu
Jln Kemuning
Lorong King Edward
Jln Stesyen
Jln Barrack
Jln Taming Sari
Jln Kota
Jln Pasar
Jln Masjid
Jln Panggong Wayang
Jln Convent
Jln Stephens
Jln Air Terjun
Jln Taming Sari
Jln Padang Bola
Jln Residen
Jln Iau
Jln Berek
Jln Lengkungan

ACCOMMODATION

Aun Chuan	3
Lake View	4
Legend Hotel	6
New Rest House	1
Panorama	2
Peking	5

N

0   100   200m

▽ *Penang, Ipoh*

opment of the Federated Malay States. For years, tin was its life force, mined and traded by a largely Chinese population. The miners were superstitious: the mere presence of a European close to a tin mine was disliked and resented, while Ambrose B. Rathborne, off tramping again, noted that, "No greater offence can be given to a gang of miners than by descending their mine with boots on and an umbrella opened overhead, as it is popularly supposed that such a proceeding is an insult to the presiding spirits, who, out of revenge will make the tin ore disappear." The actual reason for the eventual depletion of the tin deposits was rooted more in geological reality, but the diminished market for tin did later take its toll on the wealth of the town. Nowadays, bypassed by the north–south highway and replaced in administrative importance by Ipoh, Taiping has started to decline gracefully, its tattered two-storey shop fronts symptomatic of the run-down atmosphere that pervades the town. Although the main reason people visit is to relax at Maxwell Hill, allow yourself at least half a day to explore the sights of Taiping – the gardens, Perak Museum and fine buildings which line the wide roads. Its quiet charm will grow on you.

The Town

Taiping is easily walkable, and since the central streets are laid out on a grid system there's no problem finding your way around. The four main streets which run parallel to each other are Jalan Taming Sari, Jalan Pasar, Jalan Kota and Jalan Panggong Wayang. The gardens – Taman Tasik – spread to the northeast of town, close to the foot of Maxwell Hill, with the museum a little to the northwest.

A wander around the shop-lined streets surrounding Taiping's **central market** does little to detract from its reputation as a seedy old mining town; wizened *towkays* lurk at the rear of musty shophouses and dingy *kedai kopis*, while numerous food markets add a welcome splash of colour. On the southwestern outskirts of the town, you can visit the three **temples** representing the Hindu, Chinese and Muslim communities, before heading up Jalan Pesar to the **padang** and the sparkling white **District Office**, which marks the northern limit of the Chinese district.

North of here up Jalan Taming Sari is **All Saints' Church**, founded in 1887, making it the oldest Christian church in Malaysia. It cuts a forlorn figure these days: termites are slowly destroying the wooden structure, and there's talk of completely demolishing and rebuilding the church to "preserve" it for future generations. In some ways, the tiny churchyard is more interesting, providing a pertinent reminder of the hidden costs of building an empire. It contains the graves of the earliest British and Australian settlers, many of whom died at an unusually early age. Others, after many years of service to the Malay states, failed to gain a pension to allow them to return home.

Another hundred metres further on, the **Perak Museum** (daily 9.30am–5pm; closed noon–2.45pm Fri; free), housed in a cool and spacious colonial building, boasted as many as thirteen thousand exhibits when it opened in 1883. Often billed as the best museum in Malaysia, it's difficult to understand the accolade. Even the collection of stuffed rare snakes fails to excite much interest, although there is an extensive collection of ancient weapons and Orang Asli implements and ornaments. Opposite the museum, the **prison** was built in 1885 and was used by the Japanese during World War II – today it carries out most of the executions of Malaysia's drug offenders. To the left, the **Ling Nam Temple** is one of Taiping's main Chinese centres of worship.

Backtracking down Jalan Taming Sari takes you to the padang, from where it's a ten-minute stroll to **Taman Tasik**, the extensive lake gardens which are landscaped around two former tin-mining pools. At the height of the industry's success, large areas of countryside were being laid to waste, creating unsightly muddy heaps and stagnant pools. In Taiping, at least, the Resident kept a colonial sense of propriety and turned this area into a park in 1880. It's still immaculately kept, with a gazebo, freshwater fish in the lakes, and a profusion of flowers. There's also a nine-hole golf course and even a small zoo (daily 10am–6pm; $2).

A short walk to the northeast of the park, past the lotus pond, is the **Commonwealth War Cemetery**, a serene memorial to the casualties of World War II. Split in two by the road to Maxwell Hill, the cemetery is all-too-neatly divided, with Indians on one side and British and Australians on the other. There are the graves of 866 men, many of whom could not be identified. The cemetery also has the grave of Taiping's recipient of the Victoria Cross. Close by are the **Burmese Pools**, a series of natural rock pools that are not nearly as inviting as they sound. A much better bet for a cool dip are the more traditional **Coronation Pools** ($1), just at the base of Maxwell Hill, where the chlorine-free water comes straight from the hills.

Practicalities

The **train station**, just over a kilometre west of the centre of Taiping, is behind the hospital, on Jalan Stesyen: a fifteen-minute walk to the nearest hotel. The **express bus station** in the centre of town, is in a small square between Jalan Kota and Jalan Iskander, with the **taxi station** right next door. The **local bus station** is further down Jalan Panggong Wayang on the left, but you probably won't need to use this; there's another agency for KL/Singapore buses nearby.

Accommodation

For a town of its size, Taiping has a remarkable number of **hotels**, which is just as well because in high season it often has to cater for the overspill from Maxwell Hill. For those on a tight budget, or who prefer a bit more action, the town rather than the hill station is definitely the place to stay. One or two of the places are old-style wooden Chinese houses with shutters, full of character but rather grotty.

Aun Chuan, cnr of Jalan Halaman Pasar and Jalan Kota (☎05/807 5322). The best of the budget options, above *KFC* – it's clean and spacious with wooden floors. ③.

Lake View, 1a Circular Rd (☎05/807 4911). In the northeastern part of town, just south of Taman Tasik, this is a run-down basic hotel with a noisy karaoke bar. ②.

Legend Inn, cnr of Jalan Convent and Jalan Masjid (☎05/806 0000, fax 806 6666). The best hotel in town, comfortable with a pleasant air-conditioned café in the lobby. Handy for the express bus station. ⑥.

New Rest House, Taman Tasik (☎05/807 2044). This run-down modern building stands on the site of the former official quarters of the British Resident in Perak State. The rooms are large, and there's a restaurant which overlooks the Lake Gardens. ②.

Panorama, 61–79 Jalan Kota (☎05/808 4111, fax 808 4129). A slightly old-fashioned but pleasant, reasonably priced and centrally located hotel. ④.

Peking, Jalan Idris Taiping, close to the express bus station (☎05/807 2975). Has a traditional wooden exterior (though modern rooms); it's good value and the management is friendly. ②.

Eating and drinking

The most entertaining meals to be had in town are those at Taiping's numerous **food markets**. One of the best is *Larut Matang* on Jalan Iskander, a big bright eating hall with every kind of rice and noodle dish imaginable. *Kedai Kopi Tai Chen* on Jalan Pasar, one block west of the clocktower, has very good *popiah*, *mee goreng* and fruit juices; it also has a surprisingly explosive ice-crunching machine. For a more upmarket meal, try the *Nagaria Steak House* on Jalan Pasar, where Western meals go for around $20.

Maxwell Hill

MAXWELL HILL – 12km northeast of Taiping – is Malaysia's smallest (and oldest) hill station, named after the first Assistant Resident of Perak, George Maxwell. At approximately 1035m above sea level the climate is wonderfully cool, and on a clear day there are spectacular views of the west coast. Unfortunately its reputed status as the wettest place in Malaysia, with five metres of rain, also means that it's frequently too cloudy at the top to see much at all. Nevertheless, the air of colonial nostalgia makes Maxwell Hill well worth visiting. There are a few tame forest **walks**, but they're not marked so you'll have to use your initiative if you want to depart from the road. The climb to The Cottage – a stone bungalow built in the 1880s for British officialdom – leads through groves of evergreens and the largest variety of flowers in the country to the only accessible **summit**. Leeches can be a problem in the forest: wear long trousers, and socks and shoes not sandals.

The narrow road up to the hill station twists and turns round some terrifying bends and is only accessible by government Land Rover; private vehicles are not allowed. The service begins at the foot of the hill, ten minutes' walk from the lake gardens in Taiping (hourly 8am–6pm; $2 one-way) and takes 35 minutes to reach the top. If you're only making a day-trip, it's advisable to **book your seat** there in advance (☎05/807 7243), otherwise at busy times you could find yourself hanging around waiting for a space. Book the return journey up at the hill station itself in the booth by the *Rumah Beringin Resthouse*.

Many people prefer to **walk** up from Taiping instead, which takes from two-and-a-half to three hours. You'll need to be quite fit, but this way you get more time to take in the views and you can still make it down again by early evening; the marked path starts at the Land Rover pick-up point. About midway to the summit is the Tea Garden House, which was once part of an extensive tea estate. It's an ideal place to stop for a rest, as the view at this point is superb with the town of Taiping and the mirror-like waters of the gardens visible below.

Practicalities

The choice for **accommodation** is between resthouses and bungalows, and since there is only room for a total of 53 people you'll need to **book in advance** (☎05/807 7241 for all the places mentioned below). The **resthouses**, which are all situated along the road beyond the Land Rover drop-off point, are the cheapest choice: *Rumah Beringin* (②), *Rumah Rehat Bukit Larut*, the only place with a single room (①), or *Rumah Rehat Gunung Hijau*, which is the furthest up (①). **Bungalow** prices are for the whole building rather than for individual rooms, and you can choose from *Rumah Cendana* ($100) and *Rumah Tempinis* ($100) or the VIP-class *Rumah Anykasa* ($150) and *Sri Kayangan* ($200) – all sleep four to six people.

Food is available at each of the resthouses, while at the bungalows, the caretaker can arrange for food to be prepared for you, or you can do your own cooking – buy provisions in Taiping.

Penang

PENANG, 370km from Kuala Lumpur on Malaysia's northwestern coast, is a confusing amalgam of state and island. Everything of interest in Penang State is on Penang Island – **Pulau Pinang** (Betel Nut Island) in Malay – a large island of 285 square kilometres upon which the first British settlement on the Malay Peninsula was sited. Butterworth (see below), has ferry services across to the island. The confusion gets worse – as the island's likeable capital and Malaysia's second largest city, **Georgetown**, is also often referred to as "Penang". Georgetown is a fast-moving, go-ahead place, and has a reputation as a duty-free shopping mecca that accords with its history as a trading port. The epitome of its commercial development is the gigantic high-rise KOM-TAR building, visible even from the mainland.

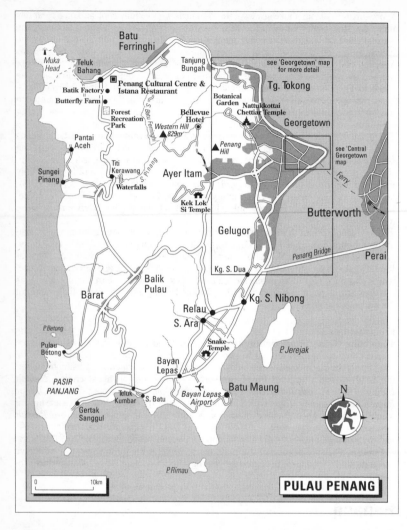

PULAU PENANG

Nonetheless, Georgetown has sacrificed few of its traditional buildings and customs to modernity. In one of Malaysia's most vibrant Chinatowns, faded two-storey shop-houses and ornate temples predominate, legacies of the massive influx of immigrants attracted here by the early establishment of a colonial port. Hot on their heels were the Indian merchants, bringing with them spices, rich cloths and religious customs, nowhere more evident in the city than during the annual festival of Thaipusam (see p.64). Georgetown also has some of the best British colonial architecture in the country in the area surrounding crumbling Fort Cornwallis, the island's oldest building. To the northwest of the centre of town, huge mansions and elegant gardens bear witness to the rewards gained by early entrepreneurs.

While the city is likely to be your base during a stay on Pulau Penang, most visitors make day-trips out, traditionally to the beaches at **Batu Ferringhi** and **Tanjung Bungah** along the north coast. No longer the hippy hang-out of the 1970s, this is now five-star resort territory, and although pollution and over-development have taken their inevitable toll, the beaches themselves aren't bad and the nightlife keeps most people happy. It's easy though, to run away with the idea that the beaches are the only reason to come to Penang, and you'll get a much more balanced picture of the island if you make the effort to spend some time away from the coast. There are enough markets, temples and historic buildings in the busy Georgetown streets to occupy at least a couple of days, and journeys to the south and west reveal a startlingly rural and mountainous interior, with a population that retains many of its traditions and industries. There are also about thirty hiking trails around the island, well described in *Nature Trails of Penang Island* published by the Malaysian Nature Society.

The island is the focus of several important **festivals** throughout the year, starting with Thaipusam in February. Perhaps the best known of the rest is the Penang Bridge Run held in May, when thousands of competitors hurtle across the bridge to Butterworth at dawn as part of a half-marathon. June is also a busy month, with the International Dragonboat Race, the Equestrian Carnival and a beach volleyball tournament on the northern coast. In July the flower festival and Grand Parade provide colour, while the Cultural Festival provides a showcase for the various ethnic groups – the Malays, Chinese and Indians – who make up Penang's population.

Some history

Until the late eighteenth century, Pulau Pinang was ruled by the **Sultans of Kedah**. For many years Kedah had been harassed by enemies, which meant that its Sultan, Mohammed J'wa Mu'Azzam Shah II, was prepared to afford trade facilities to any nation that would provide him with military protection. Enter **Francis Light** in 1771, a ship's captain of the European trading company of Jourdain, Sullivan and de Souza, who was in search of a regional trading base for both his company and the East India Company. According to contemporary accounts, Captain Light was a charming man, well trained in the art of diplomacy, and it was not long before the Sultan had housed the captain in his fort at Kuala Kedah, conferred upon him the honorary title of "Deva Raja" (God-king) and taken him into his confidence.

Light knew that the East India Company wanted to obtain a strategic port in the region to facilitate its trade with China, and as a refuge from its enemies in the Bay of Bengal. In forwarding the Sultan's offer of the island of Penang to the Company, Light drew particular attention to its safe harbour, and to the opportunities for local commerce. In 1772 the Company sent its own agent, Edward Moncton, to negotiate with the Sultan, but the talks soon broke down and it was another twelve years before agreement was reached, spurred by the accession of a new Sultan, Abdullah, and the East India Company's mounting concern that other countries were gaining a regional foothold – the French, at war with Britain, had acquired port facilities in northern Sumatra having already made a pact with Burma, and the Dutch were consolidating their position in the Straits of Melaka.

In accordance with an agreement arranged by Light, the Company was to pay Sultan Abdullah $30,000 a year. Unfortunately for the Sultan, the Company's new governor-general Charles Cornwallis firmly stated that he could not be party to the Sultan's disputes with the other Malay princes, or promise to protect him from the Burmese or Siamese. This rather pulled the rug from under Light's feet because it was on the basis of these promises that the Sultan had ceded the island of Penang in the first place. Undeterred, Light decided to conceal the facts from both parties and formally **established a port** at Penang on August 11, 1786 on his own initiative. For the next five years Light adopted stalling tactics with the Sultan, assuring him that the matter of protection was being referred to authorities in London. The Sultan eventually began to suspect that the company had reneged on the agreement, and he attempted to drive the British out of Penang by force, but the effort failed and the subsequent settlement imposed by the British allowed the Sultan an annual payment of only $6000, and no role in the future government of the island.

So it was that Penang, then inhabited by less than a hundred indigenous fishermen, became the **first British settlement** in the Malay Peninsula. Densely forested, the island was open to settlers to claim as much land as they could clear – in somewhat debonair mood, Light encouraged the razing of the jungle by firing coins from a cannon into the undergrowth. After an initial, late-eighteenth century influx, mainly of Chinese immigrants attracted by the possibilities of new commerce, Penang quickly became a major colonial administrative centre – within two years, four hundred acres were under Cultivation and the population had reached ten thousand. Francis Light was made superintendent and declared the island a free port, renaming it "Prince of Wales Island" after the British heir apparent, whose birthday fell the day after the founding of the island. Georgetown was, unsurprisingly, named after the king at that time, George III; it has retained its colonial name, even after the island reverted to the name of Penang.

For a time, all looked rosy for Penang, with Georgetown proclaimed as capital of the newly established **Straits Settlements** (incorporating Melaka and Singapore) in 1826. But the founding of Singapore in 1819 was the beginning of the end for Georgetown, and as the new colony overtook its predecessor in every respect (replacing it as capital of the Straits Settlements in 1832), Penang's fortunes rapidly began to wane. In retrospect, this had one beneficial effect, since with Georgetown stuck in the economic doldrums for a century or more, there was no significant development within the city; many of its colonial and early Chinese buildings survive to this day. Although occupied by the Japanese in 1942 during World War II and placed under the authority of a Japanese governor, the strategic significance of Singapore once more proved to be Penang's saving grace, and there was little or no bomb damage to the island.

Butterworth

Heading north from Taiping towards the coast, the landscape becomes increasingly flat and arid, as the road eases away from the backbone of mountains that dominate the western seaboard. Sitting 94km north of Taiping is the dusty, industrial town of **BUTTERWORTH**, the port for the island of Penang and the island's capital Georgetown.

The **bus station**, **port complex**, **taxi stand** and **train station** are all next door to each other, lying right on the quayside, so you shouldn't have to venture any further. Although on a branch line from the main north–south rail line, there is only one daily train that does not pass through Butterworth. This stops instead at the nearby main line station of Bukit Mertajam, a short bus or local train ride to the southeast.

Realistically, the only reason to spend any time at all in Butterworth is to sort out your **transport to Penang** – which can usually be done within half an hour of arrival. If you get stuck, there are plenty of **places to stay**, although many of the hotels are a fair way from the port. The nearer options include *G7 Lodge* (☎04/331 2662; ②), on Jalan Pantai – turn left immediately out of the bus station. Just before on Jalan Pantai is the *Beach Garden* (☎04/332 2845; ②), which is overpriced and basic. Otherwise, the *Ambassadress* (☎04/344 2788; ③) is just one of many places along Jalan Bagan Luar, the main road running out of Butterworth; facilities are better here, but it's more than walking distance from the terminals.

Georgetown

Visiting **GEORGETOWN** in 1879, stalwart Victorian traveller Isabella Bird called it "a brilliant place under a brilliant sky" and it's hard to improve on this simple statement –

Malaysia's most fascinating city retains more of its cultural history than virtually anywhere else in the country. Fort Cornwallis, St George's Church and the many buildings on and around Lebuh Pantai all survive from the earliest colonial days, and the communities of Chinatown and Little India have contributed some fine temples. Later Thai and Burmese arrivals left their mark on the city, but its predominant character is formed by the rows of peeling two-storey **Chinese shophouses** which have shutters painted in pastel colours, bright red Chinese lettering covering their colonnades, and cheerfully designed awnings to shield the goods from the glaring sun. While the confusion of rickshaws, buses, lorries and scooters make parts of Georgetown as frenetic and polluted as most other places in the region, life in the slow lane has changed very little over the years. The rituals of worship, eating out at a roadside stall, the running of the family business, have all continued with little concern for Georgetown's contemporary technological development. It may no longer be a sleepy backwater – most of the island's one-million strong population now lives here – but the city's soul is firmly rooted in the past.

Strategically sited Georgetown is no stranger to visitors, since ships from all over the world have been docking at present-day Swettenham Pier since Francis Light first established his port here in 1786. Over the years, not surprisingly, it acquired a rather

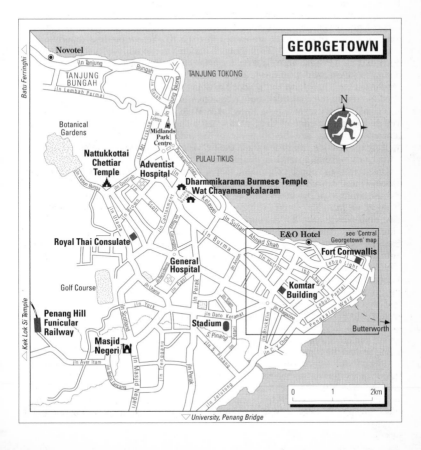

dubious reputation for backstreet dives frequented by boisterous sailors on shore leave. Where once ships' chandlers and supply merchants ran thriving businesses, modern-day maritime trade is of an entirely different nature: neon-lit bars and dingy brothels help to boost the spirits of foreign navy crews who make regular forays around the city's streets. There's been a gradual change though, especially since the late 1970s, when foreign tourists first descended upon Penang in significant numbers. Nowadays, parts of downtown Georgetown sparkle with the state-of-the-art hotels and air-con shopping malls familiar to much of modern Malaysia. But perhaps more than any other place in the country Georgetown is a magnet for budget travellers – the city is something of a hang-out, a place not only to renew Thai visas, but to relax and observe street life from a pavement café – in between trips to the beach.

Arrival, information and getting around

The most convenient approach from the mainland is on the 24-hour passenger and car **ferry service from Butterworth** (see box opposite), which takes fifteen minutes and docks at the centrally located terminal on Pengkalan Weld in Georgetown. The **Penang Bridge**, the longest in Asia at 13km, crosses from just south of Butterworth at Perai to a point on Jalan Udini, 8km south of Georgetown on the east coast; there's a one-way toll of $7 payable on the mainland – if you are coming over by **long-distance taxi** from any point on the Peninsula, check whether or not the toll is included in the fare. The **airport**, at Bayan Lepas on the southeastern tip of the island, handles some direct international flights, though most are routed through KL. Yellow bus #83 (hourly on the hour, 6am–midnight; $1.40) takes about 45 minutes to run into Georgetown, dropping you next to the Pengkalan Weld ferry terminal; otherwise a taxi costs around $19 – buy a coupon beforehand from inside the terminal building. Finally, **ferries** from Medan (Indonesia) and Langkawi (p.192) dock in Georgetown at Swettenham Pier, a few hundred metres up the dockside from Pengkalan Weld. Arriving at either the bus station, taxi stand or ferry terminals on **Pengkalan Weld** or nearby **Swettenham Pier**, puts you at the eastern edge of Georgetown, just a short walk from the hotels and major amenities. **Driving** into the city is not for the traffic-shy, though the major routes are well signposted. It's easiest to park in the KOMTAR building on Jalan Penang, which is within easy walking distance of the hotel area.

On arrival, the most convenient tourist office is the **Penang Tourist Centre** (Mon–Thurs 8.30am–1pm & 2–4.30pm, Fri 8.30am–12.30pm & 2.30–4.30pm, Sat 8.30am–1pm; ☎04/261 6663), on the ground floor of the Penang Port Commission building on Jalan Tun Syed Sheh Barakbah, which produces an excellent island and city **map** which costs $1. A couple of doors down at no. 10 is **Tourism Malaysia** (Mon–Thurs 8am–12.45pm & 2–4.15pm, Fri 8am–12.15pm & 2.45–4.15pm, Sat 8am–12.45pm; ☎04/262 0066), which is more helpful. Best of all is the **Tourist Information Centre** (daily 10am–6pm; ☎04/261 4461) on the third floor of the KOMTAR building, which is really clued up on local information and also operates half- and full-day tours of the city, from around $29. These are not a bad way to see Penang if your time is limited.

The best way of **getting around the city** is on foot. It's fairly small – you could walk from Pengkalan Weld to the top of the main street, Lebuh Chulia, in about twenty minutes – and in any case, unless you're pavement-pounding you'll miss most of the interesting and otherwise inaccessible alleyways. For longer journeys in town, and for travelling around the island, you'll need to master the excellent **bus service**. From the station next to the ferry terminal on Pengkalan Weld, blue buses service the north of the island, and yellow buses the south and west, while green buses also run from here on routes through the city out towards Ayer Itam. For buses **around the city** and its immediate environs, MPPP (red-stripe) buses run from a station on Lebuh Victoria, a block north of Pengkalan Weld. In addition, all buses stop at the station by the KOM-

---

LEAVING PENANG

Details of airline offices, travel agencies and the Thai consulate (for Thai visas) in Georgetown are given in "Listings", below.

Airport
Bayan Lepas International Airport (flight information on ☎04/643 0811); take yellow bus #83 (hourly on the hour, 6am–midnight) from Pengkalan Weld or the KOMTAR building. MAS operates a daily morning flight to Medan in Sumatra, a busy and popular route. Other direct flights are to Singapore, Bangkok, Phuket and Madras.

Ferries
The 24-hour passenger and car ferry from Pengkalan Weld to Butterworth (daily every 20min, 6am–midnight; hourly, midnight–6am; passengers 60 sen return, cars $1 return) is free on the return leg. Express ferries to Medan depart 9am daily. Both ferries leave from Swettenham Pier. Tickets for either route can be purchased in advance from the office next to the Penang Tourist Association, or for Langkawi from the Kuala–Perlis–Langkawi Ferry Service (☎04/262 5630) at the PPC Shopping Complex; travel agencies on Lebuh Chulia will also book for you.

Across the bridge: trains and buses
The nearest train station is in Butterworth (information on ☎04/331 2796), but there is a booking office in the Pengkalan Weld ferry terminal (☎04/261 0290) where you can reserve tickets to anywhere on the Peninsula. Unless you're driving, it doesn't make much sense to use the Penang Bridge to get back to the mainland given the existence of the ferries; taxis from Pengkalan Weld charge at least $10 to Butterworth station. Although some buses depart from Pengkalan Weld for destinations on the Peninsula, most use the terminal at Butterworth. This isn't as awkward for onward travel as it sounds, since there are any number of travel agencies on Lebuh Chulia who can book seats for you – in any case, services are so numerous throughout the day that you can just turn up without booking beforehand.

To Thailand
In addition to the train routes to Hat Yai, Surat Thami and Bangkok which can be picked up in Butterworth, long-distance taxis depart from several hostels (like the *New China* on Lebuh Leith) to Hat Yai, although unless there are four of you this isn't particularly economical. Try the travel agents on Lebuh Chulia for other options.

TAR building on Jalan Ria. **Fares** are rarely more than a dollar and services are frequent, though by 8pm in the evening they become more sporadic, stopping completely at midnight.

The traditional way of seeing the city is by **rickshaw** and there are drivers touting for custom outside the major hotels and all along Lebuh Chulia. Negotiate the price in advance; a ride from the ferry terminal at Pengkalen Weld to the northern end of Lebuh Chulia costs around $3. Otherwise, there are **taxi** stands by the ferry terminal and on Jalan Dr. Lim Chwee Long, off Jalan Penang. Drivers rarely use their meters, so fix the fare in advance – a trip across town runs to about $5, while a ride out to the airport or Batu Feringghi costs $19. To book a taxi in advance, call Georgetown Taxi Service on ☎04/261 7098. For **bike or car rental** – useful if you plan to see the rest of the island – check the list of addresses on p.181.

Accommodation
Despite the profusion of hotels and guesthouses, Georgetown is one of the few places in the whole country where you might experience difficulty in finding a **room**, partic-

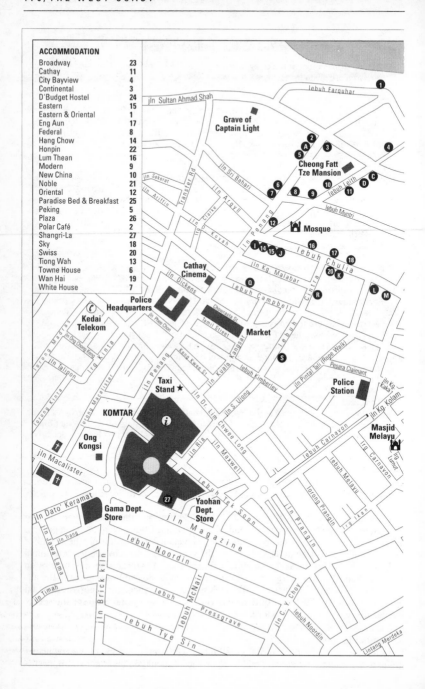

ACCOMMODATION

Broadway	23
Cathay	11
City Bayview	4
Continental	3
D'Budget Hostel	24
Eastern	15
Eastern & Oriental	1
Eng Aun	17
Federal	8
Hang Chow	14
Honpin	22
Lum Thean	16
Modern	9
New China	10
Noble	21
Oriental	12
Paradise Bed & Breakfast	25
Peking	5
Plaza	26
Polar Café	2
Shangri-La	27
Sky	18
Swiss	20
Tiong Wah	13
Towne House	6
Wan Hai	19
White House	7

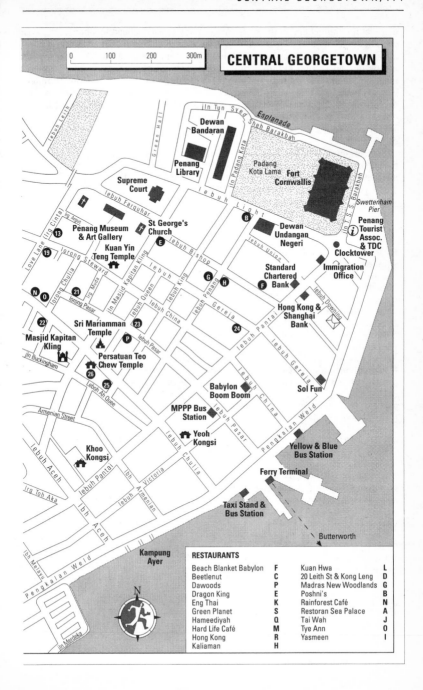

CENTRAL GEORGETOWN

0   100   200   300m

Esplanade

jln Tun Syed Sheh Barakbah

Dewan Bandaran

Penang Library

Supreme Court

lebuh Farquhar

Padang Kota Lama **Fort Cornwallis**

Swettenham Pier

Penang Museum & Art Gallery

St George's Church

Kuan Yin Teng Temple

lebuh Bishop

lebuh Light

Dewan Undangan Negeri

Penang Tourist Assoc. & TDC

Clocktower

Standard Chartered Bank

Immigration Office

lebuh Queen

lebuh China

Sri Mariamman Temple

lebuh Pasar

Hong Kong & Shanghai Bank

Masjid Kapitan Kling

jln Buckingham

Persatuan Teo Chew Temple

Lebuh Ah Quee

Babylon Boom Boom

Sol Fun

Armenian Street

MPPP Bus Station

Khoo Kongsi

Yeoh Kongsi

Yellow & Blue Bus Station

lebuh Aceh

lebuh Pantai

lebuh Armenian

lebuh Chulia

Ferry Terminal

Taxi Stand & Bus Station

Butterworth

Kampung Ayer

Pengkalan Weld

jln Merdeka

N

RESTAURANTS

Beach Blanket Babylon	**F**	Kuan Hwa	**L**
Beetlenut	**C**	20 Leith St & Kong Leng	**D**
Dawoods	**P**	Madras New Woodlands	**G**
Dragon King	**E**	Poshni's	**B**
Eng Thai	**K**	Rainforest Café	**N**
Green Planet	**S**	Restoran Sea Palace	**A**
Hameediyah	**Q**	Tai Wah	**J**
Hard Life Café	**M**	Tye Ann	**O**
Hong Kong	**R**	Yasmeen	**I**
Kaliaman	**H**		

ularly at the budget end of the scale. Arrive early or book ahead by phone; otherwise you either face a great deal of traipsing around or reliance on a rickshaw driver who'll usually be able to find you a room (though for a commission). The budget places are mostly on and around **Lebuh Chulia**, usually within ramshackle wooden-shuttered mansions, often with a portico and elegant internal staircase. Most have **dorm beds** as well as rooms and offer other useful services, such as selling bus tickets to Thailand and obtaining Thai visas. Given the choice it barely seems worth mentioning the two official **youth hostels**, the *YMCA*, 211 Jalan Macalister (☎04/229 2349; ②), and the *YWCA*, 8 Jalan Mesjid Negeri (☎04/828 1855; ②), which are a long way from the city centre.

In Georgetown's mid-range places – mostly in the same noisy area – you're often just paying for air-con and more modern furniture. Top-of-the-range hotels are more or less all located on **Jalan Penang** and **Lebuh Farquhar**, west of the centre, at all of which fifteen percent tax is added to the quoted price.

All the places to stay listed below are keyed on the map on pp.170–71.

ALONG LEBUH CHULIA

Lebuh Chulia starts with no. 1 at the eastern end (nearest the ferry terminal).

Eastern, no. 509 (☎04/261 4597). Tiny box-like rooms with "saloon" doors. It's next to the mosque, so expect it to be noisy. ①.

Eng Aun, no. 380 (☎04/261 2333). Long-running friendly backpackers' haunt with cheap rooms (though you get what you pay for). Laundry service and pleasant café, too. ①.

Hang Chow, no. 511 (☎04/261 0810). Basic and not terribly welcoming hotel, with both large and small rooms, and minuscule bathrooms. ①.

Honpin, no. 273b (☎04/262 5243). Above *Hsiang Yang* restaurant, the rather average rooms don't quite live up to the promise of the grand marble lobby. ③.

Lum Thean, no. 422 (☎04/261 4117). Modern frontage but with an interesting inner courtyard and a grand staircase. The large scruffy rooms have luxurious sprung mattresses. ①.

Paradise Bed and Breakfast, no. 99 (☎04/262 8439). Clean place though rooms are rather small and internal ones have no windows. There's a helpful information board, and breakfast is included. ①.

Sky, no. 348 (☎04/262 2323). Basic and the management can be unfriendly, but the air-con rooms are good value. Dorms $8. Rooms ②.

Swiss, no. 431 (☎04/262 0133). Another popular hostel (no dorm) that tends to get full before noon. Set back from the road with parking and an airy café. Also has laundry and travel and visa services. ②.

AROUND LEBUH CHULIA

Broadway Hostel, 35f Jalan Masjid Kapitan Keling (☎04/262 8550, fax 261 9525). Small clean dorm and inexpensive rooms make this hostel a popular option, though it's on a noisy major road. Dorms $8. ②.

Cathay, 15 Lebuh Leith (☎04/262 6271, fax 263 9300). Stylish colonial mansion dating from 1910. The cool greys of the decor, spacious rooms and courtyard fountain make for a tranquil environment. ③.

D'Budget Hostel, 9 Lebuh Gereja (☎04/263 4794). Five minutes' walk from the ferry terminal, with plenty of dorm space and small partitioned rooms, but clean, well kept and secure. Shared bathroom with hot showers and Western-style toilets, and the usual ticket service and notice board. ①.

Modern, 179c Lebuh Muntri (☎04/263 5424). On the corner of Lebuh Leith, this standard hotel gets some good reports. Top-floor rooms have balconies. ①.

New China, 22 Lebuh Leith (☎04/263 1601). Old-style hotel with seedy rear bar and a steady flow of regular and backpacking clientele. Roomy with some basic dorm space. ①.

Noble, 36 Lorong Pasar (☎04/261 2372). Tucked away on a small side street, this lacks the atmosphere of those places on Lebuh Chulia but is cheap. ①.

Plaza Hostel, 32 Lebuh Ah Quee (☎04/263 2388). The cheaper rooms are small with no windows, but the dorm is large and airy with a long balcony and pleasant view. Offers all the usual hostel services and has an air-conditioned lounge/lobby. ①.

Tiong Wah, 23 Lorong Cinta (☎04/262 2057). Cell-like rooms in a quiet area. Air-conditioned bar adds a little interest. ①.

Wan Hai, 35 Lorong Cinta (☎04/261 6853). A good place, run by the same management as the *Rainforest Café* with dorms and lower prices for single people occupying rooms. Also has a rooftop garden and bike rental. Dorms $8. ①.

ALONG JALAN PENANG, LEBUH FARQUHAR AND ELSEWHERE

City Bayview, 25a Lebuh Farquhar (☎04/263 3161, fax 263 4124). Modern highrise hotel close to the sea with a pool, a good range of restaurants and fantastic views over the bay and town. ⑦.

Continental, 5 Jalan Penang (☎04/263 6388, fax 263 8718). Impersonal and squeaky-clean hotel with a very central location; price includes breakfast. ⑤.

Federal, 39 Jalan Penang (☎04/263 4179). Reasonably attractive hotel with an Art Deco feel to it, but the rooms above the street are noisy and the bathrooms very small. ③.

Oriental, 105 Jalan Penang (☎04/263 4211, fax 263 5395). Excellent-value mid-range hotel with particularly good low-season rates Nov–Feb. ⑥.

Peking, 50a Jalan Penang (☎04/263 6191). Large, clean rooms in this moderately priced, but bland hotel. ③.

Polar Café, 48a Jalan Penang (☎04/262 2054, fax 262 9611). Comfortable rooms, sprung mattresses and inclusive continental breakfast make this a good choice – the only drawback is the sing-along bar at the front that can keep you awake till the small hours. ②.

Shangri-La, Magazine Rd (☎04/262 2622, fax 262 6526). The most luxurious hotel in Georgetown, conveniently placed next to the KOMTAR centre. All the facilities you would expect. ⑨.

Towne House, 70 Jalan Penang (☎04/263 8621, fax 262 3541). Plush and well-appointed rooms at a reasonable rate. ④.

White House, 72 Jalan Penang (☎04/263 2385). Very clean, large rooms – all with hot showers – although ones at the front tend to be a bit noisy. It's near the bottom end of this price category, and consequently very good value for money. ②.

The city centre

The main area of interest in Georgetown is the central square kilometre or so bordered by the sharply curving coast, the north–south Jalan Penang and east–west Jalan Magazine. The most prominent, if not most aesthetically pleasing, landmark is the Komplex Tun Abdul Razak (or KOMTAR), a huge highrise of shops and offices towering over the western corner of the city centre. The whole of this area could effectively be termed **Chinatown**, since the entire centre of Georgetown is dominated by shuttered two-storey shophouses and a liberal scattering of *kongsis* (clan associations) that have stood here in various forms since the late eighteenth century. Struggling to sur-

---

STREET NAMES IN GEORGETOWN

The most confusing thing about finding your way around Georgetown is understanding the **street names**. They all used to reflect the city's colonial past, but the current political climate encourages either a Malay translation of existing names or complete renaming. Thus, Penang Road has become Jalan Penang, Penang Street is Lebuh Penang, Weld Quay has become Pengkalan Weld, and Beach Street is now Lebuh Pantai. This would be relatively straightforward were it not for the fact that the new names have not always been popularly accepted, and even on official maps you'll sometimes see either name used. For example, Lebuh Cinta is almost universally known as Love Lane, while the most awkward name is Jalan Mesjid Kapitan Kling, the clumsy new title for the erstwhile Pitt Street, which more often than not is referred to simply as Lebuh Pitt.

vive this cultural domination is tiny **Little India** between Lebuh King and Lebuh Queen, while the remnants of the city's **colonial** past – Fort Cornwallis, St George's Church and the building housing the Penang Museum – are all clustered relatively close together at the eastern end of town, not far from Swettenham Docks. For a reminder of Penang's past economic success, typified by millionaire's row and the *Eastern and Oriental (E&O) Hotel*, the area around **Jalan Penang**, west of the central area, is worth exploring.

FORT CORNWALLIS AND THE WATERFRONT

The site of **Fort Cornwallis** (daily 8am–7pm; $1) on the northeastern tip of Pulau Penang marks the spot where the British fleet, under Captain Francis Light, disembarked on July 16, 1786. A fort was hastily thrown up, fronting the blustery north channel to provide barracks for Light and his men, and was named after Lord Charles Cornwallis, governor-general of India. The present structure dates from around twenty years later, but for all its significance little remains to excite the senses, just peeling walls and the seventeenth-century **Sri Rambai cannon**, sited in the northwest corner of the citadel. Presented to the Sultan of Johor by the Dutch, this was later confiscated by the British in 1871 during their attack on Selangor – they loaded 29 guns including the cannon onto the steamer "Sri Rambai" and on reaching Penang, threw it overboard where it remained submerged for almost a decade. According to local legend, the cannon refused to leave the sea bed during the subsequent salvage operation and only floated to the surface when Tunku Qudin, the former Viceroy of Selangor, tied a rope to it and ordered it to rise. Since then it's been considered a living entity with mystical powers and the local belief is that barren women can conceive by laying flowers on its barrel.

Inside the fort, there's a craft shop, a replica of a traditional Malay house and, close to the cannon, a claustrophobic underground bunker detailing the history of Penang – unimaginatively presented, but informative. An open-air auditorium hosts local music and dance festivals – keep an eye on the local press for details of shows.

The large expanse of green that borders the fort, the **Padang Kota Lama**, was once the favourite promenade of the island's colonial administrators and thronged with rickshaws and carriages. On the south side, opposite the grand sweep of the Esplanade, was a bandstand where Filipino groups played to strolling passers-by. Now used for sports and other public events, the padang is bordered by some superb examples of Anglo-Victorian architecture: the **Dewan Undangan Negeri** (State Legislative Building) with its weighty portico and ornate gables, and the **Dewan Bandaran** (town hall) of equal aesthetic if not political merit, the city's affairs now being conducted from the KOMTAR tower.

Turning left past the food stalls outside the fort brings you to the Moorish-style **clocktower**, at the junction of Lebuh Light and Lebuh Pantai, which was presented to the town in 1897 to mark Queen Victoria's Diamond Jubilee – it is sixty feet high, each foot representing a year of her reign. Turn to the right here and you're at the top of one of Georgetown's oldest streets, **Lebuh Pantai**, the heart of the business district. This narrow and congested road once fronted the beach – its swaying palms providing the first sight of the island to anyone approaching from the mainland. But the scores of moneylenders squeezed cheek-by-jowl between the imposing bank and government buildings, not to mention the constant buzz of the motor scooters, are a far cry from this. Gracefully lining an otherwise ill-proportioned street are some of Georgetown's best colonial buildings, including the Standard Chartered Bank and the Hong Kong Bank, the heavy pillars of the former providing an elegant archway and a welcome escape from the traffic.

A left turn down any of the adjoining streets leads to the **waterfront**, but there's little of interest here except the passage of the lumbering yellow ferries to and from

Butterworth. Much is made of the quaint lifestyle of the inhabitants of the stilted settlement, known as **Kampung Ayer**, close to the ferry terminal. This is also known as "Clan Piers", since each of the jetties is named after a different Chinese clan (see below). The unsanitary and semi-derelict properties here are home to the hundreds of harbour workers and their families who can not move anywhere else because of the high cost of land.

ST GEORGE'S CHURCH TO LEBUH CHULIA

On the western side of Lebuh Pantai you're in Chinatown again, a leisurely five-minute stroll through which leads onto Jalan Masjid Kapitan Kling (or Lebuh Pitt), one of the city's main thoroughfares. At its northern end, the Anglican **St George's Church** (Tues–Sat 8.30am–12.30pm & 1.30–4.30pm, Sun 8.30am–4.30pm) comes into view, one of the oldest buildings in Penang and as simple and unpretentious as anything built in the Greek style in Asia can be. It was constructed in 1817–1819 by the East India Company using convict labour, and its cool, pastel-blue interior must have been a welcome retreat from the heat for the new congregation. In 1886, on the centenary of the founding of Penang, a memorial to Francis Light was built in front of the church in the form of a Greek temple – Victoriana at its most eclectic.

Next to the church on Lebuh Farquhar (which takes its name from a former lieutenant-governor of the settlement) is the **Penang Museum and Art Gallery** (closed for renovations; check with the Tourist Information Centre if it has reopened), housed in a building dating from 1821 that was first used as a school. It has an excellent collection of memorabilia: rickshaws, press cuttings, faded black-and-white photographs of early Penang's Chinese millionaires and a panoramic photograph of Georgetown taken in the 1870s – note just how many buildings still survive. The art gallery upstairs displays temporary exhibitions of contemporary paintings and photographs – it's a bit hit-and-miss.

A few minutes' walk south of St George's Church along Jalan Masjid Kapitan Kling, the **Kuan Yin Teng Temple** is dedicated to the Buddhist Goddess of Mercy and while not the finest example of a *kongsi* – that honour goes to the Khoo Kongsi (see below) – it can claim the title of the oldest Chinese temple in Penang. Originally constructed in 1800, it was completely ravaged during World War II; what you see today, including the massive roof dominated by two guardian dragons, is a renovation.

The area east of here, enclosed by the parallel roads of Lebuh King and Lebuh Queen, forms Georgetown's compact **Little India** district. Despite being surrounded on all sides by Chinatown, it's a vibrant, self-contained community comprising saree and incense shops, banana leaf curry houses, and the towering **Sri Mariamman Temple** (open early morning to late evening) on the corner of Lebuh Queen and Lebuh Chulia. A typical example of Hindu architecture, the lofty entrance tower teems with brightly coloured sculptures of gods and swans, as well as the hundreds of pigeons that make it their home. At times, the compound becomes quite frenetic with the activities of the devotees of the main deity, Mariamman; the inner sanctum has a nine-metre-high dome, with statues of forty other deities and lions. Within a few metres of here, across Lebuh Chulia, the **Persatuan Teo Chew Temple** features fearsome guardians painted on the insides of the temple doors.

Lebuh Chulia itself – the central artery of Chinatown – was the area the southern Indian immigrants chose to establish their earliest businesses (*chulia* being the Malay word for "South Indian merchant"), and Indian shops here still deal in textiles. But the area (like much of central Georgetown) looks predominantly Chinese, its shophouses and arcades selling everything from antiques and bamboo furniture to books, photographic services and foreign holidays.

Back on Jalan Masjid Kapitan Kling, follow the road along for 500m past lines of jewellery stores, each one guarded by a sleepy octogenarian armed guard. You'll see the

Masjid Melayu ahead, tucked away on Lebuh Acheh, and although this is the oldest mosque in Penang, it's only unusual in having an Egyptian-style minaret.

THE KHOO KONGSI

Across Lebuh Acheh, where, in a secluded square at the end of an alleyway, stands the **Khoo Kongsi**. Kongsi is the Hokkien word for "clan-house", the building in which Chinese families gather to worship their ancestors. In Penang, the *kongsi* were originally formed for the mutual help and protection of nineteenth-century immigrants, who naturally tended to band together in clans according to what district they came from. This led to rivalry and often violence between the different Chinese communities, though these days the *kongsi* have reverted to their supportive role, helping with the education of members' children, settling disputes between clan members or advancing loans. Consequently, they are an important means of solidarity, although traditionally women have been excluded from many of the functions and are rarely represented in the hierarchy.

Many of the *kongsis* in Penang are well over a hundred years old and are excellent examples of traditional Chinese architecture. The **Khoo Kongsi** (Mon–Fri 9am–5pm, Sat 9am–1pm; free) is no exception. It has a spacious courtyard in front of the clan-house, opposite which is a stage for theatrical performances, and two halls in the main building itself, one with the shrine of the clan deity, the other for the display of the ancestral tablets (the equivalent of gravestones). The original building was started in 1894, an ambitious and extensive project with a roof styled in the manner of a grand

---

THE PENANG RIOTS

Chinese immigrants in Penang brought their traditions with them, including the establishment of triad (secret society) branches that had evolved in China during the eighteenth century as a means of overthrowing Manchu rule. Once in Penang, the societies provided mutual aid and protection for the Chinese community, their position later bolstered by alliances with Malay religious groups which had originally been established to assist members with funerals and marriages. As the societies grew in wealth and power, gang warfare and extortion rackets became commonplace. The newly appointed governor-general Sir Harry Ord and his inefficient police force, largely composed of people outside the Chinese community, proved ineffective in preventing the increasing turmoil, and in 1867 matters came to a head in the series of events known subsequently as the **Penang Riots**.

For nine days Georgetown was shaken by fighting between the **Tua-Peh-Kong** society, supported by the Malay **Red Flag**, and the **Ghee Hin**, allied with the Malay **White Flag**. Police intervention resulted in a temporary truce, but a major clash seemed inevitable when, on August 1, 1867, the headman of the Tua-Peh-Kong falsely charged the Ghee Hin and the White Flag societies with stealing cloth belonging to the Tua-Peh-Kong dyers. All hell broke loose and fighting raged around Armenian, Church and Chulia streets. Barricades were erected around the Khoo Kongsi, where much of the fiercest fighting took place, and you can still find bullet holes in the surrounding shops and houses. The authorities were powerless since the battery of artillery normally stationed at Fort Cornwallis had just left for Rangoon and the relief forces had not yet arrived. Countless arrests were made but the police soon had to release many from custody as there was no more room for them in the overflowing jails.

The fighting was eventually quelled by *sepoys* (Indian troops) brought in from Singapore by the governor-general, but by then hundreds had been killed and scores of houses burned. As compensation for the devastation suffered by the city, a penalty of $5000 was levied on each of the secret societies, some of which was later used to finance the building of four police stations to deal with future trouble.

palace. It took eight years to complete but was immediately gutted in a mysterious fire. Suspecting sabotage, the clan members rebuilt the house on a lesser scale, with the public excuse that the previous design had been too noble to house the ancestral tablets of ordinary mortals. Less extensive it may be, but the present structure was still meticulously crafted by experts from China. The saddle-shaped roof itself reputedly weighs 25 tons, while the central hall is dark with heavy, intricately carved beams and pillars and bulky mother-of-pearl inlaid furniture. An Art Deco grandfather clock stands somewhat incongruously in the corner. Behind this is a separate chamber, with delicate black-and-white line drawings depicting scenes of courtly life. The hall on the left is a richly decorated shrine to Tua Peh Kong, the god of prosperity; the right-hand hall contains the gilded ancestral tablets. Connecting all three halls is a balcony minutely decorated in bas-relief, whose carvings depict episodes from folk tales – even the bars on the windows have been carved into bamboo sticks.

ALONG JALAN PENANG

East of St George's Church, **Jalan Penang** separates the traditional commercial district from the residential quarter further to the west, an elegant part of town formerly frequented by colonial types.

At the far northern end of the road, on Lebuh Farquhar, stands the legendary **Eastern and Oriental Hotel** (closed for renovation until 1998), once part of the Sarkies brothers' select chain of colonial retreats (together with the *Raffles* in Singapore; see p.528). Rudyard Kipling and Somerset Maugham both stayed here, taking tiffin on the terrace and enjoying the cooling sea breeze. Continuing west along Lebuh Farquhar; after about five minutes the road merges with sea-facing Jalan Sultan Ahmad Shah, across which you'll find the overgrown churchyard where Francis Light is buried. Further along, the huge stylish mansions set back from the road in acres of manicured lawn give the road it's nickname – "millionaires' row" – and though the preposterous upkeep costs of the houses have seen several fall into disrepair, the road is a reminder of the ostentatious wealth of colonial Penang.

Backtracking towards Jalan Penang, five minutes' walk east brings you to Lebuh Leith, on the corner of which is the stunning **Cheong Fatt Tze Mansion**, whose outer walls are painted in a striking rich blue. It's the best example of nineteenth-century Chinese architecture in Penang, built by Thio Thiaw Siat, a Cantonese businessman. The elaborate halls of ceremony, bedrooms and libraries, separated by cobbled courtyards, small gardens and heavy wooden doors have been restored; sadly, much of the house's furniture and antiques disappeared long ago, but there is a plan to replace these with faithful reproductions.

Back on Jalan Penang, don't let the sophisticated shop fronts put you off bargaining a little, something that's a necessity in the cramped tourist **market** opposite the police station, a little further along. This is the place to pick up leather goods – particularly bags and wallets. Further along still, you'll come to the ordered calm of the **KOMTAR** building, the nucleus of Penang's business and government administration, comprising five levels of air-conditioned shops, offices and fast-food joints, topped by a gigantic circular tower which provides a handy orientation point.

The outskirts

There are several sights on the western and northern **outskirts** of Georgetown worth exploring, most of which provide a welcome break from the frenetic city. Trips to Ayer Itam and Penang Hill especially are a cool alternative to heading for the northern beaches for the day. MPPP buses run to all the destinations below from the station on Lebuh Victoria, though you can also pick them up at the station at the KOMTAR building on Jalan Ria.

THREE TEMPLES AND THE BOTANICAL GARDENS

A fifteen-minute bus ride on MPPP #2 or blue buses #93, #94 or #95 (towards Batu Ferringhi) brings you to **Wat Chayamangkalaram** on Lorong Burma, a Thai temple painted in yellow and blue and flanked by two statues, whose fierce grimaces and weighty swords are designed to ward off unwanted visitors. Inside, a 33-metre-long statue of the Reclining Buddha, is surrounded by other, elaborately decorated Buddha images covered with gold leaf. The **Dharmmikarama Burmese Temple** across the road is less spectacular, although the white stone elephants at the entrance are attractive and the temple's two stupas are lit to good effect at night. Entrance to both temples is between sunrise and sunset, and is free.

Further west on Jalan Kebun Bunga is the **Nattukkottai Chettiar Temple**, a seven-kilometre bus ride from the city centre on MPPP #7. This is the focus of the Hindu Thaipusam festival in February, in honour of Lord Subramanian, when thousands of devotees walk through the streets bearing *kavadis* (sacred yokes) fixed to their bodies by hooks and spikes spearing their flesh. The biggest such event in Malaysia is at Kuala Lumpur's Batu Caves (see p.120); if you can't catch that, the festivities here are a similar blend of hypnotic frenzy and celebration. At other times of the year, you're free to concentrate on the temple itself, in which an unusual wooden colonnaded walkway with exquisite pictorial tiles leads up to the inner sanctum. Here, a life-sized solid silver peacock – featured as a theme throughout the temple – bows its head to the deity, Lord Subramanian.

Just five more minutes along Jalan Kebun Bunga (Waterfall Road) from the temple, the **Botanical Gardens** (daily 7am–7pm; free) lie in a lush valley. It's a good place to escape the city and enjoy some fresh air, although the waterfall that gives the road its name has been cordoned off.

AYER ITAM AND THE KEK LOK SI TEMPLE

A thirty-minute bus ride west on MPPP #1, Ayer Itam is an appealing wooded hilly area (almost 250m above sea level), spread around the **Ayer Itam Dam**, built in the early 1960s. Despite its 550-million-litre capacity, the dam is rather dwarfed by the vertiginous surroundings, through which several short trails snake. If you're looking for a stroll outside the city, you'll do better at Penang Hill (see below), although you might come on up to the dam after visiting the nearby Kek Lok Si Temple, a couple of kilometres back down the road.

The sprawling, fairy-tale complex of **Kek Lok Si Temple** (open morning to late evening; free) is an intriguing sight as you approach Ayer Itam, the tips of its colourful towers peeking cheekily through the tree tops. Supposedly the largest Buddhist temple in Malaysia, its sheer exuberance makes it hard to dislike – bedecked with flags, lanterns and statues, its fantastic temples and pagodas linked by hundreds of steps. The entrance to the complex is approached through a tunnel of trinket stalls stretching a few hundred metres uphill, but as well as being a major tourist spot, it's a serious place of worship. The "Million Buddhas Precious Pagoda" is the most prominent feature of the compound, with a tower of simple Chinese saddle-shaped eaves and more elaborate Thai arched windows, topped by a golden Burmese *stupa*. It costs $2 to climb the 193 steps to the top, where there is a great view of Georgetown and the bay.

PENANG HILL

The other major trip outside Georgetown is to the small hill station of **Penang Hill** (Bukit Bendera), an 821-metre-high dome of tropical forest due west of Georgetown. This was once the retreat for the colony's wealthiest administrators, but nowadays is a popular weekend excursion for the locals. The cooler climate encourages flowering trees and shrubs, and there are several gentle, well-marked walks through areas whose names (Tiger Hill, Strawberry Hill) conjure up colonial days. You can also walk from here down to the Botanical Gardens, a steep descent which takes about an hour.

Take MPPP bus #1 to the end of the line and then #8 for the total 45-minute journey which terminates at the base of Penang Hill, the final climb up which is made by **funicular railway** (departures every 30min; daily 6.30am–9.30pm, Wed & Sat until midnight; $4 return). This takes thirty minutes and deposits you at the top, where there's a post office, police station and a few food stalls, as well as a hotel – the *Bellevue* (☎04/829 9500, fax 829 2052; ⑨) – five minutes from the station, which has a terrace with the best view of Georgetown. You can have a drink or a meal here – perfect at sunset when the city's lights flicker on in the distance. It's also possible to rent out a couple of government bungalows (☎04/828 3263) on the hill for just $60 a night.

Eating

Georgetown's status as Malaysia's second city means there is no shortage of cafés and restaurants. Surprisingly though, it's only really standard Malay, Chinese and Indian cuisine which is significantly represented, though a few places serve seafood, north Indian and Nonya specialities. **Hawker stalls** dish out the cheapest meals and are located either in permanent sites, in which case they're open all day and evening, or spring up by the roadside or down an alleyway at meal times. In addition, a roving **pasar malam** (night market) is held every two weeks at various venues around town (near the stadium is a favourite) – any of the tourist offices will have the latest details.

Of the **cafés** (usually open 8am–11pm), the ubiquitous Chinese *kedai kopis*, sometimes hard to distinguish from stalls when their tables spill out onto the pavement, serve reliable rice and noodle standards, although many also specialize in fine Hainan chicken rice. The other local favourite is Penang *laksa*, noodles in thick fish soup, garnished with vegetables, pineapple and *belacan* (shrimp paste). The Indian *kedai kopis* around Jalan Penang and Little India offer *murtabaks*, *rotis* and *biriyanis* as well as a bewildering array of curries, but none serve alcohol. The main travellers' hang-outs are dotted on or around Lebuh Chulia, often little more than hole-in-the-wall joints, serving Western breakfasts, banana pancakes and milkshakes, for less than a couple of dollars each. These tend to open from around 9am to 5pm; the exceptions are noted below. For **Western fast foods**, the KOMTAR building on Jalan Penang (10am–10pm) has a *KFC*, *McDonald's* and a *Pizza Hut*.

Jalan Penang is home to a handful of more upmarket **restaurants**, mainly specializing in seafood, while for high-class Western, Malay, Japanese or Chinese food you should head to the top hotels. Set meals here can sometimes work out quite reasonably and give a good opportunity to sample more unusual dishes, often with some sort of cultural entertainment thrown in; you only need to book in advance on Saturday night.

Note that during **Ramadan** (Feb/March) some places only open after sunset and can be very busy coping with the burst of activity from Penang's hungry Muslims.

HAWKER STALLS

Chinatown, Lebuh Kimberley and Lebuh Cintra.

Food Court, ground floor and roof of the KOMTAR building.

Jalan Tun Syed Shah Barakah, near Fort Cornwallis at the End of the esplanade.

Midlands Park Centre, *One-Stop International Food Garden* on the sixth floor has the full range of Eastern and Western cuisine with self-service and service sections. Most dishes are around $6. Take any bus from KOMTAR heading for Batu Ferringhi.

CAFÉS

Eng Thai, Lebuh Chulia. Close to the junction with Lebuh Cintra, this is popular for breakfasts, great milkshakes and snacks. The *Seng Hin* across the road is a similar set-up.

Green Planet, 63 Lebuh Cintra. Roomy and comfortable, with tasteful rattan and bamboo decor, this café serves international veggie food (falafel, quiche, waffles, pizza), with some ingredients organically grown, and wonderful baguettes and wholemeal bread. Also has a book exchange. Open 9.30am–3pm & 6pm–midnight.

Hard Life Café, 363 Lebuh Chulia. Bob Marley and co plastered across the walls and the sound system make this a laid-back spot for drinks, snacks and beers. They also run the *Reggae Club* further up the street, but avoid the extremely basic dorm above the café – you'll be kept up all night by the noise.

Tai Wah, Lebuh Chulia. At the eastern end, near Jalan Penang, this regular all-hours café has fast and efficient service and becomes a bar in the evening (see below).

Tye Ann, 282 Lebuh Chulia, beneath the hostel of the same name. Light and airy with the usual travellers' food, although the service is sometimes very slow.

Rainforest Restaurant, 294a Lebuh Chulia. Run by the friendly Mr Tan who also owns the *Green Planet*. Similar set up, with good food and drinks, a book exchange system and Internet terminal to send E-mails home or just surf the net.

RESTAURANTS

Beach Blanket Babylon, 16 Lebuh Bishop. Very tasteful and friendly place with a European feel, where you can linger over coffee and read a magazine. The evening set meal is good value at $25 for three courses, and the cakes are delicious. Open Mon–Sat 11am–midnight.

Beetlenuts, 9 Lebuh Leith. Tex-Mex cuisine and beers at this "funcafé" next door to *20 Lebuh Leith*. Interior decoration includes a carved up Volkswagon.

Dawoods, 63 Lebuh Queen. A well-known South Indian restaurant with a limited menu. The speciality is *curry kapitan* – spicy chicken with ginger and coconut milk.

Dragon King, 99 Lebuh Bishop. Upmarket restaurant that specializes in Nonya cuisine – try any of the *assam* fish dishes. Expensive, and service can be slow.

Eliza, thirteenth floor, *City Bayview Hotel*, 25a Lebuh Farquhar. The set meal ($18 per head) in "authentic" Malay atmosphere is accompanied by live traditional music, and the food is surprisingly tasty and well presented. The hotel also has the *Revolving Restaurant* on the fourteenth floor, serving Western and Oriental dishes, with an all-you-can-eat buffet for $25.

Hameediyah, 164 Lebuh Campbell. They'll try and haul you in from the street if you look remotely interested. Let them: it's great Indian food at reasonable prices, around $4 a head for a full meal.

Hong Kong, 29 Lebuh Cintra. Although this looks like any number of *kedai kopis* in the area, the food is of much better quality than usual, something reflected in the prices. There's an extensive Chinese menu with "specials" at $6–8 per main dish, and the portions are huge.

Kaliaman, Lebuh Penang. North and south Indian food, which arrives quickly. Standard *korma, jalfrezi* and *biriyani* dishes for around $6 each.

Kashmir, basement of *Oriental Hotel*, 105 Jalan Penang. Very popular high-class north Indian restaurant; you'll need to book at weekends. Expensive – $7 per dish and upwards – but chic.

Kong Lung, 11A Lebuh Leith. Good value Japanese restaurant that shares premises with the *20 Leith St* pub. You can choose to eat outside or beside the sushi bar, watching the chef at work. Around $20 a head.

Kuan Hwa, Lebuh Chulia. One of the many places claiming to serve the best Hainan chicken rice in Penang; around $4 a head.

Madras New Woodlands, 60 Lebuh Penang. Excellent Southern Indian cuisine at bargain prices. *Thalis* – spicy dishes with crispy pancakes – for lunch cost $4.

Poshni's, 3–5 Lebuh Light. Neat and clean Thai restaurant with fiery dishes for around $4.

Restoran Sea Palace, 50 Jalan Penang. One of the least expensive of the many seafood restaurants in this part of town, with meals averaging $15 a head.

Sky Café, 348 Lebuh Chulia. Very popular with the locals and one of the few places serving Chinese/Malay food until late (11.30pm). Fish-head *bee hoon* (a hot noodle dish) is a speciality.

Yasmeen, 117 Jalan Penang. Busy and friendly neighbourhood Indian café-restaurant that does excellent *roti canai*.

Drinking, nightlife and entertainment

Most of Georgetown's **bars** are comfortable places in which to hang out – some of the best are detailed below. With the arrival of the fleet, though, a good many turn into rowdy meat markets, and a place that may have been fine the night before could become unpleasant for women visitors, so choose carefully. Usual opening hours are 6pm–2am and occasional **happy hours** (usually 6–8pm) make the cost of beer more reasonable. In Georgetown's **discos** you'll be unlikely to hear the latest Western club sounds, but several seem to be gripped by the drag-show craze that has swept down from Thailand. This said, they do at least stay open until the early hours; there's usually a cover charge of around $10. Other entertainment is thin on the ground: the *Cathay* (Jalan Penang) and *Rex* (Jalan Burma) **cinemas** show recent releases of English-language movies; check the *New Straits Times* for details. There's no cultural centre in Penang, so it's up to the five-star hotels both in town and at Batu Ferringhi to put on shows; this is expensive as you have to pay for a meal in order to watch them.

Babylon Boom Boom, Lebuh China Ghaut. Gay and straight disco and café, whose main attraction is the twice-nightly drag cabaret show, which would give some Vegas shows a run for their money. Good fun.

Carmen Inn, basement, *City Bayview*, 25a Lebuh Farquhar. One of the better of the hotel clubs, this concentrates on Sixties and Seventies sounds.

Cheers, 22 Jalan Argyll. Not much like its American counterpart; it has a happy hour 6–8.45pm.

Hong Kong Bar, 371 Lebuh Chulia. Tiny, long-running serviceman's bar with none-too-recent hits on the jukebox and a stupefyingly sexist visitors' book.

Hotlips, cnr Jalan Penang and Jalan Sultan Ahmed Shah. A tasteless pair of giant red lips glows like a beacon outside this tacky club. It's open 8pm–2am and plays karaoke and disco.

No name bar, Lebuh Chulia. Further up from the *Hong Kong Bar* by the bus stop, this basic place always hosts a steady stream of travellers.

Polar Café, 48a Jalan Penang. Family-run sing-along bar with organist and music machine, bright lighting and TV. A hamburger stall operates outside at night.

Sol Fun, Pengkalan Weld. Techno makes it to Penang at this gay disco in a converted warehouse. There's also a nightly "Funky Divas" show and a cinema in case you get bored of the music.

Tai Wah, Lebuh Chulia. This daytime café turns into a lively bar in the evening with the cheapest beer in town. The resident Tom Waits impersonator provides musical diversion until the small hours.

20 Lebuh Leith. This renovated 1930s Straits-style mansion is littered with film memorabilia; it has a large video screen and plenty of tables in the beer garden. Slightly pricey, but interesting.

Listings

Airlines Cathay Pacific, AIA Building, 88 Lebuh Bishop (☎04/226 0411); Malaysia Airlines, third floor, KOMTAR, Jalan Penang (☎04/262 0011); Qantas, 28 Beach St (☎04/263 4428); Singapore Airlines, Wisma Penang Gardens, Jalan Sultan Ahmed Shah (☎04/226 3201); Thai International, Wisma Central, Jalan Macalister (☎04/226 8000).

American Express 274 Lebuh Victoria (Mon–Fri 8.30am–5.30pm, Sat 8.30am–1pm; ☎04/262 3724, fax 261 9024). Credit card and travellers' cheque holders can use the office as a poste restante/general delivery address.

Banks and exchange Major banks (Mon–Fri 10am–3pm, Sat 9.30–11.30am) are along Lebuh Pantai, including Standard Chartered and the Hong Kong Bank, but since they charge a hefty commission, the licensed moneychangers on Lebuh Pantai and Lebuh Chulia (daily 8.30am–6pm) are preferable – they charge no commission and the rate is often better.

Bike rental Outlets on Lebuh Chulia rent out motorbikes and pushbikes: $20 a day for a motorbike (you need a valid driving licence – in practice, you'll rarely be asked to show it); $8 for a pushbike.

Bookshops *United Books Ltd*, Jalan Penang, has a large selection of English-language books including travel books; there are several outlets in KOMTAR, including *Times Books* in the *Yaohan* department store. There are also lots of second-hand bookshops on Lebuh Chulia.

Car rental Avis, at the airport (☎04/643 9633) and Batu Ferringhi (☎04/811 1522); Hertz, 38 Lebuh Farquhar (☎04/263 5914) and at the airport (☎04/643 0208); National, at the airport (☎04/643 4205).

Consulates Bangladesh: 15 Lebuh Bishop (☎04/262 1085); Denmark: Bank Chambers, Lebuh Pantai (☎04/262 4886); France: Wisma Rajab, 82 Lebuh Bishop (☎04/262 9707); Indonesia: 467

Jalan Burma (☎04/262 4686); Japan: 2 Jalan Biggs (☎04/226 8222); Netherland: c/o Algemene Bank Nederland: 9 Lebuh Pantai (☎04/261 6471); Norway: Standard Chartered Bank Chambers, Lebuh Pantai (☎04/262 5333); Sweden: Standard Chartered Bank Chambers, Lebuh Pantai (☎04/248 5433); Thailand: 1 Jalan Tunku Abdul Rahman (☎04/226 9484); Turkey: 7 Pengkalan Weld (☎04/261 5933); UK: Standard Chartered Bank Chambers, Lebuh Pantai (☎04/262 5333). There is no representation for citizens of the USA, Canada, Ireland, Australia or New Zealand – KL has the nearest offices (see p.119).

Hospitals Adventist Hospital, Jalan Burma (☎04/226 1133) – take blue buses #93, #94 or #95 or MPPP #2; General Hospital, Jalan Western (☎04/229 3333) – green bus #92, blue buses #136 or #137, or MPPP #1, #5 or #10.

Immigration office Pejabat Imigresen, Lebuh Pantai, on the corner of Lebuh Light (☎04/644 2255). For on-the-spot visa renewals.

Pharmacy There are several pharmacies along Jalan Penang; open 10am–6pm.

Police In emergencies dial ☎999; the police headquarters is on Jalan Penang.

Post office The GPO is on Lebuh Downing (Mon–Sat 8am–6pm). The efficient poste restante/general delivery office is here, and parcel-wrapping is available from shops on Lebuh Chulia.

Sport You can play golf at Bukit Jambul Country Club, 2 Jalan Bukit Jambul (☎04/644 2255; green fees $100, $150 weekends), or the Penang Turf Club Golf (☎04/226 6701; green fees $84); there's racing at the Penang Turf Club, Jalan Batu Gantung (☎04/3226 6701) – see the local paper for fixtures and you can swim at the Chinese Swimming Club at Tanjung Tokang (☎04/899 0813).

Telephone offices Calls within Penang made from public telephone booths cost a flat rate of 10 sen and can be dialled direct. For international calls it is better to use a Telekom office at either the GPO, on Lebuh Downing, or Kodai Telekom, first floor, Jalan Burma; both are open 24 hours.

Travel agents Try MSL Travel, 340 Lebuh Chulia (☎04/226 6701) for student and youth travel. There are a large number of other agencies along Lebuh Chulia. Look for one that is TDC registered.

The northern beaches

The 15km or so along Pulau Penang's **north coast** have been aggressively marketed since the early days of package tourism, and even more so in recent years with the growth in popularity of condominiums, particularly among the Japanese. The narrow strip of coastline, hemmed in by the densely forested interior, is punctuated by a series of bays and beaches, linked by a twisting road lined with resort hotels which advertise themselves as being part of the "Pearl of the Orient". The filthy ocean rather detracts from this image, but while the water may flunk the pollution tests, the sand is crunchy, golden and relatively clean – although it's fair to say that if you've visited the east coast of Malaysia, you'll see nothing here to touch it. More worrying, though, is that the area is still being developed. Huge apartment buildings are springing up all over the place, their rooms often sold before they've even been completed. It makes you wonder how much more a short stretch of beach, reached through already congested streets, can take.

There are three main developments strung out along the northern coast: Tanjung Bungah, Batu Ferringhi and Teluk Bahang. The first two have arisen purely to serve tourism's needs, rather than growing out of a local community; this is particularly obvious at **Tanjung Bungah**, which lacks a focus. Occupied for the most part by a string of deluxe resorts, **Batu Ferringhi** is the biggest of the three, and has gone a fair way towards establishing a community and spirit of its own, while **Teluk Bahang**, with just one modern hotel, is the only place to maintain its fishing village roots. If you want to stay at any of the beaches, it's wise to ring the hotels and guesthouses first from Georgetown to check on space, especially during Christmas, Easter and Hari Raya.

Tanjung Bungah

Although there are beaches closer to Georgetown, **TANJUNG BUNGAH**, 12km and twenty minutes' bus ride (blue buses #93, #94 or #202; every 20min) from KOMTAR, is really the first decent place. That said, it's a largely uncoordinated string of properties and the beach is not as good as the one further west, just before the bus station on the way to Batu Ferringhi. There's little in the way of budget **accommodation**, the best option being the *Seaview Hotel* (☎04/896 2582; ③) further out towards Batu Ferringhi up some steps on the left-hand side of the road; it has a bearable beach, but is fairly isolated. Of the upmarket options the *Novotel*, Jalan Tanjung Bungah (☎04/890 3303, fax 890 3303; ④) offers the best deals and has the *Shock! Videotheque*, done out entirely in an Egyptian theme.

For **eating**, you're pretty much restricted to the hotels; the *Seaview* serves fairly inexpensive food. The upmarket hotels along here offer a variety of food, although all at five-star prices.

Batu Ferringhi

BATU FERRINGHI (Foreigner's Rock), a ten-minute bus ride further west on #93, earned its name from the foreigners who hung out here in the early Seventies when the island's waters really were jewel-like. Although it is almost unrecognizable since its hippy heyday, for most visitors it still provides the right mix of relaxation and excitement – the beach during the day, shopping and eating in the evening, and drinking at night in the bars and discos.

Orientation is very simple: the road runs more or less straight along the coast for 3km, along which all the hotels and restaurants are lined up side by side. The centre, such as it is, lies between two bridges a couple of kilometres apart and has a Telekom office, post office and police station, opposite which is the mosque and clinic; it is here that the bus from Georgetown stops. The **beach** is remarkably clean and since every major hotel has a pool, with luck you'll never have to swim in the sea. The trinket stalls, tailors' shops and street hawkers remain fairly unobtrusive during the day, but become the main focus when the sun goes down and the road comes alive with brightly lit stalls selling batik, T-shirts and fake designer watches.

ACCOMMODATION

Towards the western end of Batu Ferringhi there's a small enclave of **budget guesthouses** facing the beach – take the road by the *Guan Guan Café*. *T*he standards of accommodation are good, but don't expect any great bargains – rooms are generally

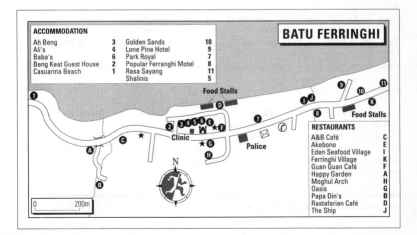

ACCOMMODATION

Ah Beng	3	Golden Sands	10
Ali's	4	Lone Pine Hotel	9
Baba's	6	Park Royal	7
Beng Keat Guest House	2	Popular Ferranghi Motel	8
Casuarina Beach	1	Rasa Sayang	11
		Shalinis	5

BATU FERRINGHI

RESTAURANTS

A&B Café	C
Akebono	E
Eden Seafood Village	I
Ferringhi Village	K
Guan Guan Café	F
Happy Garden	A
Moghul Arch	H
Oasis	G
Papa Din's	B
Rastafarian Café	D
The Ship	J

Food Stalls

Clinic

Police

N

0   200m

more expensive than in Georgetown. Independent travellers don't get particularly good deals in the expensive hotels, most of whose business is with tour groups, but it's worth enquiring about discounts out of the busy holiday season. The *Casuarina Beach* at the far western end is the most tasteful.

Ah Beng (☎04/881 1036). One of the nicest guesthouses, with polished wood floors, a sea-facing communal balcony and a washing machine. ②.

Ali's (☎04/881 1316). Very popular, with a pleasant open-air café and garden. The cheaper rooms are at the back. ②.

Baba's (☎04/881 1686). Spotless and friendly guesthouse. Has spacious air-con rooms too. ②–③.

Beng Keat Guest House (☎ & fax 04/881 1987). Set away from the beach, this has clean, comfortable rooms with showers, a garden and a small kitchen for self-catering. ②.

Casuarina Beach (☎04/811 1711, fax 881 2155). At the far western end of the beach – an intimate, low-rise, open-plan hotel that tends to be quiet. ⑧.

Golden Sands Resort (☎04/881 1911, fax 881 1880). The active social programme here, and the pool, make it one of the most lively upmarket places. There are lush gardens. ⑧.

Lone Pine (☎04/881 1511, fax 881 1282). Rather dated lowrise complex, but with large rooms right by the beach. ④.

Park Royal (☎04/881 1133, fax 881 2233). An elegant hotel with a good pool and an excellent range of restaurants. ⑧.

Popular Ferringhi Motel and Restaurant, (☎04/881 3454, fax 881 3457). A new operation just on the main road, with small but good-value rooms. ④.

Rasa Sayang (☎04/881 1966, fax 881 1984). Another classy hotel which makes the biggest concession to traditional Malay architecture. ⑧.

Shalini's (☎04/881 1859). A popular guesthouse, with cheap basic rooms and a balcony overlooking the beach. ②.

EATING AND DRINKING

There are some budget **restaurants** in Batu Ferringhi, but most places cater for the overspill from the large hotels, all of which have several restaurants of their own. By the beach there are some cheap food stalls, including the *Rastafarian Café*. There are also some fine seafood restaurants, and a few interesting Malay places. The roadside **stalls** (evenings only) by the *Guan Guan Café* sell inexpensive local food, or try *A&B Café*, by the western bridge, for tasty banana leaf curries.

Akebono. By the *Guan Guan Café*, a large Japanese restaurant where the set lunches are good value at $12.

Eden Seafood Village. At this huge beachfront place the boast is "Anything that swims, we cook it"; a cultural show accompanies the meal. Far from cheap at around $20 a dish.

Ferringhi Village. The bright and bustling place at the eastern end of the beach serves a good range of Chinese food, seafood and steaks.

Guan Guan Café. By the beach, just behind the food stalls. Moderately priced with a wide selection of food.

Happy Garden. At the western end of the main strip, this is set just off the road in a colourful flower garden and serves cheapish Chinese and Western food.

Moghul Arch. Set just back from the main cluster of beachfront hotels and restaurants, this serves excellent North Indian cuisine. Dishes are around $9.

Oasis. Centrally located on the main road, this place does Malay dishes from as little as $2.

Papa Din's Bamboo Restoran. Hidden at the end of an unlikely looking path over the western bridge, this features the septuagenarian *bomoh* (medicine man) Papa Din, who subjects you to a well-rehearsed self-adulation session as you tuck into an inexpensive and excellent three-course set meal.

Ship. Next door to the *Eden Seafood Village* is this unmissable, huge black boat with sails and rigging, serving steak at $25 a head.

Teluk Bahang

Another 5km west, the small fishing kampung of **TELUK BAHANG** is the place to come to escape the development. The long spindly pier towards the far end of the village with its multitude of fishing boats is the focus of daily life. Beyond the pier, a small path disappears into the forest and it's a two-hour trek west to the lighthouse at **Muka Head**. The beaches around this rocky headland are better than the ones at Teluk Bahang itself, but since the big hotels run boat trips out here, it's unlikely that you'll have them to yourself. Other diversions are to the south, up the road into the interior, where the Butterfly Farm and Forest Recreation Park (see overleaf) are just 200m from the village.

Accommodation is somewhat limited. Friendly *Rama's Guest House* (☎04/885 1179; ①) is about the cheapest place, with some basic dorm beds as well as rooms; take the left turn at the roundabout and it's about 50m down the road on the right. Further along the beach is the *Fisherman's Village* (no phone; ①) – simple rooms in a family home. *Madame Loh's* is another option but it's a bit more expensive ①; ask at the *Kwong Tuck Hing* shop on the main road. At the other end of the scale the beautifully decorated *Penang Mutiara*, on the main road (☎04/885 2828, fax 885 2829; ⑨), has a good range of restaurants and a well-kept beach.

Tanjung Bungah's real attraction is its plethora of inexpensive **places to eat** on the little stretch of main road, including an excellent seafood restaurant called the *End of the World*, just by the pier. The huge fresh prawns are a particular speciality. At the other end of the scale is the *Istana Malay Theatre Restaurant* (☎04/885 1175), part of the Penang Cultural Centre – a mini-Malaysia type park which incorporates traditional buildings from the nation's states. Dinner will set you back at least $45 and the nightly dance show starts at 8.30pm.

The rest of the island

If you're going to see the **rest of the island**, you'll have to get round it in one day, because apart from the hotels on the north coast and near the airport, there is no other accommodation on Penang. The trip *can* be done by bus which takes in most of the points of interest picked out below. But this route rather misses the point, which is to get away from the main road and explore the jungle, beaches and kampungs at leisure. Yellow bus #66 heads southwest from Georgetown to Balik Pulau, from where yellow bus #76 continues to Teluk Bahang. Change to blue bus #93 through Batu Ferringhi and back to town; make sure you leave Georgetown by 8 or 9am in order to get round the island. However, it's much better to **rent a motorbike**, or even a **pushbike**, from one of the outlets on Lebuh Chulia – it's a seventy-kilometre round trip so you have to be fairly fit to accomplish it using pedal-power, especially since some parts of the road are very steep. Once clear of the outskirts of Georgetown the roads are blissfully traffic-free. **Taxis** should charge around $50 for the round-island trip.

South to Gertak Senggal

The road south from Pengkalan Weld in Georgetown heads past the university to the **Snake Temple**, 12km out of town. This is a major attraction for bus tour parties (and their video cameras), and the usual bunch of stalls clutters up the otherwise impressive entrance which is guarded by two stone lions, the doors featuring brightly painted warrior gods. The temple was founded in memory of Chor Soo King, a monk who came from China over a hundred years ago and gained local fame as a healer. His statue sits in the main square in front of the temple, clothed in red and yellow. Inside, draped lazily over parts of the altar, is a handful of poisonous green snakes, which – legend has it

– mysteriously appeared upon completion of the temple in 1850 and have made the temple their refuge ever since. They're fairly lethargic (apparently drugged by incense) and most have been doctored, so it's considered safe enough to have your photograph taken with the snakes curled over you.

Continuing south, the road leads past the airport at Bayan Lepas to **BATU MAUNG**, 13km from the Snake Temple. There's not much here but pretty coastal scenes and an expensive Chinese seafood restaurant. You'll have to backtrack a couple of kilometres to the main road, which runs on 3km to **TELUK KUMBAR**, where the sea looks particularly uninviting and the beach, though reasonable, gets very crowded at weekends. West of here, the stretch of road along the south coast towards **GERTAK SANGGUL** is one of the most attractive spots on the island: gently winding and tree-lined, with the odd tantalising glimpse of glittering ocean. The road ends at a scenic bay where you can watch the local fishing boats at work.

North to Teluk Bahang

Backtracking almost to Teluk Kumbar, the road north winds steeply up to the village of **Barat**, where you have the choice of heading northeast to **BALIK PULAU** or southwest to **PULAU BETONG**. Neither are particularly enthralling, though there's something attractive in the quiet pace of life and the friendliness of the local people. Balik Pulau is probably the best choice, simply because of the string of good cafés along the main road. If you want to cut the trip short, you can head back to Georgetown via Ayer Itam.

The road north from Balik Pulau continues the circuit of the island. Next stop, and a small detour off the main road to the west, are **SUNGEI PINANG** and **PANTAI ACHEH**, Chinese fishing villages built along a narrow and largely stagnant river. If you don't mind feeling conspicuous – and can stand the pervasive rotting fish smell – they are a good place to watch the fishermen, painstakingly maintaining their wooden boats.

Back on the main road, the route once more climbs very steeply as it winds round the jungle-clad hillside, offering the occasional view over the flat, forested plain, which stretches towards the sea. A couple of kilometres from the junction for Sungei Pinang are the disappointing **Titi Kerawang Waterfalls**, for most of the year little more than a dismal, rubbish-strewn trickle. However, there is fresh fruit on sale at stalls by the roadside.

The road then levels and straightens out before reaching the **Forest Recreation Park** (Tues–Thurs & Sat–Sun 9am–1pm & 2–5pm, Fri 9am–noon & 2.45–5pm; free) on the right-hand side of the road. A museum introduces visitors to the different types of forest on Penang and there are several well-marked forest trails and a children's playground. Further along the road to Teluk Bahang is the **Butterfly Farm** (Mon–Fri 9am–5pm, Sat, Sun & holidays 9am–6pm; $4). This has all manner of creepy-crawlies including frogs, snakes, stick insects and scorpions, as well as four thousand butterflies of around 120 species, and is well worth a visit. The **batik factory**, less than 1km from the park, provides an uninspiring end to the island circuit; it is more a shop than a factory, with prices hiked up in expectation of the descending bus tours. Within sight, around 200m away, is the roundabout at Teluk Bahang. A right turn here brings you onto the northern coastal road, 20km or so from Georgetown.

Sungei Petani and around

From Butterworth, rail line and highway run north, into the state of **Kedah** and through the small town of Sungei Petani, 35km away. Few people stop, but those who do are drawn by the **archeological remains** at Lembah Bujang (Bujang Valley) 10km northwest, and the beacon of Gunung Jerai (Kedah Peak) 20km to the north, rather than any delights the town itself has to offer. Even these attractions are fairly specialist in nature – particularly the archeological site – and if you're at all short on time, keep going north.

The Town

SUNGEI PETANI is the nearest point from which to reach both sites. A clocktower dominates the main road through town – Jalan Ibrahim – to the right of which is a road leading to the **train station**. Long-distance buses depart from the stand marked "MKDM" by the clocktower. The local **bus station** and **taxi stand** are next door to each other on Jalan Puteri, which branches off left from the main road, about 200m south of the clocktower.

If you plan to visit both Lembah Bujang and Gunung Jerai in one day, you'll need to stay overnight in Sungei Petani at one of its three **hotels**, all within easy reach of the bus station. The first is the *Duta* (✆04/421 2040; ②), with reasonably priced air-con rooms; less expensive options are the optimistically named *Bright Hotel* further along on the opposite side (no phone; ①), and the nearby *Lih Pin* (no phone; ①) – the same price but very dingy. Out of town on Jalan Kolam Air, and in another price league altogether, is the *Sungei Petani Inn* (✆04/421 3411; ⑤), which is incongruously flash for the area.

There's a very popular Chinese **restaurant** at the *Bright Hotel*, and a small but lively night market a few blocks to the north.

Lembah Bujang

Lying between Gunung Jerai to the north and the Sungei Muda to the south, **Lembah Bujang** is the site of some of Malaysia's most important archeological discoveries. Much of the country's history before 1400 AD had been somewhat sketchily pieced together from unreliable, and often contradictory, contemporary accounts, until the early nineteenth century when "the relics of a Hindoo colony" were discovered in the Bujang Valley. This important find by Colonel James Low, a member of the Madras Army stationed at Penang and a keen amateur archeologist, gave credence to the prevailing theory that Hinduism was the dominant ideology in early Malaya. But since then, early twentieth-century excavations have revealed fifty or so **Buddhist temples** (known as *candis*) in the Bujang basin, creating controversy in academic circles which continues today.

Candi Bukit Batu Pahat, one of the tenth-century temples now reconstructed on the Lembah Bajang site, embodies the styles of Mahayana Buddhism as well as of the cults of Shiva and Vishnu. The argument runs that because there is no direct equivalent of the structure in India – the birthplace of Hinduism and Buddhism – this signifies that the religions adapted to the local culture, creating a new modified theology.

Since excavations are still taking place, most of the site is off limits to the public, but there is an **archeological museum** (daily 9am–5pm; free) which displays photographs of some of the finds *in situ*, as well as a number of relocated stone pillars, pots and jewels. The historical information is fairly turgidly written and there are precious few contextual comments on the artefacts, but behind the museum, eight *candis* (including Candi Bukit Batu Pahat) have been reconstructed using original materials.

Since the whole project is in its infancy, it is still quite difficult to reach the museum. From Sungei Petani take a local bus to the small village of Bedong, 8km north; here you'll see a signpost giving the direction of the museum. Another, rather infrequent, bus from Bedong takes you the final 15km, but it only drops you on the main road – the museum is a two-kilometre walk away. A taxi is a better bet; to charter one from Bedong should only cost \$8–10 one-way.

Gunung Jerai

Gunung Jerai (1200m), a massive limestone outcrop 10km north of Lembah Bujang as the crow flies, dominates the landscape. It's the highest peak in Kedah, and on clear days offers panoramic views over the rolling rice fields stretching up to Perlis in the north, and along the coastline from Penang to Langkawi. While it is stretching things to call the settlement on the peak a "hill station" – there's no colonial tradition here – there is one hotel, which can provide a pleasant overnight stop (though it's cheaper to stay at Sungei Petani). Wherever you stay, a few hours is enough to stroll around the **Sungei Teroi Forest Recreation Park** halfway up the mountain, with its rare orchids and animals including the lesser mouse deer and the long-tailed macaque for which the conservation area is renowned.

Gunung Jerai is replete with history and legend. Tales abound of the infamous **Raja Bersiong** ("the king with fangs") who once held court over the ancient kingdom of Langkasuka. Archeological digs revealed the existence of a water temple (Candi Telaga Sembilan) which many believe was the private pool of Raja Bersiong. A **Museum of Forestry** (daily 9am–3pm; free), at the top of the path leading to the recreation park, is of limited interest.

The jumping-off point for Gunung Jerai is just north of the town of Gurun on the Butterworth–Alor Setar road. Local bus #2 from Sungei Petani (every 30min) drops you at the bottom of the mountain after a thirty-minute ride. If you don't want to walk to the summit, a gentle two-hour climb, **jeeps** make the journey every 45 minutes (daily 8.30am–5pm; $5 return). At the top, you can stay at the *Peranginan Gunung Jerai* (☎04/423 4345; ⑤), which has a restaurant as well as comfortable chalets – the owners provide tents for $30 if you prefer sleeping *al fresco*.

Alor Setar

ALOR SETAR (pronounced "Alor Star"), the tiny state capital of Kedah, is the last major stop before the Thai border. It's a city that is keen to preserve its heritage – witness the many royal buildings and museums – and since Alor Setar has useful transport links to the east coast as well as to Thailand, you might well spend at least a short time here.

Kedah's history is a sad catalogue of invasion and subjugation, mainly by the Thais, lasting more or less up until the beginning of the twentieth century. But even from the earliest days, the state was noted for its independent spirit of resistance: an eleventh-century Chola-dynasty tablet inscription mentions "Kadaram (Kedah) of fierce strength". By the thirteenth century, Kedah was already asserting its own economic power over that of the Srivijaya empire, by sending ships to India to trade jungle products for such exotic goods as Arabian glass and Chinese porcelain. As a vassal state of Ayuthaya – the mighty Thai kingdom – during the mid-seventeenth century, Kedah still managed to express its defiance. For decades, the Malay states had been left to get on with their own affairs, provided they sent monetary tributes from time to time. But when, in 1645, the Kedah ruler was summoned to appear at the Thai court in person – an unprecedented request – he refused point-blank, claiming that it was beneath the dignity of a sultan to prostrate himself before another ruler. In a climb-down, the king of Ayuthaya sent a statue of himself to Kedah, instructing the court, rather hopefully, to pay homage to it twice a day. At the beginning of the nineteenth century, Kedah's relationship with its Thai conquerors degenerated into a *jihad*, or "holy war", led by Sultan Ahmad. The strength of religious feeling frightened the Bangkok government which deposed Ahmad, but in 1842 the British, anxious to see peace in the region and realizing the strength of Ahmad's hold over his people,

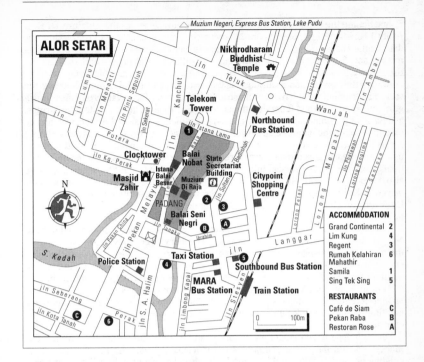

△ Muzium Negeri, Express Bus Station, Lake Pudu

ALOR SETAR

Nikhrodharam
Buddhist
Temple

Telekom
Tower

Northbound
Bus Station

WanJah

Clocktower

Balai
Nobat

State
Secretariat
Building

Citypoint
Shopping
Centre

Masjid
Zahir

Istana
Balai
Besar

Muzium
Di Raja

PADANG

Balai Seni
Negri

Langgar

ACCOMMODATION

Grand Continental	2
Lim Kung	4
Regent	3
Rumah Kelahiran Mahathir	6
Samila	1
Sing Tek Sing	5

RESTAURANTS

Café de Siam	C
Pekan Raba	B
Restoran Rose	A

S. Kedah

Police Station

Taxi Station

Southbound Bus Station

MARA
Bus Station

Train Station

0   100m

forced the sultan's reinstatement. Even this gesture had little effect on stubborn Kedah: as recently as the beginning of this century, when Kedah was transferred by the Thais to British control, it adamantly refused to become part of the Federated Malay States.

Something of Kedah's past is evident in Alor Setar today since many Thais still live here, worshipping in the splendidly restored Thai temple and running businesses and restaurants. For all that, Alor Setar is one of most Malay towns you'll find on the west coast, sustained in part by the predominance of Islam which, throughout the years of Kedah's external domination, played an important part in the maintenance of traditional Malay values. It is also the hometown of two of Malaysia's prime ministers: Tunku Abdul Rahman and Mahathir Mohammed.

The Town

Sungei Kedah runs along the western and southern outskirts of Alor Setar. The main sights are located to the west of the town around the padang, which has a large modern fountain at its centre. The **Masjid Zahir** dominates the western side of the square, its Moorish architecture highlighted at night by thousands of tiny lights. Facing the mosque, on the opposite side of the square, the elegant **Istana Balai Besar** (Royal Audience Hall) – the principal official building during the eighteenth century – stands serene amid the roaring traffic. The present two-storey, open-colonnaded structure only dates back to 1904, when the original hall was rebuilt to host the marriages of Sultan Abdul Hamid's five eldest children. So grand was the refurbishment and so lavish the ceremony, that the state was nearly bankrupted.

Just behind the Balai Besar, the old royal palace now serves as the **Muzium Di Raja** (daily 10am–6pm; Fri closed noon–2.30pm; free), an excellent way of preserving this dainty little 1930s building. The museum has its fair share of eulogistic memorabilia – medals and fond recollections of the current sultan's salad days – and some of the rooms have been kept exactly as they were used by the sultan and his family.

Across the way stands a curious octagonal tower, the **Balai Nobat**, housing the sacred instruments of the royal orchestra. Played only during royal ceremonies – inaugurations, weddings and funerals – the collection consists of three ornate silver drums, a gong, a long trumpet and a double-reeded instrument similar to the oboe, which combine to produce the haunting strains of "nobat" music. The word nobat is derived from a Persian word for a very large kettle drum, played in royal palaces. Since the instruments are regarded as the most treasured part of the sultan's regalia, so the musicians themselves are given a special title, Orang Kalur, relating to the time when they were also keepers of the royal records. The Kedah Nobat, the oldest and most famous, played at the installation of independent Malaysia's first constitutional monarch in 1947. Unfortunately, the tower, together with its priceless contents, remains closed to the public.

However, you are free to wander round the grandiose, white stucco **Balai Seni Negeri** (same hours as Muzium Di Raja), an art gallery directly across the padang from the tower, which displays largely uninspiring and derivative works showing the influence of traditional Malay culture on contemporary artists: rural scenes abound, as you might expect. South of the padang, across the Sungei Kedah, at 18 Lorong Kilang Ais, is **Rumah Kelahiran Mahathir** (Tues–Sun 9am–6pm; Fri closed noon–3pm; free), the birthplace and family home of Dr Mahathir Mohammed. It's now a museum, documenting the life of the local doctor who became the most powerful Malaysian prime minister of modern times.

For a glimpse of contemporary culture head for the **Pekan Rabu**, or "Wednesday Market", now a daily affair, running from morning to midnight. Situated in a large building on Jalan Tunku Ibrahim, there's a large collection of stalls selling everything from local farm produce to handicrafts – it's also a good place to sample traditional Kedah food like the "dodol durian", a sweetcake made from the notoriously pungent durian fruit.

The most modern sight in Alor Setar is the **Telekom Tower** (daily 10am–10pm) on Jalan Kanchut, just north of the padang, a mini-version of the one in KL, with a fast-food restaurant and viewing gallery. Walk east from here along Jalan Telok Wanjah and you'll see the **Nikhrodharam Buddhist Temple**, just beside the roundabout. The building of this glittering temple complex, decorated with many colourful statues, mosaics and paintings, began in the 1950s and was only finished in 1995; it's a match for many in Thailand and testament to the continuing influence of Thai culture in the city.

The Muzium Negeri and Lake Pudu

Hop on bus #31 heading north from Jalan Raja, adjacent to the padang, and after about 1.5km you'll pass the **Muzium Negeri** (daily 10am–6pm; Fri closed noon–3pm; free) on Jalan Lebuhraya Darulaman. There is some background information on the archeological finds at Lembah Bujang (see p.187), but the exhibits fail to ignite much interest, except for the delicate silver tree close to the entrance, known as the *bunga mas dan perak* ("the gold and silver flowers"). This refers to a practice, established in the seventeenth century, of honouring the ruling government of Thailand by a triennial presentation of two small gold and silver trees, about 1m in height, meticulously detailed even down to the birds nesting in their branches. The cost of these little sculptures was estimated at over a thousand Spanish dollars, no mean sum for those times. While the tradition was seen by Ayuthaya as a recognition of its suzerainty, the gift was considered by the Kedah rulers as a show of goodwill and friendship – a typical refusal to acknowledge their vassal status.

The extensive **Lake Pudu**, 90km from Alor Setar and near the Thai border, is the latest area of Kedah to receive the tourism treatment. To date this has stretched rather unimaginatively to a luxury resort and golf course, but the surrounding jungle and the lake itself, rich with wildlife, could offer far more to those seeking a back-to-nature experience. The only accommodation is at the well-equipped *Holiday Inn Resort Pudu Lake* (☎ & fax 04/730 4888; ⑨), which is built on two islands.

Practicalities

Alor Setar has a rather confusing array of bus stations, each serving different areas. The **express bus station** for services to Hat Yai and destinations within Malaysia is north of the centre, down an unsignposted left turning off Jalan Pekan Melayu, past a piece of waste ground around which the ticket booths are arranged – it's a ten-minute walk from here to the padang. **Northbound local buses** go from the station off Jalan Sultan Badlishah – there are more long-distance booking booths and departure points here too. For **southbound buses**, there's a station on Jalan Langgar, right in the centre of town (also the station for bus #106 for the 30min journey to Kuala Kedah for the ferry to Langkawi), and a smaller station for the MARA buses to Sungei Petani, a little further south behind the Hankya Jaya supermarket. The **taxi station** is in front of the MARA bus station. The **train station** is a five-minute walk east of the centre on Jalan Stesyen. Alor Setar is a principal station on the west coast route and a place to pick up the twice-daily express train to Hat Yai and Bangkok (5.37am & 3.30pm) on its way from Butterworth; strangely though, it doesn't stop here on the return leg. The domestic **airport** (MAS office; ☎04/721 1186), 11km north of town, is accessible by the hourly "Kepala Batas" bus from the northbound bus station. By taxi it costs $12.

The State Tourist Office (Mon–Fri 8am–4pm; ☎04/730 1957) is in the State Secretariat Building on Jalan Sultan Badlishah. Most of the major **banks** are on Jalan Raja.

Accommodation

Most **budget hotels** are close to the southbound bus station along Jalan Langgar. Furthest away from the station, but by far the best value, is the *Lim Kung* (☎04/732 8353; ①). The dark corridors look unpromising but the rooms are the largest you'll find in town for the price, and the manager is exceptionally friendly. The *Sing Tek Hotel Sing*, right above the bus station (☎04/732 5482; ①), is slightly more upmarket; the rooms are large and have bathrooms. Amongst the mid-range places try the comfortable *Regent* (☎04/731 1900, fax 731 1291; ④) on Jalan Sultan Badlishah. Most of the top-class hotels are inconveniently situated on the outskirts of town – exceptions are the landmark *Grand Continental* on Jalan Sultan Badlishah (☎04/733 5917, fax 733 5161; ⑥) and the *Samila* (☎04/731 8888, fax 733 9934; ⑤), just north of the padang, which has more character and is at the bottom end of its category – excellent value for the plush, well-appointed rooms.

Eating

You'd do well to sample some regional **Thai cuisine** while in town – try *Café de Siam* on Jalan Kota Tanah, for Thai seafood. One of the best-value places is the *Restoran Rose*, on Jalan Sultan Badlishah, which serves excellent and filling Indian food. For a variety of dishes under one roof head for the Pekan Rabu market, while if your budget can stand it, the restaurant at the *Samila* gets good reports for its Western cuisine.

Langkawi

Situated 30km off the coast at the very northwestern tip of the Peninsula is a cluster of 104 tropical islands, dotted liberally throughout the Straits of Melaka, known collectively as **LANGKAWI**. Most are little more than deserted, tiny scrub-clad atolls, and only two are inhabited, including the largest of the group, **Pulau Langkawi**, once a haven for pirates and now a sought-after refuge for wealthy tourists. With the encouragement of it's biggest fan, Dr Mahathir, who once worked as a doctor here, Pulau Langkawi has seen unparalleled development in recent years, enhanced by its duty-free status, making it Malaysia's premier island retreat. Some of the country's most luxurious hotels are here, and a new airport has been built to cope with the increasing number of visitors. Perhaps because of Pulau Langkawi's size (around 500 square kilometres), most of its inhabitants still live a traditional way of life, and its natural attractions – a mountainous interior, white sands, limestone outcrops and lush vegetation – have remained relatively unspoiled. The archipelago's beauty has fostered traditional stories of the "Islands of Legends" and in true Malay fashion almost every major landmark has a myth associated with it – each ruthlessly hijacked by the tourist authorities to promote the islands. The charms of Pulau Langkawi consist largely of lazing around on beaches and enjoying the sunshine, although you can visit the ancient **Makam Mahsuri**, various splendid waterfalls and the **Telaga Air Panas** hot springs on a day-trip or by bike or taxi. Designated **wildlife and marine parks** on neighbouring Pulau Singa Besar and Pulau Payar provide a little extra interest. You can also explore other, **uninhabited islands** in the archipelago, though the only way to do this is by taking an expensive day-trip, organized either by the tourist office or one of the hotels on Pulau Langkawi.

The principal town on Pulau Langkawi is **Kuah**, a boom town of hotels and shops in the southeast of the island, where you'll find most of the duty-free bargains. The main tourist development has taken place around three bays on the western side of the island, at **Pantai Tengah**, **Pantai Cenang** and **Pantai Kok**. Of these, Cenang is by far the most commercialized, although there is still some budget accommodation available. More recent building work has taken place at two beaches on the north coast, **Pantai Datai** and **Tanjung Rhu**, where accommodation is limited to top-class resorts. Be warned: Langkawi is not a budget destination and to appreciate all the islands have to offer, you need to spend quite a bit of money.

Getting there

Langkawi is most commonly reached from Kuala Perlis (see p.201), adjacent to the Thai border, from where there are nine **fast boats** every day (45min; $13 one-way). **Ferries** also operate eight times daily from **KUALA KEDAH** (1hr 10min; $15 one-way), 51km to the south, just 8km from Alor Setar (see p.188). There's rarely any need to book tickets in advance – just turn up when you want to go. Both services run to the jetty on the southeastern tip of the island, about five minutes' drive from Kuah itself. There are also ferry services **from Thailand**: three times daily from Satun on the border (1hr 30min; $15) – the ferries dock at Kuah. Buses supposedly run from the jetty into Kuah, but in practice it's easier to get a **taxi**, which should cost around $4. Alternatively, there's a once-daily direct express boat **from Penang** (2hr 30min; $35 one-way) which also docks at Kuah jetty. The **airport** (☎04/955 1311) is 20km west of Kuah, near Pantai Cenang, served by internal flights from KL, Penang and Ipoh, and international services from Singapore and Kansai Airport in Japan. Again, you'll have to take a taxi – it'll cost less than $10 to any of the western beaches or $12 to Kuah.

The Langkawi **tourist office** (daily 9am–5pm; ☎04/966 7789) located opposite the mosque on the way into Kuah is very helpful. There's also an information booth at the jetty terminal. The MAS office (☎04/966 6622) is in the Tabung Haji building in Kuah town.

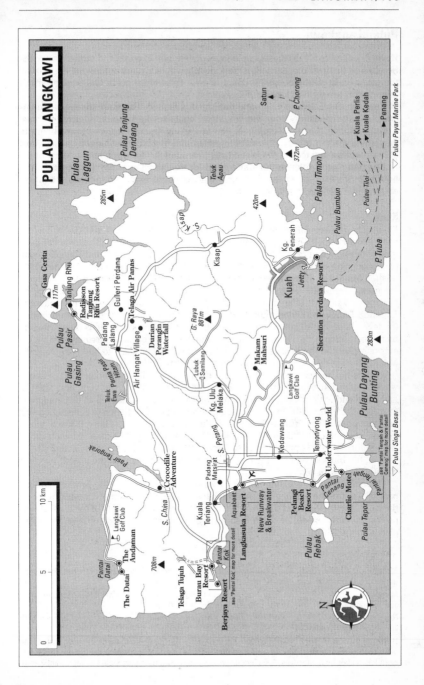

PULAU LANGKAWI

Pulau Laggun

Pulau Tanjung Dendang

Satun

P. Chorong

285m

Gua Cerita

117m

Tanjung Rhu

Radisson Tanjung Rhu Resort

Pulau Pasir

Padang Lalang

Gulleri Perdana

Telaga Air Panas

S. Kisap

420m

Teluk Apau

372m

Palau Timon

Kuala Perlis
Kuala Kedah
Penang

Pulau Gasing

Teluk Pasir Pasir
Ewa Hitam

Air Hangat Village

Durian Perangin Waterfall

G. Raya 881m

Lubuk Semilang

Kisap

Kg. Penerah

Kuah

Jetty

Pulau Bumbun

P. Tuba

▽ Pulau Payar Marine Park

Pulau Tilot

Makam Mahsuri

Kg. Ulu Melaka

Langkawi Golf Club

Sheraton Perdana Resort

283m

Pasir Tengorak

Crocodile Adventure

S. Perang

Padang Matsirat

Kedawang

Temonyong

Underwater World

Pulau Dayang Bunting

▽ Pulau Singa Besar

S. China

Langkawi Golf Club

The Andaman

708m

The Datai

Pantai Datai

Telaga Tujuh

Burau Bay Resort

Berjaya Resort

Pantai Kok

see "Pantai Kok" map for more detail

Kuala Teriang

Aquabeat

Langkasuka Resort

New Runway & Breakwater

Pelangi Beach Resort

Charlie Motel

Pantai Cenang

Pantai Tengah

see "Pantai Tengah & Pantai Cenang" map for more detail

Pulau Rebak

Pulau Tepor

▽ Pulau Singa Besar

10 km

5

0

N

Pulau Langkawi

Having docked at Kuah, most people immediately hop in a taxi and strike out for the beaches on the west coast. There is basically one circular route around the island, with the other main road cutting the island in two, connecting north and south; various minor roads are well surfaced and signposted.

However, public transport around the island is limited. There are three **bus** routes out of Kuah, departing from the bus stand opposite the hospital: hourly to Pantai Cenang (8am–6.15pm); a similar service to Padang Lalang; and every two hours to Pantai Kok (8am–4.30pm). It's easier to get around by **taxi**: most longer journeys cost $12–15, while a taxi tour of the island runs to around $50 for three hours. Many of the chalets and motels offer **motorbike rental** for around $35 per day. It takes at least a full day to see everything, but there are plenty of places to stop for a drink or a bite to eat, and fuel stops at regular intervals.

Kuah

Lining a large sweep of bay in the southeastern corner of the island, **KUAH**, with a population of thirteen thousand, is easily the largest town on Langkawi. The town has been greatly developed in recent years, with a new ferry terminal, hotels and shopping complexes popping up all along the bay. Land has been reclaimed, marooning the whitewashed **Masjid Al-Hana** mosque – which used to dominate the waterfront – behind a car park. Beside the ferry terminal is **Dataran Lang** "Eagle Square", graced by an enormous sculpture of an eagle (Langkawi means red eagle). Next to the square is **Lagenda Langkawi Dalan Taman** (daily 9am–9pm; $5), a "theme park" based around the legends of the islands with twenty hectares of landscaped gardens punctuated by more giant sculptures. There are vantage points over the bay and surroundings but it's expensive, and in the heat of the day there is no shade or place to buy refreshments. Most of the hotels and shopping complexes are further around the bay.

Kuah is not an unattractive place, but despite the multitude of hotels it's not somewhere you're likely to want to stay. However, it will probably be your first sight of Langkawi and is the place to sort out any business matters. As well as the numerous duty-free shops along the main road, selling everything from hooch to handbags, you'll find the **post office** (Mon–Wed, Sat & Sun 9.30am–3.30pm, Thurs 9.30am–noon), **police station** (☎04/966 6222) and **hospital** (☎04/966 3333) close to each other. Behind the MAYA shopping complex, also on the main road, are three parallel streets with all the **banks** (virtually the only places to change money on the island) together with the **Telekom** centre.

There are numerous eating houses of various standards, from the **hawker stalls** – past the post office heading towards the jetty – to the pricier seafood **restaurants** on the front, like the *Sari* and the *Orchid*. Despite the ready availability of fresh fish, these places are fairly expensive, each dish setting you back at least $8 – there are better places on the island.

ACCOMMODATION

Malaysia (☎04/966 6298). About halfway along the main road heading west; scruffy but with a helpful information board. Can arrange motorbike rental. ②.

Langkawi, at nos. 6–8 on the main road, close to the tourist office (☎04/966 6248). Another clean and reasonable option, though the rooms are quite basic. ②.

Region (☎04/966 7719, fax 966 7700). Down a turning opposite the mosque, a real bargain with very comfortable rooms. ④.

Beringin Beach Resort (☎04/966 6966, fax 966 0468). As you make towards the jetty, just off the main road is this small cluster of well-appointed chalets in a tiny bay, where part of the beach has been taken over by mangroves. A secluded spot, so you're own transport would be an advantage. ⑤.

Tiara Langkawi (☎04/966 2566, fax 966 2600). The unmissable pink fairy-tale castle complex on the waterfront is tacky and its rooms are poorly finished. ⑤.

Sheraton Perdana Resort (☎04/966 2020, fax 966 6414). Follow the road to the left of the jetty to this luxury place. Set in landscaped grounds, with a private beach, sports facilities and several swimming pool, the hotel commands a spectacular view of island-dotted Langkawi Bay. ⑨.

Towards the west coast beaches

Heading west from Kuah just past the Langkawi Golf Club, whose dress code for women states – alarmingly – that "skirts should not be higher than six inches from the shoulder", a signpost about 10km from town directs you to **Makam Mahsuri** (the tomb of Mahsuri), in Kampung Mawat, the site of Langkawi's most famous legend. It tells of a young woman named Mahsuri, born over two hundred years ago, whose beauty inspired a vengeful accusation of adultery from a spurned suitor – or, as some versions have it, a jealous mother-in-law – while her husband was away fighting the invading Siamese. Mahsuri protested her innocence but was found guilty by the village elders who sentenced her to death. She was tied to a stake, but as the ceremonial dagger was plunged into her, she began to bleed white blood, a sign that proved her innocence. With her dying breath, Mahsuri muttered a curse on Langkawi's prosperity to last seven generations – judging by the island's increasing income in recent years, this must be beginning to wear off at last. The white marble tomb (daily 10am–6pm; $2) stands alone in a shady garden, and the entrance fee also gains you access to a reconstruction of a traditional Malay house.

Pantai Tengah

Back on the main road, a further 8km brings you to a junction where a left turn, clearly signposted, takes you to the first of the western beaches, **PANTEI TENGAH**, 6km away. It's a quiet beach and the sand itself isn't at all bad, but the secluded nature of the bay means that the water isn't renewed by the tide and is murky. There are also jellyfish, so take local advice before you swim.

Accommodation is limited to a couple of smart resorts and a handful of low-key chalet places, about the best of which is the popular *Charlie Motel* (☎04/955 1200; ③), with chalets and a beachfront patio restaurant. A bit further along the beach, the *Sugary Sands Motel* (☎04/955 1755; ②) is one of three plots unimaginatively bunched together on a bare piece of ground; the others are *Green Hill Beach Motel* (☎04/955 1935; ②) and the *Tanjung Malie* (☎04/955 1891; ②), both of a similar standard. Close by, and much better, is the *Sunset Beach Resort* (☎04/955 1751; ③), a pretty place with good rooms, gardens and a beachfront restaurant and bar. Finally, closer to the road, are the adjacent *Langkawi Village Resort* (☎04/955 1511, fax 955 1531; ⑥) and *Langkawi Holiday Villa* (☎04/955 1701, fax 955 1504; ⑦); both are in a secluded position at the very end of the beach and there's very little to choose between them.

Eating is largely limited to the restaurants attached to the various motels and resorts. Both *Charlie* and *Sunset* have mellow beachside restaurants, hosting the occasional **barbecue** at around $15 a head. Alternative options are *Oasis* opposite *Charlie*, a colourful beach bar that does Chinese and Indian dishes, and *Sheela's* near the *Langkawi Holiday Villa*, which mixes Malay and German cuisine.

Pantai Cenang

Five hundred metres north of Tengah, the development at **PANTAI CENANG** is the most extensive on the island, with cramped chalet sites side by side. By and large though, the buildings themselves are unobtrusive, mainly because of the government's requirement that beachfront accommodation must not exceed the height of a coconut tree. The bay forms a large sweep of wide, white beach with crisp, sugary sand, but again the water here won't win any prizes for cleanliness. Less dedicated sun-worship-

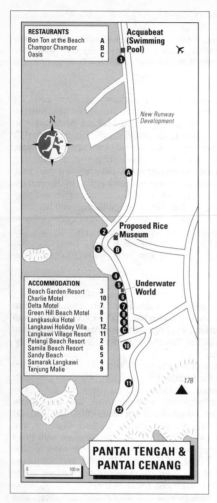

RESTAURANTS
Bon Ton at the Beach A
Champor Champor B
Oasis C

Acquabeat
(Swimming
Pool)

New Runway
Development

N

Proposed Rice
Museum

Underwater
World

ACCOMMODATION
Beach Garden Resort 3
Charlie Motel 10
Delta Motel 7
Green Hill Beach Motel 8
Langkasuka Hotel 1
Langkawi Holiday Villa 12
Langkawi Village Resort 11
Pelangi Beach Resort 2
Samila Beach Resort 6
Sandy Beach 5
Samarak Langkawi 4
Tanjung Malie 9

178

**PANTAI TENGAH &
PANTAI CENANG**

0   100 m

pers will find the lack of shade on the beach a problem, but its sheer length and breadth means that, despite the package-tour clientele, it never gets too crowded. Plenty of places offer **watersports** and **boat rental**, otherwise only available at the large resorts elsewhere on the island. One of the more organized centres is *Langkawi Marine Sports* (☎04/955 1389), where costs are negotiable depending on the season – expect to pay around $180 per boat (which can take eight people) for a round-island boat tour, $110 for a day's fishing or $25 for ten minutes' waterskiing.

The main attraction along Pantai Cenang is **Underwater World** (daily 10am–6pm; $12), which boasts that it's the largest aquarium in Asia, housing over five thousand marine and freshwater fish. Although the attached duty-free shopping complex seems like the main reason for the operation, the fish are well presented, the highlight being a walk-through aquarium where sharks, turtles and hundreds of other sea creatures swim around and above boggle-eyed visitors. There's also a touch pool where you can get feely with starfish, sea slugs and sea cucumbers. There are plans to build a **rice museum** opposite the *Pelangi Beach Resort*, which has its own mini-golf course, based around the legends of Langkawi, open to the public.

ACCOMMODATION

There are dozens of **places to stay**, although not many good options at the budget end of the scale – if money's tight, you're unlikely to be able to afford a sea view.

AB Motel (☎04/955 1300). A friendly and attractive development with gardens, hammocks and a terrace restaurant. ②.

Delta Motel (☎04/955 1891). At the promontory, has a fine location with good-value chalets. ②

Pelangi Beach Resort (☎04/955 1001, fax 955 1122). Pantai Cenang's finest accommodation, which hosted the 1989 Commonwealth Conference – a luxurious, two-storey timber development which echoes traditional Malay architecture. ⑧.

Samila Beach Resort (☎04/955 1964). One of the cheaper places on this stretch, but don't expect much. It has corrugated-roof A-frames with bathrooms. ②.

Sandy Beach Resort (☎04/955 1308). Has a wide variety of accommodation, although you'll pay more for the beachfront bungalows. ②–④.

Semarak Langkawi Beach Resort (☎04/955 1377). The is the best place in its price range and boasts spacious, wooden-floored bungalows in a large garden compound. ④.

Suria Beach Motel (☎04/955 1776). About 100m north from the promontory which separates Cenang from Tengah, with small, ramshackle rooms. ②.

EATING AND DRINKING

Most of the resorts also have attached **restaurants**, with the emphasis on Westernized local dishes. The *Delta* is good value, but doesn't serve alcohol, and the *Semerak Langkawi* has a pleasant, if slightly expensive, terrace restaurant; the *AB Motel* is better value. The *Beach Garden Resort Bistro* is a pretty beachside operation catering to the tastes of German visitors, as do many of the places along the beach. On the opposite side of the road is the excellent, but pricey *Champor Champor*. Meaning "mix mix", this small bar and restaurant combines Western and Oriental influence to successful effect in an enchanted grove atmosphere: meals are around $20. For top-notch food, head for the *Pelangi Beach Resort* – eating in its excellent Chinese or Thai restaurants could set you back around $50 a head.

North to Pantai Kok

Immediately north of the *Pelangi Beach Resort*, major development of the airport and surroundings is afoot. The extension of the runway into the bay has effectively ruined what beach there was, and the long-term plan is to turn this area into yet another golf course. It is unlikely that outlets such as the restaurant and trendy crafts shop *Bon Ton at the Beach* (☎04/955 3643), will survive. Currently this restaurant is worth visiting for its well-presented food and homemade cakes, and for the seven traditional kampung houses that stand beside it. The now defunct thousand-room *Delima Resort* further up the coast is eloquent testament to development run amok – it had to be abandoned when the chalets starting falling to pieces because of shoddy workmanship. Further up the coast, next to the *Langkasuka Resort* (☎04/955 6888, fax 955 5888; ⑥) is the *Aquabeat* indoor water theme park (daily except Tues 9am–9pm; $20), which includes wave pools and a range of water slides.

Heading north, skirting around the airport, a right turn brings you to the **Padang Matsirat** (The Field of Burnt Rice). Shortly after Mahsuri's death, the Siamese conquered Kedah and prepared to attack Langkawi. The inhabitants of the island set fire to their staple crop and poisoned their wells in order to halt the advance of the invaders, and to this day, so the legend goes, traces of burnt rice resurface in the area after a heavy downfall of rain.

Continuing round the island road, another couple of kilometres uphill you pass the *Sheraton Langkawi* (☎04/955 1901, fax 955 1968; ⑦) perched on a cliff top, before reaching **PANTAI KOK**, which lies on the far western stretch of Langkawi. It's the best beach on the island, a large sweep of powdery white sand with relatively clear and shallow water – quieter and more secluded than Cenang, more intimate in feel, and with little to do in the evening except swing in a hammock looking up at the stars. In addition, you're also only 2km from the splendid falls at Telaga Tujuh, just to the north (see below).

ACCOMMODATION

There are plans to develop a golf course here, and all the **budget chalets** have been given their marching orders; because of the uncertainty, many of the chalets have let themselves become run-down. It's possible that there will be no cheap accommodation by now, so check with Tourism Malaysia before deciding to stay here. In spite of its name, the *Last Resort* is the best option.

Berjaya Langkawi Beach and Spa Resort (☎04/959 1888, fax 959 1886). This large and luxurious operation has several grades of upmarket accommodation, a range of restaurants and a Japanese-style outdoor spa set in the woods. ⑧.

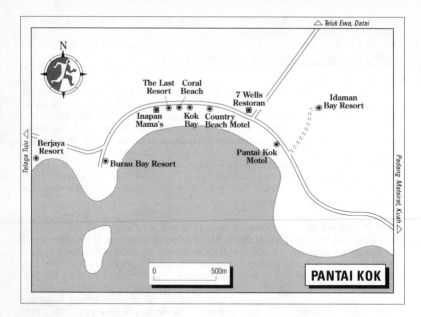

Burau Bay Resort (☎04/955 1601, fax 955 1172). This upmarket place is at the western end of the beach, and is aimed at the family market. The cabana-style chalets are quite spacious. ⑤.

Coral Beach (☎04/955 1000). Neat and tidy, if rather regimented, rows of huts. ②.

Country Beach Motel (☎04/955 1212). Riding somewhat on its reputation. Some of the chalets are fine, but the place is generally run-down. ①–③.

Idaman Bay Resort (☎04/955 1066). For something a bit out of the ordinary, the reasonably priced chalets are arranged around a freshwater pool reached by wooden walkways, and come with air-con, hot water, TV and phone. ②.

Kok Bay (☎04/955 1407). Neat rows of chalets – nothing special. ②.

Last Resort (☎04/955 1046). A great place with timber and *atap* rooms; the luxury detached beachfront bungalows here are in the next price category up. ②–③.

Pantai Kok Motel (☎04/955 1048). Very cheap rooms, but run-down. ①.

EATING AND DRINKING

Most of the chalets again have their own **restaurants**. The best food around also happens to be the cheapest, at the tiny *7 Wells Restoran*, on the corner of the road to Datai – it has wonderful home cooking with either chicken or fish dishes cooked to order. Another good option is at *The Last Resort*, which has an attractive, airy restaurant, though it's a little on the expensive side. At the lively *Idaman Bay*, the restaurant overlooks the pool and serves hot, Thai-influenced dishes; the bar balcony is built on stilts over the river which whirls underneath you when the tide comes in. Finally, *Inapan Mama's* has hamburgers on the menu and is a good spot for drinking late into the night.

Telaga Tujuh

The road after the turn-off to the *Berjaya Resort* leads up to the island's most wonderful natural attraction, **Telaga Tujuh** or "Seven Pools", a cascading freshwater stream that has pounded large recesses into the rock. The mossy surface covering the rock enables you to slide rapidly from one pool to another, before the fast-flowing water disappears over the cliff to form the ninety-metre **waterfall** you can see from below – it's only the depth of the water in the last pool that prevents you from shooting off the end too. This being Langkawi there's an associated legend, suggesting it is the playground of mountain fairies; a special kind of lime and the *sintuk* (a climbing plant with enormous pods) found around these pools are believed to have been left behind by the fairies, and the locals use them as a hair wash to rinse away bad luck.

It's a steep two-hundred-metre climb to the pools from the inevitable cluster of souvenir stalls at the base of the hill – in total, it's about a 45-minute walk from the road near the *Burau Bay Resort*. Look out for the long-tailed macaque monkeys that bound around the trail; they are playful, but can be vicious if provoked. If you're lucky, you may spot a cream-coloured giant squirrel (famed in these parts) scampering up the trunks, or a great hornbill hanging out in the tree tops. The great hornbill is the most distinctive of all Malaysian birds, with its huge, hooked orange beak and cackle-like call.

The north coast
From Pantai Kok the main road heads north to Pulau Langkawi's **north coast**. On the way you'll pass *Crocodile Adventure* (daily 9am–6pm; $6) which has daily "man vs crocodile" shows at 11.15am and 2.45pm. After 10km you'll reach a new road off to the left which leads a further 12km to **DATAI**, the site of Langkawi's newest resort development. The road curves and climbs to reveal a couple of secluded coves from where you can see several Thai islands in the distance. The sea at this point is a clear jewel-blue – perfect for a dip after the hot, dusty ride. Just before you reach the resort area there's more development close to the top-notch Datai Bay Golf Club. Private villas here go for a million dollars.

In the short time that the *Datai* (☎04/959 2500, fax 959 2600; ⑨) has been open, it has become one of Malaysia's most exclusive resorts. Volcanic rock and wood has been used with stunning effect to create architecture that is in tune with the forest surroundings. The views across the bay to Thailand are stunning. The same company also runs *The Andaman* (☎04/959 1099, fax 959 1168; ⑨), which shares the beach at Datai Bay. To reach either of these resorts on arrival on Langkawi you'll pay around $25 for a taxi from the airport, and $40 from the jetty at Kuah.

Backtracking from Datai, further round the coast, past Teluk Ewa, a couple of reasonable stretches of undeveloped beach look inviting, but the otherwise panoramic view from here is marred by an unsightly factory belching out large clouds of concrete dust. A little further on is **Pantai Pasir Hitam** (Black Sand Beach), where the cliff drops down away from the road to the black sands.

Five kilometres further east the road intersects with the main north–south route across the island at the village of **Padang Lalang**. Turn left, and a couple of kilometres through some swampy land will bring you to **TANJUNG RHU**, also known as "Casuarina Beach" because of the profusion of these trees here. The only development here is the *Radisson Tanjung Rhu Resort* (☎04/959 1091, fax 959 1211; ⑥). Close to the beach, past the sign that warns "Alcohol is the root of all evil", are some food and drink stalls – which don't sell beer. Although the sand here is a bit gritty, the sea, sheltered by the curve of the bay, is unusually tranquil, almost lagoon-like. The tide goes out far enough for you to walk to the nearby islands of **PULAU PASIR** and **PULAU GASING**, only a few metres across the sand and perfect for a bit of secluded sunbathing. On a promontory accessible only by boat from Tanjung Rhu ($80), you'll find the isolated **Gua Cerita** (Cave of Tales), facing the Thai coastline. Despite the profusion of bat droppings, it's worth looking closely inside the cave as you can make out verses of the Koran written in ancient script.

Back at the crossroads, it's another 2km east to the site of **Telaga Air Panas** (Hot Springs), reputedly formed during a quarrel between the island's two leading families over a rejected offer of marriage. Household items were flung about in the fight: the spot where gravy splashed from the pots became known as Kuah (gravy), and here, where the jugs of boiling water landed, hot springs spouted. There's not much to see and what there is has been subsumed within the **Air Hangat Village** (daily 10am–6pm; $4), which now encompasses the hot springs and an arts pavilion, designed in traditional Malay kampung style. There are demonstrations of folk and classical dance, kick boxing and *silat* at various times of the day. There is also an expensive restaurant that puts on a cultural show every evening, catering inevitably for tour groups.

Next along the road is the *Galleri Perdana* (Tues–Sun 10am–5pm; $2) which contains over ten thousand state gifts and awards presented to Prime Minister Dr Mahathir – there are plans afoot to create a prime ministerial art gallery on the island too. Further on is the turn-off for **Durian Perangin**, a waterfall reached along a difficult and rocky path, and fairly disappointing unless you happen to catch it after the wet season when the water level is high. Shortly after this the road curves to the south for the remaining 10km to Kuah.

Other islands

While most of the Langkawi archipelago is uninhabited (and uninhabitable), expensive day-trips are run to some of the nearer islands – fine if you're into snorkelling and fishing, but otherwise providing little incentive to leave the main island. Apart from an island-hopping boat that leaves from Kuah jetty twice a day (9am & 2.30pm; $35), trips are organized by various hotels at Pantai Tengah or Pantai Cenang and are expensive.

Mountainous **PULAU TUBA**, 5km south of Langkawi, is the only island with accommodation and has only one option – the *Sunrise Beach Resort* (☎04/966 0003, fax 966 0054; ④), with its own swimming pool. There's barely enough space around the rim of the island for the dirt track which encircles it, though it does take in some deserted beaches. It's awkward to get to Tuba – a matter of hanging round the Kuah jetty until someone offers to take you across in one of the small speedboats; a return trip costs $6.

PULAU DAYANG BUNTING (Island of the Pregnant Maiden) is the second largest island in the archipelago, about fifteen minutes' boat ride from Pulau Langkawi. It's the exception to the rule in having at least a couple of specific points of interest, but you'll have to visit on a day-trip as there's nowhere to stay. **Tasik Dayang Bunting**, a large and tranquil freshwater lake, is reputed to have magical properties believed to make barren women fertile. The area is overwhelmed by massive, densely forested limestone outcrops, which are at their most dramatic around the **Gua Langsir** (Cave of the Banshee), a towering 91-metre-high cave on the island's west coast, which is said to be haunted – probably because of the sounds of thousands of bats which live inside. The island-hopping boat (see above), drops you at a jetty near the lake, before continuing on to the cave, 8km to the north.

Langkawi's most recent attempt at green tourism is realized on **PULAU SINGA BESAR**, a wildlife sanctuary 3km off the southern tip of Pantai Tengah and also a stop for the island-hopping boat. The organized day-trip includes the services of a guide, since for obvious reasons you're not allowed to roam around at will. Monkeys, mouse deer, iguanas and peacocks are among the wildlife to have been freed on the island, although how many animals you actually see is inevitably a matter of luck.

There are three companies which organize trips to the **PULAU PAYAR MARINE PARK**. *Langkawi Coral* which has an office at Kuah Ferry Terminal (☎04/966 7318) is the most expensive at $220 for the day, but this does include hotel pick-ups, lunch, the use of their reef-viewing platform and all snorkelling equipment. *Island and Sun* at Kelanas in Kuah town (☎04/955 2745) has the cheapest trip at $150 in small speedboats (doesn't include hotel transfers). In the marine park there are great schools of tropical fish, and south of the island, 13km west of the Peninsula, lies a coral garden supporting the largest number of coral species in the country. Again, no accommodation is available, and to camp you must first obtain permission from the Fisheries Department at Alor Setar (☎04/732 5573).

North to the Thai border

The tiny state of **Perlis** – at 800 square kilometres the smallest in Malaysia – lies at the northwestern tip of the Peninsula bordering Thailand. Together with neighbouring Kedah, it's traditionally been viewed as the country's agricultural heartland, something reflected in the landscape which is dominated by lustrous, bright green paddy fields. There's no special reason to stop here and most people pass quickly through the state's dull towns on their way to Thailand. Although both main roads and train line cut inland to the border, it's easy enough to catch local buses to the coastal villages covered below.

Kuala Perlis

Boats to and from Langkawi dock at the little town of **KUALA PERLIS**, 45km north of Alor Setar, and although it's the second largest settlement in the state it only has two streets. Buses drop you at an unmarked stand adjacent to the jetty, from where a wooden footbridge connects with the older, more interesting part of town, a ramshackle collection of buildings on stilts. The Kuala Perlis–Langkawi Ferry Service has an office here (☎04/985 4494), but it's just as easy to turn up and board, with five departures throughout the day.

There are two **banks** in the main part of town, near the jetty. While express buses to Padang Besar, Alor Setar and Butterworth are fairly frequent, there are a couple of **hotels** if you need to stay, the cheapest of which is the *Asia* (☎04/985 5392; ②), signposted a short five-minute walk out of town. An upmarket alternative is the antiseptic *PENS Hotel* (☎04/985 4122; ④), just along from the jetty on the road towards Kangar. A few *kedai kopis* provide **snacks**, but don't expect much here.

You can reach Satun in **Thailand** directly from Kuala Perlis: small boats leave from the jetty when they are full and charge $4 for the thirty-minute journey. This is the quickest cross-border option if you're coming from Langkawi (otherwise, you have to cross by bus or train; see below). At weekends you'll be charged an additional $1 for the immigration officers' overtime payment.

Kangar, Arau and Kaki Bukit

Buses north run on to **KANGAR**, 12km from Kuala Perlis, the state capital and another unremarkable modern town, and stop at the centrally located bus station where you have to change buses for the border. The nearest **train station** is at **ARAU**, 10km east. This is the least interesting of all Malaysia's royal towns – the Royal Palace (closed to the public) on the main road looks little more than a comfortable mansion. The town is only really handy for the daily train to Hat Yai and Bangkok (which doesn't stop here on the return journey), and there are less convenient daily connections to Butterworth, Alor Setar, Sungei Petani, Taiping, Ipoh, Tapah Road and Kuala Lumpur.

With your own transport, and time to kill before crossing the border, you could visit **Gua Kelam Kaki Bukit**, a 370-metre-long limestone cave once part of a working tin mine, 14km before the border checkpoint at Padang Besar. Its name literally means "at a foothill lies a cave of darkness". The subterranean stream that runs through the cavern was once used to carry away excavated tin ore to the processing plant near the cave's entrance. Access through the cave is by way of a suspended wooden walkway so visitors can look down into the former mine, though it is also used by locals – and their motorbikes – as a means of getting to the other side of the valley. **KAKI BUKIT** itself is easily reached by bus from Kangar, but since this means carting your luggage with you through the mine and back again, you'll probably want to give it a miss and carry straight on to Padang Besar.

Crossing the border

The two land **border crossings** are at the villages of Padang Besar and, further south-east, Bukit Kayu Hitam.

The **train** comes to a halt at **PADANG BESAR**, where a very long platform connects the Malaysian service with its Thai counterpart. You don't change trains here although you must get off and go through customs at the station. By **bus**, frequent services from Kangar drop you on the road at the border, which is open from 6am to 6pm. The first train gets to Padang Besar at 7.40am, the last at 4.20pm, while buses run regularly throughout the day. The **North–South Highway** runs to the border at **BUKIT KAYU HITAM**, from where it is about a five-hundred-metre walk to Danok on the Thai side.

Once you've passed through immigration, there are regular bus connections from both places with Hat Yai, 60km away – southern Thailand's transportation hub. The train passes through here, too, on its way north to Bangkok.

travel details

Note that connections for overland transport from Penang are from Butterworth; see p.169 for details of leaving Penang.

Trains

Alor Setar to: Arau (3 daily; 30min–1hr); Bangkok (daily; 18hr 15min); Butterworth (daily; 2hr 45min); Hat Yai (daily; 2hr 20min); Ipoh (daily; 4hr 30min); Kuala Lumpur (daily; 8hr 50min); Padang Besar (2 daily; 1hr 15min); Sungei Petani (2 daily; 50min–1hr 10min); Taiping (daily; 3hr); Tapah Road (daily; 5hr 40min).

Butterworth to: Alor Setar (2 daily; 1hr 40min–2hr 20min); Bangkok (daily; 19hr 55min); Hat Yai (daily; 4hr); Ipoh (5 daily; 2hr 55min–4hr 22min); Kuala Kangsar (5 daily; 2–3hr); Kuala Lumpur (5 daily; 7hr 10min–10hr); Sungei Petani (daily; 2hr 15min); Taiping (5 daily; 1hr 30min–2hr 10min); Tapah Road (5 daily; 3hr 50min–6hr 10min).

Ipoh to: Butterworth (5 daily; 3hr 25min–5hr 10min); Kuala Kangsar (5 daily; 1hr–1hr 30min); Kuala Lumpur (6 daily; 4hr 15min–5hr); Taiping (6 daily; 1hr 40min–2hr 30min); Tapah Road (6 daily; 55min–1hr 45min).

Kuala Kangsar to: Butterworth (5 daily; 2hr 30min–3hr 40min); Ipoh (5 daily; 50min–1hr 15min); Kuala Lumpur (5 daily; 4hr 10min–7hr); Taiping (5 daily; 40min–1hr); Tapah Road (5 daily; 1hr 45min–3hr).

Padang Besar to: Alor Setar (daily; 3hr 25min); Bangkok (daily; 17hr 15min); Butterworth (daily; 2hr 40min); Hat Yai (daily; 1hr 20min); Ipoh (daily; 8hr); Kuala Lumpur (daily; 12hr 15min); Sungei Petani (2 daily; 1hr 40min–4hr 15min); Taiping (daily; 6hr 30min); Tapah Road (daily; 9hr).

Taiping to: Alor Setar (daily; 3hr 30min); Butterworth (5 daily; 1hr 50min–2hr 40min); Ipoh (6 daily; 1hr 25min–2hr 10min); Kuala Kangsar (5 daily; 30min–1hr); Kuala Lumpur (6 daily; 5hr 40min); Padang Besar (daily; 4hr 45min); Sungei Petani (daily; 2hr 45min); Tapah Road (6 daily; 2hr 20min–4hr).

Tapah Road to: Alor Setar (daily; 7hr); Butterworth (5 daily; 4hr 20min–6hr 20min); Ipoh (6 daily; 1hr 10min); Kuala Kangsar (5 daily; 1hr 50min–2hr 45min); Kuala Lumpur (6 daily; 3hr 20min–3hr 50min); Padang Besar (daily; 8hr 10min); Sungei Petani (daily; 6hr); Taiping (6 daily; 2hr 30min–3hr 40min).

Buses

Alor Setar to: Butterworth (every 30min–1hr 30min; 2hr 30min); Hat Yai (2 daily; 3hr); Ipoh (2 daily; 6hr); Johor Bahru (2 daily; 16hr); Kota Bharu (2 daily; 8–9hr); Kuala Lumpur (2 daily; 8hr); Kuala Perlis (every 30min; 1hr 30min); Kuala Terrenganu (2 daily; 8hr); Kuantan (daily; 9hr 30min); Tapah (3 daily; 6hr).

Butterworth to: Alor Setar (every 30min–1hr; 2hr 30min); Bangkok (2 daily; 18hr); Hat Yai (2 daily; 5hr 30min); Ipoh (6 daily; 3hr 45min); Kota Bharu (2 daily; 6hr); Kuala Lumpur (at least 15 daily; 7hr); Kuala Perlis (5 daily; 3hr 45min); Kuala Terengganu (2 daily; 8hr); Kuantan (3 daily; 12hr); Lumut (4 daily; 4hr); Melaka (1 daily; 6–10hr); Padang Besar (5 daily; 4hr); Singapore (at least 2 daily; 16hr); Seremban (4 daily; 8–9hr); Sungei Petani (10 daily; 1hr 15min); Surat Thani (2 daily; 10hr 30min); Taiping (14 daily; 2hr 15min); Tapah (3 daily; 4hr 30min).

Ipoh to: Alor Setar (2 daily; 6hr); Butterworth (6 daily; 3hr 45min); Kangar (2 daily; 6hr); Kuala Kangsar (every 45min; 1hr); Kuala Lumpur (every 30min–1hr; 4hr); Kuala Terrenganu (2 daily; 11hr); Kuantan (5 daily; 8hr); Lumut (every 30min–1hr; 1hr 30min); Penang (5 daily; 4hr 30min); Singapore (5 daily; 10–11hr); Taiping (every 30min; 45min); Tapah (hourly; 1hr 20min).

Lumut to: Butterworth (4 daily; 4hr); Ipoh (every 30min–1hr; 1hr 30min); Kuala Lumpur (6 daily; 5hr 30min); Kuantan (5 daily; 9hr 30min); Taiping (every 30min; 1hr 10min); Tapah (2 daily; 2hr).

Tapah to: Alor Setar (3 daily; 6hr); Butterworth (3 daily; 4hr 30min); Hat Yai (daily; 10hr); Ipoh (hourly; 1hr 20min); Kuala Lumpur (at least 10 daily; 2hr–2hr 30min); Kuala Terrenganu (daily; 7hr); Kuantan (2 daily; 6hr); Lumut (2 daily; 2hr); Melaka (2 daily; 3hr 30min); Singapore (2 daily; 10hr).

Ferries

Butterworth to: Penang (every 20min–1hr, 24hr service; 15min).

Kuala Kedah to: Langkawi (6 daily; 1hr 10min).

Kuala Perlis to: Langkawi (9 daily; 45min).

Langkawi to: Kuala Kedah (8 daily; 1hr 10min); Kuala Perlis (9 daily; 45min); Penang (daily; 2hr 30 min); Satun (3 daily; 1hr).

Penang to: Butterworth (every 20min–1hr, 24hr service; 15min); Langkawi (1 daily; 2hr); Medan (Indonesia; daily; 4hr).

Planes

Ipoh to: Johor Bahru (at least 4 daily; 55min); Kuala Lumpur (at least 6 daily; 35min); Langkawi (2 weekly; 45min).

Langkawi to: Ipoh (2 weekly; 45min); Johor Bahru (daily; 2hr 20min); Kuala Lumpur (at least 7 daily; 55min); Penang (at least 3 daily; 30min); Phuket (1 daily; 40min); Singapore (at least 7 daily; 1hr 25min).

Penang to: Bangkok (3 daily; 1hr 40min); Johor Bahru (at least 6 daily via KL; 1hr 5min–3hr 45min); Kota Bharu (daily; 40min); Kuala Lumpur (at least 19 daily; 45min); Kuding (2 weekly; 2hr); Langkawi (4 daily; 30min); Medan (daily; 20min); Phuket (daily; 30min); Singapore (at least 12 daily; 1hr 10min–3hr 55min).

CHAPTER THREE

THE INTERIOR

T he **interior** states of Pahang and Kelantan were the last regions of Peninsular Malaysia to excite the interest of the British colonial authorities. Until the 1880s the Bendahara (Prince) of Pahang, Wan Ahmed, ran his southern central state as a private fiefdom, unvisited by outsiders except for a hundred or so Chinese and European gold prospectors who had established contacts with a few remote Malay villages and **Orang Asli** settlements. When explorer and colonial administrator Sir Hugh Clifford visited, he noted that the region "did not boast a mile of road and it was smothered in deep, damp forest, threaded across a network of streams and rivers . . . flecked here and there by little splashes of sunlight." What Clifford also noted – indeed the reason for his visit – was that Pahang was, "wonderfully rich in minerals". Wan Ahmed gave the British mining and planting rights, in exchange for military protection against the incursions of the Siamese and Kelantanese.

First to arrive were British officials, then tin and gold prospectors, followed by investors in rubber and other plantation enterprises. The new arrivals initially used the rivers to get around, though the larger companies soon began to clear tracks into the valleys and along the mountain ridges, the forerunner of today's roads. Development was made much easier when the jungle railway opened in the 1920s (see below). Slowly, small towns like **Temerloh**, **Raub** and **Kuala Lipis** grew in size and importance, while new settlements like Gua Musang were established to cater for the influx of Chinese merchants and workers.

Since the 1980s, when the only highway into the interior (Route 8 from Bentong to Kota Bharu) was finished, the whole region has been transformed. If still not entirely accessible – there are corners whose "utter remoteness from mankind" have changed little since Clifford's day – the impact of the **timber, rubber and palm-oil industries** cannot be underestimated. Much of the primeval landscape, hitherto the preserve of Orang Asli, a few Malays and the odd Chinese trader, has been rapidly tamed, providing economic incentives for people from both east and west coasts to move into these areas. This encroachment has had a huge effect on the indigenous tribes of the interior, and since the late 1950s the greater part of the Orang Asli have opted out of their traditional lifestyle. It's probable that only a few hundred truly nomadic tribespeople remain, and even those have been tainted by economic progress. Orang Asli expert, Iskandar Carey, wrote in the 1970s, "There are groups of Senoi in the deep jungle who have never seen a road, although they are familiar with helicopters, a word for which has been incorporated into their language." The Centre of Orang Asli Affairs coordinates a variety of policies, including health and educational drives. Though inevitably diluting the purity of Asli culture, these initiatives have lifted their standard of living and begun the process of integrating the Orang Asli into mainstream, multiracial Malay culture.

Banjaran Titiwangsa (Main Range) forms the western boundary of the interior; to its east is an H-shaped range of steep, sandstone mountains with knife-edge ridges and luxuriant valleys where small towns and kampungs nestle. The rivers which flow from these mountains – Pahang, Tembeling, Lebir, Nenggiri and Galas – provide the northern interior's indigenous peoples, the Negritos and Senoi, with their main means of transport. Visitors, too, can travel by boat to perhaps the most stunning of all Peninsula Malaysia's delights, **Taman Negara** – the country's first national park which straddles

THE EMERGENCY, THE ORANG ASLI AND LAND RIGHTS

During the **Emergency** years (1948–60), Chinese Communist guerrillas – many originally members of the Malayan Communist Party – built jungle camps deep in the forested interior from which to operate against both British and Malayan forces. The effect of this on the way of life of the Sakai – the Orang Asli groups inhabiting areas north of the Kuantan Highway (Route 2) as far as Kuala Kerai in Kelantan – was dramatic. All but the most remote tribes were subject to intimidation and brutality, from guerrillas on one side and government forces on the other. In effect, the Orang Asli's centuries-old invisibility ended. The population of Malaysia was now aware of their presence, and the government of their strategic importance.

The Orang Asli had no choice but to grow food, act as porters for the guerrillas and, most important of all, provide an intelligence service to warn them of the approach of the enemy. In turn, government forces built eleven jungle forts, some near the towns of Raub and Tanjung Malim. In near desperation they implemented a disastrous policy – soon abandoned – of removing Orang Asli from the jungle and relocating them in new **model villages** near Raub and Gua Musang, which were no more than dressed-up prison camps. Thousands were placed behind barbed wire and hundreds died in captivity before the government dismantled the camps. By then, not surprisingly, more of the Orang Asli actively supported the insurgents – though they switched their allegiance to the security forces when the guerrillas' fortunes waned and defeat became inevitable.

At the peak of the conflict, around **ten thousand guerrillas** were hiding out in dozens of camouflaged jungle camps. For a long time they milked a support network of Chinese-dominated towns and villages in the interior, in many cases cowing the inhabitants into submission by means of public executions – although in some areas many of the poor rural workers identified with the struggle to wrest the ownership of the large rubber plantations away from the British. It was only when the government successfully started to plant informers that the security services started to get wind of guerrilla operations.

As far as the impact on the Orang Asli was concerned, government attempts to control them during the Emergency led inexorably to the imposition of a framework of laws, social strategies and programmes during the 1960s and 1970s. This has ranged from providing basic health and education facilities to subjecting the Orang Asli to Islamic proselytising, but in recent years Asli activists and legal experts have begun to contest a number of these government-sponsored initiatives. The **land rights** issue is now considered by a growing number of people to be the most urgent affecting the Orang Asli. According to one commentator, Lim Heng Seng, "the Asli find themselves virtually squatters on state land" and as long as the problem of legal entitlement to land remains unresolved, encroachment on Asli land will continue. Land is everything to the Orang Asli – in the Semai language, land is called *nerng-rik*, which means "country". Life has changed very rapidly for most Orang Asli since the Emergency years, and it pays to remember that what is seen as progress for many other Malaysians, could all too easily be a cultural trap that is closing in on the indigenous people.

the borders of Pahang, Kelantan and Terengganu states. Further south, two lake systems, **Tasek Chini** and **Tasek Bera**, are home to the Jakun and Semelai groups – Orang Asli who still live in a quasi-traditional way.

The new **Route 8** cuts up through the interior; the **drive** takes around twelve hours from KL to Kota Bharu (not allowing for the occasional landslide or rock fall). However, unless you're in a real hurry to get to either coast, consider a trip on the **jungle railway** which winds through the valleys and round the sandstone hills from Mentakab in southern Pahang to Kota Bharu, 500km to the northeast. There are interesting stops at Kuala Lipis (the former capital of Pahang), at the **Kenong Rimba** and **Jelawang** parks, and the **caves** at Dabong and Gua Musang. The train was originally known as the "Golden Blowpipe", but it runs at a snail's pace and is seldom less than two hours

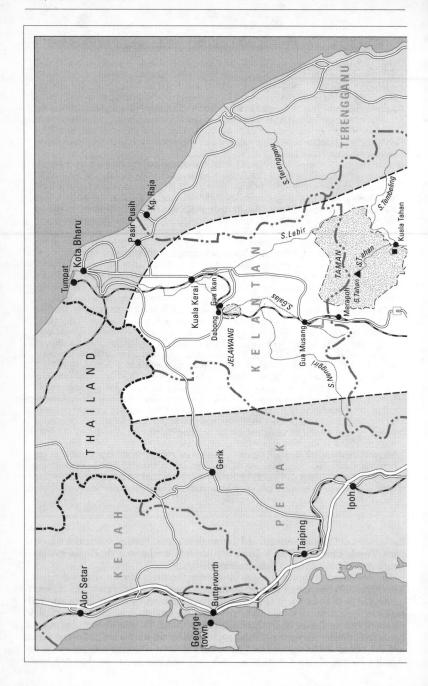

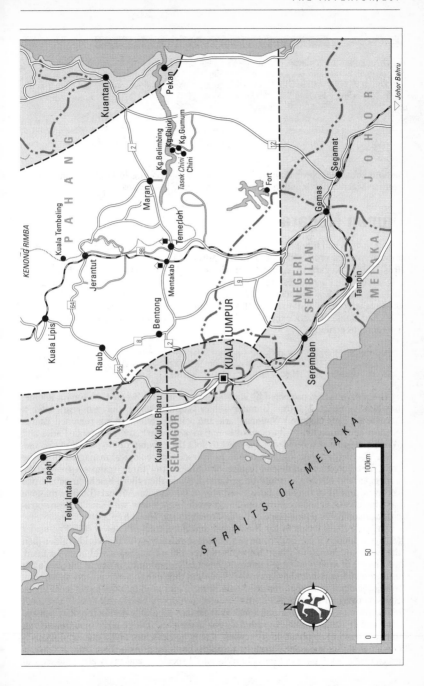

ACCOMMODATION PRICE CODES

Throughout the Malaysia chapters we've used the following **price codes** to denote the cheapest available room for two people. Single occupancy should cost less than double, though this is not always the case. Some guesthouses provide dormitory beds, for which the dollar price is given.

① $20 and under	④ $61–80	⑦ $161–240
② $21–40	⑤ $81–100	⑧ $241–400
③ $41–60	⑥ $101–160	⑨ $401 and above

behind schedule. Nevertheless, it's a great way of meeting local people and seeing remote Malay villages and the interior's spectacular landscapes.

Taman Negara

Two hundred and fifty kilometres northeast of KL is Peninsular Malaysia's largest and most important protected area, **TAMAN NEGARA**, spread over 4343 square kilometres. Taman Negara (meaning "the national park") comprises dense lowland forest, higher-altitude cloud forest enveloping the highest peak **Gunung Tahan**, numerous hills, Orang Asli settlements, hides, campsites and a chic jungle retreat. From the streams which snake down from the mountains feeding fierce waterfalls, to the lush flora and fauna, the park experience (as the tourist brochures never tire of telling you) is second to none.

There's a map of Taman Negara park on p.219.

The area was first protected by state legislation in 1925, when 1300 square kilometres was designated as the Gunung Tahan Game Reserve; thirteen years later it became the King George V National Park, and at independence it was renamed Taman Negara and extended to its current boundaries. In 1991, the Malaysian Parks and Wildlife Department decided it was best to split the running of the park into two sections. The department would continue to oversee the ecological management of the park, but accommodation and eating facilities at the three main sites – Tahan, Trenggan and Keniam – would be privatized. Since then there has been substantial **redevelopment** by the Singapore-based *Pernas* hotel chain. At Kuala Tahan a massive cash injection has financed over one hundred deluxe chalets, with smaller, less obtrusive developments taking place at Kuala Trenggan and Kuala Keniam.

The park itself forms by far the largest undivided tract of rainforest in Peninsular Malaysia; indeed it contains some of the **oldest rainforest** in the world – older than the Congo or Amazon – which has evolved over 130 million years. Although for many the chance of seeing sizeable mammals, especially **elephants**, is one of the park's big draws, very few visitors have any success unless they either make a three- or four-day trek, or journey upriver to remote Kuala Keniam and head into the forest from there. But stay overnight in the hides – tree houses positioned beside salt licks – and you'll often spot mouse deer, tapir and *seladang* (wild ox), especially during the rainy season. That said, it's quite possible to spend a week in the park and see nothing more exciting than a mound of elephant dung, armies of ants and leeches, and a colourful shape – maybe an argus pheasant – bashing through the undergrowth. **Bird life**, at least, is ever present – the park has over three hundred species – and many are quite easy to spot with good binoculars and patience. For a full rundown of the park habitats and species on view, see the wildlife account in Contexts, p.617.

Every **trek** into the forest has its fascinations. For those unfamiliar with the tropical rainforest environment, just listening to the bird, insect and animal sounds, smelling the rich, intoxicating air, wondering at the sheer size of the dipterocarp trees and peering into the **rainforest canopy** is bound to be a memorable experience. There's a myriad of entrancing sights: **flowering lianas**, giant bamboo stands with fungi which glow in the dark and chattering **macaque monkeys** rattling across the tree tops. A few dozen nomadic Batek Orang Asli, a subgroup of the Negritos, remain in the park and on the paths which weave along the west side of Sungei Tembeling and curl off north into the jungle. You may pass their vine and forest brush shelters, built to stand only for a few days before the inhabitants move on again – but you'll seldom see the Asli themselves. The Batek are mostly hunters and gatherers and the authorities generally turn a blind eye to them hunting game here. Some Batek work for the park authorities at the resort.

The undoubted success of the *Taman Negara Resort* – over sixty thousand people a year now visit the park – brings its own problems. According to some Malaysian environmentalists, the increasing number of visitors is having an impact on the park's ecosystem: the popular trail to Gunung Tahan is suffering accelerated **erosion** due to the large number of hikers who also leave rubbish on the trail, littering a formerly pristine environment. Also of concern is the effect on the biological food chain of the gradual migration of large mammals from the noisy Kuala Tahan area around the resort.

The best time to **visit** the park is between February and October, during the "dry" season, although it still rains most days even then. The park used to close in the wet season (mid-Oct to Feb), but under the new management is now staying open during this period, when there may be restrictions on the trails and boat trips. Those who want a tranquil, at-one-with-nature experience may well not take to **Kuala Tahan** and would be better advised to stay upstream at **Nusa Camp**, which is smaller and more basic. Alternatively head straight for the upriver camps at **Kuala Keniam** and **Kuala Trenggan**, or camp at one of the twelve designated sites dotted around the park.

Access to the park

The vast majority of visitors take a bus to **Tembeling jetty**, from where it's a three-hour boat trip up Sungei Tembeling to the park headquarters at **Kuala Tahan**. By jungle railway, there's access from one of two stops – either **Jerantut**, a small town 10km from the jetty, or **Kuala Tembeling**, a kampung further north; the jetty is only a thirty-minute walk. As there is no accommodation at Kuala Tembeling, many stay the night at Jerantut (see below for details), and it's also possible to take a **bus** into the park.

From KL

There are no scheduled **flights** into the park, but Kris Air (☎03/746 5210; $190 return) operates irregular services between KL and the **Sungei Tiang airstrip**, from where it's a further thirty minutes north by boat to Kuala Tahan (around $80). There is a daily shuttle bus (8am; $25) from the *Istana Hotel* in KL's Golden Triangle on Jalan Raja Chulan which also houses the **booking office** for the Taman Negara Resort. You don't need to be staying at the resort to use this bus, which arrives at Tembeling jetty in time for the 2pm boat departures. Additionally, tickets can be bought from many of the hostels in KL.

The scheduled **bus route** to the park involves two stages. First, take the Temerloh–Jerantut bus from KL's Pekeliling station (p.85), which leaves six times a day, for the three-hour trip to Jerantut ($9). From there, there are three options: either take a taxi ($16) or a local bus (40min; around $3) for the sixteen-kilometre trip to

Tembeling jetty, or take the bus tour to Kuala Tahan. As the buses only leave at 8am, 11am and 1.30pm, many visitors stay overnight in Jerantut and catch the 8am bus the next day. The 7am or 8am bus from KL gets you to Jerantut in time to catch the 11am bus to the jetty, but, as only two boats a day depart for the park headquarters – at 9am and 2pm – this leaves you with a long wait. Note that the 1.30pm Jerantut–Tembeling bus doesn't arrive at the jetty in time for the 2pm boat.

The second option is to take the **bus trip** organized by the management of the *Jerantut Resthouse* and *Sri Emas Hotel* (see below). This leaves Jerantut daily around 7am and includes visits to cocoa, palm oil and rubber plantations along the way to Kuala Tahan, arriving around 10.30am and returning to Jerantut at around 12.30pm. The cost ($23 one-way) is the same as the combined cost of a shared taxi and boat. It's certainly worth taking this bus either in or out of the park since it saves on taking the three-hour boat trip twice over.

The **train** from KL involves travelling to Gemas (trains leave KL at 8am & 2.45pm), where you change to the jungle train, which leaves Gemas at 2.20am, getting to Jerantut at 5.30am. The train arrives at the tiny station at **Kuala Tembeling** thirty minutes later at 6am (tell the guard if you want to get out at Kampung Tembeling as it's an unscheduled stop), which leaves plenty of time to walk the 2km west to the jetty for the 9am boat – there are unlikely to be any taxis as this is a very remote stop. The total price for the train trip from KL is around $12.

From the east coast

Trains leave **Wakaf Bharu**, 7km from Kota Bharu (see p.241), daily at 8.10am, reaching Kuala Tembeling at around 1pm (if the train is on time, you will be able to catch the 2pm boat departure; if not you'll have to spend the night in Jerantut). Alternatively, the 3.50pm from Wakaf Bharu arrives at Jerantut at around 9.25pm; the 7.25pm at 12.40am. **From Kuantan**, two daily buses (8am & noon; $12) go straight to Jerantut, or there's an hourly service to Temerloh, where you change for Jerantut (usually within the hour).

Jerantut

JERANTUT is a small, busy town with only one major street, Jalan Besar, lined with Chinese cafés and houses. From Jerantut's **bus station** – where the buses arrive from KL and Kuantan and leave for Tembeling jetty – it's a five-minute walk south to Jalan Besar and the centre of town. The **train station** is off Jalan Besar, just behind *Hotel Sri Emas*.

Jerantut has plenty of good-value **accommodation** and places to eat. One kilometre west of the train station on Jalan Besar is the excellent *Jerantut Resthouse* (☎09/266 4499 fax 266 4801; ②), which has comfortable dorms ($8) and twin-bed chalets with bathrooms. Managers Steven and Angie are extremely friendly and helpful, organizing the bus transfer to the park and holding a nightly briefing on what you can do in Taman Negara; you can attend these sessions even if you're not staying at the hotel. They also run *Hotel Sri Emas* (☎09/266 4499, fax 266 4801; ②), in the middle of town, at the junction of Jalan Besar and the road which leads to the train station. A third option is the *Hotel Jerantut*, 100m east on Jalan Besar from the junction (☎09/266 5568; ①), which usually has rooms available. There's an excellent **hawker centre** (daily 5pm–1am) opposite the bus station, which sells particularly good Thai food, and the Chinese cafés serve the usual dishes.

Tembeling jetty to the park headquarters

Many motorized sampans depart for the park from **Tembeling jetty** (daily 9am & 2pm, except Fri 2.30pm; $19 one-way), so that the area has become something of a mini-

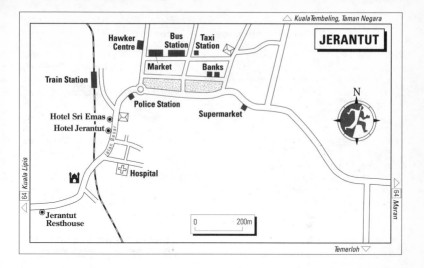

bazaar, with a hundred or more visitors waiting for a connection at any one time. At the jetty there is a handicraft shop (daily 9am–6pm), three cafés (same hours) selling *nasi campur*, noodles and snacks and, up some nearby steps, the *Taman Negara Resort* **ticket office** where you must buy a park entry permit ($1) and a licence ($5) if you're taking a camera. The Nusa Camp kiosk is to the left of the jetty. Boats to both the resort and Nusa Camp leave at the same time.

The sixty-kilometre, three-hour boat trip starts on wide Sungei Pahang, but after 300m or so the sampans branch off into the narrower **Sungei Tembeling**. At first, you'll see huts high up on the bank beside small pepper orchards and oil palm plantations, but soon the moss-draped trees reach down to the water, the forest canopy thickens, and a dab of brown leaves or a sporadic outbreak of red flowers interrupts the various shades of green. Occasionally white-horned cows and buffalo can be seen wallowing in the water, and birds skeet across the bows of the sampan, swooping into the trees.

The sampans run to two separate points: *Taman Negara Resort* at Kuala Tahan – the park headquarters – and Nusa Camp, a private initiative, 2km further northeast on Sungei Tembeling, but outside the park boundary on the east side of the river. If you arrive by road in Kuala Tahan it's no problem getting across to register at the park offices on the other side of the river – just wait for a boat from any one of the floating restaurants.

Kuala Tahan

The increasing popularity of Taman Negara as a holiday destination has led to a fair bit of development in recent years at **KUALA TAHAN**. Visitors can stay either at the resort or in the village itself on the other side of the river. The attractive park site nestles in the forest, at the confluence of the Tahan and Tembeling rivers. After disembarking at the jetty you climb the steps to the *Taman Negara Resort* **office**, where you sign in and get taken to your accommodation. An excellent site and park **map** is available here for no charge – and if you are staying in a resort chalet, you'll also get a glossy brochure giving details about the park and listing the on-site facilities. The information desk in the office

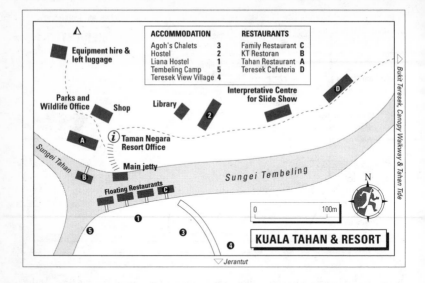

ACCOMMODATION
Agoh's Chalets	3
Hostel	2
Liana Hostel	1
Tembeling Camp	5
Teresek View Village	4

RESTAURANTS
Family Restaurant	C
KT Restoran	B
Tahan Restaurant	A
Teresek Cafeteria	D

KUALA TAHAN & RESORT

deals with queries from all park visitors, regardless of whether you're staying in Kuala Tahan itself, or at Nusa Camp. You also have to book your return boat trip at this office, although there is nearly always room on the sampans for anyone making a snap decision.

Most of the **chalets** lie east of the *Taman Negara Resort* office, while just along the path which runs through them, there's the **hostel**, a small library and annex – where slide shows about the park take place every day at 8.45pm. The **library** (daily 9am–11pm) has a diverse selection of geographical journals and accounts of the park; the slide show gives an entertaining, if out-of-date, rundown of the park's main features. Behind the office is the official **Parks and Wildlife Department** headquarters and a **shop**, selling basic provisions. The path beside the shops leads up some steps to the **campsite** where there is an office renting out everything you'll need for trekking and camping, including backpacks and light-weight jungle boots. You can also store your luggage here ($1 per day).

Accommodation

For **accommodation** at the resort you need to book in KL, either at MATIC (Malaysian Tourist Information Complex, 109 Jalan Ampang; daily 9am–9pm; ☎03/264 3929) – or in the *Hotel Istana* office (☎03/245 5585, fax 245 5430). Alternatively, call the *Taman Negara Resort* direct (☎09/266 3500, fax 266 1500). It's best to book around two weeks in advance of your trip if possible, though if you're planning to camp it isn't necessary to reserve in advance. The two-storey, two-bedroom **bungalows** are the height of luxury (⑨), with balcony, bathroom with hot showers and kitchen. Next down in price, the hundred-plus twin-bed **chalets** with bathroom (⑤–⑥) are also highly impressive, with fiercer air-con than in most expensive hotels. Significantly less expensive is the hundred-bed **hostel** ($8), a long brick building, with rather cramped four-berth rooms, at the back of which are washbasins and toilets but no cooking facilities. Lastly, there is the **campsite**, 300m from the resort office, which looks directly onto the jungle (campers are advised not to leave any food outside their tents otherwise the monkeys will get it). You can rent tents from $8 a night from the camping shop, and there's a small site charge of $2 per person.

In Kuala Tahan itself, the *Teresek View Village* (☎09/266 3065; call in the morning) provides the most comprehensive range of accommodation, from pretty chalets (①–③) to dorm rooms ($12) and tents. There's a café that does set meals for around $7 and a supermarket with much cheaper prices than the one in the resort – worth visiting to stock up on provisions before any trek. The next option is *Agoh's Chalets*, set in landscaped gardens and fronted by concrete fashioned into logs. These sweat boxes (①–②) are overpriced, but there are cheaper ($10) dorm rooms. If you're looking for an authentic kampung experience, your best bet is *Tembeling Camp*, which overlooks the river at the end of the village. Here, the four-bed *atap* huts (①) have fans, mosquito nets, outdoor cooking facilities and even a pet deer. The last, and most basic, option is *Liana Hostel* (①), on the hill just above the floating restaurants (see below).

Eating and drinking

On the resort side of Kuala Tahan there are three different **places to eat**. The *Tahan Restaurant* (daily 8am–11pm) charges around $40 a head, but the buffet is good and worth a splurge. Cheaper, but much more basic, is the *Teresek Cafeteria* (daily 8am–9pm) which is a lovely, quiet spot serving fried noodles and mixed rice, with free hot water; bring your own tea or coffee. By far the best-value food at the site is at the *KT Restoran* (daily 7am–11pm), which you'll find on a secure raft just west of the jetty. It's a private enterprise offering excellent food, both Malaysian and Western, at low prices: around $6 for a full meal. It's also the best place to order an inexpensive **packed lunch**. The last option is to cross Sungei Tembeling by sampan from the jetty and eat at the floating restaurants beside the shingle beach or in the kampung itself. All the floating restaurants do set meals for around $9 – the best range of food is at the *Family Restaurant*, which also organizes tours around the park.

Nusa Camp

The far smaller **Nusa Camp** is 2km further upstream on Sungei Tembeling. Boats from Tembeling jetty will take you straight there, stopping briefly at Kuala Tahan first. Although accommodation and food is cheaper, the disadvantage of staying here is that you are dependent on the sampans to ferry you over the river to the park proper, or down to Kuala Tahan. These trips add up, as the boatmen charge around $4 each way. There aren't any official hikes starting from the east side of the river, which is outside the park boundary, but you can walk to the **Abai waterfall**, about an hour from the camp, or up the nearby peak of **Gunung Warisan** which is two hours' hike away from Nusa.

For accommodation, it's best to book in advance at MATIC (☎03/262 7982, fax 262 7682) in KL, or call SPKG Tours (☎09/266 2369, fax 266 4369) in Jerantut. There's also an office by the jetty at Kuala Tembeling (☎09/266 3043). The most expensive accommodation is in the twin-bed **chalets** (②), which are a lot more basic than the ones at the resort, but have attached bathrooms. The tiny **tepee**-like pyramid buildings (①) have an external toilet and shower; the four-bed dorm rooms cost $10.35 a night. Nusa Camp has one small **cafeteria** (daily 8am–10pm) which does cheap set meals.

Other sites

There is also accommodation available at lodges, hides and campsites throughout the park, the sites of which are covered in more detail in the relevant accounts below. The **lodges** (③–④) upriver at Trenggan (30min from Kuala Tahan by sampan) and Keniam (2hr) are built along the same lines as the chalets at Tahan, although they're less luxurious. They should be booked in advance if you're planning to go straight there; otherwise leave booking until you arrive in Tahan. There isn't an official campsite at either of these places, but you can pitch your own tent. Along Sungei Keniam in the remote northeast of the park is *Perkai Lodge* (①), run by the Parks and Wildlife Department. It's very basic, with just eight beds, and you don't need to book – though you will need to take your own bedding. Both Trenggan and Keniam have **cafeterias**, although stocks of food are usually low unless a group is expected, when a boatful of provisions will be brought in from Kuala Tahan. Staying at *Perkai Lodge*, you have to bring your own food which you can cook on the rudimentary barbecue at the back of the lodge.

There's a $5 charge to stay overnight in the various **hides** (see box on p.216) dotted around the park; you have to reserve a place at the resort office in Kuala Tahan as each can only accommodate four to six people. Although you don't need to reserve a spot at any of the twelve **campsites**, check with the Parks and Wildlife Department office on which are actually open, since they're rotated to avoid overuse. All the campsites, with the exception of the one at Kuala Tahan, have no facilities whatsoever – you'll even have to take your own bottled water.

Inside the park

If your stay at Taman Negara is a short one, **essential places to visit** close to the resort include the steep hike up nearby **Bukit Teresek**; the **canopy walkway** where you can observe jungle life close up; and **Gua Telinga**, a large limestone cave. With three days to spare, your itinerary could also include a guided forest walk, or a night in one of several **hides**. These are positioned deep in the jungle overlooking salt licks, where you can spy animals drinking the salty water.

Naturally, all these places and activities tend to be among the most frequented in the park because of their proximity to Kuala Tahan, and to get into the undisturbed forest you really need to stay for a week or more. A week's visit, for example, could start with the thirty-kilometre **Rentis Tenor trail**, a lasso-shaped trek leading west from Kuala Tahan to Gua Telinga, then northwest into deep forest to the campsite at Sungei Tenor, where you stay in a small clearing beside a river. Back at base, you could catch a **sampan** upriver to Kuala Keniam, visit *Perkai Lodge*, and walk along the wild **Keniam trail** – where elephants are sometimes spotted – spending the night in a hide at Kumbang before taking a sampan from Kuala Trenggan back to park headquarters. Unless the park is very busy you're unlikely to see more than a handful of people during the week.

The most adventurous activity of all is the nine-day, sixty-kilometre **trek to Gunung Tahan**; for this you must plan to be in the park at least eleven days, and all groups have to be accompanied by a guide from the Parks and Wildlife Department. The trail involves **crossing Sungei Tahan** numerous times – quite a challenge if the waters have been swollen by rain – and some **steep climbing** towards the end. One of the chief thrills of the route is that it passes through various terrains, from lowland jungle to cloud forest, before reaching the 2187-metre summit.

The account of the park below is divided into three sections: day-trips that you can make from Kuala Tahan, longer trails – the Rentis Tenor and Gunung Tahan – which require a certain commitment, and trips made from the upriver sites at Trenggan and Keniam. For some treks you'll require specific equipment and resources, which are detailed where appropriate. None of the trails themselves, however, require any special skills, beyond an average level of fitness. Whether you're going on a day hike or a longer trail you should **inform park staff** first, so they know where you are if you get into any difficulty. Despite the trails being well marked, people do fall over tree roots and sometimes get lost. There's a map showing the area around Kuala Tahan on p.212, and a map of the whole park on p.219.

Getting around

Transport around the park is by sampan, which come in varying sizes depending on the depth of the river. The smaller, lighter craft run along the shallow tributaries like Sungei Tahan and Sungei Tenor, with the more powerful boats used to reach Trenggan and Keniam upriver on Sungei Tembeling. Sampans belonging to the floating cafés also **cross the river** at Kuala Tahan, and are free.

To **rent a boat** either ask the staff at the *Taman Negara Resort* office, who will arrange a trip on your behalf, or – the less expensive option – speak to the boatmen at the jetty, and sort out a price with them. In general, you can expect to spend at least $30 a day per person on boat expenses, an amount which will get you as far as the upriver sites or to Lata Berkoh on Sungei Tahan. To reach the furthest navigable spot in the park, *Perkai Lodge*, will cost around $100 per person for the return trip. When renting a sampan to the upriver sites, remember to book your return trip at the same time, since the boatmen only operate out of Kuala Tahan and Nusa Camp.

Day-trips

From Kuala Tahan, there are various **day-trips** involving **trail walking**, **river and waterfall excursions** and **hide visits**. T-shirts, shorts and strong sports shoes (although hiking boots are better) are adequate, but always have a hat, mosquito repellent and water to hand. Whether you're an ornithologist or not, it's a good idea to take **binoculars** to get the best possible look at birds from the jungle floor. A **magnifying glass** can open up a whole new world of insects, leaf and bark formations.

BUKIT TERESEK

Although undoubtedly the most heavily used trail in the park, the route to **Bukit Teresek** (which also leads on

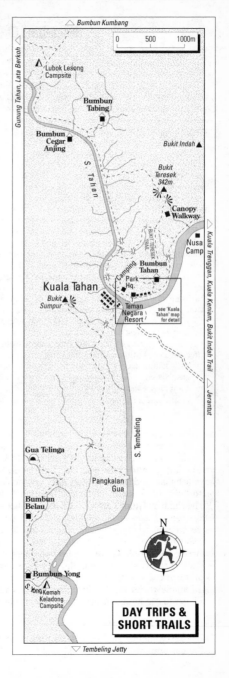

DAY TRIPS & SHORT TRAILS

THE HIDES

Spending a night in one of the park's six **hides** (known as *bumbuns*) doesn't guarantee sightings of large mammals, especially in the dry season when the **salt licks** – where plant-eating animals come to supplement their mineral intake – are often so waterless that there's little reason for deer, tapir, elephant, leopard or *seladang* to visit. But it'll be an experience you're unlikely to forget. Not only are the hides at the very roughest end of the accommodation scale – the mattresses are sometimes sodden and not without the odd flea, there's a simple chemical toilet and no washing or cooking facilities – but you're deep in the jungle with only a torch (an indispensable item) for illumination.

It's best to go in a group and take turns keeping watch, listening hard and occasionally shining the **torch** at the salt lick – if an animal is present its eyes will reflect brightly in the torch beam. Many people leave scraps of food below the hide, although environmentalists disapprove since this interferes with the animals' naturally balanced diet. As well as a torch, take rain gear, hat and sleeping bag, and all the food and drink you will need – and bring all your rubbish back for proper disposal at the resort. You have to book your bunk in the hide at the wildlife office, next to the supermarket in the resort. For a full rundown of the wildlife you might see from the hides, turn to Contexts, p.617.

There are four hides north of the *Taman Negara Resort* and two to the south. Of the northern ones, the closest is the six-bed **Bumbun Tahan** which is situated just south of the junction with the Bukit Teresek trail. However, much more promising are the eight-bed **Bumbun Tabing**, on the east bank of Sungei Tahan (see "Bukit Teresek" for directions), and the eight-bed **Bumbun Cegar Anjing**, an hour further and slightly to the south, on the west bank of Sungei Tahan, beside the old airstrip. It is reached by fording the river, but in the wet season is only accessible by boat as the river's too powerful to wade across. The most distant hide to the north of the resort is the six-bed **Bumbun Kumbang**, an eleven-kilometre walk from Kuala Tahan, which, because of its remote location, is the best place to catch sight of animals.

To the south, there's the six-bed **Bumbun Belau** on the Gua Telinga trail, and beyond the cave, the eight-bed **Bumbun Yong**, at either of which there's only a small chance of spotting wildlife as the hides are quite close both to the traffic on Sungei Tembeling and the resort's vast electricity generator – the combination of these noises has frightened most animals away.

to Bukit Indah; see below) is an excellent starter, and enables you to acclimatize to the heat and humidity. Follow the path which weaves between the chalets east of the resort office, beyond which a trail heads northeast away from the river. It's wide and easy to follow, hitting **primary jungle** almost immediately; for around 500m most of the tree types have been labelled along the way. After around twenty minutes the trail divides, straight on to Bukit Teresek and left for the Tabing hide (see box) and Bukit Indah.

The climb up **Bukit Teresek** – a 342-metre hill – is best negotiated early in the morning, before 8am. It takes about one hour at an even pace to reach the top where there's a shelter set on exposed sandstone, and marvellous views north over the valley to Gunung Tahan and Gunung Perlis (1279m). Along the trail you might hear **gibbons** or **hill squirrels** in the trees. The **monkeys** are relentless pursuers of any type of food, so keep it out of sight.

Back at the base of the hill, the canopy walkway is just 300m to the north along a clearly marked, springy path of slippery tree roots. The resort also organizes popular night jungle walks ($15), which run part of the way along the Bukit Teresek trail – you'll get to see luminous plants and insects, if nothing else.

THE CANOPY WALKWAY

About thirty minutes' walk east from Kuala Tahan along the riverside Bukit Indah trail is the **canopy walkway**. Only a small group of people can gain access to the walkway (daily 11am–3pm, except Fri 9am–noon; $5) at any one time, so you're often likely to have a wait at the start. The walkway, a 450-metre swaying bridge made from aluminium ladders bound by rope and set 30m above the ground, takes around thirty minutes to negotiate. It's reached by climbing a sturdy wooden tower – 250-year-old tualang trees support the walkway at twenty- to sixty-metre intervals and you return to terra firma by another wooden stairwell at the end of the third section. Once you've got used to the swaying, it's a pleasurable experience taking in the fine views of Sungei Tembeling and observing the insect life and tree parasites which abound at that height. Geckos, cicadas, crickets and grasshoppers hop and fly about, often landing on the walkway before leaping back onto a branch or leaf. Other species usually visible include the grey **banded leaf monkey**, with a call that sounds like a rattling tin can, and the white-eyed **dusky leaf monkey**, with its deep, nasal "ha-haw" cry; both lope about in groups of six to eight.

THE BUKIT INDAH TRAIL

Past the canopy the route divides, north and slightly uphill to the Tabing hide, another 1km further on, or northeast – heading marginally downhill and cutting back towards Sungei Tembeling – along the lovely **Bukit Indah trail**. Initially, this follows the riverbank, and you are bound to see monkeys, plenty of bird life, squirrels, shrews, a multitude of insects and (if it's early or late in the day) perhaps **tapir** or **wild ox** (*seladang*). The path to Bukit Indah itself leaves the main riverside trail (which continues to Kuala Trenggan, 6km away) and climbs at a slight gradient for 200m; the top of the hill offers a lovely view over Sungei Tembeling. It's a three-kilometre, three-hour return trip from the resort office.

GUA TELINGA AND KEMAH KELADONG

Another major trail leads south alongside the river, with branches off to the limestone outcrop of Gua Telinga, the Belau and Yong hides, and the campsite at Kemah Keladong.

From the jetty by the *KT Restoran*, take a sampan across Sungei Tahan. On the other side, follow the trail through a small kampung (where some of the resort and Park and Wildlife Department staff live) into the trees and dense foliage. The undulating trail heads across some steep spurs and traverses magnificent lowland rainforest, before descending to the flat land of the river terrace along Sungei Tembeling. The forest here has a quite different appearance from that on the hill slopes, partly the effect of flooding, notably that of 1926 which devastated extensive areas of forest around Kuala Tahan. After 3km, you follow the sign north for a further 200m to reach **Gua Telinga**.

The limestone cave looks small and unassuming, but it's deceptively deep – something you only really discover when you slide through it. Although in theory it's possible to follow a guide rope through the eighty-metre cave, in practice only small adults or children will be able to tug themselves through the narrow cavities. Be warned – most people will have to crawl along dark narrow passages in places to negotiate areas of deep, squishy guano. Thousands of tiny roundleaf and fruit bats reside in the cave, as well as giant toads, black-striped frogs and whip spiders (which aren't poisonous). You're most likely to see roundleaf bats, so called because of the shape of the "leaves" of skin around their nostrils, which help direct the sound signals transmitted to assist the bat in navigation.

From Gua Telinga, it's another 500m to the Belau hide through beautiful tall forest, and another kilometre to that at Yong (for both, see box above), where the trail divides, north to Kemah Rentis (see below) and left to the tranquil **Keladong campsite**, 500m further on, on the terraced bank of Sungei Yong. Given an early start, it's quite possible to reach this point, have a swim in the river, and get back to the resort before dusk, but bring at least a litre of water per person and a packed lunch.

LATA BERKOH

Most people visit the "roaring rapids" of **Lata Berkoh** by boat, as it's an eight-kilometre, three-hour trip on foot. You could, however, walk the trail there and arrange for a boat to pick you up for the return journey, getting the best of both worlds.

Sampans from the jetty at Kuala Tahan cost around $20 each (provided you can get a group of four together) and take roughly thirty minutes, heading upstream on Sungei Tahan, the busiest of the parks' tributaries. The jetty at the other end is just 100m from the rudimentary *Berkoh Lodge*, a small building set back from the river in a clearing. If you're intending to sleep here, check first on space with the Parks and Wildlife Department office in Kuala Tahan, and bring your own bedding and food – mattresses and a barbecue frame are provided. On the opposite bank is the Melantai **campsite** (see also "The Gunung Tahan trail" below); you can ford the river to reach this most of the year, but in the rainy season you'll have to use the trail which runs from the *Taman Negara Resort*.

The **waterfall** itself is 50m north of the lodge. There's a deep pool for swimming, and the rocks overlooking the swirling water are ideal for a picnic. If you ask the boatman to cut his engine, you'll improve your chances of hearing the sounds of the forest, and of seeing kingfishers with their yellow-and-red wings and white beaks, large grey and green fish eagles, multicoloured *bulbul* birds and, on the rocks, camouflaged monitor lizards.

The **trail** from the resort to Lata Berkoh starts at the campsite and leads through dense rainforest, past the turning for the Tabing hide to the east. After around 3km you reach the campsite at **Lubok Lesong**, just to the left of which there's a broad, pebbled beach leading down to a deep pool in Sungei Tahan. The route to the waterfall veers west from the main trail around thirty minutes after the campsite, crossing gullies and steep ridges, before reaching the river, which must be forded. The final part of the trail runs north along the west side of Sungei Tahan before reaching the falls.

Longer trails

The two main long trails in the park are the nine-day trek to **Gunung Tahan** and back, and the four-day, circular **Rentis Tenor** trail, which reaches the beautiful Sungei Tenor before dipping back east. For either, you'll need loose-fitting, lightweight cotton clothing with long sleeves, long trousers to keep insects at bay, a raincoat or poncho, and a litre bottle of water plus water-purifying equipment or tablets. Also take a lightweight tent, a powerful torch and spare batteries, a map, cooking equipment and compass, all of which can be rented from the camping shop at Kuala Tahan; check with your guide (see below) how much food you'll need to take. For Gunung Tahan you will also need a sleeping bag for the two nights spent at a high-altitude camp. To keep out the leeches – a serious problem after heavy rain – wear walking boots, or sports shoes, with your trousers tucked into heavy-duty socks, and spray on insect repellent liberally every hour or so. The Orang Asli approach is to go barefoot and flick off the leeches as they begin to bite, but this requires an advanced-level jungle temperament.

Perhaps the most important advice on all long-distance trails is to know your limitations and not run out of time. Slipping and sliding along in the dark is no fun and can be dangerous – it's easy to fall at night and impossible to see snakes or other forest-floor creatures which might be on the path.

THE GUNUNG TAHAN TRAIL

The 55-kilometre trek to Peninsular Malaysia's highest peak, **Gunung Tahan** (2187m), is the highlight of any adventurous visitor's stay in Taman Negara – but you have to allow at least nine days to accomplish it: seven to complete the trek and one day either side to get in and out of the park. Although in peak season hundreds of people trudge along the trail every week, the sense of individual achievement after fording Sungei

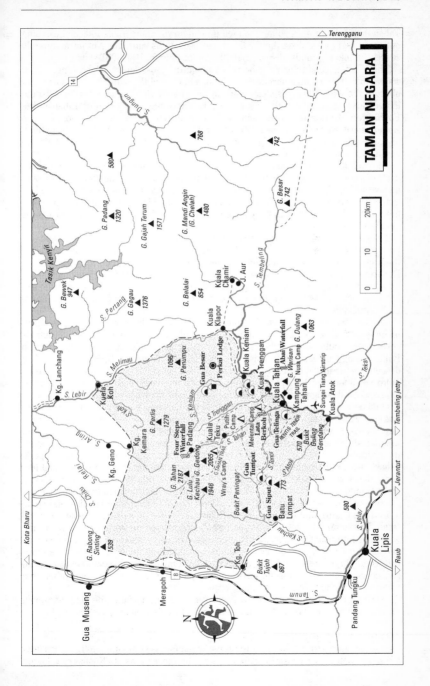

Tahan dozens of times, hauling yourself up and down innumerable hills and camping out every night – let alone the final, arduous ascent – is supreme. Not for nothing do successful hikers proudly display their "I climbed Gunung Tahan" T-shirts.

The weather conditions can't be relied upon: the moss forest, which ranges from 4000m to 6000m, is often shrouded in cloud, and even at the summit, cloud cover can obscure the view. But if it's clear, you can see at least 50km in all directions. To the indigenous inhabitants of the region, the Batek Orang Asli, Gunung Tahan is the **Forbidden Mountain**; in their folklore the summit is the home of a vast monkey, who stands guard over magic stones. Because of this, they venture to the foothills on hunting expeditions, to find wild pig, monkey or squirrel, but rarely head further up the mountain.

To reach the summit you have to follow precarious ridges which weave around the back of the mountain, since the most obvious approach from Sungei Tahan would involve scaling the almost sheer one-thousand-metre-high Teku gorge – which the first expedition, organized by the Sultan of Pahang, tried and failed to do in 1863. The summit was finally reached in 1905 by a combined British-Malay team led by the explorer Leonard Wray.

The Gunung Tahan trail is the only one in the park where you must be accompanied by a **guide** (which costs around $500 per guide for the seven days), although in truth the trail is easy to follow with a compass and map. Head first for the Parks and Wildlife Department office, where you can discover if a trek has already been planned – you may be able to join up with a group, and split the cost. Most trekkers go in groups of between four and ten; groups of twelve or more have to take two guides, according to park regulations.

The first day involves an easy six-hour walk to **Melantai**, the campsite on the east bank of Sungei Tahan, across the river from Lata Berkoh. On the second day more ground is covered, the route taking eight hours and crossing 27 hills, including a long trudge up Bukit Malang ("unlucky hill"). This section culminates at **Gunung Rajah** (576m), before descending to **Sungei Puteh**, a tiny tributary of the Tahan. Before the campsite at **Kuala Teku** you'll ford the Tahan half a dozen times – if the river's high, extra time and energy is spent following paths along the edge of the river, crossing at shallower spots.

On the third day you climb from 168m to 1100m in seven hours of steady, unrelenting trekking which takes you up onto a ridge. Prominent among the large trees along the ridge is *seraya*, with a reddish-brown trunk, as well as oaks and conifers, but the *seraya* thin out when the ridge turns to the west. Here, the character of the landscape changes dramatically, to montane oak forest where elephant tracks are common. Park experts believe that elephants live around this point – where the forest is more open and less dense than lower down but is still rich enough in foliage to provide food. The night is spent at the Gunung Tahan base camp, **Wray's Camp**, named after the explorer Leonard Wray.

The fourth day's trek takes six hours of hard climbing along steep gullies, ending up at **Padang Camp**, on the Tangga Lima Belas ridge, sited on a plateau sheltered by tall trees. The summit is now only two-and-a-half hours away, through open, hilly ground with knee-high plants, exposed rocks, and peaty streams, which support thick shrubs and small trees. The trail follows a ridge into moss forest and soon reaches the **summit** where there's a stupendous view, though thick mists often envelop the plateau and reduce visibility. It's a pristine environment: pitcher plants, orchids and other rare plants grow in the crevices and gullies of the summit.

On the return trip, the fifth night is spent back at the Padang, the sixth at Sungei Puteh, and by the end of day seven you're back at Kuala Tahan.

TO FOUR-STEPS WATERFALL

The seven-day (50km) trail to **Four-Steps Waterfall**, east of Gunung Tahan, follows the same route as that described above for the first three days. At Kuala Teku, hikers take the right fork instead, which after eight hours of following the course of the Sungei Tahan reaches the foot of the falls. Although the falls are only thirty metres high, the gorgeous setting is what makes the trek worthwhile: flat stones by the path are a good point to rest, listen to the sound of the water and look out for birds and monkeys. You can camp below the falls at **Pasir Panjang** (Panjang pass), which can be reached in around three hours along a clear path to the right of the falls.

THE RENTIS TENOR TRAIL
The other major long-distance trail is the four-day, thirty-kilometre, circular **Rentis Tenor**, which leads south to Sungei Yong, then northwest to the campsite at Kemah Rentis and southeast back to Kuala Tahan. The initial route is the same as that to Gua Telinga (see p.214), bearing north at the Yong hide (2hr from the resort), before following the course of Sungei Yong and reaching the campsite at **Kemah Yong**, just under 10km from the resort. Two hundred metres south of the campsite a side trail leads off to the left to **Bukit Guling Gendang** (570m), a steep, two-hour climb best undertaken in the morning, after a good night's rest. From the top, there's a lovely view north to Gunung Tahan, west to Gua Siput and beyond that to Bukit Penyengat (713m), the highest limestone outcrop in Peninsular Malaysia. Towards the summit the terrain changes from lowland tropical to montane forest, where tall conifer trees allow light to penetrate to the forest floor and **squirrels** predominate, with the black giant and cream giant the main species. Both are as big as the domestic cat, their call varying from a grunt to a machine-gun burst of small squeaks.

On day three the main trail continues on into the upper catchment of Sungei Yong, then over a low saddle into the catchment of Sungei Rentis. The path narrows through thick forest alongside the river, crossing it several times, until it joins **Sungei Tenor** three hours later. Here there is a remote and beautiful clearing, **Kemah Rentis**, beside the river, where you camp. It's a fifteen-kilometre hike back to the resort from here; some trekkers go easy and spend a fourth night at **Kemah Lameh** (4km from Kemah Rentis) or the campsite at **Lubok Lesong** (8km from Renuis) on Sungei Tahan.

As for the trail itself from Sungei Tenor, follow the river downstream through undulating terrain to the rapids at **Lata Keitiah** (which takes around 1hr), beyond which another tributary stream, Sungei Lameh, enters the Tenor. You are now in lowland open forest where walking is fairly easy and after four hours the trail leads to **Bumbun Cegar Anjing** (another possible overnight stop) from where it's 3km back to the resort.

Trenggan, Keniam and Perkai lodges
The **upriver lodges** are excellent bases for exploring less visited parts of the park. The boat journey along the rapid-studded **Sungei Tembeling** is exciting, while the lodges are set in tranquil surroundings, with various hikes which take in visits to caves, and bird-watching and fishing areas.

The closer lodge, at **KUALA TRENGGAN**, is 11km upstream from *Taman Negara Resort* and you can go either by boat, which takes less than an hour, or by one of two trails, which take between six and eight hours. The shorter and more direct **trail** runs alongside Sungei Tembeling (9km) on a well-trodden, lowland forest path which can be quite hard going; the easier inland route (12km) runs north past the campsite at Lubok Lesong, bearing right into dense forest where elephant tracks may be seen, and then crosses the narrow Sungei Trenggan 500m to the north, to reach the lodge. The **river trip** costs around $70 per boat; on the way, look out for water buffalo on the east bank of the river. **Trenggan Lodge** itself – a collection of wooden chalets – is partially hidden by forest on a bend in the river; in the largest chalet, an elevated building with a verandah, there's a small café.

A further 20km north along Sungei Tembeling is **KUALA KENIAM** (2hr from the resort; $140 per boat); **Keniam Lodge** comprises several more chalets and another small café. If you plan to stay a couple of nights at Keniam, ending with the trek back to Trenggan (see below), then hike upstream on your first day along Sungei Perkai (which cuts away from Sungei Tembeling, 200m north of the lodge) for 3km to *Perkai Lodge*, a popular spot for fishing and bird-spotting. The two-hour **Perkai trail** runs roughly parallel to the river; in places it's possible to leave the main path and find a way down to the water. This far from Kuala Tahan the region is rich in wildlife, including banded and dusky leaf monkeys, long-tailed macaques and white-handed gibbons, all of which are relatively easy to spot, especially with binoculars. As for big mammals, elephants certainly roam in these parts and park staff say there are tigers too, though there hasn't been a sighting for several years. Smaller animals like tapirs, civets and deer are best seen at night or early in the morning.

The trail ends at a small clearing on the river's edge, where **Perkai Lodge** stands. There are eight bunk beds here in all and the lodge doesn't have any resident staff (unlike Trenggan and Keniam), so you must bring food, drink and bedding if you intend to stay. There's at least a barbecue area and some crockery out the back. Very few people use the lodge but you still need to book with the wildlife office at the resort.

THE KENIAM–TRENGGAN TRAIL

After Gunung Tahan, the thirteen-kilometre **Keniam–Trenggan trail** is the great highlight of the park, combining the possibility of seeing elephants with visits to three caves, one of which is big enough for an army to camp in. It's generally a full day's hike, but in dry conditions can be covered in around six hours. Some people take two days instead, pitching a tent either in one of the caves or on a stretch of clear ground near a stream – there aren't any designated campsites in this remote corner of the park. The trail is a tough one, with innumerable streams to wade through, hills to circumvent, and trees blocking the path.

The trail cuts southwest from *Keniam Lodge* along a narrow, winding path through dense forest dominated by huge meranti trees with red-brown fissured bark. It's two hours before you enter limestone cave country, first reaching **Gua Luas** which, although impressive, has no large internal cavity. One hundred metres south is **Gua Daun Menari** (Cave of the Dancing Leaves), which does have a large chamber through which the wind blows leaves and other jungle debris. Climb up the side of the cave and you'll see small dark holes leading into the cave chamber where, in the pitch darkness, thousands of roundleaf bats live.

To regain the main trail, go back 50m towards Gua Luas and look for an indistinct path on the left; follow this for another 30m, at which point you should see the main trail ahead. Bear left here – the third cave, **Gua Kepayang**, is around ten minutes' walk further on. This has a very large chamber at the eastern side of the outcrop which is easy to enter and is an excellent place to put up a tent. The fourth cave, **Kepayang Kecil**, is the last limestone outcrop on the trail. A line of figs drops a curtain of roots down the rock and behind this lies a small chamber, with a slightly larger one to the right, with stalactites and stalagmites.

After passing Kecil you are about halfway along the trail but there are plenty more streams to cross, with armies of ants, flies and leeches. The trail is illuminated in places by patches of sunlight highlighting tropical mushrooms on the trees and plants, though you're soon back in the gloom again. Parts of the path are wide and easy to follow, while other sections are far narrower, passing through tunnels of bamboo. The final two hours comprise more boggy crossings as the trail descends slightly to the Trenggan valley, arriving at *Trenggan Lodge*.

LEAVING THE PARK

Most people **leave the park** the way they came, by boat down Sungei Tembeling – book your seat on the **sampan** at the resort office unless you're staying at Nusa Camp, which has its own Tembeling jetty-bound boat. You can also take the **minibus** back to Jerantut from Kuala Tahan – it's best to make a booking at the *Teresek View* in the village, or at the floating *Family Restaurant*. For the more adventurous there are two **treks** which lead out of the park. One route heads upstream on Sungei Tembeling and then branches off east into the jungle through Terengganu State; the other leaves the Gunung Tahan trail at the Padang and heads west out of the park to Merapoh in Kelantan, a village which is accessible by jungle railway and Route 8.

The Terengganu Route
To reach **Terengganu State** you'll need to take a guide to the beginning of the trail (around $100 a day), or at least make sure that the boatman knows where to drop you. You will need camping gear and food for two days. The sampan costs around $70 to take you the four hours upstream on Sungei Tembeling to the start of the trail at Kampung Besar, on the east bank of the river. From here there is a trail through the jungle, where after around four hours' walking there's a site where you can make camp, and the next day continue west for another six hours until you reach a laterite road. Going east on this road you will arrive at a small kampung, where you can camp overnight, and then get a bus out to the south–north Highway 14 (Kuantan to Kuala Terengganu).

The Kelantan Route
The route to **Kelantan** is reached from the Gunung Tahan trail – you will need a guide to get you onto the trail, which runs west northwest before joining a four-wheel drive track to **Merapoh**, two day's walk from the Tahan trail's Padang Camp (see p.220) and lying on the bus and train route between Kuala Lipis and Gua Musang. More traffic, however, tends to go the other way, and it's possible to take a landcruiser from Merapoh to the end of the track, where you camp, reaching the Padang Camp in a day's walk.

KL to the Northeast Coast

Two routes cut across the interior from KL to the northeast coast: the jungle railway and Route 8. The main stopping points are the former tin-mining town and erstwhile capital of Pahang, **Kuala Lipis** which is 170km northeast of KL, the state park at **Kenong Rimba**, the caves at **Gua Musang** and **Jelawang park**. But the chief reason for making the trip to the northwest coast is to spend time in the forests and sandstone hills of this region, an environment far from the economic expansion of the west coast and the beach-dominated muggy east coast. In this lush and rugged region, Senoi Orang Asli still live semi-nomadic lives along inaccessible river basins.

Many **Senoi** live in the wide catchment area of the jungle railway. The lifestyles of the two main Senoi groups, the Temiar and the Semai, revolve around a combination of shifting cultivation (where there is still enough accessible land left for this to be feasible), the trading of forest products, fishing and animal trapping. The **Temiar** are mountain dwellers, though the Temiar of southern Kalantan sometimes raft timber down Sungei Kelantan to **Kuala Kerai**, selling the wood on to Chinese middlemen. Although the Temiar are increasingly exploiting the forest for timber, their logging practices are marginal compared to those of the State Forestry Department. The **Semai**, in contrast, prefer to live in lowland jungle or open flat country, and there are several Semai communities close to Merapoh in southern Kelantan.

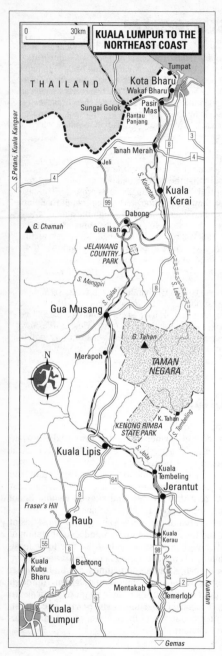

KUALA LUMPUR TO THE NORTHEAST COAST

Rail and road routes

It took indentured Tamil workers eight years to built the five-hundred-kilometre **jungle railway** from Gemas, southeast of KL, to Tumpat on the northeast coast. The line has been in full operation since 1931 (the first section from Gemas to Kuala Lipis was opened in 1920) and much of its rolling stock has not been upgraded since. Initially it was used exclusively for freight – first for tin and rubber, and later for oil palm, before a passenger service opened in 1938. If you want to cross the interior quickly, you should avoid the train – it takes fourteen hours to get from Gemas to Kota Bharu, five hours longer than by bus. But as a way of encountering rural life it can't be beaten: for the Malays, Tamils and Orang Asli who live in these remote areas, the railway is the only alternative to walking. Fellow passengers range from cheroot-smoking old men in sarongs to fast-talking women hauling kids, poultry and rice to and from the nearest market. The ancient carriages are always packed to bursting point as the trains rumble through the isolated kampungs of Pahang and Kelantan, crossing iron bridges over wide rivers, with craggy mountains rearing up on either side.

From KL, there are two **road routes** into the interior. The first leaves Route 1 at the Kuala Kubu Bharu turning (Route 55) and heads northeast past Fraser's Hill, joining Route 8 at Raub. Otherwise, take Route 2 past the Genting Highlands and turn north at Bentong, where Route 8 begins. From Taman Negara, Route 64 connects Jerantut with Route 8 north of Raub. Beyond Kuala Lipis, **Route 8** heads due north, running parallel with the railway for 100km until it bears east at Gua Musang, meeting the railway again 80km further on at Kuala Kerai. The final section of Route 8, onwards to Kota Bharu, intersects with the east–west Route 4, and later the Kuala Terengganu road, Route 3.

To Kuala Lipis: via Mentakab and Raub

The most common approach to the jungle railway from KL is to take a bus to **MEN-TAKAB**, a small town on the Kuantan Highway (Route 2), less than 100km east of KL. These run twice an hour from KL's Pudu Raya terminus and the trip takes two-and-a-half hours. Although it's unlikely you'll want to stay if you're heading north, you might need to on the return trip, heading south, as one of the four daily trains reaches Mentakab at 10.12pm, and another around 1.30am. To reach the train station walk from the bus station out onto the main road, Jalan Tun Razak, and bear left for 100m to a big junction. Turn left again on Jalan Ponniah, walk another 200m and watch for a narrow road on your right, marked to the train station – a fifteen-minute walk. There are numerous budget **hotels** behind the bus station, including *Hotel Continental*, 90 Jalan Haji Kassim (☎09/277 2622; ②), *London Café and Hotel*, 71 Jalan Temerloh (☎09/277 1119; ①), and the best option, the friendly if very basic *Hotel Hoover*, 25 Jalan Moh Hee Kiang (☎09/277 1622; ①). The best place to **eat** is the North Indian *Malabar Restoran* (8am–midnight), on Jalan Ponniah.

Leaving Mentakab by train, the route passes through Jerantut and Kuala Tembeling (see p.210 for both), access points for Taman Negara before reaching Kuala Lipis. Note that Temerloh (p.237), just to the east, is another overnight option if Mentakab doesn't appeal.

Raub

By road to Kuala Lipis, the route leaves KL and heads northeast on Route 55 to Kuala Kubu Bharu, a two-hour trip and departure point for buses to Fraser's Hill (see p.134). Beyond Kuala Kubu Bharu, the scenery gets ever more spectacular, the road following ridges along the sides of large hills, with small plantations and forests below. Kampungs become fewer and so do cars.

The only stop worth making by car or bus is at **RAUB**, on Route 8, a gold-mining town which acquired a reputation in the 1950s as one of the main areas sympathetic to the Communist guerrillas. Overlooking the padang is the two-storey resthouse and the 1910 Courthouse and District Office. The bus station is adjacent to the town's main street, where there are several elegant Chinese shophouses.

Kuala Lipis

It's hard to believe that **KUALA LIPIS** was the state capital of Pahang from 1898 to 1955, for today it's a sleepy, inconsequential place of only seven thousand people, situated at the confluence of Sungei Lipis and Sungei Jelai (a tributary of the Pahang), dwarfed by steep hills and surrounded by forest and plantations. There's none of the tin-mining fervour which characterized the town's peak years (1910–30), although the recent re-mining of gold in the area (see box on p.277) is causing a mini boom. Kuala Lipis still has frontier town charm; each Friday night the bus station disappears under a hundred stalls for the pasar malam, when rural Malays and Semai tribespeople arrive with their produce on the train from as far afield as Kuala Kerai.

Kuala Lipis started life as a small riverside settlement in the early nineteenth century; the population grew from a few dozen to around two thousand by the 1890s. By then it was a **trading centre** for *gaharu* (a fragrant aloe wood used to make joss sticks) and other jungle products, collected by the Semai and traded with Chinese *towkays*. Until the first road was built from Kuala Lumpur in the 1890s – a 170-kilometre journey by bullock cart – the river was the only means of transport; the trip from Singapore by ship and then sampan took over two weeks. Nevertheless, because of its central geographical position and early importance as a transit point on Sungei Pahang for locally mined tin, the colonial government set up its state administrative quarters here. However the

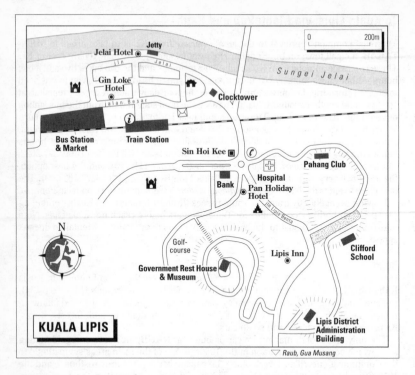

KUALA LIPIS

△ Raub, Gua Musang

tin deposits soon evaporated and the fabled gold never materialized. The rise of Kuantan marginalized Kuala Lipis, which slipped into genteel obscurity, and today there's a disproportionately large number of fine period buildings for a town whose main street is only 400m long. Nearby Kenong Rimba State Park (see p.228) is the main reason most travellers stop in Lipis; it promises rainforest hikes without the crowds which frequent nearby Taman Negara.

The Town

Heading left from the train station takes you down narrow Jalan Besar past a jumble of Chinese shophouses, which incorporate busy bars, general-purpose shops and the town's hotels. Each Friday, the buses are moved from the **market** area, next to the bus station, and the whole district is transformed into a vibrant pasar malam, when everybody in town turns out. Stalls here sell everything from pet birds to cleaning utensils, and hawkers prepare massive trays of cooked noodles, seafood, pies, deep-fried prawn cakes and superb cornmeal puddings.

Pahang's most famous Resident, Hugh Clifford, lived on Bukit Residen, a four-hundred-metre-high hill overlooking the town, and his house – a graceful one-storey colonial building – is now the Government Rest House, with a **museum** detailing the town's cultural history. The exhibits – mostly bric-a-brac – originally belonged to British and Malay colonial civil servants and include oblong brass boxes for betel leaf, coconut oil lamps and embroidered sashes. The photographs are more interesting, with one showing the resthouse at the time of the great flood of 1926, when the level of the flood waters was recorded on the outside wall. In the drawing-room to the right of the main

GOLD MINING

The upturn in the world price of **gold** has made it profitable to mine gold in Malaysia again. A gold mine in Raub which stopped operating in the 1980s reopened in 1996 and the Penjom Project, based just fifteen minutes' drive from Kuala Lipis, will be the Peninsula's largest gold mine. Its positive economic impact is already being felt in the mini construction boom in the town. However, this is no gold rush, since only the use of modern technology and mining methods extract sufficient gold from the land to make the project viable. Indeed, Kuala Lipis will have to shoulder the environmental cost of the project for long after the mining ceases, since a toxic lake of rock and cyanide – a nasty by-product of gold mining – will be created in the process.

entrance is a collection of *kris* daggers with highly ornate handles, spears and *parangs*, ceramic vases, cups and plates. Upstairs are more photographs, of Pahang's royal family, and the grand bedroom with its marvellous views over the town and beyond to Kenong Rimba and Taman Negara parks.

On the hill opposite stands the town's largest colonial structure, the **Lipis District Administration Building**, around ten minutes' walk from the train station. Dating from 1919, it's been beautifully maintained, and now serves as the local law court. The other central hill, Bukit Lipis, also has two period buildings: the Pahang Club (1867) with its distinctive sloping roof, and Clifford School (1913). Now fallen into disrepair, the **Pahang Club** is every bit the archetypal colonial club in the tropics. It was the first building constructed by the British in the town, later serving as a temporary residence for Hugh Clifford. The occasional large function is still held in the main room with its dark mahogany floor, but most of the action these days takes place in the musty, tobacco-stained bar, through the hall to the right. The once-tended gardens have now been almost reclaimed by the jungle, but the billiard room is still in use. The Pahang Club has only kept afloat by opening its doors to anyone who can pay the $100 annual membership, while visitors to the area are welcome in the club for dinner ($10 a steak) or for drinks (the bar closes when the last customer has left). There's also an indoor badminton court and tennis court attached to the club.

Directly below the Pahang Club, the **Clifford School** was built in 1913, part-funded by Hugh Clifford, and maintained as the first multiracial private school in Malaysia, admitting both British and Chinese boys. A grandiose group of buildings painted deep crimson, with a long low verandah beneath a magnificent grey-tiled roof, the school is perhaps the most famous in Malaysia – one of a select group where the country's leaders and royalty are educated.

Practicalities

Both **train and bus stations** are very central, close to the town's inexpensive hotels, but a fifteen-minute walk from the Government Rest House. The **jetty** – from where boats leave on Saturdays for Kenong Rimba State Park – lies 50m northeast of the market on Jalan Jelai. There are two **Tourist Information** offices: one is a private concern (☎09/312 3277) tucked away to the left of the train station exit, opposite the ticket booth. It's owner Hassan Tuah provides an informative map of the town and a colourful brochure on nearby Kenong Rimba State Park with details of his own tour to the park. Just outside the station is another tourist office – neither seem to keep official opening hours, but it's that kind of town.

ACCOMMODATION

The finest place **to stay** is the *Government Rest House*, on Jalan Bukit Residen (☎09/312 2600; ②–③), which has twenty bedrooms, all with shower, toilet and air-con or fan. On foot, from the train station, turn right along Jalan Besar and right again on the round-about, 100m ahead. Directly in front of you is the missable *Pan Holiday Hotel*, where you should follow the road to its left marked "To the Golf Course". After 50m take the path along the western flank of the golf course to a flight of concrete steps overgrown with weeds, which lead up through the trees – this is the most direct way up the hill to the resthouse at the top. The *Lipis Inn*, 1 Kompleks Taipan, Jalan Benta Lips (☎ & fax 09/312 5888; ⑤) is a modern and nicely furnished hotel just outside the centre of town.

Two inexpensive hotels in the town itself draw most of the budget travellers. The *Gin Loke Hotel*, 64 Jalan Besar (☎09/312 1654; ①) is very friendly, with clean rooms, shared toilet and shower and a book exchange system. The owner, Harry Tan also runs trips into Kenong Rimba park. The other budget option is the *Jelai Hotel* at 44 Jalan Jelai (☎09/312 1574; ①) overlooking the river, one street north of Jalan Besar. The twin-bed rooms are small, with shared toilet and shower.

EATING AND DRINKING

There is a smattering of below-average Chinese **cafés** on Jalan Besar, but the best bet is the lively *Sin Hoi Kee*, just by the roundabout on Jalan Lipis. The resthouse has a restaurant (Mon–Sat 8–10am, noon–2pm & 8.30–11pm) which specializes in traditional Pahang dishes like river trout in durian sauce and chicken in coconut and lemon grass. They don't serve alcohol here; for a beer, head for one of the noisy **bars** on Jalan Besar.

Kenong Rimba State Park

KENONG RIMBA STATE PARK is one of the best reasons to travel the jungle rail-way into the interior and, if coupled with a visit to Kuala Lipis, makes for a perfectly balanced three- to five-day stop-off en route from KL to Kota Bharu. Rimba's main attraction is that it offers a compact version of the Taman Negara experience – jungle trails, riverside camping, mammal-spotting and **excellent bird-watching** – at much reduced prices and without the hype which characterizes the larger park, sharing its south-western border. The park is one tenth of the size of Taman Negara, stretching over 128 square kilometres of the **Kenong Valley**, east of Banjaran Titiwangsa. It's dotted with limestone hills, which are riddled with caves of varying sizes, and crossed by trails which snake along the forest floor. The park is also a promising place to spot **big mammals**, many of which have been driven away from Taman Negara by the increase in tourism, and have ventured across into Rimba. That said, it's still unlikely you'll catch sight of a tiger or elephant, although there's certainly more of a chance here than in Taman Negara.

As Rimba is small, you can see most of the main sights within three days: one day to check out the caves, which are all within 2km of each other, another to get to the Kenong campsite and the third to return to base via the Batek Orang Asli village. No special equipment is needed, besides a tent and blanket for sleeping. Be sure, though, to take lots of mosquito repellent and always carry at least one litre of water with you on the trails.

Practicalities

The easiest way to get there is to travel **from Kuala Lipis** on Saturday, when a sampan ($15) leaves the Jalan Jelai jetty at 2pm (returning people to their kampungs from the pasar malam), arriving at the Tanjung Kiara jetty (see below) at around 4pm. On other days of the week, you can charter a sampan directly from Kuala Lipis, at around $60 per boat. However, it's cheaper to take the 6.30am local train to **BATU SEMBI-LAN**, (30min; $1) just four stops to the south of Kuala Lipis, where you walk left (east) along a narrow road 50m to the jetty on Sungei Jelai. Here, sampans take you on the

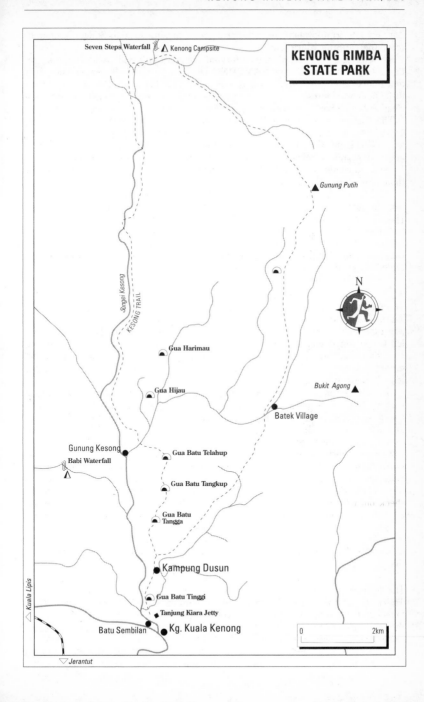

Seven Steps Waterfall
Kenong Campsite

KENONG RIMBA STATE PARK

Gunung Putih

Songei Kesong

KESONG TRAIL

N

Gua Harimau

Gua Hijau

Bukit Agong

Batek Village

Gunung Kesong
Babi Waterfall

Gua Batu Telahup

Gua Batu Tangkup

Gua Batu Tangga

Kampung Dusun

Kuala Lipis

Gua Batu Tinggi

Tanjung Kiara Jetty

Batu Sembilan
Kg. Kuala Kenong

0   2km

Jerantut

thirty-minute trip downstream ($15 per person), turning left into Sungei Kenong to reach the **Tanjung Kiara jetty**.

However you get here, it's then a forty-minute walk on a wide road from the jetty through the rather spread-out **KAMPUNG DUSUN**, past a small store on your right to a bridge where the park proper begins. After a further hour along a narrow path through lowland forest, you reach the **park headquarters** at **GUNUNG KESONG**, a clearing beside Sungei Kesong where chalets and park office are situated.

There are several people in Kuala Lipis who organize **treks** into the park. Hassan Tuah, at the information office at Kuala Lipis (see above), runs three-day **tours** to the park ($150 inclusive), including obtaining the necessary permit. Appu, another local guide who can be contacted at the hotel next to the *Gin Loke*, also runs his own tours. If you are travelling independently, you need to go to the park office on arrival and buy the **permit** (around $1).

The twelve self-contained wooden **chalets** (③–④) in the Gunung Kesong have two beds in each, and it's advisable to book in advance at the information office in Kuala Lipis. The **campsite** is close to the chalets, and it only costs a few dollars to put up your tent; there are toilets and showers on site but no cooking facilities. Some campers use Kesong as a base and then head further into the park to camp, often at the Kenong campsite, four hours' walk away in the north of the park (see below). **Eating** options are very limited at Kesong with just one café serving basic, inexpensive meals of rice, meat, vegetables, soup and *roti canai*.

The caves

The first of the six **caves** in Rimba is outside the park proper, close to the Tanjung Kiara jetty. About ten minutes' walk from the jetty along the road look out for a path on your left (west) which leads to **Gua Batu Tinggi**, a small cave which has a cavity just big enough to clamber into. Inside, there's a surprising variety of plant life – including orchids and fig trees. There's a waterfall 100m further along the trail which is an excellent place for swimming.

Gua Batu Tangga (Cave of Rock Steps) can be reached direct from the camp at Gunung Kesong, though you can also get there from Tinggi by returning on the same trail and crossing the road, following the path to the left of a house – there's a sign pointing to the cave, another twenty minutes' walk further on. Shaped like an inverted wok, the large limestone cave has a wide, deep chamber and in the northwest corner a row of rocks forms ledges or steps, which give the cave its name. The cave is sometimes occupied by elephants – the trail through the cave narrows between rocks rubbed smooth over time, probably by the passage of the great creatures – but you're more likely to catch sight of mouse deer or porcupine scurrying away. Two smaller caves, **Gua Batu Tangkup** and **Gua Batu Telahup**, are just a few hundred metres beyond Tangga on the same trail.

The last two caves are close to the park headquarters: **Gua Hijau** (Green Cave) just five minutes' walk away is home to thousands of bats, while **Gua Harimau** is a little further along on the right, scarcely more than an overhang and reputedly the lair of tigers.

The trails

The main trail in the park, the Kesong trail, is to **Seven Steps Waterfall** (10km), which heads north from the headquarters. If you don't want simply to retrace your steps on the return trip, there's an alternative route which runs back to the southeast and passes close to the Batek village.

From park headquarters, the three-hour trail to the waterfall runs along Sungei Kesong in lowland forest, through which little sunlight penetrates. Over the years, the

Batek have cleared portions of forest around this trail for agricultural purposes; this could account for the jungle's impenetrability, as secondary forest tends to grow back more thickly than primary. The trail crosses several bridges; 1km before the waterfall you cross Sungei Kesong for the final time to reach the Kenong **campsite**. From here, you're very close to the waterfall, the trail continuing through high forest to a set of rapids, with jungle closing in all around. There's nowhere to rest except on the boulders, but sitting on these, close to the edge of the river, you can listen to the loud hiss of the water dropping over the nearby falls.

Returning on the southeastern loop of the trail takes longer – around five hours – so it's best tackled after staying the night at the waterfall campsite. This trail is harder going as it traverses small hills – Gunung Putih (884m) is the largest – and follows a less well-defined path. After three hours you pass close to a **Batek village**, where someone may invite you to their hut or display some wares to sell or trade. Although this isn't an official campsite, ask if you want to pitch a tent near the huts, especially if you decide to climb **Bukit Agong** (1800m), a stiff ascent which takes around two hours each way from the village. Returning to headquarters from the village takes around another two hours on the main trail (there is no connecting path from Bukit Agong).

Gua Musang

Back on the road and train route, the jungle landscape changes near Merapoh, 80km north of Kuala Lipis, where it is dominated by large, round sandstone hills. From Merapoh, it's another hour to **GUA MUSANG**, the largest town in the interior of Kelantan. It's a largely unappealing place which expanded fast over the last decade as logging money flowed in, accelerated by the arrival of Route 8, which has made remote tracts of forest accessible to the timber saws. Most of the timber merchants and their employees are Chinese and there's a distinct frontier spirit here, typical of many towns in rural Malaysia. Gua Musang positively churns with Toyota landcruisers and motor-bikes, cheap hotels and cafés full of people making business deals day and night. At weekends, dozens of young Chinese promenade up and down the two-street town, flocking to karaoke bars or to kung fu movies at the only cinema.

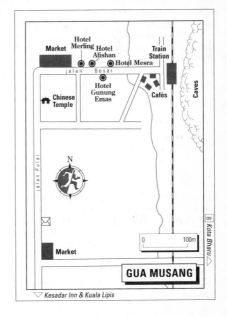

The main reason tourists stop is to visit the **caves** that riddle the mass of limestone above the town. Both the caves and the town are named after a small creature, the *musang*, which looks like a civet and used to live up in the caves; they're now almost extinct. Cross the railway track and walk through the tiny, cramped kampung in the shadow of the rock behind. Here you'll have to ask for a guide; it is possible to reach the caves on your own, but the trail – which is directly at the back of the huts – is difficult to negotiate after rain, when it's likely to be extremely slippery. Wear strong shoes and take a torch for inside the cave.

Once you've climbed almost vertically up 20m of rock face you'll see a narrow ledge; turn left and edge carefully along until you see a long slit in the rock which leads into a cave – you'll need to be fairly thin to negotiate this. Inside, the cave is enormous, 60m long and 30m high in places, and well lit. The main cave leads to lesser ones, which have rock formations jutting out from the walls and ceilings. The only way out is by the same route, which you'll need to take very carefully, especially the near-vertical descent off the ledge and back down to the kampung.

Practicalities

There are four trains a day from Kuala Lipis to Gua Musang, the first leaving at 4.30am and arriving just after 6am, the last at 3.30pm arriving at 5.10pm. The **train station** is situated directly below the limestone rock, in front of which is the town's main street, Jalan Besar, where most of the **hotels** are located. Three Chinese cheapies – *Hotel Merling* (①), *Hotel Alishan* (①) and *Hotel Mesra* (☎09/910 1813; ①) – lined along the right-hand side of the street, are owned by the same people; the slightly more upmarket *Hotel Gunung Emas* (☎09/910 2892; ②) is on the left. There's a small **day market** where the street forks left and becomes Jalan Pulai, 200m along which, past the Chinese temple, is a right-hand turn to *Kesadar Inn* (☎09/910 1229; ③–⑤). This stylish hotel comprises chalets set in a lovely lawn beside Sungei Galas, with meals served on a patio overlooking the river. If you're planning to come at the weekend it's a good idea to book ahead.

Gua Musang is not particularly renowned for its food, but the stalls near the station cook good *nasi campur* and the Chinese **cafés** on Jalan Besar serve hearty meals.

Dabong and around

From Gua Musang the next stop – 50km north – is **DABONG**, a quintessentially Kelantanese Malay village, sited on Sungei Galas and surrounded by flat-topped limestone peaks and dark green forest. Simple wooden kampung huts line the two narrow unpaved streets, and three café-cum-shops look out over the only concrete building, the school. It's not an uninteresting place to pass the time: timber-stilted houses peep out from between banana trees and a brightly painted, single platform train station looks like it hasn't changed in fifty years. The main reason for getting out of the train here is to visit **Gua Ikan**, a deep cave, 3km to the southwest, or – more excitingly – the **Jelawang Country Park**, on a mountain further south.

There is only one **place to stay** in Dabong, two rooms with bunk beds at the back of a shop on the main street ($8). Ask at the train station or at one of the shops opposite the school about availability.

Gua Ikan

The caves at **Gua Ikan** – distinguished by a stream running through a wide cavity – are a little way south of Dabong. To get there on foot, cross the railway track and walk east for 3km along a wide, paved road, or ask at the train station about a van-taxi ($10). The limestone caves are clearly marked off to the right, set in a small, unmaintained park. In the main cave – 40m long and 20m high – a small river runs along the bed, which you can follow provided you've brought a torch and watertight boots (the rocks are too slippery to go barefoot). This leads out to the other side of the cave to a small rock-enclosed area, a lovely spot to rest and listen to the birds and monkeys.

Jelawang Country Park

The **Jelawang Country Park** has much in common with Kenong Rimba. Its facilities are very basic – visitors should expect to rough it – but the trade-off is its easy access to beautiful hiking country and the distinct possibility of seeing **large mammals** and **rare birds**. It also boasts Peninsular Malaysia's highest waterfall, **Lata Jeri**.

To get here from Dabong, walk south through the village to the jetty (where boats arrive from Kuala Kerai; see below), take a sampan across Sungei Galas and catch the van-taxi which will be waiting on the other bank; it's then a four-kilometre ride east to Kampung Jelawang ($3). At the point where the van drops you, walk to the left along a small road towards the vast limestone hill, **Gunung Stong** (1421m), directly ahead – you can actually see the cascade of Lata Jeri from the road.

The hike up Gunung Stong to the park's waterfall campsite takes around ninety minutes and is fairly gruelling, involving some sheer, muddy sections, though rocks at the side of the trail allow you to rest and look back over the forest. The **campsite** is snugly sited beside the waterfall amid large trees. There are two chemical toilets close by, but no showers, so most visitors make good use of the waterfall's small rock pools instead.

The site is a reasonably pleasant spot at which to soak aching feet, after which you'll require a guide to strike out on one of the local **trails**. The three-hour **Seven Waterfalls** hike takes you up the west side of the waterfall in a roundabout way to the top then heads down the east side. The longer trail is the **Elephant Trek**, which follows the main path up the mountain for two hours to reach the top of Gunung Stong, before winding along the ridge and crossing over onto neighbouring Gunung Ayan. Although it's possible to return to the waterfall campsite the same day on this trek, it's preferable to camp for the night at a clearing along the trail, near a small stream – you'll need some warm clothing and a sleeping bag. People have seen elephants here, and there's a high chance of encountering **tapir**, **monkey** and **deer** in the early morning or early evening.

PRACTICALITIES
Tours of the country park are promoted fairly vigorously in Kota Bharu (p.241) as the "Jelawang Jungle Trail"; travel agencies and guesthouses can arrange trips, which are not bad value at around $30 per day. If you're **travelling independently** from the northeast coast, you'll need to leave Kota Bharu by 9am, taking bus #5 from the local bus station for the ninety-minute journey to Kuala Kerai ($4). From there, the journey to Dabong is either by train or boat, though since there are only two trains a day, both in the afternoon, the boat is best. The two-hour journey costs $5; see "Kuala Kerai" below for details. Heading back to Kota Bharu, you can take the evening train to Wakaf Bharu. The *Town Guesthouse* in Kota Bharu (see p.247) is planning chalets 4km from Jelawang, otherwise the overnight option is to stay at Dabong.

On to Tumpat

Moving on from Dabong, there's a choice of transport. A **boat** from the jetty (Thurs–Sat 2pm; $5) runs as far as **Kuala Kerai**, which takes ninety minutes, as does the daily **train** service which heads north at 7.57am and 9.50am (south at 4.59pm and 8.33pm; there are a couple of slower local trains during the day). From Kuala Kerai, this continues to **Tumpat**, at the end of the line, though most people get off at Wakaf Bharu, the nearest station to Kota Bharu.

The train ride is splendid, chugging along valley floors where trees and plants almost envelop the track, and then climbing steeply to cross long, metal bridges over a network of rivers. The train passes through seven tunnels; when the minimal lighting malfunctions, the swaying carriages are plunged into darkness. The few stations along the way are hardly more than lean-tos and if there is anywhere left in the Malay Peninsula that is truly remote it's here. Obscure little settlements, squeezed into the dense green cloak of jungle, have Senoi Orang Asli names like Renok, Kemubu and Pahi, from where local people board the train with their massive bundles of goods.

For the final section of the jungle railway – the 75km from Kuala Kerai to Tumpat on the northeast coast – the geography changes from mountainous, river-gashed jungle to rubber, pepper and palm oil plantations. This is also **cattle country**, where cows are a constant problem for train drivers, as they graze along the railway sidings, often straying onto the track. The trains usually travel slowly enough to avoid hitting the cows, but occasionally there's a collision. Along the route, villages become more numerous and the train swells with Malay traders and saree-clad Indian women heading for Kota Bharu. The penultimate stop is Wakaf Bharu, for Kota Bharu, 7km away by bus, with the end of the line at Tumpat, another thirty minutes northwest of Wakaf Bharu.

Kuala Kerai

The only town of any size between Gua Musang and Kota Bharu, **KUALA KERAI**, on the east bank of the two-hundred-metre-wide Sungei Kelantan, is a busy commercial centre serving inland Kelantan. Once, great barges laden with goods were floated from here down to the coast, but nowadays most of the local traffic is confined either to Route 8 which runs close to the town centre, or to the jungle railway which passes south of the town. But despite Kerai's regional importance, the pace of life here is slow, and there's very little going on through the baking hours of the early afternoon.

The town consists of an east–west street, Jalan Sultan Yahya Petra, and the north–south Jalan AN Sang, where you'll find most hotels and services. About the only distraction is to take a walk up to the Mini Zoo and Museum (daily 9am–12.30pm & 2–5pm; $1), ten minutes out of town on a well-marked road. The **zoo** is eminently missable, a sad array of ill-kept and unkempt animals. Further up the hill in a large Malay house, the **museum** commands a fine view of the town. Besides the ubiquitous stuffed animals, there are photographs of town dignitaries, markets, street life and Orang Asli in traditional dress, while other exhibits include a church organ whose chair is decorated with intricate Kelantanese symbols, various musical instruments, and a large wall hanging displaying the Kelantan royal family tree.

PRACTICALITIES

The **train and bus stations** are at the northern end of Jalan AN Sang, with the **jetty** just 50m to the west. **Trains** north leave at 7.57am, 9.23am and 7pm for the two-hour trip to Wakaf Bharu (the stop for Kota Bharu), and at 5.40am, 4.59pm and 8.33pm for the trip south. **Buses** north to Kota Bahru leave every thirty minutes from 6.30am to 6pm (around $5), and there are also services to Gua Musang (around $3) every hour, and one daily to KL at 10.30 am (around $25).

Boats to Dabong leave at 10.45am daily except Friday ($5), for the ninety-minute journey down Sungei Kelantan into Sungei Galas. There's no need to book, but get to the jetty at least fifteen minutes before departure – from Jalan AN Sang, take the left turn at the junction with Jalan Sultan Yahya Petra, and keep going until the road peters out. The jetty consists of a leaky bamboo raft connected to the river bank by a single, bowed plank – not practical if you're carrying any luggage.

For **accommodation**, there's *Hotel Kerai*, 190 Jalan AN Sang (②), which, despite its fading shutters and red-tiled kampung-style roof, has little atmosphere and only basic facilities. Opposite, the *Joomui Hotel*, 189 Jalan AN Sang (②), is a better bet, with industrial fans, TV and bucket-over-the-head showers. There are good Muslim **cafés** on the corner of the two streets, where tasty *nasi campur* and *roti canai* are served until about 9pm. Further along Jalan AN Sang on the right, the busy Chinese **hawker centre**, *Jade Garden*, serves superb seafood dishes, including Kelantese specialities like river trout and perch. At the other end of town, on the approach from Route 8 along Jalan Sultan Yahya Petra, just past the zoo and museum, there's a line of **satay stalls**.

Tasek Chini and Tasek Bera

The main interest in the southern part of the interior, below the KL–Kuantan road (Route 2), lies in its two lake systems, **Tasek Chini** and **Tasek Bera**, beautiful areas where Orang Asli groups live and work. Chini is much more developed than Bera with a small resort and a large village at its northern end, offering inexpensive accommodation and the chance to buy excellent handicrafts. The larger lake system at Bera is sparsely populated and has fewer facilities for visitors but if anything, it's even more stunning than Chini. Access to Tasek Bera is via **Temerloh**, the main town on Route 2, which is of slight interest but has reasonable hotels and places to eat.

The **Jakun** Orang Asli around Tasek Chini live in settled communities and occasionally do seasonal work. At more remote Tasek Bera, the **Semelai** cultivate tapioca, rice, vegetables, sugar cane, sweet potatoes and peppers, trap fish and collect forest products for a living. There are **crocodiles** in the lake here, and the Semelai believe their ancestors concluded a pact with the mythic supreme crocodile of the lake, forging a relationship of mutual respect. The Semelai live on the edge of the jet-black lake in elevated houses built of wood, tree bark and *atap* leaves; their sturdy boats are made from hollowed-out tree trunks, although these days they tend to buy them from the Malays, rather than make them themselves. Along Tasek Bera's seemingly endless passages through the rushes, a loud and eerie sound emanates from the *berbeling* – crude windmills made of bamboo which guide the Semelai through the swamps.

Tasek Chini

TASEK CHINI is a conglomerate of twelve connecting lakes of varying sizes spanning an area of around twenty square kilometres. The lakes have given rise to a plethora of **myths and legends**, which is hardly surprising given their serene beauty. The waters here are deep black, though from June to September their surface is brightened by shimmering pink-and-white **lotus blossoms**. The creation legend of the indigenous Jakun tells that they were planting crops one day, when an old woman with a walking stick appeared and said that the group should have sought her permission before clearing the land. But she allowed them to stay, and to legitimize their right she stabbed her stick into the centre of the clearing and told them never to pull it out. Years later, during a particularly ferocious rainstorm, a tribe member accidentally pulled out the stick, leaving a huge hole which immediately filled with water, creating the lake. Another legend tells of an ancient city which, when threatened with external attack, was flooded by its inhabitants using a system of aqueducts, with the intention of draining it later. Curious Malaysian scientists have embarked upon several research projects over the years, but nothing has ever been found. Some Jakun believe a serpent – or *naga* – guards the lakes, but the serpent has remained as elusive as the lost city.

All the lakes in the system can be explored by boat, either from *Chini Resort* in the south, or nearby Kampung Gumum. During the summer months *Chini Resort* attracts enough visitors to support a small-scale tourist industry, including a growing number of Orang Asli **carvers** who live and display their work here.

Arrival and accommodation

From KL, catch the hourly KL–Kuantan bus from either Pekeliling or Pudu Raya bus station to the small town of **Maran**, 180km (3hr; $10) east of KL on Route 2. You'll have to take a taxi to **Kampung Belimbing**, then on Sungei Pahang. From Belimbing jetty, close to the road, you can rent a boat (around $50) to take you to the lake, a trip of around forty minutes up Sungei Pahang, then south along small Sungei Chini for the final 4km to the lake. Along the way, lianas cloak the giant trees leaning across the narrow river; the boat may well pass a group of Jakun fishermen pulling up their nets.

From Kuantan, the easiest option is to take a taxi or tour – contact the Tourist Office (☎09/513 3026) which can arrange return transport and boats from $75 for two people. Otherwise, any non-express Kuantan–KL bus can drop you at the Chini turn-off where you can try and hitch a lift. The other way to get to Chini from Kuantan is to take bus #121 ($5) to **Felda Chini**, an uninteresting village set in a monotonous landscape of oil palms 16km east of the lake. The bus leaves Kuantan six times daily and takes ninety minutes to reach the kampung, from where you will have to take a motorbike-taxi (around $20) to Kampung Gumum or *Chini Resort*. From Chini, the bus back to Kuantan leaves at 5pm. Tours of Chini can also be arranged in **Cherating** at several of the hotels and the *Travel Post* in the kampung.

Most boats take you to the jetty below **Chini Resort** (☎09/456 7897, fax 456 7898), a quiet development tucked into the forest on the edge of the main lake, and the only place with a range of accommodation. It can get very busy at weekends when large groups often make block-bookings, so it's best to go in the week – during the wet season (October to January) you may have the place to yourself. The five small **dormitories** have ten beds in each ($8), while the nine two-bed **chalets** (④) can also be equipped with extra mattresses for around $20 extra per person. There's a **café**, which serves meals throughout the day, a **restaurant** (noon–2pm & 7–11pm) and a **ranger's camp** where you can rent inexpensive tents, calor-gas stoves and sleeping bags.

Five minutes by boat east of the *Chini Resort* is **KAMPUNG GUMUM**, a Jakun Orang Asli village of sixty kampung-style huts, a small store and one place to stay. The village hasn't got a jetty, so boats just pitch up on the beach. Walk along the beach for a few metres to the south (right) and up a path into the forest which leads to *Rajan Jones' Shop*, the only place in Gumum to get a meal. Jones also has a guesthouse in the village (③). Again, food is included in the price if you're staying; a well at the bottom of the garden provides the only means of washing. Jones also organizes treks round the lake.

Boat trips and trails

The shortest **boat trip** is to the Orang Asli **show village**, only twenty minutes away from the *Chini Resort*. The Jakun have built a traditional house here, made of bamboo and *atap* leaves and elevated on wooden stilts, but most of the people actually live in Gumum – there's the same range of carvings and blowpipes on sale as at *Nadia's Shop*. Better are the two-hour trips west and south to **Laut Melai**, the lake where the lotuses are most plentiful, and to **Laut Babi**, the biggest lake in the system. If the water is low, clumps of spiky pentenas grass can be seen protruding from the water, and gulls often swoop down to pluck fish from the water. In May, the few resident Chini turtles lay their eggs and the boatmen may know where to find them.

The most popular **trail** is the one leading along the side of Tasek Chini, from the resort to Gumum, a two-kilometre trip. The path can be hard to follow after heavy rain, and may involve wading through water. A longer, four-hour trail from the resort goes to a **campsite** at **Laut Terembau**, the path weaving in and out of mangrove, forest and oil palm plantations. The campsite is merely a clearing and doesn't have any facilities, so bring food and water with you. The trail continues beyond the camp and after 5km leads to a secondary road; travel east along this for 20km and you arrive at the Segamat–Kuantan road (Route 12).

There is a further campsite on the west side of the lake system at **Palau Babi**, which can only be reached by boat, and another where Sungei Chini divides off from Sungei Pahang at the top of the lake complex, not far from Belimbing.

Tasek Bera

Twenty-seven kilometres long and five kilometres wide, **TASEK BERA** is the most extensive lake system in Malaysia. Like Chini, Bera's warren of channels lead from one lake to another through waterways where nemkung rasau, a sharp, high grass with a sticky yellow fruit, grows with abandon, and reeds sprout from the water. The main lake is incredibly beautiful, its peat-edged watercourse and peat-floored bed rendering the waters jet black in places. At the edges, the centuries-old Semelai Orang Asli practice of shifting cultivation has helped create a forest of great diversity, in which large trees have been thinned and a wide variety of edible plants such as pepper and root vegetables have been sown. Apart from the Semelai, the only visitors the lake has seen in recent years are staff from Pahang's Fisheries Department, who come to take samples of the water and fish to ensure the Orang Asli aren't using chemicals or poisons to boost their catch. There's not a great deal to do at the lake beyond taking boat rides around the channels – the local Parks and Wildlife Department is planning a headquarters within the lake system, which will include visitor facilities. Its management will be a test of Malaysia's environmental credentials, since Tasek Bera was declared the country's first "wetland of international importance" in 1995.

A Semelai hut belonging to Sham Sudin marks the only point on Bera where **boats** can be rented; Sudin charges $100 for a two- to three-hour trip around the lake. He speaks some English and can answer questions on local flora and fauna. It's possible to stay in the family home for $10 a night including meals. The best way to find Sudin is to enquire at the shop on the hill just before the bridge over Sungei Bera.

Access from Temerloh

You may have no choice but to spend the night at **TEMERLOH** on your way to Tasek Bera. The best day to arrive is Tuesday, when a pasar malam is set up on Jalan Tengku Baku. There's also a market every Sunday morning by the river, close to the bus station. The helpful **Tourist Information Office** (Mon–Sat 9am–4.30pm; ☎09/296 0812) at the bus station provides information on getting to the lake.

Accommodation is easy to find and generally inexpensive, with the hotels located north of the bus station on Jalan Tengku Baku. There's little to choose between the *Hotel Isis* (☎09/296 3136; ①) at no. 12, and *New Ban Hin Hotel* (☎09/296 2331; ①-②) at no. 40, as both have communal showers and toilets, and are equipped with fans. There are also slightly more expensive air-conditioned rooms, with attached bathrooms. The *Government Resthouse* (☎09/296 3254; ③), on Jalan Humzah, is a fifteen-minute walk from the bus station. For **eating** in the evening the only option is the Malay hawker centre next to the bus station, though there are some good Indian **cafés** open during the day on Jalan Tengku Baku.

To reach the lake, the best option is to hire a taxi for the day (around $50). Otherwise, take any **bus** from the terminus south to Teriang (hourly service 7am–5pm, except 11am & noon; $3) and get off at Kereyong, a thirty-minute ride. From here, you'll have to hitch to a point 20km east where the route to Bera leaves the road – the track through oil palm plantations sees quite a lot of traffic, including plantation staff vans and motorbikes belonging to the Semelai (who charge around $10 to take you to the lakeside).

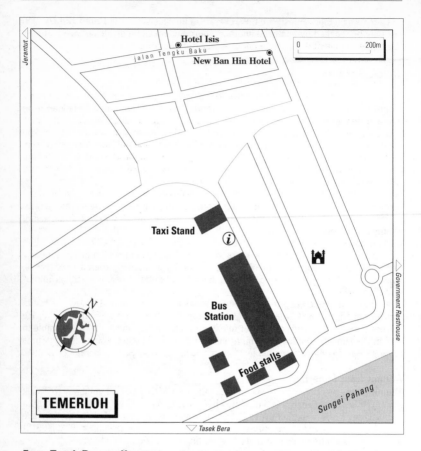

Map of TEMERLOH showing Hotel Isis, New Ban Hin Hotel, Jalan Tengku Baku, Jerantut, Taxi Stand, Bus Station, Food stalls, Government Resthouse, Sungei Pahang, Tasek Bera

From Tasek Bera to Kuantan

The only way of reaching the southern sections of Tasek Bera is by car. Pass through Teriang, and 30km further on turn east just before Bahau on Route 11, which leads to the southernmost point on the lake, a small kampung called **FORT ISKANDER**. This far south in the interior, the land is flat and most areas have been deforested, making way for agricultural plantations. There are a number of Semelai villages along the river banks here and it may be possible to find a house to spend the night, although taking a tent is more sensible. Travelling on east from Iskander, Route 11 joins Route 12; 50km north is the left turn to Kampung Chini. On Route 12, buses from Segamat to Kuantan pass hourly, and, once the road meets the Kuantan Highway, they become very frequent.

travel details

Trains

Gemas to: Gua Musang (1 daily; 11hr); Jerantut (1 daily; 3hr); Kuala Lipis (2 daily; 8hr); Mentakab (1 daily; 4hr); Tumpat (1 daily; 13hr 20min); Wakaf Bharu (2 daily; 14hr 30min).

Kuala Lumpur to: Gemas (5 daily; 3hr).

Wakaf Bharu to: Dabong (2 daily; 3hr); Gemas (2 daily; 13hr); Gua Musang (2 daily; 6hr); Jerantut (2 daily; 10hr 30min); Kuala Kerai (3 daily; 2hr); Kuala Lipis (2 daily; 9hr); Kuala Tembeling (2 daily; 10hr); Mentakab (2 daily; 12hr 30min).

Buses

Gua Musang to: Kuala Kerai (hourly; 3hr).

Jerantut to: Kuala Lipis (hourly; 1hr 30min); Tembeling jetty (3 daily; 40min); Kuala Tahan (1 daily; 2hr 30min).

Kuala Kerai to: Kota Bharu (every 30min; 2hr 30min); Kuala Lumpur (1 daily; 8hr).

Kuala Lipis to: Gua Musang (hourly; 3hr).

Kuala Lumpur to: Gua Musang (4 daily; 6hr); Kota Bharu (6 daily; 10hr); Kuala Kerai (4 daily; 8hr); Kuala Lipis (6 daily; 3hr); Mentakab (hourly; 1hr 15min); Raub (10 daily; 90min); Temerloh (every 30min; 1hr 30min).

Temerloh to: Jerantut (every 30min; 1hr).

Ferries

Dabong to: Kuala Kerai (1 daily; 2hr).

Kuala Lipis to: Kenong Rimba (Sat at 2pm; 3hr).

Tembeling jetty to: Taman Negara (daily at 9am & 2pm except Fri at 2.30pm; 3hr).

CHAPTER FOUR

THE EAST COAST

T he four-hundred-kilometre stretch from the northeastern corner of the Peninsula to Kuantan, roughly halfway down the east coast, displays a quite different cultural legacy to the more populous, industrialized western seaboard. For hundreds of years, the Malay rulers of the northern states of Kelantan and Terengganu were vassals of the Thai kingdom of Ayuthaya, suffering repeated invasions as well as the unruly squabbles of their own princes. Nevertheless, the relationship forged with the Thais allowed the Malays a great deal of autonomy which, together with the adoption of Islam in the seventeenth century, gave the region a strong sense of identity and independence. The Persatuan Islam Sa-Tanah Melayu (PAS), the Pan-Malayan Islamic Party, has dominated local politics in Kelantan since the 1950s. It's still the most "Malay" region in Malaysia, with strong cultural traditions.

Remaining free of British control until 1909, the region escaped the economic and social changes that rocked the western Malay Peninsula during the nineteenth century. Cut off by the mountainous, jungle interior from technological advances taking place in the Federated Malay States, Kelantan, Terengganu and Pahang retained their largely rural character. While immigrants poured into the tin and rubber towns of the west, the east remained underdeveloped and, as a result, still lacks the ethnic diversity of the rest of the country. The recent discovery of oil off the shores of Terengganu has dramatically increased the standard of living for some east coast residents, whose per capita income was previously well below the national average. But for the most part, the economy – one of the poorest in the federation – is still based on small-scale sea and river fishing and rice farming.

For the visitor, the east coast provides a welcome contrast to the entrepreneurial west coast. The casuarina-fringed beaches and coral reefs on three of the most beautiful islands in the South China Sea, **Pulau Perhentian**, **Pulau Redang** and **Pulau Kapas**, are the greatest attraction, but two of the three main cities have some appeal. In **Kota Bharu**, the last major town before the Thai border, the inhabitants still practise ancient Malay crafts such as kite-making and top-spinning; **Kuala Terengganu**, 160km to the south, is an up-and-coming oil-rich town with an old Chinese quarter and a traditional boat-building industry. Both are infinitely preferable to the urban disaster that is **Kuantan**, though you may find it hard to avoid passing through, since it is connected to the nation's capital by the congested and perilous Route 2, which runs across the Peninsula (and which boasts the highest accident rate in the whole country).

Much of the east coast – from Kota Bharu to Kuantan – is virtually out of bounds between November and February because of the annual **monsoon**, and the heavy rains and sea swell are too great to allow boats to reach any of the islands. Since there are no rail links, travel throughout the region is limited to the relatively traffic-free Route 3, hugging the coast, and Route 14 which runs virtually parallel a little way inland, that links Kuala Terengganu with Kuantan. It's the coastal road that's the most interesting, connecting a whole string of blissfully laid-back fishing kampungs like **Merang**, **Marang** and **Cherating**. In addition, between May and September, the beaches surrounding **Rantau Abang** are one of only five places in the world where giant leatherback turtles come to nest.

Kota Bharu

At the very northeastern corner of the Peninsula, close to the Thai border, **KOTA BHARU** is the capital of Kelantan State and one of the most important cultural centres in Malaysia. Despite this, some people find the town's initial appearance something of a disappointment. It doesn't take long, though, for Kota Bharu's charm to work, and many people stay much longer than they planned. The town is a showcase for skills and customs little practised elsewhere in Malaysia. Kota Bharu is proud of its traditions, nurtured by the town's **Gelanggang Seni** (Cultural Centre) and the various **cottage industries** that thrive in the outlying areas. There are regular festivals, and if you arrive in September after the rice harvest you'll be treated to celebrations in the surrounding villages. During the month of **Ramadan**, early in the year, strongly Muslim Kota Bharu virtually shuts up shop.

Isolation not only fostered a unique culture here – so much so that a traveller in the 1820s noted distinct differences between the dialect and dances of Kelantan and those of the rest of the Malay Peninsula – but also allowed Kota Bharu greater political autonomy than other state capitals. The railway only arrived in the region in 1931, skirting the state capital – the journey to Kuala Lumpur at that time involved thirteen ferry crossings. Kelantan's embrace of **Islam** helped preserve its isolation, and its long coastline encouraged trading contacts with the Arab world, enabling a free-flow of new ideas and customs from as early as the 1600s. Travel to Mecca was common by the nineteenth century and, unlike the rest of the country, Kelantan's legal system operated according to Islamic law – an important factor in the maintenance of national pride under Thai overlordship. Kota Bharu's most famous son, **To' Kenali**, a renowned *ulama*, or religious teacher who spent some years studying in Cairo which was then a centre for modernist ideas. He returned to his home town to establish *pondoks* – "hut schools" next to the mosque – in order to spread Islamic doctrine throughout the state. The twentieth-century equivalent of this is the reliance of the radical conservative Persatuan Islam Sa-Tanah Melayu (PAS) – the largest party in opposition in the federal parliament since 1959 – on Muslim schools to spread its message in the villages.

PAS won a landslide victory in Kelantan in the 1990 election, wiping out UMNO, the ruling party. Despite clinging on to power in the 1995 election, PAS's popularity has been sliding as it has sought to run the state along more religious lines, halting, for example, certain cultural activities, and introducing separate check-out lines at supermarkets for men and women. The break-up of its coalition with former opposition party Parti Melayu Semangat '46 in 1996, and a falling out with Kelatan's sultan who still holds considerable political sway, means PAS's days in power may be numbered, though the *Menteri Besar* (chief minister) Nik Aziz Nik Mat, is a crowd-pleasing politician.

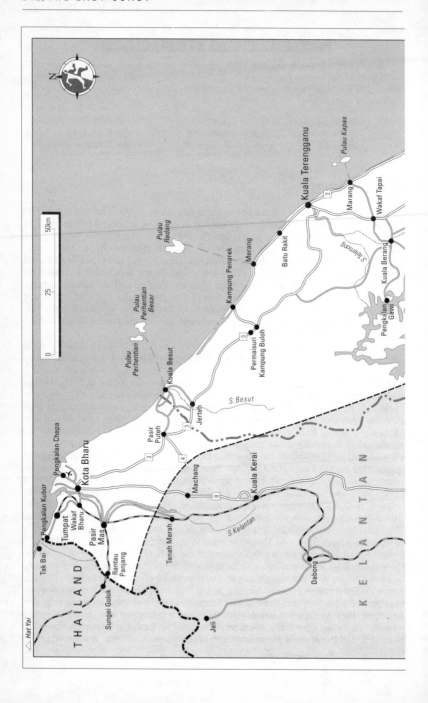

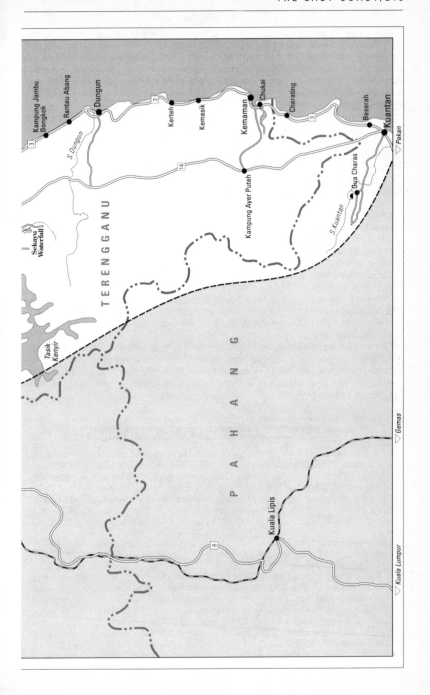

Kota Bharu's is one of only three towns in Malaysia (together with Kuala Terangganu and Dungun) to have a Malay majority. This is evident the minute you enter town – women are dressed much more circumspectly than elsewhere, and attending the mosque is a prominent feature of the day. Foreign women sometimes complain about feeling uncomfortable in Kota Bharu, but while it's not a place to sport beach wear, there's a relaxed air about the town which belies its political conservatism and mitigates its male-dominated outlook.

While you might well be drawn away from the centre by the opportunity to witness the various trades at first hand – kite and top construction, batik-printing and weaving – this shouldn't distract you from Kota Bharu's **historical buildings**, sited around Padang Merdeka, or its fine markets. Using the town as your base, you can also head out to the local **beaches** and to the temples in the surrounding countryside on the Thai border.

Arrival, information and getting around

Long-distance **buses** arrive at one of the two bus stations, inconveniently situated on the southern outskirts of Kota Bharu: the state bus company, SKMK, operates from the Langgar bus station on Jalan Pasir Puteh, as does the MARA company, which runs buses to KL and Singapore; other companies use the larger bus station on Jalan Hamzah, which also has a left-luggage facility. If you arrive at night, you're at the mercy of the unofficial taxis at the stations, whose drivers can charge up to $15 for the two-kilometre drive to the centre: the daytime charge is around $4. The **local bus station**, where you'll arrive if coming from Kuala Terengganu, is on Jalan Padong Garong, SKMK also operates some services from here and has an information counter (daily 8am–9pm; closed Fri 12.45pm–2pm). The **long-distance taxi** stand is behind the bus station on Jalan Doktor.

The nearest **train station** to Kota Bharu is 7km to the west at Wakaf Bharu, the penultimate stop on the "Jungle Railway" through the interior from Gemas. From here it's a twenty-minute ride into town on bus #19 or #27 – they run to and from the local bus station. The local **airport** is 9km northeast of the centre – a taxi into town costs $11 – buy a coupon from the taxi counter in the airport.

CROSSING THE BORDER INTO THAILAND

From Kota Bharu, you can cross the Thai border by river or by land. If you're going to stay in Thailand for more than a month, you'll need a **visa**, easily obtainable from the town's consulate (see "Listings", p.250). Both **border posts** are open daily between 6am and 6pm – remember that Thai time is one hour behind Malaysian time.

The coastal access point is at **Pengkalan Kubor**, 20km northwest of Kota Bharu, which connects with the small town of Tak Bai on the Thai side. Take bus #27 or #43 from the local bus station for the thirty-minute journey ($1.70), then the car ferry (50 sen).

More convenient however is the land crossing at **Rantau Panjang**, 30km southwest of Kota Bharu. Bus #29 departs from the local bus station in Kota Bharu every thirty minutes (6.45am–6.30pm) for the 45-minute trip ($2.60) or you can take a shared taxi from Kota Bharu for $3.50 each; from Rantau Panjang, it's a short walk across the border to Sungei Golok on the Thai side. Trains depart from there at noon and 3pm for the 23-hour trip to Bangkok via Hat Yai and Surat Thani. Buses leave at 9am and 12.30pm; buses to Hat Yai take four hours. Train information can be checked with the State Railway of Thailand in Sungei Golok (☎073/611162), although they're unlikely to accept a seat reservation over the phone. If you want to be sure of a seat, tickets can be booked for a small commission ($30) at the *Town Guesthouse* (see "Accommodation", below).There's no longer a Malaysian train service from Wakaf Bharu to Rantau Panjang.

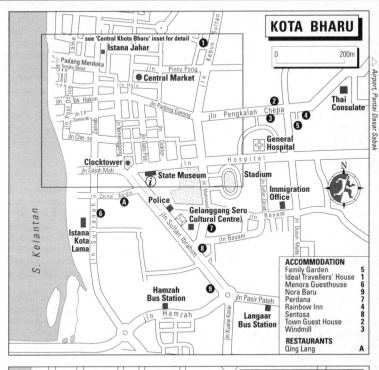

KOTA BHARU

0   200m

see 'Central Khota Bharu' inset for detail

Istana Jahar

Padang Merdeka

Central Market

Thai Consulate

General Hospital

Clocktower

State Museum

Stadium

Immigration Office

Police

Gelanggang Seru Cultural Centre

Istana Kota Lama

Hamzah Bus Station

Langaar Bus Station

S. Kelantan

ACCOMMODATION

Family Garden	5
Ideal Travellers' House	1
Menora Guesthouse	6
Nora Baru	9
Perdana	7
Rainbow Inn	4
Sentosa	8
Town Guest House	2
Windmill	3

RESTAURANTS

Qing Lang	A

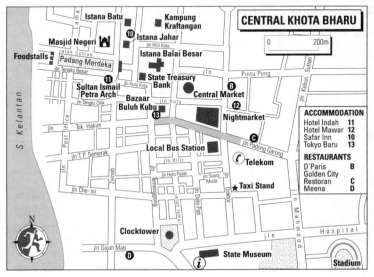

CENTRAL KHOTA BHARU

0   200m

Istana Batu

Kampung Kraftangan

Masjid Negeri

Istana Jahar

Foodstalls

Padang Merdeka

Istana Balai Besar

Sultan Ismail Petra Arch

State Treasury Bank

Central Market

Bazaar Buluh Kubu

Nightmarket

Local Bus Station

Telekom

Taxi Stand

Clocktower

State Museum

Stadium

S. Kelantan

ACCOMMODATION

Hotel Indah	11
Hotel Mawar	12
Safar Inn	10
Tokyo Baru	13

RESTAURANTS

D'Paris	B
Golden City Restoran	C
Meena	D

For details of **leaving Kota Bharu**, see the relevant entries in "Listings", p250. For **Thailand**, see the box on p.244.

The **Tourist Information Centre** (Mon–Wed & Sat 8am–4.45pm, Thurs 8am–1.15pm; ☎09/748 5534, fax 748 6652) close to the clocktower on Jalan Sultan Ibrahim, is very helpful. **Tours** of various local craft workshops and homestays (see below) can be booked here.

Although most of the sights in Kota Bharu are within easy walking distance of each other, you may want to opt for a **trishaw**. Trishaws can be found along the roads around the bus station and night market, and the normal fare for a ten-minute journey is $3 – make sure you agree the price beforehand. For longer journeys, a **taxi** is more convenient; they operate from a stand behind the local bus station on Jalan Doktor: the rate is roughly $25 per hour per taxi (not per person) for sightseeing.

Accommodation

Competition between the many **guesthouses** in Kota Bharu ensures some of the cheapest (if basic) accommodation in Malaysia; the rates often include breakfast. Some places let you do your own cooking, although given the cost of eating out this hardly seems worth while. All guesthouses have dorms as well as ordinary rooms, unless otherwise stated; common rooms, TV and laundry facilities are standard, while a few places offer batik workshops, bike rental and cultural tours. An alternative option is the **homestay programme** run by Roselan Hanafiah at the Tourist Information Centre, which offers the chance to stay with a family, often expert in a particular craft ($220 per person, minimum of 2 people for 2 nights/3 days, including all meals).

The budget hotels are poor value, and are often dirty, noisy and located in seedy areas. However, you'll find quite a few mid-range bargains, and while luxury options are very limited, the choice is wider if you stay out of town at one of the beach resorts (see "Around Kota Bharu", p.250). All the places listed below are keyed on the map on p.245.

Family Garden, 4945d Lorong Islah Lama (☎09/747 5763). Near the Thai consulate, this homely place offers free breakfast and transport to the out of town bus stations. ②.

Ideal Travellers' House, 3954f Jalan Kebun Sultan (☎09/744 2246). Down a quiet lane off the main road to the northeast of town, and often full. Good atmosphere, with a beer garden. ①.

Indah, 236b Jalan Tengku Besar (☎09/748 5081, fax 748 2788). Reasonably priced but old-fashioned rooms with good views over the river and padang. No dorm. ③.

Mawar, Jalan Parit Dalam (☎09/744 8888, fax 747 6666). A Baroque lobby – all gilt, wood and mirrors – and small but comfortable rooms. It has it's own café, and is situated right by the pasar malam. ⑥.

Menora Guest House, 3338d Jalan Sultanah Zainab (☎09/748 1669). Delightful guesthouse, with large, brightly painted rooms. The roof garden has a fantastic river view and the café is very popular. Dorm beds are $5. ①.

Nora Baru, 5229h Jalan Sultan Ibrahim (☎09/744 8455). Best of the bunch in the price range, with carpeted rooms and dorms, fifteen minutes' walk from the town centre. Dorms $7. ②.

Perdana, Jalan Mahmood (☎09/748 5000, fax 744 7621). A monstrosity of a building housing all the features you'd expect for the price, including a swimming pool and a good sports centre. ⑤.

Rainbow Inn, 4423a Jalan Pengkalan Chepa (no phone). Interesting paintings and laid-back atmosphere make up for basic rooms. There's a garden, batik workshop and bikes for rent. ①.

Safar Inn, Jalan Hilir Kota (☎09/747 8000, fax 747 9000). The best mid-priced hotel in Kota Bharu, close to all the cultural sights. The pleasantly furnished rooms are a good deal: the rate includes breakfast. ⑤.

Sentosa, 3180a Jalan Sultan Ibrahim (☎09/744 3200). Close to the Cultural Centre, this friendly hotel has fresh, comfortable rooms, though no other facilities (and no dorm). ③.

Tokyo Baru, 3945 Jalan Tok Hakim (☎09/744 4511, fax 744 9488). The management is welcoming at this upgraded hotel close to the pasar malam. Top-floor rooms have great balconies overlooking the town centre. ③.

Town Guest House, 4959a Jalan Pengkalan Chepa (☎09/748 5192, fax 744 9403). Conscientious management and a warm welcome make this one of the best guesthouses in town. Clean and comfortable, with a rooftop café. Will make train reservations ($30) to Thailand for guests. ①.

Windmill, 286 Jalan Pengkalan Chepa (☎ & fax 09/748 3207). A notch above most in this category, with classy timber decor and a coffee shop. Bike rental ($5 a day), as well as organized cultural trips. ①.

The Town

The centre of Kota Bharu, hugging the eastern bank of Sungei Kelantan, is based on a grid pattern, its busy roundabout sporting a curious pink rocket-like clocktower marking the junction of the town's three major roads, Jalan Hospital, Jalan Sultan Ibrahim and Jalan Temenggong. The area surrounding the clocktower is where you'll find most of the shops, banks and offices, while around Jalan Padang Garong, a few blocks to the north, are Kota Bharu's **markets**. Further north still, close to the river, the quiet oasis of **Padang Merdeka** marks Kota Bharu's historical centre, a compact square of fascinating buildings. The **State Museum** and the **Gelanggang Seni** (Cultural Centre), south of the clocktower, document Kota Bharu's cultural inheritance. Most of these sights are within easy walking distance of each other; you could complete a tour in a day, and take in a show in the evening.

Around Padang Merdeka

Small **Padang Merdeka** to the north of Khota Baru, is the town's historical heart. Despite its grand title – Independence Square – it's not much more than a grassy patch of land, on which the British displayed the body of the defeated Tok Janggut (Father Long Beard), a peasant spiritual leader who spearheaded a revolt against the colonial system of land taxes and tenancy regulations in 1915, one of the few specifically anti-colonial incidents to occur on the east coast.

The padang is bordered on its northern side by the white **Masjid Negeri**, known as *Serambi Mekah* – or "Verandah of Mecca" – because of its prominent role in the spread of Islam throughout Kelantan. Dominating the eastern end of the square, the immense **Sultan Ismail Petra Arch** is a recent timber building commemorating the declaration of Kota Bharu as a cultural city; beyond lies a pedestrianized area and the royal palaces. Half-hidden behind high walls and entrance gates, the single-storey **Istana Balai Besar** was built in 1844 and contains the Throne Room and State Legislative Assembly, but is now used primarily for ceremonial functions and is closed to the public. To the right of the palace gates is the former Kelantan **State Treasury Bank**, an unobtrusive stone bunker no more than two metres high, which remained in use until well into this century and which gives the square its unofficial name of "Padang Bank".

Adjacent to the former treasury, the **Istana Jahar** (daily except Fri 8.30am–4.45pm; $2) houses the Royal Customs Museum. Although not the oldest building in the square – it was constructed in 1887 – it is certainly the most traditional in style, with a timber portico and highly polished decorative panels adorning the exterior. The building takes its name from the *jahar* tree, the burnt-orange "flame of the forest", a specimen of which was planted outside in the courtyard by Sultan Mohammed IV. The sultan ordered extensive renovations to the palace in 1911, adding an Italian marble floor, which cools the interior, and a wrought-iron spiral staircase. The ground floor of the palace is given over to a display of exquisite textiles – intricate henna-coloured *ikat* weaving and lustrous *songkets* – together with samples of the ornate gold jewellery belonging to the Royal Family. Upstairs you'll see life-size reconstructions of various traditional royal ceremonies, from weddings to circumcisions. In the childbirth ritual, the mother is made to sit over a hot stove, supposedly to encourage the delivery of the afterbirth. Behind the istana is a **Weapon's Gallery** ($1), with an impressive collection of spears, daggers and *kris*, and traditional clothing.

As you leave the museum, turn the corner to your left and after a few metres you'll see the sky-blue **Istana Batu** (daily 10am–6pm; $2), an incongruous 1930s' villa built as the sultan's residence. One of the first concrete constructions in the state (its name means "stone palace"), it's now the Kelantan Royal Museum, with the rooms left in their original state. Portraits of the ruler and his family survey the vast amounts of English crockery and glassware which crowd the dining-room table – kitsch and clutter beyond belief. Still, it's worth a half-hour wander, from reception rooms to scullery, if only for comparison with the relatively humble standards of previous rulers.

Directly opposite, another large pedestrianized square is the site of the **Kampung Kraftangan** (daily except Fri 10am–5pm), or "Handicraft Village", mainly a collection of gift shops and a café. The Handicraft Museum (daily except Fri 8.30am–4.45pm; $1) occupies one of several authentic timber houses in the compound, though it displays a disappointingly limited range of crafts.

The markets

To the south, away from Padang Merdeka, are two of the most vibrant markets in Malaysia. The **Central Market** (daily 8am–6pm), in an octagonal warehouse, is the focus of the town, buzzing with stalls selling produce of all kinds, from meat and fresh vegetables to cooking pots and batik sarongs. Virtually all the stall-holders are female, the coloured headscarves of their traditional Muslim dress augmenting the vivid display. The scene is best viewed from the third floor, with the yellow perspex roof casting a soft light over the geometric piles of vegetables below. Look out for the local fish speciality, *keropok batang*, greyish brown and sausage-like in its raw state, but delicious fried and dipped in chilli sauce.

One block to the south, hundreds of brightly lit food stalls set up each evening in a car park, forming a **night market** of epic proportions. As well as offering a gastronomic experience (see "Eating", below), this performs a social function, too, as it's the place to catch up on all the local gossip.

The State Museum and the Gelanggang Seni

Situated on the corner of Jalan Hospital and Jalan Sultan Ibrahim, the **State Museum** (Thurs–Sat 8.30am–4.45pm; $2) houses an odd collection – romantic rural Malay paintings and lots of earthenware pots. Better is the collection of musical instruments on the first floor, among which is the *kertok*, a large coconut with its top sliced off and a piece of wood fastened across the opening to form a sounding board. Decorated with colourful pennants and hit with a cloth beater, it's one of the percussion instruments peculiar to Kelantan. To see these in action, visit the **Gelanggang Seni**, Kota Bharu's Cultural Centre, on Jalan Mahmood, one block behind the museum, reached via either Jalan Sultan Ibrahim or Jalan Hospital. Free performances here (March–Oct Mon, Wed & Sat except during Ramadan; check details with the Tourist Information Centre), feature many of the traditional pastimes of Kelantan – using *gasing* (spinning tops) and *rebana* (giant drums). On Wednesday evenings there are Wayung Kulit (shadow play) performances. The traditional shows on Saturday nights are unique to Kelantan. They combine singing, dancing, romance and comedy, derived from nineteenth-century court entertainments and strongly influenced by Thai culture. A visit to the centre is still the easiest way to see many of the arts that are dying out elsewhere in Malaysia, and the standard is consistently high.

Eating

Easily the most exciting place to eat at is Kota Bharu's **night market** (daily 6.30pm–midnight; closed for evening prayers 7.30–8pm), with an amazing variety of food – although vegetarians could find themselves limited to vegetable *murtabaks*. If you ask, you'll get a spoon and fork; otherwise use the jug of water and roll of tissue on

TRADITIONAL PASTIMES IN KELANTAN

Gasing Uri or **top-spinning** is one of the most vigorous of the sports played in the state and, with none of the childish connotations it has in the West, is taken very seriously, requiring a great deal of strength and dexterity. There are two types of competition: the straightforward spin, in which the winner is simply the one whose top spins the longest – the record time in Kelantan is 1 hour 47 minutes – and the striking match whereby one top has to knock out the other. The launching process is the same, however. A long length of rope is tightly wound around the top, the loose end of which is fastened to a tree trunk, and the top is flung from shoulder-height rather like a shot put – no mean feat when you consider that it weighs about 5kg. The spinner then has to rely on the nimble fingers of his partner, the "scooper", to whip up the top from its landing place and transfer it to the arena where its progress is judged. Competition is fierce, particularly in the knockout game, which takes place in an atmosphere almost like a boxing match; try to see it in a local village context if you can – the Tourist Information Centre can tell you when a competition is being held (usually September).

Kite-flying (*wau ubi*) is a hugely popular activity, so much so that the emblem for the national airline, MAS, features the *wau bulan*, or "moon kite", the most common of all the designs. Originally regarded as a means of contacting the gods, the kites are highly decorated for their benefit. The contest in which a kite-flyer had to cut the string of an opponent's kite was banned some time ago since it caused so many heated disputes – quite apart from the fact that the string, which contained ground glass to make it sharp, was also highly dangerous. Nowadays, competitions are a much more muted affair, with participants being judged purely on their handling skills and the height achieved.

The playing of *rebana* – **giant drums** – might not seem like a sport, but once you witness the energy required to produce the thunderous roll on these massive instruments, you'll begin to understand why it's classified as such. The brightly coloured drums have a diameter of over 1m, weigh 100kg, and are decorated with bamboo sticks that fan out from the rim like bicycle spokes. During a festival held every July, there is a competition to determine the most skilful group of players. Each team comprises six players who play different-sized drums nonstop for around thirty minutes, maintaining fast and complex rhythms using a combination of hands and sticks – the winner is the group with the most consistent and harmonious technique. Again, the spectacle is best seen outdoors, conducted in the traditional costume of tunic, *songket* and headdress.

each table to clean your hands before and after – and eat with your right hand only. Try the local speciality *ayam percik* (barbecued chicken with a creamy coconut sauce) or the delicious *nasi kerabu* (purple, green or blue rice with a dash of vegetables, seaweed and grated coconut), finish off with a filling *pisang murtabak* (banana pancake), and you won't have parted with much more than $5. The town's **restaurants** are a letdown after the night market and many close in the evenings in the face of such stiff competition. Note that the only places which serve alcohol are the Chinese *kedai kopis*.

D'Paris, Jalan Doktor. Passable attempt at a European café, serving freshly baked pastries, sandwiches and cappuccinos.

Golden City Restoran, Jalan Padang Garong. Lively and brightly lit *kedai kopi* serving standard Chinese food. Try the *wan tan mee* or *curry mee* – spicy noodle dishes for around $3.

Golden Jade Seafood Restoran, *Hotel Perdana*, Jalan Mahmood. A pricey outlet lacking in atmosphere, although the Shanghai and Cantonese dishes are recommended. Around $15 per dish.

Meena, Jalan Gajah Mati. Excellent, inexpensive banana leaf curries; *Meena* is frequented by locals.

Pata Seafood Restoran, *Hotel Indah*, 236b Jalan Tengku Besar. Wide-ranging menu including crab and prawns from $2.50–4 per dish.

Qing Lang, Jalan Zainal Abidin. A totally meat-free menu with prices a touch above average (around $3 per dish), but worth it. Air-con too.

Listings

Airlines MAS, Komplek Yakin, Jalan Gajah Mati (☎09/744 7000).

Airport Sultan Ismail Petra Airport is 9km northeast of town, operating a domestic service only. Flight information ☎09/743 7000.

Banks and exchange Bank Bumiputra, Jalan Doktor; Hong Kong Bank, Jalan Padong Garong; Standard Chartered Bank, Jalan Padang Garong.

Bookshops *Johan Bookshop* on Jalan Padang Garong has a small selection of English-language books; *Central Bookstore* on Jalan Temenggong by the clocktower has a larger choice, as does *Muda Osman*, Jalan Tengku Chik.

Buses The SKMK information counter (daily 8am–9pm, Fri 8am–12.45pm & 2–9pm; ☎09/744 0114) at the local bus station gives the rundown on local and long-distance services. SKMK services and MARA routes to KL and Singapore depart from the Langgar bus station on Jalan Pasir Puteh; for other companies and destinations, head for the station on Jalan Hamzah.

Car rental Avis, *Hotel Perdana* lobby (☎09/748 5000).

Hospital The General Hospital is on Jalan Hospital (☎09/748 5533).

Immigration On-the-spot visa renewals at the Immigration Department, second floor, Wisma Persekutuan, Jalan Bayan (daily 8am–4pm except Thurs 8am–12.45pm; ☎09/748 2120).

Left luggage At the bus station on Jalan Hamzah (daily 8am–10pm).

Police Headquarters on Jalan Sultan Ibrahim (☎09/748 5522).

Post office The GPO is on Jalan Sultan Ibrahim (Mon–Thurs & Sun 8am–4.30pm; ☎09/748 4033). Efficient poste restante/general delivery at counter 20.

Shopping Kota Bharu offers a vast range of home-produced items in several modern multistorey shopping complexes. The *Bazaar Bulu Kubu* on Jalan Hulu, south of Padang Merdeka, houses a cinema, as well as souvenirs and handicrafts. *Syarikat Kraftangan* at Kampung Kraftangan has higher prices compared to other markets, but better-quality kites, weaving and puppets. The shops along Jalan Sultanah Zainab are good for antiques and silverware.

Taxis The long-distance taxi stand is behind the local bus station on Jalan Doktor (☎09/744 7104); fares (per person) are around $12 to Kuala Terengganu, $25 to Kuantan and $35 to KL.

Telephones The Telekom centre is on Jalan Doktor (daily 8am–4.30pm).

Thai visas From the Royal Thai Consulate, 4426 Jalan Pengkalan Chepa (☎09/748 2545; Mon–Thurs & Sun 9am–noon & 1.30–4pm). Visas are issued within two working days and cost $33.

Trains From the station at Wakaf Bharu (information ☎09/749 6986), services run south on the Jungle Railway to Kuala Lipis and the interior. For the route into Thailand by train, see "Crossing the Border into Thailand" on p.244.

Around Kota Bharu

While there's plenty in Kota Bharu itself to keep you occupied for at least a couple of days, the outlying areas offer relaxation at the **beaches** to the north and east of town, and a look at the **cottage industries** producing local crafts. The area north of town towards the border is unsurprisingly Thai in character, boasting a few **temples** dotted among the emerald green rice paddies.

It's also worth noting that some travel agencies and a number of guesthouses in Kota Bharu arrange trips south into Kelantan's obscure interior, on the Jelawang Jungle trail – all the details are given on p.232.

The beaches and the border region

The **beaches** around town are popular with the locals, often becoming crowded at weekends, although the conservative attitudes within the state are not, on the whole, conducive to relaxed sunbathing. Compared to what's on offer further south, the sands are nothing special. The wistfully romantic names are often better than the beaches themselves.

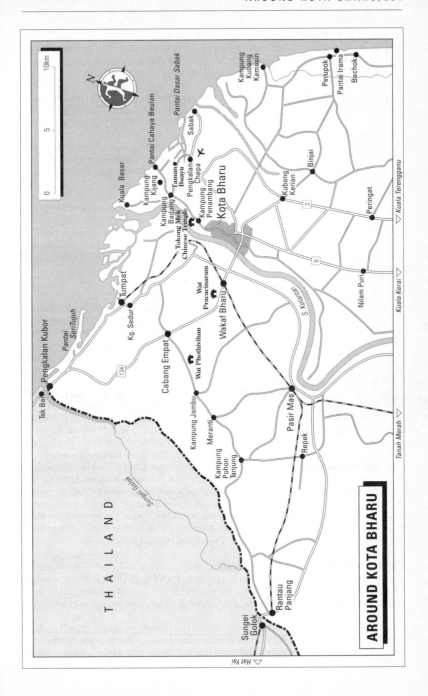

AROUND KOTA BHARU

Pantai Cahaya Beulan

Kota Bharu's best-known and most-visited beach is more commonly known as **PAN-TAI CINTA BERAHI** (shortened to PCB), 11km north of Kota Bharu, a thirty-minute ride on bus #10 from outside the Central Market. As every guidebook tells you, it's called the "Beach of Passionate Love", though the Muslim government has officially changed its name to the less suggestive "Moonlight" beach. About 100m back from the beach, off the main road, the entrance fee to the signposted **Taman Buayu** (Crocodile Farm; $2) includes the "House of Mirrors", a small zoo, a snake farm and, of course, the lolling crocodiles.

The **Tokong Mek Chinese Temple** is on the way to PCB, about 6km outside Kota Bharu to the left of the main road. It's a peaceful little temple, with some unusually dramatic three-dimensional wall sculptures featuring tigers and dragons. Bus #10 passes right by the turn-off.

There are several **places to stay** at Pantai Cahaya Beulan, although there's not much action here during the week. The best place is the *Perdana Resort* (☎09/774 4000; ⑤–⑦), with a wide range of A-frames and chalets, together with a beachfront restaurant. A marginally more comfortable option is the *Longhouse Beach* (☎09/773 1090; ③), right next to the final bus stop, also with its own restaurant. For complete luxury, stay at the *PCB Resort* (☎09/773 2307; ⑥), a very pleasant, if slightly old-fashioned, complex, with well-appointed chalets, pool and a restaurant.

Pantai Seri Tujuh, Wakaf Bahru and the Tumpat region

Buses #19 or #43 depart regularly from the local bus station in Kota Bharu for the trip to **PANTAI SERI TUJUH**, a two-kilometre stretch of coastline that looks far more idyllic on the map than it actually is – its lagoons have now turned into muddy puddles. The bus passes several Thai temples en route, in various states of disrepair. One of the most glamorous is **Wat Pracacinaram**, easily spotted just outside Wakaf Bharu, on the road to Cabang Empat. It's a brand new building, with an elaborate triple-layered roof decorated in gold, sapphire and red.

WAKAF BAHRU itself is the site of the nearest train station to Kota Bharu, but otherwise a nondescript little town. The end of the line is 12km further north at **TUMPAT**, a small town at the edge of a lush agricultural area, where tumbledown Thai temples punctuate field upon field of jewel-green rice paddies. At the **Wat Pothivihan**, 15km west of Kota Bharu, a forty-metre-long Reclining Buddha is said to be the second largest in the world (although this is not a unique claim in these parts). The colossal, if rather insipid, plaster statue contains ashes of the deceased, laid to rest here according to custom – although there's a popular rumour that it is actually a secret cache for the temple's funds. Other pavilions within the complex, somewhat dwarfed by the central structure, are of little interest, except for a small shrine to the left which honours a statue of a rather wasted-looking hermit. You can reach Wat Pothivihan by bus from Kota Bharu – #19 or #27 from the local bus station brings you to Cabang Empat, from where it's a three-and-a-half-kilometre walk, or a short taxi ride ($4 per car).

Pantai Dasar Sabak and Pantai Irama

Back on the coast, 13km northeast of Kota Bharu, **PANTAI DASAR SABAK** is of historical interest – it was the first landing place of the Japanese in 1941, prior to their invasion of the Peninsula. It's a desolate place, a rough, windswept stretch of coast with a crumbling World War II bunker.

PANTAI IRAMA, a further 12km south, strikes a less solemn note as the "Beach of Melody", and it would indeed be relatively harmonious were it not for the tidemark of rubbish along the water's edge. That said, it *is* the nicest beach within easy reach of Kota Bharu, a quiet, tree-fringed stretch of white sand, freshened by the sea breeze, but you should bear in mind that this is a conservative Muslim village, and stripping off is likely to offend people. To get here, take the #23 or #39 bus to Bachok from Kota Bharu's local bus station (the buses leave every 30min and the journey takes 45min); the beach is about 500m north of the bus station at Bachok.

Local cottage industries

The **workshops** that lining the road from Kota Bharu to Pantai Cahaya Beulan let you see master craftsmen at work. **KAMPUNG PENAMBANG** is particularly good for *songket* weaving and batik, while **KAMPUNG KIJANG** specializes in kite-making. There's always an opportunity to buy at the end of each demonstration; most workshops are open daily from 9am to 5pm. Both villages are barely beyond the town suburbs on the #10 bus, which leaves from beside the Central Market.

The making of the *gasing* (spinning top) – resembling a discus except for a short steel spike inserted in one side – is an art. The process of carefully selecting the wood which must be delicately planed and shaped, together with the precise balancing of the metal spike, can take anything up to three weeks. An intricate *wau* (kite), typically about 1.5m long by 2m across, takes around two weeks to complete, the decorations being unique to each craftsman, although tradition dictates leaf patterns and a pair of birds as the principal elements in the design. The most unusual aspect of the kite's structure is the long projection above its head, supporting a large bow that hums when the kite is flying, the musical quality of which can be judged in competition. Finally, batik-printing and weaving are the commonest crafts in Malaysia, and most of the workshops here will allow you to experiment with the techniques and create your own designs.

Pulau Perhentian

PULAU PERHENTIAN, just over 20km off the northeastern coast, remained a very well-kept secret until the late 1980s. Actually two islands rather than one – Perhentian Kecil (Small Island) and Perhentian Besar (Big Island) – both are textbook tropical paradises, neither more than 4km in length, with almost no electricity, modern plumbing or phones (bar a few mobiles). There's no doubt, however, that the Perhentians' cover has been well and truly blown: they are a popular getaway for KL and Singaporean weekenders, and see a regular stream of backpackers. Nevertheless, low-budget chalet accommodation has not been forced out by upmarket resorts – as has happened on some of Malaysia's other islands – the big money so far put off by the lack of any kind of infrastructure, although there is talk of relocating Kampung Paris Hantu on Perhentian Kecil to the mainland to make way for development.

In the meantime, although the islanders say that the place has changed beyond belief in recent years, life on Pulau Perhentian is delightful, with only flying foxes, monkeys and lizards for company as you draw up the well water for your daily shower. Be warned though, during peak season in August, the accommodation at the popular Long Beach fills up, making some hostels less than idyllic, especially if their water supply dries up. Neither island boasts a raging nightlife – in fact, with no electricity or alcohol in most places, you'll probably be tucked up in bed by 10pm. The local people are Muslim, but seem to have no objection to you bringing your own booze from the mainland. Don't be tempted to bring drugs, though – there are frequent police road checks on the way to the islands. The harsh east coast **monsoon** means that the islands, reached by slow and unsophisticated fishing boats from Kuala Besut, are accessible only between March and October. Conversely, during the middle of the dry season, from June to August, some places can suffer from a shortage of fresh water.

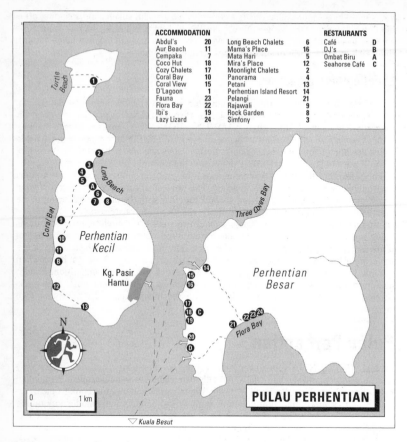

ACCOMMODATION

Abdul's	20	Long Beach Chalets	6
Aur Beach	11	Mama's Place	16
Cempaka	7	Mata Hari	5
Coco Hut	18	Mira's Place	12
Cozy Chalets	17	Moonlight Chalets	2
Coral Bay	10	Panorama	4
Coral View	15	Petani	13
D'Lagoon	1	Perhentian Island Resort	14
Fauna	23	Pelangi	21
Flora Bay	22	Rajawali	9
Ibi's	19	Rock Garden	8
Lazy Lizard	24	Simfony	3

RESTAURANTS

Café	D
DJ's	B
Ombat Biru	A
Seahorse Café	C

Turtle Beach

Long Beach

Coral Bay

Perhentian Kecil

Three Coves Bay

Perhentian Besar

Kg. Pasir Hantu

Flora Bay

N

0   1 km

PULAU PERHENTIAN

▽ Kuala Besut

It's better to have some idea of which island you want to stay on, and where, before you arrive. Only Perhentian Besar's western and southern beaches and Long Beach on Perhentian Kecil have a choice of **chalet** operations. The interiors of both islands consist of largely inaccessible, tree-covered rocky hills, although a few well-trodden paths offer some unchallenging **walks** through the jungle. **Boats** will drop you at the bay of your choice, although those without a jetty entail a bit of wading to reach the shore. Most chalet operations have small speedboats for getting around the islands. Facilities are fairly basic, though almost all the places to stay have their own **restaurant** – you don't have to be resident to eat at them. The food comprises infinite but monotonous variations on rice and noodles. On balance, despite the popularity of Kecil's Long Beach, there's a more lively scene at the beach cafés on Besar. It's worth noting that new chalets are springing up all the time.

You'll get a chance to spot turtles if you go **snorkelling** – equipment can be rented from most chalets, and boat trips around either island to undeveloped coves cost around $10 per person – just ask at your accommodation. The conditions are superb: gentle currents and visibility of up to 20m, although the seasonal sea lice can be a problem, inflicting an unpleasant but harmless sting not unlike that of a jelly fish. A foray around the rocks at the ends of most bays turns up a teeming array of brightly coloured fish and live coral. Don't break any off – it's razor-sharp, and you'll also be damaging the subaqua ecosystem.

For the more adventurous still, there are several operations on both islands running **dive courses**. Most chalets offer a single dive for qualified divers for around $85. If all this sounds too energetic, you can take a **fishing trip** with local fishermen for around $30 per person, a chance to see the way of life that sustains most islanders – though the swell of the water, combined with the smell of the landed fish, can make you queasy.

Getting there: Kuala Besut

The ragged little town of **KUALA BESUT**, 45km south of Kota Bharu just off the coastal Route 3, is the departure point for Pulau Perhentian. It's reached by bus #3, which leaves Kota Bharu's local bus station every fifteen minutes throughout the day for the hour's ride to Pasir Puteh. Then take the #96 (every 30min) for the remaining half-hour journey to Kuala Besut itself. It's simpler to take a share taxi, ($5), organized by most guesthouses in Kota Bharu.

There are no banks in Kuala Besut, or on the islands, so **change money** before you go. If you're desperate, the *Kadai Kopi* will exchange cash only, but the rate is lousy. There's always a chance that unfavourable weather conditions may force you to spend the night in town and though there's not much choice, one of the better **places to stay** is *D'Rizan Resort* (no phone; ④), a beachside place with basic A-frames, first on the left over the bridge on the main road, about 1km from the centre. If you're feeling flush, try the *Primula Besut Beach Resort* (☎09/695 6311, fax 695 6322; ⑤), a white concrete complex a couple of kilometres further south; you'll have to take a taxi.

In season, **boats** depart from the Kuala Besut quayside, just behind the bus station. Services operate roughly every two hours (1hr 30min) between 9am and 5pm – morning departures are preferable, since the weather tends to be more reliable. Tickets cost $20 one-way though it's better to buy a return ticket ($30); the boat is then obliged to bring you back on request, even if you're the only passenger. There are many travel agents in town selling boat tickets and advising on accommodation on the islands, including: Bonanza Express (☎009/691 0290), Tunjang Speedy Enterprises (☎09/691 0189) and Perhentian Pleasure Holidays (☎09/691 0313) – all within walking distance of the quay.

Perhentian Kecil

On the southeastern corner of **PERHENTIAN KECIL** is the island's only village, **Kampung Pasir Hantu**, with its only jetty, police station, school and clinic – but the littered beach and scruffy houses don't encourage you to stay. The west-facing coves have the advantage of the sunsets, a major event in the Perhentian day, try **Coral Bay**, about halfway down the island. East-facing **Long Beach** has been the target of most development on Kecil, not surprisingly, since it boasts a wide stretch of uncluttered, glistening white beach, with deep, soft sand. However, it's more exposed to the elements, forcing the chalet owners to close up from the end of October to April, since boats are unable to approach safely. Throughout the rest of the season, the water's pretty tame and shallow at low tide, giving easy access to the coral-like rocks at either end of the bay, perfect for snorkelling. The best accommodation here is at *Mata Hari*.

Coral Bay accommodation

Coral Bay (☎010/984 7636). Secluded, beach-facing chalets, the first on this side of the island. ③.
Mira's Place (☎011/976603). Located on a tiny bay, popular *Mira's Place* is a small cluster of chalets with a communal TV and radio – not the place if you *really* want to get away from it all. ③.

Aur Beach (no phone). Basic but popular chalets; nearby is *DJ's*, the only restaurant on this side of Kecil. ①.

Petani (☎01/881 2444). South-facing just around the headland from *Mira's* (accessible by a small overgrown track), *Petani* has upmarket chalets, but like *Mira's*, it can have problems with fresh water in the height of the dry season. ③.

Rajawali (☎010/980 5244). High up on the rocky headland, this chalet operation takes mainly package bookings. ①.

Long Beach accommodation

Cempaka (☎010/984 9889). A basic but friendly place – the A-frames have been built on tall stilts against the hillside to ensure an uninterrupted panorama. ①.

D'Lagoon. At the very northeast tip of the island, set in a tiny and isolated cove, with tents, rooms and chalets. From here, you can clamber across the narrow neck of the island to the turtle-spotting beach on the other side (though the best place to see turtles is on Besar – see below). ①.

Long Beach Chalets (☎010/985 9889). Has its own restaurant right beside the beach, but it's chalets are not as good as those at *Mata Hari*. ①.

Mata Hari. Eighteen simple but well-designed chalets, complete with mosquito nets and hammocks, and a good restaurant. ①–②.

Moonlight Chalets (☎010/982 8135). A wide range of chalets, and the best place for food – it is set at the northern end of the beach. The café does wild "special shakes" with Mars Bars and M&Ms, and the upstairs restaurant is about as stylish as the Perhentians get, with a good view across the beach. ①–②.

Panorama (☎010/984 1181). Set back from the beach in the shady jungle. Has a good restaurant, with Western and local dishes. ①–②.

Rock Garden. The cheapest and most basic accommodation at Long Beach. This is the place that people stay when everything else is full, and leave as quickly as they can. ①.

Perhentian Besar

The best place on the islands for **turtle-watching** is undoubtedly Three Coves Bay on the north coast of Besar. A stunning conglomeration of three beaches, separated from the main area of accommodation by rocky outcrops and reached only by speedboat, it provides a secluded haven between May and September for green and hawksbill turtles to come ashore and lay their eggs (see also "Rantau Abang", p.269).

Most of the accommodation on **PERHENTIAN BESAR** is on the western half of the island – there's a lot to choose from so it shouldn't be too difficult to find somewhere suitable if your first option is full. The beach improves as you go further south and the atmosphere is slightly more laid-back than that at Long Beach. Many of the chalets have cafés, but it's worth splashing out for the hearty pizzas ($10) at the *Seahorse Café*, just behind the *Seahorse Dive Shop*, which also has a book exchange. There is more accommodation on the island's south beach. Continuing south from *Abdul's*, a set of wooden steps traverses the rocky outcrop to a beach café serving breakfasts, snacks and set meals ($4–6). The trail across to the bay on the southern side of the island begins just past the second jetty, behind some disused private villas. A steep 45-minute climb brings you to the first of the developments on the island's south side.

Abdul's (☎010/983 7303). At the southern end of the west coast beach. the chalets are very basic but the operation receives more praise from visitors than nearby *Ibi's*. ①–②.

Coral View (☎ & fax 09/691 0943). Just around the corner from the *Perhentian Island Resort*, these are rather regimented chalets. The restaurant, overlooking two bays, is worth the outlay, offering tasty chicken and beef dishes. ③–⑥.

Cozy Chalets (☎09/697 7703). A rocky headland, difficult to pass unless the tide is low, separates this from the beach to the south of Besar. It has modern huts and a café with a good view perched on top of the rocks. ②.

Fauna (☎011/971 1843). These chalets at Flora Bay all face the beach and are set in a neat garden. ②.

Flora Bay (☎011/977266). Smart A-frame huts, and a dorm ($8); this place appeals to a more upmarket crowd. ②.

Lazy Lizard (no phone). The only truly budget accommodation on this windswept expanse of smooth, powdery sand on Flora Bay, a pleasant little encampment of ramshackle A-frames. ①.

Mama's Place. *Mama's Place*, just south of *Coral View*, is popular and has pastel-coloured chalets by the beach and cheaper ones below. The beach here is liberally scattered with coral, making a dip in the sea a bit hazardous. ①.

Perhentian Island Resort (☎013/244 8530, fax 243 4984). Has by far the best beach of the whole island group – a majestic sweep of sand, fringed by jungle, and offset by glassy, turquoise water. The family chalets are comfortable enough, and the dive centre is popular. A flat trail leads from behind the resort to the large bay in the south (see below), taking thirty minutes. ⑤–⑧

Pelangi Chalets (no phone). Laid-back place at the end of Flora Bay; good value, if slightly unimaginative in layout. ②.

Merang and Pulau Redang

There's absolutely nothing to do in **MERANG** (not to be confused with Marang, 57km further down the coast) – and that's the attraction. A tiny coastal kampung 120km south of Kota Bharu, Merang began to attract foreign travellers in the 1970s. The only places to stay were in the homes of the villagers and soon this became the very reason people wanted to come here – to get away from bland and impersonal hotels. During the 1980s a few enterprising locals turned this into a more formal arrangement, with the intro-duction of **homestays**. Unfortunately, at the time of writing, none were in operation. The reason for this is perhaps linked with the development of **Pulau Redang** (see below) as a major resort. A jetty has been built beside Merang's lighthouse, ruining what used to be the best spot for swimming. Ironically, the harbour is already silting up, making rebuilding in the future necessary. However, Merang is still beautifully tran-quil, and for the time being, the fishing community remains virtually unchanged by its visitors.

The kampung at Merang is clustered around a small T-junction close to the beach, with rough yellow sand sloping steeply towards the sea. It gets more littered the clos-er you get to the village, but it's reasonable for swimming. To the north of the main vil-lage, dominating this sweep of bay, a large mound serves as an ideal lookout across the blustery coastline – Pulau Bidong, a former refugee camp for Vietnamese boat people, and Pulau Redang are clearly visible from here. Just before the start of Ramadan in February, the beach sometimes becomes the focus of a local festival and visitors are invited to join in with traditional games and music. For the rest of the year, fishing forms the mainstay of village life – if you get up early enough (around 6am), you'll see the fishermen returning with the day's catch.

Practicalities

Coming from the north, take any bus bound for Kuala Terangganu as far as **Permaisuri**, just before Kampung Buloh on the main route through the coastal flat-lands. From here, taxis ($15 per car) or a regular minibus service (known as an econo-van; $6) go on to Merang, a further 33km. From Kuala Terengganu, a direct bus leaves the local bus station (daily 2.30pm & 8.30pm). Otherwise you can catch a bus as far as **Batu Rakit**, one of a string of pretty coastal kampungs, from where you may be able to catch a lift for the remaining 16km to Merang. It's safer to take a taxi ($20) from Kuala Terengganu if you don't want to get stuck. Returning to Kuala Terengganu is easier since econovans ($5) are at the jetty to meet visitors and workers returning from Pulau Redang. It's worth noting that because of these convoluted transport arrangements Merang is *not* a convenient stopover en route to or from Kota Bharu and the Perhentian Islands.

With all the homestays out of operation, the only budget place **to stay** is the *Kenbara Resort* (☎09/623 8771, fax 624 8772; ①). This friendly, spotless place is a fifteen-minute walk from the jetty, right by the beach. It has cooking facilities, handy as there are few dining-out options in Merang. Closer to the jetty are the *Merang Inn Village Resort* (☎09/624 3435; ②), which has standard chalets set back from the road, and the *Merang Beach Resort* (☎09/623 9018; ③), also known as the resthouse, with a hilltop café and A-frame huts close to the beach. At the opposite end of town is the tasteful and luxurious *Aryani* (☎09/624 1111, fax 624 8007; ⑨), where for a mere $680 you can sleep in a hundred-year old traditional Malay house on stilts and swim in a pool that looks like the stage set for a Hollywood musical.

There's little in the way of separate **restaurants**, but there are two basic *kedai kopis*, at the junction and on the sea front, and two or three provision stores for other snacks. There's also a pasar malam every Sunday on the main road.

Pulau Redang

Northeast of Merang lies the island of **PULAU REDANG**, just 5km by 8km, and the latest of Malaysia's government-designated **marine parks**, designed to minimize the damage to the spectacular coral reefs. The island boasts abundant marine life sustained by the **coral reef** which thrives in the mangrove-sheltered waters of the estuary. The reef had barely recovered from the havoc wreaked by a large-scale attack of "crown of thorns" starfish in the mid-1970s, when agricultural development and the building of a road to the upper reaches of the river in the late 1980s deposited silt and caused more massive damage to the coral. Happily, coral reefs have remarkable properties of self-renewal, and through the regulation of harmful activities such as spear-fishing, trawling and watersports, may be preserved. The best snorkelling is off the southern coast around the islets of Pulau Pinang and Pulau Ekor Tibu, while **scuba diving** is best around Redang's northeastern region. Among the most common fish are batfish, angel fish, box fish and butterfly fish, luminous multicoloured creatures which feed off the many anemone, sponges and bivalves to be found around the rocks. Towards the north of the island itself, an area sandwiched between the two rocky hills that run the length of Redang has been set aside for recreational purposes, allowing for some easy walks through the forest.

In recent years, Redang has been extensively redeveloped by the luxury Berjaya hotel group. Forests have been felled and hillsides levelled to make way for a golf course, a freshwater pipeline from the mainland and new roads. Despite winning Tourism Malaysia's "Best Tourist Attraction" award in 1994/95, Redang is a big disappointment if you're looking for an unspoilt island paradise. A **new village** is being built inland for the two-thousand-strong fishing community which lives on stilted houses in the estuary to the Sungei Redang. The local government wants the village to be relocated so a new jetty and more resort developments can be built, but the villagers, who were shifted once before from the nearby Pulau Pinang, are understandably reluctant. However, with pollution from the village visibly killing off the fragile reef in the estuary, the issue is by no means clear cut.

It is necessary to book accommodation on Redang in advance; there is no budget accommodation but there are campsites. Although there are several hotel and dive operations along the southeast side of the island, the main focus of tourist activity are the two *Berjaya* operations: the *Beach Resort* (☎09/697 1111, fax 697 3899; ⑧) which has the sand bay at Teluk Dalam in the north all to itself, and the *Golf and Spa Resort* (☎09/697 3988, fax 697 3899; ⑧) overlooking the fishing village. Apart from the *Berjaya* resorts and a couple of campsites within walking distance of the fishing village, the other accommodation is located around the beach at Pasir Pinjang. The most pleasant place to stay is the *Coral Redang Island Resort* (☎09/669 6923; ⑧), with its own pool, restaurant and dive centre. The cheapest place is the *Redang Lagoon* (☎09/827 2116;

⑤) where all meals are included. Other options include the *Redang Beach Resort* (☎09/622 2599), *Redang Bay* (☎09/623 6048) and *Redang Pelangi* (☎09/623 5202). All these operations have offices in Kuala Terengganu, where packages costing from around $300 per person for two nights, inclusive of meals and transport, are available. If you can get out to Pulau Pinang, the Marine Park Centre (☎011/971125) also has a campsite and a some facilities for visitors.

The *Berjaya* resorts run a daily ferry (1hr; $80 return) from Merang to Redang leaving at 10am, 2pm and 6pm, and returning at 8am, noon and 4pm. It's also possible to charter boats out to the island from the Merang jetty from around $100 one-way.

Kuala Terengganu and around

As you approach **KUALA TERENGGANU**, 160km south of Kota Bharu, a huge hillside sign in Malay and Arabic reads "God Save Terengganu" – or as locals wryly remark, "God Save the Oil". The discovery of oil in the South China Sea, just off the coast here, has undoubtedly been the main factor in Terengganu State's recent prosperity, and evidence of the new wealth is immediately apparent as you enter Kuala Terengganu, the state capital, where highrise office buildings and banks jostle for position in the busy commercial sector.

As recently as the early 1970s though, Kuala Terengganu was little more than an oversized fishing village that just happened to be the seat of the sultan, whose descendants established themselves here in the early eighteenth century. There was a certain amount of trade from the town, with neighbouring states and countries particularly interested in Kuala Terengganu's local crafts – boat-building, weaving and brassware – but economic development was slow, and what wealth there was accrued only to the rulers. A short-lived **peasants' revolt** in 1928 (see box below) resulted from the imposition of new taxes on an already overburdened populace. It was the only rebellion in the Peninsula to be led by religious leaders, taking on the character of a *jihad* (holy war) against infidels, and one of the few involving the normally passive peasantry.

Even in these nouveau riche times for Kuala Terengganu, the outward trappings of modernity have not changed the essence of this tiny Muslim metropolis, sited in what is still a conservative, strongly Islamic state. For the casual visitor, there's plenty of appeal, from the istana and Chinatown district, to the lively market and waterfront. Handicraft skills thrive in the surrounding areas, such as offshore Pulau Dayong. The **Istana Tengku Long Museum** is one of the best cultural complexes in Malaysia, and well worth a visit. Using the city as a base, you can also venture inland to **Tasik Kenyir** and the **Sekayu Waterfall**, to experience something of the outdoor life for which the state's interior is renowned.

Arrival, information and accommodation

Opposite the **taxi stand** on Jalan Masjd Abidin, is the **local bus station**; the **express bus station** is across town on Jalan Sultan Zainal Abidin. The **airport** is 13km northeast of the centre, a $12–15 taxi ride away; the city bus marked "Kem Seberang Takir" picks up from the road directly outside and runs to the local bus station. Once in the centre, you can easily get around on foot.

The **Tourism Malaysia Office** (Mon–Wed, Sat & Sun 8.45am–12.45pm & 2pm–4pm, Thurs 8am–1pm; ☎09/622 1433) is inconveniently situated at the eastern end of Jalan Sultan Zainal Abidin, on the ground floor of the Wisma MCIS building. The helpful **Tourist Information Centre** (Mon–Wed, Sat & Sun 9am–12.45pm & 2–5pm, Thurs 9am–1pm; ☎09/622 1553) is on the same road, but more centrally located near the GPO. The town is easy to get around on foot.

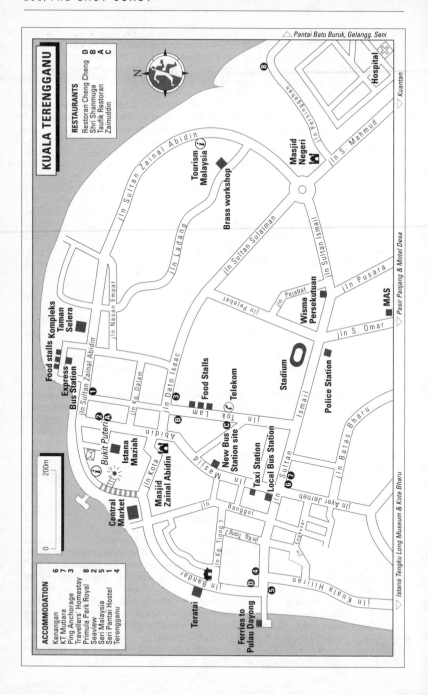

KUALA TERENGGANU

RESTAURANTS
Restoran Cheng Cheng D
Shri Shanmuga B
Taufik Restoran A
Zainuddin C

ACCOMMODATION
Kenangan 6
KT Mutiara 7
Ping Anchorage 3
Travellers' Homestay 8
Primula Park Royal 2
Seaview 5
Seri Malaysia 1
Seri Pantai Hostel 1
Terengganu 4

△ *Pantai Batu Buruk, Gelangg. Seni*

▷ *Kuantan*

▷ *Pasir Panjang & Motel Desa*

▷ *Istana Tengku Long Museum & Kota Bharu*

Hospital

Masjid Negeri

MAS

Wisma Persekutuan

Police Station

Stadium

Tourism Malaysia

Brass workshop

Telekom

Food Stalls

New Bus Station site

Taxi Station

Local Bus Station

Express Bus Station

Food stalls Kompleks Taman Selera

Bukit Puteri

Istana Maziah

Masjid Zainal Abidin

Central Market

Teratai

Ferries to Pulau Dayong

Jln Sultan Zainal Abidin
Jln Ladang
Jln Sultan Sulaiman
Jln Nesan Empat
Jln Sultan Zainal Abidin
Jln Kg Dalam
Jln Dato Isaac
Tok Lam
Jln Pejabat
Jln Pusara
Jln S. Omar
Jln Sultan Ismail
Jln S. Mahmud
Jln Persinggahan
Jln Kota
Jln Abidin
Jln Masjid Abidin
Jln Banggol
Jln Bandar
Jln Kg Tiong 1
Jln Kg Tiong 2
Jln Engku
Jln Sultan Ismail
Jln Batas Baharu
Jln Ayer Jerneh
Jln Kuala Hiliran

0   200m

N

THE TERENGGANU PEASANTS' REVOLT

In the first three decades of the twentieth century, major changes were being wrought on the **Terengganu peasantry**. The introduction by the Malay rulers of the system of *cap kurnia*, or royal gifts of land, created a new class of absentee landlords, and reduced farmers who had previously been able to sell or mortgage their land to the status of mere tenant cultivators. Furthermore, the installation of the British Advisory system in 1910 sought to **consolidate colonial power** by imposing new land taxes, a costly registration of births, deaths and marriages, and permits for everyday things like collecting wood to repair houses.

These ploys were greatly resented by the peasantry, whose response was expressed primarily in **religious terms** – the deterioration of their living conditions signalled to the faithful the imminent coming of the *Imam Mahdi* who would restore tradition and true faith. Consequently, their actions were directed against all *kafir* (unbelievers) including the Malay rulers, who were seen to be in collusion with the colonists.

The campaign of resistance began in 1922 with a series of anti-tax protests, organized by the village *imams* and spearheaded by two charismatic *ulamas* (Islamic scholars), **Sayyid Sagap** and **Haji Drahman**. As the peasants' courage and militancy increased, so relations with the government deteriorated, until one incident in April 1928 triggered a **full-scale revolt**. A group of around five hundred armed men angrily confronted three officials investigating an illegal felling near Tergat, deep in the Terengganu interior, in an attempt to provoke the British into defending their interests. Instead, Sultan Sulaiman himself travelled upstream to hear the crowd's grievances, which he duly promised to consider. The resulting legislation was a compromise that failed to satisfy the peasantry, who decided on a major assault on Kuala Terengganu. Moving upriver, they first captured the District Office at **Kuala Berang** and then proceeded to **Kuala Telemong** where they were to join forces with a local band. But the rendezvous never happened. Impatient to capitalize on previous successes, the gang at Kuala Telemong, a motley crew by comparison with the well-armed band at Kuala Berang, decided to attack the government installation alone, walking straight into the line of fire. Many of their leaders, who had previously been considered invulnerable, were killed, taking the wind out of the sails of the deeply disillusioned peasants.

However, it was the behaviour of the two *ulamas* that dealt the most powerful blow to the rebellion. Sayyid Sagap denied that he had ever been involved, claiming to be a loyal subject of the sultan; luckily for him, he had remained too far in the background to be successfully implicated. On hearing about the Kuala Telemong shooting, Haji Drahman fled to Patani, although he eventually returned voluntarily to face trial. Malay and British officials alike not only feared him personally but realized that he was too influential a figure to imprison, and so persuaded him to call off the hostilities in return for **comfortable exile to Mecca** and a healthy stipend from the government to keep him there. The peasants, having had their collective will broken, were not only deserted by their leaders but then subject to the unfettered and strangling effects of British bureaucracy.

Accommodation

There isn't a great deal of choice, or quality, when it comes to **hotels** in Kuala Terengganu – the cheap ones around the local bus station are downright seedy and unwelcoming. Fortunately, there are several good **hostels** that increase the options for the budget-conscious. Those who prefer to stay away from the action can always hole up at Pulau Dayong: *Awi's Yellow House* (☎ & fax 09/624 7363; ①–②) is a delightful timber complex of huts and walkways built on stilts over the water – it offers a variety of accommodation from basic huts to a spacious dorm, complete with mosquito nets. If you arrive by boat follow the river south as closely as possible – *Awi's* is known to all the locals. From the bus station, ask for the Duyong bus (50 sen) or take a taxi ($5), and get off at the base of the Sultan Mahmud Bridge, from where *Awi's* is a short walk. Buses across the bridge are infrequent, and the ferries stop running at around 10pm, so *Awi's* is not an ideal base, but it has its own cooking facilities and is beautifully peaceful.

Kenangan, 65 Jalan Sultan Ismail (☎09/622 2688, fax 623 3268). A little run-down and musty, but comfortable. ③.

KT Mutiara, 67 Jalan Sultan Ismail (☎09/622 2652, fax 623 6895). Recently renovated, with spacious rooms. Centrally located, next to the *Kenangan*. ③.

Motel Desa, Bukit Pak Api (☎09/622 3033, fax 622 3863). Quite a distance from the centre, set in quiet gardens on a hill overlooking town. Well-appointed rooms and a swimming pool. ⑥.

Primula Park Royal, Jalan Persinggahan (☎09/622 2100, fax 623 3360). Luxury hotel with a swimming pool that's reasonably priced. It's too far to walk; a taxi from town should cost around $3. ⑥.

Ping Anchorage Travellers' Homestay, 77a Jalan Dato' Isaac (☎09/622 0851, fax 623 9933). Budget hostel with excellent information boards, laundry facilities and a travel agency. The rooms and dorm are very basic, and the rooftop café is a welcome retreat. ①.

Seaview, 18a Jalan Masjid Abidin (☎09/622 1911, fax 622 3048). This modern, comfortable hotel has great views of the istana and the waterfront, but its cheaper rooms are at the back. ③.

Seri Malaysia, Jalan Hiliran (☎09/623 6454, fax 623 8344). An upmarket hotel, part of a national chain, set on the river. Rates include breakfast. ⑤.

Seri Pantai Hostel, Jalan Sultan Zainal Abidin (☎09/623 2141). With 24-hour check-in, this is convenient for the express bus station, though a little overpriced. Has a dorm and bicycle rental. ①.

Terengganu, 12 Jalan Sultan (☎09/622 2900). Close to the jetty, with spacious rooms with comfortable fittings, although the atmosphere is fairly sterile. ②.

The City

The centre of Kuala Terengganu is located within a compact promontory formed by Sungei Terengganu – a wide, fast-flowing river – and the South China Sea, and is connected to Route 3 by a large, modern bridge. The main artery through the commercial sector is Jalan Sultan Ismail, where you'll find the banks and government offices, while the **old town** spreads back from Jalan Bandar and the waterfront. The various crafts for which the town is renowned are all practised in **workshops** on the outskirts, and there are regular buses to most from the local bus station. The **Gelanggang Seni** (Cultural Centre) and the **Istana Tengku Long Museum** reflect the state's cultural heritage, while just across the estuary, **Pulau Duyong** is the last place in Malaysia where a unique boat-building technique is still practised.

The old town

The neat and precise **Istana Maziah** (closed to the public) is one of Kuala Terengganu's few historic monuments, set back from the sea in manicured gardens on Jalan Sultan Zainal Abidin. Now used only for official royal functions, it's reminiscent of a French chateau, with a steeply inclined red-tile roof and tall, shuttered windows.

Continuing west along the pedestrianized promenade, **Bukit Puteri** or "Princess Hill" (daily 9am–5.45pm; $1), rises 200m above the town. Relics of its time as a stronghold during the early nineteenth century – when the sultans Mohammed and Umar were fighting each other for the Terengganu throne – include a fort, supposedly built using honey to bind the bricks, and several cannons imported from Spain and Portugal. The hill is a popular spot, always crawling with school children; the lighthouse at the top is still in use.

Turn to your left after you've descended the steps from Bukit Puteri to walk along **Jalan Bandar**, the continuation of Jalan Sultan Zainal Abidin. The dusty, narrow street forms the centre of **Chinatown**, its decaying shophouses providing a sharp contrast to the highrises of the modern city. Efforts are being made to revitalize the area, and there are some excellent shops, such as *Teratai*, no.151, selling local arts and crafts. Kuala Terengganu's **Central Market** (daily 8am–9pm), a little further down on the

THE KRIS

The **kris** occupies a treasured position in Malay culture, a symbol of manhood and honour believed to harbour protective spirits. All young men crossing the barrier of puberty will receive one, which remains with them for the rest of their lives, tucked into the folds of a sarong; for an enemy to relieve someone of a *kris* is tantamount to stripping him of his virility. The weapon itself is intended to deliver a horizontal thrust rather than the more usual downward stab. When a sultan executed a treacherous subject, he did so by sliding a long *kris* through his windpipe, just above the collar bone, thereby inflicting a swift – though bloody – death.

The daggers can be highly decorative. While the iron blade is often embellished with fingerprint patterns or the body of a snake, it is the hilt, shaped like the butt of a gun to facilitate a sure grip, which is the distinguishing feature of the dagger. The hilt can be made from ivory, wood or metal; designs are usually based on the theme of a bird's head. The hilt can also be used in combat if the owner has not had time to unsheath the weapon, inflicting a damaging blow to the head.

right, close to the junction with Jalan Kota is in a modern multistorey building which backs onto the river and oozes vitality and prosperity. Upstairs, above the crowded and claustrophobic wet market, is the best place to search out batik, *songkets* and brassware.

After leaving the market, either continue south along Jalan Bandar through the remainder of Chinatown, or head east along Jalan Kota, at the far end of which you'll pass the **Masjid Zainal Abidin**, an unremarkable modern structure built in 1972 on the site of the original nineteenth-century wooden mosque.

Gelanggang Seni and the craft centres

At the far southeastern end of town, a two-kilometre walk or trishaw ride from the centre, is the **Gelanggang Seni**, a modern cultural complex facing the town's beach, Pantai Batu Buruk. Traditional dances and *silat* are performed (Fri & Sat 5–7pm & 9pm–11pm, except during Ramadan; free) by amateur groups – check with the tourist office for current details.

Of perhaps greater interest – certainly if you're looking to buy souvenirs – are the various arts and crafts centres scattered around town. Terengganu artisans have long been known for their **brassware**, working in a metal alloy called "white brass" unique to the state, a combination of yellow brass, nickel and zinc. The small **workshop** (daily 8.30am–6pm) on Jalan Ladang, close to the Tourism Malaysia office, uses the traditional "lost-wax" technique, whereby a wax maquette is covered with clay, placed in a kiln to fire the clay and melt the wax, leaving a mould in which to pour the molten metal. When the metal hardens, the clay is chipped off and the metal surface is polished and decorated. White brass, formerly the preserve of the sultans, is now used to make decorative articles such as candlesticks and large gourd-shaped vases.

The *mengkuang* style of **weaving** is practised in Terengganu: using the long thin leaves of pandanus trees, similar to bulrushes, women fashion delicate but functional items like bags, floor mats and fans. *Ky Enterprises*, about 3km due south of the centre on Jalan Panji Alam, is a good place to watch the process; take the Gong Pak Maseh or Gong bus for the fifteen-minute ride from the local bus station.

There are several other craft workshops in neighbouring Pasir Panjang, about 500m west of Jalan Panji Alam. Perhaps the most famous is that belonging to Abu Bakar bin Mohammed Amin, a **kris** maker on Lorong Saga (call to make an appointment; ☎09/622 7968). Here you can watch the two-edged dagger and its wooden sheath being decorated with fine artwork, a process which, together with the forging, can take several weeks to complete. Take minibus #12 from the local bus station and get off at the sign marked "Sekolah Kebangsaan Psr. Panjang".

Pulau Duyong

Accessible by a five-minute ferry ride (60 sen) from the jetty at the end of Jalan Sultan Ismail, **Pulau Duyong** is the largest of the islets dotting the Terengganu estuary. This community is famous for its **boat-building**, an old skill that has developed into a commercial enterprise. In the island's dry docks, old-fashioned deep-sea fishing boats line up alongside state-of-the-art luxury yachts – but whatever the price tag, the construction method is the same. The craftsmen work from memory rather than from set plans, building the hull using strong hardwood pegs to fasten the planks, then applying special sealant derived from swampland trees, which is resistant to rot. Unusually, the frame is fitted afterwards, giving the whole structure strength and flexibility. There's not much to do on Pulau Duyong other than stroll up and down the sea front, passing from workshop to workshop, but the village is pleasant, with a myriad of brightly painted wooden houses.

The Istana Tengku Long Museum

The new **Istana Tengku Long Museum** (daily 10am–6pm; Fri closed noon–3pm; $5), 3km west of the town centre in an idyllic riverside site, is among Malaysia's most exciting cultural complexes. Its landscaped gardens by the wide Sungei Terengganu feature imposing modern interpretations of the triple-roofed houses common to the area. Inside the main **Bangunan Utama** building, the first floor houses displays of exquisite fabrics, the second floor various crafts, and the third floor details the history of Terengganu. In the attached building to the left is the **Petronas Oil Gallery**, and behind this the **Islamic Gallery**, with fine examples of Koranic calligraphy. Beside the river are two examples of the **sailing boats** for which Kuala Terengganu is famed, unique combinations of European ships and Chinese junks, which you can climb into. A small **Maritime Museum** is close by, as is an excellent outdoor gallery of smaller, beautifully decorated fishing boats. There are also ancient timber palaces which have been rebuilt within the grounds.

The supreme example of these is the **Istana Tunku Long**, originally built in 1888 entirely without nails (which to Malays signify death because of their use in coffins). Like the majority of traditional east coast houses, the hardwood rectangular building has a high pointed roof and a pair of slightly curved wooden gables at either end. Each gable is fitted with twenty gilded screens, intricately carved with verses from the Koran and designed to admit air but also provide protection from driving rain.

The museum is easily reached by a twenty-minute journey on the Losong minibus (50 sen) which departs regularly from the local bus station, passing through some attractive kampungs – on the way look out for the traditional high-gabled stilted houses. There are plans to run a ferry from the jetty close to the central market – enquire at the Tourist Information Centre for details.

Eating

There are excellent **food stalls** on Jalan Tok Lam and behind the express bus station, serving the usual Malay dishes (11.30am–midnight). By comparison other restaurants are poor value, although there are one or two notable exceptions.

Restoran Cheng Cheng, Jalan Bandar. Excellent buffet in this authentic, but tourist-orientated, Chinese *kedai kopi*. Your plate is price-coded with coloured pegs – lunch costs around $5. Closes at 8.30pm.

Shri Shanmuga, Jalan Tok Lam, by the junction with Jalan Dato' Isaac. Great banana leaf curries.

MALAY DOMESTIC ARCHITECTURE

The **traditional Malay house** is now found only in rural areas – hence the generic term **kampung architecture** – with the best examples being in the states of Kelantan and Terengganu. Since they are made of wood, you won't see any over a hundred years old – weather and termites take their toll. Raised on stilts to afford protection from floods and wild animals, the walls have many windows to let in the maximum amount of light and air, and are often embellished with elaborate carvings. Inside, a large, rectangular room acts as the principal family area and as a reception room for guests, with bedrooms and storerooms behind, while the kitchen is connected to the main part of the house by an open courtyard. The roof is covered by *atap* (palm thatch), though these days tiles or corrugated iron are just as common. Regional variations in these village houses are most pronounced in the state of Negeri Sembilan, between KL and Melaka, whose Minangkabau settlers from Sumatra brought with them their distinctive saddle-shaped roofs – sweeping, curved structures called "buffalo horns". The states of Kelantan and Terengganu share cultural influences with their Thai neighbours to the north in their gables and tiled roofs, with fewer windows and more headroom, while those in Melaka are characterized by a decorative, tiled stairway leading up to an open-sided verandah. The simple, airy kampung architectural style, with its emphasis on timber, is being adopted by many new hotels and public buildings to evoke a more informal atmosphere and to emphasize Malay traditions, often to award-winning success.

Taufik Restoran, Jalan Masjid Abidin. A popular Indian place serving *murtabak*s and curry dishes starting from $2. Closed in the evening.

Zainuddin, Jalan Tok Lam. Offers a Thai-influenced menu that's surprisingly cheap at around $3 per dish, and very popular with locals.

Listings

Airlines The MAS office is at 13 Jalan Sultan Omar (☎09/622 1415).

Airport Sultan Mohammed Airport is 13km northeast of town; flight information ☎09/666 4204.

Banks and exchange Standard Chartered, UMBC and Maybank are all on Jalan Sultan Ismail.

Buses Kuala Terengganu has regular buses to all points on the Peninsula. Local buses go every 30min to Marang (7am–6pm; $1) and to Dungun and Rantau Abang (7.30am–6pm; $2).

Hospital The state hospital is off Jalan Sultan Mahmud on Jalan Peranginan (☎09/632 3333), 1km southeast of the centre.

Immigration The Wisma Persekutuan office on Jalan Pejabat (Mon–Wed & Sat 8.30am–6pm, Thurs 8.30am–1pm) issues on-the-spot-visa renewals.

Left luggage Express bus station on Jalan Sultan Zainal Abidin ($1).

Police Main police station is on Jalan Sultan Ismail (☎09/622 2222).

Post office The GPO (for poste restante/general delivery) is on Jalan Sultan Zainal Ibrahim.

Telephones There's a Telekom office on Jalan Tok Lam (8.30am–4.15pm).

Tours and travel agents The Tourist Information Centre on Jalan Sultan Zainal Abidin near the GPO arranges tours to most local places including Tasik Kenyir and Sekayu Waterfall (from $60), and can also recommend other agencies. Ping Anchorage Travel and Tours, 77a Jalan Dato' Isaac (☎09/622 0851), is very informative and efficient.

Around Kuala Terengganu

You can make excursions from Kuala Terengganu to **Tasik Kenyir**, a vast hydro-electric dam, and to the **Sekayu Waterfall**. There are also trips (around $240 for three days) to **Pulau Redang**, the stunning marine park 45km off the Terengganu coast (see p.259). With the exception of Sekayu, visits generally have to be arranged through a travel agent (see "Listings", above), as these are protected areas. This makes exploring not only expensive but also rather regimented.

Tasik Kenyir

Malaysia's largest hydro-electric dam may not seem a promising start for a "back-to-nature" experience, but on the other side of the immense concrete wall is **Tasik Kenyir**, a lake of some 360 square kilometres with 340 islands, created when the valley was flooded. Currently being developed as an alternative gateway to Taman Negara, it was once an area of lush jungle – partially submerged trees still jut out of the waters. In fact, the rotting trunks have contributed to the reduction in oxygen levels in the water, causing fish to look for food elsewhere. Otherwise, the water is clear; tours take in the many waterfalls with plunge pools for swimming, as well as the limestone Bewah Caves, deep in the hills that surround the lake.

There are two types of **accommodation** available at Tasik Kenyir: upmarket floating chalets, with full facilities, or more basic houseboats. The latter are cheaper and provide better access to the lake. Typical packages for a one-night stay cost from $135 per person in a houseboat and $150 in a floating chalet, including bus transfer from Kuala Terengganu, meals and a guided tour. You can go on a day-trip for $75, including lunch and snacks. Contact *Uncle John's Resort* (☎09/622 9564, fax 622 9569) for details. There's currently no budget accommodation, but camping facilities may be available in the future.

Sekayu Waterfall

If you can't face parting with the money for the Tasik Kenyir experience, then a trip to **Sekayu Waterfall** is a good compromise – you can include a visit to the dam on the way. Part of a government park complex, known as **Hutan Lipur Sekayu** (daily 9am–6pm; $1), the park is a busy weekend picnic spot, even if the environment has been somewhat tamed, with rustic shelters, a bird park, mini zoo and an "all-you-can-eat" fruit farm.

Take a local bus for the 45-minute journey to Kuala Berang ($2.20), and after taking a look at the dam, take a taxi for the fifteen-minute drive to the park ($10 one-way per taxi). Don't forget to arrange a pick-up time with your driver as there is no taxi stand at the park.

However, if you want to stay at the park, there are a number of **chalets** (②) and a **resthouse** (②) which must be booked in advance at the Forest Department in Kuala Berang (☎09/681 1259). Travel agents in Kuala Terengganu can arrange a day-trip costing around $40 for four people.

Marang and Pulau Kapas

Times are changing in **MARANG**, a tiny coastal village 17km south of Kuala Terengganu. Its conservative residents have long been used to the steady trickle of foreign visitors, drawn to the place by the promise of "old Malaysia", as well as the delights of nearby **Pulau Kapas**, 6km offshore. But the village, home to a handful of guesthouses and batik shops as well as local traders, and nicknamed "Cowboy Town" because of its dusty one-horse feel, is having a face-lift. Some of the ramshackle wooden shops and houses that lined the road have been demolished and replaced by a car park. A new jetty complex and walkways have also been built. While visitors might bemoan Marang's loss of character, local people welcome the improved safety and sanitation that the new buildings bring. Shades of the old Marang linger in the sleepy back-

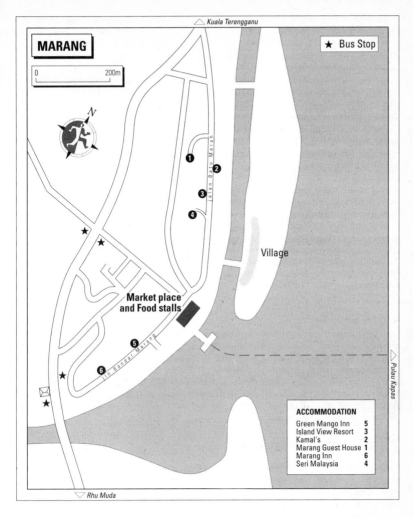

★ Bus Stop

0   200m

N

Jalan Batu Merah

❶

❷

❸

❹

Village

**Market place
and Food stalls**

❺

Jln Bandar Marang

❻

△ Kuala Terengganu

▷ Pulau Kapas

▽ Rhu Muda

ACCOMMODATION

Green Mango Inn	5
Island View Resort	3
Kamal's	2
Marang Guest House	1
Marang Inn	6
Seri Malaysia	4

water to the north of the main street, with coconut trees by a lovely clear lagoon, and colourful fishing boats. There are long empty stretches of beach here, and 2km further to the south at **Rhu Muda**.

Practicalities

Any Dungun- or Rhu Muda-bound **bus** (every 30min) from Kuala Terengganu, will drop you on the main road at Marang, from where a five-minute walk down one of the roads off to the left brings you into the centre. Although the northern end of Rhu Muda is easy enough to walk to, you can also pick up a bus on the main road.

There are no banks in Marang, though there is a police station and post office just before the bridge at the south end of the village. The **ferry companies** running boats over to Pulau Kapas have their offices on the main road, all offering the same deal of $15 for a return trip, but arrangements can just as easily be made through most of the guesthouses. The **jetty** is just off the main street. Sailings are dependent on the tide, since the harbour is very shallow – mid-morning is the usual departure time. During the monsoon months (November to February), Pulau Kapas is completely inaccessible.

Accommodation and eating

It's likely you'll want to **stay** a night or so in Marang. Most guesthouses have their own **restaurants**, serving Western food, and the food stalls near the market are worth checking out, particularly *Din Canai*, which does excellent *roti canai*.

Green Mango Inn (☎09/618 2040). One of the best places – a laid-back kampung-style guesthouse on a hill just by the jetty. ①.

Island View Resort (☎09/618 2006). A mishmash of different chalets, but the new, pricier rooms are very good value. ①–③.

Kamal's (☎09/618 2181). A long-running and cheap establishment, with some reasonable chalets, a dorm, communal showers and a café-bar. ②.

Marang Guest House (☎09/618 1976). Fresh, comfortable rooms and A-frames, and a restaurant with an excellent vantage point over the lagoon and sea. ②.

Marang Inn (☎09/618 2132). Close to the main road, this place is cheap and very basic. There's a batik shop downstairs. ①.

Seri Malaysia (☎09/618 2889, fax 618 1285). The most upmarket accommodation, where the rate includes breakfast. ⑤.

Rhu Muda

Unless you have your own transport, staying at Rhu Muda puts you out on a limb, for although there are a whole string of beach resorts, there's not the same sense of community that there is in Marang itself. About the best of the cheaper **accommodation** is the *Angullia Beach House Resort* (☎09/618 1322; ②) 2km south of Marang, a spacious grassy compound with variously priced chalets, all with their own verandahs. Better, but much pricier, is the award-winning *Marang Resort and Safaris* (☎09/618 2588, fax 618 2334; ⑥) 8km south of Marang, where traditional huts sit in the mangroves between the river and the sea.

Pulau Kapas and Pulau Gemia

A thirty-minute ride by fishing boat from Marang takes you to **PULAU KAPAS**, less than 2km in length and one of the nicest islands on the east coast. Most of the guesthouses in Marang can arrange transport out to the island, which can easily be visited in a day. Expect to pay $15 return. It's a fine spot, with coves on the western side of the island accessible only by sea or by clambering over rocks – you'll be rewarded by excellent sand and aquamarine water. Access to the remote eastern side is via a track that leads back from the jetty, taking around 45 minutes, but the sheer cliffs which plummet to the water's edge make it unwelcoming. Like many of its neighbours, Kapas is a designated marine park, the best snorkelling being around rocky Pulau Gemia, just off the northwestern shore of Pulau Kapas, while the northernmost cove is ideal for turtle-spotting.

On Kapas, the only **accommodation** is at the two western coves that directly face the mainland. The best value is *Zaki Beach Chalet* (☎010/619 5258; ①), a laid-back place set in a shady grove, with comfortable A-frames, though its cheaper rooms near the generator are very noisy. Its restaurant is definitely the place to be in the evenings. Close by, the welcoming *Pulau Kapas Garden Resort* (☎010/984 1686, fax 624 5162; ③)

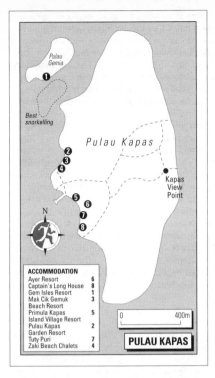

ACCOMMODATION
Ayer Resort	6
Captain's Long House	8
Gem Isles Resort	1
Mak Cik Gemuk	3
Beach Resort	
Primula Kapas	5
Island Village Resort	
Pulau Kapas	2
Garden Resort	
Tuty Puri	7
Zaki Beach Chalets	4

PULAU KAPAS

is worth checking out, with more luxurious rooms; it has a beachside restaurant and a resident diving instructor – courses start from $950. The cramped *Mak Cik Gemuk Beach Resort* (☎010/984 0972; ①–②) is the last choice. A wooden walkway over the rocks leads to the jetty in the next bay (it's possible to camp on the beach you'll pass on the way, but there are no facilities here), and to the *Primula Kapas Island Village Resort* (☎09/623 6100; ⑤), exclusive Malay-style chalets, with a swimming pool and extensive watersports facilities. Next along is the ramshackle *Ayer Resort* (☎011/971958; ②). The *Tuty Puri Island Resort* (☎09/624 6090; ⑤) is a much better operation, with a delightful beachside restaurant and well-designed chalets. At the far end of the bay, the *Captain's Longhouse* (☎09/618 1529; ③) is an attractive building of dark, polished timber, with some budget dorm beds – with only a well shower, however it's a touch overpriced.

The *Gem Isles Resort* (☎ & fax 09/624 5109) on Pulau Gemia can only be visited as part of a package deal, starting at $170 for two days and one night, all meals included. It's a well-designed place with all the chalets built on stilts at the water's edge. The snorkelling around the island is excellent and there's even a turtle hatchery.

Rantau Abang

Coastal Route 3 continues south, passing through numerous fishing kampungs before reaching **RANTAU ABANG**, 43km from Marang. Although the village is no more than a collection of guesthouses strung out at regular intervals along a couple of kilometres of dusty road, it has made its name as one of a handful of places in the world where the increasingly rare **giant leatherback turtle** comes to lay its eggs, returning year after year between May and September to the same beaches. While other species, including the hawksbill, the Olive Ridley and green turtles, are also to be found in these parts, it is the sight of the huge, ponderous leatherbacks, with their unusual coat of black, rubbery skin, lumbering up the beach, that is the real attraction.

Measuring 1.5m, and weighing on average of about 400kg, only the female ever comes ashore, heaving herself out of the water at night with her enormous front flippers until she reaches dry sand. The turtle's back flippers make digging movements to create a narrow hole 50–80cm deep in which she deposits up to a hundred eggs. The turtle then covers the hole with her rear flippers, while disguising the whole nest site by churning up more sand with the front ones. It is this action which causes the turtle to wheeze and shed tears in order to remove the kicked-up sand from her eyes and nose – although a more romantic explanation has it that the creature is grieving for her lost eggs.

Although a single turtle never lays eggs for two consecutive seasons, it can nest three or four times within the same season at two-weekly intervals. The eggs incubate for fifty or sixty days, the temperature of the sand influencing the sex of the hatchlings – warm sand produces more females, cooler sand favours males. The hatchlings – no more than a hand-span length – then crawl to the surface of the sand, leaving their broken shells at the bottom of the pit. The first few hours of a hatchling's life are particularly hazardous, for if it doesn't get destroyed by larvae or fungi in the sand, it can be picked off by crabs, birds and other predators before even reaching the sea. Usually emerging under the cover of night, they propel themselves rapidly towards the water's edge using their outsize flippers, the element of the turtle's behaviour that most baffles scientists. While it was once thought that they headed towards the lightest area in their vision (other sources of light such as torches were known to disturb their progress), other studies showed that the hatchlings were also moving away from the land's higher horizon. In so doing, it is thought that the turtles somehow memorize the beach on their scuttle towards the water, which could account for their ability to relocate Rantau Abang in later life. This theory is supported by the observation that, once in the water, turtles swim in the direction from which the waves are coming, as if guided by a magnetic sense of direction. But really, nobody knows why a mature fifty-year-old turtle, swimming in waters as far away as South America, can find its way back to nest on the coast of Terengganu. Outside of the egg-laying season, the long, unspoilt beach is a tranquil place to hang out for a day or two.

Turtle-watching

Turtle-watching was once something of a sport, with tourists riding the creatures for the sake of a good photograph – behaviour that, not surprisingly, was scaring the turtles away. The coastline 10km either side of Rantau Abang has now been set aside as a **sanctuary** for nesting turtles by the state government with the support of the Worldwide Fund for Nature, and specific nesting areas have been established on the beach, fenced off from the curious human beings. Also off-limits are the **hatcheries** set up to protect the eggs from theft or damage; the eggs are dug up immediately after the turtle has laid them and reburied in a safe site surrounded by a wire pen tagged with a date marker. When the hatchlings have broken out of their shells, they are released at the top of the beach (4–6am), and their scurry to the sea is supervised to ensure their safe progress.

The **Turtle Information Centre** (May–Aug daily 9am–1pm, 2–6pm & 8–11pm, except Fri 9am–noon & 3–11pm; Sept–April daily 8am–12.45pm & 2–4pm; free), to the north of the central two-kilometre strip, is informative and interesting, with a video and other displays relating to the turtles.

Although there are specific places where the public are allowed to watch the nesting turtles, you are asked to keep at least 5m away and refrain from using torches, camera flashes and fires, as well as making a noise. Unfortunately, not everyone follows these rules. In order to protect the turtles, the guesthouses will arrange for you to be woken during the night if one is sighted, for a fee of $3. By the time you arrive, the eggs will have been taken away by rangers, for safety.

Practicalities

Local buses from Kuala Terengganu and Marang run every thirty minutes (7.30am–6pm; 1hr) to Rantau Abang. If you're coming by express bus from the south, you have to change at Dungun, 13km to the south (see below), from where you can eas-

THE MARINE TURTLE - AN ENDANGERED SPECIES

While the striking leatherback turtle is an emotive cause for concern, the population of all marine turtles – green, black, Olive Ridley, Kemp's Ridley, hawksbill, loggerhead – is at risk. Although the authorities have gone some way towards controlling the on-shore conditions for visiting turtles at Rantau Abang, the real damage is inflicted elsewhere. Harmful fishing methods, such as the use of trawl nets, are responsible for the deaths of more than 100,000 marine turtles each year – a figure that explains the dramatic reduction in turtles nesting on the Terengganu coast from 10,155 in 1956, to a mere 27 in 1995. This figure rose slightly in 1996, but experts reckon there are as few as six turtles laying eggs on the beach. With a survival rate of only fifty percent among hatchlings, this is bound to have drastic consequences for the survival of the species: current estimates reckon on a figure of between 70,000 and 75,000 females left in the world.

But in Southeast Asia in particular, the turtles have a far more menacing predator – human beings. While its meat is forbidden by religious law in Malaysia, neighbouring nations such as Indonesia and the Philippines have traditionally relied on the turtle as an important source of nutrition. More worrying was the deliberate slaughter of turtles for their shells – each worth around US$375 – which were fashioned into ornaments, such as bowls and earrings, primarily for the Japanese market. Until 1992, when a ban was enforced, Japan imported 20 tons of hawksbill shells annually for this purpose, which involved killing over 30,000 turtles.

ily get a local bus for the remainder of the journey. Buses drop you on the main road, at the R&R Plaza, just a short walk from all the accommodation and the Turtle Information Centre.

There are surprisingly few **accommodation** options, all of them close to the beach. Prices double when the turtles are in town, from May to September; the price codes refer to the high season rate. The best place is the upmarket *Rantau Abang Visitor Centre* (☎09/844 1533; ④), 1km north of the Turtle Information Centre, with timber chalets complete with fridge and TV arranged around a peaceful lagoon. Of the budget options, *Dahimah's Guest House* (☎09/845 2843; ①–③), at the far southern end of the strip, rates highly, with very comfortable rooms and chalets surrounding a central courtyard; many of the rooms are a good deal cheaper than this category suggests, making them excellent value. Costing still less, and with much more of a backpackers' feel, is the long-running and central *Awang's* (☎09/844 3500; ①–②), a little run-down but friendly, with a variety of simple rooms as well as some overpriced air-con chalets. *Ismail's* (☎09/845 4202; ①), next door, is very basic and not as good. Both places are handily located, near the Turtle Information Centre.

All guesthouses have their own **restaurants**, serving the usual traveller-orientated food. In addition, there are **food stalls** near *Awang's*, and the excellent *Kedai Makan Rantau Abang*, 750m further south, a cheerful local eating house offering substantial rice and noodle dishes. For **midnight snacks** while turtle-watching, try the modern R&R Plaza (open 24hr), on the main road opposite the Turtle Information Centre, with a wide-ranging menu featuring Western and Malay dishes.

South to Cherating

The **route south** from Rantau Abang is a further indictment of the rampant development that has accompanied Terengganu's economic success: ugly oil refineries and huge residential complexes for their workers, built with little or no regard for the local environment. This rapid industrialization hasn't deterred the growth of tourism however, as illustrated by the success of the award-winning *Tanjung Jara Beach Hotel*

(☎09/844 1801; ⑧), a luxury resort in the style of a Malay palace, 8km south of Rantau Abang. This is easily the most attractive of the resorts along this stretch, though the sight of the offshore rigs in these parts may be off-putting for sun-seekers. It's only when you reach the secluded bay of Cherating that the scenery takes a distinct upturn.

Dungun to Chukai

The backwater town of **KUALA DUNGUN**, a further 5km south, is predominantly Chinese, with a handful of shophouses and a weekly night market each Thursday; there's no reason to spend much time here. The local bus station (for services to Rantau Abang) is in the town, on the west side of the padang, while express buses (to KL and Singapore) depart from outside the hospital on Route 3 itself – tickets can be purchased from either the *A.A.* or *Aziz* restaurants on the main road. With local buses leaving every thirty minutes to Rantau Abang (25min) en route to KL (2hr) and every thirty minutes to Kemaman (2hr), you probably won't need to spend the night. If you do, the *Kasanya* at 223–227 Jalan Tumbun (☎09/844 1704; ②), the town's main street, is the best option.

Continuing south, the highway swerves suddenly inland to avoid a small promontory before rejoining the coast at **Paka**, a small fishing village now dwarfed by the immense power plant just to the south. This marks the beginning of a dreary string of developments including Kerteh and Kemasik that are best passed through swiftly. **Kemaman**, an untidy, sprawling town halfway between Dungun and Kuantan – and barely distinguishable from its neighbour, **Chukai** – is significant only in that it's here that you'll have to change buses to reach any of the small kampungs along the road to Kuantan, including Cherating.

Cherating

The fast-expanding travellers' hangout of **CHERATING**, 47km north of Kuantan, hugs the northern end of a windswept bay, protected from the breeze by the shelter of a rocky cliff. Although most of the locals have long since moved to a small village further south, the settlement still tries to reflect kampung life by offering simple chalets and homestays at a modest charge to visitors. Ramshackle stilted huts nestle in palm groves, while a handful of beach bars lead the gentle carousing well into the night. The sum total of Cherating's billing as a "cultural village" seems to be the opportunity to learn batik-printing – though even this seems to be a thinly disguised front for marketing off-the-peg clothes at inflated prices. However, Cherating is a good place in which to unwind, with a nightlife that comes as close as the east coast gets to raging.

Any express or local bus between Kuala Terengganu and Kuantan will drop you off at Cherating, which lies within easy walking distance of Route 3. Two rough tracks lead from the road down into the main part of the village, about five minutes' away, although the one nearest the bridge is the most direct. Chalets shaded by tall, gently swaying palm trees are dotted either side of the path, increasing in density when you reach the main drag, a tiny surfaced road that runs roughly parallel to the beach. This is where you'll find most of the restaurants and bars, as well as the provisions stores and *Travel Post* (☎09/581 9134), which rents out everything from a mountain bike ($20 a day) to a boat. It also acts as a travel agency where you can book bus tickets around Malaysia and to Singapore, tours to Gua Charas (see p.279) and Tasek Chini (p.235), as well as local river and snorkelling trips ($15 including equipment).

With a reliable sea breeze, Cherating is ideal for **windsurfing**, and some of the beach bars and chalets rent out equipment, from $15 an hour. If that's a bit too active for your liking, try a brisk walk west along the **beach** to where the rippling tide makes

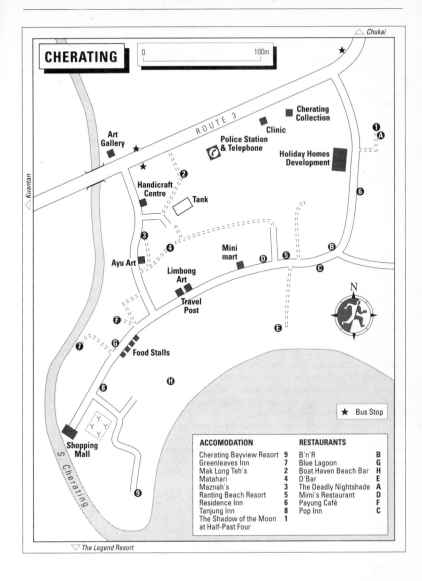

CHERATING

0   100m

△ Chukai

ROUTE 3

Art
Gallery

Cherating
Collection

Clinic

Police Station
& Telephone

Handicraft
Centre

Tank

Holiday Homes
Development

△ Kuantan

Ayu Art

Mini
mart

Limbong
Art

Travel
Post

N

Food Stalls

★ Bus Stop

Shopping
Mall

S. Cherating

ACCOMODATION

Cherating Bayview Resort	9
Greenleaves Inn	7
Mak Long Teh's	2
Matahari	4
Maznah's	3
Ranting Beach Resort	5
Residence Inn	6
Tanjung Inn	8
The Shadow of the Moon at Half-Past Four	1

RESTAURANTS

B'n'R	B
Blue Lagoon	G
Boat Haven Beach Bar	H
D'Bar	E
The Deadly Nightshade	A
Mimi's Restaurant	D
Payung Café	F
Pop Inn	C

▽ The Legend Resort

fascinating patterns on the sand. Sungei Cherating, whose brown waters run into the bay here, is really only passable at low tide, effectively cutting off the route further west. Clambering over the rocks at the eastern end of the bay brings you to a tiny secluded cove, though the beach isn't as good as that belonging to the exclusive *Club Med* over the next outcrop. Low tide is less of a problem here than in the main part of the bay, where you'll have to walk out at least 200m to reach the sea, and still further to get deep enough to swim.

Accommodation

Cherating has no shortage of **places to stay** and new accommodation is springing up all the time. Some aren't yet on the phone; the best are listed below and marked on the map above.

Greenleaves Inn (☎010/337 8242). There's a real "jungle getaway" feel to this place, with basic chalets hidden away in the groves by a river. A relaxed atmosphere with breakfast included in the price. ①.

The Legend Resort (☎09/581 9818, fax 581 9400). Top-class accommodation to the south of the main village, but accessible from the beach. Includes some good restaurants and a pool. ⑧.

Mak Long Teh's (☎09/581 9290). Set back from the main road, this is one of the original "homestays", offering set meals in a warm family environment. ②.

Matahari. Spacious, sturdy chalets each with a fridge and large verandah, as well as a separate communal area with a TV room and cooking facilities. A good place to learn batik. ①–②.

Maznah's. Wacky decor and a lively atmosphere make up for the dilapidated A-frames, most without attached bathrooms. All-day breakfast included in the price. ①.

Ranting Beach Resort. (☎09/581 9068) Well-appointed and centrally located chalets surrounding an airy restaurant. ②.

Residence Inn (☎09/581 9333, fax 09/581 9252). The most upmarket place within the village, has comfortable rooms ranged around a pleasant swimming pool and lobby area. ⑦.

Shadow of the Moon at Half-Past Four (☎09/581 9186). Ten well-designed timber chalets with attached bathroom, tucked away in a beautiful wooded area. *The Deadly Nightshade* bar and lounge are the real attraction. ②.

Tanjung Inn (☎09/581 9081). The garden compound that stretches down to the beach houses well-spaced, comfortable but slightly pricey huts. Good restaurant. ②.

Eating and drinking

Eating is the main focus of nightlife in Cherating, though unusually for Muslim Malaysia, there are many lively **bars**. Most chalet operations have their own restaurants – with monotonously similar menus. The evening **food stalls** on the road through the village offer Malay standards like *nasi lemak*, *rojak ayam* and *cendol*. For breakfast the *roti canai* stall just past the *Travel Post* can't be beat.

B'n'R. Attractively designed restaurant, though the chicken and fish dinners for around $6 don't quite live up to the promise of the decor.

Blue Lagoon. Busy bar and restaurant whose Chinese-based menu attracts the expat crowd from the local oil refineries; averages $6 per dish.

Boat Haven Beach Bar. An imaginatively constructed bow of a ship forms this beachfront bar, with tables and logs in the sand. Interesting sculptures, volleyball competitions and camp fires.

D'Bar. On the beach opposite Ranting Beach Resort. Laid-back bar which keeps late hours and serves decent Western food.

Deadly Nightshade, at the *Shadow of the Moon at Half Past Four*. One of the most imaginatively designed bars you'll come across on the east coast, if not in all of Malaysia. Fairy lights, piles of books and homemade furniture add to the atmosphere. Excellent set meals for around $7.

Mimi's Restaurant. Standard Malaysian food; nothing to get excited about.

Payung Café. Good value Indian food, in a riverside setting. Also open for breakfast and lunch, with Western dishes.

Pop Inn. Overpriced German cuisine, including grills at $20. The daily specials for $9 are worth trying, though. Closed Mon.

Kuantan and around

It's virtually inevitable that you'll pass through **KUANTAN** at some stage, since it's the region's transport hub, lying at the junction of Routes 2 (which runs across the Peninsula to KL), 3 and 14. The brash state capital of **Pahang**, sprawling out from its

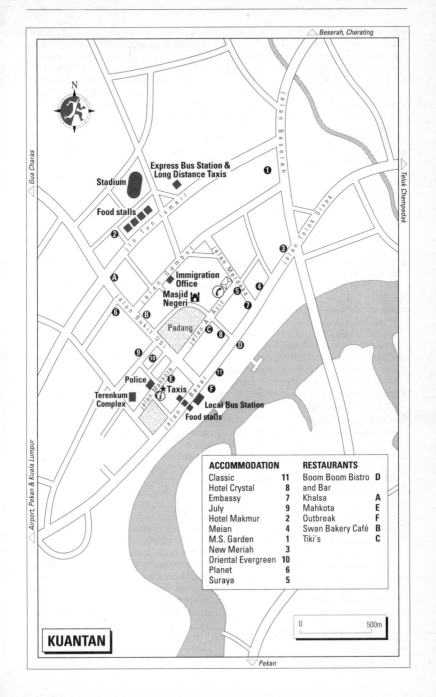

KUANTAN

ACCOMMODATION
Classic	11
Hotel Crystal	8
Embassy	7
July	9
Hotel Makmur	2
Meian	4
M.S. Garden	1
New Meriah	3
Oriental Evergreen	10
Planet	6
Suraya	5

RESTAURANTS
Boom Boom Bistro and Bar	D
Khalsa	A
Mahkota	E
Outbreak	F
Swan Bakery Café	B
Tiki's	C

thriving commercial centre, Kuantan's situation on a promontory means that traffic up the east coast faces a significant diversion inland along Sungei Kuantan before reaching the town, a factor which many consider has played its part in the failure to capture business from Singapore. This has changed, with the completion of a new bridge connecting the centre of Kuantan directly to the southern Route 3 – though this has done little to alleviate traffic congestion. Land prices in the vicinity of the bridge have soared, however, fuelled by developers keen to take advantage of the improved transport links. This is leading to the eviction of traditional communities no longer able to meet the inflated rents.

While there's little to capture your imagination in the dull, concrete buildings of the town centre – aside from the magnificent **Masjid Negeri** – the fishing communities to the south of town make an interesting diversion. The beach satellites of **Teluk Chempedak** and **Beserah** just to the north are more pleasant places to stay than the centre itself, and those with more time to spare should not miss out on **Gua Charas**, a limestone cave temple within easy reach of the town. The trip here is worth it for the stunning setting alone, dramatic outcrops in virtually deserted plantation country.

The Town

The commercial part of Kuantan is relatively small, clustered around Jalan Besar, Jalan Makhota and Jalan Tun Ismail. The former, running close by Sungei Kuantan and leading into Jalan Telok Sisek, is home to most of the budget hotels and restaurants, while, one block behind, Jalan Makhota (which changes to Jalan Haji Abdul Aziz after the junction with Jalan Bank) is where you'll find the GPO, Telekom and police station.

While most of Kuantan's urban architecture is distinctly unmemorable, its one real sight, the **Masjid Negeri** on frenetic Jalan Makhota, is stunning. Built in 1991, its pastel exterior (green for Islam, blue for peace and white for purity) is more reminiscent of a huge birthday cake than a place of worship. Despite its conventional design – a sturdy square prayer hall with a looming central dome and minarets at all four corners – it's one of the most impressive modern mosques in Malaysia, particularly at dusk when the plaintive call to prayer and the stunning lighting combine to magical effect.

The riverside villages

Most people's priority will be to escape the centre of Kuantan, a short hop south across the river by bus or long-tailed boat – though these services have dwindled since the bridge has been completed. In the communities of Kampung Tanjung Lumpur, Kampung Cempaka and Peramu you'll find plenty of peace and quiet.

KAMPUNG TANJUNG LUMPUR, reached by bus from the local bus station, is an impoverished fishing community consisting mainly of illegal Indonesian immigrants, to whom the authorities have long turned a blind eye. The rocketing land prices however are forcing families to relocate. Still, it's a good place to visit for seafood restaurants. **PERAMU**, a couple of kilometres up the road, is changing more visibly, with new housing and the recent installation of mains water. It also boasts a lively afternoon market, a long line of stalls a few minutes' walk away from the riverside.

The coastline to the south of the town is in many ways more appealing than the beach at Teluk Chempedek to the north, not least because it is still relatively undeveloped. The beach at **KAMPUNG CEMPAKA**, about 3km south of Kampung Tanjung Lumpur, is particularly good: a wide sweeping expanse of sand and shallow sea, whose currents are a whole lot safer than the buffeting waves further north. Although close enough to town for a day-trip, a good alternative would be to stay at the *Sanubari Beach Resort* (☎011/952518; ⑤), a delightful, family-run operation with comfortable chalets, a swimming pool and excellent cuisine. To get here, take a bus to Peramu, followed by an exhilarating motorbike-taxi ride ($5) for the remaining 6km.

Practicalities

The **local bus station** is on Jalan Basar, beside Sungei Kuantan, and the **express bus station** is on Jalan Stadium, in front of the Darulmakmur stadium. **Taxis** (☎513 4478) can be found between Jalan Besar and Jalan Makhota, while long distance taxis leave from the express bus station. The **airport** is 15km east of town – a taxi there from the centre costs $15.

The **Tourist Information Centre** (Mon–Fri 9am–5pm, Sat 9am–1pm; ☎09/513 3026), in a large glass and wood booth at the end of Jalan Makhota facing the playing fields, can help you out with accommodation in and around Kuantan, and also organizes **day-trips** to the surrounding area.

Accommodation

Kuantan has no shortage of **hotels**, though at the bottom end of the market the basic Chinese-run boarding houses are poor value. If you can stretch to a few extra dollars, those in the middle range are a much better.

Classic, 7 Jalan Besar (☎09/554599, fax 09/5134141). One of the best hotels in town, with large bright rooms, a café, huge bathrooms and great views of the river. ⑤.

Crystal, 59 Jalan Makhota (☎09/526577). This nicely furnished hotel has reasonably priced air-con rooms and a lounge area with TV. ②.

Embassy, 60 Jalan Telok Sisek (☎09/524406). Standard but clean Chinese hotel; all rooms have attached bathrooms. ②.

July, 73 Lorong Rusa 1, off Jalan Bukit Ubi (☎09/513 0760). This spotless hotel near the new bus station offers small but comfortable rooms, though the decor is a little twee. ①.

Makmur, Lorong Pasar Baru (☎09/514 1363, fax 09/514 2870). Clean, budget option handy for the express bus station, supermarkets and local food stalls. ②.

Meian, 78 Jalan Teluk Sisek (☎09/520949). Basic, neat and clean, though only one cheap room – the rest are a little overpriced. ②–③.

M.S. Garden, Jalan Beserah (☎09/554 0201, fax 09/554 558). Kuantan's newest luxury hotel has a grand entrance, a swimming pool and expensive rooms. ⑧.

New Meriah, 142 Jalan Telok Sisek (☎09/525433). Large, carpeted, though slightly dingy rooms and bathrooms with hot water make this a very good option. ②.

Oriental Evergreen, 157 Jalan Haji Abdul Rahman (☎09/500168). Tucked down a side street off the main road, this is surprisingly plush, with well-appointed rooms and good facilities. ⑤.

Planet, 77 Jalan Bukit Ubi (no phone). Budget hostel with 24-hour check-in and flexible check-out. The rooms are small and rock-bottom basic. ①.

Suraya, 55 Jalan Haji Abdul Aziz (☎09/554266, fax 554028). Not quite international standard, but this place still rates highly, with tasteful, subtly lit rooms and a health club. ④.

Eating and drinking

Kuantan's **restaurants** win no gastronomic awards; the **food stalls** near the mosque on Jalan Makhota behind the Ocean Shopping Complex on Jalan Tun Ismail are the best bet, and those by the river behind the bus station. Many restaurants close in the evenings, but a couple of Western-style bars have recently opened in the centre of town, catering to young affluent Malays and expats. Teluk Chempedak (see below) generally has a livelier scene, for an evening out.

Boom Boom Bistro and Bar, Jalan Teluk Sisek. A yellow and blue painted prewar bungalow, formerly a 1920 gentleman's club and a Japanese interrogation centre during the war, now serves Mexican and American food, beers and other drinks to Kuantan's smart set. There's a quieter coffee shop attached for meals during the day.

Khalsa, Jalan Bukit Ubi. One of several on this road serving Malay/Indian food. Busy and cheerful.

Makhota, 67 Jalan Makhota. Tasty banana leaf curries with all the trimmings for around $6. Open only for lunch.

Out Break, behind the *Samudra Riverview Hotel*, Jalan Besar. Large glitzy fun pub, disco and karaoke lounge, with an attached swimming pool. Happy hour is 8–10.30pm.

Swan Bakery Café, Jalan Bukit Ubi. Large air-conditioned café serving cakes, Western and Chinese food.

Tiki's, Jalan Makhota. Good-value Western breakfasts; relax with a paper and eat your eggs, tea and toast.

Listings

Airlines MAS, 7 ground floor, Wisma Bolasepak Pahang, Jalan Gambut (☎09/515 7055).

Airport The Sultan Ahmad Shah airport is 15km west of town; flight information ☎09/538 1291.

Banks OCBC and UMBC are on Jalan Telok Sisek. Standard Charter Bank, Maybank and Hong Kong Bank are all situated around the intersection of Jalan Besar and Jalan Bank.

Buses Express services run from the station on Jalan Stadium to most points on the Peninsula, including services hourly (8am–5pm) to Temerloh (for Tasik Chini and Tasik Bera), twice daily to Kuala Lipis and four daily to Jerantut (for Taman Negara).

Car rental Avis, 102 Jalan Telok Sisek (☎09/523666); Hertz, c/o Samudra River View Hotel, Jalan Besar (☎09/515 6333); National, 49, Jalan Telok Sisek (☎09/527303).

Immigration The immigration office is on the first floor, Wisma Persekutuan, Jalan Gambut for on-the-spot visa renewals (Mon–Fri 9am–4.15pm; ☎09/521373).

Post and communications The GPO, with poste restante, is on Jalan Haji Abdul Aziz; the Telekom office is next door (9am–4.15pm).

Taxis The long-distance taxi stand is above the express bus station (☎09/504478); fares per person are $20 to Kuala Terengganu, $25 to KL, $25 to Mersing and $35 to JB.

Teluk Chempedak

TELUK CHEMPEDAK, around 5km east of Kuantan, is a leafy suburb of wide roads and grand houses. Sitting on the tip of the Peninsula, the beaches have spawned a small collection of resort hotels and pricey trinket shops, all eager to capitalize on the urban disaster that is Kuantan, and edging out all but the most tenacious of the budget hostels. The narrow, sloping beach on the eastern side is reasonable, even if the sea, churned up by the constant wind into a grey broth, is less than inviting.

Bus #39 runs regularly from near the mosque on Jalan Makhota to Teluk Chempedak – the last bus is sound 9.30pm. The bus stops at the beach on the eastern side of the Peninsula and most of the **hotels** are off to the right, while a number of restaurants and snack bars face the sea to the left. The nicest place to stay is the *Hyatt* (☎09/566 1234, fax 567 7577; ⑧), whose open walkways and restaurants are pleasantly freshened by the sea breeze. It has a couple of pools and some good restaurants. The quaint *Hotel Kuantan* (☎ & fax 09/568 0026; ③), opposite the *Hyatt*, is somewhat chaotic but oozing with charm, while the cheapest rooms to be had are at the *Sri Pantai Resort* (☎09/568 5250, fax 567 7268; ②), rather grandly named for the facilities on offer, though with a wide variety of rooms ranging from grotty to reasonable. The western side of the promontory has fewer options: the government-run *Rumah Rehat* (☎09/567 4414; ④) isn't bad, but it's often full, while the *Samudra Beach Resort* (☎09/513 5933; ④), with twenty motel rooms, is very run-down – call first to see if it's open.

The **places to eat** in Teluk Chempedak are considerably more inspiring than those in Kuantan, although they are limited to the busier eastern side. The *Hyatt* has several restaurants, including a pizzeria, but you won't get away with less than $20 a dish. Facing the beach at the far end of the row of shops are some basic **food stalls**, while a few doors up, the *Massafalah* and *Pattaya* restaurants serve good seafood and steamboats for around $12 a head.

Beserah

Ten kilometres north of Kuantan on the road to Kuala Terengganu, the small village of **BESERAH** is famous for its salted fish and *keropok* (fish crackers). Fishermen still haul the day's catch to the processing areas by buffalo cart – a mode of transport that is becoming increasingly rare in techno-conscious Malaysia. Although it functions as yet another "cultural village" for Kuantan's tourists, supplied with a few handicraft workshops looking remarkably like souvenir outlets, Beserah is on the whole an unassuming place.

A few guesthouses have popped up in Beserah, making it a convenient and altogether more pleasant place to stay than Kuantan, particularly since buses (60 sen) from the local bus station ply the route regularly from 7am to 6pm. Get off at the "Pantai Beserah" sign on the right and follow the road past the sign round to the left for about 25m, where you'll find the friendly *Belia Perkasa* (☎09/544 8178, fax 544 8179), affiliated to the IYHF, with cheap dorms ($8). The *Beserah Guesthouse* (☎09/555203, fax 552831; ②) is about 100m further on, past the post office, an old-fashioned wooden boarding house facing a grey sand beach, with strict house rules and shabby rooms. If you turn right instead of left at the "Pantai Beserah" sign and walk for 1km, you'll come to *La Chaumiere* (☎09/544 7662; ①), the last house on the beach and considerably more laid-back. The price includes breakfast and, if convenient, the helpful owner will collect you from the town for $10. Further up the main road, a sign on the left points you to *Jaafar's Guest House* (no phone; ①), about 500m down a well-marked trail. Tranquil woodland is the setting for the longest-running homestay in the area, a relaxed family home where the price includes breakfast and dinner and free tea. Places **to eat** are rather thin on the ground, but the guesthouses generally offer evening meals and there's a pasar malam on Monday by the Mobil station.

Gua Charas

If you have any time to spare in Kuantan, you should visit **Gua Charas**, a cave temple 25km northeast of Kuantan, built into one of the great limestone outcrops surrounding the town. It can be seen as a leisurely day-trip: bus #48 from the local bus station departs every hour for the thirty-minute journey to the village of Panching; look to the right about halfway along for the well-kept Chinese cemetery on the hillside. At Panching, a sign to the caves points you down a four-kilometre track through overgrown rubber plantations and rows upon rows of palm oil trees – agricultural legacies responsible for the large numbers of Tamils living in the area, descendants of the indentured workers brought from southern India in the nineteenth century. It's a long, hot walk – take plenty of water with you.

Once you've reached the outcrop and paid your $1 donation, you're faced with a steep climb to the Thai Buddhist **cave temple** itself. About halfway up, a rudimentary path strikes off to the right, leading to the entrance of the main cave. Descending into the eerie darkness is not for the faint-hearted, even though the damp mud path is dimly lit by florescent tubes. Inside the vast, echoing cavern with its algae-stained vaulted roof and squeaking bats, illuminated shrines gleam from gloomy corners, guiding you to the main shrine deep in the cave. Here, an nine-metre sleeping Buddha is almost dwarfed by its giant surroundings. Back through the cave, steps lead to another, lighter hollow. It's nothing special, but if you go as far as you can to the back, the wall opens out to give a superb view of the surrounding countryside, stubby palm oil trees marching in regimented rows towards the horizon.

Pekan

Just 45km south of Kuantan lies the unassuming royal town of **PEKAN**, meaning "small town". Although the state capital of Pahang until 1898, Pekan's sleepy complacency gives the impression that nothing much has happened here for a very long time. Its neat and sober streets are lined with palaces, some modest, some vulgar – all products of the state's rapid turnover of sultans – and a handful of colonial buildings in varying states of decay.

At the edge of the tiny commercial sector, Jalan Tengku Ahmad faces the languid riverfront and leads past a row of turn-of-the-century shophouses shaded by huge rain trees, to the **Muzium Sultan Abu Bakar** (daily 9.30am–5pm; closed Fri 12.15pm– 2.45pm; free). The museum is housed in a well-proportioned Straits colonial building that has been used for various purposes down the years: as the sultan's istana, as the centre of British administration, and as the headquarters of the Japanese army during the occupation. Today it houses the State Museum of Pahang, and a collection including splendid Chinese ceramics recently salvaged from the wreck of a junk in the South China Sea, and an impressive display of royal regalia in the new east wing.

Further west long Jalan Tengku Ahmad is the unusual **Masjid Abdullah** which was built during the reign of Sultan Abdullah (1917–32). No longer used for active worship, this Art Deco structure, whose blue domes look more Turkish than Southeast Asian, is now home to the Pusat Dakwah Islamiah, the state centre for the administration of religious affairs. Next door, the current mosque, **Masjid Abu Bakar** is more conventional, with gold, bulbous domes.

Round the corner at the end of the road, past the unremarkable former offices of the sultan, is a crossroads. An archway built to resemble elephants' tusks marks your way

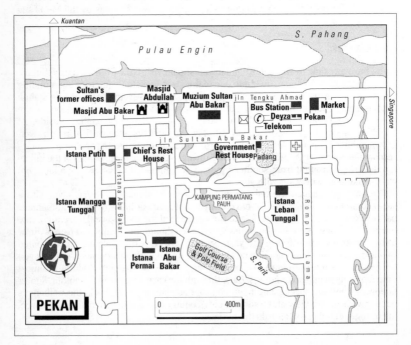

ahead to the royal quarter of the town, past the fresh, white **Istana Putih** on the corner. Opposite, the **Chief's Resthouse** of 1929 seems rather bereft, its wooden terraces gradually decaying. Just south of here is the sky-blue **Istana Mangga Tunggal**, and the **Istana Permai** (closed to the public), a tiny blue-roofed subsidiary palace that is home to the Regent of Pahang. Here you'll also see the rectangular facade of the **Istana Abu Bakar**, the palace currently occupied by the royal family. It's garish opulence is generally untypical of the buildings to be found in Pekan; the expansive grounds are now a royal golf course and polo ground.

North of the nearby sports field, a narrow winding lane brings you into **Kampung Permatang Pauh**, the secluded village area of Pekan with simple wooden stilted houses. A ten-minute walk across Sungei Parit leads to the most impressive of Pekan's royal buildings, the **Istana Leban Tunggal** – a refined wooden structure fronted by a pillared portico, with an unusual symmetrical hexagonal tower.

Practicalities

From Kuantan, Pekan is a 45-minute journey on bus #31, which leaves every 45 minutes from the local bus station. If you want to continue south, it's better to backtrack to Kuantan to pick up one of the many express buses than wait around for the infrequent local services. If you're coming from the south, just ask your bus driver to drop you off in town – all buses pass through Pekan on their way to Kuantan.

Places to stay in town are limited, and with regular connections to Kuantan, you shouldn't need to stop. The best place is the *Government Resthouse* (☎09/422 1240; ②), on the corner of the padang, where the rooms and bathrooms are vast, and the service good. Close to the bus station at 102a Jalan Tengku Arrif Bendahara is the *Deyza* (☎09/422 3690; ①), which is basic but clean – the *Pekan* next door is not as good. The choice of **restaurants** is grim, the best being the couple of Indian places along Jalan Tengku Arrif Bendahara. The food stalls near the bus station are very uninspiring.

travel details

Trains

Kota Bharu to: Gemas (2 daily; 9hr 30min–12hr 50min); Kuala Lipis (2 daily; 4hr 15min–5hr 20min); Singapore (3 weekly; 11hr 55min). For trains into Thailand see box on p.244.

Buses

Kota Bharu to: Alor Setar (2 daily; 8hr); Butterworth (2 daily; 6hr); Johor Bahru (2 daily; 12hr); Kuala Lumpur (2 daily; 7hr); Kuala Terengganu (6 daily; 3hr); Kuantan (5 daily; 6hr 30min); Melaka (1 daily; 12hr).

Kuala Terengganu to: Alor Setar (2 daily; 9hr 30min); Butterworth (2 daily; 9–10hr); Ipoh (1 daily; 11hr); Johor Bahru (2 daily; 10hr); Kota Bharu (6 daily; 3hr 30 min); Kuala Lumpur (2 daily; 8–9hr); Kuantan (8 daily; 3hr 30min); Marang (every 30min; 30min); Melaka (3 daily; 7hr);

Mersing (2 daily; 6hr); Rantau Abang (every 30 min; 1hr).

Kuantan to: Alor Setar (3 daily; 12hr); Butterworth (3 daily; 10hr); Ipoh (5 daily; 8hr); Johor Bahru (6 daily; 6hr); Kota Bahru (5 daily; 6hr); Kuala Lipis (2 daily; 6hr); Kuala Lumpur (at least 6 daily; 5hr); Kuala Terengganu (6 daily; 4hr); Melaka (2 daily; 5hr); Mersing (6 daily; 3hr 30min); Singapore (3 daily; 7hr); Temerloh (hourly; 2hr).

Planes

Kota Bharu to: Alor Setar (1 daily; 35min); Kuala Lumpur (8 daily; 50min); Penang (2 daily; 40min).

Kuala Terengganu to: Kuala Lumpur (at least 2 daily; 45min).

Kuantan to: Kuala Lumpur (at least 5 daily; 40min); Singapore (4 weekly; 50min).

CHAPTER FIVE

THE SOUTH

The south of the Malaysian Peninsula, below Kuala Lumpur and Kuantan, has some of the most historically and culturally significant towns in the country. The foundation of the west coast city of **Melaka** in the fifteenth century led to a Malay "Golden Age" under the Muslim Melaka Sultanate. During this period, the concept of *Melayu* (Malayness), still current in Malaysia, was established. For all its influence, the sultanate was surprisingly short-lived, and its fall in the early sixteenth century to the Portuguese marked the start of centuries of colonial interference in Malaysia. The Dutch and British followed the Portuguese in Melaka; British colonial rule was an essential part of the eighteenth- and nineteenth-century development of the country. The colonial inheritance is one of the main reasons people come to Melaka; other attractions include the unique culture of the Peranakan, or Baba-Nonya, the society that resulted from the intermarriage of early Chinese traders and Malay women.

Johor Bahru (or JB) at the tip of the Peninsula, dates back only to 1855, and is linked to the establishment of a settlement (originally called Tanjung Puteri) across the Johor Straits from Singapore. Elsewhere, while other foreigners came and went, the intrepid **Minangkabau** tribes from Sumatra settled in what is now the state of Negeri Sembilan, between KL and Melaka, making their mark in the spectacular architecture of **Seremban** and **Sri Menanti**, just over an hour south of the capital.

Melaka – in the centre of a small state of the same name and just two hours by bus from KL – makes a logical starting point for exploring the south. While its sights will keep you absorbed for several days, other local destinations make good day-trips: the easy-going towns of **Muar** and **Segamat**, **Pulau Besar**, and the coastal villages of **Tanjung Bidara** and **Tanjung Kling**. Most people head for the active little seaport of **Mersing** in order to reach **Pulau Tioman** and the other islands in the **Seribuat archipelago** – a draw for divers and snorkellers as well as those who simply like the idea of sandy beaches and transparent waters.

Other than these destinations, visitors tend to travel the east or west coasts, between KL, Kuantan and JB, avoiding the mountainous interior where the road network is poor. The North–South Highway (and the train line) connects KL with Singapore via the west coast. Its counterpart, the narrow Route 3 on the east coast, is a good deal more varied, winding for 300km through palm oil country and past luxuriant beaches. Increasingly,

---

ACCOMMODATION PRICE CODES

Throughout the Malaysia chapters we've used the following **price codes** to denote the cheapest available room for two people. Single occupancy should cost less than double, though this is not always the case. Some guesthouses provide dormitory beds, for which the dollar price is given.

① $20 and under	④ $61–80	⑦ $161–240
② $21–40	⑤ $81–100	⑧ $241–400
③ $41–60	⑥ $101–160	⑨ $401 and above

visitors are getting off the beaten track to see the primeval **Endau Rompin National Park**, the southernmost tropical rainforest in the Peninsula. It's a worthy and more rugged alternative to the much-visited Taman Negara, further north.

Negeri Sembilan: Seremban and Sri Menanti

The Minangkabau tribes from Sumatra established themselves in the Malay state of **Negeri Sembilan**, whose modern-day capital is the town of **Seremban**, 67km south of Kuala Lumpur. The cultural heart of the state though, is the royal town of **Sri Menanti**, 30km further east of Seremban. Centres of Minangkabau civilization (see box on p.288) since the early years of the Melaka Sultanate, both towns showcase traditional Minangkabau architecture, typified by distinctive, buffalo-horn peaked roofs.

The modern state of Negeri Sembilan is based on an old confederacy of nine districts (hence its name – *sembilan* means nine in Malay), whose early origins are uncertain. By the middle of the nineteenth century, British control over the area and its thriving **tin trade** was virtually complete, with the colonial authority administered from Sungei Ujong (today's Seremban). Wars between rival Malay and Minangkabau groups for control over the mining and transportation of tin were commonplace, most notably between the Dato Kelana, the chief of Sungei Ujung, and the Dato Bandar, who controlled the middle part of Sungei Linggi, further to the south. The heavy influx of Chinese immigrants – who numbered about half the total population of Negeri Sembilan by the time of the first official census in 1891 – only had the effect of prolonging the feuds, since their secret societies, or triads, attempted to manipulate the situation to gain local influence.

The most significant figure to emerge from this period was **Yap Ah Loy**, a charismatic leader who helped orchestrate clan rivalry in a series of violent skirmishes, one of which resulted in the sacking of Sri Menanti. He later moved to the newly established tin-mining town of Kuala Lumpur, where he quickly became an influential figure (see p.81). In an attempt to control a situation that was rapidly sliding out of control, the British Governor Jervois installed Abu Bakar of Johor as overlord, a man not only respected by the Malays but who also appeared sympathetic to the colonists' aims. However, two prominent British officials, Frank Swettenham (later Resident at the time of KL's early meteoric expansion) and Frederick Weld, weren't convinced about Abu Bakar's loyalty and bypassed his authority with the use of local British officials. Learning from the mistakes in Perak, where the hurried appointment of a British advisor had caused local uproar, their approach was cautious. Eventually a treaty was signed in 1895, which narrowed the divide between the British government and the Minangkabaus that had been the cause of so much strife.

Seremban

An hour south of the capital, **SEREMBAN** is a bustling town. In the commercial centre, decorative Chinese shophouses sit by faceless concrete structures, while further out, imposing colonial mansions line the streets. However, by far the best reason to come to Seremban is to visit the **Taman Seni Budaya Negeri** (Tues, Wed, Sat & Sun 10am–6pm, Thurs 8.15am–1pm, Fri 10am–12.15pm & 2.45–6pm; free), the state's museum and cultural centre, 3km northwest of the centre, close to the North–South Highway. It's the best introduction that you could have to the principles of Minangkabau architecture. The new museum building is of traditional construction, and the grounds contain three original timber houses, reconstructed in the 1950s. The first of these, the **Istana Ampang Tinggi**, was built forty years before the palace at Sri Menanti (see p.287), passing through successive generations of royalty until 1930, after

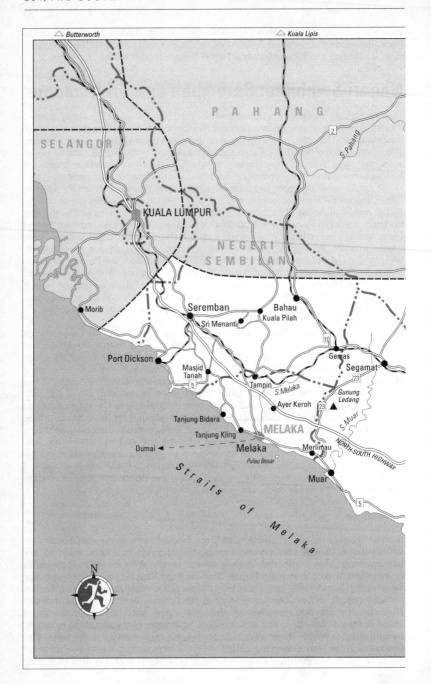

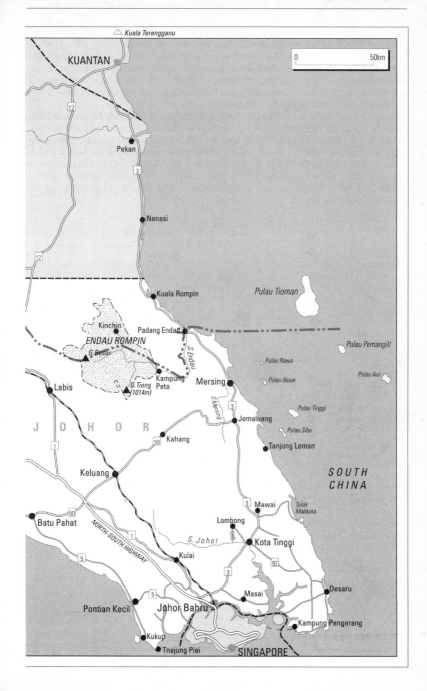

which it began to fall into disrepair. The interior of the verandah, used for entertaining male guests, displays a wealth of exuberant and intricate leaf carvings, with a pair of unusual heavy timber doors. The two other houses nearby are similar, though less elaborate, their gloomy interiors only relieved by shutters in the narrow front rooms. Inside the museum proper, the lower floor contains an exhibition of village handicrafts, as well as some moth-eaten stuffed animals; the old photographs are considerably more lively, though little of the commentary is in English.

North of the river from the bus and taxi stations, past the **Wesley Church** of 1920, is the business district, where most of the hotels, restaurants and banks are located, including the hulking Oriental Bank, with its Minangkabau inspired roof. East along Jalan Dato' Sheikh Ahmad, a right turn leads to the recreation ground, across which the nine pillars supporting the scalloped roof of the grey concrete **Masjid Negeri** come into view. Each pillar represents one of the nine states of the administration and is topped by a crescent and star, symbols of Muslim enlightenment. Beyond this lies the artificial **Lake Garden**, the focus of Seremban's parkland area.

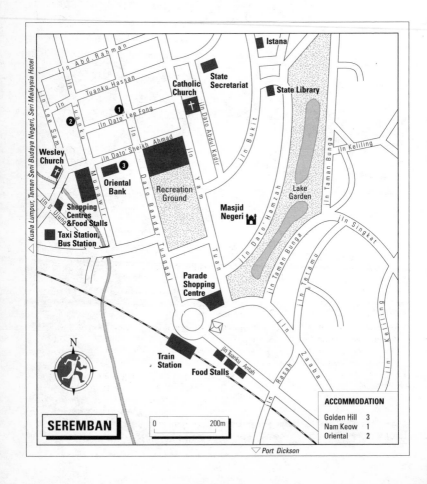

Head north along Jalan Dato' Hamzah and after a ten-minute walk you'll see the white stucco Neoclassical **State Library**, once the centre of colonial administration, with its graceful columns and portico. Past the black and gilt wrought-iron gates of the istana (closed to the public), and a left turn leads to the current **State Secretariat** which reflects the Minangkabau tradition. Its hillside position ensures that the layered, buffalo-horn roof is one of the first sights you see in town.

Practicalities

Seremban has regular train connections with Kuala Lumpur and express bus connections to both Melaka and KL. The **bus and taxi stations** are about five minutes' walk from the town across the river, while the **train station** is just to the south of the centre. You may want to stay in Seremban, though bear in mind that the town has a chronic shortage of decent, inexpensive **hotels** and many of the cheaper ones are brothels. There's no shortage of cafés in town, however and although none particularly recommend themselves, the *Bilal* at 100 Jalan Dato' Bandar Tunggal serves reliable Indian dishes. There are **food stalls** along Jalan Tuanku Munawir and close to the train station.

ACCOMMODATION

Golden Hill, 42 Jalan Dato' Sheikh Ahmad (☎06/763 5760). One of the better places, centrally located; double rooms have air-con. ①.

Oriental, 11 Jalan Tuanku Munawir (☎06/763 0119). Easily visible on your left as you walk up from the railway and bus stations. Its rooms are spartan and clean, but don't tempt you to linger. ②.

Nam Keow, 61–62 Jalan Dato' Bandar Tunggal (☎06/763 5578). More upmarket but definitely worth it, this spotless place is at the very bottom of it's price range. ④.

Seri Malaysia, Jalan Sungai Ujung (☎06/764 4181, fax 764 4179). If you're after more luxury this is the best bet, 1km away from the bus station on the road to the State Museum, with very good rooms, and breakfast included in the price. ⑤.

Sri Menanti

SRI MENANTI, 30km east of Seremban, was the royal capital of Negeri Sembilan, whose palaces – ancient and modern – are set in lush, mountainous landscape. The only reason to visit this little town is to seethe **Istana Lama**, a jewel of Minangkabau architecture. This timber palace, set in geometric gardens, was the seat of the Minangkabau rulers, whose migration to the Malay Peninsula began in the fifteenth century during the early years of the Melaka Sultanate. The sacking of Sri Menanti during the Sungei Ujong tin wars destroyed the original palace – this four-storey version was designed and built in 1902 by two Malay master craftsmen who, as the tradition dictates, used no nails or screws in its construction. The palace was used as a royal residence until 1931, with the first floor functioning as a reception area, the second as family quarters, and the third as the sultan's private apartments. The tower, once used as the treasury and royal archives, can only be reached by ladder from the sultan's private rooms and is not open to the public.

The forked projection at the apex of the central tower, known as "open scissors" is now seen very rarely, but is reproduced in the roof of the Muzium Negara in Kuala Lumpur (see p.97). The whole rectangular building is raised nearly 2m off the ground by 99 pillars, 26 of which have been carved in low-relief with complex foliated designs. The main doors and windows are plain, but a long external verandah is covered with a design of leaves and branches known as *awan larat*, or "driving clouds". The most elaborate decoration is above the front porch – a pair of fantastic creatures with lions' heads, horses' legs and long feathery tails – the style of which suggests that the craftsmen were Chinese.

THE MINANGKABAU

The **Minangkabau** people, whose cultural heartland is in mountainous western central Sumatra (Indonesia), established a community in Malaysia in the early fifteenth century. Their **origins** are somewhat sketchy since they had no written language until the arrival of Islam. Their own oral accounts trace their ancestry to Alexander the Great, while the *Sejarah Melayu* (Malay Annals) talk of a mysterious leader, Nila Pahlawan, who was pronounced king of the Palembang natives by the spittle of an ox, which had magically turned into a man. Oxen feature prominently, too, in the legend surrounding the origins of the name of the group. Their original home in Sumatra had been under attack from the Javanese, which led the native people to agree to a contest whereby the outcome of a battle fought between a tiger (representing the Javanese) and a buffalo (representing the locals) would determine who controlled the land. Against all the odds, the buffalo killed the tiger, and henceforth the inhabitants called themselves Minangkabau, meaning "the victorious buffalo".

In early times the Minangkabau were ruled in Sumatra by their own overlords or *rajas*, though political centralization never really rivalled the role of the strongly autonomous *nagari* (Sumatran for village). Each *nagari* consisted of numerous **matrilineal clans** (*suku*), each of which took the name of the mother and lived in the *adat* house, the ancestral home. The *adat* house was also in control of ancestral property which was passed down the maternal line. The *sumando* (husband) stayed in his wife's house at night but was a constituent member of his mother's house, where most of his day was spent. But although the idea that the house and clan name belonged to the woman remained uppermost, it was the *mamak* (mother's brother) who was the administrative figurehead, the authority for the proper distribution of ancestral property, and who took responsibility for the continued prosperity of the lineage. Political and ceremonial power was in the hands of men, with women dominating the domestic sphere.

While population growth and land shortage encouraged **migration**, it was the lack of ties to his wife's family, and his traditional role as an entrepreneur that facilitated the *sumando*'s wanderlust. The society encouraged a man's desire to further his fame, fortune and knowledge, and, when Islam became more established, this was achieved by religious studies under famous teachers or visits to Mecca. When and why the Minangkabaus initially emigrated to what is now **Negeri Sembilan** in Malaysia is uncertain, but – frequently called upon to supplement the armies of ambitious Malay princes and sultans – their history is closely bound up with that of Melaka and Johor.

Little is known of their interaction with the native population, although evidence of intermarriage with the region's predominant tribal group, the Sakai, indicates acceptance by the Malays of the matrilineal system. What *is* certain is that the Minangkabaus were a political force to be reckoned with. Their dominance in domestic affairs was aided by their reputation for supernatural powers, rumours of which were so widespread that the early eighteenth-century trader Alexander Hamilton noted, "Malays consider the Minangkabau to have the character of great sorcerers, who by their spells can tame wild tigers and make them carry them whither they order on their backs."

Although migration remained standard practice, after the mid-nineteenth century the drift was towards urban centres, and communal living in the *adat* house became relatively rare. This century, two important adaptations to the matrilineal system have been documented: the tendency for families from the various clans to migrate rather than just the husband; and a change in the hereditary customs, whereby individually earned property can be given to a son, becoming ancestral property only in the next generation. However, although certain matrilineal ties have weakened, most aspects of Minangkabau society have remained virtually unchanged. As a Minangkabau proverb says:

The old adat, ancient heritage,
Neither rots in the rain,
Nor cracks in the sun.

Inside, the Istana Lama is of little or no decorative interest. The palace now houses the lacklustre **Muzium Di Raja** (Tues, Wed, Sat & Sun 10am–12.45pm & 2–6pm, Thurs 8am–12.45pm, Fri 10am–12.15pm & 2.45–6pm; free) and the reconstructed state rooms bedecked in yellow (the royal colour) lack atmosphere. There are old costumes, ceremonial *krises*, golfing memorabilia and photographs of past sultans and British administrators, all of which fail to excite.

Reaching Sri Menanti is relatively straightforward. From Seremban, take a United **bus** for the 45-minute journey to Kuala Pilah. Either wait for an infrequent local bus to Sri Menanti, or take a shared taxi, a ten-minute ride costing no more than $4 per person. You'll be dropped at a dilapidated row of shops, not far from a small mosque, and walking past this you'll spot the Istana Lama. Don't be misled by the sign for the Istana Besar, the rather imposing current royal palace, topped by a startling blue roof.

The coastal route to Melaka

The rather dismal coast stretching south of the capital to Melaka is a major draw for KL weekenders, who are attracted by the populous resort of **Port Dickson** and turn a blind eye to its polluted sea. Things improve marginally the further south you go, in the smaller beach satellites of **Tanjung Bidara** and **Tanjung Kling**, though it's unlikely that you'll stay here too long given the lure of nearby Melaka. Regular bus connections with KL ensure ease of access to all points en route. The coastal road gets a little tortuous in places – but it's a more varied journey than travelling the monotonous highway.

Port Dickson

It's hard to see why **PORT DICKSON**, 34km southwest of Seremban, is so popular. The port town/beach resort itself is not much more than a few shops and banks. Port Dickson's beach, stretching as far as the Cape Richardo lighthouse, 16km to the south, is marred by passing oil tankers, sludgy brown sand, dishwater-grey sea and an enormous sewage pipe spilling out into the north of the bay. Yet it attracts a growing number of regular weekenders, to whom the town is affectionately known as PD. Whatever the reason, Port Dickson's hoteliers are rubbing their hands with glee. To cope with the increasing demand, new hotels and condominiums are constantly springing up along the length of the coastline – most developers have sensibly built swimming pools.

The best places to stay are strung out along Jalan Pantai, which runs south of Port Dickson, their locations marked out in milestones. Buses from KL stop at the bus station in the commercial part of town, but it's easy enough to hop on any Melaka-bound bus until you reach the hotel of your choice; buses from Melaka go down the coastal road before reaching the bus station, so you can get off at any time. Most chalets and hotels have their own **restaurants** but there are many others lining the road, of which the nicest is the Muslim *Pantai Ria*, near the seven-mile marker; it specializes in seafood and Chinese cuisine at around $8 a dish. **Food stalls** at the four- and five-mile markers offer everything from burgers to freshly caught fish.

Accommodation

Asrama Belia (☎ 06/64 72188). A comfortable place, affiliated to the IYHF, behind a row of shops and restaurants at the four-mile marker, with clean, newly renovated chalets and dorms – a wholesome environment. Dorms $8. ①–②.

Kong Ming (☎06/662 5683). At the five-mile marker, right by the beach, this is basic but bearable, about the least expensive hotel on this stretch. ②.

Ming Court Vista (☎06/662 5244). Located near the seven-mile marker, this is one of the longest-running upmarket resorts; it doesn't match up to the *Regency*. ⑥.

Moon Chalets (☎06/640 6944). At the seven-mile marker, this has small but plush chalets. The area has little shade. ④.

Regency (☎06/647 4090, fax 647 5016). PD's most upmarket hotel, located towards the beach. It is built in striking Minangkabau style and has facilities for watersports and tennis. ⑦.

Rotary Sunshine Camp (☎06/647 3798). The cheapest accommodation in PD, a cheerful turquoise- and yellow-painted complex of basic chalets on a hill at the third-mile marker. There are only dorm beds available here. ①.

Tanjung Bidara

The road south of Port Dickson follows the coast closely for about 20km before heading inland to a junction at the town of Masjid Tanah. The small beachside village of **TANJUNG BIDARA** is a short detour through lush paddy fields off the Port Dickson–Melaka road (Route 5; take bus #47 from Masjid Tanah) – the beach is much better than those at Port Dickson and Tanjung Kling (see below). There are two fine **places to stay**: the *Tanjung Bidara Beach Resort* (☎06/542990; ⑤), with pleasant rooms, family chalets and a pool, and the budget *Bidara Beach Lodge* (☎06/543340; ②), a delightful guesthouse a little further along.

Tanjung Kling and beyond

As route 5 heads south it becomes increasingly narrow and winding, though there's plenty to catch your eye in the small towns and kampungs en route. Around 18km from the turn-off to Tanjung Bidara, you'll reach the village and beach resort of **TANJUNG KLING** – "kling" now being a derogatory term for the Tamil immigrants who first populated this village. New developments are popping up all around this area, despite the fact that the dingy beach is less than inviting, and the community lacks facilities.

A right turn at the mosque, following the signpost to the *Malacca Club*, brings you to **Makam Hang Tuah**, the grave of the famous fifteenth-century warrior. It was formerly known locally only as *Makam Tua* or "Old Grave" in order to conceal its presence from the Portuguese who went about destroying all buildings connected with the Melaka Sultanate on their takeover in 1511.

Back on the main road, a string of small resorts begins, of which the most appealing is *Shah's Beach Resort* (☎06/315 3121, fax 315 2088; ⑤), whose intriguingly designed chalets incorporate elements of Portuguese architecture, and genuine antique furniture. The facilities include an open-air *atap*-roofed restaurant, tennis courts and a pool. Next door is the *Riviera Bay Resort* (☎06/315 1111, fax 315 3333; ⑧), an enormous complex with an arched entrance. The rooms are large and comfortable, there's a decent range of restaurants and, fortunately, a good pool, since the beach is appalling.

Route 5 heads southeast through Melaka's suburbs of stylish Peranakan mansions, passing the **Masjid Tranquerah** on the left about 2km out of town, another of the pagoda-like Melakan mosques dating from the eighteenth century, where Sultan Hussein, who ceded Singapore to Stamford Raffles in 1819, is buried.

Melaka and around

Happy is a nation that has no history.
Anon.

When Penang was known only for its oysters and Singapore was just a fishing village, **MELAKA** (formerly "Malacca") had already achieved worldwide fame. Under the aus-

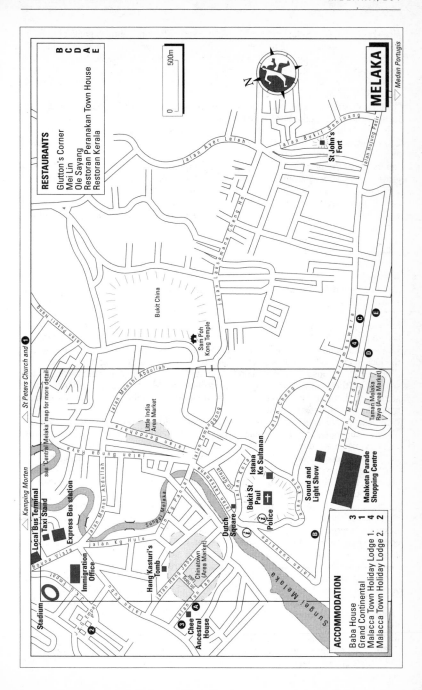

MELAKA

RESTAURANTS

Glutton's Corner   B
Mei Lin   C
Ole Sayang   D
Restoran Peranakan Town House   A
Restoran Kerala   E

ACCOMMODATION

Baba House   3
Grand Continental   1
Malacca Town Holiday Lodge 1.   4
Malacca Town Holiday Lodge 2.   2

pices of the Melaka Sultanate, founded in the early fifteenth century, political and cultural life flourished, helping to define what it means to be Malay. Yet beginning in 1511, there was a series of takeovers and botched administrations by the Portuguese, Dutch and British, causing the humiliating subjugation of the Malay people. But because of its cultural legacy, there's something about Melaka that smacks of over-preservation, all too easily apparent in the brick-red paint wash that covers everything in the so-called "historical centre". At its core, the **Dutch Square** sports a fake windmill and nineteenth-century fountain, bordering on pastiche.

For a more authentic encounter with the past, it's better to strike out into **Chinatown**, where the rich Baba-Nonya heritage is displayed in the opulent merchants' houses and elegant restaurants that line the narrow thoroughfares. There are reminders of the human costs of empire building in the many Christian churches and graveyards scattered around the town, where tombstones tell of whole families struck down by fever and of young men killed in battle. The **Portuguese Settlement** to the east of the centre has something of the decaying colonial heritage that typifies Melaka, while land reclamation in the new town area, **Taman Melaka Raya**, southeast of the centre, points to the urban regeneration that the city badly needs. Out of the centre, there are a couple of places of interest including the green-belt area of **Ayer Keroh**, 14km north of the city, and the beach resort at **Pulau Besar**.

A little history

The foundation of Melaka had its roots in the fourteenth century struggles between Java and the Thai kingdom of Ayuthaya for control of the Malay Peninsula. The *Sejarah Melayu* (Malay Annals) record that when the Sumatran prince Paramesvara from Palembang in the Srivijaya empire, could no longer tolerate subservience to Java, he fled to the island of Temasek (later Singapore), where he set himself up as ruler. The Javanese subsequently forced him to flee north to Bertam where he was welcomed by the local community. While his son, Iskandar Shah, was out hunting near modern-day Melaka Hill, a mouse deer turned on the pursuing hunting dogs, driving them into the sea. Taking this courageous act to be a good omen, Shah asked his father to build a new settlement there and in searching for a name for it, he remembered the melaka tree, which he had been sitting under.

Melaka rapidly became a cosmopolitan market town, **trading spices** from the Moluccas in the eastern Indonesian archipelago and textiles from Gujarat in northwest India. A levy exacted on all imported goods made it one of the wealthiest kingdoms in the world. Melaka's meteoric rise was initially assisted by its powerful neighbours, Ayuthaya and Java, who made good use of its trading facilities. But they soon had a serious rival, since Melaka started a campaign of **territorial expansion**. By the time of the reign of its last ruler, Sultan Mahmud Shah (1488–1530), Melaka's territory included the west coast of the Peninsula as far as Perak, the whole of Pahang, Singapore and most of east coast Sumatra. By the beginning of the sixteenth century, Melaka's population had increased to one hundred thousand, and it would not have been unusual to count as many as two thousand ships in its port. **Culturally**, too, Melaka was held to be supreme – its sophisticated language, dances and literature were all benchmarks in the Malay world. The establishment of a court structure (see p.298) defined the nature of the Melaka state and the role of the individuals within it, a philosophy which remained virtually unchanged until the nineteenth century. The linchpin of the state was the ruler, the sultan, who by virtue of his ancestry, which could be traced back to the mighty empire of Srivijaya, embodied the mystique which set Melaka apart from its rivals. With the adoption of **Islam** in the early fifteenth century, Melaka consolidated its influence. It was said that to become a Muslim was to enter the society of Melaka Malays.

But a sea change was occurring in Europe which was to end Melaka's supremacy. The **Portuguese** sought to establish links in Asia by dominating key ports in the region, and in 1511 Afonso de Albuquerque led the **conquest of Melaka**. Eight hundred officers were left to administer the new colony, and although subject to constant attack, the Portuguese – or "white Bengalis" as they were known by the Malays – maintained their hold on Melaka for the next 130 years, introducing Catholicism to the region through the efforts of **St Francis Xavier**, the "Apostle of the East". Little tangible evidence of the Portuguese remains in Melaka today – bar the Eurasian community to the east of town – a reflection of the fairly tenuous nature of their rule, which relied on the internal squabbles of local leaders to dissolve any threats to their position.

The formation of the Vereenigde Oostindische Compagnie (VOC), or **Dutch East India Company**, in 1602, spelled the end of the Portuguese. Having already founded Batavia (modern-day Jakarta), the VOC set its sights on Melaka, for the saying was, "Whoever controls Melaka has his hands on the throat of Venice". The ascendancy of Johor, an enemy of the Portuguese, gave the Dutch a natural ally, but although they made several attempts on Melaka from 1606 onwards, it wasn't until January 14, 1641, after a five-month siege, that they finally captured the city. While the Portuguese had tried to impose rule on the Malays, the Dutch sought to integrate them, finding them useful in matters of etiquette when negotiating with other Malay rulers. Chinese immigrants were drawn to the city in large numbers, often becoming more successful in business than their European rulers; many of the Chinese married Malay women, creating a new racial mix known as **Peranakan** or Baba-Nonya (see p.58). The Protestant Dutch made half-hearted attempts at religious conversion, including translating the Bible into Malay, but on the whole the attitude to the Catholic Melakans was tolerant. However, the settlement never really expanded in the way the VOC had hoped. High taxes drove merchants away to more profitable ports like the newly founded Penang, and the Dutch relied ever more on force to maintain their position in the Straits – which lost them the respect of their Malay subjects. A ditty put about by their British rivals at that time had it that: "In matters of commerce, the fault of the Dutch/Is offering too little and asking too much".

The superior maritime skills and commercial adroitness of the British East India Company (EIC) provided serious competition for the control of Melaka. Weakened by French threats on their posts in the Indies, the Dutch were not prepared to put up a fight and handed Melaka over to the British on August 15, 1795, initially on the understanding that the EIC was to act as a caretaker administration until such a time as the Dutch were able to resume control. For a while Melaka flew two flags and little seemed to have changed: the language, the legal system and even some of the officials remained the same as before. But the EIC was determined upon the supremacy of Penang, and against the advice of the resident, **William Farquhar**, ordered the destruction of Melaka's magnificent fort to deter future settlers. In fact, the whole population of Melaka would have been forcibly moved to Penang had it not been for Thomas Stamford Raffles, convalescing there at the time, who managed to impress upon the London office the impracticality – not to mention the cruelty – of such a measure.

Despite the liberalizing of trade by Farquhar, the colony continued to decline, and with the establishment of the free-trade port of Singapore in 1819, looked set to disintegrate. British administrators – just thirty in number, rising slowly to around 330 by 1931 – attempted to revitalize Melaka, introducing progressive agricultural and mining concerns; while the **Chinese** continued to flock to the town, taking over former Dutch mansions. However, investment in new hospitals, schools and a railway did little to improve Melaka's spiralling deficit and it wasn't until a Chinese entrepreneur, Tan Chey Yan, began to plant **rubber**, that Melaka's problems were alleviated. The industry boomed during the early years of the twentieth century, but after World War I, even that commodity faced mixed fortunes. When the **Japanese occupied Melaka** in 1942, they found a town exhausted by the interwar depression.

Modern-day developments, such as the **land reclamation** in Taman Melaka Raya and the reorganization of the chaotic road network, are still working to reverse Melaka's long-term decline. Whatever damage was wrought during its centuries of colonial mismanagement, nothing can take away the enduring influence of Melaka's creation of a Malay language, court system and royal lineage – a powerful legacy established in a mere hundred years that was to permanently affect development in the Peninsula.

Arrival, information and city transport

Both bus stations are located on the northern outskirts of the city, off Jalan Hang Tuah. The **local bus station** operates services to most destinations within the conurbation, and to Singapore. The chaotic **express bus station** is beyond the **taxi station**, a block to the south, in a tiny square by the river. From either, it's just a ten-minute walk to the town centre.

Many people arrive by **ferry** on the four-hour daily service from Dumai in Sumatra, which docks at the Shah Bandar jetty on Jalan Merdeka, within easy walking distance of both the historical centre and the budget hostel area. Melaka's **airport**, Batu Berendam, is 9km north of the city and handles Pelangi Air services from Singapore, Ipoh, Kuantan, Langkawi, Tioman and Pekan Baru in Sumatra. Buses from the airport into the centre are irregular, so it's best to take a taxi (around $10). There's no **train station** in Melaka itself, the nearest being at Tampin, 38km away; buses from Tampin drop you at the local bus station.

The **Tourist Information Centre** is on Jalan Kota (Mon–Thurs & Sat 8.45am–5pm, Fri 8.45am–12.15pm & 2.45–5pm, Sun 9am–5pm; ☎06/283 6538), 400m from the Shah Bandar jetty. The information board outside displays the times of the river trips to Kampung Morten (see p.303). English-language papers give details on events in the city.

LEAVING MELAKA

Airport

Batu Berendam Airport is 9km from the city centre, and caters only for small aircraft. Pelangi Air (☎06/282 2648) runs a service to both Singapore ($150 one-way) and Ipoh ($120 one-way) from Monday to Saturday, and there are Tuesday and Saturday flights to Pekan Baru ($145) and Medan ($258), both in Sumatra. For tickets contact MAS, on the first floor of the *City Bayview Hotel*, Jalan Bendahara (☎06/283 5722).

Buses

Melaka runs buses to all points on the Peninsula. There are frequent departures from the express bus station to KL, Ipoh, Butterworth and Alor Setar, while most express services to Singapore leave from the local bus station. There's rarely any need to book in advance; just turn up before departure and buy a ticket from one of the booths in the bus station.

Ferries

Two companies combine to offer a daily service to Dumai in Sumatra (4hr; $80 one-way): Madai Shipping at 321a Jalan Tun Ali (☎06/284 0671), near the bus station, and Tunas Rupat at 17a Jalan Merdeka (☎06/283 2506).

Trains

The nearest train station is in Tampin (☎06/411 1034), 38km north of the city. The Peninsular Line is a regular luxury train service that runs between Singapore and Tampin (for Melaka) – see p.37 for details. There are regular buses to Tampin from the local bus station.

City transport

Most of the places of interest are located within the compact historical centre, and are best visited **on foot**. For longer journeys, **taxis or trishaws** are the best bet, both costing roughly the same (though trishaw drivers are more difficult to negotiate with). A trip from the bus station to the centre costs around $4. A sightseeing tour by trishaw, covering all the major sights including Medan Portugis, costs from $20 per hour for two people. You should be able to get a trishaw around the Dutch Square and outside the Mhkota Parade Shopping Centre. Taxis are quite hard to find on the street, but you can always get one from the taxi station.

The **town bus service** has several useful routes for visitors, departing the local bus station: #17 runs to Taman Melaka Raya and Medan Portugis, and #19 out to Ayer Keroh (50 sen–$1.20). Many of the streets are very narrow and the one-way system is awkward so **drivers** should park their cars at the first possible opportunity and get around the city by bus, trishaw or taxi. **Car rental** outlets are given in "Listings" on p.307.

Accommodation

Melaka has a huge selection of **hotels**, although prices are a little higher than in other Malaysian towns. Most in the lower price bracket are, needless to say, located in the noisiest areas, around the bus stations or main shopping streets. Standards are generally high though, compared to KL or Georgetown. In the Taman Melaka Raya area there's a rapidly growing number of budget **hostels**, all offering broadly the same facilities; touts often wait at the local bus station. Town bus #17 from the local bus station takes you there, a taxi or trishaw costs around $5. All the hotels and hostels below are marked on the Central Melaka map.

Baba House, 125 Jalan Tun Tan Cheng Lock (☎06/281 1216, fax 281 1217). These beautifully restored Peranakan houses have been turned into an atmospheric hotel, although the lobby area is better than the rooms themselves. ④.

Chong Hoe, (☎06/282 6102) 26 Jalan Tokong Emas. One of the few hotels in Chinatown offering standard rooms with air-con, but in a noisy location opposite the mosque. ①–②.

Eastern Heritage, 8 Jalan Bukit China (☎06/283 3026). One of the best budget hostels in Melaka, set in an imaginatively decorated house that makes the best of its original architectural features. The dorms and rooms are spotless and there are nice touches such as a plunge pool and a batik workshop. Dorms $6. ①.

Grand Continental, 20 Jalan Tun Sri Lanang (☎06/284 0048, fax 284 8125). Standard hotel that is very reasonably priced. Its facilities include a pool and coffee house. ⑥.

Heeren House, 1 Jalan Tun Tan Cheng Lock (☎06/281 4241, fax 281 4239). An ideal location in Chinatown and tasteful rooms, some with four-poster beds, makes this the best choice for a small upmarket hotel. Prices, which include breakfast, are slightly higher at weekends. ⑤.

Majestic, 188 Jalan Bunga Raya (☎06/282 2367). A fading colonial hotel, with musty air-con rooms, antediluvian bathrooms and Raj-like service in the bar and restaurant. ②.

Malacca, 27a Jalan Munshi Abdullah (☎06/282 2252). A noisy, basic hotel close to the bus station, housed in an elegant old building. ②.

Malacca Town Holiday Lodge, 148b Taman Melaka Raya (☎06/284 8830). The original guesthouse run by the Lee family, who now have another closer to the bus station. Friendly place, but a bit of a walk from the main sights. ①.

Malacca Town Holiday Lodge 2, 52a Kampong Empat (☎06/284 6905). Occupying the three floors of the Wine and Spirit Association building, this spotless hostel's rooms are all named after famous brands of liquor. Apart from being in a quieter area, there's some antique Chinese furniture to add to the atmosphere, plus bicycle rental and kitchen facilities. ①.

May Chiang, 59 Jalan Munshi Abdullah (☎06/282 2101). Modest hotel with small but very clean rooms that are a delight; the double glazing helps, too. Well worth the money. ③.

Renaissance Melaka, Jalan Bendahara (☎06/284 8888, fax 284 9269). The town's major luxury hotel, with an imposing lobby complete with huge chandeliers, and elegant, well-furnished rooms. ⑥.

Robin's Nest, 205b Taman Melaka Raya (☎06/282 9142). This friendly, family-run hostel has small rooms but two pleasant lounges, video, hot showers and kitchen facilities. Dorms $7. ①.

Sunny's Inn, 270a Taman Melaka Raya (☎06/283 7990). A clean and homely place with hot showers, car, bicycle and motorbike rental and lots of information on local attractions. ①.

Traveller's Lodge, 214b Taman Melaka Raya (☎06/281 4793). Small and well-kept hostel, which has cable TV, a floor-cushioned lounge and roof garden. Dorms $7. ①.

The City

The centre of Melaka is split in two by the murky **Sungei Melaka**, the western bank of which is occupied by **Chinatown** and, 700m to the north, **Kampung Morten**, a small collection of stilted houses. On the eastern side of the river lies the colonial core – the main area of interest – with **Bukit St Paul** at its centre, encircled by Jalan Kota. Southeast of here is a section of reclaimed land known as **Taman Melaka Raya**, a new town that is home to a giant shopping centre and most of the budget hotels, restaurants and bars. There are a few sights further east of the centre: **Medan Portugis** (Portuguese Square), **St John's Fort** and **Bukit China**, the Chinese community's ancestral burial ground. They're all a little too far flung to be comfortably covered on foot – but town bus #17 runs regularly to Medan Portugis 3km from town, from where St John's Fort is only about a kilometre's walk. Take a taxi or trishaw from there to Bukit China (around $6).

Central Melaka's historic buildings are denoted as such by being painted a uniform brick-red. Intended to symbolize the red laterite from which many of Melaka's original structures were constructed, this practice actually destroys the individual character of each building. That said, it has at least meant that the area has been maintained. At a push you could get around the colonial core in a day, although to take things at a more leisurely pace and see Chinatown and the outskirts, it's better to spend three days in Melaka. Many visitors find that the city that grows on them the longer they stay.

The Istana and around

The **Istana Ke Sultanan** (daily 9am–6pm; closed Fri 12.15pm–2.45pm; $2) on Jalan Kota is not only in the geographical centre of town but stands at the very centre of Malaysian history. This imposing dark timber palace, in neatly manicured gardens, is a contemporary reconstruction of the original fifteenth-century istana based on a description in the *Sejarah Melayu*. In the best Malay architectural tradition, its multi-layered and sharply sloping roofs contain no nails. It was here that the administrative duties of the state were carried out, and also where the sultan resided when in the city – for the most part he lived further upriver at Bertam, safe from possible attacks on Melaka. Inside, after you've removed your shoes to ascend the wide staircase to the verandahed first floor, spend some time in the cultural museum which houses a rather tired display of life-sized re-creations of scenes from Malay court life, including the epic duel of Melaka's most famous warriors, Hang Tuah and Hang Jebat (see box), as well as costumes and local crafts. The building alone though is worth the entrance fee.

At the time of their conquest of Melaka, the Portuguese used the forced labour of 1500 slaves to construct the mighty **A Famosa** fort. All that is left today is a single gate, the crumbling whitewashed **Porta de Santiago**, just to the right as you leave the palace museum. The hillside site was chosen not only for its strategic position but also because it was where the Sultan's istana was located – its replacement by the Portuguese stronghold a firm reminder of who was now in charge. Square in plan with walls nearly 3m thick, its most striking feature was the keep in the northwestern corner, which loomed 40m and four storeys high over the rest of the garrison. This was no mean feat of engineering, even if the design of the fort as a whole was considered old-fashioned by contemporary European observers. When the Dutch East India Company

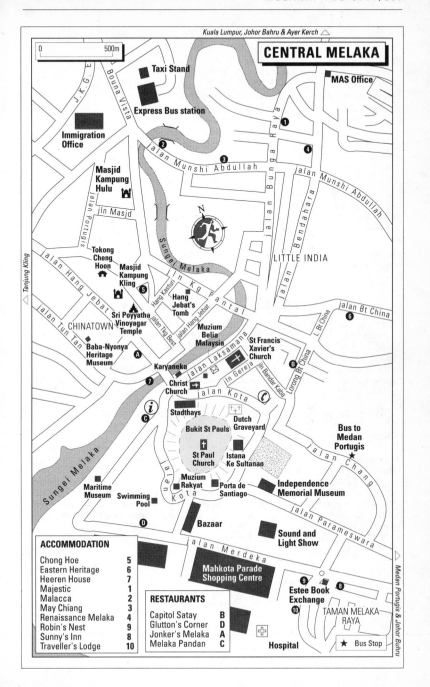

Kuala Lumpur, Johor Bahru & Ayer Kerch

CENTRAL MELAKA

MAS Office

0 — 500m

Taxi Stand

Express Bus station

Immigration Office

Jalan Munshi Abdullah

Masjid Kampung Hulu

Jalan Bunga Raya

Jalan Munshi Abdullah

Jalan Bendahara

Jln Masjid

Jalan Portugis

LITTLE INDIA

N

Tokong Cheng Hoon

Sungei Melaka

Masjid Kampung Kling

Jln Kg Pantal

Hang Jebat's Tomb

Jalan Bt China

Jalan Hang Jebat

Sri Poyyatha Vinoyagar Temple

Muzium Belia Malaysia

St Francis Xavier's Church

L Bt China

Jalan Hang Jebat

CHINATOWN

Jalan Tun Tan

Baba-Nyonya Heritage Museum

Jalan Laksamana

Jln Bandar Kaba

Karyaneka

Jln Gereja

Christ Church

Jalan Kota

Stadthays

Dutch Graveyard

Bukit St Pauls

Bus to Medan Portugis

St Paul Church

Istana Ke Sultanan

Maritime Museum

Muzium Rakyat

Porta de Santiago

Independence Memorial Museum

Jalan Chang

Swimming Pool

Jalan Kota

Jalan Parameswara

Bazaar

Sound and Light Show

Jalan Merdeka

Mahkota Parade Shopping Centre

Estee Book Exchange

TAMAN MELAKA RAYA

Hospital

★ Bus Stop

Medan Portugis & Johor Buhru

ACCOMMODATION

Chong Hoe	5
Eastern Heritage	6
Heeren House	7
Majestic	1
Malacca	2
May Chiang	3
Renaissance Melaka	4
Robin's Nest	9
Sunny's Inn	8
Traveller's Lodge	10

RESTAURANTS

Capitol Satay	B
Glutton's Corner	D
Jonker's Melaka	A
Melaka Pandan	C

defeated the Portuguese in 1641, it used the fort as its headquarters, later modifying it and adding the company crest and the date 1670 to the Porta de Santiago – features which are just about distinguishable today.

The fort stood steadfast for 296 years and probably would have survived, were it not for the arrival of the British in 1795. With their decision to relocate to Penang, orders were given in 1807 to destroy the fort in case it was later used against them. The task of demolition fell to Resident William Farquhar, who reluctantly set about the task with gangs of labourers armed with spades and pickaxes. Failing to make an impression on its solid bulk, he resorted to gunpowder, blowing sky-high pieces "as large as elephants and even some as large as houses". Sultan Munshi Abdullah said that the fort "was the pride of Melaka and after its destruction the place lost its glory, like a woman bereaved of her husband, the lustre gone from her face".

Turning your back on the gate, and facing **Padang Pahlawan** (Warrior's Field), a large open green that forms the centre of the downtown area, you'll see the **Independence Memorial Museum** (Tues–Thurs, Sat & Sun 9am–6pm, Fri 9am–noon & 3–6pm; free). Built in 1912, this elegant mansion of classic white stucco with two golden onion domes on either side of its portico, formerly housed the colonial **Malacca Club**, whose most famous guest was the novelist Somerset Maugham. This is where the author was told the story which was the basis of *Footprints in the Jungle*, in which both the Club and Melaka itself (which he calls Tanah Merah) feature

MALAY COURT STRUCTURES

One of the most outstanding achievements of the Melaka Sultanate was to create a **court structure**, setting a pattern of government that was to last for the next five hundred years, and whose prominent figures are still reflected in the street names of most towns in the country.

At the top of the tree was the **sultan**, who could trace his ancestry back to the revered leaders of Srivijaya. Far from being an autocratic tyrant, a form of social contract evolved whereby the ruler could expect undying loyalty from his subjects in return for a fair and wise dispensation of justice – the crux of the confrontation between Hang Juah and Hang Tebat. Sultans were not remote ceremonial figures: many supervised the planting of new crops, for instance, or wandered freely in the streets among the people, a style that may explain the relative humility of the palaces they occupied.

Below the ruler was a clutch of **ministers**, who undertook the day-to-day administration of government. The most important of these was the **Bendahara**, who dealt with disputes both among traders and the Malays themselves. In effect, he was the public face of the regime, wielding a great deal of power, backed by his closest subordinate, the **Penghulu Bendahari**, who supervised the *syahbandars* (harbour masters) and the sultan's domestic staff. Potential Bendaharas were trained in the office of the **Temenggung**, who was responsible for law and order, working in close partnership with the **Laksamana**, the military commander whose strongest arm was the navy.

Wide-ranging consultation regarding new measures took place in a **council of nobles**, who had earned their titles either through land ownership or from blood ties with royalty. However, given the consensual nature of politics between men of rank and power, it became necessary to emphasize the position of the ruler. The colour yellow was only allowed to be used by royalty and no one but the ruler could wear gold – unless it was a royal gift. In addition, commoners could not have pillars or enclosed verandahs in their houses or windows and reception rooms in their boats. Nevertheless, despite these methods of distinction, threats to the throne were commonplace – particularly from the Bendahara. Although little is known of the **common people** of Melaka, it is certain that they had no part in the decision-making process; though the *Sejarah Melayu* nevertheless speaks of them with some respect: "Subjects are like roots and the ruler is like the tree; without roots the tree cannot stand upright."

prominently. The museum depicts the fascinating events surrounding the lead up to independence in 1957, but unfortunately it's poorly laid out, and the sequence is hard to follow.

Bukit St Paul

Walking back through the Porta de Santiago, either climb the steps behind, past the trinket and picture sellers, up to **Bukit St Paul** (see below), or skirt round the base of the hill to the left along Jalan Kota, where Melaka's newest museums are situated. The **Muzium Rakyat**, or People's Museum (daily 9am–6pm; Fri closed 12.15pm–2.45pm; $2), is the first, and houses several displays. On the ground and first floors are exhibits showing the development and successes of Melaka during the last decade – fine if you're into housing policy and the structure of local government. On the third floor is the much more interesting – and at times gruesome – **Museum of Enduring Beauty**. Taking as its theme the word "endure" in the sense of to suffer, the exhibits show how people have always sought to alter their appearance, no matter how painful it might be. Head deformation, dental mutilations, tattooing, scarification and foot-binding are just some of the beauty processes on display. For some light relief, the top floor displays **kites** from Malaysia and around the world.

There have long been plans to establish an **Islamic and Martial Arts Museum** in a renovated Dutch building on Jalan Kota, though as yet the plans haven't come to anything. Near the proposed site is a steep set of steps which is the alternative route up to St Paul's Church on the summit of Bukit St Paul.

The shell of **St Paul's Church** – roofless, desolate and smothered in ferns – has been a ruin for almost as long as it was a functioning church. Constructed in 1521 by the Portuguese, who named it "Our Lady of the Mount", the church was visited by the Jesuit missionary **St Francis Xavier** between 1545 and 1552, and on his death in 1553 his body was brought here for burial – a brass plaque on the south wall of the chancel marks the spot where he was laid. A grisly story surrounds the exhumation of the saint's body in 1554 – allegedly showing very few signs of decay after nine months of burial – for its transferral to its final resting place in Goa in India. In response to a request for canonization, the Vatican demanded the right arm from the body which, when severed, appeared to drip blood. A related tale concerns the marble statue of St Francis that has stood in front of the church since 1952. On the morning following its consecration ceremony, a large casuarina tree was found to have fallen on the statue, severing the right arm.

The Dutch Calvinists changed the denomination of the church when they took over in 1641, renaming it St Paul's Church, and it remained in use for a further 112 years until the construction of Christ Church at the foot of the hill (see below). The British found St Paul's more useful for military than for religious purposes, storing their gunpowder here during successive wars, and building the lighthouse that guards the church's entrance. The tombstones that lie against the interior walls, together with those further down the hill in the **graveyard** itself, are worth studying. As the only major port in the Straits, many visitors were buried here, including Bishop Peter of Japan, who was a missionary in Melaka in 1598, as well as large numbers of Portuguese, Dutch and British notables, whose epitaphs have long been partly obscured by lichen. Note the tomb of the Velge family, in the graveyard on the slopes below, five members of which died within twenty days of each other during the diphtheria epidemic of 1756.

The Dutch Square and around

A winding path beside St Paul's Church brings you down into the so-called **Dutch Square**, one of the oldest surviving parts of Melaka, although two of its main features date from much later times. The Victorian marble fountain was erected in 1904 to commemorate Queen Victoria's Diamond Jubilee, the clock tower in 1886 in honour of Tan Beng Swee, a rich Chinese merchant.

Presiding over the entire south side of the square is the sturdy **Stadthuys**, now housing the **Museum of Ethnography** (daily 9am–6pm; closed Fri 12.15pm–2.45pm; $2). The simple, robust structure – more accurately a collection of buildings dating from between 1660 and 1700 – was used as a town hall throughout the whole period of Dutch and British administration. Although the long wing of warehouses projecting to the east is the oldest of the buildings here, recent renovations revealed remains of a Portuguese well and drainage system, suggesting that this was not the first development on the site. The wide, monumental, interior staircases, together with the high windows that run the length of the Stadthuys, are typical of seventeenth-century Dutch municipal buildings, though they are less suited to the tropical climate than they are to European winters. Look out of the back windows onto the whitewashed, mould-encrusted houses that line the courtyard and you could be in a Vermeer scene. The museum itself displays an array of Malay and Chinese ceramics and weaponry; the reconstruction of a seventeenth-century Dutch dining room is an exception. The rooms upstairs have endless paintings giving a blow-by-blow account of Melakan history, and old photographs showing how little the town has changed over the last hundred years.

Turn to the right as you leave the Stadthuys and you can't miss **Christ Church** (Thurs–Tues 9am–5pm; free), also facing the fountain. Built in 1753 to commemorate the centenary of the Dutch occupation of Melaka, its simple design, with neither aisles nor chancel, is typically Dutch – the porch and vestry were nineteenth-century afterthoughts. The cool, whitewashed interior has decorative fanlights high up on the walls; the roof has heavy timber beams, each cut from a single tree, and there are elaborate, two-hundred-year-old hand-carved pews. The plaques on the walls tell a sorry tale of early deaths by epidemics, and a wooden plaque to the rear of the western wall of the church commemorates local planters who were killed in World War II. A small detour down the lane on the left of the church, forking right at the old Courthouse to skirt round the foot of Bukit St Paul, leads to the overgrown remains of the **Dutch Graveyard**. This was first used in the late seventeenth century, when the VOC was still in control, hence the name, though British graves easily outnumber those of their predecessors. The tall column towards the centre of the tiny cemetery is a memorial to two of the many officers killed in the Naning War in 1831, a costly attempt to include the Naning region as part of Melaka's territory under the new Straits Settlements.

North to St Peter's Church

Back at Christ Church, moving quickly past the **Muzium Belia Malaysia** (daily 9am–6pm; closed Fri 12.30pm–2.45pm; $1) – replete with pictures of smiling, wholesome youths shaking hands with Dr Mahathir – Jalan Laksamana leads north towards **St Francis Xavier's Church**, a twin-towered nineteenth-century neo-Gothic structure. Further up from here, skirting the busy junction with Jalan Temenggong and taking Jalan Bendahara directly ahead, you're in the centre of Melaka's tumbledown **Little India**, a rather desultory line of incense and saree shops, interspersed with a few eating houses. After about five minutes' walk, you'll come to a sizeable crossroads with Jalan Munshi Abdullah, beyond which is **St Peter's Church** set back from the road on the right. The oldest Roman Catholic church in Malaysia, it was built in 1710 by a Dutch convert as a gift to the Portuguese Catholics, and has an unusual barrel-vaulted ceiling. The church really comes into its own at Easter as the centre of the Catholic community's celebrations.

The river and docks

If you feel like a rest from pavement pounding, take a **boat trip** up Sungei Melaka, leaving from the small jetty behind the Tourist Information Centre (hourly, depending on the tide, 10am–2pm; $7) – buy your tickets at the office, or on the boat itself. The 45-minute trip takes you past "Little Amsterdam", the old Dutch quarter of red-roofed *godowns*, which back directly onto the water. Look out for the slothful monitor lizards that hang out on either side of the bank, soaking up the sun, and the local fisherman who line the route, mending boats and nets. The boat turns round without stopping at Kampung Morten (see p.303), opposite which, on the right bank, you can just make out a few columns and a crumbling aisle poking out from beneath the undergrowth, all that remains of the late-sixteenth-century Portuguese church of St Lawrence. On the return journey, you're taken beyond the jetty to the **docks**, crowded with low-slung Sumatran boats, heavy wooden craft that are still sailed without the aid of a compass or charts, bringing in charcoal and timber which they trade for rice. The best time to catch the activity at the docks is around 4.30pm, when the multicoloured fishing boats leave for the night's work. From here, you can also see the new **Maritime Museum** (daily 9am–9pm; closed Fri 12.15pm–2.45pm; $2) on the quayside off Jalan Merdeka, housed in a towering replica of the Portuguese cargo ship, the *Flor De La Mar*, which sank in Melaka's harbour in the sixteenth century. Lots of model ships and paintings, inside the hull of the ship, chart Melaka's maritime history from the time of the Malay Sultanate to the arrival of the British in the eighteenth century. Across the road, another section of the museum houses some of the recovered items from the wreck of the *Diana*, which sunk in the Straits of Melaka while on route to Madras in 1817. The salvage operation began in 1993 and eventually yielded eighteen tons of chinaware. This building also has a drab display about the Malaysian navy.

Chinatown

Melaka owed a great deal of its nineteenth-century economic recovery to its Chinese community: Tan Chey Yan first planted rubber here, and one Tan Kim Seng established an early steamer company, which later became the basis of the great Straits Steam Ship Company, providing regular communication between different parts of the colony. Most of these early entrepreneurs settled in what became known as **Chinatown**, across Sungei Melaka from the colonial district. Turn left after the bridge by the Tourist Information Centre, then first right to follow the one-way system, and you'll come to **Jalan Tun Tan Cheng Lock**, fondly known as "Millionaires Row". The elegant townhouses that line the narrow road are the ancestral homes of the **Baba-Nonya** community (see box below), descendants of the original Chinese pioneers who married local Malay women – it is said that Chinese women of high class were reluctant to emigrate. The wealthiest and most successful built long, narrow-fronted houses, and minimized the "window tax" by incorporating several internal courtyards, also designed for ventilation and the collection of rainwater.

At nos. 48–50, the **Baba-Nyonya Heritage Museum** (daily 10am–12.30pm & 2-4.30pm; $7), is an amalgam of three adjacent houses belonging to one family, and an excellent example of the Chinese Palladian style. Typically connected by a common covered footway, decorated with hand-painted tiles, each front entrance has an outer swing door of elaborately carved teak, while a heavier internal door provides extra security at night. Two red lanterns, one bearing the household name, the other with messages of good luck, hang either side of the doorway, framed by heavy Greco-Roman columns. But the upper level of the building is the most eye-catching: a canopy of Chinese tiles over the porch, frames the shuttered windows – almost Venetian in character – whose glass is protected by intricate wrought-iron grilles, with eaves and fascias covered in painted floral designs. Inside, the homes are filled with gold-leaf fittings, blackwood furniture inlaid with mother-of-pearl, delicately carved lacquer screens and Victorian chandeliers. The 45-minute tour is informative.

Further up the road, at no. 107, the **Restoran Peranakan Town House** is another former mansion that is now a restaurant specializing in Nonya cuisine (see "Eating", p.306). Beyond, at no. 117, you can't fail to notice the **Chee Ancestral House**, an imperious Dutch building of pale green stucco topped by a gold dome, and home to one of Melaka's wealthiest families, who made their fortune from tapioca and rubber.

The parallel Jalan Hang Jebat – formerly named "Jonkers Street" or "Junk Street" – is Melaka's **antiques** centre (see "Shopping", p.306) and it's worth a wander even if you don't intend to buy. Crammed between the Chinese temples and shophouses, is the small, whitewashed tomb of **Hang Kasturi**, one of the "Five Companions" (see box on p.304). Turning into Jalan Hang Lekiu (still signposted as Fourth Cross Street), and then into Jalan Tokong Emas, you come to **Masjid Kampung Kling**, dating back to 1748, and displaying an unusual blend of styles. The minaret looks like a pagoda, there are English and Portuguese glazed tiles, and a Victorian chandelier hangs over a pulpit carved with Hindu and Chinese designs. Next door, the Hindu **Sri Pogyatha Vinoyagar Temple** also has a minaret, decorated with red cows, but its gloomy interior is disappointing.

The nearby **Tokong Cheng Hoon**, the "Merciful Cloud Temple", back over the junction with Jalan Hang Lekiu, is reputed to be the oldest Chinese temple in the country – though several others would dispute the title. Dedicated to the Goddess of Mercy, the main prayer hall's heavy saddled roof and oppressive dark timber beams are reminiscent of its counterpart in Georgetown. The temple authorities act as the trustees for Bukit China, the ancestral burial ground to the northeast of town (see "Bukit China" below). Smaller chambers devoted to ancestor worship are filled with small tablets bearing a photograph of the deceased and strewn with wads of fake money and papier-mâché models of luxury items, symbolizing creature comforts for the dead.

From the temple, a right turn into Jalan Portugis and then a second right brings you to **Masjid Kampung Hulu**, thought to be the oldest mosque in Malaysia. Constructed around 1728 in typical Melakan style, it's a solid-looking structure, surmounted by a bell-shaped roof with green Chinese tiles and, again, with more than a hint of pagoda in its minaret. Such architecture has its origins in Sumatra, perhaps brought over by the Minangkabaus who settled in nearby Negeri Sembilan.

From here, an alternative route back to the centre of town is to walk to the end of the road, turning right into Jalan Kampung Hulu as it follows the river and merges into

---

THE BABA-NONYAS

Tales of Melaka's burgeoning success brought vast numbers of merchants and entrepreneurs to its shores, eager to benefit from the city's status and wealth. The Chinese, in particular, came to the Malay Peninsula in droves, to escape Manchu rule – a trend that began in the sixteenth century, but continued well into the nineteenth. Many Chinese married Malay women; descendants of these marriages were known as **Peranakan** or "Straits-born Chinese". While their European counterparts were content to while away their time until retirement, when they could return home, the expatriate Chinese merchants had no such option and so became the principal wealth-generators of the thriving city. The **Babas** (male Sino-Malays) were unashamed of flaunting their new-found prosperity in the lavish townhouses which they appropriated from the Dutch and transformed into veritable palaces. They filled their houses with Italian marble, mother-of-pearl inlay blackwood furniture, hand-painted tiles and Victorian lamps. The women, known as **Nonyas** (sometimes spelt Nyonya), held sway in the domestic realm and were responsible for Peranakan society's most lasting legacy – the **cuisine**. Taking the best of both Malay and Chinese traditions, dishes rely heavily on sour sauces and coconut milk. The social etiquette of eating is Malay – using fingers, not chopsticks.

Jalan Kampung Pantai. At the junction with Jalan Hang Kasturi, a couple of minutes further on, you can pause for a moment at **Hang Jebat's Tomb**, another tiny mausoleum to one of the great warriors of the Golden Age.

Kampung Morten
The village of **Kampung Morten**, named after the British District Officer who donated $10,000 to buy the land, is a surprising find in the heart of the city. It's easiest to explore this community on foot: take the footbridge down a small path off Jalan Bunga Raya, one of the principal roads leading north out of town. The wooden stilted houses here are distinctively Melakan, with their long, rectangular living rooms and kitchens, and narrow verandahs approached by ornamental steps. On the left as you cross the footbridge the **Villa Sentosa** (daily 9am–5pm; voluntary donation), with its kampung doll's house and mini lighthouse, acts as a beacon for disorientated visitors. The warm and welcoming family will gladly show you artefacts and heirlooms handed down by the old patriarch, Tuan Haji Hashim Hadi Abdul Ghani, who died at the age of 98.

Medan Portugis and St John's Fort
The road east of Taman Melaka Raya leads, after about 3km, to Melaka's Portuguese Settlement; turn right into Jalan Albuquerque, clearly signposted off the main road, and you enter its heart. The government was prompted by increasing levels of poverty and the depletion of the population (barely any higher than the two thousand recorded in the first census in 1871) to establish this village in 1933, on the historic site of their original community. Today you're likely to recognize the descendants of the original Portuguese settlers only by hearing their language which is **Kristao**, a unique blend of Malay and old Portuguese, or seeing their surnames – Fernandez, Rodriguez and Dominguez all feature as street names.

Although there's no longer anything in the domestic architecture to indicate the heritage of the inhabitants, the **Medan Portugis** (Portuguese Square), at the end of the road, is European to the hilt, and you could be forgiven for thinking that its whitewashed edifice, worn by the salty winds, was a remnant from colonial times. Progressing through the archway, the souvenir shop and tourist-orientated restaurants surrounding the central courtyard soon make it clear that this is a purpose-built "relic", dating only from 1985. Having said that, the square is a good place for a quiet beer at sunset, cooled by the sea breeze, and the local restaurateurs make an effort to conjure up a Portuguese atmosphere, though the food is Malay in character. At the end of June a **fiesta** is held in the square with traditional food, live music and dancing. To get here, get bus #17 or #25 from Jalan Parameswara, just outside Taman Melaka Raya.

Heading back into town, make a brief detour to **St John's Fort** by turning left at the traffic lights about 500m after the settlement. Just before the next roundabout, a right turn, followed by another up an easily missable track, brings you to the base of the hill. The fort itself, a relic of the Dutch occupation and somewhat dwarfed by the adjacent water tower, isn't terribly exciting, but it offers good views over the Straits and the town.

Bukit China
Northeast of the colonial heart of Melaka, et the end of Jalan Temenggong, is **Bukit China**, the ancestral burial ground of the town's Chinese community. It is the oldest and largest such graveyard outside China. Although Chinese contacts with the Malay Peninsula probably began in the first century BC, it wasn't until the Ming Emperor Yung-Lo sent his envoy Admiral Cheng Ho in 1409 that commercial relations with Melaka were formally established, according the burgeoning settlement with vassal status. The **temple** at the foot of the hill is dedicated to Cheng Ho, upon whom was con-

ferred the title of "Sam Poh" or "Three Jewels" in 1431. Contemporary accounts are vague about the arrival of the first Chinese settlers, though the *Sejarah Melayu* recounts that on the marriage of Sultan Mansur Shah (1458–77) to the daughter of the Emperor, Princess Hang Liu, the five hundred nobles accompanying her stayed to set up home on Bukit China. It was supposedly these early pioneers who dug the well behind the temple; also known as the **Sultan's Well**, it has been of such importance to the local inhabitants as a source of fresh water that successive invading armies all sought to poison it. The Dutch enclosed it in a protecting wall, the ruins of which still remain.

At the top of Bukit China, horseshoe-shaped **graves** stretch as far as the eye can see. On the way up, you'll pass one of the oldest grave in the cemetery, belonging to Lee Kup who died in 1688. He was the first Chinese *kapitan*, a mediatory position created by the VOC which made it possible for them to rule the various ethnic communities. He was succeeded by Captain Li, whose grave on the other side of the cemetery is the subject of local myth. A fortune teller, asked to advise on the location and construction of the grave, prophesied that if it were to be dug three feet deep, Li's son would benefit, but any deeper and all profit would go to his son-in-law. Whether by accident or design, the grave was made three-and-a-half feet deep, and the son-in-law, Chan Lak

---

A CLASSIC CONFRONTATION

If any ruler puts a single one of his subjects to shame, that shall be a sign that his kingdom will be destroyed by Almighty God. Similarly it has been granted by Almighty God to Malay subjects that they shall never be disloyal or treacherous to their rulers, even if their rulers behave evilly or inflict injustice on them.

From the *Sejarah Melayu*

The tale of the duel between **Hang Tuah** and **Hang Jebat**, recounted in the *Hikayat Hang Tuah*, a seventeenth-century epic, stands as a symbol of the conflict between absolute loyalty to the sovereign and the love of a friend. These two characters, together with Hang Kasturi, Hang Lekir and Hang Lekiu, formed a band known as "The Five Companions", because of their close relationship since birth, and were highly trained in the martial arts. When they saved the life of the Bendahara Paduka Raja, the highest official in the Malay court, Sultan Mansur Shah was so impressed by their skill that he appointed them court attendants. Hang Tuah rapidly became the Sultan's favourite and was honoured with a beautiful *kris*, **Taming Sari**, which was said to have supernatural powers. This overt favouritism rankled with other long-serving officials who, in the absence from court of the rest of the companions, conspired to cast a slur on Hang Tuah's reputation by spreading the rumour that he had seduced one of the sultan's consorts. On hearing the accusation, the sultan was so enraged that he ordered the immediate execution of Hang Tuah. But the Bendahara, knowing the charge to be false, hid Hang Tuah to repay his debt to him, reporting back to the sultan that the deed had been carried out.

When Hang Jebat returned to the palace, he was shocked to discover Hang Tuah's supposed death and rampaged through Melaka, killing everyone in sight as retribution for the life of his treasured friend. The sultan, in fear of his own life, soon began to regret his decision, at which point the Bendahara revealed the truth and Hang Tuah was brought back to protect the sultan from Hang Jebat's fury and to exact justice for the murders committed. Hang Tuah wrestled hard with his conscience before deciding that the sultan had the absolute right to dispose of his subjects how he wished. So, with a heavy heart, Hang Tuah drew his *kris* against Hang Jebat and, after a protracted fight, killed him – a much-recounted episode whose moral was considered to set the seal on the Malay system of government.

Koa, went on to found the elaborate Cheng Hoon Teng temple as an expression of gratitude for his prosperity.

In the 1980s the burial ground was the subject of a bitter legal battle between the its trustees and the civil authorities. Competing plans to develop the area into a cultural and sports centre provoked a claim by the government for a $2 million bill for rent arrears, stating that the exemption over the previous centuries had been a "clerical error". This outraged the Chinese community who flatly refused to pay. The controversy was only settled in the early 1990s when the decision was made to develop Melaka's waterfront area instead, and the trustees agreed to improve the maintenance of the graveyard. Today, Bukit China is more an inner-city park than burial ground, where you're likely to encounter locals jogging, practising martial arts or simply admiring the view.

Eating

Surprisingly, there are very few quality restaurants in the centre of town – in fact, aside from a few places in Chinatown, it's hard to find much open at night. Instead, **Taman Melaka Raya** is fast becoming the favoured food centre, featuring Chinese, Nonya, Malay, Indian and seafood restaurants. Budget meals are hard to find – even the city's principal **food stalls** on Jalan Taman Melaka Raya, known as "Gluttons' Corner", are overrated and expensive: seafood is unpriced on the menu but calculated according to weight. It's far better to try the stalls just off Jalan Parameswara. Sampling **Nonya cuisine** is a must at some stage in your stay, though it is generally more expensive than other types of food. Specialities are mentioned below, but the emphasis is on spicy dishes, using sour herbs like tamarind, tempered by sweeter, creamy coconut milk. By contrast, the city's few remaining **Portuguese** restaurants are generally disappointing, expensive and tourist-orientated.

Usual restaurant **opening hours** are daily 9am–11pm, unless otherwise stated; phone numbers are given where it's necessary to book (usually only on Saturday nights).

Capitol Satay, Jalan Bukit China. Experience the Melaka version of fondue – *satay celup* – at this lively cafe where you take your pick of assorted fish, meat and vegetables skewered on sticks and cook them in a spicy peanut sauce at your table. Each stick is 35 sen and you'd be hard pressed to spend more than $5.

Gluttons' Corner, Jalan Merdeka. More a collection of permanent restaurants than food stalls, the city's highest profile eating area also has high prices and aggressive service. One of the better restaurants is *Bunga Raya*, which is popular with the locals. A full meal is at least $10 a head.

Heeren House, 1 Jalan Tun Tan Cheng Lock. This stylish, air-conditioned cafe and gift shop beneath the hotel is open for breakfast, offers salads, sandwiches and pasta dishes as well as set Nonya lunches at the weekends for $15. Open 8am–6pm.

Jonkers Melaka, 17 Jalan Hang Jebat. In a beautiful Peranakan house, this café is also a gift shop and art gallery. Good for vegetarians – set meals, including Nonya cuisine, start at $16. Homemade desserts too. Open 10am–5pm.

Long Feng Chinese Restaurant, *Renaissance Melaka Hotel*, Jalan Bendahara. Excellent Cantonese and Szechuan dishes in a classy setting. It's not cheap – around $20 per dish.

Mahkota Parade, Jalan Merdeka. Apart from the full range of Western fast food outlets and supermarket in the basement of the *Parkson Grand*, this mega-mall has a decent air-conditioned food court with dishes around $5.

Mei Lin, 542 Taman Melaka Raya. The menu of this friendly vegetarian restaurant lists items like Lemon Chicken and Sizzling Pork Ribs – but they're all made of soya. Most dishes are $3–5.

Melaka Pandan, Jalan Kota. Behind the tourist office and with a shady garden, this is the only open-air café in Melaka. A wide-ranging menu features Western and local cuisine; snacks average $4, and there's a set breakfast for $7. Open 9am–10pm.

Ole Sayang, 198–199 Jalan Taman Melaka Raya (☎06/283 4384). A moderately priced Nonya restaurant with re-created Peranakan decor. Try the beef *goreng lada*, in a rich soya-based sauce, or the *ayam lemak pulut*, a spicy, creamy chicken dish; both cost around $7. Open 11.30am–2.30pm & 6–9.30pm.

Restoran Kerala, 668 Taman Melaka Raya. Cheap and cheerful South Indian food in a sparkling clean establishment. Excellent banana leaf curries as well as tandoori set meals for about $5.

Restoran D'Nolasco, Medan Portugis. A Mediterranean atmosphere with Oriental food such as crabs in tomato and chilli sauce with soy. Around $20 a head.

Restoran Peranakan Town House, 107 Jalan Tun Tan Cheng Lock (☎06/284 5001). Marble tables with white-lace tablecloths, and a reasonably priced Nonya menu. Try spicy *rendang* dishes ($7) or *clay pot ayam* ($8). Open 8am–4pm.

Nightlife and entertainment

While the centre of town is dead at night – except for the discos in the top hotels – **Taman Melaka Raya** comes alive. There's no shortage of karaoke bars (usually 8pm–2am), though both these and the discos are expensive and somewhat lacking in character. You might be better off eschewing the Western-style bars in favour of one of the grotty Chinese bottle shops in the centre of town.

Mahkota Parade includes a 24-lane bowling alley , an amusement arcade and a three-screen cineplex. Otherwise the only source of entertainment is the nightly **Sound and Light Show**, Padang Pahlawan. A must for fans of high drama ("Something is rotten in the state of Melaka" intones the soundtrack), at an hour in length it drags a bit, but provides a one-stop introduction to the city's history. The buildings are well lit and the sound system is used imaginatively; take lots of mosquito repellent. Shows are in English (daily 9.30pm, 8.30pm during Ramadan; $5) and you can buy tickets from the booths at each end of the padang.

Shopping

Melaka is famed for its **antiques**, and there are many specialist outlets along Jalan Hang Jebat and Jalan Tun Tan Cheng Lock. Prices are usually fixed, although it does not hurt to bargain, and you can find anything from Nonya tableware to HMV gramophones in the musty shop interiors. If it's a genuine antique – and many shops fill their windows with colourful but inauthentic clutter – then check that it can be exported legally and fill in an official clearance form; the dealer should provide you with this. Jalan Bunga Raya and Jalan Munshi Abdullah comprise the modern shopping centre, where you'll find a variety of Western and local goods.

Abdu Co., 79 Jalan Hang Jabat. A good place for china and glass.

Dragon House, 65 Jalan Hang Jebat. The best value for old coins and banknotes, with helpful staff.

Karyaneka, Jalan Laksamana. Opposite the post office, this is the place to go for fixed-price crafts such as brassware, lacquerware and rattan articles.

Koo Fatt Hong, 92 Jalan Tun Tan Cheng Lock. Specialists in "Asia Spiritual and Buddha images".

Orang Utan, 59 Lorong Hang Jebat. Here, local artist Charles Cham sells his paintings, and T-shirts printed with witty cartoons and sayings.

Parkson Grand, Jalan Merdeka. A huge air-con department store, connected to the Mahkota Parade Shopping Mall; food in the basement.

Ringo, 12 Jalan Hang Jebat. British bikes and old biker artefacts, as well as unusual toys; pricey.

Tribal Arts Gallery, 10 Jalan Hang Rebat. Specialists in Sarawakian crafts, including woodwork and weaving.

Wah Aik, 92 Jalan Hang Jebat. Renowned for making silk shoes for bound feet, a practice that happily no longer exists – they're now lined up in the window as souvenirs, at a mere $75 per pair.

Listings

Banks and exchange Bank Bumiputra, Jalan Kota; Hong Kong Bank, 1a Jalan Kota; Overseas Chinese Banking Corporation, Jalan Hang Jebat. Moneychangers are often more convenient and offer as good rates as the banks: Malaccan Souvenir House and Trading, 22 Jalan Tokong; Sultan Enterprise, 31 Jalan Laksamana.

Bookshops *Estee Book Exchange*, Taman Melaka Raya, has a good selection of English-language classics and other fiction; *Lim Bros*, 20 Jalan Laksamana, has books on the Malaysian economy and politics, as well as colonial memoirs and expensive travel guides. *MPH* in Mahkota Parade also has an excellent range of books.

Car rental Avis, 27 Jalan Laksamana (☎06/283 5626); Thrifty, G5 Pasar Pelancong, Jalan Tun Sri Lanang (☎06/284 9471).

Cinema *The Cathay* and the *Rex* on Jalan Bunga Raya both show English-language films as does the *Cineplex* in Mahkota Parade. Check in English-language papers for what's on where and when.

Hospital The Straits Hospital is at 37 Jalan Parameswara (☎06/283 5336).

Immigration The immigration office is on the second floor, Bangunan Persekutuan, Jalan Hang Tuah (☎06/282 4958) for on-the-spot visa renewals.

Police The tourist police office (☎06/282 2222) is on Jalan Kota and is open 24 hours.

Post office The GPO is inconveniently situated on the way to Ayer Keroh on Jalan Bukit Baru – take town bus #19. A minor branch on Jalan Laksamana sells stamps and aerograms.

Sport The Merlin Melaka sports centre on Jalan Munshi Abdullah offers ten-pin bowling, snooker, squash, and roller skating.

Swimming There's a public swimming pool on Jalan Kota which costs $2 (daily 10am–1pm, 2–4.15pm, 6–10pm).

Telephones The Telekom building is on Jalan Chan Koon Cheng (daily 8am–5pm).

Travel agents Try Atlas Travel at 5 Jalan Hang Jebat (☎06/282 0777) for plane tickets.

Around Melaka

While there's more than enough to keep you occupied in Melaka itself, you may well fancy a break from sightseeing for more relaxed pleasures, using the city as a base. Heading north to the more rural area of **Ayer Keroh** or to the resort island of **Pulau Besar** you are guaranteed leisurely traffic-free pursuits.

Ayer Keroh

Fourteen kilometres north of the centre, **AYER KEROH** – despite its position adjacent to the North–South Highway – is a leafy recreational area that provides a pleasant alternative to staying in the city itself. Town bus #19 runs every thirty minutes from the local bus station. The major attractions are all within a few hundred metres or so of one another.

Apart from the **Hutan Rekreasi** (daily 7am–6pm; free), an area of woodland set aside for walking and picnicking, all the attractions are somewhat contrived: the **Taman Buaya**, or Crocodile Farm (Mon–Fri 9am–6pm, Sat & Sun 9.30am–7pm; $3); the **Melaka Zoo** (Mon–Fri 9am–6pm, Sat & Sun 9.30am–6.30pm; $4), purportedly the oldest and second largest in the country; and the **Taman Rama Rama** or Butterfly Farm (daily 8.30am–5.30pm; $4), with its walk-through aviary and small marine centre. The only display that demands more than fleeting attention is the **Taman Mini Malaysia** and mini **ASEAN** (Mon–Fri 10am–6pm, Sat & Sun 9.30am–6.30pm; $3), a large park fifteen minutes' walk north of the Crocodile Farm, with full-sized reconstructions of typical houses from all thirteen Malay states and the other five members of the Association of South East Asian Nations – Brunei, Indonesia, the Philippines, Singapore and Thailand. The specially constructed timber buildings are frequently used as sets for Malaysian films and soap operas, while cultural shows featuring local music and dance are staged at the park's open-air arena – ask at the ticket office for details.

The area around the lake, just off the main road, is where you'll find most of the **places to stay**, limited exclusively to upmarket resort accommodation. The best of the bunch is the *Paradise Malacca Village Resort* (☎06/232 3600, fax 232 5955; ⑨), a sprawling complex which partly uses traditional timber and rattan decor, with comfortable rooms around the swimming pools. Next door, *D'Village Resort* (☎06/232 8000; ⑥), is the least attractive option, with hot, blue-roofed chalets crammed together, though it does have the cheapest rooms. **Places to eat** are more or less limited to those in the resorts, save for a few tourist-orientated food stalls at the main attractions.

Pulau Besar

Long before it was turned into an exclusive beach resort, **PULAU BESAR**, about 5km off the coast of Melaka, was known as the burial ground of passing Muslim traders and missionaries, tales of whom live on in distorted local legends. Although its historic sites have been vigorously promoted by the tourist authorities, they consist of little more than a few ancient graves, several wells and remnants of the Japanese occupation, such as a bunker and dynamite store. However, the island's beaches and hilly scenery are pleasant enough, and its compact size makes it easy to stroll around in a day – the name "Big Island" is misleading, since Pulau Besar covers only about sixteen square kilometres.

Pulau Besar is easily reached by air-con **ferry** ($10 return), departing from the Shah Bandar jetty in town. You can also get there by fishing boat from the **Pengkalan Pernu jetty** in Umbai (on request; $8 return for a group of 12, otherwise $50 for the boat). Umbai is 6km southeast of Melaka, a twenty-minute journey from the city on bus #2. You might want to stay overnight in the luxury *Pandonusa Resort* (☎06/281 5939; ⑦), the only available **accommodation**. There is more choice when it comes to **eating**; aside from the pricey restaurant at the resort, there are a couple of local *kedai kopis* serving rice and noodle dishes.

Inland: Gunung Ledang and Segamat

Heading **inland** from Melaka into the state of Johor, a maze of minor roads covers the sparsely populated lowland. The only feature on the horizon is the conical **Gunung Ledang**. Further inland still, you'll meet up with the sweep of Route 1, connecting a string of lifeless towns, of which the least dull is **Segamat**.

Gemas, 25km northwest of Segamat, is a grubby little place, whose merit is its importance to the train network; it's here that you'll have to change if you want to venture into the interior on the so-called Jungle Railway (see p.224 for all the details). Transport connections throughout inland Johor are uncomplicated, with a good network of buses serving all destinations.

Gunung Ledang

Formerly called Mount Ophir by the British, **Gunung Ledang** (1276m) is the highest mountain in the state of Johor and is believed by the animist Orang Asli to be inhabited by spirits. The best-known legend associated with Gunung Ledang concerns the betrothal of Sultan Mansur Shah to the mountain's beautiful fairy princess. A lengthy list of requirements was presented to the sultan, on fulfilment of which the princess would consent to marry him, and while the sultan was not daunted by such items as trays of mosquito hearts and a vat of tears, he drew the line at a cup of his son's blood, and withdrew his proposal.

Gunung Ledang features a dramatic **waterfall** and challenging **treks**, though the latter are restricted to experienced climbers with their own camping equipment. You have to pay $1 to enter the area and once you're past the hotel and clutter of trinket stalls at the approach to the waterfall, the surroundings become gradually more leafy and refreshing, leading to the start of the trail to the summit. A series of rapids, which the main path follows closely, form natural pools, ideal for a cooling dip, though the water is a bit murky in places. Reaching the waterfall's source requires stamina and is disappointing in the dry season. *The Gunung Ledang Resort* (☎06/977 2888, fax 977 3555; ⑥) has rooms available, though they are nothing special. It also has set up the *Kem Rimba* adventure camp, which includes an obstacle course, adjoined by thirty unfurnished metal boxes or "jungle huts" where you can stay for $50 a night. There are various packages on offer that combine a stay at the resort with expeditions up the mountain, from around $150 — contact the resort and the national rail company KTM (☎03/272 7267, fax 273 6527) for details. There are plans to add a golf course at the foot of the mountain in the future.

The mountain is easily reached by a Segamat-bound express bus from Melaka – ask to be dropped at **SAGIL**, 11km north of Tangkak on Route 23. Here, the waterfall is clearly signposted ("Air Terjun") off the main road, from where it is a one-and-a-half-kilometre walk to the beginning of the rapids.

Segamat

While there's no real reason to continue on to **SEGAMAT**, 52km northeast of Tangkak, it's not an unpleasant town and if you're driving through on Route 1, stop for a drink and a wander around the grassy padang. This is bordered by some elegant old colonial buildings, such as the **Sekolah Tinggi**, formerly the English High School, as well as the District Office and an ill-proportioned Catholic church. The more modern, anonymous commercial centre is more than 1km to the south.

Central Segamat offers plenty of **accommodation**, including the comfortable *Pine Classic Inn* at 30 Jalan Genuang (☎07/932 3009; ③) on the main thoroughfare, the basic *Tai Ah* (☎07/931 1709; ①) over the road at nos. 42–25, and the *Segamat Inn* (☎07/931 1401; ②) in the UMNO building next to the GPO on Jalan Awang.

South to JB

It's 206km southeast from Melaka to Johor Bahru (see p.311) and the first 45km, to the Malay town of **Muar**, is through verdant countryside dotted with neatly kept timber stilted houses with double roofs. These houses – in some of the prettiest kampungs in Malaysia – are especially numerous along Route 5 and, with time to spare en route between Melaka and Maur, you could stop to visit one of them, **Penghulu's House**. Further south, the towns of **Batu Pahat** and **Pontian Kecil** are of scant interest; Batu Pahat, slightly inland, has a reputation as a red-light resort for Singaporeans. If you do want to stop anywhere else before JB and Singapore, aim for **Kukup**, right at the southern end of the west coast, and terrific for seafood. Just off the main road on the right, 2km south of the village of **MERLIMAU**, striking **Penghulu's House** was built in 1894 for a local chieftain. Elaborate wood carvings adorning the verandah and eaves, and the front steps are covered in colourful Art Nouveau hand-painted tiles. It is still inhabited by the chieftain's descendants, who will show you around.

Muar

The old port town of **MUAR** – also known as Bandar Maharani – exudes an elegance and calm that attracts surprisingly few tourists. Legend has it that Paremesvara, the fifteenth-century founder of Melaka, fled here from Singapore to establish his kingdom on the southern bank of Sungei Muar, before being persuaded to choose Melaka.

Although rejected by the Sumatran prince, Muar later became an important port in the Johor empire (see p.601), as well as a centre for *ghazal* music (see p.622), which originated in Africa – and the place whose dialect is considered the purest Bahasa Malaysia in the Peninsula.

Today, Muar's commercial centre looks like any other, with Chinese shophouses and *kedai kopi*s lining its parallel streets, Jalan Maharani, Jalan Abdullah and Jalan Meriam. But turn right out of the bus station on Jalan Maharani, following the river as the road turns into Jalan Petri, and you'll see an altogether different part of town. Under the shade of huge rain trees, Neoclassical colonial buildings, the **Custom House** and **Government Offices** (Bangunan Sultan Abu Bakar) on the right, and the **District Police Office** and **Courthouse** on the left, still have an air of confidence and prosperity from their days as a British administrative centre. The graceful **Masjid Jamek** successfully combines Western and Moorish styles or architecture.

Practicalities

Bus #2 runs frequently from Melaka's local bus station, arriving in Muar at the station on Jalan Maharani. It's less than an hour and a half away, but if you prefer to stay, there are plenty of reasonable **hotels**, the best-value place being the initially unpromising *Park View*. Aside from **eating** houses in the commercial centre of town, none of which can be particularly recommended, the *Medan Selera* near the bridge on Jalan Maharani serves Malay snacks, while the *Park View* has a bearable restaurant with a wide-ranging menu averaging $5 per dish.

ACCOMMODATION

Kingdom, 158 Jalan Meriam (☎06/952 1921). Two blocks back from the bus station, this reasonable place has small, modern rooms. ②.

Park View, Jalan Petri (☎06/951 6655). This tower block by the rover has good views over town and the river; the rooms are rather tatty but basically good value. ②.

Riverview, 29 Jalan Bentayan (☎06/951 3313, fax 951 8139). Large, comfortable rooms with decent attached bathrooms. ④.

Rumah Persingghan Tanjong Emas, Jalan Sultanah (☎06/952 7744, fax 953 7933). A ten-minute taxi ride away from the town centre in a countryside setting. This place has the quietest, most upmarket accommodation in town, with huge rooms complete with TV and telephone, a children's play area, as well as some family chalets. ③.

Batu Pahat and Pontian Kecil

Heading south, Route 5 hugs the palm-fringed coast as far as **BATU PAHAT**, which has a reputation as a venue for "dirty weekends". A more noteworthy association is with a couple of important political events. UMNO, a coalition of organizations opposed to the British-inspired Malayan Union, had its origins here in 1946. Years later, during the Constitutional Crisis of 1983, Prime Minister Dr Mahathir held a mass rally in the town to protest against the position taken by the hereditary rulers, urging the people to assert their constitutional rights and elect him. The choice of Batu Pahat as the venue for this conscience-stirring symbolized Dr Mahathir's desire to remind the rulers of UMNO's role in reversing their original acquiescence with the Malayan Union many years before. The Art Deco **Masjid Jamek** and Straits Chinese **Chamber of Commerce** are the only buildings of note.

Further south, you head into plantation country – in this case pineapples, piled high on roadside stalls in season, filling the air with their sweet smell. The next place of any consequence is the unassuming town of **PONTIAN KECIL**, 70km southeast of Batu Pahat, where you can stop off for a cup of tea or lunch at the cutesy, old-world *Resthouse* (☎06/951 6655; ②), just up from the bus station (regular services to JB) on the seafront.

Kukup

Signs featuring giant king prawns flank the roadside at **KUKUP**, waving their tentacles in eager expectation at the money you're about to part with. This small fishing community, just 19km from Pontian Kecil, has opened its doors to the Singapore package-tour trade, whose clients come to see the ancient, stilted houses built over the murky river and to sample Kukup's real attraction: the **seafood**. The town's single tumble-down street is packed with restaurants.

Tours usually include an appetite-inducing trip to the offshore **kelong**. This huge fish trap has rickety wooden platforms, from where the nets are cast, which float on their moorings, rather than being anchored to the sea bed. The agency right by the jetty or any one of the restaurants can sell you a ticket for the 45-minute tour ($5).

There's a dearth of transport from Pontian Kecil to Kukup, so you're better off catching a **taxi** for around $2 per person. There are at least half a dozen places to **eat**, from the enormous *Makanan Laut*, closest to the jetty, where you can see the food being prepared in a vast array of woks, to the more modest *Restoran Zaiton Hussin* immediately opposite, where the emphasis is on Malay rather than Chinese-style seafood. Expect to pay $13 for fish, $12 for prawns and $6 for mussels.

Connections to Indonesia and Singapore

Kukup is a little-known exit point from Malaysia to **Tanjung Balai in Indonesia**, a 45-minute ferry ride leaving from the jetty daily at 11am and 3pm, except Friday when there are no services and Sunday when only the 3pm ferry operates ($45 one-way). The problem with **arriving** in Kukup from Indonesia is that onward travel connections are sketchy – you'll have to catch a ferry to Pontian Kecil. You don't need to arrange a visa in advance for this trip.

A kilometre back towards Pontian Kecil from Kukup, you'll see a turn-off for **Tanjung Piai**. A gradually narrowing road through lush tropical fruit plantations takes you to the "southernmost tip of the mainland Asia continent" as the advertising for the *Tanjung Piai Resort* (☎ & fax 07/696 9000; ③) puts it. This string of large wooden chalets, on concrete pylons at the edge of the mangrove swamps, commands a dramatic vista of the ships coming to and from Singapore, clearly visible on the horizon. There's a seafood restaurant and the management are friendly. Apart from eating, there's little to do here other than chill out, perhaps watch the fireflies at night and enjoy the view.

Johor Bahru

The southernmost Malaysian city of any size, **JOHOR BAHRU** – or simply **JB** – is the gateway into Singapore, linked to the city-state by a 1056-metre causeway carrying a road, a railway, and the pipes through which Singapore imports its fresh water. Around fifty thousand people a day travel across the causeway, and the ensuing traffic, noise and smog affects most of unsightly downtown Johor Bahru. The town has long had to tolerate unflattering comparisons with squeaky-clean Singapore, for which it has served as a red-light haunt for many years, but things do at last seem to be changing. The past two decades have seen the state of Johor – of which JB is the capital – become one of the three sides of an economic "Growth Triangle", together with Singapore and Batam island in the Indonesian Riau archipelago. Confronted by mounting production costs in their own country, Singaporean investors have flooded across the causeway to take advantage of low labour costs, and JB has prospered accordingly. Today, the air of decay which hangs over much of downtown JB is slowly being dispelled, as the manufacturing boom finances new international hotels and ever more dazzling shopping

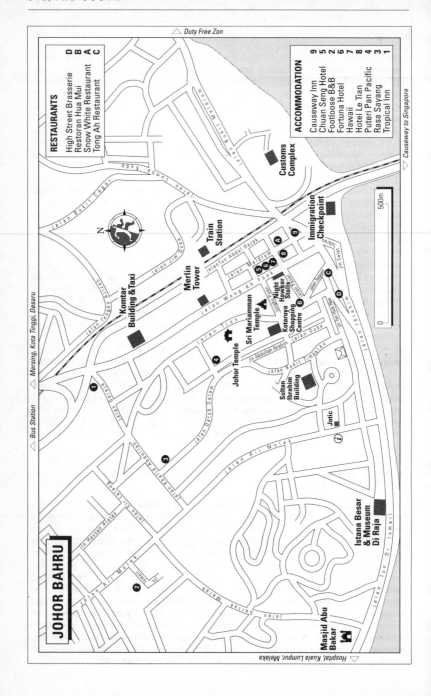

JOHOR BAHRU

RESTAURANTS

High Street Brasserie	D
Restoran Hua Mui	B
Snow White Restaurant	A
Tong Ah Restaurant	C

ACCOMMODATION

Causeway Inn	9
Chuan Seng Hotel	5
Footloose B&B	2
Fortuna Hotel	6
Hawaii	7
Hotel Le Tian	8
Puteri Pan Pacific	4
Rasa Sayang	3
Tropical Inn	1

△ Duty Free Zon

▽ Causeway to Singapore

Customs Complex

Immigration Checkpoint

Train Station

Merlin Tower

Komtar Building & Taxi

Sri Mariamman Temple

Johor Temple

Night Hawker Stalls

Kotaraya Shopping Centre

Sultan Ibrahim Building

Jotic

Istana Besar & Museum Di Raja

Masjid Abu Bakar

△ Bus Station

△ Mersing, Kota Tinggi, Desaru

▽ Hospital, Kuala Lumpur, Melaka

Jalan Ibrahim
Jalan Tun Dr Ismail
Jalan Gereja
Jalan Air Molek
Jalan Datok Dalam
Jalan Trus
Jalan Wong Ah Fook
Jalan Tun Abdul Razak
Jalan Meldrum
Jalan Bukit Timbalan
Jalan Abdullah Ibrahim
Jalan Duke
Jalan Ungku Puan
Jalan Tun Hussein
Jalan Bukit Cagar
Jalan Jim Quee
Jalan Tangku Azizah
Jalan Hassan Alatas
Jalan Gertak Merah
Jalan Selat

0   500m

N

malls. Development is particularly evident among the arcades of **Taman Century Estate**, a couple of kilometres north of the city centre along the Tebrau Highway. A huge duty-free complex and ferry terminal has been built a couple of kilometres east of the city centre and there are plans to develop the seafront area beside the causeway. To the west a new causeway is being constructed which will bypass the city completely, hopefully easing the chronic traffic that snarls up central JB's roads.

Despite these improvements, JB remains ill equipped to win the hearts of visitors. By day, it's a hectic city whose only real attraction is the royal **Istana Besar**; by night, its main streets are lit by the neon lights of its hostess bars and night clubs. If you've arrived from Singapore, there's little to detain you from the quick getaway provided by the North–South Highway to the considerable attractions of Melaka and Kuala Lumpur.

Historically though, JB stands with Melaka as one of the most important sites in the country. Chased out of its seat of power by the Portuguese in 1511, the Melakan court decamped to the Riau archipelago, south of modern-day Singapore, before upping sticks again in the 1530s and shifting to the upper reaches of the Johor river. A century of uncertainty followed for the infant kingdom of Johor, with persistent offensives by both the Portuguese and the Acehnese of northern Sumatra, forcing the court to shift its capital regularly. Stability was finally achieved by courting the friendship of the Dutch in the 1640s; the rest of the seventeenth century saw the kingdom of Johor blossom into a **thriving trading entrepôt**. By the end of the century, though, the rule of the wayward and tyrannical Sultan Mahmud had halted Johor's pre-eminence among the Malay kingdoms, and piracy was causing a decline in trade. In 1699, Sultan Mahmud was killed by his own nobles and with the Melaka-Johor dynasty finally finished, successive power struggles crippled the kingdom. Buginese immigrants, escaping the civil wars in their native Sulawesi, eventually eclipsed the power of the Sultans, and though the Buginese were finally chased out by the Dutch in 1784, the kingdom was now a shadow of its former self.

The Johor-Riau empire – and the Malay world – was split in two, with the Melaka Straits forming the dividing line following the Anglo-Dutch treaty of 1824. As links with the court in Riau faded, Sultan Ibrahim assumed power, amassing a fortune based upon hefty profits culled from plantations in Johor. The process was continued by his son Abu Bakar, who in 1885 was named Sultan of Johor, and is widely regarded as the father of modern Johor. It was Abu Bakar who, in 1866, named the new port across the Johor Straits *Johor Bahru*, or "New Johor".

The City

JB is a sprawling city, with most places of interest located close to the causeway. **Downtown JB** is undeniably scruffy, a fact born out by a stroll through the claustrophobic alleys of the sprawling **market**, below the Komtar Building on Jalan Wong Ah Fook, where machetes, silk and "one-thousand-year-old eggs" (actually preserved for a year in lime, ash and tea leaves) are sold. This area is being cleared though, as new shopping and office developments sprout up in the hilly downtown area. A little way south, the **Sri Mariamman Temple** lends a welcome splash of primary colour to the cityscape. Underneath its *gopuram*, and beyond the two gatekeepers on horseback who guard the temple, is the usual collection of vividly depicted figures from the Hindu pantheon. There's another temple, just west of the Sri Mariamman, on Jalan Trus, the nineteenth century **Johor Temple** which is JB's oldest, its murals of Chinese life darkened by years of incense smoke.

After the cramped streets of the city centre, the open western **seafront** comes as a great relief. From here, there are good views of distant Singapore, and of the slow snake of traffic labouring across the causeway. On Jalan Timbalan is the austere, grey-bricked **Sultan Ibrahim Building**, which today houses the state government offices.

THE SULTANS AND THE LAW

The British Royal Family may hog the limelight when it comes to juicy scandals, but their antics are nothing compared to what some of the nine royal families in Malaysia get up to. Nepotism, meddling in state politics and flagrant breaches of their exemption from import duties are among the lesser misdemeanours that generally go unreported in the circumspect local press. But the most notorious of them all is Johor's Sultan Iskandar Ibni Al-Marhum Sultan Ismail and his son, the Tunku Ibrahim Ismail. The sultan is alleged to have beaten his golf caddy to death in the Cameron Highlands after the unfortunate man made the mistake of laughing at a bad shot. His son, too, was convicted of shooting dead a man in a JB nightclub. Because his father was sultan, the prince was immediately pardoned. Such behaviour had long incensed Prime Minister Dr Mahathir who was itching to bring the lawless royals into line. He got his chance in 1993 when yet another beating incident involving the Sultan of Johor was reported in parliament along with 23 other similar assaults since 1972. In 1993, the federal parliament voted in the Constitutional Amendment Bill, removing the sultans' personal immunity from prosecution. Naturally, the royal families were not too happy about this, but following a stand-off with Mahathir, they agreed to compromise – no ruler would be taken to court without the Attorney General's approval. To underline their victory against the sultans, Mahathir introduced another constitutional amendment in 1994 that the king could only act on the advice of the government. Despite this, the Sultan of Johor retains considerable influence in the state and is the only one of the Malay royal families to have a private army.

It was completed in 1940, and was used by the Japanese to command their assault on Singapore in February 1942.

Walk west along the water, past the garlanded facade of the **High Court** and the impressive JB Tourism Information Centre (JOTIC) next door, and you'll soon reach the grey arch marking the entrance into the expansive gardens of the **Istana Besar** – the former residence of Johor's royal family. Ornate golden lamps line the path to the istana, a magnificent building with chalk-white walls and a low, blue roof, set on a hillock overlooking the Johor Straits. Nowadays, the royal family lives in the Istana Bukit Serene, a little further west of the city, which means that the Istana Besar is open to the public. To the right of the building is the ticket booth of the **Museum Di Raja Abu Bakar** (daily 9am–5pm, last entry 4pm; $18, children $8). The bulk of the pieces on show are gifts from foreign dignitaries, including exquisite ceramics from Japan, crystal from France and furniture from England, as well as Southeast Asian items like stuffed tigers, ornate daggers and an umbrella stand crafted from an elephant's foot.

Further west, the four rounded towers of the **Abu Bakar Mosque** make it the most elegant building in town. Completed in 1900, the mosque can accommodate two thousand worshippers; as at the istana, Sultan Abu Bakar himself laid the first stone, though he died before the mosque was completed.

Practicalities

The **bus station** is 3km away from the centre of JB on Jalan Geruda. Plenty of buses run from here to the causeway or you catch a taxi for around $5. The **train station** is to the east of the city centre, off Jalan Tun Abdul Razak. Flights to JB land at **Senai airport**, 25km north of the city, from where a regular bus service ($1.40) runs to the bus station. Heading out to the airport, MAS passengers can take the $4 shuttle bus from outside the *Puteri Pan Pacific*, which connects with all major flights. Alternatively, you can get a taxi to the airport for about $25. The MAS office is at Level 1, Menara Pelangi, Jalan Kuning Taman Pelangi (☎07/334 1001). If you want to explore Malaysia out of Singapore, it's far cheaper to **rent a car** in JB. Contact either Avis, at the *Tropical Inn*

Practicalities

Buses from JB run every thirty minutes on the 45-minute trip to Kota Tinggi, stopping at the centrally situated bus station, which caters for both express and local services. Bus #43 leaves hourly from Kota Tinggi (7am–7pm; $2), winding up through rubber-plantation country to the entrance to the waterfall.

The hotels **in Kota Tinggi** are located around the bus station, the best value of which is the modern and spotless *Sin May Chun* at 26 Jalan Tambatan (☎07/833 3573; ①); the *Bunga Raya* further along at 12 Jalan Jaafar (☎07/883 3023; ①) is also well kept. The *Nasha* at 40 Jalan Tambatan (☎07/883 8000; ②) is the most upmarket option, but its rooms are small and musty. Seafood is a speciality in the town, with a number of flashy **restaurants** close to the river, including the *Sin Mei Lee* and the *Mui Tou* – prices are surprisingly reasonable at around $6–8 per dish, so this is the place to try out crab, lobster and prawns.

Desaru

DESARU is the first major beach resort outside Singapore and as beaches go, it's not that bad, with its sheltered, casuarina-fringed bay. But there are better places further up the coast, and the wide, well-kept but rather soulless streets don't inspire any lengthy stays. It's nearly 100km by road from JB, so most visitors from Singapore come by sea from Changi Point (see "Leaving Singapore", pp.506–507). The transport system is geared towards this, with shuttle buses running the 45 minutes from the Malaysian port of Kampung Pengerang to Desaru itself. In addition, the PGB company runs bus #5 from JB, and there are also local connections with Kota Tinggi.

The three **places to stay** in Desaru are all under the auspices of the *Desaru Garden Beach Resort* (☎07/882 1101). It has a full range of accommodation from a fairly poor campsite ($5 per person) and dorms ($12), chalets (④), through to two hotels, the *Desaru View* (☎07/822 1221; ⑤), and the newer and more pleasant *Desaru Hotel* (☎07/822 1101; ⑤), both with pools. Be warned that rates rise dramatically at weekends. All the places have **restaurants**, predominantly Chinese and Japanese, and a very average meal costs a minimum of $15 a head.

Mersing

The fishing port of **MERSING**, 130km north of Johor Bahru, lies on the languid Sungei Mersing. A bustling and industrious little town, it's the main gateway to **Pulau Tioman** and the smaller islands of the Seribuat archipelago, and is unlikely to delay you longer than one night. Hotels, restaurants and travel agencies have sprung up to cater for the seasonal flood of tourists – it pays to work out exactly what you want to do before arriving in Mersing, or you may be swamped by the touts that hang around the jetty.

Mersing is grouped around two main streets, Jalan Abu Bakar and Jalan Ismail, fanning out from a roundabout on Route 3. Mersing's Chinese and Indian temples, just south of the roundabout, are unremarkable. The only real sight in town is the square **Masjid Jamek**, on a nearby hilltop, its cool, pastel-green tiled dome and minaret lit to spectacular effect at night, when it appears to hang in the sky. In the centre of town, by a mini-roundabout on Jalan Abu Bakar, is a historic Chinese **shophouse**, built by Poh Keh, a Mersing pioneer, its verandah and floral wall motifs a little too prettily renovated.

Practicalities

Express buses from Singapore, JB or Kuantan drop you off just before the round-about, and at the R&R Plaza near the jetty. The **local bus station** for services to Kota

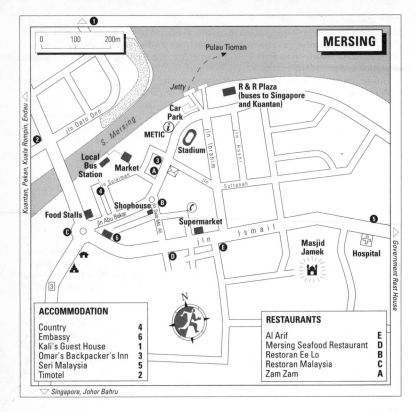

Tinggi, Endau and elsewhere is on Jalan Sulaiman, close to the riverfront. The **Mersing Tourist Information Centre** (METIC; ☎07/799 5212) is in a new building on Jalan Abu Bakar. The staff are very helpful and offer impartial advice on the many different island deals.

The **jetty** is about ten minutes' walk from the roundabout along Jalan Abu Bakar – for details of getting to the islands, see "Leaving for the islands" below. One problem with **leaving Mersing** is that few buses originate here, so there can be a fight for seats in the peak season. Express tickets can be bought in advance from *Restoran Malaysia* and R&R Plaza. You may experience problems buying a ticket at the *Restoran Malaysia* – if so the assistants at METIC will help you. Singapore-bound services depart from the R&R Plaza near the jetty.

Leaving for the islands

Mersing is the main departure point for Tioman. For details of departures from Tanjong Gemuk see p.322. At the jetty there's a cluster of agency booths representing various islands, boats and resorts, known collectively as the **Tourist Centre**. For impartial information you're better off going to METIC (see above).

If you're heading to **Pulau Tioman** itself, rather than any of the smaller islands, you may as well take your chances with accommodation once there and just buy a boat tick-et – even in the busiest season (May to October) you're unlikely to have difficulty finding a place to stay. Inside the nearby R&R Plaza – a collection of restaurants, money-changers and more resort offices – you'll find a large signboard indicating which company's boats sail at what time that day – the latest departure will normally be no later than about 4pm, depending on the tide. You can then buy your ticket from the agency booth whose timings suit you best. For the **other islands**, it's better to head for the particular island office itself, each of which is based around the jetty, or to one of the many **travel agencies** in town – mostly along Jalan Abu Baker – to book in advance, since boat services are less regular and accommodation more at a premium.

Whatever you decide, make sure that you **change money** before you leave as rates on the islands are lousy; there are branches of Maybank and Bank Bumiputra on Jalan Ismail. If you have your own transport, there's a secure **car park** by the jetty which charges $7 per day.

Accommodation

If you've missed the day's sailings, you'll have to spend the night in Mersing. There's no shortage of low-budget **hotels**; to get to either of the two places to the north of town, take the local bus which runs every thirty minutes. Taxis cost $3.

Country, Jalan Sulaimen (☎07/799 1799). Near the bus station, this hotel is more upmarket than its price suggests; each carpeted room has comfortable furniture, a bathroom and balcony. ②.

Embassy, 2 Jalan Ismail (☎07/799 3545). Clean and comfortable, this relatively quiet and well-run place has two or three beds to a room, in addition to ordinary doubles. ①.

Kali's Guesthouse (☎07/799 3613). A charming place by the sea, 2km north of town, with a peaceful garden and a choice of A-frames, chalets or dearer cottages. Phone for collection from town or take the Endou-bound bus. ①–③.

Merlin Inn (☎07/799 1312) Set on a hill 3km north of the roundabout, this run-down hotel has a good view of the islands, a pool and elegant restaurant, though rather musty rooms. ⑤.

Omar's Backpackers' Hostel, Jalan Abu Bakar (☎07/793125). Opposite the GPO, this is one of the cheapest places in Mersing, with dorm beds and excellent-value double rooms. Dorms $7. ①.

Seri Malaysia, Jalan Ismail (☎07/799 1876, fax 799 1886). Opposite the hospital, a ten-minute walk from the jetty. Another in this nationwide chain of reasonably priced good quality hotels, where the price includes breakfast. ⑤.

Timotel, 839 Jalan Endau (☎07/799 5888, fax 799 5333). Just across the river this new hotel has tastefully furnished rooms with huge double beds. The rates include breakfast and there's an attached karaoke pub. ⑥.

Eating

Mersing is a great place for **eating**, with seafood topping the menu. The **food stalls** near the roundabout are particularly good – try the satay and banana fritters.

Al Arif, Jalan Ismail. Opposite the Parkson Ria supermarket, this Indian café serves cheap, good-quality food.

Golden Dragon, *Embassy Hotel*, 2 Jalan Ismail. The widest-ranging Chinese and seafood menu in town, though a touch more expensive than some. Averages $8 per dish.

Mersing Seafood Restaurant, Jalan Ismail. One of the best seafood (and air-con) restaurants in town, with a good selection of crab, prawn and mussel dishes at around $8 each.

Restoran Ee Lo, Jalan Dato Md. Ali, on the Jalan Abu Bakar mini-roundabout. A variety of Chinese-based dishes, as well as a limited range of seafood.

Zam Zam, Jalan Abu Bakar. Always busy, this serves tasty Indian food including great *roti canai*.

Pulau Tioman

Shaped like a giant apostrophe in the South China Sea, **PULAU TIOMAN**, 30km east of Mersing, has long been one of Malaysia's most popular holiday islands. Thirty-eight kilometres in length and nineteen kilometres at its widest point, it is the largest of the

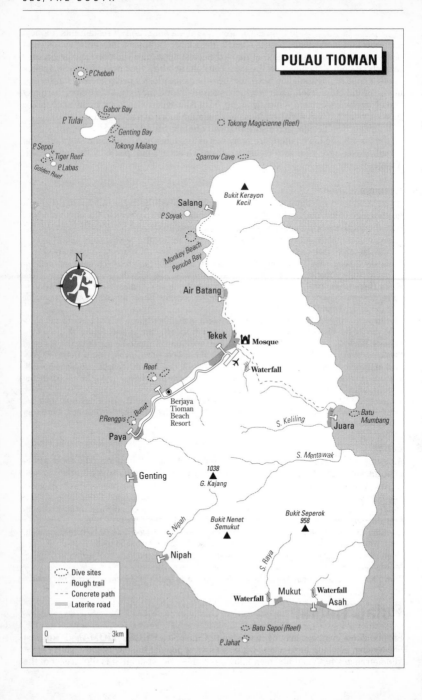

PULAU TIOMAN

P. Chebeh

Gabor Bay

P Tulai

Genting Bay

Tokong Malang

P. Sepoi

Tiger Reef

Golden Reef

P Labas

Tokong Magicienne (Reef)

Sparrow Cave

Salang

Bukit Kerayon Kecil

P Soyak

Monkey Beach

Penuba Bay

Air Batang

Tekek

Mosque

Reef

Waterfall

Bunut

Berjaya Tioman Beach Resort

P.Renggis

S. Keliling

Batu Mumbang

Paya

Juara

S. Mentawak

Genting

1038

G. Kajang

Bukit Seperok

958

Bukit Nenet Semukut

S. Nipah

S. Raya

Nipah

Waterfall

Mukut

Waterfall

Asah

Dive sites
Rough trail
Concrete path
Laterite road

0   3km

Batu Sepoi (Reef)

P. Jahat

N

64 volcanic islands that form the Seribuat archipelago. The sheer size and inaccessibility of its mountainous spine has preserved its most valuable asset – the dense, variegated **jungle**. As you approach, Tioman looms above you, shrouded in cloud; the two peculiar granite pinnacles of Bukit Nenek Semukut on its southern tip are known as *chula naga* (dragon's horns). According to legend, the origins of Pulau Tioman lie in the flight of a dragon princess on her way to China, who fell in love with the surrounding waters and decided to settle here permanently by transforming her body into an island. First mention of the island in official records dates back to 1403, when a Chinese trading expedition to Southeast Asia and Mecca found Tioman, with its abundant supplies of fresh water, a handy stopping place. Shipping charts called it Zhumaskan, though local inhabitants believe the island to be named after the *tiong* (Hill Mynah bird) that is commonly found here.

Ever since the 1970s, when it was voted one of the ten most beautiful islands in the world by *Time* magazine, crowds have been flocking to its palm-fringed shores, in search of the mythical Bali H'ai for which it was the chosen film location in the Hollywood musical, *South Pacific*. But twenty-odd years is a long time in tourism. Where slow fishing vessels used to ply the seas for the arduous five-hour journey to Tioman, noisy express boats now complete the trip in less than two hours and these, combined with the several daily flights from Singapore and other parts of the Peninsula, have helped destroy the sense of romantic isolation that once made the island so popular. Those in search of unspoilt beaches will also be disappointed – though there are some superb exceptions. Damage has been inflicted on the surrounding coral and marine life, but Pulau Tioman displays a remarkable resilience, and to fail to visit it is to miss out – the greater part of the island has still not lost its intimate, village atmosphere.

Tioman has plenty of **activities**, particularly diving (see p.323) and watersports, though you can also go **wildlife**-spotting on its few easy hikes. You should see mouse deer, flying lemur, long-tailed macaques and monitor lizards. Look out for the clusters of greater frigate birds that gather on the surrounding islands and rocks; occasionally you'll see Christmas Island frigate birds, breeding only on the island after which they are named, more than 2000km south of Tioman. Like the rest of the Peninsula's east coast, Tioman is affected by the **monsoon**, making the island virtually unreachable by sea between November and February, while July and August are the busiest months, when prices increase and accommodation must be booked well in advance. Even in the dry season, it rains almost daily; cloud seems to hang permanently around the island's mountainous ridge.

Accommodation possibilities range from the island's one international-standard resort, through to chalet developments and simple beachfront A-frames – the latter being gradually edged out by identical, tin-roofed box chalets. Most of the habitation on Tioman is along the west coast, with the popular budget places being in the main village of **Tekek** and the bay of **Air Batang**; while the east coast's sole settlement, **Juara**, is less developed – you'll easily find a place to stay in the latter two villages for under

---

SANDFLIES

Sandflies can be a real problem on all of the Seribuat islands, though reputedly Juara, on the east coast of Tioman, is the worst place, depending on the season. These little pests look like tiny fruit flies, with black bodies and white wings and, though harmless, can suck blood and cause an extremely itchy lump, which can sometimes become a nasty blister, especially if scratched. Short of dousing yourself all over with insect repellent or hiding out in the sea all day long, there's virtually nothing you can do, although using suntan oil rather than lotion or cream is supposed to help.

$20 per head. **Genting** and **Salang** are noisy, more upmarket resorts, while **Paya** and **Nipah**, together with **Mukut** on the island's southern coast are just opening up to tourism. Long gone are the days when you had to resort to a hurricane lamp at night – everywhere has electricity, albeit from a local generator. Nightlife has still to take off, however, though beer is available everywhere on the island.

Getting there

Thirteen companies operate **express boats from Mersing** (see p.318), which take roughly two hours or less, depending on the tide; tickets are $25 for the one-way trip, though travel agents in Mersing may offer discounts if you buy an open-return ticket (see "Leaving Tioman" box below). Whichever service you use, it's important to decide in advance which bay or village you want to stay in, since the boats generally make drops only at the major resorts of Genting, Tekek, Air Batang and Salang (in that order); there are only occasional boats from Mersing to Juara on the east coast. At **Tanjong Gemuk**, 38km north of Mersing on the Pahang side of the border with Johor, is a new ferry terminal from which there are daily services at 9am and 2pm ($25 one-way). The journey time is slightly faster at just over an hour to the *Berjaya Tioman Beach Resort*, the first stop on the island. For more details call ☎07/794 2053.

From **Singapore**, there's a daily catamaran service (March–Oct; $143 return; see "Leaving Singapore", pp.506–507 for details), which takes four and a half hours and runs directly to the Berjaya Tioman Beach. Arriving **by air**, you'll land at the airstrip in Tekek, from where there's a half-hourly shuttle bus to the *Berjaya Tioman Beach Resort*, 2km to the south, along the only proper road on the island. Otherwise, you'll have to make your own way from the airport to the other beaches, involving a trip on the sea bus or sea taxi (see below) from the nearby Tekek jetty.

Getting around the island

The only road wide enough for vehicles other than motorbikes is between Tekek and the *Berjaya Tioman Beach Resort*, while a two-metre-wide concrete path runs north from Tekek to the promontory, a twenty-minute walk, commencing again on the other side of the rocks for the length of Air Batang. **Trails** are limited, though crossing the island has been made a lot easier by the building of cement steps beginning around ten minutes' walk from Tekek jetty and running as far as Juara (see "Juara", p.327, for details of the route). Less obvious trails connect Genting with Paya, and Air Batang with Penuba Bay, Monkey Beach and Salang – details are given below in the relevant sections. The ridge of mountains running the length of the island culminates in an impressive cluster of peaks in the south, of which the highest, **Gunung Kajang** (1038m), is inaccessible to all but the most experienced and well-equipped climbers.

For everyday transport around the coast of the island, use the **sea bus**, a slow service that hops from jetty to jetty. From Tekek, there are six boats a day to the *Berjaya*

LEAVING TIOMAN

Although many of the travel agencies in Mersing may try to sell you an open-return boat ticket to Tioman, tickets are readily available from outlets at any of the bays on the island. **Express boats** all leave at around 7–8am daily, making their pick-ups from each jetty. Slower boats usually leave before midday, picking up from every bay – check with your chalet-owner. The ferry to Tanjung Gemuk leaves at 11am and 4pm from the *Berjaya Tioman Beach Resort*. There are also daily **flights** to Kuala Lumpur ($141), Singapore ($167) and Kuantan ($72) with Berjaya Air (☎03/244 1718), Pelangi Air (☎03/746 3000 or ☎02/336 6777) and Tradewinds (☎02/225 4488). You can make reservations for Berjaya Air and Pelangi Air at the *Berjaya Tioman Beach Resort* (☎09/445445).

Sungei Palas Tea Estate, Cameron Highlands

Wall sculpture in the Rose Centre, Cameron Highlands

Fisherman, Beserah

Woman fanning herself, Kota Bharu

Drum festival, Kota Bharu

Christ Church with national flag, Melaka

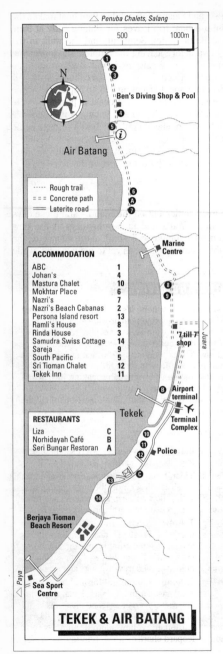

△ Penuba Chalets, Salang

| 0 | 500 | 1000m |

N

Ben's Diving Shop & Pool

Air Batang

- ····· Rough trail
- = = = Concrete path
- ═══ Laterite road

Marine Centre

'7 till 7' shop

△ Juara

Airport terminal

Terminal Complex

Tekek

Police

△ Paya

Berjaya Tioman Beach Resort

Sea Sport Centre

TEKEK & AIR BATANG

ACCOMMODATION

ABC	1
Johan's	4
Mastura Chalet	10
Mokhtar Place	6
Nazri's	7
Nazri's Beach Cabanas	2
Persona Island resort	13
Ramli's House	8
Rinda House	3
Samudra Swiss Cottage	14
Sareja	9
South Pacific	5
Sri Tioman Chalet	12
Tekek Inn	11

RESTAURANTS

Liza	C
Norhidayah Café	B
Seri Bungar Restoran	A

the beach south of the jetty is pretty decent, with good budget accommodation. However, the incessant stream of chugging ferries, the roar of aeroplanes and the churning of concrete mixers all combine to make Tekek one of the least inspiring parts of Tioman.

For a break from the beach, pop into the **Tioman Island Museum** (daily 9.30am–5pm; $1) on the first floor of the Terminal Complex next to the airport. Displaying some twelfth- to fourteenth-century Chinese ceramics, which were lost overboard from early trading vessels, it also outlines the facts and myths concerning the island. North of the main jetty, at the very end of the bay, it's hard to miss the government-sponsored **Marine Centre** with its hefty concrete jetty and dazzlingly blue-roofed buildings. Set up to protect the coral and marine life around the island, and to patrol the fishing taking place in its waters, it also contains an aquarium and samples of coral (daily 9.30am–5pm; free).

Accommodation

There are lots of **places to stay** in Tekek, though choices are significantly better south of the jetty. Tioman's only true resort is the *Berjaya Tioman Beach Resort* which has excellent sports facilities. North of the jetty, along the path, are a whole string of down-at-heel A-frames. *Ramli's House* ($20) has run-down chalets close to the beach in a little garden; you'd do better opting for the slightly more expensive *Sareja* (no phone, ②) next door.

Berjaya Tioman Beach Resort (☎09/414 5445, fax 414 5718). Two kilometres south of Tekek. Facilities include two pools, tennis courts, horse riding, watersports and a golf course – though the cheaper rooms aren't up to much. ⑦.

Mastura Chalet (☎09/715283). Simple wooden chalets; also has a diving operation. ②.

Persona Island Resort (☎ & fax 09/414 6213). Set back from the beach, next to the post office. A pleasant upmarket operation with solid hotel-style rooms and an airy restaurant. ⑤.

Samudra Swiss Cottage (☎07/224 2829). The first place north of the resort, this lies in a shady jungle setting, with a dive shop and small restaurant. ②.

Sri Tioman Chalets (☎011/224 2829). Good atmosphere and value, with solid hotel-style rooms and an airy restaurant, set back from the beach. Further north, hill-facing or sea-facing chalets sit in a secluded, leafy compound with its own small restaurant. ②.

Tekek Inn (☎011/358395). More unspectacular wooden chalets by the beach – a second choice after the *Sri Tioman Chalets*. ②.

Eating and drinking

One of Tekek's nicest **restaurants**, *Liza*, is at the far southern end of the bay, with a wide-ranging menu specializing in seafood and Western snacks – it's popularity has pushed the prices up to around $20 a meal, though. Most of the other places are attached to the chalet groups; the best are those with beachside settings, such as *Sri Tioman Chalet*. A rickety bridge crosses a small, stagnant lagoon just past the airstrip, over which you'll find *Norhidayah Café*, serving snacks, fried rice and noodles; it's also good for sunset drinks.

Air Batang

Despite its ever-increasing popularity, **AIR BATANG**, 2km north of Tekek from jetty to jetty, is still one of the best areas on Tioman, competing with Juara for the budget market. Although there's plenty of accommodation, it has a more spacious feel than Tekek or its northern neighbour Salang, and what development there is tends to be relatively tasteful and low-key. The cement path that runs its length is interrupted by little wooden bridges over streams, overhung with greenery. A jetty divides the bay roughly in half; the beach is better at the southern end of the bay, close to the promontory, though the shallow northern end is safer for children. A fifteen-minute **trail** leads over the headland to the north which, after an initial scramble, flattens out into an easy walk, ending up at **Penuba Bay**. This secluded cove is littered with dead coral right up to the sea's edge, which makes it impossible to swim comfortably, though many people still prefer its peace and quiet to the beach at Air Batang. From here, it's an hour's walk to Monkey Beach, beyond which is Salang; see below for both.

Accommodation

As you get off the boat, a signpost helpfully lists the direction of the numerous places to stay in the bay; the best are listed below. Not all have fans or their own bathrooms, though mosquito nets are usually provided. All these places are marked on the map.

ABC (☎011/349868). At the far northern end of the bay, this long-running operation is still the best in Air Batang: basic but pretty chalets in a well-tended garden with its own freshwater stream. More expensive chalets, up on the rocks, have a great view over the bay. ①–②.

Johan's (no phone). A good choice with well-spaced chalets and new, larger ones up the hill. ①.

Mokhtar's Place (☎09/414 6665). South of the jetty, this place is more upmarket, though the chalets are a little close together and face inwards, rather than out to sea. ①.

Nazri's Beach Cabanas (☎011/333486, fax 07/799 5405). Located at the northern end of Air Batang, this is a truly spectacular outfit (affiliated to *Nazri's*), with large, air-con cottages set in spacious grounds, and some ordinary, cheaper chalets at the back. ②–③.

Nazri's Place (☎011/333 486, fax 07/799 5405). At the southern end of the bay, this rides rather on its long-standing reputation, with shabby, overpriced rooms. It does have the best bit of beach on the strip, though. ①–③.

Penuba Chalets (☎011/952963). The only place to stay in Penuba Bay, and you're committed to eating here every night, too, unless you fancy a scramble over the headland in the dark. Its stilted chalets are high up on the rocks and have fantastic views out to sea. ②.

Rinda House (no phone). A good spot in a neat and shaded setting at the northern end of Air Batang, perfect for watching the sun go down from one of their hammocks. ①.

South Pacific (no phone). Close to the jetty. A little run-down these days, though all the chalets have bathrooms, and some are right on the beach. ①.

Eating, drinking and nightlife

Air Batang likes to keep its **nightlife** low-key, unlike Salang, which can get rowdy during the season. Most of the chalets have their own **restaurants**, though you don't have to be staying there to eat at them. Menus tend to reflect Western tastes and fish is a staple feature.

ABC. Good-quality food – chicken and fish dishes average $10 – and fresh fruit juices. There's an informal bar, and a good sound system means this friendly joint is always rocking.

Nazri's Place. Does a very hearty breakfast for $8.50 and does lots of Western-style food for lunch and dinner (around $7 a dish). Good location on the beach.

Nazri's Beach Cabanas. The food is slightly more expensive than elsewhere – things like chicken-in-a-basket and burgers, averaging $8; its balcony is great for a sunset beer.

Seri Bungur Restoran. Serves traditional Malay food; you won't part with more than about $4.

Salang

No longer a secluded idyll as it's often claimed, **SALANG** has been subject to the sort of merciless development that is uncharacteristic of the island as a whole. The stretch along the beach front is now completely chock-a-block with new buildings, and the jungle is being torn down to make way for uniform rows of overpriced chalets, mostly without a view of the sea. This is a shame, as Salang actually has one of the loveliest beaches on Tioman (its northern half excepted, where rocks and coral debris prohibit all sunbathing and swimming). Things look set to get worse with the development of *Nadia's Inn* resort at the southern end of the beach.

A rough trail takes you over the headland to the south for the 45-minute scramble to **Monkey Beach**. There are few monkeys around these days, but the well-hidden cove is more than adequate compensation. It's a popular spot for trainee divers because of its clear, calm waters, and you may want to base yourself here to take advantage of the two good **dive schools**, Dive Asia and Ben's Diving Centre, both of which run daily courses ($625–1200), with instruction in English and German.

Accommodation and eating

On the right as you leave the jetty are a little cluster of budget **places**, the best of which is *Zaid's* (③), with attractive hillside chalets; there are some dorm beds ($10) too. *Nora's Café* is a friendly family operation, whose well-kept chalets (①) with bathroom, fan and mosquito nets make them the best value, set behind the little lagoon. *Khalid's Place* (☎011/953421; ②) is set back from the beach in landscaped gardens. The management are friendly and some of the rooms have air-con. The largest outfit, towards the centre of the bay, is *Salang Indah* (☎011/730230; ①–④), with well-appointed chalets to suit

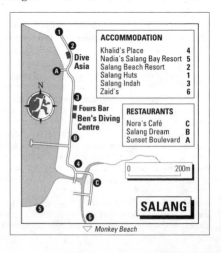

ACCOMMODATION

Khalid's Place	4
Nadia's Salang Bay Resort	5
Salang Beach Resort	2
Salang Huts	1
Salang Indah	3
Zaid's	6

RESTAURANTS

Nora's Café	C
Salang Dream	B
Sunset Boulevard	A

Dive Asia

Fours Bar
Ben's Diving Centre

0   200m

SALANG

▽ Monkey Beach

every budget, from run-of-the-mill sea-facing boxes to double-storey family chalets. The *Salang Beach Resort* (☎07/799 2337; ②) has upmarket pretensions, with comfortable, hillside chalets; the sea-facing ones are double the normal price. At the far end of the bay, the standard chalets at *Salang Huts* (②) are considerably quieter than others along the stretch, though they overlook unattractive piles of rocks and there's no beach to speak of.

There's a polarized choice when it comes to **eating**, from the expensive restaurants at *Salang Dream* and *Salang Beach Resort*, where the emphasis is on Malay cuisine and seafood at around $8 per dish, to the more informal *Zaid's* and *Nora's Café*, serving excellent Western and Malay dishes for no more than $2–3. For **nightlife**, there are several choices: *Four S Bar*, a candle-lit beer bar, the *Dive Bar* next to Ben's Diving Centre and the more upmarket *Sunset Boulevard*, which has the best views of the bay.

Juara

As Tioman's west coast becomes more and more developed, many people are making their way to **JUARA**, the only settlement on the east coast. Life is simpler here, the locals speak less English and are much more conservative than elsewhere on the island: officially alcohol isn't served. There's only one sea bus to the kampung from the east coast of Tioman, so at any other time the journey to this isolated bay must be made **on foot** through the jungle, a moderate trek that takes under two hours from Tekek. The start of the trail (a five-minute walk from the airstrip) is easy enough to identify since it's the only concrete path that heads off in that direction, passing the local mosque before hitting virgin jungle after about fifteen minutes. There's no danger of losing your way: cement steps climb steeply through the greenery, tapering off into a smooth, downhill path once you're over the ridge. Here there are unusual blue ferns, and some of the rarer trees are labelled. After 45 minutes, there is a **waterfall** – it's forbidden to bathe here, since it supplies Tekek with water. From the waterfall, it's another hour or so to Juara village.

Although Juara's seclusion may have saved it so far from the excesses all too apparent on the west coast, everywhere has electricity and new chalets are already springing up. For the time being, however, Juara is refreshingly free from the buzz of speedboats and motorbikes, while its wide sweep of beach is far cleaner and less crowded than anywhere on the other side. A constant sea breeze means that fans aren't necessary, though the downside to this is that the water is always choppy, and the bay, facing out to the open sea, is the most susceptible on the island to bad weather.

Juara in fact consists of two bays; the northern has a jetty, opposite which the cross-island path emerges. Most of the accommodation and restaurants are here too, within a five-minute walk of the jetty. Although the southern bay does have a few chalets, you'll face a long scramble over the rocks or a dark walk along the concrete path that runs behind all the developments to get to the nearest restaurants.

JUARA

RESTAURANTS

Aliputra	**A**
Beach Café	**B**
Bushman's	**D**
Happy Café	**C**

ACCOMMODATION

Atan's	2
Basir	4
Juara Bay Resort	7
Mutiara	3
Paradise Point	1
Rainbow	6
Sunrise	5

Tekek

N

0   200m

▽ South Bay

Accommodation and eating

Starting at the northern end, the best options are *Paradise Point* ($15) about 100m down the beach from the jetty, which has the cheapest A-frames, and chalets a little apart from the rest of the clutch. *Atan's* (②), past the cross-island path, boasts an interesting, two-storey guesthouse, rather like a Swiss chalet; while *Mutiara* (☎07/799 4833; ①–③) is the biggest operation, with a wide variety of room types and prices – these are also the people to see if you want to arrange a boat trip for fishing or snorkelling. A little further south, *Basir* has good sea-facing chalets (②), with some cheaper huts as well, while at the very end of the strip, *Sunrise* and *Rainbow* have characterful, painted A-frames right on the beach (both ①). You'll pass the *Juara Bay Resort* at the end of the northern bay as you follow the path round to the even quieter southern bay. The beach here is even better than that on the northern bay and there are several cheap places to stay, including *Mezanie Chalet* (☎09/547 8445; ②), which has its own restaurant.

While there's less choice for **eating**, portions tend, on the whole, to be larger and the menus more imaginative than on the west coast. *Paradise Point* does good *rotis* and unusual dishes, such as fish with peanut sauce and fried rice with coconut, averaging around $5. Two simple places nestle side by side at the jetty, *Ali Putra* and *Beach Café*, both with a huge range of local and Western dishes. To the south, *Happy Café* is always busy, has good music and serves ice cream among other things, while *Sunrise* is open for breakfast and lunch only with muesli, home-baked bread and cakes. At night try *Bushman's*, a shack next to *Sunrise*, and the only place serving alcohol at Juara.

Asah and Mukut

South of Juara are the deserted remains of the village at **ASAH**; the round-the-island boat trip (see "Getting around the island", p.322) calls here, or take a sea taxi from Genting ($60 per person), the nearest point of access. These days, the only signs of life are the trails of litter left by day-trippers dropping by to visit the famous **waterfall**, the setting for the "Happy Talk" sequence from *South Pacific*. A fifteen-minute walk from the ramshackle jetty, the twenty-metre-high cascade is barely recognizable from the film, though certainly photogenic enough. While the deep-plunge pool at the foot of the waterfall provides a refreshing dip, there's not much to detain you in Asah but the stunning view of the dramatic, insurmountable twin peaks of **Bukit Nenek Semukut**.

Mukut

It's far better to spend time at nearby **MUKUT**, a tiny fishing village just five minutes from Asah by sea taxi, in the shadow of granite outcrops. Shrouded by dense forest, and connected to the outside world by a solitary card phone, it's a wonderfully peaceful and friendly spot to unwind, though be warned that this is still a conservative place, unused to Western sunbathing habits.

Having paid handsomely to get here, you'll probably want to make it worth your while by staying for some time. The nicest position is occupied by *Chalets Park* (③), with secluded chalets shaded by trees. Those at *Sri Tanjung Chalets* (②) at the far western end of the cove overlook a patch of beach – ask at the house in the village where the name is painted on a tyre. The places to **eat** are few and basic. The *Sri Sentosa* is a bit on the dingy side, though popular with the locals, while the views from *Mukut Coral Resort* and the *7-Eleven* café just by the jetty make up for their lack of variety.

Nipah

For almost total isolation, head to **NIPAH** on Tioman's southwest coast. Comprising a clean, empty beach of coarse, yellow sand and a landlocked lagoon, there's no village to speak of here, but there is a Dive Centre and canoeing. You might be lucky enough to get a ferry from the mainland to drop you here since there is an adequate jetty, but it's more likely that you'll have to come by sea taxi from Genting, costing around $30 per person.

There's only one **place to stay**: the *Nipah Resort* (☎011/764184; ②), offering basic chalets and more expensive A-frames, as well as a nicely designed restaurant; the food can get a little monotonous. The air-con longhouse, *Nipah Paradise*, at the far end, caters only for pre-booked packages from Singapore.

Genting

Usually the first stop from the mainland, **GENTING**, at the western extremity of the island, is hardly a heartening welcome, an ugly blot on the landscape. The cramped developments cater largely for Singaporean tour groups and the settlement is awash with discos and karaoke bars. Except on weekends and holidays when prices rise dramatically, it has a rather gloomy feel.

The southern end of the beach is the best, which is also where most of the low-budget **accommodation** is situated. There's little to choose between *Genting Jaya* (☎07/799 4811; ②) and the many more similar, unnamed places nearby. At the far northern end of the concrete path, the *Sea Star Beach Resort* (☎011/718334; ②) is not bad for the price, though *Sun Beach* (☎07/799 4918; ③), the largest enterprise just north of the jetty, has the widest variety of rooms and a large balcony restaurant. Places to eat are generally limited to large, open-plan **restaurants** attached to the resorts; the emphasis is on catering for large numbers rather than providing interesting, quality meals. Prices are predictably inflated, though the *Yonghwa Restaurant* in front of the jetty has more moderately priced dishes on its Chinese-based menu.

Paya

In contrast to its noisy neighbour, the understated developments at **PAYA**, further up the west coast (and just 5km from Tekek), seem relatively peaceful. Once again, package tours are the norm, and individual travellers turning up at this narrow stretch of pristine beach will find their options somewhat limited. **Jungle walks** are worth exploring here, as the greenery is at its most lush, despite the minor inroads made by the resorts. You can even walk to Genting from Paya, a tough, overgrown and at times steep trek taking about an hour from jetty to jetty. The easier thirty-minute trail north to Bunut ends up at a fantastic, deserted beach – though the rumours are that the Pahang royal family, who own it, are planning a new resort here. From here it's a hot 45-minute walk through the golf course to the *Berjaya Tioman Beach Resort* and a further half-hour to Tekek.

The only budget **accommodation** in Paya is at the *Paya Holiday* (☎011/716196; ②), right in the centre of the small bay. A little further to the north, the *Paya Beach Resort* (☎07/799 1432, fax 799 1436; ⑤) has reasonable facilities, including sea sports and snooker, though its chalets are shoddily built. By far the best operation is the *Paya Tioman Resort* (☎011/324121; ④), set back in the woodland, with open-air restaurant and barbecue facilities.

The other Seribuat islands

Though Pulau Tioman is the best known and most visited of the 64 volcanic islands which form the **SERIBUAT ARCHIPELAGO**, there are a handful of other accessible islands whose beaches and opportunities for seclusion outstrip those of their larger

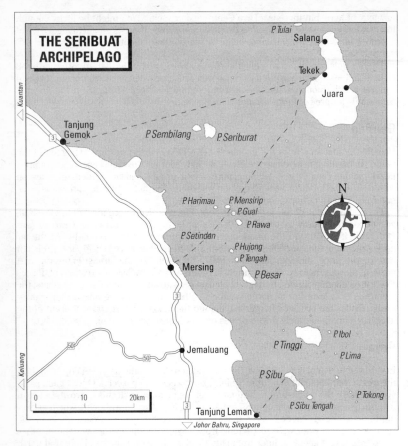

THE SERIBUAT
ARCHIPELAGO

Kuantan

P. Tulai
Salang

Tekek

Juara

Tanjung
Gemok

P. Sembilang   *P. Seriburat*

N

P. Harimau   *P. Mensirip*
    P. Gual
    P. Rawa

P. Setindan

    P. Hujong
    P. Tengah

Mersing

    P. Besar

Keluang

Jemaluang

P. Tinggi   *P. Ibol*

    P. Lima

P. Sibu

    P. Tokong

0   10   20km

Tanjung Leman   *P. Sibu Tengah*

▽ *Johor Bahru, Singapore*

rival. For archetypal azure waters and table-salt sand, four in particular stand out:
Pulau Besar, **Pulau Tinggi**, **Pulau Sibu** and **Pulau Rawa** – though none of them are
particularly geared to a tight budget. All the islands are designated **marine parks** and,
like Tioman, belong to the state of Pahang, unlike their port of access, Mersing, which
lies in Johor. *Omar's Backpackers' Hostel* (see p.319) offers a one-day island hopping trip
aboard its "Black Sausage" traditional Malay fishing boat. At $60 per person (minimum
four people), this takes in either three islands to the south of Mersing (Pulau Hujung,
Tengah and Besar) or four islands to the north (Pulau Harimau, Mensirip, Gual and
Rawa). The price includes lunch and snorkelling equipment and is the only cheap way
of seeing several islands at the same time.

Pulau Besar

The long and narrow landmass of **PULAU BESAR**, 4km by 1km, is also known as Pulau
Babi Besar, or "Big Pig Island". Just over an hour's ferry ride from Mersing (departs
daily around midday; $30 return), it's one of the most developed islands, with a variety
of resorts and chalets, but despite this, outside the main holiday periods, you're still like-

ly to have the place to yourself. The island claims to be sheltered from the worst of the monsoon, but there's a strong undertow and constant sea breeze even in the dry season. Topped by two peaks, Bukit Atap Zink (225m) and Bukit Berot (275m), the island is crossed by three relatively easy **trails**: a ten-minute stroll from behind the *Hillside Chalet Island Resort* at the northern end of the island brings you to the Beach of Passionate Love; while an hour's walk starting either from behind the central jetty or from just beyond the *Perfect Life Resort* leads to secluded bays. However, neither beach is as good as the west-facing one where all the accommodation is situated.

Accommodation and eating

The **resorts** on Besar are all well spaced out facing the mainland. The *Radin Island Resort* (☎07/799 4152; ⑥), more or less in the middle of the bay, is the best place on the island, with superbly designed chalets. The only budget-orientated place is a set of four A-frames (②) right by the sea, not far from the *Radin Island* – ask at the small shop by the phone and post box. The *Perfect Life Resort* (☎07/793948; ⑤), at the far southern end of the bay, has its own jetty and the best bit of beach on the island; its clapboard buildings look a bit motley at first sight, but they're quite comfortable inside. Next door is *Suntam Island Resort* (☎07/799 4995; ②), with simple but homely chalets set far apart from each other in a well-tended flower garden. Right at the far northern end of the island, the exclusive *Hillside Chalet Island Resort* (☎07/799 4831; ⑤) has an isolated setting, a good thirty-minute walk from the rest of the developments. Its beach isn't that special, but the chalets are comfortable and arranged in flourishing green gardens.

All the places to stay have their own **restaurants**; that at the *Hillside* is the most expensive at around $30 per head, although the room rates include breakfast. The *Radin* has an elegant open-air restaurant designed to catch the sea breezes, while *Suntam Island Resort* serves reasonable meals, such as *nasi goreng* for around $4.

Pulau Tinggi

One of the largest of the island group, **PULAU TINGGI** is also the most distinctive, with its towering volcanic peak sticking up like a giant upturned funnel (*tinggi* actually means "tall" or "high"). You can climb the mountain, an arduous four-hour trip, though you will need a local guide to help you as the route can be quite dangerous. A gentler excursion is to the **waterfall**, pretty disappointing outside the rainy season, about thirty minutes over the headland along a well-worn path – but with a splendid beach.

The island is a two-hour boat ride from Mersing ($50 return). **Accommodation** is currently limited to two resorts, *Nadia's Inn* (☎011/799 5582; ⑧), but with a good swimming pool, and the friendly *Tinggi Island Resort* (☎011/766018; ⑥) with basic chalets but good watersports facilities. You can **eat** at both of the resorts, for about $10 for a meal, or try the local food stalls by the jetty, where *nasi goreng* is served.

Pulau Sibu

PULAU SIBU lies closest to the mainland, the most popular – if the least scenically interesting – of the islands after Tioman, though the huge monitor lizards and the butterflies here make up for the lack of mountains and jungle. Like the rest of the islands, Sibu boasts fine beaches, though the sand is yellower and the current more turbulent than some. Shaped like a bone, the island's narrow waist can be crossed in only a few minutes, revealing a double bay known as Twin Beach. Most of the coves have good offshore coral.

Most of the resorts on Sibu operate their own boats **from Tanjung Leman**, a tiny village about 30km down the coast from Mersing and an hour's boat ride from the island. It's not an established route, so you must ask the resort in advance to pick you up. *O&H*'s boat, the distinctive "Black Pudding", runs the one-hour journey to and from Tanjung Leman daily ($16). Tanjung Leman is awkward to get to without your own transport, though it's clearly marked off Route 3. If you're taking *O&H's* boat, a free bus ride from Mersing is included – if not you can pay $10 for the journey. A taxi from Johor Bahru or Mersing costs around $60, but since there is no stand at Tanjung Leman, you must arrange a pick-up in advance. Secure parking is available for $7 per day.

Accommodation and eating

Halfway along the eastern coast, *O&H Kampung Huts* (☎011/354 322; ②–③) is the best place to stay on the island if you're on a budget, a friendly and relaxed set-up of A-frames and some dearer but still fairly basic chalets. Also on the eastern side, the *Sea Gypsy Village Resort* (☎07/222 8642, fax 238 7305; ⑥) is much more exclusive, aiming for the diving market, with all-inclusive packages costing around US$100 per night for two people. It's a tasteful place, with simple chalets and an attractive lounge and dining area. For something more unusual, try *Rimba Resort* (☎011/711528; ⑥), on the north coast, whose simply furnished cottages have an African theme and whose communal areas are scattered with floor cushions. They offer a package including boat transfer and all food. *Sibu Island Cabanas* (☎07/331 1920; ④) is one of the lower-priced options – its chalets are shabby, but it has a good stretch of beach. Head back from the *Cabanas*, over the small ridge in the centre of the island, to get to *Twin Beach Resort* (☎03/948 8966; ③), the only place with sunrise- *and* sunset-viewing; its A-frames and pricier chalets are run-down, but you can also camp here.

Eating on Pulau Sibu is a pleasure. *O&H* has excellent fish and chicken curries with rice, vegetables and salad, as well as Western options, at around $15 for a full meal. *Sea Gypsy* also offers great cuisine, but for resort guests only. The restaurant at *Twin Beach* specializes in (reasonably priced) Chinese food.

Pulau Rawa

PULAU RAWA is a 75-minute boat ride ($30 return) from Mersing; its sugary sands and transparent waters get uniformly rave reviews although the sand flies are unavoidable. There's only one **place to stay**, the deluxe *Rawa Safaris Island Resort* (☎07/799 1204, fax 799 3848; ③–⑦), where there are cheap *atap*-roofed A-frames as well as comfortable, well-equipped chalets, and every facility for watersports. Try to book a couple of days in advance, especially at weekends. Rawa is close enough to visit as a day-trip – but you'll have to charter a boat from Mersing, and you're not allowed to bring your own food and drink onto the island.

Endau Rompin National Park

One of the few remaining areas of lowland tropical rainforest left in Peninsular Malaysia, the **ENDAU ROMPIN NATIONAL PARK** covers approximately 870 square kilometres – about one and a half times the area of Singapore. Surrounding the headwaters of the lengthy Sungei Endau and sitting astride the Johor–Pahang state border, the region was shaped by volcanic eruptions more than 150 million years ago. The force of the explosions sent up huge clouds of ash, creating the quartz crystal ignimbrite that's still very much in evidence along the park's trails and rivers, its glassy shards glinting in the light. Endau Rompin's steeply sloped mountains level out into sandstone plateaux. The park is valued by conservationists for the richness of both **flora and fauna**. It is the habitat of the increasingly rare **Sumatran rhinoceros** – who hide out in the far western area of the park, off-limits to visitors – this dense, lush habitat has also nurtured several species new to science, including at least three trees, eight herbs and two mosses, documented by the Malaysian Nature Society during its 1985–86 expedition, which itself helped to establish the need for a properly controlled park. The restrictions imposed as a result of Endau Rompin's establishment as a National Park in 1989 at last ensure its protection from the damaging logging that took place here in the 1970s. For the less specialized nature-lover, there's plenty on offer, from gentle **trekking** to more strenuous mountain-climbing and **rafting**. Although gradually becoming accustomed to tourists, Endau Rompin still has a long way to go before it suffers the over-use that afflicts Taman Negara, and for the time being at least, its trails remain refreshingly untrampled.

The aboriginal people of the Endau Rompin area are commonly referred to by the generic term **Orang Ulu**, meaning "upriver people". Traditionally collectors of forest products such as resins, rattan and camphor wood, their lives revolve around the rivers – you can still see dug-outs made from a single tree trunk and canoes made of lengths of bark sewn together with twine. In recent years, these nomadic peoples have become more settled, living in permanent villages such as Kampung Peta, accessible only by an old logging track two hours' drive from the nearest tarmac road.

Acquiring a permit for the park can require a certain degree of determination (see "Practicalities" on p.335), and once there, conditions are fairly primitive and you'll need a guide. All this means that its best to book a tour. During the monsoon, the park is completely inaccessible, since many of its waterways are swollen and the trails are too boggy to use. Take loose-fitting, lightweight cotton clothing that will help to protect you from scratches and bites and is quick to dry – even in the dry season you're bound to get wet from crossing rivers. Waterproofs will come in handy, and you'll need tons of insect repellent – and a lighter to burn off leeches.

Approaching the park

Travelling north of Mersing along Highway 3, past **Kampung Air Papan**, reputed to have the best local beach, you'll eventually reach **Padang Endau**, on the Johor side of the Sungei Endau. There's nothing to keep you here, although across the bridge in Pahang state, is the Tanjung Gemuk jetty for Tioman, a largely empty development of shops and a *Seri Malaysia Hotel* (☎07/794 4723, fax 794 4732; ⑤) which organizes trips into the park. About 10km further up the coast, on the way to sleepy Kuala Rompin, is the *Watering Hole Bungalows* (☎011/411 894; ①–②), set 2km off the main road by the beach. There's little to do at this attractively laid-out complex of *atap*-roofed A-frames and huts, run by a Swiss-Malaysian couple, but it makes for a pleasant rest. The price includes breakfast, and hearty meals are available for $10. If you call in advance, they will pick you up from the bus station in Kuala Rompin. The owners also help run treks into the Endau Rompin National Park in conjunction with Wilderness Experience.

The park

The park is watered by three **river systems** based around the main tributaries of Sungei Marong, Sungei Jasin and Sungei Endau, reaching out to the south and east. At the confluence of the latter two rivers, at the eastern end of the park, lies Endau Rompin's base camp at **KUALA JASIN**. Although the park's boundaries lie some distance beyond the rivers, it is only in these valleys that you can roam freely. **Rafting** down the peaty Sungei Endau is a possibility, too, with short stretches of stony bed and relatively sluggish flow interspersed by white-water rapids and huge boulders. After the river merges with Sungei Kinchin, the flow becomes slower and the scenery generally less exciting. Ask at the Visitor Control Centre at Kampung Peta for advice on arranging a rafting trip.

The Janing Barat plateau

The accessible area of the park includes the **Janing Barat plateau** (710m), to which a relatively easy four-hour trail leads southeast of the base camp. Topped by a giant sandstone slab, the outcrop marks an abrupt change from the lush growth of wild ginger, characterized by its bright crimson flowers, and the ever-present betel-nut palm, in favour of tough fan palms. On the ridge of the mountain, at around 450m, is a boggy, waterlogged area, producing a small patch of heath forest, though it is past this, in the taller forest, that most of the wild animals can be found – look out for the occasional group of pigs, or a solitary **tapir** chewing at the bark of the trees.

The waterfalls

Each river boasts a major waterfall, the best of which are along Sungei Jasin, southwest of base camp. Two routes lead from the base camp to the head of the river, where the spectacular **Buaya Sangkut** cascades in a forty-metre torrent, almost as wide as it is high. A track along the northern bank leads directly to the falls, a six-hour hike across the multiple ridges of Bukit Segongong (765m). An Orang Ulu legend tells of an old crocodile who lived in the pools above the waterfall, and one day got stuck between some rocks, its body transforming itself into the white-water rapids – the translation of the waterfall's name in fact means "trapped crocodile". A longer, less-defined trail branches off south, about ten minutes out of base camp, crossing Sungei Jasin to reach the estuary, Kuala Marong, about 45 minutes later. From here, you can head east along Sungei Marong as far as Kuala Bunuh Sawa (2hr), or continue along Sungei Jasin to the **Upeh Guling** waterfall, ten minutes further on. Although initially less impressive than Buayu Sangkut, one striking feature is the collection of deep potholes near the top of the falls, whose steep sides have been eroded by the water into smooth, natural bath tubs – a good place to soothe aching feet. Following the river closely for a further two hours will bring you to **Batu Hampar** waterfall, where you can either pitch a tent, or continue the additional three hours to Buaya Sangkut.

Flora and fauna in the park

At the upper levels of the jungle, epiphytes are common: non-parasitic plants which take advantage of their position on tree branches to get the light they need for photosynthesis. Here, too, are massive palms, but it's mostly orchids and ferns that flourish. Lower down in the forest shade, moths and spiders camouflage themselves among the greyish brown lichen that covers the barks, and squirrels and lizards scurry up and down. Much closer to eye level, where most of the light is cut out by the virtually impenetrable canopy, are **birds** like babblers and woodpeckers. You'll also see **tree frogs**, whose expanded disc-like toes and finger tips, sticky with mucus, help them cling to leaves and branches. The forest floor is mostly covered by **ferns and mosses**, as well as tree seedlings struggling to find a chink in the canopy.

There are at least seven species of **hornbill** (see box on p.414) in the park, which are hard to miss, particularly in flight, when their oversized, white-tipped wings counterbalance their enormous curved orange bills. Early in the morning, the hooting of the male **gibbon** joins the dawn chorus of insects, cuckoos and babblers. This is the time of day when the wildlife is most active; by noon all the action has died down. The late afternoon cool heralds a second burst of activity, and is a particularly good time for bird-watching, and at night, owls, frogs, rats and pythons are about. If you're on a tour with a guide (see below), you've a better chance of spotting tiger or elephant **footprints**, though wild pigs, mouse deer and colourful toads are far more usual sightings.

Practicalities

At present, there are two ways of entering **Endau Rompin National Park**, both requiring your own transport to get you as far as the main access points. **From Mersing**, take Route 3 south as far as Jemaluang, then the smaller and windier Route 50 west for a further 42km. Take a right turn just after a bridge, signposted to the Kahang palm oil mill, 5km before Kahang itself. Continue north for 48km along logging tracks until you reach the Orang Asli settlement of Kampung Peta, the site of the Visitor Control Centre where you will have to register with the park rangers. There are basic A-frame huts (③). From here, it's another 15km to the base camp at Kuala Jasin, taking close to three hours on foot, though by boat it's just 45 minutes (departures on request; $10 per person). If this isn't adventurous enough for you, then you can take a trip upriver **from Endau**, 33km north of Mersing – a six-hour trip on a motorboat as far as Kampung Peta, costing around $200.

Endau Rompin covers areas of both Johor and Pahang, but only Johor requires visitors to arrange a **permit** before they enter the park. This costs $20 and is available on the spot from Johor State Economic Unit, Level 2, Bangunan Sultan Ibrahim, Johor Bahru (Mon–Fri 8am–4.15pm, Sat 8am–12.45pm; ☎07/223 7471, fax 223 7472). However charges don't stop there; once inside the park it costs $40 per person per day to visit the Upeh Guling waterfalls, Kuala Marong or the Janing Barat plateau, and $35 for the Buayu Sangkut waterfalls. You'll also be charged an extra $10 to use your camera. None of these charges apply if you enter the park from Pahang. Although new chalets are planned, for now the only facilities available are at the designated **camping grounds** at the Upeh Guling, Batu Hampar and Buaya Sangkut waterfalls, which cost $10 per person per night. If you're on a tour, your guide cooks **food** for you, but take energy-giving snacks as well. If you're not on a tour, you'll have to fend for yourself – remember that carrying cooking pots in addition to the rest of your gear can get very tiring in dense jungle.

Both the Johor and Pahang authorities and the Malaysian Nature Society advise you to book an **organized tour** through a travel agency, which will spare you the hassle of arranging permits and travel. Packages organized by the *Seri Malaysia* (see above) start at $160 (minimum four people) for a day-trip into the park, including a night's stay at the hotel, and run to $260, which includes camping out in the park itself at **Jeram Gerugul**. This compares to $440 for the four-day/three-night trip organized by Wilderness Experience (☎03/717 8221) based in Petaling Jaya. Other tour operators who can arrange trips into the park include Memories Holiday Resort (☎03/245 0746) in Kuala Lumpur, New Asia Holiday Tours and Travel (☎07/233 7392) in Johor Bahru, and Giamso Travel (☎07/799 2253) in Mersing. Further information on current conditions in the park can be obtained from Mr Danapal, a tour guide, by E-mail on davana@tm.net.my.

travel details

Trains

Johor Bahru to: Gemas (7 daily; 3–5hr); Kuala Lipis (3 weekly; 7hr); Kuala Lumpur (5 daily; 6hr 20min–7hr 10min); Seremban (5 daily; 4hr 20min–7hr 20min); Singapore (8 daily; 25min); Tumpat (3 weekly; 12hr).

Kuala Lumpur to: Gemas (5 daily; 3hr 40min–4hr 15min); Johor Bahru (5 daily; 6hr 45min–9hr); Segamat (5 daily; 3hr 35min–5hr 10min); Seremban (5 daily; 1hr 50min–2hr 10min).

Seremban to: Gemas (5 daily; 1hr 45min–2hr 20min); Johor Bahru (5 daily; 5–7hr); Singapore (5 daily; 6hr); Kuala Lumpur (5 daily; 2hr–2hr 45min).

Buses

Johor Bahru to: Alor Setar (2 daily; 16hr); Butterworth (at least 2 daily; 14hr); Ipoh (4 daily; 9hr); Kota Bharu (2 daily; 12hr); Kuala Lumpur (every 30min; 7hr); Kuala Terengganu (2 daily; 10hr); Kuantan (6 daily; 6hr); Melaka (5 daily; 4hr); Mersing (at least 2 daily; 2hr 30min); Singapore (every 30min; 1hr).

Melaka to: Alor Setar (11 daily; 8hr); Butterworth (11 daily; 6hr); Ipoh (11 daily; 4hr); Johor Bahru (5 daily; 4hr); Kota Bharu (1 daily; 11hr); Kuala Lumpur (14 daily; 2hr); Kuala Terengganu (1 daily; 8hr); Kuantan (1 daily; 6hr); Mersing (2 daily; 5hr); Singapore (9 daily; 5hr).

Mersing to: Johor Bahru (at least 2 daily; 2hr 30min); Kluang (every 45min; 2hr); Kuala Lumpur (2 daily; 7hr); Kuantan (3 daily; 3hr 30min); Melaka (2 daily; 5hr); Singapore (4 daily; 3hr 30min).

Seremban to: Butterworth (4 daily; 9hr); Ipoh (2 daily; 5hr); Johor Bahru (3 daily; 5hr 30min); Kota Bharu (4 daily; 10hr); Kuala Lumpur (every 10min; 1hr); Mersing (2 daily; 5hr).

Ferries

Melaka to: Dumai (1 daily; 2hr 30min).

Mersing to: Pulau Besar (1 daily; 1hr 10min); Pulau Rawa (1 daily; 1hr 15min); Pulau Sibu (1 daily; 2hr 30min); Pulau Tinggi (1 daily; 2hr), Pulau Tioman (at least 4 daily; 1hr 30min–5hr).

Pulau Tioman to: Singapore (6 weekly; 4hr 30min).

Planes

Johor Bahru to: Ipoh (1 daily; 2hr 10min); Kota Kinabulu (1 daily; 2hr 20min); Kuala Lumpur (at least 7 daily; 45min); Kuching (at least 2 daily; 1hr 25min); Langkawi (1 daily; 2hr 20min); Penang (2 daily; 1hr).

Melaka to: Ipoh (6 weekly; 50min); Medan (2 weekly; 1hr); Pekan Baru (2 weekly; 30min); Singapore (6 weekly; 55min).

Pulau Tioman to: Kuala Lumpur (up to 8 daily; 45min); Kuantan (1 daily; 45min); Singapore (3 daily; 30min).

CHAPTER SIX

SARAWAK

S ix hundred kilometres across the South China Sea from Peninsular Malaysia, the two East Malaysian states of Sarawak and Sabah occupy the northwest flank of the island of Borneo (the rest of which, save the enclave of Brunei, is Indonesian Kalimantan). **Sarawak** is the larger of the two states, and a more different place to Peninsular Malaysia is hard to imagine. Clear rivers spill down the jungle-covered mountains to become wide, muddy arteries nearer the sea, while the surviving rainforest, highland plateaux and river communities combine to form one of the most complex and diverse ecosystems on earth. Monkeys, deer and lizards abound, although deforestation, caused by both the logging industry and indigenous farming, has had a serious effect on mammals like the orang-utan, proboscis monkey and rhino, which are now all **endangered species**. Ironically, even Sarawak's official state emblem, the eccentric-looking hornbill, is at risk – the bird's beak has been used for centuries by indigenous tribespeople to carve images from the natural and supernatural worlds.

The most convincing reason for hopping across the sea to Sarawak is the possibility of contact with the **indigenous peoples**, who make up around half the state's population. They fall into groups known historically either as Land Dyaks, Sea Dyaks or Orang Ulu (people of the interior). The indigenous peoples have for centuries lived in massive longhouses, visits to which are the highlight of most trips to Sarawak. Journeys through the interior often take days, and travellers have traditionally been dependent on the goodwill of longhouse residents for food, accommodation and safe passage. Tour operators based in Kuching and Miri now pay certain longhouses an annual stipend in exchange for bringing in foreign travellers, sums which pay for structural renovations, and travel and education costs for the longhouse children. But increasing contact with the outside world has undoubtedly had a detrimental effect on several of the communities. Visits to the semi-nomadic Penan especially, who number no more than two thousand in total, have forced the modern age upon them with alarming rapidity. It's argued that contact with tourists can leave groups like this expecting, if not dependent on, food and consumer items from outside.

Other factors also endanger the survival of the indigenous peoples. The Malaysian government wants the semi-nomadic Penan, and others like them, to move into permanent settlements, despite strong resistance form these forest-dwelling hunter-gatherers. However, the main reason for encouraging tribes to "reap the dividends of development" in this way is to take the sting out of the **anti-forestry campaigns** currently being waged in Sarawak. Timber barons and politicians are afraid that an increase in the number of successful court cases, proving the indigenous groups' customary ownership of the forest, could prevent the lucrative trade in exporting hardwood to the developed world. Although the timber cartels have been successful in buying off some local communities with money and extravagant promises (especially along the Baram river in the north), native tribes backed by environmental groups are resisting the loggers. There's more on the politics of logging and the environment in Contexts on p.613.

Most people start their exploration of Sarawak in the capital **Kuching**, in the southwest. This is the starting point for visiting Iban longhouse communities on the Batang Ai river system, and the Bidayuh dwellings near the Indonesian border, south of the

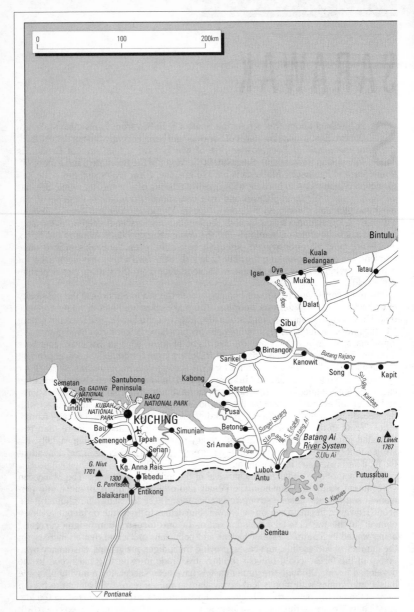

city. Kuching is also a base for seeing nearby **Bako National Park**. Although Sarawak is not noted for its beaches, there are decent ones along its **southwestern seaboard**, accessible from the capital by bus. A four-hour boat ride north of Kuching, **Sibu** marks

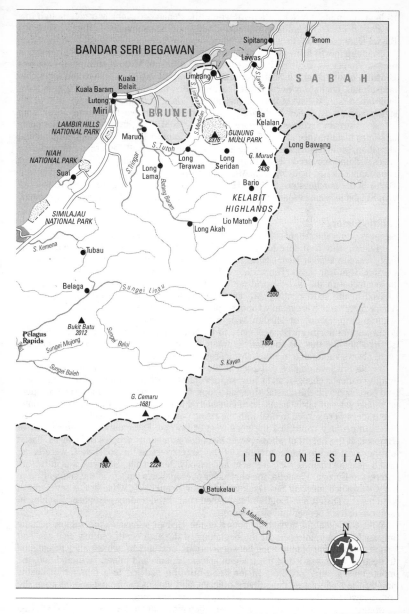

the start of the popular route along **Batang Rajang**, Sarawak's longest river. Most people stop at **Kapit** and from there visit longhouses along the Katibas and Baleh tributaries. Until recently, more adventurous souls continued as far along the river as

Belaga, a remote interior settlement where the Penan occasionally trade, though this area was declared off-limits to tourists in 1996, pending completion of the controversial Bakun Dam (see p.384).

The route north from Sibu is by bus, along Sarawak's only main road – even this is unpaved in places. You pass near the backwater retreat of **Mukah**, through the town of **Bintulu**, before reaching **Niah National Park** with its vast cave system and accessible forest hikes. On its way north to the Brunei border, the road goes to **Miri**, a busy town built on oil money. East of here, thousands of kilos of hardwood logs – the fruit of the state's aggressive policy of deforestation – are floated down the **Baram** river from forests upstream. Express boats go as far upriver as **Marudi**, from where smaller boats or planes head further east to **Gunung Mulu National Park**. Sarawak's chief natural attraction, Mulu features astonishing limestone **pinnacles** and numerous extraordinary caves and undiscovered passageways under its three mountains, and is nowadays most commonly reached by flying from Miri. Flights from Miri and Marudi also connect with **Bario** in the northeastern **Kelabit Highlands**, a forested plateau from where you can visit Kelabit longhouses, and perhaps even encounter the Penan, who roam these parts.

A little history

Sarawak's first inhabitants were cave-dwelling **hunter-gatherers**, distant ancestors of the Penan, who lived here forty thousand years ago. Evidence of their existence was discovered in 1958 at Niah Caves, by a team from the Sarawak Museum headed by its curator, Tom Harrisson. The various tribes lived fairly isolated lives and there was little contact with the wider world until the first trading boats from Sumatra and Java arrived in the sixth century AD, exchanging cloth and pottery for jungle produce. These merchants were mainly Hindus, some of whom subsequently settled in Sarawak, while a larger group of Muslim Malays from Java and Sumatra founded the city of Vijayapura in northern Borneo, close to Brunei, in the eleventh century. But isolated settlements like this, on the northernmost fringes of the Sumatran Srivijaya empire, were always vulnerable to attack from pirates and Muslim rivals.

As the Srivijaya empire collapsed at the end of the thirteenth century, so regional trading patterns changed and **Chinese merchants** became dominant, bartering beads and porcelain with the coastal Melanau people for *bezoar* stones (from the gall bladders of monkeys) and birds' nests, both considered aphrodisiacs by the Chinese. In time, the traders were forced to deal with the rising power of the Malay sultans, who by the fifteenth century controlled the northwest of Borneo. Paramount was the **Sultan of Brunei**, at the height of whose power even the indigenous peoples of Sarawak, based on the coast and in the headwaters of the large rivers in the southwest, were being taxed heavily; clashes were frequent and bloody. Meanwhile, Sarawak was attracting interest in Europe. Pigafetta, the chronicler of Magellan's voyage in the sixteenth century, described meeting Sea Dyak groups near Brunei Bay, while in the seventeenth century the **Dutch** and **English** established short-lived trading posts near Kuching in order to extract pepper and other spices.

With the eventual decline in power of the Brunei sultanate, the region became impossible to administrate. At the beginning of the eighteenth century civil war had erupted as a result of to feuding between various local sultans, while piracy threatened to destroy what was left of the trade in spices, animals and minerals. In addition, the indigenous groups' predilection for **head-hunting** had led to a number of deaths among the traders and the sultan's officials, and violent confrontations between the more powerful ethnic groups over territory were increasing.

Matters were at their most explosive when Englishman **James Brooke** took an interest in the area. Born in India, Brooke joined the Indian army and was wounded in the First Anglo-Burmese War, before being sent to his family home in Devon to convalesce. Returning to the East, he arrived in Singapore in the 1830s, where he learned of the Sultan of Brunei's troubles in Sarawak. The sultan's uncle, Hashim, had recruited Dyak workers to mine high-grade antimony ore in the Sarawak valley near present-day Kuching, but conditions were intolerable and the Dyaks, with the support of local Malays, rebelled. Brooke – having chartered a schooner in Singapore and gathered together a small but well-armed force – quelled the rebellion and, as a reward, demanded sovereignty over the area around Kuching. The sultan had little choice but to relinquish control of the difficult territory and in 1841 Brooke was installed as the first **White Rajah** of Sarawak, launching a dynastic rule which lasted for a century.

Brooke signed treaties with the sultan and tolerated the business dealings of the Chinese, though his initial concern was to stamp out piracy and pacify the warring tribal groups. Displaying an early environmental awareness, Brooke also opposed calls from British and Singapore-based businessmen to exploit the region commercially which, he believed, would have been to the detriment of the ethnic groups, whom he found fascinating. In the 1840s he wrote, "Sarawak belongs to all her peoples and not to us. It is for them we labour, not for ourselves." Laudable words, which didn't prevent him from building a network of **forts** to strengthen his rule, or from sending officials into the malarial swamps and mountainous interior to contact the inaccessible Orang Ulu tribes.

Brooke's administration was not without its troubles. In one incident his men killed dozens of Dyaks, who were part of a pirate fleet, while in 1857 Chinese **Hakka goldminers**, based in the settlement of Bau on the Sarawak river, opposed Brooke's attempts to eliminate their trade in opium and suppress their secret societies. They attacked Kuching and killed a number of officials; Brooke got away by the skin of his teeth. His nephew, **Charles Brooke**, assembled a massive force of warrior Dyaks and followed the miners, and in the battle that ensued over a thousand Chinese were killed.

The acquisition of territory from the Sultan of Brunei continued throughout Charles Brooke's reign, which started in 1863. River valleys, known as divisions, were bought for a few thousand pounds, the Dyaks living there either persuaded to enter into deals or crushed if they resisted. Elsewhere, Brooke set the warrior Iban against the Kayan, whose stronghold was in the central and northern interior, and by 1905 his fiefdom encompassed almost all of the land traditionally occupied by the coastal Malays, as well as that of the Sea Dyaks along the rivers and the Land Dyaks in the mountains. Brunei itself had shrunk so much it was now surrounded on all three sides by Brooke's Sarawak.

During the 1890s Charles Brooke encouraged Chinese **immigration** into the area around Sibu and along the Rajang river, where pepper, and later rubber, farms were established. Bazaars were set up and traders travelled the rivers bartering with the ethnic groups. Brooke thought that these few intrepid Chinese traders – mostly poor men forever in debt to the *towkays* (merchants) in the towns who had advanced them goods on credit – might undermine the indigenous way of life, so he banned them from staying in longhouses and insisted they report regularly to his officials.

The third and last rajah, **Vyner Brooke**, consolidated the gains of his father, Charles, but was less concerned with indigenous matters. Although the new constitution, which he proposed in 1941, would have helped to bring the sub-colonial backwater of Sarawak into the twentieth century, it was the **Japanese invasion** which effectively put an end to his control. Brooke escaped but most of his officials were interned, and some were subsequently executed. With the Japanese surrender in 1945, Australian forces temporarily ran the state; Vyner returned the next year and ceded Sarawak to the British government. Many Malays opposed this, believing that **British rule** was a backward step. Their protest reached its peak in 1949 when the British governor was murdered. With Malaysian independence in 1957, attempts were made to include Sarawak, Sabah and Brunei in the **Malaysian Federation**, inaugurated in 1963, with Brunei exiting at the last minute. Sarawak's inclusion in the federation was opposed by Indonesia, and skirmishes broke out along the Sarawak–Kalimantan border, with Indonesia arming

SARAWAK PRACTICALITIES

It matters little what time of year you travel to Sarawak. The riverine **climate** and humid rainforests aren't seriously affected by the monsoon, though you can depend upon it raining steadily most days, with the odd persistent outburst, more often at night than during the day. What will affect your travel plans is the **budget factor**. Flights from Peninsular Malaysia to Sarawak can dig deep into the pocket, and accommodation and internal travel – cost more than on the mainland. However, food and soft drinks are always a bargain, and ethnic artefacts bought in longhouses are usually good value too.

Getting there

MAS flights to **Kuching** are the most straightforward approach. The most regular service is from **Kuala Lumpur** (at least 10 daily; $262 one-way); otherwise, there are MAS flights from **Johor Bahru** (4 daily; around $170). There are MAS flights from **Singapore** (3 daily; around $230), but you'd do better skipping over the causeway to JB and flying from there. The other main service is from **Kota Kinabalu** (5 daily; around $230). From elsewhere in the region, MAS flies from the Kalimantan city of **Pontianak** on Monday and Thursday ($170 plus), and the Indonesian carrier Merpati has a weekly flight for around $150; Royal Brunei flies from **Bandar Seri Begawan** on Monday, Tuesday and Friday ($250).

Reaching **Miri**, in the north, usually involves taking an MAS internal flight from Kuching ($165 one-way), though there are two direct flights daily from KL ($422). There are also flights to Miri from Kota Kinabalu (4 daily; around $100).

By boat and overland

There are daily boat services **from Brunei** to both Lawas and Limbang, the two far northern divisions of Sarawak – see "Leaving Bandar Seri Begawan", p.486.

The main **overland** route into Sarawak is by bus or taxi **from Kuala Belait** in Brunei to Miri, a very straightforward crossing involving a ferry across the Belait river; see p.497 for all the details. The other main crossing is via **Sipitang** in Sabah (see p.450) to Lawas, either by local bus or taxi or by the daily Lawas Express which originates in Sabah's capital Kota Kinabalu (see p.426).

From Indonesian Kalimantan, there are remote border crossings to villages in the northeastern Kelabit Highlands (see p.414), though you're unlikely to be approaching from this direction. More straightforward is the overland route from **Pontianak** into southwest Sarawak, crossing **from Entikong** to Tebedu, around 100km south of Kuching.

Getting around

Boats – the main mode of transport – come in three sizes and nearly always run to a reliable timetable. Sea-bound **launches** ply the busy stretch from Kuching to Sarikei, at the mouth of Batang Rajang; turbo-charged express **boats** shoot up and down the main rivers; and smaller, diesel-powered **longboats** provide transport along the tributaries.

Occasionally it may be necessary to **rent a longboat**, particularly for travel along the more remote tributaries, though it can be prohibitively expensive if you aren't travelling

communist guerrillas inside Sarawak, who opposed both British and Malay rule. The insurgency, known as the **Konfrontasi**, continued for three years, but was eventually put down by Malaysian troops aided by the British.

Throughout the 1960s and 1970s reconstruction programmes strengthened regional communities and provided housing, resources and jobs. These days, Sarawak is a predominantly peaceful, multiracial state, though in recent years social tensions have been triggered by the government's economic strategy, chiefly the promotion of the **timber industry** over the indigenous groups' claims to the land. Despite progress on as part of a group: it's common to pay in excess of $100 a day to visit the more distant longhouses. In addition, although the distances travelled from one longhouse to another are often not great (around 30km on average), travelling upstream against the current, in shallow waters and through rapids is hard going. You may have to get out of the boat and help pull it over the rocks.

In some areas, you'll need a **permit** before you can visit, though it's usually a straightforward matter to obtain one; all the details are given where necessary.

Accommodation

Most towns in Sarawak have mid-range hotels, lodging houses and cut-price *rumah tumpangan* (guesthouses); the only places with top-class **hotels** are Kuching, Miri, Bintulu, Sibu and Gunung Kulu National Park.

Budget travellers often head as quickly as possible to the **longhouses**, where gifts or a small cash donation (around $10 a night) take the place of a room rate. The more remote the longhouse, the more basic the gifts can be and local foodstuffs will usually do, though if you plan to stay at a longhouse for a few days then more exotic gifts from Kuching or from your home country are the order of the day. Although it's possible, in theory, to stay for a while at a longhouse, most visitors only remain for a day or two, and you certainly shouldn't base your budget on plans to stay for next to nothing at a longhouse every night. A trip to a longhouse is very much a hit-or-miss experience; some tourists literally have the time of their lives, others leave Sarawak sorely disappointed. If you plan to spurn the tour groups and go it alone, your first step should be to ask around at coffee shops, hotels, jetties and riverside petrol stations, to ascertain which longhouses tend to be welcoming . If you're on a river that's not served by express boats, find out which longhouses have boats returning to them in the near future. Unannounced visits to longhouse communities *can* work out perfectly agreeably, but it's always wise to have an introduction: before you board a boat, ideally you'll have already been invited to a longhouse by someone you've met around town. Should you turn up totally on spec, ask to meet the *tuai rumah* (headman); under no circumstances should you waltz up the stairs and into a longhouse uninvited. Finally, bear in mind that if you're keen to witness costumery and festivities you'll need either to travel as part of a tour (in which case your guide can arrange a cultural itinerary with the locals), or visit during the *gawai dayak* period (see p.67).

Don't expect to save funds by **camping** either. There are no campsites and locals seldom, if ever, sleep out in the open. To do so would at the very least invite much curiosity, and at worst, increase the chances of contracting an unpleasant disease or attracting unfriendly wildlife.

Throughout the Malaysia chapters we've used the following **price codes** to denote the cheapest available room for two people. Single occupancy should cost less than double, though this is not always the case. Some guesthouses provide dormitory beds, for which the dollar price is given.

① $20 and under	④ $61–80	⑦ $161–240
② $21–40	⑤ $81–100	⑧ $241–400
③ $41–60	⑥ $101–160	⑨ $401 and above

the question of land rights, communities usually lose the battle for the forests, often forfeiting their former economic autonomy and ending up worse off as wage earners in seasonal employment. Although the rate of deforestation is slowing down, and the state government is now processing more timber in the state rather than exporting whole trunks, hopes for sustainable management of the remaining fifty percent of Sarawak's rainforest cover seem unrealistic – largely because the powerful timber lobby and the state's politicians go hand in glove, unwilling to relinquish control of the highly lucrative logging industry.

SOUTHWEST SARAWAK

Southwest Sarawak is the most densely populated part of the state, supporting around one and a half million people. It's also the only part of the state to be well served by road, a reflection of its long-standing trading importance. Malays from Sumatra and Java first arrived 1300 years ago, Chinese traders have been visiting the region since the eighth century, while Iban tribes migrated here from the Kapuas river basin in present-day Kalimantan around three hundred years ago, supplanting the original Bidayuh population. A second wave of Chinese immigrants settled here in the eighteenth century, initially to mine gold and antimony, a mineral used in medicines and dyes which was in great demand in Europe. Later, when the bottom dropped out of the antimony market, the Chinese switched their endeavours to growing pepper and rubber.

A visit to **Kuching** – set upriver from the swamp-ridden coastline – is likely to be a starting point for the more adventurous travelling to be done beyond Sibu, four hours away by boat. But the city and surroundings contain enough to occupy a couple of weeks' sightseeing. Kuching's **Sarawak Museum** holds the state's best collection of ethnic artefacts, antique ceramics, brassware and natural history exhibits, while easy day-trips include visits to the **Semanggoh Wildlife Rehabilitation Centre** and **Jong's Crocodile Farm**, both to the south, and the **Sarawak Cultural Village**, on the Santubong Peninsula to the north. You'll need more time for **Bako National Park** – at least a couple of days – as you will to see either the **Bidayuh longhouses** near the remote Kalimantan border or the languid coastal village of **Sematan** to the west. Visiting the Iban longhouses on the **Batang Ai river system**, east of the capital, is more complicated altogether, but it's a trip that's mostly rewarded by the warm reception.

Kuching

Despite modernisation, **KUCHING** – the capital of Sarawak – is a highly attractive place, it's elegant colonial buildings decaying under the fierce equatorial sun and lashing rains. The restored courthouse and istana still serve their original purpose, while the commercial district – in the heart of the old town – is a warren of crowded lanes in which Kuching's **Chinese community** run cafés, hotels, general stores and laundries. Main Bazaar, the city's oldest street, sports the remains of its original **godowns**, now converted into shops but still overlooking Sungei Sarawak, Kuching's main supply route since the city's earliest days. In 1841 James Brooke came up the river, arriving at a village known as "Sarawak", which lay on a small stream called Sungei Mata Kuching (cat's eye), adjoining the main river. It seems likely that the stream's name was shortened by Brooke and came to refer to the fast-expanding settlement, though a much-repeated tale has the first rajah pointing to the village and asking its name. The locals, thinking Brooke was pointing to a cat, replied – reasonably enough – "kuching" (a cat). Either way, it wasn't until 1872 that Charles Brooke officially changed the settlement's name from Sarawak to Kuching.

Until the 1920s, the capital was largely confined to the south bank of Sungei Sarawak, stretching only from the Chinese heartland around Jalan Temple, east of today's centre, to the Malay kampung around the mosque to the west. On the north bank, activity revolved around the fort and a few dozen houses reserved for British officials. It was the prewar **rubber boom** which financed the town's expansion: Jalan Padungan, an elegant tree-lined avenue, 1km east of the centre, became the smart place in which to live and work. The kampung areas increased in size, too, as the population was swollen by the arrival of a new bureaucracy of Malay civil servants, as well as by Dyaks from

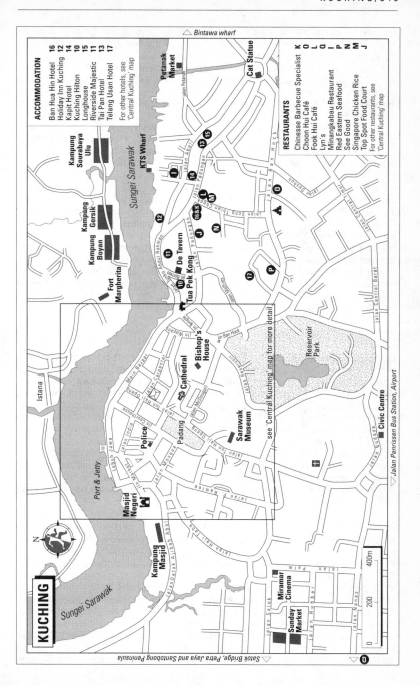

KUCHING

ACCOMMODATION
Ban Hua Hin Hotel	16
Holiday Inn Kuching	12
Kapit Hotel	14
Kuching Hilton	10
Longhouse	15
Riverside Majestic	11
Tai Pan Hotel	13
Telang Usan Hotel	17

For other hotels, see 'Central Kuching' map

RESTAURANTS
Chinesse Barbecue Specialist	K
Choon Hui Café	O
Fook Hui Café	Q
Lyn's	P
Minangkabau Restaurant	I
Red Eastern Seafood	N
See Good	M
Singapore Chicken Rice	
Top Spot Food Court	J

For other restaurants, see 'Central Kuching' map

the interior and immigrants from Hokkien province in mainland China looking for work. The city escaped serious destruction during World War II, since Japanese bombing raids were mainly intent on destroying the oil wells in the north of Sarawak – the few bombs that were dropped on Kuching missed the military base at Fort Margherita and set fire to a fuel store. Since independence business has boomed, and though many of the impressive **nineteenth-century buildings** were restored, others have been destroyed to make way for new roads and office developments. However, the planners cast a sympathetic eye over perhaps the most important part of Kuching. Following a large-scale renovation of the river esplanade, a spacious **riverwalk** once again integrates the city with the waters to which it owes its growth. Yet despite the inevitable structural changes, Kuching still feels like a colonial outpost, albeit one tattered at the edges and lazily acquiescing to benign takeover bid by a cosmopolitan alliance of Chinese businesses, urbanized Dyaks and curious tourists.

On the whole, Kuching is underrated by visitors. Most stop only for a day or two to organize trips to Bako National Park, the longhouses and the interior. But there's a fair amount to keep you occupied. The city's 250,000 inhabitants are divided between Chinese, Malays, Indians and the various **indigenous groups** (mostly Iban, Bidayuh and Melanau) with the Chinese forming the largest group. Indeed, Chinese enterprise has been pivotal to Kuching's economic success, while Chinese clan houses play a central part in the **cultural life** of the city; at the main temple, there are musical events, theatrical performances and religious rituals most weekends (and non-stop at Chinese New Year). Despite the Iban accounting for around thirty percent of the state population, indigenous people have little impact in Kuching, although they come out in force on Saturday (market day) and at the annual festivals.

Arrival and information

Kuching **airport** is 11km south of the city, from where you either take a taxi into the centre (coupons from a booth outside the arrivals hall; $16.50) or the #12a bus, from directly outside the terminal (every 40min, daily 7am–6pm; 90 sen); it's a thirty-minute ride into the city. Long-distance **buses** from Sibu and further north, and from Pontianack (in Kalimantan), halt at the Jalan Penrissen bus station 5km south of downtown Kuching. Buses #3 or #3a (50 sen) will take you up to waterfront Lebuh Jawa. Buses from around Kuching and southwestern Sarawak will drop you at one of the four central bus-stopping points (see "City Transport" below).

The **boats** from Sibu and Sarikei dock at the Bintawa Wharf (also known as the Express Association Wharf), 5km east of the city centre in the suburb of Pending. Walk down to the main road, 100m away, and catch bus #17 or #19 into the centre (every 30min, daily 6am–11pm; 60 sen), a thirty-minute trip. These buses run along Main Bazaar before reaching the bus station at Jalan Masjid.

Information

There is a small **Sarawak Tourist Association** (STA) desk in the airport (daily 8am–5pm; ☎082/456266), but the main office is next to the Sarawak Steamship Building on Main Bazaar, at the junction with Jalan Tun Haji Openg (Mon–Thurs 8.30am–12.45pm & 2–4.15pm, Fri 8.30–11.30am & 2.30–4.45pm, Sat 8am–12.45pm; ☎082/240620). This has plenty of maps, bus timetables, hotel listings and dozens of glossy leaflets on everything from weaving to tattooing. Although city maps here are free, for a detailed map of Sarawak state you'll need to ask for the "Periplus" Sarawak map at one of the city's specialist booksellers (see p.358).

There's another tourist office on Jalan Mosque, the newly formed **Sarawak Tourism Board** Visitor Information Centre (Mon–Thurs 8am–2.15pm, Fri 8am–4.45pm, Sat 8am–12.45pm; ☎082/410942). Besides giving general information, this has the booking

LEAVING KUCHING

For details of airline offices, the national parks office and Indonesian consulate in Kuching, see "Listings", p.358. For tour operators see box on p.359.

Airport
Take a taxi, or the #12a bus from the station on Lebuh Jawa out to the airport (flight enquiries on ☎082/457373). There are services to Bandar (5 weekly; $360), Bintulu (9 daily; $117), Johor Bahru (4 daily; $170), Kota Kinabalu (5 daily; $228), KL (at least 10 daily; from $262), Miri (9 daily; $165), Sibu (10 daily; $75), Singapore (3 daily; $230) and Pontianak (3 weekly; $170).

Boats
Fast boats to Sarikei and Sibu leave from the Bintawa Wharf at Pending. *Express Bahagia*, 50 Jalan Padungan (☎082/421948), runs daily direct trips to both Sarikei ($29) and Sibu ($33), departing at 1pm. On Monday, Wednesday and Friday they also have an 8.15am service stopping at both destinations. *Concord Marine* (☎082/412551), based at the *Metropole Hotel* on Jalan Green Hill, runs up to Sibu via Sarikei on Tuesday, Thursday, Saturday and Sunday at 8.30am ($33). The much slower cargo boat run by *Rajah Ramin Shipping* (☎082/411082) departs from the KTS Wharf on Wednesday and Saturday at 6pm ($15). To reach Bintawa, take buses #17 or #19 from Jalan Masjid (see "Buses", below). Since tickets are available on board, you needn't book in advance – though it can't do any harm.

Buses
Long-distance **buses** to points north in Sarawak, and southwards to Kalimantan, depart from the Jalan Penrissen Bus Station south of town. Sarawak Transport Company buses #3 and #3a (50 sen) run half-hourly from 6.30am until 6pm, from waterfront Lebuh Jawa. Alternatively, take a taxi ($10). Larger express bus companies operating out of the Jalan Penrissen terminal include Biaramas Express (☎082/452139); PB Express (☎082/461277), whose downtown agent is Natural Colour, in Lebuh Khoo Hun Yeng's Electra House; and Borneo Highway Express (☎082/453190), for whose services tickets are available at Yong Ngee Loong, 43 Jalan Gambir (☎082/243794). For departures to greater Kuching and southwestern Sarawak, see "City Transport", below.

desk of the National Parks and Wildlife Office, which issues permits for Semengoh, Bako, Gading and Kubah parks (call ☎082/248088 for booking enquiries).

You can also gen up on Kuching by picking up a copy of the excellent *Official Kuching Guide*, available in all city hotel lobbies and free.

City transport

You can **walk** around much of downtown Kuching with ease and will have little use for the city buses. However, some of the **local buses** are more useful. Rather than a single, integrated local bus service, Kuching has four distinct companies which run out to the city's satellite tourist attractions, and around southwestern Sarawak. The Sarawak Transport Company's green-and-red buses depart from their terminal at the western end of Lebuh Jawa for the airport, Bau and Lundu to the west, and Semengoh, Jong's Crocodile Farm, Anna Rais, Serian, Sri Aman and Lubok Antu to the east. Originating from Jalan Mosque, Chin Lian Long's blue-and-white buses trundle out to the Indonesian consulate, the immigration office and Bintawa Express Wharf; while Petra Jaya Transport travels the road northward to Damai, Santubong and Bako, from below the open-air market on Lebuh Market. Finally, Matang Transport Company buses serving Matang and Kubah depart from the northern end of Jalan P. Ramlee.

The main **taxi rank** is at the western end of Jalan Gaumbier, although you can usually flag one down in front of the plush hotels along Jalan Tunku Abdul Rahman; avoid going into any of the hotel concourses, however, as the fixed prices charged by the taxis are a lot steeper there. You should always negotiate the price before starting the trip – often the "fixed rate" lowers after a bit of haggling, and to get across the city from, say, the *Holiday Inn Kuching* to Lebuh Jawa shouldn't cost more than $6. Note that fares increase significantly after midnight.

Noisy, diesel-operated **sampans** (every 15min, daily 6am–10pm; 20 sen) depart from the jetty opposite the courthouse on the waterfront, crossing Sungei Sarawak to reach Fort Margherita in the northern part of Kuching. The boat trip only takes a few minutes. Should you wish to cruise the river at greater leisure, you can rent your own sampan (locals call them *tambangs*) for $15–20 per hour.

Accommodation

Finding inexpensive **accommodation** in Kuching is not easy – be prepared to pay around $30 for a double room if the budget places are full. Moving up a grade, the mid-range lodging houses are reliable enough; there are quite a number in the Jalan Green Hill area. At the top end of the scale, most of the expensive hotels have great views over the river, as well as swimming pools and 24-hour service. If you want to stay on the coast, head for the resorts of the Santubong Peninsula (see p.361). All the hotels below are marked either on the map of greater Kuching on p.345 or central Kuching on p.350.

Ah Chew, 3 Lebuh Jawa (☎082/286302). Noisy, as it overlooks the bus station. Used by a mostly young Chinese clientele, the rooms have communal bathrooms and paper-thin walls. ①.

Anglican Rest House, Jalan McDougall (☎082/240188). Kuching's best deal is set in the gardens of the Anglican Cathedral. It's often full (particularly in August), so call to book ahead. The main two-storey, wooden colonial building has comfortable, twin-bed rooms with high ceilings and shared bathrooms, and there are also two self-contained apartments with bedroom, verandah and bathroom. The resthouse has had a few security problems, so don't leave valuables unattended. ②.

Arif, Jalan Haji Taha (☎082/241211). Snug and friendly place, handily positioned for the night market. A variety of rooms are available, with fan, air-con and bath. ②.

B&B Inn, first floor, 30–31 Jalan Tabuan (☎082/237366). Kuching's only backpacker-oriented address has dorm beds for $14, a handful of bare but tidy private rooms sharing common facilities, and a dull breakfast thrown in for good luck. ②.

Ban Hua Hin, 36 Jalan Padungan (☎082/242351). Aimed at Chinese workers rather than tourists; basic and friendly. ①.

Borneo, 30 Jalan Tabuan (☎082/244122). Comfortable hotel – Kuching's oldest – whose lovely rooms have polished wooden floors, air-con, bath or shower, and TV. ⑥.

Fata, junction of Lebuh Temple and Jalan MacDougall (☎082/248111). Excellent location a few metres from Reservoir Park. The small rooms have air-con, showers and TV. ③.

Holiday Inn Kuching, Jalan Tunku Abdul Rahman (☎082/423111, fax 426169). Overlooking the river with some of the rooms (for an extra $20) looking directly out onto the fort on the opposite bank; has a pool, restaurant and bookshop. ⑧.

Kapit, 59 Jalan Padungan (☎082/420961). Away from the centre and popular with a Malaysian business clientele. Rooms have air-con, shower and TV. ②.

Kuching Hilton, Jalan Tunku Abdul Rahman (☎082/248200). Another top-class hotel, whose front rooms have a great view of the river. There's a pool and a mouthwatering range of food and drink outlets. ⑧.

Kuching, 6 Jalan Temple (☎082/413985). About the best budget option if the resthouse is full. That said, it's very basic, spartan and a bit dirty, with one shower and toilet on each floor, although each room has a fan and sink. ①.

Longhouse, Jalan Abell (☎082/419333). East of the centre, and frequented mainly by visiting business people. Rooms have air-con, shower and TV. ②.

Mandarin, 6 Jalan Green Hill (☎082/418269). One of the most promising places in Green Hill. Full facilities – air-con, shower, toilet and TV – but most rooms are rather small. ②.

Orchid Inn, 2 Jalan Green Hill (☎082/411417). Like the *Mandarin*, this is fairly comfortable and is close to some excellent cafés; it has particularly friendly staff. ②.

Riverside Majestic, Jalan Tunku Abdul Rahman (☎082/247777). One of Kuching's priciest and most opulent hotels, this ten-floor marble extravaganza offers all the comforts and amenities you could wish for: several classy restaurants and bars, full sporting facilities, business centre and adjoining shopping complex. Views from the river-facing rooms are breathtaking. ⑧.

Tai Pan, 93 Jalan Padungan (☎082/082/417363). Cosy, family-run place, situated on a lane just off the main street. The small rooms have air-con, shower and TV. ②.

Telang Usan, Bon Hok Rd (☎082/415588, fax 425316). A real gem of a place, mid-range but well-appointed, run by exceptionally friendly staff and possessing a harmonious style that reflects its Kenyah name, meaning Sweet River. The *Dullit Coffee House* is a likeable escape from the bustle of downtown Kuching. Recommended. ⑤.

The City

The central area, sandwiched between Jalan Courthouse to the west, Jalan Temple to the east and Reservoir Park to the south, is usually referred to as **colonial Kuching**. The courthouse, the post office and the Sarawak Museum are the most impressive buildings here, with the museum itself the city's most absorbing attraction. Set within this small area is **Chinatown**, which incorporates the main shopping streets – Main Bazaar and Jalan Carpenter. To the east of Jalan Temple lie Jalan Green Hill and Jalan Tunku Abdul Rahman, the principal accommodation districts. Further south from the old town's narrow, busy streets – yet only fifteen minutes' walk from the river – is **Reservoir Park**; while bordering the colonial area, on the western edge of the centre, is the state **mosque** and main Malay residential area, dominated by detached kampung-style dwellings with their sloping roofs, intricate carvings around the windows and elevated verandahs. From the mosque it's a short hop east to Lebuh India, another shopping hot spot and home, as the name suggests, to several of the city's Indian restaurants. Southwest, Satok bridge leads to Kuching new town and the timber museum, while north, across the river, is **Fort Margherita** – now the Police Museum – and the **istana**, still the residence of Sarawak's head of state.

Colonial Kuching and the esplanade

If you exclude the Sarawak Museum, Kuching's colonial buildings will occupy only an hour or two of your time. The most obvious place to start is at the square white **Courthouse**, overlooking the river on the south bank at the junction of Main Bazaar and Jalan Tun Haji Openg. Built in 1874, and sporting impressive Romanesque columns and a balcony, the courthouse is fronted by the **Charles Brooke Memorial**, a six-metre-high granite obelisk erected in 1924, at whose four corners are stone figures representing the four largest ethnic groups in Sarawak: the Chinese, Dyaks, Malays and Orang Ulu. Today the four-room court still holds sessions to which the public are admitted (Mon–Thurs 10am–noon) – and it's worth going inside the main court chamber in any case to see the **murals** on the ceiling and walls. The traditional designs were painted by artists from various tribal groups, the vividly coloured paintings with scenes from longhouse life: a woman weaving *pua kumba* cloth on her loom, men hunting with blowpipes, and celebrations after the rice harvest.

When the rebellious Chinese gold-miners who nearly ended James Brooke's tenuous rule in the 1830s ran amok through the streets of Kuching, they razed the riverside wooden fort that used to stand directly north of the courthouse. The miners were sentenced to death across the road, and the site of the fort was redeveloped. Today, the

CENTRAL KUCHING

RESTAURANTS

Chin Heng Café	H
Green Vegetarian Café	D
Jubilee Restoran	B
Madinah Restoran	C
National Islamic Café	E
Nam Sen Coffee Shop	A
River Café	F
Tiger Garden Coffee Shop	G

For other restaurants, see 'Kuching' map

ACCOMMODATION

Ah Chew Hotel	1
Arif Hotel	2
Anglican Rest House	3
B & B Inn	8
Borneo Hotel	7
Fata Hotel	9
Kuching Hotel	4
Mandarin Hotel	5
Orchid Inn	6

For other hotels, see 'Kuching' map

★ Bus Stop

0   200m

▽ *Kuching Airport*

single-turreted **Square Tower** (daily 10am–2pm & 4–9.30pm; free) that sprang from the ashes of the fort in 1879 houses a multimedia information centre and a video theatre which describes to tourists all that Sarawak has to offer. The tower's renaissance formed just one element of the recent restoration and reclamation which created Kuching's delightful new **esplanade**. Stretching almost a kilometre from the waterfront markets to the *Holiday Inn*, the esplanade has quickly become *the* place to see and be seen in the evening, its manicured lawns enlivened by sculptures, seating areas and, around the Square Tower, jolly musical fountains. Several of the *godowns* (warehouses) that once fronted onto the river were sacrificed during the development, but two fine buildings – the lovingly restored Sarawak Steamship Building, and the former Chinese General Chamber of Commerce (see below) – have survived. Early-morning strollers in the esplanade will see elderly Sarawakians going about their daily tai chi routines.

Away from the river, directly below the courthouse, the **Round Tower** was originally built as a dispensary in the 1880s, its austere dimensions explained by the fact that it was designed to double as a fort in an emergency. Straight across Jalan Tun Haji Openg, you'll have no difficulty in picking out the absurdly grand **post office**, whose massive ornamental columns, semicircular arches and decorative friezes were outmoded almost as soon as they were completed in 1931. Continue on down Jalan Tun Haji Openg, skirt the well-groomed grassland known as **Padang Merdeka**, turn left onto Jalan McDougall and you'll see the modern Anglican **Cathedral**. A walk through the grounds leads to the oldest consecrated grounds in Borneo, the European **cemetery**. An unassuming plot of land, and very easily missed, the cemetery nevertheless manages to conjure the ghosts of old Kuching. Of the few stones still legible, one recalls Charles James Fox and Henry Steel, "officers of the Sarawak Government, who were treacherously murdered at Kanowit" in 1859. "Justice", the stone reassures us, "was done". A few steps further east stands another Kuching landmark, the large, two-storey wooden **Bishop's House**, built in 1849, which makes it the oldest surviving building in the city.

Chinatown and further east

The grid of streets running eastwards from Jalan Tun Haji Openg to the main Chinese temple, Tua Pek Kong, constitutes Kuching's **Chinatown**. On busy Main Bazaar and, one block south, on Jalan Carpenter, there are numerous cafés, restaurants, laundries and stores operating out of renovated two-storey shophouses, built by Hokkien and Teochew immigrants who arrived in the 1890s. The shophouses were originally divided into three sections: the front room was where the merchant conducted business and stored his goods (salt, flour, jungle products collected by indigenous peoples, and salted fish caught and prepared by Malay fishermen), the back room was the family quarters, and the loft was where the business partners would sleep.

Overlooking the river on Jalan Temple stands **Tua Pek Kong**, the oldest Taoist temple in Sarawak (1876), whose position – in accordance with Chinese tradition – was carefully divined through geomancy. Plenty of people drop by during the day to pay their respects to the temple deity, Tua Pek Kong, the patron saint of business who is much in demand in this dynamic city. Supplicants burn paper money and joss sticks, and pray for good fortune. The temple maintains an immensely busy cultural life, especially during Chinese New Year, when there are theatrical and musical performances, readings and rituals.

Tua Pek Kong may have taken care of all matters spiritual in the Chinese community for much of the past century, but matters temporal were long the domain of the squat, cream-coloured edifice below on the waterfront, once the Chinese General Chamber of Commerce. The building now houses the **Chinese History Museum** (daily except Fri 9am–6pm; free), which makes use of paintings, black-and-white photographs and a modest selection of artefacts to chart the migration and integration of Sarawak's Chinese community.

Jalan Tunku Abdul Rahman heads east from the temple, past several of the swankier hotels, becomes **Jalan Padungan**, and runs to a roundabout on the eastern edge of the city, separating Kuching proper from its outskirts. The one-kilometre walk along the tree-lined avenue takes you past some splendidly ornate shophouses (whose elaborate decor was paid for by the rubber boom of the 1930s), and you can't fail to spot the avenue's **cat statue**, a 1.5-metre-high white plaster effigy, her paw raised in welcome. Created by local artist Yong Kee Yet as a nod to the supposed derivation of the city's name, it's a popular spot for family photos.

West of Chinatown: market, kampung and mosque

Heading west along the riverfront from Main Bazaar puts you on Jalan Gambier, fronting which is the **cargo port** – less important than it once was, but still a fascinating place. In the late afternoon you'll see cargo boats from West Kalimantan unloading tons of tropical fruits to be sold in the nearby **markets**. One block back from Jalan Market, a series of open-air food stalls are very much the focal point for Kuching's traders and buyers, who tuck in to noodle soups and stir fries, *roti canai* and *daal* throughout the day. East of here a handsome arch leads into **Jalan India**, the busiest pedestrian thoroughfare in Kuching and the best place to buy shoes and cheap clothing. The street is named after the Indian coolies who arrived in the early part of this century to work at the docks; at 37 Jalan India, a dim passageway leads to the oldest of the Indian community's mosques dating back to the mid-nineteenth century.

Follow the curve of the river southwest for 300m or so and you reach Jalan Datuk Ajibah Abol's **Kampung Masjid**, which retains many well-preserved family houses, built at the turn of the century by well-to-do government officials, and with traditional features such as floor-level windows fronted by carved railings.

On the steep hill above stands the **Masjid Negara**, whose gold cupolas glint in the dying sun at evening prayers. There's been a mosque on this site for around two hundred years, though this one only dates from the 1960s. If you want to go inside (9am–3pm; closed Fri), men must wear long trousers and women skirts and a headdress; a headscarf for women is provided by the mosque at the entrance.

The Malay enclave's southern boundary is the wide, traffic-clogged **Jalan Satok**. At its junction with Jalan Palm, opposite the *Miramar Cinema*, lies the site of Kuching's **Sunday market**, which actually kicks off on Saturday afternoon; it continues until about 2am on Sunday morning, picks up again at 6am and finally ends around midday. Buses #4a and #4b get you there from the Matang Transport Company bus station, or from outside the post office, in five minutes. This is the place for picking up supplies of everything from rabbits to knives; other stalls sell *satay*, curry pie, sweets and *lycheesank*, a soft drink made with beans, rice pellets, sugar and lychees. Amid the congested confusion, look out for the alley where Dyaks sell fruit, vegetables and handicrafts – a good place to pick up inexpensive baskets and textiles. Note that the market is the one place in Kuching where you should watch your bag and keep your money in a secure place.

The Sarawak Museum

Back on central Jalan Tun Haji Openg, set just below the padang, is Kuching's prime tourist attraction, the **Sarawak Museum** (daily except Fri; free), whose main building (the largest colonial structure in Kuching) was built in the 1890s and is set back from the road in lovely gardens. A new wing, opened in 1983, lies on the other side of Jalan Tun Haji Openg – connected to the main building by the bridge over the road. Charles Brooke first conceived the idea of a museum in Kuching, prompted by the nineteenth-century naturalist Alfred Russell Wallace, who spent two years in Sarawak in the 1850s; Wallace's natural history exhibits now form the basis of the collection on show in the main building. The museum's best-known curator was **Tom Harrisson**, whose discovery of a 39,000-year-old skull in the caves at Niah in 1957 prompted a radical reappraisal of the origins of early man in Southeast Asia. Under the museum's auspices, Harrisson frequently visited remote Orang Ulu tribes, bringing back the ceremonial artefacts that comprise some of the museum's greatest assets, on display in the new wing.

THE MAIN BUILDING

There's an information desk at the main entrance, beyond which is the **natural science** section, whose varied exhibits include a massive hairball from a crocodile's stomach and fairly pedestrian displays highlighting the diverse range of plant, animal and bird species in Borneo. The **ethnographic** section on the upper floor is of an altogether different standard, despite the occasionally vague labelling. Here you can walk into an authentic wooden Iban longhouse and climb up into the rafters of the *sadau* (loft), which is used to store bamboo fish baskets, ironwork and sleeping mats; you're also free to finger the intricately glazed, sturdy Chinese ceramic jars and fine

LONGHOUSE LIFE

In the last century observers described Sarawak's **longhouses** as being up to one kilometre long, but these days few have more than one hundred doors – representing the number of families living there. Traditionally, longhouses were erected by rivers (the main means of transport for Sea Dyaks – the Iban and Melanau – and Orang Ulu groups like the Kenyah, Kayan and Kelabit), though the predominant Land Dyak group, the Bidayuh, built their dwellings away from rivers, in the hills. Most longhouses are made from timber laced with bamboo and rattan cord. A communal verandah runs parallel to the private section where the families eat, sleep and keep their artefacts, some of which (like the ceramic jars) can be centuries old. On the verandah the inhabitants socialize, dry rice, weave baskets and textiles, and greet visitors. A near vertical ladder is often the only way up, while underneath the longhouse, pigs and chickens rummage around, eating the various bits of debris thrown from above. Outlying huts, set away from the main house, are used to store grain. In the more hierarchical ethnic groups, like the Kayan, natives not born in the longhouse who desire entry, live in nearby huts, until the *tuai* (headman) decides that they have achieved higher status and can be allowed into the house.

woven *pua kumbu* cloth. The Penan hut here is a much simpler affair, constructed of bamboo and rattan creeper, within which are blowpipes and *parangs* (machetes), animal hides, coconut husks used as drinking vessels, and hardy back-baskets, made from the pandanus palm and the bemban reed. At the other end of the floor, there's a collection of fearsome Iban war totems, and woodcarvings from the Kayan and Kenyah ethnic groups who live in the headwaters of the Rajang, Baram and Balau rivers. One carving – a ten-metre-high ceremonial pole made of hardwood – sports a pattern of grimacing heads and kneeling bodies stretching up in supplication. Towering above all of this, on one of the walls, is a massive mural of images from longhouse life: sowing and reaping rice, hunting, fishing, dancing and playing music. Elsewhere, you'll also find **musical instruments** used by the various tribes: the Bidayuh's heavy copper gongs, Iban drums and the Kayan *sape*, a stringed instrument looking a little like a lute. Also, keep an eye out for the small collection of Iban *palangs* – two-centimetre-long rhinoceros-bone penis pins – which were once a popular method of re-energizing a wilting love life in the longhouse: inserted horizontally, in case you were wondering.

THE NEW WING

Across the road, in the new wing, the **ground floor** has a book and gift shop, paintings by local artists, and a section detailing the history of Sarawak from James Brooke's time until the present day. The real interest, though, is upstairs, where there's an unparalleled collection of antique ceramics and brassware, prehistoric relics and early trading goods.

Heading round anticlockwise, you come first to the **prehistoric artefacts**, including ceramic fragments found at Tom Harrisson's Niah and Santubong excavation sites – in particular remnants of plain, globular Neolithic vessels used in funerary rites. Early **Chinese ceramics** are well represented, too. Typical of the Song Dynasty is the dish decorated with carved lotus petals, and there's also a vase in the shape of two joined fishes with one mouth. The Tang and Yuan Dynasty wares show a qualitative step forward – look for the beautiful blue-and-white glazed teapot decorated with a pair of dragons whose heads form the spout, tails the handle and legs the feet. Later fifteenth-century wares – the products of larger, more complex kilns – are more elaborate still. There are wonderful examples of work adorned with sprig moulding; one dish is decorated with a four-clawed dragon pursuing a flaming pearl.

From the tenth century onwards, Borneo's tribal groups traded rhinoceros horn, ivory and spices for Chinese ceramics, most notably colourful **storage jars**, which became closely linked to tribal customs and beliefs. The status and wealth of a person depended on how many jars they possessed, with the most valuable ones only used for funeral purposes or for ceremonies like the *gawai kenyalang* (the rite of passage for a mature, prosperous man). Other jars would be used for storage, to brew rice wine and to pay dowries, fines for adultery and divorce settlements. Among the Berawan in northern Sarawak, when a person died, the corpse was packed into a jar in a squatting position; as decomposition took place, the liquid from the body was drained away through a bamboo pipe. Jars – it is said – can also possess the power of foretelling future events and can summon spirits through the sounds they emit when struck.

Many of the hundreds of jars here are magnificent objects, in brown, black and vivid green glazes, with dragon-emblazoned motifs. One spectacular giant is almost a metre high, coloured blue and white, and adorned with scenes of real and mythical Chinese life, incorporating the intricate detail of plant petals, houses and epic landscapes. Contemporary ceramics take their influence from these early jars, with skilled Chinese potters – mainly immigrants from Kwantung Province – adopting the traditional decorative patterns of the ethnic groups, in animist images of birds, plants and fish.

The other major section is devoted to a exquisite **brassware** collection. Many of these superbly wrought cannons and kettles were crafted in Brunei and, again, many found their way into interior longhouses through exchange with traders and merchants, where they were traditionally used to store wealth and as currency. Both kettles and cannons are strikingly ornate, adorned with miniature animals – which, in the case of the dragon cannons, comprise the very body of the object.

From the Sarawak Museum to Reservoir Park

Behind the new wing of the museum, the **Islamic Museum** (daily except Fri 9am–6am; free) is housed in the Madrasah Melayu Building, a former Arabic school, painted in brilliant white and with a cool tiled interior. The museum's seven galleries represent diverse aspects of Islamic culture, from architecture to weaponry, history to coinage, and textiles to prayer.

Back across the road at the Sarawak Museum's main building, a path through the sloping garden leads to the **Heroes Memorial** (commemorating the dead of World War II and the Konfrontasi – less than five minutes' walk away. You'll pass the **Kuching Aquarium** (daily 9am–6pm; free) on the way, which contains a small collection of marine life, including turtles from Sipidan in Sabah (see p.466). Following the path past the memorial takes you to the corner of the museum gardens and out onto narrow Jalan Reservoir, across which lies **Reservoir Park**, a beautiful, if artificial, tropical environment with many resident bird species and wildlife. Quiet during the day, it perks up in late afternoon; there's a café (daily 8am–4.30pm), a drinks kiosk, boats for rent, a playground and stretching frames for work-out enthusiasts. The other road bordering the park, Lorong Park, leads up to the **Civic Centre** on Jalan Budaya, an ultra-modern building with a **planetarium** (Tues only) and space for temporary exhibitions. The Sarawak Tourist Association office can provide information on current events here, though most visitors come for the restaurant on the top floor which has fine views over the city and – on a good day, as far as Kalinmantan.

Across Sungei Sarawak

There was a Malay kampung on the north side of the river before the arrival of James Brooke, and within forty years – during the reign of Charles Brooke – two of Kuching's most important buildings were built here. Boats cross from a number of waterfront jetties, including the one opposite the courthouse on Main Bazaar, on the south side (every 15min, daily 6am–10pm; 20 sen), and once across the river, you can follow a marked path towards the **istana**, built by Charles Brooke in 1869 and still the official home of Sarawak's head of state. It is an elegant, stately building with a distinctive shingle roof, set in a long, sloping garden with an excellent view of the courthouse on the opposite bank. Various pieces of Brooke memorabilia and other relics are kept in one of the rooms, but unfortunately you can only visit the istana on two days of the year, over the Hari Raya holiday at the end of Ramadan (see p.63).

Along the river bank, 1km to the east, is **Fort Margherita**; retrace your steps back to the jetty and you can follow a marked path there. The first fort built on this site was James Brooke's most important defensive installation, commanding the view along Sungei Sarawak. However, the fort was burned to the ground in 1857 by rebel Chinese gold-miners and was rebuilt by Charles Brooke in 1879, who named it after his wife. It is the finest example of the Brookes' system of fortifications; there are around twenty other river forts of humbler construction throughout Sarawak, strategically placed to repel pirates and Dyak or Kayan war parties. Looking for all the world like a defensive English castle, Fort Margherita is the only one of the forts open to the public, and renovations have ensured that it looks much as it did last century; the grounds and interior now house a **Police Museum** (Tues–Sun 10am–6pm; free but take your passport). Outside the central keep stand old cannons and other pieces of artillery, while inside there is a solid collection of swords, guns and uniforms. There's even a reconstructed opium den, and exhibits on illegal games and drugs, while photographs recall the communist insurgency and Konfrontasi, which required the small Sarawak army to call upon British military aid to help defend the bazaar towns in the interior.

From the fort, it's easy to thread your way eastwards and down to the Malay kampungs over which it stands guard: **Kampung Boyan** segues into **Kampung Gersik**, which in turn is assimilated by **Kampung Sourabaya Ulu**. All three kampungs feature wonderful clapboard stilthouses, some in cheery pastel blues and greens, others gloriously dilapidated, teetering on knock-kneed stilts and accessed by bowed promenades. From this side of the fort, boats will deposit you near the *Riverside Majestic Hotel* on the east side of the city centre.

Petra Jaya, the Timber Museum and Cat Museum

Across Satok bridge, southwest of the centre, the road careers round to the northern part of Kuching and the new town, known as **Petra Jaya**. This is an ugly area, devoid of any real interest and, compared to the older parts of Kuching, apparently devoid of life, too. Still, it's where you'll find most of the government offices, including the national headquarters of the Parks and Wildlife Department (see "Listings", p.358), as well as two contrasting museums.

The appropriately log-shaped **Timber Museum** (Mon–Thurs 8.30am–4pm, Fri 8.30–11.30am & 2.30–4.30pm, Sat 8am–12.30pm; free) is next to the stadium on Jalan Wisma Sumbar Alam, which is the main thoroughfare in Petra Jaya; bus #8 runs here from the Matong Transport Company terminal. Built in 1985 for the express purpose of putting across the timber industry's point of view in the increasingly acrimonious debate on tropical deforestation, the museum does its job well, with informative displays and exhibits, and plenty of facts and figures about tree types and the economic case for logging. Hardly surprisingly, the other side of the argument – the devastation of land which has been farmed for generations by the tribal groups – isn't addressed. The rationale that economic development must come before all other considerations fails to address the simple fact that most of the timber-related wealth either goes into the pockets of big business tycoons, or is siphoned off in state taxes to the national government. The displays even suggest that the Dyaks, who have lost much of their customary land through deforestation, have ultimately gained as they now live in less remote areas with health and education facilities nearby. But many ethnic groups, who have recently set up representative committees, would say the forests are their liveli-hood: remove the forests and tribal culture eventually withers and dies.

There's some light relief in the **Cat Museum** (Tues–Sun 9am–5pm; free) in Petra Jaya's DBKU Building, visible from just about all over Kuching. Claiming to be the only such museum in the world, the exhibits take as their starting point the supposed derivation of the city's name from the Malay word for "cat" – which means photos of cats from around the world, *Garfield* comic strips, feline-related art and folklore that's strictly for cat freaks. Take bus #2b from the Petra Jaya terminal.

Eating and nightlife

Many of the **cafés** and **hawker stalls**, especially those along Jalan Carpenter, close at around 7pm; even the top restaurants close early, with last orders at around 10pm. This aside, Kuching is a great city for food – but you've got to know what to ask for. Local specialities such as wild boar and deer sometimes crop up on Chinese menus; and the jungle fern vegetables, *midin* and *paku*, are available throughout the city. In addition, Kuching has its own versions of *kuey teow* (thick rice noodles, with meat and vegeta-bles in gravy), and of *laksa*, a rich soup where rice vermicelli is combined with shred-ded chicken, prawns and beansprouts in a spicy coconut gravy. Sarawakians often slurp down a bowl of *laksa* for breakfast, though some prefer *kolok mee*, an oily, tasty dish fea-turing dry noodles. Seafood is also splendid here: beside oysters, prawns, crab and squid, look out for more unusual ingredients like slipper lobsters and *ambal* (bamboo clams), and for *umai*, a raw fish salad lent considerable zing by the addition of shallots and lime. Though Kuching can't boast a very happening **nightlife**, places *do* exist where you can have a beer without being deafened by karaoke. The city's best bar is *De Tavern*, a Kayan-run watering-hole opposite the *Hilton* on Jalan Borneo, whose owner-manager is happy to pour a free glass of *tuak* for first-time visitors. From here, it's a short stagger to the *Hilton*'s *Peppers* disco, where you can opt for dancing or shooting pool. Should you develop a taste for *tuak*, try the range at the *Telang Usan Hotel*'s *Dulit Terrace and Tuak Bar*.

Food centres and hawker stalls

Jalan Carpenter Hawkers, Jalan Carpenter. Opposite the Chinese temple, a compact centre with a range of dishes including excellent *laksa*. Popular with Kuching's young Chinese.

Gerail Anekarasa Hawker Centre, Jalan Satok, under the bridge. Famous for its barbecued chicken and steaks. It's a bit of a trek, but a whole chicken plus rice and vegetables only costs around $10 for two. Take any Petra Jaya bus, but check it goes as far as the bridge.

Open-air market, Jalan Market. Massive hawker centre that's very cheap and popular with locals for basic rice, noodle and curry dishes; a handful of stalls sell seafood and beer into the early hours.

Petanak Market, Jalan Petanak. West of the *Longhouse Hotel*, this early-morning market has a food centre that kicks off at 4am, making it an excellent option after a night out; all regional cuisines rep-resented.

Top Spot Food Court, sixth floor, Taman Keret, Jalan Padungan. Set above a car park, the stalls in this open-sided food court offer everything from seafood to *satay*, and claypot to steak; all bene-fit from a fine view out over the city.

Restaurants and cafés

Chin Heng Café, 5 Jalan Green Hill. Taxi drivers' haven and local café for those who stay in the nearby inns. No real food served until 11am, when delicious chillied beans, sweet and sours, and stir fries appear for around $3 a portion. Run by a very friendly family.

Chinese Barbecue Specialist, Jalan Padungan. Barbecued duck, chicken and back meat of pork is hacked up unceremoniously and laid on rice at the front of this bustling, rough and ready shop-house; while a Cantonese kitchen operates out the back.

Choon Hui Café, Jalan Ban Hock. Storming *laksa* and filling *kolok mee* make this plain coffee shop near Kuching's Hindu temple a huge breakfast-time hit with locals.

City Tower, Civic Centre, Jalan Budaya. Decent Chinese food, though outshone by the marvellous city views.

Fook Hui, Jalan Padungan. Famed coffee shop whose reputation depends, in part, on its *ha kau* pork dumplings.

Green Vegetarian Café, 16 Main Bazaar. Indian vegetarian food, including *biriyanis* and veggie *thalis* (lunchtime only; $3).

Jubilee Restoran, 49 Jalan India. Excellent Malay restaurant set amid busy textile stores. The *kacang goreng* (peanuts in fish paste), *sayur* (green beans in chilli and lemon) and *tahu* (fried bean-curd) are particularly tasty house specials – or simply make do with a *roti canai* or a *murtabak*. Full meals from $8 for two.

Lyn's, 10, Lot 62, Lorong 4, Jalan Nanas (☎082/234934). *Tandoori* specialist, a short taxi ride from the town centre, but worth seeking out for its excellent North Indian menu. Closed Sun.

Madinah, 47 Jalan India. Dependable (mainly) Malay food, next door to the *Jubilee*; the beef *rendang* is particularly good, as is the fish curry.

Meisan Restoran, ground floor, *Holiday Inn Kuching*, Jalan Tunku Abdul Rahman. Spicy Szechuanese food. Although the Sunday-lunchtime *dim sum* is reasonably priced, evening meals are expensive, at $50 for two including beer, but worth splashing out for.

Minangkabau, 168 Jalan Chan Chin Ann. Excellent Indonesian restaurant with a range of dishes which you can't find anywhere else in Kuching – and only at lunchtime, even here. It specializes in chilli-hot fish curries and beef *rendang*, all for the very reasonable cost of around $10–15 for two.

Nam Sen, 17 Jalan Market. Highly cool old coffee shop, complete with varnished chairs, marble tables and "No spitting" signs. Popular with boiler-suited workers from the nearby docks and handy for snatching an early-morning coffee or noodle soup before catching a bus.

National Islamic Café, Jalan Carpenter. Serves halal food, curries and unleavened bread from mid-morning until around 9pm. Very popular with visitors and inexpensive at $3–4 a head.

Red Eastern Seafood, Jalan Ban Hock. Cracking steamboat place which also offers fruit and ice cream. One of a gaggle of popular seafood restaurants around Ban Hock.

River Café, Main Bazaar. Breezy waterfront café serving quite divine *popiah*, and a challenging *laksa*.

See Good, Jalan Bukit Mata Kuching. Don't be fooled by this seafood eating house's inauspicious surrounds: standards of cooking are high, and the owners friendly. Slipper lobster in pepper, bamboo clams (known locally as "monkeys' penises") and *midin* make for a fine dinner. Two can eat heartily for $60, including beer. Evenings only; closed on the 14th and 18th of every month.

Singapore Chicken Rice, Jalan Song Thian Cheok. Tasty fast food Southeast Asian style; ignore the tacky decor.

Tiger Garden Coffee Shop, Jalan Temple, Green Hill. The best Chinese dumplings in town and great for other Chinese staples, too – $3 a head, including coffee or tea. Stalls outside on the pavement whip up delicious noodle dishes.

Shopping

Kuching is the best place in Sarawak to buy just about anything, although it would be unwise to stock up on tribal textiles and handicrafts here if you are visiting Sibu, Kapit or the longhouses in the interior. Most of the **handicraft** and **antique** shops are along Main Bazaar, Jalan Temple and Jalan Wayang. There are some **ceramic stalls** on the road to the airport, but it's better to visit the **potteries** (open daily 8am–noon & 2–6pm) themselves, clustered together on Jalan Penrissen, 8km from town – take STC bus #3, #3a, #9a or #9b from Lebuh Jawa. You can walk around and watch the potters in action at the wheel and firing kilns; each pottery also has a shop on site, though the work isn't particularly innovative.

Adventure Images, 55 Main Bazaar. This showroom has the best postcards you can buy in Sarawak.

Arts of Asia, 68 Main Bazaar. One of the most comprehensive private galleries in town, it sells naturalistic paintings and sculpture, which tend to be expensive.

Eeze Trading, just past the *Holiday Inn Kuching* on Jalan Tunku Abdul Rahman. Souvenirs for the person who has everything – the only shop in the city selling dried insects.

Galeri M, *Hilton Hotel*. Besides beadwork, hornbill carvings and Sarawakian antiques, *Galeri M* stocks a massive range of contemporary local art.

Sarakraf, 14 Main Bazaar. Decent stock of baskets, textiles and ironwork.

Sarawak Batik Art Shop, 1 Jalan Temple. A fine collection of Iban *pua kumbu* textiles (see box on the Iban on pp.370–371).

Sarawak House, 67 Main Bazaar. Flashy and expensive but usually worth a look.

Sarawak Plaza, Jalan Tunku Abdul Rahman, close to the *Holiday Inn Kuching*. This mall is the major focus for Western products – fashion accessories, shirts and shoes, and dance music cassettes. The handicraft store has a good range of bags, T-shirts and ethnic jewellery; though perhaps the most useful stop is the pharmacy on the first floor.

Sing Ching Loon, 57 Main Bazaar. Pricey handicrafts and antiques, but good for a browse.

Tan Brothers, Jalan Padungan, close to junction with Jalan Mathies. Baskets, carvings and bags.

Talan Usan, Jalan Ban Hock. Lobby sells superb Penan and Orang Ulu crafts.

Yeo Hing Chuan, 46 Main Bazaar. Interesting carvings and other handicrafts; a quality carved hardwood figure 30cm tall costs about $400.

Listings

Airlines MAS, Lot 215, Jalan Song Thian Cheok (☎082/246622); Merpati, c/o Sin Hwa Travel Service, 8 Lebuh Temple (☎082/246688); Royal Brunei Airlines, first floor, Rugayah Bldg, Jalan Song Thian Cheok (☎082/243344); SAEGA Airlines, Level 16, Wisma Ting Pek Khiing, 1 Jalan Padungan (☎082/236905); Singapore Airlines, Wisma Bukit Maja Kuching, Jalan Tunku Abdul Rahman (☎082/247777).

Banks and exchange Hong Kong, 2 Jalan Tun Haji Openg; Overseas Union Bank, junction of Main Bazaar and Jalan Tun Haji Openg; Standard Chartered, Wisma Bukit Maja Kuching, Jalan Tunku Abdul Rahman. There are moneychangers at the airport (daily 8am–8pm) and in the city: *Majid & Sons*, 45 Jalan India and *Mohamad Yahia & Sons*, in the basement of Jalan Abell's Sarawak Plaza; both offer good rates.

Bookshops *Mohamad Yahiah & Sons*, with branches in the *Holiday Inn* and the basement of the Sarawak Plaza, offer the best range of books in Sarawak, and also stock the best maps of the state; in addition, they sell the English-language *Borneo Post*, which features international news and a small section on events in the state. *Sky Book Store*, 57 Jalan Padungan, and *Star Books*, 30 Main Bazaar, are good for geographical, cultural and anthropological material; there is also a bookshop within the Sarawak Museum. For fiction, make for the Riverside Complex's *Times Books*.

Car rental Pronto Car Rental, first floor, 98 Jalan Padungan (☎082/236889); Mayflower Car Rental, fourth floor, Bangunan Satok, Jalan Satok (☎082/410110).

Hospitals Sarawak General Hospital, Jalan Ong Kee Hui, (☎082/257555), charges $1 for A & E consultations; for private treatment, go to Norman Medical Centre, Jalan Tun Datuk Patinggi (☎082/440055), or the Timberland Medical Centre, Rock Rd (☎082/234991).

Immigration First floor, Bangunan Sultan Iskander, Jalan Simpang Tiga, (Mon–Fri 8am–noon & 2–4.30pm; ☎082/245661), for visa extensions; take Chin Lian Long bus #11.

Indonesian consulate At 5a Jalan Pisang (Mon–Thurs 8.30am–noon & 2–4pm; ☎082/241734) – take bus #5a or #6 from Jalan Mosque. Visas cost $10; allow at least two working days – though you may no longer need one to cross at Entikong (see p.368).

Laundry *All Clean Services*, 175g Jalan Chan Chin Ann (☎082/243524); *Mr Dobi*, Jalan Abell.

National parks and wildlife office Permits for Sarawak's National Parks are issued at the left-hand desk in the Visitor Information Centre (see p.346).

Pharmacy *Apex Pharmacy*, Electra House, Lebuh Power (☎082/246011), and second floor, Sarawak Plaza, Jalan Tunku Abdul Rahman.

Police Drop by the Central Police Station on Jalan (☎082/241222). Come here to report stolen and lost property.

Post office The main post office is on Jalan Tun Haji Openg (Mon–Sat 8am–6pm, Sun 10am–1pm); poste restante/general delivery can be collected here – take your passport.

TOUR OPERATORS IN KUCHING

The standard of the tours on and around Sungei Lupar and Sungei Skrang, 300km east of Kuching, is high. Most of the Iban longhouses here aren't over-commercialized, though it's best to go in small groups – no more than eight people – so always check how many are going on your tour. Most companies charge around $100 a day per person which is quite steep, but the tours are packed with activity, and especially good if you're short on time.

Asian Overland, 286a first floor, Westwood Park, Jalan Tubuan (☎082/ 251163). Good longhouse trips in the Kuching vicinity and on the Batang Ai river system (see pp.368–371 for details). Also arranges trips further afield to Mulu National Park and on the "Head-hunters Trail" from Mulu to Lawas.

Borneo Adventure, 55 Main Bazaar (☎082/245175). Award-winning operation running excellent trips throughout Sarawak and Sabah, including some splendid treks around the Kelabit Highlands. Its jungle lodge, set beside the Batang Ai longhouse of Nanga Sumpa, is a triumph of eco-tourism.

CPH Travel Agencies, 70 Jalan Padungan (☎082/243708). Sarawak's oldest operator, with good contacts in the native communities.

Ibanika Expedition, first floor, Lot 464, Sec. 10 KTLD, Jalan Nanas (☎082/ 424022). Operates longhouse tours and supplies guides who can speak French, German and Japanese.

Interworld, 85 Jalan Rambutan (☎082/252344). Guides expeditions up the Skrang and Batang Ai rivers, plus Niah and Mulu adventures.

Telang Usan Transportation, second floor, 127a Bangunan Kelolong, Jalan Nagor (☎082/254787). Slick outfit whose well-informed guides run dependably good trips around Kuching and beyond.

Tour Exotica, first floor, 1–3 Jalan Temple (☎082/254607). Run by Winston Marshall, whose best deal is the one-day tour to a Bidayuh longhouse. No other company visits the Gunung Braang region near the Kalimantan border, south of Kuching, or offers a day package (around $140 for two) to a traditional Bidayuh community.

Tropical Adventure, 17 Main Bazaar (☎082/413088). Adventures on offer include trekking around Bario, exploring Mulu and trips to Iban longhouses.

Swimming There's a pool at MBKS Building, Jalan Pending (Mon–Fri 2.30–9pm, Sat 6.45–8.45pm, Sun 9.30am–9pm; ☎082/426915); $2 adults, $1 children. Closed on public holidays.

Telephones International calls can be made at the Telekom office, Jalan Batu Lintang (Mon–Fri 8am–6am, Sat 8am–noon), from most public card phones, and from all major hotels.

Day-trips from Kuching

The area **around Kuching** is well served by road, and two days' worth of interesting excursions can be made by bus and boat, without the trouble of hiring guides and porters. Within an hour's bus ride of the capital you can visit a crocodile farm, a wildlife rehabilitation centre deep in the forest, and the riverside villages of the Santubong Peninsula. Some people stay out at one of the peninsula's luxury resort hotels, near to which is the Sarawak Cultural Village, a showpiece community where model longhouses are staffed by guides from each of the ethnic groups.

Semengoh Wildlife Rehabilitation Centre

The **Semengoh Wildlife Rehabilitation Centre** (daily 8am–12.45pm & 2–4.15pm; free), some 30km south of Kuching, was established in 1976 to rehabilitate wild animals and birds – mostly endangered species confiscated from apprehended poachers or found injured in the forest. You need a permit from the Parks and Wildlife desk in Kuching's Visitor Information Centre to visit Semengoh – staff here will inform you as to whether plans to move the centre lock, stock and barrel to Kubah National Park (see below) have gone ahead or not. It's a twenty-minute walk from the entrance to the centre's headquarters (closed 12.30–2pm), where you can pick up a free, detailed information pack, and buy snacks and drinks.

At the centre, the animals are first put into cages and later released into the **forest reserve**, after which they can be returned to the wild proper – usually to the area where they were first found. Because of this system, it's best to coordinate your visit with the feeding times (8.30am & 3pm), when the "advanced stage" animals out in the reserve sometimes return for their papaya, bananas and melons.

Along an elevated wooden walkway, a minute from the headquarters, are various animals and birds undergoing the first stage of rehabilitation. In the dozen cages there are usually proboscis monkeys, orang-utans (a protected species in Sarawak), gibbons, hornbills, porcupines, honey bears and eagles. It doesn't take long to stop by all the cages. After seeing the animals, you can return to the road by one of the **trails** which cut into the forest from the track leading to the headquarters. Here the tree and plant species are labelled, so you can identify dipterocarp tree types, including meranti and engkabang species, and wild fruit trees, among them cempedak and durian. To reach Semengoh, take an STC bus #6 from Lebuh Jawa.

Jong's Crocodile Farm

To reach **Jong's Crocodile Farm** (daily 9am–5pm; $5), 29km south of Kuching on the Serian Highway, take a STC bus #3, #3a or #9 to Siruban Village (departures at 8.20am, 10.30am, noon & 1.30pm, returning to Kuching at 10am, noon, 2pm & 4pm.) The journey takes 25 minutes. Crocodiles are an endangered species in Sarawak and various species are bred on the premises – though some of those are killed at a tender age and their skins sold. The farm is hardly an essential trip since, apart from at feeding times (daily 9am & 3pm), there isn't a great deal to see. But it's worth a quick look in, especially if you haven't got time to head upriver into Sarawak's interior, where you might have a more authentic, heart-stopping meeting with a crocodile. Just to keep you on your toes, the farm features some grisly photographic reminders that people are frequently attacked by crocodiles; one photo shows a dead croc whose stomach has been cut open, revealing an assortment of masticated animals.

Kubah National Park and the Matang Wildlife Centre

Located just 20km west of Kuching, the dipterocarp forest of **Kubah National Park** offers a pleasing and manageable day-trip out of Kuching. There are three modest mountains – **Selang**, **Sendok** and **Serapi** – criss-crossed with the waterfalls and streams for which Kubah is noted. Staff at park headquarters will point you in the direction of Kubah's trails, among them the **Palmarium Trail**, where you'll see many of the hundred-odd species of palm known to thrive here; the **Waterfall Trail**, a ninety-minute hike to impressive, split-level falls; and the **Bukit Selang Trail**, less than an hour's walk from headquarters and boasting some grand views. Kubah's best views, however, are from the three-hour **Gunung Serapi Summit Trail**. Serapi's natural beauty featured in Nick Nolte's 1988 jungle adventure movie, *Farewell to the King*; from its summit, you can see Kuching and much of southwestern Sarawak. A final path, the Rayu Trail, leads, after a couple of hours, to the **Matang Wildlife Centre**. The centre, which should be fully operational by the start of 1998, aims to provide a safe-house for endangered species of indigenous wildlife, and may even house some of the animals presently at Semengoh (see above). In addition, there are walking trails, a picnic site and a freshwater stream that's ideal for a cooling dip.

Though most visitors to Kubah return to the capital at the end of the day, there is some **accommodation**. In Kubah itself you can stay one of five four-bed chalets (⑤–⑦). At Matang, there are hostels (③) and chalets (③–⑥), and tents are available for $4 per night. Note that overnight guests must register at Kuching's Visitor Information Centre. Matang Transport bus #18 runs past the entrance to Kubah National Park, before continuing on to Matang Wildlife Centre.

The Santubong Peninsula

The **Santubong Peninsula**, 30km north of Kuching, is dominated by 810-metre Gunung Santubong, which looms over the peninsula at the point where Sungei Sarawak meets the sea. Once the site of an early trading settlement, the peninsula is a region full of strangely shaped rocks within patches of secondary forest. Stretches of the river and coastline are being rapidly developed as a retreat for tourists and city-weary locals, with the *Damai Lagoon Resort* and the *Holiday Inn Damai Beach* setting the pace. Other than *Holiday Inn* punters, most people come out to the peninsula to explore the small riverside villages of Buntal and Santubong, or to visit the much-hyped **Sarawak Cultural Village**, next to the *Holiday Inn*.

Buntal, Santubong and the resorts

From Kuching's Petra Jaya depot, the #2b bus (every 40min, daily 6.40am–6pm) makes the forty-minute trip through housing developments and small rubber and pepper plantations, leaving the main road and running along the edge of the river to **Buntal**. This quiet riverside kampung is bordered by forest and is famed in these parts for its **seafood restaurants**, which stand on stilts in the seaside shallows; *Lim Hok An* is the pick of the bunch. There's a small beach, too, while locals offer short boat trips along Sungei Sarawak.

From Buntal, the bus returns to the main road and weaves up the lower reaches of Gunung Santubong, before turning east down a narrow road for 2km to **KAMPUNG SANTUBONG**, a very pretty place, set on an inlet with fishing boats hauled up onto the beach. Two Chinese cafés, *Son Hong* and the *Santubong*, whip up tasty stir-fry and rice dishes, and one of the houses opposite the *Santubong* takes lodgers (①); very few tourists actually stay on the peninsula unless it's at one of the resorts up the road (see below). There's some interesting **rock graffiti** near Santubong – head back along the Kuching road for 200m and turn left just before the six-kilometre sign. Thirty metres down the track you'll see a path running between two rocks leading to some curiously carved boulders, one featuring a prone human figure; the other forms are hard to decipher. An exact dating hasn't been made, although archeologists think the rock images could be around a thousand years old.

The bus continues from Santubong for another 5km and, after winding further up the densely forested mountain road, dips down to the **Holiday Inn Damai Beach** (☎082/846999; ⑦) nestling in a natural hollow at the end of the road. "Sarawak's best-kept secret" is in fact a mini-resort, with pool and tennis courts alongside a private palm-fringed, yellow sand beach. There's also a fleet of vans available to take you anywhere – at a price – though the #2b bus stops right outside the hotel gates. The splendid *Damai Lagoon Resort* (☎082/846900; ⑧), sister hotel to Kuching's *Riverside Majestic* – to which it is linked by regular daily bus shuttles – out-swanks the *Holiday Inn*. Sculpted around a magnificent, lagoon-style swimming pool with sunken bar, this compact resort boasts its own private cove, a range of good restaurants, plus health centre, sauna, jacuzzi and watersport facilities.

The handful of trails skeining the peninsula offer ample scope for **trekking**. The trail that loops from the *Santubong Mountain Trek* restaurant (a few minutes' walk south of the resorts) around to the entrance of the Cultural Village (see below) makes for a pleasant ninety-minute forest stroll. The *Mountain Trek* is also the place to kick off the much heavier **Gunung Santubong Trek** ($1), for whose final ascent you'll need to rely upon ropes and rope ladders. Allow at least three hours for your ascent, plus a couple more to return to sea level.

Sarawak Cultural Village

Beside the entrance to the *Holiday Inn Damai Beach* is the **Sarawak Cultural Village** (daily 9am–5.30pm; stage shows at 11.30am & 4.30pm; adults $45), a kind of theme park for the state's varied communities, where seven authentically built **ethnic dwellings** stand in a dramatic setting: the sea to one side, a lake in the middle of the site and Gunung Santubong looming behind. There's no substitute, of course, for viewing longhouse life out in the sticks, but as an overview of the costumes, traditions and daily lives of Sarawak's peoples, the cultural village is a valuable experience, and one which has garnered several tourist industry awards. As well as Iban, Orang Ulu and Bidayuh longhouses, there's a Malay townhouse, a Chinese farmhouse, a Melanau "tall house" (*rumah tinggi*) and a Penan jungle settlement. Though the tribespeople working here live in Kuching, all settlements are functioning daytime communities, demonstrating weaving, cooking and instrument-playing, along with more idiosyncratic pursuits like top-spinning (in the Malay townhouse), drilling blowpipes (in the Penan settlement) and processing sago (at the Melanau tall house). The **shows** put on twice daily are understandably touristy, and some visitors have complained at their trivialization of ancient forest skills – the Penan segment, for instance, has a man moving in slow motion, mimicking the practice of hunting with a blowpipe and aiming it at the audience, before turning his sharpshooting to balloons dangling from the roof of the auditorium. Unless you've got unlimited time to explore Sarawak's river systems, this is about as close as you'll get to witnessing tribal culture.

Bako National Park

BAKO NATIONAL PARK, a two-hour bus and boat journey northeast of Kuching, is Sarawak's oldest national park, occupying the northern section of the Muara Tebas Peninsula at the mouth of Sungei Bako. The area was once part of a forest reserve – a region set aside for timber growing and extraction – but in 1957 it became a national park, fully protected from exploitation. Although relatively small, Bako is spectacular in its own way: its steep rocky cliffs, punctuated by deep bays and lovely sandy beaches, are thrillingly different from the rest of the predominantly flat and muddy Sarawak coastline. The peninsula is composed of sandstone which, over the years, has been worn down to produce delicate pink iron patterns on cliff faces, honeycomb weathering and contorted rock arches rising from the sea. Access to some of the beaches is difficult, requiring tricky descents down nearly vertical paths. Above, the forest contains various species of wildlife, and rivers and waterfalls for bathing. The hike to the highest point, **Bukit Gondol** (260m), is among the most popular of the trails which crisscross Bako, its peak offering a wide view over the park to the South China Sea.

Practicalities

First stop for the trip to Bako is the Parks and Wildlife Department desk at the Visitor Information Centre in Kuching (see p.346), where you need to get a **permit** and reserve your accommodation (see below). This is done over the counter and only takes a few minutes. Once at the park, it's generally a straightforward business to extend your stay if you want to. Note that day-trippers can miss out the Visitor Information Centre and arrange their permit in Kampung Bako.

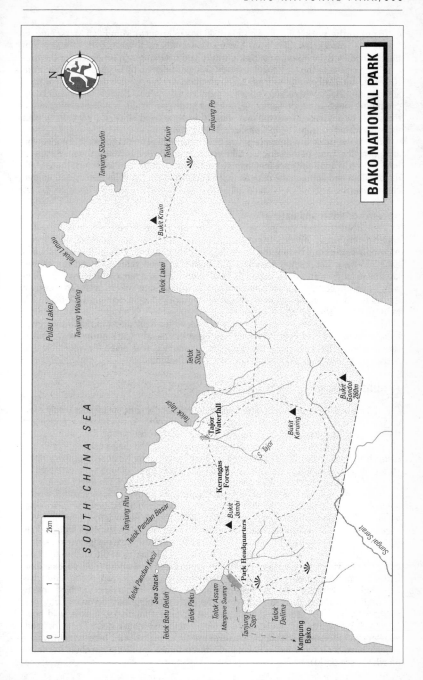

BAKO NATIONAL PARK

N

SOUTH CHINA SEA

Pulau Lakei

Telok Limau

Tanjung Waiding

Tanjung Sibudin

Tanjung Po

Telok Kruin

Bukit Kruin

Telok Lakei

Telok Sibur

Telok Tajor

Tajor Waterfall

Kerangas Forest

S. Tajor

Bukit Kerung

Bukit Gondol 260m

Bukit Jambi

Tanjung Rhu

Telok Pandan Besar

Telok Pandan Kecil

Sea Stack

Telok Batu Belah

Telok Paku

Telok Assam

Mangrove Swamp

Park Headquarters

Tanjung Sapi

Telok Delima

Kampung Bako

Sungai Serait

2km

0   1   2km

To **get to the park**, take the Petra Jaya #6 bus ($3 return) from Jalan Market or use one of the **minibuses**, also from Electra House ($3 each way), both of which run hourly to the jetty at **Kampung Bako**, where you have to rent a **longboat** for the thirty-minute cruise to the park headquarters ($30 per boat; up to 10 people). By car from Kuching, the 37-kilometre journey takes around forty minutes, and there's a car park at Kampung Bako where you can leave your vehicle safely. There's rarely a delay in catching a longboat at the kampung, unless a large tour group is being relayed out to the park. In any case, you wouldn't want to hang around since it's very dirty, with garbage scattered from the line of shops to the river.

Once at the **park headquarters** you need to sign in. The ranger will then give you an informative **map** of the park and take you to your accommodation. You may want an hour to look around the excellent displays and exhibits at the headquarters; these identify the flora and fauna in the park as well as describing in detail its history and unique characteristics.

Accommodation and eating

At park headquarters, various types of **accommodation** have been built along the edge of the forest, divided from the beach 50m away by a row of coconut trees. Although seldom full during the week, Bako tends to get very busy at weekends and bank holidays. For budget travellers the **hostel** is good value (①) and the shared kitchen is fully equipped. Going up the scale, there's also a range of **lodges** (③), all of which provide bed linen, fridge and cooking facilities. Some hikers prefer to **camp** on the trails – tents can be rented from the headquarters for $4, although it's not much more to stay at the hostel.

The **café** at park headquarters is very simple, with a daily menu of rice with vegetables, meat or fish and egg dishes, all at budget prices. The park **shop** has a limited range of goods but can keep you supplied with tins, rice, fruit and a few vegetables, so there's no need to lug basic provisions out from Kuching.

Around the park

Given the easy access and cheap accommodation within the park, many people stay a few days longer than planned at Bako, taking picnics to one of the seven **beaches**, relaxing at the park headquarters itself, or going slow on the trails to observe the flora and fauna. In all, you'll come across seven different **vegetation** types, including peat bog, scrub and mangrove; most of the sixteen trails run through an attractive mixture of primary dipterocarp forest and *kerangas* (in Iban, "poor soil"), a sparser type of forest characterized by much thinner tree cover, stubbier plants and more open pathways. On top of the low hill on the Lintang trail, the strange landscape of Padang Baut is covered in rock plates, where, among the shrubs, you'll find **pitcher plants**, whose deep, mouth-shaped lids open to trap water and insects which are then digested in the soupy liquid. Elsewhere, on the cliffs, delicate plants cling to vertical rock faces or manage to eke out an existence in little pockets of soil, while closer to park headquarters the coastline is thick with mangrove trees.

You're more likely to catch sight of the **wildlife** while lazing at the chalets than out on the trails. Monkeys are always lurking around on the lookout for food, so it's important to keep the kitchen and dormitory doors locked. Even the rare flying lemur has been sighted swinging from the trees around the park headquarters. The best time to see wildlife on the trails is at night or in the early morning and, if you're lucky, you might catch sight of proboscis, macaque and silver leaf monkeys, snakes, wild boar, giant monitor lizards, squirrels, bearded pigs, otters and mouse deer. The park headquarters and the open paths in the *kerangas* are the best places for **bird-watching**: 150 species have been recorded in Bako, including two rare species of hornbills (for more on which, see p.414).

The trails

It's best to get an early start on the **trails**, taking much-needed rests at the strategic-ally positioned viewpoint huts along the way. The sixteen trails are all colour-coded: every twenty metres, paint splashes denoting the trail are clearly marked on trees and rocks. You'll need to carry a litre of water per person (you can refill your bottle from the streams), a light rainproof jacket, mosquito repellent and sunscreen. Wear com-fortable shoes with a good grip (there's no need for heavy-duty walking boots), light clothing like T-shirt and shorts, and take a sunhat. Don't forget your swimming gear either, as cool streams cut across the trails, and beaches and waterfalls are never far away. The park map clearly shows the trails, which all start from park headquarters.

Probably the most popular trail is the 3.5-kilometre hike to **Tajor Waterfall**, a hike estimated at two and a half hours, though it can easily be done in ninety minutes if you don't linger too long for rests or plant study. The initial half -hour climb from the jetty, on a steep and circuitous, root-bound path up the forested cliff is the hardest section. At the top you move swiftly through scrubland into *kerangas* – a section without much shade, where pitcher plants are profuse. The path leads to a simple wooden hut with a fine prospect of the peninsula. Moving on, you return to sun-shielded forest, where the dry, sandy path gives way to a muddy trail through peat bog, leading eventually to the waterfall itself, a lovely spot for swimming and eating your picnic.

Alternatively, if you leave the main trail at the wooden hut and viewpoint and turn west, a path descends to two beautiful **beaches**, Telok Pandan Kecil and Telok Pandan Besar, each around a thirty-minute hike from the viewpoint. During the week you'll probably be the only person at either, with Kecil in particular involving a steep, rugged descent down sandstone rocks to reach the refreshingly clean water. The other two beaches at Bako – Sibur and Limau – are much harder to reach, but enjoyable once you've got there. To find **Telok Sibur** beach, continue past Tajor Waterfall, following the main trail for around forty minutes, before turning west on the black-and-red trail. The demanding descent to the beach takes anything from twenty minutes to an hour to accomplish. You'll have to drop down the cliff face using creepers and roots to help you, and your troubles aren't over when you reach the bottom either, since you're then in a mangrove swamp and must tread carefully so as not to lose your footing among the stones. After wading across a river, you reach the beach – the longest on the peninsu-la and, not surprisingly, seldom visited.

The hike to **Telok Limau**, estimated at seven hours, can be done in five at a push. The terrain alternates between swampland and scrub and primary and secondary for-est, and provides fabulous views round the whole peninsula. The beach itself marks the most northerly point in the park; it's not really possible to get there and back in a day. Either bring a tent and food and camp on the beach, as perfect a spot to lay your head as you will ever find, or arrange with park headquarters for a boat to pick you up for the return trip, which costs around $200. Once out at Limau you could detour on the way back along the marked trail to **Kruin**, at the eastern end of the park – an area where you're most likely to spot wildlife. There is a secluded freshwater pond on the way and, from the top of the nearby hill, a grand view of the park's eastern edges.

Far western Sarawak

Compared with Niah, Mulu and the Kelabit Highlands, Sarawak's far western corner is bereft of spectacular attractions. The **caves** a short distance from the town of Bau are worth a look if your schedule doesn't have space for the altogether more impressive systems further north; otherwise the only sight of real note is **Gunung Gading National Park**, located just north of the one-horse town of Lundu. The best beaches in the area are also close to Lundu, although Bako National Park (see above) is a better bet for sun, sea and sand. From Lundu, infrequent buses run out to the diminutive fishing community of **Sematan**, the most westerly inhabited point in Sarawak, and a likeable enough backwater.

Bau, Lundu and the Gunung Gading National Park

STC #2 buses ($3) depart from Kuching's Lebuh Jawa throughout the day, pulling into the nondescript market town of **BAU** an hour later. Nineteenth-century prospectors were drawn here by the gold that veined the surrounding countryside, but drab modern-day Bau doesn't live up to its romantic past. The largest and best of the caves around Bau is the **Fairy Cave**, 10km south of town. Tour agents in Kuching will arrange adventure caving here, but as long as you pack a torch, you can take a taxi from Bau and have a wander through the cave yourself.

A less frequent STC service, the #2b, leaves Kuching for **LUNDU** via Batu Kawa at 8am, 11.15am, 12.30pm, 2.15pm and 4pm ($7.80), clattering through a landscape which gradually transforms from plantation to forest, with jungle-clad hills close by. For most visitors who stray out this far, Lundu is a staging-post en route to either the jungle or the coast. Waiting for an onward connection, there may be time to walk around its small **market**, where you can buy fresh fruit, or to go into one of the **cafés** bordering the town square; the *Jouee* serves excellent noodles.

From Lundu's central bus terminal, you'll need to catch an STC #17 "Pandan" bus (40 sen) to cover the 2km up the road north of town to the park headquarters of **Gunung Gading National Park**, where rafflesia, the world's largest plant, grows. Discovered by – and named after – Sir Stamford Raffles, its flowers grow up to one metre across, smell of rotting meat, and are pollinated by carrion flies. With no predictable flowering season, there's a certain amount of luck involved in seeing this strange plant: call park headquarters (☎082/735714) for advice. Upon arrival, a ranger will lead you out to the plant or (if you are really in luck) plants in bloom.

Besides Gunung Gading itself, the park has three other mountains, **Perigi**, **Lundu**, and **Sebuloh**. It's possible to climb both Gading and Perigi on the colour-coded **trails** that trace the forest. Both are full-on hikes, not to be undertaken lightly; for lesser mortals, the two-hour round trip offered by the Waterfall Trail is a more sedate alternative. Waterfall 7, where it ends, offers good, refreshing swimming. As elsewhere, day-trippers can **register** on arrival at the park; over nighters must first check in at the Visitor Information Centre in Kuching.

Accommodation in the park takes the form of a hostel (①) and chalets (③–⑥); or you can stay back in Lundu, at either the *Lundu Gading Hotel* (☎082/735299; ③), or the cheaper *Cheng Hak Boarding House* (contact *Goh Joo Hak Store*, near the *Lundu Gading* at 51 Bazaar; ①). Beyond the park entrance, the road from Lundu continues northward until it reaches the coast, some 8km later, at **Pandan Beach**. Considered by many locals to be the best in the area, Pandan is a half-kilometre-long stretch of white sand near a beachfront kampung; a little way out to the east, shorter **Siar Beach** is another pleasing spot.

Sematan

Some 25km northwest of Lundu, the few quiet shophouses of **SEMATAN** are located at the end of the road from Kuching. The town's mostly deserted long **beach** has reasonably clean yellow sand with coconut palms – but be aware that sandflies are notoriously bad here, and the water is shallow. A coastal track runs for several miles northwest of Sematan; an hour's walk from town is rugged **Cape Belinsah**, where there's nothing to do but clamber around on the rocks. From here it may soon be possible to visit the island of **Talang Talang**, clearly visible a few kilometres north of the cape, where there is a small turtle sanctuary. Already listed as a conservation zone, the island may soon be gazetted as a national park: enquire at the Visitor Information Centre in Kuching for the current state of play.

As well as laid-back beaches, Sematan also has several local **trails**, starting from the wood just a couple of minutes across the bay, 200m away. Ask one of the men hanging around the small jetty to take you over – it should only cost a few dollars. Once across the water, the boatman can point out the start of a circular trail which runs through plantations and a tiny kampung, before winding around to join the road on which the bus comes in. All in all, it's a two-hour trip.

For **accommodation** in Sematan, the *Sematan Hotel* (☎082/711162; ②), on Sematan Bazaar, is a friendly place with small, clean rooms, or you can make do with the grim beachfront *Lai Sematan Bungalows* (☎082/711133, ②). The detached chalets are fairly basic and sleep four; it's necessary to reserve in advance, since the janitor needs to make a special journey to Sematan to give you the keys. Two or three Chinese **cafés** in the village serve hot meals; local crabs are particularly tasty.

The Kalimantan border: Bidayuh longhouses and Gunung Penrissen

One hundred kilometres south of Kuching, up in the mountains straddling the border with Kalimantan, are several authentic **Bidayuh longhouses**, which offer a fascinating insight into the culture of the only remaining Land Dyaks in Sarawak. Unlike other ethnic groups, the Bidayuh built their multi-levelled, elevated longhouses at the base of hills rather than rivers and, as a consequence, endured violent attacks during the last century from other more aggressive groups, especially the Iban, who were migrating across the mountains from the Kapuas river region in west Kalimantan. Bidayuh longhouses were frequently raided, the men's heads severed, the children taken as slaves, and the women offered a choice between becoming the victors' wives or losing their heads too. The Bidayuh, for their part, weren't exactly passive victims: they are the only ethnic group which traditionally erected a separate structure in each community called a **head-house**, where the heads of their enemies were kept and which served as a focus for male activities and rituals. Given the constant attacks, it's not surprising that the Bidayuh are among the more introverted of Sarawak's ethnic groups, yet they welcome sensitive visitors just as much as the more demonstrative Iban or Kelabit. Many Bidayuh traditions are thriving; they make the best **bamboo crafts** of all the indigenous groups and also excellent mats. But only a small percentage of the remaining Bidayuh population in Sarawak, which totals around fifty thousand, still live in the longhouses. Most of the young men prefer seasonal employment in logging, or work on the rubber and pepper plantations, while many of the children go on to further education before taking jobs in the burgeoning clerical and service industries.

The longhouses

From Lebuh Jawa, STC bus #6 runs south of Semengoh Rehabilitation Centre to the longhouse at **BENUK** several times a day, but the better longhouses are to be found 20km further south at **ANNA RAIS**, the largest Bidayuh settlement in the area, served by STC #9 (every 30min, daily 6.40am–5.55pm). The two-hour journey to Anna Rais takes you past the **market gardens** bordering Jalan Serian – whose Hakka farmers cultivate pumpkins, tomatoes and so on – before veering onto southbound Jalan Padawan, at **Tapah**. Jalan Padawan is quite a rocky ride, but looking at the pepper plantations and small churches along the way may take your mind off your discomfort. Given its proximity to the capital, the place is inevitably touristy (a $3 entry fee is levied, and there are public toilets for visitors outside the village), but don't be unduly discouraged: Anna Rais is a user-friendly and colourful initiation into longhouse life, hemmed by groves of bamboo and fruit trees, and still very much a living community. As you wander around, you'll be offered food and drink, possibly even betel nut, and invited to watch and participate in craft demonstrations. Outside several longhouse chambers are bell-shaped ironwood rice mortars, some of which are said to be a century old. Villagers might show you round the **skull house** (*panggah*), outside which stands a British cannon from 1756, though don't take this part of your "tour" for granted.

The best time to go is at the weekend when the children are back from school and the wage-earners back from their logging and city jobs. Most visitors stay a couple of hours, returning to Kuching the same day, but you can stay the night, though if you want to do this, remember to bring some gifts. Alternatively, you can sleep in the community hall at **KAMPUNG ABANG**, a ten-minute drive beyond Anna Rais, and a useful overnight stop if you want to trek up nearby Gunung Penrissen the next day. While you're here, you might test your nerves on the nearby **hanging bridge**. South of Abang, a new development provisionally called the Borneo Highlands Resort is presently under construction; the Visitor Information Centre in Kuching can update you on this.

Gunung Penrissen

The most accessible of the mountains on the Malaysia/Kalimantan is the spectacular 1300-metre **Gunung Penrissen**, the hike up which involves tough walking along narrow paths and crossing fast-flowing streams which descend from the source of Sungei Sarawak; vertical ladders help you on the last section. This and other nearby peaks are criss-crossed by narrow paths, known only to locals and a few trained trackers, so it's inadvisable to venture on to them without a **guide**. William Nub (☎082/410858) will arrange a guide for you, starting from either of the longhouses detailed above or from Kampung Abang. Although the ascent and descent of Penrissen can be done in one hard day, you may prefer to set up camp at the foot of the summit, so bring a lightweight tent and food supplies.

Gunung Penrissen was strategically important in the 1950s border skirmishes between the Malaysian and Indonesian armies, and there's still a Malaysian **military post** close to the summit from where exhausted walkers gaze over the rainforest into Kalimantan to the south and east, and to the South China Sea over the forests to the north.

Serian and the border crossing

Some 20km southeast of Gunung Penrissen is the **border crossing** at TEBEDU, 120km from Kuching. Buses to Tebedu leave from **SERIAN**, a workaday town with an excellent fruit and vegetable market on the main Kuching–Sri Aman road. You'll need to set off first thing, as local buses from Tebedu which run south across the border to the Indonesian town of **ENTIKONG** and on to Pontianak stop running in the early afternoon. Tebedu is tiny, little more than an administrative centre, with a couple of dispiriting hotels. The border crossing at Entikong is open from 6am to 5pm and you need a valid Indonesian visa, available in Kuching (though this may soon no longer be necessary).

Batang Lupar and Batang Ai

Although Sibu – and Batang Rajang – is only four hours by boat from Kuching, the most popular destination for **longhouse visits** from the capital remains the **Batang Ai river system**, 200km east of the city, a distance which takes at least six hours to cover. Many of the tour operators in Kuching have established good relations with the friendly Iban communities here; indeed many of the operators' staff are Iban from the longhouses themselves. It's quite possible, however, to try your luck without travelling under the protective wing of a tour group. Access is via the town of **Sri Aman**, 150km southeast of Kuching, reached either by STC buses from Lebuh Jawa (7.30am, 9.30am, noon, 3pm & 7.30pm; $15), or on the Biramas Express (1pm; $15) from the Penrissen Road terminal; the journey takes three or four hours. All buses bound for Sri Aman stop at Serian, where you can stock up with drinking water and provisions.

Sri Aman

SRI AMAN is the second biggest town in southwest Sarawak and is the administrative capital of this part of the state. It sits upriver on Sungei Lupar, whose lower reaches are over 1500 metres wide, though the river narrows dramatically as it meanders through the flat alluvial plain. Just before Sri Aman, a small island in the river obstructs the flow of the incoming tide, producing the town's renowned "tidal bore". At regular intervals, when enough water has accumulated, a billowing wave rushes by with some force: longboats are hauled up onto the muddy bank and large vessels head for mid-stream in an attempt to ride the bore as evenly as possible. At its most impressive, the bore rolls up like a mini-tidal wave, rocking boats and splashing the new Chinese temple which is set back from the pier. Somerset Maugham was caught by the wave in 1929 and nearly drowned, a tale he recounted in "Yellow Streak" in his *Borneo Tales*.

The busy town itself has a central defensive fort, **Fort Alice**, built by Charles Brooke in 1864 and thus predating Fort Margherita in Kuching. More compact than the one in the capital, the fort (now a government office and not open to the public) has turrets, a courtyard and, oddly, a drawbridge. Charles Brooke based himself in this region for many years, heading a small force which repelled the downriver advances of pirates and intervened in the upriver conflicts between warring Iban factions.

There are several **hotels** in town: the *Champion Inn*, 1248 Main Bazaar (☎083/320140; ②), is the most central; *Hoover Hotel*, 139 Jalan Club (☎083/321985; ②) the best value; while the smartest is the *Alishan Hotel*, 120 Jalan Council (☎083/322578; ③).

Visiting the longhouses

The **Batang Lupar** and **Batang Ai region**, around 40km southeast of Sri Aman, is Iban territory. Although there was a major displacement here in the 1960s, caused by the building of the Batang Ai reservoir, most Iban still maintain their traditional lifestyles. It is common to meet young men and women who have done a stint in a logging camp or at a hawker stall in Sri Aman or Kuching, and yet have returned to the longhouse life. Nevertheless, many people have moved away permanently, and the onus on keeping the essentially agricultural way of life going is being increasingly placed on the women and adolescents.

The numerous **Iban longhouses** (the Skrang, Lemanak, Engkari and the Delok) on the main tributaries of the Lupar and its continuation beyond the Batang Ai reservoir, the Ai, are fairly accessible from Sri Aman. All the Kuching-based tour operators (see p.359) offer two- to five-day trips, and some – Borneo Adventures and Asian Overland, for instance – have "adopted" a longhouse. For travellers on a short stay, tours like this are ideal, but check that the size of the group doesn't exceed six to eight people as things can get a bit congested. For a three-day tour booked through a Kuching outfit, you can expect to pay around $500. If you want to make your own way to a longhouse, in the first instance you need to head for one of the number of **jetties** around this part of Sarawak. At these sites, get talking to some of the locals who go back and forth along the rivers and with any luck you'll get an invitation to a longhouse – or, at the very least, lots of advice regarding forthcoming departures. Bear in mind, though, that the logis-

THE IBAN

The **Iban** – one of the ethnic groups categorized as Sea Dyaks – comprise nearly one-third of the population of Sarawak, making them easily the most numerous of Sarawak's indigenous peoples. They originated in the Kapuas river basin of West Kalimantan, on the other side of the mountains which separate Kalimantan and Sarawak, but having outgrown their lands they migrated to the Lupar river in southwest Sarawak in the early sixteenth century, looking for **new land** to cultivate. Once in Sarawak, the Iban soon clashed with the coastal Melanau, and by the eighteenth century they had moved up the Rajang into the interior, into areas that were traditionally Kayan lands. Inevitably, great battles were waged between these two powerful groups, with one contemporary source recording seeing "a mass of boats drifting along the stream, while the Dyaks were spearing and stabbing each other; decapitated trunks and heads without bodies, scattered about in ghastly profusion."

Head-hunting become established during the Iban migrations, a practice generally sponsored by the need to top up the spiritual reserve in a new longhouse, though revenge too played a part. It didn't matter how the head was taken or to whom it belonged. An account which appeared in the *Sarawak Gazette* in 1909, just when Charles Brooke hoped his policy of stopping head-hunting was at last becoming effective, reported that:

> *Justly are the Dyaks called head-hunters, for during the whole of their life, from early youth till their death, all their thoughts are fixed on the hunting of heads. The women, in their cruelty and blood-thirstiness, are the cause. At every festival the old trophies are taken from the fireplace and carried through the house by the women who sing a monotonous song in honour of the hero who cut off the head, and in derision of the poor victims whose skulls are carried around. Everywhere, the infernal chorus, "Bring us more of them", is heard.*

Although conflict between the various ethnic groups stopped with the slowing down of the migrations, heads were still being taken as recently as the 1960s during the Konfrontasi skirmishes, when Indonesian army units came up against Iban fighters in the Malaysian army.

After the Melanau, the Iban are the most "modernized" of Sarawak's ethnic groups. Around ten percent live in towns – mostly Kuching, Sri Aman and Sibu – and work in a variety of trades, from handicrafts to manufacturing. Even the bulk of the rural Iban, the vast majority of whom still live in longhouses, undertake seasonal work in the rubber and oil industries, and it is no small irony that **logging** – the business which most devastates their own customary lands – provides plentiful and lucrative work.

Unlike most of the other groups, the Iban are a very egalitarian people – the longhouse *tuai* (headman) is more of a figurehead than someone who wields power. Women in the community have different duties to men; they never go hunting or work in logging, but are considered to be great weavers. Indeed, it's an Iban woman's weaving prowess that determines her status in the community. In this context, they're most renowned for their

tics of travel in this area mean that you might be wiser settling for a tour: there's no developed express boat scene such as exists on the Rajang (see p.378), so upriver travel can sometimes only be speedily achieved by chartering your own vessel.

The **Skrang** is reached by taking a Betong bus from Sri Aman and getting off just short of Entabau, at Pais, where you can check out imminent upriver departures at the jetty. Be warned, though, that of all the tributaries in this region of Sarawak, the Skrang is the most touristy, and you may find that longhouses won't take you in unless you've booked through the operator which has "adopted" them. To reach either the Lemanak, or the Batang Ai and its tributaries you'll need to take an STC bus from Sri Aman southeast to **LUBOK ANTU**, a small town 50km away which has a predominantly Iban beautiful **pua kumbu** (blanket or coverlet) work, a cloth of intricate design and colour. The *pua kumbu* once played an integral part in Iban rituals, when they were hung prominently during harvest festivals and weddings, or used to cover structures containing charms and offerings to the gods. And, when head-hunting was still a much-valued tradition, the women would wear the *pua kumbu* to receive the "prize" brought home by their menfolk. The cloth is generally made by using the *ikat* technique, which involves binding, tying and dyeing the material so as to build up complex patterns.

The Iban are extremely gregarious and love an opportunity to throw a **party**, drinking *tuak*, eating piles of meat and fish and cracking jokes (the Iban lexicon is rich with double entendres). The games visitors find themselves playing when visiting the Iban are often designed to get as many laughs at their expense as possible. The best time to visit is during June when the **gawai** (harvest) **festival** gets into swing – the months of May and June after the rice harvest are customarily a time for relaxing, hunting, craft-making and merrymaking.

Of all the customs maintained by the Iban, perhaps the most singular is their style of **tattooing**, which is not just a form of ornamentation, but also an indication of personal wealth and other achievements. Many designs are used, from a simple circular outline for the shoulder, chest or outer side of the wrists, to more elaborate designs (dogs, scorpions or dragons) for the inner and outer surfaces of the thigh. The two most important locations for tattoos are considered to be the hand and the throat. A tattoo on the hand indicates that you have "taken a head" – some elders still have these – while one on the throat means that you are a fully mature man, with wealth, possessions, land and family. Tattooing is usually carried out by an experienced artist, either a longhouse resident or a travelling tattooist who arrives just prior to the *gawai* season. A carved design on a block of wood is smeared with ink and pressed to the skin, the resulting outline then punctured with needles dipped in dark ink, made from a mixture of sugar juice, water and soot. For the actual tattooing a hammer-like instrument is used that has two or three needles protruding from its head. These are dipped in ink, the hammer placed against the skin and hit repeatedly with a wooden block, after which rice is smeared over the inflamed area to prevent infection.

Each longhouse hosts at least one open weekend during *gawai* when visitors are welcome as long as they bring **gifts**. Anything will do, from basic food supplies like meat, salt and sugar to Western clothes and cassettes – gifts of toys are guaranteed to endear you to the kids. But as you are supposed to socialize with the chief's family first – unless you've met someone else en route – the gifts should be given to the chief to distribute accordingly. Other **house rules** include never walking straight into a longhouse unless you are following your guide – wait to be invited. Shake hands with everybody who wants to shake yours but don't touch the locals anywhere else; for example, don't tousle the heads of the children. Eat as much as possible and don't worry if it looks like you are eating the family's entire supply of food – it is the custom to stuff visitors, whether foreigners or next-door neighbours, and there is usually more in reserve. You should also accept the offer to swim in the river – everybody goes, usually in small groups, for a wash at the start of the day and at dusk – but be careful not to reveal your anatomy; wear a sarong or shorts.

population. Here, you'll need to ask for the local shuttle ($1.50) down to the **Batang Ai reservoir jetty**, about 10km to the northeast, in order to explore the tributaries of the Batang Ai; this is not a very regular service, and if you get to Lubok Antu late, you'll have need of the decent rooms at the *Kelingkang Inn* (☎083/584331; ③) and of the *kolok mee*, *nasi goreng* and other meals served up beside the bus station in the *Oriental Café*. The only other accommodation alternative in the area is the luxurious *Hilton Batang Ai Resort* (☎082/248200, fax 428984; ⑦) on the banks of the reservoir, one of Sarawak's new breed of quirky, out-station resorts. If you want to try your luck along the pretty, but muddier Sungei Lemanak, get off the Sri Aman–Lubok Antu bus at **Rumah Bareng**, and make enquiries at the jetty there.

SIBU AND THE RAJANG BASIN

The 560-kilometre-long **Batang Rajang**, known as *batang* (big river) rather than *sungei*, because of its great width and length, lies at the very heart of Sarawak. In many ways, it's changed little since the nineteenth century, when Chinese and Malay adventurers took boats from Sibu wharf to the bazaar town of **Kapit**, before heading up the Rajang to the frontier settlement of **Belaga** to trade with the nomadic Penan. This is the world of isolated colonial forts, and of longboat trips to stately longhouses, where massive woodcarvings guard the entrance. Once the little town of **Song** on the Rajang has been reached, **Iban longhouses** along the Katibas and Baleh tributaries become easily accessible; while guides in Kapit and Belaga can lead you on jungle treks to **Kayan longhouses** or visits to **Penan** communities.

Approaching along the coast from Kuching, initial impressions of the Rajang are of a wide, dirty channel, used to transport logs from the interior of the state to the outside world. From the small town of Sarakei, near the mouth of the Rajang, to beyond Kapit over 200km to the east, hundreds of log-laden barges chug downstream past dozens of processing factories and storage depots. Despite the state government's commitment to slowing down the pace of deforestation, there are few signs of this along the lower reaches of the Rajang. Around ninety minutes upriver from the coast, the major port of **Sibu** is the headquarters of the timber cartels – indeed, now that the accessible forests of the north have been thoroughly logged, Sibu has overtaken Miri and Marudi as the focal point of Sarawak's timber industry.

A little history

For centuries, the Rajang was rife with tribal conflict. In the fifteenth century – the height of power of the Malay sultanates – Malays living in the estuaries of southern Sarawak pushed the immigrant Iban up the rivers towards present-day Sibu. This antagonized the indigenous people of those regions, especially the Baleh and upper Rajang Kayan, and throughout the seventeenth and eighteenth centuries they fought amongst themselves for territory and heads. Occasionally, when they felt threatened, the Malays and the Iban would form an uneasy alliance to attack inland Kayan tribes and carry out piratical raids on passing Indonesian and Chinese ships.

With the arrival of the British, it was clear that no serious opening up of the interior could go ahead until the region was made relatively safe – which meant controlling the land and subjugating, or displacing, many of the indigenous inhabitants. James Brooke bought a section of Batang Rajang from the Sultan of Brunei in 1853, while his successor, Charles, asserted his authority over the Iban and Kayan tribes, and encouraged **Chinese pioneers** to move into the interior. Some of the more intrepid Chinese pioneers started to trade upriver with the Iban and, with support from the Malay business community and Brooke officials, built settlements at Kanowit and Sibu in the late nineteenth century, hacking out farms in the jungle, on which, with varying degrees of success, they grew rice, vegetables, pepper and rubber. Indeed, Sibu's early growth was largely financed by the proceeds of rubber cultivation. But the pioneers faced numerous disputes with the Iban, who, historically in conflict with the Malays who pushed them away from the estuaries, now resented the Chinese for clearing and growing crops on land the Iban believed belonged to them.

The life of the upriver pioneers was a dangerous one: most lived on their *atap*-roofed boats, never leaving them, even while trading with the Iban. Some, however, learned the tribal languages and customs and, although banned from doing so by Brooke, would spent nights in the longhouses; a few even took Dyak wives. The traders would spend a month or more plying the tributaries, leaving cloth, salt and shotgun cartridges on credit with the Dyaks and then returning to pick up **jungle produce** in exchange, like birds' nests, camphor, beeswax, honey and *bezoar* stones. But it was a risky life for these pioneers, especially when they were faced with an Iban tribesman, whose only way out of a credit impasse was to do away with the trader.

Sibu

SIBU, 60km from the coast up Batang Rajang, is Sarawak's second largest city and the state's biggest port. It seethes with activity, most of the action taking place on the long jetties, with their separate bays for passenger boats, commercial craft and logging barges. Most of the local population are Foochow Chinese (the town is known locally as New Foochow) and its remarkable modern growth is largely attributed to these industrious and enterprising immigrants. Sibu, unlike Kuching or Miri, never retained a large contingent of Brooke officials, which means its Chinese character has never really been diluted. Following the success of the early rubber plantations, manufacturing industries (largely textiles and consumer items) were established here, while later, after independence, Chinese businessmen moved into the lucrative trade in **timber**. But it wasn't all untrammelled expansion. In 1928 the Chinese *godowns* along the wharf and many of the cramped lodging houses and cafés were destroyed by fire. The town was devastated again in World War II by advancing Japanese forces, and was occupied for three years, during which time much of the Chinese population was forced into slave labour.

There is still a wild edge to Sibu: the traders are louder and more persuasive, the locals more assertively friendly, while everywhere are signs of the timber cartels' wealth . Multistorey commercial buildings sit on the outskirts of town, there are brand new Toyota pick-ups on the streets, and crowds of Chinese in the cafés, surrounded by beer and whisky bottles, slapping down twenty-dollar notes during a session of mahjong. The town's most striking landmark is the towering, seven-storey pagoda, next to the temple, while behind it is the old Chinatown, with its warren of narrow streets, along which are most of the cheap hotels, the hawker stalls and the cramped fish, meat and vegetable markets. Beyond simply soaking up the town's vibrant atmosphere, there's little for visitors to do in Sibu, though you'll want to check out the bustling pasar malam and the small museum on the edge of town, which focuses on the Chinese migration and the displaced ethnic communities. Most people are here because it's the first stage of an expedition upriver – though don't be surprised if you end up feeling sorry to leave.

Arrival and information

Flights from Kuching, Bintulu and Miri arrive at the **airport** is 25km east of the city centre. The taxi drivers at the airport will tell you not to bother with the bus, and then charge you $20 for the journey into the centre. Otherwise, make your way out of the tiny terminal and on to the main road where there is a bus stop for the #3a into town (every 40min, daily 7am–6pm). This takes you to the **bus and taxi station** on Jalan Khoo Peng Loong, 200m west of Chinatown, where several of the city's budget hotels are located; this is also where the long-distance buses from Bintulu and points north arrive.

Travelling by boat from Sarikei, you dock at the **upriver boat wharf**, 100m northwest of the bus terminal. This is where you come to catch the express boat on to Kapit and Belaga, while for **downriver boats** – the ones from Kapit and to Sarikei – there's another jetty, 100m further northwest, just beside the Chinese temple. Walking directly behind the pagoda you come to Jalan Tukang Besi and on to Jalan Central, another main street with accommodation and restaurants. For more **departure details**, see the relevant sections in "Listings", p.377.

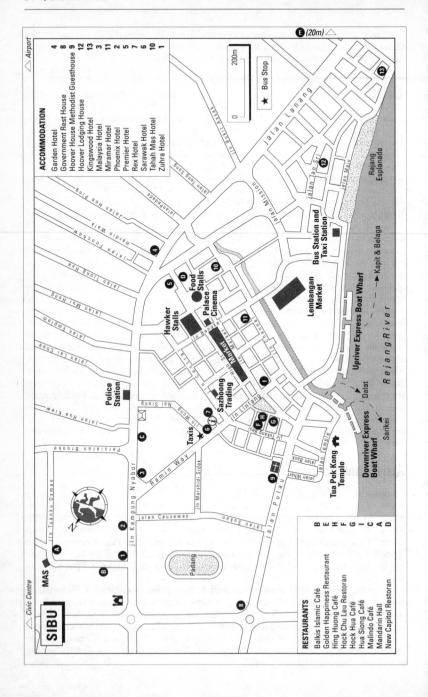

SIBU

△ *Civic Centre*

△ *Airport*

E *(20m)* △

ACCOMMODATION

Garden Hotel	4
Government Rest House	8
Hoover House Methodist Guesthouse	9
Hoover Lodging House	12
Kingswood Hotel	13
Malaysia Hotel	3
Miramar Hotel	11
Phoenix Hotel	2
Premier Hotel	5
Rex Hotel	7
Sarawak Hotel	6
Tanah Mas Hotel	10
Zuhra Hotel	1

★ **Bus Stop**

0   200m

RESTAURANTS

Balkis Islamic Café	B
Golden Happiness Restaurant	E
Hing Huong Café	H
Hock Chu Leu Restoran	F
Hock Hua Café	G
Hua Siong Café	I
Malindo Café	C
Mandarin Hall	A
New Capitol Restoran	D

Jalan Tuanku Osman

Persiaran Brooke

Jalan Hua Kiew

Jalan Lai Chee

Jalan Empiam

Jalan Mui Hong

Jalan Tiong Hua

Jalan Toochow

Hardin Walk

Jalan Hoe Ping

Jalan Tiong Seng

Ramin Way

Jalan Kampung Nyabor

Jln Kai Peng

Jalan Mission

Jalan Lanang

Jalan Tan Sri

Jalan Maju

MAS

Police Station

Taxis

Jln Wong Nai Siong

Jln Central

Hawker Stalls

Food Stalls

Palace Cinema

Sazhoong Trading

Market

Jln Lintang

Jln Maju

Jln Tukang Besi

Jln Bengkel

Jalan Masjid Sidek

Jalan Bank

Jalan Temple

Jln Wharf

Jalan Pulau

Jalan Sukan

jalan Causeway

Tua Pek Kong Temple

Lembangan Market

Bus Station and Taxi Station

Downriver Express Boat Wharf

Upriver Express Boat Wharf

Rejang River

Rejang Esplanade

→ *Kapit & Belaga*

← *Dalat*

← *Sarikei*

Padang

△ E ▲ F △ H ▲ G ▲ I

A **B** **C** **D**

1 2 3 4 5 6 7 8 9 10 11 12 13

Sibu's Visitor Information Centre is at the back of the *Sarawak Hotel*, off Ramin Way. Here you can get leaflets, an accommodation list and a map of greater Sibu. For **information** on town and longhouse tours, call in at Frankie Ting's office, *Sazhong Trading*, at 4 Jalan Central (Mon–Sat 8am–4.40pm; ☎084/336017).

Accommodation

It is fairly easy to find **accommodation** in Sibu, though many hotels are in the old town, where the day market, hawker stalls and cafés – open from before dawn – makes a lie-in difficult. The pasar malam makes going to bed early tricky too, though things quieten down around 11pm. Prices are cheaper than in Kuching, though the standard of the rooms is not as high.

Garden, 1 Jalan Hoe Ping (☎084/317888). Likeable 40-room hotel just a stone's throw from the city centre, with in-house coffee shop and business centre. Recommended. ⑤.

Government Rest House, Jalan Pulau (☎084/330406). Fifteen minutes' walk from the wharf in a large colonial building at the far end of Jalan Pulau. The double rooms are pricey but comfortable, and some overlook a tranquil garden at the back. Visiting officials take priority, so you are more likely to get a room here at the weekends. ③.

Hoover House Methodist Guesthouse, Jalan Pulau (☎084/332491). Quiet situation, basic double rooms with communal bathrooms, and a friendly caretaker. Book in advance, asking for Mr Naing Unju. ①.

Hoover Lodging House, 34 Jalan Tan Sri (☎084/334490). Unobtrusively positioned in a cramped side street close to the bus station, and surprisingly clean for this price bracket. Cheapest rooms are tiny, with fan and shared facilities, but $8 more secures you a window and your own bathroom. ①.

Kingwood, Lorong 4, Lanang Rd (☎084/335888). Really plush place, counting rooftop pool, health centre, fine river views and several food and drink outlets among its many assets. ⑦.

Malaysia, Jalan Kampung Nyabor (☎084/332299). A popular, but fairly shabby place, located on a busy main road, with small rooms, shared toilet and shower; it's family-run and friendly. ②.

Miramar, 47 Jalan Channel (☎084/332433). Grubby, not very friendly, but centrally located, looking directly down on the night market. ②.

Phoenix, Jalan Ki Peng, off Jalan Kampung Nyabor (☎084/313877). Smart and friendly; one of the best upmarket hotels, with spacious modern rooms, some with baths, and TV. ④–⑤.

Premier, Jalan Kampung Nyabor (☎084/323222). Top-class hotel; you can tell by the chill of the air-con as you approach the doorway. ⑥.

Rex, 32 Jalan Cross (☎084/330625). Cheap, functional rooms with fan and shared facilities. Air-con rooms are more expensive. ②.

Sarawak, 34 Jalan Cross (☎084/333455). Recently had a facelift and now with an elevator to the tastefully decorated rooms on four floors. Predictably, more expensive than in the old days; the large rooms now equipped with TV, air-con and shower. ③.

Tanah Mas, Block 5 Jalan Kampung Nyabor (☎084/333188). Another decent and central hotel in the *Premier* mould, though somewhat pricier. ⑦.

Zuhra, Jalan Kampung Nyabor (☎084/310711). This quality hotel has smallish, modern rooms with air-con, TV and shower. ③.

The Town

For a century or more, Batang Rajang has been the Sibu's commercial and industrial lifeline. Along the **wharf**, on Jalan Khoo Peng Loong, plankways lead to several points where boats dock, while the stalls lining the road sell basic provisions for river journeys. At the western edge of the harbour is the **Rajang Esplanade**, a small park built in 1987 on reclaimed land. It's a popular place to sit and enjoy the evening breeze, and occasionally cultural events, too, like ethnic dancing and Chinese firework displays.

Head back past the boat wharf and Jalan Khoo Peng Loong merges with Jalan Pulau close to the **Tua Pek Kong Temple**. There was a small, wooden temple on this site as early as 1870, though soon afterwards it was rebuilt on a much grander scale, with a tiled roof, stone block floor and decorative fixtures imported from China. Two large concrete lions guard the entrance, while the fifteen-metre-wide main chamber is always busy with people paying respects to the deity, Tua Pek Kong, a prominent Confucian scholar. The statue of Tua Pek Kong, to the left of the front entrance, is the most important image in the temple and survived both the fire of 1928 and Japanese bombardment. Elsewhere, the roof and columns are decorated with traditional dragon and holy bird statues, while emblazoned on the temple wall to the left of the entrance are murals depicting the signs of the Chinese zodiac. For a small donation, the caretaker, Tan Teck Chiang, will tell you the story of the temple and give you a brief rundown on the significance of these and other images. In 1987 the rear section of the temple was replaced by the $1.5-million, seven-storey **pagoda**, from the top of which there's a splendid view of the Rajang snaking away below.

Across the way, in the network of streets between Jalan Market, Jalan Channel and Jalan Central, is **Chinatown** with its plethora of hardware shops, newspaper stalls, rowdy cafés, textile wholesalers, cassette sellers, food and fruit juice vendors and hotels. The central artery, **Jalan Market**, runs from Jalan Pulau beside the temple, and forms the hub of possibly the most vibrant pasar malam in Sarawak. At dusk, hundreds of stalls are set up, offering a wide variety of foods, many of them specific Sibu delicacies like stuffed dumplings, grilled fish and chicken wings, or – not for the faint-hearted – pig or duck's head and a range of offal. The pasar malam operates nightly from dusk until 10pm.

On the southwestern edge of the old town, in beside Jalan Channel, the daily **Lembangan Market** opens before dawn and closes around 5pm. There are hundreds of stalls here, many of the hawkers are Iban from nearby longhouses, selling anything from edible delicacies like flying fox, squirrel, snake, turtle, snail, jungle ferns and exotic fruits, to rattan baskets, beadwork, charm bracelets and leather belts and thongs.

The Civic Centre

On the outskirts, the one place worth visiting is the modern **Civic Centre**, 2km north of the centre, which contains a small but high-quality collection in its **Cultural Exhibition Hall** (Tues–Sun 10.30am–5.30pm; free) on the ground floor. Take the Jalan Tun Abang Haji Openg bus from the bus terminal and ask for the Civic Centre. In a series of display chambers, the hall details the varied peoples of the Rajang by means of well-chosen photographs, artefacts and paraphernalia. Among the costumes, backpacks and instruments in the Orang Ulu chamber, look out for some evocative old snaps of headmen, and an amazing photograph of a peace-making ceremony between Kayan and Iban tribespeople on November 16, 1924, at which representatives from both tribes killed pigs to authenticate their truce. There are more atmospheric pictures – of tattooing and cock-fighting – in the adjacent Iban chamber, plus a scale model of an Iban longhouse that was made using bark, ironwood and bamboo. The mocked-up Malay wedding room falls somewhere short of interesting, but the Chinese display has a good stab at charting the history of the Foochow migration to the region (a bust of Wong Nai Siong, the Methodist minister who led the original pioneers, takes centre stage), alongside records of the numerous cultural associations which were the immigrants' first port of call when they arrived. In exchange for voluntary labour, the associations would find the new arrivals paid work and lodgings and induct them into the business and cultural life of the city.

Eating

Throughout town there are Chinese cafés selling Sibu's most famous dish, Foochow noodles – steamed and then served in a soy and oyster sauce with spring onions and dried fish. Other local favourites include *midin* (a type of wild fern), *kang puan mee* (noodles cooked in lard) and *kong bian* (oriental bagels, sprinkled with sesame seed). Prawn and crab are of a high quality and, in season, tropical fruit like star fruit, rambutan and guava are available from market stalls. Although Sibu has some fine air-con **restaurants**, most people prefer to be outside when the weather's good; even the well-off opt to eat at **hawker stalls**. Busiest in the morning are those at the Lembangan Market, but in the evening everyone congregates at the pasar malam in the town centre, though you can't sit down and eat here – if you buy *dim sum* or other snacks, you'll have to wander down to the esplanade to eat. Also popular are the stalls in the block immediately west of the *Premier Hotel*, and those in the two-storey, circular building next door. Most cafés are **open** throughout the day, from around 7am to 8pm, with the Chinese coffee houses staying open until around midnight. Restaurants open from around 11am until 11pm.

Balkis Islamic Café, 69 Jalan Osman. Very good North Indian staples like *roti canai, murtabak* and curries. It's near the MAS office and post office and costs around $3 a head. Open 7am–8pm.

Golden Happiness Restaurant, Jalan Chengal. Two-level Foochow restaurant that's always packed to the rafters, owing to such culinary delights as frogs' legs coated in cashews, venison with ginger and sublime Foochow noodles.

Hing Huong Café, off Jalan Tukang Besi. This spit-and-sawdust shop has been cooking up *tien pien hu* (soup laced with a "skin" that's achieved by steaming a mixture of rice powder and water, and much more palatable than it sounds) for decades. Breakfast at the *Hock Hua* opposite and they'll bring a bowl over to you.

Hock Chu Leu Restoran, 28 Jalan Tukan Besi. Well-known Foochow restaurant with great baked fish and fresh vegetables. Around $25 for two, including beer.

Hock Hua Café, off Jalan Tukang Besi. Nondescript coffee shop famed for its awesome breakfast-time *kong bian*, which come either plain or oozing with pork and garlic stuffing; *kang puan mee* is also excellent here, or you can sample the *Hing Huong*'s *tien pien hu* (see above).

Hua Siong Café, Jalan Market. Busy place popular with locals, near the market and jetty. Great for drinking beer or tea and watching frenetic Sibu go by.

Malindo Café, 20 Jalan Kampung Nyabor. Tasty, spicy Indonesian food – the stuffed crab is particularly good and cheap at $4–5 a head.

Mandarin Hall, Wisma See Hua, Jalan Tuanku Osman. Excellent Foochow restaurant that turns its hand to breakfast each morning, when stalls serving *bubor cha cha, dim sum, laksa* and *kang puan mee* do a roaring trade in the dining room.

New Capitol Restoran, Jalan Workshop. Expensive Chinese restaurant though worth the splurge: it costs $25–30 a head, including drinks. The nearby hawker stalls are popular, too, specializing in Malay food – crisp green bean and chilli, and curried chicken and beef dishes – with plenty of tables protected from the elements.

Peppers Café, *Tanah Mas Hotel*, Jalan Kampung Nyabor. A wide menu including Western dishes as well as Malay fish curries. The international flavour is very popular with Sibu business people, but it's not cheap at around $40 for two.

Listings

Airport Flight information ☎084/334351; MAS is at 61 Jalan Tunku Osman (☎084/326166). There are services to Bintulu (4 daily), Kuching (11 daily) and Miri (5 daily).

Banks Bumiputra, Lot 6 & 7, Jalan Kampung Nyabor; Public Bank, 2–6 Jalan Tuanku Osman.

Boats Upriver express departures to Kanowit ($7), Song ($12) and Kapit ($15) leave at least hourly (5.30am until mid-afternoon) from Sibu's upriver wharf. Destinations are displayed on signs in the windows of all boats, and cardboard "clocks" are set to their estimated departure times. Only the first two departures carry on to Belaga, and even then only if the water of the Pelagus Rapids (p.383) is deep enough. From the downriver wharf, Express Bahagia, 20a Jalan Tukang Besi (☎084/319228), run a daily direct service to Kuching at 11.30am, plus a 6.45am boat via Sarikei on Sunday, Tuesday and Thursday; Concorde Marine, 1 Bank Rd (☎084/331593) boats leave for Kuching via Sarikei on Monday, Wednesday and Friday at 6.45am, and on Saturday at 11am

($29/35); and Rajah Ramin, 18 Jalan Khoo Peng Loong (☎084/321531), runs a slow-boat ($15) to the capital on Monday and Friday at 11am. Dalat boats (for Mukah; see p.388) depart in the early morning, tide permitting ($12). Otherwise, speedboats ($18) depart when full from beside the downriver wharf. For more on upriver departures, see the section following.

Buses Departures to Kuching, Mukah, Bintulu and Miri through the day – book through one of the several bus companies scattered along Jalan Khoo Peng Loong and Jalan Maju, among them locally based Lanang Rd Co, 6 Jalan Maju (☎084/335973); also a couple of daily connections to Kalimantan. Bus #3a runs out to the airport ($2) from the foot of the esplanade, on Jalan Maju.

Handicrafts *Chai Chiang Store*, 5 Jalan Central, for woodcarvings, beadwork, bamboo and rattan baskets, and mats; prices are cheaper than in Kuching. There are also stalls selling basketware where Jalan Channel hits the wharf. There are several ceramic factories close to Sibu: buses leave every hour from Jalan Khoo Peng Loong to *Toh Brothers*, Jalan Ord Ulu Oya.

Hospital Lau King Hoe, Jalan Pulau, next to the RPA building (☎084/343333).

Laundry *Dobi Sibu*, 5g Jalan Bindang.

Police Jalan Kampung Nyabor (☎084/336144).

Post office The main office is on Jalan Kampung Nyabar (Mon–Fri 8am–6pm, Sat 8am–noon).

Taxis ☎084/320773.

Tour operators Ibrahim Tourist Guide, 1 Lane One, Jalan Bengkel (☎084/318987). As Sibu is usually the first stop on trips up the Rajang, few people organize tours from here. But if you're not going any further, Ibrahim's overnight tour to an Iban longhouse close to Sibu is good value at around $200 for two. Frankie Ting at Sazhong Trading (see above) organizes a similar trip to nearby Rumah Sawai.

Up the Rajang: Kanowit, Song and Sungei Katibas

From Sibu the express boats head up the Rajang, stopping first at **Kanowit** and then **Song** – from where explorations of **Sungei Katibas** are possible – before heading onwards to Kapit (see below). The distance between each wood-processing yard steadily lengthens until Song is reached; they rarely disturb the thick jungle thereafter. Along the way, small Iban boats can be seen hugging the sides of the river to get as far away as possible from the swell that the fast boats create.

The express **boat** from Sibu (daily, at least once an hour, 5.30am–2.30pm; $15) takes three hours to reach Kapit. The two earliest departures from Sibu go beyond Kapit, water levels permitting, right the way to the upper reaches of the Rajang and Belaga. You can't book in advance – seats are on a strictly first-come, first-served basis – so always arrive at least fifteen minutes early to get a seat, and then nip off to buy any provisions you require for the journey.

Kanowit

An hour from Sibu, the boat reaches the sleepy settlement of **KANOWIT**. There are two hotels on waterfront Jalan Kubu, the *Kanowit Air Con* (☎084/752155; ②) and the *Harbour View Inn* (☎084/753188; ③). There are also a few cafés and the fiery red **Hock Ann Teng Temple**, but the only real reason to get out here is to see **Fort Emma**, one of the first defensive structures built by James Brooke. It's just a couple of hundred metres to the west of the jetty in front of the town's two hotels – en route you'll pass the lurid green mosque and a gaily flowered waterfront park. Built in 1859 of timber and bamboo, the fort took its name from James's beloved sister, its presence intended to inhibit the numerous raids by the local Iban on the remaining Rajang Melanau tribes. However, soon after the fort was built it was overrun; future attacks were only repulsed by stationing a platoon here, mostly comprising Iban and Malays in the pay of Brooke's officials. Up until the Japanese occupation, Fort Emma was the nerve centre of the entire district, but with the passing of colonial rule the building fell into disuse as there were no more pirates to repulse, head-hunters to pursue, or rebellious Chinese miners to suppress. Despite years of neglect, the fort, perched on raised ground, is still impressive. There are plans to turn the it into a museum – ask at the Sibu Visitor Information Centre for details.

Song and Sungei Katibas

The next stop is at **SONG**, another hour upstream, at the head of one of the Rajang's major tributaries, Sungei Katibas, which winds and narrows as it runs south towards the mountainous border region with Kalimantan. There's not much to the place, which is little more than a few blocks of waterfront shophouses (some of them 1920s wooden affairs, their shutters painted in cheery blues and greens), a jetty, a small Chinese temple and two waterfront hotels: the *Capital Hotel* (☎084/777252; ①) and much smarter *Katibas Inn* (☎084/777323; ②). Along the riverside are the usual Chinese stores, plus several **coffee shops** knocking out simple noodle dishes. In addition, stalls on the upper floor of the market facing the *Capital* serve *nasi lemak* and other Malay staples; you'll have to head up to the nearby *Happy Garden Seafood Restaurant* for a meal of any sophistication. Song does have a helpful **guide**, Richard Kho, who can arrange visits to Iban longhouses on the Katibas (see below); ask at the hotel or try calling ☎084/777228.

Sungei Katibas

To explore **Sungei Katibas**, you need to catch the passenger longboat which leaves Song twice each morning; departure times change so ask at the jetty. On the Katibas are several Iban longhouses worth visiting, including the large community at the junction of the Katibas and one of its own small tributaries, Sungei Bangkit. It takes between two and three hours to reach **Nanga Bangkit**, which comprises an impressive fifty-door longhouse and a dozen smaller dwellings on the opposite bank. This is the boat's final port of call, so most of your fellow passengers will get off here, and one is bound to invite you to visit. The longhouse women are excellent weavers, and you can buy a wall hanging or thin rug here for around $300. There are another twelve or so Iban longhouses along the banks of the river, each with its own rice fields, which cling to the inclines. To travel further down Sungei Bangkit may mean **renting a boat**, though if you're lucky you'll be able to tag along with a smaller longboat heading your way. Negotiate the fare before you start the trip – going to **Rumah Guyang**, Sungei Bangkit's uppermost longhouse, should cost around $60 each way. Passenger boats on the Kabitas, on the other hand, push on from Bangkit as far as **Nanga Enkuah**, an Iban community with three sizeable longhouses an hour further south. To access the border region from here – say, to reach idyllic **Rumah Api**, at the end of the river – requires chartering a vessel in Engkuah (an extremely expensive business).

Despite their proximity to big-town Sibu, the river communities still hold their customs dear. Along the banks of the Katibas and the Bangkit you'll catch sight of small **burial houses** set back on the banks. For a good 300m either side of the burial spots, the jungle is left undisturbed; these areas are strictly out of bounds to locals from neighbouring longhouses and other visitors. The surrounding areas also remain uncultivated out of respect to the ancestors.

For more details on visiting longhouses, see Sarawak practicalities on p.343.

Kapit and around

KAPIT – around three hours east of Sibu – is a fast-growing town with a frontier atmosphere, a riverside settlement in the middle of thick jungle being made more accessible by the day. It started life as a remote bazaar for a small community of British officials and Chinese *towkays* trading with the region's indigenous population, but these days, the signs of rapid expansion are everywhere: heavy boxes of rifle cartridges, machine parts and provisions are unloaded from the tops of the express boats, and local landowners drive around in Toyotas, picking up workers to clear land or build houses. There is still a strong native presence; the fruit sellers are much more forthright here than in Sibu or Kuching because (for the time being at least) this is still their territory. The timber trade employs native workers from distant longhouses on short-term contracts, and the bright lights of Kapit are where they come to spend their wages – karaoke lounges, snooker halls and brothels are all much in evidence.

Although most travellers stay just one night, waiting for boats either way along the Rajang or for connecting longboats along **Sungei Baleh** (see p.383), it's easy to get to like Kapit. The place itself is tiny – little more than a few streets cleared out of the luxuriant forest which threatens to engulf it. However, there are lots of good cafés in which to while away the time, a decent museum collection, and – out of town – the chance to visit Sebabai Park, 10km away along a track. Kapit is also a good place to organize trips to nearby the Pelagus Rapids and to local Iban communities, with one of the legitimate **tour operators** based in town (see "Around Kapit" on p.382 for details).

The Town

Close to the jetty is Kapit's main landmark, **Fort Sylvia**, built in 1880 (and renamed in 1925 after Vyner Brooke's wife) in an attempt to prevent the warring Iban attacking smaller and more pacific groups such as the upriver Ukit and Bukitan. The fort also served to limit Iban migration along the nearby Sungei Baleh, and confine them to the section of the Rajang below Kapit. Its most famous administrator was **Domingo de Rozario** who was born in the istana kitchen in Kuching, the son of James Brookes' Portuguese chef. De Rozario's memoirs record that life in Kapit was pleasant and that he got on well with the natives, but he found it most troublesome when dealing with "cases of heads taken on raids". These days the fort houses administrative offices; there's little of period interest inside, though if you're curious, the officials will let you take a look.

Along Kapit's oldest riverside street, **Jalan Temenggong Koh**, the rows of simple shophouses which once nestled between patches of jungle are now giving way to stores and cafés housed in concrete buildings, which can withstand the fires and deluges which regularly occur. The **jetties** are always a hive of activity, too, with dozens of longboats bobbing up and down at their moorings and scores of people making their way back and forth between the express boats and smaller craft with bulky bundles of goods. Merchants, timber employers and visitors watch the goings-on from marble-topped tables in the *Chuong Hin Café*, opposite the jetty.

Kapit's main square, simply called **Kapit Square**, is surrounded by shops selling everything from noodles to rope. The walk westwards along Jalan Temenggong, which forms the square's northern edge, leads to the **day market** where tribespeople rail at you until you buy a cluster of tropical fruit, and other traders point out boxes of wriggling eels and shrimps. Occasionally frogs, turtles, birds and monkeys are sold. There's a wet fish section too, and textile and shoe stalls upstairs in the main building. The stalls in front of the market sell great Sarawakan fast food – prawn cakes, *pau*, curry pies and sweet pastries. The only place in town to buy ethnic artefacts is *Lai Lai*

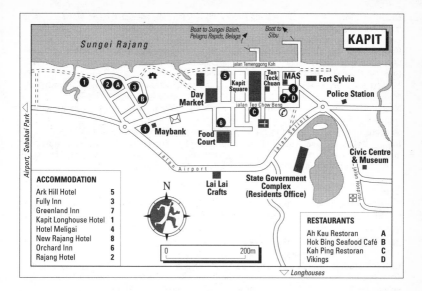

Crafts on Jalan Airport, which has an excellent collection of rugs, sarongs, baskets, *pua kumbu* textiles, woodcarvings, beads and ceramics.

Back from the jetty, near the pond, is the **Civic Museum** (Mon–Fri 2–4.30pm; free), which has a collection of interesting exhibits on the tribes in the Rajang basin, including a well-constructed longhouse and a mural painted by local Iban; Timothy Chua's sketches and watercolours of Kapit, Belaga and Song portray a life which is slowly disappearing. The museum also describes the lives of the Hokkien traders who were early pioneers in the region.

Practicalities

The **airport** is 4km south of town, from where you should be able to jump in a Toyota van for the ride to central Kapit Square ($2). If not, taxis into the centre charge $10. The MAS agent (☎084/796484) is in the centre of town. The express **boats** dock at the town jetty, from where it is a few minutes' walk to anywhere in town. The only **information** available is from Tan Teck Chuan, whose office is at 11 Jalan Sit Leong; he supplies accommodation details. The Maybank, beside the *Hotel Meligai*, changes travellers' cheques.

You need a **permit** to travel beyond Kapit, available from the **Resident's Office** (Mon–Fri 8am–12.30pm & 2.15–4.15pm), on the first floor of the State Government Complex which is 100m north of the jetty on Jalan Selinik. Take your passport with you; the process is a formality (from the government office you can proceed to the police station, and then back again) and there's no charge.

Accommodation

Ark Hill, 10 Jalan Airport (☎084/796168). On the edge of the centre with small, clean rooms, including air-con and shower. ③.

Fully Inn, Jalan Temenggong (☎084/797366). All eighteen rooms are inexpensive and appealing; some have views over the river, and a few have tiny balconies. ②.

Greenland Inn, Jalan Teo Chow Beng (☎084/796388). Recently opened, the *Greenland* is cashing in on Kapit's growth. The rooms are small and clean, some with good views over the Rajang. Facilities include air-con and bathroom. ③.

Kapit Longhouse, 21 Jalan Berjaya (☎084/796415). The cheapest hotel in town with a lovely position at the river's edge. Although grubby, only the *Rajang* is more popular with travellers. The rooms have fans but are basic; bathrooms are shared. ②.

Meligai, Jalan Airport (☎084/796817). The only upmarket hotel in town which is full of brash businessmen. There is a good restaurant here, and the large rooms have full facilities. ③.

New Rajang Inn, 104 Jalan Teo Chow Beng (☎084/796600). Small rooms which are all fully equipped with air-con, shower and TV. ②–③.

Orchard Inn, 64 Jalan Airport (☎084/796325). Rooms with air-con, shower and TV. ③.

Rajang, 28 Jalan Temenggoh, New Bazaar (☎084/796709). One of Sarawak's best-known travellers' hotels, where the guys at reception strum guitars and have sing-songs during siesta. The large rooms, many overlooking the river, have efficient fans and good bathrooms. ①.

Eating

Kapit is a great place to **eat** on the hoof – which is ironic as it's one town where you may spend a lot of time just sitting around. The food from **hawker** stalls and **markets** is great and, as a rule, can be better than in the few sit-down **restaurants**.

Ah Kau Restoran, Jalan Berjaya. Specializes in local recipes: wild boar, steamed fish, jungle vegetables, and as much rice as you can eat, with beer, at $25 for two.

Covered Market, Jalan Airport. A dozen separate stalls serving Chinese, Malay and Dyak dishes. *Gerai Islam* sells *roti canai* and various noodle dishes with local vegetables, seafood and meat. The optimum time to eat here is between noon and 3pm, though it's open until 9pm.

Day market Stalls, Jalan Teo Chow Beng. Sarawak fast food like curry puffs, prawn cakes, cornmeal cake and tofu buns. Open 7am–5pm.

Hock Bing Seafood Café, west of the temple. There are tables along the pavement at this bustling café, which serves the best prawn dishes in Kapit. Friendly, atmospheric and excellent value at around $20 for two, including beer.

Kah Ping Restoran, Kapit Square, Jalan Teo Chow Beng. Good spot to watch Kapit life go by; the best options are the Chinese noodle and rice dishes.

Vikings, eastern end of Jalan Teo Chow Beng. It had to come to Kapit: Western fast food including fried chicken, french fries and hamburgers, all at local prices.

Around Kapit

Although the roads around Kapit don't go very far in any direction, worthwhile trips can be made to Sebabai Park, and to the few **longhouses** accessible by road (although these don't compare with visiting the traditional Iban communities along Sungei Baleh; see next section). You might also consider a trip to the spectacular **Pelagus Rapids**, an hour upstream.

You'll need a **guide**, or to be part of a small **tour group**, to take a day-trip to Pelagus (see below), for the more inaccessible longhouses. When approached – as you will be early on in your stay – ask whether the person is registered with the Sarawak Tourist Association (STA); some unregistered guides are unreliable and since many charge over $100 a day just to take you to their longhouses, you want to be sure you're getting a good deal. It's always best to haggle a little, as well as checking exactly what the price includes. There shouldn't be any extra costs, like contributions for food, once the trip has started. Hotel receptions can help with arranging tours, but the best person to consult in Kapit is the fully licensed **Tan Teck Chuan** (11 Jalan Tan Sit Leong, Kapit Square; ☎084/796352, fax 796655), a *towkay* and explorer who knows Sungei Baleh and its tributaries very well. He organizes one- and two-night tours to longhouses (two pay $500 for a two-day, one-night trip), has good contacts with Iban *tuais*, and also runs inexpensive (around $80 for the day) trips to the Pelagus Rapids. Tan can also arrange much more expensive four-day trips to a Kayan longhouse, Long Singut, far up Sungei Baleh, or three-day trips along the Baleh's Gaat and Mujong tributaries to visit **Iban communities** which still perform the *mering* ceremony. This is the procedure for welcoming strangers, where the *tuai* sings a song before touching eggs, tobacco and rice cakes and the visitors copy his actions, after which everyone can sit down and informal conversation, tea-drinking and eating can commence. Top of the range is Tan's seven-day tour into the forest to meet the Penan.

Sebabai Park

To reach **Sebabai Park**, take the irregular Toyota van to Sebabai longhouse, a ten-kilometre trip east ($5 return); the Toyota stop is in front of the day market on Jalan Teo Chow Beng. Although the park is a popular picnic spot for locals at weekends, in the week you will have the place to yourself. The bus weaves up and down the hilly road through the forest, passing houses and occasionally stopping for locals carrying wood or bringing sacks of rice from the market. At the end of the road by the longhouse, a sign points up a hill to the park. The path leads down into dense primary forest, crosses streams and, after about fifteen minutes, ends at a small **waterfall**, surrounded by insects, birds and monkeys and perfect for swimming. There aren't any facilities here so bring water and some food if you're going to stay a while. Returning, note that vans don't run between noon and 2pm, when the drivers are taking a break in the longhouse.

Pelagus Rapids

Upstream of Kapit lie the churning waters of the **Pelagus Rapids**, a deceptively shallow stretch where large, submerged stones make your through passage treacherous. According to local belief, the rapids' seven sections represent the seven segments of an enormous serpent which was chopped up and floated downriver by villagers to the north.

It's only recently that running the rapids has become entirely safe. The old boats weren't powerful enough and, when the water was too low or too high, would drop you off before the rapids so you could walk along the river bank and get into another boat waiting further on. But the latest express boats are turbo-charged with reinforced steel hulls; their immense thrust does the trick unless the water level is so low that the boat's bottom is scraping the riverbed.

Express boats take an hour to reach the rapids, but the snazzy launch maintained by the *Pelagus Resort* (☎084/796050; ⑨) which is immediately above the rapids, can manage the journey in a death-defying 45 minutes. Many of the resort's forty comfortable rooms overlook the rapids; and there are day- and night-time hikes into the surrounding rainforest, as well as trips ($100 a head) to local longhouses available upon request. The resort's riverfront dining room serves three meals a day, and has a menu that runs to exotic local dishes like *pangsoh* (chicken baked in bamboo). The boat transfer from Kapit to the resort and back costs $50 return per person, but you can economize by hopping on a Belaga-bound express boat instead.

Along Sungei Baleh

Sungei Baleh branches off from the Rajang 10km east of Kapit, at the point where the main river twists north towards to the Pelagus Rapids. Several boats leave Kapit for Sungei Baleh between 7am and noon. Some ply only the 20km to **NANGA BALEH** (90min; $8), a large, modern longhouse, where there is also a logging camp; some push on to the junction with the tributaries of Sungei Gaat and Sungei Merirai, two and a half hours from Kapit ($10); while others follow the shorter stretch to the Sungei Mujong junction (1hr; $6) – a large tributary closer to Kapit.

The most authentic **Iban longhouses** in the Baleh region are on the Gaat and Merirai tributaries, and can only be reached by renting a longboat, although you may be able to tag along with one of the locally owned boats heading up the tributaries. The longhouse wharves at the junctions of the Baleh and these smaller rivers are the places to ask for advice on how to travel further, and to find out which longhouses are good to visit; almost anyone who invites you to their home will be trustworthy. **Renting longboats** to take you along the tributaries is expensive at around $100 per day, but during good weather, quite a number traverse the upper reaches of the rivers, to longhouses which (for the moment at least) lie just beyond the boundaries of the timber zone.

Wherever you head, the **scenery** is magnificent – the land is covered in dense jungle, with the mountains on the Sarawak–Kalimantan border, 50km to the south, peeping out of the morning mist. Occasionally you'll hear sounds of conversation, hammering and splashing as you round a corner and catch sight of an Iban family pulling their bamboo fish traps out of the water, or cooking their catch over an open fire.

For the moment, some of the express boats from Kapit go as far as the **Putai** logging camp, way up the Baleh at the junction with Sungei Putai (a four-hour trip). You'll have to check in Kapit that the boat still operates, as some camps in this area have recently closed down. Beyond Putai, the Baleh narrows and is no longer navigable by regular express boat – all onward travel is by longboat. One place to make for on the upper Baleh is the river's only **Kenyah longhouse**, established by a group of Indonesian Kenyah, two hours beyond Putai by longboat. Although not a large wooden beauty like some of the Iban longhouses along the Baleh, the people here are friendly and the location breathtaking. The river brims with fish, while the surrounding forest supports deer, buffalo and wild boar. You're close here to the Kalimantan border and within sight of the remote peak, **Batu Tiban**, reached by explorer Redmond O' Hanlon, and described in his book *Into The Heart Of Borneo*.

To Belaga and beyond

Owing to governmental sensitivity surrounding the Bakun Dam Project (for which hundreds of square kilometres of timber are to be lopped, and thousands of indigenous people displaced), Belaga and Sungei Balui were in 1996 declared **off-limits** to non-Malaysians. We've included the following information in the hope that the local authorities will be persuaded by the Sarawakian tourist industry to back down; ask in Kapit for the current state of play. In the meantime, tourists are still permitted to venture as far upstream as the Pelagus Rapids.

In the nineteenth century, the 150-kilometre trip from Kapit to **Belaga**, on the furthest reaches of the Rajang, took two weeks in a longboat, a treacherous trip which involved negotiating rapids and dodging Iban raids on longhouses which belong to the original inhabitants of the upper Rajang, the **Kenyah** and the **Kayan**. After Charles Brooke purchased the region from the Sultan of Brunei in 1853, a small bazaar was built in Belaga and Chinese pioneers arrived to trade with both the Kayan and the nomadic **Punan** and **Penan** who roamed over a wide swathe of the forest. The British presence in this region was tiny – officials would occasionally brave the trip from Kapit but no fort was built this far up the river.

These days the trip takes up to six hours, depending on the river level. Occasionally the boat companies cancel departures: if the water level is very low, the Pelagus Rapids can be particularly hazardous, but if the level is high, the Rajang becomes a raging torrent. However, if the conditions are right, it's an excellent trip. Logging camps are scarcer in this stretch of the river, and as you near the centre of Sarawak, wispy clouds cloak the hills and the screech of rainforest monkeys and birds can be heard.

Longhouses are dotted along the river bank. As far as **Long Pila**, ninety minutes from Kapit, the people are all Iban, though between here and Belaga there are many tribes, including the Ukit, Bukitan, Tanjong and Sekapan. Before the 1860s the Kayan were numerous here, too, but when they protected the killers of two government officials, Charles Brooke led a punitive expedition against them, driving them back to the Belaga river, upstream of Belaga itself.

Belaga

BELAGA, which lies at the confluence of the Rajang and Sungei Balui, is as remote as you can get in the Sarawak interior but it's not uncharted territory by any means. As early as 1900, Chinese *towkays* had opened up Belaga to trade and were supplying the tribespeople with kerosene, cooking oil and cartridges, in exchange for beadwork and mats, beeswax, ebony and tree gums. In more recent years it's been possible to cut northwest to the coast, via Tubau, from this isolated spot, by getting rides in loggers' vehicles from a camp just to the north on the Belaga river, but timber production is slowing down in the area and consequently there are fewer four-wheel drives going to and forth between the camps. This means that the only real reason for coming to Belaga these days is to travel along **Sungei Balui**, which weaves and curls east for over 200km until it reaches its headwaters in the mountains which divide Sarawak from Kalimantan. This requires a certain amount of planning though, and a great deal of money since fuel prices are inflated this far away from the urban centres: diesel is three times more expensive here than on the coast and renting a longboat is really only feasible if you're in a group of four to six. There is a guide in Belaga (see "Practicalities" below) while solo travellers wanting to visit the Kayan communities (see box below) on the Balui may be able to join a larger group, paying just a single share of the tour price.

There's nothing particular to do in Belaga itself except watch the comings and goings. Sometimes the Penan arrive to sell things – their uniquely carved knives can be picked up for a third of the price you would pay in Sibu. A seasonal appearance is also made by the **wild honey collectors** from Kalimantan, who arrive in March and again in September to trade their jungle produce for supplies. Other faces on Belaga's small network of streets include Kayan and Kenyah, with their fantastic tattoos and elongated ear lobes wandering through the bazaar, and eating wild boar and fried ferns in the Chinese cafés.

From the jetty, everything is fairly close by: market, shops selling provisions, a few nondescript houses and, beyond, a small track snaking towards the formidably dense forest, a few hundred metres away. Twenty minutes' walk along a small path which runs south and adjacent to the river, there's a pretty kampung where the Kejaman (a small ethnic group related to the Kayan, now almost extinct) burial pole – currently on display outside the Sarawak Museum in Kuching – was found in the early years of this century. The path weaves through pepper gardens and past wooden, stilted houses, to a school where curious children stop their games to stare at strangers. Looking over the river, just before the playing field beyond the kampung, you can see a Kayan *salong* or **burial tomb** on the opposite bank – a small wood construction with a multicoloured wooden sculpture sporting the image of a face. It's taboo for anyone other than the dead person's family to go within a hundred metres of the tomb. As the Kayan prefer to build their longhouses on tributaries, yet position *salongs* on the main rivers, they are often all you see for many kilometres when you travel along Sungei Balui.

Practicalities

Belaga's three **hotels** all offer similar rooms, which are of quite a high standard considering how isolated the town is. *Hotel Belaga*, 14 Main Bazaar (☎086/461244; ②), is

THE KAYAN AND KENYAH

The **Kayan** and the **Kenyah** are the most numerous and powerful of the Orang Ulu groups who live in the upper Rajang, and along Sungei Balui and its tributaries. The Kayan are the more numerous, at around forty thousand people, while the Kenyah population is around ten thousand (though there are substantially more over the mountains in Kalimantan). Both groups migrated from East Kalimantan into Sarawak approximately six hundred years ago, although during the nineteenth century, when Iban migration led to clashes between the groups, they were pushed back to the lands they occupy today. The Kayan and the Kenyah have a lot in common: they are class-conscious, with a well-defined social hierarchy (unlike those of the Iban or Penan), and their language, with Malay-Polynesian roots, is completely different to the other groups. Traditionally, the **social order** was topped by the *tuai rumah* (chief) of the longhouse, followed by a group of three or four lesser aristocrats or *payin*, lay families and slaves (slavery no longer exists). Both groups take great pride in the construction of their **longhouses** which are very impressive. Tom Harrisson, of the Sarawak Museum, learned of a longhouse on the upper Balui which was nearly one kilometre long, and in the Kenyah town of Long Nawang across the border in Kalimantan, you can visit a longhouse as high as a three-storey building and hundreds of metres long. Artistic expression plays an important role in longhouse culture, the Kayan especially maintaining a wide range of **musical traditions** including the lute-like *sape*, which is used to accompany long voice epics. **Textiles** are woven by traditional techniques in the upriver longhouses, and Kayan and Kenyah **woodcarvings**, which are among the most spectacular in Southeast Asia, are produced both for sale and for ceremonial uses. Potent **rice wine** is still drunk by some Kayan, although many communities have now converted to Christianity, and alcohol has been successfully banned by the missionaries.

the favourite – the rooms have bathroom and fan. Owner Andrew Tiong and his family run a café downstairs which is the best place to eat in town. The *Bee Lian Inn*, 11 Main Bazaar (☎086/461416; ①), and *Hotel Sing Soon Huat*, 27 New Bazaar (☎086/461257; ②), are the alternatives, both with small, basic rooms.

Officially, you need a **permit** to travel onwards on the Balui, or to attempt the overland route to Tubau (see below). The government office (Mon–Fri 8am–noon & 2–4.15pm) is the first building on your right along the path from the jetty.

If Belaga's only **guide**, Eddie John Balarik, is in town, he'll soon find you, though you can leave a message for him at the *Bee Lian Inn*. Eddie's the acknowledged local expert, with excellent contacts with the Penan. He organizes a three-day expedition to Long Akah, a Kayan settlement a day's travel northeast of Belaga on Sungei Linau; as well as a jungle trek, which follows an ancient trade path, staying overnight with the Penan and with an option to go hunting and fishing. These trips cost around $100 a day all in. He will go as far as Long Busang, too (see "River Expeditions from Belaga", below), but this kind of trip requires lightweight camping gear, medicines, food and gifts for the locals. To get to Long Busang and back takes a week, and costs $3000–4000 per group for longboat rental and Eddie's fee.

River expeditions from Belaga

Visiting longhouses and trekking into the forest are the only reasons why visitors come this far into the interior, but even if you're not up for a full expedition, you can see some nearby places without a guide. The express to the north along Sungei Balui leaves in the late morning, passing the Bakun construction site before reaching its first main stop at **Long Murum**, a large Kayan longhouse for the chief of the region. There is a charge (around $10) for spending the night here, so you don't need to take gifts. The second stop is at the mouth of **Sungei Linau**, at the small Kayan settlement of **Long Linau**, three hours from Belaga, though if you want to explore any further along the Linau, it's best to ask about longboats in Belaga as little traffic comes this way.

The express boat terminates an hour beyond Linau, at the large, traditional Lahanan longhouse, **Long Panggat**, from where you'll need to charter a longboat (around $120 per day) to travel any further. Another very rewarding place to try and reach is **Long Daro**, a Kayan community a full day's outboard motoring from Lahanan. Daro's architecture is spectacular, the whole of the communal verandah one huge mural with Kayan designs. Four hours further along the Balui lies **Long Aya**, the only **Ukit** longhouse in Sarawak. As well as the local Balui express boats, the Sibu-Belaga services push on to Linau, departing daily from Belaga at around 1.30pm.

The last but one settlement eastwards on the Balui, **Long Jawe**, lies in the foothills leading to the Kalimantan border. From here, British troops led operations against the Indonesians during the Konfrontasi in 1963, and most of the debris from the fighting is still around and used in ingenious ways: ammunition boxes for trunks and bridge strips as floorboards. Although most of the five-hundred-plus population are Kayan, other Orang Ulu people live here and there's occasional trade with the Penan, Ukit and the timber personnel: a new track has been hacked out of the jungle to facilitate logging in this previously pristine region of primary rainforest. The last village on the Balui, **Long Busang**, takes a full two days to reach from Belaga.

On to Kalimantan, Tubau and Bintulu

It's possible to reach Indonesian Kalimantan from Belaga, although it's an expensive trip because of the cost of **chartering longboats**. You'll also need to get your passport stamped at the Resident's Office in Kapit (see p.381), as there's no immigration department in Belaga. The guide, Eddie John, will know if any boats are heading in the right direction, via Long Busang (see above), two days' southeast of Belaga, and then leaving the Balui at the junction with Sungei Aput, which flows to the border. You'll need to a guide to show you where the trail leaves the river, leading over the unmarked border to **Long Nawang**, a large Kenyah settlement, where there's an Indonesian immigration post. It's a fascinating area in which to trek, but few organized tours are available from the Kalimantan side, so travellers have to rely on local guides, initiative and luck.

It's now much harder to reach the coastal port of Bintulu (see p.390) from Sungei Belaga, a route which entails taking logging vehicles northwest through a deforested area to **TUBAU**, and then boats west down Sungei Kemena to Bintulu. After five years of sustained timber harvesting in this area, demand has lessened and fewer four-wheel drives make the rough, overland trip. It's best to ask Eddie John Balarik in Belaga or Tan Teck Chuan in Kapit before setting out or else you might waste a day at a logging camp before having to retrace your steps to Belaga. Coming **from Bintulu** you could take the express to Tubau (see "Listings" p.393, for details), which is a pleasant enough trip, and ask around there if trucks are going to Kastima camp and beyond to Sungei Belaga. This route aside, the only other way out of Belaga is to get the 6am express to Sibu which connects with the 2pm bus to Bintulu, another four hours away ($18).

THE COAST FROM SIBU TO LAWAS

The route along the western flank of Sarawak from Sibu towards the Bruneian border is one of the most travelled in the state. Although dense mangrove swamp deprives the 150km of inland road linking Sibu with Bintulu of a clear view of the South China Sea, a lone chink in the vegetation yields access to the charming and peaceful Melanau backwater of **Mukah**, which is perfect for a few days' relaxation. Further northeast, the

Sibu–Brunei road offers diversions into some of Sarawak's – indeed Malaysia's – best national parks. **Similajau National Park**, 20km northeast of the industrial town of **Bintulu**, is a long thin strip of beach and forest; **Lambir Hills National Park**, further up the main highway, 30km south of Miri, is more established, and scientific reports have suggested that its vegetation types and tree species are more numerous than anywhere else so far studied across the globe. However these places are just preparation for Sarawak's most famous park, **Niah National Park**, halfway between Bintulu and Miri. Noted for its formidable **limestone caves** – the mouth of the main cave is the largest in the world – the park was put on the map in the mid-1950s when the curator of the Sarawak Museum, Tom Harrisson, discovered human remains and rock graffiti inside the caves; subsequent dating has suggested that Southeast Asia's earliest inhabitants were living in Sarawak as long as forty thousand years ago.

After Niah it's another two hours to **Miri**, which, like Sibu, is a predominantly Chinese town and an important administrative centre – though there the similarities end. The region developed commercially much later than southwestern Sarawak, with Miri's rapid expansion stimulated by the discovery of massive oil reserves. Since World War II, Bintulu has grown to rival Miri, specializing in the tapping of abundant pockets of natural gas on its doorstep. Both towns have a smaller percentage of indigenous inhabitants than Sarawak's other main settlements and although Iban and Melanau live in the area, there are very few longhouses to visit. However, you will need to pass through Miri en route to Batang Baram for flights, river trips to Marudi and Gunung Mulu park, or to catch a flight to the Kelabit Highlands (for all of which see "The Northern Interior", p.405). It's also the starting point for the onward trip to Brunei: from Miri the road runs along the coast to Kuala Baram (the mouth of the Baram river) and on to Kuala Belait and the **Brunei border**. East of here, tucked into the folds of Brunei are two peculiar "divisions" of Sarawak: finger-shaped **Limbang**, and **Lawas**, the most northerly strip of Sarawak, stretching north to meet Sabah.

Mukah

Should racing up and down the waterways of the Rajang Basin leave you temporarily too exhausted to countenance the walking trails and sapping heat of Sarawak's northerly national parks, a couple of days' easy living in laid-back **MUKAH** is sure to provide the perfect tonic. Accessed by a poor track that strikes north from Sarawak's main highway, passing oil palms, sago and ship-shape longhouses before veering west along the coast, Mukah is a charmingly sleepy seaside bolt hole in a traditionally Melanau-dominated area. Indeed, as you approach town, you'll see an impressive **mosque** to your left, its spiked roof themed upon the conical hat traditionally worn by the Melanau. All Mukah's accommodation is clustered 500m north of here in the **old town**, a simple grid of streets running roughly east–west along the south bank of **Sungei Mukah**, with new shophouses and older, more charismatic wooden versions, some brightened by striped screens.

Sights are few and far between in downtown Mukah: the best the town can offer is the garish, river-facing **Tua Pek Kong Temple**, from whose verandah you can view the river's stilthouses and boats. Bearded Tua Pek Kong, patron saint of businessmen, sits at the head of the temple's main hall, while on its walls are finely painted murals of Buddhist and Taoist deities, among them the Monkey God, Quan Yin and – bottom on the right on the right-hand wall – the patron saint of beggars Ji Gong, who you'll recognize by his dishevelled clothing and the bottle he clutches. Just east of the temple, there's a weathered old **smokestack** that testifies to Mukah's colonial sago trade. And that's about it in the centre of town, though there's a gem of a water village, **Kampung Tellian**, just 3km from town. Straddling Sungei Tellian, which at its wider points is

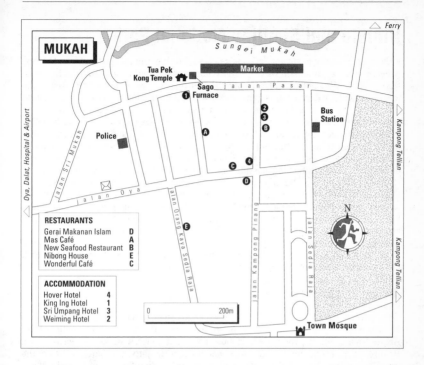

clogged with jolly blue fishing boats, Tellian is a veritable spaghetti junction of winding paths, precarious crisscrossing boardwalks and bridges. The friendly Melanau residents of its many stilthouses still wring a living from processing sago the traditional way.

Practicalities

Mukah's **bus station** lies on the eastern edge of the old town. From here, there are daily buses for Sibu and Bintulu, and for Dalat, the departure point for launches to Sibu. The airport is 3km west of town, and best reached in one of the taxis that buzz around town; tickets can be purchased at MAS, on the waterfront at 6 Jalan Pasar.

The *Hover Hotel* (☎084/871251; ②) is Mukah's cheapest **hotel**, its grubby rooms redeemed by the characterful old wooden shophouse which houses it. The *Sri Umpang* (☎084/871888; ②) on Main Bazaar is far more appealing, with tidy air-con rooms and attached bathrooms; the *Weiming Hotel* (☎084/872278; ②), directly across the road, and the *King Ing Hotel* (☎084/871400; ②), opposite the temple on Jalan Boyan, run it a close second. Otherwise, there are two modest resorts on a scruffy strip of beach a few kilometres southwest of town, the *Pantai Harmoni Resort* (☎084/872566; ②) and the *Mukah Kaul Resort* (③–④), currently being built, which promises to be the better of the two.

Mukah's best **restaurant**, the *Nibong House*, a five-minute walk from the old town, represents your best chance of sampling one of the area's specialities, *umai* (raw fish in lime and onions) and fried sago worms. Other options are more workaday: for Islamic food, there's the *Gerai Makanan Islam*, opposite the *Hover Hotel*, or the *Wonderful Café and Bakery*, further down the road. The *Mas Café*, around the corner, is clean and inviting, and does good *laksa sarawak* and *nasi campur*, while the tidy *New Seafood Café*, beside the *Sri Umpang*, does passable *kuey teow*.

Bintulu and Similjau National Park

BINTULU is at the centre of Sarawak's fastest growing industrial area. Up until twenty years ago, the settlement was little more than a convenient resting point on the route from Sibu to Miri, but when large **natural gas** reserves were discovered offshore in the 1960s, speedy expansion began. Since then Bintulu has followed in Miri's footsteps as a primary resources boom town, with a population that has tripled in a decade to sixty thousand, and an industrial output that uses over six million tonnes of liquefied natural gas a year, and around a thousand tonnes of ammonia and 1500 tonnes of urea for fertilizers per day. All this is a long way from the town's origins. Before Bintulu was bought by Charles Brooke from the Sultan of Brunei in 1853, Melanau pirates preyed on the local coast, attacking passing ships and decapitating their crews. The name Bintulu is derived from the Malay *Menta Ulau* – "the place for gathering heads".

Modern Bintulu is very ordinary, a flat, compact rectangle of streets bordered by the airfield to the east and Sungei Kemena to the west, with nothing much of interest in between. But inexpensive accommodation is easy to find, the restaurants are excellent and the markets sell local delicacies like fresh fish grilled with *belacan* (shrimp paste). Although most people just stay overnight to await a bus connection to Niah National Park, longer stays can take in **Taman Tumbina Park** (see opposite page), just north of the centre, and nearby **Simulajau National Park** (p.394).

Arrival and accommodation

The **airport**, incredibly, is right in the town centre, within 100m of most of the hotels and restaurants. The long-distance **bus station** is over the road, a block north of Jalan Abang Galau, with the riverside local bus station ten minutes' walk west across town. Boats for trips up Sungei Kemena to Tubau dock at the **jetty**, two blocks south of the long-distance bus station. The town's main **taxi rank** is directly in front of the local bus station. There is no tourist office, although some leaflets on the town can be picked up from the **Bintulu Development Authority**, on Jalan Sommerville (Mon–Fri 8.30am–4.30pm; ☎086/332011).

ACCOMMODATION

There's quite a wide range of **accommodation** in Bintulu, though the only real budget choices are the *rumah tumpangans* down by the river, basic lodging houses with dormitory-style rooms catering for timber camp workers and oil company employees. They're often full and in any case, there have been complaints from solo women travellers about conditions and behaviour in several of them; the places listed below are all a grade up and much nicer.

Capital, Jalan Keppel (☎086/331167). This is a popular travellers' hotel: cheap, basic and noisy. The shared bathrooms have bucket-over-the-head showers. ②.

City Inn, 149 Jalan Masjid (☎086/337711). The rooms here are small but do come with air-con, TV and shower; after dark, the din from the nearby *La Bamba* karaoke joint can make sleeping difficult. ③.

Fata Inn, 113 Jalan Masjid (☎086/332998). Amiable staff and pleasant air-con rooms with attached bathrooms make the *Fata* an appealing choice; ask for a room with hot water. ②.

Hoover, Jalan Abang Galau (☎086/337166). Smart but overpriced rooms equipped with air-con and shower. ④.

Kemena Inn, 78 Jalan Keppel (☎086/331533). This is a popular place, with decent rooms, run by a friendly family. A good first choice. ③.

King's Inn, Jalan Masjid (☎086/337337). Modern, clean and cool rooms with all the usual facilities. ②.

National Inn, Jalan Abang Galau (☎086/337222). Small rooms with ferociously cold air-con. ③.

Plaza, Jalan Abang Galau (☎086/35111). The top end of the hotel spectrum, with a swimming pool, and large modern rooms with full facilities; their brochure has the audacity to boast airport shuttles. ⑦.

Royal, 10 Jalan Padada (☎086/332166). Lent an air of some distinction by its varnished wood trimmings, the *Royal* offers considerable privacy and comfort. ④.

The Town

Bintulu's main commercial streets, **Main Bazaar** and **Jalan Keppel** (the latter named after an early British official who did a long stint here), are lined with cafés spilling over with boisterous beer-drinkers, while the stores overflow with shoes, clothes and electrical equipment. A couple of blocks to the west of the commercial hub, Main Bazaar passes the **Kuan Yin Tong temple**, less impressive than the Chinese temples in Kuching or Sibu, but a rallying point for the town's Hokkien-descended population in the evening. Fifty metres west of here across Main Bazaar is the **day market** – two large, open-sided circular buildings with blue roofs overlooking the river; seafood and vegetables are sold on the ground floor, while a variety of Malay and Chinese cafés can be found upstairs. Although the market stalls stay open until 5pm, the cafés close at 2pm. Adjacent is the **Pasar Tamu**, where locals still bring in small quantities of goods and lay them on rough tables to sell. Bintulu witnessed a little bit of history in September 1867, when the first ever Council Negri, or legislative assembly meeting, of any of the states that were later to comprise Malaysia, was convened here. Chaired by Charles Brooke, and attended by five British officers and sixteen local chiefs, the event is today commemorated by the **Council Negri Monument**, 200m northwest of the Pasar Tamu. Across town, meanwhile, the **pasar malam** starts up at around 6pm in the long-distance bus station and gets very crowded by 9pm. It's a great place to browse, eat grilled fish, meat pastries, *umai* and sweets, and it's almost impossible to avoid talking to locals who want to practise their English.

Within view of the boat jetty, across the wide Sungei Kemena, lies **KAMPUNG JEPAK**, the traditional home of the local Malay and Melanau-descended population. It's well worth the hour's trip, if only to escape the hustle and bustle of the town centre for a short while, since the kampung has a completely different atmosphere to Bintulu itself, with few cars, lots of children and old people, and a much slower pace of life. Small diesel-powered boats (every 20min; $1) make the crossing from the jetty. As well as its *cencaluk* or salted shrimps, Jepak is famous for its pungent shrimp paste, *belacan*, which you will find on sale all over Sarawak and Peninsular Malaysia; and although most *belacan* is produced in factories, cottage industries still proliferate here – the production season is December to January. Another major kampung activity used to be sago-processing, stemming from the days when sago, together with fish, was the staple food, though most of the production these days takes place in factories at the Kidurong Industrial Estate, 20km north of town.

Taman Tumbina park

Two kilometres north of town is **Taman Tumbina** (daily 8am–6pm; $2), a hundred-kilometre tropical recreation area, whose name (a hybrid of *tumbuhan*, meaning plant, and *binatang*, animal) reflects its sizeable collection of wildlife and vegetation. Take bus #1 from the local bus station, get off at the *Sing Kwong* supermarket, then cross over the roundabout in front of you and head uphill – it's a pleasant five-minute walk north from the main road, Jalan Tanjung Batu.

Extending across a hill with lovely views over the sea, the park is criss-crossed with walkways and wooden steps and has a small wood with bougainvillea plants, fruit trees and ferns, its paths running alongside streams and dipping under creepers. Mynah birds tackle passers-by with greetings – "hello, goodbye and how-are-you" – while other

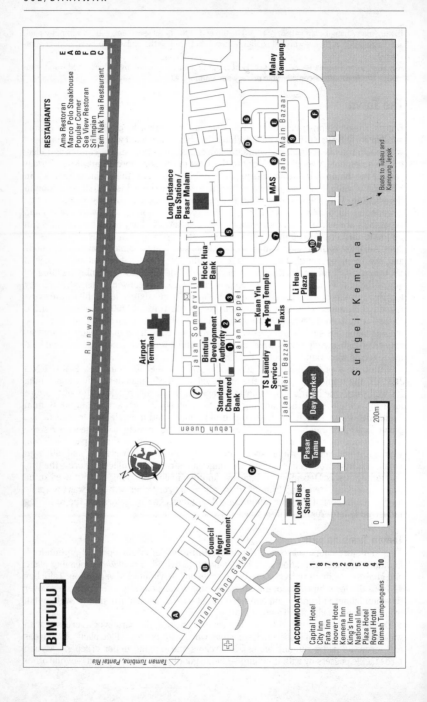

BINTULU

Taman Tumbina, Pantai Fila

Runway

Airport Terminal

Jalan Abang Galau

A
B
Council Negri Monument
C

Lebuh Queen

Jalan Sommerville

Standard Chartered Bank

Bintulu Development Authority
1
2
3

Jalan Keppel

Hock Hua Bank

4

TS Laundry Service

Kuan Yin Tong Temple
Taxis

Long Distance Bus Station / Pasar Malam

5

7

MAS

8
D

9
E
6

F

Jalan Main Bazzar

Malay Kampung

10

Li Hua Plaza

Jalan Main Bazzar

Day Market

Pasar Tamu

Local Bus Station

Sungei Kemena

Boats to Tubau and Kampung Jepak

0   200m

RESTAURANTS

Ama Restoran   E
Marco Polo Steakhouse A
Popular Corner   B
Sea View Restoran   F
Sri Impian   D
Tam Nak Thai Restaurant C

ACCOMMODATION

Capital Hotel   1
City Inn   8
Fata Inn   7
Hoover Hotel   3
Kemena Inn   2
King's Inn   9
National Inn   5
Plaza Hotel   6
Royal Hotel   4
Rumah Tumpangans   10

inhabitants include orang-utans, crocodiles, gibbons, deer, a lion, two tigers donated several years ago by a circus passing through town, a variety of Southeast Asian birds, flamingos and ducks. Unfortunately the **beach** opposite the entrance to the park is dirty and no effort is made to maintain it.

Eating

Although no culinary capital, Bintulu has a number of fine north Indian and Chinese **restaurants**. There are **hawker stalls** at both the day market and the pasar malam, the latter in particular serving great steamed seafood, stir-fried noodles, *umai, satay* and *pisang goreng*, though as in Sibu, there aren't any tables – the locals take food home to eat. Tables are set along the alley between the *City Inn* and the *Sri Impian*, where you can buy night-time beer and seafood. The waterfront stalls 2km north of town at **Pantai Ria** are another night-time snacking option – either walk or take bus #1.

Ama Restoran, Jalan Keppel. This place has excellent curries, and is particularly busy at lunchtime.

Marco Polo Steakhouse, Jalan Abang Galau. This upmarket steakhouse (200m northwest of the day market) has an in-house band which makes talking impossible, though at least it's better than the karaoke which starts up later in the evening.

Popular Corner, Lebuh Raya Abang Galau. Several outlets under one roof, selling claypots, seafood, chicken rice and juices; out front is a capacious forecourt.

Sea View Restoran, 254 Esplanade. An atmospheric Chinese café, pleasantly positioned overlooking Sungei Kemena and away from the traffic. The food is of a high standard and meals go for around $15 a head, including beer.

Sri Impian, Jalan Keppel. If you can't find anything you fancy among the *Sri Impian*'s expansive spread of Malay food, there's an in-house *murtabak*-and-*roti canai* stall.

Tam Nak Thai Restaurant, Jalan Main Bazaar. Curries, tom yam soups and all the other Thai classics, served in a pleasing dining room.

Listings

Airport Flights to Kuching (9 daily; $117), Sibu (4 daily; $64) and Miri (3 daily; $69). Also, two planes fly daily to Sabah's capital, Kota Kinabalu. Call ☎086/331963 for flight information. MAS is at 129 Jalan Masjid (☎086/331554).

Banks Standard Chartered, 89 Jalan Keppel; Hock Hua Bank, Jalan Keppel.

Boats Express boats to Tubau, 60km east, leave daily at 7am, 9am, 10.30am, noon and 1.30pm (2hr 30min; around $16). From here it's possible to cut through the forest to Belaga; see p.385 for more details. Boats return from Tubau at 6am, 7.30am, 9am, 10.30am and noon.

Buses Suria Bus Company (☎086/335489) is at the long-distance bus station, running eight daily air-con services north to Miri via Batu Niah (for Niah National Park, see below). Many other bus companies operate here, meaning that there are at least ten daily departures for Kuching ($52), eight to Sibu ($17) and several to Miri ($18). In addition, Borneo Highway Express (☎086/339855) runs a daily 5.30pm service to Pontianak ($86.50) in Kalimantan.

Government offices Jalan Tun Razak: Forestry Department (☎086/331117); Immigration Department (☎086/312211); Resident's Office (Mon–Fri 8.30am–noon & 2–4.15pm; ☎086/331896).

Hospital Jalan Abang Galau (☎086/331455).

Laundry *Teo Soon*, 48 Main Bazaar; same-day service costs around $5.

Police Branch on Jalan Sommerville (☎086/331129).

Post office Main office on Jalan Tun Razak (☎086/332375).

Telephone Telekom office at the western end of Jalan Sommerville (Mon–Sat 8.30am–4.30pm).

Tour operators Similajau Adventure Tours, lobby floor, *Plaza Hotel* (☎086/331552) will arrange hiking trips to the nearby national parks, plus boat excursions along Sungei Kemena.

Similajau National Park

The recent opening of **Similajau National Park**, 20km northeast along the coast from Bintulu, might well persuade you to stop in the region a bit longer. The park has a lot in common with Bako, near Kuching, with its long, unspoiled sandy beaches broken only by rocky headlands and freshwater streams. Beach walks and short hikes are possible, either along the 30km of coastline or following the trails which run alongside small rivers winding into the forest, their source in the undulating hills which rise only a few hundred metres from the beach. Shrubs grow on the cliff faces, pitcher plants can be found in the ridges and orchids hang from the trees and rocks. Twenty-four species of mammal have been recorded in the park, including gibbons and long-tailed macaques, mouse deer, wild boar, porcupines, civets and squirrels. The monkeys are quite friendly but sightings of anything else are quite rare unless you're very patient. Salt-water crocodiles are found occasionally wallowing in some of the rivers, especially after rain – one good reason for not swimming in the river close to the park centre – and there have even been sightings of dolphins and porpoises out in the waves.

Speedboats rented from Bintulu jetty cost $300 per day, an almost prohibitive sum unless there are at least six people sharing the cost. Boats arrive at the headquarters on the jetty the starting point for the short trail north to the beach. You can also get to Simulujau by **road** by leaving the trunk road to Batu Niah (see below) after 15km and bearing left along a newly paved road to a small kampung, Kuala Likau, at the entrance to the park. Buses don't yet come out this way, though the Parks and Forestry Department in Bintulu (see "Listings" above) will have the latest transport details; a taxi from town shouldn't cost more than $40.

Accommodation at the park ranges from chalets with rooms (②), to the hostel (beds $10, rooms ②) and the **campsite**, where rented tents cost only a few dollars. As well as the chalets, the park headquarters has a canteen that presently serves only drinks (the Forestry Office in Bintulu will be able to tell you whether this is still the case), and an **information centre** (daily 8am–5pm), with a small display on the local flora and fauna. You can book accommodation through the Bintulu Forestry Department (see p.393).

The trails

At just 30km by 1.5km, the park hasn't any particularly arduous trails but it's as well to wear light boots, a long-sleeved shirt and long trousers on the trails, as well as a hat, as the sun is very fierce in this part of Sarawak. A water bottle is useful although the river water is quite drinkable.

By far the greatest attractions are the beaches, on which turtles occasionally nest in April and May. The two-and-a-half-hour walk north to the two **turtle beaches** starts from the park headquarters, the first stage involving crossing Sungei Likau in a motorized longboat. The trail ascends into the forest and soon reaches the turning to the **Viewpoint Trail**, which after, some forty minutes from the headquarters, delivers superb views of the South China Sea. Meanwhile the main trail follows the coastline to the turtle beaches, an hour beyond which is **Golden Beach**, noted for its fine sand. Walk north along Golden Beach for ten minutes, and you reach the trail which runs inland along the side of Sungei Sebubong. Although the park offers a boat trip from the headquarters to this point, it's much more enjoyable to walk – the route into the forest is especially gratifying after the heat and lack of shade of the open beach. After fifteen minutes the trail reaches **Kolam Sebubong**, a freshwater pool, whose waters are stained a remarkable ruby red by harmless tannin acid from the nearby peat swamp.

The other worthwhile trail leads to the **Selansur Rapids**. Follow the Turtle Beach trail for one hour and look for a marked trail which heads into the forest parallel to a small river, Sungei Kabalak. It passes through sparse *kerangas* forest and towering dipterocarp forest before climbing the sides of hills, where you'll hear monkeys high up in the trees and the omnipresent chainsaw-like call of the cicadas. After around ninety minutes you reach the rapids, a pleasant place to rest and take a dip.

Niah National Park

Visiting **NIAH NATIONAL PARK**, 131km north of Bintulu, is a highly rewarding experience – in less than a day you can see one of the largest caves in the world, as well as prehistoric rock graffiti in the remarkable Painted Cave, and hike along primary forest trails. The park consists of 31 square kilometres of lowland forest and limestone massifs, the highest of these **Gunung Subis**, rising to nearly 400m and riddled with caves. Although the region wasn't designated a National Park until 1975, it has been a National Historic Monument since 1958, when Tom Harrisson discovered evidence that early man had been using Niah as a cemetery. In the outer area of the present park, deep excavations revealed **human remains**, including skulls which dated back forty thousand years and artefacts like flake stone tools, sandstone pounders, mortars, bone points and shell ornaments – the first evidence that people had lived in Southeast Asia that long ago.

Some of the caves at Niah are frequented year-round by **bird's nest** harvesters (after swiftlet nests for soup), a state of affairs that has worried the park authorities who are concerned about the effect on the bird population. Officially, the nests should only be collected during two specific seasons: before the swifts lay their eggs, and after the departure of the young, when the nests are no longer needed. Consequently, Niah National Park has been **closed** for several months at a time on recent occasions in an attempt to stop the collectors' activities – check to see if Niah is still open for visitors before going.

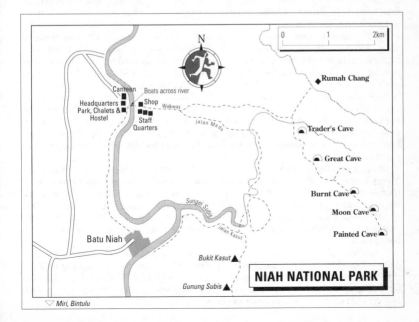

Practicalities

The park is roughly halfway between Bintulu and Miri, 11km off the main road close to the small town of **Batu Niah**, which you can reach by regular Syarikat Bas Suria services from either Bintulu or Miri (see p.390 and p.397). There are a few average Chinese cafés here, and the *Niah Cave Inn* (☎085/737333; ③) is the best **accommodation** option. The caves are 3km north of Batu Niah, and reached either by a pleasant walk along the forest path – which takes thirty minutes – or by **longboat** (daily 8am–4pm; $10) or taxi ($10).

The path from Batu Niah leads straight to the **park headquarters**, beautifully located on the western bank of Sungei Niah, with the forest deep and thick on the other side of the river. **Hostel** beds in salubrious rooms sleeping up to four cost $10, though of course it's perfectly possible to rent an entire room if you don't relish sharing digs with strangers. Otherwise, you might splash out on one of the smart new **chalets** (④) constructed beside the park headquarters. You'll only need to book accommodation in advance (at the Parks and Wildlife Department offices in Bintulu or Miri) if you intend to visit at weekends, when the park is at its busiest. There's a **shop** (daily 7am–10pm) where you can buy basic foodstuffs, and a **canteen** (daily 7.30am–10pm) which has a limited range of dishes, such as stir fries, noodles and omelettes, at very reasonable prices.

The caves and trails

From the park headquarters it's a thirty-minute walk to the **caves**, heading east on the only trail into the park. After crossing the narrow Sungei Niah by *sampan*, the trail strikes off from beside a general store that stocks chocolate, drinks, batteries and torches, and follows a wooden walkway through dense rainforest where you are likely to see monkeys, hornbills, birdwing butterflies, tree squirrels and flying lizards. A clearly marked path leaves the walkway on the left after forty minutes, running to an Iban longhouse, **Rumah Chang**, where you can buy soft drinks and snacks if you did not stock up at the head of the trail.

Further along the main walkway, a rock- and creeper-encrusted jungle wall looms up ahead and the path takes you up through the **Trader's Cave** (so called because early nest-gatherers would congregate here to sell their harvests to merchants) to the mind-blowing, 60m by 250m west mouth of the **Great Cave**. Crude steps have been dug out of the rock for the final ascent. From within the immense, draughty darkness disembodied voices can be heard above the squeal of masses of bats. The voices come from the **bird's nest collectors** who, despite official scrutiny, are close to exhausting the fragile stocks of swiftlet nests, used to make the famous bird's-nest soup; three species of swiftlet breed here, co-existing in the cave's voluminous rafters with the bats. Thin beanstalk poles snake up from the cave floor and the collectors can just be made out on top of them.

Once inside, the walkway continues on to the Painted Cave, via **Burnt Cave** and **Moon Cave**. The smell of guano intensifies as the path leads around extraordinary rock formations, and the sounds – of your voice, of dripping water, of bat-chatter and the nest collectors' scrapes – are magnified considerably. As the walkway worms deeper into the darkness, the light through the cave mouth ebbs and artificial lighting takes over. As the planks are often slippery with guano, it's best to wear shoes with a grip and take a torch.

After thirty minutes you reach the **Painted Cave**, in which early Sarawak communities buried their dead in **boat-shaped coffins**, or "death ships", arranged around the cave walls; when Harrisson first entered, the cave had partially collapsed, and the contents were spilled all around. Subsequent dating proved that the caves had been used as a cemetery for tens of thousands of years.

One of these wooden coffins is still perched on an incline, as though beached after a monumental journey, its contents long since removed to the Sarawak Museum for safe-keeping. Despite the light streaming from an opening at the far end of the cave, it's hard to distinguish the **wall paintings** that give the cave its name (especially as they are now fenced off), but they stretch from the dark right-hand corner behind the coffin – a thirty-metre-long tableau depicting boats on a journey, the figures apparently either jumping on and off, or dancing. This image fits various Borneo mythologies where the dead undergo water-bound challenges on their way to the afterlife. The markings, although crude, can be made out, but the brown paint strokes are now extremely faded.

The only way back to the entrance is by the same route – try to be there at dusk when the swiftlets return and the bats swarm out for the night. Even if you miss this, there's plenty to keep you occupied on the march back, including fireflies and luminous fungi visible from the walkway – switch off your torch and let your eyes accustom themselves to the dark.

There are two **trails** in the park which, after the claustrophobic darkness of the caves, offer a much-needed breath of fresh air. The first, **Jalan Madu**, splits off to the right from the plank walkway around 800m from the park headquarters and cuts first east, then south, across a peat swamp forest, where you see wild orchids, mushrooms and pandanus. The trail crosses Sungei Subis and then follows its south bank to its confluence with Sungei Niah, from where you'll have to hail a passing boat to cross over to Batu Niah ($1). The other, and more spectacular trail, is that to **Bukit Kasut**, its starting point at the confluence of the two rivers. After crossing the river, the clearly marked trail winds through *kerangas* forest, round the foothills of Bukit Kasut and up to the summit – a hard one-hour slog, at the end of which there's a view both of the impenetrable forest canopy and Batu Niah.

Miri and around

With a population of 400,000 and rising, **MIRI** is a real boom town, and, despite historic links with Western businesses – specifically the oil producer Shell – and a significant expatriate community, it retains a strong Chinese character. Some of the town's earliest inhabitants were pioneering Chinese merchants who set up shops to trade with the Kayan who lived in longhouses to the northeast along Batang Baram. But Miri remained a tiny, unimportant settlement up until the time oil was discovered in 1882, though it wasn't until 1910 that the black gold was drilled in any quantity. Since then, over six hundred wells have been drilled in the Miri area, on and offshore, and the main refineries are just 5km up the coast at Lutong. Miri is congested with traffic, bursting out of the constraints of its topography – sea to the north and hills to the south – but after a week or two spent trekking in wild northeastern Sarawak, you may well think favourably of the place. For a quick escape from the city, there are regular buses south to nearby **Lambir Hills National Park**, not a bad place for a picnic and a swim.

Arrival, information and accommodation

Miri's **airport** is 8km west of the town centre: bus #9 (every 45min, daily 6.15am–8pm; $1) runs from outside the terminal to the **bus station**, which is located next to the town's original shopping centre, Wisma Pelita. Long-distance buses also terminate here. It's a five-minute walk from here east to Jalan China and the old town. For all **departure details**, see "Listings", below.

The new **Visitor Information Centre** (☎085/434181) next to the bus station at 452 Jalan Melayu, has maps and leaflets, and is also the place to go if you need to book accommodation at the local national parks. You'll need a **permit** to visit Marudi on the Baram and the Kelabit Highlands, which can be obtained by going to the **Resident's**

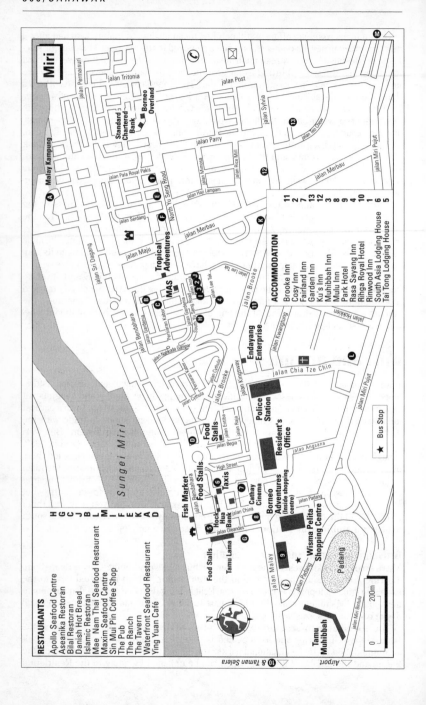

Miri

RESTAURANTS

Apollo Seafood Centre	H
Aseanika Restoran	G
Bilal Restoran	C
Danish Hot Bread	J
Islamic Restoran	B
Mae Nam Thai Seafood Restaurant	L
Maxim Seafood Centre	M
Sin Mui Pin Coffee Shop	I
The Pub	F
The Ranch	E
The Tavern	K
Waterfront Seafood Restaurant	A
Ying Yuan Café	D

ACCOMMODATION

Brooke Inn	11
Cosy Inn	2
Fairland Inn	7
Garden Inn	13
Ku's Inn	3
Muhibbah Inn	8
Mulu Inn	9
Park Hotel	4
Rasa Sayang Inn	10
Rihga Royal Hotel	1
Rinwood Inn	6
South Asia Lodging House	5
Tai Tong Lodging House	5

Office (see "Listings") on Jalan Raja, and picking up the relevant form. Fill in the form, take it to the **police** headquarters next door, get it stamped, then photocopied (along with your passport) in the shop opposite the police station, and head back to the Resident's Office for the permit. If you're going on an arranged tour to any of these places, the operator will obtain the permit for you, but otherwise allow two hours for the whole rigmarole.

ACCOMMODATION

Lodging houses with dorm beds offer the cheapest deal, but these are really basic and none too clean. If you're prepared to pay a bit more, Miri has lots of regular hotels.

Brooke Inn, 14 Brooke Rd (☎085/412881). Quiet and clean hotel whose cosy rooms have TV, air-con and smartly tiled bathrooms; should you find yourself at a loose end, the friendly reception staff will pipe up to your room your choice of movie from the local video shop. Recommended. ③.

Cosy Inn, South Yu Seng Rd (☎085/415522). Well positioned close to the MAS office and a string of excellent Indian cafés. The rooms are small, though all have air-con, TV and bathroom. ③.

Fairland Inn, Jalan Raja, at Raja Square (☎085/413981). Excellent hotel with a perfect roof for drying laundry on. Clean, well-equipped rooms, and friendly and helpful staff. ②

Garden Inn, Lot 290, Jalan Teo Chew (☎085/419822). This is a quiet hotel, family-run and hence very hospitable, with small rooms in the middle of the new town. Family rooms are available for $80. ③.

Ku's Inn, 3 Jalan Sylvia (☎085/413733). Located on a busy street, the rooms are cosy, with air-con and shower. ③.

Muhibbah Inn, Lot 548 South Yu Seng Rd (☎412003). Uncharismatic but polished rooms, the least expensive of them box-like with shared outside amenities. ②.

Mulu Inn, Jalan Melayu, opposite Wisma Pelita Tunku (☎085/417168). Though not always as clean as it might be, this place is still very popular with tourists and is good value with large rooms, some of which hold three beds. Ask for a room at the back, away from the busy road. ②.

Park, Jalan Raja (☎085/414555). With so many other mid-range hotels in town, the *Park* has felt the pinch recently, and its heavily discounted, extensive rooms are a snip. ③.

Rinwood Inn, Lot 826, North Yu Seng Rd (☎085/415888). Upmarket place which is popular with business people. The rooms are large with full facilities – air-con, showers and TV. ⑥.

Rasa Sayang Inn, Lot 566, Jalan Lee Tak (☎085/413880). Located in a quiet spot with small rooms and full facilities. Comfortable, and a pleasant place to stay. ③.

Rihga Royal, Jalan Temenggong Datuk Oyong Lawai (☎085/421121, fax 425057). Unimpeachable resort-style hotel that also prides itself on its excellent business facilities; within its manicured grounds you'll find a giant pool, fitness centre and full range of restaurants and bars. If you can afford to stay here, you'll probably roll up in a taxi. For the record though, bus #1 from the station passes the front gates. ⑨.

South East Asia Lodging House, Jalan Raja, at Raja Square (☎085/416921). This is very cheap (and a little sleazy), with dorm beds and shared facilities. $18.

Tai Tong Lodging House, Jalan China (jetty end). Situated in the old part of town, it has men-only dorms, and more expensive private rooms are also available. Dorms $8. ②.

The Town

The **old town** around Jalan China was once the commercial hub of Miri and is still the most enjoyable area to wander around. It's packed with cafés and shops, and there's a **wet fish market** at the top of Jalan China, next to which is the **Chinese temple**, a simple red-and-yellow building whose bottle-green roof is patrolled by fearsome dragons. From its small, river-facing forecourt where devotees burn joss sticks and paper money, you can watch the boats being unloaded at the fish market next door. The wide road running parallel to the river, **Jalan Bendahara**, is the simplest route into the new town area; if you push on past the central **mosque** you'll pass the old Malay kampung, between Jalan Bendahara and the river. The houses here are now extremely dilapidated.

The **shops** in Miri are some of the best on this side of the state and there are even a few malls, the first of which to be constructed, **Wisma Pelita**, is on Jalan Padang. *Pelita Book Centre*, on the first floor has a wide selection of English-language books on Sarawak culture and geography; while *Longhouse Handicraft Centre*, on the top floor, sells rattan bags, *pua kumbu* textiles, wooden carvings, jars, hats and beads. At *Syarikat Unique Arts and Handicrafts Centre*, Lot 2994, Jalan Airport, 4km out of Miri, native crafts can be bought at lower prices than in town.

Directly south of the bus station is the padang, on whose border lies **Tamu Muhibbah**, (daily 6am–2pm), the town's jungle produce market, where Orang Ulu come downriver to sell rattan mats, tropical fruits, rice wine and even jungle animals. Further afield, buses #1, #5 and #11 (40 sen) from the bus station go to **Taman Selera**, 4km west of town, whose tranquil beach is one kilometre long. It's a fine place to watch the sun go down, eat *satay* and drink beer from the hawker stalls.

Eating, drinking and nightlife

You can hardly go wrong for food in Miri, although the *Apollo*, *Maxim's* and *Bilal* are a cut above the other **restaurants** for value and quality. As for stalls, the ones next to the *Cathay Cinema* on Jalan China are known for their delicious *laksa* noodles and *congee* (Chinese rice porridge). There's Malay food in the Tamu Lama on Jalan Oleander, and at night you can dine at the stalls in the market at the junction of Jalan Entiba and Jalan Begia. At the *Danish Hot Bread* bakery, next to the *Cosy Inn* on South Yu Seng Road, you can buy a creamy, cakey treat to round off your meal. Along North Yu Seng Road in the new town are two of the rowdiest watering-holes in Sarawak, including *The Ranch* and *The Pub* – rock-music-playing, hard-drinking **bars** where expat oil personnel and other Europeans meet. The *Tavern*, a little way south in the *Pacific Orient Hotel*, is a shade more upmarket. Keep an eye out for the Filipino bands that often play live around town.

Apollo Seafood Centre, 4 South Yu Seng Rd. Very popular with expats and visitors alike. The grilled stingray and pineapple rice is exquisite, although eating here is not cheap at around $40 for two, including beer.

Aseanika Restoran, Jalan Melayu. Malay café serving excellent *rotis* and curries. Closed during Ramadan.

Bilal Restoran, Lot 250, Persiaran Kabor, Beautiful Jade Centre. Superb North Indian food: *rotis*, *naan*, *murtabak*, and outstanding tandoori chicken at around $6 for each giant-sized portion.

China Street Food Stalls, near the temple. Known for their delicious *laksa* noodles and *congee* (Chinese rice porridge).

Islamic Restoran, 233 Jalan Maju. Around the corner from the *Bilal*, this is another decent place whose speciality is spiced Malay dishes.

Mae Nam Thai Restaurant, *Dynasty Hotel*, Jalan Pujt Lutong. Authentic Thai cuisine at around $20 a head for a filling meal.

Maxim Seafood Centre, Lot 342, Blk 7, Jalan Miri-Pujut. Although it's a bit of a trek to get there (take a taxi), *Maxim's* is still Miri's most popular restaurant. Serves a superb array of grilled fish with *blanchan;* and delicious vegetable dishes with chilli, herbs and garlic. It costs roughly $40 for two, including beer.

Sin Mui Pin Coffee Shop, 5 South Yu Seng Rd. A high-quality fish restaurant, with a vibrant atmosphere. The stingray is excellent – order your rice and vegetables from the people at the rear. Get here before 8pm to avoid a long wait.

Tanjong Seaview, Taman Selera beach. This food centre is very popular with young Miri couples and families, and offers superb *satay* at low prices.

Waterfront Seafood Restaurant, Jalan Pala Roya Pakis. Overlooking Sungei Miri and the shambolic Malay kampung, and set above the hubbub of downtown Miri, the *Waterfront* cooks up dependably delicious seafood.

Ying Yuan Café, Lot 55, Jalan Bendahar. Busy Chinese café noted for its mixed rice which includes prawns, chicken, baby sweetcorn and okra: cheap, filling and delicious.

Listings

Airport Daily flights to Kota Kinabalu (6 daily; $104), Kuala Lumpur (8 daily; $422), Kuching (9 daily; $165), Sibu (5 daily; $115), Marudi (4 daily; $30), Gunung Mulu (3 daily; $70), Bario (1 daily; $70), Bintulu (3 daily; $69), Limbang (6 daily; $45), Lawas (3 daily; $60), Long Lellang (2 weekly; $80) and Pontianak (2 weekly; $300). For flight enquiries call ☎085/414242. MAS is on South Yu Seng Rd (☎085/414144).

Banks and exchange Standard Chartered, Jalan Merpati; Bank Bumiputra, Jalan Bendahara (11am–3pm only). There is a moneychanger in the *Magnum 4-digit* shop at 12 Jalan China.

Buses All buses leave from the bus station. Bus Suria (☎085/412173) for Bintulu and other locations south including Kuching and Pontiak; Miri Transport (☎085/418655) for Lambir Hills; Miri Belait Transport (☎085/419129) for Kuala Belait in Brunei (daily 7am, 9am, 10.30am, 1pm & 3.30pm; $12.20; last departure from Belait to BSB in Brunei is around 3.30pm, so set off early) and Limbang (7am; $26).

Car rental Mega Services, 3, Lorong 1, Sungei Krokop (☎085/427436).

Hospital Miri's General Hospital is on the airport road (☎085/420033).

Immigration office At Jalan Kipas (Room 3; Mon–Fri 8am–noon & 2–4.15pm). You can extend your Sarawak visa here, but only by a few days. The officials insist that you have to leave the state and then return if you want to spend more time in Sarawak.

Laundry There are no downtown laundries, so ask at your hotel reception.

Parks and wildlife department Booking for National Parks accommodation is now handled by the Visitor Information Centre (see p.397).

Police headquarters On Jalan King (☎085/433677).

Post office On Jalan Post.

Resident's office On Jalan Raja (Mon–Fri 8.15am–noon & 2–4.15pm; ☎085/33203).

Telephones Telekom office on Jalan Post (daily 7.30am–10pm).

Tour operators If you are going it alone into Mulu, it's well worth while contacting Endayang Enterprise, second floor, Judson Clinic, 171a Jalan Brooke (☎085/438740, fax 661927), whose Berawan owner, Thomas Ngang, is experienced at arranging cut-price accommodation, boat transfers and guides for independent travellers in the park, as well as meals at his affordable restaurant. Borneo Adventures, ninth floor, Wisma Pelita (☎085/414935), a branch of the excellent Kuching operation, manages trips out to any of northern Sarawak's attractions, and has excellent guides in the Kelabit Highlands. Tropical Adventures, ground floor, *Mega Hotel* (☎082/419337), specializes in treks to the Baram, Gunung Mulu Park and the Kelabit Highlands; expect to pay at least $800 for two for a five- or six-day trek. Borneo Overland (☎082/430255), beside the Standard Chartered Bank on Jalan Merpati, does similar tours at roughly the same prices.

Lambir Hills National Park

Situated 32km south of Miri, **Lambir Hills National Park** is perfect for a day-trip and is particularly popular with Miri locals at the weekends. The contours of the region were formed sixty million years ago, when a vast area of sedimentary rock was laid down, stretching from present-day western Sarawak to Sabah. There is limestone and clay at lower levels, and sandstone and shale closer to the surface. Subsequent upheavals created the hills and the rich soil substrata, and gave rise to the local rainforest, with its distinctive vegetation types. Mixed dipterocarp forest makes up over half the area with the vast hardwood trees – meranti, kapur and keruing – creating deep shadows on the forest floor; the kerangas forest, with its peaty soils, low-lying vegetation and smaller trees, is lighter and drier.

Fourteen well-marked **trails** criss-cross the south part of the park, several leading to **waterfalls**. The longest trail – the four-hour trek to the summit of **Bukit Lambir** – is tough but rewarding, with a wonderful view across the park, the sounds of insects and birds echoing below. The trail cuts across deceptively steep hills, where gnarled roots are often the only helping hand up an almost vertical incline – you may well catch sight of monkeys, lizards or snakes on the trail.

To reach the three **Latak waterfalls**, 1.5km from park headquarters, follow the trail marked "Latak", which branches off north from the Bukit Lambir trail. The furthest of the falls (Latak itself) is the best, its 25-metre cascade feeding an alluring pool, but given its proximity to park headquarters, it is inevitably overrun at the weekends. There are more spectacular falls further afield; it takes two and a half hours to reach the **Pantu** and **Pancur** waterfalls – watch for the narrow paths which lead down to the rivers from the main Bukit Lambir trail. These are fine places to stop and eat, and take a deliciously cool swim. The most remote waterfall, **Tengkorong**, is a further thirty minutes' walk from Pancur.

Practicalities

Buses leave Miri's bus station every thirty minutes (daily 6.30am–4.30pm) for the forty-minute trip – any bus bound for Batu Niah, Bakong or Bekenu will do. Approaching from Niah National Park, you can take the Batu Niah–Miri bus which takes ninety minutes; ask for the Lambir Hills stop.

Accommodation at the park is limited, so it's best to book in advance at Miri's Parks and Wildlife Department office (see "Listings" above). The two options are the chalets (③), which have cooking facilities, and the campsite ($4). Both are close to the road, next to the **park headquarters** (daily 9am–5pm), which issues permits and park maps, and the **canteen** (daily 8am–7pm). If you intend to go on the longer trails, bring hiking boots, water bottle, torch, sun hat and insect repellent.

North of Miri: the border region

The trip by road from Sarawak **to Brunei** is complicated and, if you head on to Sabah, can take up to two days – many people prefer to fly straight from Miri to Kota Kinabalu. The only advantage – and not a particularly compelling one at that – of the land and sea route is that you can visit the territorial divisions of **Limbang** and **Lawas**, which contrast greatly with the land around Miri as they are sparsely populated by an ethnic mix of Iban, Murut, Berawan and Kelabit. This is a hard area to get around, though, as there are few boats and no roads.

Heading straight for Brunei from Miri, the trunk road north runs a few kilometres in from the coast alongside rubber plantations to **KUALA BARAM**, 30km away, a small town situated at the mouth of Batang Baram. Here, all vehicles and pedestrians have to cross the river by ferry (every 20min, daily 6am–8pm) and then make their way on towards the **border** at the Bruneian town of Kuala Belait (see p.497), another 6km further.

At Kuala Belait, you hop on board a Bruneian bus which runs to Seria, for connections to the capital, Bandar Seri Begawan. All legs of the journey from Miri to Kuala Belait are included in the price of a Miri Belait Transport Company ticket. The last bus from Kuala Belait that will get you to the Bruneian capital the same day leaves at around 3.30pm; from Seria, the first bus to the capital leaves at 7am, after which the service is very regular.

Limbang and around

Just to the south of Bandar is **Limbang**, a strip of Sarawak roughly 30km wide and 50km deep, sandwiched between the two parts of Brunei. It's a seldom-visited, inaccessible district, though travel is possible along Sungei Limbang, which snakes into the interior from the mangrove-cloaked coast, and provides access to Gunung Mulu National Park by an adventurous river trip along Sungei Medalam (see "Limbang Town", below). For centuries, Limbang was a trading centre run by Malays, who bartered the jungle produce collected by the Berawan, Kelabit, Besayak and Murut peoples with fellow

Chinese and Malay merchants. Although the White Rajahs never actually bought Limbang from the Sultan of Brunei, as they did the areas to the south, Charles Brooke occupied the region in 1890, following demonstrations by the ethnic groups against the increasingly decadent rule of the sultan. However, Brooke's main reason for interceding was to acquire as large a slice of what was left of Brunei as possible, before his Sabah-based rivals in the British North Borneo Chartered Company overran it.

Limbang town

The only building of note in the only settlement, **LIMBANG TOWN**, is the riverbank

fort, the most northerly of Charles Brooke's defensive structures. Constructed in 1897, it was renovated in 1966 when much of the woodwork was replaced by more durable materials like concrete and *belian* of "iron wood". It was originally designed to serve as an administrative centre, but was instead used to monitor native insurgency in the early years of this century; now it's the departure point for boats to Lauan and Brunei (see below). The rest of the small town is composed of a few streets set back from the river; the main street, Jalan Bangsiol, leads to the **market**, which is at its busiest on Friday when fruit, animals and vegetables are brought in from the forest to be sold.

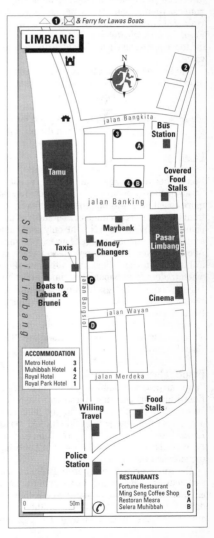

The **airport** is 2km south of the town and you'll need to get a **taxi** (around $6) into the centre. There are daily flights to and from Miri and Lawas, which cost around $25; Willing Travel on Jalan Bangsiol is the local ticket agent. The **jetty** for boats to Labuan and Brunei is behind the fort on Jalan Bangsiol: two boats leave early in the morning for Labuan ($20), and there are hourly departures to Brunei ($15) until 6pm. The daily Lawas boat (7.30am; $20) leaves from the jetty 400m north of the old town. Several daily boats also travel the 50km upstream on Sungei Limbang to Nanga Medamit, a couple of hours away, from where Sungei Medalam veers south into Mulu Park, passing the Iban longhouses of **Melaban** and **Bala** en route, as well as the rangers' lodge at **Mentawai**. Independent visitors to Mulu normally enter town from Miri. Still, as long as all your paperwork is in order (including, in this case, the entry permit), there's nothing to stop you from entering Limbang-side; call George (☎085/231189) to arrange a boat, but expect to fork out several hundred dollars. There are buses to Nanga Medamit, too, from Jalan Tarap, every two hours from 9am until 3pm, the trip taking around ninety minutes, twice as long as the boat. Also originating from Jalan Tarap's bus terminal is the daily Mirah bus (9.30am; $26). There are no buses to Lawas, though many services run up to the border with the Bruneian district of Temburong.

The cheapest **accommodation** in town is inappropriately named *Royal Hotel* (☎085/215690; ①) on Jalan Tarap, where all rooms share common amenities. The *Muhibbah Inn* (☎085/212488; ②) on nearby Jalan Banking also has a number of economical rooms, and represents far better value than the neighbouring *Metro Hotel* (☎085/211133; ③), where you'll have to pay $20 extra for the luxury of a window. At the *Royal Park Hotel* (☎085/212155; ④), opposite the Lawas jetty some 400m north of the old town, prices take a further hike, though the well-presented rooms still afford decent value.

The hawker stalls on the breezy first floor of the market offer the most affordable **food** in town, as well as good views of the water village across the river. There are more stalls in the covered building below the bus terminal, and still more on the open ground below Jalan Merdeka. The pick of Limbang's restaurants are the friendly Malay joints, the *Mesra*; the *Selera Muhibbah* – good for *rotis* and *biriyanis*; the *Fortune Restaurant*, serving quality Chinese food; and the plain *Ming Seng Coffee Shop*.

Lawas

Boxed between Sabah and Brunei's sparsely inhabited Temburong District is Sarawak's most northwesterly district, **Lawas**, a little larger than Limbang and with more coastline. It was bought by Charles Brooke from the Sultan of Brunei in 1905, and from its origins as a remote bazaar and trading centre for Berawan, Kelabit and Chinese pioneers, **LAWAS TOWN** – the only settlement of any size in the area – has grown into a bustling centre on Sungei Lawas, becoming prosperous from its timber industry. Above the river is a posh new market which is the town's main focal point, selling tropical fruits and vegetables, and with several food stalls upstairs. Saturdays are busiest, when traders from Sabah sometimes arrive to sell clothes and textiles. Otherwise, the only diversion in town is the Chinese temple five minutes north of the market, on Jalan Bunga Teratai, remarkable only for the unusual fact that a large portion of it is open to the elements.

North of town, Jalan Punang leads, after around 7km, to **PUNANG** itself, the site of a reasonably attractive beach – minibuses ($2) make the trip from the bus station on Jalan Pengiran.

Practicalities

Lawas **airport** is around 3km south of town – a bus usually meets the daily flights from Kota Kinabalu, Limbang, Bario and Ba Kelalan in the Kelabit Highlands. The MAS agent is Eng Huat Travel Agency, on Jalan Law Siew Ann (☎085/285570). **Boats** arrive and depart from the jetty beside the old mosque, 400m east of the town: the *Pertama Lawas* leaves daily for Brunei (7.30am; $20) and there are also boats to Sabah's Pulau Labuan (daily at 7.30am; $20) and to Limbang (daily at 9am; $20). Tickets are sold at the jetty just before departure.

The trip **overland** to and from Brunei's Temburong District is by taxi ($80 for a full car), while minibuses and taxis run to the **border with Sabah**, where you can pick up another bus or taxi to Sipitang (see p.450), an hour's journey all told. There's also a daily through-bus to Kota Kinabalu, the *Lawas Express*, which leaves at 7.30am ($20), and also passes through Sipitang. The only other way out of Lawas is by **land cruiser** (daily; around $35) to the lowland Kelabit settlement of Pa Kelalan (see p.000), 90km south; most of the five-hour trip is on a rough unpaved road – go to the parking space in front of the *Mee Yan Hotel* for details.

The *Mee Yan Hotel* (①), at the bottom of the town, offers the least expensive **accommodation** in Lawas, but it's a dark, sleazy place, and you'd do well to head upmarket, and make for either the *Federal Hotel* (③) on Jalan Punang, or the top-of-the-range *Shangsan Hotel* (⑤) on Jalan Trusan.

For inexpensive **food**, try the upper floor of the market. There's no menu at the tidy *Soon Yeng* restaurant below the hotel of the same name, but the Chinese food there is good. Otherwise, most of the best eating places cluster around the *Mee Yan Hotel*. Across the road from it is the Malay *Restoran Hj Narudin Bin Matusop*, while one block away in the other direction the *Bee Hiong* restaurant specializes in *dim sum*. The *Mee Yan*'s next-door neighbour, the *Ho Peng* though, is by far the best Chinese coffee shop in town, serving up sensational noodle dishes.

THE NORTHERN INTERIOR

The **northern interior**, loosely defined as the watershed of **Batang Baram** – the wide river to the northeast of Miri – incorporates both the wildest, most untouched areas of Sarawak, and the most environmentally degraded. At the northernmost point of the White Rajahs' reach (and almost completely ignored by the Sultan of Brunei) the Baram had a number of Brooke fortifications, but the tribal groups living along the river's reaches were largely left to their own devices. More recently though, Baram was the first part of Sarawak to be heavily logged, and timber yards now line the river for 50km from **Kuala Baram** to **Marudi**, the largest town in the region, and for 20km to the east. The scale of the industry can be judged by the number of timber rafts which float down the wide, silt-clogged river. Although the state government is cutting back production in the north, the forests are still being harvested at the rate of over 300,000 hectares a year: some estimates suggest that over half of Sarawak's inland forests have already gone. The very obvious environmental problems apart, there's great concern at the impact that **logging** has had on the region's indigenous inhabitants, mostly Kayan, Kenyah, Kelabit and Penan. Soil erosion as a result of the deforestation has damaged their lands, water catchments are murky and often unfit for drinking, and the food supply – either game in the forest or from agricultural land – is diminishing. Disease is rife, too, spread principally by contact with timber personnel and water-born parasites. The Penan are the worst affected because, as hunters and gatherers, they rely solely on the forest for survival. However, resistance to logging has been vigorous, with various groups constructing barricades in disputed territories. Some local communities have applied to set up **Communal Reserves**, both to protect the remaining areas of primary rainforest and to maintain the secondary areas where they practise shifting cultivation, harvest fruit trees and plants, and hunt. The state government has refused most of these applications, and the communities have reacted by taking their cases to the courts.

Despite the despoliation, the northern interior holds many of Sarawak's most renowned natural delights. One of Batang Baram's tributaries, **Sungei Tutoh**, branches off east to **Gunung Mulu National Park**, which contains the famous pinnacles and many impressive cave systems. Further east still, straddling the border with Kalimantan and only accessible by plane, lies the magnificent **Kelabit Highlands**, a lush, sparsely populated mountain plateau, whose pleasing climate and low humidity, makes it the best place in the state for long treks in the rainforest.

Travel in the region is very efficient, due to the excellent rural air service and reliable river boats. In a ten-day trip you cover visit Gunung Mulu, the Kelabit Highlands, the bazaar town of Marudi, and a Kenyah longhouse on the Tutoh.

Marudi and around

MARUDI, 80km southeast of Miri on Batang Baram, is the only bazaar in the whole Baram watershed, supplying the interior with consumer items, from outboard engines to plastic buckets. Marudi's **jetty**, where dozens of express boats and larger vessels crowd the water, is the centre of the community; stalls and cafés here do a brisk trade as the boats disgorge those who come to visit or barter. Timber magnates in jeans and dark glasses drive by in brand new Toyota vans – even the mobile phone has made it here – while groups of young men wait for temporary labour in the timber camps, processing yards and nearby rubber estates. Marudi was acquired by Charles Brooke from the Sultan of Brunei in 1882, and he renamed it Claudetown, after the first official sent by James Brooke to administer the area. Brooke encouraged Iban tribespeople from the middle Rajang to migrate here, to act as a bulwark against Kayan war parties who, at their peak in the mid-nineteenth century, amassed up to three thousand warriors on expeditions downriver in search of human trophies.

The town is dominated by two features, the jetty and the hilltop fort, **Fort Hose**, which is reached by walking past the main Bazaar Square, west of the jetty, and following Jalan Fort to the top of the hill. The fort was named after the most well-known of the Residents to have occupied the position here, the naturalist Charles Hose. Built in 1901, its ironwood tiles are still in perfect condition, as are the ceremonial brass cannons at the front. The fort is now a government office, but part of it houses a **Penan handicraft centre** (Mon–Fri 9pm–2am), selling baskets, metalwork and textiles. Five minutes' further along the hilltop road is the old Resident's house, which, though sturdy and quite habitable, is currently vacant and beginning to become tatty in the tropical climate.

Practicalities

It only takes a few minutes to walk from Marudi's **airport** into town, although **taxis** usually meet the morning flights from Gunung Mulu, Bario and Miri. The boat **jetty** is north of the centre and only five minutes' walk from the main hotel, the *Grand* (☎085/55712; ①), which is just off the airport road, Jalan Cinema, and provides far and away the best **accommodation** in town. The hotel is massive with clean and quiet rooms, and at the reception you'll find details of Gunung Mulu tours and visits to longhouses. The *Alisan*, on Jalan Queen, off Jalan Cinema (☎085/55601; ②), is a very good deal, too. Other options include the *Hotel Zola*, a stone's throw from the jetty on Jalan Cinema (☎085/755311; ②); *Jaya Hotel*, Lot 950, Jalan Newshop (☎085/756425; ③), which has small, clean air-con rooms; and the most expensive place in town, the *Victoria Hotel*, Lot 961, in Bazaar Square (☎085/756067; ③), which has good views over the river.

There are two excellent **restaurants**: the Indian *Restoran Koperselara*, just past the *Alisan* hotel on Jalan Cinema, sells *roti canai*, curries and refreshing *teh tarek* (a full meal costs around $4); while *Boon Kee Restoran*, set behind the main street in Jalan Newshop, is a great place for dinner, with outdoor tables. A favourite meal here is sweet and sour prawns, greens in garlic and rice, plus beer – all for around $15 a head. Otherwise, a couple of cafés beside the jetty and on the square do adequate rice and noodle dishes.

River trips from Marudi

The upriver Baram express (daily at 8.30am, 10am & 2.30pm; $15) goes to the settlement of **Long Lama**, 80km southeast, returning to Marudi at 6.45am and 10am. The longhouse at Long Lama has sleeping facilities and it's possible to arrange trips further down the Baram to **Long Akah**, another 60km east, although renting a longboat for this journey is expensive.

Another daily departure from Marudi is the Tinjar express (8am), which takes two hours to reach the Kayan longhouse at **Long Teru**, where most of the inhabitants work in a timber camp. The only boat along the Tutoh river to **Long Terawan** (where there's a connection for Gunung Mulu National Park) leaves at noon. Although most people travel this route specifically to go to the park, on the way you pass a number of traditional Kayan longhouses which are worth visiting. An hour from Marudi along the Tutoh, you reach the periphery of the loggers' activities; from here on, the river is clear, the jungle closing in around the river banks.

Finally, the boat (hourly 7am–3pm; $12) west from Marudi to Kuala Baram (see p.402) takes three hours, with numerous buses waiting at the other end for onward travel to Miri or Brunei.

Gunung Mulu National Park

GUNUNG MULU NATIONAL PARK is Sarawak's premier national park and largest conservation area, located deep in the rainforest. Until 1992, when commercial flights began to cover the route, Gunung Mulu was accessible only by a full-day trip from Marudi along the Baram, Tutoh and Melinau rivers, but the region has been a magnet for explorers and scientists since the 1930s. New discoveries are still being made, but at the last count, Mulu featured 20,000 animal species and 3500 plant species. Quite apart from the park's primary rainforest, which is characterized by clear rivers and high-altitude vegetation, there are has three mountains dominated by dramatically eroded features, including fifty-metre-high razor-sharp limestone spikes known as the **pinnacles**; there's also the largest limestone **cave system** in the world, much of which is still being explored. The two major hikes, to the pinnacles on Gunung Api and to the summit of **Gunung Mulu**, are daunting, but you're rewarded with stupendous views of the rainforest, stretching as far as Brunei.

Most of the world's limestone landscapes have been modified by glaciation within the last two million years and although Mulu is far older (the region formed over twenty million years ago) and has been weathered by a combination of rainfall, rivers and high temperatures, it has never been moulded by ice. The caves, which penetrate deep into the mountains, were created by running water and are very ancient: the oldest formed around five million years ago, the youngest during the last fifty thousand years. The surface water driving down the slopes of Mulu has eroded vast amounts of material, shaping the landscape outside, as well as carving cave passages within, dividing the great chunks of limestone into separate mountains.

Modern **explorers** have been coming for well over a century, starting in the 1850s with Spenser St John, who – although he didn't reach the summit of Gunung Mulu – wrote inspiringly about the region in his book *Life in the Forests of the Far East*. A more successful bid was launched in 1932 when the South Pole explorer Lord Shackleton got to the top during a research trip organized by Tom Harrisson, who would later become the curator of the Sarawak Museum. After his successful ascent Shackleton recorded that:

> *Although it was steep, the going during the first day or two was comparatively good, for the forest still consisted of big timber rising to a height of over one hundred feet. But it grew colder and soon we entered at around four thousand feet that extraordinary phenomenon, the moss forest. Sometimes we found ourselves plunging deeper and deeper, not knowing whether we were walking on the top of the wood or on the forest floor and occasionally having to cut tunnels through the squelching moss.*

More recently, a Royal Geographical Society trip in 1976, led by Robin Hanbury-Tenison, put forward a quite overwhelming case for designating the region a national

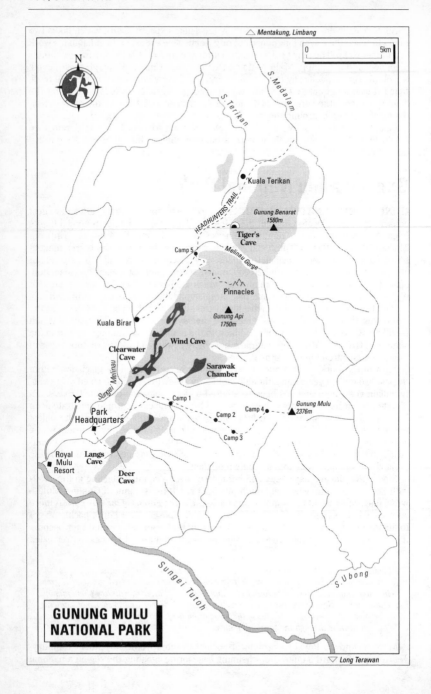

△ *Mentakung, Limbang*

0   5km

N

S. Terikan

S. Medalam

● Kuala Terikan

Gunung Benarat
1580m ▲

HEADHUNTERS TRAIL

Tiger's
Cave

Camp 5 ●

Melinau Gorge

Pinnacles

Gunung Api
1750m ▲

Kuala Birar ●

Wind Cave

Clearwater
Cave

Sarawak
Chamber

Sungei Melinau

Camp 1 ●

Camp 4 ●   *Gunung Mulu*
       2376m ▲

Park
Headquarters

Camp 2 ●

Camp 3 ●

Royal
Mulu ■
Resort

Langs
Cave

Deer
Cave

Sungei Tutoh

S. Ubong

GUNUNG MULU
NATIONAL PARK

▽ *Long Terawan*

TOURS IN THE PARK

The **minimum costs** per group for a guide and the various activities are as follows: for the **pinnacles** (2 nights/3 days) around $80; **Mulu summit** (3 nights/3 days) around $110; adventure caving $60–120 per trip; adventure caving in Sarawak Chamber $80; Deer Cave and Lang's Cave $20; and Clearwater Cave and Wind Cave $40. If you need a porter the charge is an extra $25 for one day and night. You've also got to shell out for **boat travel** (ranging from $85 for 1–4 people for the trip to Clearwater Cave, and up to $350 for 1–4 people for the journey to Long Birar, en route to the pinnacles), but once there it's possible to hitch rides along Sungei Melanau, the main thoroughfare through the park, connecting the airport with the headquarters, the caves and the main trails.

park, based on studies of the flora, fauna, caves, rivers and overall tourist potential. Over 250 kilometres of the caves have now been explored, yet experts believe this is only around thirty percent of the total. By 1985 the park was open for tourists, and it now attracts twenty thousand visitors a year. While there are still no roads into the area, Mulu is under threat from **developers**. The *Royal Mulu Resort* is now up and running, and there are plans to cut down acres of forest to build a golf course and an international airstrip.

Practicalities

You'll need three **permits** to visit Mulu: one from the Visitor Information Centre, one from the Resident's office, and a police clearance permit. If you're on a tour, the operator will obtain them on your behalf. Independent travellers should wait until they arrive at park headquarters to get them, since the offices in Miri (see p.397) may ask to see evidence that you are travelling with a tour operator before issuing the permits.

Among the **equipment** you'll need is a large plastic water bottle, comfortable walking shoes with a good tread, sun hat and swimming gear, a poncho/rain sheet, torch, mosquito repellent, headache pills, salt solution, ointment for bites, and a basic first aid kit. On the trails it's best to wear light clothing – shorts and T-shirts – rather than fully cover the body; this way, if the conditions are wet, it'll be easier to see any leeches that might be clinging to you. For the pinnacles, Mulu and Head-hunter's Trail, bring long trousers and long-sleeved shirts for the dusk insect assault, and for the occasional cool nights. A thin mat is also useful on the trails.

Getting there

Although you can arrive unannounced and book into the park hostel, most visitors come to Mulu as part of a **tour group** (see "Kuching", p.359; "Miri", p.401, and "Kuala Lumpur", p.119, for addresses). With a tour, all the incidental costs, including the guides which are mandatory for the treks and cave visits, are taken care of. But prices are high – around $600 per person, for example, for a three-night, four-day trip to climb the pinnacles and see the caves. Going independently, preferably in a group of two to four people, you should be able to undercut these costs, but allow yourself an extra day at the beginning of the visit to discuss options and prices with one of the guides based at the park headquarters or the nearby independent lodges (and try to avoid arriving at the weekend or on a public holiday when the park is at its busiest).

To **fly** to Mulu from Miri (daily at 8.40am, 10.10am, 11.50am & 3pm; around $70) or Marudi (daily at 9.20am; around $40) you must book ahead, as the tiny Twin-Otters carry only nineteen passengers each. The **airport** is 2km east of park headquarters, and longboats and minibuses meet the planes to take you to the headquarters or wherever you have arranged accommodation (see below).

LEAVING THE PARK

Return **flights** to Miri leave the park three times daily, and there are also two weekly flights to Marudi. For the return trip **by boat** you have to arrange with the park headquarters for the longboat to pick you up at 6am. This connects with the express or longboat at Long Terawan at 7.15am, which gets you to Marudi between 10.30am and 11am, in time to get the noon boat to Kuala Baram.

Reaching Mulu **by boat** from Miri involves four separate stages and takes all day. The first step is to take an early bus ($3) or taxi ($20) to Kuala Baram, at the mouth of Batang Baram, which takes thirty minutes. From there, take the hourly express boat upriver to Marudi ($12) – you'll need to catch the 7am or 8am to be in time to connect with the noon express to Long Terawan (around $20). When the river is low, this boat may only go as far as Long Panai-Kuala Apoh ($12), though you can then take a longboat ($10) from there to Long Terawan.

Soon after leaving Marudi the boat turns into the narrow Sungei Tutoh and the scenery changes from lines of timber yards to thick forest, with occasional settlements stretching down to the bank. It takes about three hours to reach Long Terawan where there'll be a **longboat** ($25–50 per person, depending on the number of passengers) to take you on the final two-hour trip, down Sungei Tutoh and into its tributary, Sungei Melanau, to the park. It's along the Melanau that the scenery really becomes breathtaking, the multiple greens of the forest deepening in the early-evening light, the peaks of Gunung Mulu and Api peeping through a whirl of mist.

Arrival, eating and accommodation

Upon arrival at the **park headquarters** you must sign in and show – or acquire – your permit and pay your park fees ($3 per person; $5 for a camera permit; $10 for a video camera). If you have arranged to sleep at one of the tour groups' lodges a few hundred metres upstream, then the longboat will take you there after a brief stop at the headquarters. The parks office (no phone) has got surprisingly little information on Mulu, but the **tour lodges** are better equipped. Some have books on the caves, and their guest diaries makes for fascinating reading.

Next to park headquarters you'll find various **places to stay**, ranging from a hostel with dorm beds ($10) and cooking facilities, through to chalets (②–③) of various shapes and sizes. The park's last word in comfort and sophistication, the *Royal Mulu Resort* (☎085/421122, fax 421088; ⑦) stands on the bank of the Melinau a five-minute boat ride downriver from park headquarters, and boast a sun deck, swimming pool and satellite TV. Its smart rooms are raised off the ground on wooden promenades. Further up the river, the lodges owned by the tour operators sometimes have spare rooms, where independent travellers can often stay cheaply (①); get back on the longboat and ask to be dropped off at *Endayang Inn* in Miri (☎085/438740; ②) which is one of the best. Staff there can also help with boat transport around the park. The *Melinau Canteen* (☎011/291641) has dorm beds for $10.

The air-con **café** (daily 8am–8pm) at the headquarters serves a range of meals, consisting of mostly rice, meat and vegetables. Next door is a small shop which sells basic provisions like rice, tins of fish and curry, and dried meat and fish. Across the bridge stretching from park headquarters to the far side of Sungei Melinau, the *Buyun Sipan Lounge* is an excellent venue, selling Western and Asian meals, breakfasts, packed lunches, beers and cold drinks; the *Royal Mulu Resort*'s coffee house also cooks up decent Western and Malaysian food, though at more inflated prices. Meals at the **lodges** are included in the tour price, though independent travellers can pay a fixed rate of around $12 for a three-course meal, and around $6 for breakfast – higher than the café prices but then the food is substantially better.

The park

Everyone's itinerary at Mulu includes a visit to the **show caves** – and, if you have the time and the money, either trekking to the **pinnacles**, scaling **Gunung Mulu** or undertaking some **adventure caving**. You will need three full days to trek to the pinnacles and the caves, and four or five to reach Mulu summit. If you really are a stickler for punishment (and unaffected by cost), then you can end your trip to Mulu by caving into the Sarawak Chamber – altogether, an action-packed and fairly unforgettable ten days' worth of activities. When planning your itinerary, consider leaving Mulu by the **Headhunter's Trail** to Limbang (see opposite), which is easily combined with a trip to the pinnacles.

The show caves

Only four of the 25 caves so far explored in Mulu are open to visitors – Deer Cave, Lang's Cave, Wind Cave and Clearwater Cave. As these so-called **show caves** are Mulu's most popular attractions, they can sometimes get quite crowded, and there's the occasional log-jam along the plankway to the two closest to park headquarters, Deer Cave and Lang's Cave. If you want to be sure of having a cave all to yourself, it's possible to arrange a foray out to one of Mulu's many other caves, though this sort of customized trip doesn't come cheap. Another more challenging means to escape the crowds is to work some adventure caving into your tour itinerary – the Sarawak Chamber, and the passages connecting Wind Cave to Clearwater Cave are just two of the park's more popular routes.

The most immediately impressive cave in the park is **Deer Cave**, the nearest to the headquarters, which is believed to contain the largest cave passage in the world. Once inhabited by deer, which used to shelter in its cavernous reaches, Deer Cave would have been known to the Berawan and Penan but was never used for burial purposes, unlike the smaller caves dotted around the park. From the headquarters, there's a well-marked three-kilometre plankway which runs through a peat swamp forest and passes an ancient Penan burial cave in which were found fragmented skulls, now in the Sarawak Museum. Once in Deer Cave itself, the statistics become unfathomable: the cave passage is over 2km long and 174m high, while up above, hundreds of thousands of bats live in the cave's nooks and crannies. You follow the path through the cave for an hour to an area where a large hole in the roof allows light to penetrate. Here, in the so-called **Garden of Eden**, scientists of the 1976 RGS expedition discovered luxuriant vegetation undisturbed for centuries; Robin Hanbury-Tenison noted that "even the fish were tame and gathered in shoals around a hand dipped in the water". It's an incredible spot: plants battle for the light, birds and insects celebrate the warm, bright air, giant ferns cluster around pebbles and families of grey leaf monkeys scuttle about unafraid. The best – and the busiest – time to visit Deer Cave is in the late afternoon: wait around the cave entrance at dusk and you'll see vast swarms of bats streaming out of the cave into the darkening skies, off in search of food. The entrance to **Lang's Cave** (named after the local guide who first found it) is close to that of Deer Cave. The smallest of the show caves, it still merits a look, if only to gaze at the waxen, weird and wonderful rock formations, especially the curtain stalactites and coral-like growths – helictites – that grip its curved walls.

Probing some 107km through Mulu's substratum, **Clearwater Cave**, thought to be the longest in Southeast Asia, is reached by a fifteen-minute longboat journey ($80) along Sungei Melinau from park headquarters. Longboats moor at a small jungle pool, after which the cave is named, at the base of the two-hundred-step climb to the cave mouth. Discovered in 1988, the cave tunnels here weave deep into the mountain. Ordinary visitors can only explore the small section close to the entrance, where lighting has been installed along a walkway leading 300m on to **Young Lady's Cave**, which ends abruptly in a fifty-metre-deep pothole. Deep inside the main body of the cave is subterranean **Clearwater River**, which flows through a five-kilometre passage reaching heights and widths of as much as 90m. En route to Clearwater Cave, most visitors halt at the **Wind Cave**. Fairly small in comparison with the other caves, it nevertheless contains a great variety of golden, contorted rock shapes, stalactites and stalagmites, which are best seen in the subtly illuminated King's Room. It's another five minutes from Wind Cave to Clearwater Cave, either by boat or via the walkway joining them; the alternative is to adventure cave between them, an exhausting and muddy five-hour trip involving lots of wading and swimming in icy Clearwater River. Wind Cave and Clearwater Cave can be incorporated with a trip to or from the pinnacles (see below).

The pinnacles

Five million years ago a constant splatter of raindrops dissolved Gunung Api's limestone and carved out the **pinnacles** – fifty metres high with the cutting edge of samurai swords – from a solid block of rock. The erosion is still going on and the entire region is pockmarked with deep shafts penetrating far into the heart of the mountain: one-third of Gunung Api has already been washed away and in perhaps another ten million years the whole of it will disappear. From 1200m up on Gunung Api, it's impossible not to be overawed by the sheer size and grandeur of the pinnacles, especially when the setting sun causes them to cast shadows far across the top of the trees growing from the soil caught in the crevices near their base.

From park headquarters the first part of the trip is by longboat upstream along Sungei Melinau; you may have to help pull the boat through the rapids if the water level is very low. After landing at Kuala Birar, there's a two-and-a-half-hour trek through lowland forest to reach **Camp 5**, close to the Melinau gorge, with nearby **Gunung Api** (1750m) and **Gunung Benarat** (1580m) casting long shadows across it in the fading afternoon light. Most pinnacle climbers spend two nights at Camp 5, where there's a large hut for sleeping and cooking facilities partially protected by a rocky overhang. A bridge straddles the river and on the other side a path disappears into the jungle; this is the first stage of the Head-hunter's Trail (see below).

The demanding **ascent** up the south face of Gunung Api to get a good view of the pinnacles takes around seven hours, there and back. The trail is honeycombed with holes and passages through which rainwater immediately disappears, and it's vital to bring a litre of water per person at the very least, as there's none on the trail. Carry little else with you – wear light clothing and a hat, and bring a snack – or you'll be too weighed down. Indeed, tour operators are being economical with the truth when they describe the climb as "moderate" – to the less than fully fit, climbing to the pinnacles can be extraordinarily taxing. Only a few metres from Camp 5 the track quickly leads to the face of the mountain where it disappears among tree roots and slippery limestone debris. After two hours' climb, including rests, a striking vista opens up: the rainforest stretches below as far as the eye can see and wispy clouds drift along your line of vision. The climb gets tougher as you scramble between the rocks and the high trees give way to **moss forest**, where pitcher plants feed on insects, and ants and squirrels dart in and out of the roots of trees.

The last thirty minutes of the climb is almost a sheer vertical manoeuvre. Ladders, thick pegs and ropes help you on this final ascent and just when your limbs are finally giving way, you arrive at the top of the **ridge** which overlooks the pinnacles. The ridge is itself a pinnacle, although sited across a ravine from the main cluster, and if you tap the rocks around you, they will reverberate because of the large holes in the limestone underneath. The vegetation is sparse, but includes the balsam plant with pale pink flowers, and pitcher plants full of nutrient-rich liquid. After taking in the stunning sight of the dozens of fifty-metre-high grey limestone shapes, jutting out from their perch in an unreachable hollow on the side of the mountain, it's time for the return slog, which takes three to four hours, longer when the route is particularly slippery.

Walks from Camp 5

Once back at the camp, most people rest, swim, eat and sleep, preferring to start the return trip to park headquarters the following day. But there are a few interesting options if you want to stay longer and explore the area. A path from the camp follows the river further upstream and ends below the **Melinau gorge**, where a vertical wall of rock rises 100m above the river, which vanishes into a crevice on the way back to its underground source. This is a beautiful spot although there is nowhere other than slippery rocks to rest before returning to Camp 5, a return trip of around two hours. Another short trail from Camp 5 begins on the other side of the rope bridge, where you take the path to the right to the base of **Gunung Benarat** and to the lower shaft of **Tiger's Cave**, a return trip of around three hours.

A third, much longer option from Camp 5 is to follow the so-called **Head-hunter's Trail**, a route supposedly traced by Kayan war parties in days gone by. Once across the bridge you turn left and walk along a wide trail passing a large rock, Batu Rikan (around 4km). From here the trail is clearly marked to **Kuala Terikan**, four hours (11km) away, a small Berawan settlement on the banks of Sungei Terikan, where you'll find basic hut accommodation. From here the trail continues for two hours to Sungei Medalam, along which you can take a longboat to the Iban longhouse at **Bala**. It's best to stay here and then continue next day down Sungei Medalam in a longboat into Sungei Limbang and on up to Limbang Town (see p.403), an all-day trip. This is a particularly good route for those wanting to get to Brunei from Mulu, as boats run frequently from Limbang to Bandar.

Gunung Mulu

The route to the summit of **Gunung Mulu** (2376m) was first discovered in the 1920s by Tama Nilong, a rhinoceros-hunter. Earlier explorers hadn't been able to find a way around the huge surrounding cliffs, but Nilong discovered the southwest ridge trail by following rhinoceros tracks, enabling Lord Shackleton in 1932 to become the first mountaineer to reach the summit. It's a more straightforward climb these days, though much of the route is very steep; any reasonably fit person can complete it.

The first stage is from park to **Camp 3**, an easy three-hour walk on a flat trail which crosses from the park's prevalent limestone to the sandstone terrain of Gunung Mulu en route. **Hornbills** (see box below) fly low over the jungle canopy and, if you watch the trail carefully, you may see wild boar and mouse deer tracks. The first night is at the open hut at Camp 3, which has cooking facilities. Day two comprises a hard, ten-hour, uphill slog; there are two resting places on the way where you have time to wash your tired limbs in small rock pools. From here onwards you're in a moss forest where great clumps of dripping vegetation cover the trees and rocks, small openings revealing lovely views of the park. The next part of the trail is Nilong's **southwest ridge**, a series of small hills negotiated by a narrow, twisting path. When the rain has been heavy, there are lots of little swamps to negotiate, one known as "Rhino's Lake" because it was here that the last rhinoceros in the area was shot in the 1950s. For some decades the rhino was believed to be extinct in Sarawak although what appear to be rhino tracks have recently been discovered on the slopes of Mulu. The hut at **Camp 4** is at 1800m. It can be cool here, so you'll need a sleeping bag.

Most climbers set off well before dawn for the hard ninety-minute trek to the **summit**, if possible timing their arrival to coincide with sunrise. After an hour's climbing – just before dawn – you pass an overgrown helicopter pad. Now the forest is waking up, the insect and bird chorus reverberating in the thin, high-altitude air. On this final

HORNBILLS

HORNBILLS

Hornbills are those bizarre, almost prehistoric-looking, inhabitants of tropical forests, whose presence (or absence) is an important ecological indicator of the health of the forest. You should have little difficulty in identifying the hornbill: they are large, black-and-white birds with disproportionately huge (often decurved) bills, topped with an ornamental casque – a piece of generally hollow horn attached to the upper mandible of the bill. The function of the casque is unknown, but it may play a role in attracting a mate and in courtship ceremonies. In addition to this, the birds have a long tail and broad wings which produce a loud "whooshing" sound as they glide and flap across the forest canopy.

Hornbills are heavily dependent upon large forest trees for nesting, using natural tree cavities as nest sites. The female seals herself into the cavity by plastering up the entrance to the nest hole with a combination of mud, tree bark and wood dust. This prevents snakes, civets, squirrels and other potential predators from raiding the nest. She spends up to three months here, totally dependent on the male bird to provide her and the offspring with a diet of fruit (mainly figs), insects and small forest animals by means of a narrow slit in the plaster wall. When the young bird is old enough to fly, the female breaks open the mud wall to emerge back into the forest. Given their nesting habits, it is essential that large, undisturbed, good-quality tracts of forest are retained in order to secure a future for hornbills. Sadly, populations in many parts of Asia have declined or been driven to the point of extinction by human encroachment, overhunting and deforestation.

Ten of the world's 46 species of hornbill are found in Malaysia, many of the species endangered or only present in small, isolated populations. Two of the most commonly seen species are the pied hornbill and the black hornbill. The **pied hornbill** can be identified by its white abdomen and tail, and white wing tips in flight. It's the smallest hornbill you're likely to see, reaching 75cm in length. It appears more tolerant to forest degradation than other species and during the non-breeding season gathers in noisy flocks which are generally heard well before they are seen. The **black hornbill** is only slightly larger and black, save for the white tips to the outer tail feathers. Some individuals also show a white patch behind the eye. Two of the larger species of hornbill found in Malaysia are the **helmeted hornbill** and the **rhinoceros hornbill**. Both of these are over 120cm in length, mainly black, with white tails and bellies. The rhinoceros hornbill has a bright orange rhino horn-shaped casque (hence the name), whereas the helmeted hornbill has a bright red head, neck and helmet-shaped casque. The call of the helmeted is a remarkable series of "took" notes which start off slowly and then accelerate to reach a ringing crescendo of cackles.

Other than Gunung Mulu National Park, good places to spot the birds **elsewhere in Malaysia** are Taman Negara, Fraser's Hill, Langkawi, Sabah's Danum Valley, and Mount Kinabalu National Park.

stretch there are big clumps of pitcher plants, though it's easy to miss them as by this point you are hauling yourself up by ropes onto the cold, windswept, craggy peak. From here, the view is exhilarating, looking down on Gunung Api and, on a clear day, far across the forest to Brunei Bay. Below Sungei Melanau can just be made out, a pencil-thin wavy light-brown line, bisecting the deep-green density of the forest carpet.

It's just possible to do the whole **return trip** from the summit to park headquarters in one day. This takes around twelve hours and cuts out the last night at Camp 4. The red-and-white marks on the trees marking the trail are easy to see, so you shouldn't lose your way in fading light.

The Kelabit Highlands

One hundred kilometres southeast of Mulu and effectively accessible only by air, the long, high plateau of the **Kelabit Highlands** runs along the border with Kalimantan.

The home of the Kelabit people for hundreds of years, Western explorers had no idea of the existence of this self-sufficient mountain community until the turn of this century, when Brooke officials made a few brief visits. But the Highlands were (literally) not put on the map until World War II, when British and Australian commandos, led by Major Tom Harrisson, used a number of Kelabit settlements as bases for waging a guerrilla war against the occupying Japanese forces. After parachuting into the forest, Harrisson and his team were taken to the largest longhouse in the area, in the village of **Bario**, to meet the chief. With his help Harrisson set out to contact the region's other ethnic groups, and within twelve months was in a position to convince Allied Command in Manila that the tribes were thirsty for retaliation.

Before Harrisson's men built the airstrip at Bario, trekking over the inhospitable terrain was the only way to get there – it took two weeks from Marudi to the west, which, according to early accounts, required hacking through moss forests and circumnavigating sharp limestone hills and savage gorges. It was another seven days through similar conditions to the furthest navigable point on Batang Baram, **Lio Matoh**, just off the edge of the plateau. After the war, missionaries arrived and converted the animist Kelabit to Christianity, with the consequence that many of their traditions, like burial rituals and the promiscuous parties called *iraus* (where Chinese jars full of rice wine were consumed) disappeared. What's more, the magnificent Kelabit **megaliths** – associated with these traditions – were soon swallowed by the jungle: dolmens, urns, rock carvings of human faces and ossuaries containing bones and skulls used in funereal processes, were all lost to the elements. Carvings of human faces celebrated feats of valour, like a

successful head-hunting expedition, and birds were also popular images – a motif that still survives in the bead- and craftwork of neighbouring ethnic groups. Now the three most populous Kelabit settlements – Bario, Long Lellang to the southwest and Ba Kelalan to the north – have a daily air service in tiny 21-seater Twin-Otter planes, giving the highland people the chance of daily contact with the world beyond, and curious tourists the opportunity to visit them with relative ease.

For all the recent contact, the highlands remain a gloriously unspoiled region, with its dazzlingly vivid flora, abundant game and a cool refreshing climate. Not surprisingly, these factors have made this a popular target for walkers, attracted by jungle **treks** and meetings with friendly local people, many of whom live in sturdy **longhouses** surrounded by their livestock, fruit trees and wet paddy fields. Visiting the longhouses is an unmissable part of any trip to the highlands and the Kelabit aren't as concerned as the Iban or Kayan with formality. Once you've attracted the attention of an adult longhouse dweller, you'll inevitably be invited in, soon after which the chief will arrive and take charge, urging you to eat with his family and, probably, insisting that you stay in his rooms. But if you've already made friends with another family, no harm is done by turning the chief down and staying with them. Your arrival will usually be an excuse for a mini-party, with much laughing, joking and cross-cultural leg-pulling. Swimming in the river below the longhouse is a delight, and if a hunter offers to take you on a night trek – go.

A number of excellent **tours**, which include trekking and visits to longhouses, are run by companies based in Miri, whose itineraries range from four-day tours to Bario, including short walks to Pa Umor and Pa Berang, to more strenuous five-day visits to longhouses around Ramudu, Pa Dalih and Long Dano. There's also an adventurous trip which follows Penan forest trails through Long Ugong, Long Semadoh and Long Uping. All these tours work out at around $170 per night for two people.

Bario

The central settlement of **BARIO** is approximately 15km west of the border with Indonesian Kalimantan, and a few days' hard hike from Long Lellang to the south or Ba Kelalan to the north. It's a small but widely dispersed community, set among the plateau's rolling hills, surrounded by rice fields and comprising six distinct settlements – Ullong Pallang, Bario Assal, Padang Pasir, Arur Dalan, Pa Ramapuh and Pa Derong. Although Bario's new airfield is now 2km away to the east, **Padang Pasir**, the site of the former landing strip (now a buffalo pasture), is still the closest the place gets to a "centre", its small cluster of buildings yielding a lodging house, a handful of dwellings and a new block of shops. With no telephones and next to no motorized vehicles, the pace of life could hardly be slower, with only arriving planes disturbing the tranquillity.

Practicalities

The daily **flights** from Miri and Marudi bring in pieces of machinery, food, household and agricultural utensils as well as visitors. The planes don't land when the weather's bad so you may well get stuck in Bario – bring enough funds, as there are no banks. Trying to get on the flight from Miri in the first place can be hard as Bario people tend to book ahead and the flights fill up quickly: ask to be put on the reserve list and call back the day before you want to fly. It's best to avoid Friday and Saturday, when Kelabit in Miri go home for the weekend.

Unless you are invited to stay in one of its Kelabit longhouses, Bario only has two **places to stay**. One hundred metres north of the old airfield is *Tarawe's*, a relaxed lodging house (①) run by John Tarawe and Englishwoman Karen Hedderman. It has four rooms with three beds in each, and mats for occasions when large groups arrive. Inexpensive, hearty meals are available here, including wild boar, ferns in garlic, rice and other seasonal dishes (around $8), and breakfasts of noodles and eggs (around $5). Run by Munney Bala, the *Bario De Plateau Lodge* (①; walk for ten minutes from the new airport, and turn right at the T-junction whose left turn leads into Padang Pasir) is a similar set-up, though the downside of its idyllic rural location is that it's a little isolated. The only other place to stay, *Bario Lodging House*, is no longer open to the general public, as the owners don't need to look any further than their own extended family to fill the two spare rooms.

There are two **cafés** in Padang Pasir which sell soft drinks, noodles, cakes and rice dishes in the daytime, and there's an MAS office (daily 10am–noon) just above *Tarawe's*. Several **guides** operate out of Bario, and it's worth hiring one if you want to explore the highlands without fear of getting lost. Shep Bala, of Ullong Pallang, is one; others can be contacted by enquiring at *Terawe's*. You should pay around $60 a day for a guide, but bear in mind that if you take the guide part of the way along a one-way trip, you'll be expected to pay for his return to Bario. Should you reach a longhouse unaided, you can always hire a local guide to highlight its more localized attractions – suggestions below.

Day-trips from Bario

A good way to acclimatize to the high-altitude conditions is to embark on short treks from Bario – the walk to the longhouse at Pa Umor is especially rewarding. Follow the track past *Tarawe's* for thirty minutes, then turn down a narrow path to the right, and after about an hour you'll reach **Pa Umor**, a modern longhouse, where someone's bound to invite you in. From Pa Umor the path leads past the fork to the Kalimantan frontier post at Lembudud (six hours away) and over a precarious bridge, past remnants of an earlier longhouse, into a lovely copse, from where there are fine views of the lush highlands. Watch out for a right fork along a buffalo track, which leads into a thick, aromatic forest. At the end of this path is one of only two functioning **salt licks** on the highlands. Extracting fine grey salt from the muddy water at the bottom of the small well is a traditional Kelabit industry which goes back centuries. The salt is then cooked and dried, and heaved back on the narrow trail to the longhouses.

Two other longhouses, **Pa Ukat** and **Pa Lungan**, lie further along the main track. Ignore the right turn to Pa Umor and keep walking; it takes around forty minutes to get to Pa Ukat, and Pa Lungan is three hours further along the winding road. Both are pleasant, easy walks, but get in an early start if you're heading to the latter as there's little shade.

A twenty-minute stroll west of Bario along the road adjacent to the airstrip, leads to one of the larger longhouses in the area, hilltop **Ullong Pallang**. The residents' grandparents decamped here from Pa Main (see below) during the confrontation.

South of Bario

To get to the thriving Kelabit longhouses of **Ramudu**, **Pa Dalih** and **Long Dano**, you'll have to hike through secondary forest. The longhouses, which provide accommodation, can be linked up in the **Bario Loop**, a demanding four- or five-day trek that starts and finishes on the old airstrip. From Ramudu, it's possible to continue for the gruelling six- to eight-day trip south, on the **Harrisson trail** to the Baram river settlement of **Lio Matoh**.

The Bario loop

Tracing the **Bario Loop** is the perfect way to experience the natural beauty and see the attractive longhouses of the Kelabit Highlands. The loop takes you in a vague oval through the settlements of Kampung Baru, Long Dano, Pa Dalih, Ramudu and Pa

Berang – the clockwise journey described below gets the longest leg out of the way while you're still fresh, but of course you can go anti-clockwise. All walkers stop over in Long Dano, Ramudu and Pa Berang, and many also spend a fourth night at Pa Dalih. Some sections of the journey (Long Dano to Pa Dalit, for instance) are easier to follow than others, and longhouse residents do occasionally report seeing unaccompanied tourists popping out of the jungle. Nevertheless it's wise to hire a guide for the trip: the cost shouldn't be more than $400, including a $10–20 courtesy charge at each longhouse to cover food and lodging. See previous page for tips on hiring a guide in Bario. Comfortable shoes with a good grip are essential, as are waterproofs and a light pack.

The first leg is the nine-hour slog from Bario to Long Dano. The initial route is across the airfield and along a wide, stream-side track to the longhouse settlement of **Kampung Baru**, which appears some 45 minutes later. One kilometre beyond Kampung Baru, you follow a path to the left over a wobbly steel-and-bamboo bridge, which leads onto a narrow, undulating buffalo path. If it's been raining, mud will have collected in troughs along the route. The path weaves up and down the sides of the hills and occasionally drops into the mud pools which provide bathing holes for the buffalo, the most valuable livestock of the Kelabit. There are several resting places en route; you'll see Kelabit families carrying produce back and forth to Bario, including generators and rolls of wire to bring electricity to isolated longhouses. Four or five hours out of Kampung Baru, you'll pass through the area where the longhouse of **Pa Main** used to stand, until its residents relocated to the Bario settlements of Pa Ramapuh and Ullong Pallang during the uncertain times of the Konfrontasi. Your guide should be able to lead you to the hillside site of the British Army outpost that oversaw Pa Main, where empty shell canisters and other such detritus remain to this day.

From here, another three hours' walking brings you to the Kelabit longhouse community of **Long Dano**, which nestles in fields beside a small brook, with the forest crowding in around. Visitors spend most of their time on the communal bamboo verandah, from where you can see tiny apartments, one for each family. Below the verandah are storerooms for the stocks of rice, other grains and fried fish. A Christian community, Long Dano incorporates a Methodist church and even a tiny shop, and is surrounded by tended fields. The river nearby is full of fish and hunting is abundant. Jobs like rice harvesting, mat-making and textile-weaving are dictated by the time of year – the rice cycle starts in August with the clearing and planting of the fields, and the crop is cultivated in February. After the hard labour required in processing the rice, the Kelabit women turn their attention to crafts and the men to hunting or fishing, going on trips to other longhouses or to big towns like Miri and Marudi. Some Dano Kelabit leave to work in Miri or in the logging industry, but most return for the **iraus**, which centre on massive feasts of wild boar, crackers, rice and traditional games. The conversion to Christianity since the war has meant that rice wine has been banned – there are copious jugs of lemonade and *milo* instead. If you wish to learn more about the *iraus*, or about any of the other facets of Kelabit cultural life, then English-speaking Elvis is the man to contact. In any case, his mother cooks a mean batch of *bus keran*, or "jackfruit chewing gum".

The track from Long Dano to Pa Dalih is in very good nick, and the journey takes just two hours. It's tempting to push on to Ramudu, but since this next leg is arguably the most exacting of the loop, you might want to catch your breath before the rigours of the five-hour hike. Comprising three longhouses, a school and a football field, **Pa Dalih** is a springboard to several highland adventures, among them the half-day hike to see the village's huge stone drums, once used as caskets for the dead. You could also try the two-day, one-night round-trip to **Pa Diit waterfall**, and the full-on trek east to

Long Layu and **Lembudud**, over the Kalimantan border. If you need local expertise in planning any of these trips, the man to contact in Pa Dalih is called Andreas.

The journey from Pa Dalih to Ramudu kicks off by skirting Pa Dalih's paddy fields. Shortly after you emerge into buffalo pasture, where to your left is a large rock in whose carved niches the remains of the village's dead were once left in jars; one collapsed example is still apparent. Four or five hours of steep ups and downs ensue, before you reach ten-door **Ramudu**, set behind groves of pineapple trees and sugar cane, vegetable gardens and a grassy airstrip. The people of Ramudu are famed for their skilfully woven rattan back baskets and they may have a surplus of stock which you can bargain for. They also make deliciously more-ish *gula tapur*, or sugar cane candy. Paran Belaan is the man to speak to if you intend to push south to Long Beruang and beyond (see below), though you won't need a guide to see the **carved boulder** ten minutes out of the village on the Pa Dalih side, with intriguing representations of a face, a buffalo and a human figure. Pa Berang is seven and a half hours away, along a path that sets off past Ramudu's rice mill shed and across a hanging bridge spanning Sungei Kelapang. The trail follows the Kelapang for an hour, then plunges into the forest for several hours of crisscrossing Batang River, finally reaching Pa Berang after a last couple of hours' splashing through swampland.

Pa Berang is home to eight Penan families, who live in somewhat grottier conditions than those enjoyed by the residents of the loop's other longhouses. Food isn't forthcoming here, so you'll need to have brought rice and tinned food with you from Bario, which you'll be able to prepare in the kitchen of the chief, Tama Simun. Tama doubles as village pastor, and his banging on a bamboo chime each morning at 5am, to call the village together for some vociferous hymn-singing, provides trekkers with a jarring morning call. Since Tama can't speak any English, you'll need to speak to Balang Ibun if you need any information, or want to push on to Long Lellang (see below). Baths are taken in the river.

The last section of the loop, which takes between four and five hours, threads around a few gentle slopes and crosses a half-sunk bridge over Sungei Drapur, before coming to a lengthy stretch of swamp forest that becomes a quagmire in the rainy season. The going is made fractionally easier by the lengths of bamboo that locals have laid along portions of the path, but you'll still be glad to surface in the pastures that border on Bario's old runway.

Further south: Lio Matoh and Long Lellang

From Ramudu, a southerly trail runs right the way down to the head of Batang Baram, at **Lio Matoh**. The trail follows the watershed of Sungei Kelapang, taking a full day to reach the jungle shelter at **Long Okan**, which hasn't any facilities, so you'll need a light blanket for sleeping. The next day it's four more hours along a hard, hilly trail to **Long Beruang**, a large Penan settlement, whose inhabitants are semi-nomadic, preferring sago-collecting and hunting to the settled rice-growing of the Kelabit. Have a few little gifts, like food or tobacco, at hand.

A day's walk on from Long Beruang gets you to the longhouse at **Long Banga**, from where it's a two-hour walk downhill off the plateau to the timber camp and longhouse at Lio Matoh, the most easterly settlement on Batang Baram. For the Kelabit especially, this seems like a thriving, busy community in contrast with the jungle longhouses up the track. From Lio Matoh, small longboats travel downriver daily – it's a question of asking around and negotiating a price. You should pay no more than $120 to Marudi if you are sharing a boat, but if you can't find other people to travel with, it will cost about $800 for the three-day journey. If there's no alternative, rent a boat to the next busy point, Long Palai, which is less than a day away, and try either to join a boat there or backtrack to Long Banga for a flight to Marudi. There is a trail that leads from Long Peluan westwards to **Long Lellang**, though it's quicker to go via Pa Berang.

North to Pa Kelalan via Pa Lungan

The last of the main trails from Bario is the four-day trail due north through the villages of Pa Lungan and Pa Rupai to the large Kelabit village of **Ba Kelalan** which has an airstrip, from where it's possible to travel overland to Lawas (see p.404). You can make side trips to climb **Batu Lawi** (2039m) or **Gunung Murud** (2438m), the twin peaks of the former making it the most impressive mountain in the area. The Kelabit traditionally believed Batu Lawi had an evil spirit and so never went near it, and although animist beliefs don't play much part in Kelabit life these days, climbers will still have difficulty finding a local prepared to act as a guide to Lawi. The lower peak can be climbed without equipment, but the other sheer-sided peak requires proper gear – it was only scaled for the first time in 1986. Gunung Murud is the highest mountain in Sarawak, an extremely hard climb and only accessible to highly experienced mountaineers.

Bario to Pa Kelalan via Pa Lungan

The time required for this difficult trek depends on fitness and finances. Although a Kelabit could pull it off in ten hours, it's best to allow three days – this is some of the richest, thickest forest in Borneo.

The route from Bario heads past the longhouse at Pa Ukat (see "Day-trips from Bario" on p.417): watch out for the **trailside boulder** a few kilometres along the trail, on which human faces are carved, the only known example of funerary art remaining in the highlands. After about eight hours you reach **Pa Lungan**, which consists of detached family units around a large rectangular field for pigs and buffalo. Visitors stay in the longhouse, usually in the chief's quarters.

On the second day, it takes around four hours to get to the abandoned village of **Long Rapung**. On the way, before the forest closes in around you, look out for Gunung Murud on your left, if it's not shrouded in mist. A small shelter still exists at Long Rapung, which is nothing more than just an intersection of paths and a place to rest – you could spend the night here, allowing for a less strenuous third day. Otherwise, press on to **Pa Rupai**, four to five hours away on a hard narrow trail infamous for its leeches. A long downward slope passes through irrigated rice fields to the village. You're now in Kalimantan, although there are no signs to prove it.

It takes two more hours before the village of **Long Medan** comes into sight; here you can rent a motorcycle to the town of Long Nawang in Kalimantan and fly onto Tarakan (provided you have a visa). The last stage of the trail to Ba Kelalan curves out of Long Medang and climbs a short, steep hill – this point marks the frontier with Kalimantan. You then walk alongside rice fields to the army outpost outside Ba Kelalan where you need to show your passport.

Ba Kelanan is smaller and more compact than Bario, comprised of single dwellings, a large longhouse and a few shops selling basic provisions. As in Bario, the airport is right in the centre of town, with the main street running parallel. There's a small **hotel**, the *Green Valley Inn* (①) and two coffee shops. **Flights** leave mid-morning to Lawas or else you can trek north to Buduk Aru for two hours, where a Land Rover travels the logging road, taking four dusty (or mud-splattered) hours to reach Lawas. Along much of the road the signs of deforestation are only too apparent: wide gashes in the forest open out the scenery and piles of timber await collection.

travel details

Buses

Batu Niah to: Bintulu (4 daily; 2–3hr); Miri (4 daily; 2–3hr).

Bintulu to: Batu Niah (5 daily; 2–3hr); Sarikei (3 daily; 4hr); Sibu (4 daily; 4hr).

Kuching to: Bako (12 daily; 1hr); Damai beach (every 40min; 1hr); Lundu (4 daily; 2hr); Sarikei (3 daily; 5–6hr); Serian (4 daily; 1hr); Semanggoh (4 daily; 1hr); Sri Aman (3 daily; 3hr); Tebedu (1 daily; 10hr).

Miri to: Batu Niah (4 daily; 2–3hr); Bintulu (4 daily; 4hr); Kuala Baram (every 15min; 45min); Kuala Belait (6 daily; 3hr); Lambir Hills (every 30min; 40min).

Sarikei to: Bintulu (4 daily; 4hr); Kuching (3 daily; 5–6hr).

Sibu to: Bintulu (4 daily; 4hr).

Boats

Belaga to: Kapit (2 daily, at same time; 4hr).

Bintulu to: Tubau (5 daily; 2–3hr).

Kapit to: Belaga (2 daily; 4–5hr); Sungei Gaat (1 daily; 2hr); Mujong (1 daily; 2hr); Nanga Baleh (2 daily; 4hr).

Kuala Baram to: Marudi (7 daily; 3hr)

Kuching to: Sarikei (2 daily; 2–3hr); Sibu (2 weekly; 14hr).

Long Lama to: Marudi (3 daily; 3hr).

Marudi to: Kuala Baram (7 daily; 2–3hr); Lapok (1 daily; 2hr); Long Lama (3 daily; 3hr).

Sarikei to: Kuching (2 daily; 2–3hr); Sibu (2 daily; 1–2hr); Sibu (8 daily; 1–2hr).

Sibu to: Kapit (9 daily; 3–4hr); Kuching (2 weekly; 14hr).

Tubau to: Bintulu (5 daily; 2hr).

Planes

Bandar Seri Begawan (Brunei) to: Kuching (3 weekly; 1hr 10min).

Bario to: Marudi (1 daily; 50min); to Miri (1 daily; 1hr 15min).

Bintulu to: Kuching (9 daily; 1hr); Miri (4 daily; 35min); Sibu (7 daily; 1hr).

Johor Bahru to: Kuching (4 daily; 1hr 20min).

Kapit to: Sibu (2 weekly; 40min).

Kota Kinabalu to: Kuching (5 daily; 2hr 20min); Miri (5 daily; 40min).

Kuala Lumpur to: Kuching (9 daily; 1hr 40min).

Kuantan to: Kuching (1 weekly; 1hr 20min).

Kuching to: Bandar (3 weekly; 1hr 10min); Bintulu (9 daily; 1hr); Johor Bahru (4 daily; 1hr 20min); Kota Kinabalu (5 daily; 2hr 20min); Kuala Lumpur (9 daily; 1hr 40min); Kuantan (1 weekly; 1hr 20min); Miri (13 daily; 1hr); Pontianak (3 weekly; 1hr); Sibu (11 daily; 40min) Singapore (3 daily; 1hr 20min).

Marudi to: Bario (1 daily; 50min); Miri (4 daily; 20min).

Miri to: Bario (1 daily; 1hr 15min); Bintulu (4 daily; 35min); Kapit (2 weekly; 40min); Kota Kinabalu (5 daily; 40min); Kuching (8 daily; 1hr); Lawas (4 daily; 45min); Limbang (7 daily; 45min); Marudi (4 daily; 20min); Sibu (7 daily; 1hr).

Pontianak to: Kuching (3 weekly; 1hr).

Sibu to: Bintulu (6 daily; 35min); Kuching (11 daily; 40min); Miri (7 daily; 1hr).

Singapore to: Kuching (3 daily; 1hr 20min).

CHAPTER SEVEN

SABAH

Sabah, bordering Sarawak on the northwestern flank of Borneo, boasts an ethnic and geographical make-up every bit as idiosyncratic as its neighbour's. Until European powers began to gain a foothold here in the last century, the northern tip of this remote landmass was inhabited by tribal peoples who had only minimal contact with the outside world, so that their costumes, traditions and languages were quite unique to the region. Although mention of Borneo typically evokes images of head-hunters and impenetrable jungle, the state of Sabah, part of the Malaysian Federation since its foundation in 1963, has undergone rapid, if patchy modernization. The **logging** industry, which reached its destructive peak in the 1970s and 1980s, has raped vast portions of the natural forest cover; World War II bombs and hurried urban redevelopment have conspired to produce a capital city and a chain of towns almost devoid of architectural worth; while a lack of funding from Kuala Lumpur has left the state's infrastructure and economy in a state of disrepair.

It's a bleak picture, but one which neglects the natural riches on parade in a fertile region, whose name – according to some sources – means "the land below the wind", its 72,500 square kilometres falling just below the typhoon belt. Sabah encompasses various **terrains** from swampy, mangrove-tangled coastal areas, through the dazzling greens of paddy fields and rainforests to the dizzy heights of the Crocker Mountain Range – home to the highest mountain peak between the Himalayas and New Guinea. These surroundings maintain an astounding range of indigenous **wildlife**, from forest-dwelling proboscis monkeys, orang-utans, bearded pigs and hornbills, to the turtles who swim ashore to lay their eggs on Sabah's east coast.

Among Sabah's **ethnic** groups, more than eighty dialects are spoken by over thirty races, though with traditional costumes increasingly losing out to T-shirts and shorts, it would take an anthropologist to distinguish one tribe from another. The peoples of the Kadazan/Dusun tribes constitute the largest indigenous racial group, along with the Murut of the southwest, and Sabah's so-called "sea gypsies", the Bajau. More recently, Sabah has seen a huge influx of Filipino and Indonesian immigrants, particularly on the east coast. The best time to witness the music, dance, food and handicrafts of tribal Sabah is during the *Sabah Fest* every May, a week-long celebration that's the climax of *Pesta Kaamatan*, the Kadazan/Dusun harvest festival. Otherwise, try to visit one of the **tamus**, or market fairs, held (usually weekly) in towns and villages across the state. The *tamu* has long been an important social focal point of tribal life in Sabah, and each draws crowds of people from the surrounding region, who come to catch up with local goings-on as much as to buy and sell produce.

Its relative inaccessibility and expense make Sabah a place to visit with a specific purpose in mind, the classic reason being to climb 4101-metre Mount Kinabalu in the northwest. Most trips start in the friendly capital **Kota Kinabalu**, from where Sabah's main road heads south to **Beaufort**, beyond which the state's only railway takes advantage of the swathe cut through the Crocker Mountain Range by the broad Sungei Padas to head into the rural **interior**. Here, southeast of the towns of **Tenom** and **Keningau** is Murut territory, isolated enough to allow a taste of the adventures that travelling in Sabah once entailed; while a short way north, Kadazan/Dusuns tend the patchwork of paddy fields that quilts **Tambunan Plain**.

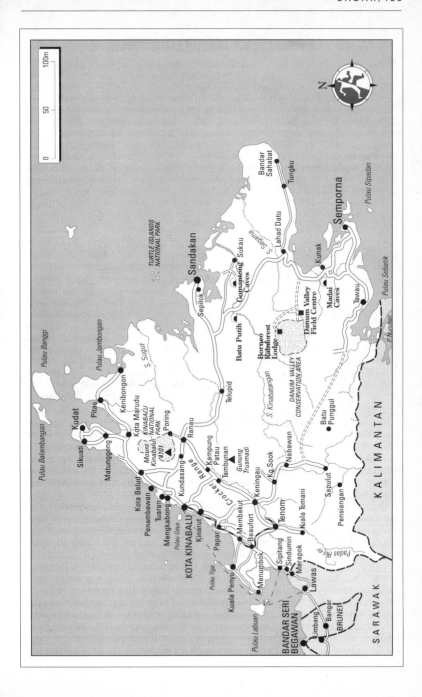

SABAH PRACTICALITIES

Sabah is just north of the equator which means its **climate** is hot and humid. Temperatures can reach 33°C, but an average of 27–28°C throughout the year is more typical. The **wet season** lasts from November until February, but you'll experience rain at most times of the year – especially if you're in the rainforest or up Mount Kinabalu. Perhaps a more important consideration is what you can afford to do when you get there. Sabah is 600km and a pricey air ticket away from the mainland, while several of its highlights will cut large chunks out of your **budget**, so it's worth doing some sums before committing yourself.

Getting there
Kota Kinabalu (KK) is almost certain to be your first port of call in Sabah. MAS flies from **Kuala Lumpur** (at least 11 daily; from $437) and from **Johor Bahru** (5 daily; $347) – only one flight a day out of JB is direct. There are also departures out of **Kuching** (5 daily; around $230), with direct flights every day except Tuesday and Friday. From the Bruneian capital **Bandar Seri Begawan**, services are with Royal Brunei (3 weekly; $117). From **Manila**, Philippine Airlines (3 weekly) tickets to KK are undercut by MAS (3 weekly; $450). A Cathay Pacific subsidiary, Dragon Air, makes the trip from **Hong Kong** to KK (3 weekly; $940). Finally, from Tarakan in **Kalimantan**, there are Bouraq (3 weekly; $185) and MAS (2 weekly; $210) flights to Tawau.

Daily **boats** from **Brunei** (p.486), and from **Lawas** and **Limbang** in northern Sarawak, run to Pulau Labuan, from where there are regular connections with KK. There's a ferry from northeastern **Kalimantan** to Tawau (see p.473) once or twice a week. The only **overland route** into Sabah is from Lawas which is a short bus ride away from the border at Merapok; see p.404 for more.

Getting around
Unless you rent your own transport in KK (see p.435), or can afford to take internal flights, you'll rely almost exclusively upon **buses**, **minibuses** and **landcruisers** for getting around. Though the going can get rather bumpy if you head south of Sandakan, the state's roads have been much improved in recent years. A sealed road now stretches

North of Kota Kinabalu, the main road strays into Bajau country, before turning eastwards through lowland dipterocarp forest and the awesome granite shelves of **Mount Kinabalu**. The mountain is a joy, its challenging but manageable slopes seemingly tailor-made for amateur climbers; from the jagged summit there are staggering views of Sabah's west coast, through the clouds below. Further north are the beaches and coconut groves of **Kudat**, where the few remaining **longhouses** of the Rungus tribe can be visited.

The towns of the eastern seaboard are unlikely to win you over. Impoverished and still troubled by pirates, they are collectively known as Sabah's "wild east". Nevertheless, most people go as far as **Sandakan**, a busy community built with timber money, and base for visiting the **Turtle Islands Park**. Indeed, if wildlife is your main reason for coming to Sabah, you'll doubtless be keen to continue around the east coast since more close-ups are possible at **Sepilok Orang-utan Rehabilitation Centre**, as well as along the lower reaches of **Sungei Kinabatangan**, which support groups of proboscis monkeys. Further south, the **Danum Valley Conservation Area** has embarked on a programme of eco-tourism intended to let the surrounding virgin rainforest pay its way, its *Borneo Rainforest Lodge* offering visitors the chance to get to grips with nature. Of more specialized interest is Sabah's only oceanic island, **Pulau Sipadan**, just off Semporna on the southeastern coast. It's touted as one of the world's top diving havens, though sky-high prices make it a destination for serious divers only.

from Beaufort around to Tawau, from where logging roads complete the loop. Minibuses are by far the most common form of public transport, following both local and long-distance routes, always at breakneck speed. Angered by the recklessness of minibus drivers, and in particular by their tendency to slow to a halt without warning when flagged down, other road users are lobbying to have these vehicles outlawed, but for the moment they remain a necessary evil. Roomier, though much slower buses operate locally in Kota Kinabalu, Sandakan and Tawau, as well as making scheduled, early-morning trips across the state. Outsize jeeps, called landcruisers, are fastest of all, though these are more expensive. Sabah is crisscrossed by a good **plane** network, with daily flights between Kota Kinabalu, Sandakan and Tawau. There's no equivalent in Sabah to Sarawak's express boats, and you'll have to rent your own **boat** if you're intent on a river trip – usually a substantial outlay.

Accommodation

Accommodation in Sabah generally means locally run Chinese hotels, ranging from seedy lodging houses that double as brothels to charming enough mid-range establishments. That said, the last few years have seen a perceptible rise in the number of beach and jungle resorts popping up around the state. **Hostels** catering specifically for budget travellers are few and far between – dormitory beds are available only in Kota Kinabalu, Sandakan and Mount Kinabalu Park. There's less of a **longhouse** scene in Sabah than there is in Sarawak, though it's quite feasible to stay overnight in one of the longhouses around Sapulut, or on the Kudat Peninsula. If you do, the etiquette is the same as in Sarawak – see p.370 for all the details.

Throughout the Malaysia chapters we've used the following **price codes** to denote the cheapest available room for two people. Single occupancy should cost less than double, though this is not always the case. Some guesthouses provide dormitory beds, for which the dollar price is given.

① $20 and under	④ $61–80	⑦ $161–240
② $21–40	⑤ $81–100	⑧ $241–400
③ $41–60	⑥ $101–160	⑨ $401 and above

A little history

Little is known of Sabah's **early history**, though archeological finds in limestone caves in the east indicate that the northern tip of Borneo has been inhabited for well over ten thousand years. Chinese merchants were trading with local settlements by 700 AD, and by the fourteenth century, the tract of land now known as Sabah came under the sway of the sultans of Brunei and Sulu, though its isolated communities of hunter-gatherers would have been generally unaware of this fact. In 1521, Europe's superpowers first arrived, when the ships of the Portuguese navigator Ferdinand Magellan stopped off at Brunei and later sailed northwards. But it was to be almost 250 years before any significant development occurred, when – in 1763 – one Captain Cowley established a short-lived trading post on Pulau Balambangan, an island north of Kudat, on behalf of the British East India Company. Further colonial involvement came in 1846, when Pulau Labuan (at the mouth of Brunei Bay) was ceded to the British by the Sultan of Brunei. In 1878 the Austrian, **Baron von Overbeck** – with the financial backing of British businessman Alfred Dent – agreed to pay the Sultan an annuity of $15,000 to cede northern Borneo to him. Shortly afterwards a further annual payment of $5000 was negotiated with the Sultan of Sulu, who also laid claim to the region. Von Overbeck hastened to England to finalize matters and in 1881 the **British North Borneo Chartered Company** was registered, with full sovereignty over northern Borneo. Shortly afterwards, von Overbeck sold his shares to Dent.

With the company up and running, the first steps were taken towards making the territory pay its way: rubber, tobacco and, after 1885, timber, were commercially harvested. By 1905 a **railway** linked Jesselton (later called Kota Kinabalu) on the coast, with the resource-rich interior. When the company introduced taxes the locals were understandably ill pleased and native resistance followed – **Mat Salleh**, the son of a Bajau chief, and his followers sacked the company's settlement on Pulau Gaya in 1897. Another uprising, in **Rundum** in 1915, resulted in the slaughter of hundreds of Murut tribespeople by British forces.

No other major disturbances troubled the Chartered Company until New Year's Day, 1942, when the Japanese Imperial forces invaded Pulau Labuan. Less than three weeks later Sandakan fell, and over two years of occupation followed, before the Japanese surrendered on September 9, 1945. The years of **World War II** were devastating ones for Sabah: occupied by the Japanese, it was bombed by Allied forces eager to neutralize its harbours. By the time of the Japanese surrender, next to nothing of Jesselton and Sandakan remained standing. Even worse were the hardships that the captured Allied troops and civilians endured – culminating in the Death March of September 1944, when 2400 POWs made a forced march from Sandakan to Ranau. Only six men, all Australians, survived.

Unable to finance the rebuilding of North Borneo, the Chartered Company sold the territory in 1946 to the British Crown, and Jesselton was declared the new capital of the **Crown Colony of North Borneo**. However, within fifteen years, plans had been laid for a federation consisting of Malaya, Singapore, Sarawak, North Borneo and Brunei. Although Brunei pulled out at the last minute, the **Federation** was still declared and at midnight on September 15, 1963, colonial rule ended in North Borneo – which was quickly renamed Sabah. Objecting to the inclusion of Sarawak and Sabah in the Federation, Indonesia's president Sukarno initiated his anti-Malaysian Konfrontasi policy, and sporadic skirmishes broke out along the Sabah–Kalimantan border for the next three years.

In 1967, Jesselton was renamed Kota Kinabalu; the decade that followed saw Sabah's **timber industry** reach its destructive peak. More recently, there have been moves to establish a secondary industry in timber-processing, a move that gained in urgency when the federal government limited the state's exporting of logs in 1991. Relations with Kuala Lumpur have been strained since the mid-1980s. Sabah toed the UNMO party line until 1985, but then the Parti Bersatu Sabah (PBS), led by the Christian **Joseph Pairin Kitingan**, was returned to office in the state elections – the first time a non-Muslim had attained power in Malaysia. Subsequently, Sabahans have complained of minimal funding of their state's infrastructure and a corresponding loss of foreign investment – and of blatant pro-Muslim propaganda, which has run as far as offering Christians cash incentives to convert to Islam. Anti-federal feelings are worsened by the fact that 95 percent of the profits from Sabah's flourishing crude petroleum exporting industry are syphoned into KL. More recently, Pairin himself was charged with corruption, accused of awarding a lucrative contract to a relative, with many Sabahans interpreting the charge as an attempt to discredit his Christian government. Whatever the truth, early 1994's **state elections** saw Pairin and the PBS retain power, only to yield it to the Barisan Nasional just weeks later, when first three, and then many more of his assemblymen defected to the opposition – a defection that made many in KK suspicious of corruption, though so far without proof. Sabah's new chief minister is Tan Sri Sakaran Dandai; Pairin's case is yet to be resolved.

Kota Kinabalu and around

Since 1946, Sabah's seat of government has been based at **KOTA KINABALU**, halfway up the state's western seaboard. KK (as it's universally known) certainly isn't one of the

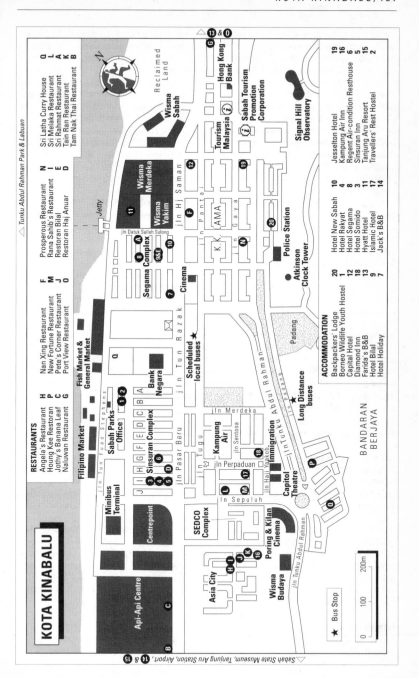

KOTA KINABALU

RESTAURANTS

Angela's Restaurant	H
Houng Kee Restoran	P
Jothy's Banana Leaf	C
Naluwan Restaurant	G

Nan Xing Restaurant	F
New Fortune Restaurant	J
Pete's Corner Restaurant	O
Port View Restaurant	

Prosperous Restaurant	N
Rana Sahib's Restaurant	I
Restoran Bilal	E
Restoran Haj Anuar	D

Sri Latha Curry House	Q
Sri Melaka Restaurant	L
Sri Rahmat Restaurant	A
Tain Ran Restaurant	K
Tam Nak Thai Restaurant	B

ACCOMMODATION

Backpackers' Lodge	20
Borneo Wildlife Youth Hostel	1
Capital Hotel	12
Diamond Inn	18
Farida's B&B	13
Hotel Bilal	9
Hotel Holiday	7

Hotel New Sabah	10
Hotel Rakyat	4
Hotel Segama	8
Hotel Somido	3
Hyatt Hotel	11
Islamic Hotel	17
Jack's B&B	14

Jesselton Hotel	19
Kampung Air Inn	16
Regent Air-condition Resthouse	6
Sinsuran Inn	5
Tanjung Aru Resort	15
Travellers' Rest Hostel	2

★ Bus Stop

0   100   200m

world's magical cities – World War II bombing all but robbed it of charismatic buildings, and first impressions are of a grim concrete sprawl – but the friendliness of its citizens and its proximity to a clutch of idyllic islands still charm visitors, which is lucky, since you'll be hard pressed to avoid KK on a trip to Sabah.

Modern-day Kota Kinabalu can trace its history back to 1882, the year the British North Borneo Chartered Company first established an outpost on nearby **Pulau Gaya**. After this was burned down by followers of the Bajau rebel, Mat Salleh, in 1897, the Company chose a mainland site for a new town which was known to locals as *Api Api*, or "Fire, Fire". One explanation is that the name referred to the firing of the original settlement; another, that it reflected the abundance of fireflies inhabiting its swamps. Renamed **Jesselton**, after Sir Charles Jessel, the vice-chairman of the Chartered Company, the town prospered. By 1905, the Trans-Borneo Railway reached from Jesselton to Beaufort, meaning that for the first time, rubber could be transported efficiently from the interior to the coast.

The Japanese invasion of North Borneo in 1942 marked the start of three and a half years of **military occupation**: of old Jesselton, only the Atkinson Clock Tower and the post office (today's tourist office) survived the resulting Allied bombing. However, progress since the war has been startling and today, with a population approaching 200,000, Kota Kinabalu (the name, meaning simply Kinabalu City, was coined after Malaysian independence in 1963) is a thriving seaport once more.

Most of downtown KK has been reclaimed from the sea during the past century – so ruthlessly in some places that pockets of stilt houses have been left stranded in stagnant land-bound lakes. On the resulting new patches of land, large complexes of interconnecting concrete buildings – the Sinsuran and Segama complexes and Asia City are three – have been constructed, their ground floors taken up by shops, restaurants and businesses, the upper floors turned into apartments. In addition, the ambitious Sutera Harbour project will add swish shopping centres, big name hotels, a marina and a bus station to the waterfront. The city has a limited number of sights, best of which are its **markets** and the **State Museum**, while south of the centre a series of kampungs provide a glimpse into the region's relatively recent tribal past. But KK's highlight is, without doubt, offshore **Tunku Abdul Rahman Park**, whose five unspoilt islands (including Pulau Gaya), are just ten minutes by speedboat from the city centre.

Arrival, information and getting around

KK's **airport** is 6km and fifteen minutes south of the centre. Six yellow-and-red Luen Thung Company buses a day travel from the airport into town (first bus approximately 6.30am, last bus 5.30pm; 65 sen), stopping opposite the GPO on Jalan Tun Razak. Otherwise, walk out to the main road – a five-minute stroll – and catch a minibus ($1–1.50) into town; or take a taxi, for which you need to buy a $12 coupon in the arrival hall.

Trains from Tenom and Beaufort pull in close to the airport at **Tanjung Aru Station**, which is beside Jalan Kepayan, the main road to points south of KK, so you'll have no trouble catching a bus heading into town. **Long-distance buses** from Sandakan and elsewhere congregate on the open land east of Jalan Padang, from where it's no more than a five-minute walk to any of KK's central hotels. **Ferries** to and from Labuan dock in front of the *Hyatt Hotel*, on Jalan Tun Fuad Stephens. For all **departure information**, see the box on "Leaving KK".

Information
At the **Sabah Tourism Promotion Corporation** (STPC; Mon–Fri 8am–4.15pm, Sat 8am–12.45pm; ☎088/212121), in the old GPO at 51 Jalan Gaya, the staff are friendly and

LEAVING KK

See "Listings", pp.434–35 for details of airline offices, tour operators and the Indonesian consulate in KK.

Airport
From KK's **airport** there are regular connections with the mainland, Singapore, Manila, Brunei and Hong Kong. Six buses a day run from opposite the GPO (first bus 6.30am; 65 sen); otherwise take a Putatan- or Petagas-bound minibus from the terminal behind the Centrepoint Shopping Centre and tell the driver your destination – he might charge an extra $1 for the detour.

Buses
Long-distance buses for points north, south and east of KK leave from the open land east of Jalan Padang. Apart from a number of very early morning buses to Sandakan, one or two to Kudat, and one each to Tawau and Beaufort, buses leave when full; turn up by 7am to ensure a seat. This terminus is also the departure point for the daily *Lawas Express* (1pm) to Lawas in Sarawak.

Trains
Although there is a rail link from KK to Beaufort, the bus gets you there in half the time. The stretch of line between Beaufort and Tenom (see p.442) is the most picturesque part of the Sabahan train system. Call ☎088/252536 for up-to-date timetable information.

Ferries
Services to Pulau Labuan (see p.447) seem to change with the wind, but you can bank on at least three daily departures. The *Ming Hai* departs from KK at 8am, returning at 1pm; while the *Express Kinabalu* makes the same journey at 10am, returning at 3pm. The *Duta Muhibbah* and the *Hoover Express* leave for Labuan on alternate days, at 1pm. One-way tickets cost $28 second class. All tickets are sold at the jetty and it's worth booking ahead if you plan to travel at the weekend or over a holiday. Alternatively, you could drop by at Jasa Samudra Shipping, first floor, Block E, Segama Complex (☎088/219810), or Rezeki Murni, first floor, Block D, Segama Complex (☎088/236835).

will inform you of any forthcoming events, though their $2 **map** is now rather outdated. **Tourism Malaysia** (Mon-Fri 8am–12.45pm & 2–4.15pm, Sat 8am–12.45pm; ☎088/211732), across Jalan Gaya in the EON CMG Building, can answer questions about Peninsular Malaysia or Sarawak.

If you're travelling to Mount Kinabalu and Poring (see p.457), you need to go to the **Sabah Parks** office (Mon–Fri 8.30am–4pm, Sat 8.30am–noon; ☎088/211881), in Block K of the Sinsuran Complex, Jalan Tun Fuad Stephens, to book your accommodation; this is also the place to come to arrange accommodation in Tunku Abdul Rahman (see below) and Pulau Tiga (p.446). For reservations at the Danum Valley Conservation Area (p.471), drop by the offices of the **Innoprise Corporation**, 1km southwest of the centre in Block D, Sadong Jaya Complex (Mon–Fri 8am–12.45pm & 2–4.15pm, Sat 8am–12.45pm; ☎088/243245), where reservations can be made. Finally, enquiries for the *Batu Punggul Resort* (see p.442) can be made at Korporasi Pembangunan Desa, 9 Tuaran Road (☎088/428910 ext 240).

What's on information is in short supply in KK, though you'll find details of cultural events in any of Sabah's English-language newspapers – the *Borneo Mail, Sabah Times, Morning Post* and *Daily Express*. Otherwise, the **notice boards** at the *Travellers' Rest Hostel* and *Jack's B&B* (see below) are valuable sources of information.

City transport

The city centre is compact enough to traverse on foot in fifteen minutes; even the museum is only a further twenty minutes' hike southwest of town, though you'll probably want to take a bus or taxi. **Taxis** are inexpensive provided you agree a price before setting off. It'll cost no more than $5–6 to travel right across the city centre; you'll find taxi ranks outside the *Hyatt Hotel* on Jalan Datuk Salleh Sulong, at the GPO on Jalan Tun Razak, and at Centrepoint shopping centre on Lebuh Raya Pantai Baru. See "Listings" for taxi booking numbers.

Taking a **bus** is more complicated, since until the planned terminal materializes, there's no central station in KK, just one patch of land for minibuses and another for scheduled buses, in addition to the long-distance bus area beside the padang. Buses leave when full from the **minibus terminal**, behind the Centrepoint Shopping Centre on Jalan Datuk Salleh Sulong for the suburbs and the airport. The bus stop opposite the GPO on Jalan Tun Razak is the starting point for **scheduled buses** travelling through KK's suburbs as far as Tuaran in the north and Penampang in the south. Marginally cheaper – and much safer – than minibuses, these leave at set times, empty or full, but take far longer to reach their destinations.

Accommodation

Compared to mainland Malaysia or Indonesia, the price of a room in Kota Kinabalu comes as an unpleasant surprise. Few of the capital's **hotels** are budget-rated and many of the cheaper ones double as brothels. Fortunately there's a handful of backpackers' hostels in the city centre, and two more just on the outskirts. The bulk of the possibilities – most of them Chinese-run hotels – are in the Sinsuran Complex on the west side of town, and the adjacent Kampung Air. The area around Jalan Pantai has several places too. While there's nowhere to **camp** in central KK, it's possible to set up a tent on the nearby islands in Tunku Abdul Rahman Park (p.608). The nightly rate on all islands is $5 for adults and $2 for under-18s, payable at the Sabah Parks office (see p.429) in the Sinsuran Complex – where you'll also need to secure written permission. If you're camping to save money, bear in mind that there's the boat to the island to pay for, too.

Bilal, Lot 1, Block B, Segama Complex (☎088/256709). Set above an excellent Indian restaurant, the *Bilal* is a respectable establishment, offering basic but clean rooms; an extra $5 gets you your own bathroom. ②.

Capital, 23 Jalan Haji Saman (☎088/231999). This recently renovated hotel boasts few amenities, though its 102 rooms are spacious, light and comfortable. ⑤.

Diamond Inn, Block 37, Kampung Air (☎088/213222). A great deal of effort has gone into this comfortable hotel, where the smart rooms have TV, air-con and fridge. ③.

Gayana Resort, Pulau Gaya; contact Lot 16, ground floor, Wisma Sabah (☎088/245158). This posh resort's range of chalets and rooms nestle into a scenic bay on Gaya's northern coast; guests can pick from a selection of watersports (including scuba-diving courses), or simply opt for nature walks around the island. At dinner time, either make for the excellent *Gayana Seafood Restaurant* or splash out on a dinner cruise on the luxury yacht. ⑥.

Holiday, Lot 1/2, Block F, Segama Complex (☎088/213116). A friendly hotel, whose well-groomed rooms have TV, air-con and bathroom. ④.

Hyatt, Jalan Datuk Salleh Sulong (☎088/221234). All the comforts you might imagine – swimming pool, business centre, choice of restaurants – and at a central location. ⑧.

Islamic, 8 Jalan Perpaduan, Kampung Air (☎088/254325). Unappealing, no-frills option – but undeniably cheap. ②.

Jesselton, 69 Jalan Gaya (☎088/223333). Lady Mountbatten and Mohammed Ali are just two of the illustrious guests to have sampled the old-world charm of this, KK's oldest hotel, set square in the centre of the city; a good Western grill and a harmonious coffee shop complement the sophisticated rooms. ⑧.

Kampung Air Inn, Block A, Ruang Singgah Mata 1, Asia City Complex (☎088/256622). Smart new mid-range address offering all the embellishments of a top-flight hotel – restaurants, business centre, airport transfers – at a fraction of the price. Recommended. ⑥.

New Sabah, Lot 3/4, Block A, Segama Complex (☎088/224590). Ordinary hotel, slightly tattier than the near by *Holiday*, whose tiled rooms (all with attached bathroom) are functional but soulless. ③.

Pulau Manukan Chalets, Pulau Manukan (also through Sabah Parks). Twenty attractive chalets – each has two double rooms and is let as a unit – are located on or overlooking an idyllic beach, and have use of a restaurant and swimming pool; prices increase by a third at the weekend. ④.

Rakyat, Lot 3, Block I, Sinsuran Complex (☎088/222715). The nine pleasant rooms offer a modicum of comfort; a few extra dollars secure you air-con, TV and a private bathroom. ③.

Segama, Lot 1, Block D, Segama Complex (☎088/221327). Decent renovations have done the *Segama* the power of good, and its compact rooms are now really rather inviting; inside bathrooms cost an extra $15. ②.

Shangri-La Tanjung Aru Resort, Tanjung Aru Beach (☎088/225800). Superior luxury hotel, set in delightful seaside gardens, and boasting two pools, watersports and fitness centres, several food outlets (including the superb *Peppino's* for Italian cuisine) – and prices to match. Hourly shuttle buses ensure easy access into the city, and there are also free runs up to its sister-hotel, the *Rasa Ria* (p.451). Recommended. ⑧.

Sinsuran Inn, Lot 1, Block I, Sinsuran Complex (☎088/211158; ③). Though undecorated, the rooms are capacious and clean, and have TV, bathroom and air-con. ③.

Somido, Lot 8, Block I, Sinsuran Complex (☎088/211946). Not a very distinguished budget place, though clean enough. ②.

HOSTELS

Backpackers' Lodge, Lot 25 Lorong Dewan, Australia Place (☎088/261495). New, spotlessly clean dorms-only operation below Signal Hill; guests have access to common showers, TV and laundry facilities, and breakfast is included. $18.

Borneo Wildlife Youth Hostel, Lot 4 Block L, Siswan Complex (☎088/213668). Dormitory class house, next door to the *Travellers' Rest Hostel* (see below), but forgoing its neighbour's free breakfasts and movies to keep costs to a minimum; downstairs are the friendly staff of Borneo Wildlife (see box on p.435). $15; $10 with YHA or student card.

Farida's B&B, 413 Jalan Saga, Mile 4.5, Kampung Likas (☎088/428733). A delightful family-run concern, fifteen minutes away from the minibus terminal – catch a "Kg Likas" bus – and perfect if you want a quiet life. Rooms and dorms are wonderfully airy, and fitted out in varnished wood. Dorms $12. ②.

Jack's B&B, no. 17, Block B, Jalan Karamunsing (☎088/232367). One kilometre southwest of the minibus terminus (take a Sembulan bus), *Jack's* is as spotless and as friendly a place as you could want, its dorms fitted with air-con and fan. Breakfast is included, there are heaps of latest-release videos, and Jack will also lay on island and fishing trips on request: recommended. Dorms $18. ②.

Regent Air-Condition Resthouse, Lot 5, Block G, Sinsuran Complex (☎088/224594). Situated above the *New Azura* restaurant, the *Regent* lacks the same eye for travellers' needs as the city's longer-established places, but the rooms themselves are fresh and smart, all sharing bathrooms. ②.

Travellers' Rest Hostel, Lot 5/6, Block L, Sinsuran Complex (☎088/224264). KK's original guesthouse, and still the city's best budget choice: dorms and rooms are simple but clean enough (prices include breakfast), the owners are friendly and helpful, and there's an informative notice board, which includes details of the hostel's own tours. Recommended. Dorms $12. ②.

The City

Downtown KK was almost totally obliterated by World War II bombs, and only in the northeastern corner of the city centre – an area known as **KK Lama**, or old KK – are there even the faintest remains of its colonial past. KK Lama is bordered by **Jalan Pantai** (Beach Road), formerly the waterfront, and **Jalan Gaya**, where the attractive old general post office building houses the STPC. A lively **street market** is held along Jalan Gaya every Sunday morning, with stalls selling herbal teas, handicrafts, orchids and rabbits, and streetside coffee shops doing a roaring trade in *dim sum* and noodles.

A block east, under the shadow of Bukit Bendera (Signal Hill), stands the **Atkinson Clocktower**, a quaint wooden landmark built in 1905 in memory of a district officer in the Chartered Company. From here, you can take the fifteen-minute walk up to breezy **Signal Hill Observatory**, which provides a good overview of KK's matrix of dreary buildings and of the infinitely more attractive bay. Early photographs of the city show colonial officers playing cricket on the **padang**, which you'll pass on your way to the observatory.

It's a five-minute stroll from the padang west across town to KK's waterfront markets, the most diverting of which is the **Filipino Market**, opposite blocks K and M of the Sinsuran Complex. Its numerous stalls are run by Filipino immigrants, who stock Sabahan ethnic wares beside their Filipino baskets, shells and trinkets. Next door is the dark and labyrinthine **general market** and, behind that, the manic waterfront **fish market** – worth investigating if you can stomach the vile stench.

To the Sabah State Museum

Head southwest along Jalan Tunku Abdul Rahman, past the pyramidal Catholic **Sacred Heart Cathedral** and – slightly further on – the **Sabah State Mosque**, whose eye-catching dome sits, like a Fabergé egg, on top of the main body of the complex.

After twenty minutes walk (if you can't face the walk from the centre, take a bus from opposite the GPO) you reach the **Sabah State Museum** (Mon–Thurs 10am–6pm, Sat & Sun 9am–6pm; free), KK's most rewarding sight whose buildings are styled on Murut and Rungus longhouses and set in exotic grounds that are home to several splendid steam engines. Its highlight is its ethnographic collection which features a *bangkaran*, or cluster of human skulls, dating from Sabah's head-hunting days; and a *sininggazanak*, a totemic wooden figurine which would have been placed in the field of a Kadazan man who had died leaving no heirs. Photographs in the history gallery trace the development of Kota Kinabalu – look out for an intriguing picture of Jesselton at a time when Jalan Gaya still constituted the waterfront, lined with lean-tos thatched with nipah palm leaves. There are old snaps of Chartered Company officials, Sabahan natives and Chinese pioneers, while beyond, in the Merdeka Gallery, contemporary newspaper cuttings trace the story of Malaysia's path to independence. Of rather less interest is the tired collection of stuffed animals in the natural history section, while only a fine old wooden coffin from Batu Putih (see p.469) stands out among the clay shards of the archeology gallery. As for the Islamic Civilisation Gallery, most of its collection comprises photographs of objects from other museums around the world, though it does boast an exquisite nineteenth-century Ottoman chess board crafted from mother-of-pearl, ebony and ivory, and several antique Korans. There is a souvenir shop with a good selection of literature.

The **Science and Technology Centre** (same hours as museum; free), next door to the museum, houses less-than-gripping exhibitions on oil-drilling and broadcasting technology, so head upstairs to the **Art Gallery** (Mon–Thurs 10am–4.30pm, Sat & Sun 9.30am–5pm; free) instead. Many of the works on display are unadventurous, postcard images of Sabah, though there are exceptions – notably the impressionistic paintings of Suzie Majikol and a dreamlike work in oil of four women dancing by Nazric Said. The gallery's centrepiece is a giant, eye-catching string of Rungus beads hanging from the ceiling, created by Chee Sing Teck.

Fronting the museum is an **Ethnobotanic Garden** (daily 6am–6pm), whose huge range of tropical plants is best experienced on one of the free guided tours (9am & 2pm except Fri). Exquisitely crafted, traditional houses representing all Sabah's major tribes border the garden, in the Kampung Warisan, or Heritage Village.

Past the museum, Jalan Tunku Abdul Rahman continues on for another 2.5km (becoming Jalan Mat Salleh) to the beach at **Tanjung Aru**, site of the swanky *Shangri-La Resort*, a superb development and bolt hole of Nick Leeson (see p.546) before his arrest in Frankfurt. The beach itself is reasonable – it's long and fairly narrow, and has several food and drink stalls – but with so many beautiful islands just off the coast, there's no great incentive to visit. To reach Tanjung Aru direct from the centre, take a red Luen Thung Company bus from opposite the GPO.

Eating, drinking and nightlife

Finding somewhere to eat in KK causes no headaches, with a big range of Malay, Chinese and Indian **restaurants**, and a good selection of central **hawker stalls**. Problems arise, though, if you want to sample Sabahan cuisine: while the indigenous peoples all have their own dishes, their total absence from the menus of KK is a big disappointment. Note that quite a few restaurants are closed by mid-evening, so be prepared for an early dinner; specific opening hours (daily unless otherwise stated) are given below. Opening hours for hawker stalls listed below are usually daily 6–11pm; the exception is the general market, whose stalls operate daily 9am–6pm. KK only has a handful of **bars** and **clubs**, the best of which are listed below.

Hawker stalls

General Market, Jalan Tun Fuad Stephens. The *nasi campur* stalls on the upper floor provide filling, good-value meals.

Night Market, behind the Filipino Market, Jalan Tun Fuad Stephens. Fried chicken and barbecue fish are the specialities here.

SEDCO Square, SEDCO complex. Restaurant-lined square, with outdoor tables; a fine place for barbecued meat and fish.

Tanjung Aru Beach. Busiest and best at the weekend, when large numbers of locals come for satay and barbecued seafood.

Cafés and restaurants

Angela's, Block G, Asia City (☎088/252281). Ignore the gooey pink decor and endless cat pictures; the Nonya cooking here is really rather good – try *otak otak* (fishhead curry), or plump for a less exotic choice from the Western menu. Mon–Sat 11.30am–2.30pm & 6.30–10.30pm.

Restoran Bilal, Block B, Segama Complex. A classic North Indian Muslim eating house, with a buffet-style range of tasty and inexpensive curries. Daily 6am–9pm.

Restoran Haj Anuar, Block H, Sinsuran Complex. Cosy, open-fronted place opposite the *Sinsuran Inn*, with a Malay menu including *soto, nasi lemak* and *nasi campur*. Daily 7am–7pm.

Houng Kee Seafood Restaurant, 5 Mosque Valley, Jalan Padang. The garden fronting this charming restaurant makes it an appealing place to relax over a meal. The house speciality is steamed fish; two people can feast for $40. Daily 7am–10.30pm.

Jothy's Banana Leaf, 1/G9 Api Api Centre (☎088/261595). Beside its mountainous *daun pisang* (banana leaf) meals, *Jothy's* has *biriyanis* and curries, though for proper *naan* you're better off at *Rana Sahib's* (below). Daily 10am–10pm.

Naluwan, 16–17 Jalan Haji Saman. A huge, cavernous place, and a porker's paradise: a modest outlay ($7 lunch, $15 dinner) buys you all you can eat from a buffet that's constantly replenished with all manner of tasty Asian dishes. Daily 11am–2.30pm & 6.30–11.30pm.

Nan Xing Restaurant, 33–35 Jalan Haji Saman. A decent Cantonese menu that includes a range of *dim sum* as well as steaks and chops. Daily noon–2.30pm & 6–9pm.

New Fortune Eating House, Block 36, Jalan Laiman Diki, Kampung Air. A busy place housing several stalls, the best of which serves superb *dim sum* at breakfast and later. Open 6am–7pm.

Pete's Corner, Block B Asia City. Neatly tiled, open-fronted corner shop serving egg, sausage and baked-bean breakfasts, omelettes and sandwiches, as well as more substantial Western meals such as steaks and chops, at very affordable prices. Daily 7am–5.30pm.

Phoenix Court Restaurant, *Hyatt Hotel*, Jalan Datuk Salleh Sulong (☎088/221234). Superior Cantonese and Szechuan food, and elegant surroundings. Expect to pay $30–40 a head, and reserve in advance. Daily 11am–2pm & 7–11pm.

Port View Restaurant, Jalan Haji Saman. Lively at night, when the roadside tables fill up with locals choosing from a wide range of (live) seafood. Daily 6pm–2am, Sat until 3am.

Prosperous Szechuan Restaurant, 103 Jalan Gaya (☎088/264666). Hot and spicy Chinese food, pleasing decor, smartly attired staff and a good range of set meals from $36. Daily 11.30am–2.30pm & 5.30–10.30pm.

Rana Sahib's, Block G Asia City (☎088/231354). The owner used to work in Singapore's celebrated *Moti Mahal*, and his pedigree shines through in the princely North Indian menu in this fresh, air-conditioned establishment; *sag gost* and *chicken kashmir* are both superb, and there's a mango *lassi* to die for. Daily 11.30am–2.30pm & 6.30–10.30pm.

Restoran Sri Rahmat, Lot 7, Block D Segama Complex. A basic Malay restaurant – though with an air-con room – that's worth frequenting for the delicious *laksa* alone. Open Mon–Sat 7am–9pm, Sun 7am–5pm.

Sri Melaka, 9 Jalan Laiman Diki, Kampung Air. A popular establishment that's great for Malay and Nonya food; try the excellent *assam fishhead* ($8 portion feeds two). Open 8.30am–9.30pm.

Sri Latha Curry House, Jalan 4 no. 33, Bandaran Berjaya. The banana leaf curry in this no-frills South Indian restaurant, is a mountainous, all-you-can-eat feast ($3.50 for vegetarian, $6 for meat), served by really friendly staff. There's chicken *biriyani* on a Saturday, and *masala dosai* on Sunday mornings. Daily 6.30am–2am.

Tain Ran Vegetarian Restaurant, Block A, Ruang Singgah Mata 1, Asia City Complex. Spartan coffee shop with a mouthwatering array of veggie dishes served from a tin-tray buffet counter. Daily 9am–7pm.

Tam Nak Thai, 5/G5 Api-Api Centre (☎088/257328). Authentic Thai cuisine unavailable elsewhere in the city, and a pleasing ambience. Daily 11.30am–3pm & 6–10pm.

Bars and clubs

Crash, below *New Sabah Inn*, Jalan Pantai. Lively enough place which has a midweek bikini parade, set behind a facade crafted to resemble the chassis of a jet-plane.

Next Door, *Shangri-La Tanjung Aru Resort*, Tanjung Aru Beach. Likeable (if pricey) bar with good pool table and decent choice on the jukebox.

Rocky Fun Pub & Café, Lot 52, Jalan Gaya. Good-time bar favoured by expats and featuring a karaoke area, dance floor and café. Daily until 2am.

Shenanigan's, *Hyatt Kinabalu*, Jalan Datuk Salleh Sulong. Slick and central bar whose overall-wearing staff pull English pints as well as local lagers. Features live music. Mon–Thurs 11am–1am, Fri & Sat 11am–2am, Sun 4pm–midnight.

Tiffiny Discotheatre, Block A, Jalan Karamunsing. Glitzy disco where live bands play nightly, and Happy Hour runs from 8.30 to 9.30pm; cover charge $12–15. Open till 2am, Sat till 3am.

Listings

Airlines Dragon Air, ground floor, Block C, Kompleks Kuwasa, Jalan Karamunsing (☎088/254733); MAS, Kompleks Karamunsing, Jalan Tuaran (☎088/213555); Philippine Air, Kompleks Karamunsing, Jalan Tuaran (☎088/239600); Royal Brunei, ground floor, Block C, Kompleks Kuwasa, Jalan Karamunsing (☎088/242193); Singapore Airlines, ground floor, Block C, Kompleks Kuwasa, Jalan Karamunsing (☎088/255444); Thai Airways, ground floor, Block C, Kompleks Kuwasa, Jalan Karamunsing (☎088/232896).

American Express Lot 3.50 & 3.51, third floor, Kompleks Karamunsing (Mon–Fri 8.30am–5.30pm; ☎088/241200).

Banks and exchange Hong Kong & Shanghai Bank, 56 Jalan Gaya; Sabah Bank, Block K, Sinsuran Complex; Standard Chartered Bank, 20 Jalan Hj Saman. Moneychangers (Mon–Sat 10am–7pm) in Wisma Merdeka include Ban Loong Money Changer and Travellers' Money Changer, both on the ground floor; there's also an office in the Taiping Goldsmith, Block A, Sinsuran Complex.

Bookshops *Arena Book Centre* (Block L, Sinsuran Complex), *Iwase Bookshop* (Wisma Merdeka) and the *Yaohan* bookstore (second floor, Centre Point) all have a few shelves of English-language novels. For an unparalleled array of books on Southeast Asia, head for *Borneo Crafts* (Wisma Merdeka), or to their branch at the Sabah State Museum; the *Hyatt*'s bookshop stocks a modest range of international newspapers and magazines.

Car rental Ais Rent-A-Car, Lot 1, Block A, Sinsuran Complex (☎088/238954); Kinabalu Rent-A-Car, Lot 3.60, third floor, Kompleks Karamunsing (☎088/232602), and at the Hyatt Hotel; Sabah Holiday Rent-A-Car, Lot 20, Wisma Sabah, Jalan Tun Razak (☎088/245106). Rates start from around $170 per day, though four-wheel drives (from $250) are advisable if you plan to get off the beaten track.

Cinemas The *Poring and Kilan Cinema*, and the *Capitol Theatre*, below the SEDCO Centre at the western edge of downtown KK, both have regular screenings of English-language movies. Programme listings are in the *Borneo Mail* or *Daily Express*.

Consulates The nearest consular representation for most nationalities is in KL; see p.119.

Danum Valley Reservations for the Danum Valley Conservation Area (see p.471) can be made at the Innoprise Corporation, Block D, Kompleks Sadong Jaya (☎088/243245).

Hospital Queen Elizabeth Hospital is beyond the Sabah State Museum, on Jalan Penampang (☎088/218166). In an emergency, dial ☎999.

Immigration Office fourth floor, Wisma Dang Bandang, Jalan Hj Yaakob (Mon–Fri 8am–12.30pm & 2–4.15pm, Sat 8am–12.45pm; ☎088/216711). Visa extensions up to a month are available and cost $2.

Indonesian Immigration The Konsulat Jenderal Indonesia, Jalan Kemajuan (☎088/218600), issues one-month visas for Kalimantan.

Laundry *Bright Laundry*, Wisma Merdeka; Daily Clean Laundry, Block B, Sinsuran Complex.

Pharmacies *Centre Point Pharmacy*, Centre Point; *Farmasi Gaya*, 122 Jalan Gaya; *Metropharm*, Block A, Sinsuran Complex.

Police The main police station, Balai Polis KK (☎088/258191 or ☎088/258111), is below Atkinson Clocktower on Jalan Padang.

TOUR OPERATORS IN KK

A large number of **tour operators** are based in KK, and though prices are often high, many of the adventure tours on offer are only possible through an agency; some of the best are listed below. Expect to pay around $40 for a half-day KK city tour; $100 for day-trips to Tunku Abdul Rahman Park, the Rafflesia Centre or Kinabalu National Park; $180 for a day's white-water rafting; and $600 upwards for extended tours into the forested interior, depending on the size of the group.

Api Tours, 13 Jalan Punai Kedut, Mile 5 Jalan Tuaran (☎088/421963). For rafting, and more demanding trips like longhouse tours and the Mount Trusmadi Trek.

Borneo Expeditions, *Shangri-La Tanjung Aru Resort* (☎088/222721). A white-water rafting specialist, but organizes inland tours, too.

Borneo Divers, fourth floor, Wisma Sabah (☎088/222226). The most prestigious outfit for diving trips and scuba courses; three days (two nights) on Sipidan with them costs US$700.

Borneo Sea Adventures, first floor, 8A Karamunsing Warehouse (☎088/230000). One-day trips to Sipadan out of Semporna ($200) for groups of four or more.

Borneo Wildlife Adventure, Block L, Sinsuran Complex (☎088/213668). Tailor-made adventure tours along the Sarawak and Kalimantan borders.

Discovery Tours, Shopping Arcade, *Shangri-La Tanjung Aru Resort* (☎088/221224). Half- and full-day tours in the KK area.

Journey World Travel, Taman Fortuna, Jalan Penampang (☎088/221586). Imaginative operator devising tailor-made adventure tours along the Sarawak and Kalimantan borders.

Sipadan Dive Centre, tenth floor, Wisma Merdeka (☎088/240584). A newish organization, but already one of the top dogs on Sipadan. Two-day, one-night excursions cost $1495 per person, and an extra day and night is a further $275 a head; prices include return transfer from KK to Sipadan by air, land and sea, three daily boat dives plus unlimited shore dives. Recommended.

Travellers' Rest Hostel, Block L, Sinsuran Complex (☎088/240625). Provides the most competitive rates for trips out of Sandakan.

Post office The GPO (Mon–Sat 8am–5pm, Sun 10am–1pm) lies between the Sinsuran and Segama complexes, on Jalan Tun Razak; poste restante/general delivery is just inside the front doors.

Sabah Parks Block K, Sinsuran Complex (Mon–Fri 8.30am–4pm, Sat 8.30am–noon; ☎088/211881).

Shopping *Borneo Handicraft* (first floor, Wisma Merdeka) has a good choice of woodwork, basketry and gongs; *Borneo Handicraft & Ceramic Shop* (ground floor, Centre Point) stocks ceramics, antiques and primitive sculptures; also good are the souvenir shops at the Sabah State Museum and the STPC; while the Filipino Market's scores of stalls sell both local and Filipino wares.

Telephones There are IDD facilities at Kedai Telekom (daily 8am–10pm), in Kompleks Sadong Jaya. Phone cards, available at the GPO and any shops displaying the "Uniphone Kad" sign, can be used for international calls in orange, but not yellow, public phone booths – there are some in Centre Point.

Taxis Book a taxi on either ☎088/52113 or 51863.

Tunku Abdul Rahman Park

Named after Malaysia's first prime minister, and situated just a stone's throw from central Kota Kinabalu, the **five islands** of **Tunku Abdul Rahman Park** (sometimes written as TAR Park) represent the most westerly ripples of the undulating Crocker Mountain Range (see p.439). Gazetted as a national park in 1974, since then their forests, beaches and coral reefs have been the salvation of tourists stuck in the capital. All five islands lie within an eight-kilometre radius of downtown KK, with park territory just 3km off the mainland at its closest point, but unless you've got your own boat, or you're prepared to charter one for the whole day, you'll have to opt for just one island at a time.

Largest of the park's islands – and the site of the British North Borneo Chartered Company's first outpost in the region – is **Pulau Gaya**, whose name is derived from *goyoh*, the Bajau word for "big". Today, a large stilt village housing thousands of KK's Filipino immigrants sits off its east coast. Although a native chief granted the island's timber rights to a certain Mr White in 1879, they were never fully exploited. Lowland rainforest still blankets Gaya, a twenty-kilometre system of trails snaking across it. Most of these trails start on the southern side of the island at **Camp Bay**, which is adjacent to a mangrove forest whose crabs and mudskippers can be viewed from the boardwalk that intersects it. While Camp Bay offers pleasant enough swimming, a more secluded and alluring alternative is **Police·Beach**, on the north coast. Boatmen demand extra for circling round to this side of Gaya, but it's money well spent: the bay is idyllic, its dazzling white sand running gently down to the water, lined by trees. Wildlife on Gaya includes hornbills, wild pigs, lizards, snakes and macaques – which have been known to swim over to nearby **Pulau Sapi** (Cow Island), a 25-acre islet off the northwestern coast of Gaya that's popular with swimmers, snorkellers and picnickers. Though far smaller than Gaya, Sapi too is ringed by trails and home to macaques and hornbills.

The park's three other islands cluster together 2.5km west of Gaya. The park headquarters is situated on crescent-shaped **Pulau Manukan** – site of a former stone quarry and now the most developed of all the park's islands – though you'll have no cause to visit it, since all the literature available can be picked up at KK's Sabah Parks office. Manukan's fine beaches and coral have led to the construction of chalets, a restaurant, swimming pool, tennis and squash courts, which draw large numbers of locals. Across a narrow channel from Manukan is tiny **Pulau Mamutik**, which can be crossed on foot in fifteen minutes and has excellent sands on either side of its jetty. **Pulau Sulug** is the most remote of the islands and consequently the quietest. Its good coral makes it popular with divers and on its eastern side is a long sand spit that ends in a sharp drop-off.

Practicalities

The **boat service** initiated by Sabah Parks makes getting out to the islands straight-forward. Boats depart for the islands at 8am, 9am, 10am, 11am, noon, 2pm and 4.30pm, returning at 7.30am, 9.30am, 10.30am, 11.30am, 3pm and 4pm; the return fare is $10 (children $5), regardless of how many takers there are. Chartering a boat to go island-hopping costs $20 a head (minimum six people). Contact Sabah Parks for details, or make directly for the waterfront behind the *Hyatt* on Jalan Tun Fuad Stephens. Otherwise, numerous speedboats gather daily behind the *Hyatt*; be prepared for some intensive haggling. Boats won't leave for less than $40–50, but if you're in a group, you shouldn't pay more than $10–12 per person for a return journey. Once you've arrived at your chosen island, don't forget to arrange a pick-up time. It's also wise, if you're trav-elling with a private boatman and not through Sabah Parks to pay only when you're safely back in KK – there have been reports of tourists being left on islands overnight. If you don't have **snorkelling gear** with you, the boatmen will rent you some ($5 a day), but try it out before they speed back to KK.

The $2 **entry fee** presently charged on landing at Sapi, Manukan and Mamutik will in time apply to all the islands. **Accommodation** in the park – island camping and the *Manukan Chalets* – must be booked through the Sabah Parks office (Mon–Fri 8.30am–4pm, Sat 8.30am–noon; ☎088/211881), except the *Gayana Resort*, on the north-eastern side of Gaya, which lies in the one patch of the island outside the park perime-ters. There's a **restaurant** serving the chalets on Manukan, and the *Gayana Resort*'s seafood restaurant, but otherwise nowhere to eat, so take a picnic.

South of KK

Regular minibuses from Jalan Tun Fuad Stephens leave the city for the suburb of **DONG-GONGON**, around 10km to the south. From the bus station here, it's only a ten-minute local bus ride past rice fields and winding streams to **Kampung Monsopiad**, where 39 of the 42 skulls cleaved by legendary Kadazan warrior, Monsopiad provide the centre-piece of the **Monsopiad Cultural Village** (call ☎088/761336 for an appointment; $15), a Kadazan theme park nestled in an attractive rustic setting. The village comprises a muse-um, handicraft workshop, granary, and a main hall, in which cultural performances and native feasts are held (by prior arrangement). Monsopiad's grisly harvest of skulls remains in his ancestral house; as resident guide Wenidy Moujadi shows you arouns, he will recount legends that have been passed down about the great man. Among the skulls, displayed in a row along a rafter like a coconut shy, and decked with *hisad* (palm) leaves signifying the victims' hair, a thigh bone testifies to one such story. Visiting a neighbour-ing village for a large feast, Monsopiad ended up in a dancing competition with a relative, called Gantang. When this ended unresolved, they had a drinking competition, before finally beginning to fight. His head fuzzy from the rice wine, Monsopiad forgot himself and resorted unfairly to using a bamboo spear, instead of his sword, to kill Gantang, whose thigh bone – rather than his head – was awarded to Monsopiad to remind him of his moment of dishonour. Monsopiad eventually grew too fond of harvesting heads and constituted a public menace; killed by a group of friends, he was buried beneath a stone that still stands near the house, with his own head left intact out of respect. Once a year (usually in May), a Kadazan priestess, or *bobohizan*, is called in to communicate with the skulls' spirits, whose job it is to watch over Monsopiad's descendants.

Once you're out in Donggongon, you might as well take the opportunity to see Sabah's oldest church, **St Michael's Catholic Church**, only a twenty-minute walk (or short bus ride) beyond the bus terminus and along the main road. Built in 1897, the sturdy granite building stands on a hillock above peaceful Kampung Dabak, its red roof topped by a simple stone cross; inside, the church is undecorated, save a mural depict-ing the Last Supper and framed paintings of the Stations of the Cross.

Kinarut to Papar

Further down the main road south, KK's suburbs yield to a carpet of paddy fields that stretches away to the foothills of the Crocker Mountain Range. From the minibus terminal in town, there are frequent departures to the village of **Kinarut**, 21km away, the starting point for an enjoyable half-hour stroll along a quiet road to **Kampung Tampasak**, where there's a replica of the *sininggazanak* in the State Museum (see p.432). From the two faded old shophouses that form the centre of Kinarut, walk across the rail line, cross the bridge to your left and turn right – the turning to the kampung is signposted by an overgrown tyre. On your way, you'll see two or three mysterious menhirs, upright stones, thought to have been erected centuries ago either as status symbols or boundary stones, or to mark the burial places of shamans.

Two to three kilometres away at **Kinarut Laut** (take a Papar minibus from KK), the *Seaside Travellers' Inn* (☎088/750313; ③) has become a popular retreat for KK weekenders, its dorms ($25)and rooms a little overpriced but otherwise hard to fault; a balcony off the dining room looks out to the nearby islands of Dinawan and Muntukat, and over the inn's own unspectacular stretch of beach. The slightly plusher *Langkah Syabas Beach Resort* (☎088/752000; ⑥), next door, has fourteen welcoming chalets around a swimming pool, just 100m from the shore. A kilometre back towards KK, the *Kindawan Riding Centre* offers **horseback** trips through the surrounding countryside ($60 for 90min; call Dale Sinidol, ☎088/225525).

The one town of any size between KK and Beaufort (see p.444), **Papar**, is another 20km or so further south; buses run here all through the day from KK's minibus terminal. Unless you're here on Sunday for the decent weekly market, the only reason to break your journey is to visit the nearby beach – **Pantai Manis** – reached by minibus ($1) from the centre of Papar.

Southwestern Sabah and the interior

Sabah's **southwestern** reaches are dominated by the ridge of the **Crocker Mountain Range**, which divides the state's west coast and swampy Klias Peninsula from the area christened the **interior** in the days of the Chartered Company. At one time, this sparsely populated region was effectively isolated from the west coast by the mountains. This changed at the turn of the century, when a railway was built between Jesselton (modern-day KK), and the interior in order to transport the raw materials being produced by the region's thriving rubber industry. Today, logging has taken precedence, though the Kadazan/Dusun and Murut peoples still look to the interior's fertile soils for their living, cultivating rice, maize and cocoa.

Travelling by bus and train, it's possible to circumnavigate the region from KK, starting with a drive southeast over the mountains to the Kadazan/Dusun town of **Tambunan**, which sits on a plain chequered with paddy fields. From Tambunan, the road continues further south to **Keningau**, the centre of the interior's timber industry. Following the circular route to KK entails travelling on to **Tenom**, but Keningau is also the launch pad for more adventurous detours deeper into the heart of the interior. Both Tenom and Keningau mark the start of Murut territory, which stretches down to the Kalimantan border. The traditional ways of the Murut are fast dying out, but those prepared to venture into the less accessible areas south of Keningau and Tenom – using remote **Sapulut** as a base – will come across isolated tribes to whom home is still a longhouse, albeit a modernized one.

Tenom itself sits on the bank of the Sungei Padas, whose turbulent waters you'll have to negotiate if you sign up for a white-water rafting tour. The train line connects Tenom with **Beaufort**, from where you can head one of three ways: north to KK; south to

Sipitang, the terminus for buses and taxis into Sarawak; or west into the **Klias Peninsula**, an infertile former swamp forest that forms the northeastern reach of Brunei Bay. From Kuala Penyu, in the northern corner of the peninsula, boats travel to **Pulau Tiga Park**; ferries and speedboats connect Menumbok, on the peninsula's southern side, with the duty-free island of **Pulau Labuan**.

The Crocker Mountain Range

Unless you take a Tenom-bound train from Beaufort (see p.444), the only way to reach the interior of Sabah is to follow the 80km of road from KK, southeast to Tambunan (see below); buses leave regularly from beside the padang in KK. Ten kilometres out of the city, paddy fields give way to the rolling foothills of the **Crocker Mountain Range** and buses start the long, twisting haul up to the 1649-metre-high Sinsuron Pass. You'll have views of mighty Mount Kinabalu, weather permitting. The occasional lean-to shack sits by the side of the road, piled with pineapples, bananas and vegetables; often there's no one attending them, as some locals believe that anyone pilfering risks death by black magic. Should you wish to dally for a little longer in the bracing chill of the Sinsuron Pass, you might consider spending a night at the *Gunung Emas Highlands Resort* (☎011/811562), at the 52km mark of the KK–Tambunan road: guests choose between dormitory beds ($21), double rooms sharing common toilets (③), treetop cabins "for those who want to experience the lifestyle of Tarzan and Jane" (④), and more luxurious suites (⑥). Jungle trails from the resort lead to a picturesque waterfall, and to a viewpoint from which KK is visible on a clear day.

A few kilometres beyond the pass, the **Rafflesia Complex** (Mon–Fri 8am–12.45pm & 2–5pm, Sat & Sun 8am–5pm; free) houses examples of the rafflesia flower, a parasitic plant whose rubbery, liver-spotted blooms can reach up to one metre in diameter – making it the world's largest flower. Its full name, Rafflesia Arnoldii, recalls its discovery, in Sumatra in 1818, by Sir Stamford Raffles and his physician, the naturalist Dr Joseph Arnold. "The petals", Raffles recorded, "are of a brick-red with numerous pustular spots of a lighter colour. The whole substance of the flower is not less than half an inch thick, and of a firm fleshy consistence." There's no need to hire one of the guides ($20) advertised at the complex's Visitor Centre, as the park's paths are simple to follow and you're not going to miss a plant that size; someone at the centre should be able to direct you to one in bloom, though it's a good idea to phone the Visitor Centre's hotline (☎011/861499) before leaving KK to avoid a wasted journey – each flower only lasts a few days before dying.

Tambunan Plain

Seventeen kilometres short of Tambunan, a kink in the road reveals the gleaming emerald paddy fields of **Tambunan Plain** below. Flanked by groves of bamboos – the result of a colonial regulation that for every pole cut, twenty more be planted – and threaded by the Sungei Pegalam, the plain is thought to have been named after two warriors, Tamadons and Gombunan, whose peoples joined forces centuries ago to expel invading tribes. **Gunung Trusmadi**, Sabah's second highest mountain (2642m), towers above the plain's eastern flank.

If you want to visit the forest-framed, fifteen-metre-high **Mawah Waterfall**, you'll have to get off the bus when you hit the main Ranau–Tambunan road, and catch another bus ($2) going northeast (to Ranau). After 7km, you reach the wide gravel trail leading to the waterfall from **Kampung Patau**, from where it's another two-hour hike through an idyllic bowl of hills stepped with groves of fern and bamboo.

Tambunan

After such a wonderful approach, the small Kadazan settlement of **TAMBUNAN**, centred on an ugly square of modern shophouses, is bound to disappoint. The most generous thing that can be said about Tambunan, administrative centre of Tambunan District, is that it's a quiet and spacious town; the site, every Thursday, of a lively *tamu*, for which a smart new market building has been erected.

Although now a sleepy agricultural district, Tambunan featured in one of the more turbulent periods in Sabah's history, when it witnessed the demise of folk hero and rebel, **Mat Salleh**, who in 1897 burned down the British settlement on Pulau Gaya, in protest at taxes being levied by the Chartered Company. Branded an outlaw with a price on his head, Salleh finally negotiated a deal with William Clarke Cowie of the Chartered Company that allowed him and his men to settle in Tambunan. Such a humiliating outcome outraged other members of the company and Salleh hurriedly withdrew to Tambunan Plain, where he erected a fort of bamboo and stone. Sure enough, government forces descended into the plain at the beginning of 1900 and besieged Salleh's fort; by the end of January, Salleh was dead, killed by a stray bullet. It's said that had Salleh been wearing his "invulnerable jacket", inscribed with Koranic tracts and exhibited in the Sabah State Museum, he would have lived to fight another day. At **Kampung Tibabar**, a few kilometres north of Tambunan, a stone memorial marks the site of his fort.

Buses to and from KK, Ranau and Keningau stop in the main square, around which are several unspectacular eating houses. There are also two **places to stay** in town: the *Government Rest House* (☎087/774339; ③), a five-minute walk from the main road up a small hill which overlooks the Tambuan Plain; or the *Tambunan Village Resort Centre* (TVRC; ☎087/774076; ③), 1km north of town, the fruit of a 1987 Operation Raleigh venture. As well as a restaurant, the centre boasts a cottage industry producing *lihing* – the rice wine for which Tambunan is locally renowned.

Keningau

A fifty-kilometre jaunt down the road from Tambunan brings you to the rapidly expanding town of **KENINGAU**, the interior's forestry capital. It's a hectic, noisy place, streets crammed with tooting buses and taxis, pavements lined by women hawking cigarettes and children offering "shoeshine, boss" from morning to night. At the weekend, the town attracts crowds of labourers from the sawmills and logging camps that have scarred the hills around it – a phenomenon in part responsible for a burgeoning prostitution trade which puts several of the town's hotels off-limits.

Keningau's single attraction is its **Chinese temple**, situated right beside the bus terminus. The brightly painted murals that cover its walls and ceilings are more reminiscent of those in a Hindu temple, while in the forecourt is a statue of a fat, smiling Buddha, resplendent in red and yellow gown. If you're in town on **market** day (Thursday), check out Keningau's *tamu*, a short walk up the main Keningau–Tambunan road. The only other distraction is the minibus ride twenty minutes northeast of town, through paddy fields and small kampungs, to **Taman Bandukan**. This pleasant riverside park is packed with picnicking locals on Sundays, but at other times grazing cows and scores of butterflies are your only company; the river is clean and good for swimming, while from above its far banks – reached by a wobbly suspension bridge – there's a good view of the surrounding hills. Take a minibus from the central square to Bingkor, telling the driver where you're headed.

Rather than **heading on**, to either Tenom or Tambunan, a more exciting alternative is to head for Sapulut (see below) to explore Sabah's Murut heartland; this remote region is effectively a dead end and accessible only from Keningau, to which you'll have to backtrack afterwards. It's also possible to take a landcruiser and strike east along the logging roads which connect the interior with Tawau, the largest town in southern Sabah though this really is a tough route.

Practicalities

Buses and **taxis** terminate in and around the town's central square. It isn't possible to reserve a seat on a **landcruiser** to Tawau ($80) and drivers only set off with a full load, so turn up as early as you possibly can.

A couple of adequate **hotels** – *Hotel Hiap Soon* (☎087/331541; ②) and the pricier *Hotel Tai Wah* (☎087/332092; ②) – are near the centre, though the majority are found in the new part of town, five minutes' walk behind the Chinese temple, up Jalan Masuk Spur. It's here that you'll find Keningau's friendliest budget choice, *Wah Hin* (☎087/332506; ②); others nearby are brothels. Keningau's poshest address is the *Hotel Perkasa* (☎087/331045, fax 334800;⑥), 1km out of town on the Tambunan road, which runs to an in-house health centre and restaurants.

Locals swear by the boiled duck at the *Yung On* coffee shop, a five-minute walk to the right of the Chinese temple's neighbour, the Yuk Yin School, at the northeastern edge of town. Nearby are *Restoran Shahrizal*, which serves fine *rotis* and curries behind its bamboo facade; and Keningau's best **restaurant**, the *Mandarin*, where one of the specialities is freshwater fish. Across town, near the *Hotel Wah Hin*, the *People Restaurant* dishes up *dim sum* and noodles. For a more economical meal, try the cluster of **food stalls** beside the bus stop, bearing in mind that most are closed by dusk.

The interior: Sapulut and beyond

One or two buses ($20) a day make the 116-kilometre journey from Keningau southeast to **Sapulut**, deep in the heart of Murut country – the departure point for some exhilarating river expeditions. The time-honoured customs of Sabah's indigenous peoples are dying out at an alarming rate, but along the rivers around Sapulut you can still witness traditional longhouse community life, little changed over the centuries. Moreover, the experience of sitting at the prow of a boat that's inching up a churning Bornean river under a dense canopy of forest is one that's hard to beat. If you do make the trip, bear in mind that it will take a few days and that you'll have to retrace your steps to Keningau, as the road runs out at Sapulut.

The trip starts inauspiciously: the terrain towards Sapulut has been so scarred by logging that, for much of the journey, you'll wonder why you bothered coming. Moreover, you'll be lucky if you make it to Sapulut without the bus suffering buckled suspension or a puncture: the scraps of tyre and inner tube littering the length of the unsealed road testify to its treacherousness. To make matters worse, endless logging trucks loom terrifyingly out of the dust cloud that hangs permanently over the route.

Around an hour out of Keningau is tiny **Kampung Sook**, barely more than a wide stretch of the road, with a few stalls and split bamboo houses and a huge district office. Beyond Sook, keep your eyes peeled for roadside shelters, erected by the Murut over their buried dead and draped with painted cloths. While crosses decorate several of these cloths, others feature more unorthodox designs, such as portraits of football players.

Sapulut

It takes four hours to reach **SAPULUT**, situated at the convergence of the Sapulut and Talankai rivers, and hemmed in by densely forested hills. It remains an appealing place in spite of its ugly tapioca mill, and though the main reason for coming here is to continue up- or downriver, there's enough of interest to warrant a day in the village itself. Across the pedestrian suspension bridge that spans Sungei Talankai is Sapulut's former schoolhouse (dating back to Japanese occupation, and now overgrown) and its **Mahkamah,** or native court building. The hollowed sandstone rock you can see outside the court is the *batu kelasan,* or spirit stone, by which men who were accused were entitled to test their innocence, the theory being that if they touched it and took an oath of honesty (a *sumpah*), and didn't subsequently die, they were telling the truth. A two-hour climb through the secondary forest above the mill brings you to a panoramic view of the surrounding kampungs and countryside.

The one **place to stay** in Sapulut is at the home of Lantir Bakayas (②), the boatman who arranges trips to Batu Punggul (see below). Lantir's wife serves up simple but filling **meals** ($5) throughout the day, and Lantir himself will happily show you around the village. Minibus drivers will drop you at Lantir's house, which is on the left-hand side of the road, beyond the mill.

Beyond Sapulut

The best trip out of Sapulut is up Sungei Sapulut to **Batu Punggul,** a 250-metre-high limestone cliff that rears out of virgin jungle. The climb to the summit is rewarded by outstanding views of the forest, while another few minutes' walk brings you to the impressive **Tinahas Caves,** whose walls are lined with swifts' nests and roosting bats. The Korperasi Pembangunan Desa (KPD), which controls Sapulut's tapioca mill, operates the *Batu Punggul Resort,* twenty minutes' walk from the cliff. As well as its resthouse (①–②), guests can stay in a traditional Murut longhouse (①), or can camp out, and there's a canteen, too. For an extra charge, villagers from a nearby longhouse will lay on a Murut cultural evening, complete with jars of lethal *tapai* (rice wine). A six-berth **boat** to Batu Punggul costs $250; the trip takes around two and a half hours (though it could be three times as long, depending on the weather) and passes isolated riverside kampungs and longhouses on the way. Both the boat and accommodation should be booked ahead in KK (see p.426), but arrangements can be made directly with Lantir, subject to there being space at the resort.

The going gets tougher – and pricier – if you travel downriver from Sapulut to visit one of the kampungs towards the Kalimantan border. The first settlement of any size, forty minutes south of Sapulut, is **Kampung Pagalongan,** a surprisingly large community, where local villagers pick up supplies. It's another ten minutes to the bend in the river commanded by **Kampung Silungai's** huge 120-metre longhouse. Despite its jarring zinc roof, the longhouse is an appealing construction of green and white wooden slats, centring on a ceremonial hall, and home to around six hundred extremely friendly villagers. More traditional longhouses can be seen at nearby **Pensiangan,** but their future is uncertain since the logging industry is moving unerringly towards this settlement – already there's reputed to be a track from Sapulut, though minibuses don't run this far. Finally, provided you have an Indonesian visa, it's possible to follow the Sungei Sapulut **into Kalimantan,** though renting a boat for such a journey is prohibitively expensive.

The person to contact if you want to explore the territory south of Sapulut is Lantir, who arranges **tailor-made trips** to these parts, though at a price: chartering a boat for a day's river meandering – say to Pensiangan and back – costs $400 for up to six people. Very occasionally, much cheaper **passenger launches** ply this stretch of the river – ask Lantir to check with the KPD office in Salong, 5km south of Sapulut, before you charter a boat, though bear in mind that you could have a long wait for a boat back again.

Tenom and around

After Keningau, the small town of **TENOM,** 42km to the southwest, comes as a great relief. The heady days when Tenom was the bustling headquarters of the Interior

District of British North Borneo are now long gone, and today it's a peaceful, friendly backwater. It has its fair share of dreary concrete buildings, but is given a certain grace by its mantle of lushly forested hills, while the centre boasts a selection of charismatic wooden shophouses and mansions, and a blue-domed mosque. The surroundings are extremely fertile, supporting maize, cocoa and soya beans – predominantly cultivated by the indigenous Murut people.

The **Tenom Agricultural Research Station** (Mon–Thurs 7am–3pm, Fri 7am–noon, Sat 7am–12.30pm) in Lagud Sebran, a 25-minute bus ride from below the padang, is where the state's Agricultural Department carries out feasibility studies on a wide range of crops. The research station is renowned for its **Orchid Centre** where a profusion of orchids cascade from trees and tree trunks. Less tempting, but actually much better than it sounds, is the nearby **Crop Museum** (free), where you can easily spend an hour strolling through the groves of exotic fruit trees and tropical plants, like durian, rambutan, jackfruit, coffee and okra – all tended by women in wide-brimmed hats. Views from the research station's own **resthouse** (☎087/735661; ②–③) are beautiful, though it's a fair walk from the station headquarters.

Murut villages

A string of tiny **Murut villages** runs along the road south of Tenom, most of them accessible by catching a bus bound for Kuala Tomani, 37km from Tenom. The Murut are Christians – the result of some fairly vigorous missionary work early this century – which accounts for the area's several powder-blue churches, made of wood and with names like True Jesus Church. Traditional longhouses have disappeared from the region, but a few **ceremonial halls** still stand, inside which you'll find *lansaran*: Murut trampolines, made of planks and pliant logs, and used for dancing jigs on special occasions. To see one, ask your bus driver to stop at **Kampung Mamai Tom** (around 28km from Tenom) or, better still, at **Kampung Kaparungan**, close to Kuala Tomani, where the bamboo benches in the ceremonial hall have gaps in them to take *tapai* jars. Sadly, the Murut rarely don their traditional costumes these days, unless tourists pay them to do so. The proposed **Murut cultural village**, to be built between Tenom and Melalap, may or may not materialize – if you're interested, contact the STPC in KK, or ask around in Tenom.

Practicalities

Buses north to Keningau ($5) – from where you can continue on to KK – and south to Kuala Tomani ($4), circle around Tenom all day long, looking for takers; you can always pick one up on the main street, at the western edge of the padang. **Shared taxis** to Keningau also cost $5 and leave from the main street whenever they've assembled four passengers. The journey northwest to Beaufort is best done by **train** – Tenom marks the end of Sabah's only stretch of railway and the track skirts the southeast edge of town. Tenom Station is on the southern edge of the padang – call for reservations to be sure of a railcar seat (see "Beaufort" below for timetable and details).

If friendly *Hotel Kim San* (☎087/735485; ②) at the southwestern end of town is full, all is not lost: **rooms** at the *Hotel Sri Jaya* (☎087/735077; ②), on Tenom's main street, are spick and span, or there's the simpler and less expensive *Hotel Sabah* (☎087/735534; ②), off a side road by the market. The classiest place in town though, is the *Hotel Perkasa* (☎087/735811; ④–⑤), a $3 taxi ride (or strenuous hike) up the hill above town, its pleasing rooms affording great views of the surrounding countryside. **Places to eat** are plentiful, with a clutch of coffee shops and restaurants in the area around the *Hotel Kim San*. For a tasty *mee* soup, try the *Restoran Double Happiness*, below the padang; or, for something a bit more lavish, head 2km south of town along the Tomani road to the cavernous *YNL Restaurant* (daily 6pm–1am), where the speciality is fresh fish caught in the nearby Sungei Padas. There's decent Chinese food at the *Perkasa*, and at the market on Saturday evenings, hawker stalls are set out on the hotel's front lawn.

Beaufort

Named after the elaborately named Leicester P. Beaufort, one of the early governors of British North Borneo, **BEAUFORT** is a well-to-do, uneventful town, normally only used by tourists taking a train to Tenom, or on their way to the white-water rafting on nearby Sungei Padas. Beaufort's commercial importance has declined markedly since the laying of a sealed road from KK into the interior lessened the importance of its rail link with Tenom. The town's position on the banks of the Sungei Padas leaves it prone to flooding, which explains why its shophouses are raised on steps – early photographs show Beaufort looking like a sort of Southeast Asian Venice. But once you've poked around in the town market, inspected angular St Paul's Church at the top of town and taken a walk past the stilt houses on the river bank, you've exhausted its sights.

The **train** station is next to Sungei Padas at the southern side of town, from where it's a minute or so on foot into the centre – walk up the road opposite the station forecourt. **Buses** stop in the centre itself, beside the market, while taxis congregate outside the train station.

Beaufort's two **hotels** are the *Beaufort* (☎087/211911; ②), east of the market, and the *Mandarin Inn* (☎087/212798; ②), five minutes' walk across the river – they're practically identical, though rooms at the *Mandarin* just have the edge in terms of freshness. When it comes to **eating**, you could do a lot worse than *Christopher's Corner Parking*, across from the train station, whose friendly owner will rustle you up a really good Western breakfast – toast, marmalade, sausage, beans and egg. *Restoran Kim Wah*, a sizeable establishment below the *Hotel Beaufort*, serves simple Chinese food, though better is to be found at the *Foh Chuan*, sited in one of the new blocks just north of the *Beaufort*, which is famed locally for its noodle dishes. The *Loong Hing*, 250m over the bridge and out of town, is another establishment that comes highly recommended, though if it's curries and *rotis* you're after, the *Bismillah* in the town centre is hard to beat. There are also hawker stalls – including a meatball soup-seller that locals rave about – upstairs in the town market and more next to the bridge.

Taking the train

Over the metals all rusted brown,
Thunders the "Mail" to Jesselton Town;
Tearing on madly, reck'ning not fate,
Making up time – she's two days late
See how the sparks from her smokestack shower,
Swaying on wildly at three miles an hour.

As this 1922 rhyme illustrates, Sabah's only railway line is more a curio than a practical mode of transport. Although the line runs all the way from KK to Tenom, travelling between Beaufort and the capital is far quicker by **bus**, and it's only the two-and-a-quarter-hour journey from Beaufort to Tenom – a boneshaking ride tracing the twists and turns of the Sungei Padas – that's really worth making. The train passes tiny stations and winds through dramatic jungle that at times arches right over the track. Three types of train – diesel, cargo and railcar – ply the route daily; the fastest, most comfortable and most expensive option is the compact railcar, whose front windows afford an unimpeded view of the oncoming countryside; but it only holds a handful of passengers, so phone or call in at the station to book ahead.

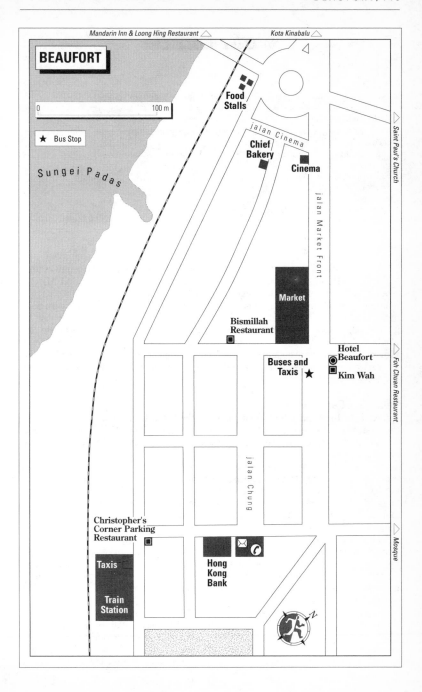

BEAUFORT

Mandarin Inn & Loong Hing Restaurant △

Kota Kinabalu △

Food Stalls

0   100 m

★ Bus Stop

S u n g e i   P a d a s

jalan Cinema

Chief Bakery

Cinema

Saint Paul's Church ▷

jalan Market Front

Market

Bismillah Restaurant

Hotel Beaufort

Buses and Taxis ★

Kim Wah

Foh Chuan Restaurant ▷

jalan Chung

Christopher's Corner Parking Restaurant

Taxis

Mosque ▷

Hong Kong Bank

Train Station

N

TRAIN TIMETABLE

Beaufort–Tenom
Mon–Sat: 8.25am (railcar); 10.50am (diesel); noon (cargo); 1.55pm (diesel); 3.50pm (railcar).
Sun: 6.45am (diesel); 10.50am (diesel); 2.30pm (diesel); 4.05pm (railcar).

Tenom–Beaufort
Mon–Sat: 6.40am (railcar); 7.30am (diesel); 8am (cargo); 1.40pm (diesel); 4pm (railcar).
Sun: 7.20am (railcar); 7.55am (diesel); 12.10pm (diesel); 3.05pm (diesel).

Railcar: $8.35 one-way.
Diesel & Cargo: $2.75 one-way.

Information on ☎087/221518 (Beaufort) or ☎087/4735514 (Tenom).

West of Beaufort: the Klias Peninsula and Pulau Tiga Park

Immediately west of Beaufort and served by regular minibuses from the centre of town is the **Klias Peninsula**, from whose most westerly settlement, tiny **MENUMBOK**, several ferries depart daily for Pulau Labuan (see below). Meanwhile, it's a jarring, hour-long bus ride from Beaufort northwest to **KUALA PENYU**, at the northern point of the peninsula, the departure point for **Pulau Tiga Park** and not a place to visit for its own sake. If you get stuck here, your only hope is a room at the *Government Rest House* (☎087/884231; ③), five minutes beyond the Shell garage on the waterfront. **Moving on**, if there are no buses leaving Penyu for major destinations, take a local bus to nearby Kampung Kayul and wave down a bus coming from Menumbok heading either for KK or Beaufort.

Pulau Tiga Park

Pulau Tiga Park – north of Kuala Penyu in the South China Sea – once comprised three islands, but wave erosion has reduced one of them, Pulau Kalampunian Besar, to a sand bar. The remaining two, Tiga and Kalampunian Damit, offer good **snorkelling**, plus the chance to see some unusual **wildlife**.

Pulau Tiga itself was formed by erupting mud volcanoes; you can still see smaller versions, occasionally squirting strings of mud into the air, at the top of the island. Circled by fine sand beaches and good coral, and crisscrossed by lengthy trails, Tiga's forested interior harbours wild pigs and monitor lizards; if you're down on the sands, look out for Tiga's most famous inhabitants, its megapodes, or rotund incubator birds – so called because they lay their eggs in mounds of sand and leaves.

Pulau Kalampunian Damit, 1km northeast of Pulau Tiga, is known locally as Pulau Ular, or "Snake Island", as it attracts a species of sea snake called the yellow-lipped sea krait in huge numbers – on an average day, at least a hundred of these metallic grey and black creatures come ashore to rest, mate and lay their eggs. Though dozy in the heat of the day, the sea kraits are poisonous, so you're best off accompanied by a ranger if you want to see them.

To **get to the park**, speak to the Sabah Parks office in KK (see p.429), or call Mr Simbaluk or Mr Salim (☎011/818321), Sabah Parks' representatives in the park. The return journey costs a minimum of $150 for one to five people, and $30 for each extra passenger – though there's no harm in bargaining. From Tiga, bank on $30 more for a boat to visit Kalampunian Damit. The only **accommodation** is on Tiga itself, where a night in either the hostel or one of three cabins costs $30 a head. If that's too pricey, there's space for camping. Bookings are handled by Sabah Parks in KK.

Pulau Labuan

PULAU LABUAN, around 10km west of the Klias Peninsula, is a small, arrowhead-shaped island, whose size bears no relation to its significance. The terms of a treaty with the Sultan of Brunei yielded the island to the British Crown long before neighbouring Sabah was procured by the Chartered Company, and on Christmas Eve, 1846, Captain G.R. Mundy took possession of it in the name of Queen Victoria. In addition to Labuan's fine anchorage and consequent potential as a trading post, it was its **coal deposits** – the northern tip of the island is still called Tanjung Kubong, or Coal Point – which attracted the British, keen to establish a coaling station for passing steamships. With trade in mind, the island was made a free port in 1848; by 1889, it had been incorporated into British North Borneo, a state of affairs that lasted until it joined the Straits Settlements a few years into the new century.

World War II brought the focus of the world upon Labuan. Less than a month after the bombing of Pearl Harbour, the island was occupied by the invading Japanese army, on New Year's Day, 1942, and it was through Labuan that the Japanese forces penetrated British North Borneo. During the war years the island was known as **Maida Island**, in memory of General Maida, commander-in-chief of the Japanese forces in British Borneo, who was killed in a plane crash near Bintulu on his way to declare its airport open. In June 1945, the men of the Ninth Australian Infantry Division landed on Labuan and three and a half years of occupation came to an end; having witnessed the arrival of Japanese forces, it was only fitting that Labuan should also witness their surrender, which took place on September 9, 1945. Labuan, along with Sabah, reverted to the British Crown in July 1946, though it was a further seventeen years before it actually became part of Sabah. Then, in 1984, the island was declared part of Malaysian Federal Territory, governed directly by Kuala Lumpur. Today, Labuan – with a population fast approaching fifty thousand – is still a duty-free port, though its present status as both a sordid getaway for Bruneians and Sabahans after prostitutes and cheap beer, and a base for Filipino smugglers, is at odds with its pretensions to becoming an offshore banking centre and tourist hot spot. Still, with ferries from KK and Brunei interconnecting at Labuan, you may well end up spending some time here.

The island

The centre of Labuan, previously known as Victoria but now referred to simply as **LABUAN TOWN**, lies on the southeastern side of the island, its central streets thronging with Malaysian businessmen and Russian sailors, Bruneian shoppers and Filipino traders. The *gerai*, or permanent **market**, at the far western end of town, is rather downbeat, though its upper level affords good views of Kampung Patau Patau, the modest **water village** northwest of town whose surrounding waters bristle with rotting foundations. Below the market is a gathering of tin shacks, where Filipinos sell seashell models, stuffed turtles, leather bags, brassware, cloths and silks.

Just 500m north of town, the dome of the **An 'Nur Jamek Mosque** resembles a concrete shuttlecock; from there you'll have to travel further afield to amuse yourself. Layang Layangan minibuses from the bus area (see below) will drop you at Labuan's **war memorial**, next to a sleepy kampung 4km north of town. Occupying a serene seaside site within the aptly named **Peace Park**, the memorial – a concave concrete bridge covered in grass – commemorates all those who died in Borneo in World War II; just below, an enclosure marks the site of the Japanese surrender of 1945. Locals swim on the narrow **beach** beside the memorial, strewn with driftwood and coconut husks, though there's a better stretch around 1km further north. There's another

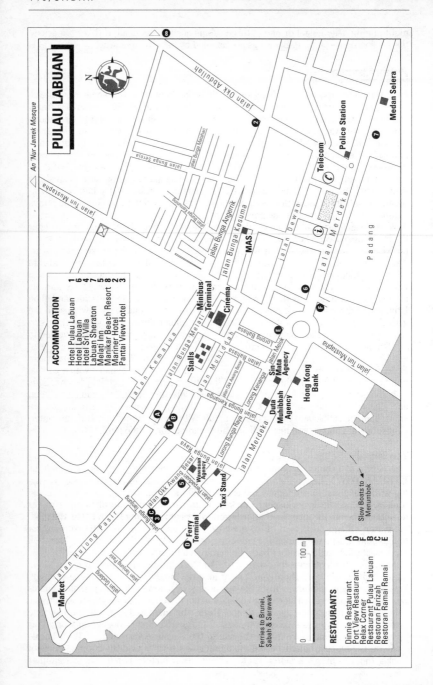

PULAU LABUAN

ACCOMMODATION

Hotel Pulau Labuan	1
Hotel Labuan	6
Hotel Sri Villa	4
Labuan Sheraton	7
Melati Inn	5
Manikar Beach Resort	8
Mariner Hotel	2
Pantai View Hotel	3

RESTAURANTS

Dinnie Restaurant	A
Port View Restaurant	D
Relax Corner	F
Restaurant Pulau Labuan	B
Restoran Farizah	C
Restoran Ramai Ramai	E

decent beach across the island, below the **chimney**, all that remains of Labuan's coal industry. On the way out to the airport is a large **Allied war cemetery**.

That's about it for land-bound tourists, but scuba divers will find more to entertain them offshore. Several World War II and postwar **shipwrecks** lie in the waters off Labuan's southern coast, among them the *USS Salute* (scuppered by a mine in 1945), and a passenger steamer commandeered by the Japanese and sunk by the Australian airforce, also in 1945. *Borneo Divers* (☎087/415867) charge $100 for one wreck dive, $185 for two dives, and just $65 for a reef dive off **Pulau Kuraman**, one of several picturesque islands off Labuan's southern coast; they also offer more expensive three-day/two-night packages out of KK.

Practicalities

Jalan Merdeka, running along the seafront below the town centre, forms the spine of Labuan Town; along it, you'll find a branch of the Hong Kong Bank and the **tourist information office** (☎087/423445). Running north from the middle of Jalan Merdeka, and effectively splitting the town in two, is Jalan Tun Mustapha, home to the new post office building and to the local **Borneo Divers** office. **Ferries** from Kota Kinabalu, Menumbok, Limbang and Lawas in Sarawak, and Bandar Seri Begawan (in Brunei) dock at the ferry terminal, below Jalan Merdeka; see below for all departure details. Labuan's **airport** is 3km north of town and connected to it by regular, inexpensive **minibuses**, which run from the eastern end of Jalan Bunga Melati; there's a MAS office in the *Federal Hotel*, on Jalan Bunga Kesuma (☎087/412263).

ACCOMMODATION

There are plenty of **places to stay** in Labuan, though unless you're prepared to brave one of the places over at the east end of town, which double as brothels, none is in the budget price range. The best deal in town is a room with a fan in the Indian-run *Pantai View Hotel*, while the *Manikar Beach Resort* is the plushest option.

Labuan, Jalan Tun Merdeka (☎087/412311). One of the more expensive options, which has its own swimming pool. ⑥.

Labuan Sheraton, Jalan Tun Merdeka (☎087/422000). A new place, with fine rooms and a range of stylish restaurants and bars. ⑧.

Manikar Beach Resort, (☎087/418700). Set in 15 acres of private beach and gardens up on the northwestern tip of the island, this is Labuan's last word in swank. Its 250 ocean-view rooms allow access to classy business, recreational and watersports facilities. ⑨.

Mariner, Jalan Tanjung Purun (☎087/418822). The well-appointed rooms represent excellent value, so long as long-term price cuts still apply. ⑤.

Melati Inn, (☎087/416307). Right opposite the terminal on is the, where double rooms come with TV, air-con and (for an extra $3) bathroom. ③.

Pantai View, Jalan Bunga Tanjung (☎087/411339). Good value Indian-run hotel. ②.

Pulau Labuan, Jalan Perpaduan (☎087/416288). A comfortable, if rather overpriced option. ④.

Sri Villa, Jalan OKK Awang Besar (☎087/416369). Good value, though slightly pricer than the *Pantai*, which is in the same bracket. ②.

EATING

Along Jalan Merdeka and Jalan OKK Awang Besar you'll find a number of no-frills, Chinese and Indian **restaurants** – the latter featuring American wrestling videos day and night. Particularly good for *rotis*, *murtabaks* and curries is *Restoran Farizah*, next to the *Pantai View* (see above) – though many locals swear by the *Faizal*, a short way west along the same street. Two blocks north, facing each other on Jalan Bunga Mawar, there's the Muslim *Dinnie Restaurant* and the *Restaurant Pulau Labuan*, an air-con restaurant with a wide Chinese menu. For great *dim sum* and Chinese tea, try *Restoran Ramai Ramai* at the intersection of Jalan Merdeka and Jalan Tun Mustapha;

also good for Chinese cuisine is Jalan Merdeka's waterfront *Port View Restaurant* where diners enjoy great sea views. At night, make a beeline for the stalls west of the town cinema, above Jalan Muhibbah, where you'll find *nasi campur* and delicious barbecued chicken wings. Altogether more upmarket is the *Hotel Labuan*'s *Nagalang Chinese & Japanese Restaurant*, while below it is the 24-hour *Kiamsam Terrace* coffee shop. Should you want a quick sharpener before dining, *Relax Corner* opposite *Hotel Labuan* is a friendly pub serving cold and incredibly cheap beer.

FERRIES FROM LABUAN
Tickets are sold sporadically at the arrival points at the ferry terminal area, though if the booth is closed, there are three outlets nearby: Duta Muhibbah Agency (daily 8am–4pm; ☎087/413827) and Sin Matu Agency (Mon–Sat 8am–5pm, Sun 8am–noon; ☎087/412261), at 52 and 55 Jalan Merdeka respectively, and Wawasan Agency (daily 8am–4pm; ☎087/422236), at 88 Jalan OKK Awang Besar.

Although schedules are susceptible to change, there are presently three departures a day to **Kota Kinabalu**, at 8.30am, 1pm and 3pm ($28); and four to **Brunei** at 8am, 12.15pm, 2pm & 3pm ($24). For **Limbang**, a ferry leaves daily at 12.30pm, while a **Lawas** ferry departs at 12.30pm – both cost $20. Finally, there are plenty of speedboats ($10) to **Menumbok**, from where it's a two-hour bus ride to Kota Kinabalu, as well as two daily car ferries ($5 for foot passengers) that depart from the jetty behind the Hong Kong Bank at 8am and 1pm.

To Sarawak: Sipitang

On the bumpy gravel road 47km southwest of Beaufort, **SIPITANG** is a sleepy seafront town worth bearing in mind if you need a place to stay en route to Sarawak. Approaching from the north, a bridge marks the start of town – look out for the pretty stilt houses to your left as you cross. Just over the bridge, there's a jetty from where a **boat** leaves (daily 7am; $20) for Labuan; 250m beyond that, you're in the town centre. Buses for Beaufort, KK and Lawas (see below) congregate in the centre of town; right next to the bus terminus is the taxi stand. Except for a trip to **Taman Negara** – a beachside picnic spot a few kilometres south of town, and favoured by locals at the weekend, when there'll probably be a minibus service – there's nothing to do in Sipitang. On the bright side, there are stacks of **restaurants** and eating houses in the centre of town, of which a couple, the *Kami* and the *Rina*, have used their magical, sunset-facing positions on the shore of Brunei Bay to good advantage by erecting balconies over the water's edge. Across the main road, *Restoran Bismillah* does good curries and breakfast *rotis*; a minute or so further south, the *Asandong* puts on a superb Malay buffet every night. A number of satay- and fried-chicken sellers set up stalls on the waterfront at dusk. Of the **hotels** along the main road, the *Hotel Asanol* (☎087/821506; ②) is the friendliest and most affordable; failing that, nearby *Hotel Shangsan* (☎087/821800; ④) is tidy enough, though substantially pricier.

Crossing into Sarawak

The easiest way to travel from Sipitang **to Lawas in Sarawak** is to take a minibus or taxi (both $10) from the centre of town, which takes one hour. It's cheaper to wait for the *Lawas Express* ($6), which leaves KK daily at 1pm, passing through Sipitang around 4pm and getting to Lawas some time after 5pm; you can catch a $2 minibus to Sindumin, on the Sabah side of the border, and then connect with a Sarawak bus. Whichever you choose, the driver will wait while you pass through the passport controls flanking the border – one in Sindumin, the other a couple of hundred metres away at Merapok in Sarawak.

North of Kota Kinabalu

North of Kota Kinabalu, Sabah's trans-state road hurries through the capital's drab suburbs and past the timber yards of **Tepilok**, en route to the more pastoral environs of **Tuaran**. From here, the *atap* houses of the Bajau water villages, **Mengkabong** and **Penambawang**, are both a stone's throw away. Although the main road veers eastwards to Ranau (see p.459) just outside Tuaran, a lesser fork runs north, through the foothills of Mount Kinabalu before reaching **Kota Belud**, the site of a weekly market that attracts tribespeople from all over the region. The landscape really hots up north of Kota Belud: jewel-bright paddy fields line the road for much of the way up to the **Kudat Peninsula**, with Mount Kinabalu beyond. Journey's end is signalled by the coconut groves and beaches of **Kudat**, formerly capital of British North Borneo, but now a focal point for the Rungus people who dwell in modernized longhouses in the surrounding countryside.

Buses for Tuaran and Kota Belud leave KK throughout the day, and both destinations make for decent day-trips out of the capital. However, it's worth thinking twice before committing yourself to the longer trip to the Kudat Peninsula, as the region's inaccessible beaches and modern longhouses leave many visitors disappointed.

Tuaran, Mengkabong and Penambawang

It takes just under an hour to travel the 34km from Kota Kinabalu to **TUARAN**, from where it's possible to visit two water villages. On the way, you'll pass the **Yayasan Sabah Building** – a vast glass cylinder in Likas Bay, which houses the Sabah Foundation, an organization that channels profits from its huge timber concession into schools, hospitals and a flying doctor service.

Of the two villages, **MENGKABONG**, ten minutes out of Tuaran on a local bus, is the most accessible and is a favourite destination with KK's tour agencies. The sight of a village built out over the sea on stilts is usually a compelling one, but Mengkabong is a noisy, charmless example, and you'd do well to make the extra effort to reach **PENAMBAWANG**. Minibuses to Kampung Surusup – the tiny settlement from where you can catch a boat to Penambawang – leave from the road west of Tuaran's brown clocktower: it's a twenty-minute drive (on a nightmarish road) through idyllic paddy fields. Once in Surusup, you'll need to ask around for a boat – Penambawang is fifteen minutes northeast, across a wide bay skirted with mangroves, and the return ride shouldn't cost more than $10–15. Except for a handful of zinc roofs, it's a timeless village, with houses of *atap*, bamboo and wood interconnected by labyrinthine boardwalks – called *jambatan* – along which fish are laid out to dry. The village's welcoming inhabitants are Muslim Bajau.

While **hotels** in Tuaran are nothing to write home about, the *Shangri-La Tanjung Aru*'s (see p.431) sister resort, away to the west on Dalit Bay, is as classy a place to stay as any on Sabah and worth considering if you've got money to spare. The *Rasa Ria Resort* (☎088/792888; ⑨), sandwiched between its own 400-acre forest and the South China Sea, has over three hundred luxury rooms, most with sea views. Within its grounds are a superb 18-hole golf course, and a private nature reserve that has orangutans, orchids and pitcher plants among its natural assets. Several shuttle buses leave daily from the *Tanjung Aru Resort*, taking around 45 minutes to reach Dalit Bay.

Kota Belud and on to Kota Marudu

For six days of the week, **KOTA BELUD**, 75km northeast of KK on the road to Kudat, is a drab little town, its main street the haunt of listless teenagers and packs of scraggy dogs. Each Sunday, though, it springs to life, as hordes of villagers from the surrounding countryside congregate at its weekly market, said to be the biggest in Sabah, ten minutes' walk out of town along Jalan Hasbollah. The *tamu* fulfils a social, as much as a commercial, role, and tribes represented include the Rungus, Kadazan/Dusun and Bajau, who occasionally ride in on horseback and in traditional apparel.

Kota Belud's popularity among KK's tour operators means it always has tourists; even so, you're far more likely to see dried fish, chains of yeast beads (used to make rice wine), buffalo, betel nut and *tudung saji* (colourful food covers) for sale, than souvenirs. At Kota Belud's annual *tamu besar*, or "big market", in addition to the more typical stalls, there are cultural performances, traditional horseback games and handicraft demonstrations. The *tamu besar* usually takes place in November. For more details, call in at the STPC in KK.

To catch the weekly *tamu* at its best, plan to leave KK by 7am at the latest. Buses ($5) leave from the far side of the Shell garage near the GPO; or catch a Kudat-bound bus ($5) from the long-distance station; it's a scenic ninety-minute trip.

Practicalities

Buses stop beside the smashing new district office in the centre of town, and with onward connections so good, there's really no need to spend the night here. A far better idea is to book a bed at the Kinabalu National Park (see p.454), which can be reached via Tamparuli, or to carry on to Kudat. If you do **stay**, there's only the diminutive *KB Resthouse Resort* (☎088/265842; ⑤), sited on a small hill on the outskirts of town, just a short stroll from the site of the *tamu*. The resort also maintains a lodge 8km away in the countryside called the *Kulambai Homestead*, which offers visitors the chance to enjoy kampung living in an idyllic location, ringed by paddy fields. Staff here can arrange trips to see otters, egrets and proboscis monkeys. There's not much in the way of **restaurants** either; for Malay food, try *Restoran Rahmat* below the district office, or one of the lean-to stalls beyond the far side of the office. Otherwise, *Kedai Makan Sin Hing*, on the main KK–Kudat road serves up basic Chinese meals. Of the coffee shops over in the newer portion of KB (to the left of the Kudat road as you enter town), the *Restoran Zam Zam* does good curries and fried chicken.

Kota Marudu and around

The 26km from Kota Belud north to Kampung Timbang takes in some of Sabah's most dramatic scenery, with the grand peaks of Mount Kinabalu reflected – rice harvest allowing – in the still waters of the paddy fields to the east. At the base of Marudu Bay, the road forks, the right turn leading to **KOTA MARUDU** – a town with two hotels and several restaurants, but with nothing to entice you to stop and try them out. East of Kota Marudu, a potholed road passes seaside kampungs and huge sawmills before reaching Pitas, from where it's possible to catch a bus to Kenibongon, the departure point for boats to Pulau Jambongon, though the activities of pirates in its waters currently make the island unsafe to visit.

The Kudat Peninsula

Coconut groves and paddy fields line the upper portion of the badly surfaced road that runs northwest of Marudu Bay. Many of the coconuts end up at the desiccated coconut plant 9km out of **KUDAT**, right on Borneo's northern tip – from the bus, you'll see piles of discarded husks, resembling bleached skulls.

Kudat lies on the western shore of Marudu Bay; its good natural harbour meant it was declared the administrative capital of British North Borneo in 1881, though control was switched to Sandakan two years later. Although it is lively and indisputably friendly, there's not much to bring you here, save for a peek at the town centre's lurid orange **Chinese temple**, a stroll around the busy **waterfront** – where wiry old men carry sacks to and from the *godowns* which back Jalan Lo Thien Chock's shophouses – and a visit to the adjacent **stilt village** at the southern end of town.

The Kudat Peninsula is home to the Rungus people, and until recently their **long-house** dwellings, or *binatang*, were the region's main attraction. They still exist, and their size still impresses, but today they're often made with sheets of corrugated zinc, whose durability makes it preferable to traditional materials like timbers, tree bark, *rattan* and *nipah* leaves. **Kampung Tinanggol**, set back from the KK road, 37km south of Kudat, boasts three 25-family longhouses and a quaint white church. The STPC has constructed an authentic *binatang* in the village which allows visitors to spend a night in a traditional Rungus environment. Contact the STPC in KK for more details. Further south, at **Kampung Mattungong**, a footpath leads eastwards over a wire suspension bridge, through bamboo groves, to **Kampung Mompilis**, which has two dilapidated longhouses; it's really the walk that makes the trip worth while.

The beaches

Kudat's most famous beach is **Bak Bak**, 12km north of town, though **Tajau**, a few kilometres to the north, is favoured by some locals. Across on the west coast, there's **Bangau Beach**, near the town of **Sikuati** – any bus headed for KK can drop you at the turning, but then it's a six-kilometre hike to the beach. Sikuati itself is only a small coastal settlement, some 20km west of Kudat, though it hosts a good-sized Sunday *tamu*. Further south, green turtles are said to come ashore to lay their eggs, at attractive **Kelambu Beach**. To reach Kelambu, turn right onto Jalan Indarasan Laut, some 39km south of Kudat, and push on for another 6km.

Quite a few locals visit Bak Bak on a Sunday; otherwise local buses to kampungs near Kudat's beaches are so erratic as to be totally impractical. Taking a taxi is the only practical solution, but prices start at around $16 for the return journey.

It's also possible to take a ferry to **Pulau Banggi**, off Sabah's north coast, though only if you've got a few days to spare, as departures are unpredictable, and the only way to get around the island once you're there is to hitch on local boats. The island boasts forest and beaches, and there's a small government **resthouse** (☎088/612511; ③) at Kampung Kalaki, the main settlement – contact the *Urusetia* in Kudat (see below) for details.

Practicalities

Downtown Kudat centres on the intersection of Jalan Ibrahim Arshad and Jalan Lo Thien Chock – the latter is Kudat's main street, with most of its shops and a Standard Chartered Bank. **Minibuses** congregate a few yards east of the intersection, as do the town's **taxis**, though the two main KK-bound **buses** (daily at 7.30am & noon) stop along Lorong Empat west of Jalan Lo Thien Chock. For **ferries** to Pulau Banggi, head for the jetty at the southern end of Jalan Lo Thien Chock.

Accommodation starts with the *Hotel Oriental* (☎088/611045; ②), at the portside end of Jalan Lo Thien Chock, whose bright and clean rooms are only marred by an insalubrious hallway, shared toilets and a noisy snooker hall downstairs. For a bit more comfort, best bet is the *Hotel Greenland* (☎088/613211; ③), five minutes' east of the town centre, in Block E of "New Kudat", the SEDCO shophouse development. *Hotel Sunrise* (☎088/611517; ②), in the middle of Jalan Lo Thien Chock, is another decent establishment; here, an extra $16 or so gets you your own bathroom and TV. Finally, enquiries about Pulau Banggi's resthouse can be made at Kudat's *Urusetia*, or District Office (☎088/611511), beyond the golf course.

Restoran Sungei Wang, two minutes beyond the *Greenland Hotel*, is the best **restaurant** in town, serving such delights as scallops in black bean sauce and tofu with crabmeat for around $6; there are tables outside on the patio, which is strung with fairy lights. Back in the town centre, *Sri Mutiara*, opposite the *Sunrise* on Jalan Lo Thien Chock, is a spruce joint that serves tasty Malay food and finger-licking fried chicken. At the *Keng Nam Tong Coffee Shop*, opposite the *Silver Inn*, you can have coffee and cake on a marble-topped table, and there's passable north Indian food at *Restoran Mawar* near the turning to Lorong Empat.

Kinabalu National Park

There's no more astounding sight in Borneo than the cloud-encased summit of **Mount Kinabalu** – at 4101 metres, half the height of Everest – shooting skywards from the 750 square kilometres of **KINABALU NATIONAL PARK**. Eighty-five kilometres north-east of KK and plainly visible from Sabah's west coast, Kinabalu's jagged peaks appear impossibly daunting at first sight, but in fact, the mountain is relatively easily climbed, by means of a well-defined, 8.5 kilometre path which weaves up its southern side to the bare granite of the summit, passing a vast range of flora and fauna. Limbs that are weary from the climb up the mountain will welcome the warm, sulphurous waters of the **Poring Hot Springs**, around 40km away, just outside the park's southeastern border, while between these two sites is the small town of **Ranau**, an accommodation option if you arrive too late to reach the springs.

A TUT bus leaves KK's long-distance terminal for the park daily at 7.30am, after which minibuses depart when they're full; don't forget to arrange your accommodation at the Sabah Parks office before you board (see "Practicalities", p.459, for all the details).

Practicalities

It's a good idea to book a **place to stay** in the park as soon as possible – especially if you're planning to go at the weekend, when it's at its busiest. If you're really organized, you can book by post or phone: postal bookings should be addressed to the Park Warden, Sabah Parks Office, Lot 1-3, Block K, Sinsuran Shopping Complex, PO Box 10626, Kota Kinabalu (☎088/211585). Otherwise, drop in at the office, where the friendly staff will help you plan your ascent. You'll need at least two days to climb Mount Kinabalu – three if you want to carry on by bus to Poring – though you'll be glad of a spare day or two, in case cloud cover spoils the view from the summit. Only accommodation is paid for in KK – permits and guide fees are levied at the park itself (see below). Note that, while prices in this section are given for two people sharing, some of the lodge and cabin accommodation requires that you book for a minimum of four to eight people.

Upon **arrival**, buses stop at the extended cluster of lodgings, restaurants and offices known as park headquarters, depositing you outside the **park reception** office (daily 7am–7.30pm), where you go to check into your accommodation. Staff here will provide you with useful maps and information sheets, while at the neighbouring souvenir shop there's a wide range of T-shirts, postcards and Borneo-related books. The staff at the park reception can also arrange charter buses ($60) to Poring.

Most climbers spend their first night at the mountain around the **park headquarters** and set off early the next morning. Exploring the twenty kilometres of **trails** that loop the montane forest around the headquarters is as good an introduction as any to the park – you can join the free guided tour that leaves daily from the administration office at 11.15am. Less dramatic, but still interesting, are the labelled plants of the **Mountain Garden** (Mon–Fri 8am–4.30pm, Sat 8am–5pm, Sun 9am–4pm), below the administration office. The **Multivision Show** (daily at 1.30pm; $1), screened in the office itself, and the **Slide Show** (Mon & Fri–Sat at 7.30pm; $1) are less informative – instead, go upstairs for the photos, visuals and mounted exhibits of the **Exhibit Centre**, where you should look out, in particular, for the monster stick insect.

A cluster of **hotels** has sprung up along the main road outside the park, but there's a perfectly adequate range of choices in the park itself. For those on tight budgets, the *Old* or *New Fellowship* **hostels** are basic but salubrious dormitory set-ups ($10) with cooking facilities. From there, prices take a hike, with a variety of cabins all working out at roughly $40 a head. The twin-bed **cabins** (④) command magnificent views and are convenient for the park's administration office, while the four-person **annexe rooms** (②) are in the office itself. Top of the range are the *Nepenthes Villas* (⑥) – tasteful wooden chalets, each sleeping four people – and the swish *Kinabalu Lodge* (⑤).

Huts on the mountain couldn't be more basic – with the exception of *Laban Rata Rest House* (③) which has its own restaurant, as well as central heating and hot water showers. Otherwise, *Gunting Lagadan*, *Panar Laban* and *Waras* huts (all ①) have electricity and cooking facilities. *Sayat-Sayat Hut* (①) is an hour further up the mountain, and lacks even an electricity supply.

The park's best **restaurant** is the *Kinabalu Balsam* (daily 6am–10pm, Sat until 11pm), whose balcony has fine views of the mountain top; inside the entrance is a shop which sells chocolate, corned beef and biscuits for the climb. Alternatively, make for the administration office and the *Liwagu Restaurant* (daily 6am–10pm, Sat until 11pm), which, despite having all the ambience of a school canteen, serves well-cooked dishes, both Western and Asian. Higher up, unless you're catering for yourself, the only option is the restaurant in the *Laban Rata Rest House* (daily 7am–8pm & 2am–3.30am), where the food is fortifying, if on the pricey side.

Mount Kinabalu

Conquering **Mount Kinabalu** today is far easier than it was in 1858, when Spenser St John, British consul-general to the native states of Borneo, found his progress blocked by Kadazan "shaking their spears and giving us other hostile signs". Hugh Low, at the time British colonial secretary on Pulau Labuan, had made the first recorded ascent of the mountain seven years earlier, though he baulked at climbing its highest peak, considering it "inaccessible to any but winged animals". The peak – subsequently named after Low, as was the mile-deep gully that cleaves the mountain top – was finally conquered in 1888 by John Whitehead. **Low's Gully** splits the summit into a U-shape, which led early explorers to conclude that Kinabalu was volcanic; in fact, the mountain is a granite pluton – an enormous ball of molten rock which has solidified and forced its way through the Crocker Mountain Range over millions of years. This process continues today, with the mountain gaining a few millimetres annually.

The origin of the mountain's name is uncertain; one legend tells how a Chinese prince travelled to Borneo to seek out a huge pearl, guarded by a dragon at the summit of the mountain. Having slain the dragon and claimed the pearl, the prince married a Kadazan girl, only to desert her and return to China. His wife was left to mourn him on the slopes of the mountain – hence *Kina* (China) and *balu* (widow) – where she eventually turned to stone. Another idea is that the name derives from the Kadazan words *Aki Nabalu* – "the revered place of the dead". Nineteenth-century climbs had to take into account the superstitions of local porters, who believed the mountain to be a sacred ancestral home. When Low climbed it, his guides brought along charms, quartz crystals and human teeth to protect the party, and Kadazan porters still offer up chickens, eggs, cigars, betel nut and rice to the mountain's spirits at an annual ceremony.

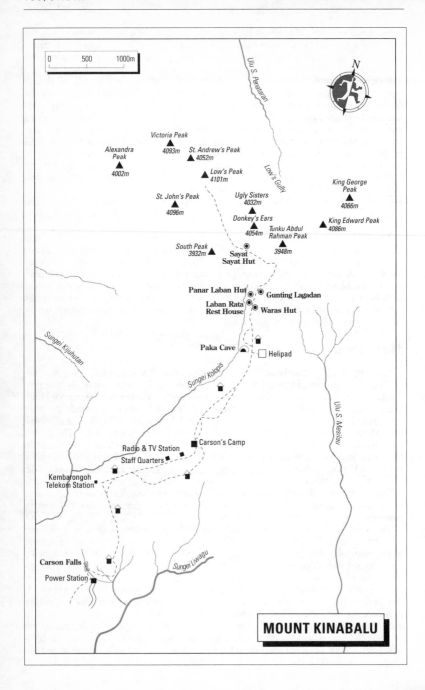

LOW'S GULLY

Mount Kinabalu grabbed the world's headlines in March 1993, when two British army officers and three Hong Kong soldiers went missing on a training exercise down Low's Gully – described by Spenser St John as "a deep chasm, surrounded on three sides by precipices, so deep that the eye could not reach the bottom. . . . There was no descending here. " Defeated by impassable waterfalls and boulders, the men set up camp in a mountain cave and left out an SOS marked out with white pebbles. Treacherous weather conditions and inhospitable terrain repeatedly thwarted rescue attempts, but they were finally found, on day thirty of what should have been a ten-day mission – by which time they were surviving on a diet of Polo mints.

Climbing the mountain

Aim to be at the park reception by 7am, where, besides your climbing **permit** ($10, $2 for under-18s) and your $3.50 "Climber's Personal Accident Insurance", you'll be asked to pay for an obligatory **guide** – an outlay that can be minimized by tagging along with other climbers: guides cost $25 a day for one to three people, but only $30 for seven or eight people. Porters are also available ($25 a day for loads up to 24lb), though the **lockers and saferoom** at reception make this an unnecessary expense. Useful things to take with you include a torch, headache tablets (for altitude sickness), suntan lotion and strong shoes or hiking boots. Bring warm clothes to combat the bitter cold on the summit. Adequate raincoats are sold at the park's souvenir shop. It's over an hour's walk from the reception to the power station that marks the start of the mountain trail proper, so you might prefer to take the **shuttle bus** ($2).

Climbing to your first night's accommodation, at around 3350m, takes between three and six hours, depending on your fitness. Roots and stones along the **trail** serve as steps, with wooden "ladders" laid up the muddier stretches. The air gets progressively cooler as you climb, but the walk is still a hard and sweaty one, and you'll be glad of the regular water tanks and **sheltered rest points** en route.

Two or three hours into the climb, incredible views of the hills, sea and clouds below you start to unfold (if the weather is kind); higher up, at just above 3000m, a detour to the left brings you to **Paka Cave** – no more than a large overhanging rock, and the site of overnight camps on early expeditions. The end of your first day's climbing is heralded by the appearance of the mighty granitic slopes of the **Panar Laban** rock face, veined by trickling waterfalls. From the resthouses (see below) at the foot of Panar Laban – the name is a corruption of a Dusun word meaning "place of sacrifice" – views of the sun setting over the South China Sea are exquisite. It's here that you'll spend your night on the mountain.

Plan to get up at 2.30am the next morning to join the pseudo-religious candle-lit procession to the top. Although ropes have been strung up much of this segment of the trail, none of the climbing is really hairy. That said, the air is quite thin, so headaches, nausea and breathlessness are a possibility. The spectacle of sunrise will rob you of any remaining breath, and then it's back down to Panar Laban for a hearty breakfast before the two-hour amble down to park headquarters. When you finally arrive back at headquarters, reflect on the fact that Kusang Gurung, the Nepalese runner and winner of the 1991 **Kinabalu Climbathon**, ran up and down the mountain in a staggering 2 hours, 42 minutes and 33 seconds.

Poring Hot Springs

Sited 43km from park headquarters, on the southeastern side of Kinabalu National Park, are the **Poring Hot Springs** ($2, free for overnight guests). The complex was

FLORA AND FAUNA IN THE PARK

If you dash headlong up and down Mount Kinabalu and then depart, as some visitors do, you'll miss out on many of the region's natural riches. The national park's diverse terrains have spawned an incredible variety of plants and wildlife, and you are far more likely to glimpse some of them by walking its trails at a leisurely pace.

Flora

Around a third of the park's area is covered by **lowland dipterocarp forest**, characterized by massive, buttressed trees, allowing only sparse growth at ground level. The world's largest flower, the parasitic – and very elusive – Rafflesia (see p.366), occasionally blooms in the lowland forest around Poring Hot Springs. Between 900m and 1800m, you'll come across the oaks, chestnuts, ferns and mosses (including the Dawsonia – the world's largest moss, which can reach a height of 1m) of the **montane forest**.

The higher altitude of the **cloud forest** (1800–2600m) supports a huge range of flowering plants: around a thousand orchids and 26 varieties of rhododendron are known to grow in the forest, including Low's Rhododendron, whose yellow flowers can attain a width of 30cm. The hanging lichen that drapes across branches of stunted trees lends a magical feel to the landscape at this height. It's at this level, too, that you're most likely to see the park's most famous plants – its nine species of cup-shaped **pitcher plants**, which secrete a nectar that first attracts insects and then drowns them, as they are unable to escape the slippery sides of the pitcher. Early climber Spenser St John is alleged to have seen one such plant digesting a rat.

Higher still, above 2600m, only the most tenacious plantlife can survive – like the agonizingly gnarled Sayat-Sayat tree, and the heath rhododendron found only on Mount Kinabalu – while beyond 3300m, soil gives way to granite. Here, grasses, sedges and the elegant blooms of Low's Buttercup are all that flourish.

Fauna

While **mammals** that dwell in the park include orang-utans, Bornean gibbons, tarsiers and clouded leopards, you're unlikely to see anything more exotic than squirrels, rats and tree shrews. You might just catch sight of a mouse deer or a bearded pig, if you're lucky. The higher reaches of Mount Kinabalu boast two types of **birds** seen nowhere else in the world – the Kinabalu Friendly Warbler and Kinabalu Mountain Blackbird. Lower down, look out for hornbills and eagles, as well as the Malaysian Tree Pie, identifiable by its foot-long tail. You're bound to see plenty of **insects**: butterflies and moths flit through the trees, while down on the forest floor are creatures like the Trilobite Beetle, whose orange-and-black armour plating lend it a fearsome aspect.

developed by the Japanese during World War II, though the wooden tubs they installed have since been replaced by a clutch of round and square outdoor hot tubs, set in well-landscaped grounds, and large enough to seat two people at a time. After a few days' hiking up the mountain, a soak in its hot (48–60°C) sulphurous waters is just the ticket. The baths are a couple of minutes from the main gates, across a suspension bridge that spans Sungei Mamut; there's a plunge pool adjacent and two enclosed baths (from $15 an hour) with jacuzzi.

A fifteen-minute walk beyond the baths brings you to Poring's **canopy walk** (daily 10.30am–3.30pm, $2; 6pm–6am, $30 for 1–3 people, $10 for each extra person; 6–10.30am, $60 1–3 people, $20 extra; camera $5), where five tree huts connected by suspended walkways afford you a monkey's-eye view of the surrounding lowland rainforest. Views from the walkways – at their highest point, 60m above ground – are tremendous, though the shouts of giddy tourists negotiating them thwart your chances of seeing anything more interesting than birds, butterflies and ants. If you're set on witnessing some wildlife, arrange a more expensive trip **at night** or in the **early morning**, when it's cooler and quieter – or make do with the low-key but beautiful residents of the newly constructed **butterfly enclosures**.

A more conventional trail strikes off to the right of the baths, reaching 150-metre-high **Langanan Waterfall** about an hour and a half later. On its way, the trail passes smaller **Kepungit Waterfall** – whose icy pool is ideal for swimming – and a cave lined with squealing, fluttering bats, as well as groves of towering bamboo (*poring* means "bamboo" in Kadazan). Be warned: if it's been raining, there'll be leeches on the trail. A strong flick with the finger sometimes despatches them, though often you'll only end up transferring the leech onto your hand; a more foolproof method is to burn them off with a cigarette.

Practicalities

If you're in a group, it's best to charter a **minibus** to take you from Kinabalu Park head-quarters to Poring – the alternative is to wave down a passing Ranau-bound minibus (see below) and change there. The journey takes around half an hour. Minibuses drop you beside Poring's **reception** hut, inside the complex gates, where you can arrange an onward minibus when you leave. The springs' new café is now the best **place to eat** at Poring; the only alternatives are the two unspectacular operations just outside the gates: the *Poring Restoran* (daily 8am–8pm), which serves uninspiring Chinese food, and the *Kedai Makanan Melayu* (daily 8am–6pm), three doors along, whose simple Malay dishes take an age to reach your table.

No permit is needed to visit Poring, though you'll have to book your accommodation at the Sabah Parks office in KK. Unless you're camping ($5 per person) on the grounds beyond the reception, the most affordable **place to stay** is at one of the two dorm units comprising the *Poring Hostel* (①), both of which have good cooking facilities. Two more upmarket **cabins** are also available: the *New Cabin* (④), which accommodates four, and *Old Cabin* (⑤), sleeping up to six.

Ranau

Set in a pleasant valley, the small town of **RANAU** huddles around a square on the south side of the main KK–Sandakan road, 20km from Kinabalu National Park. There's nothing to do here, but it's a handy stopping point if it's too late to travel the extra 19km to Poring. Like KK, Ranau is based around a grid of ugly, lettered blocks; street names are in short supply, though one exception is Jalan Kibarambang – the first turning on the right if you're coming from KK, and home both to a rickety old market and a new Chinese temple, its pale cream walls striped by red pillars. The first day of every month sees a lively *tamu*, around one kilometre out of town, towards Sandakan.

Incidentally, between Kinabalu Park headquarters and Ranau is **KUNDASANG**, where a war memorial 150m off the main road commemorates the victims of the "Death March" of September 1944, when Japanese troops marched 2400 POWs from Sandakan to Ranau (see p.606).

Practicalities

Minibuses stop at the eastern edge of town, on a patch of land beside Block A. At present, **long-distance buses** from KK to Sandakan stop briefly across town, on Jalan Kibarambang – also the site of Ranau's **shared taxi** stand – though there is talk of incorporating them both at the minibus terminus.

Ranau has three **hotels**, the best of which is the quiet, six-room *View Motel* (☎088/876445; ③) in Block L. The *Hotel Ranau* (☎088/875661; ②), next to the *Bank Bumiputra* at the top of the square, has a range of rooms from box-like singles to more spacious air-con doubles with bathrooms. The *Kinabalu Hotel* (☎088/876028; ②), below the square in Block A, is a smartly painted place with cosy rooms and shared bathrooms.

Jalan Kibarambang has several **restaurants and coffee shops**, including the excellent *Restoran Muslim* (daily 6.30am–10pm), where you can feast on great fried chicken to the strains of WWF wrestling videos on the TV; the next-door *Yeong Hing* is good for snatching a quick *pow* on pitstops between KK and Sandakan. Interesting Chinese food is in short supply in Ranau, though the *Sin Mui Mui Restoran* (closed Fri afternoon) at the southern edge of the square has a good menu. Also recommended is the *Mien Mien Restoran*, opposite. For Malay food, make for the *Restoran Sugut* (daily 7am–10pm), below the *View Motel*.

Sandakan and around

Sandwiched between sea and cliffs, and lacking Kota Kinabalu's sense of space, **SANDAKAN** isn't an immediately appealing city. Like Sabah's capital, Sandakan was all but destroyed during World War II, and its postwar reconstruction was worked around an unimaginative – and, in Sabah, all too familiar – grid system of indistinguishable concrete blocks. That said, the town is the springboard to several of Sabah's most fascinating destinations, including the **Turtle Islands Park** (p.466) and the **Sepilok Orang-utan Rehabilitation Centre** (p.465). The town centre itself is not without redeeming features.

Although eighteenth-century accounts exist of a trading outpost called Sandakan within the Sultanate of Sulu (whose epicentre was in what is now the Philippines), the town's modern history began in the early 1870s, with the arrival of a group of European adventurers. Except for one – a moustachioed Scot called William Clarke Cowie, who ran guns for the Sultan of Sulu – nothing is known about these men, though Kampung German, the name of the settlement they established on Pulau Timbang, does point to

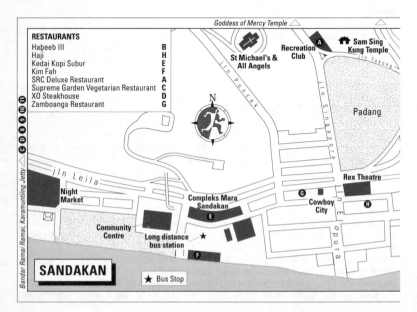

their predominant nationality. The area of northeast Borneo between Brunei Bay and Sungei Kinabatangan had been leased by the Sultan of Brunei to the American Trading Company in 1865. The company's attempt to establish a settlement here failed after a year, and in 1877 the Anglo-Austrian partnership of Baron Von Overbeck and Alfred Dent took up the lease, naming Englishman **William Pryer** as the first Resident of the east coast. After Kampung German burned down a year later, nearby Buli Sim-Sim was chosen by Pryer as the site of his new town, which he named *Elopura*, or "Beautiful City", although locals persisted in referring to it as Sandakan (in Sulu, "to be pawned"). By 1885, Sandakan was the capital of British North Borneo, its natural harbour and proximity to sources of timber, beeswax, rattan and edible birds' nests transforming it into a thriving commercial centre. Sabahan timber was used to build Peking's Temple of Heaven and much of Sandakan's early trade was with Hong Kong; there's still a strong Cantonese influence in the town.

In January 1942, the Japanese army took control, establishing a POW camp from where the infamous Death March to Ranau commenced. What little of the town was left standing after intensive Allied bombing was burned down by the Japanese, and the end of the war saw the administration of Sabah shift to KK. Nevertheless, by the 1950s a rebuilt Sandakan had become the economic engine of the state, while the **timber** boom of the 1960s and 1970s generated such wealth that the town was reputed to have the world's greatest concentration of millionaires. When the region's good timber ran out in the 1980s, Sandakan looked to oil palm and cocoa, crops which now dominate the surrounding landscape.

Arrival, information and city transport

The **long-distance bus station** is below Jalan Leila, ten minutes' walk west of the town centre; long-distance taxis and land cruisers also operate from this area. The **airport** is 11km north of town; minibuses ($1.50) run there from the southern end of Jalan

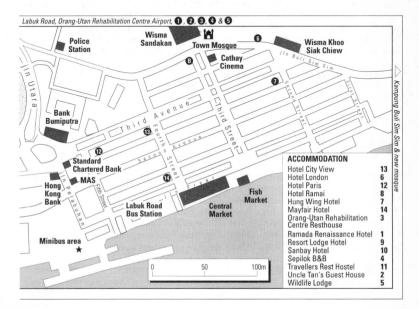

ACCOMMODATION
Hotel City View	13
Hotel London	6
Hotel Paris	12
Hotel Ramai	8
Hung Wing Hotel	7
Mayfair Hotel	14
Orang-Utan Rehabilitation Centre Resthouse	3
Ramada Renaissance Hotel	1
Resort Lodge Hotel	9
Sanbay Hotel	10
Sepilok B&B	4
Travellers Rest Hostel	11
Uncle Tan's Guest House	2
Wildlife Lodge	5

Pelabuhan throughout the day, or you can get a taxi for around $12. The boat from Zamboanga (see "Listings", p.464) docks at **Karamunting Jetty**, 3km west of town – buses await new arrivals. Downtown Sandakan's **addresses** take a little getting used to, as they rely on numbers rather than street names; indeed, less central addresses are pinpointed according to their distances out of the downtown area, hence "Mile 1 1/2", "Mile 3", and so on (given below). There's no tourist office as such, though the Sabah Parks office (see "Listings", p.465 for address) hands out **free maps** for tourists. You may need to visit the office in any case, if you want to go to the Turtle Islands Park.

Sandakan's two local bus stations are within a couple of minutes' walk of each other, in the centre of town. The scheduled services of the Labuk Road Bus Company leave from the waterfront **Labuk Road Station** – blue-and-white buses travel up Labuk Road itself, while those sporting red, yellow and green stripes are bound for points west, along Jalan Leila. A short walk west along Jalan Pryer brings you to the **minibus area**. The two stations have many destinations in common, so it's worth checking both to find the earliest bus to your destination.

Taxis speed around town throughout the day, but if you can't spot one, make for the southern end of Fourth Street, where they gather in numbers.

Accommodation

Sandakan's only central budget hostel is in the suburb of **Bandar Ramai-Ramai**, though there are a few dormitory set-ups way out of town – one on the Labuk Road, another three near the Sepilok Orang-utan Rehabilitation Centre (p.465). The majority of hotels are in the blocks forming the town centre, with several also in Ramai-Ramai, which can be reached in five minutes on any westbound bus.

City View, Block 23, Third Avenue (☎089/271122). Central hotel whose spacious and appealing rooms, furnished with TV and mini-bar, lie off rather gloomy corridors; downstairs on the ground floor is the smart *Hawaii* coffee shop. ⑥.

Hung Wing, Block 13, Third Avenue (☎089/218034). The absence of a lift means rooms get less expensive as they get higher: top-floor rooms, smallish but tidy, are a bargain. ②.

London, Block 10, Jalan Buli Sim-Sim (☎089/216366). The bare but presentable rooms in this friendly hotel next to Wisma Khoo have air-con and private bathrooms. ②.

Mayfair, 24 Jalan Pryer (☎089/219855). Clean but spartan rooms, situated over the Malaysian Textile Centre. ③.

Orang-utan Rehabilitation Centre Resthouse, Sepilok Road (☎089/215189). Just 100m from the rehabilitation centre's reception, the jolly, varnished-wood resthouse is the best placed (if not the most charismatic) of the Sepilok accommodation options; there are a handful of fresh rooms, if a dorm bed ($15) doesn't appeal. All room rates include breakfast, but for other meals you'll need to make for the rehabilitation centre's canteen. ③.

Paris, Third Avenue (☎089/218488). Tatty Chinese hotel with budget-rated fan rooms; air-con rooms are 50 percent more expensive. ②.

Ramada Renaissance, Jalan Utara (☎089/213299). Sandakan's five-star finest, with swish restaurants, business centre, swimming pool and sports facilities. ⑧.

Ramai, Mile 1 1/2 Jalan Leila (☎089/273222). Real effort has been made in this excellent mid-range hotel, whose 44 spacious rooms, complete with bathrooms, TV and air-con, are within striking distance of downtown Sandakan; recommended. ④.

Resort Lodge, Mile 1 1/2 Jalan Leila (☎089/45211). Like the *Hung Wing*, more affordable as you climb to the higher floors; not a budget choice, but good if you want a little comfort. ③.

Sanbay, Mile 1 1/2 Jalan Leila (☎089/275000). Smart new hotel west of the town centre. ⑦.

Sepilok B&B, Sepilok Road (☎089/532288). Rougher and rather more basic than the *Resthouse* (above), the *B&B*'s dorms and rooms are signposted down a dirt track, fifteen minutes' stroll from the centre. Breakfast is included, and the canteen has a limited range of meals and snacks. Dorms $15. ②.

Travellers' Rest Hostel, second floor, Apartment 2, Block E, Bandar Ramai-Ramai (☎089/221460). Sister hostel to the well-established KK namesake, offering clean, bargain-priced dorms and rooms with breakfast included. Owner Chris Perez can arrange trips to his jungle camp ($130 return, then $15 a day) and elsewhere. Dorms $10. ②.

Uncle Tan's, Mile 17 1/2 Labuk Road (☎089/531639). Perennially popular guesthouse some thirty minutes' bus ride from town, where the $20 charge for a bed in a basic wooden hut includes three meals. Uncle Tan himself arranges tours of the surrounding area, including trips to his jungle camp ($130 return, then $15 a day). Coming from KK by bus, ask to be dropped at *Tan's*, which is around 28km west of Sandakan. ②.

Wildlife Lodge, Sepilok Road (☎089/533031). Welcoming, family-run operation, set in delightful grounds a five-minute walk from the rehabilitation centre; dorm beds ($20) represent better value than the slightly overpriced rooms: a private bathroom costs $10 on top of the basic double room rate, while air-con costs a whacking $25 surcharge. The on-site *Banana Café* serves burgers, hot dogs, curries and noodle soups. ③.

The Town

Sandakan town stands on the northern lip of Sandakan Bay – much of it on land reclaimed from the sea early this century. Stretching west of the dense maze of numbered streets and avenues that makes up the downtown area is Jalan Leila, while to the east, running up round the bay, is Jalan Buli Sim-Sim. The heart of the town centre is its **padang** – one of the few reminders of Sandakan's colonial heritage.

First stop should be the uproarious **waterfront markets** (daily 7am–6pm) along Jalan Pryer, down whose dark aisles you'll find exquisite conches and turtle eggs, illegally imported from the Philippines. A row of weather-beaten old fishing boats moors behind the fish market, Sabah's largest. Despite the strong police presence along this stretch of Jalan Pryer, pickpocketing is rife, so be vigilant.

A fifteen-minute walk east of the town centre, along Jalan Buli Sim-Sim, deposits you in front of Sandakan's modern, minimalist **mosque**, which stands on a promontory and commands fine views of the bay. Flanking its eastern side is **Kampung Buli Sim-Sim**, the water village around which Sandakan expanded in the nineteenth century, whose countless photogenic shacks spread like lilies out into the bay, crisscrossed by walkways. There's a marked contrast between the dilapidation of the water village and the well-tended surroundings of Sandakan's colonial remnants, especially the quintessentially English **St Michael's and All Angels Church**, a five-minute walk north up Jalan Puncak, one block west of the padang. Here, varnished pews, memorial plaques and faded photographs give a sense of the past rarely felt in Sabah. Steps lead down from the far side of the church grounds to Jalan Singapore, across which, on Jalan Tokong, the **Sam Sing Kung Temple** rears up above the padang. Inside, its smoke-stained walls are lined with wooden boards etched with gold Chinese characters; above the entrance hangs a wonderful woodcarving of a boatful of people coursing through an ocean teeming with prawns, crabs and fish. Sandakan's oldest temple is the **Goddess of Mercy Temple**, five minutes further north up Jalan Singapore in a grove of magnificent palms; unfortunately modernization has robbed it of any character.

A ten-minute walk north up Jalan Utara, across on the eastern side of the padang brings you to the foot of Jalan Istana, from whose **Observation Point** are good views of the town, boats and islands below. Turn right down the road beyond the observation point, and bear left after Sandakan's half-Tudor, half-kampung-style **istana**, and you're in the huge town **cemetery**, its thousands of green and sky-blue gravestones banked impressively up a hillside. You can continue along the path to the **Japanese cemetery** where, besides the graves of Japanese soldiers killed in action in World War II, are those of Japanese girls sold into prostitution in the late nineteenth and early twentieth centuries.

There's another pleasing view of Sandakan Bay from the **Puu Jih Shih Temple**, a new complex high up on the cliffs, 4km west of town. Inside, three tall statues of Buddha, carved from imported teak and embellished with gold foil, stand on the altar, ringed by 32 dragon-entwined pillars – also of teak. Come early in the morning and your visit will be accompanied by the songs of scores of birds that swoop around the temple's rafters. Sibuga buses from the Labuk Road Station drop you off nearby.

Speedboats from below Jalan Pryer run across to **Pulau Berhala** 4km offshore, below whose vertical sandstone cliffs is a decent beach; with a lot of bargaining, the return journey should come to $20. Berhala once housed a leper colony, and in World War II was used as a POW camp by the Japanese, housing American author Agnes Keith (see "Books", p.627) and her son George, amongst others.

Eating

Sandakan may not be able to match KK's variety of **restaurants**, but there's still enough choice here to suit most people, with Malay, Chinese, Indian and Western food all well represented. Most places are in the town centre or along Jalan Leila, though several renowned **seafood** restaurants open every evening on Trig Hill, high up above the town, with fine views of Sandakan Bay. For **hawker stalls**, the market on Jalan Pryer and the night stalls that operate on open land in front of the post office are unbeatable, or there's the grandstand on Jalan Singapore, under which a makeshift cluster of *satay* stalls sets up every evening. Unless you've got the money for a night at the *Illusions Discotheque* at the *Renaissance Hotel*, **nightlife** in Sandakan is limited to Jalan Lelia's *Cowboy City*, a big, bare air-con bar that gets lively and raucous late in the evening. Beer is widely available in Chinese restaurants and coffee shops.

Habeeb III, corner of Jalan Buli Sim-Sim and Third St. Despite a menu that's full of tempting Indonesian Malay and Western dishes (including breakfasts), only a handful of choices seems to be available at any one time in this cheap and cheerful air-con restaurant, so keep you fingers crossed as you order.

Haji, Second Avenue. South of the padang, this is one of several restaurants below the *Rex Cinema*. It's a popular Muslim Indian place with an air-con dining room upstairs; fresh juices and *rotis* are memorable, as is the creamy chicken korma. Daily 8.30am–9.30pm.

Kedai Kopi Subur, Compleks Mara Sandakan, Jalan Leila. No-frills coffee shop specializing in *coto makassar* – a tasty, meaty broth with chunks of rice cake. Daily 8am–9pm.

Kim Fah, behind the long-distance bus station, off Jalan Leila. Rough and ready Chinese seafood restaurant, with views of the bay. Daily 11am–2pm & 5pm–3am.

SRC Deluxe Restaurant, *Sandakan Recreation Club*, Jalan Singapore. Cantonese dishes include delicious whole baked duck in plum sauce ($35), which serves three. At night steamboat ($9 a head) is served on the second-floor terrace. Daily 11.30am–2pm & 5–10pm.

Supreme Garden Vegetarian Restaurant, Block 30, Bandar Ramai-Ramai, Jalan Leila. Affordable and welcoming establishment, where the imaginative menu runs to mock-meat dishes like fried vegetarian frog with black bean sauce; a vegetarian steamboat ($3 per person) is available Monday–Friday. Daily 10am–2pm & 5.30–9pm.

XO Steakhouse, Hsiang Garden Estate, Mile 1 1/2 Jalan Leila. Sandakan's premier Western food restaurant, serving fish and seafood as well as Australian steaks. Daily 11am–2pm & 6–10pm.

Zamboanga Restaurant, Jalan Lelia, between Jalan Puncak and Jalan Singapore. Faceless Malay coffee shop that's enlivened by the arrival of a Filipino chef after 7pm. Daily 10am–10pm.

Listings

Airlines MAS, Sabah Building, Jalan Pelabuhan – formerly Jalan Edinburgh – open Mon–Fri 8am–4.30pm, Sat 8am–3pm, Sun 8am–noon (☎089/273966).

Banks and exchange Bank Bumiputra, opposite Standard Chartered Bank, Third Avenue; Hong Kong, corner of Third Avenue and Jalan Pelabuhan; Standard Chartered Bank, Sabah Building, Jalan Pelabuhan.

Boats to the Philippines The passenger boat ($140 one-way) to Zamboanga in the Philippines leaves at 3pm every Thursday from the Karamunting jetty, 3km west of the city centre; tickets should be bought at the jetty at least a day before departure. Tourists are currently issued a three-week visa upon arrival, but check this by phoning the Filipino embassy in KL.

Laundry *Sandakan Laundry*, Third Avenue, between Third and Fourth streets.

Pharmacy *Borneo Dispensary*, corner of Fifth Street and Second Avenue.

Police The main police station is on Jalan Sim Sim (☎089/211222).

Post Sandakan's GPO is five minutes' walk west of town, on Jalan Leila (Mon–Fri 8am–5pm, Sat 10am–1pm).

Sabah Parks Nineth floor, Wisma Khoo (Mon–Fri 8am–12.45pm & 2–4.15pm, Sat 8am–12.45pm; ☎089/273453).

Telephones At the Telekom office, sixth floor, Wisma Khoo (daily 8.30am–4.45pm); IDD calls can presently only be made on card phones.

Tour operators SI Tours, third floor, Yeng Yo Hong Building, arranges tours of the sights around Sandakan, as do Wildlife Expeditions, 903, nineth floor, Wisma Khoo Siak Chiew (☎089/219616), and Discovery Tours Lot 908, Wisma Khoo Siak Chew (☎089/274106). For budget trips to the Turtle Islands Park, Gomantong and the Kinabatangan, contact the *Travellers' Rest Hostel*, or *Uncle Tan's*.

Sepilok Orang-utan Rehabilitation Centre

One of only three orang-utan sanctuaries in the world, the **Sepilok Orang-utan Rehabilitation Centre** (daily 9–11am & 2–3.30pm; feeding times 10am & 3pm; $10, use of camcorder $10; ☎089/531180), 25km west of Sandakan, occupies a 43-square-kilometre patch of lowland rainforest. The centre was established in 1964 as a retraining centre for orangs liberated by a law prohibiting the catching and keeping of them as pets – though the timber boom has meant that Sepilok's more recent arrivals come from regions where logging has robbed them of their homes. At the centre, young and domesticated orang-utans (the name means "man of the forest" in Malay), whose survival instincts are undeveloped, are trained to fend for themselves. Although not always successful, this process has so far seen around a hundred orangs reintroduced to their natural habitat. To aid the integration process, bananas and milk are made available to those still finding their forest feet at two **feeding stations**; the diet is never varied, as a way of encouraging orangs to forage for other foodstuffs in the trees.

Orang-utans – tailless, red haired apes – can reach a height of around 1.65m, and can live to be as old as thirty. Solitary, but not aggressively territorial animals, they live a largely arboreal existence, eating fruit, leaves, bark and the occasional insect. At the **information centre** that fronts the Sepilok sanctuary, a blackboard outlines the day's events, while inside there's an exhibition on forest preservation. A **video** outlining the work carried out at the centre is shown here twice daily and, since it's sometimes screened before feeding time, it's wise to turn up early if you want to catch it. Close to feeding time a warden leads you for ten minutes along a wooden boardwalk to **Station A**, passing the **nursery**, where baby orang-utans are taught elementary climbing skills on ropes and branches (it's occasionally possible to visit the nursery in the morning – enquire at reception). Nothing prepares you for the thrill of seeing young orangs swinging, shimmying and strolling towards their breakfast, jealously watched by gangs of macaques that loiter around for scraps. Once replete, more cunning orangs take away enough bananas for a picnic lunch in the trees. There's a better chance of seeing semi-mature and more independent orangs a thirty-minute hike from the visitor information centre at Station B, though this feeding station is only open to tourists sporadically; ask at reception when you arrive. Sepilok is also a halfway house for honey bears, elephants and other wild animals that are either sick or en route for other reserves in Sabah. You can't see any of these, though the four extremely rare **Sumatran rhinos** kept for breeding at the centre can be viewed by up to fifteen people at a time, at 10am, 10.30am and 11.30am ($2).

Buses leave for the centre daily at 9.20am, 11.30am, 1.30pm and 3pm from Sandakan's Labuk Road Station, but if you want an earlier start, head for the minibus area and take a "Batu 14" bus.

Stall selling paper replica offerings, Singapore

Lapau Diraja, Bandar Seri Begawan

Buddhist temple, Singapore

Raffles Hotel, Singapore

Tamu Kianggeh, Bandar Seri Begawan

First floor window of a Chinatown shophouse, Singapore

Temple monks, Phor Kark See Temple, Singapore

Veeramakaliammam Temple, Singapore

LESLEY READER

JO PEGGIE

Terrace of Singapore shophouses

The Gateway building, designed by
I.M. Pei, Singapore

SIMON RICHMOND

Antique shop, Chinatown

Travellers' Rest charges $220 per person (minimum three people), or $200 if you don't mind sleeping in the boat that takes you out. Tan's fees are substantially lower, at $180 a head (minimum six people), though guests stay not on Selingaan, but at Tan's lodge on nearby less idyllic Pulau Libaran, where sightings are not guaranteed. There have been complaints that the promised shuttle to Selingaan has not been forthcoming. Otherwise, go to the Sabah Parks office in Wisma Khoo in Sandakan where, subject to availability, you'll be able to arrange a lift with the next group out and pay for your accommodation, all for around $200. If you book through an agency you'll be looking at upwards of $250 for the same package. Sabah Parks allows no more than twenty visitors a night onto Selingaan, all of whom are put up in the island's four comfortable **chalets** and eat at *Roses' Café* inside the visitor centre; set breakfasts, lunches and dinners are available, but sticking to the menu ensures better value.

Gomantong Caves

Further afield, the **Gomantang Caves**, south of Sandakan Bay, are inspiring enough to warrant a visit at any time of the year, though you'll get most out of the trip when the edible nests of their resident swiftlets are being harvested. The caves are administered by Sabah's Wildlife Department, which permits just two harvests a year – one between February and April, allowing the birds time to rebuild before the egg-laying season, the other between July and September, when the young have hatched and left. Bird's-nest soup has long been a Chinese culinary speciality and Chinese merchants have been coming to Borneo to trade for birds' nests for at least twelve centuries.

Of the two major caves, **Simud Hitam** is easiest to visit. The cave is reached by following the trail that runs off behind the staff quarters to the right of the reception building, taking a right fork after five minutes, and continuing on for a further ten minutes – the stench of ammonia will tell you when you are getting near. Reaching a height of 90m, with bug-ridden piles of compacted guano on the floor, Simud Hitam supports a colony of black-nest swiftlets, whose nests – a mixture of saliva and feathers – sell for US$40 a kilogram. Come at the right time and you'll see the harvesting (see p.470). Above Simud Hitam is the larger but less accessible **Simud Putih**, home to the white-nest swiftlet, whose nests are of pure, dried saliva and can fetch prices of over US$500 a kilogram. Harvesting is a dangerous business: workers scale impossibly precarious rattan ladders and ropes – some up to 60m high – to collect the nests, and there are occasional fatalities. To reach Simud Putih, take the left fork, five minutes along the trail originating from the reception building, and start climbing. Outside the caves there's a picnic site and canteen, and an **information centre** that will fill you in on the caves' ecosystem. Ringing the whole area is a patch of virgin jungle supporting orang-utans and elephants – neither of which you're likely to see.

It's easiest to go with a tour agency (anywhere from $60–300 per person), but under your own steam, one minibus a day (6am) leaves Sandakan's long-distance bus station for **Sukau**, a riverside town some 20km beyond the turning to Gomantong. This drops you on the main road, from where it's 5km down a former logging road to the caves. Alternatively, you could take any bus bound for Lahad Datu (see below), get off at the turning for Sukau, and try your luck from there. If you travel here independently, be sure to bring a torch, so that you can experience the full effect of the caves. Should you get stranded, you should be able to find a bed in the *Gomantong Rainforest Lodge* (Sabah Travel Services ☎089/221089; ③–④), located right beside Gomantong's reception building.

Sungei Kinabatangan

East of the entrance to Sandakan Bay, Sabah's longest river, the 560-kilometre **Kinabatangan**, ends its northeasterly path from the interior to the Sulu Sea. The dual

PROBOSCIS MONKEYS

For many naturalists, a trip to Borneo would not be complete without an encounter with a **proboscis monkey**, a shy animal confined to riverine forests and mangrove swamps of the Bornean coast and found nowhere else in the world. It derives its name from the enlarged, drooping, red nose of the adult male monkey; females and young animals are snub-nosed. The role of the drooping nose, which seems to straighten out when the animal is issuing its curious honking call note, is unclear, although it is likely to help in attracting a mate. The monkeys are reddish-brown in colour, with a dark red cap; in addition, the adult males have a cream-white collar (or neck ruff). All of them have long, thick, white tails and white rumps, and the adult males in particular have large bellies, giving them a rather portly, "old gentleman" appearance. Males are significantly heavier than females, weighing up to 23kg, compared with a maximum female weight of 10kg. All in all, this combination of features has earned male proboscis monkeys the (not entirely complimentary) name of *orang belanda*, or "Dutchman", in parts of Borneo.

The monkeys live in loose groups, spending their days in trees close to the water, feeding on young leaves, shoots and fruit. They are most active at dawn and dusk, when moving to and from feeding sites. Although they are mostly arboreal (tree-living), they will walk across open areas when necessary, and are proficient swimmers, aided by partly webbed feet. They are quite choosy feeders, preferring the leaves of the Sonneraita mangrove tree, a rather specialist diet which means that large areas of forest need to be protected to provide groups of monkeys with sufficient food. This fact, coupled with the restricted range of the proboscis monkey, makes the species vulnerable to habitat loss and hunting pressure.

Visitors can hope to see proboscis monkeys in several of the national parks in Sabah and Sarawak, apart from the admittedly remote Kinabatangan area: in Sarawak in particular, the animals can be seen in Bako National Park (p.362) and in the Mangroves Forest Reserve near Kampung Salak.

threats of piracy and flooding have kept its lower reaches largely free of development, and the area consequently has a wealth of Bornean wildlife. Elephants, orang-utans, gibbons, macaques and crocodiles all dwell in the forest flanking the river, and the resident **bird life** is equally impressive. With luck, you'll glimpse hornbills, Brahming kites, crested serpent eagles, egrets, exquisite blue-banded and stork-billed kingfishers, and oriental darters, which dive underwater to find food and then sit on the shore, with their wings outstretched to dry. The Kinabatangan's greatest natural assets, however, are its **proboscis monkeys** (see box), found beside the water's edge each afternoon; they are instantly recognizable, looking not unlike Batman's arch-foe, the Penguin.

Again, the only effective way to see the Kinabatangan is through a tour operator, who can arrange afternoon boat and monkey-spotting trips out of Sandakan. To appreciate the full beauty of the river though, it's best to stay in one of the several **jungle lodges** on its banks. Those run by *Uncle Tan's* and the *Travellers' Rest Hostel* in Sandakan (see pp.462–63) boast the most competitive prices: both charge $130 for the return journey, then $15 a night expenses. It should be stressed that these options are real back-to-nature experiences, and if you value your creature comforts they won't be to your liking. If this is the case, you can arrange a more expensive – and more salubrious – tour through one of the handful of operators that now maintain lodges in Sukau (see above) – these are Sipadan Dive Centre (p.435), Borneo Eco Tours ☎088/234005, Discovery Tours (p.435), SI Tours (p.465) and Wildlife Expeditions (p.465). Tours include overland travel to Sukau, plus a boat cruise from there to see the proboscis monkeys.

Batu Putih

Within the limestone outcrop of **Batu Putih** (known locally as Batu Tulug), 1km north of the Kinabatangan Bridge on the road between Sandakan and Lahad Datu, small caves contain wooden coffins well over a hundred years old. When the former curator of the Sarawak Museum, Tom Harrisson, explored the caves in the 1950s, he found many hardwood coffin troughs and lids, as well as a wooden upright, grooved with notches that were thought to represent a genealogical record. It was from here that the two-hundred-year-old coffin lid with a buffalo's head carved into its handle, displayed at the Sabah State Museum, was taken; other coffins are still in their original spots, though unless archeology is your passion, think twice about making the detour to see them. All buses to Lahad Datu pass by the caves.

South of Sandakan

Below Sandakan Bay, the horseshoe of Sabah's main road continues southwards over the Kinabatangan Bridge to the towns of **Lahad Datu** and **Tawau**. This far east, the state's central mountain ranges taper away, to be replaced by lowland – and sometimes swampy – coastal regions lapped by the **Sulu** and **Celebes** seas, and dominated by oil palm plantations. Archeological finds around **Madai**, off the road between Lahad Datu and Tawau, prove that this area of Borneo has been inhabited for well over ten thousand years. Nowadays, this is Sabah's "wild east", where streets teem with Filipino and Indonesian immigrants trying to scratch a living, and where pirates working out of islands in the nearby Filipino waters pose a real threat to fishermen. You'll sense a profound change of mood if you arrive direct from KK. Filipinos and Indonesians have been migrating into Sabah since the 1950s, when they were drawn in search of work on Sabah's plantations, but the influx of Filipinos rose sharply in the 1970s, as a result of the civil unrest in Mindanao.

The lowland rainforest runs riot at the **Danum Valley Conservation Area**, which can be reached via Lahad Datu and best enjoyed by staying at the splendid *Borneo Rainforest Lodge*. Closer to Kalimantan, and around the southern lip of wide **Darvel Bay**, the oceanic island of **Sipadan** is acclaimed as one of the world's top diving spots, its flawless coral ablaze with exotic fishes and sea creatures. More prosaically, you'll find yourself this far around the state if you're **heading to Indonesia**: a boat from Tawau is the cheapest way to reach northeastern Kalimantan.

If you're heading back to KK, there is an alternative to retracing your steps around the crown of the state. From Tawau, land cruisers depart daily for Keningau (p.440), travelling on logging roads that complete a **ring road** of sorts around Sabah.

Lahad Datu

A discomfiting sense of lawlessness prevails in **LAHAD DATU**, 175km south of Sandakan, on shallow Darvel Bay. In recent years, this unattractive boom town has been flooded by immigrants – many of whom you'll see eking out a living by hawking cigarettes and nuts – while pirates are known to work the adjacent coastline. In 1986, a mob of heavily armed pirates stormed the Standard Chartered Bank and MAS office on Jalan Teratai, Lahad Datu's main street, making off with almost $100,000.

Buses stop at the terminus on Jalan Bunga Raya, a couple of minutes east of the town centre – look inland and you'll see the tall, green and white building that marks the northeastern end of Jalan Teratai, in which (in the *Hotel Mido*) you'll find Lahad Datu's MAS office (☎089/881707). The **airport** is a short taxi ride north of town.

As Lahad Datu is the jumping-off point for trips to the Danum Valley Conservation Area (see below), your first port of call will probably be the **Innoprise office**

(☎089/881092), in Block 3 of the Fajar Centre, a $2 taxi-ride north of the town centre. Here you can book trips to the valley, if you haven't already done so in KK, or pick up the bus (Mon, Wed & Fri at 3pm; $30) if you have. The only tourist sight in town is **Kampong Panji**, a run-down water village on the western edge of town.

Budget **accommodation** centres the northeastern (bus terminus) end of Jalan Teratai: the *Ocean Hotel* (☎089/881700; ②) has reasonably spruce rooms, but for rock-bottom prices, head up the side street 20m southwest of it, to seedy *Rumah Tumpungan Malaysia* (☎089/883358; ②), where the absence of a lift makes the rooms on higher floors cheaper. Opposite, the *Malaysia Venus Hotel II* (no phone; ②) the best deal in town, has clean but spartan rooms with attached bathrooms. You could also try the well-furnished *Hotel Jago Kota* (☎089/882000; ③) on Jalan Kampong Panji, or Jalan Teratai's slightly shoddier *Hotel Mido* (☎089/881800; ③). Top of the tree is the new *Executive Hotel* (☎089/881333; ⑥), whose gleaming white colonnades and welcoming rooms stand proudly beside the entrance to Kampong Panji, at the southwestern end of Jalan Terati.

A handful of decent **restaurants** make a stay in Lahad Datu more bearable. There's the cave-like Chinese *Restoran Melawar*, a block southwest of the *Hotel Mido*; the *Restoran Auliah* (closes at 7pm), 50m away on Jalan Kiambang, does a fine *biyriani*. Otherwise, go for the *Executive Hotel's* harmonious *Spring Palace Chinese Restaurant*, which specializes in Cantonese and Szechuan cuisine, and boasts a memorable *dim sum* menu. The town's swish new **market** has upstairs stalls commanding pleasant views out to sea.

To Sahabat

Although good stretches of beach do exist along the coastline east of Lahad Datu, the threat of piracy puts them off limits. The only exception is the beach at **TUNGKU**, a seaside village that has its own police station – though 70km is a long way to go for a dip in the sea; look for a Tungku minibus at Lahad Datu's terminus.

A wiser plan is to continue east into **Sahabat**, a vast area of land which Sabah's Federal Land Development Agency (FELDA), has blanketed with oil palms. Here, the plantation settlement of **BANDAR SAHABAT** provides the unlikely backdrop to a tasteful seafront hotel, the *Sahabat Beach Resort* (⑤). While the hotel's palm-fringed beach can't be called idyllic – abutting it is a jetty where boats are loaded with palm oil – it's breezy and clean enough. Plans afoot include a watersports complex and tours of local plantations. Those on a tighter budget should stay instead at the adjacent *Sahabat Resort Annexe* (③), whose rooms are perfectly cheery – though bear in mind that prices here may increase as the resort's amenities improve. Bookings at both places can be made on ☎089/776533.

Madai Caves

If you didn't get to Gomantong Caves (see p.467), it's worth breaking your journey to Tawau for a trip to the **Madai Caves**, 13km west of the unremarkable coastal town of Kunak. Although humans have dwelt in them for over ten thousand years, the caves of the Madai limestone massif are most remarkable for the bird life they support; here, as at Gomantong, the nests of swiftlets are harvested for bird's-nest soup. The entrance to the cave system is marked by a motley gathering of fragile stilt huts – home, in season, to Idahan nest-harvesters. Once beyond the front aperture, you'll discover a succession of vast chambers in which swiftlets dive, bats squeak and guano lies ankle-deep. In season, harvesters will offer to show you the remnants of old Idahan coffins in the caves – but at a price. The caves are pitch-black, so a torch is essential.

Tawau-bound minibuses will drop you in the Madai area for $5, though with the caves 3km off the main road, it's worth paying an extra $2 to be driven all the way.

Danum Valley Conservation Area

Sabah's **Danum Valley Conservation Area** (DVCA) spans 438 square kilometres of primary lowland rainforest west of Lahad Datu, and lies within the boundaries of the **Yayasan Sabah Concession Area** (YSCA), the vast tract of forest whose sustained-yield logging subsidizes the Sabah Foundation's charitable works across the state (see p.451). Established in 1981 for the purpose of rainforest-related "conservation, research, education and recreation", the DVCA supports a wealth of wildlife from bearded pigs to orang-utans, Sumatran rhinos to Asian elephants, and hornbills to pheasants. Until recently, the hub of all tourist activity in the area was the **Danum Valley Field Centre**, 85km west of Lahad Datu, on the DVCA's eastern edge. Now, though, the centre is off-limits to anyone unable to produce evidence that their visit is scientifically motivated, and as a tourist attraction it has been all but superseded by the **Borneo Rainforest Lodge**, a major new initiative aiming to show that eco-tourism can positively aid the protection of the rainforests. Sited on a bend in Sungei Danum and staffed by guides who possess a mind-boggling knowledge of the environment, the lodge specializes in what it calls a "high-quality natural history interpretative service", giving visitors the chance, "not only to experience the Borneo rainforest, but to understand today's conservation realities": wildlife treks and marked nature trails weave through the surrounding forest, while a canopy walkway, video and slide shows illustrate how the rainforest functions. Other activities include trips to the field centre and night safaris by jeep; or you can see the recently unearthed coffins and jars of a Dusun burial site at a two-hundred-metre escarpment near the lodge. If you have the money, you'll find that the *Borneo Rainforest Lodge* is quite the best way to experience Sabah's forest firsthand.

Practicalities

Guests of the *Borneo Rainforest Lodge* transfer ($100 return per person) from Lahad Datu to the lodge by air-conditioned jeep – staff can pick you up either at the airport, or at the Innoprise office (see p.469). Buses to the Field Centre leave from the Innoprise office on Monday, Wednesday and Friday at 3pm ($60 return); at other times you'll have to charter your own transport ($260). Though it's sometimes possible to arrange a visit to the DVCA once you reach Lahad Datu, it's wiser to do so in Kota Kinabalu. Upon arrival at either site, there's a $25 entrance fee. At the Field Centre it's obligatory to hire a guide ($20 for a half-day) for your first foray into the forest; while at the *Rainforest Lodge* the fee for jungle activities is $50 a day.

If you can sweet-talk your way into the Field Centre, much the cheaper **accommodation** option in the DVCA, you'll have the choice of a tidy resthouse whose seven twin rooms have attached bathrooms (③), and dorm beds ($36 per person) where bathrooms are shared. Camping (☎088/243245) costs $15 per person, and you'll need your own tent. As for the *Borneo Rainforest Lodge* (☎088/243245; ⑨), its comfortable (but not lavish) twin rooms are built around a central lodge whose first-floor bar-cum-restaurant affords breathtaking views across Sungei Danum; prices include three hearty set meals a day, a mixture of Western and Asian dishes.

Semporna

Like Lahad Datu, **SEMPORNA** is worth visiting only as a springboard to better things – in this case, Pulau Sipadan (see below); boats depart for the island most days. Sited

108km to the east of Tawau, the whole of this Bajau fishing town seems in danger of spilling into the sea. Stilt houses are clustered either side of the town, and its one concession to tourism, the Semporna Ocean Tourism Centre (SOTC), balances on a causeway jutting out into the sea – even its chaotic market, where buses stop, is built half on land and half on stilts.

The rectangular sails of Bajau boats drift across the bay east of Semporna, which is studded by many small **islands**; some have good beaches, though none to compare with those of Pulau Sipadan. Still, Pulau Gaya, Pulau Sibuan and Pulau Mabul are all recommended locally for snorkelling and swimming – staff at the *Dragon Inn Hotel* (see below) can arrange boats for the day for $200–250, though you may pay less by haggling with a fisherman at the water's edge beyond the market. The chances are that the company taking you to Sipadan will have booked you in at the SOTC's *Dragon Inn Hotel* (☎089/781088; ④). If not, one economical option, the adequate *Hotel Semporna* (☎089/781378; ④), sits right in the centre of town. Three **tour operators** – Borneo Divers, Sipadan Dive Centre and Borneo Sea Adventures – have offices at the SOTC, as does Today Travel Service, Semporna's MAS agent.

Barring the uninspiring restaurants downtown, Semporna's only **eating** options are both on the same causeway as the SOTC: the classy *Pearl City Restaurant*, which has views out to sea, and the nearby, more decrepit *Floating Restaurant*.

Pulau Sipadan

In the past few years, a trip to tiny **Pulau Sipadan** – 30km south of Semporna in the Celebes Sea – has become *de rigueur* for the hardcore scuba diving fraternity. Acclaimed by marine biologist Jacques Cousteau as "an untouched piece of art", Sipadan is a cornucopia of marine life, its waters teeming with turtles, moray eels, sharks, barracuda, vast schools of gaily coloured tropical fish, and a diversity of coral that's been compared to that at Australia's Great Barrier Reef.

Pulau Sipadan is at the crown of a limestone spire rising 600m from the sea bed and widening at the top to form a coral shelf shaped like an artist's palette. The diving highlights include a network of marine caves – the most eerie being **Turtle Cavern**, a watery grave to the skeletal remains of turtles which have strayed in and become lost. **White-tip Avenue** and **Barracuda Point** are frequented, respectively, by basking white-tip sharks and spiralling shoals of slender barracuda, while the **Hanging Gardens** is an extraordinarily elegant profusion of soft coral hanging from the underside of the reef ledge. Snorkellers accompanying divers to the island can expect to see reef sharks and white-tips, lion fish, barracudas and scores of turtles, without having to leave the surface; the **Drop-off**, just beyond the jetty, is a good place to wade out and don goggles. Be aware, though, that if you go out on a boat dive, divemaster and divers will quickly disappear below the surface, leaving you to your own devices for forty minutes.

The island itself is carpeted by lush forest, and fringed by flawless white sand **beaches**, up which green turtles drag themselves to lay their eggs. Spare moments between dives are spent idling in the sun on hammocks or loungers, playing a little badminton or joining one of the ad hoc volleyball matches that evolve from time to time. A sunset walk around Sipadan takes around twenty minutes. Recently, Malaysia's ownership of the area has been disputed by the Indonesian government; the outcome of this could alter the face of marine tourism on Sipadan.

With limited **accommodation** on the island, the only way to stay on Pulau Sipadan is by booking through a **tour operator** – all but one of the companies selling diving trips operate out of Kota Kinabalu (see p.435 for details), the exception being *Pulau Sipadan Resort*, which is based in Tawau (see below). It is possible to make independent day-trips to the island: locals with boats (and snorkelling equipment) for rent are plentiful on the SOTC causeway in Semporna, though you're looking at around

$350–450 for the day for the boat and a few dollars more for the snorkelling equipment. An **underwater filming company**, Scuba zoo, recently set up by two English entrepreneurs, will accompany you on a dive and produce a video ($50) of you swimming amidst Sipadan's marine life.

Tawau

Beyond the Madai Caves, 150km southwest of Lahad Datu, is **TAWAU**, Sabah's southernmost town of any size. Tawau was originally a small Bajau settlement, until the British North Borneo Chartered Company, attracted by its fine harbour and the rich volcanic soil, transformed it into the thriving commercial port it is today. As in so many regions of Sabah, while the town's prosperity relied at first upon the cultivation of cocoa, nowadays oil palm plantations and timber logging are in the ascendancy, attracting many Filipino and Indonesian immigrants. Tawau is also a major departure point for Kalimantan – the Indonesian portion of Borneo (see box on p.475).

Central Tawau is an orderly blend of wooden shophouses and concrete buildings. There's little to see or do here, though the **market** beside *Hotel Soon Yee* is worthy of a browse. That apart, you might stroll along Tawau's backbone, Jalan Dunlop; its Teo Chew Association building is crowned by a Chinese temple, while the sprawling provisions market on the square of reclaimed land opposite is mildly diverting.

An hour's drive north of town is the **Tawau Hills State Park**, a patch of lowland rainforest with trails, hot springs and a waterfall, though reaching it is trickier than it's worth; public buses only make the trip on a Sunday.

Practicalities

Long-distance **buses** terminate below the eastern end of Tawau's main street, Jalan Dunlop, with land cruisers to Keningau (see below) leaving from the same site; the **local bus** terminus is on Jalan Stephen Tan, in the centre of town, while **shared taxis** park at the foot of Jalan Domenic. The **airport** is only a little over a kilometre northwest of town – take one of the hotel courtesy buses waiting there, or hail a taxi ($3). The sole **Sipadan operator** not based in KK is *Pulau Sipadan Resort*, Block P, Bandar Sabindo (☎089/765200). **Ferries** to Indonesia depart from Customs Wharf, 150m south of Jalan Dunlop's Shell station.

As well as several **banks**, the commercial estate known as the Fajar Centre, east of Jalan Masjid, houses both the Telekom building in Block 35, and the MAS office in Wisma Sasco; you'll find the **post office** across the southern side of Jalan Dunlop.

ACCOMMODATION

Most of Tawau's budget **hotels** are along Jalan Stephen Tan or Jalan Chester, the best of which is *Hotel Soon Yee*.

Belmont Marco Polo, Jalan Stephen Tan (☎089/777988). The classiest address in town is still this swish place above the mosque. ⑥.

Kinabalu Rest House, Jalan Chester. Bare, seedy – but extremely low-priced – lodgings over a Muslim Indian restaurant. ①.

Loong, 3868 Jalan Abaca (☎089/765308). Another bargain, with good facilities, friendly staff and a great location – central, yet off the busy main drags. ②.

Murah, Jalan Stephen Tan. All the rooms have air-con, TV and bathrooms. ②.

North Borneo, Jalan Dunlop (☎089/763060). A mid-range establishment located behind Tawau's cinema. ④.

Sanctuary, 4263 Jalan Chester (☎089/751155). A smart place, with spacious rooms furnished with TV, hot showers and air-con. ④.

Soon Yee, Jalan Stephen Tan (☎089/772447). A very friendly Chinese hotel, and the best bargain option in town. ①.

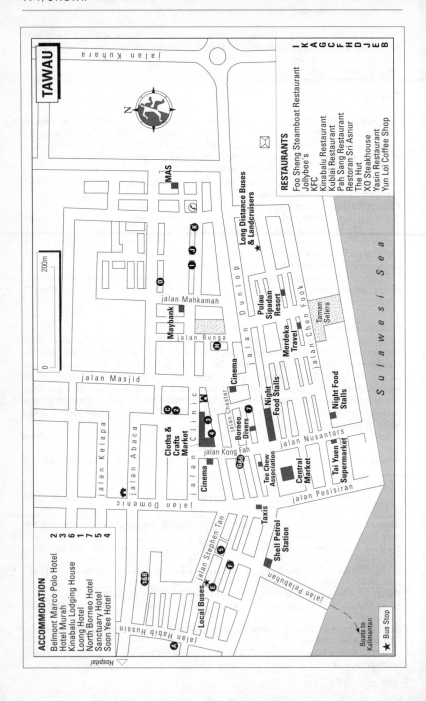

TAWAU

ACCOMMODATION

Belmont Marco Polo Hotel	2
Hotel Murah	3
Kinabalu Lodging House	6
Loong Hotel	1
North Borneo Hotel	7
Sanctuary Hotel	5
Soon Yee Hotel	4

RESTAURANTS

Foo Sheng Steamboat Restaurant	I
Jollybee's	K
KFC	A
Kinabalu Restaurant	G
Kublai Restaurant	C
Pah Sang Restaurant	F
Restoran Sri Asnur	H
The Hut	D
XO Steakhouse	J
Yasin Restaurant	E
Yun Loi Coffee Shop	B

Sulawesi Sea

★ Bus Stop

Boats to Kalimantan

ON TO INDONESIA

Tawau is the main stepping stone for onward **travel to Kalimantan**. Presently there are two ferries plying the route daily. At the time of writing, the *Samudra Express* was departing early in the morning, and the *Samudra Indah* in the early afternoon – though with the schedule notoriously subject to change, it's worth checking at the ticket booth north of the jetty on Jalan Pelabuhan on arrival. Nunukan ($25) is an hour from Tawau, after which it's a further two hours to Tarakan ($65).

The only **airlines** making the half-hour flight to Tarakan are MAS (Mon & Sat; $210) and the Indonesian Bouraq (Tues, Thurs & Sat; $185), whose agent in Tawau is Merdeka Travel, south of Jalan Dunlop in Block M, Bandar Sabindo (☎089/772531).

Since Indonesian **visas** aren't issued in Nunukan or Tarakan, you'll need to arrange one in advance. This can either be done in KK (see p.435), or by taking a bus from Tawau's local station to the **Indonesian Consulate** (☎089/777252), at Mile 1 1/2, Jalan Apas. The price of a visa is $75. The Malaysian immigration office is on the first floor of the Persekutuan Tawau (Tawau Federal Building), 200m southeast of the long-distance bus station.

EATING

Two blocks below Jalan Dunlop in the Sabindo Complex, the two-hundred-metre stretch of open-air **restaurants** and **stalls** collectively known as *Taman Selera* sets up daily; best-value are the Malay stalls, though bargain seafood is available at night, along with cold beer and *satay*. You'll find several good Indian Muslim restaurants above Jalan Dunlop in the town centre, among them the *Yasin* and the *Kinabalu*; as well as the excellent *Pah Sang Restaurant*, which specializes in aromatic *bak kut teh*. North of here, below the *Loong Hotel*, the extensive (English) menu at the *Yun Loi Coffee Shop* includes good claypot dishes, and at night there's a BBQ seafood stall out on the covered forecourt. However, the Fajar Centre, east of the town centre, has a virtual monopoly on more stylish venues. Pick of the bunch is the *Hut* in Block 29, which has generous Western set meals. The open-fronted *Foo Sheng Restaurant*, in Block 41, couldn't be more basic, but is still a good option if you fancy a steamboat pig-out; the *XO Steakhouse*, on the opposite corner, provides a protein fix. Otherwise, you might try the *Restoran Sri Asnur*, Block 38, if you want to go Thai or Malay. Finally, the *Marco Polo Hotel*'s elegant *Kublai Restaurant* has a *dim sum* breakfast on Sunday morning. The cakes and pastries at *Jolly Bee*'s bakery make fine desserts. Tawau's only bar of note is the *Marco Polo*'s pleasant lobby bar.

Circling Sabah: west of Tawau

A network of **logging roads** spanning the southern portion of Sabah makes it possible to travel back to KK overland, without having to retrace your steps. While not cheap, the journey by **land cruiser** (vehicles leave when full; $80) from Tawau's long-distance bus terminus to Keningau, along a track that parallels the Kalimantan border, is worth taking for excitement value alone.

The journey feels comfortable enough as you leave Tawau, as passengers are taken in two vehicles past the police roadblock outside town that checks on overcrowding – but then you're all transferred into one land cruiser. At **Merotai**, some 20km out of Tawau, the sealed road ends and the jolting ride begins, taking you past cocoa and palm plantations, lush forest and vast timber mills. Two-thirds of the way to Keningau, a quarry marks the left turn for Sapulut (see p.441), though if it's dark you're better off going on to Keningau, as vehicles are few and far between. Closer to **Kampung Sook**, look out for Murut graves by the roadside. Assuming your land cruiser doesn't experience difficulties – and the assumption is an optimistic one – you should reach Keningau in the early evening.

travel details

Trains

See box on p.429.

Beaufort to: KK (2 daily; 4hr); Tenom (5 daily; 2hr 30min).

KK to Beaufort (2 daily; 4hr); Tenom (2 daily; 7hr).

Tenom to: Beaufort (5 daily; 2hr 30min); KK (2 daily; 7hr).

Buses

Sabah's long-distance buses run to schedules, normally departing early in the morning. Minibuses and land cruisers leave as soon as they can muster a full quota of passengers. The list below is of the approximate number of buses travelling daily between the major towns, but schedules and services change constantly.

Beaufort to: KK (15 daily; 2hr); Kuala Penyu (8 daily; 1hr); Menumbok (8 daily; 1hr 30min); Sipitang (9 daily; 50min).

Keningau to: KK (15 daily; 2hr 30min); Sapulut (2 daily; 4hr); Tambunan (10 daily; 1hr); Tawau (2 daily; 6–8hr); Tenom (20 daily; 50min).

KK to: Beaufort (15 daily; 2hr); Keningau (15 daily; 2hr 30min); Kinabalu National Park (8 daily; 1hr 45min); Kota Belud (16 daily; 2hr 10min); Kudat (10 daily; 4hr); Lawas, Sarawak (1 daily; 4hr); Menumbok (6 daily; 2hr 30min); Papar (20 daily; 40min); Ranau (10 daily; 2hr); Sandakan (12 daily;

5hr 30min); Tambunan (11 daily; 1hr 30min); Tawau (2 daily; 9hr); Tuaran (10 daily; 50min).

Sandakan to: KK (12 daily; 5hr 45min); Lahad Datu (6 daily; 2hr 30min); Ranau (8 daily; 3hr 30min); Tawau (6 daily; 4hr 30min).

Tawau to: Keningau (1–2 daily; 6–8hr); KK (2 daily; 9hr); Lahad Datu (8 daily; 2hr); Sandakan (6 daily; 4hr 30min); Semporna (14 daily; 1hr 30min).

Tenom to: Beaufort (20 daily; 50min).

Ferries

KK to: Labuan (3 daily; 2hr).

Labuan to: Brunei (4 daily; 1hr 30min); KK (3 daily; 2hr); Menumbok (at least 10 daily; 25min); Sipitang (1 daily; 1hr 10min).

Tawau to: Nunukan (2 daily; 1hr); Tarakan (2 daily; 3hr).

Planes

KK to: Kudat (2 weekly; 40min); Labuan (7 daily; 30min); Lahad Datu (3 daily; 50min); Sandakan (6 daily; 50min); Tawau (7 daily; 45min).

Sandakan to: KK (6 daily; 50 min): Kudat (5 weekly; 45min); Lahad Datu (1 weekly; 1hr 5min); Tawau (2 weekly; 1hr 40min).

Tawau to: Tarakan (5 weekly; 30min).

CHAPTER EIGHT

BRUNEI

The tiny Islamic **Sultanate of Brunei** perches on the northwestern coast of Borneo, surrounded, and at one point even split in two, by the meandering border of Sarawak. At its peak in the sixteenth century, Brunei was the seat of the proudest empire in Borneo, its sultans receiving tribute from as far away as Manila. But by the end of the nineteenth century, its glory days were long past, and Brunei was a country which feared for its very existence. European adventurers methodically chipped away at its territory, absorbing it into their new colonies, eventually leaving the sultanate confined within only 5765 square kilometres.

Today, however, the Sultanate of Brunei is thriving. Its 280,000 inhabitants (Malays account for seventy percent of these; the rest are Chinese, Indians, indigenous tribes and expatriates) enjoy a quality of life almost unparalleled in Southeast Asia. Education and healthcare are free; houses, cars, and even pilgrimages to Mecca are subsidized; taxation on personal income is unheard of; and the average per capita income is around US$19,000. The explanation for this dramatic turn around is simple: **oil**, first discovered in 1903, at the site of what is now the town of Seria. Although it took until 1931 for the reserves to yield solid financial returns, the sultanate's natural resources (oil was later joined by natural gas) have produced a national wealth that's the envy of surrounding states.

Despite such lucrative resources, much of Brunei has remained unchanged for centuries. It lies on a slim coastal plain, threaded by several substantial rivers. Most of the country lies below 150 metres on an alluvial coastal plain, its lowland rainforest, peat swamp and heath forest running down to sandy beaches and mangrove swamps. The country is divided into four districts: **Brunei Muara**, which contains the capital, Bandar Seri Begawan; agricultural **Tutong**; oil-rich **Belait**; and **Temburong**, a sparsely populated backwater, severed from the rest of Brunei by the Limbang district of Sarawak. Because of the oil, Brunei has never needed to exploit its forestry to any great degree, with the result that primary and secondary tropical forest still cover around seventy percent of the total land area.

Oil has made Bruneians rich, none more so than Brunei's 29th **sultan**, Hassanal Bolkiah (his full title is 31 words long). The *Guinness Book of Records* and *Fortune Magazine* have both credited the present sultan as the richest man in the world, with assets estimated to be as high as US$37 billion. The sultan himself disputes such claims, asserting that he doesn't have unlimited access to state funds. Nevertheless, he has managed to acquire hotels in Singapore, London and Beverly Hills; a magnificent residence, the US$350-million Istana Nurul Iman; a collection of three hundred cars and a private fleet of aircraft; and over two hundred fine polo horses, kept at his personal country club. For his 50th birthday bash in 1996, sufficient funds were available to lure Michael Jackson into performing.

Their quality of life has engendered in Bruneians an acquiescence towards the royal family's extravagance that extends to the country's **political climate**. Sleepy Brunei certainly doesn't seem like a place under a state of emergency, but it has been since 1962, when the last recorded democratic elections resulted in an attempted coup (see below); provisions still exist for the detention, without trial, of citizens. Furthermore, popular involvement in government decision-making remains minimal: the sultan fulfils

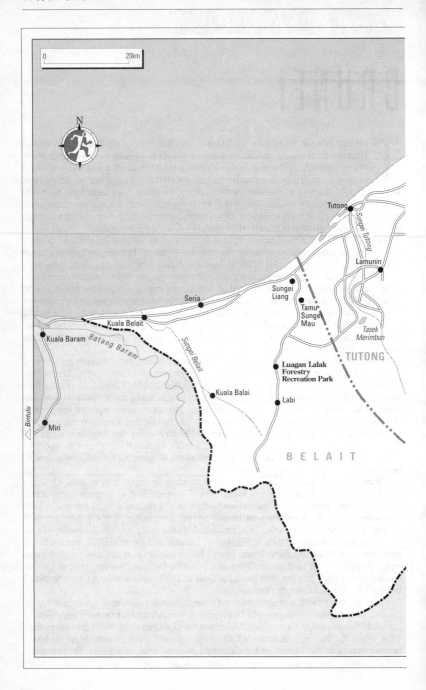

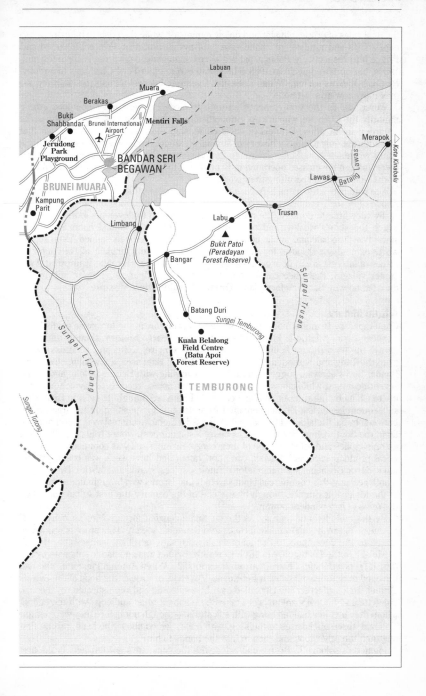

the dual roles of prime minister and defence minister, while the posts of minister of foreign affairs and minister of finance are held by his brothers, Prince Mohamed and Prince Jefri respectively. Political parties were countenanced for three years in the mid-1980s, but outlawed again in 1988. The sultan is quoted in Lord Chalfont's biography, *By God's Will*, as saying, "When I see some genuine interest among the citizenry, we may move towards elections."

Worse still is the government's attitude towards Brunei's most populous ethnic minority, the **Chinese**, who are not automatically classed as citizens. To enjoy the perks accorded to all other Bruneians, their citizenship must be proven, a process that demands not only a lengthy history of familial residence, but also a rigorous and humiliating written test in Malay language and customs. The discrimination doesn't end there: foreign businesses operating in Brunei tend to show favouritism towards Malays over Chinese when recruiting their workforce.

The sultanate's full name is *Negara Brunei Darussalam*, the "Country of Brunei, the Abode of Peace", and peaceful is a fair, if rather polite, description of the state. There's really very little to do here, the result of a disinclination to develop a tourist industry which the state's wealth renders unnecessary. Nightlife is almost nonexistent, and since 1991, the sale and public consumption of liquor have been banned. Even so, it's worth extending a stopover for a glimpse of the capital alone. Virtually all the country's places of interest are in or around **Bandar Seri Begawan**. Here the **Kampung Ayer** (water village), that once constituted the core of the Bruneian Empire still exists, dwarfed now by Bandar's formidable **Omar Ali Saifuddien Mosque**.

A little history

Contemporary Brunei's modest size belies its pivotal role in the formative centuries of Bornean history. Little is known of the sultanate's **early history**, though trade was always the powerhouse behind the growth of its empire. Coins and ceramics dating from the Tang and Sung dynasties found in the Kota Batu area, a few kilometres from Bandar Seri Begawan, suggest that China was trading with Brunei as long ago as the seventh century, while allusions in ninth-century Chinese records to payments of tribute to China by the ruler of an Asian city called Puni are thought to refer to Brunei. In subsequent centuries, Brunei benefited from its strategic position on the trade route between India, Melaka and China, and exercised a lucrative control over merchant traffic in the South China Sea. As well as being a staging post, where traders could stock up on supplies and off-load some of their cargo, Brunei itself was commercially active. Local produce such as beeswax, camphor, rattan and brasswork was traded by the *nakhoda*, or Bruneian sea traders, for ceramics, spices, woods and fabrics. By the fourteenth century, this commercial clout saw to it that Brunei was brought under the sway of the Majapahit Empire, though by the end of the century the first sultan had taken the reins of independent power.

By the mid-fifteenth century, as the sultanate courted foreign Muslim merchants' business, **Islam** began to make inroads into Bruneian society. This process was accelerated by the decamping to Brunei of wealthy Muslim merchant families after the fall of Melaka to the Portuguese in 1511. Certainly, Brunei was an Islamic sultanate by the time it received its first **European visitors** in 1521. When Antonio Pigafetta, who had travelled to Southeast Asia with Ferdinand Magellan, arrived at the head of the Sungei Brunei, he found a thriving city ruled over by a splendid and sophisticated royal court. Pigafetta and his companions were taken by elephant to an audience with the sultan, whom they met in a hall "all hung with silk stuffs" – though not before they were taught "to make three obeisances to the king, with hands joined above the head, raising first one then the other foot, and then to kiss the hands to him".

Pigafetta's sojourn in Brunei coincided with the sultanate's **golden age**. In the first half of the sixteenth century, Brunei was Borneo's foremost kingdom, its influence stretching along the island's northern and western coasts, and even as far as territory belonging to the modern-day Philippines. Such was the extent of Bruneian authority that Western visitors found the sultanate and the island interchangeable: the word "Borneo" is thought to be no more than a European corruption of Brunei. The fall of Melaka did much to bolster the importance of Brunei, though the foundation of its success was a strong and efficient form of government based upon traditional Islamic frameworks, headed by the sultan himself and represented in the outer regions of Bruneian territories by his *pengiran*, or noblemen. But by the close of the sixteenth century, things were beginning to turn sour for the sultanate. Trouble with Catholic Spain, now sniffing around the South China and Sulu seas with a view to colonization, led to a sea battle off the coast at Muara in 1578; the battle was won by Spain, whose forces took Brunei Town, only to be chased out days later by a cholera epidemic. The threat of piracy caused more problems, scaring off passing trade. Worse still, at home the sultans began to lose control of the *pengiran*, as factional struggles ruptured the court.

Western entrepreneurs arrived in this self-destructive climate, keen to take advantage of gaps in the trade market left by Brunei's decline. One such fortune-seeker was **James Brooke**, whose arrival off the coast of Kuching in August 1839 was to change the face of Borneo for ever. For helping the sultan to quell a Dyak uprising, Brooke demanded and was given the governorship of Sarawak; Brunei's contraction had begun. Over subsequent decades, the state was to shrink steadily, as Brooke and his successors used the suppression of piracy as the excuse they needed to siphon off more and more territory into the familial fiefdom. This trend culminated in the cession of the Limbang region in 1890 – a move which literally split Brunei in two.

Elsewhere, more Bruneian land was being lost to other powers. In January 1846, a court faction unsympathetic to foreign land-grabbing seized power in Brunei and the chief minister was murdered. British gunboats quelled the coup and Pulau Labuan was ceded to the British crown. A **treaty** signed the following year, forbidding the sultanate from ceding any of its territories without the British Crown's consent, underlined the decline of Brunei's power. Shortly afterwards, in 1865, American consul Charles Lee Moses negotiated a treaty granting a ten-year lease to the American Trading Company of the portion of northeast Borneo that was later to become Sabah. By 1888, the British had declared Brunei a **protected state**, which meant the responsibility for its foreign affairs lay with London.

The turn of the twentieth century was marked by the **discovery of oil**: given what little remained of Bruneian territory, it could hardly have been altruism that spurred the British to set up a Residency here in 1906. Initially, though, profits from the fledgling oil industry were slow to come and the early decades of the century saw rubber estates springing up at Berakas, Gadong and Temburong. However, by 1931, the Seria Oil Field was on stream and by 1938 oil exports, engineered by the British Malayan Petroleum Company, had topped M$5 million. Despite the hefty slice of profits appropriated by the British, the sultanate was still able to pay off debts from the lean years of the late nineteenth century.

The **Japanese invasion** of December 1941 temporarily halted Brunei's path to recovery. As in Sabah, Allied bombing over the three and a half years of occupation that followed left much rebuilding to be done. While Sabah, Sarawak and Pulau Labuan became Crown Colonies in the early postwar years, Brunei remained a **British protectorate** and retained its British Resident. Only in 1959 was the Residency finally withdrawn and a new constitution established, with provisions for a democratically elected legislative council. At the same time, Sultan Omar Ali Saifuddien (the present sultan's father) was careful to retain British involvement in matters of defence and foreign affairs – a move whose sagacity was made apparent when, in 1962, an armed coup led by Sheik Azahari's pro-democratic Brunei People's Party (PRB) was crushed by British

BRUNEI PRACTICALITIES

Brunei's **climate**, like that of neighbouring Sabah and Sarawak, is hot and humid, with average temperatures in the high twenties throughout the year. Lying 440km north of the equator, Brunei has a tropical weather system, so even if you visit outside the official **wet season** (usually November to February) there's every chance that you'll see some rain. Brunei is most commonly visited as a stepping stone to either Sabah or Sarawak, but if you are having to watch your **budget** carefully, you may find an internal MAS flight between the two Malaysian states a less expensive alternative. Flying from Miri to Labuan and proceeding from there to Sabah, for instance, can work out only marginally pricier – and far more time-effective – than bussing through Brunei and taking to the sea from there, once you've taken into account the inevitable overnighter in Bandar.

For **general information** on visiting Brunei, see the relevant sections of Basics.

Getting there

Air services are either with Royal Brunei or MAS. From Kuala Lumpur, there are six Royal Brunei flights a week to Bandar (M$600), though their prices are substantially undercut by MAS (2 daily; M$450). MAS flights also compare well from Kota Kinabalu (2 daily; M$90) and Kuching (5 weekly; M$250); the equivalent Royal Brunei flights cost around M$120 and M$360 respectively. The once-daily Singapore Airlines flights from Singapore's Changi Airport cost around S$400. Royal Brunei also has flights from Hong Kong (3 weekly) and Jakarta (4 weekly), while there are services from Manila with Philippine Airlines (3 weekly) and from Bangkok with Thai Airways.

Boats to Brunei depart daily from Lawas and Limbang in northern Sarawak, and from Pulau Labuan (see p.447), itself connected by boat to Kota Kinabalu in Sabah. From Miri (see p.397) in Sarawak, several **buses** travel daily to Kuala Belait, in the far western corner of Brunei. The overland route from Sabah to Brunei necessitates taking a bus to Lawas, and then a taxi into Temburong District, from where it's only a short boat trip (see p.494) to Bandar.

Getting around

If you intend to explore Brunei in some depth, you've got little option but to **rent a car**. South of the main coastal roads, **bus** services are nonexistent, while **taxis** are expensive if you want to cover much ground outside the capital. Apart from short hops across Sungei Brunei in Bandar's river taxis, the only time you're likely to use a **boat** is to get to Temburong District (see p.494), which is cut off from the rest of Brunei by the Limbang area of Sarawak.

Accommodation

The country's natural resources mean it has no need to court tourists and with one exception, **hotels** in Bandar are all up in the mid- to upper-range price brackets. While **longhouses** do exist in the interior, their inaccessibility means you aren't at all likely to stay at them.

Throughout the Singapore and Brunei chapters we've used the following **price codes** to denote the cheapest available room for two people. Single occupancy should cost less than double, though this is not always the case. Some guesthouses provide dormitory beds, for which the dollar price is given.

① $25 and under	④ $61–100	⑦ $201–300
② $25–40	⑤ $101–150	⑧ $301–400
③ $41–60	⑥ $151–200	⑨ $401 and over

Army Gurkhas. Since the coup, the result of Sultan Omar's refusal to convene the first sitting of the legislative council, Brunei has been ruled by the decree of the sultan, in his role as non-elected prime minister, and the government's emergency powers (see p.477) have been in place.

Despite showing interest in joining the planned **Malaysian Federation** in 1963, Brunei suffered a last-minute attack of cold feet, choosing to opt out rather than risk losing its new-found oil wealth and compromising the pre-eminence of its monarchy. Brunei remained a British Protectorate until January 1, 1984, when it attained full **independence**. Meanwhile, **oil reserves** have fulfilled all expectations; in 1956, onshore oil fields yielded 114,000 barrels a day and by the end of the decade offshore fields were yielding further profits. But it was only in the 1970s, the decade that saw oil prices shoot through the ceiling, that the money really began to roll in, by which time the state's **liquefied natural gas** (LNG) reserves were also being fully exploited. Nevertheless, Brunei's hydrocarbon resources are finite – estimates suggest that they'll sputter out a few decades into the next millennium – and as the government casts around for alternative sources of income for the future, it may well start to invest in tourism. Until then, Brunei remains of only limited interest to tourists.

Bandar Seri Begawan

BANDAR SERI BEGAWAN, or Bandar as it's known locally, is the capital of Brunei and the sultanate's only settlement of any real size. Until 1970, Bandar was known simply as Brunei Town; the present name means "Town of the Seri Begawan" – the title Sultan Omar Ali Saifuddien took after abdicating in favour of his son Hassanal Bolkiah in 1967. Straddling the northern bank of a twist in the Sungei Brunei, the city is characterized by its unlikely juxtaposition of striking modern buildings (the latest and most impressive being the twin malls of the Yayasan Sultan Haji Hassanal Bolkiah shopping complex) and traditional stilt houses. Brunei's original seat of power was **Kampung Ayer**, the water village which is still home to around half the city's population; the sultan's palace is the only building on dry land. With the arrival of the British Residency in 1906 came an attempt to coax the kampung people onto dry land, but although the streets which form downtown Bandar were laid out, the kampung dwellers stayed put, preferring to retain their traditional way of life. More recently, the Brunei government has tried to entice its water villagers onshore by means of modern housing projects, though Kampung Ayer still accounts for some thirty thousand of Bandar's population in 1986.

As recently as the middle of this century, Brunei's capital was a sleepy water village. Posted here as a teacher in the late 1950s, the novelist Anthony Burgess discovered that onshore Bandar comprised "a single street of shops, run by Chinese, which sold long-playing records and old copies of the Daily Mirror Weekly". That contemporary Bandar has become the attractive, clean and modern waterfront city it is today is due, inevitably, to oil. With the new-found wealth of the 1970s came large-scale urbanization north of the Sungei Brunei, resulting in housing schemes, shopping centres and, more obviously, the magnificent **Omar Ali Saifuddien Mosque**, which dominates the skyline of Bandar. First-time visitors are pleasantly surprised by a sense of space that's rare among Southeast Asian cites. Unfortunately, the contrasts with neighbouring capitals don't end there: lacking the frenetic vitality of other cities, Bandar is not a place which normally engenders much affection. Nor is it cheap to visit; the fact that most visitors to Brunei are business people means room prices can be prohibitively high. Nevertheless, the sights of Bandar are interesting enough to warrant a day or two's stopover.

Arrival, information and city transport

Flying into Bandar, you'll arrive at plush **Brunei International Airport**. If you need to book a room upon arrival, there are free public phones to your right beyond passport control. To the left, as you walk out of the arrivals concourse and into the car park,

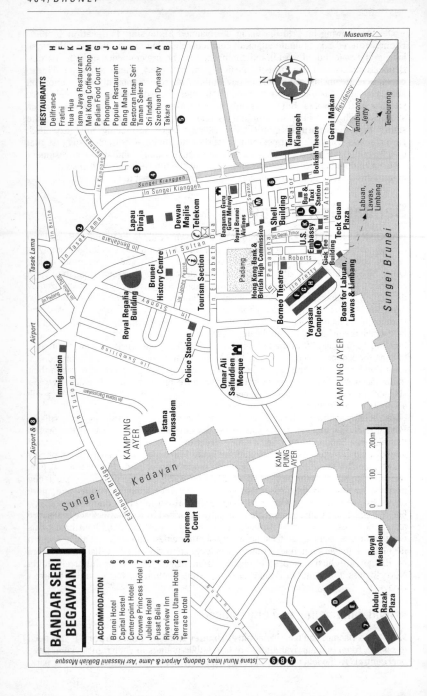

BANDAR SERI BEGAWAN

ACCOMMODATION

Brunei Hotel	6
Capital Hostel	3
Centerpoint Hotel	9
Crowne Princess Hotel	7
Jubilee Hotel	5
Pusat Belia	4
Riverview Inn	8
Sheraton Utama Hotel	2
Terrace Hotel	1

RESTAURANTS

Delifrance	H
Fratini	F
Hua Hua	K
Isma Jaya Restaurant	L
Mei Kong Coffee Shop	M
Padian Food Court	G
Phongmun	J
Popular Restaurant	C
Rang Mahel	E
Restoran Intan Seri	D
Taman Selera	I
Sri Indah	A
Szechuan Dynasty	B
Takara	

is a **tourist information booth**, whose staff will furnish you with the glossy and rather vague 100-page *Explore Brunei* booklet. Taking a taxi to cover the 11km into Bandar costs $15–20, so if you have time, you can make a huge saving by bearing right as you exit arrivals, into the free parking zone, where you can catch a bus (every 15min, 8am–8pm; $1) into town. You can get change for the fare at the airport branch of the Islamic Bank of Brunei (Mon–Thurs 9am–noon & 2–3pm, Fri 8–11am & 2.30–3.30pm, Sat 9–11am). **Boats** from Pulau Labuan, Lawas and Limbang all dock centrally, at the foot of Jalan Roberts, while buses from Sarawak and the west of Brunei terminate at the **bus station** below Jalan Cator.

City transport

With as much as half of Bandar's population living in the villages that make up Kampung Ayer, it makes sense that the most common form of **public transport** in the city should be its **water taxis**. A veritable armada of these skinny speedboats plies the Sungei Brunei night and day, charging only $1–2 for a short hop – pay your fare on board. If you want a longer tour of the water villages, or want to see the Sultan's Palace from the river, a half-hour round trip will cost around $15–20 per person – but prices are negotiable, especially if you're in a group. The jetty below the intersection of Jalan Roberts and Jalan MacArthur is the best place to catch a water taxi, though it's also possible to hail one from Jalan Residency.

Following a recent overhaul, Bandar's local **bus** network is now infinitely more user-friendly. Services to points north, east and west of the city centre now leave (every 15–20min, 6.30am–6pm; $1) from the bus station, underneath the multistorey car park just south of the eastern end of Jalan Cator. Three bus services ply the roads around the capital, their names pilfered from London's Underground system. Central Line buses run between the airport and the Brunei and Malay Technology museums, crossing the city en route; while the Circle Line loops up to the new Jame 'Asr Hassanil Bolkiah Mosque, and Gadong. Of the Northern Line's three routes, #1 and #2 run from Bandar northwards to the airport and Berakas, and #3 to the Technology Museum. Relevant bus details to destinations outside the capital are given throughout the rest of the chapter.

Taking a **taxi** to and from Bandar's points of interest is easier, though obviously more expensive than taking a bus. As with the buses, the city's taxi service had a recent makeover, and two distinct types now co-exist. Regular, metered taxis congregate beside the bus station and outside swisher shopping centres and hotels; fares start from $3, and a short journey – say, from the city centre to the Brunei Museum – costs $5–7. A nighttime surcharge applies between 9pm and 6am, there's a $5 charge on trips to the airport, and each piece of luggage loaded in the boot costs a further $1. For longer journeys, out to Seria or Kuala Belait for instance, drivers will be prepared to haggle for a fixed price. The new CTS service, whose purple cars run around the city, as far afield as Gadong and Batu One – but not, infuriatingly, to either the museums or the airport – charge a flat rate of $3. For the addresses of car rental agencies, see "Listings", p.491.

Accommodation

Brunei is almost bereft of budget **accommodation**, with the *Pusat Belia* (youth hostel) the only real option. Some visitors have resorted to taking a bus to the coast and sleeping on the beach, though this is hardly advisable. If you've got money, there's a fair selection of comfortable hotels to choose from, though most are firmly mid- to upper-range in price, with double rooms starting at $80.

Brunei, 95 Jalan Pemancha (☎02/242372). Comfortable and well appointed, this is Bandar's most central commercial hotel. ⑥.

LEAVING BANDAR SERI BEGAWAN

For addresses and details of airlines, travel agents and consulates in Bandar, see "Listings", p.491.

Airport

Buses ($1) run to the Lapangan Terbang Antarabangsa airport at least every fifteen minutes between 6.30am and 6pm, from the station below Jalan Cator. All Central Line and Northern Line buses ply this route. Taxis ($15–20) congregate at the bus station. For **flight information** call ☎02/331747. Don't forget the **airport tax**: $5 for flights to Malaysia and Singapore, $12 for all other destinations.

By boat

For the moment, boats for Labuan, Lawas and Limbang leave from beside the Customs and Immigration Station at the junction of Jalan Roberts and Jalan MacArthur. There's been talk of shifting Labuan and Lawas services up to Muara (see p.493); when or whether this will happen is anyone's guess, but the city's ticket agencies will be able to put you in the picture. Tickets for **Labuan** (daily at 8am, 8.30am, 1pm & 2pm; $20–25) and **Lawas** (daily at 11.30am; $15) are sold by New Island Shipping, first floor, Giok Tee Building, Jalan MacArthur (☎02/243059), and Halim Tours, Lorong Gerai Timor, off Jalan MacArthur (☎02/226688); for **Limbang** (frequent departures 7am–5.30pm according to demand; $10), tickets are sold at the open stalls opposite Lorong Gerai Timor, on Jalan MacArthur. From Labuan, there are daily connections on to Kota Kinabalu and Menumbok in Sabah, though to ensure you catch one, it's wise to leave Bandar early in the day. Note that tickets to Labuan should be booked as early as possible – especially if you want to travel over a weekend or a holiday. Also be aware that schedules change, so double-check departure times to all destinations.

Boats to Bangar in **Temburong** (every 45min, 6.30am–4.30pm; $7) depart from Jalan Residency; tickets are sold beside the jetty. From Temburong's largest settlement, Bangar, it's possible to travel overland to both Lawas and Limbang (see below).

By road

The most obvious means of exiting Bandar overland is to take a bus to Seria (hourly 7am–3pm), change there for Kuala Belait and catch another bus or taxi to Miri, in Sarawak. Alternatively, from Bangar (p.494) you can take a taxi to Lawas, from where buses depart daily for Sabah. There are buses from the Brunei/ Sarawak border, in Temburong District, to Limbang (see p.403).

Capital Hostel, Jalan Kampung Berangan (☎02/223561). A budget option by Bruneian standards, and a useful standby if you can't get into the neighbouring *Pusat Belia*. ④.

Centrepoint, Abdul Razak Complex, Gadong (☎02/430430). Excellent business and recreational facilities in luxury service apartments; within the building are several good restaurants. ⑦.

Crowne Princess, Jalan Tutong (☎02/241128). With 117 well-appointed rooms, situated away over Edinburgh Bridge; regular shuttle buses run to and from the city centre. The in-house restaurant has decent Asian food. ⑤.

Jubilee, Jubilee Plaza, Jalan Kampung Kianggeh (☎02/228070). East of Sungei Kianggeh, a well-groomed, mid-range hotel set opposite a patch of traditional kampung houses. ⑤.

Pusat Belia, Jalan Sungai Kianggeh (☎02/222900). Brunei's youth hostel, and by far the cheapest option in town, providing you can get in – you may need an ISIC or IH card. Rooms are shared with three others, and there's a pool ($1) downstairs. $10 for three nights.

Riverview Inn, Km 1, Jalan Gadong (☎02/238238). Just as good as the *Brunei*, but an annoying distance from the centre. ⑥.

Sheraton Utama, Jalan Tasek Lama (☎02/244272). Brunei's first international-standard hotel, with 156 swanky rooms and suites, plus a well-equipped business centre. ⑨.

Terrace, Jalan Tasek Lama (☎02/243554). Reasonable hotel, whose rooms are slightly worn and dated; outside is a quiet pool. ⑦.

The City

Downtown Bandar is hemmed in by water: to the east is Sungei Kianggeh; to the south, the wide Sungei Brunei; and to the west, Sungei Kedayan, which runs up to the **Edinburgh Bridge**. The **Omar Ali Saifuddien Mosque**, overlooking the compact knot of central streets, is Bandar's most obvious point of reference, sitting in a cradle formed by **Kampung Ayer** (water village), which spreads like water lilies on a pond across large expanses of the river. Over Edinburgh Bridge, **Jalan Tutong** runs westwards and past the Mile 1 area (a grid of shopping complexes and hotels), reaching Istana Nurul Iman 3km later; in the other direction, **Jalan Residency** hugs the river bank on its way to the **Brunei Museum** and its neighbouring attractions.

The Omar Ali Saifuddien Mosque

At the very heart of both the city and the sultanate's Muslim faith is the magnificent **Omar Ali Saifuddien Mosque** (Mon–Wed, Sat & Sun 8am–noon, 1–3.30pm & 4.30–5.30pm, Thurs closed to non-Muslims, Fri 4.30–5.30pm). Built in classical Islamic style, and mirrored in the circular lagoon, it's a breathtaking sight, whether viewed in a dazzling sunlight or seen illuminated a lurid green at night. The mosque was commissioned by and named after the father of the present sultan, and completed in 1958 at a cost of US$5 million. It makes splendid use of opulent yet tasteful fittings – Italian marble, granite from Shanghai, Arabian and Belgian carpets, and English chandeliers and stained glass. Topping the cream-coloured building is a 52-metre-high golden dome whose curved surface is adorned with a mosaic comprising over three million pieces of Venetian glass. Anthony Burgess described the mosque's construction in his autobiography, *Little Wilson and Big God*: "The dome had been covered with gold leaf," he wrote, "which, owing to the contraction and expansion of the structure with comparative cool and large heat, fell to the ground in flakes and splinters which were taken by the fisherfolk to be a gift from Allah." It is sometimes possible to obtain permission to ride the elevator up the 44-metre-high minaret, and look out over the water village below. A replica of a sixteenth-century royal barge, or *mahligai*, which stands in the lagoon is used on special religious occasions. The usual dress codes – modest attire, and shoes to be left at the entrance – apply when entering the mosque.

Kampung Ayer

From the mosque, it's no distance to Bandar's **Kampung Ayer**, or water village, whose sheer scale makes it one of the great sights of Southeast Asia. Stilt villages have occupied this stretch of the Sungei Brunei for hundreds of years: Antonio Pigafetta, visiting Borneo in 1521, described a city, "entirely built on foundations in the salt water . . . it contains twenty-five thousand fires or families. The houses are all of wood, placed on great piles to raise them high up". Today, an estimated thirty thousand people live in the scores of sprawling villages that compose Kampung Ayer, their dwellings connected by a maze of wooden promenades. These villages now feature their own clinics, mosques, schools, a fire brigade and even a police station; the homes have piped water, electricity and TV. Despite all these amenities, Kampung Ayer's charm lessens as you get closer. Its waters are distinctly unsanitary, and the houses are susceptible to fire. Even so, a strong sense of community has meant that attempts to move the inhabitants onto dry land and into housing more in keeping with a state that has the highest per capita income in the world, have met with little success.

The meandering ways of Kampung Ayer make it an intriguing place to explore on foot. For a real impression of its dimensions though, it's best to charter one of the water taxis that zip around the river (see "City transport", above). A handful of traditional **cottage industries** continue to turn out copperware and brassware (at Kampung Ujong Bukit), and exquisite sarongs and boats (Kampung Saba Darat); the boatmen should know the whereabouts of some of them.

Along Jalan Sultan

Just to the east of the Omar Ali Saifuddien Mosque, Bandar's main drag, broad **Jalan Sultan**, runs north past several of the city's lesser sights. First is the **Brunei History Centre** (Mon–Thurs & Sat 7.45am–12.25 & 1.30–4pm; free), a research institution whose dull displays (maps showing Brunei's changing shape, and tables outlining the genealogy of past sultans) will have you hurrying on to the **Royal Regalia Building** (Mon–Thurs 8.30am–5pm, Fri 9–11.30am & 2.30–5pm, Sat & Sun 8.30am–5pm; free) next door, opened in 1992 as part of the sultan's silver jubilee celebrations. The exhibition, which is housed in a magnificent semicircular building fitted out with lavish carpets and marble, uses photographs and exhibits to chart the life of the present sultan. The sycophantic labelling apart ("Since childhood His Majesty has a very cheerful, generous and benign personality"; of schooldays, "He picked up his lessons very fast within a short time"; of Sandhurst, "popular with fellow cadets as well as higher officers"), there's some quite interesting stuff here, including a surprisingly happy, smiling shot of the sultan taken during his circumcision ceremony, as well as a golden hand and forearm used to support his chin during the coronation, and a beautifully ornate crown. The **Constitutional Gallery** in the same building is inevitably drier, but its documents and treaties are worth a scan. Fronting the whole collection is the **coronation carriage**, or *usungan*, ringed by regalia from the coronation ceremony – which took place right across Jalan Sultan in the **Lapau Diraja** (Royal Ceremonial Hall), on August 1, 1968. The hall's slightly tacky exterior belies the grandeur of its huge inner chamber, whose western side is approached by a mini escalator. Beyond this, rows of red, black, pink and white pillars run up to the golden *patarana*, or royal throne. Although the hall is not officially open to the public, it's usually possible to take a peek at its lavish interior. Next door is the parliament building, the **Dewan Majlis**, which used to house the Legislative Assembly.

East of the Lapau Diraja and parallel to Jalan Sultan is Jalan Sungai Kianggeh, which runs past the daily market **Tamu Kianggeh**, and Bandar's most central **Chinese temple**, before arriving at Jalan Tasek, the turning to tranquil **Tasek Lama Park** which is five minutes' walk from the main road. Bear left and pass through the pretty gardens to a small waterfall; bear right along the sealed road and right again at the fork and you'll end up at a bottle-green reservoir.

East to the Brunei Museum

Jalan Residency runs eastwards from Sungei Kianggeh, bordered to the right by the Sungei Brunei and to the left by a hillside Muslim cemetery whose scores of decrepit stones are shaded by an orchard of gnarled frangipani trees. After a little less than a kilometre, the road reaches the **Brunei Arts and Handicrafts Training Centre** (Mon–Thurs & Sat 7.45am–12.15pm & 1.30–4.30pm, Fri & Sun 8.30am–2pm; free), an organization dedicated to perpetuating the sultanate's cultural heritage. Here, young Bruneians are taught traditional skills, such as songkok matting, basketry and bamboo-working, brass casting and the crafting of the *kris* (traditional dagger). Apart from the occasional weaving demonstration though, the training process is off-limits unless you've applied in advance for written permission. You'll probably have to make do with browsing through the **craft shop**'s decent selection of reasonably priced basketry, silverware and spinning tops.

From here it's 4km to the Brunei Museum (eastbound buses run, occasionally, from the stop opposite the handicrafts centre), shortly before which is the **tomb** of **Sultan Bolkiah** (1473–1521), Brunei's fifth sultan, who held sway at the very peak of the state's power. It's worth setting aside an hour or two for the **Brunei Museum** (Tues–Thurs 9am–5pm, Fri 9.30–11.30am & 2.30–5pm, Sat & Sun 9am–5pm; free), which has several outstanding galleries. In the inevitable Oil and Gas Gallery, set up by Brunei Shell Petroleum, exhibits, graphics and captions recount the story of Brunei's oil reserves, from the drilling of the first well in 1928, to current extraction and refining techniques. Also interesting, though tantalizingly sketchy, is the Muslim Life Gallery, whose dioramas allow glimpses of social traditions, such as the sweetening of a new-born baby's mouth with honey or dates, and the disposal of its placenta in a *bayung*, a palm leaf basket which is either hung on a tree or floated downriver. At the back of the gallery, a small collection of early photographs shows riverine hawkers trading from their boats in Kampung Ayer. The museum's undoubted highlight, though, is its superb Islamic Art Gallery where, among the riches on display are beautifully illuminated antique Korans from India, Iran, Egypt and Turkey, exquisite prayer mats, and quirkier items like a pair of ungainly wooden slippers.

Steps around the back of the museum drop down to the riverside **Malay Technology Museum** (9am–5pm except Fri 9–11.30am & 2.30–5pm; closed Tues; free), whose three galleries provide a mildly engaging insight into traditional Malay life. Of greatest interest is Gallery Three, whose exhibits include the *pelarik gasing*, a machine which evenly cuts spinning tops, the *lamin keleput*, used for boring blowpipes, and other devices worked from forest materials by Brunei's indigenous people. In the same gallery are authentic examples of Kedayan, Murut and Dusun dwellings, while elsewhere in the building, you'll see dioramas highlighting stilt-house and *atap*-roof construction, boat-making and fishing methods.

The Jame 'Asr Hassanil Bolkiah Mosque

Many people reckon that the **Jame 'Asr Hassanil Bolkiah Mosque** (Mon–Wed, Sat & Sun 8am–noon, 1–3.30pm & 4.30–5.30pm; Thurs & Fri closed to non-Muslims), set in harmonious gardens in the commercial suburb of Gadong, has a distinct edge over the Omar Ali Saifuddien Mosque both of style and grandeur. Droves of Bangladeshi workers busily clip and sweep outside, below the mosque's sea-blue roof, golden domes and slender minarets, while silk-clad Bruneians go about their daily prayer. This is Brunei's largest mosque, constructed to commemorate the silver jubilee of the sultan's reign in 1992. It's referred to as the Kiarong Mosque (after a neighbouring kampung) by locals, who find its full name rather a mouthful. Circle Line buses skirt the grounds of the mosque en route to Gadong, though you'll get an impression of the building on your way to and from the airport.

The Istana Nurul Iman

The **Istana Nurul Iman**, the official residence of the sultan, is sited at a superb riverside spot 4km west of the capital. Bigger than either Buckingham Palace or the Vatican, the istana is a monument to self-indulgence. Its design, by Filipino architect Leandro Locsin, is a sinuous blend of traditional and modern, with Islamic motifs such as arches and domes, and sloping roofs fashioned on traditional longhouse designs, combined with all the mod cons you'd expect of a house whose owner earns an estimated US$5 million a day.

James Bartholomew's book, *The Richest Man in the World*, lists some of the mind-boggling figures relating to the palace. Over half a kilometre long, it contains a grand total of 1778 rooms, including 257 toilets. Illuminating these rooms requires 51,000 light bulbs, many of which are consumed by the palace's 564 chandeliers; simply getting around the rooms requires 18 lifts and 44 staircases. The throne room is said to be particularly sumptuous: twelve one-ton chandeliers hang from its ceiling, while its four grand thrones stand against the backdrop of a eighteen-metre arch, tiled in 22-carat gold. In addition to the throne room, there's a royal banquet hall that seats 4000 diners, a prayer hall where 1500 people can worship at any one time, an underground car park for the sultan's hundreds of vehicles, a state-of-the-art sports complex, and a helipad. Inevitably, the palace is rarely open to the general public, though the sultan does declare open house every year during *Hari Raya*. Otherwise, nearby **Taman Persiaran Damuan**, a kilometre-long park sandwiched between Jalan Tutong and Sungei Brunei, offers the best view, or you can fork out for a boat trip and see the palace lit up at night from the water. Opposite the park is **Pulau Ranggu**, where proboscis monkeys congregate on the shore towards dusk.

All westbound buses travel along Jalan Tutong, over the Edinburgh Bridge and past the istana, though it is possible to walk. En route you'll pass the city's **Mile 1** area, in the southwestern corner of which the **Royal Mausoleum and Graveyard** are tucked away. Sultans have been buried at this site since 1786, though only the last four were laid to rest in the mausoleum.

Eating and drinking

Fortunately, Bandar's **restaurants** are more reasonably priced than its hotels; there's a modest range of decent establishments, reflecting the multicultural make-up of the city's population. Several of Bandar's better eating places are situated in the area west of Edinburgh Bridge, a short taxi-ride – or an interesting walk beyond the Omar Ali Saifuddien Mosque and through Kampung Ayer – from downtown. Though several kilometres northwest of downtown Bandar, the booming suburb of Gadong has a number of interesting restaurants too, as well as branches of *McDonald's* and *Pizza Hut*, and is within range of CTS taxis. If you're on a tight budget, head for the night **stalls** behind the Chinese temple on Jalan Sungei Kianggeh, where the bursting flames and billowing smoke of chicken being barbecued over charcoal fires have a hellishly dramatic aspect. Malay favourites are laid out buffet-style here, but the lack of tables and chairs makes life difficult. Alternatively, there's a cluster of stalls behind the Temburong jetty on Jalan Residency, whose lack of panache is somewhat redeemed by good and cheap *soto ayam, nasi campur* and other Malay staples.

One thing you won't find downtown is a bar. Drinking **alcohol** in public has been outlawed in Brunei since New Year's Day, 1991, though if you're gasping for a beer, the local expats will tell you to ask discreetly at any of the city's Chinese restaurants. The *Brunei International Club*, a ten-minute taxi ride from the city at Simpang 197, Jalan Berakas, seems to have served its last can of lager, though given its history of closings and reopenings, this rough and ready expat haunt could be operational in the near future.

Café Melati, *Sheraton Utama Hotel*, Jalan Sungei Kianggeh. The generous buffet lunch ($25) in this bright and breezy establishment fills you up for the day; buffet dinner ($30) features a different international culinary theme every night. Mon–Sat noon–2pm & 7–10pm, Sun 7–10pm.

Delifrance, ground floor, Yayasan Complex, Jalan Kumbang Pasang. Sleekly run, French-style coffee and croissant joint. Daily 9am–9pm.

Fratini, G24 Block C, Yayasan Complex, Jalan Kumbang Pasang (☎02/232892). Italian-run expat oasis, adding a welcome dash of sophistication to Bandar's dining scene; choose from a decent range of pizzas and pastas ($11–15), then round things off with a cappuccino. Daily 11.30am–2pm & 6–10pm.

Hua Hua Restaurant, 48 Jalan Sultan. Steamed chicken with sausage is one of the highlights in this hole-in-the-wall Chinese establishment, where $15 feeds two people. Daily 7am–9pm.

Isma Jaya, 27 Jalan Sultan. Lip-smacking *korma* and *biriyani* sell well here; this is one of several good Indian restaurants along Jalan Sultan. Daily 6am–8pm.

Mei Kong Coffee Shop, 108 Jalan Pemancha. Coffee shop, fronted by a chicken rice bar, serving noodles, *rotis* and *panggang* (rice and prawns cooked in banana leaves). The unmarked *Mei Kong* is stationed right beside the Hong Kong Bank. Daily 5am–8pm.

Padian Food Court, first floor, Yayasan Complex, Jalan Kumbang Pasang. Snow-bright, air-con food court whose spotless stalls serve Thai, Arabic, Japanese, Indian and several other regional cuisines. Daily 9am–10pm.

Phongmun Restaurant, second floor, Teck Guan Plaza, Jalan Sultan. Classy and centrally located Chinese restaurant, with wall panels depicting roses and dragons; you can get *dim sum* here. Daily 6.30am–11pm; *dim sum* served 6.30am–4.40pm.

Popular Restaurant, Shop 5, Block 1, Putri Anak Norain Complex, Batu 1, Jalan Tutong. Bare but clean Indian restaurant, serving peerless *dosai*, tandoori breads and curries. Mon 4–10pm, Tues–Sun 8am–10pm.

Rang Mahel, first floor, 3a Bangunan Mas Panchawarna, Batu 1, Jalan Tutong. Cosy and well-respected North Indian place; below is the *Regent's Den*, where cheaper Indian snacks are available. Both open daily 7.30am–10.30pm.

Restoran Intan Seri Taman Selera, 1–2 Bangunan Mas Panchawarna, Batu 1, Jalan Tutong. Popular, buffet-style Malay restaurant with a *satay* stall outside at night. Daily 7am–9.30pm.

Restoran Melayu Selasik, top floor, Bangunan Guru Guru Melayu, Jalan Sungei Kianggeh. Malay/Bruneian restaurant that verges on the chintzy, but boasts friendly staff and well-cooked dishes for $4–5. The house speciality, the *set ambuyat* ($19 for two), offers fish, vegetables, shrimp and beef dishes, arranged around a bowl of *ambuyat*, a sago glue which is wrapped, candy-floss style, around chopsticks, and dipped in *sambal belacan*.

Snoopy Corner & Fast Food, 108 Bangunan Guru Guru Melayu, Jalan Sungei Kianggeh. Small and simple Indian joint, producing good curries and a delicious chicken *biryani*. Mon–Sat 6am–8.30pm, Sun 6am–1.30pm.

Sri Indah, 66 Jalan MacArthur. Sweaty, cramped place churning out *murtabaks* and *rotis* that hit the spot. Daily 7am–9pm.

Szechuan Dynasty, *Centrepoint*, Abdul Razak Complex, Gadong. A truly elegant dining experience, though one which won't necessarily be to all tastes – the prevalence of chilli, pepper and ginger means the emphasis here is firmly on hot, spicy Chinese food. Daily noon–2.30pm & 6–10pm.

Takara, *Centrepoint*, Abdul Razak Complex, Gadong. Top-rank Japanese restaurant serving such classics as *sashimi* and *teppanyaki*; groups might consider dining the authentic Japanese way – cross-legged on the floor, in a *tatami* room. Daily 11.30am–2.30pm & 6–10pm.

Listings

Airlines MAS, 144 Jalan Pemancha (☎02/224141); Philippine Airlines, first floor, Wisma Haji Fatimah, Jalan Sultan (☎02/222970); Royal Brunei Airlines, RBA Plaza, Jalan Sultan (☎02/242222); Singapore Airlines, 49–50 Jalan Sultan (☎02/227253); Thai Airways, fourth floor, Komplek Jalan Sultan, 51–55 Jalan Sultan (☎02/242991).

American Express Unit 401–03, fourth floor, Shell Building, Jalan Sultan (Mon–Fri 8.30am–5pm, Sat 8.30am–1pm, ☎02/228314).

Banks and exchange Hong Kong Bank, Jalan Sultan; International Bank of Brunei, Jalan Roberts; Overseas Union Bank, RBA Plaza, Jalan Sultan; Standard Chartered Bank, Jalan Sultan. Banking hours are Mon–Fri 9am–3pm, Sat 9–11am. In addition, there are many cash-only moneychangers along Jalan MacArthur.

Bookshops *Best Eastern Books*, G4 Teck Guan Plaza, Jalan Sultan, stocks a modest range of English-language books and magazines; *Times Bookshop*, first floor, Yayasan Complex, isn't bad either.

Car rental Avis, *Sheraton Hotel*, Jalan Sungai Kianggeh (☎02/227100); National, first floor, Hasbullah 4, Jalan Gadong (☎02/224921); Roseraya Car Rental, Unit 105, Wisma Hj. Mohd Taha, Mile 2, Jalan Gadong (☎02/241442).

Cinemas *Borneo Theatre*, on Jalan Roberts, and *Bolkiah Theatre*, on Jalan Sungai Kianggeh, both screen English-language movies; tickets around $4.

Embassies and consulates Australia, fourth floor, Teck Guan Plaza, Jalan Sultan (☎02/229435); Indonesia, Simpang 528, Lot 4498, Sungei Hanching Baru, Jalan Muara (☎02/330180); Malaysia,

437 Kampung Pelambayan, Jalan Kota Batu (☎02/228410); Philippines, fourth & fifth floor, Badi'ah Building, Mile 1, Jalan Tutong (☎02/241465); Singapore, fifth floor, RBA Plaza, Jalan Sultan (☎02/227583); Thailand, no. 1, Simpang 52-86-16, Kampung Mata-Mata, Jalan Gadong (☎02/229653); UK, third floor, Hong Kong Bank Chambers, Jalan Sultan (☎02/222231); USA, third floor, Teck Guan Plaza, Jalan Sultan (☎02/229670).

Hospital The Raja Isteri Pengiran Anak Saleha Hospital (RIPAS) is across Edinburgh Bridge on Jalan Putera Al-Muhtadee Billah (☎02/222366); or there's the private Hart Medical Clinic at 47 Jalan Sultan (☎02/225531). For an ambulance, call ☎991.

Immigration The Immigration Office (Mon–Thurs & Sat 7.45am–12.15pm & 1.45–4.30pm) is opposite Jalan Sumbiling, on Jalan Tutong.

Laundry *Superkleen*, opposite *Brunei Hotel*, Jalan Pemancha.

Pharmacies *Khong Lin Dispensary*, G3A, Wisma Jaya, Jalan Pemancha; *Sentosa Dispensary*, 42 Jalan Sultan.

Police Central Police Station, Jalan Stoney (☎02/222333).

Post office The GPO (Mon–Thurs & Sat 8am–4.30pm) is at the intersection of Jalan Elizabeth Dua and Jalan Sultan. Poste restante/general delivery is at the Money Order counter.

Telephones Telekom (daily 8am–midnight) is next to the GPO on Jalan Sultan; international calls can be made from here, or else buy a phone card (in $5, $10, $20 or $50 denominations) and use a public booth.

Travel agents A number of travel agents around the city offer tours around the state; Zura Travel Service, Room 101, Bangunan Guru Guru Melayu, Jalan Kianggeh (☎02/225812); and Freme Travel Services, fourth floor, Wisma Jaya, Jalan Pemancha (☎02/234277), are central. Both offer three-hour city ($40) and countryside ($50) tours.

Brunei Muara

Once you've exhausted all that Bandar has to offer, you may consider going further afield in **Brunei Muara** – the district of Brunei that contains the capital. It's worth knowing that, with the obvious exception of **Jerudong Park Playground**, Brunei's own little Disneyland, none of Brunei Muara's destinations are unmissable and few are served by direct buses. Unless you are willing to pay through the nose for taxis or rent a car, think twice before planning a trip to these destinations. Principal among the attractions that ring the capital are **Kampung Parit** and **Bukit Shahbandar Forest Recreation Park**, the former an evocation of how Bruneians lived in the days before oil and concrete, the latter a sizeable nature reserve; both make pleasant day-trips. For a glimpse of Brunei's countryside, with a little determination it's possible to see the cultivated land that flanks Jalan Mulaut. You may prefer simply to head for one of the area's several **beaches**.

Along Jalan Mulaut

Some 15km west of Bandar along the road to Tutong, a mosque marks the turning southwards onto **Jalan Mulaut**. From here, it's a further 10km to **KAMPUNG PARIT** (daily 8am–6pm; free), where a number of old-style Bornean dwellings have been erected to shed light on traditional Bruneian village life. Amongst the exhibits, which were built by artisans from local villages using only forest materials, is a replica of Kampung Ayer, pre-manufactured timber and zinc. The park's playground, picnic site and cluster of food stalls make it popular with Bruneian weekenders. Even so, access is not easy: unless you take a taxi, the only public transport access is by bus to Tutong; you have to get off after 15km, at the turning, and make your own way from there.

South of the park, Jalan Mulaut continues across some fine countryside, on its way to the Sarawak border. Rice cultivation dominates this region of Brunei, much of which belongs to the **Wasan Rice Project**, a rice farm established in the late 1970s to promote rice self-sufficiency through cultivation and research. Around 6km beyond the farm, Jalan Mulaut reaches an immigration checkpoint, from where it's possible to push on into Sarawak.

Muara and around

Northeast of the city, beyond the Brunei Museum, Jalan Kota Batu stretches all the way up to **MUARA**, an oil town and Brunei's main port. The town was originally established to serve the now-defunct Brooketon Coal Mine, which was situated a few kilometres to the west. While there's nothing to bring you to Muara itself, nearby **Muara Beach** boasts a reasonable stretch of sand, as well as food stalls and changing rooms. At Serasa Beach a few kilometres south of Muara town, a recently built watersports complex has facilities for sailing, windsurfing, water-skiing and fishing. Buses ($2) to Muara from the capital pass along Jalan Kota Batu, skirting Sungei Brunei's north bank. En route is **Pulau Chermin**, a tiny island whose unremarkable royal tombs are all that remain of the fortress which stood here three centuries ago. The island has been a protected archeological site since pieces of Ming and Tang Dynasty pottery were unearthed, and is off-limits unless you have permission to visit from the state museum. Pulau Chermin is opposite Kampung Sungei Besar, around 10km out of Bandar. Five kilometres further up the road to Muara, the chain of pools at **Mentiri Falls** offers good swimming amid lush forest. The path to the falls starts at the side of a river on the left-hand side of the road, beyond Simpang 378.

The coast: Crocodile Beach, Bukit Shahbandar and Jerudong Park Playground

From Muara, a highway more or less follows the northern coast for 18km to Tutong. A few kilometres out of town, there's a turning to Pantai Meragang, known locally as **Crocodile Beach**, and considered by many to be the best in the area; a major international hotel chain plans to construct a resort here. The beach is 1km west of the intersection of Jalan Muara and the Muara–Tutong Highway.

Around 20km west of Muara is the **Bukit Shahbandar Forest Recreation Park** (daily 8am–6pm; free), its seventy hectares of acacia, pine and heath forest scored by unchallenging trails, and dotted with shelters and lookout points over Bandar and the South China Sea. Marking the entrance into the park is an information centre with displays on the surrounding terrain. **Camping** is allowed, provided you have permission from the Director of Forestry's office on Jalan Roberts. Unfortunately, Bukit Shahbandar is tricky to reach; unless you're prepared to pay for a taxi, you'll have to take a bus to Berakas and try to hitch from there.

Several kilometres west of Bukit Shahbandar on the road to Tutong, the district of **Jerudong** was long remarkable only for being the playground of the sultan, whose polo stadium and stables are located here. The soft opening of the **Jerudong Park Playground** (grounds open daily 2pm–2am; games and rides Mon, Tues & Wed 5pm–midnight; Thurs & Sat 5pm–2am; Fri & Sun 2pm–midnight; during Ramadan daily 8pm–2am; free) on the occasion of the sultan's 48th birthday, in 1994, changed all this. Conceived as a "lasting testimony to His Majesty's generosity to his *rakyat* (people)", the park has since been improved and expanded into a cracking funfair/adventure park whose scores of rides make it that rarest of treats, a Bruneian must-see. Daily gates average two thousand, there's very little queuing for rides, and enough of interest to keep you amused for a long evening. For strong stomachs there's the **Boomerang** rollercoaster or the heart-in-the-mouth vertical fall, the **giant drop**, while those of a more delicate constitution might enjoy the **Supakarts**, shooting galleries, boat rides, space-ride simulators, bumper cars and carousels. Beyond the excellent **hawker centre** that abuts the park are the yellow towers and green floodlights of the polo stadium.

Jerudong Park Playground is tricky to reach, and trickier to get back from once buses have stopped in the early evening, so taking a taxi is your best bet – a return fare shouldn't exceed $50, but you'll have to haggle.

Temburong District

Hilly **Temburong District** has been isolated from the rest of Brunei since 1884, when the strip of land to its west was ceded to Sarawak. Sparsely populated by Malay, Iban and Murut groups, the region is swathed in rainforest that can be explored in the forest reserves at Peradayan and Batu Apoi. Temburong is an important source of gravel for Brunei; timber is also culled from its land, though not on a large scale. The district is accessible only by a hair-raising **speedboat journey** from Bandar (see p.486). The boats, whose shape and speed has earned them the name "flying coffins" scream through a network of narrow mangrove estuaries that are home to crocodiles and proboscis monkeys, swooping around corners and narrowly missing vessels travelling the opposite way, before shooting off down Sungei Temburong. Boatmen don't mind if you sit on top of the cabin, but think twice before doing so.

All boats terminate at Bangar, the crossroads for the district's two main roads. Temburong has over sixty kilometres of good roads, providing links into Sarawak, with Limbang (see p.403) to the west, and Lawas (p.404) to the east.

Bangar: crossing to Sarawak

Temburong's one settlement of any size, **BANGAR** stands beside the bridge where the district's main road crosses Sungei Temburong. After the thrilling boat trip from the capital, the town is a disappointment. Its main street, which runs west from the jetty to the ugly town mosque, is lined only by a handful of nondescript **coffee shops** and provision stores. Across the bridge is Bangar's grandest building, its new District Office, whose waterfront café is the town's most salubrious **place to eat**. There are no places to stay in Bangar.

If you're planning to cross **into Sarawak** – either to Limbang or to Lawas – you'll first have to make for the **immigration post** beside the turning for Kampung Puni, 5km west of Bangar. Limbang is easiest and cheapest to reach: after a \$5–10 taxi ride from Bangar, take a ferry (\$1) across the river which marks the border with Malaysia, and then catch one of the connecting buses (\$2) which run into Limbang until 5pm. Lawas is accessible by road, via Labu (see below), but only by a very expensive taxi-ride from Bangar.

Around Bangar

On its way to Lawas, the road east of Bangar trundles past a few small settlements and the occasional sawmill, reaching the **Peradayan Forest Reserve** after 15km. From the road, it's a ninety-minute walk through the reserve's dipterocarp rainforest, to the top of 310-metre **Bukit Patoi**, whose plateau affords excellent views of the surrounding terrain, and of Lawas in Sarawak. Camping on Bukit Patoi is possible, though there are no facilities. A few kilometres beyond the reserve, the road reaches **Labu**, a mysterious place whose existence amounts only to a sign reading "Labu 0km". From here, it's only a few kilometres to the border with Sarawak – but bear in mind that the immigration outpost is way back beyond Bangar (see above).

The end of the seventeen kilometres of road running south of Bangar is marked by **Batang Duri**, whose smart Iban longhouse is occupied by around two hundred people. A short walk beyond the longhouse leads to a small waterfall whose cool waters make for a refreshing swim. There's more river-swimming a couple of kilometres back up the road, at **Taman Batang Duri**, a well-manicured park that's blighted by its very sad mini zoo. With permission from Bangar's District Office, you can camp at the park.

Much of the area south of Batang Duri now makes up the **Batu Apoi Forest Reserve**, which spans around five hundred square kilometres and incorporates the **Kuala Belalong Field Centre**, built as a joint venture between the *Universiti Brunei*

Darussalem and Brunei Shell to facilitate research into the surrounding rainforest. Several trails lead into the reserve and there's also a canopy walk and observation tower; visitors can stay at one of the field centre's chalets, provided there's not a full house of researchers. Bookings should be made through the Department of Biology, at the university (☎02/427001). Bear in mind, though, that the five-kilometre, two-hour boat trip up Sungei Temburong from Batang Duri to reach the field centre is an expensive one.

Taxis are available in Bangar to all of these places, with return fares starting at around $15.

Tutong District

West of Muara District is wedge-shaped **Tutong District**, whose main settlement, **Tutong**, is a little over 40km west of Bandar. Though a coastal highway now connects Tutong with Muara District, buses ($3) from the capital still make the one-hour journey via inland Jalan Tutong, which is skirted by scrublands and grasslands. The wide range of mountains that runs down through Borneo from Sabah misses all but the Temburong District of Brunei; accordingly, the terrain of Tutong District never manages more than a gentle roll, making it ideal for the heightened agriculturalism the government is presently trying to develop in the area, in preparation for the eventual demise of the oil reserves.

Tutong
Bruneian settlements don't come any sleepier than **TUTONG**. The town has witnessed none of the development that the discovery of oil has caused further west, but though Tutong makes no real demands upon tourists' time, it's an amiable enough place to break the trip between Sarawak and Bandar. Tutong's one street of any size, Jalan Enche Awang, is flanked by rows of shophouses on one side, and on the other by broad Sungei Tutong, its far bank massed with palm trees.

You won't find anywhere to stay in Tutong, but there are several **restaurants**: try the *Haji K-K-Koya* at Jalan Enche Awang 14, or the Chinese *Ho Yuen* at no. 12. If you're in town on a Friday morning, you should visit the animated **Tamu Tutong**, which draws fruit and vegetable vendors from the interior of Brunei. The market takes place on a patch of land 1km from central Tutong at Kampung Serambagaun, and is reached by walking out of town along Jalan Enche Awang and taking a left turn at the fork in the road.

Ignoring this fork and continuing on across the coastal highway brings you, after fifteen minutes, to the best stretch of beach in the area, the peninsular **Pantai Seri Kenangan** whose yellow sands divide Sungei Tutong from the South China Sea. Its name translates as "Unforgettable Beach" and though this may be rather stretching the point, it's pleasant enough.

Tasek Merimbun
Tutong District's most impressive geographical feature is **Tasek Merimbun**, an S-shaped lake, the largest in Brunei. Wooden boardwalks run from the attractively landscaped shore across to Pulau Jelandung, a tiny wooded island, and around the lake itself are pathways and picnic spots. It would be a charming place to visit, if it wasn't so awkward to reach: unless you've rented a car, you aren't likely to get here, since the lake is around 25km inland from Tutong and not served by buses; a return taxi fare costs well over $50. If you're driving, follow Jalan Tutong out of Bandar and after around 30km take the left turn to Lamunin. From there, signposts lead you to Tasek Merimbun, along roads that traverse glistening paddy fields.

Belait District

Belait District, west of Tutong and over Sungei Tutong, is oil and gas country, and has been the economic heart of the sultanate ever since the Seria Oil Field was established in 1931. The oil boom led directly to the rise of the region's two main coastal towns, **Seria** and **Kuala Belait**. Inland, though, it's a different story: down fifty-kilometre-long **Labi Road**, Iban **longhouses** and tiny kampungs survive in the face of the tremendous changes brought about by the sultanate's sudden wealth and the substantial population shift to the coast.

Labi Road

Flat scrublands line the road westwards from Tutong to Seria. The sands along this stretch of Brunei's coast are a brilliant white due to their high silicon content. In time, as Brunei looks for moneymaking alternatives to its finite oil reserves, these sands could well spawn a glass industry. A few kilometres over Sungei Tutong, a south turning marks the start of **Labi Road**, which offers the chance to explore the state's interior. First stop, 500m up the road, is the **Sungei Liang Forest Reserve**, whose 14 hectares of thick lowland forest can be explored by following one of the well-kept walking trails leading from the lakes, information centre and picnic shelters clustered around the entrance. With your own car, it's possible to push on down Labi Road from the reserve. Come on a Sunday morning and you'll pass by bustling **Tamu Sungai Mau**, several kilometres south of Sungei Liang, while beyond this is the 270-hectare **Luagan Lalak Forestry Recreation Park**, whose freshwater swamp swells into a lake with the onset of the monsoon rains, flooding the sedges that grow around it. Some 35km south of Sungei Liang is **LABI** itself, a small agricultural settlement whose surrounding hills have refused to yield up their oil riches, despite much speculative drilling. In the meantime, Labi relies on harvests of durian and rambutan for its livelihood. It was Labi's oil potential which led to the construction of Labi Road; shortly after Labi, it peters out, though a passable track pushes on towards the border with Sarawak, passing several modern Iban longhouses, the biggest of which, **Rumah Panjang Mendaram Besar**, houses around a hundred people. Just beyond the longhouse, a footpath to the left leads, after twenty minutes, to **Wasai Mendaram**, a low waterfall with a pool you can swim in. Another longhouse, **Rumah Panjang Teraja**, marks the end of Labi Road, with only swamp forest beyond.

Seria

At the very epicentre of Brunei's oil and gas wealth is **SERIA**, 65km west of Bandar. Until oil was first discovered here at the turn of the century, the area where the town now stands was nothing more than a malarial swamp, known locally as Padang Berawa, or "Wild Pigeon's Field": an oil prospector researching in the area in 1926 reported that, "walking here means really climbing and jumping over naked roots, and struggling and cutting through air roots of mangroves of more than man's height". It took until 1931 for S1, the sultanate's first well, to deliver commercially, after which Seria expanded rapidly, followed in more recent times by offshore drilling, the construction of a gas-processing plant in 1955 and the opening of an oil refinery in 1983. Despite its mineral wealth, Seria remained an isolated settlement for several decades, unlinked by road with the capital. Driving along the shore on their way here four decades ago, Anthony Burgess and his wife "misjudged the table of the tides. We raced the incoming waves but lost. . . . Crocodiles, which had adapted themselves to shore life in order to prey on monkeys, lazily considered swimming across the sungei that joined the sea to examine us. The water had risen to our waists and was still rising. Lynne, always courageous, stripped and swam to the nearest kampung. Twenty men produced a rope and hauled us out. This sort of thing had happened before." At this time, Shell were still employing crocodile hunters to safeguard drilling sites.

As you approach from Tutong, you'll see numbers of small oil wells called "nodding donkeys" because of their rocking motion, though they actually bear a closer resemblance to praying mantises. Around the town are green-roofed housing units and bungalows, constructed by Brunei Shell for their employees, while on the waterfront is the **Billionth Barrel Monument**, whose interlocking arches celebrate the huge productivity of the first well. Seria town centre is a hectic place, dominated by the Plaza Seria shopping mall, across from the bus station.

Though there are no places to stay, budget **restaurants** and coffee shops abound. On Jalan Sultan Omar Ali (left of the plaza if viewed from the bus station), you'll find the *Universal Café* at no. 11, a sleepy retreat that's good for coffee while you wait for a bus. Next door, the air-con *Restoran Sayang Merah* sells Asian and Western dishes such as bolognaise, Spanish omelettes and T-bone steaks. For a more upmarket meal, try the *New China Restaurant* in Plaza Seria.

Kuala Belait and on Sarawak

It's a little under 20km from Seria to the neighbouring oil town of **KUALA BELAIT**. There's nothing very enticing about Kuala Belait, but with all buses to and from Miri in Sarawak stopping here, it's a place you may have to visit. The town is ringed by suburban development that caters for the expat community, while central Kuala Belait is characterized by the many workshops and businesses that the local oil industry has spawned. If Kuala Belait seems sleepy today, pity the poor expats consigned to its drilling stations in the early part of the century. A contemporary rhyme encapsulated the torpor and isolation they felt:

> *Work of course gets sometimes weary*
> *Up in Belait*
> *And the evenings long and dreary*
> *Up in Belait*
> *But when again New Year draws nigh*
> *Let's go to Miri, they all cry.*

Buses stop at the intersection of Jalan Bunga Raya and Jalan McKerron, across which is the town's **taxi** stand. Jalan McKerron houses several good **restaurants** – the best of which are the tastefully decorated *Buccaneer Steakhouse* at no. 94, whose mid-priced international food is aimed squarely at the expat market; and the *Akhbar Restaurant*, at no. 99a, with a Malay and North Indian menu which includes excellent *dosai*. Of KB's handful of other restaurants, two in particular, the first-floor *Healthy Way Tandoori* at 30 Jalan Pretty (the town's main drag, a block east of McKerron), and Jalan Bunga Raya's *Orchid Room*, are worth a visit – the former for its storming *naans*, *tikka masalas* and *lassis*, the latter for it's good value three-course Western set lunches (Mon–Fri; $5). Next door to Jalan McKerron's *Buccaneer* at no. 93, is one of Kualal Belait's two **hotels**, *Hotel Sentosa* (☎03/ 331345; ④), with capacious, well-appointed and welcoming rooms. The alternative is the slightly more expensive *Sea View Hotel* (☎03/332651; ⑤), 3–4km back along the coastal road towards Seria. You can **change money** in town at the Hong Kong Bank (Mon–Fri 9am–3pm, Sat 9–11am).

Buses to Sarawak leave Kuala Belait's bus station at 7.30am, 9.30am, 11am, 1.30pm and 3.30pm; the price ($10.20) includes the ferry across Sungei Belait and the connecting Sarawakian bus over the border. **Taxi** drivers charge around $100 for a full car to Miri, though you should be able to haggle them down substantially.

Upriver: Kuala Balai

Kuala Belait squats on the eastern bank of calm **Sungei Belait**, and motorboatmen whose craft are moored at the back of the central market on Jalan McKerron will take you upriver – it'll cost at least $100 for the return trip. Unless it's the river travel itself you're interested in, there's very little reason to make the trip. After around forty minutes, **KUALA BALAI** comes into sight. Once a thriving centre for sago-processing, Kuala Balai has seen its population dwindle from hundreds to just a handful, as its inhabitants have left in search of work on the oil fields; it's now little more than a ghost town. As you approach Balai, look out for the wooden cage of human skulls on stilts over the river – a grim remnant of Borneo's head-hunting days.

t r a v e l   d e t a i l s

Buses

Brunei has a generous ratio of cars to citizens, so its bus network is skimpy. If you want to make a day-trip out of Bandar, you'll have to start early in the morning.

Bandar Seri Begawan to: Muara (every 30min until 4.30pm; 30min); Seria (hourly until 3pm; 1hr 45min); Tutong (hourly until 3pm; 1hr).

Kuala Belait to: Miri (every 2hr, 7.30am–3.30pm; 1hr 30min); Seria (every 30min until 6.30pm; 45min).

Seria to: Bandar Seri Begawan (every 45min until 2pm; 1hr 45min); Kuala Belait (every 30 min; 45min);

Miri (every 2hr, 7am–3pm; 2hr).

Ferries

Bandar Seri Begawan to: Bangar (every 45min; 50min); Lawas (1 daily; 2hr); Limbang (at least 8 daily; 30min); Pulau Labuan (4 daily; 1hr 30min).

CHAPTER NINE

SINGAPORE

Singapore is certainly the handiest city I ever saw, as well planned and carefully executed as though built entirely by one man. It is like a big desk, full of drawers and pigeon-holes, where everything has its place, and can always be found in it.

W. Hornaday, 1885.

Despite the immense changes the past century has wrought upon the tiny island of **Singapore**, natural historian William Hornaday's succinct appraisal is as valid today as it was in 1885. Since gaining full independence from Malaysia in 1965, this absorbing city-state – which measures just 580 square kilometres and is linked by a kilometre-long causeway to the southern tip of Malaysia – has been transformed from a sleepy colonial backwater to a pristine, futuristic shrine to consumerism. It's one of Southeast Asia's most accessible destinations, its downtown areas dense with towering skyscrapers and gleaming shopping malls, while sprawling new towns ring the centre, with their own separate communities and well-planned facilities. Yet visitors prepared to peer beneath the state's squeaky-clean surface will discover a profusion of age-old buildings, values and traditions that have survived in the face of profound social and geographical change. And the island has not been overwhelmed by development – even as you make your way in from the airport, you'll be struck immediately by Singapore's abundance of parks, nature reserves, and lush, tropical greenery. Inevitably, given its geographical position, the state is seen by most people as a mere stopover and, because of its size, you can gain an impression of the place in just a few hours. However, a lengthier stay is easily justified. Quite apart from the cultural highlights, you'll find several days spent in Singapore invaluable for arranging financial transfers, seeing to medical problems and generally gathering strength before continuing on to the region's less affluent – and often more demanding – areas.

Singapore's progress over the past three decades has been remarkable. Lacking any noteworthy natural resources, its early prosperity was based on a vigorous **free trade** policy, put in place in 1819 when Sir Stamford Raffles first set up a British trading post here. Later, mass industrialization bolstered the economy, and today the state boasts the world's second busiest port after Rotterdam, minimal unemployment, and a super-efficient infrastructure. Almost the entire population has been moved from unsanitary kampungs into swish new apartments, and the average per capita income is over US$12,000. Yet none of this was achieved without considerable compromise – indeed, the state's detractors claim it has sold its soul in return for prosperity.

Put simply, at the core of the Singapore success story is an unwritten bargain between its government and population, which stipulates the loss of a certain amount of personal freedom, in return for levels of affluence and comfort that would have seemed unimaginable thirty years ago. Lee Kuan Yew (former prime minister and now senior minister) has gone on record as saying, "When you are hungry, when you lack basic services, freedom, human rights and democracy do not add up to much." Outsiders often bridle at these sentiments, and it's true that some of the regulations in force here can seem extreme: neglecting to flush a public toilet, jaywalking, chewing gum and eating on the subway all carry sizeable fines. The case of American teenager, Michael Fay, caught the world's headlines in early 1994, when he was given four strokes of the *rotan* (cane) for vandalizing cars. But far more telling is the fact that

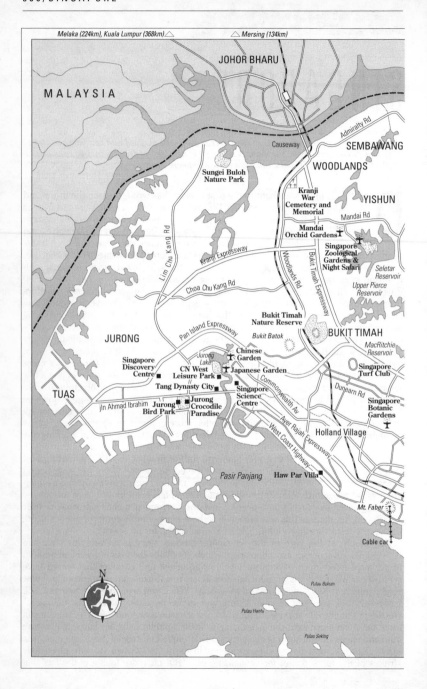

Melaka (224km), Kuala Lumpur (368km) △   △ Mersing (134km)

JOHOR BHARU

MALAYSIA

Causeway

Admiralty Rd

SEMBAWANG

WOODLANDS

Sungei Buloh
Nature Park

Kranji
War
Cemetery and
Memorial

YISHUN

Mandai Rd

Mandai
Orchid Gardens

Singapore
Zoological
Gardens &
Night Safari

Seletar
Reservoir

Kranji Expressway

Lim Chu Kang Rd

Woodlands Rd

Bukit Timah Expressway

Upper Pierce
Reservoir

Choa Chu Kang Rd

Pan Island Expressway

Bukit Timah
Nature Reserve

Bukit Batok

BUKIT TIMAH

MacRitchie
Reservoir

JURONG

Chinese
Garden

Jurong
Lake

Japanese Garden

Singapore
Turf Club

Singapore
Discovery
Centre

CN West
Leisure Park

Dunearn Rd

Tang Dynasty City

Commonwealth Av

Singapore
Science
Centre

TUAS

jln Ahmad Ibrahim

Jurong
Bird Park

Jurong
Crocodile
Paradise

Ayer Rajah Expressway

Singapore
Botanic
Gardens

Holland Village

West Coast Highway

Pasir Panjang

Haw Par Villa

Mt. Faber

Cable car

N

Pulau Bukum

Pulau Hantu

Pulau Seking

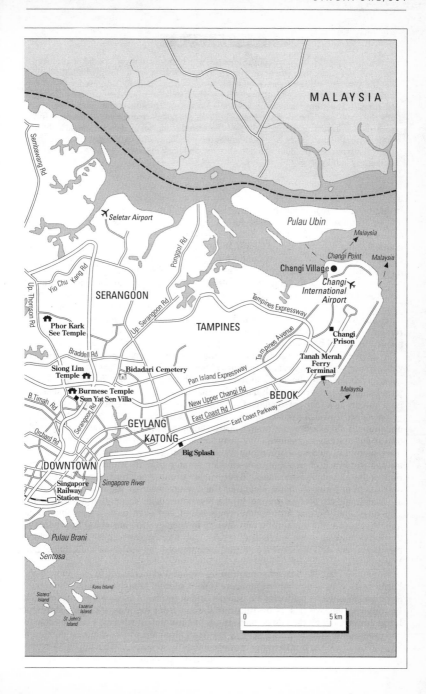

MALAYSIA

Sembawang Rd

Seletar Airport

Pulau Ubin

Malaysia

Changi Point

Changi Village

Malaysia

Changi International Airport

Up. Thomson Rd

Yio Chu Kang Rd

Ponggol Rd

SERANGOON

Up. Serangoon Rd

Tampines Expressway

Phor Kark See Temple

TAMPINES

Tampines Avenue

Braddell Rd

Changi Prison

Siong Lim Temple

Bidadari Cemetery

Pan Island Expressway

Tanah Merah Ferry Terminal

Serangoon Rd

Burmese Temple

Sun Yat Sen Villa

New Upper Changi Rd

Malaysia

B Timah Rd

BEDOK

East Coast Rd

East Coast Parkway

Orchard Rd

GEYLANG

KATONG

DOWNTOWN

Big Splash

Singapore Railway Station

Singapore River

Pulau Brani

Sentosa

Sisters' Island

Kusu Island

Lazarus Island

St John's Island

0   5 km

WHEN TO GO

Singapore is just 136km north of the equator, which means that you should be prepared for a hot and sticky time whenever you go. **Temperatures** are uniformly high throughout the year, but it's the region's humidity levels – what Anthony Burgess termed "the hot wet dishrag atmosphere of Singapore" – which make the heat really uncomfortable. Be prepared for **rain** during your stay, too – November, December and January are usually the coolest and the wettest months, but rain can fall all year round. On average, July records the lowest annual rainfall. See the introduction for a detailed climate chart. Otherwise, the only other consideration is the possibility of coinciding with one of the many **festivals** (see p.66), of which the liveliest and most extensive is Chinese New Year, in January and February

these punishments are rarely, if ever, inflicted, as Singaporeans have learned not to break the law. The population, trusting the wisdom of its leaders, seems generally content to acquiesce to a paternalistic form of **government** that critics describe as soft authoritarianism. Consequently, Singaporeans have earned a reputation for cowed, unquestioning subservience, a view that can be overstated, but which isn't without an element of truth. The past has taught Singaporeans that, if they follow their government's lead, they reap the benefits. In addition, they take a pride in their country that occasionally extends to smugness – witness the huge celebrations that accompany National Day, Singapore's annual collective pat on the back. Yet there is good reason to be proud: Singapore is a clean, safe place to visit, its amenities are second to none and its public places are smoke-free and hygienic. And as the nation's youth (who don't remember a time before the improvements they take for granted) begin to find a voice, public life should become increasingly, if gradually, more liberal and democratic.

Whatever the political ramifications of the state's economic success, of more relevance to the seven million annual visitors to Singapore is the fact that improvements in living conditions have been shadowed by a steady loss of the state's **heritage**, as historic buildings and streets are bulldozed to make way for shopping centres. Singapore undoubtedly lacks the personality of some southeast Asian cities, but its reputation for being sterile and sanitized is unfair. Shopping on state-of-the-art Orchard Road is undoubtedly a major draw for many tourists, but under the long shadows cast by giddy towers and spires you'll still find the dusty temples, fragrant medicinal shops, and colonial buildings of old Singapore, neatly divided into enclaves, each home to a distinct ethnic culture. Much of Singapore's fascination springs from its **multicultural population**: of the 2.8 million inhabitants, 76 percent are Chinese (a figure reflected in the predominance of Chinese shops, restaurants and temples across the island), 15 percent are Malay, and 6.5 percent are Indian, the remainder being from other ethnic groups. This diverse ethnic mix textures the whole island, and often turns a ten-minute walk into what seems like a hop from one country to another. One intriguing by-product of this ethnic melting pot is **Singlish** (see p.635), or Singaporean English, a patois which blends English with the speech patterns, exclamations and vocabulary of Chinese and Malay.

The entire state is compact enough to be explored exhaustively in just a few days. Forming the core of downtown Singapore is the **Colonial District**, around whose public buildings and lofty cathedral the island's British residents used to promenade. Each surrounding enclave has its own distinct flavour, from the aromatic spice stores of **Little India**, to the tumbledown backstreets of **Chinatown**, where it's still possible to find calligraphers and fortune tellers, or the **Arab Quarter**, whose cluttered stores sell fine cloths and silks. **North** of the city, you'll find the country's two nature reserves – Bukit Timah Nature Reserve and the Central Catchment Area – and the splendid

Singapore Zoological Gardens. In the **west** of the island, the East meets Disneyworld at **Tang Dynasty City** and **Haw Par Villas**, while the **east coast** features good seafood restaurants, set on long stretches of sandy beach. In addition, over fifty islands and islets lie within Singaporean waters, all of which can be reached with varying degrees of ease. The best day-trips, however, are to **Sentosa**, the island amusement arcade which is linked to the south coast by a short causeway (and cable car), and to **Pulau Ubin**, off the east coast, where the inhabitants continue to live a kampung life long since eradicated from the mainland.

A little history

What little is known of Singapore's ancient history relies heavily upon legend and supposition. Third-century Chinese sailors could have been referring to Singapore in their account of a place called Pu-Luo-Chung, or "island at the end of a peninsula". In the late thirteenth century, Marco Polo reported seeing a place called Chiamassie, which could also have been Singapore: by then the island was known locally as Temasek – "sea town" – and was a minor trading outpost of the Sumatran Srivijaya empire. The island's present name – from the Sanskrit **Singapura**, meaning "Lion City" – was first recorded in the sixteenth century, when a legend narrated in the Malay annals, the *Sejarah Melayu*, told how a Sumatran prince saw a lion while sheltering on the island from a storm; the annals reported that the name had been in common use since the end of the fourteenth century.

Throughout the fourteenth century, Singapura felt the squeeze as the Ayuthaya and Majapahit empires of Thailand and Java struggled for control of the Malay Peninsula. Around 1390, a Sumatran prince called **Paramesvara** threw off his allegiance to the Javanese Majapahit Empire and fled from Palembang to present-day Singapore. There, he murdered his host and ruled the island until a Javanese offensive forced him to flee north, up the Peninsula, where he and his son, Iskandar Shah, subsequently founded the Melaka Sultanate. A grave on Fort Canning Hill (see p.533) is said to be that of **Iskandar Shah**, though its authenticity is doubtful. With the rise of the Melaka Sultanate, Singapore devolved into an inconsequential fishing settlement; a century or so later, the arrival of the Portuguese in Melaka forced Malay leaders to flee southwards to modern-day Johor Bahru for sanctuary. A Portuguese account of 1613 described the razing of an unnamed Malay outpost at the mouth of Sungei Johor to the ground, an event which marked the beginning of two centuries of historical limbo for Singapore.

By the late eighteenth century, with China opening up for trade with the West, the British East India Company felt the need to establish outposts along the Straits of Melaka to protect its interests. Penang was secured in 1786, but with the Dutch expanding their rule in the East Indies (Indonesia), a port was needed further south. Enter **Thomas Stamford Raffles** (see p.530 for biography). In 1818, the governor-general of India authorized Raffles, then lieutenant-governor of Bencoolen (in Sumatra), to establish a **British colony** at the southern tip of the Malay Peninsula; early the next year, he stepped ashore on the northern bank of the Singapore River accompanied by Colonel William Farquhar, former resident of Melaka and fluent in Malay.

At the time, inhospitable swampland and tiger-infested jungle covered Singapore, and its population is generally thought to have numbered around 150, although some historians suggest it could have been as high as a thousand. Raffles recognized the island's potential for providing a deep-water harbour, and immediately struck a treaty with **Abdul Rahman**, *temenggong* (chieftain) of Singapore, establishing a British trading station there. The Dutch were furious at this British incursion into what they considered their territory, but Raffles – who still needed the approval of the Sultan of Johor for his outpost, as Abdul Rahman was only an underling – disregarded Dutch sensibilities. He approached the sultan's brother, Hussein, recognized him as the true sultan, and concluded a second treaty with both the *temenggong* and **His Highness the Sultan Hussein Mohammed Shah**. The Union Jack was raised, and Singapore's future as a free trading post was set.

With its strategic position at the foot of the Straits of Melaka, and with no customs duties levied on imported or exported goods, Singapore's expansion was meteoric. The population had reached ten thousand by the time of the first census in 1824, with Malays, Chinese, Indians and Europeans arriving in search of work as coolies and merchants. In 1822, Raffles set about drawing up the demarcation lines that divide present-day Singapore. The area south of the Singapore River was earmarked for the Chinese; a swamp at the mouth of the river was filled and the commercial district established there. Muslims were settled around the Sultan's Palace in today's Arab Quarter. The Singapore of those times was a far cry from the pristine city of the late twentieth century. "There were thousands of rats all over the district" wrote Abdullah bin Kadir, scribe to Stamford Raffles, "some almost as large as cats. They were so big that they used to attack us if we went out walking at night and many people were knocked over."

In 1824, Sultan Hussein and the *temenggong* were brought out, and Singapore ceded outright to the British. Three years later, the fledgling state united with Penang and Melaka (now under British rule) to form the **Straits Settlements**, which became a British crown colony in 1867. For forty years the island's *laissez-faire* economy boomed, though life was chaotic, and disease rife. More and more immigrants poured onto the island; by 1860 the population had reached eighty thousand, with each ethnic community bringing its attendant cuisines, languages and architecture. Arabs, Indians, Javanese and Bugis all came, but most populous of all were the **Chinese** from the southern provinces of China, who settled quickly, helped by the clan societies (*kongsis*) already establishing footholds on the island. The British, for their part, erected impressive Neoclassical theatres, courts and assembly halls, and in 1887 Singapore's most quintessentially British establishment, the *Raffles Hotel*, opened for business.

By the end of the nineteenth century, the opening of the Suez Canal and the advent of the steamship had consolidated Singapore's position at the hub of international trade in the region, with the port becoming a major staging post on the Europe–East Asia route. In 1877, Henry Ridley began his one-man crusade to introduce the **rubber plant** into southeast Asia, a move which further bolstered Singapore's importance as the island soon became the world centre of rubber exporting. This status was further enhanced by the slow but steady drawing of the Malay Peninsula under British control – a process begun with the Treaty of Pangkor in 1874 and completed in 1914 – which meant that Singapore gained further from the mainland's tin- and rubber-based economy. Between 1873 and 1913 trade increased eightfold, a trend which continued well into the twentieth century. Singapore's Asian communities found their political voice in the 1920s. In 1926, the Singapore Malay Union was established, and four years later, the Chinese-supported Malayan Communist Party (MCP). But grumblings of independence had risen to no more than a faint whisper before an altogether more immediate problem reared its head.

The bubble burst in 1942. In December 1941, the Japanese had bombed Pearl Harbour and invaded the Malay Peninsula. Less than two months later they were at the top of the causeway, safe from the guns of "Fortress Singapore", which pointed south from what is now Sentosa island. The inhabitants of Singapore had not been prepared for an attack from this direction and on February 15, 1942, the **fall of Singapore** (which the Japanese then renamed Syonan, or "Light of the South") was complete. Winston Churchill called the British surrender "the worst disaster and the largest capitulation in British history"; cruelly, it later transpired that the Japanese forces had been outnumbered and their supplies hopelessly stretched immediately prior to the surrender.

Three and a half years of brutal **Japanese** rule ensued, during which thousands of civilians were executed in vicious anti-Chinese purges and Europeans were either herded into **Changi Prison**, or marched up the Peninsula to work on Thailand's infamous "'Death Railway". Less well known is the vicious campaign, known as Operation Sook Ching, mounted by the military police force, or *Kempeitai*, during which upwards of 25,000 Chinese males between 18 and 50 years of age were shot dead at Punggol and Changi beaches as enemies to the Japanese. Following the atomic destruction of Hiroshima and Nagasaki in 1945, Singapore was passed back into British hands, but things were never to be the same. Singaporeans now wanted a say in the government of the island, and in 1957 the British government agreed to the establishment of an elected, 51-member legislative assembly. Full internal **self-government** was achieved in May 1959, when the **People's Action Party** (PAP), led by Cambridge law graduate **Lee Kuan Yew**, won 43 of the 51 seats. Lee became Singapore's first prime minister, and quickly looked for the security of a merger with neighbouring Malaya. For its part (despite reservations about aligning with Singapore's predominantly Chinese population) anti-Communist Malaya feared that extremists within the PAP would turn Singapore into a Communist base, and accordingly preferred to have the state under its wing.

In 1963, Singapore combined with Malaya, Sarawak and British North Borneo (modern-day Sabah) to form the **Federation of Malaysia**. The alliance, though, was an uneasy one, and within two years Singapore was asked to leave the federation, in the face of outrage in Kuala Lumpur at the PAP's attempts to break into Peninsular politics in 1964. Hours after announcing Singapore's **full independence**, on August 9, 1965, a tearful Lee Kuan Yew went on national TV and described the event as "a moment of anguish". One hundred and forty-six years after Sir Stamford Raffles had set Singapore on the world map, the tiny island, with no natural resources of its own, faced the prospect of being consigned to history's bottom drawer of crumbling colonial ports.

Instead, Lee's personal vision and drive transformed Singapore into an Asian economic heavyweight, a position achieved at a price. Heavy-handed **censorship** of the media was introduced, and even more disturbing was the government's attitude towards **political opposition**. When the opposition Worker's Party won a by-election in 1981, the candidate, J.B. Jeyaretham, found himself charged with several criminal offences, and chased through the Singaporean law courts for the next decade. The archaic **Internal Security Act** still grants the power to detain without trial anyone the government deems a threat to the nation, which has kept political prisoner Chia Thye Poh under lock and key since 1966 for allegedly advocating violence. Population policies, too, have brought criticism from abroad. These began in the early 1970s, with a **birth control campaign** which proved so successful that it had to be reversed: the 1980s saw the introduction of the "Go For Three" project, which offered tax incentives for those having more than two children in an attempt to boost the national – and some say, more specifically the Chinese Singaporean – birth rate. Lee Kuan Yew also made clear his conviction that Singapore's educated elite should intermarry.

At other times, Singapore tries so hard to reshape itself that it falls into self-parody. "We have to pursue this subject of fun very seriously if we want to stay competitive in the twenty-first century" was the reaction of former Minister of State George Yeo, when confronted with the fact that some foreigners find Singapore dull. The government's annual courtesy campaign, which in 1996 urged the population to hold lift doors open for neighbours and prevent their washing from dripping onto passers-by below, appears equally risible to outsiders. Whether Singaporeans will continue to suffer their government's foibles remains to be seen. Adults beyond a certain age remember how things were before independence and, more importantly, before the existence of the Mass Rapid Transit (MRT) system, housing projects and saving schemes. But their children and grandchildren have no such perspective, and telltale signs – presently nothing more extreme than feet up on MRT seats and jaywalking – suggest that the government can expect more **dissent** in future years. Already a substantial brain drain is afflicting the country, as skilled Singaporeans choose to move abroad in the pursuit of heightened civil liberties. The man charged with leading Singapore towards the millennium is **Goh Chok Tong**, who became prime minister upon Lee's retirement in 1990. Goh has made it clear that he favours a more open form of government, though

LEAVING SINGAPORE

For Changi airport flight enquiries, and the addresses and telephone numbers of airlines, travel agencies and the Malay, Indonesian and Thai consulates in Singapore, see "Listings", p.592.

Trains
You can make free seat reservations up to one month in advance of departure at the information kiosk (daily 8.30am–2.30pm & 3.00–7pm; ☎2225165) in the train station. The 10.30pm *Express Senandung Malam* gets into KL early the next morning; the 7.30am *Express Rakyat* arrives in the early afternoon – this continues to Butterworth, arriving at 11pm. The new Peninsula Line service (☎2242588) is similar to the E&O (see box on p.509), but rather more affordable: a return trip from Singapore to Melaka on the charming old steam train, the *Temerloh*, costs $590.

Buses and taxis
To Malaysia: the easiest way across the causeway is to get the #170 JB-bound bus from the Ban San Terminal (every 15min, 6am–12.30am; $1.10) or the plusher air-con Singapore–JB Express (every 10min, 6.30am–11.30pm; $2.10), both of which take around an hour (including border formalities); both stop at JB bus terminal. From the taxi stand next to the terminal, a car to JB (seating four) costs $30. The Singapore–KL Express leaves from the Ban San Terminal daily at 9am, 1pm and 10pm (6hr; $17.30–22); the afternoon departure doesn't leave much time to find a room on arrival. Buy your KL ticket from the booth in the terminal, a couple of days in advance at holiday times. For other destinations, go to the Lavender Street Terminal, where buses to Butterworth ($29), Penang ($30), Kota Bharu ($30) and Ipoh ($27) tend to leave in the late afternoon; those to Melaka ($11), Mersing ($11) and Kuantan ($17) depart in the early morning and afternoon. For KL ($17) there are both morning and night departures from this terminal. Book as far in advance as possible – operators at the terminal include Pan Malaysia Express (☎2947034), Hasry Ekoba Express (☎2926243), Malacca–Singapore Express (☎2935915) and Masmara Travel (☎2947034). It's slightly cheaper to travel to JB and then catch an onward bus from the bus terminal there – though it still pays to make an early start from Singapore.

To Thailand: buses leave early morning from Beach Road Golden Mile Complex. You can buy a ticket all the way to Bangkok (though it may be cheaper just to buy one as far as Hat Yai and pay for the rest of the journey in Thai currency once there). Fares to Hat Yai (16hr) start at around $30, while Bangkok will set you back around $70. Try whether he will be able to break the mould set by Lee – who still looms over the political scene in his role as senior minister, and whose son, Brigadier-General Lee Hsien Loong, is deputy prime minister – remains open to question.

Recent events suggest that Goh has the mandate to do so. Though in 1991's elections he suffered the relative setback of seeing an unprecedented four opposition members voted into parliament. In the campaign of December 1996 however (which the PAP had won even before the polling stations opened as opposition candidates contested fewer than half of the seats), he clawed back two of these seats – partly thanks to insinuations that constituencies failing to return their PAP candidate would drop down the waiting list for housing estate renovations.

Orientation

The diamond-shaped island of Singapore is 42km from east to west at its widest points, and 23km from north to south. The downtown city areas huddle at the southern tip of the diamond, radiating out from the mouth of the **Singapore River**. Two northeast–southwest roads form a dual spine to the central area, both of them traversing the river. One starts out as **North Bridge Road**, crosses the river and becomes

---

Phya Travel Service (☎2945415) or Sunny Holidays (☎2927927), and don't forget to allow two working days for securing a Thai visa (needed for stays of over 15 days).

Boats

To Malaysia: From Changi Point (bus #2 to Changi Village), bumboats run to Kampung Pengerang, on the southeastern tip of Johor (for access to the beach resort of Desaru; p.317) boats leave when they're full (daily 7am–4pm; $5 one-way) and the trip takes 45 minutes. A newer, more reliable service departs for Tanjung Belungkor, also in Johor, daily at 8.15am, 11.15am, 2.15pm and 5.15pm from the new Changi Ferry Terminal (bus #2 to Changi Village, and then a taxi). Run by Ferrylink (☎5453600), the service takes 45 minutes and costs $24 return; check in one hour before departure. Finally, from the Tanah Merah Ferry Terminal (bus #35 from Bedok MRT), there's a 7.30am service (March–Oct daily except Wed; $140 return) to Tioman Island (p.319). Information and tickets from Auto Batam (☎2714866). Again, check-in is one hour before departure.

To Indonesia: Boats to Batam in the Riau archipelago depart throughout the day from the World Trade Centre (7.45am–6.20pm; $16 one-way), docking at Sekupang, from where you take a taxi to Hangnadim airport for internal Indonesian flights. There are also four boats a day ($49 one-way; info and tickets from Dino Shipping/Channel Holidays ☎2702228), or Auto Batam/Kalpin Tours (☎2714866) from the WTC to Tanjung Pinang on Pulau Bintan, from where cargo boats leave three times a week for Pekanbaru in Sumatra. There are also boat services from Kijang Port, south of Tanjung Pinang, to Jakarta.

Planes

There are good deals on plane tickets from Singapore to Australia, Bali, Bangkok and Hong Kong. However, if you're planning to head for either Malaysia or Indonesia by air, it might be worth going to JB (p.311), across the causeway, or Batam, the nearest Indonesian island (see "Boats" below), and buying a flight from there.

Bus #16 (daily 6am–midnight; $1.10) runs frequently, down Orchard Road and Brah Basah Road, and is joined by the #16e between 6am and 9am. You can also use the Airbus (7am–midnight; £5) which calls at all central hotels. Flagging down a taxi on the street will cost around $12–15. For **Seletar Airport**, from where Silkair and Pelangi Air fly to Tioman island in Malaysia ($125 one-way), take bus #103 from Eu Tong Sen Street, Hill Street or Serangoon Road, or take a taxi ($10). Note that there's a **departure tax** of $15 levied on all flights from Singapore.

South Bridge Road; the other begins as **Victoria Street**, becomes Hill Street and skirts Chinatown as **New Bridge Road**.

At the very heart of the city, on the north bank, the **Colonial District** is home to a cluster of buildings that recall the days of early British rule – Parliament House, the cathedral, the Supreme Court, the Cricket Club and, most famously, *Raffles Hotel*. Moving west, the fringes of **Fort Canning Park** has several attractions, including Singapore's National Museum. From here, it's a five-minute stroll to the eastern end of **Orchard Road**, the main shopping area in the city. North from Fort Canning Park you soon enter **Little India**, whose main drag – Serangoon Road – is around fifteen minutes' walk from *Raffles Hotel*. Ten minutes southeast from Little India, Singapore's traditional **Arab Quarter** squats at the intersection of North Bridge Road and Arab Street.

South, across the river, the monolithic towers of the **Financial District** cast long shadows over **Chinatown**, whose row of shophouses stretches for around one kilometre, as far as Cantonment Road. Singapore's **World Trade Centre** is a fifteen-minute walk southwest of the outskirts of Chinatown, and from there cable cars run across to **Sentosa**.

The various sights and attractions around **the rest of the island** fall neatly into distinct geographical areas: north, east and west. The island is developing a system of expressways, of which the main ones are the east–west **Pan Island Expressway** and the **East Coast Parkway/Ayer Rajah Expressway**, both of which run from Changi to Jurong, and the **Bukit Timah Expressway**, which branches off north from the Pan Island Expressway at Bukit Timah new town, running north to Woodlands. At Woodlands, the road (shadowed by the train from the railway station near Chinatown) crosses the **causeway** linking Singapore with Malaysia.

Arrival and information

Most people's first glimpse of Singapore is of Changi Airport, and a telling glimpse it is. Its two terminals, connected by the Skytrain monorail, are modern, efficient and air-conditioned – a Singapore in microcosm. Other arrivals are from over the causeway from the Malaysian city of Johor Bahru (p.311), or by boat from the Indonesian archipelago. Wherever you arrive, the well-oiled infrastructure means that you'll have no problem getting into the centre. For **departure information**, see the box on pp.506–7.

By air
Changi Airport is at the far eastern end of Singapore, 16km from the city centre. As well as duty-free shops, moneychanging and left-luggage facilities, the airport boasts a 24-hr post office and telephone service, hotel reservations counters, day rooms, saunas, and business and internet centres. There's also a *McDonald's*, a *Swenson's* ice cream parlour and, in Terminal One's basement, a food centre – the cheapest and most authentically Singaporean option. That said, the likelihood is that you'll barely get the chance to take in the place at all – baggage comes through so quickly at Changi that you can be on a bus or in a taxi within fifteen minutes of arrival. Be sure to pick up one of the free maps and weekly "What's On" guides that the Singapore Tourist Promotion Board (STPB) leaves at the airport.

Since Singapore's underground train system doesn't yet extend as far as the airport, you'll have to take either a taxi or a public bus into the centre. The **bus** departure points in the basements of both terminals are well signposted – but make sure you've got the right money before you leave the concourse, as Singapore bus drivers don't give change; take the #16 (every 10min, 6am–midnight; $1.10–1.40). The bus heads west to Stamford Road (ask the driver to give you a shout at the Suntec City stop for Beach Road, and at the YMCA stop if you plan to cross over Bras Basah Park to Bencoolen

THE EASTERN AND ORIENTAL EXPRESS

If you've got money to burn, there's no more luxurious way to cover the 1900km from **Singapore to Bangkok** than on the sumptuous **Eastern & Oriental Express**, a fairytale trip that unashamedly re-creates for passengers the pampered days of the region's colonial past.

Departing once or twice weekly from Singapore, the Express takes approximately 41 hours to wend its unhurried way to Bangkok's Hualamphong Station, stopping at Kuala Lumpur, Ipoh and Butterworth en route. At Butterworth, passengers disembark for a whistle-stop **tour of Penang** by bus and trishaw. On board, guests enjoy breakfast in bed, lunch, tea and dinner, all served by attentive Thai and Malaysian staff in traditional or period garb. There are two bars – one is in the observation carriage at the rear of the train – as well as two luxurious restaurant cars serving Western and Oriental cuisine of a high standard; fortune tellers, Chinese opera singers and musicians keep you entertained. A word of warning: many guests dress up lavishly for the occasion so be sure to have suitably **smart clothes** with you or you'll feel decidedly uncomfortable.

Prices start at £260 per person for the hop up to KL; £470 will get you as far as Penang, while the full two-night Singapore–Bangkok experience weighs in at a hefty £740 per person. **Bookings** can be made in Singapore at E&O Services, 05-01 Carlton Building, 90 Cecil St (☎3234390), or in Bangkok through Sea Tours Co. Ltd, Room 413-4, fourth floor, Siam Centre, 965 Rama I Rd (☎02/2514862). Alternatively, contact the specialist tour operators listed in Basics before leaving home.

Street) before skirting the southern side of Orchard Road. If you arrive in the early evening, you could also take advantage of the faster #16e (every 12min, 5–8pm: $1.40), though in this case you'll need to alight at Stamford Road's *Capitol Cinema* to be within striking distance of Beach Road. A private company, Airbus, also plies the road into town (every 20min, 7am–midnight; $5), its air-con buses zooming straight into the centre before circuiting one of three hotel enclaves: Western Orchard Road, Eastern Orchard and Victoria Street, and the Beach Road–Raffles Boulevard area. You'll find Airbus counters in terminals one and two, or call ☎5421721 for further details. **Taxis** from the airport levy a $3 surcharge on top of the fare. Again, pick-up points are well signposted: a trip into downtown Singapore costs around $15 and takes twenty minutes or so. There are also **car rental agencies** at the airport (see "Listings", p.592), though you'd be advised not to travel around Singapore by car (see "City transport", p.511, for better alternatives).

By road and rail

Singapore is linked to Johor Bahru by a 1056-metre-long **causeway** which runs across the Strait of Johor to Woodlands town, in the far north of the island. All buses and trains **from Malaysia** currently pass over the causeway, though there is talk of a second connection being constructed further east.

Buses stop at one of two terminals in Singapore. Local buses **from Johor Bahru** (JB) arrive at **Ban San Terminal** at the junction of Queen and Arab streets, from where a two-minute walk along Queen Street, followed by a left along Rochor Road takes you to Bugis MRT station. Buses from elsewhere **in Malaysia** and **from Thailand** terminate at **Lavender Street Terminal**, at the corner of Lavender Street and Kallang Bahru, around five minutes' walk from Lavender MRT. Alternatively, walk a short way in the other direction to the end of Jalan Besar and hop on bus #139, which travels along Bencoolen Street. In addition, bus #145 passes the Lavender Street Terminal on its way down North Bridge and South Bridge roads.

Trains from Malaysia end their journey at the **Singapore Railway Station** on Keppel Road, southwest of Chinatown. Oddly, you haven't officially arrived in Singapore until you step out of the station – which is owned by Malaysia – and into the street, as a sign above the main station entrance saying "Welcome to Malaysia" testifies. The grounds of Singapore's railway system were sold lock, stock and barrel to the Federal Malay States in 1918, though recently the Singapore government has been buying back segments of it piecemeal. From Keppel Road, bus #97 travels past Tanjong Pagar MRT and on to Selegie and Serangoon roads.

By sea

Boats from the Indonesian archipelago of **Riau** (through which travellers from Sumatra will approach Singapore) dock at the World Trade Centre, off Telok Blangah Road, roughly 5km east of the centre. From Telok Blangah Road, bus #97 runs to Tanjong Pagar MRT, the #65 goes to Selegie and Serangoon roads via Orchard Road, or for Chinatown take bus #166. It's also possible to reach Singapore by boat **from Malaysia**. Bumboats from Kampung Pengerang on the southeastern coast of Johor moor at Changi Village, beyond the airport, from where bus #2 travels into the centre, via Geylang, Victoria and New Bridge roads. Swisher ferries from Tanjung Belungkor, also in Johor, dock at the Changi ferry terminal, a little way east of Changi Village, from where you'll have to take a taxi and then connect with the #2. Finally, ferries from Tioman Island dock at the new Tanah Merah Ferry Terminal, from where bus #35 will run you up to Bedok MRT station.

Information

The Singapore Tourist Promotion Board (STPB) maintains two **Tourist Information Centres**, both of which operate very useful toll-free information lines. One is at 02-34 Raffles Hotel Shopping Arcade, 328 North Bridge Rd (daily 8.30am–8pm; ☎1-800/3341335 or 1-800/3341336); the other below Orchard Road's western end at Tourism Court, 1 Orchard Spring Lane (daily 8.30am–6pm; ☎1-800/7383778 or 1-800/7383779). It's worth dropping in to pick up the free hand-outs, the biggest of which – the *Singapore Official Guide* – is very informative and features some handy maps. Other **maps** worth having include the slender *Map of Singapore* endorsed by the Singapore Hotel Association, and the *Singapore Street Directory* – a snip at $6 and invaluable if you're going to rent a car.

A number of publications offer **what's on** listings and recommendations. The *Singapore Visitor* and *This Week Singapore* are available free at hotels all over the island, but are really nothing more than advertising vehicles for Singapore's swankier shops. The "Life!" section of the *Singapore Straits Times* has a decent listings section, but best of all is *8 Days* magazine, published weekly ($1.50), and the newer *IS*, a free paper published fortnightly. Finally, scanning **notice boards** in guesthouses can also be helpful.

FINDING AN ADDRESS

With so many of Singapore's shops, restaurants and offices located in vast highrise buildings and shopping centres, deciphering **addresses** can sometimes be tricky. The numbering system generally adhered to is as follows:

#02-15 means room number 15 on the second floor; #10-08 is room number 8 on the tenth floor. Bear in mind that in Singapore, ground level is referred to as #01, or the first floor.

City transport

All parts of the island are accessible by bus or MRT – the underground rail network – and fares are reasonable; consequently, there's little to be gained by renting a car. However you travel, it's best to avoid rush hour (8–9.30am & 5–7pm) if at all possible; outside these times, things are relatively uncongested. A Transitlink Guide ($1.40), available from bus interchanges, MRT stations and major bookshops, outlines every bus and MRT route on the island in exhaustive detail – there's even a five-step explanation of how to board a train. Singapore also has thousands of **taxis** which are surprisingly affordable. Getting around **on foot** is the best way to do justice to the central areas. Bear in mind, though, that you are in the tropics: apply sun screen and stay out of the midday sun. Strolling through the remaining pockets of old Singapore entails negotiating uneven five-foot ways (the covered pavements that front Singapore's old shophouses) and yawning storm drains.

The MRT (Mass Rapid Transit) System

Singapore's **MRT** system was officially opened on March 12, 1988, and now boasts over 75 kilometres of track passing through 48 stations. In terms of cleanliness, efficiency and value for money, the system is second to none – compared to London's tubes or New York's subways, a trip on the MRT is a joy. Nor is there any possibility of delays owing to a passenger falling on the line – the automatic doors dividing the platform from the track open only when a train arrives and is stationary. The system has two main lines: the recently extended north–south line, which runs a vaguely horseshoe-shaped route from Marina Bay up to the north of the island and then southwest to Jurong, and the east–west line, connecting Boon Lay to Pasir Ris; see the MRT map below for more details. Trains run every four to five minutes on average, daily from 6am until midnight. For **information**, enquire at the Station Control Room on any ticket concourse, or call the **MRT Information Centre** (toll-free; ☎1-800/3368900). A **no-smoking** rule applies on all trains, and eating and drinking is also outlawed. Another policy appears from signs in the ticket concourse to ban hedgehogs from the MRT. In fact, it means "no durians" – not an unreasonable request if you've ever spent any time in a confined space with one of these pungent fruits. **Tickets** cost between 60c and $1.50 for a one-way journey. If you don't have any coins for the ticket machines (inside the main hall at each station), change machines will break $1 and $2 notes; larger notes can be changed at the information counter.

Most Singaporeans avoid the rigmarole of buying a ticket every day by purchasing a **Transitlink Farecard** – a stored-value card that's valid on all MRT and bus journeys in Singapore, and is sold at MRT stations and bus interchanges for $12 (including a $2 deposit). The cost of each journey you make is automatically deducted from the card when you pass it through the turnstile; any credit on the card when you leave Singapore will be reimbursed if you take it to a Farecard outlet. An **MRT Tourist Souvenir Ticket** is also available for $6 from leading hotels and central MRT stations. Note, though, that it only has a stored value of $5.50.

Buses

Singapore's **bus** network is slightly cheaper to use than the MRT system, and far more comprehensive – you'll probably spend more time on buses than on trains and there are several routes which are particularly useful for sightseeing (see box below). Two bus companies operate on the roads of Singapore: the **Singapore Bus Service** (SBS) and **Trans-Island Bus Services** (TIBS). Most of their buses charge distance-related fares, ranging from 50c–$1.10 (60c–$1.40 for air-con buses). Others charge a flat fare as displayed on the destination plates on the front of the bus. Unless you are on a route

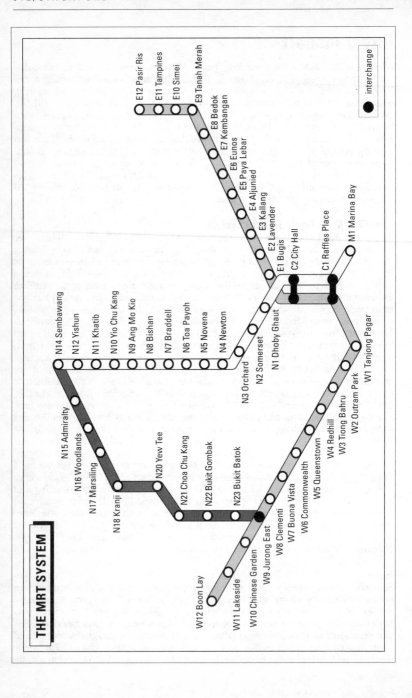

THE MRT SYSTEM

● interchange

USEFUL BUS ROUTES

Below is a selection of bus routes which connect Singapore's major points of interest; note that many of the services from the Orchard Road area actually leave from Penang Road or Somerset Road.

#2 passes along Eu Tong Sen Street (in Chinatown) and Victoria Street (past the Arab Quarter) en route to Changi Prison and Changi Village.

#7 runs along Orchard Road, Bras Basah Road and Victoria Street; its return journey takes in North Bridge Road, Stamford Road, Penang Road and Somerset Road en route to Holland Village.

#14 takes in Orchard Road and Bras Basah Road, then heads east through Geylang and beyond – alight when you cross Tanjong Katong Road for *Big Splash*; stay on until Bedok South Avenue 1 for the Europa Sailing Centre.

#16 passes down from Orchard Road and Bras Basah Road, before heading east for Changi Airport; returns via Stamford Road and skirts below Orchard Road.

#16e runs from Orchard Road and Bras Basah Road to the airport (6–9am), and from the airport to Stamford, Penang and Somerset roads (5–8pm).

#51 travels along North Bridge Road and South Bridge Road en route to Haw Par Villa.

#65 terminates at the World Trade Centre, after passing down Jalan Besar, Bencoolen Street, Penang Road and Somerset Road.

#97 runs along Stamford Road to Little India, then on to Upper Serangoon Road; returns via Bencoolen Street and Collyer Quay.

#103 runs between New Bridge Road Terminal (Chinatown) and Serangoon Road (Little India).

#105 runs along Stevens Road and Scotts Road on its way to Holland Road (for Holland Village).

#124 connects Scotts Road, Orchard Road and North Bridge Road with South Bridge Road, Upper Cross Street and New Bridge Road in Chinatown; in the opposite direction, travels along Eu Tong Sen Street, Hill Street, Stamford Road and Somerset Road.

#139 heads past Tai Gin Road, via Dhoby Ghaut, Selegie Road, Serangoon Road and Balestier Road.

#167 passes down Scotts Road, Orchard Road and Bras Basah Road, Collyer Quay, Shenton Way and Neil Road (for Chinatown).

#170 starts at the Ban San Terminal at the northern end of Queen Street, passing Bukit Timah Nature Reserve and Kranji War Cemetery on its way to JB in Malaysia.

#190 is the most direct service between Orchard Road and Chinatown, via Scotts Road, Orchard Road, Bras Basah Road, Victoria Street, Hill Street and New Bridge Road; returns via Eu Tong Sen Street, Hill Street, Stamford Road, Penang Road, Somerset Road and Scotts Road.

rarely frequented by tourists, the driver is likely to know of anywhere you could possibly be heading for, and signs at bus stops will alert you. For bus route **information**, call ☎1-800/2872727 (SBS) or ☎4823888 (TIBS).

Tell the driver where you want to go, and he'll tell you how much money to drop into the metal chute. Change isn't given, so make sure you have coins. If you are in town for a while, buy a **Transitlink Farecard** (see "The MRT System"), which you insert into the validator as you board; press the button to select your fare. Another ticket option is the **Singapore Explorer Ticket** ($5 one-day, $12 three-day), though you'd have to do an awful lot of travelling to make these tickets pay. The same is true of using the **Singapore Trolley**, a mock-antique bus that loops between the Botanic Gardens,

Chinatown and the World Trade Centre throughout the day. One day's unlimited travel is $9, while a "point to point" fare is $3 – not much cheaper than a taxi.

Taxis

There are more than ten thousand **taxis** on the streets of Singapore, so you'll hardly ever have trouble hailing a cab, day or night. Taxis are all metered, the fare starting at $2.40 for the first 1500m: after that it rises 10c for every 240 metres. However, there are **surcharges** to bear in mind, most notably the 50 percent charged on journeys between midnight and 6am. Journeys from Changi or Seletar airports incur a $3 surcharge, there's a $2.20 surcharge for taxis booked over the phone and a 50c peak period surcharge (Mon–Fri 7.30–9.30am & 4.30–7pm, Sat 7.30–9.30am & 11.30am–2pm).

More confusingly still, there's a **Central Business District** (CBD) surcharge, introduced to alleviate jams on the island's most central roads. The area encompassing Chinatown, Orchard Road and the financial zone is no-go (Mon–Fri 7.30am–6.30pm, Sat 7.30am–2pm), unless drivers have a CBD license. The license costs $3 daily and, unless another passenger has already taken your taxi into the CBD zone on the day you are travelling, you are liable for the charge.

On the whole, Singaporean taxi drivers are a friendly enough bunch, but their English isn't always good, so it's a good idea to have your destination written down on a piece of paper if you are heading off the beaten track. If a taxi displays a red destination sign on its dashboard, it means the driver is changing shift and will accept customers only if they are going in his direction. Finally, tourists confined to **wheelchairs** should note that TIBS Taxis (☎4811211) have ten wheelchair-accessible cabs.

Renting cars and bikes

The Singapore government has introduced huge disincentives to driving in order to combat traffic congestion. If you want to drive into the CBD (see above) you'll have to buy a licence, available at post offices and licence booths at entrances to the district. Parking, too, is expensive and requires that you purchase coupons from a licence booth, post office or shop. In fact, the only real reason for **renting a car** in Singapore is to travel up into Malaysia – and even then it's far cheaper to rent from a company based over the causeway (in JB), as Singaporean firms levy a $25 Malaysia surcharge. If you're still keen on driving in Singapore itself, you'll find rental companies listed on p.592. For details of prices, documentation and road rules, see Basics, p.40.

Bike rental is possible along the East Coast Parkway, where the cycle track that skirts the seashore is always crowded with Singaporeans zooming around in full cycling gear. Expect to pay around $4–8 an hour for a mountain bike, and bring some form of ID to leave at the office. The dirt tracks that crisscross Pulau Ubin, off Changi Point at the eastern tip of the island, are ideal for biking – a day's rental at one of the cluster of shops near the jetty again costs $4–8, though the price doubles in school holidays. Finally, there's a range of bikes – including tandems – available for rent next to the ferry terminal on Sentosa Island ($2–5 an hour), providing by far the best way to see the island.

Organized tours

If you're pushed for time, there are several reputable operators in Singapore offering **sightseeing tours**. The main ones are listed on p.593, or ask at your hotel or the tourist office. Tours vary according to the operator, but four-hour city tours typically take in Orchard Road, Chinatown and Little India, and cost around $25. For a Round the Island Tour (8hr) – visiting places of interest on all of Singapore's coasts, and including a trip to a modern housing project – expect to pay $70. There are also **specialist tours** on Raffles, horse racing, Singapore by night and World War II sights, costing $30–80 per

SINGAPORE RIVER, ISLAND AND HARBOUR CRUISES

Fleets of **cruise boats** ply Singapore's southern waters every day and night. The best of these, the Singapore River cruises, cast off from North Boat Quay and Clarke Quay (hourly 9am–7pm) for a $7 cruise on traditional bumboats, passing the old *godowns* upriver where traders once stored their merchandise. Several cruise companies also operate out of Clifford Pier and the World Trade Centre, offering a whole host of seaborne possibilities, from luxury catamaran trips around Singapore's southern isles to dinner on a *tongkang* (Chinese sailing boat). On average, a straightforward cruise will set you back around $20, and a dinner special $35–80. The companies below are all recommended by the STPB. It is quite possible to **charter** your own boat – a few companies are listed below – but you can bank on forking out up to $1000 a day for the privilege. If you don't relish the idea of an organized cruise, you can haggle with a bumboat man on Clifford Pier: if you're lucky, he might take a group of you around the southern isles for $25 an hour.

Cruise companies
Eastwind Organisation (☎5333432).
J&N Cruises (☎2707100).
Singapore Explorer (☎3396833).
Singapore River Boat (☎3389205).
Singapore River Cruises (☎3366119).
Watertours (☎5339811).

Charter companies
Amaril Cruises (☎4759688).
Fantasy Cruises (☎2840424).
J&N Cruises (☎2707100).
Pacific Seacraft (☎2706665).

person. For more details, contact the STPB. For **nature trips** and **bird-watching**, contact R. Subharaj at 8 Jalan Buloh Perindu (☎7874733), whose tours range from three-hour birding sessions ($20) to personalized nature trips spanning Singapore and Malaysia, for around $600 a day for a group of up to five people.

Members of the Registered Tourist Guides Association (☎7383265) charge $25–50 an hour (minimum 4hr) for a **personalized tour**. Finally, **free sightseeing tours** of Singapore, arranged by the STPB, are available to transit passengers at Changi Airport – call in at the tour desk in the transit lounge if you're interested.

Trishaws – three-wheeled bicycles with a carriage on the back – were once a practical transport option in Singapore, though they're a bit of an anachronism these days. You'll still see a few trishaws providing a genuine service around Little India and Chinatown, but most drivers now congregate along Waterloo Street between Bras Basah and Stamford roads waiting for the arrival of the next bus load of tourists, who'll happily pay $25–40 for a 45-minute sightseeing ride.

Accommodation

Room rates take a noticeable leap when you cross the causeway from Malaysia into Singapore, but good deals still abound if your expectations aren't too high or, at the budget end of the scale, if you don't mind sharing. Singapore's status as one of the main gateways to southeast Asia means that occupancy rates are permanently high. Even so, you shouldn't encounter too many difficulties in finding a room, and advance booking isn't really necessary unless your visit coincides with Chinese New Year (usually January/February) or *Hari Raya* (usually March/April).

The **Singapore Hotel Association** has booking counters at Changi Airport (daily 8am–11.30pm; ☎5426955 or 5459789) which will find you a room in the city free of charge, though they only represent Singapore's official hotels, all of which are listed in a free STPB booklet. Touts at the airport also hand out flyers advertising rooms, but things can get a bit embarrassing if you arrive and then don't like the place they represent.

The cheapest beds are in the communal **dormitories** of many of Singapore's rest-houses, where you'll pay $10 or less a night. The next best deals are at **guesthouses**, most of which are situated along Bencoolen Street and Beach Road, with an increasing number in nearby Little India and some also south of the river, in Chinatown. Singapore's classic guesthouse address is *Peony Mansions* on Bencoolen Street, where a cluster of establishments is shoehorned into several floors of a decrepit apartment building, though the Bencoolen area is becoming less fashionable with every passing year. Guesthouses aren't nearly as cosy as their name suggests: costing $20–30, the rooms are tiny, bare, and divided by paper-thin partitions, toilets are shared, and showers are cold. However, another $10–20 secures a bigger, air-con room, and often TV, laundry and cooking facilities, lockers and breakfast are included. Always check that the room is clean and secure, and that the shower and air-con work before you hand over any money. It's always worth asking for a discount, too, though you stand the best chance of a reduction if you are staying a few days. Finally, since guesthouses aren't subject to the same safety checks as official hotels, without sounding alarmist, it's a good idea to check for a fire escape.

The appeal of Singapore's **Chinese-owned hotels**, similar in price to guesthouses, is their air of faded grandeur – some haven't changed in forty years. Sadly, faded grandeur is something the government frowns upon, with the result that there are not too many left. In more **modern, mid-range hotels**, a room for two with air-con, private bathroom and TV will set you back around $60–90 a night. From there, prices rise steadily and at the top end of the scale, Singapore boasts some extraordinarily opulent hotels, ranging from the colonial splendour of *Raffles* to the awesome spectacle of the *Westin Stamford* – currently the world's tallest hotel. Though you'll find the greatest concentration of upmarket hotels around Orchard Road, most of the new breed of boutique hotels – which use antique furniture and fittings to create an air of Oriental nostalgia – are based in Chinatown.

Camping is not really a practical option in Singapore: the few sites are inconveniently located. The *Universal Adventure* shop (☎7206639) on Pulau Ubin, off the east coast (see p.561), rents out two- and four-person tents ($20/30), which can be pitched on open land on the island. The only other option is to go to Sentosa island (see p.566), where a four-person tent costs $16 (including the island entrance fee), pitched on a site with toilets and barbecue pits (details on ☎2707888).

Bencoolen Street and around

Bencoolen Street has long been the mainstay of Singapore's backpacker industry – so long, in fact, that its buildings are beginning to show their age, while others have already fallen to the demolition ball. Still, the location is handy for all parts of central Singapore, and the proliferation of guesthouses makes it a great place for meeting people. All the places listed here are keyed on the map on the opposite page.

Bayview Inn, 30 Bencoolen St (☎3372882, fax 3382880). Bencoolen Street's poshest hotel, with very comfortable rooms, a compact rooftop swimming pool and a friendly, modern café. ⑤.

Bencoolen Hotel, 47 Bencoolen St, (☎3360822). Great-value, fairly upmarket option, with business centre, laundry service, air-ticketing facilities and smart rooms equipped with all mod cons. ④.

Bencoolen House Traveller's Centre, seventh floor, 27f Bencoolen St (☎3381206). Bearable at the price, though dorms are grottier than most. Guests have use of the kitchen. Dorms $7. ①.

Goh's Homestay, fourth floor, 169d Bencoolen St (☎3396561, fax 3398606). The smartest guest-house in town (at the top of its price category), with fresh and inviting (if slightly cell-like) rooms, pricier dorm beds than usual, laundry service, a bright, comfortable lounge/canteen area serving great breakfasts, and a pet python. Recommended. Dorms $14. ③.

Hawaii Hostel, second floor, 171b Bencoolen St (☎3384187). Small, tidy, air-con rooms with breakfast included. Dorms $10. ②.

Latin House Home Stay, 03-46 Peony Mansions, 46–52 Bencoolen St (☎3396308). The budget-priced dorms are adequate, but the rooms are a little run-down. Dorms $7. ①.

ACCOMMODATION

Ah Chew Hotel	11	Hawaii Hostel	5	Raffles Hotel	26
Allson Hotel	22	Landmark Mercure Hotel	1	San Wah Hotel	20
Backpackers' Cozy Nest	23	Latin House Homestay	19	Shang Onn Hotel	25
Backpackers' Cozy Corner	10	Lee Boarding House	19	South East Asia Hotel	4
Bayview Inn	21	Lee Traveller's Club	15	Strand Hotel	18
Beach Hotel	13	Metropole Hotel	24	Summer View Hotel	3
Bencoolen Hotel	16	New Backpackers' Lodge	9	Sun Sun Hotel	7
Bencoolen House Travellers Centre	17	New 7th Storey Hotel	2	Waffles Home Stay	12
Goh's Homestay	6	Peony Mansion Green Curtains	19	Willy's Guest House	15
Intercontinental Hotel	14	Peony Mansion Travellers' Lodge	8		

Lee Boarding House, 07-52 Peony Mansions, 46–52 Bencoolen St (☎3383149). The brightest place in Peony Mansion: clean, simple dorms (a dollar more for air-con) and rooms, a pleasant breakfast area and laundry facilities. There's another *Lee*'s on Beach Road (see below). Dorms $8. ①.

Peony Mansion Green Curtains, No 04-46 Peony Mansions, 46–52 Bencoolen St (☎3385638). A travel consultant's desk and notice board make this a handy place to stay. The dorms are cramped, while rooms range from basic to more comfortable doubles with TV, fridge, air-con and toilet. ①.

Peony Mansions Travellers' Lodge, second floor, 131a Bencoolen St (☎3348697). Actually a couple of hundred metres down the road from its parent guesthouse, *Green Curtains* (see above), this branch has lots of clean featureless rooms (the cheapest share common showers) but no dorm beds; the Airpower travel agency operates right beside the lodge's friendly reception area. ①.

San Wah Hotel, 36 Bencoolen St (☎3362428). Shabby but rather charming Chinese hotel which benefits from being set back slightly from the road. $5 surcharge for air-con. ③.

South East Asia Hotel, 190 Waterloo St (☎3382394). Spotless doubles with air-con, TV and phone for those yearning for a few creature comforts. Downstairs is a vegetarian restaurant serving Western breakfasts, and right next door is Singapore's liveliest Buddhist temple. ③.

Strand Hotel, 25 Bencoolen St (☎3381866, fax 3363149). Excellent-value hotel with clean, welcoming rooms and a variety of services. ④.

Summer View Hotel, 173 Bencoolen St (☎3381122, fax 3366346). The future face of Bencoolen street: a smart but unpretentious 100-room hotel with all the facilities the budget-minded business traveller or tourist might need (café, car rental facilities, valet services, currency exchange and tour desk), but none of the needless frills that push up prices. ⑤.

DORM BEDS

The places listed below offer the **cheapest beds** in Singapore. For full details, see the relevant reviews.

Bencoolen House,	p.516.	*Lee Traveller's Club,*	p.518.
Canton Guest House,	p.521.	*Peony Mansions Travellers' Lodge,*	p.517.
Cavenagh Gardens,	p.519.	*Sandy's Place,*	p.520.
Chinatown Guest House,	p.521.	*Waffles Homestay,*	p.519.
Goh's Homestay,	p.516.	*Willy's Guest House,*	p.519.
Latin House,	p.516.	*YMCA International House,*	p.520.

Sun Sun Hotel, 260–262 Middle Rd (☎3384911). Housed in a splendid 1928 building, the *Sun Sun* isn't overpriced – decent rooms and plenty of communal bathrooms. Air-con rooms are also available, while downstairs is the wonderful *L.E. Café & Confectionery.* ③.

Beach Road to Victoria Street

A few blocks east of Bencoolen Street, **Beach Road** boasts a mixture of charismatic old Chinese hotels and smart new guesthouses. What's more, you can brag about having stayed down the road from *Raffles Hotel* (or even in it) when you get home. These hotels are keyed on the map on p.517.

Ah Chew Hotel, 496 North Bridge Rd (☎3375285). Simple but charismatic rooms with "Wild West" swing doors, crammed with period furniture and run by a gang of T-shirted old men lounging on antique opium couches. Despite its address, it's just around the corner from North Bridge Road, on Liang Seah Street. ②.

Allson Hotel, 101 Victoria St (☎3360811, fax 3397019). Reasonable 450-room hotel with shopping arcade, health and business centres and a clutch of restaurants. Some effort has been made to cater for the disabled: there are low counters and phones and adapted toilets, but you'll need to book well ahead for the hotel's one specifically designed bedroom. ⑦.

Backpackers' Cozy Corner, 2a Liang Seah St (☎3348761). Newish operation that springs a few surprises, its standard flophouse rooms sharing common facilities. Dorms $7. ①.

Backpackers' Cozy Nest, 28c Seah St (☎3399095). The better of Singapore's "cozy" twins, with dorms and tiny, inexpensive rooms. From the roof garden there are views over its more auspicious neighbour, *Raffles*. Recommended. Dorms $7. ①.

Beach Hotel, 95 Beach Rd (☎3367712). The Lee empire's latest addition: professionally run and really tidy, though you'd expect a few more amenities for the price. ④.

Intercontinental, 80 Middle Rd (☎3387600, fax 338 7366). Smashing new hotel within the thriving Bugis Junction development, convenient and sumptuously furnished, with business centre, swimming pool, health club and an array of excellent restaurants including *Pimai Thai* and *Olive Tree*; see "Eating". ⑦.

Landmark Mercure Hotel, 390 Victoria St (☎2972828, fax 2982038). Very pleasant, once you get past the dated shopping centre downstairs; handy for Bugis MRT Station and Arab Street. ⑦.

Lee Travellers' Club, 06-02 Fu Yuen Building, 75 Beach Rd (☎3395490). Like its Bencoolen Street counterpart, clean and friendly, with bright dormitories and spick and span communal toilets. Dorms $7. ①.

Metropole Hotel, 41 Seah St (☎3363611, fax 3393610). Friendly, great-value establishment just across the road from *Raffles*, with roomy lodgings served by the intriguing *Imperial Herbal Restaurant*. ⑤.

New Backpackers' Lodge, 18a Liang Seah St (☎3387460). Cheerily painted, shuttered shophouse with 21 dorm beds, and tiny rooms – request one with a window. Breakfast and hot drinks included. Facilities include lockers, laundry, notice board and a companionable seating area. Dorms $8. ①.

New 7th Storey Hotel, 229 Rochor Rd (☎3370251, fax 3343550). Despite its rather old-fashioned exterior, this is a clean hotel with perfectly respectable rooms, all with TV. Rooms with en-suite bathrooms are available, though the communal ones are fine. ③.

Raffles Hotel, 1 Beach Rd (☎3371886, fax 3397650). The flagship of Singapore's tourism industry, *Raffles* takes shameless advantage of its reputation: $21 buys you a Singapore Sling and a glass to take home, while the souvenir shop stocks *Raffles* golf balls, socks and cuddly tigers. Still, it's a beautiful place, dotted with frangipani trees and palms, and the suites (there are no rooms) are as tasteful as you would expect at these prices. See p.529 for more details. ⑦.

Shang Onn Hotel, 37 Beach Rd (☎3384153). Set in a quaint old building sporting attractive green shutters, the *Shang Onn* has reasonable rooms and a friendly manager/owner. ②.

Waffles Home Stay, third floor, 490 North Bridge Rd (☎3341608). French-run crashpad, pleasantly tiled and painted following recent renovations, whose prices include breakfast and a free flow of hot drinks. There are discounts if you introduce new guests; oodles of advice are pinned up on notice boards around the walls. Recommended. Dorms $8. ①.

Willy's Guest House, 04-02 Fu Yuen Building, 75 Beach Rd (☎33788826). Box-like but tidy enough rooms at competitive prices that include breakfast and hot drinks taken in a cramped day-room; there are few bathrooms, so expect queues. Dorms $8. ①.

The Colonial District

A handful of expensive hotels squat at the edges of the Padang, just north of the Singapore River. Several of them – including the *Marina Mandarin*, *Oriental* and *Pan Pacific* hotels – stand on the reclaimed land which robbed Beach Road of its beach. All the places below are marked on the "Colonial District" map on p.527.

Excelsior Hotel, 5 Coleman St (☎3387733, fax 3393847). Sister to the *Peninsula* (whose gymnasium guests can use), the *Excelsior*'s 271 rooms enjoy a swimming pool, 24-hour room service, TV, safe and secretarial service, and are as handy for the Financial District as for Orchard Road's shopping centres. The excellent *Annalakshmi* Indian vegetarian restaurant is the best of the hotel's several food outlets. ⑦.

Marina Mandarin Hotel, 6 Raffles Blvd (☎3383388, fax 3394977). Top-flight hotel, architecturally interesting and affording great harbour views; the atrium is particularly impressive. ⑧.

Oriental Singapore, 5 Raffles Ave (☎3380066, fax 3399537). Housed, like the *Marina Mandarin*, in what's claimed to be southeast Asia's largest shopping centre and hotel complex, Marina Square, the *Oriental* is one of Singapore's priciest hotels, but with very good reason: rooms are exquisitely furnished, views out over Marina Bay are breathtaking, and all the luxuries you could want are on hand. For a real treat, try their *Oriental Club*, whose two floors of luxury rooms have complimentary breakfast, evening cocktails and laundry service. Recommended. ⑨.

Pan Pacific Hotel, Marina Square, 7 Raffles Blvd (☎3368111, fax 3394852). The place to go if you prefer your pool to have an underwater sound system; facilities for the disabled. ⑧.

Peninsula Hotel, 3 Coleman St (☎3372200, fax 339 3580). Like the neighbouring *Excelsior*, a good mid-range choice. ⑦.

Westin Plaza, 2 Stamford Rd (☎3388585, fax 3365117). Top-of-the-range hotel whose amenities are shared with the *Westin Stamford*. Located right above City Hall MRT. ⑧.

Westin Stamford, 2 Stamford Rd (☎3388585, fax 3365117). Upper-floor rooms aren't for those with vertigo, though the views are as splendid as you'd expect from the tallest hotel in the world. There are 1253 classy rooms here, 16 restaurants and an MRT station downstairs; recommended. ⑧.

Orchard Road and around

Sumptuous hotels abound in and around **Orchard Road** and unless you opt for a dorm bed at the YMCA or tiny *Cavenagh Garden*, you have to be prepared to spend a bare minimum of $80 double. You can multiply that figure by four or five, though, if you decide to treat yourself. See the map on p.536 for the location of hotels in this district.

Cavenagh Garden, 03-376, Block 73 Cavenagh Rd (☎7374600). A homestay in the literal sense of the word: two dorm beds are available on a balcony off the family living room, and various rooms are dotted around the house. A steep $20 extra is demanded for a private shower. At the end of Cuppage Road, cross the Expressway bridge and walk to the left for 300m. Dorms $10. ②.

Cockpit Hotel, 6/7 Oxley Rise (☎7379111, fax 7373105). Renamed in 1960 due to the frequent patronage of airline crews, the Georgian facade of this 176-room hotel harks back to its beginnings in 1941 as the *London Hotel* on Beach Road. Its pastel-shaded rooms are serviced by several decent restaurants and bars. ⑦.

The Elizabeth, 24 Mount Elizabeth (☎7381188, fax 7324173). Within its toytown exterior, this bou-tique hotel oozes panache; delightful and well-appointed rooms. ⑧.

Goodwood Park Hotel, 22 Scotts Rd (☎7377411, fax 7328558). Don't be surprised if this opulent hotel reminds you of *Raffles* – both were designed by the same architect. The building is a study in elegance, its arching facades fronting exquisitely appointed rooms. ⑨.

Holiday Inn Park View, 11 Cavenagh Rd (☎7338333, fax 7344593). Guests of this smart hotel with all the trimmings are next-door neighbours of Singapore's president for the duration of their stay – the istana is just across the road. ⑧.

Hyatt Regency, 10–12 Scotts Rd (☎7381234, fax 7321696). Classy hotel, with access facilities for the disabled, and a good option if you like your nightlife: within the hotel are the trendy *Brannigan's* bar and *Chinoserie* discotheque. ⑨.

Imperial Hotel, 1 Rumbia (☎7371666, fax 7374761). Tucked away at a peaceful hillside location off Clemenceau Avenue, a stone's throw from Chinatown, the 600 spacious and appealing rooms of the *Imperial* are amongst the best placed in Singapore. What's more, the peerless *Rang Mahal* Indian restaurant is only an elevator ride away. Recommended. ⑧.

Lloyd's Inn, 2 Lloyd Rd (☎7377309). Motel-style building boasting attractive rooms and a fine loca-tion, just five minutes from Orchard Road. ④.

Mandarin Hotel, 333 Orchard Rd (☎7374411, fax 7322361). Every luxury you could hope for; even if you don't stay, take a trip up to the top floors for the magnificent view of central Singapore. ⑨.

Metropolitan YMCA, 60 Stevens Rd (☎7377755, fax 2355528). Not as central as the YMCA on Orchard Road, but perfectly adequate, and suitable for travellers in wheelchairs. ④.

Mitre Hotel, 145 Killiney Rd (☎7373811). Reasonable old Chinese hotel, set amid overgrown grounds, and with an endearingly shabby air about it; there's a great lobby bar downstairs. ②.

Sandy's Place, 3c Sarkies Rd (☎7341431). Rooms are a touch overpriced in this friendly, laid-back place, set across a field from Newton MRT, but the dorms are tidy, and the price includes a fruit breakfast. It's best to phone ahead. Dorms $30.

Sheraton Towers, 39 Scotts Rd (☎7376888, fax 7371072). Faultless hotel voted one of the top ten in the world by *Business Traveller* magazine; the lobby area is dazzling and there's even a waterfall out the back. ⑧.

Singapore Marriott, 320 Orchard Rd (☎7349900, fax 7335251). A superior hotel and a Singapore landmark, housed in a 33-storey pagoda-style building next to *C.K.Tangs Department Store*. ⑨.

Sloane Court Hotel, 17 Balmoral Rd (☎2353311, fax 7339041). As close to a Tudor house as you get in Singapore, the *Sloane Court* is tucked away in a prime residential area, near Newton MRT. ④.

Supreme Hotel, 15 Kramat Rd (☎7378333, fax 7337404). A budget hotel, well placed at the eastern end of Orchard Road, which levies a hefty $200 deposit at check in. ④.

VIP, Balmoral Crescent (☎2354277, fax 2352824). Within walking distance of Orchard Road, a quiet, affordable hotel with swimming pool. ④.

YMCA International House, 1 Orchard Rd (☎3366000, fax 3373140). Plush but overpriced rooms, excellent sports facilities (including rooftop pool) and free room service from the *McDonald's* down-stairs. Dorm beds are the most expensive in town, though, and there's a first-day charge of $5 for non-members. Buses #16 and #16e from the airport stop right outside. Dorms $25. ④.

Little India

Buses along Jalan Besar connect **Little India** with the rest of central Singapore. Little India's hotels and guesthouses used not to attract many Western visitors, though many more backpackers have been holing up here of late. All the places below are marked on the map on p.548.

Albert Court Hotel, 180 Albert St (☎3393939, fax 3393252). This charmingly conceived new bou-tique hotel, designed around the restaurants of lively *Albert Court Mall*, is just a short walk from both Bugis Village and Little India; rooms have all the standard embellishments. ⑦.

Ali's Nest, 23 Robert's Lane (☎2912938). Popular among the backpacker fraternity, if the graffitied plaudits on the reception walls are taken as authentic, though it's not particularly clean or spacious. Dorms $8. ①.

Boon Wah Hotel, 43a Jalan Besar (☎2991466, fax 2942176). This decent Chinese hotel offers clean, if slightly cramped, rooms with TV, air-con and shower. The entrance is around the corner, on Upper Dickson Road. ④.

Broadway Hotel, 195 Serangoon Rd (☎2924661, fax 2916414). Ugly-looking hotel in the heart of Little India, boasting pleasant enough rooms with air-con, bathroom and TV. ④.

Dickson Court, 1 Dickson Rd (☎2977811, fax 2977833). With smart, well-furnished rooms off light courtyard corridors, the *Dickson Court* represents pretty good value; most corners of central Singapore are accessible from the bus stop across the road on Jalan Besar. ⑤.

Fortuna Hotel, 2 Owen Rd (☎295 3577). New mid-range hotel offering brilliant value for money; facilities include a health centre and secretarial services. ⑤.

Kerbau Hotel, 54–62 Kerbau Rd (☎2976668). Friendly place, if somewhat vault-like, with spruce and welcoming rooms; discounts for stays of three days or more. ④.

Little India Guest House, 3 Veerasamy Rd (☎2942866, fax 2984866). A smart guesthouse with excellent, fresh-looking rooms and spotless toilets. ③.

Mount Emily Hotel, 10a Upper Wilkie Rd, Mount Emily Park (☎3389151, fax 3396008). Rooms here are pricey and just starting to show their age, but the hotel's location beside a lovely park above the city makes it a quiet, relaxing option. ⑤.

Palace Hotel, 407a Jalan Besar (☎2983108). Friendly hotel with spacious rooms, some of which have little balconies. Recommended. ②.

Perak Lodge, 12 Perak Rd (☎2969072, fax 3920919). One of the new breed of upper-bracket guest-houses, set within a smashing blue-and-white shophouse in a back street behind the Little India arcade. The rooms are secure, well-appointed and welcoming, and the price includes a continental breakfast. Downstairs there's an airy, residents-only living area. Recommended. ④.

Pin Guan, 80 Owen Rd (☎2935750). Old-style Chinese hotel housed in a charming colonial villa; simple but clean rooms with shared toilet facilities. ②.

Chinatown and around

Despite being such a big tourist draw, **Chinatown** isn't very well furnished with budget accommodation. On the other hand, the area does contain a mass of upmarket hotels which benefit from their proximity to the business district. The following places are all keyed on the map on p.540.

Canton Guest House, 42 Smith St (☎3231275). A bed in one of the series of cheery, carpeted, air-con dorms in this prewar shophouse bases you in the bustling heart of Chinatown. Dorms $10.

Chinatown Guest House, fifth floor, 325d New Bridge Rd (☎2200671). This friendly, no-frills place is a popular choice, offering varied rooms, free breakfast and luggage storage. However, the cheapest rooms are tiny, the dorms pretty cramped and there are just three bathrooms. Dorms $12. ②.

Chinatown Hotel, 12–16 Teck Lim Rd (☎2255166, fax 2253912). Decent boutique hotel with very smart rooms but few extra frills. ⑤.

Chinese YMCA, 70 Palmer Rd (☎2224666). There are fewer amenities here than in Singapore's other Ys, but the rates are lower and it's handy for the train station. ④.

Damenlou Hotel, 12 Ann Siang Rd (☎2211900, fax 2258500). Given its lovingly restored 1925 facade, the 12 compact but well-appointed rooms in this friendly hotel are surprisingly modern. After a pre-dinner drink overlooking Chinatown on the rooftop garden, head down to the excellent *Swee Kee* restaurant (p.573). ⑤.

Dragon Cityview, 18 Mosque St (☎2239228). Sizeable, comfortable double rooms in the middle of Chinatown, all with air-con, TV, fridge and bathroom, and set in attractive shophouses. ④.

The Duxton, 83 Duxton Rd (☎2277678, fax 2271232). Elegant rooms in the renovated shophouses that make up this hotel don't come cheap; it's in the Tanjong Pagar redevelopment zone. ⑧.

Inn of the Sixth Happiness, 9–37 Erskine Rd (☎2233266, fax 2237951). Delightful boutique hotel renovated from fourteen shophouses and named after a 1958 film starring Ingrid Bergman. Rosewood furniture, porcelain lamps and silk robes give an air of Chinese nostalgia, and the VIP suites boast antique opium beds. Its a shame the rooms aren't more spacious. Recommended. ⑤.

Majestic Hotel, 31–37 Bukit Pasoh Rd (☎2223377). Unspectacular but scrupulously clean, old-style hotel. All rooms have air-con, while those at the front boast little balconies; for a private bathroom add on $10, and for a TV, $5. ③.

Royal Peacock Hotel, 55 Keong Saik Rd (☎223 3522, fax 221 1770). Keong Saik Road was once a notorious red light district, and the silky, sassy elegance of the *Royal Peacock* recalls those days. Sculpted from ten shophouses, it's a superb boutique hotel, with great rooms, a bar, café and business services. ⑥.

Geylang and Katong

Geylang and Katong, along Singapore's southeastern coast, have traditionally both been Malay-dominated areas. If you can't face the noise and the bustle of central Singapore, this region might appeal – certainly its cool sea breezes and Malay markets are an advantage. MRT and buses connect you quickly with downtown Singapore.

Amber Hotel, 42 Amber Rd (☎3442323). Comfortable rooms with TV, air-con and bathroom just a short walk from the east coast. ④.

Hotel 81, 305 Joo Chiat Rd (☎3488181). Housed in a beautifully restored Peranakan building in cream and burgundy, *Hotel 81* offers rooms pleasant enough for any self-respecting business person, but at the fraction of the prices of the heavyweights downtown. Great place. ④.

Malacca Hotel, 97–99 Still Rd (☎3457411). Good value if you want a few luxuries: every (smart) room has air-con, phone, TV and bathroom. ④.

Sing Hoe Hotel, 759 Mountbatten Rd (☎4400602). Beautifully kept colonial house, with attractive reliefs on its external walls, but overpriced for its unmemorable, air-con rooms. Look out for the amazing "gingerbread house" next door. ③.

Soon Teck Hotel, 57a Koon Seng Rd (☎3440240). A peaceful Chinese hotel with just five air-con rooms. Communal facilities are clean, and downstairs is a sleepy coffee shop. Recommended. ③.

Sentosa Island

Two luxury hotels on the island of **Sentosa** allow you to bypass the bustle of downtown Singapore. If you aren't too keen to negotiate any of the more long-winded means of transport to the island (for details and an island report, see p.566), it's possible to get a taxi direct from the airport to Sentosa (though note that from 7am to 10pm a $6 surcharge is levied).

The Beaufort (☎2750331, fax 275 0228). A swanky hotel, elegantly appointed and fitted out in varnished wood and bounded by two 18-hole golf courses and a beach. A $40 price increase applies on Friday and Saturday. ⑧.

Rasa Sentosa Shangri-La's Resort (☎2750100, fax 2750355). Opened in 1993, the *Rasa Sentosa* is the first hotel in Singapore to have its own beach front, and its situation on Sentosa island makes it a good option if you've got kids to amuse. As at the *Beaufort*, a $40 price rise applies on Friday and Saturday; and rooms with a sea view also cost an extra $40. ⑦.

Downtown Singapore

Ever since Sir Stamford Raffles first landed on its northern bank, in 1819, the area around the Singapore River, which strikes into the heart of the island from the island's south coast, has formed the hub of Singapore. All of Singapore's central districts lie within a three-kilometre radius of the mouth of the river – which makes **Downtown Singapore** an extremely convenient place to tour. Although buses do run between these districts (see bus routes information on p.513), you might find that you prefer to explore the whole central region on foot. You'll need at least two days to do full justice to the main areas: the **Colonial District**, **Chinatown** and the **Financial District**, **Little India** and the **Arab Quarter**; while Singapore's commercial mecca, **Orchard Road**, can occupy a single morning, or several days, depending on how much you enjoy shopping.

The Colonial District

North of the Singapore River, take a walk down to where Coleman Street abuts Saint Andrew's Road, and look across the Padang towards the city. Laid out before you is a panorama that defines Singapore's past and present. In the foreground is the Singapore Cricket Club – the epitome of colonial man's stubborn refusal to adapt to his surroundings. Behind that, the river snakes westwards and inland, passing the last few surviving *godowns* from Singapore's original trade boom. Towering high above all this, are the spires of the modern business district. The Padang is the very nexus of the **Colonial District**, flanked by dignified reminders of British rule. To the south are Empress Place Building and Parliament House, to the north, the grand old *Raffles Hotel*, beyond which a string of nineteenth- and twentieth-century churches leads to Singapore's most famous entertainment centre, Bugis Village. Heading west, you pass City Hall and the Supreme Court before climbing the slopes of Fort Canning Hill, ten minutes' walk from the Padang, and one of the few hills in Singapore not yet lost to land reclamation. The late twentieth century seems strangely absent amid all these echoes of the past, though the district's most notable modern building doesn't do things by half – the *Westin Stamford*, on Stamford Road, is the world's tallest hotel.

Along the northern bank of the Singapore River

As the colony's trade grew in the last century, the **Singapore River** became its main artery, clogged with bumboats – traditional cargo boats with eyes painted on their prows, as if they are looking where they are going. The boat pilots ferried coffee, sugar and rice to the *godowns*, where coolies loaded and unloaded sacks. Indeed, in the 1880s the river itself was so busy it was practically possible to walk from one side of it to the other without getting your feet wet. A recent campaign to clean up the waters of the river relocated the bumboats to the west coast, though a handful still remain and offer trips downriver and around Marina Bay (see "Organized Tours" on p.514). These days, with the bumboats gone, the river is quieter, cleaner and inevitably less charismatic, though parts of both banks are undergoing a profound commercial revitalization as new restaurants and bars move into formerly abandoned buildings.

From Raffles Place MRT it's just a couple of minutes' walk past the former GPO, to the elegant suspension struts of **Cavenagh Bridge** – a good place to start a tour of Singapore's colonial centre. Named after Major General Orfeur Cavenagh, Governor of the Straits Settlements from 1859 to 1867, the bridge was constructed in 1869 by Indian convict labourers using imported Glasgow steel. Times change, but not necessarily on the bridge, where a police sign still maintains: "The use of this bridge is prohibited to any vehicle of which the laden weight exceeds 3cwt and to all cattle and horses."

Stepping off the bridge, you're confronted by **Empress Place Building**, a robust Neoclassical structure named for Queen Victoria and completed in 1865. It served for ten years as a courthouse before the Registry of Births and Deaths and the Immigration Department moved in. Latterly, it has housed cultural exhibitions; when renovations are completed, the building will reopen with a permanent **Asian Civilization** collection – ask at the STPB for further details. The pyramid-shaped time capsule in the grounds in front of the building was sealed in 1990 as part of Singapore's silver jubilee celebrations and is due to be opened in 2015. It contains "significant items" from Singapore's first 25 independent years: the clever money says that when opened it'll yield a Lee Kuan Yew speech or two.

Next door to Empress Place Building, two fine, off-white examples of colonial architecture, the **Victoria Concert Hall** and adjoining **Victoria Theatre**, are home to some of Singapore's most prestigious cultural events. The theatre was originally completed in 1862 as Singapore's town hall, while the Concert Hall was added in 1905 as a tribute to the monarch's reign. During the Japanese occupation, the clocktower here was

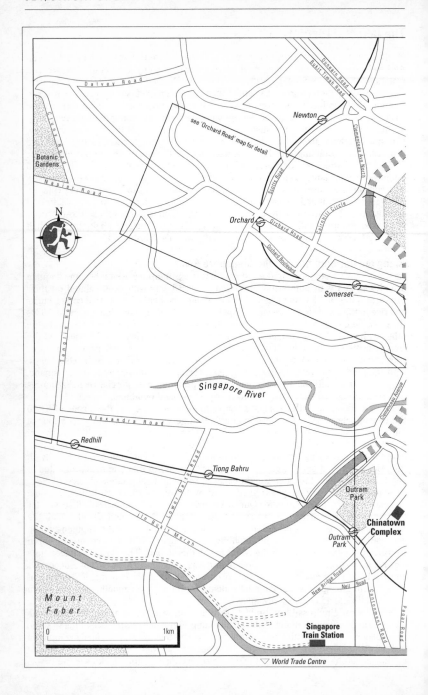

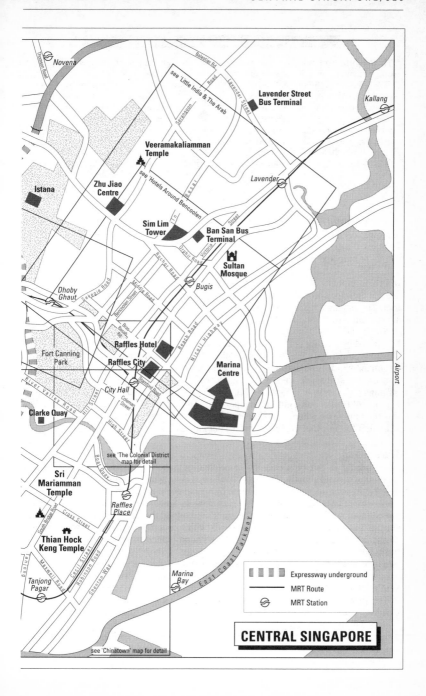

CENTRAL SINGAPORE

altered to Tokyo time, while the statue of Raffles that once stood in front of the tower narrowly escaped being melted down. As luck would have it, the newly installed Japanese curator of the National Museum – where the statue was sent – valued it sufficiently to hide it and report it destroyed.

Further inland, along North Bank Quay, a copy of the statue marks the **landing site** where, in January 1819, the great man apparently took his first steps on Singaporean soil. Sir Stamford now stares contemplatively across the river towards the business district. The Singapore River cruise boats (see p.515) depart from a tiny jetty a few steps along from Raffles' statue.

North of the statue up Parliament Lane, the dignified white Victorian building on the left ringed by fencing is **Parliament House**, built as a private dwelling for a rich merchant by Singapore's pre-eminent colonial architect, the Irishman George Drumgould Coleman, who was named the settlement's Superintendent of Public Works in 1833. It is sometimes possible to watch Singapore's parliament in session from up in the Strangers' Gallery – call ☎3368811 for details. The bronze elephant in front of Parliament House was a gift to Singapore from King Rama V of Thailand (whose father was the king upon whom *The King and I* was based) after his trip to the island in 1871 – the first foreign visit ever made by a Thai monarch.

The Padang

The **Padang** is the very essence of colonial Singapore. Earmarked by Raffles as a recreation ground shortly after his arrival, such is its symbolic significance that its borders have never been encroached upon by speculators and it remains much as it was in 1907, when G.M. Reith wrote in his *Handbook to Singapore*, "Cricket, tennis, hockey, football and bowls are played on the plain . . . beyond the carriage drive on the other side, is a strip of green along the sea-wall, with a foot-path, which affords a cool and pleasant walk in the early morning and afternoon." Once the last over of the day had been bowled, the Padang would have assumed a more social role: the image of Singapore's European community hastening to the corner once known as Scandal Point to catch up on the latest gossip is pure Somerset Maugham. Today the Padang is still kept pristine by a bevy of gardeners mounted on state-of-the-art lawnmowers.

The brown-tiled roof, whitewashed walls and dark green blinds of the **Singapore Cricket Club**, at the southwestern end of the Padang, have a nostalgic charm. Founded in the 1850s, the club was the hub of colonial British society and still operates a "members only" rule, though there's nothing to stop you watching the action from outside on the Padang. The Singapore Rugby Sevens are played here, as well as a plethora of other big sporting events and parades; a timetable of forthcoming events is

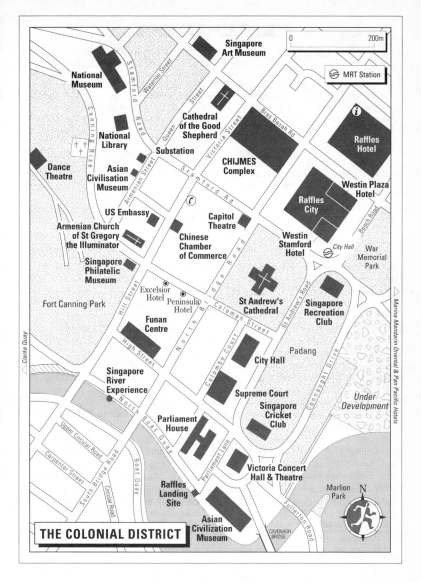

THE COLONIAL DISTRICT

available at the club's reception. Eurasians who were formerly ineligible for membership of the Cricket Club founded their own establishment instead in 1883: the **Singapore Recreation Club**, which lies across on the north side of the Padang, and is presently undergoing profound renovations.

Just to the west of the Cricket Club, Singapore's Neoclassical **Supreme Court** (formerly the site of the exclusive *Hotel de L'Europe*, whose drawing rooms allegedly pro-

THE SEPOY MUTINY

Plaques on the west wall of St Andrew's Cathedral commemorate the victims of one of Singapore's bloodiest episodes, the **Sepoy Mutiny** of 1915. The mutiny began when a German warship, the *Emden*, was sunk by an Australian ship off the Cocos Islands: its survivors were brought to Singapore and imprisoned at Tanglin Barracks, at the western end of Orchard Road. With almost all of Singapore's troop contingent away in Europe fighting the Kaiser, soldiers of the Fifth Light Infantry, called sepoys – whose members were all Muslim Punjabis – were sent to guard the prisoners. Unfortunately, these men's allegiance to the British had recently been strained by the news that Muslim Turkey had come out against the Allies in Europe. A rumour that they were soon to be sent to Turkey to fight fellow Muslims upset them still further, and the German prisoners were able to incite the sepoys to mutiny. In the ensuing rampage through the city on February 15, 1915, the sepoys killed forty soldiers and civilians before they were finally rounded up by some remaining European sailors and a band of men led by the Sultan of Johor. All were court-martialled and 36 sepoys were executed before huge crowds. As for the Germans, they took the opportunity to effect an escape. Nine of them finally got back to Germany via Jakarta and one, Julius Lauterbach, received an Iron Cross in recognition of his daring and rather convoluted flight home through China and North America.

vided Somerset Maugham with inspiration for many of his southeast Asian short stories) was built between 1937 and 1939, and sports a domed roof of green lead and a splendid, wood-panelled entrance hall – which is as far as you'll get unless you're appearing in front of the judges, as it's not open to the public. Next door is older **City Hall**, whose uniform rows of grandiose Corinthian columns lend it the austere air of a mausoleum and reflect its role in recent Singaporean history. Wartime photographs show Lord Louis Mountbatten (then Supreme Allied Commander in southeast Asia) on the steps announcing Japan's surrender to the British in 1945. Fourteen years later, Lee Kuan Yew chose the same spot from which to address his electorate at a victory rally celebrating self-government for Singapore. Nowadays, rather less dramatic photographs are taken on the steps as newlyweds line up to have their big day captured in front of one of Singapore's most imposing buildings.

The final building on the west side of the Padang, **St Andrew's Cathedral** on Coleman Street, gleams even brighter than the rest. The third church on this site, the cathedral was built in high-vaulted, Neo-Gothic style, using Indian convict labour, and was consecrated by Bishop Cotton of Calcutta on January 25, 1862. Its exterior walls were plastered using Madras *chunam* – an unlikely composite of eggs, lime, sugar and shredded coconut husks which shines brightly when smoothed – while the small cross behind the pulpit was crafted from two fourteenth-century nails salvaged from the ruins of England's Coventry Cathedral, razed to the ground during World War II. Closed-circuit TVs have been installed, which allow the whole congregation to view proceedings up at the altar – a reflection of the Chinese fascination with all things hi-tech, which the cathedral's size hardly requires.

Land reclamation has widened the Padang to the east, but much of the waterside **Esplanade Park** is presently off-limits, while work continues on the ambitious **Theatres by the Bay** project, aimed at making Singapore the arts capital of the east by the end of the millennium.

Raffles City and Raffles Hotel

Immediately north of St Andrew's Cathedral, across Stamford Road, is **Raffles City**, a huge development comprising two enormous hotels – one of which is the 73-storey *Westin Stamford* – a multi-level shopping centre and floor upon floor of offices.

Completed in 1985, the complex was designed by Chinese-American architect I.M. Pei – the man behind the glass pyramid which fronts the Louvre in Paris – and required the highly contentious demolition of the venerable Raffles Institution, established by Raffles himself and built in 1835 by George Drumgould Coleman. The **Westin Stamford** holds an annual vertical marathon, in which hardy athletes attempt to run up to the top floor in as short a time as possible: the current record stands at under seven minutes. Elevators transport lesser mortals to admire the view from the *Compass Rose* bar and restaurant on the top floor. On the open land east of Raffles City stands the imposing **Civilian War Memorial**. Comprising four seventy-metre-high white columns, it's known locally as the chopsticks.

If the *Westin Stamford* is the tallest hotel in the world, the one across the way is perhaps the most famous. The lofty halls, restaurants, bars, and peaceful gardens of the legendary **Raffles Hotel**, almost a byword for colonialism, prompted Somerset Maugham to remark that it "stood for all the fables of the exotic East". Oddly, though, this most inherently British of hotels started life as a modest seafront bungalow belonging to an Arab trader, Mohamed Alsagoff. After a spell as a tiffin house run by an Englishman called Captain Dare, the property was bought in 1886 by the Sarkie brothers, enterprising Armenians who eventually controlled a triumvirate of quintessentially colonial lodgings: the *Raffles*, the *Eastern and Oriental* in Penang, and the *Strand* in Rangoon.

Raffles Hotel opened for business on December 1, 1887, and quickly began to attract some impressive guests. It is thought that Joseph Conrad stayed in the late 1880s, and certainly Rudyard Kipling visited soon after, though at that stage the hotel couldn't, it seems, boast such sumptuous rooms as in later years. "Let the traveller take note," wrote Kipling, "feed at *Raffles* and stay at the *Hotel de l'Europe*". The hotel had its heyday during the first three decades of the new century, decades which saw it firmly establish its reputation for luxury and elegance – it was the first building in Singapore with electric lights and fans. In 1902, a little piece of Singaporean history was made at the hotel, according to an apocryphal tale, when the last tiger to be killed on the island was shot inside the building. Thirteen years later another *Raffles* legend, the "Singapore Sling" cocktail, was created by bartender Ngiam Tong Boon. The rich, famous and influential have always patronized the hotel, but despite a guest list heavy with politicians and film stars, the hotel is proudest of its literary connections. Herman Hesse, Somerset Maugham, Noel Coward and Günter Grass all stayed at *Raffles* at some time – Maugham is said to have written many of his Asian tales under a frangipani tree in the garden.

During World War II, British expatriates who had gathered in *Raffles* as the Japanese swept through the island in 1942, quickly found themselves to be POWs, and the hotel became a Japanese officers' quarters. After the Japanese surrender in 1945, *Raffles* became a transit camp for liberated Allied prisoners. Postwar deterioration earned it the affectionate but melancholy soubriquet, "grand old lady of the East", and the hotel was little more than a shabby tourist diversion when the government finally declared it a national monument in 1987. A $160-million facelift followed and the hotel reopened on September 16, 1991.

The new-look *Raffles* gets a very mixed reception. Though it retains much of its colonial grace, a shopping arcade which now curves around the back of the hotel lacks class, selling *Raffles*-related souvenirs, exclusive garments, leatherware and perfume. Still, if you're in Singapore, there's no missing *Raffles* and, assuming you can't afford to stay here, there are plenty of other ways to soak up the atmosphere. A free **museum** (daily 10am–9pm) located upstairs, at the back of the hotel complex, is crammed with memorabilia, much of which was recovered in a nationwide heritage search which encouraged Singaporeans to turn in souvenirs that had found their way up sleeves and into handbags over the years. In the Jubilee Hall, you can catch a 25-minute film, *Raffles Revisited* (daily at 11am, 1pm & 2pm; $5). Otherwise, a Singapore Sling in one of the hotel's several bars will cost you around $17.

Brah Basah Road and the Singapore Art Museum

Brah Basah Road cuts west from *Raffles*, crossing North Bridge Road and then passing Singapore's newest and most aesthetically pleasing eating place, the **CHIJMES** complex. Based around the Neo-Gothic husk of the former Convent of the Holy Infant Jesus (from whose name the complex's acronymic title is derived), CHIJMES is a rustic version of London's Covent Garden, whose lawns, courtyards, waterfalls, fountains and sunken forecourt give a sense of spacial dynamics that is rare indeed in Singapore. CHIJMES' shops and boutiques open between 9am and 10pm, the restaurants and bars from 11am to 1am. Beyond CHIJMES, Bras Basah crosses Victoria and Queen Street, where elderly trishaw drivers in yellow T-shirts tout for custom, before arriving at the new **Singapore Art Museum** (Tues–Sun 9am–5.30pm; $3) on 71 Bras Basah Rd. A long-overdue replacement for the tired art wing of the National Museum, the Art oric: by 1807 he was named chief secretary to the governor in Penang and soon Lord Minto, the governor-general of the East India Company in India, was alerted to his Oriental expertise. Meeting Minto on a trip to Calcutta in 1810, Raffles was appointed secretary to the governor-general in Malaya, a promotion quickly followed by the governorship of Java in 1811. Raffles' rule of Java was wise, libertarian and compassionate, his economic, judicial and social reforms transforming an island bowed by Dutch rule.

Post-Waterloo European rebuilding saw the East Indies returned to the Dutch in 1816 – to the chagrin of Raffles, who foresaw problems for British trade should the Dutch regain their hold on the area. From Java, Raffles transferred to the governorship of Bencoolen, on the southern coast of Sumatra, but not before he had returned home for a break, stopping at St Helena en route to meet Napoleon ("a monster"). While in England he met his second wife, Sophia Hull (his first, Olivia, had died in 1814), and was knighted.

Raffles and Sophia sailed to Bencoolen in early 1818, Sophia reporting that her husband spent the four-month journey deep in study. Once in Sumatra, Raffles found the time to study the region's flora and fauna as tirelessly as ever, discovering the Rafflesia arnoldii – "perhaps the largest and most magnificent flower in the world" – on a jungle field trip. By now, Raffles felt strongly that Britain should establish a base in the Straits of Melaka; meeting Hastings (Minto's successor) in late 1818, he was given leave to pursue this possibility and in 1819 duly sailed to the southern tip of the Malay Peninsula, where his securing of Singapore early that year was a daring masterstroke of diplomacy.

For a man whose name is inextricably linked with Singapore, Raffles spent a remarkably short time on the island. His first stay was for one week, and the second for three weeks, during which time he helped delineate the new settlement. Subsequent sojourns in Bencoolen ended tragically with the loss of four of his five children to tropical illnesses, and his own health began to deteriorate. Raffles visited Singapore one last time in late 1822; his final public duty there was to lay the foundation stone of the Singapore Institution (later the Raffles Institution), an establishment created to educate local Malays, albeit upper-class ones.

By August 1824, he was back in England. Awaiting news of a possible pension award from the East India Company, Raffles spent his free time founding the London Zoo and setting up a farm in Hendon. But the new life he had planned for Sophia and himself never materialized. Days after hearing that a Calcutta bank holding £16,000 of his capital had folded, his pension application was refused; worse still, the company was demanding £22,000 for overpayment. Three months later, the brain tumour that had caused him headaches for several years took his life on July 4, 1826. Buried at Hendon, he was honoured by no memorial tablet – the vicar had investments in slave plantations in the West Indies and was unimpressed by Raffles' friendship with William Wilberforce. Only in 1832 was Raffles commemorated, by a statue in Westminster Abbey.

Museum has a peerless location in the venerable St Joseph's Institution, Singapore's first Catholic school, whose impressive semicircular front facade and silvery dome rang to the sounds of school bells and rote learning until 1987. Though extensions have been necessary, many of the original rooms survive, among them the school chapel (now an auditorium), whose holy water receptacles, stations of the cross and mosaic floor remain intact. In the school quad, the former gymnasium, glass sculptures by the American designer Dale Chihuly sprout off the walls like luminescent mushrooms.

The Art Museum's rolling schedule of visiting collections brings work by such acclaimed artists as Marc Chagall and the sculptor Carl Milles to Singapore. But greater emphasis is placed on contemporary local and southeast Asian artists and artwork. Indeed, the museum's real strength lies in the mapping of the Asian experience – from Bui Xian Phai's *Coalmine*, an unremittingly desolate memory of his labour in a

Vietnam re-education camp, to Srihadi Sudarsono's *Horizon Dan Prahu*, in which traditional Indonesian fishing boats ply a Mark Rothko-esque canvas. Boonma's *The Pleasure of Being, Crying, Dying and Eating* comprises a tall stack of ceramic bowls decorated with jawbones and fronted by a scattering of broken pottery.

Guides conduct free **tours** (Tues & Fri 11am, Wed & Thurs 11am, 2pm & 3pm, Sat & Sun 11am & 2.30pm) around the museum's major works. Outside these times, you can better get to grips with exhibits by visiting the **E-Mage Multimedia Gallery**, which gives background to the ASEAN artists and artworks featured. Outside the museum, the souvenir shop stocks prints and postcards, and there's a classy branch of *Dôme*, where you can have a coffee under the watchful gaze of a statue of the seventeenth-century saint John Baptist de la Salle, which stands over the museum's porch.

Waterloo Street to Bugis Village

Sunday sees **Waterloo Street**, the street that flanks the Art Museum's western wall, at its best, springing to life as worshippers throng to its temples, churches and synagogue. The modern **Kuan Yim Temple**, named after the Buddhist Goddess of Mercy, may not have the cluttered altars, dusty rafters and elaborate roofs of Chinatown's temples, but is still extremely popular; all along the pavement outside, old ladies in floppy, wide-brimmed hats sell fresh flowers from baskets. Religious artefact shops on the ground floor of the apartment building opposite are well placed to catch worshippers on their way out – one shop specializes in small shrines for the house: the deluxe model boasts flashing lights and an extractor fan to expel unwanted incense smoke. **Fortune-tellers** and street traders operate along this stretch of the road, too, and look out for the cage containing turtles and a sleepy old snake: make a donation, touch one of the creatures inside, and it's said that good luck will come your way.

One block east of Waterloo Street's shops and temples, at the junction of Rochor Road and Victoria Street sits **Bugis Village** – a rather tame manifestation of infamous Bugis Street. Until it was demolished to make way for an MRT station, Bugis Street embodied old Singapore: after dark it was a chaotic place, crawling with rowdy sailors, transvestites and prostitutes – anathema to a Singapore government keen to clean up its country's reputation. However, Singaporean public opinion demanded a replacement, though when Bugis Village opened in 1991 with its beer gardens, seafood restaurants and pubs, it was a shadow of its former self. Although local reaction has been largely negative, a steady stream of tourists passes through nightly. The transvestites are notable only by their absence, the sole reminder of their heritage a weak cabaret show in the *Boom Boom Room* nightclub.

Along Hill Street to Fort Canning Park

From Stamford Road, **Hill Street** heads south to the river, flanking the eastern side of Fort Canning Park. **The Singapore Chinese Chamber of Commerce** (at 47 Hill St), a brash, Chinese-style building from 1964 featuring a striking pagoda roof, lies 30m down on the left. Along its facade are two large panels, each depicting nine intricately crafted porcelain dragons flying from the sea up to the sky. By way of contrast, the tiny Armenian **Church of St Gregory the Illuminator**, across the road and next to the former American Embassy, was designed by George Drumgould Coleman in 1835 (which makes it one of the oldest buildings in Singapore). Inside is a single, circular chamber, fronted by a marble altar and a painting of the Last Supper. Among the white gravestones and statues in the church's grounds is the tombstone of Agnes Joaquim, a nineteenth-century Armenian resident of Singapore, after whom the national flower, the delicate, purple Vanda Miss Joaquim Orchid is named; she discovered the orchid in her garden, and had it registered at the botanic gardens. The **Singapore Philatelic**

Museum (Tues–Sun 9am–4.30pm; $2), straight across Canning Rise at 23b Coleman St, makes a valiant stab at lending universal appeal to the wacky world of stamp collecting, aided by interactive games, an audio-visual theatre, and "mail-maze". There are free tours daily at 11am and 2pm.

Around the corner at 45 Armenian St, the **Substation**, a disused power station, has been converted into a multimedia arts centre. Even if you don't have time to check out its classes, discussions and performances (see p.590 for more details), the coffee shop is a pleasant place to hang out for a while. A market takes place in the courtyard every Sunday afternoon, with stalls selling everything from local crafts to secondhand Russian watches. The spectacular property next door, built in 1910 and fronted by two black eagles, is shortly to open as an **Asian Civilization Museum** (whose annexe will be housed in the Empress Place Building: see p.523).

Fort Canning Park and around

When Raffles first caught sight of Singapore, **Fort Canning Park** was known locally as Bukit Larangan (Forbidden Hill). Malay annals tell of the five ancient kings of Singapura, said to have ruled the island from here six hundred years ago, and archeological digs have unearthed artefacts which prove it was inhabited as early as the fourteenth century. The last of the kings, Sultan Iskandar Shah, reputedly lies here, and a *keramat*, or auspicious place, on the eastern slope of the hill marks the supposed site of his grave. It was out of respect for and fear of his spirit that the Malays decreed the hill forbidden, and these days the *keramat* still attracts a trickle of Singaporean Muslims, as well as childless couples who offer prayers here for fertility.

However, when the British arrived, Singapore's first British Resident William Farquhar displayed typical colonial tact by promptly having the hill cleared and building a bungalow on the summit. Named Government House, it stood on what was then called Government Hill. The bungalow was subsequently replaced in 1859 by a fort named after Viscount George Canning, governor-general of India, but of this only a gateway, guardhouse and adjoining wall remain today. An early European **cemetery** survives, however, upon whose stones are engraved intriguing epitaphs to nineteenth-century sailors, traders and residents, among them pioneering colonial architect George Coleman.

History apart, Fort Canning Park is spacious and breezy and offers respite from, as well as fine views of, Singapore's crowded streets. There's a "back entrance" to the park which involves climbing the exhausting flight of steps that runs between the Hill Street Building and Food Centre, on Hill Street. Once you reach the top, there's a brilliant view along High Street towards the Merlion. The hill, which houses two theatres, is ringed by two walks, signs along which illuminate aspects of the park's fourteenth- and nineteenth-century history. The **underground bunkers**, from which the Allied war effort in Singapore was masterminded, are also due to be opened to the public.

River Valley Road skirts the southwestern slope of Fort Canning Park, passing the **River Valley Swimming Complex** (daily 8am–9.30pm; $1; bus #32 from North Bridge Road or #54 from Scotts Road). Evidence of the recent Singapore River development drive which initiated the beautification of Boat Quay itself can be seen across the road, where **Clarke Quay**, a chain of nineteenth-century *godowns*, has been renovated into an attractive shopping and eating complex. Housed in one of the five blocks comprising the complex is Clarke Quay Adventure (daily 11am–10.30pm; $5), an indoor boat journey past working models that illuminate Singapore's formative historical events and characters. Despite a cast of eighty animatronic figures from cackling pirates and hissing snakes to familiar figures like Raffles and Conrad, the ride is an exercise in kitsch and, clocking in at just ten minutes, rather pricey. Most laughable of all is the opium den, where you share the clientele's drug-induced hallucinations of dragons. A river taxi for Clarke Quay (daily 11am–11pm; $2 return) departs every five minutes from the quayside above the Standard Chartered Bank, two minutes' walk from Raffles Place MRT.

The **Chettiar Hindu Temple** (daily 8am–noon & 5.30–8.30pm), a minute's walk further west, at the intersection of River Valley and Tank roads, is the goal of every participant in Singapore's annual Thaipusam Festival (see p.64 for more details of Thaipusam festivities). This large temple, dwarfed by the pink *Imperial Hotel*, is dedicated to Lord Subramaniam and boasts a wonderful *gopuram* or bank of sculpted gods and goddesses. Built in 1984, it replaced a nineteenth-century temple built by Indian Chettiars (moneylenders); inside, 48 glass panels etched with Hindu deities line the roof.

The National Museum

An eye-catching dome of stained glass tops the entrance to Singapore's **National Museum** (Tues–Sun 9am–5.30pm; $3), on Stamford Road. The museum's forerunner, the Raffles Museum and Library, was opened in 1887 and soon acquired a reputation for the excellence of its natural history collection. In 1969, the place was renamed the National Museum in recognition of Singapore's independence, and subsequently altered its bias towards local history and culture. It's a fairly low-key collection, but one from which you can expect to wring an hour or two's enjoyment. Following a recent shake-up, the only permanent exhibition is now the **History of Singapore Gallery**, which features twenty dioramas depicting formative events in the state's history – from the arrival of Raffles in 1819 up to the first session of parliament in 1965. Other exhibitions come and go: recent ones have focused on the Hakka people, the life of the Straits Chinese community and nineteenth-century botanical prints; check the local press for details. Free **guided tours** start downstairs at the ticket counter (Tues–Fri 11am), and the free film shows in the **AV Theatrette** (daily at 10am, noon, 2pm & 4pm), examining subjects like old Chinatown and Little India, the Singapore River and traditional kampung life, are also worth catching.

Orchard Road

It would be hard to conjure an image more diametrically opposed to the reality of modern-day **Orchard Road** than C.M. Turnbull's description of it during early colonial times as "a country lane lined with bamboo hedges and shrubbery, with trees meeting overhead for its whole length". One hundred years ago, a stroll down Orchard Road would have passed row upon row of nutmeg trees, and would have been enjoyed in the company of merchants taking their daily constitutionals, followed at a discreet distance by their trusty manservants. Today, Orchard Road is synonymous with shopping – indeed, tourist brochures refer to it as the "Fifth Avenue, the Regent Street, the Champs Elysées, the Via Veneto and the Ginza of Singapore". Huge malls, selling everything you can imagine, line the road, though don't expect shopping to be relaxing; hordes of dawdling tourists from the numerous hotels along the road make browsing difficult. The road runs northwest from Fort Canning Park and is served by three MRT stations – Dhoby Ghaut, Somerset and Orchard; of these Orchard MRT is the most central for shopping expeditions.

Orchard Road does have one or two other diversions if you get tired of looking at CDs, watches and clothes. Towards the eastern end, the President of Singapore's abode – the **Istana Negara Singapura** – is open to the public a few times a year, and rows of houses that hark back to old Singapore flank Cuppage Road and Emerald Hill Road. The latter road also contains a museum depicting life in a turn-of-the-century Peranakan house. And, way up beyond the most westerly point of the road, the **Singapore Botanic Gardens** make for a relaxing stroll in beautiful surroundings. On the whole, though, visitors really only come to Orchard Road in the daytime to shop and at night for a whole host of clubs and bars.

ORCHARD ROAD SHOPPING CENTRES

The main Orchard Road shopping centres are detailed below; see map on pp.536–37.

Centrepoint Dependable all-round complex, whose seven floors of shops include *Marks and Spencers* and *Robinsons* – Singapore's oldest department store.

C.K. Tang's Singapore's most famous department store, whose pagoda-style construction provides Orchard Road with one of its most recognizable landmarks.

Delfi Orchard Good for crystalware, glassware and art galleries.

Forum the Shopping Mall Kids' clothes, toyshops, modelling specialists and clothes stores.

Lucky Plaza Crammed with tailors and electronics, this is Orchard Road's classic venue for haggling.

Ngee Ann City A brooding twin-towered complex – Singapore meets Gotham City – with a wealth of good clothes shops.

Orchard Plaza Tailors, leather jackets and silks galore, as well as a glut of audio, video and camera stores where haggling is par for the course.

Palais Renaissance One of Singapore's classiest complexes, featuring Ralph Lauren, Gucci, Karl Lagerfeld, Christian Dior and other heavyweights.

Plaza Singapura Sportswear and sports equipment, musical instruments, audio, video and general electrical equipment, and the *Yaohan* department store, to boot.

Tanglin Shopping Centre Unsurpassed for art, antiques and curios.

Tudor Court Fashion shops, including Asian designers Dick Lee, Esther Tay and Arthur Yen.

Wisma Atria Like *Centrepoint*, a safe bet, whatever it is you're after.

Dhoby Ghaut to Emerald Hill

In the **Dhoby Ghaut** area (at the eastern tip of Orchard Road), Indian *dhobies*, or laundrymen, used to wash clothes in the Stamford Canal, which once ran along Orchard and Stamford roads. Three minutes' walk west along Orchard Road from Dhoby Ghaut MRT takes you past Plaza Singapura, beyond which stern-looking soldiers guard the gate of the **Istana Negara Singapura**. Built in 1869, the istana, with its ornate cornices, elegant louvred shutters and high mansard roof, was originally the official residence of Singapore's British governors, though on independence it became the residence of the president of Singapore – currently Ong Teng Cheong, whose portrait you'll see in banks, post offices and shops across the state. The shuttered istana is only open to visitors on public holidays and is probably worth a visit if your trip coincides with one – the president goes walkabout at some point during every open day as thousands of Singaporeans flock to picnic on the well-landscaped sweeps and dips of its lawns, and brass bands belt out jaunty tunes. The **changing of the guard** ceremony, takes place at 5.45pm every first Sunday of the month.

The **Tan Yeok Nee Mansion**, across the road at 207 Clemenceau Ave, is currently closed and its future is unclear. Built in traditional south Chinese style for a wealthy Teochew merchant who traded in pepper and gambier (a resin used in tanning), and featuring ornate roofs and massive granite pillars, the mid-1880s mansion served as headquarters to the Singapore Salvation Army from 1940 until 1991. Further along Orchard Road, two-thirds of **Cuppage Road** have been pedestrianized, making it a great place to sit out and have a beer or a meal. **Cuppage Terrace** itself, halfway along on the left, is an unusually (for Orchard Road) old row of shophouses, containing tailors and souvenir shops, as well as several antique shops upstairs. A number of even more architecturally notable houses have also survived the bulldozers in Emerald Hill Road, parallel to Cuppage Road. Emerald Hill was granted to Englishman William Cuppage in 1845 and for some years afterwards was the site of a large nutmeg plantation. After Cuppage's death in 1872, the land was subdivided and sold off, much of it

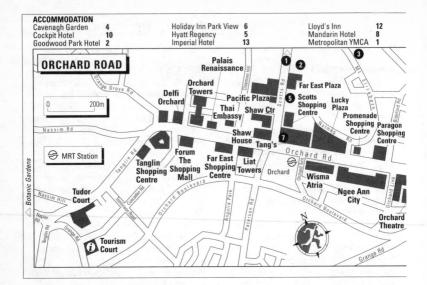

ACCOMMODATION

Cavenagh Garden	4	Holiday Inn Park View	6	Lloyd's Inn	12
Cockpit Hotel	10	Hyatt Regency	5	Mandarin Hotel	8
Goodwood Park Hotel	2	Imperial Hotel	13	Metropolitan YMCA	1

bought by members of the Peranakan community, which evolved in Malaya as a result of the intermarriage between early Chinese settlers and Malay women. A walk up Emerald Hill Road takes you past a number of exquisitely crafted houses dating from this period, built in a decorative architectural style known as Chinese Baroque, typified by highly coloured ceramic tiles, carved swing doors, shuttered windows and pastel-shaded walls with fine plaster mouldings.

Through the swing doors of 2 Emerald Hill Rd, the **Show House Museum** (Mon–Sat 10.30am–2.30pm; $4 includes guided tour) gives you a brief insight into Peranakan culture, the house's four furnished rooms highlighting the lifestyle and traditions of the Straits Chinese. The museum's dining room boasts a fine collection of seventeenth-century Ching dynasty porcelain, but no chopsticks – Peranakans ate with their hands at home. Look out, too, for the birdcage-like food container which could be hoisted up to the ceiling to keep the food away from rats. Meals were in three sittings: the first for the men (served by their daughters-in-law), the second for the elder women and daughters (again served by the daughters-in-law), and only when all the others had eaten did the daughters-in-law dine with the servants. It's no wonder parents presented their daughters with black veils, symbolizing mourning, when they married.

West to the Botanic Gardens

West of Emerald Hill Road, the **shopping centres** of Orchard Road begin to come thick and fast; a list of good shops is given on p.545. A couple of minutes' north of Orchard Road along Scotts Road, the impressive **Goodwood Hotel** started life in 1900 as the Teutonia Club for German expats. With the start of war across Europe in 1914, the club was commandeered by the British Custodian of Enemy Property and it didn't open again until 1918, after which it served for several years as a function hall. In 1929 it became a hotel, though by 1942 the Goodwood – like *Raffles* – was lodging Japanese officers. Fitting, then, that the hotel was chosen, after the war, as one of the venues for a war crimes court.

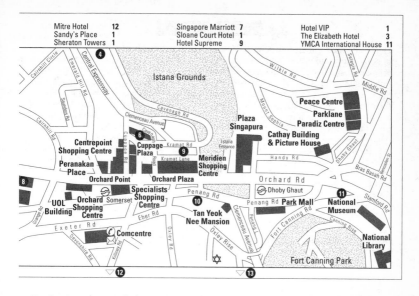

Mitre Hotel	12	Singapore Marriott	7	Hotel VIP	1
Sandy's Place	1	Sloane Court Hotel	1	The Elizabeth Hotel	3
Sheraton Towers	1	Hotel Supreme	9	YMCA International House	11

By the time you reach the western end of Orchard Road, you'll be glad of the open space afforded by the **Singapore Botanic Gardens** (Mon–Fri 5am–midnight; free) on Cluny Road. Founded in 1859, it was here, in 1877, that the Brazilian seeds from which grew the great **rubber plantations** of Malaysia were first nurtured. Henry Ridley, named director of the botanic gardens the following year, recognized the financial potential of rubber and spent the next twenty years of his life persuading Malayan plantation-owners to convert to this new crop, an obsession which earned him the nickname "Mad" Ridley. The fifty-odd hectares of land feature a mini-jungle, rose garden, topiary, fernery, palm valley, and lakes that are home to turtles and swans. There's also the **National Orchid Garden** (daily 8.30am–6pm; $2) with sixty thousand plants; orchid jewellery, made by plating real flowers with gold, is on sale here –around $100 per piece. At dawn and dusk, joggers and students of tai chi haunt the lawns and paths of the gardens, while at the weekend, newlyweds bundle down from church for their photos to be taken – a ritual recalled in Lee Tzu Pheng's poem, *Bridal Party at the Botanics*, whose bride's "two hundred dollar face/is melting in the sun", while beside her is her groom, "black-stuffed, oil-slicked, fainting/in his finery, by the shrubbery". You can pick up a free **map** of the grounds at the ranger's office, a little to the right of the main gate.

The Botanic Gardens are a ten-minute walk from the western end of Orchard Road, or catch bus #7, #106 or #174 from Orchard Boulevard. The #106 passes down Bencoolen Street before heading on towards the gardens, while the #174 originates in New Bridge Road in Chinatown.

Chinatown

The two square kilometres of **Chinatown**, bounded by New Bridge Road to the west, Neil and Maxwell roads to the south, Cecil Street to the east and the Singapore River to the north, once constituted the focal point of Chinese life and culture in Singapore. Nowadays the area is on its last traditional legs, scarred by the wounds of demolition and dwarfed by the Financial District (see p.545), in which the island's yuppies oversee

the machinations of one of Asia's most dynamic money markets. Even so, a wander
through the surviving nineteenth-century streets unearths aged craft shops, restaurants unchanged in forty years and provision stores crammed with birds' nests, dried
cuttlefish, ginger, chillies, mushrooms and salted fish.

  The area was first earmarked for settlement by the Chinese community by Sir
Stamford Raffles himself, who decided on his second visit to the island in June 1819 that
the ethnic communities should live separately. As increasing numbers of immigrants
poured into Singapore, Chinatown became just that – a Chinese town, where new
arrivals from the mainland, mostly from the Kwangtung (Canton) and Fukien provinces,
would have been pleased to find temples, shops and, most importantly *kongsi* (clan associations), which helped them to find food and lodgings and work, mainly as small traders
and coolies. The prevalent architectural form was the **shophouse**, a shuttered building
whose moulded facade fronted living rooms upstairs and a shop on the ground floor. By
the mid-twentieth century, the area southwest of the Singapore River was rich with the
imported cultural heritage of China, but independence brought ambition. The government regarded the tumbledown slums of Chinatown as an eyesore and embarked upon
a catastrophic **redevelopment campaign** that saw whole roads bulldozed to make way
for new shopping centres, and street traders relocated into organized complexes. Only
recently did public opinion finally convince the Singaporean authorities to restore, and
not redevelop, Chinatown. Renovated buildings remain faithful to the original designs,
though there's a tendency to render once characterful shophouses improbably perfect.
The latest problem to threaten the fabric of Chinatown is spiralling rents, which in time
will drive out the last few remaining families and traditional businesses, leaving the area
open for full exploitation by bistros, advertising agencies and souvenir shops. All of
which means that Chinatown is best visited soon. And go early in the morning, when the
sun isn't yet hot enough to make walking around unpleasant.

Along Telok Ayer Street

Follow the signs for Maxwell Road out of Tanjong Pagar MRT and you'll surface on the
southern edge of Chinatown. Take the left-hand path in front of the station and cross

Maxwell Road; after about fifty metres you'll hit **Telok Ayer Street**, whose Malay name – Watery Bay – recalls a time when the street would have run along the shoreline of the Straits of Singapore. Nowadays it's no closer to a beach than is Beach Road, but alongside the shops and stores there are still a number of temples and mosques that have survived from the time when immigrants and sailors stepping ashore wanted to thank the gods for their safe passage.

Facing you as you approach Telok Ayer Street is the square **Chinese Methodist Church**, established in 1889, whose design – portholes and windows adorned with white crosses and capped by a Chinese-style pagoda-style roof – testifies to its multi-cultural nature. Further up, shortly beyond McCallum Street, the enormous **Thian Hock Keng Temple**, the Temple of Heavenly Happiness, is a hugely impressive Hokkien building. Built on the site of a small joss house where immigrants made offerings to Ma Chu Por (or Tian Hou), the Queen of Heaven, the temple was started in 1839 using materials imported from China. By the time the temple was finished in 1842 a statue of the goddess had been shipped in from southern China, and this still stands in the centre of the temple's main hall, flanked by the God of War on the right and the Protector of Life on the left. From the street, the temple looks spectacular: dragons stalk its broad roofs, while the entrance to the temple compound bristles with ceramic flowers, foliage and figures. Two stone lions stand guard at the entrance, and door gods, painted on the front doors, prevent evil spirits from entering. Look out, too, for the huge ovens, always lit, in which offerings to either gods or ancestors are burnt.

A block west of Telok Ayer Street is **Amoy Street**, which – together with China and Telok Ayer streets – was also designated as a Hokkien enclave in the colony's early days. Long terraces of shophouses flank the street, all featuring characteristic **five foot ways**, or covered verandahs, so called simply because they jut five feet out from the house. Some of the shophouses are in a ramshackle state, while others have been marvellously renovated, only to be bought by companies in need of some fancy office space. It's worth walking down to the **Sian Chai Kang Temple**, at 66 Amoy St, painted a shade of red as fiery as the dragons on its roof – it's a musty, open-fronted place dominated by huge urns, full to the brim with ash from untold numbers of burned incense sticks.

Telok Ayer Street continues north over Cross Street to another former waterfront temple, the well-hidden **Fuk Tak Ch'i Temple**, at no. 76. A dark, claustrophobic place, its two shrines are jam-packed with tiny smoke-ringed effigies of Chinese deities. As you walk inside, on your left is the God of Wealth with his horse. Two doors along, the Seong Moh Trading Company sells prayer books and incense sticks.

Wak Hai Cheng Bio Temple on Philip Street completes Chinatown's string of former waterfront temples, fronted by an ugly concrete courtyard crisscrossed by a web of ropes supporting numerous spiralled incense sticks. Its name means "Temple of the Calm Sea", which made it a logical choice for early worshippers who had arrived safely in Singapore; an effigy of Tian Hou, the Queen of Heaven and protector of seafarers, is housed in the temple's right-hand chamber. This temple, too, has an incredibly ornate roof, crammed with tiny models of Chinese village scenes. The temple cat meanders across here sometimes, dwarfing the tableaux like a creature from a Godzilla movie.

From China Street to Ann Siang Hill

Around **China Street** and its offshoots, Chinatown becomes more residential, the roads affording at least an insight into how the area might have appeared in its prime. The old ways still survive – though only just – in this part of Singapore. In the upper windows of tumbledown shophouses, wizened old men in white T-shirts and striped pyjama trousers stare out from behind wooden gates, flanked by songbird cages and laundry poles hung with washing. Down at street level, the trishaw is still a recognized form of transport.

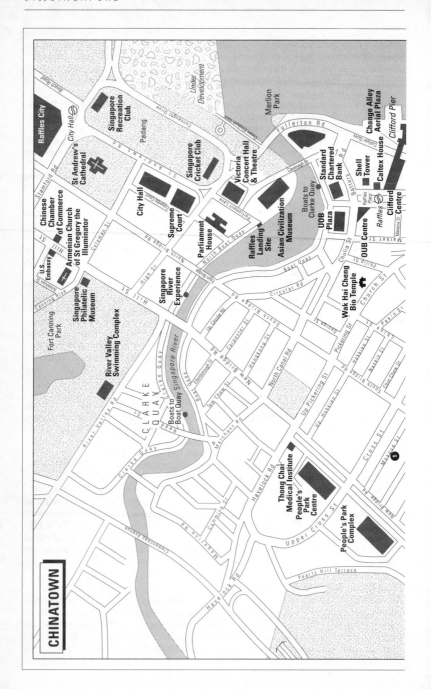

CHINATOWN

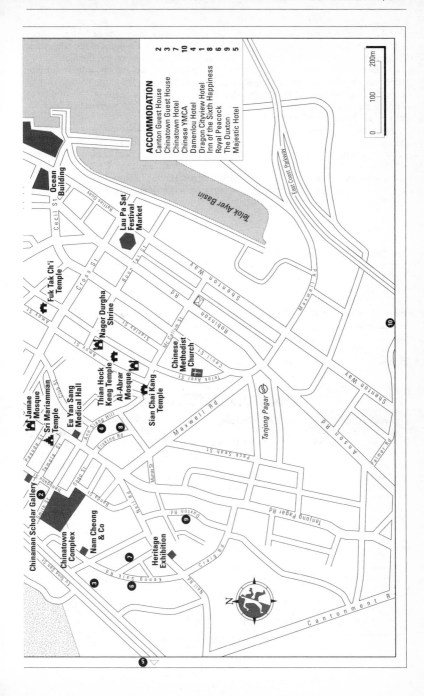

ACCOMMODATION

Canton Guest House	2
Chinatown Guest House	3
Chinatown Hotel	7
Chinese YMCA	10
Damenlou Hotel	4
Dragon Cityview Hotel	1
Inn of the Sixth Happiness	8
Royal Peacock	6
The Duxton	9
Majestic Hotel	5

But the traditional trades and industries – medicine shops, bakers, popiah skin makers – which operated here as recently as the mid-1990s, are now a thing of the past, their shophouses converted into architects' studios, marketing agencies and the like.

At the southern end of China Street, Club Street rises up steeply, a thoroughfare once noted for its **temple-carving shops**, although these too fell to the demolition ball a couple of years ago. An impromptu **flea market** often takes shape on the far side of the car park opposite, where traders squat on their haunches surrounded by catalogues, old coins, sleeveless records and phone cards.

Even the **clan associations** and **guilds** that gave Club Street its name are fast disappearing, though there are still a few to be seen, higher up the hill. These are easy to spot; black-and-white photos of old members cover the walls, and behind the screens which almost invariably span the doorway, old men sit and chat. From upstairs, the clacking sound of mahjong tiles reaches the street. Having laboured up Club Street to the brow of Ann Siang Hill, you may be ready for a refreshing drink in the *Ann Siang Hill Chinese Teahouse*.

Tanjong Pagar

The district of **Tanjong Pagar** at the southern tip of South Bridge Road, between Neil and Tanjong Pagar roads, is another area that's changed beyond recognition in recent years. Once a veritable sewer of brothels and opium dens, it was earmarked by the authorities as a conservation area, following which over two hundred shophouses were painstakingly restored, painted in sickly pastel hues and converted into bars catering to the Financial District crowd, or restaurants and shops which prey on passing tourists. A bazaar at 51 Neil Rd has several touristy shops, while the **Heritage Exhibition** (daily 11am–6pm; free) in the same building is a rather grand name for what is essentially just a small room of old photographs.

The highlight of a trip around Tanjong Pagar is a stop at one of the traditional **teahouses** along Neil Road. At *Tea Chapter*, at nos. 9a–11a (daily 11am–11pm), you can

---

TAKING CHINESE TEA

If you're in need of a quick, thirst-quenching drink, avoid **Chinese teahouses**: the art of tea-making is heavily bound up in ritual, and the unhurried preparation time is crucial to the production of a pleasing brew. What's more, when you do get a cup, it's barely more than a mouthful and then the whole process kicks off again.

Tea drinking in China goes back thousands of years. Legend has it that the first cuppa was drunk by Emperor Shen Nong, who was pleasantly surprised by the aroma produced by some dried tea leaves falling into the water he was boiling. He was even more pleased when he tasted the brew. By the eighth century, the art form was so complex that Chinese scholar Lu Yu produced a three-volume tome on the processes involved.

Tea shops normally have conventional tables and chairs, but the authentic experience involves kneeling at a much lower traditional table. The basic procedure is as follows: the server places a towel in front of himself and his guest, with the folded edge facing the guest, and stuffs leaves into the pot with a bamboo scoop. Water, boiled over a flame, has to reach an optimum temperature, depending on which type of tea is being made; experts can tell its heat by the size of the bubbles rising, which are described variously, and rather confusingly, as "sand eyes", "prawn eyes", "fish eyes", etc. Once the pot has been warmed inside and out, the first pot of tea is made, transferred into the pouring jar and then, frustratingly, poured back *over* the pot – the thinking being that over a period of time, the porous clay of the pot becomes infused with the fragrance of the tea. Once a second pot is ready, a draught is poured into the sniffing cup, from which the aroma of the brew is savoured. Only now is it time to actually drink the tea and if you want a second cup, the complete procedure starts again.

have tea in the very chair in which Queen Elizabeth sat when she visited in 1989 – the shop is plastered with photographs of the occasion. The Chinese take tea-drinking very seriously – buy a bag of tea here and one of the staff will teach you all the attached rituals (see box); 100g bags go for from $5 to over $65. Tea sets are also on sale, though they don't come cheap.

Along South Bridge Road

During the Japanese occupation, roadblocks were set up at the point where **South Bridge Road** meets Cross Street and Singaporeans were vetted at an interrogation post for signs of anti-Japanese feeling. Those whose answers failed to satisfy the guards either ended up as POWs or were never seen again. Nowadays – in stark contrast to the Tanjong Pagar conservation area – South Bridge Road is lined with numerous dingy shops that look as if they've seen no custom since the war.

Turn right out of Ann Siang Hill and you'll see **Eu Yan Sang Medical Hall** (Mon–Sat 8.30am–6pm) at 267–271 South Bridge Rd, first opened in 1910 and geared up, to an extent, for the tourist trade – some of the staff speak good English. The shop has been beautifully renovated: the smell is the first thing you'll notice (a little like a compost heap on a hot day), the second, the weird assortment of ingredients on the shelves, which to the uninitiated look more likely to kill than cure. Besides the usual herbs and roots favoured by the Chinese are various dubious remedies derived from exotic and endangered species. Blood circulation problems and external injuries are eased with centipedes and insects, crushed into a "rubbing liquor"; the ground-up gall bladders of snakes or bears apparently work wonders on pimples; monkey's gallstones aid asthmatics; while deer penis is supposed to provide a lift to any sexual problem. Antlers, sea horses, scorpions and turtle shells also feature regularly in Chinese prescriptions, though the greatest cure-all of Oriental medicine is said to be **ginseng**, a clever little root that will combat anything from weakness of the heart to acne and jet lag. If you need a pick-me-up, or are just curious, the shop administers free glasses of ginseng tea.

Across the road from the front doors of *Eu Yan Sang*, the compound of the **Sri Mariamman Hindu Temple** bursts with primary coloured, wild-looking statues of deities and animals, and there's always some ritual or other being attended to by one of the temple's priests, drafted in from the subcontinent and dressed in simple loincloths. A wood and *atap* hut was first erected here in 1827, on land belonging to Naraina Pillay – a government clerk who arrived on the same ship as Stamford Raffles, when Raffles first came ashore at Singapore. The present temple was completed in around 1843 and boasts a superb *gopuram* over the front entrance. Once inside the temple, look up at the roof and you'll see splendidly vivid friezes depicting a host of Hindu deities, including the three manifestations of the Supreme Being: Brahma the Creator (with three of his four heads showing), Vishnu the Preserver, and Shiva the Destroyer (holding one of his sons). The main sanctum, facing you as you walk inside, is devoted to Goddess Mariamman, who's worshipped for her powers to cure disease. Smaller sanctums dotted about the open walkway circumnavigating the temple honour a host of other deities. In that dedicated to Goddess Periachi Amman, a sculpture portrays her with a queen lying on her lap, whose evil child she has ripped from her womb. Odd, then, that the Periachi Amman should be the Protector of Children, to whom babies are brought when one month old. Sri Aravan, with his bushy moustache and big ears, is far less intimidating. His sanctum is at the back on the right-hand side of the complex.

To the left of the main sanctum there's an unassuming patch of sand which, once a year during the festival of **Thimithi** (see p.68), is covered in red-hot coals, which male Hindus run across to prove the strength of their faith. The participants, who line up all the way along South Bridge Road waiting for their turn, are supposedly protected from the heat of the coals by the power of prayer, though the presence of an ambulance parked round the back of the temple suggests that some aren't praying quite hard enough.

West: Chinatown Complex and beyond

After crumbling Telok Ayer and China streets, much of the section of Chinatown **west of South Bridge Road** seems far less authentic. This is tour-bus Chinatown, heaving with gangs of holidaymakers plundering souvenir shops. However, until as recently as the 1950s, **Sago Street**, across South Bridge Road from Ann Siang Hill, was home to several death houses – rudimentary hospices where skeletal citizens saw out their final hours on rattan camp beds. These houses were finally deemed indecent and all have now gone, replaced by lifeless restaurants and shops stacked to the rafters with cheap Chinese vases, teapots, cups and saucers. Sago, Smith, Temple and Pagoda streets only really recapture their youth around the time of Chinese New Year, when they're crammed to bursting with stalls selling festive branches of blossom, oranges, sausages and waxed chickens – which look as if they have melted to reveal a handful of bones inside.

At other times of the year, give yourself an hour or so for the few things worth seeing. The hideous concrete exterior of the **Chinatown Complex**, at the end of Sago Street, belies the charm of the teeming market it houses. Walk up the front steps, past the garlic, fruit and nut hawkers, and once inside, the market's many twists and turns reveal stalls selling silk, kimonos, rattan, leather and clothes. There are no fixed prices, so you'll need to haggle. Deep in the market's belly is *Kan Meng* (shop 01-K6) – a calligraphers' stall, where you can have an oriental ink sign quickly drawn for you – while the *Capitol Plastics* stall (01-16) specializes in mahjong sets. There's a food centre on the second floor, while the wet market within the complex gets pretty packed early in the morning, when locals come to buy fresh fish or meat. Here, abacuses are still used to tally bills, and sugar canes lean like spears against the wall.

Sago Street skirts to the right of the Chinatown Complex, and its name changes to **Trengganu Street**. Despite the hordes of tourists, and the shops selling Singapore Airlines uniforms, presentation chopstick sets and silk hats with false pony tails, there are occasional glimpses of Chinatown's old trades and industries. At 30 Smith St, soya sauce is still dispensed from huge bins, while the *Fook Weng* store at no. 34 offers shirts, watches, mobile phones, money and passports – all made out of paper – which the Chinese burn to ensure their ancestors don't want for creature comforts in the next life. *Nam Cheong and Co*, off nearby Kreta Ayer Street, takes this industry to its logical conclusion, producing huge houses and near life-size safes, servants and Mercedes for the self-respecting ghost about town; the shop is at 01-04, Block 334, Keong Saik Road, between Chinatown Complex and New Bridge Road.

The area around Trengganu Street is best appreciated by wandering aimlessly, but there is one permanent museum that warrants a special trip. The **Chinaman Scholar Gallery**, at 14b Trengganu St (Mon–Fri 9am–4pm; $6), is more junk shop than museum, housed in a single room within a 120-year-old shophouse. Most of its artefacts date from the early twentieth century, and the owner Vincent Tan talks his guests around them with great pride, pointing out pedestrian pieces like vases and furniture, as well as the more fascinating exhibits, like the tiny pairs of shoes worn by young girls to stop their feet growing and thus render them more beautiful.

Trengganu's cross streets – Smith, Temple and Pagoda – run west to Chinatown's main shopping drag, comprising southbound **New Bridge Road** and northbound **Eu Tong Sen Street**, along which are lined a handful of large malls. Try to pop into one of the barbecue pork vendors around the intersection of Smith, Temple and Pagoda streets with New Bridge Road – the squares of red, fatty, delicious meat that they cook on wire meshes over fires produce an odour that is pure Chinatown.

The **Thong Chai Medical Institute** has been sited at the top of Eu Tong Sen Street since 1892, when it first opened its doors with the avowed intention of dispensing free

SHOPPING IN CHINATOWN

As well as the markets and stores covered in the text, look out for the following, all either on or near to New Bridge Road and Eu Tong Sen Street.

Chinatown Point, 133 New Bridge Rd. One of its two buildings houses bright, fashionable, Orchard Road-style shop units; the other is a handicraft centre, with scores of tourist-orientated businesses.

Hong Lim Complex, 531–531a Upper Cross St. Several Chinese provisions stores, fronted by sackfuls of dried mushrooms, cuttlefish, chillies, garlic cloves, onions, fritters and crackers. Other shops sell products ranging from acupuncture accessories to birds' nests.

Lucky Chinatown Complex, 11 New Bridge Rd. Fairly upmarket place with lots of jewellery shops, even an Oriental-style *McDonalds*.

New Bridge Centre, 336 Smith St. The *Da You Department Store* (second floor) sells Chinese religious artefacts, tea sets and crockery.

Pearl's Centre, 100 Eu Tong Sen St. A centre for Chinese medicine. The Chinese Patent Medicines and Medicated

Liquors Centre at 03-19 (daily 10am–9.30pm) and TCM Chinese Medicines at 02-21 (daily 10am–9pm) both have a Chinese clinic, where a consultation will cost you $5.

People's Park Centre, 101 Upper Cross St. Stall-like shop units selling cheap shoes, cassettes, electronics and gold. Look into *Nison Department Store* (daily 9.30am–10pm), on the first and second floors, which has some beautiful statues and rosewood screens.

People's Park Complex, 1 Park Rd. The *Overseas Emporium* is at 02-70 (daily 10am–9.30pm), and warrants a browse through its shelves of Chinese instruments, calligraphy pens, lacquerwork and jade. Also interesting is *Tashing Emporium* (daily 10am–10pm), a Taiwanese shop at 01-79a, selling food, clothes and Oriental trinkets. Cobblers set up stall in the courtyard beside the complex, behind which is a market and food centre.

medical help regardless of race, colour or creed. Listed as a national monument, it has recently been taken over by the Seiawan Company, whose intentions are less charitable – when renovations are completed the beautiful southern Chinese-style building is to become a flashy souvenir shop, which seems a waste of its wonderful serpentine gables and wooden inscribed pillars. Northwest of the Thong Chai institute is a Teochew Chinese enclave based around Ellenborough and Tew Chew streets. **Ellenborough Market** incorporates a third-floor food centre serving Teochew specialities, as well as a wet market where fish-mincing machines are in constant action – a sight to be avoided if you have any intention of eating fishball soup.

The Financial District

Until an early exercise in land reclamation in the mid-1820s rendered the zone fit for building, the patch of land south of the Singapore River, where Raffles Place now stands, was a swampland. However, within just a few years Commercial Square (later renamed Raffles Place) was the colony's busiest business address, boasting the banks, ship's chandlers and warehouses of a burgeoning trading port. The square now forms the nucleus of the **Financial District** – the commercial heart of the state, home to many of its 140 banks and financial institutions. Cutting through the district is **Battery Road**, whose name recalls the days when Fort Fullerton (named after Robert Fullerton, first Governor of the Straits Settlements) and its attendant battery of guns used to stand on the site of the Fullerton Building (until recently Singapore's GPO).

Raffles Place and the south riverbank

Raffles Place was Singapore's central shopping area until Orchard Road superseded it in the late 1960s. Two department stores, *Robinsons* and *John Little*, dominated the area until then, but subsequent development turned Raffles Place into Singapore's financial epicentre, ringed by buildings so tall that pedestrians crossing the square feel like ants in a canyon. The most striking way to experience the giddy heights of the Financial District is by surfacing from Raffles Place MRT – follow the signs for Cecil Street out of the station – and looking up to gleaming towers, blue skies and racing clouds. To your left is the soaring metallic triangle of the **OUB Centre** (Overseas Union Bank), and, right of that, the heftier **UOB Building** (United Overseas Bank); in front of you are the rich brown walls of the **Standard Chartered Bank**, and to your right rise sturdy **Shell Tower** and the almost Art Deco **Caltex House**. A smallish statue, entitled *Progress and Advancement*, stands at the northern end of Raffles Place. Erected in 1988, it's a miniature version of what was then the skyline of central Singapore. Inevitably, the very progress and advancement it celebrates has already rendered it out of date – not featured is the **UOB Plaza**, a rocket of a building only recently built beside the existing UOB Building. The three roads that run southwest from Raffles Place – Cecil Street, Robinson Road and Shenton Way – are all choc-a-bloc with more highrise banks and financial houses; to the west is Chinatown.

Just north of Raffles Place, and beneath the "elephant's trunk" curve of the Singapore River, the pedestrianized row of shophouses known as **Boat Quay** is presently enjoying a renaissance. Derelict until a few years ago, it's Singapore's most fashionable hang-out, sporting a huge collection of thriving restaurants and bars, and is an excellent spot for an alfresco meal or drink.

East of Raffles Place

Branching off the second floor of the Clifford Centre, on the eastern side of Raffles Place, is **Change Alley Aerial Plaza**. The original Change Alley was a cheap, bustling street-level bazaar, which redevelopment wiped off the face of Singapore; all that remains is a sanitized, modern-day version, housed on a covered footbridge across

---

THE BARINGS BANK SCANDAL

Singapore hit the international headlines early in 1995, the City of London's oldest merchant bank **Barings**, collapsed as a result of what the London *Evening Standard* called "massive unauthorized dealings" in derivatives on the Japanese stock market. The supposed culprit – "the man who broke the bank", as the press dubbed him – was named as Nick Leeson, an Englishman dealing out of the bank's offices in the Financial District of Singapore. Leeson, it was alleged, had gambled huge funds in the hope of recouping losses made through ill-judged trading, only calling it a day when the bank's losses were approaching one billion pounds. One of his colleagues claimed that Leeson made "other fraudsters look like Walt Disney", although many have questioned the quality of Barings' management and financial controls which allowed such a catastrophe to happen.

By the time the scandal broke, Leeson was missing, and a pan-southeast Asian search was in full swing when he finally turned up – and was promptly arrested – six days later in Frankfurt. News of his capture was greeted with cheers from dealers in the Singapore Stock Exchange when it flashed across their screens. In the weeks that followed, Dutch bank ING bought out Barings for one pound sterling, while Nick Leeson languished in a Frankfurt jail. In time, Singapore's application for extradition was duly granted, and less than two weeks after being passed into Singaporean custody, on December 2, 1995, the rogue trader pleaded guilty to two charges of deceit, and received a six-and-a-half-year sentence which he is currently serving in Tanah Merah Prison.

Collyer Quay. The tailors here have a persuasive line in patter – you'll have to be very determined if you aren't going to waste half an hour being convinced that you need a new suit.

Walking through Change Alley Aerial Plaza deposits you at **Clifford Pier**, long the departure point for trips on the Singapore River and to the southern islands. There are still a few bumboats tied up here, though these days they're rented out as cruise boats rather than earning a living as cargo boats. Visible from the pier to the north is the elegant **Fullerton Building**, fronted by sturdy pillars. Built in 1928 as the headquarters for the General Post Office (a role it fulfilled until the mid-1990s) remarkably, this was once one of Singapore's tallest buildings. Old photographs of Singapore depict Japanese soldiers marching past it after the surrender of the Allied forces during World War II.

Opposite the Fullerton Building is **Merlion Park** (daily 6am–midnight; free), in which Singapore's national symbol, the statue of the mythical Merlion, presides. Half-lion, half-fish, and wholly ugly, the creature reflects Singapore's name – in Sanskrit, *Singapura* means "Lion City" – and its historical links with the sea. There are good views of Singapore's colonial buildings from the park, while beside the entrance to the park is a tacky souvenir shop shifting truck loads of Merlion T-shirts, paperweights and paperknives to passing tourists.

Back at Clifford Pier it's just a short walk to the south along Raffles Quay to Telok Ayer Market, recently renamed **Lau Pa Sat Festival Market**. Originally built in 1894 on land reclaimed from the sea, its octagonal cast-iron frame has been turned into Singapore's most tasteful food centre (daily 24hr), which offers a range of southeast Asian cuisines, as well as laying on free entertainment such as local bands and Chinese opera performances. After 7pm, the portion of Boon Tat Street between Robinson Road and Shenton Way is closed to traffic, and traditional hawker stalls take over the street.

One of Singapore's most ambitious land reclamation projects, **Marina South**, is plainly visible from Raffles Quay and Shenton Way. This has all the makings of a splendid folly – the entertainment and recreation park which was built on it during the 1980s has already gone bankrupt and the large patch of land now seems to serve no other purpose than to carry the East Coast Parkway on its journey west – making it surely the world's biggest bridge support. Marina South is a ghost town, its only real asset an imaginative children's playground within a pleasant park; access is by MRT from Raffles Place, or bus #400 from Tanjong Pagar MRT. Below Marina South, Singapore's **port** begins its sprawl westwards. Singapore is the world's busiest container port (the second busiest port overall after Rotterdam), and hundreds of ships are docked south of the island at any one time, waiting for permission from the Port of Singapore Authority to enter one of the state's seven terminals.

Little India

A tour around **Little India** amounts to an all-out assault on the senses. Indian pop music blares out from gargantuan speakers outside cassette shops and the air is heavily perfumed with sweet incense, curry powder and jasmine garlands. Hindu women promenade in bright sarees; and a wealth of "hole-in-the-wall" restaurants serve up superior curries.

Indians did not always dominate this convenient central niche of Singapore, just fifteen minutes from the colonial district. Its original occupants were Europeans and Eurasians who established country houses here, and for whom a race course was built (on the site of modern day Farrer Park) in the 1840s. Only when Indian-run **brick kilns** began to operate here did a pronouncedly Indian community start to evolve. The enclave grew when a number of **cattle and buffalo yards** opened in the area in the latter half of the nineteenth century, and more Hindus were drawn in search of work.

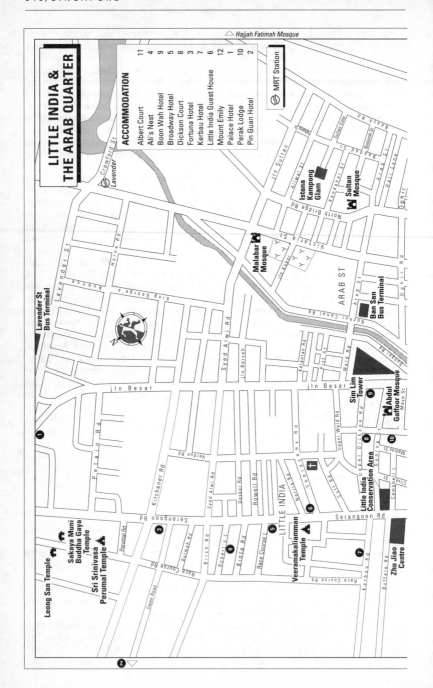

LITTLE INDIA & THE ARAB QUARTER

ACCOMMODATION

Albert Court	11
Ali's Nest	4
Boon Wah Hotel	9
Broadway Hotel	5
Dickson Court	8
Fortuna Hotel	3
Kerbau Hotel	7
Little India Guest House	12
Mount Emily	6
Palace Hotel	1
Perak Lodge	10
Pin Guan Hotel	2

△ Hajjah Fatimah Mosque

Ⓜ MRT Station

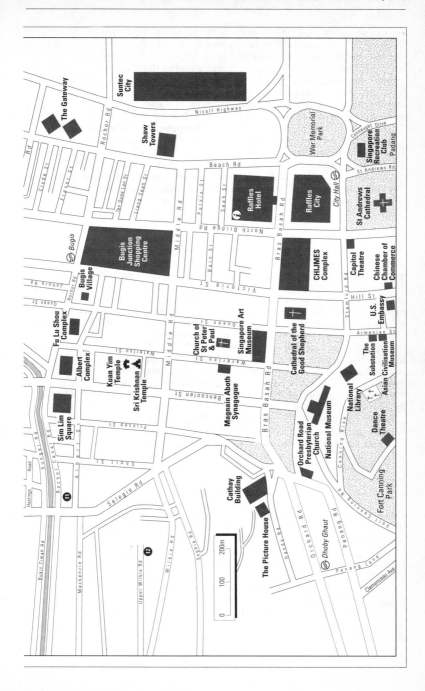

Street names hark back to this trade: side by side off the western reach of Serangoon Road are Buffalo Road and Kerbau (confusingly, "buffalo" in Malay) Road, along both of which cattle were kept in slaughter pens. Singapore's largest maternity hospital, nearby on Bukit Timah Road, is called Kandang Kerbau (Buffalo Pen) Hospital. Indians featured prominently in the development of Singapore, though not always out of choice: from 1825 onwards, convicts were transported from the subcontinent and by the 1840s there were over a thousand Indian prisoners labouring on buildings such as St Andrew's Cathedral and the istana.

The district's backbone is the north–south **Serangoon Road**, whose southern end is alive with shops, restaurants and fortune-tellers. To the east, stretching as far as Jalan Besar, is a tight knot of roads that's ripe for exploration, while parallel to Serangoon Road, **Race Course Road** boasts a clutch of fine restaurants and some temples. Little India is only a fifteen-minute walk from Bencoolen Street and Beach Road. From Orchard Road, take bus #65 or #111 and ask for Serangoon Road. Alternatively, take the MRT to Dhoby Ghaut, hop on bus #64, #65 or #111 and, again, get off at Serangoon Road.

Along Serangoon Road

Dating from 1822 and hence one of the island's oldest roadways, **Serangoon Road** is a kaleidoscopic whirl of Indian life, its shops selling everything from nostril studs and ankle bracelets to incense sticks and *kum kum* powder (used to make the red dot Hindus wear on their foreheads). Little stalls, set up in doorways and under "five foot ways", sell garlands, gaudy posters of Hindu gods and gurus, movie soundtracks and newspapers like *The Hindu* and *India Today*. Look out for parrot-wielding **fortune-tellers** – you tell the man your name, he passes your name on to his feathered partner, and the bird then picks out a card with your fortune on it.

At the southwestern end of Serangoon Road, the **Zhu Jiao Centre** combines many of Little India's ventures under one roof. Beyond its ground-floor food centre is a wet market that's not for the faint-hearted – traders push around trolleys piled high with goats' heads, while the halal butchers go to work in full view of the customers. Elsewhere, live crabs shuffle busily in buckets, their claws tied together, and there's a mouthwatering range of fruits on sale, including mangoes and whole branches of bananas. Upstairs, on the second floor, you'll find Indian fabrics, leatherware, footwear, watches and cheap electronic goods. On Sunday, the forecourt of the centre becomes an ad hoc social club for immigrant labourers working in Singapore, most of whom are actually Bangladeshi. Along the northern side of the Zhu Jiao Centre, Buffalo Road sports a cluster of provisions stores with sacks of spices and fresh coconut, ground using a primitive machine out on the road.

Little India's remaining shophouses are fast being touched up from the same pastel paintbox which has "restored" Chinatown to its present doll's house tweeness. Fortunately the colours work far better in an Indian context, and the results are really quite pleasing. In particular, check out Kerbau Road, one block north of Buffalo Road, whose shophouses have been meticulously renovated and now harbour a proliferation of Indian produce stores and a pleasant beer garden. (A right turn from Kerbau Road takes you onto **Race Course Road**, whose fine restaurants serve both north and south Indian food; several specialize in fish head curry.)

The little braid of roads across Serangoon Road from the Zhu Jiao Centre – Hastings Road, Campbell Lane and Dunlop Street – also merits investigation. Bounded by Serangoon to the west, Dunlop Street to the north and Campbell Lane to the south, the lovingly restored block of shophouses comprising the **Little India Conservation Area** was opened recently as a sort of Little India in microcosm: behind its cream walls and green shutters you'll find the Hastings Road Food Court (see p.571) and the Little India Arcade, where you can purchase textiles and tapestries, bangles, religious statuary, Indian tapes and CDs, and even traditional ayurvedic (herbal) medicines. Around Deepavali, the arcade's narrow ways are choked with locals hastening to buy decorations, garlands, traditional confectionery and fine clothes.

Dunlop Street's **Abdul Gaffoor Mosque** (at no. 41) is a little-known, crumbling beauty, bristling with small spires pointing up at the sky. Campbell Lane is a good place for buying Indian sandals, while walking along Clive Street towards Upper Dickson Road, you'll find on your right a batch of junk dealers patiently tinkering with ancient cookers, air-con units and TVs. Left along Upper Dickson Road – past an old barber's shop where a short back and sides is followed by a crunching head yank "to relieve tension" – are the *Madras New Woodlands Restaurant*, at nos. 12–14 and, around the corner, *Komala Villas* at 76 Serangoon Rd; two of Little India's best southern Indian restaurants (see p.578 for full details). Turn right when Upper Dickson Road deposits you back on Serangoon Road. Further up, opposite the turning to Veerasamy Road, the **Veeramakaliamman Temple** – dedicated to the ferocious Hindu goddess, Kali – features a fanciful *gopuram* that's flanked by majestic lions on the temple walls. Each year over Deepavali (p.68), a pulsating market takes place on the open land just above the temple.

You won't find **Pink Street** – one of the most incongruous and sordid spots in the whole of clean, shiny Singapore – on any city map. The entire length of the "street" (in fact it's merely an alley between the backs of Rowell and Desker roads) is punctuated by open doorways, inside which gaggles of bored-looking prostitutes sit knitting or watching TV, oblivious to the gawping crowds of local men who accumulate outside. Stalls along the alley sell distinctly un-Singaporean merchandise such as sex toys, blue videos and potency pills, while con-men work the "three cups and a ball" routine on unwary passers-by.

North of Desker Road

Beyond Desker Road, a five-minute walk north takes you to the edge of Little India, a diversion worth making to see three very different temples. Each year, on the day of the Thaipusam festival (January/February), the courtyard of the **Sri Srinivasa Perumal Temple**, at 397 Serangoon Rd, witnesses a gruesome melee of activity, as Hindu devotees don huge metal frames (*kavadis*) topped with peacock feathers, which are fastened to their flesh with hooks and prongs. The devotees then leave the temple, stopping only while a coconut is smashed at their feet for good luck, and parade all the way to the Chettiar Temple on Tank Road, off Orchard Road. Even if you miss the festival, it's worth a trip to see the five-tiered *gopuram* with its sculptures of the various manifestations of Lord Vishnu the Preserver. On the wall to the right of the front gate, a sculpted elephant, its leg caught in a crocodile's mouth, trumpets silently.

Just beyond the Sri Srinivasa temple complex, a small path leads northwest to Race Course Road, where the **Sakaya Muni Buddha Gaya Temple** (or the Temple of the Thousand Lights) is on the right at no. 366. It's a slightly kitsch temple that betrays a strong Thai influence – not surprising, since it was built entirely by a Thai monk, Vutthisasala. On the left of the temple as you enter is a huge replica of Buddha's footprint, inlaid with mother-of-pearl; beyond sits a huge Buddha ringed by the thousand electric lights from which the temple takes its alternative name; while 25 scenes from the Buddha's life decorate the pedestal on which he sits. It is possible to walk inside the Buddha, through a door in his back; inside is a smaller representation, this time of Buddha reclining. The left wall of the temple features a sort of wheel of fortune – spin it (for 30c) and take the numbered sheet of paper that corresponds to the number at which the wheel stops, to discover your fortune. Further along the left wall, a small donation entitles you to a shake of a tin full of numbered sticks, after which, again, you get a corresponding sheet of forecasts.

Double back onto Serangoon Road and a five-minute walk southeast along Petain Road leads to Jalan Besar, a route which takes in some immaculate examples of

Peranakan shophouses, their facades covered with elegant ceramic tiles reminiscent of Portuguese *azulejos*. There's more Peranakan architecture on display on Jalan Besar itself (turn right at the end of Petain Road), while further south a daily **flea market** takes place around Pitt Street, Weld Road, Kelantan Lane and Pasar Lane – second-hand tools, odd shoes and foreign currency are all laid out for sale on plastic sheets at the side of the road.

The Arab Quarter

Before the arrival of Raffles, the area of Singapore west of the Rochor River housed a Malay village known as Kampung Glam, after the Gelam tribe of sea gypsies who lived there. After signing a dubious treaty with the newly installed "Sultan" Hussein Mohammed Shah (see p.504), Raffles allotted the area to the sultan and designated the land around it as a Muslim settlement. Soon the zone was attracting Arab traders, as the road names in today's **Arab Quarter** – Baghdad Street, Muscat Street and Haji Lane – suggest. Even now, descendants of Sultan Hussein live in the grounds of the Istana Kampong Glam, a palace right in the centre of the district, bounded by Arab Street, Beach Road, Jalan Sultan and Rochor Canal Road. Just outside the quarter, Beach Road still maintains shops which betray its former proximity to the sea – ships' chandlers and fishing tackle specialists – and you should also take the time to walk southwest from Arab Street to see the two logic-defying office buildings that together comprise **The Gateway**. Designed by I.M. Pei, they rise magnificently into the air like vast razor blades and appear two-dimensional when viewed from certain angles. The Arab Quarter is no more than a ten-minute walk from Bencoolen Street. To get there from Orchard Road, take bus #7 to Victoria Street and get off when you spot the *Landmark Mercure Hotel* on your right; alternatively, head for Bugis MRT.

Arab Street and North Bridge Road

While Little India is memorable for its fragrances, it's the vibrant colours of the shops of **Arab Street** and its environs that stick in the memory. The street boasts the highest concentration of shops in the Arab Quarter; its pavements are an obstacle course of carpets, cloths, baskets and bags. Most of the shops have been renovated, though one or two (like *Shivlal & Sons* at no. 77, and *Uttamram & Co* at no. 73) still retain their original dark wood and glass cabinets, and wide wooden benches where the shopkeepers sit. Textile stores are most prominent, their walls, ceilings and doorways draped with cloths and batiks. Elsewhere you'll see leather, basketware, gold, gemstones and jewellery for sale, while the most impressive range of basketware and rattan work – fans, hats and walking sticks – is found at the intersection with Beach Road, in the *Rahmath Trading Corporation*, at nos. 22–26. It's easy to spend a couple of hours weaving in and out of the stores, but don't expect a quiet window-shopping session – the traders here are masters of the forced sale, and will have you loaded with sarongs, baskets and leather bags before you know it.

The quarter's most evocative patch is the stretch of **North Bridge Road** between Arab Street and Jalan Sultan. Here, the men sport long sarongs and Abe Lincoln beards, the women fantastically colourful shawls and robes, while the shops and restaurants are geared more towards locals than tourists: *Kazura Co*, at 755 North Bridge Rd, for instance, sells alcohol-free perfumes, while neighbouring stores stock rosaries, prayer mats, the *songkok* hats worn by Muslim males in mosques, and *miswak* sticks – twigs the width of a finger used by some locals to clean their teeth.

Several roads run off the western side of North Bridge Road, including Jalan Pisang (Banana Street), on which a street barber works under a tarpaulin. A walk up Jalan Kubor (Grave Street) and across Victoria Street takes you to an unkempt Muslim **cemetery** where, it is said, Malay royalty are buried. On Sundays, Victoria Street throngs with children in full Muslim garb on their way to study scripture at the Arabic school, **Madrasah Al Junied Al-Islamiah.**

Istana Kampong Glam and the Sultan Mosque

Squatting between Kandahar and Aliwal streets, the **Istana Kampong Glam** was built as the royal palace of Sultan Ali Iskandar Shah, son of Sultan Hussein who negotiated with Raffles to hand over Singapore to the British; the sultan's descendants live here to this day, and continue to share an annual government allowance. Despite its royal provenance, the istana is a modest, colonial-style building, run-down and dingy, its grounds dotted with huts. Outside there's a **stone mason's** shop on the corner of Baghdad Street and Sultan Gate, which chips out the lions that stand outside Chinese temples. Another stone mason's, nearby at 24 Baghdad St, specializes in Muslim graves – uniformly shaped stones that look remarkably like chess pawns.

A few steps further on, Baghdad Street crosses pedestrianized Bussorah Street, from where you get the best initial views of the golden domes of the **Sultan Mosque** or Masjid Sultan (daily 9am–1pm), the beating heart of the Muslim faith in Singapore. An earlier mosque stood on this site, finished in 1825 and constructed with the help of a $3000 donation from the East India Company. The present building was completed a century later, according to a design by colonial architects Swan and MacLaren: if you look carefully at the glistening necks of the domes, you can see that the effect is created by the bases of thousands of ordinary glass bottles, an incongruity which sets the tone for the rest of the building. Steps at the top of Bussorah Street lead into a wide lobby, where a digital display lists current prayer times. Beyond, though out of bounds to non-Muslims, is the main prayer hall, a large, bare chamber that's fronted by two more digital clocks enabling the faithful to time their prayers to the exact second. An exhaustive set of rules applies to visitors wishing to enter the lobby: shoes must be taken off and shoulders and legs covered; no video cameras are allowed inside the mosque and entry is not permitted during the Friday mass congregation (11.30am–2.30pm). The best time to come is in the Muslim fasting month of Ramadan – when the faithful can only eat after dusk, and Muskat and Kandahar streets are awash with stalls selling *biryiani*, barbecued chicken and cakes.

It's only a five-minute walk on to the **Hajjah Fatimah Mosque** on Beach Road, where a collection of photographs in the entrance porch show the mosque through the years following its construction in 1846 – first surrounded by shophouses, then by open land, and finally by huge housing projects. Across from the mosque, the **Golden Mile Complex** at 5001 Beach Rd attracts so many Thai nationals that locals refer to it as "Thai Village". Numerous bus firms selling tickets to Thailand operate out of here, while inside, the shops sell Thai foodstuffs, cafés sell Singha beer and Mekong whisky, and authentic restaurants serve up old favourites. On a Sunday, Thais come down here in hordes to meet up with their compatriots, listen to Thai pop music, and have a few drinks.

Northern Singapore

While land reclamation has radically altered the east coast and industrialization the west, the **northern** expanses of the island up to the Straits of Johor still retain pockets of the **rainforest** and mangrove swamp which blanketed Singapore on Raffles' arrival in 1819. These are interspersed today with sprawling **new towns** like Toa Payoh, maze-like Bishan and Ang Mo Kio, built in the 1970s. The name of the last, meaning "red-haired devil's bridge" refers to the nineteenth-century British surveyor, John Turnbull Thomson, under whose supervision the transport network of Singapore began to penetrate the interior of the island. Man-eating tigers roamed these parts well into this century, and it was here that Allied forces confronted the invading Japanese army in 1942, a period of Singaporean history movingly recalled by the **Kranji War Memorial** on Woodlands Road. What remains of Singapore's agricultural past still clings tenaciously to the far northern sweep of the island: you'll see prawn and poultry farms, orchards and vegetable gardens when travelling in these parts.

Dominating the central northern region are two nature reserves, divided by the Bukit Timah Expressway, the main road route to Malaysia. West of the expressway is **Bukit Timah Nature Reserve**, an accessible slice of primary rainforest, while to the east, the four reservoirs of the Central Catchment Area are one of Singapore's main sources of water. North of here, the zone's principal tourist attraction is the excellent **Singapore Zoological Gardens**, sited on a finger of land pointing into the Seletar Reservoir. To the east are two of Singapore's most eye-catching Buddhist temples – **Siong Lim Temple** and the **Kong Meng San Phor Kark See** temple complex – as well as tiny Tai Gin Road, which houses both the occasional residence of Chinese nationalist leader Dr Sun Yat Sen and Singapore's Burmese temple.

Exploring the north is a matter of pinpointing the particular sight you want to see and heading straight for it; the bus trip to the zoo, for instance, takes around 45 minutes. Travel between all these places is decidedly tricky unless you are driving or in a cab, so don't expect to take in everything in a day. However, Siong Lim Temple, Sun Yat Sen Villa and the Burmese Temple all nestle around the outskirts of Toa Payoh new town and could be incorporated into a single expedition; as could the zoo, Mandai Orchid Gardens and the Kranji cemetery and memorial. The Kong Meng San Phor Kark See temple complex really requires a separate journey.

Bukit Timah

Bukit Timah Road shoots northwest from the junction of Selegie and Serangoon roads, arriving 8km later at the faceless town of **BUKIT TIMAH**, which boasts Singapore's only racecourse, the **Singapore Turf Club**. Since legal gambling in Singapore outside the course is restricted to the random lottery system, the annual racing calendar here is understandably popular, typically featuring eight meetings, spaced throughout the year and held over two consecutive weekends. Call ☎4693611 for race-meeting details – the most prestigious events include the Singapore Gold Cup in September, the Lion City Cup in January, and the Singapore Derby in October. When there's no racing in Singapore, a giant video screen links Bukit Timah to various courses across the causeway in Malaysia. There's a fairly strict dress code – sandals, jeans, shorts and T-shirts are out – and foreign visitors have to take their passports with them. The day's fixtures begin after lunch, and tickets cost $5.15 or $10.30 for public stands, and $20.60 for the air-conditioned members' enclosure. **Tours** comprising an afternoon's racing viewed from the members' enclosure can be booked in advance (see p.593) but you'd do far better to just turn up, eat at the course's decent food centre and soak up the atmosphere in the stands. The bus details are the same as for the Bukit Timah Nature Reserve – see below.

Bukit Timah Nature Reserve

Bukit Timah Road continues west past Singapore's last remaining pocket of primary rainforest, which now comprises **Bukit Timah Nature Reserve** (daily 7am–7pm; free). Visiting this area of Singapore in the mid-eighteenth century, natural historian Alfred Russel Wallace reported seeing "tiger pits, carefully covered with sticks and leaves and so well concealed, that in several cases I had a narrow escape from falling into them. . . . Formerly a sharp stake was stuck erect in the bottom," he continued, "but after an unfortunate traveller had been killed by falling into one, its use was forbidden." Today the 81-hectare reserve, established in 1883 by Nathaniel Cantley, superintendent of the Botanic Gardens, yields no such hazards and provides a refuge for the dwindling numbers of species still extant in Singapore – only 25 types of mammal now inhabit the island. Creatures you're most likely to see in Bukit Timah are long-tailed macaques, butterflies, insects, and birds like the dark-necked tailorbird, which builds its nest by sewing together leaves. Scorpions, snakes, flying lemurs and pangolins (anteaters, whose name is derived from the Malay word *peng-goling*, meaning "roller", a reference to the animal's habit of rolling into a ball when threatened) can be found here too.

Recent alterations have vastly improved the reserve, which now has an informative **visitor centre** (daily 8.30am–6pm) full of displays, specimens and photos relating to the wildlife beyond. Four main paths from the centre twist and turn through the forest around and to the top of **Bukit Timah Hill**, which – at a paltry 162.5m – is actually Singapore's largest hill. The paths are all well signposted, colour-coded and dotted with rest and shelter points, and they're clearly mapped on the free leaflet handed out to all visitors. You'd do best to visit in the early morning (when it's cooler) and midweek (when there are fewer visitors).

Dramatic **Hindhede Quarry** (five minutes' walk up the slope to the left of the visitor centre) is a fine place to head for once you've explored the forest – its deep green waters are ideal for a cooling swim. Across Bukit Timah Road from the reserve is another forested hill, **Bukit Batok**, where British and Australian POWs were forced to erect a fifteen-metre-high wooden shrine, the Syonan Tyureito, for their Japanese captors. Only the steps at its base now remain. Legend has it that the shrine itself was destroyed by termites which the prisoners secretly introduced to the structure. Gone, too, is the wooden cross erected by the POWs to honour their dead.

Bus #171 passes down Somerset and Scotts roads en route to Bukit Timah Reserve, while the #181 can be picked up on North Bridge Road, South Bridge Road or New Bridge Road; a third option is to take the #170 from the Ban San Terminal on Queen Street. Take any of these buses to get to Bukit Batok, but stay on until you see Old Jurong Road on your left. The hill is located at the end of Lorong Sesuai, the next turning left, the road itself laid by the same prisoners who constructed the shrine.

Tai Gin Road: the Sun Yat Sen Villa and Burmese Temple

Between Jalan Toa Payoh to the north and Balestier Road to the south is the **Sun Yat Sen Villa** (Mon–Fri 9am–4pm, Sat 9am–3pm; free), on tiny Tai Gin Road. Built to house the mistress of a wealthy Chinese businessman, this attractive bungalow changed hands in 1905, when one Teo Eng Hock bought it for his mother. Chinese nationalist leader Dr Sun Yat Sen paid his first of eight visits to Singapore the following year, and was invited by Teo to stay at Tai Gin Road, where he quickly established a Singapore branch of the *Tong Meng Hui* – a society dedicated to replacing the Manchu dynasty in China with a modern republic. After serving as a communications camp for the Japanese during World War II, the villa fell into disrepair until 1966, when it was opened to the public. Sadly, the collection of photographs inside is fairly dull unless you are familiar with that period of Chinese history; of more interest is the second-floor gallery with photos of Singapore during World War II, and an accompanying collection of combs, keys, pipes, glasses and other personal effects of victims of the Japanese occupation.

Next door is the **Sasanaramsi Burmese Buddhist Temple** (daily 6am–10pm), reconstructed in just two years having being moved from its previous site at Kinta Road because of redevelopment. Decorated by craftsmen from Burma, the temple's ground floor is dominated by a large, white marble statue of the Buddha brought over from Burma in 1932; upstairs is another Buddha statue, this time standing, and ringed by blue sky painted on the wall behind. Tiny Buddha images are presently being "bought" by worshippers at $1000 a throw; when they're all sold they'll be mounted on the painted sky.

Bus #139 from Selegie Road comes out this way. You'll see a BP service station on the right of Balestier Road after about ten minutes – get off at the next stop, where Tai Gin Road is across the road and down a short footpath.

The Siong Lim and Phor Kark See temples

Two of Singapore's largest Chinese temples are situated in the island's central region, east of the Central Catchment Area. Both are rather isolated, but have plenty to interest temple enthusiasts, and they buzz with activity at festival times.

The name of the popular **Siong Lim Temple**, at 184e Jalan Toa Payoh (bus #8 from outside Toa Payoh MRT), means "Twin Groves of the Lotus Mountain" – a reference to the Buddha's birth in a grove of trees and his death under a Bodhi tree. The Chinese abbot, Sek Hean Wei, established the temple at the turn of the century when, passing through Singapore on his way home after a pilgrimage to Sri Lanka, he was waylaid by wealthy Hokkien merchant and philanthropist, Low Kim Pong, who supplied both land and finances for the venture. Several renovations haven't robbed the temple of its grandeur, though the urban development of Toa Payoh's outskirts around it hardly enhances its appearance. Set behind a rock garden that combines a water cascade, ponds, streams and bridges, the temple is guarded by statues of the **Four Kings of Heaven**, each posted to keep evil out of the temple, symbolized by the demons on which they are treading. The highly regarded collection of carved and sculpted gods inside the temple's several halls includes a **Laughing Buddha**, believed to grant good luck if you rub his stomach, a shrine to Kuan Yin, Goddess of Mercy (in the rear hall), and a number of Thai-style Buddha figures.

The largest temple complex in Singapore – and one of the largest in southeast Asia – lies north of MacRitchie Reservoir, right in the middle of the island. **Phor Kark See Temple** (known in full as the Kong Meng San Phor Kark See Temple Complex), at 88 Bright Hill Drive, spreads over nineteen acres and combines temples, pagodas, pavilions, a Buddhist library and a vast crematorium to such impressive effect that it has been used several times as a backdrop to Chinese kung fu movies. More modern than Siong Lim, Phor Kark See boasts none of the faded charm of Singapore's older temples, but relies instead on its sheer magnitude and exuberant decor for effect. Multi-tiered roofs bristle with ceramic dragons, phoenixes, birds and human figures, while around the complex are statues of various deities, including a nine-metre-high marble statue of Kuan Yin, Goddess of Mercy. A soaring pagoda capped by a golden *chedi* (a reliquary tower) renders the complex even more striking. Even the **crematorium** – conveniently placed for the nearby Bright Hill Evergreen Home for the elderly – doesn't do things by half. Housed below a Thai-style facade of elaborately carved, gilt wood, it's huge and can cope with five ceremonies at one time. Below the crematorium is a pair of ponds, where thousands of turtles sunbathe precariously on wooden planks that slant into the water. A nearby sign prohibits worshippers from letting new turtles into the ponds, a practice supposed to bring good luck. Old ladies beside the viewing gallery sell bunches of vegetables, which purchasers then throw to the lucky turtles.

Take bus #130 up Victoria Street to reach the complex, alighting at the far end of Sin Ming Drive.

Upper Serangoon Road: Bidadari Cemetery

One of Singapore's more offbeat attractions, **Bidadari Cemetery**, lies some 10km northeast of the city, on Upper Serangoon Road. It's a Christian graveyard and the majority of its aged gravestones are in typical Western style, but there are Chinese graves here, too, their semicircular design affording a kneeling place to pray for the well-being of one's ancestors. Buried somewhere in the area is A.P. Williams, a British sailor upon whose life Joseph Conrad based his novel, *Lord Jim*. In his travelogue *In Search of Conrad*, Gavin Young describes how he tracked down Williams' burial plot in the depths of Singapore's public records offices – but seeking out the number he quotes (2559) yields no sign of the grave. Many species of birds flourish in the long grass of the grounds, making this a good destination for ornithologists – indeed, the Nature Society of Singapore periodically visits the cemetery. A word of warning, though: don't go wading into tall grass unless you are wearing ankle-high boots, as snakes also inhabit the cemetery.

Bus #97 from Stamford, Selegie and Serangoon roads, and #106 from Orchard, Selegie and Serangoon roads both pass by the cemetery. Bus drivers aren't all familiar with the location of Bidadari, so tell them you want the more famous Youngberg Hospital, which is just across the road from the cemetery. It takes around fifteen minutes to travel from Selegie Road to Bidadari.

Singapore Zoological Gardens and Night Safari

The **Singapore Zoological Gardens** (daily 8.30am–6pm; $10.30) on Mandai Lake Road, are spread over a promontory jutting into peaceful Seletar Reservoir. The gardens attract over one million visitors a year – a fact perhaps explained by their status as one of the world's few open zoos, where moats are preferred to cages. The zoo manages to approximate the natural habitats of the animals it holds, and though leopards, pumas and jaguars still have to be kept behind bars, this is a thoughtful, humane place, described as "one of the really beautiful zoos" by the conservationist Sir Peter Scott.

There are over two thousand animals here, representing more than 240 species, so it's best to allow a whole day for your visit. A **tram** ($2) circles the grounds on a one-way circuit, but as it won't always be going your way, be prepared for a lot of footwork. Highlights include the komodo dragons, the polar bears (which you view underwater from a gallery) and the primate kingdom; also worth checking out is the **special loan enclosure**, which has recently played host to a giant panda, an Indian white tiger and a golden monkey. Two **animal shows** are featured daily – a primate and reptile show (10.30am & 2.30pm) and an elephant and sea lion show (11.30am & 3.30pm), the sea lions skidding, swimming and jumping to the theme from *Hawaii 5 'O'*. Kids tend to get most out of these shows, and **Children's World** offers them the chance to ride a camel, hold young chicks and see a milking demonstration; at 9am and 4pm daily they can even share a meal with an **orang-utan** (see p.570). The recent opening of the **Night Safari** (daily 7.30pm–midnight; $15.45) has added a further forty hectares to the grounds of the zoo. Here, over a hundred species of animals – among them elephants, rhinos, giraffes, leopards, hyenas, otters, and incredibly cute fishing cats – play out their nocturnal routines under a forest of standard lamps. Only five of the safari's eight zones are walkable – to see the rest you'll need to take a fifty-minute Jurassic Park-style tram ride ($3), and tolerate the intrusive chattering of its taped guide. A meal at one of two restaurants outside the entrance will pass the time between the zoo's closing and the safari's opening.

Buy the $1 *Guide to S'pore Zoo* on arrival: besides riding and feeding times and a helpful map, the booklet suggests itineraries which take in all the major shows and attractions. At the other end of your trip, drop by the **gift shop** next to the exit, which stocks cuddly toys and rather less tempting bags of "zoo poo" compost. Several food and drink kiosks are dotted around the zoo, or you can head for the reasonable *Makan Terrace*, bang in the centre of the grounds, where there are one or two hawker stalls.

To get to the zoo, take **bus** #171 from either Stamford Road or Orchard Boulevard to Mandai Road, then transfer to #138. Alternatively, take the MRT to Ang Mo Kio and connect with the #138.

Mandai Orchid Gardens

It's only a ten-minute walk from the zoo down Mandai Lake Road to the **Mandai Orchid Gardens** (daily 8.30am–5.30pm; $2), or you can take the #138 bus from the zoo, which stops right outside. Orchids are big business in Singapore: in 1991 alone, over $20 million of cut orchid flowers were exported from 56 orchid farms across the state. Here, four hectares of flowers are cultivated on a gentle slope, tended by old ladies in wide-brimmed hats. Unless you are a keen horticulturist, the place will be of only limited interest since little effort has been taken to make it instructive. Still, if you've been to the zoo, the gardens make a colourful detour on the way home, and the price of a gift box of orchids (under $70) compares favourably with more central flower shops.

Woodlands, Kranji War Cemetery and the Sungei Buloh Nature Park

Five kilometres north of the zoo is the bustling town of **WOODLANDS**, from where the **causeway** spanning the Strait of Johor links Singapore to Johor Bahru in Malaysia. At peak hours (6.30–9.30am & 5.30–7.30pm) and at weekends, the roads leading to the causeway seethe with cars and trucks – all full of petrol, after a law passed in the early 1990s banned Singaporeans from driving out of the country on an empty tank. Previously, people crossed into Malaysia, filled up with cut-price fuel and then headed home; now, signs line the roads approaching the causeway requesting that "Singapore cars please top up to 3/4 tank" – or risk a $500 fine.

Bus #170 from Ban San Terminal on Queen Street heads towards Woodlands on its way to JB, passing the **Kranji War Cemetery and Memorial** on Woodlands Road, where only the sound of birds and insects breaks the silence in the immaculate grounds. This is the resting place of the many Allied troops who died in the defence of Singapore; as you enter, row upon row of graves slope up the landscaped hill in front of you, some identified only as "known unto God". The graves are bare: placing flowers is banned because still water encourages mosquitoes to breed. A simple stone cross stands over the cemetery and above is the **memorial**, around which are recorded the names of more than twenty thousand soldiers (from Britain, Canada, Sri Lanka, India, Malaysia, the Netherlands, New Zealand and Singapore) who died in this region during World War II. Two unassuming **tombs** stand on the wide lawns below the cemetery, belonging to Yusof Bin Ishak and Dr Benjamin Henry Sheares, independent Singapore's first two presidents. As well as the #170, bus #181 from New Bridge Road and #182 from Stamford Road or Orchard Boulevard pass the cemetery; the journey takes at least 45 minutes.

Singapore's newest wildlife sanctuary, **Sungei Buloh Nature Park** (daily 7am–7pm; $1; ☎6690377) lies some 4–5km northwest of Kranji Cemetery, on the north coast. Beyond its visitor centre, café and video theatre (shows daily 9am, 11am, 1pm & 3pm) stretch 87 hectares of mangrove, mud flats, orchards and grassland hosting creatures such as kingfishers and mudskippers, herons and sea eagles. Visit between September and March, and you're likely to catch sight of migratory birds from around Asia roosting and feeding. Take the MRT to either Woodlands or Kranji station, then transfer to bus #925, which stops at Kranji car park from Monday to Friday, and at the park's entrance on Saturday and Sunday.

Eastern Singapore

Thirty years ago, **eastern Singapore** was largely rural, dotted with Malay kampung villages which perched on stilts over the shoreline, harbouring the odd weekend retreat owned by Europeans or monied locals. Massive **land reclamation** and development programmes have altered the region beyond recognition, wiping out all traces of the kampungs and throwing up huge housing projects in their place. Today, former seafront suburbs like Bedok are separated from the Straits of Singapore by a broad crescent of man-made land, much of which constitutes the **East Coast Park**, whose five kilometres incorporate leisure and watersports facilities, imported sand beaches and seafood restaurants. Yet despite the massive upheavals that have ruptured the communities of the east coast, parts of it, including the suburbs of **Geylang** and **Katong**, have managed to retain a strong Malay identity.

Dominating the eastern tip of the island is Changi Airport and, beyond that, **Changi Village**, in whose prison the Japanese interned Allied troops and civilians during World War II. From Changi Point, it's possible to take a boat to **Pulau Ubin**, a small island with echoes of pre-development Singapore. If your schedule allows for only one trip out of downtown Singapore, Changi and its environs should definitely be on your shortlist.

Geylang and Katong

Malay culture has held sway in and around the adjoining suburbs of **GEYLANG** and **KATONG** since the mid-nineteenth century, when Malays and Indonesians first arrived to work in the local *copra* (coconut husk) processing factory and later on its *serai*, or lemon grass, farms. Many of its shophouses, restaurants and food centres are Malay-influenced, less so the thriving trade in prostitution that carries on here, unchecked by the local authorities. **Geylang Road** itself runs east from the Kallang River and off its main stem shoot 42 lorongs, or lanes, down which are clusters of brothels, recognizable by their exterior fairy lights. At its far eastern end, Geylang Road meets **Joo Chiat Road**, which – after the restrictions of downtown Singapore – has a refreshingly laid-back and shambolic air. In the **Joo Chiat Complex**, at the northern end of the road, textile merchants drape their wares on any available floor and wall space, transforming the drab interior. More market than shopping centre, it's a prime destination for anyone interested in buying cheap silk, batik, rugs or muslin.

Before striking off down Joo Chiat Road, cross Changi Road to the north, where – east of Geylang Serai – a hawker centre and wet market provide more Malay atmosphere, from the smell of clove cigarettes to the line of sarong sellers beyond the food stalls. The contrast between this authentic slice of life, and the **Malay Village** (daily 10am–10pm; $10 for its three attractions, otherwise free) on the other side of Geylang Serai, is huge. Opened in 1990, and conceived as a celebration of the cuisine, music, dance, arts and crafts of the Malay people, the village conspicuously failed either to woo tourists or to rent out its replica wooden-kampung-style shops to locals, and seemed to be dying a slow death until a Hong Kong-based company took it over. Sadly, the three new tourist lures unveiled at the recent relaunch pack very little punch: the **Lagenda Fantasi**, an audio-visual presentation of Islamic and Malay legends such as Aladdin, Ali Baba and Nile Sang Utama, is geared squarely at kids; the **Cultural Museum** features a humdrum array of household instruments, cloths, kites and *krises*, and a mock-up of a Malay wedding scene; and the dismal **Kampung Days** exhibition reproduces a traditional Malay kampung homestead, complete with fishing and rice-pounding scenes, a *wayang kulit* stage, an open-air cinema, and the seemingly obligatory wedding scene. If you give these attractions a miss, you're left with the village's 66 **shops**, selling batik, kites, spinning tops, bird cages and textiles, and the evening **food court** with free cultural performances on Saturday and Sunday nights. For details of the village's two restaurants, the halal Chinese *Floating Seafood* restaurant and the open-air *Temenggong* restaurant, see p.579.

As you walk south down Joo Chiat Road you'll have to negotiate piles of merchandise that spill out of shophouses and onto the pavement. In particular, there's cane and wood furniture in the *Phoon Fang Cheong* shop at no. 175, while the store at no. 86 specializes in Chinese religious paraphernalia. Of the buildings, none are as magnificent as the immaculate **Peranakan shophouses** on Koon Seng Road (on your left about halfway down Joo Chiat Road), where painstaking work has restored their multicoloured facades, eaves and mouldings.

To get to Joo Chiat Road, take the MRT to Paya Lebar, from where a short walk left out of the station, across Sims Avenue and left again onto Geylang Road, brings you to the northern end of the road and the Joo Chiat Complex. Alternatively, bus #16 from Orchard and Bras Basah roads deposits you right in the middle of Joo Chiat Road.

Changi

Bus #2 from outside the *Victoria Hotel* on Victoria Street, or from Tanah Merah MRT, drops you right outside **Changi Prison**, the infamous site of a World War II POW camp in which Allied prisoners were subjected to the harshest of treatment by their Japanese jailers. The prison itself is still in use (drug offenders are periodically executed here), but on its north side, through the outer gates, is the hugely moving prison **museum** (Mon–Sat 9.30am–4.30pm, Sun 5.30pm religious service only; free), where sketches and photographs plot the Japanese invasion of Singapore and the fate of the soldiers and civilians subsequently incarcerated here and in nearby camps. Predominant are photos by George Aspinall, which record the appalling living conditions and illnesses suffered by POWs in Malaya and Thailand during the occupation. Aspinall, then a young Australian trooper, took his photographs using a folding Kodak 2 camera, later developing them with a stock of processing materials which he found while working on a labour gang in Singapore's docks. Novelist James Clavell was a young British artillery officer in Singapore at the time of the Japanese invasion; his *King Rat* evokes the "obscene forbidding prison" at Changi, describing the cells of the prison camp, where ". . . the stench was nauseating. Stench from rotting bodies. Stench from a generation of confined human bodies." Elsewhere in the museum, sketches drawn by W.R.M. Haxworth of prisoners playing bridge amongst other things betray a dry sense of humour and some stiff upper lips in the face of adversity.

Beyond the museum is a replica of a simple wooden chapel, typical of those erected in Singapore's wartime prisons; its brass cross was crafted from spent ammunition casings, while the north wall carries poignant messages, penned by former POWs and relatives.

On a lighter note, among the war-related books stocked in the souvenir shop is *The Happiness Box*, the first copy of which was written, illustrated and bound by POWs in Changi in 1942 as a Christmas present for children in the prison. The Japanese became suspicious of the POWs' motives when they noticed one of the book's central characters was called Winston, but it was buried in the prison grounds before the Japanese could confiscate it.

Changi Village

Journey's end for bus #2 is at the terminal at **CHANGI VILLAGE**, ten minutes further on from the prison. There's little to bring you out here, save to catch a boat from **Changi Point**, behind the bus terminal, for Pulau Ubin (see below), or to the coast of Johor in Malaysia (see "Leaving Singapore" on p.506). The left-hand jetty is for Ubin, the right-hand one for bumboats to Johor.

A stroll over the footbridge to the right of the two jetties takes you to **Changi Beach**, the execution site of many thousands of Singaporean civilians by Japanese soldiers in World War II. As a beach it wins few prizes, its most pleasant aspect being the view. To your left as you look out to sea is Pulau Ubin, slightly to the right is the island of Tekong (a military zone), behind which you can see a hill on mainland Malaysia. In the water you'll see *kelongs* (large fish traps), and boats galore, from bumboats to supertankers. Changi Village Road, the village's main drag, has a smattering of good restaurants, or you could try the hawker centre near the bus terminal.

Pulau Ubin

Pulau Ubin, 2km offshore, gives visitors a pretty good idea of what Singapore would have been like fifty years ago. A lazy backwater tucked into the Straits of Johor, it's a great place to head for when you get tired of shops, highrises and traffic, and it's almost worth coming for the boat trip alone, made in an old oil-stained bumboat which chugs noisily across Serangoon Harbour, belching fumes all the way. Boats depart from Changi Point throughout the day from 6am onwards, leaving whenever a boat is full. The last boat back to Changi leaves as late as 10pm depending on demand, but plan to be at the jetty by 8.30pm at the latest, just in case. The trip takes ten minutes and costs $1 each way. The boats dock at a rickety old pier in **Ubin Village**, where Malay stilt houses teeter over the sludgy, mangrove beach. The main road is lined with scores of battered old mopeds, locals sit around watching the day take its course, and chickens run free in the dirt.

The best, and most enjoyable, way to explore the dirt tracks of Ubin is by **mountain bike**. At *Universal Adventure* on the left-hand side of the road leading west from the jetty, you'll pay $5–15 for a day's rental, depending on the bike and the season (it's most expensive during school holidays). You'll be given a baffling map of the island's labyrinthine network of tracks, though it's more fun to strike off and see where you end up – Ubin is only a small island (just 7km by 2km) so you won't get lost.

Ride through the village until you come to a basketball court, where a right turn takes you past raised kampung houses and rubber trees to the eastern side of the island. Turning left instead takes you to the centre of the island. After about five minutes you'll come to a deep, impressive quarry, from which granite was taken to build the causeway linking Singapore to Malaysia (hence the name "Ubin", which is Malay for granite). Further north along this track is a rather incongruous **Thai Buddhist Temple**, complete with portraits of the King and Queen of Thailand, and a bookcase full of Thai books. Pictures telling the story of the life of Buddha ring the inner walls of the temple, along with images of various Buddhist hells – most disturbing of which is that of demons pouring molten liquid down the mouths of "those who always drink liquor". If you follow the left track out of Ubin Village for twenty or thirty minutes, you'll come to a steep slope: a right turn at the top takes you straight to the temple, just beyond which is another quarry, where you can take a swim and cool off.

Ignoring the right turn to the temple at the top of the steep slope and continuing straight ahead takes you towards the island's best restaurant, the *Ubin Restaurant*; it's a bit tricky to find, though – you'll have to look out for a taxi taking Singaporean diners there, to discover which track to turn down.

Western Singapore

Since the government's industrialization programme began in the late 1960s, far **western Singapore** has developed into the manufacturing heart of the state, and today thousands of companies occupy units within the towns of Jurong and Tuas. Manufacturing has proven the backbone of Singapore's economic success – the state presently produces more than half the world's hard disk drives for example. Despite this saturation, much of the western region – crafted from former swampland and wasteland – remains remarkably verdant, and perhaps surprisingly, given the industrial surroundings, several major tourist attractions are located here, including **Haw Par**

Villa, as garish a theme park as you'll ever set eyes on. But the pick of the bunch is fascinating **Jurong BirdPark**, closely followed by the **Tang Dynasty City**, where huge investment has resulted in a faithful reproduction of a traditional Chinese city. Slightly further east, the **Singapore Science Centre** is packed with imaginative and informative exhibitions, and is not to be missed if you've got kids to entertain.

All of these places are easily reached from the city centre, using either buses or the MRT; specific details are given where appropriate.

Telok Blangah, the World Trade Centre and Mount Faber.

A twenty-minute walk west of Chinatown is the area known as **Telok Blangah** in which stands Singapore's **World Trade Centre**, itself a splendid shopping centre-cum-marine terminal, where boats depart Singapore for Indonesia's Riau Archipelago. Lots of buses come this way: #97 and #166 travel down Bencoolen Street, #65 continues on from Bencoolen Street to Orchard Boulevard; from Scotts and Orchard roads, take bus #143. You'll know when to get off, because you'll see cable cars rocking across the skyline in front of you, on their way to and from Mount Faber.

Before catching one of these cable cars, either to Sentosa (see p.566), or up Mount Faber (see below), you might spare an hour to check out the **Singapore Maritime Showcase** (Tues–Fri 10.30am–6.30pm, Sat & Sun 10.30am–8.30pm; $4) on the WTC's Harbour Promenade – an unfocused collection of video games, Lego models and touch-sensitive TVs hung loosely around the theme of Singapore's tradition as a port and trading post. Its highlight, the lame "Maritime Odyssey" ride, which whisks you in an outsized cargo box past models depicting Singapore's seafaring history, is a pale shadow of even the Clarke Quay Adventure (p.533). The only other thing to do here is to take a walk around the **Guinness World of Records Exhibition** at 02-70 World Trade Centre, 1 Maritime Square (daily 9.30am–7.30pm; $5), a familiar trawl through the world's tallest, shortest, fattest and oldest people.

Once called Telok Blangah, **Mount Faber** – 600m north of the WTC – was renamed in 1845 after Government Engineer Captain Charles Edward Faber; the top of the "mount" (hillock would be a better word) commands fine views of Keppel Harbour and, to the northeast, central Singapore – views which are even more impressive at night, when the city is lit up. It's a long, steep walk from Telok Blangah Road up to the top of Mount Faber – its better to take the **cable car** from the World Trade Centre complex (daily 8.30am–9pm; $5.50 return). An accident in 1983, when a ship's mast clipped the cables on which the cars are suspended, cost seven passengers their lives, but today laser eyes ensure history won't repeat itself. As you'd expect, there's a correspondingly strong souvenir shop presence, though you can escape this by moving away from the area immediately around the cable car station and up into the park.

In the early days of colonial rule, Temenggong Abdul Rahman played prime minister to Sultan Hussein Shah's president, and his signature graced the treaty authorizing the East India Company to operate out of Singapore. All that's left of his settlement on the southern slopes of Mount Faber is its pillared mosque – the **State of Johor Mosque** – and, behind that, a small Malay cemetery and a portion of the brickwork that once housed the *temenggong*'s baths. The mosque lies five minutes' walk east of the World Trade Centre, and is passed by all WTC-bound buses.

Haw Par Villa

As an entertaining exercise in bad taste, **Haw Par Villa** has few equals. Located 7km from downtown, at 262 Pasir Panjang Road (daily 9am–6pm; $16.50), it describes itself as an "aesthetically arresting . . . park which promises you the unfolding of Chinese legends and mythologies", for which read a gaudy parade of rides, shows, and over a thousand grotesque statues. Previously known as Tiger Balm Gardens, the park now takes its name from its original owners, the Aw brothers, Boon Haw and Boon Par, who made a fortune early this century selling Tiger Balm – a cure-all unction created by their father. When the British government introduced licensing requirements for the possession of large animals, the private zoo which the brothers maintained on their estate here was closed down and replaced by statues.

The admission price is on the steep side, but you could easily spend the best part of a day here if you're determined to enjoy yourself. The park features a couple of **rides**: the rather tame "Wrath of the Water Gods Flume Ride" and the better "Tales of China" boat ride through a dragon's belly, in which a series of splendidly gory statues show you what happens to errant souls who end up in one of the ten courts of hell. But it's the hundreds of **statues** crammed into the park's grounds for which the park is known, and there are also various theatre and film shows to take in, retelling classic Chinese tales. Of these, the *Four Seasons Theatre* is the most fun, though if you attend a show here, be prepared to have to play a role yourself. For up-to-the-minute details of show times, ask at the ticket counter on arrival. Meals and snacks can be had at the *Artisan's Eating House* or the more upmarket *Watergarden's Restaurant*.

To get to Haw Par Villa, take the MRT to Buona Vista and change on to a #200 bus to Pasir Panjang Road. Bus #51 trundles down North Bridge Road on its way to the park, while the #143 can be picked up on Scotts, Orchard and New Bridge roads.

Holland Village

A couple of kilometres north of Haw Par Villa, **Holland Village** was previously home to some of the British soldiers based in Singapore and has now developed into an expat stronghold, with a whole row of Western restaurants and shops. The **Holland Road Shopping Centre** at 211 Holland Ave is the place to head for if you want to buy Asian art, crafts or textiles: there are shops on two levels where you can buy anything from an Indian pram to a Chinese opium pipe, while outside, cobblers, key-cutters and newsagents set up stall. The small road alongside the shopping centre is called Lorong Liput, and off it shoots Lorong Mambong, home to a thriving restaurant scene and two excellent **craft shops** – *Sin Seng Huat* at no. 16 and *Sin Huat Hing* at no. 6 – both specializing in ceramic elephants, dragon pots, porcelain, rattan and bamboo products. **Pasar Holland**, opposite the shops, is a small, tumbledown market selling fruit, flowers, fish and meat, as well as housing a handful of hawker stalls.

From Buona Vista MRT, walk up Commonwealth Avenue and then turn left onto Holland Avenue. Alternatively, buses #7 and #105 from Orchard Boulevard both pass the top of Holland Avenue – ring the bell when you see the Esso garage.

Around Jurong Lake and beyond

Several tourist destinations are dotted around the environs of tranquil **Jurong Lake**, about 4km northwest of the new town of Clementi. You're far more likely to want to come out this way if you've got children in tow. Of all the area's attractions, only the **Tang Dynasty City** is of universal appeal.

Singapore Science Centre

At the **Singapore Science Centre** (Tues–Sun 10am–6pm; $3), seven exhibition galleries hold over six hundred hands-on exhibits designed to inject interest into even the most impenetrable scientific principles. The majority of the centre's visitors are local school children, who sweep around the galleries in vast, deafening waves, frantically trying out each interactive display. The exhibits variously allow you to experience sight through an insect's eyes, to write in Braille, and to see a thermal heat reflection of yourself. The **Omnimax-Theatre** (planetarium show $6, movie $9; ☎5603316), within the centre's grounds, has entertaining features about science, space and history shown on a huge, engulfing dome screen.

It takes ten minutes at most to reach the Science Centre on foot from Jurong East MRT: walk left out of the station across the road, through a housing estate, and you'll see the centre opposite you.

Chinese and Japanese Gardens

The **Chinese and Japanese Gardens** (daily 9am–6pm; $4.50) situated below Jurong Lake, defy categorization – too expensive and too far out to visit for just a sit-down in the park and too dull to be a fully fledged tourist attraction. In the **Chinese Garden** (or Yu Hwa Yuan), pagodas, pavilions, bridges, arches and weeping willows attempt to capture the style of Beijing's Summer Palace – and fail. If you visit at the weekend, be prepared to be confronted by hordes of newlyweds scouring the garden for a decent photo opportunity. The Chinese Garden is best explored on the day of the annual Moon Cake Festival (see p.68), when children parade with their lanterns after dark.

Across the impressive, 65-metre "Bridge of Double Beauty" is the **Japanese Garden** (or *Seiwaen*, "Garden of Tranquillity"), whose wooden bridges, carp ponds, pebble footpaths and stone lanterns do much to help you forget the awful formica chairs and tables in the central pavilion. From Chinese Garden MRT Station, northeast of Jurong Lake, follow signs to the Chinese Garden's back entrance, three or four minutes down a footpath.

A short walk left along Yuan Ching Road, from the main exit out of the Japanese Garden, takes you to the Tang Dynasty City (see below). On the way you'll pass the **CN West Leisure Park** (Tues–Fri noon–6pm, Sat & Sun 9.30am–6pm; $4), a water fun park – which can also be reached direct from the centre on bus #154 from Boon Lay MRT.

Tang Dynasty City

You needn't worry about missing the entrance to the **Tang Dynasty City** (daily 10am–6.30pm; $15.45) on the corner of Yuan Ching Road and Jalan Ahmad Ibrahim: enclosing this $90-million complex is a ten-metre-high re-creation of the Great Wall, built from bricks imported from China. Indeed, practically everything inside this cultural and historical theme park is authentic, since it's the work of 85 Chinese craftsmen. As well as the scheduled shows involving such events as a traditional Chinese wedding ceremony or a duel between swordsmen, you'll find all the features of an eighth-century Chinese city: a bank (where the abacus is preferred to the computer), a teahouse, a medicine shop stacked with herbs and potions, a winery, the intriguingly named "Chamber of A Thousand Pleasures" and the courthouse, with its punishment paddles for administering beatings. Pictures and artefacts at the rather lame **House of Li** give an insight into Tang fashion, music and dance, while other attractions include the **Ghost Mansion**, which sets 3-D special effects to spookily good use; and the **Underground Palace**, in whose "Chamber of the Valiant Souls" a two thousand-strong legion of stern-looking terracotta warriors silently awaits its emperor's call to battle. Based upon the famous warriors of Xian, they're a little shorter than their Chinese counterparts due to copyright laws. It's no surprise that the city doubles as a **movie lot**, boasting three studios which specialize in period and kung-fu films: hopes are high that after 1997 Singapore might take over Hong Kong's mantle as the home of Oriental cinema. There's a buffet-style **café** on site but, if you can afford them, the set meals in the *Tai He Lou Theatre Restaurant* are great fun: you are entertained by troupes of **Chinese gymnasts** as you eat (see p.579).

To get to the Tang Dynasty City, take bus #154 or #240 from Lakeside MRT Station.

Jurong BirdPark and Crocodile Paradise

The twenty hectares of land which comprise the **Jurong BirdPark** (Mon–Fri 9am–6pm, Sat & Sun 8am–6pm; $9.27), on Jalan Ahmad Ibrahim, has more than eight thousand birds from over six hundred species, ranging from Antarctic penguins to New Zealand kiwis. This makes this it one of the world's largest bird collections, and the biggest in southeast Asia. A ride on the **Panorail** ($2.06) is a good way to get your bearings; the bullet-shaped monorail skims over, past or through all the main exhibits, with its running commentary pointing out the attractions.

Be sure at least to catch the **Waterfall Walk-in Aviary**, which allows visitors to walk amongst 1500 free-flying birds in a specially created tropical rainforest, dominated by a thirty-metre-high waterfall. Other exhibits to seek out are the colourful **Southeast Asian Birds**, where a tropical thunderstorm is simulated daily at noon; the **Penguin Parade** (feeding times 10.30am and 3.30pm); and the **World of Darkness**, a fascinating exhibit which swaps day for night with the aid of a system of reversed lighting, in order that its cute collection of nocturnal residents doesn't snooze throughout the park's opening hours. The best of the **bird shows** is undoubtedly the "Kings of the Skies" show (4pm) – a *tour de force* of speed-flying by a band of trained eagles, hawks and falcons. Entrance to this, and to the similar "World of Hawks" show (10am) and "All Star Bird Show" (11am & 3pm), is free. To get to the BirdPark, take either bus #194 or #251 from the bus interchange outside Boon Lay MRT station, a ten-minute ride.

Across the car park in front of the BirdPark, **Jurong Crocodile Paradise** (daily 9am–6pm; $6) houses the biggest gathering of crocodiles in Singapore. It's no paradise for the poor beasts forced to feature in the "Crocodile Wrestling and Snake Handling Show" (11.45am & 2pm), which has them pushed, pulled and sat on in the name of entertainment. Worse still is the "Catch-A-Croc Show" (10.45am & 3pm) – meant to showcase "the safe handling of crocodiles" – during which a character swathed in crocodile hide and dripping with crocodile teeth proceeds to tie up a croc's mouth, legs and tail, using rope and a stick. It comes as no surprise that the *Seafood Paradise Restaurant*, in the main entrance building, serves up crocs on plates.

The Singapore Discovery Centre and Tiger Brewery

The hands-on **Singapore Discovery Centre** (Tues–Fri 9am–7pm, Sat & Sun 9am–8pm; $9) at 510 Upper Jurong Rd is mainly geared towards local school parties. The emphasis is on Singapore's technological achievements, but there are three exhibits with broader appeal: **Airborne Rangers** ($4) lets you take a virtual parachute jump, there is a computer-simulated **Shooting Gallery** ($3), and a **motion simulator** ($4). In the grounds outside the centre is a cluster of military vehicles of varying vintages, and an imaginative playground complete with its own maze. To reach the Singapore Discovery Centre, take bus #192 or #193 from Boon Lay MRT station.

Tiger Beer, now the flagship brew of the **Asia Pacific Breweries Limited**, has been brewed in Singapore since 1931, though back then its home was the Malayan Breweries on Alexandra Road, where it was developed with help from Heineken. A few years later, the establishment of Archipelago Brewery by German giants Beck's seemed to set the scene for a Singaporean beer war, especially when Tiger's new rival, Anchor Beer, was priced slightly lower. But in 1941 Archipelago was bought out by Malayan Breweries, since when the organization has gone from strength to strength, moving in May 1990 into new seven-hectare holdings in Tuas, and changing its name to reflect "the new international role the company has assumed", although it's still commonly known as the Tiger Brewery.

Today, the tiger beneath a palm tree that adorns the label on every bottle of Tiger Beer can be seen in ads across the state. The original slogan for the beer was used by Anthony Burgess as the title for his debut novel, *Time for a Tiger*. As the protagonist, the embattled, debt-ridden police-lieutenant Nabby Adams gulps down another beer, ". . . fresh blood flowed through his arteries, the electric light seemed brighter, what were a few bills anyway?".

A **tour** of the brewery (☎8606483 for details) is made up of three component parts, arranged in rising order of appeal: first comes a film show which fills visitors in on the history of the set-up; next, a walk through the space-age brewing, bottling and canning halls; and finally an hour or two's free drinking in the company's own bar – Nabby would have approved. You need at least ten people in the party, though all is not lost if you are travelling alone – phone up and, if there's a tour already arranged, ask to tag along. To get to Tuas, take bus #193 from Boon Lay MRT Station.

Sentosa and the southern isles

Many little **islands** stud the waters immediately south of Singapore. Some, like Pulau Bukom, are owned by petrochemical companies and are off-limits to tourists. Three others – **Sentosa, St John's and Kusu** – are served by ferries and can be visited without difficulty, though their accessibility has geared them very much to tourism. If you crave a more secluded spot, you'll have to charter a bumboat to one of the more remote islands from the World Trade Centre or Clifford Pier (see p.515 for details) or head for Pulau Ubin, off Singapore's east coast (p.561).

Sentosa

Given the rampant development that has transformed **SENTOSA** into the most developed of Singapore's southern islands over the past twenty years, it's ironic that its name means "tranquillity" in Malay. Sentosa has come a long way since World War II, when it was a British military base known as Pulau Blakang Mati, or the "Island of Death Behind". Promoted for its beaches, sports facilities, hotels and attractions, and ringed by a speeding monorail, it's a contrived but enjoyable place. The island is linked to the mainland by a brand new five-hundred-metre causeway and a necklace of cable cars.

Sentosa is big business. In 1992, for instance, 3.32 million visitors descended on this tiny island, which measures just 3km by 1km. Nevertheless you'll hear mixed reports of the place around Singapore. Ultimately, it's as enjoyable as you make it; there's certainly plenty to do (though few of the attractions would make the grade at Disneyland), so much so that it's a good idea to arrive early, with a clear plan of action. Taking a round trip on the trans-island monorail upon arrival helps you get your bearings. **Admission** to several attractions is included in the Sentosa entry ticket (see "Practicalities", p.568), though for the more popular attractions, a further charge is levied. It's wise to avoid coming at the weekend, while public holidays should be avoided at all costs.

The attractions
Two attractions outshine all others on Sentosa. At the **Underwater World** (daily 9am–9pm; $12) near monorail station 2, a moving walkway carries you the length of a hundred-metre acrylic tunnel that snakes through two large tanks: sharks lurk menacingly on all sides, huge stingrays drape themselves languidly above you, and immense shoals of gaily coloured fish dart to and fro. This may not sound all that exciting, but the sensation of being engulfed by sea life of all descriptions is really a breathtaking one, and the nearest you'll get to being on the ocean floor without donning a wet suit. A **touchpool** beside the entrance allows you to pick up star fish and sea cucumbers – the latter rather like socks filled with wet sand – while beyond that is the **Marine Theatre**, screening educational films throughout the day.

The other major-league attraction is the **Pioneers of Singapore, Surrender Chambers and Festivals of Singapore Exhibition** (daily 9am–9pm; $5), near monorail station 2. Here, life-sized dioramas present the history and heritage of Singapore from the fourteenth century through to the surrender of the Japanese in 1945. Though some of the wax dummies look like they've been pinched from clothes shop windows, the effect is fascinating. The highlight of the exhibition is the Surrender Chambers, where audio-visuals, videos, dioramas and artefacts combine to recount the events of World War II in Singapore. There are more wax dummies on parade in the new Festivals of Singapore gallery, this time dolled up in all manner of festive costumes to showcase the various ethnic celebrations that annually rock Singapore.

A trip up to the new improved **Fort Siloso** (monorail station 3), on the far western tip of the island, ties in nicely with a visit to the Surrender Chambers. The fort – actually a cluster of buildings and gun emplacements above a series of tunnels bored into the island – guarded Singapore's western approaches from the 1880s until 1956, but was rendered obsolete in 1942, when the Japanese moved down into Singapore from Malaysia. Today, the recorded voice of Battery Sergeant Major Cooper talks you through a mock-up of a nineteenth-century barracks, complete with living quarters, laundry and assault course. You can explore the complex's hefty gun emplacements and tunnels and, during the "Sounds of Siloso" show, booming audio effects re-create the sensation of being in the tunnels during wartime.

The rest of Sentosa is crammed with less interesting options. **The Asian Village** (daily 10am–9pm; free), next to the ferry terminal, showcases Asian life by way of restaurants, craft shops and street performances – little more than a vehicle for shifting overpriced arts, crafts and food. Within the village are the fairground rides of Adventure Asia ($10) and the **Thai Pavilion Theatre**, in which the "Colours of Asia" (10.15am & 4pm; $5) and "Fascinating Asia" (6.30pm & 7.15pm; $18 including dinner) cultural shows are staged daily. Otherwise, you might consider one of Sentosa's three latest attractions: **Volcanoland** (daily 9am–9pm; $10), with a simulated eruption and trip to the earth's core; **Fantasy Island** (Mon, Tues & Fri–Sun 10am–7pm; $16), with hi-tech water rides – "Flashflood", "Blackhole" and, for small children, "Pygmy Puddle"; or **Wondergolf** (9am–9pm; $8), with 45 crazy holes. If you end up at the **Maritime Museum** (daily 10am–7pm; $2), you're really scraping the bottom of the barrel – you'd do better strolling in the elegant grounds of the **Sentosa Orchid Gardens** near monorail station 1. For something slightly more exciting head for the **Butterfly Park and Insect Kingdom Museum** (Mon–Fri 9am–6pm, Sat & Sun 9am–6.30pm; $5), near monorail station 5, which is stuffed with all sorts of creepy crawlies.

Probably the best option, though, after a trip on the monorail and a visit to one or two attractions, is to head for the three **beaches** (monorail station 2 or 5, or take bus A or bus M) on Sentosa's southwestern coast. Created with thousands of cubic metres of imported white sand and scores of coconut palms, they offer canoes, surf boards and aqua bikes for rent – as well as plain old deckchairs. The water here is great for swimming and Singapore does not demand the same modesty on its beaches as Malaysia, although topless and nude bathing are out. In recent years, Singapore's annual Dragonboat Racing Festival (see p.68) has been held off Siloso Beach.

By 7pm, many of Sentosa's attractions are closed, but not so the **Musical Fountain** (shows at 4pm, 4.30pm, 5pm, 5.30pm, 7.20pm, 8.20pm & 9.20pm), which is either cute or appalling, depending on your point of view. The fountain dances along to such classics as the *1812 Overture*, with colourful lights and lasers adding to the effect. Recently, the display has been overlooked by a new, 37-metre-high statue of Singapore's tourism totem, the **Merlion**, which itself takes centre-stage in the laser-illuminated "Rise of the Merlion" portions of the shows (7.50pm, 8.50pm & 9.50pm).

Practicalities

Basic **admission** to Sentosa costs $5, though this doesn't include the cost of actually reaching the island. From the **World Trade Centre** at 1 Maritime Square (buses #65, #97, #143 and #166), **ferries** depart every fifteen minutes (9am–9pm; $1.30 return). However, the most spectacular way there is by one of the **cable cars** (daily 8.30am–9pm) which travel on a loop between mainland Mount Faber (see p.562) and Sentosa. A one-station trip (from the WTC to Sentosa, for instance) costs $5, two stations costs $5.50, and for a round trip – from the WTC up to Mount Faber, across to Sentosa and back to the WTC, you'll pay $6.50, not including the basic $5 admission fee.

Crossing the bridge to Sentosa costs nothing if you walk, though you still have to pay the admission fee. Two **buses** operating out of the WTC bus terminal– bus A(a) and bus A(b) – run across the bridge every ten to fifteen minutes (7am–11pm; last bus back to the mainland at 11.30pm; $6). Service C, meanwhile, shuttles between Tiong Bahru MRT station and the ferry terminal on Sentosa (7am–11pm; $6), while bus M makes the same journey but continues on to the southern beaches (4–11pm; $6). In addition, bus E runs from Orchard Road to Sentosa's Gateway station (10am–10.30pm; $7).

Sentosa's basic admission fee gives unlimited rides on Sentosa's **monorail and bus systems** – bus #2 circles the island between 9am and 7pm and services A, C and M are often handy too, while the monorail runs from 9am until 10pm. But the best way to get about is to **rent a bike** for the day ($4–8 an hour depending on the machine) from the kiosk beside the ferry terminal; tandems are also available. The *Rasa Sentosa Food Centre*, beside the ferry terminal is the cheapest **eating** option; otherwise, try the near- by *Sentosa Riverboat* for fast food, or monorail station 5's *Sweetimes Café*. There's a *Burger King* and a coffee house at the ferry terminal as well as a beer garden – though the new *Sunset Bay* bar (see p.585) is a far cooler spot for a beer. Sentosa has two inter- national-class **hotels**, one budget hotel and limited camping possibilities (see p.516 for more details).

Kusu, St John's and other islands

Well kept and clean as they are, Sentosa's beaches do tend to get overcrowded and you may do better to head for either **St John's** or **Kusu** islands, which are 6km south of Singapore and connected to the mainland by a **ferry** from the WTC. This reaches Kusu in thirty minutes and then continues on to St John's, arriving shortly afterwards. On weekdays and Saturdays there are only two departures **from the WTC**, at 10am and 1.30pm; departures are **from St John's** at 11.15 am and 2.45pm, and **from Kusu** at 11.45am and 3.15pm. On Sundays and public holidays, services are more frequent, departing from the WTC at 9.45am, 11.15am, 12.45pm, 2.15pm, 3.45pm and 5.15pm ($6.20; ☎2703918).

Both islands have decent sand beaches, though the most interesting of the two is Kusu, also known as **Turtle Island**. Singaporean legend tells of a Chinese and a Malay sailor who were once saved from drowning by a turtle which transformed itself into an island; a pool of turtles is still kept on the island. Another legend describes how an epi- demic afflicting a ship moored off Kusu was banished by the God Tua Pek Kong. Whatever the truth in these tales, once a year during the ninth lunar month (October or November), tens of thousands of Singaporean pilgrims descend upon the **Chinese temple** and **Malay shrine** a few minutes' walk from the jetty on Kusu, to pray for pros- perity. The island is impossibly crowded during this time, but the rest of the year it offers a tranquil escape from the mainland. There is a modest cafeteria on St John's, but if you're going to Kusu it's wise to take a picnic.

Other southern islands

Since no regular ferries run to any of Singapore's other southern islands, you'll have to **charter a bumboat** from Jardine Steps (beside the World Trade Centre) or from Clifford Pier. Boats take up to twelve passengers, and cost at least $30–40 an hour. Unless you rent a boat for the whole day, don't forget to arrange to be picked up again.

Lazarus Island and attractive **Sisters Islands**, which lie in the same cluster of isles as St John's and Kusu, are both popular snorkelling and fishing haunts, as is **Pulau Hantu** ("Ghost Island" in Malay), 12km further west and under the shadow of Shell-owned Pulau Bukum. Most interesting of all, though, is **Pulau Seking**, three or four kilometres east of Hantu, where a handful of Malays continues to live in traditional stilt houses that teeter over the sea, their lifestyle almost untouched by the progress that has transformed the mainland. These islands are all very basic, so take a picnic and a day's supply of bottled water with you.

Eating

Along with shopping, **eating** ranks as the Singaporean national pastime and an enormous number of food outlets cater for this obsession. However, eating out is not afforded the same reverence that it receives in the West. Often, you'll find yourself eating off plastic plates in bare, unpretentious restaurants that ring to the sound of agitated conversation (invariably about food) – it's the food, and not the surroundings, that is important. Singapore offers new arrivals in Asia the chance to sample the whole spectrum of the region's dishes. What's more, strict government regulations ensure that food outlets are consistently hygienic – you don't need to worry about eating food cooked at a street stall. You may want to choreograph you visit to coincide with July's **Singapore Food Festival**, a celebration of regional cuisines during which food outlets across the island whip up interesting local specialities. You can also take **food tours**, or enrol on one of the courses run by the Raffles Culinary Academy ($90 per day; ☎3311747) and Violet Oon's Kitchen (see p.582).

The mass of establishments serving **Chinese** food reflects the fact that Chinese residents account for around 78 percent of the population. You're most likely to come across Cantonese, Beijing and Szechuan restaurants, though there's not a region of China whose specialities you can't sample. **North and South Indian** cuisines give a good account of themselves too, as do restaurants serving **Malay**, **Indonesian**, **Korean**, **Japanese** and **Vietnamese** food. One thing you won't find, however, is a Singaporean restaurant: the closest Singapore comes to an indigenous cuisine is **Nonya**, a hybrid of Chinese and Malay food that developed following the intermarrying of nineteenth-century Chinese immigrants with Malay women. Of course you can eat **Western food** in Singapore – venture beyond the ubiquitous burger chains and pizza parlours, and you'll find a host of excellent restaurants cooking anything from haggis to jambalaya. These and other dishes may be enjoyed at establishments geared to the dishes of a particular nation, or at **international restaurants**, whose menus are a patchwork of Western cuisines. A more informal alternative is to opt for a plate of **British** food – fish and chips, say – at a pub or bar.

Several specialist Chinese restaurants and a number of Indian restaurants serve **vegetarian food**, but otherwise vegetarians need to tread very carefully: chicken and seafood will appear in a whole host of dishes unless you make it perfectly clear that you don't want them. **Halal food** is predictably easy to find, given the number of Muslims in Singapore; the Arab Street end of North Bridge Road and Serangoon Road's Zhu Jiao Centre both have proliferations of restaurants and stalls. There are no **kosher** restaurants, but you could try one of the delis listed below, or the food store at the Maghain Aboth Synagogue opposite the Church of St Peter and Paul, on Waterloo Street.

By far the cheapest and most fun place to dine in Singapore is in a **hawker centre** or **food court**, where scores of stalls let you mix and match dishes at really low prices. For a few extra dollars you graduate into the realm of proper **restaurants**, ranging from no-frills, open-fronted eating houses and coffee shops to sumptuously decorated establishments – often, though not always, located in swanky hotels. Restaurant **opening hours**, on average, are 11.30am–2.30pm and 6–10.30pm daily; hawker stall owners tend to operate to their own schedules, but are invariably open at peak eating times.

Breakfast, brunch and snacks

Guesthouses sometimes include coffee or tea and toast in the price of the room but the chances are you'll want to head off elsewhere for breakfast. **Western breakfasts** are available, at a price, at all bigger hotels, most famously at the *Hilton* or *Raffles*. Otherwise, there are a number of cafés serving continental breakfasts, while *McDonald's*, *Kentucky Fried Chicken* and *Burger King* all rustle up breakfasts before reverting to burgers and chicken after 11am. For a really cheap fry-up you can't beat a Western food stall in a hawker centre. Here, $8 will buy enough steak, chops and sausage for even the most starving carnivore. Many visitors to Singapore find the **local breakfasts** a little hard to stomach, but if you shelve your Western preconceptions, there are some tasty possibilities. The classic Chinese breakfast is *congee*, a watery rice porridge augmented with chopped spring onion, crispy fried onion and strips of meat, though the titbits that comprise *dim sum* tend to be more palatable to Western tastes. An abiding favourite among Malays is *nasi lemak*, rice cooked in coconut milk and served with *sambal ikan bilis* (tiny crisp-fried anchovies in hot chilli paste), fried peanuts and slices of fried or hard-boiled egg. Otherwise, try investigating one of the scores of Indian establishments serving up curry and bread breakfasts.

Breakfast With An Orang-Utan, Singapore Zoo, 80 Mandai Lake Rd, Northern Singapore (☎3608509). A bumper American-style spread with seasonal tropical fruits, shared with whichever orang is on duty, costs $15.50. Daily 9–10am.

Breakfast With The Birds, Jurong BirdPark, Jalan Ahmad Ibrahim, Western Singapore (☎2650022). A buffet of local and Western breakfast favourites, eaten to the accompaniment of the caged songbirds hanging above you; $12. Daily 9am–11am.

Brooklyn Bagels, 235 River Valley Rd, Orchard Road District (☎7320056). Tiny takeaway joint where you choose from plain, egg, onion, garlic, sesame or pumpernickel bagels, filled with pastrami, salmon or roast beef, or make do with a plain old muffin. All produce is baked in-house daily. Open Mon–Thurs 7am–8pm, Fri & Sat 7am–midnight, Sun 7am–6pm.

Champagne Brunch At The Hilton, *Hilton Hotel*, 581 Orchard Rd (☎7372233). Around $50 buys a superb free flow of delicacies – oysters, salmon, curry and cakes – washed down with litres of champagne and orange juice. Reservations are essential. Sun 11.30am–2.30pm only.

Coffee Connection, 01-39/40 Shaw Leisure Gallery, Beach Road, Colonial District. One of a chain of coffee houses serving good-value breakfast specials, fine coffees and cakes. Daily 9–11.30am.

D.M. Moosa Restaurant, 129 Bencoolen St, Colonial District. Does a roaring trade in *roti prata* (fried bread) and curry sauce each morning.

Delifrance, *Singapore Marriott*, 320 Orchard Rd. This stylish café is one of a chain of French delis specializing in filled croissants and pastries; recommended. Daily 8am–9pm.

Dôme, 01-02 Cecil Ct, 138 Cecil St, Financial District (☎2214369). Slick café – one of a global chain – boasting an impressive list of coffees and teas. Muffins, toast and croissants are reasonable, and a selection of international papers are on hand. There is also a branch at the National Art Museum. Daily 7.30am–10pm.

Ed's Diner, 03-12 Raffles City Shopping Centre, 252 North Bridge Rd, Colonial District. American-style coffee shop where toast, scrambled eggs and bacon, with coffee or tea, costs around $4.

Famous Amos, 01-05 Specialists' Shopping Centre, 277 Orchard Rd. Sublime handmade cookies to take away.

Mirana Cake House, Chinatown Point, 133 New Bridge Rd and OUB Centre, 1 Raffles Place, Chinatown. Spick and span cake and gateaux chain.

Mr Cucumber, 02-02 Clifford Centre, 24 Raffles Place, Financial District (☎5340363). Sandwich bar with a wide variety of fillings, catering for the business crowd. Sandwiches from $3 upwards, or try one of the bagels supplied by *Brooklyn Bagels*. Mon–Fri 10am–6pm, Sat 11am–3pm.

Oriel Café, 30 Selegie Rd, Colonial District. Based in the same wedge-shaped colonial building as the *Selegie Arts Centre*, the *Oriel* draws an interesting crowd, who breakfast on muffins, croissants, toast and coffee.

Red Lantern Beer Garden, Basement, 60a Change Alley Aerial Plaza, Collyer Quay, Financial District. The continental set breakfast in this enclosed beer garden is great value at under $5. Daily 7–10.30am.

Selera Restaurant, 15 Mackenzie Rd, Colonial District (☎3385687). The best curry puffs – curried meat and boiled egg folded into pastry – in Singapore. Two will fill you up for around a dollar. Daily noon–11.30pm.

Sin Lam Tong, 181 New Bridge Rd, Chinatown. *Dim sum* served between 4am and 2pm in anodyne surroundings.

Spinelli Coffee Company, 01–15 Bugis Junction, 230 Victoria St, Colonial District. San Francisco-based outfit that's riding on the crest of Singapore's current mania for fresh coffee; the narrow bar is ideal for a quick expresso.

Tenco Food Centre, Sim Lim Square Food Court, 1 Rochor Canal Rd, Colonial District. The short stroll from Bencoolen Street's guesthouses is rewarded by a filling mixed grill (under $10), available at the Western stall on the left-hand side of the food centre.

Tiffin Room, *Raffles Hotel*, 1 Beach Rd, Colonial District (☎3371886). Have your buffet breakfast here and you won't eat again until dinner; $25 per person. Daily 7.30–10am.

Hawker centres and food courts

Avoid the peak lunching (12.30–1.30pm) and dining (6–7pm) periods, when hungry Singaporeans go to their nearest hawker centre, and you should have no problems in finding a seat. Although **hawker centres** are kept scrupulously clean, they are often housed in functional buildings which tend to get extremely hot and, if you are seated next to a stall cooking fried rice or noodles, extremely smoky. As a consequence, an increasing number of smaller, air-conditioned **food courts** are popping up, where eating is a slightly more civilized, if less atmospheric affair. Hawker centres and food courts are open from lunchtime through to dinner time and sometimes beyond, though individual stalls open and shut as they please.

Chinatown Complex, Smith St, at end of New Bridge Road, Chinatown. A huge range of dishes with a predictably Chinese bias.

Empress Place Centre, north bank, Singapore River. Spacious and central outdoor hawker centre.

Food Junction, B1, *Seiyu Department Store*, Bugis Junction, 200 Victoria St, Colonial District. Happening food court whose trendy piped music provides a stirring soundtrack to your dinner. Culinary themes as diverse as Thai, Japanese, *nasi padang* and claypot are represented, and there's a choice of local desserts or *Haagen Dazs* ice creams.

Geylang Serai Food Centre, Geylang Serai, East Singapore. In the heart of Singapore's Malay quarter, with a corresponding range of stalls. Turn left out of Paya Lebar MRT and left again onto Sims Avenue; the centre is five minutes' walk along, on your right.

Hastings Road Food Court, Little India Arcade, Serangoon Rd, Little India. Diminutive food court whose handful of stalls are labelled by region – Keralan, Mughlai, Sri Lankan and so on.

Hawker's Alley, Block D, Clarke Quay. Just a handful of stalls in an air-con hall.

Hill Street Centre, 64 Hill St, Colonial District. A number of fine Chinese and Indian stalls on two floors. On the far right-hand side as you enter is a stall serving excellent *popiah* (spring rolls stuffed with bamboo shoots, beansprouts, prawns and hot chilli paste).

Lau Pa Sat Festival Market, 18 Raffles Quay, Financial District. The smartest hawker stalls in Singapore, and now open round the clock. At lunchtime the place is full to bursting with suits from the city; at night the clubbers take over.

Nan Tai Eating House 01-29 Block 261, Waterloo St, Colonial District. Modest but varied selection of stalls, including popular seafood and *rojak* hawkers.

New Bugis Street, Colonial District. A handful of evening hawkers dishes up Asian specialities like *satay, laksa, kueh* and *sushi*.

Newton Circus Hawker Centre, north end of Scotts Road, a short walk from Newton MRT, Orchard Road District. Prices are a little higher than other centres because it's on the mainstream tourist trail, but it has the advantage of staying open until late. Noted for its seafood stalls, though these, and all the centre's other stalls may have to close down in 1997, should planned developments take place.

Orchard Emerald Food Court, Basement, Orchard Emerald, 218 Orchard Rd. Smart food court, bang in the centre of Orchard Road, where the Indonesian buffet is great value.

People's Park Complex Hawker Centre, Eu Tong Sen St, Chinatown. Lots of good stalls selling tasty Chinese specialities.

Picnic Food Court, Scotts Shopping Centre, 6 Scotts Rd, Orchard Road District. Slap bang in the middle of Orchard Road, squeaky clean, and with lots of choice.

Point Food Court, Orchard Point, 160 Orchard Rd. Expansive new basement court that's handy if you're shopping on Orchard Road.

Queen Street Hawker Centre, Block 270, Queen St, across the road from Bugis Village, Colonial District. A rough and ready centre with many Indian stalls.

Satay Club, Clarke Quay, Singapore River. A Singapore institution not to be missed, serving inexpensive chicken and mutton satay. Open evenings only, from around 7pm.

Sim Lim Square Food Centre, 1 Rochor Canal Rd, Colonial District. Convenient if you are staying on Bencoolen Street; it's under the Sim Lim Square building.

Suntec Fountain Food Terrace, Suntec City Mall, 3 Temasek Blvd, Colonial District. Appealing new court, where stalls are listed according to cuisine, and diners look out upon the thirty-metre spurts of Suntec City's mind-boggling fountain.

Taman Serasi, junction of Napier and Cluny roads, Orchard Road District. Opposite the main entrance to the Botanical Gardens, the speciality here is *roti john*.

Zhujiao Hawker Centre, corner of Bukit Timah and Serangoon roads, Little India. The bulk of its stalls, naturally enough, serve Indian food.

Coffee shops and restaurants

Below is a representative selection of the thousands of **coffee shops** and **restaurants** that span Singapore, with the **cuisines** listed alphabetically; note that the direction "off Orchard Road" means you'll find the restaurant in the area of Orchard Road (not necessarily just off the road). **Meal prices**, where quoted, are fairly arbitrary – even in the most extravagant restaurant in Singapore it's possible to snack on fried rice and a soft drink. Equally, a delicacy such as shark's-fin or bird's nest soup will send a bill soaring, no matter how unpretentious the restaurant. Individual **opening hours** are given below. If possible, try to book ahead at more upmarket restaurants, particularly on Saturday nights and Sunday lunchtimes, when they are at their busiest. Moreover, bear in mind that many restaurants close over Chinese New Year, and those that don't are often bursting at the seams. There aren't too many establishments that enforce a dress code, though it's always best to dress up a little if you're heading for a hotel restaurant.

Chinese

The majority of the **Chinese** restaurants in Singapore are Cantonese, that is, from the province of Canton (Guangdong) in southern China, though you'll also come across northern Beijing (or Peking) and western Szechuan cuisines, as well as the Hokkien specialities of the southeastern province of Fukien; and Teochew dishes from the area east of Canton. Whatever the region, it's undoubtedly the real thing – Chinese food as eaten by the Chinese – which means it won't always sound particularly appealing to foreigners: the Chinese eat all parts of an animal, from its lips to its undercarriage, and it's important to retain a sense of adventure when exploring menus. Fish and seafood is nearly always outstanding in Chinese cuisine, with prawns, crab, squid and a variety of fish on offer. Noodles, too, are ubiquitous, and come in wonderful variations. For something a little more unusual, try a **steamboat**, a Chinese-style fondue filled with boiling stock in which you cook meat, fish, shellfish, eggs and vegetables; or a **claypot** – meat, fish or shellfish cooked over a fire in an earthenware pot. The other thing to note is that in many Cantonese restaurants (and in other regional restaurants, too), lunch consists of **dim sum** – steamed and fried dumplings served in little bamboo baskets.

BEIJING

Pine Court, 35th floor, *Mandarin Hotel*, 333 Orchard Rd (☎7374411). Three elegant pine trees dominate this beautiful restaurant, where the speciality is whole Peking duck ($70) – enough for three hungry people. Cheaper set meals are available, too. You'll need to reserve in advance. Daily noon–2.30pm & 7–10.30pm.

Prima Tower Revolving Restaurant, 201 Keppel Rd, Chinatown (☎2728822). Fine duck dishes and a great view are the two highlights here. Take bus #97 from Bencoolen Street or Tanjong Pagar MRT. Daily 11am–3pm & 6.30–11pm.

CANTONESE

Bugis Village, Colonial District. Touts at the several seafood restaurants here hassle you incessantly to take a seat and a menu. The furious competition ensures prices are reasonable, despite the high proportion of tourists; all restaurants work from similar, mainstream menus. Daily 5pm–3am.

Capital, 01-207, Block 2, Cantonment Rd, Chinatown (☎2213516). The friendly staff in this spotless restaurant recommend fried deer meat with ginger; also worth a try are the fried prawns rolled in beancurd skin. A feast for two costs less than $35. Daily noon–2.30pm & 6–10.30pm.

Ever Happy Seafood Restaurant, 2 Lorong 25, Geylang Rd, Eastern Singapore (☎7421493). The outdoor terrace makes this a popular local spot. Seafood is recommended, as is the extensive claypot menu; *dim sum* is available day and night. Daily 11am–3am.

Fatty's Wing Seong Restaurant, 01-33 Albert Complex, Albert St, Colonial District (☎3381087). A Singapore institution, where every dish on the wide Cantonese menu is well cooked and speedily delivered. Around $20 a head. Daily noon–11pm.

Hai Tien Lo, 37th floor, *Pan Pacific Hotel*, 7 Raffles Blvd, Marina Square, Colonial District (☎3368111). If you have money enough for just one blow-out, come here for exquisitely presented food and stunning views of downtown Singapore. Extravagant set meals are available, while Sunday lunchtimes are set aside for *dim sum* (10.30am–2.30pm). Daily noon–2.30pm & 6.30–10.30pm.

Hillman, 01-159, Block 1, Cantonment Rd, Chinatown (☎2215073). Extremely popular for its rich-tasting earthen pots of flavoursome stews featuring various meats and seafood; small pots (around $10) fill two. Daily 11.30am–2.30pm & 5.30–10.30pm.

Mitzi's, 24–26 Murray Terrace, Chinatown (☎2220929). The cracking Cantonese food in this simple place, situated in a row of restaurants known as "Food Alley", draws crowds, so be prepared to wait in line. Two can eat for $30, drinks extra. Daily 11am–3pm & 6–10pm.

Mouth, 02-01 Chinatown Point, 133 New Bridge Rd, Chinatown (☎5344233). Beside a popular *dim sum* menu, this jam-packed restaurant offers classy Hong Kong new-wave Cantonese food, at under $20 a head. Daily 11am–4am (*dim sum* 11.30am–5pm).

Northern Palace, 10-00 Colombo Court, Colonial District (☎3384513). *Dim sum* dishes here all cost under $3, and are served in the traditional way from a trolley. Daily noon–2.30pm & 6.30–10.30pm.

Sin Lam Tong, 181 New Bridge Rd, Chinatown. Venerable teahouse, recently uprooted from its original Smith Street address, but still serving early morning *dim sum* delights (all under $3) before reverting to a lunchtime menu. Daily 4am–2pm for *dim sum*, 8am–5pm for lunch.

Swee Kee, *Damenlou Hotel*, 12 Ann Siang Rd, Chinatown (☎2211900). A Cantonese restaurant with real pedigree: Tang Swee Kee hawked the first bowl of his trademark *ka shou* fish-head noodles more than sixty years ago, and now his son sells this and other well-cooked dishes from the attractive coffee shop on the ground floor of his Chinatown hotel. Daily 11am–2.30pm & 5.30–11pm.

Thye Choon Huan Restaurant and Bar, corner of New Bridge and Upper Cross streets, Chinatown. Old-style coffee shop whose fittings ooze antiquity, from its marble-topped tables to its huge, liver-spotted mirror; *wan ton* and noodle soups, chicken, and duck rice can all be whistled up in a trice.

Tung Lok Shark's Fin Restaurant, 04-07/9 Liang Court, 177 River Valley Rd, Colonial District (π3366022). The twelve types of shark's-fin dishes (from $20 per person) inevitably constitute the highlight of this lavish restaurant. Meals up to $50 a head. Daily 11.30am–3pm & 6.30–11pm.

Ubin Seafood, 2161 Pulau Ubin (π5458202). One of the finest seafood restaurants in Singapore – and with a great view of Johor. Take bus #2 from Victoria St to Changi Village, and hop on a bumboat to Pulau Ubin. Then catch a taxi or rent a bike. Daily 11.30am–9pm.

Union Farm Eating House, 435a Clementi Rd, Western Singapore (π4662776). Until thirty years ago, this used to be a poultry farm, and palms and bamboo still surround the restaurant. The house special, *chee pow kai* (marinated chicken wrapped in greaseproof paper and deep-fried – $14 buys enough for two), is messy and wonderful. From Clementi MRT take bus #154 and get off when you see Maju army camp. Daily 11.30am–8.30pm.

Wang Jiang Lou, Block A, Clarke Quay, Singapore River (π3383001). Slick Cantonese-Teochew restaurant where the ingredients of a full seafood menu eye you suspiciously from tanks on the walls. Also available is a medley of *dim sum* (weekday lunchtime; $14), and night-time steamboat (from $11). Daily 11.30am–2.30pm & 6.30–10.30pm.

HAINANESE

Mooi Chin Palace, B1-03 Funan Centre, 109 North Bridge Rd, Colonial District (π3397766). Hainanese immigrants often worked as domestics to colonial families, resulting in crossover dishes like Hainanese mutton soup and Hainanese pork chop – both cooked to perfection in this sixty-year-old place, where whole *pomfret sambal* ($24) is a speciality, and set menus start at $32 for two. Daily 7.30–9am (*dim sum*), 11.30am–3pm & 6–10pm.

Swee Kee, 51–53 Middle Rd, Colonial District (π3385551). Venerable coffee-shop-style restaurant whose succulent Hainanese chicken rice ($3.50) is the best in Singapore. Daily 10am–9.30pm.

Yet Con Chicken Rice Restaurant, 25 Purvis St, Colonial District (π3376819). Cheap and cheerful, old-time restaurant: try "crunchy, crispy" roast pork with pickled cabbage and radish, or for $10 chicken rice, washed down with barley water, for two people. Daily 10.30am–9.30pm.

HOKKIEN

Bee Heong, 4th Floor, Pil Building, 140 Cecil St, Financial District (π2229075). Customers are pumped through at a rate of knots in this lunchtime-only, cafeteria-style place; there's no menu, but the *beggar chicken* and dried chilli prawn come recommended, or ask the friendly staff for advice. Daily 11am–3pm.

Beng Hiang, 20 Murray St, Chinatown (π2216695). The Hokkien chef relies heavily upon robust soups and sauces, though his most popular dish is a superbly cooked fried *mee*; the lack of a menu makes ordering distinctly tricky, but persistence is rewarded by well-cooked food at good-value prices – you can eat well for under $15. Daily 11.30am–2pm & 6–9pm.

Beng Thin Hoon Kee, 05-02 OCBC Centre, 65 Chulia St, Financial District (π5332818). Hidden inside the OCBC car park, this minty green restaurant is very popular at lunchtime with city slickers from the nearby business district. Big portions make it a good and filling introduction to Hokkien cuisine. Daily 11.30am–3pm & 6–10pm.

Yang Hong Kee, 72 Tanjong Pagar Rd, Chinatown. Cheap, no-frills Hokkien restaurant where the lack of spoken English stymies attempts to experiment. Daily 11am–2.30pm & 6–10pm.

SZECHUAN AND HUNANESE

Cherry Garden, *The Oriental*, 5 Raffles Ave, Marina Square, Colonial District (π3380066 ext 3538). Elegant restaurant, designed to resemble a Chinese courtyard, and serving tasty Szechuan and Hunanese dishes. Hunanese honey glazed ham is delectable, as is the Szechuan house speciality, camphor-smoked duck and beancurd crust (both under $30); the set lunch costs $44 a head. Daily noon–2.30pm & 6.30–10.30pm.

Long Jiang, *Crown Prince Hotel*, 270 Orchard Rd (π7321111 ext 1700). The daily buffet lunch here is an excellent initiation to Szechuan cuisine ($22 a head, weekends $26). Daily 11.30am–2.30pm & 6.30–10.30pm.

Min Jiang, *Goodwood Park Hotel*, 22 Scotts Rd, off Orchard Rd (☎7375337). This restaurant's reputation for fine Szechuan classics – like camphor and tea-smoked duck – makes reservations a good idea. A meal for two costs around $60. Daily noon–2.30pm & 6.30–10.30pm.

Spice Garden, 03-100 *Hotel Meridien* Shopping Centre, 100 Orchard Rd (☎7324122). The classic Hunanese dish, steamed minced pigeon in bamboo tube, is a highlight of the menu here; reasonable set lunches and dinners are also available. Daily 11.30am–3pm & 6.30–11pm.

Taikan-En Chinese Restaurant, *Hotel New Otani*, 177a River Valley Rd (☎3383333 ext 8690). A tiny replica of a Chinese teahouse is the centrepiece of the dining room; most dishes cost less than $15. Daily 11.30am–2.30pm & 6.30–10.30pm.

TEOCHEW

Ban Seng, 79 New Bridge Rd, Chinatown (☎5331471). The mid-priced dishes served here are still cooked using traditional charcoal ovens: try the steamed crayfish, braised goose or stuffed sea cucumber; mid-priced. Daily 12–2.30pm & 6–10pm.

Chui Wah Lin, 49 Mosque St, Chinatown. No-frills, open-fronted restaurant where you point to what you want from the display of inexpensive Teochew dishes. The squares of red, jellyish substance you can see in trays are solidified pig's blood, long favoured by old men for its invigorating qualities. Daily 7am–9pm.

Liang Kee, 02-406, Block 2, Tew Chew St, Chinatown (☎5341029). Unpretentious, popular local restaurant that thwarts tourists with its lack of any written clues as to the food on offer. Good quality, though. Open noon–2.30pm & 6–9.30pm; closed Wed.

Teochew City Seafood Restaurant, 05-16 Centrepoint, 176 Orchard Rd (☎7333338). Standard Teochew restaurant whose karaoke facilities are, mercifully, confined to two private rooms; $50 suffices for a meal for two. Daily 11.30am–2.30pm & 6.30–11pm.

VEGETARIAN CHINESE

Fut Sai Kai, 147 Kitchener Rd, Little India (☎2980336). Old-fashioned Cantonese restaurant with a strongly Oriental atmosphere and fiery red decor; $20 is sufficient for two. Beancurd forms the backbone of Chinese vegetarian cooking, though it reaches your table shaped to resemble meat or fish. Open Tues–Sun 10am–9pm.

Happy Realm Vegetarian Food Centre, 03-16 Pearls Centre, 100 Eu Tong Sen St, Chinatown (☎2226141). "The way to good health and a sound mind", boasts the restaurant's card; tasty and reasonably priced vegetarian dishes. Daily 11am–8.30pm.

Kwan Yim Vegetarian Restaurant, 190 Waterloo St, Colonial District (☎3382394). A huge display of sweet and savoury *pow* is the highlight of this unfussy establishment, sited close to Bencoolen Street. Daily 8am–8.30pm.

Lingzhi, B1-17/18 Orchard Towers, 400 Orchard Rd (☎7343788). A real treat, where skewers of vegetables served with satay sauce are the highlight of an imaginative menu; there's also a takeaway counter. Daily 11.30am–10pm.

OTHER SPECIALITY RESTAURANTS

Doc Cheng's, *Raffles Hotel*, 328 North Bridge Rd, Colonial District (☎3311612). East meets West in the most recent addition to *Raffles*, an ice-cool joint themed around the global travels of imagined local bon viveur, Doc Cheng. Though the menu betrays Alaskan, Japanese Cajun and Spanish influences, Chinese culinary ideology provides the backbone to much of the food; decor presents a similarly eclectic blend of Oriental, Art Deco and modernist influences. Two pay around $60. Daily noon–10.30pm.

Imperial Herbal Restaurant, third floor, *Metropole Hotel*, 41 Seah St, Colonial District (☎3370491 ext 212). The place to go if you are concerned about your Yin and Yang balance: after checking your pulse and tongue, a resident Chinese physician recommends either a cooling or a "heaty" dish from the menu. For migraine sufferers the drunken scorpions are, by all accounts, a must; rheumatics should opt for crispy black ants. Daily 11.30am–2.30pm & 6.30–10.30pm.

Moi Kong Hakka, 22 Murray St, Chinatown (☎2217758). Hakka food relies heavily on salted and preserved ingredients and dishes here, in the best Hakka food outlet in Singapore, encompass abacus yam starch beads ($6) and stewed pork belly with preserved vegetables. Daily 10.30am–2.30pm & 6–10pm.

HIGH TEA AND TIFFIN

Many of Singapore's swisher hotels advertise that most colonial of traditions, **high tea**, in the local press; below are a few of the more permanent choices. Typically, a Singapore high tea comprises local and Western snacks, both sweet and savoury. If you really want to play the part of a Victorian settler, Singapore's most splendid food outlet at the *Raffles* still serves **tiffin** – the colonial term for a light curry meal (derived from the Hindi word for luncheon).

Café l'Espresso, *Goodwood Park Hotel*, 22 Scotts Rd, Orchard Road District (☎7377411). A great array of English cakes and pastries. Daily 2.30–6pm.

Café Vienna, *Royal Holiday Inn Crowne Plaza*, 25 Scotts Rd, Orchard Road District (☎7377966). Tremendously popular among Singaporeans, so get here early and wait in line to avoid disappointment. Open Mon–Fri 3–5.30pm, Sat & Sun 3–6pm.

Coleman's Café, *Peninsula Hotel*, 3 Coleman St, Colonial District (☎3372200). Cut-price, Saturdays-only high tea of more than twenty traditional hawker favourites. Sat 3–6pm.

Fosters, 02-38 *Specialists' Shopping Centre*, 277 Orchard Rd (☎7378939). Devonshire teas ($10) served 3–6pm.

Hilton Lounge, *Hilton Hotel*, 581 Orchard Rd (☎7372233). Afternoon tea ($23) at the *Hilton* is taken overlooking Orchard Road from the second floor mezzanine lounge. Daily noon–5pm.

Tiffin Room, *Raffles Hotel*, 1 Beach Rd, Colonial District (☎3371886). Tiffin lunch (noon–2pm) and dinner (7–10pm) both cost over $30 per person, though the spread of edibles, and the charming colonial surroundings make them worth considering. Between tiffin sittings, high tea ($25) is served 3.30–5pm.

Upstairs Café, Tudor Court, 131 Tanglin Rd, Orchard Road District (☎7336586). High tea is good value at $9, though the music from the clothes shops down the corridor is intrusive. Daily 11am–7pm.

Mosque Street Taiwanese Style Steamboat House, 44 Mosque St, Chinatown (☎2229560). Take a seat at the food bar, on which 60 individual woks are set on built-in heaters, purchase your steamboat ingredients ($6 per person) – noodles, egg, prawns, pork, fish – and get cooking. Great late-night fun. Daily 6pm–5am.

Shanghai Palace Seafood Restaurant, *Excelsior Hotel*, 5 Coleman St, Colonial District (☎3393428). Authentic Shanghai dishes – drunken chicken, fried hot and sour chicken, beancurd claypot – and a smattering of Cantonese and Szechuan favourites served in unfussy surroundings; two people pay upwards of $50. Daily noon–2.30pm & 6.30–10.30pm.

Snackworld, 01-12/13 Cuppage Plaza, 5 Koek Rd, off Orchard Road. Hectic terrace restaurant where the Chinese menu is enlivened by hot-plate crocodile meat ($25) and emu. Daily 11am–midnight.

Top Flight Mongolian BBQ, 04-01 Park Mall, 9 Penang Rd, off Orchard Road (☎3344888). Create your own combination from an array of meats, vegetables and sauces and hand it in at the open kitchen, where it's cooked for you on a hot griddle. Unlimited visits to the food bar cost under $20 (lunchtime) and $25 (dinner), and include starters and desserts. Daily 11.30am–2.30pm & 6–11pm.

European and international

Bistro Chez Moi, 217 East Coast Rd, Eastern Singapore (☎4403318). Intriguing Franco-Vietnamese crossbreed which makes it possible to follow an escargot starter with a bowl of *pho* (noodle soup), or sugar-cane prawns with saddle of rabbit; French set meals start from $14, Vietnamese from $11. Daily 11.30am–2.30pm & 6–10.30pm.

Le Bistrot Delifrance, 02-00, 249 Holland Rd, Holland Village ☎4670201. The latest addition to *Delifrance*'s Singaporean chain is a fully fledged restaurant, with a selective menu of steaks, chicken and fish dishes from $14.50. Daily 11am–2.30pm & 6–10.30pm.

Compass Rose, 69th floor, *Westin Stamford Hotel*, 2 Stamford Rd, Colonial District (☎3388585). An expensive place, but one that boasts a panoramic view of central Singapore. Buffet lunch ($45) is the cheapest way to experience the international cuisine. Daily noon–2.30pm & 7–10.30pm.

Duxton Deli and Wine Bar, 21 Duxton Hill, Chinatown (☎2277716). Pleasant wine bar on fashionable Duxton Hill where a sandwich or snack outside on the terrace will cost you less than $10. Open Mon–Sat 10am–midnight.

Gordon Grill, *Goodwood Park Hotel*, 22 Scotts Rd, off Orchard Road (☎2358637). Upmarket restaurant lent a Scottish feel by the tartan decor and the haggis with tatties: excellent food – but at a price. Set lunch ($37) is your best bet; the set dinner is a mighty $85. Daily noon–3pm & 7–11pm.

Hot Stones, 53 Boat Quay, Singapore River (☎5345188). A healthy and novel twist on dining: steaks, chicken and seafood grilled at table on non-porous Alpine rock heated to 200° – no oil, but bags of flavour. Daily noon–2.30pm & 6–10.30pm. See *Restaurants and bars along Boat Quay* map.

Istanbul Corner, 01-11 Cuppage Plaza, 5 Koek Rd, off Orchard Road (☎7388115). Authentic Turkish and Middle Eastern grills: the perfect way to round off a few Tiger beers on adjacent Cuppage Terrace.

Louis' Oyster Bar, 36 Boat Quay, Singapore River (☎5330534). The Louis in question is Louis Armstrong, who beams down from all the walls. Oysters cost around $15 per half-dozen, but the High Society Platter (crayfish, crab, mussels, oysters and prawns on ice; $50 for two) is hard to resist. Open Mon–Sat 11am–11pm, Sun 6–11pm.

Maison Basque, Suntec City Mall, 3 Temasek Blvd, Colonial District (☎3385308). French food cooked with half an eye over the border into Spain: come and have a crack at the filling Paella San Sebastian (a chicken, monkfish, prawn, mussel and squid feast); or settle for the *Ttoro* (seafood soup), washed down with mouthfuls of sangria ($20 per half-litre). Daily 11am–3pm & 6–11pm.

Maxim's de Paris, The *Regent Hotel*, 1 Cuscaden Rd, off Orchard Road (☎7338888). Stunning cuisine in a classic French dining room – one for a celebration. Open Mon–Fri 12.30–2.30pm & daily 6.30–10.30pm.

Milano's, Funan Centre, North Bridge Rd, Colonial District. Their "All you can eat – all day, every day" policy makes *Milano's* unbeatable value: choose from soups, pizzas, pastas and salad. Then choose again. And again. $11 a head.

Olive Tree, *Hotel Inter-Continental*, 80 Middle Rd, Colonial District (☎3387600). Anything goes in this stylish joint as long as there's a sun-kissed, Mediterranean connection: kick off with *bruschetta* or *gambas ceviche* (prawns marinated in tomato sauce, lime juice and olive oil), move on to *merguez* sausages with couscous, complemented by a Lebanese durum wheat salad, and end with Andalucian chocolate mousse. Buffet-style set lunches ($33) and dinners ($35) ease the choosing process.

Paulaner Bräuhaus, 01-01 Millenia Walk, 9 Raffles Blvd, Colonial District (☎3377123). German theme restaurant-cum-brewery, serving generous platters of *wurst, kartoffeln* and *sauerkraut*; two pay $60, including a stein of beer each. Dinner 11am–2.30pm & 6.30–9.30pm, then drinks only (see p.584).

Pasta Fresca, 30 Boat Quay, Singapore River (☎5326283). Match up fresh pasta and a sauce from the menu, and sit out on the riverside terrace. Around $20 a head, drinks extra. Daily 11am–10pm.

Prego, third floor, *Westin Stamford*, 2 Stamford Rd, Colonial District (☎3388585). Upbeat, checked-tablecloth decor, fine soups, pastas, pizzas and meat dishes, and prices that won't break the bank; set lunch of three courses plus coffee for $30. Daily noon–2.30pm & 7–10.30pm.

Pronto, fifth floor, *Oriental Hotel*, 5 Raffles Ave, Colonial District (☎3380066). Affordable open-air restaurant beside the *Oriental's* fifth-floor pool; pastas and pizzas cost around $15, meat dishes slightly more; leave room for the delicious *tiramisu*. Daily noon–10pm.

Ristorante Bologna, fourth floor, *Marina Mandarin Hotel*, 6 Raffles Blvd, Colonial District (☎3383388). Award-winning restaurant with da Vinci prints on the walls and musicians to serenade you. Meals are fairly steeply priced – dishes average out at $40 – but the buffet lunch (noon–2.30pm; closed Sat) will fill you up for $36. Daily noon–2.30pm & 7pm–midnight.

Rosette, 22/24 Orchard Rd, opposite Dhoby Ghaut MRT (☎3386115). The Singapore Hotel Association Training & Educational Centre runs this place, the deal being that customers get good, fair-priced Continental food in return for being part of the training procedure. Set lunches from $15, and on Friday nights a five-course meal with wine costs $45. Mon–Sat noon–3pm & 7–10pm.

Victorian Café, Victoria Memorial Hall, Empress Place, Colonial District (☎3397231). The marble tables and dark wood fittings in this tasteful café are offset by bare white walls. Pasta, pizzas, soup and sandwiches, all for less than $8. Open Mon–Sat 11.30am–6.30pm.

Indian

Akbal Muslim Food Stall, 168–170 Serangoon Rd, Little India. Set within the *Thye Chong Restaurant* on the corner of Norris Road, *chapatis* are hand-cooked on a griddle in front of you. Brains, liver and goats' legs flank more conventional dishes on the accompanying curry menu.

Annalakshmi, *Excelsior Hotel* & Shopping Centre, 5 Coleman St, Colonial District (☎3399993). Terrific North and South Indian vegetarian food in sumptuous surroundings, with all profits going to Kala Mandhir, an Indian cultural association next door. Many of the staff are volunteers from the Hindu community, so your waiter might just be a doctor or a lawyer. Dishes from $10. Daily 11.30am–3pm & 6–9.30pm.

Banana Leaf Apolo, 54–58 Race Course Rd, Little India (☎2938682). Recently refurbished, and now resplendent in marble, though eating with your hands is still the order of the day; pioneering fish-head curry ($30 for two people) restaurant where a wide selection of South Indian dishes are all served on banana leaves. Daily 10.30am–10pm.

Gandhi Eating House, 29 Chandler Rd, Little India. Many locals reckon this open-fronted place on the flipside of Racecourse Road is knocking out the best chicken curries in Little India; meals come on banana leaves, water in metal jugs. Daily 9am–9.30pm.

Islamic Restaurant, 791–797 North Bridge Rd, Arab Quarter (☎2987563). Aged Muslim restaurant manned by a gang of old men who plod solemnly up and down between the tables. It boasts the best chicken *biriyani* in Singapore, cooked in the traditional way – heated from above and below with charcoal. $10 for two. Open 9.30am–9.30pm; closed Fri.

Kinara, 57 Boat Quay, Singapore River (☎5330412). Exquisite restaurant boasting antique fittings imported from the subcontinent; a marvellous view of the river from upstairs, and elegantly presented Punjabi dishes. Around $50 for two. Daily noon–2.30pm & 6.30–10.30pm.

Komala Villas, 76–78 Serangoon Rd, Little India (☎2936980). A cramped, popular vegetarian establishment specializing in fifteen varieties of *dosai*. The "South Indian Meal", served upstairs on a banana leaf, is great value at $4.50. Daily 7am–10pm.

Madras New Woodlands, 12–14 Upper Dickson Rd, Little India (☎2971594). Functional, canteen-style place serving up decent vegetarian food at bargain prices. House specialities are the Thali set meal ($4) and the VIP Thali ($6); *samosas, bahjis* and other snacks are available after 3pm, and there's a big selection of sweets, too. Recommended. Daily 8am–11pm.

Maharani, 05-36 Far East Plaza, Scotts Road, off Orchard Road (☎2358840). Orchard Road's pioneering North Indian restaurant grades each dish's "heatiness" with star ratings. Around $25 a head, with beer. Daily noon–10.30pm.

Moti Mahal, 18 Murray St, Chinatown (☎2214338). Not cheap, but one of Singapore's very best, serving tasty *tandoori* dishes in pleasant surroundings. The special is *murg massalam*, a whole chicken stuffed with rice ($50 – order in advance). Daily 11am–3pm & 6.30–10.30pm.

Muthu's Curry Restaurant, 76/78 Race Course Rd, Little India (☎2932389) Rough and ready South Indian restaurant with no menu, but famous for its fish-head curry. Daily 10am–10pm.

Nur Jehan, 66 Race Course Rd, Little India (☎2928033). Prize-winning cook Gurdayal Singh used to work at the legendary Singaporean restaurant *Omar Khayyam*, so expect fine food in this rather bare, but extremely friendly North Indian restaurant. Daily 11am–11.30pm.

Orchard Maharajah, 25 Cuppage Terrace, Cuppage Road, off Orchard Road (☎7326331). Set in a wonderful old Peranakan house, this splendid North Indian restaurant has a large terrace and a tempting menu that includes the sublime fish *mumtaz* – fillet of fish stuffed with minced mutton, almonds, eggs, cashews and raisins – worth the extra few dollars. The set lunch is good value at $16. Daily 11.30am–3pm & 6.30–11pm.

Rang Mahal, *Imperial Hotel*, 11 Jalan Rumbia, off Orchard Road (☎7371666). Quite superlative restaurant whose divine North Indian food has secured it a place in *Tatler's Singapore's Best Restaurants* guide for the past thirteen years. Cultural performances accompany your dining, there are daily set meals, and buffet lunches available Sat and Sun. Daily noon–2.30pm & 7–11pm.

Royal Bengal, 72 Boat Quay, Singapore River (☎5384329). Predominantly North Indian restaurant whose menu ranges from the dramatic (chicken *tandoori* served on a flaming sword) to the stomach-turning (lamb's testicles), and features an unusually wide selection of seafood dishes such as stingray and pomfret. Open Mon–Fri & Sun 11.30am–2.30pm & 7–11pm, Sat 7–11pm.

Sri Vijayah, 229 Selegie Rd, Little India (☎3361748). Hole-in-the-wall vegetarian banana leaf joint offering unbeatable value for money: $3 buys a replenishable mountain of rice and vegetable curries, and there's a mouth-watering display of sweetmeats at the front door. Daily 6am–10pm.

Taj Jazzaurant, 02-01 Little India Arcade, 48 Serangoon Rd, Little India (☎2914680). Fine north and south Indian food until 10pm (signature dishes: South coast prawn and *brinjal* curry at $12, and *raan pasinda*, leg of lamb in yoghurt, for $18), after which the bar continues to serve (see p.584).

Zam Zam, 699 North Bridge Rd, Arab Quarter (☎2987011). A simple curry house, though worth a visit to see the award-winning *murtabak* maker in action. Daily 7am–11pm.

Indonesian

Alkaff Mansion, 10 Telok Blangah Green, Western Singapore (☎2786979). Built in the 1920s as a weekend retreat for the Alkaff family, the splendidly restored mansion offers a superb *rijstaffel* ($66), ten dishes served by a line of ten women in traditional *kebayas*. Or just have a beer in the bar, worth the exorbitant price for an hour or two of colonial grandeur. Bus #145 from Redhill MRT. Daily noon–midnight.

House of Sundanese Food, 55 Boat Quay, Singapore River (☎5343775) and 218 East Coast Rd (☎3455020). Spicy salads and barbecued seafood characterize the cuisine of Sunda (West Java), served here in simple yet tasteful surroundings. Try the tasty *ikan sunda* (grilled Javanese fish) – an $18 fish serves two to three people. Open Tues–Sun 11am–2.30pm & 5–10pm.

Rendezvous, 02-19 Raffles City Shopping Centre, 252 North Bridge Rd, Colonial District (☎3397508). Revered *nasi padang* joint that still turns in lip-smacking curries, *rendangs* and *sambals*; the weighing machine in the corner is an unusual touch. Daily 11am–9.30pm.

Rumah Makam Minang, 18a Kandahar St, Arab Quarter. Fiery *nasi padang* – highly spiced Sumatran cuisine – in the heart of the Arab Quarter; $4 ensures a good feed, while $3 buys the popular barbecued fish. Daily noon–2.30pm & 6–10.30pm.

Sanur, 04-17/18 Centrepoint, 176 Orchard Rd (☎7342192). Hearty, reasonably priced food served by waitresses in traditional batik dress; the beef *rendang* is terrific. It's best to book ahead. Daily 11.30am–2.45pm & 5.45–10pm.

Sayna, Block D, Clarke Quay, Singapore River (☎3396388). Kampung-style *atap* roofs and bamboo screens combine to cosy effect in this affordable restaurant; the *nasi padang* buffet lunch ($15) guarantees a huge feed; or choose from the à la carte menu at night. Open noon–3pm & 6–10.30pm; closed Tues.

RESTAURANT ENTERTAINMENT

Asian Village, Sentosa Island. The *Fascinating Asian* dance show in the Thai Pavilion starts at 6.30pm and 7.15pm nightly; the $18 charge includes a buffet dinner.

Hilton-British Airways Playhouse, Hilton Hotel, 581 Orchard Rd (☎7372233). London West End plays by playwrights in the Alan Ayckbourn mould are presented periodically; tickets are expensive (over $120 per person) but include a four-course dinner.

Malay Village, Geyland Serai, Eastern Singapore. The *Floating Seafood Restaurant* stages nightly Malay Cultural shows, but those on tighter budgets can watch free singing and dancing in the village's entrance courtyard . Open Sat & Sun 7.30–9.30pm.

Mandarin, 333 Orchard Rd (☎7374411). The price – around $50 – buys you an international buffet and a viewing of the *Asean Night* cultural show, music, songs and dance from all the southeast Asian countries. Dinner at 7pm; show starts at 8pm. Book ahead.

Merlion Ballroon, *Cockpit Hotel*, 6–7 Oxley Rise, off Orchard Road (☎7379111). The nightly *Instant Asia* show is preceded by a buffet; the package costs $38, and dinner is at 7pm. Book in advance.

Singa Inn Seafood Restaurant, 920 East Coast Parkway, Eastern Singapore (☎3451111). Dinner at this well-established seafood restaurant entitles you to watch the *Asian Cultural Show*, which kicks off at 8pm, Monday to Friday. Reservations recommended.

Tai He Lou Theatre, *Tang Dynasty City*, 2 Yuan Ching Rd, Jurong Lake, Western Singapore (☎2611116). Chinese dancers and gymnasts perform as you enjoy buffet lunch (1.15pm) or dinner (7.30pm). Under $30, though this doesn't include the Tang Dynasty City entrance fee.

Sukmaindra, *Royal Holiday Inn Crowne Plaza*, 25 Scotts Rd, off Orchard Road (☎7317988). Singapore's only Bruneian restaurant, with an inevitably strong Indonesian influence. Well-cooked food, and no alcohol, which keeps the price down. Daily 11.30am–3pm & 6.30–11pm.

Tambuah Mas Indonesian Restaurant, 04-10, Tanglin Shopping Centre, 19 Tanglin Rd, off Orchard Road (☎7333333). Friendly restaurant, approached through a Minangkabau-style entrance, and offering padang food and a smattering of Chinese dishes. Daily 11.30am–2.30pm & 6–10.30pm.

Japanese

Fiesta Sushi Factory, 25 Boon Tat St, Financial District. Most business is done at the takeaway counter at the front of this affordable sushi joint (single pieces from 50c to $1), though there's limited seating at the back.

Inagiku, third floor, *Westin Plaza Hotel*, 2 Stamford Rd, Colonial District (☎3388585). More of a maze than a restaurant, with four sections serving expensive, quality *tempura*, *teppanyaki*, *sushi*, and an à la carte menu – the latter the cheapest alternative. Open Mon–Sat noon–2.30pm & 6.30–10.30pm.

Japanese stalls, *Food Junction*, B1, *Seiyu Department Store*, Bugis Junction, 200 Victoria St, Colonial District. *Sumo* has *sashimi*, *tempura* and *teriyaki* sets around $9; while nearby *Express-Teppanyaki*'s "big-value meal" ($6.20) offers your choice of meats and vegetables flash-fried on the U-shaped hot bar.

Senbazuru, *Hotel New Otani*, 177a River Valley Rd, Colonial District (☎3383333). If the wide menu proves too mind-boggling, choose from the selection of set lunches; for real gastronomes, there's the *kaiseki ryori*, or traditional eleven-course meal. Daily 11.30am–2.30pm & 6.30–10.30pm.

Sushi Kaiseki Nogawa, fourth floor, *Crown Prince Hotel*, 270 Orchard Rd (☎7323053). Tiny *sushi* bar down a spooky corridor, where food is served by demure waitresses in kimonos; a meal for two starts at around $60. Daily noon–3pm & 5–12pm.

Sushi Tei, 20 Lorong Mambong, Holland Village (☎4632310). A cross-fertilization of Tokyo sushi bar and airport baggage reclaim: diners snatch *sushi* sets ($1.50–$4) from the conveyor belt looping the bar.

Korean

Haebok's Korean Restaurant, 44–46 Tanjong Pagar Rd, Chinatown (☎2239003). All the standard dishes, served by lukewarm staff in a plain dining room. If you aren't acquainted with Korean food, plastic models of the meals available displayed in the front window lend a few pointers. Daily 11.30am–3pm & 5.30–10.30pm.

Hando Korean Restaurant, 05-01 Orchard Shopping Centre, 321 Orchard Rd (☎2358451). Classic dishes taken in a cushioned, traditional Korean chamber. At least $45 for two, more if you sink a few OB beers. Daily 11am–11pm.

Korean Restaurant Pte Ltd, 05-35 Specialists' Centre, 277 Orchard Rd (☎2350018). Singapore's first Korean restaurant, beautifully furnished and serving up a wide range of dependably good dishes at around $16–20 per dish. Daily 11am–11pm.

Seoul Garden Korean Restaurant, 03-119 Marina Square, 6 Raffles Blvd, Colonial District (☎3391339). Entertaining, busy restaurant with daily set lunches from $7.90; best value is the "all you can eat" Korean barbecue – a buffet of twenty seasoned meats, seafoods and vegetables cooked by customers at their tables. Open Mon–Fri 11am–3pm & 5.30–10.30pm, Sat & Sun 11am–10.30pm.

Malay and Nonya

Aziza's, 02-15 Albert Court, 180 Albert St, Colonial District (☎2351130). Stylish little place serving premier Malay food; set meals are available ($15–30), or try the house speciality, *ayam panggang kasturi* – chicken charcoal-grilled with black shallot sauce, lemon grass and fresh lime on a banana leaf. You'll need to book ahead. Mon–Sat 11.30am–3pm & 6.30–10.30pm, Sun 6.30–10.30pm.

Bengawan Solo. Excellent cake shop, specializing in Malay *kueh* (cakes) and with branches at Centrepoint, 176 Orchard Rd, and at Clifford Centre, 24 Raffles Place, Financial District. Daily 10am–8pm.

Blue Ginger, 97 Tanjong Pagar Rd, Chinatown (☎2223928). Housed in a renovated shophouse, this trendy Peranakan restaurant is proving a yuppy favourite, thanks to such dishes as *ikan masal assam gulai* (mackerel simmered in a tamarind and lemongrass gravy), and that benchmark of

Nonya cuisine, *ayam buah keluak* – braised chicken with Indonesian black nuts. Daily 11.30am–3pm & 6.30–11pm.

Bintang Timur, 02-08/13 Far East Plaza, 14 Scotts Rd, off Orchard Road (☎2354539). A perennial favourite, thanks to its reliable cooking; sticks of satay here are bigger than usual, so don't over-order. Around $12 a head without beer. Daily 11am–9.45pm.

Guan Hoe Soon, 214 Joo Chiat Rd, Katong, Eastern Singapore (☎3442761). Fifty years old, and still turning out fine Nonya cuisine; try the *Chen Dool* (coconut milk, red beans, sugar, green jelly and ice), a refreshing end to a meal. Around $35 for two, with beer. Open 11am–3pm & 6–9.30pm; closed Tues.

Mum's Kitchen, 314 Joo Chiat Rd, Eastern Singapore (☎3460969). Emphasis here, as you'd imagine, is on home-cooked food, Nonya-based, though with other Asian incursions. House speciality, Mum's Curry, is wonderful, and best chased down by homemade barley water; special business lunches (Mon–Fri) offer three courses at $18 for two people. Daily 11am–10pm.

Nonya & Baba, 262 River Valley Rd, Colonial District (☎7341382). Greatly respected Nonya restaurant lent character by its marble tables and tasteful decor; the *otak otak* (fish mashed with coconut milk and chilli paste, wrapped in banana leaf) and the *ayam buah keluak* (chicken with black nuts) are both terrific; other dishes cost around $7 a head. Daily 11.30am–10pm.

Peranakan Inn, 210 East Coast Rd , Eastern Singapore (☎4406195). As much effort goes into the food as went into the renovation of this immaculate, sky-blue shophouse restaurant, which offers authentic Nonya favourites at reasonable prices; around $8 a dish. Daily 11am–3pm & 6–11pm.

Spring Blossoms Café, *Bayview Inn*, 30 Bencoolen St, Colonial District (☎3372882 ext 281). This faceless hotel café's buffet lunch is a great introduction to Nonya cuisine, and very reasonable at around $14. Open Wed, Sat & Sun noon–5pm.

MARKETS AND SUPERMARKETS

Some guesthouses do have cooking facilities, and if you want to buy your own food or fancy a bag of fresh fruit, you're most likely to go to a **wet market** – so called due to the pools of water perpetually covering the floor. If you don't know a mango from a mangosteen, vendors are usually very helpful – and see food glossary on p.49. Singapore also has plenty of **supermarkets**, most of which have a delicatessen counter and bakery – some offer familiar beers from back home, too.

Markets
Little India is served by the large wet market in the *Zhujiao Centre*, at the southern end of Serangoon Road; both the *Chinatown Complex* and *Ellenborough Street* markets in **Chinatown** reward a visit, too; and you'll find other wet markets out of the city centre, in Singapore's new towns.

Supermarkets
Cold Storage, branches at Centrepoint, Orchard Rd; 293 Holland Rd; 31 Amber Rd, Katong. Local chain which stocks a wide range of Western products.

Diamaru, Liang Court Shopping Complex, 177 River Valley Rd. Japanese department store with a large food hall featuring takeaway counters.

Good Gifts Emporium, Golden Mile Complex, 5001 Beach Rd. A smallish supermarket with a leaning towards Thai produce.

NTUC Fairprice, Rochor Centre, 1 Rochor Rd. Basic supermarket that's handy for Bencoolen Street.

Sogo, Raffles City Shopping Centre, 252 North Bridge Rd. Japanese department store where you can buy groceries and takeaway snacks.

Tashing Emporium, People's Park Complex, 1 Park Rd. Taiwanese emporium whose food hall sells some interesting Chinese produce.

Yaohan, Plaza Singapura, 68 Orchard Rd. Japanese department store and supermarket similar to *Diamaru* and *Sogo*.

Violet Oon's Kitchen, 11 Bukit Pasoh Rd, Chinatown (☎2263225). Diners in this immaculately renovated shophouse are in truly safe hands – Violet Oon is one of Singapore's most renowned food writers; if you don't choose from the small but well-formed menu, try either the Nonya Feast ($30) or the Nonya Rendezvous ($20). Violet also conducts occasional cookery workshops (call ☎3237379). Open Mon–Sat 10am–11pm.

Thai, Vietnamese and Filipino

Bistro Chez Moi, 217 East Coast Rd, Eastern Singapore (☎4403318). Vietnamese (and French) cuisine, east of downtown Singapore.

Cozy Kosina, 04-76 Lucky Plaza, 304 Orchard Rd. Open-fronted, canteen-style Filipino restaurant serving local specialities like *kare kare* (Filipino-style beef stew with peanut butter) and *tinolang manok*, chicken soup with papaya. Daily 10.30am–9pm.

Cuppage Thai Food Restaurant, 49 Cuppage Terrace, off Orchard Road (☎7341116). Nondescript inside, but boasting a great outdoor terrace, this cheap and cheerful restaurant offers quality Thai dishes at around the $8 mark. Daily 11am–3pm & 6–11pm.

Pornping Thai Seafood Restaurant, 01-96/98 Golden Mile Complex, 5001 Beach Rd, Arab Quarter (☎2985016). Set in a complex known locally as "Thai Village" and always full of Thais waiting to catch buses home. All the standard dishes at cheap prices – $25 buys a meal for two, washed down with Singha beer. Daily 10am–10pm.

Saigon, 04-03 Cairnhill Place, 15 Cairnhill Rd, off Orchard Road (☎2350626). A posh yet affordable place which doesn't overdo the traditional Vietnamese decor. The baked fish with meat filling is reason enough to come; set lunches start from $15 (minimum two people). Daily 11.45am–2.45pm & 6–10.30pm.

Shingthai Palace, 13 Purvis St, Colonial District (☎3371161). Elegant little restaurant off Beach Road serving reasonably priced Thai dishes; try the *peek kai sord sai* (chicken wings with asparagus, prawns, mushrooms and meat). Around $15–20 a head. Daily 11am–3pm & 6–10.30pm.

Sukhothai, 47 Boat Quay, Singapore River (☎5381323). Chef's recommendations include fried cotton fish topped with sliced green mangoes, but you can't go far wrong whatever you plump for; the dining room is rather understated, so take advantage of the riverside tables. Daily 6.30–11pm, Mon–Fri also noon–3pm.

US

Billy Bombers, 02-52 Bugis Junction, 200 Victoria St, Colonial District (☎3378018). Shades of *Arnold's* diner in *Happy Days*: reasonably priced burgers and bowls of chilli eaten in speakeasy booths upholstered in red leather.

Bobby Rubino's, B1-03 Fountain Court, CHIJMES, 30 Victoria St, Colonial District (☎3375466). Ribs are the speciality, but steaks, burgers and other big-boy platters are available; eschew the "wine-rack" partitions and rough-hewn red-brick interior and make for the terrace, superbly located below CHIJMES' looming convent. Daily 12.30–4pm & 6–10pm.

Cha Cha Cha, 32 Lorong Mambong, Holland Village (☎46216509). Classic Mexican dishes in this vibrantly coloured restaurant range from $10 to 22; outside are a few open-air patio tables, ideal for posing with a bottle of Dos Equis beer, but book ahead for these. Daily 11.30am–10pm.

Chico's N Charlie's, 05-01 Liat Towers, 541 Orchard Rd (☎7341753). Faithfully re-created Mexican decor and food ($11–38), as well as a good-value set lunch ($15 for main course, soup, garlic bread, dessert and coffee or tea). Daily 11am–11pm.

Dan Ryan's Chicago Grill, B1-01 Tanglin Mall, 91 Tanglin Rd, off Orchard Road (☎7383800). Chug back a Budweiser and get stuck into "American portions" of ribs, burgers and chicken in a dining room that's crammed with Americana; main courses cost around $15. Daily 11am–midnight.

El Felipe's, 34 Lorong Mambong, Holland Village (☎4681520). Charming venue, with a raised bar area fitted out in weathered, light-blue wooden panels, a jukebox, and a menu embracing everything from *burritos* to *fajitas*. Daily noon–10pm.

El Pollo Loco, 01-75 Millenia Walk, 9 Raffles Blvd, Colonial District (☎3397377), branch at 2 Lorong Mambong. Surely the only Singaporean restaurant to boast an endorsement from the *American Heart Association*: flame-broiled chicken served with tortillas and salsa in the latest branch of this health-conscious, Los Angeles-based chain.

Hard Rock Café, 50 Cuscaden Rd, off Orchard Road (☎2355232). Big-boy portions of ribs, burgers and steaks served to the ear-bending accompaniment of Guns 'n' Roses, Deep Purple et al. The delicately named pig sandwich ($14) is irresistible, or there's a three-course set lunch (Mon–Fri 11am-2pm). Open 11am–10.30pm; closed Sun.

Ponderosa, 02-13-19 Plaza Singapura, 68 Orchard Rd (☎3360139). The perfect cure for vitamin deficiency – chicken, steak and fish set meals come with baked potato, sundae, and as much salad as you can eat, at a bargain $12.50. Daily 11am–10pm.

Seah Street Deli, *Raffles Hotel*, 1 Beach Rd, Colonial District (☎3371886). New York-style deli boasting the most mountainous sandwiches in Asia, at around $10 each. Huge crayons, bagels and wristwatches on the walls make this the most un-colonial establishment in *Raffles Hotel*. Daily 11am–10pm, Fri & Sat until 11pm.

Stars, 01-18 CHIJMES, 30 Victoria St, Colonial District (☎3321033). *Stars* conspired to secure prime spot in CHIJMES, and its verandahs take full advantage of this fact; the ground-floor café serves *tacos*, pizzas, salads and grilled shellfish ($10 each dish); while the tasteful pillared room upstairs features a more heavyweight menu.

Drinking and nightlife

Singapore has much more to offer in the way of **nightlife** than it's often given credit for. The island's burgeoning **bar and pub** scene means there is now a wide range of drinking holes to choose from, with the Colonial District, Boat Quay and Orchard Road areas offering particularly good pub crawl potential. With competition hotting up, more and more bars are turning to **live music** to woo punters, though this is usually no more than cover versions performed by local bands. That said, big-name groups do occasionally make forays into southeast Asia, playing Bangkok, Kuala Lumpur and Jakarta as well as Singapore. **Clubs** also do brisk business; glitzy yet unpretentious, they feature the latest imported pop, rock and dance music, though don't expect anything like a rave scene – Ecstasy isn't in the Singaporean dictionary.

Bars and pubs

With the **bars and pubs** of Singapore ranging from slick cocktail joints, through elegant colonial chambers to boozy dives, you're bound to find a place that suits you. Establishments open either in the late morning (to catch the lunchtime dining trade) or in the early evening, and usually close around midnight. On Friday and Saturday, opening hours almost invariably extend by an hour or two. Many serve snacks throughout the day, and a few offer more substantial dishes. It's possible to buy a small glass of beer in most places for around $5, but **prices** can be double or treble that amount, especially in the Orchard Road district. A glass of wine usually costs much the same as a beer, and spirits a dollar or two more. One way of cutting costs is to arrive in time for **Happy Hour** in the early evening, when bars offer local beers and house wine either at half price, or "one for one" – you get two of whatever you order, but one is held back for later.

Singaporeans adore rock **music**, and a plethora of bars panders to this, presenting nightly performances by local or Filipino covers bands. These are picked out below, but for more details see p.623. Also hugely popular is **karaoke**, which almost reaches an art form in some Singapore bars.

Boat Quay and Clarke Quay

Buzz, 88 Circular Rd. Decor is nothing special, and the music stuck in an eighties groove, but this place still rages over the weekend, with local and expat twenty- and thirty-somethings coming in their herds.

Escobar, 37 Boat Quay. Latino grooves, best enjoyed by secreting yourself among the cool people who inhabit the waterfront terrace; bar snacks are uninspiring except for the decent *calamares*.

Café@boatquay, 82 Boat Quay. On-line cyber-café enabling you to munch a sandwich and chug a beer as you surf the net (access $5 for 30min).

Crazy Elephant, 01-07 Trader's Market, Clarke Quay. The only bar with any real clout along Clarke Quay, playing decent rock music on the turntable between live sessions by the house band; decor is a rag-tag blend of tea chest panels and graffiti, but regulars prefer the tables out by the water's edge. Mon–Thurs & Sun 5pm–1am, Fri & Sat till 2am.

Emoh Café, 9–9a Circular Rd. Tremendous chill-out joint, modelled on a kid's den (*Emoh* spells "home" backwards) with guitars to strum, table footie, internet access ($7 an hour) and even a bed to recline on; Happy Hour is 6am–8pm, and snacks weigh in at under $10. Open 24hr.

Harry's Quayside, 28 Boat Quay. There's live jazz Wednesday to Saturday in this upmarket place, and a blues jam every Sunday evening. Light lunches are served and prices are lower in the early evening. Daily 1pm–1am.

Molly Malone's, 42 Circular Rd. With Kilkenny and Guinness on tap, sounds courtesy of Van Morrison and the Pogues, and a menu offering Connemara oysters and Irish stew, hardly your quintessential Singaporean boozer, but a good crack nonetheless, when full.

Rootz, 60 Boat Quay. Cramped and sweaty bar, rocking over the weekend, whose DJ's catholic tastes embrace soul, Motown, funk, hip-hop, reggae and R&B; not the place for a quiet chat.

The Colonial District

Bar and Billiards Room, *Raffles Hotel*, 1 Beach Rd. A Singapore Sling ($17), in the colonial elegance of the hotel where Ngiam Tong Boon invented it in 1915, is required drinking on a visit to Singapore. Snacks are available through the afternoon, and playing billiards costs another $15 an hour. Daily 11.30am–midnight.

Bonne Santé, 01-13 CHIJMES, 30 Victoria St. Fancy wine bar in CHIJMES' Tuscan courtyard; a yuppie magnet.

Compass Rose Bar, seventieth floor, *Westin Stamford Hotel*, 2 Stamford Rd. Tasteful bar from whose floor-to-ceiling windows you can see as far as southern Malaysia. Happy Hour 5.30–8.30pm; minimum charge $15 after 8.30pm. Daily 11am–12.30am.

Harry Keery's, 01-20 Capitol Building, 11 Stamford Rd. Slick operation, with stylish metal furnishings and music videos showing on mini-TVs set into the bar. Japanese food and imported beers (*Budweiser, Kronenbourg* and *Grolsch*) available. Happy Hour 11.30am–8.30pm; open 11am–midnight.

Lot, Stock and Barrel Pub, 29 Seah St. Frequented by an early office crowd and a late backpacker crowd (Beach Road's homestays are just around the corner), who come for the rock classics on the jukebox. Happy Hour 4–8pm; open 4pm–midnight.

Paulaner Bräuhaus, 01-01 Millenia Walk, 9 Raffles Blvd. *Wurst* and *sauerkraut* might be a priority upstairs (see p.577), but down in the bar of this themed micobrewery, lager is very much in the forefront of the punter's minds; predictably busy around Oktoberfest-time.

Somerset's Bar, Level Three, *Westin Plaza Hotel*, 2 Stamford Rd. Sterile, open-plan bar improved by top-notch live jazz. Happy Hour Mon–Fri 5–8.30pm; open 5pm–2am.

Little India and around

Bar, 202 Serangoon Rd. Set behind saloon-style swing doors, this tiny drinking den is peopled by bleary-eyed boozers; faded old beer ads and shelves lined with dusty bottles of brutal Chinese liqueurs line the walls, while crushed peanut shells litter the floor. Daily 10am–10pm.

Leisure Pub, B1-01 Selegie Centre, 189 Selegie Rd. Tame but endearing, darts-orientated establishment that's ideal for a quiet chat. Happy Hour 3–8pm; open 5pm–12.30am.

Pirate's Well Pub, 01-275 Selegie Complex, Selegie Rd. Indian-run hideaway catering to the Little India community; dim lighting conjures a moody atmosphere. Daily 5pm–midnight.

Taj Jazzaurant, 02-01 Little India Arcade, 48 Serangoon. Once the plates and cutlery have been cleared away, there's swinging Hindi and Tamil dance music deep into the night.

Orchard Road

Anywhere, 04-08/09 Tanglin Shopping Centre, 19 Tanglin Rd. Tania, Singapore's most famous covers band, plays nightly to a boozy roomful of expats that's at its rowdiest on Friday nights. Happy Hour Mon–Fri 6–8pm; open Mon–Sat 6pm–2am.

Brannigan's, *Hyatt Regency Hotel*, 10-12 Scotts Rd. Popular expat haunt where cocktails smooth the way during Happy Hour (5–8pm), and house bands are usually good. Daily 5pm–1am.

Excalibur Pub, B1-06 Tanglin Shopping Centre, 19 Tanglin Rd. Wonderfully cluttered and cramped British-style pub that's full of weatherbeaten expats. Daily 11am–10.30pm.

Fabrice's World Music Bar, Basement, *Dynasty Hotel*, 320 Orchard Rd. Hip music and decor from around the world make this Singapore's current hot spot; expect pricey cover charges after 10pm and prohibitively expensive drinks. Happy Hour 5–8pm; open 3am.

The Ginivy, 02-11 Rear Block, Orchard Towers, 1 Claymore Drive. Good-time Country & Western bar with a decent house band. Daily 8pm–3am.

Hard Rock Café, 02-01 HPL House, 50 Cuscaden Rd. Pricey drinks and a cover charge after 10.30pm make this cult bar/restaurant an expensive experience. Happy Hour Mon–Fri 4–7pm; open daily 11am–2am.

Ice Cold Beer, 9 Emerald Hill. Noisy, hectic and happening place where the beers are kept on ice under the glass-topped bar; the lamentable upstairs den is best avoided; Happy Hour daily 5–9pm, and there are regular promotions. Daily 5pm–midnight.

No 5 Emerald Hill, 5 Emerald Hill Rd. Quite a pleasant Peranakan-style bar/restaurant, if you can stomach the preening and posing of the bar staff. Happy Hour 5–8pm; open noon–2am.

Observation Lounge, 38th floor, *Mandarin Hotel*, 333 Orchard Rd. Swanky cocktail bar offering awesome views over downtown Singapore. Open 11am–1am except Fri & Sat 11am–2am.

Saxophone, 23 Cuppage Rd. The coolest address in town, and a magnet for the beautiful people, who relax on the terrace to the sounds of the house jazz band. Classy French food is served, but neither that nor the drinks come cheap – start elsewhere, or catch Happy Hour (6–8pm). Daily 6pm–2am.

Shirley's Place, 02-01 Far East Shopping Centre, 545 Orchard Rd. A current favourite among Singapore's hard-drinking expats and always lively and fun; recommended.

Snackworld, Cuppage Terrace. Buy a bottle of *Tiger* and enjoy the music drifting over from *Saxophone* without paying *Saxophone* prices – a great place to hang out. Daily 11am–midnight.

Vintage Rock Café, 03-18 Cuppage Plaza, 5 Koek Rd. Friendly staff and locals, great R&B music on the speakers and cheapish beer: recommended. Happy Hour 5–8pm; open 5pm–midnight.

Why? Pub, 04-06 Far East Plaza, 14 Scotts Rd. The budget prices in this tiny, lively pub attract big drinkers. Daily 2pm–midnight.

River Valley Road

The Mitre, 145 Killiney Rd. Marvellously shabby old hotel bar, with TV and dartboard.

Next Page Pub, 15 Mohamed Sultan Rd. Cool, popular pub, with pool table, scatter cushions and R&B sounds. Daily 3pm–1am.

Wong San's, 12 Jalan Mohamed Sultan. Stylish pub in a beautifully decorated Peranakan-style building, popular with local journalists and white-collar workers. Daily 3pm–1am.

The Yard, 294 River Valley Rd. Busy English pub with bar snacks available with a 3–8pm Happy Hour. Daily 3pm–midnight.

Sentosa Island

Sunset Bay, Siloso Beach, Sentosa (☎2750668). Sleepy straw-roofed beach bar, recalling pre-development Sentosa, where beach bums can cavort on one of seven volleyball courts down on the sand, or merely baywatch out to the twinkling lights of the ships waiting to enter Singapore's harbours. Take bus M from the mainland, and book ahead for volleyball at the weekends. Open Mon–Thurs 10am–10pm, Fri & Sun till 11pm, Sat till midnight.

Tanjong Pagar

Cable Car Saloon, 2 Duxton Hill. Modelled on a Chicago cable car, a haunt frequented by couples, with subtle jazz sounds; cocktails are a speciality, or explore the stock of over three hundred whiskeys. Mon–Sat 5pm–midnight, Sun 3pm–midnight.

Duxton's Chicago Bar, 6–9 Duxton Hill. Good live jazz and blues, Americana on the walls and a decent adjoining restaurant; Happy Hour (noon–8.30pm) prices last all day Sunday. Daily noon–1am.

Elvis' Place, 1a Duxton Hill. Elvis-devoted pub where videos of the King are screened regularly. Open Mon–Sat 3pm–midnight.

Flag and Whistle Public House, 10 Duxton Hill. Predictable British pub, complete with Bass beer, bar snacks and a large Union Jack. Daily 11am–midnight.

J.J. Mahoney Pub, 58 Duxton Rd. A popular haunt for karaoke-hungry local yuppies; the bar serves Bass beer and snacks throughout the night; Happy Hour is 11am–8pm, but doesn't include Bass. Daily 11am–1am.

Clubs

Unlike their London and New York counterparts, Singaporean **clubs** are refreshingly naive, their customers more intent on enjoying themselves than on posing. European and American dance music dominates (though some play Cantonese pop songs, too), and many feature live bands playing cover versions of current hits and pop classics. Clubs tend to open around 9pm, though some start earlier in the evening with a Happy Hour; a few include self-contained bars or restaurants that get going at lunchtime. Most have a **cover charge**, at least on busy Friday and Saturday nights, which fluctuates between $10 and $30, depending on what day it is and what sex you are, and almost invariably entitles you to a drink or two. It's worth checking the local press to see which venues are currently in favour; a scan through *8 Days* magazine will bring you up to date. Singapore also has a plethora of extremely seedy hostess clubs, in which aged Chinese hostesses working on commission try to hassle you into buying them a drink. Extortionately expensive, these joints are to be avoided, not least because they attract a decidedly unsavoury clientele. Fortunately, they are easy to spot: even if you get beyond the heavy wooden front door flanked by brandy adverts, the pitch darkness inside gives the game away.

Boom Boom Room, 02-04, 3 New Bugis St (☎3398187). The comedy and dance on show every night is tame by old Bugis Street standards, though still well attended and enjoyed by locals and tourists. Cover charge Tues–Sat; 9pm–2am.

Chinoiserie, *Hyatt Regency Hotel*, 10–12 Scotts Rd (☎7381234). Big, sleek club favoured by Singapore Airline girls and the beautiful people; dress casual smart. Daily 9pm–3am.

D'Cockpit, *Cockpit Hotel*, 6–7 Oxley Rise (☎7379111). Stars glitter on the ceiling and prisms project rainbows onto the walls in this tacky club where cha-cha-cha and samba take precedence. Daily 5pm–1am.

Fire Disco, 04-19 Orchard Plaza, 150 Orchard Rd (☎2350155). A mixed bag: downstairs is teeny-bopper paradise; upstairs, cult Singapore covers band Energy plays nightly. Daily 8pm–3am.

Modesto's, *Orchard Parade Hotel*, 1 Tanglin Rd (☎7371133). One of the hippest places in town, where R&B sounds dominate every night except Wednesday, which is 1970s retro night; cover charges rise over the weekend. Happy Hour 6–8pm; daily 5pm–3am.

Rascals, *Pan Pacific Hotel*, Marina Square, 6 Raffles Blvd (☎3388050). Generous Happy Hours (all day Mon–Fri) apply; Sunday draws a predominantly gay crowd. Daily 6pm–3am.

Sparks Disco, seventh floor, Ngee Ann City, 391 Orchard Rd (☎7356133). Soccer pitch-sized and multi-chambered nightspot whose slick Art-Deco fittings are aimed squarely at the yuppie market. Three live bands play jazz, pop and Canto-pop. Daily Mon–Sat 6pm–3am.

Suzie Wong, Block A Clarke Quay, 3 River Valley Rd (☎4330174). *Cheong sam*-clad chanteuses crooning schmaltzy numbers from a spiral staircase provide the entertainment in this stylish piano bar. Happy Hour 7–9pm; open Mon–Thurs 6pm–2am.

Top Ten, 05-18a Orchard Towers, 400 Orchard Rd (☎7323077). This glitzy, multi-tiered disco attracts expats galore, and isn't cheap. Acts like Los Lobos and Robert Palmer have played here in the past. Daily 5pm–3am.

Warehouse Disco, *River View Hotel*, 382 Havelock Rd (☎7329922). Low cover charges and prices draw teenybopper hordes. Happy Hour 5–8pm; daily 5pm–2am.

Zouk, 17–21 Jiak Kim St (☎7382988). Singapore's trendiest club, fitted out to create something akin to a Mediterranean feel. World-renowned DJs like Paul Oakenfold guest occasionally. Happy Hour 8–9pm; open Mon–Sat 6pm–3am.

KARAOKE

It's hard to avoid **karaoke** these days in Singapore – bars, discos, restaurants and even shopping centres are infested with KTV (karaoke television). Request a song from the KJ (karaoke DJ), pick up the mike, look up at the TV screen in front of you and you're away. Lounges devoted to karaoke – there are several in Cuppage Plaza and Lucky Plaza, both on Orchard Road – are prohibitively expensive, so your best bet is to scour the "Bars and Pubs" listings above for an appropriate establishment. For the true devotee, *Singsation*, in the *Plaza Hotel* on Beach Road, is Singapore's karaoke capital, boasting a number of theme rooms that allow you to croon "Sailing" in outer space, or "Everything I Do" in a log cabin.

Live music

Singapore is too far off the European and North American tour trail to attract many big-name performers, but there are occasional visits to rally the troops. Rivalling Western music in terms of popularity in Singapore is **Canto-pop**, a bland hybrid of Cantonese lyrics and Western disco beats; Hong Kong Canto-pop superstars visit periodically, and the rapturous welcomes they receive make their shows quite an experience. No matter who else is in town, you can always catch a set of cover versions at one of Singapore's bars and clubs; main venues are picked out below.

Anywhere, 04-08/09 Tanglin Shopping Centre, 19 Tanglin Rd (☎7348233). Good-time rock music by local favourites Tania.

Brannigan's, *Hyatt Regency Hotel*, 10–12 Scotts Rd (☎7331188). Contemporary sounds by southeast Asian bands.

Duxton's Chicago Bar, 6–9 Duxton Hill (☎2224096). Reputable jazz and blues club. It's a bar next door to the grill.

Fabrice's World Music Bar, Basement, *Dynasty Hotel*, 320 Orchard Rd (☎7388887). Resident bands – from all around the world – which change every two months.

Fire Disco, 04-19 Orchard Plaza, 150 Orchard Rd (☎2350155). Accomplished covers band Energy plays two sets nightly.

The Ginivy, 02-11 Rear Block, Orchard Towers, 1 Claymore Drive (☎7375702). Country and western sounds and a lively dance floor.

Hard Rock Café, 02-01 HPL House, 50 Cuscaden Rd (☎2355232). MR standards cranked up good and loud.

Harry's Quayside, 28 Boat Quay (☎5383029). Live jazz Wednesday to Saturday, and a blues jam on Sunday evening.

Molly Malone's, 42 Circular Rd. Two guitar and fiddle sets nightly.

Saxophone, 23 Cuppage Rd (☎2358385). Slick jazz played on a cramped stage behind the bar.

Singapore Indoor Stadium, Stadium Rd. The usual venue for big-name bands in town; tickets are available through Sistic or Ticketcharge (see box below).

World Trade Centre, 1 Maritime Square (☎3212717). Hosts international acts from time to time, as well as presenting free local gigs in its amphitheatre (check press for details).

The arts and culture

Of all the performing arts, **drama** gets the best showing in Singapore, the island's theatres staging productions that range from English farces to contemporary productions by local writers. **Dance** – Western or Asian – is more of a rarity, and events crop up only periodically, though if your trip coincides with the biennial **Singapore Festival of Arts** (next scheduled for 1998) you may see something memorable. **Asian culture** is showcased in Singapore's major venues from time to time, but tends to appear more often on

---

TICKETING AGENCIES

Sistic (☎3485555) and **Ticketcharge** (☎2962929) are Singapore's central ticketing agencies. The cost of a ticket to a cultural performance in Singapore usually starts at around $10–15, though international acts command substantially higher prices.

Sistic
The Forum Shopping Mall, 583 Orchard Rd
Liang Court, 177 River Valley Rd
Scotts Shopping Centre, 6 Scotts Rd
Specialists' Shopping Centre, 277 Orchard Rd
Raffles City, 252 North Bridge Rd
Cold Storage World Trade Centre, 1 Maritime Square
Parco Bugis Junction, 200 Victoria St

Takashimaya, Ngee Ann City, 391 Orchard Rd
Victoria Concert Hall
Singapore Indoor Stadium, Stadium Rd

Ticketcharge
Centrepoint, 176 Orchard Rd
Tangs, corner of Scotts and Orchard roads
Substation, 45 Armenian St

---

the street than in the auditorium, particularly around the time of the bigger festivals. Outstripping all other forms of entertainment in terms of popularity is **film**, with up-to-the-minute Asian and Western movies all drawing big crowds every day across the island, and the annual **Singapore International Film Festival** in April. For **information** on cultural events and performances, pick up a copy of either the *Singapore Straits Times* (whose daily *Life!* supplement has a good "what's on" section), *8 Days* magazine or the fortnightly and free *IS* magazine. Alternatively, phone the venue's box office – all the relevant numbers are given below. Tickets for music shows, theatre and dance are sold either at the venue itself, or through ticketing agencies.

Classical music

At the epicentre of the **Western** classical music scene in Singapore is the **Singapore Symphony Orchestra**. Performances by this 85-member, multinational orchestra take place at the Victoria Concert Hall and often feature guest soloists, conductors and choirs from around the world; occasional **Chinese** classical music shows are included in the programme. From time to time, ensembles from the orchestra also give **lunchtime concerts**. In addition, the Singapore Symphony Orchestra gives occasional free performances in Singapore's parks, while Sentosa Island also plays host to regular Sunday concerts – the shows themselves are free, but the usual Sentosa entry fee applies.

Nanyang Academy of Fine Arts Chinese Orchestra (☎3376636). Chinese classical and folk music.

Singapore Broadcasting Corporation's Chinese Orchestra (☎2560401, ext 2732 for info). Performances of traditional Chinese music played on traditional instruments.

Singapore Symphony Orchestra, Victoria Concert Hall, Empress Place (☎3381230). Performances on Friday and Saturday evenings throughout the year.

Cultural performances

If you walk around Singapore's streets for long enough, you're likely to come across some sort of streetside **cultural event**, most usually a wayang, or Chinese opera, played out on tumbledown outdoor stages that spring up overnight next to temples and markets, or just at the side of the road. Wayangs are highly dramatic and stylized affairs, in which garishly made-up and costumed characters enact popular Chinese legends to the accompaniment of the crashes of cymbals and gongs. Wayangs take place throughout the year, but the best time to catch one is during the Festival of the Hungry Ghosts, when they are held to entertain passing spooks, or during the Festival of the Nine Emperor Gods (see p.68). The STPB may also be able to help you track down a wayang, and as usual the local press is worth checking, or else you could make do with the tourist-friendly, subtitled performances at Clarke Quay (Thurs & Fri 7.45pm; free). Another fascinating traditional performance, **lion dancing**, takes to the streets during Chinese New Year, and **puppet theatres** appear around then, as well.

The Kala Mandhir cultural association, based at the *Excelsior Hotel* on Coleman Street, is dedicated to perpetuating traditional **Indian** art, music and dance. Less spontaneous displays of Asian culture can be seen at **theme parks** such as Asian Village on Sentosa Island (p.567), Tang Dynasty City (p.562) and the Malay Cultural Village (p.579). Finally, there are several restaurants which offer a free **cultural dinner show** to guests (see p.579).

Film

With over fifty **cinemas** on the island, you should have no trouble finding a movie that appeals to you, and at a price ($5–8) that compares favourably with Europe and America. As well as Hollywood's latest blockbusters, a wide range of **Chinese, Malay and Indian movies**, all with English subtitles, are screened. Chinese productions tend to be a raucous blend of slapstick and martial arts, while Malay and Indian movies are characterized by exuberant song and dance routines. Cinema-going is a popular pastime, so if you plan to catch a newly released film, turn up early – and take along a jumper, as air-con units are perpetually on full blast. Be prepared, also, for a lot of noise during shows: Singaporeans are great ones for talking all the way through the subtitled movies, and the sound of a bag of popcorn being rustled pales next to the sound of melon seeds being cracked and crunched. The most central cinemas are listed below, but check the local press for a full rundown of any special events or one-offs that might be taking place. **European** movies in languages other than English also pop up occasionally. The Alliance Française (1 Sarkies Rd; ☎7378422) screens free French movies every Tuesday (7.15pm) and Wednesday (9.15pm). There are also regular presentations at the British Council (see "Listings" on p.592 for address) and Goethe Institute (7/f1 Finlayson Green; ☎5345011). Depending on when you visit, you might coincide with the **Singapore International Film Festival**. Now an annual event, it screens over 150 films and shorts – mostly by Asian directors – over two weeks. Smaller festivals are occasionally mounted by the Singapore Film Society.

Capitol Theatre, 1 Stamford Rd (☎3379759). Statues of maidens on winged horses flank the screen in this marvellous old Art Deco cinema screening Western blockbusters.

Cathay Cinema, 11 Dhoby Ghaut (☎3383400). Singapore's oldest cinema; now a multi-screen.

Jade Classics, fourth floor, Shaw Leisure Gallery, 100 Beach Rd (☎2942568). Like the *Picture House*, this screens slightly more cerebral movies than most.

Kreta Ayer People's Theatre, 30a Kreta Ayer Rd (☎2223972). Expect a leaning towards Oriental films, due to its location in the heart of Chinatown.

Lido Cineplex, Level 5, Shaw House, 1 Scotts Rd (☎7324124). Five screens, including the luxurious *Lido Classic*.

The Picture House, Cathay Building, 11 Dhoby Ghaut (☎3383400). A new cinema, pricier than most, screening interesting new releases.

Studio City, Riverside Point, Clarke Quay (☎4382838). This cinema is just a minute's stroll from Clark Quay, across the Read Bridge.

United Artists Bugis Junction, 200 Victoria St (☎3379522). Posh and central new cinema.

Theatre and the performing arts

Singapore has a modest but thriving **drama** scene, with most local productions debuting at either the *Black Box, Substation* or *Drama Centre*, and graduating to the *Victoria Theatre* if they are successful. Foreign companies occasionally visit and usually perform at the *Victoria* or *Kallang* theatres. Performances of **dance** crop up from time to time – most notably by the *Singapore Dance Theatre* (☎3380611), which performs periodically at various venues, and even in local parks.

Singapore's biennial **Festival of the Arts** attracts class acts from all over the world. The next festival will be held in 1998, spreading over two months between June and August; a schedule of events is published a month before the festival begins so, unless you are in Singapore for quite a while, you'll probably have trouble getting tickets for the more popular events. Still, an accompanying **fringe festival** takes place concurrently, and its programme always includes free street and park performances. In addition, Singapore hosts a **Festival of Asian Performing Arts** in odd-numbered years, which showcases cultures of neighbouring nations.

The Black Box, Fort Canning Centre, Cox Terrace, Fort Canning Park (☎3384077). Local productions by the *Theatreworks Company*.

Boom Boom Room, 02-04, 3 New Bugis St (☎3398187). Stand-up comedy hasn't really taken off in Singapore, though the *Boom Boom Room*'s vaguely saucy revue, with a camp Malay comedian whose jokes are delivered in broad Singlish (Singaporean English), is worth checking out.

Drama Centre, Canning Rise (☎3360005). Drama by local companies.

Hilton-British Airways Playhouse, *Hilton Hotel,* 581 Orchard Rd (☎7372233). Light comedy from London's West End theatres.

Kallang Theatre, Stadium Walk (☎4403970). Hosts visiting companies such as the Bolshoi Ballet.

The Substation, 45 Armenian St (☎3377800). Self-styled "home for the arts" with a multipurpose hall that presents drama and dance, as well as art, sculpture and photography exhibitions in its gallery.

Victoria Theatre, 9 Empress Place (☎3377490). Visiting performers and successful local performances.

Shopping

For many stopover visitors, Singapore is synonymous with **shopping**, though contrary to popular belief prices are not rock bottom across the board, due to the consistently strong Singaporean dollar and a rising cost of living. Good deals can be found on watches, cameras, electrical and computer equipment, fabrics and antiques, and cut-price imitations – Rolexes, Lacoste polo shirts and so on – are rife, but many other articles offer no substantial saving. Choice and convenience though, make the Singapore shopping experience a rewarding one, with scores of shopping centres and department stores meaning that you're rarely more than an air-con escalator ride away from what you want to buy. What's more, come during the **Great Singapore Sale** (usually in June or July), and you'll find seriously marked-down prices in many outlets across the island. The STPB's excellent *Singapore Shopping* booklet details exhaustively what you can buy and where; another of their publications, the *Directory of Good Retailers*, lists those shops deemed fit to be members of the Good Retailers Scheme. Judged on their courteousness and reliability, these shops all display a red-and-white merlion symbol in their windows. If you have any complaints to lodge, contact CASE (Consumer Association of Singapore; ☎2705433) or, better still, go to Singapore's **Small Claims Tribunal**, Subordinate Courts, Apollo Centre, 2 Havelock Rd (☎4355937), which has a fast-track system for dealing with tourists' complaints; to have your case heard costs $10.

A goods and services **tax** (GST), introduced in 1994, has added a three percent sales tax to all goods and services, but tourists can claim a refund on purchases of $500 or over at retailers displaying a **GST Tourist Refund Scheme** sticker. It's a slightly long-winded process, but one which the tourist board's *Tax Refund for Visitors to Singapore* brochure explains very clearly.

For clothes (either by Western or local designers – the latter are far more reasonably priced), tailor-made suits, sports equipment, electronic goods or antiques, the shopping malls of **Orchard Road** will have all you could possibly want; some of the quirkier shopping centres are listed on p.535. At **Arab Street** (p.552), you'll find exquisite tex-tiles and batiks, robust basketware and some good deals on jewellery, as well as more unusual Muslim items. From here, make a beeline for **Little India** (p.547), where the silk stores and goldsmiths spoil you for choice; en route you'll pass the intersection of **Bencoolen Street and Rochor Road**, where a gaggle of shopping centres stocks electrical goods galore. As well as its souvenir shops, **Chinatown** boasts some more traditional outlets stocking Chinese foodstuffs, medicines, instruments and porcelain – Chinatown's shopping highlights are listed on p.545. For souvenirs, head for the *Singapore Handicraft Centre* in New Bridge Road (see below) or for the recently reno-vated Tanjong Pagar zone (p.542) whose restored shophouses feature Oriental goods a cut above the normal tourist tat. As well as the various shops and outlets picked out in the text, check out any of the following as you travel around Singapore. Usual **shop-ping hours** are daily 10am–9pm, though some shopping centres, especially those along Orchard Road, stay open until 10pm. The only exception to this is the Christian-owned *C. K. Tang's*, which closes on Sunday.

Antiques: *Antiques of the Orient*, 02-40 Tanglin Shopping Centre, 19 Tanglin Rd, specialists in anti-quarian books, maps and prints; *Babazar*, 31a–35a Cuppage Terrace; *Katong Antiques House*, 208 East Coast Rd, an Aladdin's cave of tiffin carriers, Peranakan slippers and cloths, and Chinese porce-lain; *Tong Mern Sern Antiques*, Block D, Clarke Quay, a potpourri of ancient bits and bobs – post-cards, abacuses, lamps, old 78s – from Singapore's past; *Wong's Collections*, 13 Ann Siang Hill, sells everything from antique furniture and wartime food coupons to matchboxes and MRT cards.

Buddhist goods *Nanyang Buddhist Culture Service*, 01-13 Block 333, Kret Ayer Rd, sells effigies, trinkets, necklaces and books.

Camping equipment *Campers' Corner*, 01-13 Paradiz Centre, 1 Selegie Rd.

Computers and software: *Funan Centre*, 109 North Bridge Rd.

Electronic equipment: Sim Lim Tower, 10 Jalan Besar, Lucky Plaza, 304 Orchard Rd.

Fabrics and silk *China Silk House*, 02-11/13 Tanglin Shopping Centre, 19 Tanglin Rd; *Malaya Silk Store*, 01-01/02 Orchard Shopping Centre, 321 Orchard Rd; *Jim Thompson Silk Shop*, 01-01 *Orchard Parade Hotel*, 1 Tanglin Rd.

Jewellery The entire first floor of the Pidemco Centre, 95 South Bridge Rd, is a jewellery mart.

Music: *Beethoven Record House*, 03-41 Centrepoint, 176 Orchard Rd, for classical sounds; *Lata Music Centre*, 42 Race Course Rd, for Indian music on tape; *Roxy Records*, 03-36 Funan Centre, 109 North Bridge Rd, for new releases; *Supreme Record Centre*, 03-28 Centrepoint, 175 Orchard Rd; *Tower Records*, fourth floor, Pacific Plaza, Orchard Rd, for a wide choice of music on CD.

Porcelain *New Ming Village*, 32 Pandan Road (Clementi MRT and then bus #78), where all the work on Ming and Qing Dynasty reproductions is done by hand, according to traditional methods – most fascinating is the painstaking work of the painters. This is not a place to come to unless you are dead set on buying some porcelain.

Rubber stamp makers Stamps from *Poh Hwa Stamp Maker*, 02-50 Hong Lim Complex, Block 531 Upper Cross St, make inexpensive gifts.

Souvenirs *Chinese Cloisonné-ware Centre*, 03-31/32 Raffles City Shopping Centre, 250 North Bridge Rd; *Eng Tiang Huat*, 284 River Valley Rd, for Oriental musical instruments, wayang cos-tumes and props; *Funan Stamp and Coin Agency*, 03-03 Funan Centre, 109 North Bridge Rd; *Royal Selangor*, 01-45 Clarke Quay, for fine pewterwork; *Singapore Handicraft Centre*, Chinatown Point, 133 New Bridge Rd, gathers around fifty souvenir shops under one roof; *Zhen Lacquer Gallery*, 17 Duxton Rd.

Listings

Airlines Aeroflot, 01-02/02-00 Tan Chong Tower, 15 Queen St (☎3361757); Air Canada, 02-43/46 Meridien Shopping Centre, 100 Orchard Rd (☎7328555); Air India, 17-01 UIC Building, 5 Shenton Way (☎2259411); Air Lanka, 13-01a/b, 133 Cecil St (☎2257233); also PIL Building, 140 Cecil St (☎2236026); Air New Zealand, 24-08 Ocean Building, 10 Collyer Quay (☎5358266); American Airlines, 04-01 Middle Rd (☎3390001); British Airways, 01-56 United Square, 101 Thomson Rd (☎2538444); Cathay Pacific, 16-01 Ocean Building, 10 Collyer Quay (☎5331333); Garuda, 01-68 United Square, 101 Thomson Rd (☎2505666); KLM, 12-06 Ngee Ann City Tower A, 391a Orchard Road (☎7377622); Lufthansa, 05-07 Palais Renaissance, 390 Orchard Rd (☎7379222); MAS, 02-09 Singapore Shopping Centre, 190 Clemenceau Ave (☎3366777); Pelangi Air, 02-09 Singapore Shopping Centre, 190 Clemenceau Ave (☎3366777); Philippine Airlines, 01-10 Parklane Shopping Mall, 35 Selegie Rd (☎3361611); Qantas, 04-02 The Promenade, 300 Orchard Rd (☎7373744); Royal Brunei, 01-4a/4b/5 *Royal Holiday Inn Crowne Plaza*, 25 Scotts Rd (☎2354672); Royal Nepal Airlines, 09-00 SIA Building, 77 Robinson Rd (☎2257575); Singapore Airlines, 77 Robinson Rd (☎2238888), and also at *Mandarin Hotel*, 333 Orchard Rd (☎2297293) and Raffles City Shopping Centre, 252 North Bridge Rd (☎2297274); Thai Airways, 02-00 The Globe, 100 Cecil St (☎2249977); Silkair, see Singapore Airlines (☎2212221); United Airlines, 01-03 Hong Leong Building, 16 Raffles Quay (☎2200711).

Airport The toll-free Changi Airport flight information number is ☎1800/5421234.

American Express Travel services at 01-06 Lucky Plaza, 304 Orchard Rd (Mon–Fri 9am–5pm, Sat 9am–1pm; ☎2355789), and 01-04/05 Winsland House, 3 Killiney Rd (☎2355788).

Banks and exchange All Singapore's banks change travellers' cheques, with the *UOB* and *Posbank* charging the lowest commission; normal banking hours are Mon–Fri 10am–3pm & Sat 11am–1pm. Licensed moneychangers also abound – particularly in Arab Street, Serangoon Road's Mustafa Centre, and the Orchard Road shopping centres – and offer more favourable rates.

Bookshops *Times* bookshops stock a wide choice of titles, and crop up all over town: branches at 04-08/15 Centrepoint, 175 Orchard Rd, and at 02-24/25 Raffles City Shopping Centre, 252 North Bridge Rd. *MPH* shops are also well stocked, especially the flagship store on Stamford Road. For second-hand books, head for *Books Paradise*, 01-15 Paradiz Centre, 1 Selegie Rd. *Select Books*, 03-15 Tanglin Shopping Centre, 19 Tanglin Rd (☎7321515), has a huge array of specialist books on south-east Asia, while *Packir Mohamed & Sons*, 01-20/21 Orchard Plaza, 150 Orchard Rd, boasts a vast selection of magazines.

British Council At Napier Road, west of Orchard Road (☎4731111).

Car rental Avis, *Boulevard Hotel*, 200 Orchard Blvd (☎7371668), airport Terminal 1 (☎5432331) and Terminal 2 (☎5428855); Hertz, 01-20 Tanglin Shopping Centre, 19 Tanglin Rd (☎7344646) – to pick up at airport, phone the downtown branch; Sintat, Terminals 1 & 2, Changi Airport (☎5459086 or ☎5427288).

Credit card helplines American Express (☎2998133); Diners Card (☎2944222); Mastercard (☎5332888); Visa (☎1800-3451345).

Dentists Listed in the Singapore Buying Guide (equivalent to the Yellow Pages) under "Dental Surgeons", and "Dentist Emergency Service".

Disabled travellers *Access Singapore*, an informative booklet published by the National Council of Social Service, details hotels, banks, shopping centres and hospitals with facilities for the disabled. For a copy of the booklet write to the Council at 11 Penang Lane (☎3361544).

Diving equipment Great Blue Dive Shop, 03-05 Holland Rd Shopping Centre, 211 Holland Ave (☎4670767), arranges local and overseas diving trips, as well as renting and selling equipment.

Embassies and consulates Australia, 25 Napier Rd (☎7379311); Brunei, 235 Tanglin Hill (☎7339055); Canada, 14-00 IBM Towers, 80 Anson Rd (☎3253200); France, 5 Gallop Rd (☎4664866); Germany, 14-00 Far East Shopping Centre, 545 Orchard Rd (☎7371355); India, 31 Grange Rd (☎7376777); Indonesia, 7 Chatsworth Rd (☎7377422); Ireland, 08-06 Tiong Bahru Rd (☎2768935); Malaysia, 301 Jervois Rd (☎2350111); New Zealand, 15-06, Ngee Ann City Tower A, 391a Orchard Rd (☎2359966); Philippines, 20 Nassim Rd (☎7373977); Sri Lanka, 13-07/13 Goldhill Plaza, 51 Newton Rd (☎2544595); Thailand, 370 Orchard Rd (☎7372644); UK, Tanglin Rd (☎4739333); USA, 30 Hill St (☎3380251); Vietnam, 10 Leedon Park (☎4625938).

Emergencies Police ☎999; Ambulance and Fire Brigade ☎995 (all toll-free); larger hotels have doctors on call at all times.

Hospitals Singapore General, Outram Road (☎2223322); Alexandra Hospital, Alexandra Rd (☎4735222); and National University Hospital, Kent Ridge (☎7795555). All are state hospitals and all have casualty departments.

Laundry *Washington Dry Cleaning*, 02-22 Cuppage Plaza, 5 Koek Rd (Mon–Sat 9am–7.45pm); *Washy Washy*, 01-18 Cuppage Plaza, 5 Koek Rd (Mon–Sat 10am–7pm).

Pharmacies *Guardian* pharmacy has over forty outlets, including ones at Centrepoint, 176 Orchard Rd; Raffles City Shopping Centre, 252 North Bridge Rd; and Clifford Centre, 24 Raffles Place. Usual hours are 9am–6pm, but some stay open until 10pm.

Police Tanglin Police Station, 17 Napier Rd, off Orchard Road (☎7330000); come here to report stolen property. In an emergency, dial ☎999.

Post offices The GPO is beside the SIA Building on Robinson Road, between its intersections with McCallum Street and Maxwell Road (Mon–Fri 8am–6pm, Sat 8am–2pm); poste restante/general delivery is here (take your passport). Branches at Raffles City and Changi Airport.

Sports Bowling: Singapore Tenpin Bowling Congress (☎2973841) will tell you which bowling centre is closest to you, or check in Yellow Pages; sailing: Europa Sailing Centre, 1210 East Coast Parkway; snooker: Academy of Snooker, Albert Complex, Albert Street (☎3395030); tennis: Singapore Tennis Centre, 1020 East Coast Parkway (☎4425966); watersports: Cowanbunga Ski Centre (☎3448813) and William Watersports (☎2826879); scuba diving: Asia Aquatic, 7 Circular Rd (☎5368116) and Pro Diving Service, 32 Bali Lane (☎2912261).

Swimming Most central public pool is on River Valley Road, though Katong Swimming Complex, on Wilkinson Road, and Buona Vista Swimming Complex, on Holland Drive, are better. For something more adventurous, try Sentosa's Fantasy Island (see p.567).

Telephones There are IDD, fax and telex services at the Comcentre, 31 Exeter Rd; otherwise, IDD calls can be made from any public card phone or credit card phone – cards are sold at post offices and newsagents.

Tour operators Explorer (☎5381677), Gray Line of Singapore (☎3318244), Holiday Tours (☎7382622), Malaysia and Singapore Travel Centre (☎7378877), RMG Tours (☎7387776) and Singapore Sightseeing (☎3323755) can all arrange sightseeing tours of Singapore.

Travel agents All the following are good for discounted air fares and buying bus tickets to Malaysia and Thailand: Airmaster Travel Centre, *Plaza Hotel*, Beach Rd (☎3383942); Airpower Travel, 131a Bencoolen St (☎3346571); Harharat Travel, first floor, 171 Bencoolen St (☎3372633); STA Travel, 02-17 *Orchard Parade Hotel*, 1 Tanglin Rd (☎7345681).

Vaccinations Vaccinations can be arranged through the Government Vaccination Centre, Institute of Health, 226 Outram Rd (☎2227711).

Visa enquiries Contact the Immigration Department, 08-26 Pidemco Centre, 95 South Bridge Rd (Mon–Fri 9am–5pm; ☎5322877).

Women's Singapore AWARE is a women's helpline (☎2931011).

THE HISTORICAL FRAMEWORK

The modern-day nations of Malaysia, Singapore and Brunei only came into existence in 1965. Before that, their history was inextricably linked with events in the larger Malay archipelago, from Sumatra, across Borneo to the Philippines. The problem for any historian is the lack of reliable source material for the region: there's little hard archeological evidence pertaining to the prehistoric period, while the events prior to the foundation of Melaka are known only from unreliable written accounts by Chinese and Arab traders.

However, there are two vital sources for an understanding of events in the formative fourteenth and fifteenth centuries: the **Suma Oriental** (Treatise of the Orient), by Tomé Pires, a Portuguese emissary who came to Melaka in 1512 and wrote a history of the Orient based upon his own observations, and the **Sejarah Melayu**, the seventeenth century "Malay Annals", which recorded oral historical tales recounted in a poetic, rather than strictly chronological, style. Although differing in many respects, not least in time scale, both volumes describe similar events.

Portuguese and Dutch **colonists** who arrived in the sixteenth and seventeenth centuries provided **written records**, though these tended to concern commercial rather than political or social matters. And the wealth of information from British colonial times, from the early nineteenth century onwards – although giving detailed insights into Malay affairs – is imprinted with an imperialistic bias. It is only in the twentieth century, when Malay sources come into play, that a complete picture can be presented.

BEGINNINGS

The oldest remains of *homo sapiens* were discovered in the Niah Caves in Sarawak in 1958 (see p.597), and are thought to be those of hunter-gatherers, between 35,000 and 40,000 years old; other finds in the Peninsular state of Kedah are only 10,000 years old. The variety of **ethnic groups** found in both east and west Malaysia – from small, dark-skinned Negritos through to paler Austronesian Malays – has led to the theory of a slow filtration of peoples through the Malay archipelago from southern Indo-China – a theory backed by an almost universal belief in animism, celebration of fertility and ancestor worship among the various peoples.

The development of the Malay archipelago owed much to the importance of the **shipping trade**, which flourished as early as the first century AD. This was engendered by the region's strategic geographical position, linking the two major markets of the early world – India and China – and by the richness of its own resources. From the dense jungle of the Peninsula and from northern Borneo came aromatic woods, timber and *nipah* palm thatch, traded by the forest-dwelling Orang Asli with the coastal Malays, who then bartered or sold it on to Arab and Chinese merchants. The region was also rumoured to be rich in **gold**, leading to its description by Greek explorers as "The Golden Chersonese" (peninsula), a phrase that was used by later travellers, bowled over by the spectacular scenery and culture. Although gold was never found in the quantities supposed to exist, ornaments made of the precious metal helped to develop decorative traditions among craftsmen, and still survive today. More significant, however, were the **tin fields** of the Malay Peninsula, mined in early times to provide an alloy used for temple sculptures. Chinese traders were also attracted by the medicinal properties of various sea products, such as sea slugs, collected by the Orang Laut (sea people), as well as the aesthetic value of pearls and tortoise shells.

In return, the indigenous peoples acquired cloth, pottery and glass from foreign traders, and came into contact with new ideas, religions and cultural practices. From as early as 200 AD, **Indian traders** brought with them their Hindu and Buddhist practices, and archeological evidence from later periods, such as the tenth-century temples at Lembah Bujang (p.187), suggests that the indigenes not only tolerated these new belief systems, but adapted them to suit their own experiences. Perhaps the most striking contemporary example of such cultural interchange is the traditional entertainment of *wayang kulit* (shadow plays), still commonly performed in the eastern Peninsular states, whose stories are drawn from the Hindu *Ramayana*.

Contact with **China**, the other significant trading source, was initially much less pronounced due to the pre-eminence of the overland silk route, further to the north. It wasn't until much later, in the eighth and ninth centuries, that Chinese ships ventured into the archipelago.

There's little evidence to reveal the **structure of society** in these early times. All that is certain is that by the time Srivijaya (see below) appeared on the scene, there were already a number of states – particularly in the Kelantan and Terengganu areas of the Peninsula – that were sending envoys to China. This suggests a well-developed social system, complete with chiefs and diplomats, who were perhaps the forebears of the later Malay nobility.

SRIVIJAYA

The calm channel of the Melaka Straits provided a refuge for ships which were forced to wait several months for a change in the monsoon winds. The inhabitants of the western Peninsula and eastern Sumatra were quick to realize their geographical advantage, and from the fifth century onwards a succession of **entrepôts** (storage ports) was created to cater for the needs of passing vessels. Gradually these evolved into kingdoms, such as that of **Langkasuka** in the Patani region of what is now Thailand, and **Vijayapura** in west Borneo, with well-developed courtly practices and traditions of government.

One entrepôt stood head and shoulders above the rest to become the mighty empire of **Srivijaya**, eminent from the beginning of the seventh century until the end of the thirteenth, and encompassing all the shores and islands surrounding the Straits of Melaka. Since records are fragmentary, the exact location of Srivijaya is still a matter for debate, although most sources point to **Palembang** in southern Sumatra. The empire's early success was owed primarily to its favourable relationship with China, which it plied with tributes to ensure profitable trade. The entrepôt's stable administration attracted commerce when insurrection elsewhere frightened traders away, while its wealth was boosted by extracting tolls and taxes from passing ships. With such valuable cargoes bound for the port, **piracy** in the surrounding oceans was rife, but was kept in check in Srivijayan waters by the fearsome Orang Laut who formed the linchpin of the navy. Indeed, they might otherwise have turned to piracy themselves had not the prestige of association with the empire been so great.

Significant political concepts developed during the period of Srivijayan rule which were to form the basis of Malay government in future centuries. Unquestioning **loyalty** among subjects was underpinned by the notion of *daulat*, the divine force of the ruler (who was called the Maharaja, further evidence of Indian influence in the region), which would strike down anyone guilty of *derhaka* (treason) – a powerful means of control over a deeply superstitious people. Srivijaya also became known as an important centre for **Mahayana Buddhism** and learning. Supported by a buoyant economy, centres for study sprang up all over the empire, and monks and scholars were attracted from afar by Srivijaya's academic reputation. When the respected Chinese monk, I Ching, arrived in 671 AD, he found more than a thousand monks studying the Buddhist scriptures.

The decision made between 1079 and 1082 to shift the capital (for reasons unknown) from Palembang to **Melayu**, in the Sungei Jambi area to the north, seems to have marked the start of Srivijaya's decline. Piracy became almost uncontrollable, with even the loyal Orang Laut turning against their rulers, and soon both local and foreign traders began to seek safer ports, with the area that is now Kedah becoming one of the main beneficiaries.

Other regions were soon able to replicate the peaceable conditions and efficient administration conducive to commercial success. One such was **Puni** in northwest Borneo, thought to be the predecessor of Brunei, which had been trading with China since the ninth century. Over the next three hundred years Puni continued to prosper until its capital numbered more than ten thousand people, drawn by the hospitable reception given to visiting merchants and by the entrepôt's considerable wealth.

Srivijaya's fate was sealed when it attracted the eye of envious foreign rivals, among them the Majapahit empire of Java, the Cholas of India and, latterly, the Thai kingdom of Ligor. In 1275, the Majapahits invaded Melayu and made inroads into many of Srivijaya's peninsular territories. The Cholas raided Sumatra and Kedah, while Ligor enforced its territorial claims by the instigation of a **tribute system**, whereby local Malay chiefs sent gifts of gold to their Thai overlords as recognition of their vassal status, a practice which continued until the nineteenth century (see "Alor Setar", p.188). Moreover, trading restrictions in China were relaxed from the late twelfth century onwards, which made it more lucrative for traders to go directly to the source of their desired products, bypassing the once mighty entrepôt. Around the early fourteenth century Srivijaya's name disappears from the record books.

THE MELAKA SULTANATE

With the collapse of Srivijaya came the beginning of the Malay Peninsula's most significant historical period, the establishment of the **Melaka Sultanate**. Both the *Sejarah Melayu* (Malay Annals) and the Portuguese *Suma Oriental* document the story of a Sumatran prince from Palembang named **Parameswara**, who fled the collapsing empire of Srivijaya to set up his own kingdom, finally settling on the site of present-day Melaka (see p.290–307 for more).

As well placed as its Sumatran predecessor, with a deep, sheltered harbour and good riverine access to its own lucrative jungle produce, Melaka set about establishing itself as an international marketplace. The securement of a special agreement in 1405 with the new Chinese Emperor, Yung-lo, guaranteed trade to Melaka and protected it from its main warring rivals: the kingdom of Samudra-Pasai in northeast Sumatra, and that of Aru further to the south. To ensure further its prosperity, Melaka's second ruler, Parameswara's son **Iskandar Shah** (1414–24), took the precaution of acknowledging the neighbouring kingdoms of Ayuthaya and Majapahit as overlords. In return, Melaka received vital supplies and much-needed immigrants which bolstered the expansion of the settlement.

New laws empowered an **effective administration** to meet the needs of passing traders, guaranteeing their safety in pirate-infested waters and offering ample space in which to store their cargo and refit their vessels. Port taxes and market regulations were managed by four **Shahbandars** (harbour masters). Each was in charge of a group of nations: one for the northwest Indian state of Gujurat alone; another for southern India, Bengal, Samudra-Pasai and Burma; the third for local neighbours such as Java, Palembang and Borneo; and the fourth for the eastern nations, including China and Japan. Intimately concerned with the physical and commercial requirements of his group, the Shahbandar also supervised the giving of gifts to the ruler and his ministers, an important method of boosting the kingdom's wealth.

Melaka began to amplify its reputation by territorial expansion which, by the reign of its last ruler **Sultan Mahmud Shah** (1488–1530), included the west coast of the Peninsula as far as Perak, Pahang, Singapore, and most of east coast Sumatra. But although this made it strong enough to reject the patronage of Java and Ayuthaya, it never really controlled the far north or east of the Peninsula, nor did it make inroads into its competitors' territories in northern Sumatra.

Hand in hand with the trade in commodities went the exchange of ideas. By the thirteenth century, Arab merchants had begun to frequent Melaka's shores, bringing with them their religion, **Islam**, which their Muslim Indian counterparts helped to propagate among the Malays. The sultanate's **conversion** helped to increase its prestige by placing it within a worldwide community which worked to maintain profitable trade links. But even those outside Melaka's jurisdiction embraced the doctrine with enthusiasm: the fourteenth-century **Terengganu Stone**, with its inscription espousing Islam's tenets, is thought to be the oldest Malay text written in Arabic script.

The legacy of **Melaka's Golden Age** reaches far beyond memories of its material wealth. One of the most significant developments was the establishment of a **court structure** (see p.298), which was to lay the foundations for a system of government which lasted until the nineteenth century. The **sultan**, as head of state, traced his ancestry back through Paramesvara to the Maharajas of ancient Srivijaya, his claimed divinity strengthened by the sultanate's conversion to Islam, which held Muslim rulers to be Allah's representative on earth. To ensure further his power, always under threat from the over-zealous nobility, the sultan embarked on a series of measures to emphasize his "otherness": no one but he could wear gold unless it was a royal gift, and yellow garments were forbidden amongst the general population.

The Melaka Sultanate also allowed the **arts** to flourish; the principal features of the courtly dances and music of this period can still be distinguished in traditional entertainments today. Much more significant, however, was the refinement of **language**, adapting the primitive Malay – itself of Austronesian roots – that had been used in the kingdom of Srivijaya, into a language of the elite. Such was Melaka's prestige that all who passed through the entrepôt sought to imitate it, and by the sixteenth century, Malay was the most widely used language in the archipelago. Tellingly, the word *bahasa*, although literally meaning "language", came to signify Malay culture in general.

THE PORTUGUESE CONQUEST OF MELAKA

With a fortune as tempting as Melaka's, it wasn't long before Europe set its sights on the acquisition of the empire. At the beginning of the sixteenth century, the **Portuguese** began to take issue with Venetian control of the Eastern market. They planned instead to establish direct contacts with the commodity brokers of the East by gaining control of crucial regional ports.

The key player in the subsequent **conquest** of Melaka was Portuguese viceroy **Alfonso de Albuquerque**, who led the assault on the entrepôt in 1511, forcing its surrender after less than a month's siege. Sultan Mahmud Shah fled to the island of Bentan in the Riau archipelago (see below), and Albuquerque himself departed a year later, leaving behind eight hundred offi-

cers to administer the new colony. There are few physical reminders of their time in Melaka, apart from the gateway to their fort, A Famosa (see p.296), and the small **Eurasian** community, descendants of intermarriage between the Portuguese and local Malay women. The colonizers had more success with religion, however, converting large numbers of locals to **Catholicism**; their churches still dominate the city. Aloof and somewhat effete in their high-necked ruffs and stockings, the Portuguese were not well liked, but despite the almost constant attacks from upriver Malays, the Portuguese controlled Melaka for the next 130 years.

CONTEMPORARY RIVALS OF MELAKA

During the period of Melaka's meteoric rise, **Brunei** had been busily establishing itself as a trading port of some renown. Ideally poised on the sea route to China, it had for a long time benefited from its vassal status to successive Ming emperors, and now with its arch rival's capture it set about filling its place. The Brunei Sultanate's conversion to **Islam**, no doubt precipitated by the arrival of wealthy Muslim merchants fleeing from the Portuguese in Melaka, also helped to increase its international prestige. When geographer Antonio Pigafetta, travelling with Ferdinand Magellan's expedition of 1521, visited Brunei, he found the court brimming with visitors from all over the world. This, indeed, was Brunei's "Golden Age", with its borders embracing land as far south as present-day Kuching in Sarawak, and as far north as the lower islands of the modern-day Philippines. Brunei's efforts, however, were soon curtailed by Spanish colonization in 1578, which, although lasting only a matter of weeks, enabled the Philippine kingdom of Sulu to gain a hold in the area – a fact which put paid to Brunei's early expansionist aims.

The ambitious Thai kingdom of **Ayuthaya** had been initially willing to strike bargains with Melaka, but by 1455 had tired of its competitor's unhindered progress and launched a full-scale attack. Sources are vague as to the outcome, though it can reasonably be assumed that Ayuthaya was emphatically defeated, since the Thai kingdom made no further attempts on the entrepôt for the next forty years. It was only when Melaka's last ruler, Sultan Mahmud Shah,

For a more detailed account of Brunei's early history and its **Golden Age**, see p.480.

sought to include the Thai vassal state of Kelantan in his own territories that he provoked Ayuthaya to retaliate with another unsuccessful foray into the Peninsula in 1500, though it was to be another 35 years – well after the fall of Melaka to the Portuguese – before they tried again.

THE KINGDOM OF JOHOR

Johor's rise to pre-eminence in the Malay world began as a direct consequence of the fall of Melaka to the Portuguese. Fleeing Melaka, Sultan Mahmud Shah made for Pulau Bentan in the Riau archipelago, south of Singapore, where he established the first **court of Johor**. When, in 1526, the Portuguese attacked and razed the settlement, Mahmud fled once again, this time to Sumatra, where he died in 1528. It was left to his son, Alauddin Riayat Shah, to found a new court on the upper reaches of the Johor river, though the capital of the kingdom then shifted repeatedly, during a century of assaults on Johor territory by Portugal and the Sumatran Sultanate of Aceh.

The **arrival of the Dutch** in southeast Asia towards the end of the sixteenth century marked a distinct upturn in Johor's fortunes. Hoping for protection from its local enemies, the court aligned itself firmly with the new European arrivals, and was instrumental in the successful siege of Portuguese Melaka by the Dutch in 1641 (see below). Such loyalty was rewarded by trading privileges and by help in securing a treaty with Aceh, the main aggressive force in Sumatra at that time, which at last gave Johor the breathing space to develop. Soon it had grown into a thriving kingdom, its sway extending some way throughout the Peninsula.

Johor was the supreme Malay kingdom for much of the seventeenth century, but by the 1690s its empire was fraying under the irrational and despotic rule of another Sultan Mahmud. Lacking strong leadership, Johor's Orang Laut turned to piracy, scaring off the trade upon which the kingdom relied, while wars with the Sumatran kingdom of Jambi, one of which resulted in the total destruction of Johor's capital, weakened it still further. No

longer able to tolerate Sultan Mahmud's cruel regime, his nobles stabbed him to death in 1699. Not only did this change the nature of power in Malay government – previously, law deemed that the sultan could only be punished by Allah – but it marked the end of the Melaka dynasty.

THE DUTCH IN MELAKA

Already the masters of Indonesia's valuable spice trade, the Vereenigde Oostindische Compagnie (VOC), or **Dutch East India Company**, began a bid to gain control of its most potent rival, Melaka. After a five-month siege, the Dutch flag was hoisted over Melaka in 1641. Instead of ruling from above as their predecessors had tried to do, the Dutch cleverly wove their subjects into the fabric of government: each racial group was represented by a *Kapitan*, a respected figure from the community who mediated between his own people and the new administrators – often becoming a very wealthy and powerful person in his own right. The Dutch were also responsible for the rebuilding of Melaka, much of which had been turned to rubble during the protracted takeover of the city. Many of these structures, in their distinctive northern European style, still survive today. The narrow houses and *godowns* backing on to the network of canals are reminiscent of Amsterdam, and the headquarters of the administration, the Stadthuys, is one of Melaka's main tourist attractions.

By the mid-eighteenth century, the conditions for trade with **China** were at their peak: the relaxation of maritime restrictions in China itself had opened up the Straits for their merchants, while Europeans were eager to satisfy the growing demand for tea. Since the Chinese had no interest in the native goods that Europe could supply in exchange, and the Dutch themselves had no knowledge of indigenous products, European traders found themselves more and more reliant on Indian items, such as cloth and opium, as bartering tools. The Chinese came to Melaka in droves and soon established themselves as the city's foremost entrepreneurs. Chinese intermarriage with local Malay women created a new cultural blend, known as **Peranakan** (literally, "Straits-born") or Baba-Nonya – the legacy of which is the opulent mansions and unique cuisine of Melaka (see box, p.302).

But a number of factors prevented Dutch Melaka from fulfilling its potential. Since the VOC salary was hardly bountiful, Dutch administrators found it more lucrative to trade on the black market, taking backhanders from grateful merchants, a situation which severely damaged Melaka's commercial standing. High taxes forced traders to more economical locations such as the newly established British port of **Penang**, whose foundation in 1786 heralded the awakening of British interest in the Straits. A more significant sign of Dutch loss of control was their reliance on military rather than governmental means to sustain their supremacy, which ultimately made them vulnerable to anyone of greater strength. In the end, given the VOC's overall strategy in the archipelago, Melaka never stood a chance: Batavia (modern-day Jakarta) was the VOC capital, and Johor's penchant for commerce suited Dutch purposes too much for it to put serious effort into maintaining Melaka's fortunes.

THE BUGIS AND THE MINANGKABAUS

Through the second half of the seventeenth century, a new ethnic group, the **Bugis** – renowned for their martial and commercial skills – had been trickling into the Peninsula, seeking refuge from the civil wars which wracked their homeland of Sulawesi (in the mid-eastern Indonesian archipelago). By the beginning of the eighteenth century, there were enough of them to constitute a powerful court lobby, and in 1721 they took advantage of factional struggles to capture the kingdom of Johor – now based in Riau. Installing a Malay puppet sultan, Sulaiman, the Bugis ruled for over sixty years, making Riau an essential port of call on the eastern trade route; they even almost succeeded in capturing Melaka in 1756. Although their ousting had long been desired by discontented Malay vassals, it was the Dutch who put paid to the Bugis supremacy in the Straits. When Riau-Johor made another bid for Melaka in 1784, the Dutch held on with renewed vigour and finally forced a treaty placing all Bugis territory in Dutch hands.

In spiritual terms, the **Minangkabaus** (see box, p.288) had what the Bugis lacked; hailing from western Sumatra, this matrilineal society could claim cultural affinity with the ancient kingdom of Srivijaya. Although this migrant group had been present in the Negeri Sembilan region since the fifteenth century, the second half of the seventeenth century brought them to the Malay Peninsula in larger numbers. Despite professing allegiance to their Sumatran ruler, the Minangkabaus were prepared to accept Malay overlordship, which in practice gave them a great deal of autonomy. Accredited with supernatural powers, the warrior Minangkabaus were not natural allies of the Bugis or the Malays, although they did occasionally join forces in order to defeat a common enemy. In fact, over time the distinction between various migrant groups became less obvious, as intermarriage blurred clan demarcations, and Malay influence, such as the adoption of Malay titles, became more pronounced.

THE END OF AN ERA

At the end of the eighteenth century, Dutch control in southeast Asia was more widespread than ever, and the VOC empire should have been at its height. Instead, its coffers were bare and it faced the superior trading and maritime skills of the British. The disastrous defeat of the Dutch in the fourth Anglo-Dutch war (1781–83) lowered their morale still further, and when the British, in the form of the **East India Company** (EIC), moved in on Melaka and the rest of the Dutch Asian domain in 1795, the VOC barely demurred.

Initially, the British agreed to a caretaker administration, whereby they would assume sovereignty over the entrepôt to prevent it falling under French control, now that Napoleon had conquered Holland. The end of the Napoleonic wars in Europe put the Dutch in a position to retake Melaka between 1818 and 1825, but in the meantime, the EIC had established the stable port of **Penang** and – under the supervision of **Sir Thomas Stamford Raffles** (see p.530) – founded the new settlement of **Singapore** as their own regional entrepôt, signing a formal agreement with the Sultanate of Riau-Johor in 1819.

The strategic position and free-trade policy of Singapore – backed by the impressive industrial developments of the British at home – instantly threatened the viability of both Melaka and Penang, forcing the Dutch finally to relinquish their hold on the former to the British, and leaving the latter to dwindle to a backwater. In the face of such stiff competition, smaller

Malay rivals inevitably linked their fortunes to the British.

THE CONSOLIDATION OF BRITISH POWER

To a degree, the British presence in Malay lands was only the most recent episode in a history of foreign interference that stretched back centuries. What differed this time, however, was the rapidity and extent of the takeover – aided by technological developments in the West that improved communications.

The British assumption of power was sealed by the **Anglo-Dutch Treaty** of 1824, which divided territories between the two countries using the Straits of Melaka as the dividing line, thereby splitting the Riau-Johor kingdom as well as ending centuries of cultural interchange with Sumatra. This was followed in 1826 by the unification of Melaka, Penang (together with its mainland counterpart Province Wellesley) and Singapore into one administration, known as the **Straits Settlements**, with Singapore replacing Penang as its capital in 1832. Even with this more cohesive power base, the official British line was minimum interference for maximum trading opportunity, a policy that was brought into sharp conflict with the desires of local empire builders by the **Naning Wars of 1831**. These erupted when the governor of the Straits Settlements, Robert Fullerton, tried to impose Melaka's tax laws on a somewhat uppity local chief, Abdul Said. A year-long battle ensued, and though the British were finally able to cede Naning to Melaka's territories, their pyrrhic victory brought home the costs of too close an involvement in complex Malay politics.

The Anglo-Dutch Treaty did not include **Borneo**, however, and though the EIC discouraged official expansion, preferring to concentrate on expanding their trading contacts rather than geographical control, its benefits did not elude the sights of one British explorer, **James Brooke** (1803–68). Finding lawlessness throughout the territories, Brooke persuaded the Sultan of Brunei to award him his own area – **Sarawak** – in 1841, becoming the first of a line of "**White Rajahs**" that ruled the state until the start of World War II. By involving formerly rebellious Malay chiefs in government, he quickly managed to assert his authority, although the less congenial Iban tribes in the interior proved more of a problem. Despite the informal association of the British with Rajah Brooke (Sarawak was not granted the status of a protectorate), trade between Singapore and Sarawak flourished – though Brooke was careful not to encourage European contacts that might challenge his hold on the state. By the mid-nineteenth century, however, the British attitude had mellowed considerably; they chose Brooke as their agent in Brunei, and found him a useful deterrent against French and Dutch aspirations towards the valuable trade routes.

Raffles had at first hoped that **Singapore** would act as a market to sell British goods to traders from all over southeast Asia, but it soon became clear that **Chinese** merchants, the linchpin of Singapore's trade, were interested only in Malay products such as birds' nests, seaweed and camphor. But passing traders were not the only Chinese to come to the Straits. Although settlers had trickled into the Peninsula since the early days of Melaka, new pepper and gambier (an astringent product used in tanning and dyeing) **plantations**, and the rapidly expanding **tin mines**, attracted floods of willing workers eager to escape a life of poverty in China. By 1845, the Chinese formed over half of Singapore's population, while principal towns along the Peninsula's west coast – site of the world's largest tin field – as well as Sarawak's capital, Kuching, became predominantly Chinese.

Allowed a large degree of commercial independence by both the British and the Malay chiefs, the Chinese carried their traditions into the social and political arena with the formation of *kongsi*s, or clan houses (see p.176), and secret societies (triads). Struggles between clan groups were rife, sometimes resulting in large-scale riots, such as those in Penang in 1867 (see p.176), where the triads allied themselves with Malay groups in a bloody street battle lasting several days.

REGIONAL CONFLICT

Malays, too, were hardly immune from factional conflicts, which frequently became intertwined with Chinese squabbles, causing a string of **civil wars**.

In **Negeri Sembilan** (1824–69), conflict was largely brought about by contending Minangkabau heirs, although most worrying to British administrators were arguments over the control of the tin trade (see p.283). **Pahang's** skirmishes (1858–63) also involved rival political claims by two brothers, Mutahir and Ahmad, although this time the British were much more directly involved. On hearing that the Thais had backed Ahmad, the Straits Governor Cavenagh hastily aligned himself with Mutahir by attacking Kuala Terengganu (a Thai vassal town), in order to ward off further foreign involvement in the Peninsula. But the British government was outraged by this decision and forbade any other action to prevent Ahmad's succession.

Perak (1861–73) was riven with the disputes of rival Chinese clans in the central region of Larut and once again, tin was a major contributing factor. In **Selangor** (1867–73), tax claims between Malay chiefs were the basis of the wars. The British again intervened, this time to support Tengku Kudin, the person they thought most likely to assure a peaceful resolution to the conflict. However, he was a weak figure, little respected by his own people, and the effect was to underline to the Malays that British help could even be secured for a lacklustre regime such as Kudin's.

Lawlessness like this was detrimental to commerce, giving the British an excuse to increase their involvement in local affairs. A meeting was arranged by the new Straits Governor, Andrew Clarke, on Pulau Pangkor, just off the west coast of the Peninsula, between the chiefs of the Perak Malays. In the meantime, Rajah Abdullah, the man most likely to succeed to the Perak throne, had written to Clarke asking for the appointment of a British **Resident** (or advisor), in return for his own guaranteed position as sultan. On January 20, 1874, the **Pangkor Treaty** (p.152) was signed between the British and Abdullah, formalizing British intervention in the political affairs of the Malay people.

BRITISH MALAYA

By 1888 the name **British Malaya** had been brought into use by Governor Clarke – a term which reflected the intention to extend British control over the whole Peninsula. Over subsequent decades, the Malay sultans' economic and administrative powers were to be gradually eroded, while the introduction of rubber estates during the first half of the twentieth century made British Malaya one of the most productive colonies in the world.

Each state soon saw the arrival of a **Resident** (see p.159), a senior British civil servant whose main function was to act as advisor to the local sultan, but who also oversaw the collecting of local taxes. The system worked reasonably well, although relations deteriorated with J.W.W. Birch's posting as Resident of Perak. Unlike the first Resident, the respected Hugh Low, Birch was not sympathetic to the ways of the Malays, and was soon out of favour. Perak's Sultan Abdullah in particular opposed Birch's centralizing tendencies, and senior British officials, fearful of a Malay rebellion, announced that judicial decisions would from now on be in the hands of the British, which was against the letter of the Pangkor Treaty. Furious Malays soon found a vent for their frustration: on November 2, 1875, Birch was killed on an upriver visit. The British brought in troops from India and Hong Kong to quell the trouble, although the attack on Birch was not followed by further assaults on colonial staff.

Agreements along the lines of the Pangkor Treaty were drawn up with Selangor, Negeri Sembilan and Pahang states in the 1880s, and in 1896 these three became bracketed together under the title of the **Federated Malay States**, with the increasingly important town of Kuala Lumpur made the regional capital.

The gradual extension of British power brought further unrest, particularly in the east coast states, where the Malays proved just as resentful of British control as in Perak. In Pahang a set of skirmishes known as the **Pahang War** took place in 1891, when Malay chiefs protested about the reduction of their former privileges. One powerful chief, Dato' Bahaman, was stripped of his title by Pahang's Resident, Hugh Clifford, as a result of which the Dato' led a small rebellion which – though never a serious military threat to the British – soon became the stuff of legends. One fighter, **Mat Kilau**, gained a place in folklore as a heroic figure who stood up to the British in the name of Malay nationalism. From this time onwards, Malays would interpret the uprisings as a valiant attempt to safeguard Malay traditions and preserve Malay autonomy. However, the only real impact the Pahang War had on the hitherto smooth extension of British power was briefly to slow down the pace of colonial administration. It also further underlined the contrasts between various regions of the Peninsula: the economies of the northern states of Pahang, Kelantan and Terengganu developed less quick

For an account of the **founding of Kuala Lumpur**, see p.81.

ly than those of the western states, which were under more effective British control.

By 1909, the northern Malay states of Kedah, Perlis, Kelantan and Terengganu – previously under Thai control – were brought into the colonial fold: along with Johor (which joined in 1914) they were grouped together as the **Unfederated Malay States** and by the outbreak of World War I, British political control was more or less complete. The Peninsula was subdivided into groups of states and regions with the seat of power split between Singapore and Kuala Lumpur. Borneo, too, had been brought under British control: the three states of Sarawak, Sabah and Brunei had been transformed into **protectorates** in 1888, a status which handed over the responsibility for their foreign policy to the British in exchange for military protection.

THE EXPANSION OF BRITISH INTERESTS IN BORNEO

The legacy of the first "White Rajah" of **Sarawak**, James Brooke, was furthered by his nephew Charles in the closing years of the nineteenth century. New regions – the Baram and Trusan valleys and Limbang – were bought, or rather wrested, from the Sultan of Brunei, while the British North Borneo Chartered Company handed over to Brooke the Lawas Valley in 1905. The Chartered Company had assumed control over Northern Borneo (later renamed Sabah) in 1878 when an Austrian, Baron von Overbeck, with the backing of British businessmen, paid the sultans of Brunei and Sulu an annuity to administer and develop the region.

Like his uncle before him, **Charles Brooke** ruled Sarawak in a paternalistic fashion, recruiting soldiers, lowly officials and boatmen from the ranks of the ethnic groups and leaving the Chinese to get on with running commercial enterprises and opening out the interior. Although the British government in London and the colonial administrators in Singapore were concerned about Brooke's territorial expansions, they accepted that the indigenous peoples were not being oppressed and that Brooke's rule was not despotic.

The rule of the last White Rajah, **Vyner Brooke**, Charles' eldest son (1916–41), saw no new territorial acquisitions, but there was a steady development in rubber, pepper and palm oil production. The ethnic peoples mostly continued living a traditional lifestyle in longhouses along the river systems and, with the end of groups' practice of head-hunting, there was some degree of integration among the country's varied racial groups.

By way of contrast, the **British North Borneo Chartered Company**'s writ in what became Sabah encountered some early obstacles. Its plans for economic expansion involved clearing the rainforest and **planting rubber and tobacco** over large areas, and levying taxes on the ethnic groups. Resistance followed, with the most vigorous action in 1897 led by a Bajau chief, **Mat Salleh**, whose men rampaged through the company's out-station on Pulau Gaya. Another rebellion by the Murut tribespeople in 1915 resulted in a heavy-handed response from British forces who killed hundreds.

By the turn of the twentieth century, the majority of the lands of the erstwhile powerful **Sultanate of Brunei** had been dismembered – the sultanate was now surrounded by Sarawak. But the sultan's fortunes had not completely disappeared and with the discovery of **oil** in 1929, the British thought it prudent to appoint a Resident. Exploitation of the small state's oil beds picked up pace in the 1930s following investment from British companies; see p.481 for more details.

ECONOMIC DEVELOPMENT AND ETHNIC RIVALRIES

In the first quarter of the twentieth century hundreds of thousands of **immigrants** from China and India were encouraged by the British to emigrate to sites across Peninsular Malaysia, Sarawak, North Borneo and Singapore. They came to work as tin miners or plantation labourers, and Malaya's population in this period doubled to four million.

The main impact of what was effectively a recruitment drive by the British was to fuel resentment among the Malays, who believed that they were being denied the economic opportunities advanced to others. The situation was made worse under the British **education system**, since schooling was offered at a very basic level to only small numbers of Malays, Chinese and Indians. The British barely noticed the deepening differences between the ethnic groups – a factor which contributed to resentment and racial violence in later years.

A further deterioration in Malay-Chinese relations followed the success of the mainland Chinese revolutionary groups in Malaya. The educated Chinese, who joined the **Malayan Communist Party** (MCP) from 1930 onwards, formed the backbone of the politicized Chinese movements after World War II, which demanded an end to British rule and to what they perceived as special privileges extended to the Malays. For their part, the Malays – specifically those influenced by radical Islamic movements – saw better education as the key to their future. The establishment of the **Singapore Malay Union** in 1926 gradually gained support in Straits Settlement areas where Malays were outnumbered by Chinese. It held its first conference in 1939 and advocated a Malay supremacist line.

Despite the argument put forward by the British in the 1930s that a Union for Malaya, (incorporating the Unfederated Malay States) would decentralize power and integrate the regional state groupings, little progress had been made on the burning issue of independence by the time Malaya was **invaded** by the Japanese in late 1941.

JAPANESE OCCUPATION

By February 1942, the whole of Malaya and Singapore was in Japanese hands and most of the British were POWs. The **surrender** of the British forces in Singapore (see p.505 for details) ushered in a Japanese regime which proceeded to brutalize the Chinese, largely because of Japan's history of conflict with China: up to fifty thousand people were tortured and killed in the two weeks immediately after the surrender of the island by the British military command. Allied POWs were rounded up into prison camps; many of the troops subsequently were sent to build the infamous "Death Railway" in Burma.

In **Malaya**, towns and buildings were destroyed as the Allies attempted to bomb strategic targets. But with the Japanese firmly in control, the occupiers ingratiated themselves with some of the Malay elite by suggesting that after the war the country would be given independence. Predictably, it was the Chinese activists in the MCP, more than the Malays, who organized **resistance** during wartime; in the chaotic period directly after the war it was the MCP's armed wing, the **Malayan People's Anti-Japanese Army** (MPAJA), who maintained order in many areas.

The Japanese invasion of **Sarawak** in late 1941 began with the capture of the Miri oil field and spread south, encountering little resistance. Although the Japanese invaders never penetrated the interior, they quickly established complete control over the populated towns along the coast. The Chinese in Miri, Sibu and Kuching were the main targets: the Japanese put down rebellions against their rule brutally, and there was no organized guerrilla activity until late in the occupation. What resistance there was prompted by the presence of Major **Tom Harrison** and his team of British and Australian commandos, who parachuted into the remote Kelabit Highlands to gauge the feelings of the indigenous tribespeople; they later managed to recruit Kayan, Kenyah and Kelabit warriors in an uprising.

In **North Borneo**, the Japanese invaded Pulau Labuan on New Year's Day, 1942 (see p.447). Over the next three years the main suburban areas were bombed by the Allies, and by the time of the Japanese surrender in September 1945, most of Jesselton (modern-day KK) and Sandakan had been destroyed. Captured troops and civilians suffered enormously – the worst single outrage being the Death March in September 1944 when 2400 POWs were forced to walk from Sandakan to Ranau. Only six prisoners survived.

The Allies had been preparing to retake Singapore, but just prior to the planned invasion the **Japanese surrendered** on September 9, 1945, on Pulau Labuan, following the dropping of atom bombs on Nagasaki and Hiroshima.

The surrender led to a power vacuum in the region, with the British initially left with no choice but to work with the MPAJA to exert political control. Violence occurred between the MPAJA and Malays, with those who were accused of collaborating with the Japanese during the occupation specifically targeted.

THE FEDERATION OF MALAYA

Immediately after the war, the British updated the idea of a Malayan **union** – a position halfway towards full independence – which would make the Chinese and Indian inhabitants full citizens and give them equal rights with the Malays.

This quickly aroused opposition among the Malays, with Malayan nationalists forming the **United Malays National Organization** (UMNO) in 1946. Its main tenet was that Malays should retain their special privileges, largely because they were the region's first inhabitants. UMNO also pushed the customary Malay line that the uniquely powerful position of the sultans should not be tampered with – indeed, they still exerted immense power despite the administrative changes wrought by the British.

UMNO supporters displayed widespread resistance to the British plan and the idea of union was subsequently replaced by the **Federation of Malaya**. Established in 1948, this upheld the power and privileges of the sultans and brought all the regional groupings together under one government, with the exception of Chinese-dominated Singapore, whose inclusion would have led to the Malays being a minority. Protests erupted in Singapore at its exclusion, with the **Malayan Democratic Union** (MDU) calling for integration with Malaya – a position that commanded little support among the Chinese population.

In **Borneo**, after the Japanese surrender, the Colonial Office in London stepped into the breach and with Vyner Brooke offering no objection, made Sarawak and North Borneo **Crown Colonies**. Britain also signed a Treaty of Protection with the Sultan of Brunei, making Sarawak's high commissioner the Governor of Brunei – a purely decorative position, as the sultan remained the chief power in the state.

Although Sarawak's ruling body, the Council Negeri (composed of Malays, Chinese, Iban and British) had voted to transfer power to Britain, some Malays and prominent Iban in Kuching opposed their country's new status. Protests reached a peak with the assassination in Sibu in 1949 of the top official in the new administration, Governor Duncan Stewart. But on the whole, resentment at the passing of the Brooke era was short-lived, and as the population gradually got used to the new political alignments, the economy expanded. The infrastructure of both Sarawak and north Borneo steadily improved, with new roads and a limited air service helping to open out the country to commercial development.

Brunei's most lucrative resource – its oil fields – sustained considerable damage during the Japanese invasion, and much of the postwar period was spent in rebuilding the installations. The British governor was withdrawn in 1959 leaving the sultan in sole charge of the region, although Britain was still responsible for defence matters and foreign relations.

THE EMERGENCY

In Peninsular Malaya many Chinese were angered by the change of the status of the country from a colony to a federation, in which they effectively became second-class citizens. According to the new laws, non-Malays could only qualify as citizens if they had lived in the country for fifteen out of the last twenty-five years, and they also had to prove they spoke Malay or English.

More Chinese began to identify with the MCP, which, under its new leader, **Chin Peng**, declared its intention of setting up a Malayan republic. Peng fused the MCP with the remains of the wartime resistance movement, the MPAJA, and using the arms supplies which the latter had dumped in the forests, he recruited a secret central committee, set up **guerrilla cells** deep in the jungle and, from June 1948, launched sporadic attacks on rubber estates, killing planters and employees as well as spreading fear among rural communities.

The period of unrest, which lasted for twelve years (1948–60), was referred to as **the Emergency**, rather than a civil war, which it undoubtedly was. This was mainly for insurance purposes – planters would have had their premiums cancelled if war had been officially declared. Although the Emergency was never fully felt in the main urban areas – life went on as normal in Kuala Lumpur – the British rubber estate owners would arrive for steaks and *stengahs* at the *Coliseum Hotel* in central KL with harrowing stories of how the guerrillas (dubbed Communist Terrorists) had hacked off the arms of rural Chinese workers who had refused to support the cause, and of armed attacks on plantations.

The British were slow to respond to the threat but once lieutenant-general Sir Harold Briggs was put in command of police and army forces, Malaya was on a war footing. The most controversial policy Briggs enacted was the **resettlement** of 400,000 rural Chinese – mostly squatters who had moved to areas bordering the jungle to escape victimization by the Japanese during the war – as well as thousands of Orang Asli seen as potential MCP sympathizers in four hundred "New Villages", scattered across the country. Although these forced migrations were successful in breaking down many of the guerrillas' supply networks, they had the effect of making both Chinese and Orang Asli more sympathetic to the idea of a Communist republic replacing British rule.

The violence peaked in 1950 with ambushes and attacks on plantations near Ipoh, Kuala Kangsar, Kuala Lipis and Raub. The most notorious incident occurred in 1951 on the road to Fraser's Hill, when the British high commissioner to Malaya, **Sir Henry Gurney**, was assassinated (see p.136). Under the new commissioner, Sir Gerald Templer, a new policy was introduced to win hearts and minds. "White Areas" were established: regions perceived as free of guerrilla activity. Communities in these areas had food restrictions and curfews lifted, a policy which began to dissipate guerrilla activity over the next three years. At the same time, the British army – bolstered by conscripted British National Servicemen and assisted by Gurkha contingents and the Malay police force – successfully hunted down most of the Chinese leaders, although not Chin Peng. The leaders were offered an amnesty in 1956, which was refused, and Peng and most of the remaining cell members fled over the border to Thailand where they received sanctuary; some still live there and only formally admitted defeat in 1989.

TOWARDS INDEPENDENCE

The Emergency had the effect of speeding up the political processes prior to independence. Although UMNO stuck to its "Malays first" policy – its founder Dato' Onn bin Jaafar resigned because his call to include non-Malays was rejected – in 1955 the new leader, **Tunku Abdul Rahman** (a royal Malay whose brother was the Sultan of Kedah), forged a united position between UMNO, the moderate Malayan Chinese Association (MCA) and the Malayan Indian Association. This merger was called the **Alliance**, and it was to sweep into power under the rallying cry of **Merdeka** (Freedom). The hope was that ethnic divisions would no

longer be a major factor if **Malayan independence** was granted, though the very real differences between the various ethnic groups' positions still hadn't been eradicated.

With British backing, *Merdeka* was promulgated on August 15, 1957 in a ceremony in Kuala Lumpur's padang – promptly renamed Merdeka Square. The British high commissioner signed a treaty which decreed that under British and Malay law the Federation of Malaya was now independent of the Crown. The first Prime Minister was Tunku Abdul Rahman. The new **constitution** allowed for the nine Malay sultans to alternate as king, and established a two-tier **parliament** – a house of elected representatives and a Senate with delegates from each of the states. Although the system was, in theory, a democracy, the Malay-dominated UMNO remained by far the most influential element in the political equation.

Under Rahman, the country was fully committed to economic expansion and full employment; foreign investment was actively encouraged. Arguments between the two dominant Alliance parties, UMNO and the MCA, were mostly over the allocation of seats in parliament and in the area of education, but Rahman refused to compromise the pre-eminent position of the Malays, and the MCA remained far less powerful than UMNO. Despite the Alliance's aim of creating a new citizen, whose loyalties would be to the country and not to their particular ethnic group, age-old communal divisions had still not been obliterated,

Similarly, in **Singapore** the process of gaining independence gained momentum throughout the 1950s. In 1957 the British gave the go-ahead for the setting up of an elected 51-member assembly, and full **self-government** was attained in 1959, when the People's Action Party (PAP) under **Lee Kuan Yew** won most of the seats. Lee immediately entered into talks with Tunku Abdul Rahman over the notion that Singapore and Malaya should be joined administratively – Rahman initially agreed, although he feared the influence of pro-Communist extremists in the PAP.

In 1961 Tunku Abdul Rahman announced that the two Crown Colonies of Sarawak and North Borneo should join Malaya and Singapore in a revised federation. Many in Borneo would have preferred the idea of a separate Borneo Federation, but the advent of the Konfrontasi, an armed struggle launched by newly independent Indonesia to wrest control of the two colonies from Malaya (see below) played into Rahman's hands – those against his proposals could see how vulnerable the states were to attack from Indonesia.

Behind Rahman's proposal was the concern that demographic trends would in time lead to Malaya having a greater Chinese population than Malay. Consequently he campaigned hard for the inclusion of the two Malay-dominated Borneo colonies into the proposed federation, to act as a demographic balance to the Chinese in Singapore.

FEDERATION AND THE KONFRONTASI

In September 1963 North Borneo (quickly renamed Sabah), Sarawak and Singapore joined Malaya in the **Federation of Malaysia** – "Malaysia" being a term first coined by the British in the 1950s when the notion of a Greater Malaya had been propounded. Both Indonesia, which laid claim to Sarawak (the border of Indonesian Kalimantan ran alongside the state), and the Philippines, which argued it had jurisdiction over Sabah as it had originally been part of the Sulu Sultanate, reacted angrily to the new federation. Although the Philippines backed down, Indonesia didn't, and border skirmishes known as the **Konfrontasi** ensued. The conflict intensified as Indonesian soldiers crossed the border, and a wider war was only just averted when Indonesian President Sukarno backed away from costly confrontations with British and Gurkha troops brought in to boost Sarawak's small armed forces.

Differences soon developed between Lee Kuan Yew and the Malay-dominated Alliance party over the lack of egalitarian policies – although the PAP had dominated recent elections, many Chinese were concerned that UMNO's overall influence in the Federation was too great. Tensions rose on the island and ugly racial incidents developed into full-scale **riots** in 1964, in which several people were killed.

These developments were viewed with great concern by Tunku Abdul Rahman and he decided it would be best if Singapore left the Federation. This was emphatically not in Singapore's best interests, since it was an island without any obvious natural resources; Lee is reported to have cried when the expulsion was announced. Singapore thus acquired full **independence** on August 9, 1965 (see p.505 for details), and the severing of the bond between Malaysia and Singapore soured relations between the countries for some years.

BRUNEI

In **Brunei**, the sultan's autocratic rule was tested in 1962 when, in the state's first ever general election, the left-wing **Brunei People's Party** (BPP) came to power. Sultan Omar, however, viewed democracy suspiciously and refused to let the BPP form a government. A rebellion followed, when the BPP – backed by the Communist North Kalimantan Army – gained control of parts of Seria, Kuala Belait, Tutong and Bandar, but the revolt was crushed within four days by British and Gurkha forces. Sultan Omar's powers remained unchanged and the autocratic royal rule of Brunei continues to this day. Although Abdul Rahman had wanted Brunei to join the Malaysian Federation, too, along with neighbouring Sarawak and Sabah, Omar refused when he realized Rahman's price – a substantial proportion of Brunei's oil and gas revenues. Brunei remained under nominal British jurisdiction until **independence** was declared on December 31, 1983.

ETHNIC CONFLICT

The exclusion of Singapore from the Malaysian Federation was not enough to quell the ethnic conflicts. Resentment built among the Chinese over the principle that Malay be the main language taught in schools and over the privileged employment opportunities offered to Malays. In 1969 the UMNO (Malay)-dominated Alliance lost regional power in parliamentary elections, and Malays in major cities reacted angrily to a perceived increase in power of the Chinese, who had commemorated their breakthrough with festivities in the streets. These triggered counter-demonstrations by Malays. Hundreds of people, mostly Chinese, were killed and injured in the **riots** which followed, with Kuala Lumpur in particular becoming a war zone where large crowds of youths went on the rampage. Rahman kept the country under a state of emergency for nearly two years, during which the draconian **Internal Security Act** (ISA) was used to arrest and imprison activists, as well as many writers and artists.

THE NEW ECONOMIC POLICY

Rahman never recovered full political command after the riots and resigned in 1971, handing over to the new Prime Minister, **Tun Abdul Razak**, also from UMNO, who took a less authoritarian stance – although still implementing the ISA. He brought the parties in Sarawak and Sabah into the political process and initiated a broad set of directives, called the **New Economic Policy** (NEP). This set out to restructure the management of the economy so that it would be less reliant on the Chinese, who previously dominated its most lucrative sectors. Ethnic Malays were to be classed as **Bumiputras** (sons of the soil) and given favoured positions in business, commerce and other professions (see p.57 for details). All schools were also required to teach Malay as a first language, rather than English, Cantonese or Tamil.

DEVELOPMENTS IN SINGAPORE

Lee Kuan Yew continued to rule **Singapore** in a similarly draconian style, also using Internal Security legislation to detain anyone thought to be a threat to the nation. Yet despite earlier doubts, Lee's transformation of the island's **economy** was amazing. Political alignments were made to maximize business opportunities – the government was non-Communist, ethnically mixed and (in theory at least) democratic, although like Malaysia's UMNO, no other party seriously rivalled the PAP.

The economy grew fast: per capita income increased an astonishing fourfold between 1965 and 1977, with huge profits being made in financial services, hi-tech manufacturing, information technology and the petroleum industry. The high taxes these boom areas produced were used to bolster the island's infrastructure and housing, and by 1980 the impossible had been achieved: Singapore stood on the verge of becoming a **Newly Industialized Economy** (NIE), along with Hong Kong, Taiwan and South Korea. Lee had converted a tiny, highly populated country with no inherent assets into a dynamic crossroads between East and West.

But these developments came at a price. Through the 1970s and 1980s the image of Singapore as a humourless, dull place where everyone worked within the confines of a Big Brother civic apparatus started to take shape,

For a full **history of Singapore** and contemporary developments, turn to p.503.

and political intolerance became a fact of life. The **Opposition Worker's Party** won a by-election in 1984 and yet the candidate, J.B. Jeyaretnam, was unable to take his seat as he found himself charged under five offences. Although cleared, further investigations sullied his chances of developing his political career – clearly even one voice proffering criticism of Lee's policies could not be tolerated.

CONTEMPORARY MALAYSIA

For the last two decades Malaysian politics has been dominated by the present prime minister, **Dr Mahathir Mohammed**, who, like all previous PMs leads the UMNO party; he has triumphed at every election since winning his party's nomination in 1981. UMNO is the dominant party in a coalition, the **Barisan National**, which includes representatives from the other mainstream Chinese and Indian parties.

Over these years, UNMO's prime concern has been to extend the concept of the New Economic Policy, which officially ended in 1990. Initially, this policy was underwritten by oil and timber revenues, while Malaysia looked away from the West, preferring to rely on other southeast Asian countries, especially Singapore, as economic partners. But as the costs of the NEP started to bite, Mahathir galvanized Western investment, offering juicy financial incentives like low-tax rates and cheap labour. The UK soon became the main foreign investor in Malaysia.

Through tax, educational and financial breaks many Malays have got richer through the NEP's blatantly racist system of opportunities, but their share of the economy still stands at just twenty percent – way below the projected thirty percent declared when the NEP began. Although the policy was understandably popular with Malays, it was deeply resented by the Chinese and Indians, although outspoken critics of the government are few.

In 1991 the **New Development Policy** succeeded the NEP. Critics say the favoured position of the Malays is just being continued under a new name, but Mahathir has been careful to remove some of the most ill-regarded elements, such as the use of quotas to push Malays into powerful positions. Despite the lighter touch, *bumiputras* are still protected, and the Chinese and Indians have to work substantially harder for a commensurate reward in most spheres of Malaysian economic and educational life.

The structure of Malaysia's expanding **economy** has changed over the last twenty years. Manufacturing output overtook agriculture as the biggest earner in the late 1980s, while the shift to export-dominated areas, notably hi-tech industries and the services sector, has changed the landscape of regions like the Klang Valley, Petaling Jaya and Johor where industrial zones have mushroomed. The development patterns which took shape last century still hold true today: the most productive areas, with the highest per capita income, remain the west coast, particularly the urban areas of Kuala Lumpur, Ipoh, Penang, Melaka and Johor, with the east coast and interior lagging far behind, although revenue from **tourism** is changing the picture slightly.

The only serious threat to Mahathir was in 1987 when Tunku Razaleigh Hamzah, the then trade and industry minister and member of the Kelantan royal family, challenged the prime minister's leadership of UMNO. In the wake of his narrow defeat, Razaleigh formed his own party **Semangat '46** (meaning Spirit of '46, after the year in which UMNO had been founded), which went on to make an alliance with the opposition Islam fundamentalist party PAS. In the October 1990 election, this combination of Semangat and PAS helped reap all 13 parliamentary and 39 state seats in Kelantan.

But by the next election in April 1995, the strains between Semangat and PAS were beginning to show. Although PAS managed to hold on to power in Kelantan, their seat numbers were cut, as the Barisan National coalition went on to its greatest victory since independence in 1957. The fall out with Semangat became public when PAS attempted to push through controversial new regulations on entertainment in the state. A year later, the split with PAS was official and Semangat was in negotiations for its members to rejoin UMNO. This reunification of the parties happened in October 1996, underlining Mahathir's skill at neutering political opposition by embracing former enemies and bringing them within the BN fold.

The battle with PAS continues, though, particularly over PAS's intention to bring strict Islamic, or *Syariat*, law into force in Kelantan. The most controversial part of this plan would be the introduction of a criminal code which dictates that for crimes such as theft, fornication and intoxication, hands and legs should be severed and people lashed, possibly even to death. Such penalties cannot become law until passed by a two-thirds majority in the Federal Parliament – a highly unlikely event. In a Muslim country, Mahathir cannot be seen to be too un-Islamic in opposing PAS outright. So he has found other ways of dealing with this political thorn, in particular, by doing little to assist the economy of Kelantan, which remains the poorest state in Malaysia.

During the 1990s Dr Mahathir's position has been unassailable, his control over his country's political destiny aided and abetted by the impressive economic performance. National revenues have continued to increase substantially as a result either of profits from timber, mostly cut from the forests in Sarawak; the expansion of palm oil plantations often in logged areas, or cleared mangrove forests; and a further widening of the manufacturing base, especially in assembly line goods like electrical products and clothes.

EAST MALAYSIA; POLITICS AND LOGGING

The two east Malaysian states have contrasting political complexions. Whereas in Sarawak the dominant Muslim party, the **Sarawak Alliance**, stands foursquare with the policies of UMNO on the mainland, in Sabah the **Parti Bersatu Sabah** (PBS) has opposed Mahathir on many issues. Led by a Christian, Joseph Pairin Kitingan, for many years – the only non-Muslim to hold political power in Malaysia – the PBS is critical of central government's bleeding of 95 percent of the profits of the state's crude petroleum exporting industry, and of its blatant pro-Muslim propaganda – Christians have even been offered cash incentives to convert to Islam. Pairin however lost power in the 1994 elections: a Muslim, Tan Sri Sakaran Dandai, is now the state's chief minister.

Although Sarawak's politics are dominated by Muslims in the Sarawak Alliance, which is part of the wider Barisan National, over the last twelve years the indigenous groups have had a small say in the political process. The **Parti Bansa Dayak Sarawak** (PBDS) was formed by defecting Iban representatives from the Sarawak Alliance, which has provided the indigenous population of the state (which makes up roughly fifty percent of the population) with an important voice.

Although Mahathir hasn't met with any substantial internal opposition, some of Malaysia's economic policies have been condemned internationally, while the issues surrounding **logging** and development projects in particular have brought severe criticism. Environmental groups in and outside the country have fought to highlight the irretrievable loss of biodiversity caused by the systematic felling of the Sarawak forests, but the angle which has most embarrassed the Sarawak state government – though less so Mahathir – is the impact of logging on the lifestyles of the **indigenous groups**. Although laws exist to prevent the logging of customary land – areas which the ethnic inhabitants can prove have been lived on or used for agriculture for no less than fifty years – they are nearly impossible to enforce. Timber concessionaries frequently overstep the legal boundaries with impunity. International criticism has been met by defensive statements and at the 1992 Earth Summit in Rio de Janeiro, Mahathir suggested that Western nations had no right to tell the developing countries what they could and couldn't do with their natural resources. Currently, logging is actually on the decrease with government targets set to reduce timber harvesting by ten percent each year. Critics counter by saying this isn't enough to save the forests, which within thirty years will cover less than twenty percent of the surface of the country, instead of the current sixty percent.

> For more on the **politics and economics of logging**, see the following feature, "Cutting Down the Rainforest".

CONTROVERSY AND DEVELOPMENT

Deforestation is not the only hot topic on the environmental agenda in Malaysia; massive **dam constructions** are another. One example in Sarawak is a M$30-billion project, the **Bakun** dam in the Belaga district, which was recently approved by Kuala Lumpur. Environmentalists who oppose the scheme say it flies in the face of an avalanche of scientific evidence indicating that the flooding of an area the size of Singapore will have numerous adverse effects, including the uprooting of five thousand ethnic people and the eradication of the region's unique biodiversity.

Yet the convoluted economic processes at work in modern Malaysia were highlighted again in early 1994 when it became clear that £1.3 billion's worth of defence contracts awarded to British companies had been linked to £234 million of British aid money for the building of a hydroelectric dam at **Pergau** in northern Kelantan. British civil servants declared the dam "a bad buy", but the British government went ahead, it was suggested, because the Malaysians had made the arms purchases conditional on the massive injection of funds to underwrite the dam. A Parliamentary Committee in Britain launched an inquiry, but the issue was firmly swept under the carpet in Malaysia where the press stood right behind Mahathir. Indeed, the British press coverage incensed the Malaysian government, which threatened to withhold contracts from British companies as a result.

Although the Pergau controversy harmed relations between the two countries, the thinking which underpins Malaysian **foreign policy** – essentially an open-arms approach, with slight favouritism showed to fellow-Islamic states – is unlikely to lead to any nation being viewed as a long-term enemy. Mahathir's chief goal throughout the last few years of his tenancy – deputy prime minister Anwar is expected to succeed him before the end of the century – has been to raise Malaysia's profile to that of a **fully developed country** by the year 2020; to all intents and purposes, Malaysia is already a Newly Industrialized Economy. But many observers wonder how Malaysia can continue to expand its economy *and* maintain full employment, and suspect that certain skeletons in the closet, particularly the ethnic distrust which has characterized the country's recent past, will return to haunt it when recession starts to bite.

CUTTING DOWN THE RAINFOREST

Although much of the sting has gone out of the global environment debate since the Earth Summit in Rio de Janeiro in 1992, rainforest depletion continues to be a highly contentious subject in Malaysia. In recent years, vociferous pressure groups have raised the profile of rainforest and wetland degradation issues among the general public, while the impact of deforestation on Sarawak's ethnic groups has kept the environment debate on the boil.

However, the government in Kuala Lumpur is quick to defend itself. It insists that modern forest management programmes are increasingly sustainable, and that factors other than timber cultivation are responsible for ecological erosion and the destruction of traditional lifestyles.

Nonetheless, the main reason why deforestation remains an issue is simply because logging is so lucrative – **timber revenues** account for thirteen percent of Malaysia's GNP and earn the nation nearly US$3 billion in export income per year. This makes Malaysia the planet's largest producer of tropical hardwood timber, and the harvesting looks set to continue, albeit at a slower pace than in the rampant days of the 1970s and 1980s.

The government has promulgated environmental laws, most notably the obligation for timber concessionaires to conduct approved **Environmental Impact Assessments** (EIAs) before cultivation can commence. Environmental groups have had some success in limiting specific concessions by using this legislation, but the forest clearance continues apace – many Malaysian forestry professionals admit, off the record, that the laws won't work properly until more staff are employed and a greater commitment is made to tackle corruption and the overharvesting of concession zones. The environmentalists themselves are fully stretched; the main group, *Sahabat Alam Malaysia*, has only a handful of full-time employees in the whole of Sarawak, and is consequently very limited in its sphere of operations.

THE HISTORICAL BACKGROUND

Malaysia's vast timber industry has important historical antecedents. The **sustainable exploitation** of forest products by the indigenous population has always played a vital part in the domestic and export economy of the region. For almost two thousand years, the ethnic tribes have bartered products like rattan, wild rubber and forest plants with foreign traders; first with Indian merchants, followed by Chinese, Malay, and more recently, British traders.

Commercial logging started in Sabah (then North Borneo) in the late nineteenth century. The British Borneo Trading and Planting Company began to extract large trees from the area around Sandakan to satisfy the demand for timber sleepers for the expanding railway system in China. By 1930 the larger **British Borneo Timber Company** (BBTC) was primarily responsible for the extraction of 178,000 cubic metres of timber, rising to nearly five million cubic metres by the outbreak of World War II, and Sandakan became one of the world's main timber ports. Most areas were logged indiscriminately, and the indigenous tribal groups who lived there were brought into the economic system to work on North Borneo's rubber, tobacco and, later, oil palm plantations. The process intensified as the main players in Sabah tapped the lucrative Japanese market, where postwar reconstruction costing billions of dollars was underway. By the early 1960s, timber had accelerated past rubber as the region's chief export and by 1970 nearly thirty percent of Sabah had been extensively logged, with palm oil and other plantation crops replacing around a quarter of the degraded forest. Timber exports had accounted for less than ten percent of all exports from Sabah in 1950; by the 1970s, this had rocketed to over seventy percent.

In **Sarawak** the development of large foreign-run plantations was hindered initially by the White Rajahs, James and Charles Brooke, who largely kept foreign investment out of their paternalistically run fiefdom. However, small indigenous timber concerns run by Chinese and Malay merchants were allowed to trade. But once the BBTC was given rights to start logging in northern Sarawak in the 1930s, timber extraction grew rapidly, especially since the third White Rajah, Vyner Brooke, was less stringent in his opposition to the economic development of the state. Timber was viewed as a vital commercial resource to be utilized in the massive reconstruction of the state, following the devastating Japanese occupation. During its short postwar period as a Crown Colony and, then after 1963, as a Malaysian state, logging in Sarawak has grown to become one of its chief revenue earners, alongside oil extraction. The state government encouraged foreign investment and issued timber concessions to rich individuals, who were encouraged to carve up ever more remote areas. Most of the Baram basin has been logged – the river is now a soupy, brown sludge due to the run off of earth and silt caused by the extraction process – and attention has switched to the remote Balui river system in the east of the state.

Peninsular Malaysia's pre-independence economy was not as reliant on timber revenues as those of Sabah and Sarawak. Although one sixth of the region's 120,000 square kilometres of forest, predominantly in Johor, Perak and Negeri Sembilan states, had been cut down by 1957, most of the logging had been done gradually and on a small, localized scale. As in Sabah, it was the demand for rail sleepers for the expansion of the Malayan train network in the 1920s which had first attracted the commercial logging companies, but wide-scale clearing and conversion to rubber and palm oil plantations in the more remote areas of Pahang, Perlis, Kedah and Terengganu didn't intensify until the 1960s. By the end of the 1970s, more efficient extraction methods, coupled with a massive increase in foreign investment in the logging industry, had led to over forty percent of the Peninsula's remaining forests being either cleared for plantation purposes or partially logged.

THE CONTEMPORARY PICTURE

During the 1980s logging slowed down as a result of new legislation being enacted. Under the **National Forestry Policy** (NFP), deforestation was reduced to 900 square kilometres a year, almost a third slower than the previous rate. The government also designated 47,000 square kilometres of land as **Permanent Forest Estates** in which a variety of valuable tree species are cultivated. But critics argue that these forest estates may not be able to

recover from the original depletion they suffered in the 1970s, and point out that the 1988 log output was over two million cubic metres higher than the 1986 figure – ie, far more than is considered sustainable and in apparent disregard of the NFP.

The largest share of contemporary logging takes place in **Sarawak** – eighty percent of the total Malaysian output in the 1990s, or 2700 square kilometres a year. In principle, **customary land tenure**, which was enshrined in law throughout the White Rajah period, protects the land claimed by the state's indigenous tribal groups and formed the basis of the 1958 **Sarawak Land Code**. However, according to the groups and their supporters, much commercial logging ignores this. Not only are locations of special importance – burial places, access routes and sections of rivers used for fishing – disregarded by loggers, but even areas in which the indigenous people can prove they have lived and farmed for generations have been abused. Forests around Bintulu, Belaga and Limbang have suffered in this way, with the seminomadic Penan at the forefront of opposition to the encroachment onto their customary lands.

Kuala Lumpur's sanctioning, in 1995, of the **Bakun Dam Project** provided clear proof that the situation isn't likely to improve in the near future. Sited upriver from Belaga at the top of the Rajang, when the dam comes to fruition early in the new millennium, more than five hundred square kilometres of forest will have been flooded out, robbing many endangered species of their habitat, and displacing several thousand indigenous tribespeople. As if to add insult to injury, much of the electricity generated is to be diverted, along undersea cables, to the Peninsula. Ekran, the company awarded the contract, is generally considered ill equipped to manage such an immense engineering project: evidently, its well-documented links with eminent Sarawakian politicians were more instrumental in its success than the competence of its tender.

THE THREAT TO TRADITIONAL LIFESTYLES

Unlike many of the ethnic groups who can base their customary land claims on a settled history of farming, the nomadic lifestyle of the **Penan**, and the particular ways in which they utilize the land, makes it hard for their land rights to be defined and recognized. An added factor has been that since the mid-1980s the Sarawak state government's avowed policy has been to bring the Penan into what it views as the development process, by urging them to move to permanent longhouses, work in the cash economy and send their children to school.

The Penan have proved resilient to these attempts to assimilate them into the wider Malaysian social system, largely because the government diktats seem to go suspiciously hand in hand with an expansion of logging in their customary land areas. Very often, there's been no warning that Penan land has been earmarked for logging until the extraction actually begins – examples in remote areas of the Belaga district have been well documented by the environmental group **Sahabat Alam Malaysia**. Subsequently, the Penan have had to watch the destruction of their traditional living areas: trees are cut down; wildlife disappears along with its habitat; and the rivers become polluted by soil erosion, topsoil run-off and siltation.

In retaliation, some Penan tribespeople have applied for **communal forest areas** (so-called "Penan zones") to be designated, so that some of their land would receive protection, but until now, all such applications have been refused. As a result the Penan, especially in the Baram watershed and Belaga, have resorted to **direct action**, with local people confronting logging companies, building barricades, removing and even destroying machinery. To stop the protests spreading, the state government amended the Forestry Act in 1987 to outlaw these actions, even when they took place on land proven to be owned by the locals. However, the blockades have continued, receiving worldwide publicity, which forced the state government to announce that they would set aside large areas as reserves where logging would not be allowed. This appears to be a step in the right direction, but the destruction of tribal areas continues.

The current picture in **Sabah** is very similar, where recent aerial photographic surveys have shown that 44,000 square kilometres (over sixty percent) of the state's 74,000 square kilometres have been exploited for timber. However, there hasn't been the same level of tribal protest, simply because fewer of Sabah's indigenous people live in the deep interior where most of the logging takes place.

PALM OIL CULTIVATION

Another hot issue in Sarawak in recent years has been **palm oil cultivation**. Increasingly, logged areas are being replanted with palm oil trees, now one of Sarawak's leading exports. The State Environment Department includes these monoculture plantations in its figure for the total amount of the state still under forest, but environment groups say that oil palm plantations sustain only a tiny proportion of the flora and fauna that a dipterocarp forest does, which they have invariably replaced. Accurate figures, however, are notoriously hard to come by. The eco-activists say that less than half of Sarawak's 124,000 square kilometres remains as forest; the state claims the figure is more like three-quarters – though it includes oil palm and other plantation zones in its calculations.

GOVERNMENT INITIATIVES

The **Malaysian government** is naturally keen to deflect attention away from the accusation that the timber concessions it grants are solely responsible for unsustainable timber production. In response, the government suggests that the **slash-and-burn** agricultural practices of the indigenous groups in Sarawak, and to a lesser degree, in Sabah and the interior of Peninsular Malaysia, are what cause substantial deforestation. But researchers have found that the bulk of this agricultural activity occurs in secondary rather than primary (untouched) forest. Indeed, environmental groups believe that only around one hundred square kilometres of primary forest – a tiny proportion compared to the haul by commercial timber companies – is cleared by the indigenous groups annually.

Whatever the truth behind the figures for east Malaysia, there is far less of an argument about rainforest degradation in **Peninsular Malaysia**, largely because timber production there has been cut by around fifty percent in the last decade. Even so, the logged output is still estimated to stand at around five million cubic metres a year throughout the 1990s, which leaves around 50,000 square kilometres of forest out of a total surface area of 131,700 square kilometres – the remainder vanishing at the rate of nearly 1000 square kilometres each year.

However, **reforestation schemes** within the Permanent Forest Estates – government-run tracts of land given over to tree cultivation – are on the increase. And organizations like the **Forest Resource Institute of Malaysia** (FRIM), which sustains an area of secondary forest on the edge of Kuala Lumpur, prove how rainforest habitats can be renewed. FRIMS' ecological management plan ensures that a comprehensive range of flora, including tree species and a wide spectrum of plants, are planted and monitored over a long period. It must be stressed, however, that FRIM is the exception rather than the rule, and most environmentalists within Malaysia don't believe that renewable forestry can offset the damage caused by current timber extraction techniques, which seldom aid regrowth. As a rule, logging devastates over seventy percent of all the flora, topsoil and root structures in a given area.

THE FUTURE

As Malaysia – its spiralling GNP based on a solid manufacturing base – gets richer, it's likely that the revenue derived from cutting down the rainforests will decrease. As a consequence, the government hopes that the controversies surrounding logging – which have pitted "Third World" leaders like Prime Minister Dr Mahathir against richer countries who argue that Malaysia should stop exploiting its dwindling forests for the future safety of the planet

– will die down. In the meantime, however, timber remains the highest export earner.

Malaysia is slowly becoming more environmentally friendly, largely as a result of well-organized and scientifically persuasive organizations within the country, but the **pace of change** is slow. There is still a lack of effective reforestation schemes, though the Malaysian government does at least claim it will not follow the example of Thailand, where only ten percent of the country remains forested, and it condemns the horrendous situation in lawless Burma and Cambodia where Thai and Japanese companies are clearing the remaining stocks of the world's teak forests at devastating speed. However, the complex system of logging **regulations** in force in Malaysia has, in recent years, lacked bite. If the logging is to be stopped, then the government has to apply teeth to what have hitherto been purely symbolic enforcement measures.

Perhaps more importantly, if Malaysia wants to continue talking about the country's cultural diversity in its tourist promotion brochures, then the land rights of the indigenous groups, particularly in Sarawak, have to be respected. The legislation, especially the EIA system, currently little more than a sham, must be made to work quickly.

WILDLIFE

There's an extraordinary tropical biodiversity on the Malay Peninsula and in Borneo, with over six hundred species of birds; more than two hundred mammal species, including the tiger, Asian elephant, orangutan and tapir; many thousands of flowering plant species, among them the insectivorous pitcher plant and scores of others of known medicinal value; and over one hundred species of brightly coloured butterflies. This enormous variety of bird, plant and animal life makes any visit to a tropical rainforest a memorable experience.

Downtown Singapore, on the other hand, is not the sort of place you would expect to find much plant or animal life. The rapid urbanization of Singapore has had a major impact on its indigenous wildlife, and the state has consequently lost many of its original forest plant species, all its large mammals and many of its ecologically sensitive bird species such as hornbills. However, two remnant patches of tropical forest still survive amid the rampant development – at Bukit Timah Nature Reserve and the Botanic Gardens.

Although Malaysia is divided into two distinct parts – Peninsular and east Malaysia (the states of Sabah and Sarawak on the island of Borneo) – the wildlife and plant communities of both areas are very similar, since Borneo was joined to the mainland by a land bridge during the ice age. Nonetheless, there are some specific differences. The forests of the Peninsula support populations of several large mammal species, such as tiger, tapir and *gaur* (a forest-dwelling wild cattle), which are absent from Borneo. Other large mammals, like the Asian elephant, and birds like the hornbill, occur both on Borneo and on the Peninsula; while Borneo features the orang-utan (the "man of the forest") and the proboscis monkey. Indeed, this latter species is endemic to the island of Borneo.

WILDLIFE SITES

Two of the most exciting – and accessible – areas in which to **view wildlife** are featured below. The round-ups of bird, plant and animal life at **Taman Negara** and **Fraser's Hill** should be read in conjunction with the general accounts of both places in the guide. In addition, there are shorter wildlife accounts and special features throughout the guide: check the page references given below. It's worth noting that Sarawak, in particular, has endless opportunities for observing wildlife in its national parks and river systems: all the practical details for visiting the region are contained in the Sarawak chapter.

Wherever you plan to go, it's important to remember that observing wildlife in tropical forests requires much patience, and on any one visit it is unlikely that you will encounter more than a fraction of the wildlife living in the forest. Many of the mammals are shy and nocturnal.

A WILDLIFE CHECKLIST	
Sites	
Botanic Gardens	(p.536)
and Bukit Timah: Singapore	(p.554)
Danum Valley Conservation	
Area: Sabah	(p.471)
Fraser's Hill: Peninsula	(p.134)
Kinabalu National Park: Sabah	(p.454)
Pulau Tioman: Peninsula	(p.319)
Rantau Abang: Peninsula	(p.269)
Semanggoh Wildlife Rehabilitation Centre:	
Sarawak	(p.344)
Sepilok Orang Utan Rehabilitation Centre:	
Sabah	(p.465)
Taman Negara: Peninsula	(p.208)
Turtle Islands Park: Sabah	(p.466)
Wildlife	
Hornbills	(p.414)
Marine turtle	(p.271)
Proboscis monkeys	(p.468)

REFERENCE BOOKS

The following **books** are useful sources of reference, most available on the ground in Malaysia and Singapore: the Sabah Society's *Pocket Guide to the Birds of Borneo* (Sabah Society, Malaysia); M. Strange & A. Jeyarajasingam's *Photographic Guide to the Birds of Peninsular Malaysia and Singapore* (Sun Tree Publishing, Singapore); J. Payne, C. Francis & K. Phillipp's *Field Guide to the Mammals of Borneo* (Sabah Society, Malaysia); M. Tweedie's *Mammals of Malaysia* (Longman, Malaysia); and Lord Medway's *Wild Mammals of Malaya and Singapore* (Oxford University Press).

TAMAN NEGARA

The vast expanse (4343 square kilometres) of **Taman Negara** contains one of the world's oldest tropical rainforests, and is generally regarded as one of Asia's finest national parks. It has an **equatorial climate**, with rainfall throughout the year and no distinct dry season. Temperatures can reach 35°C during the day, with the air often feeling very muggy. Most rain falls as heavy convectional showers in the afternoon, following a hot and sunny morning – from November to February, heavy rains may cause flooding in low-lying areas.

FOREST TREES

The natural richness of the habitat is reflected in the range of forest types found within the park. Only a small proportion of Taman Negara is true **lowland forest**, though it's here that most of the trails and hides are located. The lowlands support **dipterocarp** (meaning "two-winged fruit") evergreen forest, featuring tall tropical hardwood species and thick-stemmed lianas. There are more than four hundred dipterocarp species in Malaysia, and it's not uncommon to find up to forty in just one small area of forest. Among those present at Taman Negara are the majestic fifty-metre tall tualang, southeast Asia's tallest tree; many others have broad, snaking buttress roots and leaves the size of dinner plates. Several species of **fruit trees**, such as durian, mango, jambu and rambutan also grow wild here.

On slightly higher ground, **montane forest** predominates, mainly oak and native conifers, with a shrub layer of rattan and dwarf palm.

Higher still (above 1500m on Gunung Tahan) is **cloud forest**, where trees are often cloaked by swirling mist, and the damp boughs bear thick growths of mosses and ferns. At elevations of over 1700m, miniature montane forest of rhododendron and fan palms is found, but it will be the hardy explorer who reaches such heights.

MAMMALS

The best method of trying to see some of the larger herbivorous (grazing) **mammals** is to spend the night in a **hide** overlooking a salt lick – the animals visit these natural and artificial "salt sites" to consume salt. There are six hides in the park, and to maximize your chances of spotting mammals you will need to stay overnight at one.

Animals commonly encountered include the Malayan **tapir**, a species related to horses and rhinos, though pig-like in appearance with a short, fat body, a long snout and black-and-white colouring. The **gaur** (wild cattle) is dark in colour apart from its white leg patches, which look like ankle socks. There are also several species of **deer**: the larger *sambar;* the *kijang* or barking deer, this the size of a roe deer; and the lesser and greater mouse deer, these the last two largely nocturnal, and not much bigger than rabbits.

Primates (monkeys and gibbons) are found throughout the park, although they are quite shy since they have traditionally been hunted for food by the park's indigenous groups. The dawn chorus of a white-handed **gibbon** troupe – making a plaintive whooping noise – is not a sound which will be quickly forgotten. Other primates include the long-tailed and pig-tailed **macaques**, which come to the ground to feed, the latter identified by its shorter tail, brown fur and pinkish brown face. There are dusky (or spectacled – with white patches around the eyes) and banded **leaf monkeys**, too, which can be recognized by their long, drooping tails (gibbons have no tails) and their habit of keeping their bodies hidden amongst the foliage – whereas macaques feed on the ground, both leaf monkeys and gibbons keep to the trees.

Several **squirrel** species, including the black and common giant squirrels, are present in the park, and towards dusk there's a chance of seeing the nocturnal red flying squirrel shuffling along the highest branches of a tree before launching itself to glide across the forest canopy to an adjacent tree. This squirrel can make continuous glides of up to 100m at a time.

Other mammals you might encounter by – admittedly fairly remote – chance are the Asian **elephant,** with smaller ears and a more humped back than the African; **tigers,** of which a reasonably healthy population exists due to an abundance of prey and the relatively large size of the protected area; and **sun bears**. The bears are an interesting species: standing about 70cm high on all fours, and around 1.5m in length, they are dark brown or black, with muzzle and breast marked dirty white to dull orange. They live on fruit, honey and termites and their behaviour towards humans can be unpredictable, particularly if there are cubs nearby.

Clouded leopards are also present, a beautifully marked cat species with a pattern of cloud-like markings on the sides of the body. They live mostly in the trees, crossing from bough to bough in their search for food, eating monkeys, squirrels and birds, which they swat with their claws; they're most active at twilight. Smaller predators include the **leopard cat** (around the size of a large domestic cat) and several species of nocturnal **civet**, some of which have been known to enter the hides at night in search of tourists' food. Smooth **otters** may also sometimes be seen, in small family groups along Sungei Tembeling.

BIRDS

Over 250 species of bird – including some of the most spectacular forest-dwelling birds in the world – have been recorded in Taman Negara, though many species are shy or only present in small numbers. Birds are at their most active from early to mid-morning, and again in the late afternoon and evening periods; the areas around Kuala Keniam, and the Kumbang and Tabing hides are particularly worth visiting.

Resident forest birds include several species of **green pigeon**, which feed on the fruiting trees, along with species such as **bulbuls** (vocal, fruit-eating birds which often flock to feed). **Wintering birds** from elsewhere in Asia, such as warblers and thrushes, join resident **minivets** (slender, colourful birds with long, graduated tails, white, yellow or red bands in the wings and outer tail feathers of the same colour) and **babblers** (a short-tailed, round-winged, ground-dwelling species) from September to March, and it is during this period

that the visitor can hope to encounter the greatest diversity of birds. Up to seventy species alone can be seen near the park headquarters, particularly if the trees are in fruit.

Brilliantly coloured **pittas** in hues of red, yellow, blue and black are ground-dwelling birds, which generally occur singly or in pairs, though they are notoriously shy and difficult to approach. The resident species are the giant, garnet and banded pittas, with blue-winged and hooded pittas being winter visitors.

In addition, several species of pheasant may be seen along the trails, including the **Malaysian peacock pheasant**, a shy bird with a blue-green crest and a patch of bare, orange facial skin. The feathers of the back and tail have green *ocelli* (eye-spots). The crested and crestless **fireback** are similar species of pheasant, differing in the crested fireback's black crest, white-tail plumes, blue-sheen upper parts and orange (rather than grey) belly. The **great argus** is the largest pheasant species present in the area, with the male birds reaching a maximum of 1.7m in length including the long tail feathers, their penetrating "kwow wow" series of call notes audible most days in the park. Finally, the **mountain peacock pheasant** – very similar in plumage to the Malaysian peacock pheasant – is found high on Gunung Tahan and is endemic to Malaysia.

You'll also see birds of prey, with two of the most common species, the **crested serpent eagle** and the **changeable hawk eagle**, often spotted soaring over gaps in the forest canopy. The crested serpent eagle (with a 75cm wingspan; about the size of a buzzard) can be identified by the black and white bands on the trailing edge of the wings and on the tail.

Other species confined to tropical forests are **trogons** (brightly coloured, mid-storey birds), of which five species are present at Taman Negara, and several species of **hornbill** – large, broad-winged, long-tailed forest birds with huge, almost outlandish bills.

REPTILES AND AMPHIBIANS

Reptiles and amphibians are well represented in the area. **Monitor lizards** (which can grow to be over 2m long) can be found close to the park headquarters, as can **skinks** (a type of lizard which slithers along the ground a bit like a snake, not using its legs).

Several species of snake are present, too, including the reticulated **python** (which feeds on small mammals and birds and can grow to a staggering 9m in length), and the king and common **cobras**; king cobras, the largest venomous snake in the world, grow up to five metres long. These are all pretty rare in Taman Negara, though, and you're more likely to come across **whip snakes** (which eat insects and lizards) and – most common of all – harmless green **tree snakes** (which, not surprisingly, live in the trees, and eat lizards).

FRASER'S HILL

At **Fraser's Hill** visitors can escape the stultifying tropical heat of the lowlands and venture into the cool breezes and fogs of the mountain forests, where ferns and pitcher plants cling to damp, moss-covered branches. It's a noted area for bird-watching, with the hill itself harbouring several montane species of bird, while mammals represented in the area include those normally restricted to more mountainous regions, in addition to some lowland species.

Much of the **forest** at Fraser's Hill is in pristine condition and the route there takes you from lowland forest through sub-montane to montane forest. Higher up on the hill, there are more evergreen tree species present, while the very nature of the vegetation changes: the trees are more gnarled and stunted, and the boughs heavily laden with dripping mosses and colourful epiphytic orchids (ie, orchids which grow on other plants and trees).

MAMMALS

The more strictly montane mammal species at Fraser's Hill include the **siamang gibbon**, a large, all-black gibbon, lacking any pale facial markings, that spends its time exclusively in trees. There are also several species of **bat**, including the montane form of the Malayan fruit bat and the grey fruit bat, and several **squirrel**

species such as the mountain red-bellied squirrel and the tiny Himalayan striped squirrel. The latter species has a pattern of black-and-yellow stripes running along the length of its back. Lowland mammal species which may be encountered are the tiger, clouded leopard, sun bear and leaf monkeys, for descriptions of which see "Taman Negara" above. However, most of these are scarce here, and you can only realistically expect to encounter monkeys, squirrels and, possibly, siamangs.

BIRDS

A feature of montane forest bird flocks is the **mixed feeding flock**, which may contain many different species. These pass rapidly through an area of forest searching for and gleaning insects as they go, and it's quite likely that different observers will see entirely different species in one flock. Species which commonly occur within these flocks are the **lesser racket-tailed drongo**, a black crow-like bird with long tail streamers; the **speckled piculet**, a small spotted woodpecker; and the **blue nuthatch**, a small species – blue-black in colour with a white throat and pale eye ring – which runs up and down tree trunks. Several species of brightly coloured **laughing thrushes**, small thrush-sized birds which spend time foraging on the ground, also occur in these flocks. One sound to listen out for is the distinctive cackling "took" call of the **helmeted hornbill** – see p.414 for more on these birds.

Fraser's Hill itself peaks at 1310m at the High Pines, where there is a ridge trail. Here, there's the possibility of encountering species unlikely to be seen at lower altitudes, including the brown bullfinch and the **cutia** – a striking bird, with blue cap, black eyeline and tail, white underparts barred black and a chestnut-coloured back.

Tony Stones

MALAYSIAN MUSIC

Like many places in the region, Malaysia is rapidly becoming Westernized at the expense of its own traditions, and lacks the dynamic indigenous music scene of its neighbour Indonesia. The creation of the modern Malaysian Federation in 1963 had the effect of pushing the traditional royal court musical styles and folk music into the background and such music now tends to be heard only at festivals or in the Islamic heartland of Kelantan state, in the northeast corner of Peninsular Malaysia. In their place are the pan-Asian pop styles that have more in common with Western pop music than Malaysian traditions.

Nevertheless, when you do track down Malaysian traditional music, there's a surprising richness to it, deriving from the peculiar blend of **ethnic influences** brought by the Arab and Chinese traders, the Indian workers and colonizers from Portugal, Holland and Britain.

The Malays adopted Arabic **instruments** such as the *gendang* (double-headed drum) and *rebana* (frame drum), the harmonium from India, and the *tawak* gong from China, to make their own folk styles. The most prominent melodic instrument is the *rebab*, the spiked fiddle of Middle Eastern origin, found also in Thailand and Indonesia. A lot of contemporary musicians use the Western violin, brought originally by the Portuguese, which they play in *rebab* style, in the lap.

The **pantum** style of Malaysian singing survives, too − centuries old and still very popular. This consists of vocal duets − sometimes with drums, but more often a cappella − which are nearly always improvised. *Pantums* developed from Islamic devotional song, where sections of the Koran would be sung. Nowadays even adverts can be sung in *pantum* and can often be witty or slapstick in character. *Pantum* has become quite an informal style with its loose metre offering opportunities for the singers to be topical and satirical, and still, occasionally, devotional.

KELANTAN: SILAT AND ZIKIR BARAT

Kelantan is the heart of the country's folk culture and the place to start a musical tour of Malaysia. Malay music and dance is performed at the cultural centre (see p.248) in Kota Bharu every week, and performances usually incorporate a wide range of different styles. A small ensemble of *aderams* (long drums), *serunai* (a cross between a clarinet and an oboe) and *tawaks* generates a loose set of cross rhythms, while two Malay gents in baggy costumes perform **silat** − an ancient dance of self-defence − in a sandpit. As the music intensifies, their flowing Tai Chi-like movements change and they grip each other. The first to throw the other onto the ground is the winner. The music rises to a crescendo as the wrestling intensifies, the *serunai* screeching atonally while the drums and gongs quicken the loose rhythm.

Alongside the *silat* band are twelve men sitting in another sandpit with small, brightly coloured, wooden xylophones in front of them. The rhythm they hammer out in unison is fast and jolly, the idea being for all the players to end each piece at precisely the same time. Although a recreational activity more than an art form, this is an interesting style of communal music, known as **kertok**, which originated with the Orang Asli.

Later in the day there is usually a **wayang kulit** (shadow puppet) performance, a tradition which occurs across southeast Asia and presents tales from the Hindu epic, the *Ramayana*. In Malaysia, however, the sound is very different to the *gamelan* (court music) that accompanies Indonesian *wayang kulit*. Here, a larger version of the *silat* band, including a xylophone, hammers out the fanfare. The puppeteer sits beside the musicians onstage behind a screen, and while he chants the epic he illustrates the story with dozens of wooden shadow puppets. A different side of Malaysian music emerges at night in Kota Bharu, as people meet after evening prayers for supper at the market's outdoor stalls. Here, you can hear the distinct refrains of **zikir birat**. Singers chant rhythmically in *Bahasa Malaysia*, over a dense bed of percussion. Each player takes turns to chant a verse, which can be elaborated upon, allowing the performance to go on for many hours.

The form is basically a version of Islamic ritual and particularly of Sufic singing (known as *zikir*). In its most traditional form, two singers perform on the street outside mosques or in markets, alternating verses in praise of Allah to the rhythm of a single tambourine. As it took on a more secular slant, however, teams of men would chant newly composed texts about anything of topical interest. *Zikir birat* now has its pop stars, like Draman, Dollah and Mat Yeh, and is beginning to be recorded by Indian and Chinese singers, too.

KUALA LUMPUR: GHAZAL AND DONDANG

In **Kuala Lumpur**, traditional music doesn't seem to play the same integral part in everyday life. Most of the music you hear in the city, pounding from the cassette bars, is homegrown pop and rock. However, wandering the streets you do hear snatches of Islamic love songs – not unlike *ghazals* – performed by blind buskers, who accompany themselves on tinny keyboards.

More professional (and more strictly) **ghazal** artists are to be heard on cassette or in concert. The great star of this genre was the lamented **Kamariah Noor**, who died recently. She had a voice both intense and languid, bending and holding notes to inject maximum emotion into a song. Kamariah often sang with her husband, **Hamzah Dolmat**, Malaysia's greatest *rebab* player, whose slow, rather mournful style is characterized by a wonderful melodic creativity.

Other recent Malay stars include the **Kumpulum Sri Maharani** ensemble, which plays **dondang sayang**, a slow, intense, majestic music led by sharp percussive drum rolls, which trigger a shift in melody or a change in the pace of the rhythm. This is a quintessentially Malaysian style, bringing together Indian,

Arabic, Chinese and Portuguese instruments to create a mood of gentle intensity. *Tabla* and harmonium from India and the double-headed drum (the *gendang*) and tambourine from Arabia mark out the rhythms, while the violin and the *oud* provide the melodies.

Dondang traditionally accompanies classical singing – usually duets whose lyrics, like in ghazal, are often romantic epics. Maharani's band integrates electric keyboard and snippets of guitar into the traditional framework. Songs these days are short, starting with fast, expressive drumming. When the singers begin, the rhythm slows down, only to accelerate for dramatic emphasis towards the finale.

MELAKA: RONGGENG

Melaka makes a good musical stop, to hear the old fiddle music of the *rebab*, adapted here to the European instrument. It's a peculiarly Malaysian style of playing that is the basis of the main folk dance music across the country, **ronggeng**. Other instruments in the *ronggeng* unit include two *rebana* (frame drums) and a brass gong to mark the time.

Ronggeng fiddlers play a wide range of melodies, which, perhaps due to the music's Portuguese heritage, sound a trifle Romany or Moorish. Performances revolve around dozens of tunes that locals know instinctively. When the singers join in, the rhythm slows and the violinist switches from ebullient fiddler to plaintive accompanist.

One of the most popular dances is the **joget**. Other percussive instruments are added to the basic *ronggeng* format and most *joget* tunes end with a "chinchang passage" – the point where the drums and violin quicken and the dancers hop from one leg to another like dancing cockerels.

And then there is **zapin**, yet another musical style led by the accordion. Like in so much Malaysian folk music, Arab, European and Indian elements come together here to form something new. The *zapin* tempos start out slow but will often quicken abruptly as the accordion provides the cue for the dancers to improvise around their set steps.

COURT AND CEREMONIAL MUSIC

Nobat is almost impossible to see these days as it's the classical music of the sultan's courts and is, by definition, played to a private audience. This music is functional rather than performed as entertainment, and is an inherent part of religious (Islamic) rituals and court ceremonies like the crowning of a ruler, weddings and funerals. *Nobat* came from the Middle East and became enmeshed with the pomp of the sultanates soon after the region embraced Islam in the fourteenth and fifteenth centuries. The main instruments – the *nehara* (large drum), *serunai* (oboe) and *nafiri* (silver trumpet) – are fairly similar to those used in Thailand's small *piphat* classical ensembles.

At east coast festivals watch out for **main puteri**, a music-cum- dance style used for healing by shamens. Its trance-like beat is played on the *rebab, gengang* drums and *tetawak* (gongs). The music possesses the shamen, who is then able to extract evil spirits from, and consequently purify, his client.

Among the **ethnic groups** in Sarawak, music plays an important part in dance dramas and provides an aural backdrop for ceremonies like the rite-of-passage *Gawai Kenyaalang* festival. The main instruments are a variety of gongs, a *sape* (lute) and small drums. Long epic dramas are often sung at auspicious occasions, although among most groups, especially the Kelabits of northern Sarawak, this tradition is fast disappearing.

CROONERS, POP AND ROCK

Malaysian pop music was born in the 1950s when a young singer called **P. Ramlee** rose to fame. Very much the Harry Belafonte of Malaysian music, Ramlee set romantic lyrics to Malay melodies, bringing the *dondang sayang* style up to date in duets with his wife **Saloma**. Musically, he expanded the folk instrument repertoire, often recording with an orchestra, and reflecting the influence of Cuban mambos and cha-cha-chas in the postwar period. His singing style is a European version of classical *dondang* – an Arabic-inflected purring baritone, romantically lush but vulnerable. His great duets with Saloma are Malaysian pop music's finest hour. To hear Ramlee's work, head for the *Blue Moon* in KL's *Hotel Equatorial* (see p.91).

Ramlee launched a new movement in modernizing classical singing, shortening the songs and using Western instruments. Singers like **Zaleha Hamid** continue the tradition, singing in a more upbeat but still orthodox style, backed by kit drums, keyboards, bass and flute. Along with other stars like **Sharifah Aini** and **Herman Tino**, Hamid's material is the most popular of the older-style Malaysian music.

However, the younger generation have firmly turned their back on this kind of Malay music. In the 1960s and 1970s they looked to Indonesian pop, which was adapting Western rock ideas. These days, **Malay rock and pop** cassettes outnumber *dondang, ronggang* and *zikir* twenty to one in the stores, but there is little to be said in its favour since it is so completely derivative – the **heavy metal** music industry is second only to Brazil's among developing countries. The only Malaysian element is the lyrics which, due to legislation, have to be sung in *Bahasa Malaysia* rather than English.

The brightest light at the soft-rock end of the spectrum is **Sheila Majid**. She has become Malaysia's first international pop star, filling halls in Indonesia and Japan. Her singing style is a kind of mellow Asian soul, with a synthesized backdrop and George Benson-style guitar rhythms. Her producer and husband Roslan Aziz is keen to introduce more traditional instrumental sounds but the market at present wants things Western. Nonetheless, Majid has provided a link between the traditional and the modern in her album "Legenda", where she covers songs by P. Ramlee.

A new development is the birth of a home-grown **rap** style, which although rhythmically taking its call from the United States, is performed in Malay with lyrics geared towards particularly Malaysian experiences. One group, **4U2C**, has had some of its material banned because of the controversial nature of the lyrics.

NEW DIRECTIONS

Although Western-style pop and rock dominate the Malaysian charts and media, over the past few years a few musicians have started looking back to their roots and to traditional melodies, while still working within a Western context. It's perhaps not enough to talk of as a movement, though it does have a name – **musica nusantara** (music of the archipelago).

The two main artists involved are **Shequal** and **Zainal Abidin**, both of whom use acoustic instruments like accordions, tabla, sitar and flute. They write their songs and melodies themselves, rather than updating classics, and they both come from rock backgrounds. Abidin used to sing with soft-rock band Headwind before leaving to search for a more indigenous direction.

He found this in what he called kampung (village) music, and began to write lyrics concerned with the erosion of the old ways of life. His song "Baba" warns of the threat to the Baba culture, the Malay-speaking Chinese community in Melaka. More recently, however, he has started playing what he calls "World Music", mixing rock and traditional styles with those of the African musicians, Youssou N'Dour and Papa Wemba, whom he met at a WOMAD festival in Japan.

Shequal is well worth checking out, too. His best-known song, "Balada Nusantara", is a beautiful melody led by a lovely accordion line. The mood is upbeat but relaxed, evoking the atmosphere of the coast with its slow pace of life and traditions.

Another interesting direction is evident in the releases by a fusion group called **Asiabeat**, who are causing a stir around KL with an intriguing blend of East and West, fusing traditional Eastern instruments like the *shakuhachi* (Japanese bamboo flute), played by an American, John Kaiser Neptune, with saxophones and guitars. Asiabeat often plays in KL (see p.115 for music venues).

Other musicians pursuing individual destinies include **Kit Leee**, who records way-out electronic pieces, most recently with a talented Brazilian singer, Marilia, and his friend and some-time collaborator **Rafique**, who produces KL's only music with a political edge. He gets away with criticizing the government, he says, because he is the only person doing it. His songs include "Shut Up", about the mid-1980s Internal Security Act, and "Khalwat", about the Muslim law that forbids courting couples from getting too close before marriage.

Taken (and abridged) from
the Rough Guide to World Music.
Thanks to Jak Kilby for additional research.

DISCOGRAPHY

Malaysian music is yet to make the jump to Western labels and much good music is available on cassette only, through local labels.

TRADITIONAL

Kampulum Sri Maharani *Dondang Sayang Mambo* (EMI, Malaysia). Slow, intense music with the lovely voice of veteran singer Fadzil Ahmed and some hopping *ronggeng*.

Orkes Maharani *Ghazal Parti* (EMI, Malaysia). Lively *ghazal* singing over harmonium, violin and guitar.

Various *Album Melayu Deli* (EMI, Malaysia). Zaleha Hamid and other singers use traditional melodies in a popular context.

Mat Yeh and Dollah To'deh *Modern Zikir* (Suara, Malaysia). Leading exponents of *zikir barat*.

Keluaran Syarikat *Irama* (Irama, Malaysia). Music of the indigenous Kayan people from Sarawak: yodelling voice, drums and gongs.

Taboh Kajat Iban *Iban Music* (MSP, Malaysia). Music of the Iban people of Sarawak, singing over a variety of gongs.

POP

P. Ramlee *Kenangan Abadi Vols 1 & 2* (EMI, Malaysia). The great crooner's best-of, with lush orchestral arrangements and slushy melodies.

P. Ramlee and Saloma *Di Mana Kan Ku Cari Ganti* (EMI, Malaysia). These duets were perhaps Malaysian pop's finest hour – although there is some dross too! Not even P. Ramlee can get away with singing with kids.

Sheila Majid *Legenda* (EMI, Malaysia). Best-selling singer's classic album of Ramlee covers. Lightweight musically, but with a persuasively sweet voice.

Zainal Abidin *Zainal Abidin* (WEA, Malaysia). Kampung singer blending old styles and traditional instruments with pop.

BOOKS

There's no shortage of books written about Malaysia, Singapore and Brunei, though as the selection below demonstrates, the majority have tended to be penned by Western visitors to the region, rather than by local writers. Only in the latter part of the twentieth century has writing about Malaysia and Singapore, by Malaysians and Singaporeans themselves, begun to gather momentum.

The best selection of local writing is available in the countries themselves, though *Skoob Books Publishing* of London are doing much to introduce southeast Asian literature to the West.

In the reviews below, publishers are listed in the format, UK/US publisher – unless the title is available in one country only, in which case we've specified the country. Many books are published by local publishers – you may be able to order them from bookshops in your own country, and most are available in Malaysia, Singapore or Brunei; o/p signifies out of print.

TRAVEL, IMPRESSIONS, EXPLORATION AND ADVENTURE

James Barclay, *A Stroll Through Borneo* (Hodder & Stoughton, UK, o/p). A seminal tour of Sarawak and Indonesian Kalimantan by the doyen of travel writers; particularly perceptive on the Kayan ethnic group.

John Bastin (ed), *Travellers' Singapore* (Penerbit Fajar Bakti, Malaysia; distributed in the UK). Singapore-related vignettes from as early as 1819 and as late as the Japanese conquest of 1942.

Isabella Bird, *The Golden Chersonese* (OUP/Century, o/p). Delightful epistolary romp through old southeast Asia, penned by the intrepid Bird, whose adventures in the Malay states in 1879 ranged from strolls through Singapore's streets to elephant-back rides and encounters with alligators.

Margaret Brooke, *My Life in Sarawak* (OUP, UK, o/p). Engaging account by White Rajah Charles Brooke's wife of nineteenth-century Sarawak, which reveals a sympathetic attitude to her subjects (which extended to rubbing eau de cologne into a Dyak warrior's forehead). Her eye for detail conveys the wonder of an unprejudiced colonial embracing an alien culture.

Anthony Burgess, *Little Wilson and Big God* (Penguin/Grove Atlantic, o/p). An application for a teaching post in Malaya while drunk on cider took Burgess ("novelist, composer, traveller, teacher, raconteur, linguist, soldier, husband, boozer, and amorous adventurer") to Kuala Kangsar's Malay College in 1954. His unerring eye for extraordinary characters and customary relish for cultural and semantic detail make the Asian segment of this autobiography an entertaining time capsule of 1950s Malaysia.

Spencer Chapman, *The Jungle is Neutral*, o/p (Mayflower/Royal Publications, o/p). This riveting first-hand account of being lost, and surviving, in the Malay jungle during World War II reads like a breathless novel.

Oscar Cook, *Borneo, the Stealer of Hearts* (Borneo Publishing Company). Written by a young district officer in the North Borneo Civil Service this piece of Imperial literature that's interesting but insufferably plummy.

G.M. Gullick, *They Came To Malaya* (OUP). A cornucopia of accounts and of people, places and events, written by the governors, planters and explorers who tamed Malaya.

Eric Hansen, *Stranger In The Forest*, o/p (Abacus/Houghton Mifflin o/p). A gripping book, the result of a seven-month tramp through the forests of Sarawak and Kalimantan in 1982, that almost saw the author killed by a poison dart.

Victor T. King, *The Best of Borneo Travel* (OUP Blackwell). Compendium of extracts from Bornean travel writing since the sixteenth century; an interesting travelling companion.

Andro Linklater, *Wild People* (John Murray/ Grove-Atlantic). As telling and as entertaining a glimpse into the lifestyle of the Iban as you could pack, depicting their age-old traditions surviving amidst the T-shirts, baseball caps and rock posters of Western influence.

Redmond O'Hanlon, *Into The Heart of Borneo* (Picador/Vintage). A hugely entertaining yarn recounting O'Hanlon's refreshingly amateurish romp through the jungle to a remote summit on the Sarawak/Kalimantan border, partnered by the English poet James Fenton.

Ambrose B. Rathborne, *Camping and Tramping in Malaya* (OUP, o/p). Lively nineteenth-century account with insights into the colonial personalities and working conditions of the leading figures of the day; many of Rathborne's impressions of the country still ring true today.

The Rev G.M. Reith, *1907 Handbook to Singapore* (OUP, UK o/p). Intriguing period piece which illuminates colonial attitudes in turn-of-the-century Singapore: drill hall, gaol and docks are detailed in favour of Chinatown, while the list of useful Malay phrases includes such essentials as "harness the horse" and "off with you".

Spenser St John, *Life in the Forests of the Far East* (OUP, UK). A description of an early ascent of Mount Kinabalu is a highlight of this animated nineteenth-century adventure, written by the personal secretary to Rajah Brooke.

Michael Wise (ed), *Travellers' Tales of Old Singapore* In Print Publishing, UK. Identical in theme to Bastin's *Travellers' Singapore* (above), though Wise's selection of tales is the more catholic and more engrossing of the two.

Gavin Young, *In Search of Conrad* (Penguin, UK). In which Young plays detective and historian, tracing Joseph Conrad's footsteps around southeast Asia in search of the stories and locations that inspired him. Young's time in Singapore takes him from the National Library to Bidadari cemetery in search of A.P. Williams – Conrad's Lord Jim.

HISTORY AND POLITICS

S. Robert Aiken, *Imperial Beldeveres* (OUP, UK). Sketches, photographs and contemporary accounts enliven this compact examination of the development, landscapes and attractions of the hill stations of Malaya.

Syed Husin Ali, *Two Faces (Detention without Trial)* (Insan). In 1974, Syed, a sociology profes-

sor at Universiti Malaya, was taken from his home and detained under the Internal Security Act. For six years he languished in Kamunting, Malaysia's own Gulag. This is his harrowing, eye-opening story.

Barbara Watson Andaya and Leonard Andaya, *The History of Malaysia* (Macmillan/St Martin's Press o/p in UK). Unlike more paternalistic histories, penned by former colonists, this standard text on the region takes a more even-handed view of Malaysia, and finds time for cultural coverage, too.

Noel Barber, *War of the Running Dogs* (Arrow, UK o/p). Illuminates the Malayan Emergency with a novelist's eye for mood.

James Bartholomew, *The Richest Man in the World* (Penguin, UK). Despite an obvious (and admitted) lack of sources, Bartholomew's study of the Sultan of Brunei makes fairly engaging reading – particularly the mind-bending facts and figures used to illustrate the sultan's wealth.

David Brazil, *Street Smart Singapore* (Times Editions, Singapore). An Aladdin's cave of Singaporean history and trivia that remains fascinating throughout.

Maurice Collis, *Raffles* (Century, o/p). The most accessible and enjoyable biography of Sir Stamford Raffles on the market – very readable.

Peter Elphick, *Singapore The Pregnable Fortress* Coronet, UK. Drawing on documents only made available in 1993, Elphick has produced the definitive history of the fall of Singapore, showing the gaffes, low morale and desertion that led to it; a scholarly *tour de force*.

Stephen Fay, *The Fall of Barings* (Arrow/Norton). A fascinating and surprisingly readable tale by an authoritative financial writer, of how one of London's oldest and most prestigious banking houses was brought to ruin by the reckless though inadequately controlled derivatives trading.

Images of Asia, series: Maya Jayapal's *Old Singapore*; Sarnia Hayes Hoyt's *Old Malacca* and *Old Penang* (OUP). Concise volumes which chart the growth of three of the region's most important outposts, drawing on contemporary maps, sketches and photographs to engrossing effect.

Robert Jackson, *The Malayan Emergency* (Routledge, UK, o/p). Thorough account of the conflict between the Chinese Communist guerrillas and the security forces in postwar Malaya.

Abdullah bin Kadir, *The Hikayat Abdullah* (OUP, UK). Raffles' one-time clerk, Melakanborn Abdullah, later turned diarist of some of the most formative years of southeast Asian history; his first-hand account is crammed with illuminating vignettes and character portraits.

Nick Leeson, *Rogue Trader* (Warner/ Little.Brown). Leeson's own account of his beginnings, his ambitions and of the whirlpool of deceit in which he floundered as the result of his covert trading in Singapore. The inadequacies of Barings' systems and controls are revealed as contributing factors, though Leeson's apparent lack of penitence wins him little sympathy.

Eric Lomax, *The Railway Man* (Vintage/ Ballantine). Such is the power of Lomax's artless, redemptive and moving story of capture during the fall of Singapore, torture by the Japanese and reconciliation with his tormentor after fifty years, that many reviewers were moved to tears.

James Minchin, *No Man Is An Island* (Allen & Unwin/Paul & Co). A well-researched, and at times critical study of Lee Kuan Yew, which refuses to kowtow to Singapore's ex-PM and is hence unavailable in Singapore itself, but gleefully sold in shops throughout Malaysia.

Anthony Oei, *What If There Had Been No Lee Kuan Yew* (Mandarin Paperbacks, Singapore). Ignore its sycophantic tone, and this is a readable enough overview of the life and works of Singapore's pre-eminent statesman; for a more opinionated account, see Minchin above.

Steven Runciman, *The White Rajahs* (Cambridge University Press, o/p). A ponderous, blow-by-blow chronicle of the Brookes' private fiefdom, whose attention to detail compensates for its lack of colour.

Sterling Seagrave, *Lords of the Rim* (Corgi/ Putnam). History and hard economics are the tools Seagrave uses as he highlights the extent to which the "offshore Chinese" have shouldered their way into the vanguard of Pacific Rim economies.

C. Mary Turnbull, *A Short History of Malaysia, Singapore & Brunei* (Graham Brash, Singapore). Decent, informed introduction to the region, touching on the major issues that have shaped it. Its big brother, Turnbull's *History of Singapore 1819-1988* (OUP in UK) is, in contrast, as scholarly an approach to Singapore as you could wish to read.

C.E. Wurtzburg, *Raffles of the Eastern Isles* (OUP, UK). A weighty and learned tome that's the definitive study of the man who founded modern Singapore; not for the marginally interested, who should opt for Collis's more accessible volume (above).

WORLD WAR II AND THE JAPANESE OCCUPATION

Noel Barber, *Sinister Twilight* (Arrow, UK). Documents the fall of Singapore to the Japanese, by re-imagining the crucial events of the period.

Russell Braddon, *The Naked Island* (Penguin/ Simon & Schuster, o/p). Southeast Asia under the Japanese: Braddon's disturbing yet moving first-hand account of the POW camps of Malaya, Singapore and Siam displays courage in the face of appalling conditions and treatment; worth scouring second-hand stores for.

Chin Kee Onn, *Malaya Upside Down*. A coherent analysis of the impact of the Japanese occupation on Malaysian society; difficult to find in the UK and US, but available in Malaysian bookshops.

Agnes Keith, *Three Came Home* (Eland/Little, Brown o/p). Pieced together from scraps of paper secreted in latrines and teddy bears, this is a remarkable story of survival in the face of Japanese attempts to eradicate the "proudery and arrogance" of the West in the World War II prison camps of Borneo.

CULTURE AND SOCIETY

Salleh Ben Joned, *As I Please* (Skoob/ Atrium). Named after his occasional column in the *New Straits Times*, Salleh's articles are candid observations on Malaysian society with titles such as "The Art of Pissing" and "Kiss My Arse – In the Name of Common Humanity". Don't let this mislead you. Although he's outspoken, Salleh is thoughtful and intensely proud of his Malay roots.

Iskandar Carey, *The Orang Asli* (OUP, o/p). The only detailed anthropological work on the indigenes of Peninsular Malaysia.

Culture Shock! Malaysia/Culture Shock! Singapore (Kuperard/Graphic Arts Center

Publishing). Cultural dos and don'ts for the leisure and business traveller to the region, spanning subjects as diverse as handing over business cards and belching after a fine meal.

Tom Harrisson, *A World Within* (OUP, US, o/p). The only in-depth description of the Kelabit peoples of Sarawak, and a cracking good World War II tale courtesy of Harrisson, who parachuted into the Kelabit Highlands to organize resistance against the Japanese.

William Krohn, *In Borneo Jungles* (OUP, o/p). An interwar-years description of the infamous head-hunters of Sarawak.

Leslie Layton, *Songbirds in Singapore* (OUP, US). A delightful examination of songbird-keeping in Singapore, detailing all facets of the pastime, from its growth in the nineteenth century.

Rahman Rashid, *A Malaysian Journey*. Excellent autobiographical account by a journalist returning to Malaysia in the 1990s after self-imposed exile; look it up in KL's bookshops.

Karim Raslan, *Ceritalah: Malaysia in Transition* (Times). Collection of the young lawyer-turned-journalist's articles from local newspapers and magazines, provide an insight into modern Malaysia. Raslan may at times be sentimental and an apologist for the excesses of Malaysia's political and social set-up, but he is always entertaining. The essay "Roots", about his family, is excellent.

Owen Rutter, *The Pagans of North Borneo* (OUP, o/p). Dry, scholarly examination of the lifestyles and traditions of Sabah's non-Muslim peoples, which suffers from a tendency towards cultural chauvinism.

Sabah Women Action Resource Group, *Women in Sabah* (SAWO in Malaysia). Occasionally interesting profile of the status and contribution of women in Sabahan society; available in KK shops.

Tan Kok Seng, *Son Of Singapore* (Heinemann, US, o/p). Tan Kok Seng's candid and sobering autobiography on the underside of the Singaporean success story, telling of hard times spent as a coolie.

NATURAL HISTORY AND ECOLOGY

For specific field guides to the birds and mammals of Malaysia, Singapore, Sabah and Sarawak, see p.618.

Odoardo Beccari, *Wanderings in the Great Forests of Borneo* (OUP, o/p US). Vivid turn-of-the-century account of the natural and human environment of Sarawak.

John Briggs, *Parks of Malaysia* (Longman Malaysia). Top tips and maps for the serious naturalist or hiker in Malaysia.

Mark Cleary & Peter Eaton, *Borneo Change and Development* (Penerbit Fajar Bakti, Malaysia). A very readable composite of Bornean history, economy and society, that's rounded off by a section dealing with issues such as logging, conservation and the future of the Penan.

G.W.H. Davison & Chew Yen Fook, *A Photographic Guide to Birds of Peninsular Malaysia and Singapore* (New Holland/ R.Curtis). Well-keyed and user-friendly, these slender volumes carry oodles of glossy plates that make positive identifying a breeze. The companion volume, *A Photographic Guide to Birds of Borneo*, is also excellent.

Robin Hanbury-Tenison, *Mulu: The Rain Forest* (Arrow o/p). Hanbury-Tenison's overview of the flora, fauna and ecology of the rainforest, the result of a 1977 Royal Geographical Society field trip into Sarawak's Gunung Mulu National Park; makes enlightening reading.

Jeffrey McNeely, *Soul of the Tiger* (OUP/Doubleday). Synoptic, multi-disciplinary overview of the importance of the various facets of nature and the environment to the peoples of the region.

Alfred Russel Wallace, *The Malay Archipelago* (OUP/Dover, o/p). Wallace's peerless account of the flora and fauna of Borneo, based on travels made between 1854 and 1862 – during which time he collected over one hundred thousand specimens. Still required reading for nature lovers.

World Rainforest Movement, *The Battle For Sarawak's Forests*. A worthy collection of writings on the acrimonious, and sometimes violent, confrontations between the state government-sponsored loggers and tribespeople in east Malaysia.

ART AND ARCHITECTURE

Jacques Dumarcay, *The House in Southeast Asia* (OUP, o/p US); *Palaces of Southeast Asia* (OUP, o/p US). The former is a pocket-sized overview of regional domestic architecture, covering the rituals and techniques of house construction; the latter is more specialist, but has only ten pages on Malaysia.

Norman Edwards, *Singapore House and Residential Life* (OUP, o/p US). The development of the Singapore detached house, traced from early plantation villas, through colonial bungalows to Chinese landowners' mansions; beguiling photographs.

Roxana Waterson, *The Living House* (OUP). More authoritative than Dumarcay's slender introduction to southeast Asian dwellings, and required reading for anyone with an interest in the subject.

LITERATURE

Charles Allen, *Tales from the South China Seas* (Futura/David Charles, o/p). Memoirs of the last generation of British colonists, in which predictable Raj attitudes prevail, though some of the drama of everyday lives, often in inhospitable conditions, is evinced with considerable pathos.

Gopal Baratham, *Moonrise*; *Sunset* (Serpent's tail). When How Kum Menon's fiancée is murdered while sleeping by his side in Singapore's East Coast Park, it seems everyone he knows has a motive. How Kum turns detective, and an engaging whodunnit emerges. In A *Candle or the Sun*, Baratham swallows hard and tackles the thorny issue of political corruption.

Noel Barber, *Tanamera* (Hodder, UK). Romantic saga based in mid-twentieth century Singapore.

Anthony Burgess, *The Long Day Wanes* (Minerva/Norton). Burgess's Malayan trilogy – *Time for a Tiger*, *The Enemy in the Blanket* and *Beds in the East* – published in one volume, provides a witty and acutely observed vision of 1950s Malaya, underscoring the racial prejudices of the period. *Time for a Tiger*, the first novel, is worth reading for the Falstaffian Nabby Adams alone.

James Clavell, *King Rat* (Hodder/Dell). Set in Japanese-occupied Singapore, a gripping tale of survival in the notorious Changi Prison.

Joseph Conrad, *Lord Jim* (Penguin). Southeast Asia provides the backdrop to the story of Jim's desertion of an apparently sinking ship and subsequent efforts to redeem himself; modelled upon the sailor, A.P. Williams, Jim's character also yields echoes of Rajah Brooke of Sarawak.

Alastair Dingwall (ed.), *South-east Asia Traveller's Literary Companion* (In Print Publishing, UK). Among the bite-sized essays in this gem of a book are enlightening segments on Malaysia and Singapore, into which are crammed biopics, a recommended reading list, historical, linguistic and literary backgrounds. Excerpts range from classical Malayan literature to the nations' leading contemporary lights.

J.G. Farrell, *The Singapore Grip* (Flamingo, o/p/ Carroll & Graf). Lengthy novel – Farrell's last – of World War II Singapore in which real and fictitious characters flit from tennis to dinner party as the countdown to the Japanese occupation begins.

Henri Fauconnier, *The Soul of Malaya* (OUP, UK, o/p). Fauconnier's semi-autobiographical novel is a lyrical, sensory tour of the plantations, jungle and beaches of early twentieth-century Malaya, and pierces deeply into the underside of the country.

Lloyd Fernando, *Scorpion Orchid* (Heinemann Educational, o/p); *Green is the Colour* (Landmark Books in Singapore). Social politics form the basis of Fernando's works: in *Scorpion Orchid* he concerns himself with the difficulties of adjusting to the move towards Merdeka and new nationhood; while *Green is the Colour* is a remarkable novel, exploring the deep-seated racial tensions brought to light by the Kuala Lumpur demonstrations of May 1969.

Chin Kee Onn, *The Grand Illusion*. A novel with a difference, exploring the Emergency from the perspective of a Communist guerrilla cell; also good is *Twilight of the Nyonyas*, a historical novel about the life and culture of a Nonya family. Both are widely available in Malaysia.

K.S. Maniam, *The Return* (Skoob, UK); *In A Far Country* (Skoob in UK); *Haunting the Tiger*. The purgative writings of this Tamil-descended Malaysian author are strong, highly descriptive and humorous – essential reading.

Wong Phui Nam, *Ways of Exile* (Skoob, UK). Chinese Malaysian poet's first collection published outside Malaysia; evocative works rooted in the interaction of cultures and ethnicity.

William Riviere, *Borneo Fire* (Sceptre). As he spins his tale of family fortunes and forest fires in contemporary Sarawak, Riviere highlights both the state's staggering beauty, and its environmental plight.

Rex Shelley, *The Shrimp People*. Eurasian family saga, critically acclaimed in Singapore, that's played out against the backdrop of the years of race riots and confrontation in Singapore, Malaysia and Indonesia.

Skoob Pacifica Anthology No. 1 and No. 2. (Skoob/Antrim). These two thorough compendia of writings from the Pacific Rim together comprise an invaluable introduction to the contemporary literatures of Singapore and Malaysia.

W. Somerset Maugham, *Short Stories Volume 4* (Mandarin/Penguin). Peopled by hoary sailors, bored plantation-dwellers and colonials wearing mutton chop whiskers and topees, Maugham's short stories resuscitate turn-of-the-century Malaya; quintessential colonial literature graced by an easy style and a steady eye for a story.

Paul Theroux, *Saint Jack* (Penguin/Ballantine, o/p); *The Consul's File* (Penguin/Pocket Books, o/p). *Saint Jack* tells the compulsively bawdy tale of Jack Flowers, an ageing American who supplements his earnings at a Singapore ship's chandlers by pimping for Westerners; Jack's jaundiced eye and Theroux's rich prose open windows on Singapore's past. In *The Consul's File*, a series of short stories are recounted by the fictitious American consul to interior Malaya.

Leslie Thomas, *The Virgin Soldiers* (Penguin/Little Brown, o/p). The bawdy exploits of teenage British Army conscripts snatching all the enjoyment they can, before being sent to fight in troubled 1950s Malaya.

Beth Yahp, *The Crocodile Fury* (Women's Press, UK). Described by one reviewer as a "spicy Malaysian curry" to Amy Tan's "lightly seasoned Chinese soup", Yahp has produced a garlicky, rambunctious storytelling treat that shadows the lives of three women – grandmother, mother and daughter – in colonial and post-colonial Malaysia.

LANGUAGE

The national language of Malaysia, Singapore and Brunei is *Bahasa Malaysia*, which means, simply, "Malay language". It's an old language, with early roots in the central and south Pacific, and one which was refined by its use in the ancient kingdom of Srivijaya and during the fifteenth-century Melaka Sultanate into a language of the elite. Indeed, the very word *bahasa* (language) came to signify Malay culture in general.

The situation is slightly complicated by the presence of several other racial groups and languages in all three countries: in Singapore, for example, Mandarin, Tamil and English all have the status of official languages, as well as Malay; in Malaysia itself, Cantonese, Mandarin, other Chinese languages like Hokkien and Hakka, and Tamil all form significant minority languages. In practice, however, you'll be able to get by with **English** in all but the most remote areas, since this is the common means of communication between the different races, as well as the language of business.

Nevertheless, it always helps to pick up a few words, especially since basic *Bahasa* is simple enough to learn. Understanding the quick-fire, staccato speech is a different matter altogether, particularly since the spoken word is often corrupted. For example, Malays will often

---

MANGLISH

"To *lah* or not to *lah*, that is the question." This slogan, spotted on a T-shirt in Melaka, sums up what most visitors notice first off about English as it's spoken in Malaysia – the indiscriminate addition of the meaningless *lah* to the end of many words. But the development of **Manglish** – as the combination of Malay and English is called – doesn't stop with *lah*. Courtesy of the Chinese-Malaysian satirical writer and poet Kit Leee, Manglish has taken on a life of its own. In his book *Adoi* (meaning "ouch"), Leee explains how Manglish should be written exactly as it sounds; hence *debladigarmen* – a contraction of "the bloody government" and *olafasudden* for "all of a sudden". Leee is quick to point out that he didn't invent Manglish, but that it has been evolving ever since the end of British rule, when the previously imposed rules of spoken English were thrown out. On a more serious note, with Malaysia aiming for developed nation status, the government is aware of the need to raise the level of **English proficiency** in the country. But in the meantime, writers and performers such as Leee, Julian Mokhtar and Rafique Rashid, entertain their fellow countrymen with this unique language, some examples of which are below:

ackchwurly	"Actually", used as a sentence starter.
aidontch-main	"I don't mind"
baiwanfriwan	"Buy one and you'll get one free", a sales ploy
betayudon	"You'd better not do that!"
(doan)tokkok	"Don't talk rubbish!"
tingwat	"What do you think?"
watudu	"What can we do?", a rhetorical question
yusobadwan	"You're such a bad one!" meaning "that's not very nice!"

Leee advises that *Mat Salleh's* (white-skinned *furriners*) should not attempt to speak Manglish as it might cause offence, but that it is worth while studying the language so as to understand *wat peeple are saying about you lah*.

use -lah at the end of a word or sentence –
hence Minumlah Coca-cola – a meaningless,
though pervasive, suffix.

GRAMMAR

Nouns have no genders and don't require an arti-
cle, while the **plural** form is constructed just by
saying the word twice; thus "child" is anak, while
"children" is anak anak – occasionally you'll see
this written as if to the power of two, as in anak2.
Doubling a word can also indicate "doing"; for
example, jalan jalan is used to mean "walking".
Verbs have no tenses either, the meaning being
indicated either by the context, or by the use of
"time" words such as sedang, akan and sudah for
the present, future and past. **Sentence order** is
the same as in English, though adjectives usually
follow their corresponding nouns.

PRONUNCIATION

The **pronunciation** of Bahasa Malaysia is
broadly the same as the English reading of
Roman script, with a few exceptions:

VOWELS AND DIPHTHONGS

a as in c**u**p

e as in **e**nd

i as in bout**i**que

o as in g**o**t

u as in b**oo**t

ai as in f**i**ne

au as in h**ow**

sy as in **sh**ut

CONSONANTS

c as in **ch**eap

g as in **g**irl

j as in **j**oy

k hard, as in English, except at the end of the
word, when you should stop just short of pro-
nouncing it. In writing, this is frequently indicated by an apostrophe at the end of the word; for
example, beso' for besok.

COMMON WORDS AND PHRASES IN BAHASA MALAYSIA

CIVILITIES AND BASIC PHRASES

Selamat is the all-purpose greeting derived from Arabic, which communicates a general goodwill.

Good morning	Selamat pagi	I come from...	Saya dari...
Good afternoon	Selamat petang	England	Inggris
Good evening	Selamat malam	America	Amerika
Good night	Selamat tidur	Australia	Australia
Goodbye	Selamat tinggal	Canada	Kanada
Bon Voyage	Selamat jalan	New Zealand	Zealandia Baru
Welcome	Selamat datang	Ireland	Irlandia
Bon Appetit	Selamat makan	Scotland	Skotlandia
How are you?	Apa kabar?	Do you speak English?	Bisa bercakap bahasa
Fine/OK	Baik		Inggris?
See you later	Jumpa lagi	I don't understand	Saya tidak mengerti
Please	Tolong	I want...	Saya mahu...
Thank you	Terima kasih	I like...	Saya suka...
You're welcome	Sama sama	What is this/that?	Apa ini/itu?
Sorry/excuse me	Maaf	Can you help me?	Bolekah anda tolong
No worries/never mind	Tidak apa-apa		saya?
Yes	Ya	What?	Apa?
No	Tidak	When?	Bila?
What is your name?	Siapa nama anda?	Where?	Dimana?
My name is...	Nama saya...	Why?	Mengapa?
Where are you from?	Dari mana?	How?	Berapa?

Continues...

GETTING AROUND AND DIRECTIONS

Where is the...?	*Dimana...?*	Front	*Hadapan*
I want to go to...	*Saya mahu naik ke...*	Behind	*Belakang*
How do I get there?	*Bagaimanakah saya*	North	*Utara*
	boleh ke sana?	South	*Selatan*
How far?	*Berapa jauh?*	East	*Timur*
How long will it	*Berapa lama?*	West	*Barat*
take?		Street	*Jalan*
When will the bus	*Bila bas berangkat?*	Train station	*Stesen keratapi*
leave?		Bus station	*Stesen bas*
What time does	*Jam berapa keratapi*	Airport	*Lapangan terbang*
the train arrive?	*sampai?*	Ticket	*Tiket*
Stop	*Berhenti*	Hotel	*Hotel/rumah*
Wait	*Tunggu*		*penginapan*
Go up	*Naik*	Post office	*Pejabat pos*
Go down	*Turun*	Restaurant	*Restoran*
Turn	*Belok*	Shop	*Kedai*
Right	*Kanan*	Market	*Pasar*
Left	*Kiri*	Taxi	*Teksi*
Straight	*Terus*	Trishaw	*Becak*

ACCOMMODATION

How much is...?	*Berapa...?*	Please clean my	*Tolong bersikan bilik*
I need a room.	*Saya perlu satu bilik.*	room.	*saya.*
Cheap/expensive	*Murah/mahal*	Can I store my	*Bisa titip barang?*
I'm staying for one	*Saya mahu tinggal*	luggage here?	
night.	*satu hari.*		

SHOPPING

I want to buy...	*Saya mahu beli...*	I'll give you no	*Saya bayar tidak*
Can you reduce	*Boleh kurang?*	more than...	*lebih dari...*
the price?		I'm just looking	*Saya hanya lihat-lihat*

PERSONAL PRONOUNS AND TITLES

You'll often see the word *Dato'* placed before the name of a government official or some other worthy. It's an honorific title of distinction roughly equivalent to the British "Sir". Royalty are always addressed as *Tuanku*.

I/my	*Saya*	S/he	*Dia*	They	*Mereka*	Mrs	*Puan*
You	*Anda/awak*	We	*Kami*	Mr	*Encik*	Miss	*Cik*

USEFUL ADJECTIVES

Good	*Bagus*	Big	*Besar*
A lot/very much	*Banyak*	Small	*Kecil*
A little	*Sedikit*	Enough	*Cukup*
Cold (Object)	*Sejuk*	Closed	*Tutup*
Cold (Person)	*Dingin*	Hungry	*Laparad*
Hot	*Panas*	Thirsty	*Haus*
Sweet	*Manis*	Tired	*Lelah*
Salty	*Garam*	Ill/sick	*Sakit*

Continues...

USEFUL NOUNS

Entrance	*Masuk*	Food	*Makan*
Exit	*Keluar*	Drink	*Minum*
Toilet	*Tandas*	Boyfriend/girlfriend	*Pacar*
Man	*Lelaki*	Husband	*Suami*
Woman	*Perempuan*	Wife	*Istri*
Water	*Air*	Friend	*Kawan*
Money	*Wang/duit*		

USEFUL VERBS

Malay verbs do not conjugate, and often double as nouns or adjectives. Here, they are given in the form in which you'd use the verb, rather than in the strictly grammatical infinitive.

Come	*Datang*	Give	*Beri*
Go	*Pergi*	Take	*Gambil*
Do	*Buat*	Sit	*Duduk*
Have	*Punya*	Sleep	*Tidur*

NUMBERS

0	*Nul*	11	*Sebelas*
1	*Satu*	12	*Duabelas*
2	*Dua*	20	*Duapuluh*
3	*Tiga*	21	*Dua puluh satu*
4	*Empat*	100	*Seratus*
5	*Lima*	143	*Seratus empatpuluh tiga*
6	*Enam*	200	*Duaratus*
7	*Tujuh*	1000	*Seribu*
8	*Lapan*	1 Million	*Sejuta*
9	*Sembilan*	A Half	*Setengah*
10	*Sepuluh*		

TIME AND DAYS OF THE WEEK

What time is it?	*Jam berapa?*	Year	*Tahun*
It's...		Today	*Hari Ini*
three o'clock	*Jam tiga*	Tomorrow	*Besok*
ten past four	*Jam empat lewat sepuluh*	Yesterday	*Kemarin*
quarter to five	*Jam lima kurang*	Now	*Sekarang*
	seperempat	Ago	*Yang Lalu*
six-thirty	*Jam setengah tujuh*	Not Yet	*Belum*
	(lit. "half to seven")	Never	*Tidak Perna*
7am	*Tujuh pagi*		
8pm	*Lapan malam*	Monday	*Hari Isnin*
Second	*Detik*	Tuesday	*Hari Selasa*
Minute	*Menit*	Wednesday	*Hari Rabu*
Hour	*Jam*	Thursday	*Hari Kamis*
Day	*Hari*	Friday	*Hari Jumaat*
Week	*Minggu*	Saturday	*Hari Sabtu*
Month	*Bulan*	Sunday	*Hari Ahad/minggu*

For more Malay words, see the glossary of words and terms in the next section.

SINGLISH: AN INTRODUCTION

Upon first hearing the machine-gun rattle of Singaporean English, or **Singlish**, you could easily be forgiven for thinking you're listening to a language other than English. To begin with, **pronunciation** is so staccato that many words are rendered almost unrecognizable – especially monosyllabic words such as "cheque" and "book", which would be spoken "che-boo", or "last week", which would become "las-wee". In contrast, in two-syllable words the second syllable is lengthened, and stressed by a rise in tone: ask a Singaporean what they've been doing, and you'll variously be told "wor-king", "sho-pping", "slee-ping" and "swi-mming".

But it's the unorthodox rhythms of phrasing that make Singlish so memorable. Conventional English **syntax** is twisted and wrung, and tenses and pronouns cast to one side. If you ask a Singaporean if they've ever seen Michael Jackson you might be answered "I ever see him"; ask if they have a car, and the response might be: "last time [meaning 'before'] got, now no have"; while enquiring whether they've just been shopping might yield: "go come back already".

Indeed, **responses** are almost invariably shortened down to their bare bones, with single-word replies often repeated for stress. Thus: request something in a shop and you'll hear: "have, have", or "got, got". (If it's a Singaporean customer, he may respond with "where got?" – by which he means "where is it?") In a restaurant, if you ask whether the kitchen can rustle you up a sandwich, the reply will be either: "can, can", or "cannot".

Suffixes and exclamations drawn from Malay, Hokkien and English complete this patois, the most distinctive being "lah", as in "okay lah", and "so cheap one lah" (the latter translates as "this is really inexpensive, isn't it?"). Also commonly heard, are "is it?" (pronounced "eezeet?"), which expresses exclamations like "really?" or "you don't say"; and "ah", which means "yes" if on its own and complemented by a nod of the head, but can imply a question if set at the end of a phrase.

If Singlish still has you totally baffled, you might try raising your eyes to the Heavens, and crying either "ay yor" (with a drop of tone on "yor") or "Allama" – both expressions of annoyance or exasperation.

A GLOSSARY OF WORDS AND TERMS

ATAP Palm thatch.

AIR PANAS Hot springs.

AIR TERJUN Waterfall.

BABA Straits-born Chinese (male).

BANDAR Town.

BATANG River system.

BATIK Wax and dye technique of cloth decoration.

BATU Rock/stone.

BOMOH Traditional healer.

BUKIT Hill.

BUMBUN Hide.

BUMIPUTRA Indigenous Malay person (lit. "son of the soil").

CANDI Temple.

DAULAT Divine force possessed by a ruler that commands unquestioning loyalty.

DERHAKA Treason; punished severely even in contemporary Malaysia.

EKSPRES Express (used for boats and buses).

GASING Spinning top.

GELANGGANG SENI Cultural Centre.

GEREJA Church.

GODOWN Warehouse.

GOPURAM Sculpted deities over the entrance to a Hindu temple.

GUA Cave.

GUNUNG Mountain.

HALAL Something that's permissible by Islam.

HUTAN Forest.

IKAT Woven fabric.

ISTANA Palace.

JALAN Road.

JAMBATAN Bridge.

KAMPUNG Village.

KEDAI KOPI Coffee shop.

KELONG Large marine fish trap.

KERANGAS Sparse forest (literally "poor soil").

KHALWAT Close proximity; forbidden between people of the opposite sex under Islamic law.

KONGSI Chinese clan house/temple.

KOTA Fort.

KRIS Wavy-bladed dagger.

KUALA River confluence or estuary.

LEBUH Street.

LORONG Lane.

MAKAM Grave or tomb.

MAK YONG Epic courtly dance drama.

MANDI Asian method of bathing by dousing with water from a tank using a small bucket.

MASJID Mosque.

MEDAN SELERA Food centre.

MENARA Minaret or tower.

MERDEKA Freedom (and therefore applied to Malaysian independence).

MINANGKABAU Matriarchal people from Sumatra.

MUZIUM Museum.

NEGARA National.

NIPAH Palm tree.

NONYA Straits-born Chinese (female); sometimes *Nyonya*.

ORANG ASLI Peninsular Malaysia aborigines (lit. "original people"); also Orang Ulu (upriver people) and Orang Laut (sea people).

PADANG Field/square; usually the main town square.

PANTAI Beach.

PARANG Machete.

PASAR Market (pasar malam, nightmarket).

PEJABAT DAERAH District office.

PEJABAT POS Post office.

PEKAN Town.

PELABUHAN Port/harbour.

PENGHULU Chief/leader.

PENGKALAN Port/harbour.

PERANAKAN Straits-born Chinese.

PERIGI Well.

PINTU Arch/gate.

PONDOK Hut/shelter; used as religious schools.

PULAU Island.

PUSAT BANDAR Town centre.

RAJAH Prince (often spelled Raja).

RAMADAN Muslim fasting month.

REBANA Drum.

ROTAN Rattan cane; used in the infliction of corporal punishment.

RUMAH PERSINGGAHAN Lodging house.

RUMAH REHAT Resthouse (usually government-run).

SAREE Traditional Indian woman's garment, worn in conjunction with a *choli* (short-sleeved blouse).

SEKOLAH School.

SILAT Malay art of self-defence.

SONGKET Woven cloth.

STESEN BAS Bus station.

STESEN KERATAPI Train station.

SULTAN Ruler.

SUNGEI River.

TAI CHI Chinese martial art; commonly performed as an early-morning exercise.

TAMAN Park.

TAMU Market/fair.

TANJUNG Cape/headland.

TASIK (or Tasek) Lake.

TELAGA Freshwater spring or well.

TELUK Bay/inlet.

TOKONG Chinese temple.

TOWKAY Chinese merchant.

WAU Kite.

WAYANG KULIT Shadow puppet play.

ACRONYMS

KTM *Keretapi Tanah Melayu*, the Malaysian national railway company.

MAS Malaysian national airline.

MCP Malayan Communist Party.

MRT Singapore's Mass Rapid Transit system.

PAS *Parti Islam Sa-Melayu*, the Pan-Malaysian Islamic Party.

PAP Singaporean People's Action Party.

UNMO United Malays National Organization.

INDEX

A

Abdul Rahman 504, 562
Abdullah bin Kadir 504, 530
Accommodation 42–45
Air Batang 325
Airlines
  in Australasia 14
  in Britain 4
  in Ireland 8
  in North America 9
Airport taxes 74
Alor Setar 188–191
Animism 62
Anna Rais 367
Arau 201
Architecture, Malay 265
Asah 328
Ayer Keroh 307
Ayuthaya 188, 599–601, 503

B

Ba Kelalan 420
Baba-Nonya 293, 302, 601
Bajau 61, 422, 452
Bako National Park 362–365
Bakun Dam 612, 614
Baleh, Sungei 383
Balik Pulau 186
Bandar Sahabat 470
Bandar Seri Begawan
  483–492
Bangar 494
Banjaran Titiwangsa 139
Banks 27–28
Baram, Batang 405
Barat 186
Barings Bank 546
Bario 416–417
Barisan National 610
Batang Ai River System
  368–371
Batang Duri 494
Batang Lupar River System
  368–371
Batik 70

Batu Apoi Forest Reserve 494
Batu Caves 120
Batu Ferringhi 183
Batu Muang 186
Batu Niah 396
Batu Pahat 310
Batu Punggul 442
Batu Putih 469
Batu Sembilan 228
Bau 366
Beaufort 444
Belaga 385
Belait District 496
Benuk 367
Beserah 279
Bidayuh 60, 367–368
Bike rental 41
Bintulu 390–393
Birch J.W.W. 14
Bird's nests 395, 467, 470
Birds 619–620
Books 625–630
Brassware 71, 263, 354
Briggs, Lieutenant General Sir
  Harold 607
Brinchang 145–147
British Borneo Timber Company
  613
British North Borneo Company
  425, 473, 605
Brooke, Charles 341, 352, 369,
  372, 403, 605, 613
Brooke, James 340, 344, 372,
  378, 481, 603, 605, 613
Brooke, Vyner 341, 605, 607
BRUNEI 477–498
Brunei Muara 492
Brunei People's Party 609
Brunei, Sultan of 340–341
Bugis 602
Bukit Cahaya Sri Alam
  Agricultural Park 126
Bukit Kayu Hitam 202
Bumiputras 57, 610
Buntal 361
Burgess, Anthony 483, 487,
  565
Burial houses 379, 385, 441
Buses 34–35
Butterworth 166

C

Cameron Highlands 137–147
Cameron, William 137
Camping 44
Canto-pop 587
Car rental 40–41
Ceramics 353
Cheng Ho 303
Cherating 272–274
Children, Travelling with 74
Chin Peng 607
Chinese
  in Brunei 480
  medicine 543
  people 57
  religions 64–65
Chukai 272
Churchill, Winston 505
Clarke, Governor Andrew 604
Clavell, James 560
Clifford, Sir Hugh 204, 226, 604
Coleman, George Drumgould
  526, 532, 533
Collis, Maurice 530
Conrad, Joseph 557
Consulates, see Embassies
Contraceptives 74
Cornwallis, Lord Charles 174
Costs 27–28
Cowie, William Clarke 440, 460
Cowley, Captain 425
Credit cards 27
Crocker Mountain Range 439
Crocodiles 360, 565
Currency 27–28
Customs regulations 18–20

D

Dabong 232
Dams 612
Danum Valley Conservation
  Area 471
Datai 199
De Albuquerque, Afonso 293,
  600
De Rozario, Domingo 380
Death march 426, 459, 461,
  466, 606
Deepavali 64
Dent, Alfred 425, 461
Desaru 317

Directory 74–75
Disabled travellers 25–26
Doctors 33
Donggongon 437
Drink 48–52
Drinking water 31
Drugs 19
Dutch East India Company 293, 601
Duty free goods 18–20, 74

E

Early settlers 597
East India Company 165, 293, 530–531, 602
Eastern & Oriental, The 13, 37, 509
Embassies
  Bruneian abroad 20
  Malaysian abroad 19
  Singaporean abroad 20
Emergencies 33, 56
Emergency, the 205, 607
Endau Rompin National Park 332–335
Entikong 368
Entry requirements 18–20
Ethnic peoples 56–61
Etiquette 64–65

F

Farquhar, Colonel William 293, 298, 504, 533
Federation of Malaysia 505, 604
Felda Chini 236
Ferries 38–39
Festivals 66–68
Fireflies 129
Flight agents
  in Australasia 14
  in Britain 5
  in Ireland 8
  in North America 10
Flights
  from Australasia 13–16
  from Britain 3–7
  from Ireland 7–8
  from North America 8–13
  from Southeast Asia 16–18
Flights within Malaysia, Singapore & Brunei 39–40

Fly-drive 7, 13, 15
Food & drink glossary 49–51
Food 45–51
Forest Institute of Malaysia (FRIM) 123
Fort Iskander 238
Fraser's Hill 134–137, 620
Fraser, James 134
Gay and lesbian life 74
Genting 329
Genting Highlands 123
GEORGETOWN 166–182
  Accommodation 169–173
  Airport 168
  Ayer Itam Dam 178
  Chinatown 173
  Departure 169
  Eastern and Oriental Hotel 177
  Eating 179–180
  Ferry terminals 168
  Fort Cornwallis 174
  History 165
  Jalan Penang 177
  Kek Lok Si Temple 178
  Khoo Kongsi 176
KOMTAR 177
  Accommodation 169–173
  Airport 168
  Ayer Itam Dam 178
  Chinatown 173
  Departure 169
  Eastern and Oriental Hotel 177
  Eating 179–180
  Ferry terminals 168
  Fort Cornwallis 174
  History 165
  Jalan Penang 177
  Kek Lok Si Temple 178
  Khoo Kongsi 176
  Lebuh Chulia 175
  Lebuh Pantai 174
  Listings 181
  Little India 175
  Nattukkottai Chettiar Temple 178
  Nightlife and entertainment 180–181
  Penang Hill 178
  Penang Museum and Art Gallery 175
  St George's Church 175
  Tourist offices 168
  Transport 168–169
Gertak Sanggul 186
Glossary 635
Goh Chok Tong 506
Gold 227, 597

Gomantong Caves 467
Gua Charas 279
Gua Masang 231
Guesthouses 42
Gunung Gading National Park 366
Gunung Jerai 188
Gunung Kesong 230
Gunung Ledang 308
Gunung Mulu National Park 407–414
Gunung Penrissen 368
Gurney, Sir Henry 136, 608

H

Hakka peoples 341
Hanbury-Tenison, Robin 407, 411
Hari Raya 63
Harrisson, Tom 340, 352–353, 388, 395, 407, 415, 469, 606
Head-hunting 340, 367
Health matters 29–33
Hinduism 64
Homestays 43
Hornbills 334, 337, 413, 414
Hospitals 33
Hostels 43
Hotels 43

I

Iban 59, 370–371
Idahan people 470
Indian people 58
Indonesia departure points 311
Indonesia, border crossings 368, 475
Inoculations 29
Insurance 21–22
Ipoh 147–150
Iskandar Shah 292, 503, 599
Islam 63

J

Jelawang Country Park 232
Jerantut 210
Jessel, Sir Charles 428
Joaquim, Agnes 532
Johor Bahru 311–316

Johor, Sultans of 314
Juara 327
Jungle railway 224

K

Kadazan/Dusun people 61, 422, 452
Kaki Bukit 201
Kampung Abang 368
Kampung Bako 364
Kampung Baru 418
Kampung Belimbing 236
Kampung Cempaka 276
Kampung Dusun 230
Kampung Gumum 236
Kampung Jepak 391
Kampung Kaparungan 443
Kampung Kijang 253
Kampung Kuantan 129
Kampung Mamai Tom 443
Kampung Mattungong 453
Kampung Mompilis 453
Kampung Monsopiad 437
Kampung Morten 303
Kampung Parit 492
Kampung Patau 439
Kampung Penambang 253
Kampung Santubong 361
Kampung Sook 441, 475
Kampung Sungei Pinang Besar 157
Kampung Sungei Pinang Kecil 157
Kampung Tampasak 438
Kampung Tanjung Lumpur 276
Kampung Teluk Gedong 155
Kampung Tibabar 440
Kampung Tinanggol 453
Kangar 201
Kanowit 378
Kapit 380–382
Karaoke 587
Katibas, Sungei 379
Kayan people 60, 386, 407
Kelabit Highlands 414–420
Kelabit people 60, 414–420
Kellie's Castle 151
Kemaman 272
Keningau 440
Kenong Rimba State Park 228
Kenyah people 60, 386

Kinabalu National Park 454–459
Kinabatangan, Sungei 467–469
Kinarut 438
Kinarut Laut 438
Kipling, Rudyard 177, 529
Kite-flying 249, 253
Kitingan, Joseph Pairin 426, 611
Klang Valley 124–128
Konfrontasi 342, 355, 387, 426, 609
Kongsi 176, 538, 603
Kota Belud 451
Kota Bharu 241–250
Kota Kinabalu 426–436
Kota Marudu 452
Kota Tinggi 316
Kris 263
Kuah 194
Kuala Balai 498
Kuala Baram 402
Kuala Belait 497
Kuala Besut 255
Kuala Dungun 272
Kuala Jasin 333
Kuala Kangsar 157–159
Kuala Kedah 192
Kuala Keniam 222
Kuala Kerai 234
Kuala Kubu Bharu 136
Kuala Lipis 225–228
KUALA LUMPUR 79–120
  Accommodation 88–91
  Airport 83
  Architecture 94
  Art galleries 116
  Bangsar 108
  Brickfields 107
  Bus stations 85
  Central Market 99
  Chan See Shu Yuen Temple 101
  Chinatown 100–102
  Chow Kit Market 105
  Cinemas 116
  Coliseum Hotel 105
  Colonial District 95
  Cultural shows 117
  Dayabumi Complex 94, 96
  Departure 84
  Eating 111–113
  Golden Triangle 104
  History 81–83

  Jalan Ampang 102
  Jalan Petaling 101
  Jame Mosque 99
  Kampung Bharu 105
  Kuala Lumpur Aziz Shah
    International Airport 83
  Lake Gardens 97–99
  Lat, 116
  Listings 118–120
  Little India 104
  Markets 117
  Masjid Negara 96
  Maybank Building 94, 101
  Menara Kuala Lumpur 102
  Merdeka Square 95
  Muzium Negara 97
  National Art Gallery 97
  National Zoo 109
  Nightlife 114–115
  Nurismatic Museum 101–102
  Parliament House 99
  Petronas Towers 94, 103
  Railway station 96
  Royal Selangor Club 95
  Rubber Museum 109
  See Yeoh Temple 101
  Shopping 117–118
  Sri Mahamariamman Temple 101
  Sultan Abdul Samad Building 95
  Thean Hou Temple 107
  Titiwangsa, Lake 106
  Tourist offices 85
  Train station 84
  Transport 86–88
Kuala Penyu 446
Kuala Perlis 201
Kuala Selangor 128
Kuala Tahan 211–213
Kuala Tembeling 210
Kuala Terengganu 259–265
Kuala Terikan 413
Kuala Trenggan 221
Kuantan 274–278
Kubah National Park 360
KUCHING 344–359
  Accommodation 348
  Airport 346
  Bus station 346
  Cat Museum 356
  Chinatown 351
  Colonial district 349–351
  Courthouse 349
  Departure 347
  Eating 356
  Ferry terminals 346
  Fort Margherita 355
  History 344–346

Islamic Museum 354
Istana 355
Jalan India 352
Jong's Crocodile Farm 360
Listings 358
Longhouses 353
Masjid Negara 352
Police Museum 355
Reservoir Park 354
Round Tower 350
Sarawak Cultural Village 362
Sarawak Museum 352–354
Semenggoh Wildlife
  Rehabilitation Centre 359
Shopping 357
Square Tower 350
Sunday Market 352
Timber Museum 355
Tour operators 359
Tourist information 346
Transport 347
Tua Pek Kong 351
Kudat 452–454
Kukup 311
Kundasang 459

L
Labi 496
Labu 494
Lahad Datu 469
Lambir Hills National Park 401
Land Dyaks 337
Langkawi 192–200
Language 631–634
Laundry 74
Lawas 404, 450
Lee Kuan Yew 499, 505, 528,
  608, 610
Leeches 73
Leeson, Nick 546
Lembah Bujang 187
Lembong 316
Light, Francis 165
Limbang 403
Lio Matoh 419
Logging 322, 342, 337, 355,
  373, 405, 422, 426, 461, 612,
  613–616
Long Banga 419
Long Beruang 419
Long Dano 418
Long Jawai 387
Long Lellang 420
Long Medan 420

Long Murum 386
Long Rapung 420
Long Terawan 407
Longhouses 44, 367, 369–371,
  379, 384, 416–420
Low's Gully 455
Low, Colonel James 187
Low, Hugh 159, 455
Lubok Antu 370
Lumut 152
Lundu 366

M
Madai caves 470
Magellan 340
Magellan, Ferdinand 425, 480,
  600
Mahathir, Prime Minister Dr
  310, 610
Majapahit 503, 599
Majid Sheila 623
Malay court, social structure 298
Malay people 57
Malaya, Federation of 606,
Malayan Communist Party 606
Malayan Democratic Union 607
Malaysia, Federation of 341, 609
Manglish 631
Maps 23–25
Maran 235
Marang 266–268
Marudi 406
Mat Kilau 604
Mat Salleh 426, 428, 440, 605
Matang Wildlife Centre 360
Maugham, Somerset 177, 298,
  369, 529
Mawai 316
Maxwell Hill 162
Maxwell, Sir George 137, 159,
  162
Megaliths 415, 438
MELAKA 290–307
  A Famosa Fort 296
  Accommodation 295
  Airport 294
  Baba-Nyonya Heritage Museum
    301
  Bukit China 303
  Bukit St Paul 299
  Bus stations 294
  Chinatown 301–303

  Christ Church 300
  Departure 294
  Dutch Square 299
  Eating 305
  Ferry terminal 294
  History 292–294
  Independence Memorial Museum
    298
  Istana ke Sultanan 296
  Kampung Morten 303
  Listings 307
  Maritime Museum 301
  Medan Portugis 303
  Museum of Ethnography 300
  Nightlife and entertainment 306
  Shopping 306
  St Paul's Church 299
  St Peter's Church 300
  Stadthuys 300
  Tokong Cheng Hoon 302
  Tourist information 294
  Transport 295
Melanau 60, 388, 390
Mengkabong 451
Mentakab 225
Menumbok 446
Merang 257
Merdeka 608
Merlimau 309
Merotai 475
Mersing 317–319
Minangkabau 265, 282, 283,
  286, 287, 288, 602
Miri 397–401
Money, changing 26–28
Mosques 63
Mount Kinabalu 455–457
Mountbatten, Lord Louis 528
Muar 309
Muara 493
Mukah 388
Mukut 328
Mulu, Gunung 413
Murut people 61, 422, 441, 443
Music, Malaysian 621–624
Musical instruments 71, 97,
  190, 248–249, 353, 621–624

N
Nanga Baleh 383
Naning, wars of 603
New Villages 608
Newly Industrialised Economy
  (NIE) 610

Newspapers 54
Niah Caves 597
Niah National Park 395–397
Nipah 328
Nusa Camp 213

O

O'Hanlon, Redmond 384
Oil 397, 477, 481, 496, 605, 607
Opening hours 69–70
Orang Asli 58, 123, 204, 205, 209, 223, 235, 237, 597, 608
Orang Asli Museum 122
Orang Laut 598
Orang Ulu 60, 333, 337, 359, 376, 386, 465
Overbeck, Baron Von 425, 461, 605

P

Pa Berang 419
Pa Dalih 418
Pa Lungan 420
Pa Rupai 420
Pa Umor 417
Package tours
  from Australasia 15
  from Britain 6–7
  from North America 13
Padang Besar 202
Padang Lalang 199
Paka 272
Palangs 353
Palembang 598
Pangkor Town 154
Pangkor Treaty 152, 159, 604
Pantai Acheh 186
Pantai Cinta Berahi 252
Pantai Dasar Sabak 252
Pantai Irama 252
Pantai Seri Tujuh 252
Pantei Cenang 195
Pantei Kok 197
Pantei Tengah 195
Papar 438
Parameswara 292, 309, 503, 599
Parti Bersatu Sabah 611
Pasir Bogak 155
Paya 313
Pei, I.M. 529, 552

Pekan 280
Pelagus Rapids 383
Penambawang 451
Penan 337, 405, 419, 614–615
Penan people 60
Penang 163–186
Penang Riots 176
Peninsula Line, The 37
Pensiangan 442
People's Action Party 505
Peoples 56–61
Peradayan Forest Reserve 494
Perak Tong Temple 150
Perak, skirmishes in 604
Peramu 276
Peranakan 58, 536, 601
Pergau Dam 612
Perhentian Besar 256
Perhentian Kecil 255
Pesta Kaamatan 422
Petaling Jaya 124
Pewter 71
Pharmacies 33
Pigafetta, Antonio 340, 480, 487, 600
Pillay, Naraina 543
Piracy 598, 469
Pitcher plants 364, 394
Police 55–56
Polo, Marco 503
Pontian Kecil 310
Poring Hot Springs 457–459
Port Dickson 289
Port Klang 127
Post offices 52
Proboscis monkeys 468
Public holidays 69–70
Pulau Banggi 453
Pulau Besar 308, 330
Pulau Betong 186
Pulau Chermin 493
Pulau Dayang Bunting 200
Pulau Duyong 264
Pulau Gasing 199
Pulau Gaya 436
Pulau Gemia 268
Pulau Kalampunian Damit 446
Pulau Kapas 268
Pulau Ketam 128
Pulau Labuan 447–450
Pulau Mamutik 436
Pulau Manukan 436
Pulau Pangkor 152–157

Pulau Pangkor Laut 157
Pulau Pasir 199
Pulau Payar Marine Park 200
Pulau Perhentian 253–257
Pulau Rawa 332
Pulau Redang 258
Pulau Sapi 436
Pulau Sembilan 157
Pulau Sibu 331
Pulau Singa Besar 200
Pulau Sipadan 472
Pulau Sulug 436
Pulau Tiga 446
Pulau Tiga Park 446
Pulau Tinggi 331
Pulau Tioman 319–329
Pulau Tuba 200
Punang 404
Putrajaya 126

R

Radio 54
Raffles Hotel 528
Raffles, Sir Thomas Stamford 293, 499, 503, 526, 530–531, 602
Rafflesia 366, 439, 531
Rajah Abdullah 604
Rajang, Batang 372, 378–384
Ramadan 63
Ramayana 598
Ramlee, P. 623
Ranau 459
Rantau Abang 269–271
Raub 225
Religion 62–65
Remadu 419
Residential System, The 159
Riau 602
Ringlet 140–141
Route 8 205
Rubber 109, 293, 344, 373, 504, 537 605
Rungus 452

S

SABAH 422–476
Sagil 309
Sahabat 470
Salang 326
Sam Poh Tong Castle 151
Sandakan 460–465

Sandflies 321
Santubong Peninsula 361
Sapulut 441
SARAWAK 337–421
  Alliance 611
  border crossing 450, 494, 497
  Village 362
Sarees 71
Sea Dyaks 337
Sebabai Park 383
Segamat 309
Sejarah Melayu 292, 296, 298,
  304, 503, 530, 597
Sekayu Waterfall 266
Selangor civil war 604
Sematan 366
Semporna 471
Sepilok Orang-utan
  Rehabilitation Centre 465
Seremban 283–287
Seria 496
Serian 368
Seribuat Archipelago
  319–332
Shackleton, Lord 407, 413
Shah Alam 126
Shopping 70–71
Sibu 373–378
Sikuati 453
Silverware 71
Similajau National Park 394
SINGAPORE 499–593
  Accommodation 515–522
  Airport 508
  Arab Quarter 552
  Beach Road 553
  Bidadari Temple 556
  Bike rental 514
  Bugis Village 532
  Bukit Timah 554
  Bukit Timah Nature Reserve 554
  Bus terminals 509
  Car rental 514
  Changi 560
  CHIJMES 530
  China Street 539
  Chinatown 537–545
  Chinatown Complex 544
  Chinese and Japanese Gardens
    564
  Cinema 589
  Classical music 588
  Colonial District 523–534
  Crocodile Paradise 565
  Cultural performances 579, 588
  Departure 506

  Eating 570–583
  Ferry terminals 510
  Financial District 545–547
  Fort Canning Park 533
  Geylang 559
  Goodwood Hotel 536
  Haw Par Villa 562
  History 503–507
  Holland Village 563
  Jurong BirdPark 565
  Jurong Lake 563
  Katong 559
  Kusu island 568
  Lau Pa Sat Festival Market 547
  Lazarus island 569
  Listings 592
  Little India 547–552
  Mandai Orchid Gardens 558
  Markets and supermarkets 581
  Mount Faber 562
  National Museum 534
  Night Safari 557
  Nightlife 583–587
  Orchard Road 534
  Organized tours 514
  Orientation 507
  Padang 526
  Parliamentary System 526
  Phor Kark See Temple 556
  Pulau Hantu 569
  Pulau Seking 569
  Pulau Ubin 561
  Raffles City 528
  Raffles Hotel 529
  Raffles Place 546
  Restaurant entertainment 579
  Sakya Muni Buddha Temple 551
  Sasanaramsi Burmese Buddhist
    Temple 555
  Sentosa 566–568
  Sepoy Mutiny 528
  Serangoon Road 550
  Shopping 535, 545, 590
  Singapore Art Museum 530
  Singapore Botanic Gardens 536
  Singapore Discovery Centre 565
  Singapore River 523
  Singapore Science Centre 563
  Singapore Zoological Gardens 557
  Siong Lim Temple 556
  Sister's islands 569
  Sri Mariamman Hindu temple 543
  St Andrew's Cathedral 528
  St John's island 568
  Sultan Mosque 553
  Sun Yat Sen Villa 555
  Tang Dynasty City 564
  Tanjong Pagar 542
  Telok Ayer Street 538
  Telok Blangah 562

  Theatre and performing arts 590
  Thian Hock Keng Temple 539
  Tiffin 576
  Tiger Brewery 565
  Tourist offices 510
  Train station 510
  Transport 511–514
  Waterloo Street 532
  Woodlands 558
  World Trade Centre 562
  Zhu Jiao Centre 550
  Zoological Gardens 557
Sipitang 450
Song 379
Songbirds 538
Songket 70
South Pacific 321
Sri Aman 369
Sri Menanti 287–289
Srivijaya Empire 292, 298, 340,
  598–599
St John, Spenser 407, 455,
  457
Stadthuys 601
Stewart, Governor Duncan 607
Straits Chinese people 58
Straits Settlements 603
Sukau 467
Sultan Hassanal Bolkiah of
  Brunei 477, 488
Sultan Hussein Mohammed
  Shah 504, 562
Sultan Mahmud Shah 292,
  599–601
Sultan Omar Ali Saifuddien of
  Brunei 481, 609
Sulu, Sultanate of 425, 460
Suma Oriental 597
Sumatran Rhino 332
Sun Yat Sen, Dr 555
Sungei Balui 385–387
Sungei Petani 186
Sungei Pinang 186
Swettenham, Frank 81

T
Taiping 160–162
Taman Negara 208–223, 618
Tambun Hot Springs 151
Tambunan 440
Tanjung Piai 311
Tamus 422, 452
Tanah Rata 141–145
Tanjung Bidara 290

Tanjung Bungah 182
Tanjung Kling 290
Tanjung Rhu 199
Tapah 139
Tasek Bera 237
Tasek Chini 235–237
Tasik Kenyir 266
Tawau 473
Taxis, Long distance 38
Tea 145, 542
Tebedu 368
Tekek 323
Telaga Tujuh 198
Telephones 53–54
Television 54
Telok Mahkota 316
Teluk Bahang 185
Teluk Belanga 157
Teluk Chempedak 278
Teluk Intan 139
Teluk Ketapang 156
Teluk Kumbar 186
Teluk Nipah 156
Temburong District 494
Temerloh 237
Templer Park 121
Temples
  Chinese 65
  Hindu 64
  Indian 64
Tenom 442
Terengganu Peasants' Revolt 261
Terengganu Stone 599

Thailand, border crossings 202, 244
Thaipusam 64, 122, 534
Timithi 543
Tin 127, 134, 160–161, 283, 597, 603
Tour operators
  in Australasia 16
  in Britain 6
  in Ireland 8
  in North America 12
Tourist Board
  in Malaysia 22
  in Singapore 23
Tourist Information 22–23
Trains in Malaysia and Singapore 35–38
Travellers' cheques 26
Trekking 72–73
Trishaws 41
Tuaran 451
Tubau 387
Tumpat 252
Tun, Abdul Razak, Prime Minister 610
Tungku 470
Tunku Abdul Rahman Park 436
Tunku Abdul Rahman, Prime Minister 608–609
Tunku Qudin 174
Turtle Islands Park 466
Turtles 156, 269–271, 466
Tutong District 495

U

Ukit peoples 387
United Malay National Organization 310, 607–610

V

Visas 18–20

W

Wakaf Bahru 252
Wallace, Alfred Russell 352, 554
Wan Ahmed 204
Watersports 72, 323
Wayang kulit 588–589, 598, 621
White Rajahs 341, 603, 613
Whitehead, John 455
Wildlife 617–620
Wiring money 27
Women, travel advice for 75
Woodcarving 71, 123, 432
Working opportunities 75

X

Xavier, St Francis 293, 299

Y

Yap Ah Loy 81, 283
Young, Gavin 557
Youth Hostel associations 43

direct orders from

Amsterdam	1-85828-218-7	UK£8.99	US$14.95	CAN$19.99
Andalucia	1-85828-219-5	9.99	16.95	22.99
Australia	1-85828-220-9	13.99	21.95	29.99
Bali	1-85828-134-2	8.99	14.95	19.99
Barcelona	1-85828-221-7	8.99	14.95	19.99
Berlin	1-85828-129-6	8.99	14.95	19.99
Belgium & Luxembourg	1-85828-222-5	10.99	17.95	23.99
Brazil	1-85828-102-4	9.99	15.95	19.99
Britain	1-85828-208-X	12.99	19.95	25.99
Brittany & Normandy	1-85828-224-1	9.99	16.95	22.99
Bulgaria	1-85828-183-0	9.99	16.95	22.99
California	1-85828-181-4	10.99	16.95	22.99
Canada	1-85828-130-X	10.99	14.95	19.99
China	1-85828-225-X	15.99	24.95	32.99
Corfu	1-85828-226-8	8.99	14.95	19.99
Corsica	1-85828-227-6	9.99	16.95	22.99
Costa Rica	1-85828-136-9	9.99	15.95	21.99
Crete	1-85828-132-6	8.99	14.95	18.99
Cyprus	1-85828-182-2	9.99	16.95	22.99
Czech & Slovak Republics	1-85828-121-0	9.99	16.95	22.99
Egypt	1-85828-188-1	10.99	17.95	23.99
Europe	1-85828-159-8	14.99	19.95	25.99
England	1-85828-160-1	10.99	17.95	23.99
First Time Europe	1-85828-270-5	7.99	9.95	12.99
Florida	1-85828-184-4	10.99	16.95	22.99
France	1-85828-228-4	12.99	19.95	25.99
Germany	1-85828-128-8	11.99	17.95	23.99
Goa	1-85828-275-6	8.99	14.95	19.99
Greece	1-85828-131-8	9.99	16.95	20.99
Greek Islands	1-85828-163-6	8.99	14.95	19.99
Guatemala	1-85828-189-X	10.99	16.95	22.99
Hawaii: Big Island	1-85828-158-X	8.99	12.95	16.99
Hawaii	1-85828-206-3	10.99	16.95	22.99
Holland	1-85828-229-2	10.99	17.95	23.99
Hong Kong	1-85828-187-3	8.99	14.95	19.99
Hungary	1-85828-123-7	8.99	14.95	19.99
India	1-85828-200-4	14.99	23.95	31.99
Ireland	1-85828-179-2	10.99	17.95	23.99
Italy	1-85828-167-9	12.99	19.95	25.99
Jamaica	1-85828-230-6	9.99	16.95	22.99
Kenya	1-85828-192-X	11.99	18.95	24.99
London	1-85828-231-4	9.99	15.95	21.99
Mallorca & Menorca	1-85828-165-2	8.99	14.95	19.99
Malaysia, Singapore & Brunei	1-85828-232-2	11.99	18.95	24.99
Mexico	1-85828-044-3	10.99	16.95	22.99
Morocco	1-85828-040-0	9.99	16.95	21.99
Moscow	1-85828-118-0	8.99	14.95	19.99
Nepal	1-85828-190-3	10.99	17.95	23.99
New York	1-85828-171-7	9.99	15.95	21.99
Norway	1-85828-234-9	10.99	17.95	23.99
Pacific Northwest	1-85828-092-3	9.99	14.95	19.99

In the UK, Rough Guides are available from all good bookstores, but can be obtained from Penguin by contacting: Penguin Direct, Penguin Books Ltd, Bath Road, Harmondsworth, West Drayton, Middlesex UB7 0DA; or telephone the credit line on 0181-899 4036 (9am–5pm) and ask for Penguin Direct. Visa and Access accepted. Delivery will normally be within 14 working days. Penguin Direct ordering facilities are only available in the UK and the USA. The availability and published prices quoted are correct at the time of going to press but are subject to alteration without prior notice.

around the world

Paris	1-85828-235-7	8.99	14.95	19.99
Poland	1-85828-168-7	10.99	17.95	23.99
Portugal	1-85828-180-6	9.99	16.95	22.99
Prague	1-85828-122-9	8.99	14.95	19.99
Provence	1-85828-127-X	9.99	16.95	22.99
Pyrenees	1-85828-093-1	8.99	15.95	19.99
Rhodes & the Dodecanese	1-85828-120-2	8.99	14.95	19.99
Romania	1-85828-097-4	9.99	15.95	21.99
San Francisco	1-85828-185-7	8.99	14.95	19.99
Scandinavia	1-85828-236-5	12.99	20.95	27.99
Scotland	1-85828-166-0	9.99	16.95	22.99
Sicily	1-85828-178-4	9.99	16.95	22.99
Singapore	1-85828-135-0	8.99	14.95	19.99
Soutwest USA	1-85828-239-X	10.99	16.95	22.99
Spain	1-85828-240-3	11.99	18.95	24.99
St Petersburg	1-85828-133-4	8.99	14.95	19.99
Sweden	1-85828-241-1	10.99	17.95	23.99
Thailand	1-85828-140-7	10.99	17.95	24.99
Tunisia	1-85828-139-3	10.99	17.95	24.99
Turkey	1-85828-242-X	12.99	19.95	25.99
Tuscany & Umbria	1-85828-243-8	10.99	17.95	23.99
USA	1-85828-161-X	14.99	19.95	25.99
Venice	1-85828-170-9	8.99	14.95	19.99
Vietnam	1-85828-191-1	9.99	15.95	21.99
Wales	1-85828-245-4	10.99	17.95	23.99
Washington DC	1-85828-246-2	8.99	14.95	19.99
West Africa	1-85828-101-6	15.99	24.95	34.99
More Women Travel	1-85828-098-2	10.99	16.95	22.99
Zimbabwe & Botswana	1-85828-186-5	11.99	18.95	24.99
Phrasebooks				
Czech	1-85828-148-2	3.50	5.00	7.00
French	1-85828-144-X	3.50	5.00	7.00
German	1-85828-146-6	3.50	5.00	7.00
Greek	1-85828-145-8	3.50	5.00	7.00
Italian	1-85828-143-1	3.50	5.00	7.00
Mexican	1-85828-176-8	3.50	5.00	7.00
Portuguese	1-85828-175-X	3.50	5.00	7.00
Polish	1-85828-174-1	3.50	5.00	7.00
Spanish	1-85828-147-4	3.50	5.00	7.00
Thai	1-85828-177-6	3.50	5.00	7.00
Turkish	1-85828-173-3	3.50	5.00	7.00
Vietnamese	1-85828-172-5	3.50	5.00	7.00
Reference				
Classical Music	1-85828-113-X	12.99	19.95	25.99
Internet	1-85828-198-9	5.00	8.00	10.00
Jazz	1-85828-137-7	16.99	24.95	34.99
Opera	1-85828-138-5	16.99	24.95	34.99
Reggae	1-85828-247-0	12.99	19.95	25.99
Rock	1-85828-201-2	17.99	26.95	35.00
World Music	1-85828-017-6	16.99	22.95	29.99

In the USA, or for international orders, charge your order by Master Card or Visa (US$15.00 minimum order): call 1-800-253-6476; or send orders, with complete name, address and zip code, and list price, plus $2.00 shipping and handling per order to: Consumer Sales, Penguin USA, PO Box 999 – Dept #17109, Bergenfield, NJ 07621. No COD. Prepay foreign orders by international money order, a cheque drawn on a US bank, or US currency. No postage stamps are accepted. All orders are subject to stock availability at the time they are processed. Refunds will be made for books not available at that time. Please allow a minimum of four weeks for delivery.

Stay in touch with us!

ROUGH*NEWS* is Rough Guides' free newsletter. In three issues a year we give you news, travel issues, music reviews, readers' letters and the latest dispatches from authors on the road.

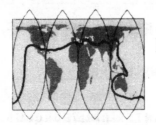

ROYAL BRUNEI

**Touching
the Middle East,
Far East and Australasia**

Contact
**Royal Brunei Airlines
in London
on
0171 584 6660 (Reservations)
0171 584 9939 (Sales)
or
Your local Travel Agent**

MAGIC
OF THE ORIENT

expert advice

> With our personal knowledge of Malaysia, we offer first hand and honest advice.

personal service

> One of our small team of consultants can help plan and organise your holiday to the finest detail.

choice

> With a wide choice of flexible and interesting tour options we can tailor-make a holiday to suit your personal requirements. From a longhouse in the depths of the Borneo Rainforest to a luxury resort on the Peninsula, the choice is yours.

hotels

fly-drive

coach tours

beach resorts

adventure trips

inclusive holidays

accommodation only

holidays for the independent minded

TEL: 01293 537700

www.magic-of-the-orient.com
AITO • ABTA V2984 • ATOL 2865